# HANDBOOK OF DEVELOPMENTAL COGNITIVE NEUROSCIENCE

**Developmental Cognitive Neuroscience**
Mark Johnson and Bruce Pennington, editors

*Neurodevelopmental Disorders,* Helen Tager-Flusberg, editor, 1999

*Handbook of Developmental Cognitive Neuroscience,* Charles A. Nelson and Monica Luciana, editors, 2001

# HANDBOOK OF DEVELOPMENTAL COGNITIVE NEUROSCIENCE

*Edited by*

Charles A. Nelson
Monica Luciana

A BRADFORD BOOK
THE MIT PRESS
CAMBRIDGE, MASSACHUSETTS
LONDON, ENGLAND

This book was set in Baskerville by Impressions Book and Journal Services, Inc., Madison, Wisconsin, and was printed and bound in the United States of America.

Library of Congress Cataloging-in-Publication Data

Handbook of developmental cognitive neuroscience / edited by Charles A. Nelson and Monica Luciana.
    p.   cm.
  "A Bradford book"
  Includes bibliographical references and index.
  ISBN 0-262-14073-X (alk. paper)
    1. Developmental neurobiology—Handbooks, manuals, etc. 2. Cognitive neuroscience—Handbooks, manuals, etc. I. Nelson, Charles A. (Charles Alexander) II. Luciana, Monica. [DNLM: 1. Nervous System—growth & development. 2. Nervous System Physiology. 3. Cognition—physiology. 4. Human Development. WL 102 H23535 2001]

QP363.5.H365 2001
612.8′2—dc21                        00-046567

# CONTENTS

# FOREWORD

The first *Handbook of Cognitive Neuroscience* appeared in 1984. According to that volume's preface, this was only 8 years after George Miller and Michael Gazzaniga coined the term "cognitive neuroscience" to describe a new research front on the border between biological and behavioral science. At the time, Miller, Gazzaniga, and a few like-minded colleagues, saw the need for a new research program that would use the techniques of both brain science and cognitive science to explore the biological foundations of human cognition. That first handbook, edited by Gazzaniga, contained only one chapter on development. For the most part, that chapter described the methods of cognitive science, what they had revealed about the human mind, and what, in combination with brain science, they might reveal about the development of the mind–brain.

Now, Charles Nelson and Monica Luciana have organized and edited the first *Handbook of Developmental Cognitive Neuroscience*. Its publication testifies to the rapid progress developmental cognitive neuroscience has made over the past 16 years. The handbook more than fulfills the vision that Miller, Gazzaniga, and other early cognitive neuroscientists had for their new research program. As one can see from the handbook's sections on sensory and sensorimotor systems, language, executive function, and cognition, the theories and methods of cognitive science have a central role in developmental cognitive neuroscience. Furthermore, cognitive neuroscience has progressed to a point where scientists can begin asking and answering fundamental questions about interactions between emotion and cognition. In these areas, methods of cognitive science allow researchers to conduct careful analyses and to develop detailed models of the mental processes that guide and regulate our behavior. Using these models, scientists can ask how the components of those models might map onto the neural structures and circuits that provide the biological substrate for cognition.

Brain imaging and recording technologies are among the central methodological paradigms of cognitive neuroscience. Imaging and recording technologies allow cognitive neuroscientists to study neural structure/mental function correlations in normal human brains. Initially recording and imaging techniques, such as PET, that required administration of radio isotopes allowed scientists to study structure–function relations only in adult brains. Developmentalists could use adult studies to frame hypotheses about what might be happening within a child's developing brain. Recent technological advances, such as functional magnetic resonance imaging and multi-electrode brain recording, have yielded methods that can be safely used to study structure–function relations and their development in children's brains. These new techniques plus more refined cognitive models account for the progress and heightened interest in developmental cognitive neuroscience.

This handbook also illustrates how the brain sciences contribute to cognitive neuroscience. Neuropsychology has a long history of the study of how brain trauma affects behavior. The power of studying normal versus impaired brains, both mature and developing, is evident in the handbook's section on neurodevelopmental aspects of clinical disorders.

Basic developmental neurobiology has elucidated developmental phenomena such as corticogenesis, neurogenesis, and synaptogenesis, as well as the role of critical and sensitive periods in development. There have also been attempts to discern how such phenomena relate to human behavior. Combining basic neurobiology with systems neuroscience, imaging, and cognitive science will no doubt expedite our understanding of how changes at the cellular and subcellular levels affect and are affected by experience. Some of the most recent, and exciting, findings in basic neurobiology establish that the human brain remains malleable and plastic throughout our lifetimes. One of the great opportunities in developmental cognitive neuroscience, as this handbook indicates, is to explore what this new understanding of lifelong, neural plasticity implies for brain and child development.

Recently, claims about what brain science might mean for parenting and early childhood have captured the public's imagination. We should encourage the public's interest in developmental brain science and applaud attempts to base early childhood policy and practice on a scientific basis. However, in some instances public enthusiasm far outstrips our scientific understanding. Too often the messages broadcast by advocates and the media do not accurately reflect what scientists currently know about synapses, critical periods, neural plasticity, and how experience affects the brain. If we wish to base policy and practice on brain science or cognitive neuroscience, it is imperative that scientists knowledgeable in the relevant disciplines engage in careful discussion of what their disciplines, alone and collectively, can contribute to better policy and practice and articulate their conclusions to the interested public. This handbook provides an excellent starting point for that discussion.

The power, promise, and importance of the attempt to understand the biological foundations of human cognition, are amply illustrated throughout the handbook's chapters.

John T. Bruer

# INTRODUCTION

Hebb's seminal volume, *The Organization of Behavior*, was instrumental in helping to organize the field of behavioral neuroscience. From the time that book was published in 1949 through the early 1980s, there was tremendous interest in the neural bases of behavior, particularly cognitive behavior. Admittedly, much of the work in this field was dominated by animal studies, but that was a product of the methods available at the time (a point repeatedly stressed to the first author of this volume by his undergraduate advisors at McGill, when he expressed interest in studying the relation between brain and behavior in the human child).

This began to change, however, in the mid 1980s as excitement grew over a noninvasive new tool believed to be capable of peering into the human brain. This tool, Positron Emission Tomography (PET), exploded into the scientific mainstream with the seminal publication by Michael Posner and Marcus Raichle and their colleagues at Washington University. In a paper this group published in 1988 (Posner, Petersen, Fox, and Raichle, 1988), it became clear that it was possible to ascertain where processes underlying complex thought (in this case, attention) were taking place in the brain.

Closely monitoring this change was the James S. McDonnell Foundation. Anticipating the partial merger of three distinctive fields—cognitive psychology, neuroscience, and computational science—the Foundation recognized the need to train scientists in the language of these three fields. To do so, they funded what became known as the *Summer Institute in Cognitive Neuroscience*. In some small way the impetus for this book began over a decade ago, in 1988, in Cambridge, Massachusetts, when the first author of this volume attended the inaugural *Summer Institute* (the agenda for which is reproduced at the end of this Introduction). This first meeting was brilliantly organized by Michael Posner, Gordon Shepherd, and Stephen Kosslyn, and graciously hosted by Harvard University. For two full weeks it brought to an audience of graduate students, postdocs, and junior faculty an outstanding panel of scientists. Labs were interspersed with lectures, which were interspersed with hallway conversation, collectively making this a very high caliber intellectual endeavor.

One element of this meeting that was particularly memorable, however, was what was *not* discussed, at least not formally: the study of development. Clearly the work of Jay McClelland, David Hubel, and many others who presented at the *Summer Institute* had implications for development, but development *as* development received little formal attention. An exception was a small breakout session on the development of memory that Stephen Kosslyn and Michael Posner (who themselves have long been interested in this topic) asked the author and a number of other attendees to organize. With this one exception, development received little discussion at the meeting.

Through the late 1980s into the 1990s, the field of cognitive neuroscience took hold. The *Summer Institutes* continued and flourished, the Cognitive Neuroscience Society and the *Journal of Cognitive Neuroscience* were launched, and psychology departments throughout the United States began to advertise for faculty positions in this field. However, interest in the neural underpinnings of development occurred very slowly. There are many reasons for this trend (for discussion, see Nelson and Bloom, 1997), but suffice to say that change began to occur on three fronts. One was that through the 1980s the field of developmental neuroscience began to yield discoveries of profound importance (e.g., the pattern of synaptogenesis; the role of experience in influencing brain development). A second was that a number of prominent cognitive neuroscientists who had historically studied mature function acknowledged the importance of studying development (e.g., in the mid 1990s a meeting of the Cognitive Neuroscience Society devoted a symposium to developmental cognitive neuroscience). Finally, a new generation of developmental psychologists began to recognize the need for considering the neurobiological underpinnings of behavioral development (again, see Nelson and Bloom, 1997 for discussion). Collectively, then, the time was right for the field of *developmental* cognitive neuroscience to be born (approximately 16 years after Michael Gazzaniga's first *Handbook of Cognitive Neuroscience* was published).

This *Handbook of Developmental Cognitive Neuroscience* represents the distillation of the best this new field has to offer; it also reflects a number of strong biases by the editors. One such bias is that the field of developmental cognitive neuroscience must be grounded in basic neurodevelopmental science, particularly developmental neurobiology. To this end, the first part of this volume (Fundamentals of Developmental Neurobiology) is devoted to basic studies and principles of neural development. Here the reader learns about pre- and postnatal neurogenesis, synaptogenesis, and myelination; the effects of sex hormones on brain development; and about development of the hippocampus and prefrontal cortex in particular (given the importance of these regions for cognitive development). A second bias is our emphasis on the importance of methodological advances. Thus, the second part of the volume (Methodological Paradigms) is devoted to describing methods that have proved so important in elucidating brain–behavior relations in the context of cognitive development. These methods include behavioral "marker" tasks, along with event-related potentials (ERPs), functional Magnetic Resonance Imaging (fMRI), and genetic and computational (neural network) modeling.

Over the past several years the area of neural plasticity has received tremendous attention by both neuroscientists and behavioral scientists. Indeed, the forces that shape and mold the brain may well represent the "new" developmental psychology, albeit a more mechanistic and reductionistic version than offered by previous generations of developmental psychologists and one that emphasizes development within a lifespan context. That is, the forces that mold the brain's structure and physiology are now recognized to operate well into adulthood (see Tanapat, Hastings, and Gould, chapter 7, this volume). To this end, the third part (Neural Plasticity of Development) is devoted to a discussion of this area, emphasizing both normative and atypical aspects of development.

Because the development of sensory and sensorimotor systems and language has played such a prominent role in both neuroscience and in developmental psychology, the fourth (Sensory and Sensorimotor Systems) and fifth (Language) parts of this volume are devoted to this area. Here we are enlightened about the development of the visual and auditory systems, the development of skilled motor movements, and several aspects of language development. Embedded within these chapters is yet another bias of the editors: the need to juxtapose the study of normative development against that of atypical development, as each mutually informs the other.

The sixth part of the book (Cognition) reflects the substance of the volume, as befits a book on *cognitive* neuroscience. Here we provide chapters on the development of attention, memory, face/object recognition, spatial cognition, number comprehension, and executive functions. Naturally, the work captured by the distinguished authors of these chapters is framed in a neuroscience context.

The seventh part of this volume (Neurodevelopmental Aspects of Clinical Disorders) returns the reader to the theme of how studies of atypical development can inform the study of typical development. However, these chapters directly target studies of atypical populations. We introduce the reader to the importance of nutrition on brain–behavioral development, on the risks of prenatal alcohol and cocaine exposure, on the development of autism, Tourette's syndrome, and schizophrenia, and on disorders of attention.

The eighth and final part of the book (Emotion and Cognition Interactions) anticipates what may well represent the next cutting edge area, that of developmental affective neuroscience and the manner in which affective experience may act to shape cognitive processes. This part begins with a tutorial on the neurobiology of attachment, and progresses to a discourse on the effects of deprivation on emotional development, on the neurobiology of temperament, and on reward-seeking behavior.

Overall, this volume possesses the breadth and depth necessary to do justice to this exciting new scientific field. It does so by drawing on internationally known experts who have graciously contributed their time and energy to bring the reader the first complete *Handbook of Developmental Cognitive Neuroscience*. We hope that you are as pleased with the result as we are.

Charles A. Nelson
Monica Luciana

## REFERENCES

Hebb, D. O., 1949. *The Organization of Behavior*. New York: Wiley Press.
Nelson, C. A., and F. E. Bloom, 1997. Child development and neuroscience. *Child Devel.* 68:970–987.
Posner, M. I., S. E. Petersen, P. T. Fox, and M. E. Raichle, 1988. Localization of cognitive operations in the human brain. *Science* 240(4859):1627–1631.

## JAMES S. MCDONNELL FOUNDATION SUMMER INSTITUTE IN COGNITIVE NEUROSCIENCE

### 13–24 June 1988, Harvard University

Lectures will be in Room 1 of William James Hall, which is located at 33 Kirkland Street (at the corner of Kirkland and Divinity Avenue) in Cambridge. Laboratories and discussion groups will meet in smaller rooms (to be announced) within William James Hall. Unless otherwise noted, lunch and dinner will be open; a booklet describing the many and varied Harvard Square restaurants will be distributed at the Institute. Coffee and donuts will be available beginning at 8:15 A.M. in Room 105 of William James Hall (off the lobby), and soft drinks and cookies will be provided in the laboratory rooms in the afternoon.

Prior reading:

*Cognition* (2nd ed.). A. L. Glass and K. Holyoak (New York. Random House). Chapters 1, 2, 4, and 9.

*Parallel Distributed Processing.* D. E. Rumelhart and J. McClelland
(Cambridge, MA: MIT Press).
Chapters 1–4; 16 and 17 optional.

*Principles of Behavioral Neurology.* M.-M. Mesulam (Philadelphia: F. A. Davis).
Chapters 3, 4, and 7.

*Neurobiology* (2nd ed.). G. M. Shepherd (New York: Oxford University Press).
Chapters 16, 29, and 30.

**WEEK 1: MEMORY**

*Monday, 13 June*

| | |
|---|---|
| 8:15 | Registration and parking permits (in Room 105 of William James Hall) |
| 9:00 | Overview (Michael I. Posner, Stephen M. Kosslyn, and Gordon M. Shepherd) |
| 10:00 | A memory system in the monkey (Mortimer Mishkin) |
| 11:30 Lab | Toward a computational model of a memory system in the monkey (Stephen M. Kosslyn and John D. E. Gabrieli) |

Lunch

| | |
|---|---|
| 2:00 | Hands-on use of computer model of a memory system |
| 3:00 Demo | Cellular and synaptic organization of cerebral cortex (Alan Peters) |
| 4:00 Demo | Interpreting scans, observing and testing amnesic patients (William Hirst and Bruce T. Volpe) |
| 5:00 | General review and discussion |

*Tuesday, 14 June*

| | |
|---|---|
| 9:00 | The anatomy of declarative memory: Focus on hippocampus (Larry R. Squire) |
| 10:30 | The anatomy of a procedural memory: Focus on cerebellum (Richard F. Thompson) |

Lunch

| | |
|---|---|
| 2:00 Demo | Circuit organization of hippocampus and cerebellum (Gordon M. Shepherd) |
| 3:00 Lab | Separating declarative and procedural memory in amnesics and normals (John D. E. Gabrieli) |
| 4:00 | Hands-on demonstrations of experimental paradigms used to test amnesics; small group discussion |
| 5:00 | General review and discussion |

Dinner

(Evening sessions during the first week are optional)

| | |
|---|---|
| 8:00 | Review of study panel on memory (Michael S. Gazzaniga) Review of study panel on higher cognitive processes (Terence W. Picton) |

*Wednesday, 15 June*

| | |
|---|---|
| 9:00 | Overview of neural computation (Tomaso Poggio) |
| 10:30 | Physiology of memory mechanisms (Gary S. Lynch) |

Lunch

| | |
|---|---|
| 2:00 Lab | Properties of connectionist systems (James L. McClelland) |
| 3:00 Disc | Making connections between real neural architectures and neural networks (Gordon M. Shepherd) |
| 4:00 | Hands-on explorations of connectionist models |
| 5:00 | General review and discussion |

Dinner

8:00      Review of study panel on motor control (Emilio Bizzi)
Review of study panel on emotion (Stanley Schachter and
Jerome E. Singer)

*Thursday, 16 June*

9:00      Possible transmitter systems in memory: Psychopharmacology
(Trevor W. Robbins)
10:30      Disorders of memory and cognition in Alzheimer's disease
(Mary Jo Nissen)
12:00      Memory from a single-cell point of view: Discussant (Robert
Desimone)

Lunch

2:00 Demo      Neurotransmitters and neuromodulators in cerebral cortex
(Gordon M. Shepherd)
3:00 Lab      Connectionist models of memory disorders (Jay G. Rueckl and
John D. E. Gabrieli)
4:00      Hand-on use of connectionist models to explore the bases of memory
disorders
5:00      General review and discussion

Dinner

8:00      Review of study panel on attention (Michael I. Posner)

*Friday, 17 June*

9:00      Cognitive psychophysiology in the study of memory: Event-related
potentials and event-related magnetic fields as tools for cognitive
science (Emanuel Donchin)
10:30      PET and related approaches to studying memory function
(Marcus E. Raichle)

Lunch

2:00 Demo      Lesion method approach to memory systems in humans
(Antonio R. Damasio)
3:00 Disc      Summary of basic principles of cortical circuits
(Gordon M. Shepherd)
4:00      Small group discussion of memory
5:00      General review and discussion

*Saturday Evening:* Clam bake
*Sunday Evening:* Lobster buffet

## WEEK 2: HIGH-LEVEL VISION

*Monday, 20 June*

9:00      Anatomy of the visual system (David C. Van Essen)
10:30      Physiology of the visual system: Single cell recordings
(Robert H. Wurtz)

Lunch

2:00 Demo      Functional organization of the visual system (David C. Van Essen)
3:00 Lab      Models of the "two cortical visual systems" (Jay G. Rueckl,
Kyle R. Cave, and Stephen M. Kosslyn)
4:00      Analysis of "hidden units" in "two cortical visual systems"
connectionist model
5:00      General review and discussion

*Tuesday, 21 June*

9:00      The anatomy and physiology of the posterior parietal lobe (Richard A. Andersen)

10:30      The functions of the visual-spatial attention system (Anne M. Treisman)

Lunch

2:00 Demo      A connectionist/control architecture for attention and skill acquisition: From potential physiology to behavior (Walter Schneider)

3:00 Lab      Studying visual attention: Pop-out, illusory conjunctions (William Prinzmetal)

4:00      Hands-on demonstrations of visual attention phenomena; small group discussion

5:00      General review and discussion

Dinner

8:00      Anatomical, physiological, and psychophysical evidence for separate pathways for form, color, movement and stereo (David F. L. Hubel)

*Wednesday, 22 June*

9:00      Neurological patients as an approach to studying spatial attention (M. Marsel Mesulam)

10:30      Cognitive studies of neurological deficits (Michael I. Posner)

Lunch

2:00 Demo      Neuropsychological examination of patients (William P. Milberg)

3:00 Demo      Anatomical methods for brain studies (M. Marsel Mesulam)

4:00 Lab      Hands-on demonstrations: Cerebral laterality experiments (Stephen M. Kosslyn and John D. E. Gabrieli)

5:00      General review and discussion

*Thursday, 23 June*

9:00      The visual agnosias (Elizabeth K. Warrington)

10:30      The anomias (Harold Goodglass)

Lunch

3:00 Demo      Neural basis of cortical maps (Gordon M. Shepherd and John S. Kauer)

4:00      Small group discussion

5:00      General review and discussion

*Friday, 24 June*

9:00      Visual object recognition (Irving Biederman)

10:30      Visual imagery and visual perception (Stephen M. Kosslyn)

Lunch

2:00 Lab      A computer simulation of neurological disorders of high-level visual recognition processes (Stephen M. Kosslyn and Gretchen Wang)

4:00      Hands-on experimentation with computer simulation of high-level visual recognition syndromes

5:00      General review and discussion

8:00 Banquet

After dinner: Brief summation by Michael I. Posner, Stephen M. Kosslyn, and Gordon M. Shepherd

# I

# FUNDAMENTALS OF DEVELOPMENTAL NEUROBIOLOGY

# 1 Neocortical Neuronogenesis: Regulation, Control Points, and a Strategy of Structural Variation

T. TAKAHASHI, R. S. NOWAKOWSKI,
AND V. S. CAVINESS, JR.

ABSTRACT Cognitive and adaptive behaviors both across and within mammalian species vary in association with variation in neocortical structure. Here we present an algorithm of neocortical histogenetic operation, based upon experiments in the mouse with an emphasis upon neuronogenesis, that defines control points at which large-scale revisions may be associated with speciation and small-scale revisions with the structural distinctions within species. We suggest that the master control mechanism for the neuronogenetic sequence occurs at the G1 restriction point and that it is at this control point that both large- and small-scale variations in numeration are coordinated with those of specification of neuronal class and regional specification. Lower amplitude and regionally diverse modulations, typical of within-species differences, will also arise from modulation of cortical development downstream from neuronogenesis.

## Introduction

The neocortex is the central and indispensable "organ" of cognitive process. It is by far the largest structure of the brain and is bilaterally represented in the cerebral hemispheres of the mammalian forebrain. It is bounded at the medial and ventral margin of the hemisphere by the hippocampal formation and amygdaloid nucleus and rostrally and ventrally by piriform cortex, the diagonal band, and septal structures. To the extent that "cognition follows form," the range and quality of cognitive processes, as these vary across and within species, are correlates of the variations in neocortical struc-

ture across and within species (Hahn, Jensen, and Dudek, 1979). That is, the study of the evolutionary and ontogenetic origins of these structural variations is a cornerstone of cognitive neuroscience.

The general structural features of the neocortex are greatly regular across mammalian species. In all species, neurons with long axons, which are excitatory, group broadly into five classes which are arrayed tangentially by class into regular laminar order (figure 1.1A; table 1.1; Cajal, 1952; Lorente de No, 1938; Peters and Jones, 1984). These general classes are, by layer, the small pyramids of layer II, the medium-sized pyramids of layer III, the granule cells of layer IV, the large pyramids of layer V, and the polymorphic neurons of layer VI. Inhibitory interneurons, a minority population, distribute without laminar grouping more or less uniformly throughout the height of the cortex (Lavdas, Mione, and Parnavelas, 1996; Peters and Jones, 1984). The general laminar structure varies regionally in terms of these cytologic details as well as the relative numbers and the packing density of the separate neuronal classes. These variations have represented the principal criteria for the regional parcellation of the neocortex into architectonic fields that form the basis for understanding the multimodal and hierarchic neocortical representations of neural and cognitive systems (Brodmann, 1909; Caviness, 1975; Zilles, 1990). Thus, the generic neocortical map places perceptual (visual, acoustic, somatosensory, and gustatory representations) in constant positions relative to each other in the posterior and lateral regions of the hemisphere and motor representations anteriorly (figure 1.1B).

The general similarity in organization of the neocortex of all mammals stands in marked contrast to the variable features that differentiate the neocortex from species to species. Most notable among these variable features is neocortical volume or, more specifically, surface area (table 1.2; Haug, 1987; Holloway, 1974;

T. TAKAHASHI Department of Neurology, Massachusetts General Hospital, Harvard Medical School, Boston, Massachusetts; Department of Pediatrics, Keio University School of Medicine, Tokyo, Japan.
R. S. NOWAKOWSKI Department of Neuroscience and Cell Biology, UMDNJ–Robert Wood Johnson Medical School, Piscataway, New Jersey.
V. S. CAVINESS, JR. Department of Neurology, Massachusetts General Hospital, Harvard Medical School, Boston, Massachusetts.

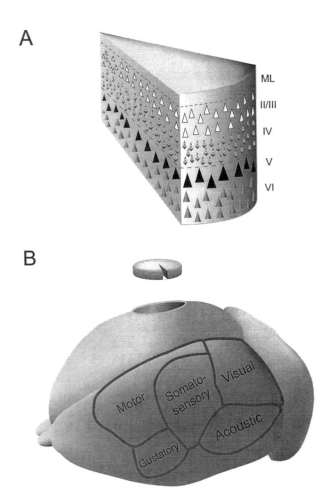

A

ML
II/III
IV
V
VI

B

Motor
Somato-
sensory
Visual
Acoustic
Gustatory

FIGURE 1.1  Generic neocortical format. (**A**) Laminar architecture from cutout in **B**. The mammalian neocortical format comprehends a range of specific neuronal classes, ordered by class into layers II–VI. (ML: molecular layer.) (**B**) Regional variations in cytologic detail and in the relative numbers and packing density of neurons distinguish architectonic fields, mapped from caudal to rostral as visual, somatosensory, acoustic, and gustatory sensory and motor representations. The map is represented bilaterally in paired cerebral hemispheres.

TABLE 1.1

*General mammalian system of neocortical specification*

| Systems Topology by Hierarchical Order | Neuronal Class by Laminar Order |
|---|---|
| Primary representations[1]<br>V–SS<br>M<br>A–G | Layers by class: Polymorphic VI, large pyramidal V, granular IV, medium and small pyramidal III/II. (Primary areas, e.g., VI are more granular than other areas.) |
| Unimodal associative areas | |
| Multimodal associative and limbic areas | |

[1] The primary visual (V), somatosensory (SS), acoustic (A), gustatory (G), and motor (M) representations are here positioned schematically to represent their relative caudal to rostral (left to right) and medial to lateral (top to bottom) spatial relationships in the cortex.

Adapted from Mesulam (1998).

tion (Krubitzer, 1995; Manger et al., 1998; Morgane, Glezer, and Jacobs, 1988; Northcutt and Kaas, 1995; Van Essen, Newsome, and Maunsell, 1984; Van Essen et al., 1986; Woolsey and van der Loos, 1970) as well as a corresponding increase in the number of neurons, which may be larger and more complex in their form and circuitry relationships (Northcutt and Kaas, 1995).

The scale of variation in neocortical structure is more muted among normal members of a species and tends to be regional rather than global in its expression (table 1.2). In particular, variation in overall neocortical volume is of relatively low order, reflecting a general constancy of neuron number and size, which are the essential determinants of volume (Andrews, Halpern, and Purves, 1997; Kennedy et al., 1998; Rademacher et al., 1993; Van Essen, Newsome, and Maunsell, 1984; Van Essen et al., 1986). Whereas the total mean volume of the neocortex of normal young adults appears to be minimally variant (Kennedy et al., 1998), the surface area of individual architectonic representations (Rademacher et al., 1993; Stensaas, Eddington, and Dobelle, 1974), the form of specific gyri (Ono, Jubik, and Abernathy, 1990), and the mapping of architectonic representations to specific gyri (Rademacher et al., 1993) may be as idiosyncratic as, perhaps, the individual fingerprint.

THE NEOCORTICAL HISTOGENETIC SEQUENCE  The structure of neocortex emerges in the course of a series of histogenetic events common to all mammals (figure 1.2; Sidman and Rakic, 1982). The histogenetic se-

Jerison, 1973, 1982, 1987; Zilles et al., 1988). The scaling (or proportionality) of neocortical volume to that of other brain regions or somatic structures (Schmidt-Nielsen, 1984) is species-specific and highly variable with, for example, a 400-fold or more greater surface areas between the brain of a human and that of a mouse. Moreover, the surface contour is smooth in smaller species but folded in species-specific gyral patterns in species with larger and more complex brains. Moreover, with the brains of larger, complex species or in species with distinctive adaptive specializations, there is an increase in the hierarchic complexity of the architectonic map and corresponding systems organiza-

TABLE 1.2

*Variation and regulation of phenotype in the neocortex*

| | Numeration (numbers of cells) | Interspecific Characteristics | Individual Characteristics | Regulation |
|---|---|---|---|---|
| Volume (surface area) | Volume | Species-typical | Regionally variable, low order | Output domain and preneuronogenetic parcellation |
| | Surface conformation | Species-typical smooth vs. gyriform conformation where general surface pattern among gyrencephalic mammals is species-typical | Regionally variable—low-order variation in gyral pattern, contour, size | |
| | Scaling | Species-typical scaling relationships respecting neocortex to other CNS structures and respecting corresponding neocortical representations | Regionally variable, low-order variation | |
| | **Architectonic Fields (maps)** | **Interspecific Characteristics** | **Individual Characteristics** | **Regulation** |
| | Cytoarchitectonic fields | Change in both size and number of fields | Low-order changes in size but *not* number | Time domain and size of TNG |
| | **Neuronal Subtypes[1] (neuron classes and laminae)** | **Interspecific Characteristics** | **Individual Characteristics** | **Regulation** |
| Specification | Laminar order by class | Species-typical by subclass and sublaminae | Invariant | |
| | Neurons by class size, and complexity of form and circuitry relationships | Species-typical in parallel with other domains of size and complexity | Invariant or only low-order regional variation | Time domain and intracortical processes |

[1]We suggest that neuronal form, laminar and sublaminar destinations, and final circuitry affiliations are ultimately directly or indirectly attributable to properties inherent in specification.

quence is initiated with the generation of neurons, or neuronogenesis, which occurs in a pseudostratified ventricular epithelium (PVE; for abbreviations, see table 1.3) at the margins of the forebrain ventricle. Prior to the formation of the earliest neurons, the epithelium proliferates exponentially (Rakic, 1988) and is already partitioned regionally with reference to expression domains of a diversity of transcription factors (Puelles and Rubenstein, 1993; Shimamura et al., 1995). In all species, once neuronogenesis is initiated, postmitotic neurons migrate across the width of the cerebral wall, where they become sorted by class into layers (Rakic, 1972; Takahashi et al., 1999b). A substantial number are then eliminated by histogenetic cell death (Ferrar et al.,

1990, 1992; Finlay and Pallas, 1989; Finlay and Slattery, 1983; Spreafico et al., 1995; Thomaidou et al., 1997; Verney et al., 1999). Surviving neurons form synapses with other neurons, grow, and further differentiate as they become integrated into neural circuitry (Bourgeois, Jastreboff, and Rakic, 1989; Bourgeois and Rakic, 1993; Rakic, 1995; Rakic, Bourgeois, and Goldman-Rakic, 1994). The progression of the sequence, expressed in terms of the origin of successive neocortical layers, is scaled identically to the overall time course of neuronogenesis in each species. As indicated in figure 1.3, progression through this temporal interval is expressed as a percentile of the duration of the interval (Caviness, Takahashi, and Nowakowski, 1995).

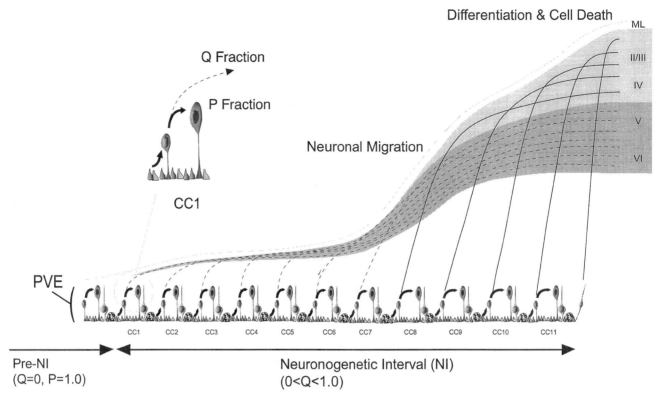

Q Fraction

P Fraction

CC1

Neuronal Migration

Differentiation & Cell Death

ML

II/III

IV

V

VI

PVE

CC1  CC2  CC3  CC4  CC5  CC6  CC7  CC8  CC9  CC10  CC11

Pre-NI
(Q=0, P=1.0)

Neuronogenetic Interval (NI)
(0<Q<1.0)

FIGURE 1.2 The principal events of neocortical histogenesis. Histogenesis of the neocortex is initiated with cell proliferation in the pseudostratified ventricular epithelium (PVE). The founder population proliferates exponentially through an extended series of cycles in the preneuronogenetic phase (pre-NI) during which no cells exit the cycle ($Q = 0$, $P = 1.0$). The onset of the neuronogenetic interval (NI) corresponds to $CC_1$, the first cycle when $Q$ becomes greater than 0 and postmitotic cells exit the cycle as young neurons. The cells of the PVE then execute a series of integer cycles ($CC_1$–$CC_{11}$ in mouse). As young neurons of the $Q$ fraction exit their respective cycles, they migrate across the embryonic cerebral wall where they are assembled into neocortex more or less in inside-to-outside order. Thus, the earliest formed are destined for layer VI of the cortex while later formed cells will take up positions in progressively more superficial layers V–II. Lines (for granular/supragranular layers) and broken lines (for infragranular layers) schematically indicate cell cycle of neuron origin in approximate relation to laminar destination). At the conclusion of migration, a substantial proportion of young neurons are eliminated by cell death while surviving neurons grow, differentiate, and become integrated into cortical circuitry.

These commonalities of sequence and scaling of sequence progression suggest that histogenesis is regulated by similar mechanisms across species (Caviness, Takahashi, and Nowakowski, 1995). Therefore, it can be inferred from comparative study that regulatory mechanisms operate at three levels: (1) a general mammalian program, which assures the generic events of specification and histogenesis; (2) a species-specific variation of the generic histogenetic program, which assures specific structural adaptations; and (3) modulatory mechanisms within species, which determine structural variations distinctive to the individual.

The execution of the histogenetic sequence must depend upon a great number of interdependent molecular and cellular biological events (Gerhart and Kirschner, 1997). These must vary in systematic ways across species to provide for the distinct structural features that distinguish species. Yet, in order to assure characteristic constancy of structure among individuals of a species, the execution of these molecular and cellular biological events must be greatly regular and stably buffered in the face of modest variations in fetal genotype and developmental conditions that must exist between individuals (Kennedy et al., 1998). With respect to neocortical development, the nature of variations in histogenetic process associated with species-specific differences is not readily tackled directly by experiment. On the other hand, the workings of histogenetic process may be elucidated through experiment as it proceeds in a given species. Through experiment in a species, one may construct a specific program or algorithm of the generic sequence in its detailed operations and with respect to control points that regulate the whole sequence. In principle, such an algorithm and,

## TABLE 1.3
*Abbreviations*

| | |
|---|---|
| PVE | Pseudostratified ventricular epithelium |
| TNG | Transverse neurogenetic gradient |
| G1 | First gap phase of the cell cycle that occurs between M and S phases |
| G2 | Second gap phase of the cell cycle that occurs between S and M phases |
| M | Mitosis phase of the cell cycle |
| S | DNA synthetic phase of the cell cycle |
| $T_C$ | Length of the whole cell cycle |
| $T_S$ | Length of the S phase |
| $T_{G2+M}$ | Length of the G2 and M phases combined |
| $T_{C-CCn}$ | Length of the whole cell cycle of cell cycle $n$ |
| $P$ | Proportion of cells that continue to proliferate |
| $Q$ | Proportion of cells that become proliferatively quiescent (or that quit the cell cycle) |
| $Q_n$ | $Q$ for that cell cycle |
| $k$ | Dimensionless constant that relates $Q$ to cell cycle number |
| $OUT_n$ | Output of the PVE at any given cell cycle $n$ |
| $OUT_{TOTAL}$ | Total neuron production from the PVE over the entire neuronogenetic interval |
| $PVE_n$ | Size of the PVE at that cell cycle |
| $CC_n$ | Cell cycle $n$ |
| LE | Leading edge of a CC domain |
| TE | Trailing edge of a CC domain |

in particular, its control points comprise both a description and a theoretical framework for the developmental origins of the cortical features common to all mammalian species and for mechanisms that regulate the global and large-scale structural differences that distinguish neocortex of different species or, on a smaller scale, those that distinguish neocortical structure among individuals of a species.

In the ensuing discussion, we construct an algorithmic framework for the neocortical histogenetic sequence in the mouse. The principal. emphasis is given to neuronogenesis, the initial step in the sequence; but this perspective is extended, in a limited fashion, to the events that both precede and follow neuronogenesis. The cell cycle—proceeding regularly in proliferative cells through the first gap (G1), the DNA synthetic (S), the second gap (G2), and finally the cell division (M) phases—is the engine that drives neuronogenesis and is the cell biological function in which control mechanisms are vested (Caviness, Takahashi, and Nowakowski, 1999a). The algorithmic construction of the operation of the neuronogenetic process is parameter-based and quantitative, which, we suggest, is essential to any meaningful model of histogenetic regulation. The central thesis of this review is that neuronogenesis, in all its

complexity of cell behaviors and individual cell biological steps, may be understood to be globally regulated by molecular events coordinated at a master control mechanism within the G1 phase of the cell cycle. For reasons to be described, this master control mechanism could readily operate to determine structural modifications in neocortex introduced with the origin of new species. Low-level modulations in the operation of this same control mechanism may also determine the lower order structural variations of the neocortex that distinguish individuals of a species. However, other mechanisms and cellular events occuring further downstream in the histogenetic sequence will be suggested as additional determinants of individual variation with species.

## The pseudostratified ventricular epithelium: Architecture and elementary operation

Neurons arise at locations that are remote from their final destinations. They arise from the pseudostratified ventricular epithelium (PVE), a specialized proliferative epithelium that lines the ventricular cavities of the embryonic telencephalic pallium (figures 1.2 and 1.4; Boulder Committee, 1970; His, 1889; Sauer, 1935, 1936). The PVE is pseudostratified, a feature that determines two complex features of its operation that are common to all proliferative pseudostratified epithelia. First, its cells, attached at the ventricular margin, vary systematically in their form with progression through the cell cycle (figures 1.2 and 1.5; Sauer, 1936, 1937; Takahashi, Nowakowski, and Caviness, 1995). M phase occurs with the cell in rounded configuration at the ventricular margin. The cell elongates through G1 phase and enters S phase in maximally elongate configuration with its nucleus in the outer half of the epithelium. It shortens again with progression during G2 (Hayes and Nowakowski, 1999). Second, proliferative activity is asynchronous. This quality has the critical implication, to which we return later, that proportionate representation of the sequential phases of the cell cycle will correspond to the duration of that phase as a fraction of the duration of the total cell cycle, $T_C$ (Nowakowski, Lewin, and Miller, 1989).

There are two systematic operational properties of the neocortical PVE that are critical to the integrated operation of this epithelium. First, neurons arise sequentially from any given region of the epithelium more or less in an inside-out order with respect to their ultimate position in the cortex (Bisconte and Marty, 1975a,b; Caviness and Sidman, 1973; Fernandez and Bravo, 1974; Hicks and D'Amato, 1968; Luskin and Shatz, 1985; Rakic, 1974; Takahashi et al., 1999b). That is, the neurons of neocortical layer VI are the first to arise while neurons of successively overlying layers arise

## Cortical Layer

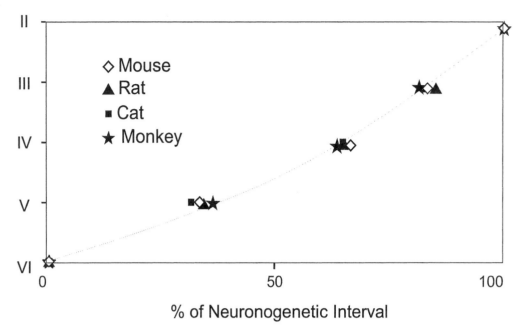

% of Neuronogenetic Interval

FIGURE 1.3  Scaling of neuronogenetic process across species. The time of production of neurons for each layer of the neocortex is compared in four different species—mouse, rat, cat, and monkey—as a function of the percentage of the neuronogenetic interval in each species that has elapsed at the time that the cortical layer is produced.

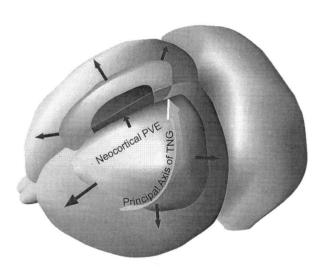

FIGURE 1.4  Embryonic brain with the PVE drawn in perspective. The proliferative process, initiated at the far rostrolateral margin of the PVE, propagates along the principal (rostrolateral to caudomedial) axis of the TNG (curved wide arrow). The neighborhood relationships of proliferative cells within the PVE generally determine the neighborhood relationships of their postmigratory progeny within the cortex (arrows projecting from the PVE to the hemispheric surface).

more or less in order. We refer to this origin of class by sequence as the *neuronogenetic sequence* (figure 1.2). Second, the proliferative process does not proceed synchronously across the epithelium, but rather is initiated at the far rostrolateral margin of the PVE where the neocortical PVE is continuous with that of the ganglionic eminence (figure 1.4; Bisconte and Marty, 1975b; Caviness and Sidman, 1973; Fernandez and Bravo, 1974; Hicks and D'Amato, 1968; McSherry, 1984; McSherry and Smart, 1986; Miyama et al., 1997; Rakic, 1974; Smart and McSherry, 1982; Smart and Smart, 1982). Neuronogenesis, once initiated, propagates from rostrolateral to caudomedial PVE. As a consequence, at any time during neuronogenesis, the progression of the neuronogenetic sequence will be spatially graded across the PVE, an operational aspect of the proliferative process in the PVE referred to as the *transverse neurogenetic gradient* or TNG (Bayer and Altman, 1991).

Once a young neuron exits the proliferative cycle, it must migrate across the developing hemispheric wall to the emerging cortex, a journey of thousands of microns in large mammals (Rakic, 1972; Sidman and Rakic, 1973). Upon arrival, each neuron is further sorted as appropriate to its class into the emerging layers VI–II/

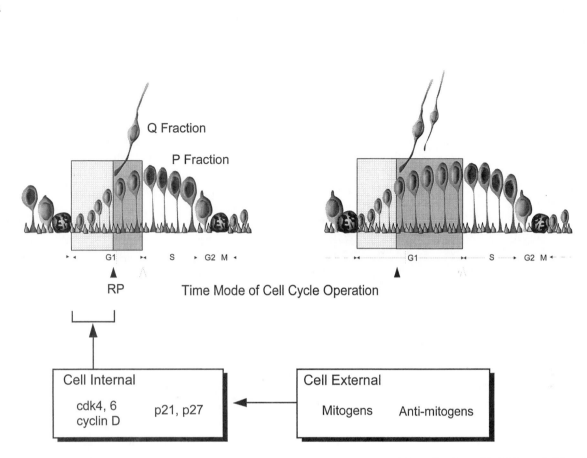

FIGURE 1.5  Time and output modes of operation of the cell cycle of the PVE. The shape of cells of the PVE correlates with phase of the cell cycle. Cells undergo mitosis (M) in a rounded configuration at the ventricular margin. Postmitotic cells in G1 phase progressively elongate as the nucleus ascends to initiate S phase in the outer half of the PVE. As cells move through G2 phases, they shorten and the nucleus descends to undergo mitosis. The proliferative cell passes through two regulatory transitions in G1 phase, the restriction point (RP, filled arrowheads) and the G1/S phase transition (open arrowheads). The decision to leave the cycle as Q fraction or to remain as P fraction corresponds to whether the cell passes RP. Such a decision will be determined by the relative balance of facilitatory (cdk4 and 6, cyclin D) and inhibitory (p27 and p21) cell-internal molecules; this balance is modulated by cell-external factors (mitogens, antimitogens). The pre-RP interval of G1 (horizontal bracket), which is fixed in duration, is thought to be the only phase of the cell cycle where the behavior of proliferative cells of the PVE may be modified by such cell-external agents. The post-RP interval is variable, increasing with successive cell cycles as the determinant of the increase in the length of G1 phase ($T_{G1}$) over the NI. $Q$ increases concurrently with $T_{G1}$. The increases in the post-RP interval and $Q$ with progression of neuronogenesis are represented in left and right panels.

III of the neocortex (Takahashi et al., 1996, 1999b). It is significant that the neighborhood relationships of the proliferative population generally determine the neighborhood relationships of the postmigratory population within the cortex (figure 1.4), and this appears to be a particularly stringent rule for the cells destined for layers V and VI (Kornack and Rakic, 1995; Misson et al., 1991; Walsh and Cepko, 1992a,b, 1993). This observation is only one component of the body of evidence suggesting that a protomap of the neocortical architectonic map is in some way represented within the developmentally primitive PVE in the course of the proliferative process (Miyama et al., 1997; Rakic, 1988).

In summary, the advance of the neuronogenetic sequence within all regions of the PVE is ordered temporally according to the TNG and spatially by the topographic organization of the PVE. This integrated operation is the principle through which the two-dimensional (rostrocaudal and mediolateral) structure of the PVE is "translated" upon what becomes the laminate—i.e., three-dimensional—structure of the neocortex. Our investigations, conducted in the mouse, have revealed that integration of these operational domains of the PVE is regulated by two parameters and that this regulation is tightly constrained. We will approach the evidence for these assertions from the vantage of a larger discussion of the proliferative operation of the epithelium.

## Neuronogenesis: An algorithm based upon experiments in mouse

EQUATIONS The cell cycle of histogenetic systems operates in two modes. The first mode is the time mode with reference to the duration of the cell cycle ($T_C$) and the durations of its successive G1, S, G2, and M ($T_{G1}$, $T_S$, $T_{G2+M}$) phases (figures 1.5 and 1.6). The second is the output mode with reference to the fraction ($Q$) of postmitotic cells that exits, as opposed to the fraction ($P$) that returns to S phase: $P + Q = 1.0$ (figures 1.2 and 1.5).

Neurons of the neocortex arise from a founder population through a discrete neuronogenetic interval, corresponding to a sequence of integer cell cycles (Caviness, Takahashi, and Nowakowski, 1999a). That is, a neuron precursor cannot execute a partial cycle (figure 1.2; Takahashi, Nowakowski, and Caviness, 1995). The equation for calculation of the size of the PVE derived from a PVE founder cell population with unit size of 1 over the course of $n$ cell cycles ($PVE_n$) is

$$PVE_n = P_1 \prod_{i=2}^{n} 2P_i \qquad (1.1)$$

where $P_i$ is the $P$ fraction at cell cycle $i$ ($2 \leq i \leq 11$ in mouse) (Caviness, Takahashi, and Nowakowski, 2000; Takahashi, Nowakowski, and Caviness, 1996). With each passing cell cycle of the neuronogenetic interval, the size of the PVE ($PVE_n$) increases when $P > 0.5$ and decreases when $P < 0.5$.

The number of neurons formed during each cycle will be equal to twice the size of the PVE at that cell cycle (each cell will have two daughter cells) times $Q$ or

$$OUT_n = 2PVE_n \times Q_n \qquad (1.2)$$

where $OUT_n$ is the output of the PVE at any given cell cycle $n$, $PVE_n$ is the size of the PVE at that cell cycle (as given in equation 1.1) and $Q_n$ is $Q$ for that cell cycle (Caviness, Takahashi, and Nowakowski, 2000; Takahashi, Nowakowski, and Caviness, 1996).

Over the entire neuronogenetic interval the total neuron production ($OUT_{TOTAL}$) corresponds to the sum of neurons produced with each cycle; or, as derived from equation 1.2:

$$OUT_{TOTAL} = Q_1 + \sum_{n=2}^{TOTAL} 2PVE_{n=1} * Q_n \qquad (1.3)$$

where TOTAL is the total number of cell cycles that constitute the neuronogenetic interval in a given species (Caviness, Takahashi, and Nowakowski, 2000; Takahashi, Nowakowski, and Caviness, 1996). $Q$ reaches 1.0 at the completion of the final cycle; that is, the entire set of cells corresponding to 2PVE of the final cycle will exit the VZ as the terminal output of the proliferative process (figure 1.2).

PARAMETERS The parameters that satisfy these equations are the numbers of cell cycles that constitute the neuronogenetic interval and $Q$ and $P$ for each cycle. These parameters, derived in mouse through experiments based upon patterns of labeling with the S phase marker bromodeoxyuridine (BUdR) or BUdR and tritiated thymidine (Takahashi, Nowakowski, and Caviness, 1992, 1995), have been found to be identical in widely separated regions of the PVE, suggesting that the neuronogenetic algorithm applies generally to the epithelium. Independently of location in the PVE, the neuronogenetic interval is 6 days in duration and $T_C$ increases from just over 8 h to approximately 20 h (figure 1.6A) with variation no greater than $\pm 5$–7% in any small area of the PVE at any time (Cai, Hayes, and Nowakowski, 1997). From the pattern of advance of $T_C$ with each day, we calculate that 11 cell cycles can be executed during the 6-day neuronogenetic interval. There is no systematic change in $T_{G2+M}$ or $T_S$ (figure 1.6A). That is, the doubling of $T_C$ reflects a near quadrupling of $T_{G1}$. In other words, G1 phase is the only phase of the cycle whose duration is regulated in the course of murine neocortical neuronogenesis. The increment in $Q$ per cycle is found to be low at first. The "pivot point" of the system where the number of postmitotic cells leaving the cycle is the same as the number returning to S phase ($P = Q = 0.5$) is achieved only during the eighth cycle (figure 1.6B). This corresponds to a point nearly 75% of the way through the full set of 11 cycles. The continued advance of the two parameters, $Q$ to 1.0 and $P$ to 0, is much more rapid over the terminal three cycles.

NEURON PRODUCTION As a correlate of the slow initial rise of $Q$, the initial rate of neuron production per cycle is low and the PVE increases approximately 50-fold in volume over the initial 8 cycles (figure 1.6C) with only a 2-fold increase in its height (Caviness, Takahashi, and Nowakowski, 2000; Takahashi, Nowakowski, and Caviness, 1996). Thus, the PVE must increase approximately 25 times in area (i.e., approximately 5-fold in each of its two tangential dimensions) between the beginning of the neuronogenetic interval (i.e., $CC_1$) and $CC_8$. With respect to a founder cell present at the outset of

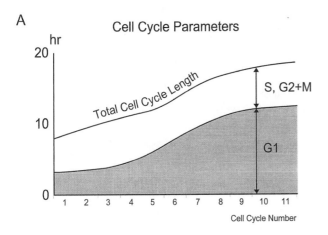

**A**

**Cell Cycle Parameters**

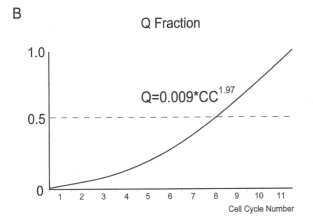

**B**

**Q Fraction**

$$Q=0.009*CC^{1.97}$$

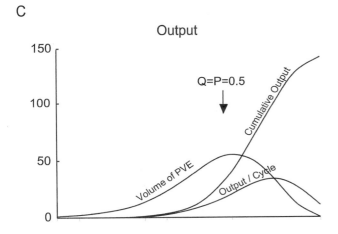

**C**

**Output**

$Q=P=0.5$

FIGURE 1.6 Parameters for cell cycle and neuron production in the PVE. (**A**) The advance in cell cycle length (ordinate) as a function of cycle (abscissa) is attributable entirely to a near quadrupling of the duration of the G1 phase. (**B**) The progression of $Q$ as a function of cell cycle is expressed as $Q = 0.009 \times CC^{1.97}$ in mouse. Note that the "pivot point" where the number of postmitotic cells leaving the cycle is the same as the number returning to S phase ($P = Q = 0.5$, broken line) is achieved only during the eighth cycle. (**C**) The volume of the PVE increases approximately 50-fold over the initial eight cycles, i.e., until the pivot point ($Q = P = 0.5$) is reached (arrow). The rate of neuron production per cycle (Output/Cycle) is initially low but rises steadily after the pivot point is passed. The multiplier effect of the proliferative process in mouse is such that the lineage arising from the average founder cell, i.e., a single cell proliferating in the PVE at the outset of the NI, will generate a cumulative progeny (Cumulative Output) of approximately 140 cells.

methods, cell death is not entered as a parameter into our equations. These estimates of neuron production based upon parameters measured experimentally in the murine neocortical PVE accord well with numbers that have been based on direct counts (Caviness, Takahashi, and Nowakowski, 2000; Rhee et al., 1998; Tan et al., 1998; Vaccarino et al., 1999).

*Two domains of neuronogenetic operation*

In the foregoing sections we introduced the cellular structure of the PVE and its modes of operation and provided the parameters that determine its proliferative behavior. Within this detail we discern two coordinate domains of regulation, each with its separate and distinct regulatory principles (Caviness, Takahashi, and Nowakowski, 1999b). Locally there is the *output domain*, which encompasses the parameters that determine neuronal output from a founder population as the neuronogenetic sequence is enacted in a given region. Globally there is the *temporospatial domain*, which encompasses those parameters governing the pace at which the neuronogenetic sequence advances down the TNG.

OUTPUT DOMAIN Neuronal output from a founder population is the expression of an iterative sequence through which the ascent of $Q$ determines the output for each respective cycle. Total output is the sum of the output for the set of cycles. That is, only two parameters, the number of cell cycles and the ascent of $Q$ with each cycle, determine the output of the proliferative process from a founder population. Time, *sensu strictu*, is not directly a parameter governing output (Caviness, Takahashi, and Nowakowski, 1995; Takahashi, Nowakowski, and Caviness, 1996) because output per cycle is deter-

the 11 cell cycle neuronogenetic period, the average total cumulative output (OUT$_{TOTAL}$) is approximately 140 cells (from equation 1.3). Of these, approximately 30% are formed through the first 7 cycles, but 70% are formed at $CC_8$ and afterwards, i.e., after $Q$ has become greater than 0.5 (figure 1.6C). Because the rate of cell death in the PVE, as estimated by reliable methods (Thomaidou et al., 1997), is less than 1% per cell cycle and within the standard error of our experimental

mined by the number of mitoses that occur, taken together with $Q$, and not the number of hours between mitoses.

The proliferative sequence is initiated from a population that is proliferating exponentially, i.e., $Q = 0$ and $P = 1$ (figure 1.2) (Caviness, Takahashi, and Nowakowski, 2000; Rakic, 1988). It terminates when $Q$ reaches 1 and $P$ becomes 0, and hence no cells re-enter the proliferative populations. In the course of the intervening interval, the progeny of the founder population will execute a mean number of integer cycles corresponding to the number of cycles required for $Q$ to traverse its obligatory path from $Q = 0$ to $Q = 1.0$ (Takahashi, Nowakowski, and Caviness, 1996). We have seen that the ascent of $Q$ with each cycle is nonlinear such that the relationship between $Q$ and cell cycle at any moment has the form

$$Q = k\text{CC}^{1.97} \qquad (1.4)$$

where $k$ is a constant corresponding to the proportionate advance of $Q$ with each cycle (Caviness, Takahashi, and Nowakowski, 2000; Takahashi, Nowakowski, and Caviness, 1996, 1997, 1999). The constant, which is dimensionless, has a value of approximately 0.009 in the mouse.

Read abstractly, this formulation states a best-fit relationship between the progression of $Q$ and cell cycle. However, when we consider the biology represented by $Q$ more closely, we realize that this formulation carries a substantially deeper significance. That is, the number of cycles that constitute the neuronogenetic sequence is determined by those molecular biological mechanisms that determine the probability at each successive cycle that postmitotic daughter cells will exit the proliferative process. In other words, the number of cycles is set by the molecular mechanism that regulates the output mode of the proliferative process.

TEMPOROSPATIAL DOMAIN  Whereas the output domain is governed by parameters that are without time dimension, global coordination of the neuronogenetic sequence across the expanse of the PVE is strictly regulated in terms of temporospatial order (figure 1.7; Caviness, Takahashi, and Nowakowski, 2000; Miyama et al., 1997). Specifically, the initiation of the neuronogenetic sequence, as it occurs with respect to the principal axis of the TNG (rostrolateral to caudomedial), is strictly regulated in time. Regulation is monotonic, we suggest, under the control of the parameter $T_C$. Temporospatial constraints are imposed by the operating properties of the pseudostratified proliferative epithelium in which cells proliferate asynchronously. Thus, in all regions of the PVE there will be cells in all phases of the cell cycle

(Sauer, 1936; Sauer and Walker, 1959; Takahashi, Nowakowski, and Caviness, 1995), and the proportional representation of cells by phase will correspond to the duration of that phase as a fraction of $T_C$.

Consider the initial temporospatial progression of $Q$ from 0 at the beginning of $\text{CC}_1$ (figure 1.7). $\text{CC}_1$ is initiated in G1 progeny of the founder cycle (designated as $\text{CC}_0$) at origin of the TNG in the rostrolateral PVE (Caviness, Takahashi, and Nowakowski, 2000). We will refer to the narrow region of the PVE where cells now operate in $\text{CC}_1$ as the $\text{CC}_1$ domain. The leading edge (LE) of this domain will advance spatially along the principal axis of the TNG at an hourly rate corresponding to the rate that cells along the LE exit $\text{CC}_0$ ($1/T_{\text{C}-\text{CC}0}$). After a time equal to $T_{\text{C}-\text{CC}1}$ has elapsed, a second LE for $\text{CC}_2$ will leave the rostrolateral edge of the PVE, and $\text{CC}_2$ cells will become intermixed with $\text{CC}_1$ cells; thereafter, a new LE will be formed for each successive CC. However, because the time between each LE lengthens as each $T_C$ lengthens, the distance between successive LE will increase. The result of this process is a wave-like sequence of progression of LEs across the PVE (figure 1.7). Between each LE are the cells of two successive CCs; thus each CC is found between the LE of both the preceding and the succeeding LE. At any given time during the neuronogenetic interval there is an overlapping mosaic pattern of CC domains where the borders of each CC domain are continuously shifting. The number of CC domains active across the PVE at any given time has not been determined experimentally; but based on the lengthening of $T_C$, we have elsewhere estimated that this number is approximately 5 at the time early in development when the LE of the $\text{CC}_1$ domain has traveled the full extent of the principal axis and when $T_C$ is short (Caviness, Takahashi, and Nowakowski, 2000). At the termination of the neuronogenetic interval when $T_C$ is maximal, we have estimated that there are only about 1.2 CC domains present at the time that trailing edge (TE) of $\text{CC}_{11}$ leaves the rostrocaudal origin of the TNG.

We have elsewhere suggested that the wave-like propagation of the CC domains across the surface of the PVE provides a plausible positional encoding mechanism by which PVE cells "know" where they are in the TNG (Caviness, Takahashi, and Nowakowski, 1999a; Miyama et al., 1997). This positional coding could provide boundary imposition for cytoarchitectural landmarks, provided that there is a synchronizing signal coupled to the wave action. Specifically, mapping information appears to reside in neurons of layers VI and V (De Carlos and O'Leary, 1992; Erzurumlu and Jhaveri, 1992; Molnar and Blakemore, 1995); and, we suggest, mapping

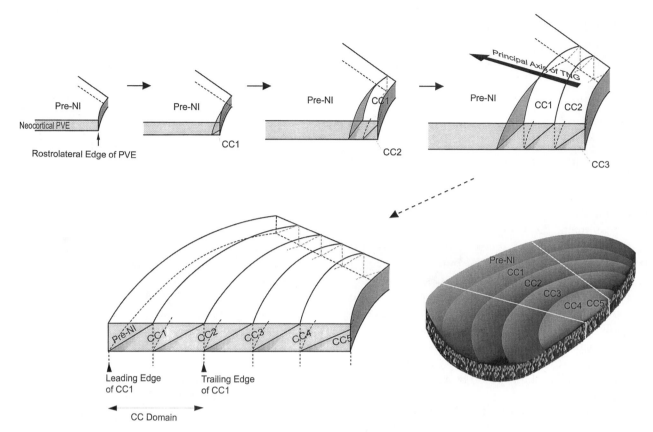

FIGURE 1.7 Temporospatial domain of neuronogenetic operation. The cell cycle domains ($CC_1$, $CC_2$, and so on) propagate across the neocortical PVE along the principal axis of the transverse neurogenetic gradient (TNG, a thick arrow on the "surface" of the PVE, upper panel) as neuronogenesis proceeds (from left to right in the upper panel, horizontal arrows, continuing to the lower panel, a broken arrow). Approximately 40 h after the onset of neuronogenesis (the lower panel), cycle domains are distributed in descending order, $CC_5$–$CC_1$, along the principal axis of the TNG, represented schematically in a wedge cutaway on the left and with respect to the full PVE surface on the right. The leading edge of a given domain corresponds to the trailing edge of the cycle that is two cycles ahead. Thus, in this diagram each domain has the form of a parallelogram, reflecting the idea that at any point there will be cells representative of two cell cycles. The size of a given domain is the distance between the leading edge and trailing edge, and the height is proportional to the relative prevalence of the cells of that CC. The size of a given domain increases with increasing cell cycle length.

information is encoded as they arise with cycles 1–7. We envision the following operating properties of such a mechanism. At any given time there are multiple CC domains spanning the TNG in overlapping fashion (figure 1.7). The critical mechanism complementary to domain propagation, we suggest, would be an encoding signal that emanates from origin as each LE passes through the origin and then is propagated rapidly (i.e., traveling across the PVE in a time much less than a single cell cycle) down the TNG. One possible mechanism for the propagation of synchronizing signal is via gap junctions between cells of the PVE (Bittman et al., 1997). The borders of a "mapping unit" encoded by a given CC domain could correspond to its LE and trailing edge (TE) where they abut the TE and LE of domains of $CC_{N-2}$ and $CC_{N+2}$, respectively (figure 1.7).

Alternatively, they might modulate the encoding process within the territory of overlap. The process would be repeated as each TE leaves the origin so that successive waves of parcellation would lead to an increasingly atomized mosaic of map units within the PVE. We suggest that this mechanism of parcellation would extend the relatively coarse-grained parcellation implicit in the domains of distribution of transcription factors, already instantiated in the PVE by the outset of the neuronogenetic interval (Puelles and Rubenstein, 1993; Shimamura et al., 1995). To the extent that such a mechanism might serve to "translate" a CC domain into an architectonic area, there will be linkage between the temporospatial domain (the set of $T_C$s plus the TNG) and the cytoarchitectonic subdivisions of the mature neocortex. Such specification of a unit of the protomap would also be closely coordinated with the same molecular events governing the numbers, and perhaps also the classes, of neurons that will populate the laminae of the corresponding region of the neocortex.

## A master integrator

The two domains of proliferative process, i.e., the output and temporospatial domains, are coordinated subroutines within the overall complexity of the proliferative activity of the PVE. As we have discussed, each is regulated in its dynamic progression by a single elementary proliferative parameter. In the case of the output domain, the main parameter is $k$ (hence $Q$), which determines for a specified founder population both the number of cells that become neurons and the expansion size of the cortex. In the case of the temporospatial domain, it is the kinetic parameter $T_C$ that determines the pace of advance of the CC domains across the PVE. $T_C$, in turn, advances systematically with cycle as $T_{G1}$ is regulated. In the following discussion, we propose that both the output and temporospatial domains are coordinated and integrated by a shared integrative mechanism.

The G1 restriction point (figure 1.5; Caviness, Takahashi, and Nowakowski, 1999a; Pardee, 1989) is an obvious candidate for the "master" integrative mechanism from its functions, which are well established in general cell biology. "Restriction point" is a short-hand designation for a sequence of molecular actions involving multiple molecular agents (Coats et al., 1996; Pardee, 1989; Zetterberg, Larsson, and Wiman, 1995). These molecular actions determine whether a cell in G1 phase will leave the cycle or advance to the G1/S transition (figure 1.5; Roberts et al., 1994; Sherr, 1993; Sherr and Roberts, 1995). Thus, from the perspective of a large population of daughter cells entering G1 phase of a given cell cycle, $P$ corresponds to the probability that the cell will pass the restriction point for that cycle, reenter S, then divide again. $Q$ for that cycle corresponds, therefore, to the probability that the cell will not pass the restriction point but instead will leave the PVE and migrate to the cortical plate (figure 1.5). The restriction point is of further interest to mechanisms regulating $Q$ in that its operation is modulated by cell external influences that are known to modulate $Q$ and also to modulate other domains of proliferative behavior.

Whether or not a cell passes the restriction point will be determined by the relative balance of facilitatory and inhibitory actions acting at the restriction point (figure 1.5; Massague and Polyak, 1995; Roberts et al., 1994; Sherr, 1993, 1994). One set of molecular operators that acts to drive the cell through the restriction point is represented by the cyclin-dependent kinases cdk4 and 6 and their regulatory subunit cyclin D (Massague and Polyak, 1995; Roberts et al., 1994; Sherr, 1993, 1994). A second set that works in opposition to the kinases, blocking passage through the restriction point and thereby forcing the cell to leave the cycle, are the inhibitors represented by p27 and p21 (Massague and Polyak, 1995; Sherr and Roberts, 1995). This balance at the restriction checkpoint is modulated by a heterogeneous array of cell external factors that are both positive (physiologic mitogens) and negative (physiologic antimitogens) with respect to restriction point passage. In nonneural cell lines maintained in vitro, the actions of physiologic mitogens include the upregulation of the expression and activity of the elements of Cdk4/6–cyclin D complexes and the downregulation of the actions of the inhibitors (Koff et al., 1993; Massague and Polyak, 1995; Roberts et al., 1994; Sherr and Roberts, 1995). The physiologic antimitogens acting in G1 phase are opposite in effect (Koff et al., 1993; Massague and Polyak, 1995; Roberts et al., 1994; Sherr and Roberts, 1995). A principal consequence of a cell passing the restriction point is activation of master transcription factors, in particular E2F (Follette and O'Farrell, 1997; Lees and Harlow, 1995; Sherr, 1994), which apparently promotes the passage through the G1/S transition. It remains to future investigations to consider whether other consequences of this transcriptional activity are those fundamental to histogenetic specification.

Mechanisms that regulate $T_{G1}$ are less completely explored. Nevertheless, the restriction point remains the plausible control point in that experimentally induced variations in $Q$ are closely coordinate with variations in $T_{G1}$. For example, overexpression of cyclin E in diploid fibroblasts not only drives $Q$ to near 0 (and $P$ toward 1), but also coordinately decreases $T_{G1}$ (Ohtsubo and Roberts, 1993; Ohtsubo et al., 1995). We are not aware of complementary studies that have considered whether upward pressure on $Q$ is associated with a corresponding increase in $T_{G1}$. Nor has it been clarified in terms of molecular mechanisms how the G1 phase becomes shortened in the models mentioned previously.

Thus, an extensive body of investigation in nonneural cells establishes the restriction point as an integrative mechanism general to proliferative vertebrate cells. Limited observations now relate more specifically to the restriction point in the proliferative cells that form the neocortical PVE. Thus, check points, which arrest the cycle of the PVE, operate adaptively within both the G2 and G1 phases according to patterns consistent with other proliferative vertebrate cells (Takahashi et al., 1999a). The principal regulatory operators, including cdk2, its regulatory subunit cyclin E (indispensable to the G1/S transition), and the cycle progression inhibitors p27 and p21 (known to operate at the restriction point of vertebrate cells), also have established activity in the PVE (Fero et al., 1996; Kiyokawa et al., 1996; Lee et al., 1996; Nakayama et al., 1996; Tsai et al., 1993). Moreover, the patterns of expression of these operators across the neuronogenetic interval are closely in accord with what would be predicted from the progression of the proliferative process itself (Delalle et al., 1999). Specifically, in the course of the early cycles when $Q$ is low and $T_{G1}$ is short, levels of cyclin E expression are maximum and those of p27 are minimum. Subsequently, as the pivot point is approached where $Q = P = 0.5$, the expression of cyclin E plummets to low asymptote while that of p27 surges to its peak levels of expression, declining only modestly thereafter as the epithelium involutes and the neuronogenetic interval ends. In addition, when dissociated cells of the PVE are cultured with the mitogen FGF, not only is $Q$ driven downward toward 0, but also $T_{G1}$ is shortened to what is essentially its minimal duration observed in the earliest cycles in vivo (Cavanagh et al., 1997). The coordinate nature of these progressions of cycle parameters, $Q$, $P$, and $T_{G1}$, and the molecular mechanisms of cycle regulation open a window upon the fundamental workings of the neuronogenetic algorithm that has been formulated here.

Thus far, in attempting to formulate a neuronogenetic algorithm our emphasis has been upon neuronal output, how it is regulated within region and throughout all regions of the PVE. Another set of critical mechanisms of histogenesis comprises those of specification, specification of cell class, and regional specification (Caviness, Takahashi, and Nowakowski, 2000). That is, cells are produced by class in appropriate numbers; cells are assigned by class to the separate neocortical fields in appropriate numbers. In that a fuller consideration of proliferative mechanisms fundamental to histogenetic specification would strain the intended scope of this review, we will limit this discussion to the suggestion that the restriction point may serve an even more elaborate master control mechanism than we have thus far postulated. That is, those mechanisms determinant of cell number may at the restriction point become coordinate with those of class and regional specification. By "coordinate" we intend that regulatory mechanisms are interlocking. Their interlocking activities may be scaled upward or downward (nonproportionately) or uniformly (proportionately) scaled. The argument for coordinate regulation is in part circumstantial in that the events of specification of both class and region are not only in effect within the proliferative epithelium but also that cell numeration is precisely coordinated with these events of specification (Caviness, Takahashi, and Nowakowski, 2000).

## Structural variation and the neuronogenetic algorithm

As described in our introduction, differences between species are characterized by variations in the surface area of the neocortex as well as in the hierarchic complexities of systems organization reflected in the neocortical map and its systems of connections. Within species, by contrast, there is constancy of overall neocortical magnitude and in the topology of the systems map, where interindividual variation is expressed regionally in terms of the size and configuration of individual gyri and in the areal extent of individual cytoarchitectonic fields. In the following sections, we suggest that the global structural variations attendant upon speciation reflect the consequences of parameter changes driving the regulatory controls of the neuronogenetic algorithm. These may be large in scale and potentially saltatory in their appearance in support of speciation. We suggest that the regionally limited, low-amplitude structural variations that distinguish individuals of a species may reflect modulatory influences acting upon these regulatory controls or, alternatively, influences that modulate the course of later-occurring intracortical events. It is our intent to propose a set of hypothetical strategic principles offered by this framework; it should be evident that these principles do not constitute a comprehensive system of origin of neocortical structural variation.

THE NEURONOGENETIC ALGORITHM AND STRUCTURAL DIFFERENCES ACROSS SPECIES In principle, species-specific changes in cortical structure could be produced by changes at any of the control points of the neuronogenetic algorithm. Here we emphasize how two important features of neocortical organization, magnitude, and cytoarchitectonic subdivisions, could be affected by variation of controls governing output and temporospatial domains, respectively.

Variations in overall neocortical magnitude are readily programmed within the context of the output domain of the neuronogenetic algorithm (figure 1.8). The focal point for such control of neocortical magnitude is encapsulated by the constant $k$ (equation 1.4) which, we have noted, is 0.009 in mouse. If $k$ is made smaller than 0.009, more cell cycles would be required to traverse the pathway from $Q = 0$ to $Q = 1$. The consequence of this change would be a cortex larger than that of mouse, with more neurons as specified by the changes in $Q$ and the number of cell cycles (using equa-

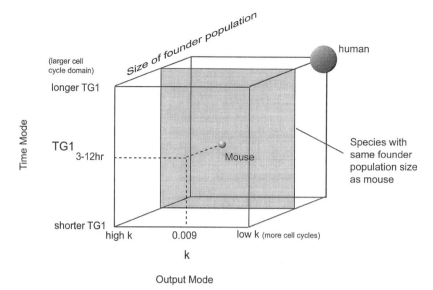

FIGURE 1.8 Neuronogenetic determinants of structural variation of neocortex. Variations in the three cardinal features of neocortical structure—size, number of mapping units, and neuronal class—are specified by variations in three developmental determinants. These are the preneuronogenetic or pre-NI events (the starting size of the PVE at the outset of neuronogenesis: "Size of founder population," $y$-axis), the output ($k$: $x$-axis), and time (length of G1 phase: $T_{G1}$, $z$-axis) modes of operation of the cell cycle. The coordinate operation of these three determinants is integrated and illustrated here as the three orthogonal axes of a cube. Each axis is orthogonal to the other two because, we suggest, the three determinants are regulated independently, but adult phenotypes are produced by an interaction of two of these three determinants. For example, the number of neurons formed, and hence the actual size of the neocortex, is influenced interactively by the output mode and the pre-NI events. The mouse neocortex occupies the center of the cube with a "moderate-sized" neocortex; the human neocortex is at one extreme corner of the cube. Variation in founder cell number is established pre-NI. Variation in the output mode arises from changes in the constant $k$, which determines the relationship between $Q$ and cell cycle number (equation 1.4). In mouse $k$ is 0.009; neuron number will vary upward or downward from that of mouse with lower or higher $k$ (more or fewer cycles during the neuronogenetic interval). The time mode is measured as variation in $T_C$ but regulated by the post-restriction point length of G1. Values for mouse $T_C$ range from about 10 to 20 h, and the size and number of mapping units will be dependent upon variation in $T_C$ (represented in the time mode) interacting with the size of the founder population (figures 1.7 and 1.9). An increasing range of specification of neuronal subclasses will correlate with increasing duration of G1 phase, related, we suggest, to an increasing range of post-restriction point transcriptional activity secondary to the release of master transcription factors including E2F. The force of any of the three determinants will reflect a balance of cell internal and cell external (e.g., mitogens, antimitogens) influences (see the text and the legend to figure 1.5).

tions 1.1, 1.2, and 1.3). An increase in $k$ greater than 0.009 would, via the same logic, produce a cortex smaller than that of mouse. These changes in size would apply to the entire neocortex and do so uniformly. This is because the number of neurons produced from equivalent founder populations will be identical as the neuronogenetic sequence is enacted sequentially along the TNG and under the regulation of $Q$.

Thus, a single change in $k$, induced at the G1 restriction point, could produce the step changes in neocortical magnitude that are necessary for speciation. This is illustrated by the consequences of knockout of the p27 gene in mice, which results in an animal that is some 30–40% larger than animals with the wild-type gene. The enlargement in this animal is a more-or-less uniformly scaled increase in body size and in (most)

internal organs, including the brain. It is pertinent to the argument that the enlargement occurs as a consequence of increase in cell number (Fero et al., 1996; Kiyokawa et al., 1996; Nakayama et al., 1996). As far as is known, p27 operates only within the cell cycle at the restriction point, and the inference from the knockout is that the "computation" governed by p27 is to determine the gating of probability that cells will pass the G1 restriction point. Importantly, the p27-governed computation can be only partially rate-limiting; otherwise, p27 knockout animals would be infinitely large. Other cycle progression inhibitors acting at the restriction point, for example p21, must complement the action of p27. These may include inhibitors that act globally, such as p27, but also others which are strictly regional in their jurisdictions. Note that the actions of either restriction point promoters or inhibitors on the mechanisms that set $k$ would, in principle, modify equation 1.4 and thereby regulate the output domain. In this way differential action mediated by a family of inhibitors might provide for uniform or nonuniform differential scaling of body and brain size, or even of neocortical and non-neocortical brain structures such as those characteristic of species diversity (Finlay and Darlington, 1995; Holloway, 1974, 1979; Jerison, 1979; Stephan, Bauchot, and Andy, 1970).

Species differences also involve variation in the size of corresponding architectonic representations that are components of the separate sensory and motor systems in the neocortex. Such variations would be expected to arise from variations in the temporospatial pace of movement of the CC domains across the principal axis of the TNG. Thus, an upward shift in $T_C$ would enlarge while a downward shift would reduce the size of corresponding map representations (figure 1.9). These changes in the time domain will interact with the num-

ber of founder cells, which sets the starting size of the TNG. If the founder cell population is unchanged, then TNG is a constant size and a change in $T_C$ would change the number of mapping units without an effect upon neuronal number. But if, for example, founder cell number is increased, producing an increased TNG, and this change occurs coordinately with an increase $T_C$, then both neuron number and the numbers of cortical areas would increase while the number of architectonic fields would not increase. Such a mechanism might underlie mapping differences that distinguish the neocortex across the range of large and small rodents, say, mouse to rat to beaver (Killackey, Rhoades, and Bennett-Clarke, 1995; Krubitzer, 1995; Northcutt and Kaas, 1995; Welker, 1990).

Variations in map unit size, dependent upon $T_C$-induced variations in the pace of progression of CC domains, would complement species characteristic variations in the preneuronogenetic size of the neocortical PVE. Thus, the number of CC domains to be

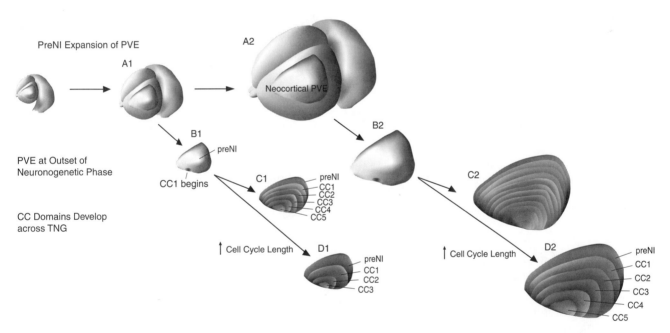

FIGURE 1.9  Schema correlating variation in the growth of the PVE and progression of cell cycle domains. Depending upon the number of cycles antedating the onset of neuronogenesis, the PVE might enlarge moderately (A1) or greatly (A2) prior to the onset of neuronogenesis (pre-NI expansion of PVE). Once neuronogenesis is initiated (B1, B2) in the far rostrolateral region of the PVE with cell cycle 1 ("$CC_1$ begins"), the PVE will become partitioned into cell cycle domains (C1, C2, D1, D2). In mouse (C1) it is estimated that five cycle domains will be established before the domain of $CC_1$ invades and replaces completely the last vestige of the preneuronogenetic PVE at the caudomedial extremity of the PVE (see also figure 1.7). In the specific instances where cell cycle length is longer

(D1, D2), the PVE would be partitioned into a smaller number of CC domains. With greater pre-NI expansion of the PVE (A2) giving rise to a larger PVE (B2), the same cell cycle length as that in mouse would result in more CC domains (C2). With greater pre-NI expansion but with longer cell cycle length the PVE would be larger PVE but partitioned in the same number of CC domains (D2). (The theoretical consequences of other possible patterns of variation in $T_C$, i.e., shorter cell cycle length, and preneuronogenetic size of PVE are not illustrated.) Mechanisms postulated here might lead to an increased number of mapping units or, alternatively, assure a common mapping pattern across the range of small to large rodents, for example, from mouse to beaver.

instantiated simultaneously in the PVE by a series of cell cycles of identical $T_C$ will vary directly with the length of the preneuronogenetic TNG. Moreover, it is conceivable that these two determinants, i.e., the progression of $T_C$ with cell cycle and the expanse of neocortical PVE (the length of the principal axis of TNG), might vary independently, providing for a great range of variation in numbers of map representations or in the sizes of corresponding representations across a range of species such as rat, cat, monkey, and man (figure 1.9; Killackey, Rhoades, and Bennett-Clarke, 1995; Krubitzer, 1995; Northcutt and Kaas, 1995).

THE NEURONOGENETIC ALGORITHM AND STRUCTURAL DIFFERENCES WITHIN SPECIES   The regional diversity of neocortical structure that distinguishes individuals of a species is expressed, for the most part, in terms of low-amplitude variation in the size of architectonic representations or gyral size and conformation projected upon a map of invariant topology. That is, each member of the species will have the identical set of map representations, but corresponding map representations will vary in the size of their surface projections and to some extent will do so independently of variations in the projection of other mapping units. Such variation can be produced by modulation of the neuronogenetic algorithm via coordinate local variation of both the pace of ascent of $Q$ and $T_C$ with cell cycle (figure 1.8). Thus, local expansion (contraction) of a "map unit," reflecting a local decrease (or increase) in $k$, must be matched with a corresponding increase (reduction) in $T_C$ so that the boundaries of mapping units are adjusted coordinately with the variation in their size.

## Postproliferative regulation of structural variation

As neurons are produced in the PVE, they migrate to the cortical plate where they begin an additional set of developmental events that culminates in their assembly into functional systems. Chief among these postproliferative events are synaptogenesis and cell death, which are the principal histogenetic cellular processes of the intracortical phase of neocortical histogenesis. It is to be anticipated that the workings of synaptogenesis and cell death determine the contributions to structural variation of this phase of neocortical histogenesis. In primates, synaptogenesis proceeds more or less at the same pace and through the same interval in all cerebral regions in a way that does not suggest a strictly regulated and systematic global ordering of the sort seen with neuronogenesis (Bourgeois, Goldman-Rakic, and Rakic, 1994; Bourgeois and Rakic, 1993; Granger et al.,

1995; Rakic, Bourgeois, and Goldman-Rakic, 1994). In the mouse, cell death also proceeds monotonically and uniformly in widely separated neocortical fields. The pattern of progression of cell death is fully dissociated from both neuronogenetic sequence and the temporospatial pattern of progression of CC domains down the principal axis of the TNG (Verney et al., 1999). That is, the pace of histogenetic process within the cortex marches to the beat of its own drummer, not to the pace set by neuronogenesis. Moreover, the amplitudes of the intracortical histogenetic processes are not only idiosyncratic with respect to cortical region, and even layer within region, but also are of relatively low amplitude, modulating population numbers by cell death, for example, by some 15–35% at most (Ferrar et al., 1990, 1992; Finlay and Pallas, 1989; Finlay and Slattery, 1983; Spreafico et al., 1995; Thomaidou et al., 1997; Verney et al., 1999). Such patterns of modulation, of variable expression in different species and in special systems, are generally appropriate to the character and magnitude of variations that distinguish the structure of neocortex among individuals. It should be recognized, further, that the post-proliferative regulatory events occur in an early time frame of life, which would favor exposure to adaptive influences imposed by experience.

## Recapitulation and synthesis

Our most general hypothesis, then, is that those mechanisms acting to produce the saltatory changes associated with speciation are not essentially different with respect to the algorithmic control points that modulate adaptive distinctions among individuals of species (see also Nijhout, 1999). For the former, potentially large in scale and expressed in terms of variations in both magnitude and topology of mapping, we look to the globally coherent, uniformly regulated mechanisms that support the neuronogenetic algorithm. Within this framework, we suggest, revisions of computations driven by just two elementary proliferative parameters—one from the output domain and one from the temporospatial domain—would readily scale the ranges of magnitudes and topologies presented by comparative study. Such revisions could act over several orders of magnitude to build the neocortical areas associated with small (e.g., mouse) and large (e.g., human) species (Caviness, Takahashi, and Nowakowski, 1995). Speculatively, one might imagine that speciation could occur in these processes via the introduction of major differences (e.g., timing, binding constants, tissue-specific expression) for the expression of molecular actions crucial for controlling events occurring at the "master integrator" associated with the G1 restriction checkpoint.

For variations that distinguish the neocortex of individuals within a species, typically regionally discrete and of relatively low amplitude, we also consider a low-amplitude modulation of the same control points of the neuronal algorithm. Here, however, we anticipate that a second source of structural distinctions respecting the neocortex of individuals within species are traceable to variations in the course of intracortical histogenetic events, synaptogenesis and cell death. Whereas no parameter-driven formulation yet characterizes these late intracortical histogenetic processes, it is clear that they operate coordinately with the adaptive process of systems matching and coordinately with large-scale systems assembly as the organism optimizes its neural apparatus to the specific offerings of situation. In keeping with this perspective, it has been found that variance of neocortical volumes is determined virtually on a gyrus-by-gyrus basis, principally by a nonlinear interaction of individual and gyrus (Kennedy et al., 1998). This general insight is consistent with other investigations, in which it was established that the neocortical volumes of gyri serving specific operations are enlarged when these functions are overlearned from early childhood (Amunts et al., 1997). By implication, the cortical phase of neocortical histogenesis is geared to serve those mechanisms by which the specific experience of the organism "builds the brain" as an adaptive response to this experience as it is acquired (Van der Loos et al., 1978).

ACKNOWLEDGMENTS Supported by NIH grants NS12005 and NS33433, NASA grant NAG2–750 and a grant from Pharmacia-Upjohn Fund for Growth and Development Research. T.T. was supported by a fellowship of The Medical Foundation, Inc., Charles A. King Trust, Boston, Massachusetts.

## REFERENCES

ANDREWS, T., S. HALPERN, and D. PURVES, 1997. Correlated size variations in human visual cortex, lateral geniculate nucleus, and optic tract. *J. Neurosci.* 17:2859–2868.

AMUNTS, K., G. SCHLAUG, L. JAENCKE, H. STEINMETZ, A. SCHLEICHER, A. DABRINGHAUS, and K. ZILLES, 1997. Motor cortex and hand motor skills: Structural compliance in the human brain. *Hum. Brain Map* 5:206–215.

BAYER, S. A., and J. ALTMAN, 1991. *Neocortical Development.* New York: Raven Press.

BISCONTE, J.-C., and R. MARTY, 1975a. Analyse chronoarchitectonique du cerveau de rat par radioautographie. I. Histogenese du telencephale. *J. Hirnforsch.* 16:55–74.

BISCONTE, J.-C., and R. MARTY, 1975b. Etude quantitative du marquage radioautographique dans le systeme nerveux du rat. II. Caracteristiques finales dans le cerveau de l'animal adulte. *Exp. Brain Res.* 22:37–56.

BITTMAN, K., D. OWENS, A. KRIEGSTEIN, and J. LoTURCO, 1997. Cell coupling and uncoupling in the ventricular zone of developing neocortex. *J. Neurosci.* 17:7037–7044.

BOULDER COMMITTEE, 1970. Embryonic vertebrate nervous system: Revised terminology. *Anat. Rec.* 166:257–262.

BOURGEOIS, J.-P., P. S. GOLDMAN-RAKIC, and P. RAKIC, 1994. Synaptogenesis in the prefrontal cortex of rhesus monkeys. *Cereb. Cortex* 4:78–96.

BOURGEOIS, J.-P., P. J. JASTREBOFF, and P. RAKIC, 1989. Synaptogenesis in visual cortex of normal and preterm monkeys: Evidence for intrinsic regulation of synaptic overproduction. *Proc. Natl. Acad. Sci. (USA)* 86:4297–4301.

BOURGEOIS, J.-P., and P. RAKIC, 1993. Changes of synaptic density in the primary visual cortex of the macaque monkey from fetal to adult stage. *J. Neurosci.* 13:2801–2860.

BRODMANN, K., 1909. *Vergleichende Lokalisationslehre der Grosshirnrinde.* Leipzig: Barth.

CAI, L., N. HAYES, and R. S. NOWAKOWSKI, 1997. Local homogeneity of cell cycle length in developing mouse cortex. *J. Neurosci.* 17:2079–2087.

CAJAL, S. RAMON Y., 1952. *Histologie du Systeme Nerveux de l'Homme e des Vertebres.* Madrid: Consejo Superior de Investigaciones Cientificas.

CAVANAGH, J., M. MIONE, I. PAPPAS, and J. PARNAVELAS, 1997. Basic fibroblast growth factor prolongs the proliferation of rat cortical progenitor cells in vitro without altering their cell cycle parameters. *Cereb. Cortex* 7:293–302.

CAVINESS, V. S., JR., 1975. Architectonic map of neocortex of the normal mouse. *J. Comp. Neurol.* 164:247–263.

CAVINESS, V. S., JR., and R. L. SIDMAN, 1973. Time of origin of corresponding cell classes in the cerebral cortex of normal and reeler mutant mice: An autoradiographic analysis. *J. Comp. Neurol.* 148:141–152.

CAVINESS, V. S., JR., T. TAKAHASHI, and R. S. NOWAKOWSKI, 1995. Numbers, time and neocortical neuronogenesis: A general developmental and evolutionary model. *Trends Neurosci.* 18:379–383.

CAVINESS, V. S., JR., T. TAKAHASHI, and R. S. NOWAKOWSKI, 1999a. The G1 restriction point as critical regulator of neocortical neuronogenesis. *J. Neurochem. Res.* 24:497–506.

CAVINESS, V. S., JR., T. TAKAHASHI, and R. S. NOWAKOWSKI, 1999b. Neocortical neuronogenesis: The G1 restriction point as master integrative mechanism. In *The Newborn Brain—Scientific Basis and Clinical Application,* H. Lagercrantz and M. Hanson, eds. Cambridge: Cambridge University Press (in press).

CAVINESS, V. S., JR., T. TAKAHASHI, and R. S. NOWAKOWSKI, 2000. Neuronogenesis and the early events of neocortical histogenesis. In *Development of the Neocortex,* A. Goffinet, and P. Rakic, eds. Berlin: Springer Verlag, pp. 107–143.

COATS, S., W. M. FLANAGAN, J. NOURSE, and J. M. ROBERTS, 1996. Requirement of p27$^{Kip1}$ for restriction point control of fibroblast cell cycle. *Science* 272:877–880.

DE CARLOS, J. A., and D. M. O'LEARY, 1992. Growth and targeting of subplate axons and establishment of major cortical pathways. *J. Neurosci.* 12:1194–1211.

DELALLE, I., T. TAKAHASHI, R. S. NOWAKOWSKI, L.-H. TSAI, and V. S. CAVINESS, JR., 1999. Cyclin E–p27 opposition and regulation of the G1 phase of the cell cycle in the murine neocortical PVE: A quantitative analysis of mRNA in situ hybridization. *Cereb. Cortex* 9:824–832.

ERZURUMLU, R. S., and S. JHAVERI, 1992. Emergence of connectivity in the embryonic rat parietal cortex. *Cereb. Cortex* 2:336–352.

FERNANDEZ, V., and H. BRAVO, 1974. Autoradiographic study of the cerebral cortex in the rabbit. *Brain Behav. Evol.* 9:317–332.

FERO, M., M. RIVKIN, M. TASCH, P. PORTER, C. CAROW, E. FIRPO, K. POLYAK, L.-H. TSAI, V. BROUDY, R. PERLMUTTER, K. KAUSHANSKY, and J. ROBERTS, 1996. A syndrome of multiorgan hyperplasia with features of gigantism, tumorigenesis, and female sterility in p27$^{Kip1}$-deficient mice. *Cell* 85:733–744.

FERRAR, I., E. BERNET, E. SORIANO, T. DEL RIO, and M. FONSECA, 1990. Naturally occurring cell death in the cerebral cortex of the rat and removal of dead cells of transitory phagocytes. *Neuroscience* 39:451–458.

FERRAR, I., E. SORIANO, J. A. DEL RIO, S. ALCANTARA, and C. AULADELL, 1992. Cell death and removal in the cerebral cortex during development. *Prog. Neurobiol.* 39:1–43.

FINLAY, B. L., and R. B. DARLINGTON, 1995. Linked regularities in the development and evolution of mammalian brains. *Science* 268:1578–1584.

FINLAY, B. L., and S. L. PALLAS, 1989. Control of cell number in the developing mammalian visual system. *Prog. Neurobiol.* 32:207–234.

FINLAY, B. L., and M. SLATTERY, 1983. Local differences in the amount of early cell death in neocortex predict adult local specializations. *Science* 219:1349–1351.

FOLLETTE, P., and P. O'FARRELL, 1997. Connecting cell behavior to patterning: Lessons from the cell cycle. *Cell* 88:309–314.

GERHART, J., and M. KIRSCHNER, 1997. *Cell, Embryos, and Evolution.* London: Blackwell Science.

GRANGER, B., F. TEKAIA, A. LE SOURD, P. RAKIC, and J.-P. BOURGEOIS, 1995. Tempo of neurogenesis and synaptogenesis in the primate cingulate mesocortex: Comparison with the neocortex. *J. Comp. Neurol.* 360:363–376.

HAHN, M., C. JENSEN, and B. DUDEK, 1979. Introduction: Toward understanding the brain-behavior relationship. In *Development and Evolution of Brain Size*, M. Hahn, C. Jensen, and B. Dudek, eds. New York: Academic Press, pp. 2–7.

HAUG, H., 1987. Brain sizes, surfaces, and neuronal sizes of the cortex cerebri: A stereological investigation of man and his variability and a comparison with some mammals (primates, whales, marsupials, insectivores, and one elephant). *Am. J. Anat.* 180:126–142.

HAYES, N., and R. NOWAKOWSKI, 2000. Exploiting the dynamics of S-phase tracers in developing brain: Interkinetic nuclear migration for cells entering vs leaving the S-phase. *Dev. Neurosci.* 22:44–55.

HICKS, S. P., and C. J. D'AMATO, 1968. Cell migration to the isocortex in the rat. *Anat. Rec.* 160:619–634.

HIS, W., 1889. Die Neuroblasten und deren Entstehung im embryonalen Mark. *Abh. Math. Phys. Cl., Kgl. Saechs. Ges. Wiss.* 15:313–372.

HOLLOWAY, R., 1974. On the meaning of brain size. *Science* 184:677–679.

HOLLOWAY, R., 1979. Brain size, allometry, and reorganization: Toward a synthesis. In *Development and Evolution of Brain Size*, M. Hahn, C. Jensen, and B. Dudek, eds. New York: Academic Press, pp. 61–88.

JERISON, H., ed., 1973. *The Evolution of the Brain and Intelligence.* New York: Academic Press.

JERISON, H., 1979. The evolution of diversity in brain size. In *Development and Evolution of Brain Size*, M. Hahn, C. Jensen, and B. Dudek, eds. New York: Academic Press, pp. 30–57.

JERISON, H., 1982. Allometry, brain size, cortical surface, and convolutedness. In *Primate Brain Evolution: Methods and Concepts*, E. Armstrong and D. Falk, eds. New York: Plenum Press, pp. 77–84.

JERISON, H., 1987. Brain size. In *Encyclopedia of Neuroscience*, G. Adelman, ed. Boston: Birkhauser, pp. 168–170.

KENNEDY, D., N. LANGE, N. MAKRIS, J. BATES, and V. S. CAVINESS, JR., 1998. Gyri of the human neocortex: An MRI-based analysis of volumes and variance. *Cereb. Cortex* 8:372–385.

KILLACKEY, H. P., R. W. RHOADES, and C. A. BENNETT-CLARKE, 1995. The formation of a cortical somatotopic map. *Trends Neurosci.* 18:402–407.

KIYOKAWA, H., R. KINEMAN, K. MANOVA-TODORAVA, V. SOARES, E. HOFFMAN, M. ONO, D. KHANAM, A. HAYDAY, L. FROHMAN, and A. KOFF, 1996. Enhanced growth of mice lacking the cyclin-dependent kinase inhibitor function of p27$^{Kip1}$. *Cell* 85:721–732.

KOFF, A., M. OHTSUKI, K. POLYAK, J. M. ROBERTS, and J. MASSAGUE, 1993. Negative regulation of G1 progression in mammalian cells; inhibition of cyclin E-dependent kinase by TGF-β. *Science* 260:536–539.

KORNACK, D. R., and P. RAKIC, 1995. Radial and horizontal deployment of clonally related cells in the primate neocortex: Relationship to distinct mitotic lineages. *Neuron* 15:311–321.

KRUBITZER, L., 1995. The organization of neocortex in mammals: Are species differences really so different? *Trends Neurosci.* 18:408–417.

LAVDAS, A., M. C. MIONE, and J. G. PARNAVELAS, 1996. Neuronal clones in the cerebral cortex show morphological and neurotransmitter heterogeneity during development. *Cereb. Cortex* 6:490–497.

LEE, M.-H., M. NIKOLIC, C. BAPTISTA, E. LAI, L.-H. TSAI, and J. MASSAGUE, 1996. The brain-specific activator p35 allows Cdk5 to escape inhibition by p27$^{Kip1}$ in neurons. *Proc. Natl. Acad. Sci. (USA)* 93:3259–3263.

LEES, E., and E. HARLOW, 1995. Cell cycle progression and cell growth in mammalian cells: Kinetic aspects of transition events. In *Cell Cycle Control*, C. Hutchison and D. Glover, eds. Oxford: Oxford University Press, pp. 228–263.

LORENTE DE NO, R., 1938. Cerebral cortex: Architecture, intracortical connections, motor projections. In *Physiology of the Nervous System*, J. F. Fulton, ed. London: Oxford University Press, pp. 274–313.

LUSKIN, M. B., and C. J. SHATZ, 1985. Neurogenesis of the cat's primary visual cortex. *J. Comp. Neurol.* 242:611–631.

MANGER, P., M. SUM, M. SZYMANSKI, S. RIDGWAY, and L. KRUBITZER, 1998. Modular subdivisions of dolphin insular cortex: Does evolutionary history repeat itself? *J. Cogn. Neurosci.* 10:153–166.

MASSAGUE, J., and K. POLYAK, 1995. Mammalian antiproliferative signals and their targets. *Curr. Opin. Gen. Dev.* 5:91–96.

McSHERRY, G. M., 1984. Mapping of cortical histogenesis in the ferret. *J. Embryol. Exp. Morph.* 81:239–252.

McSHERRY, G. M., and I. H. M. SMART, 1986. Cell production gradients in the developing ferret isocortex. *J. Anat.* 1–14.

MESULAM, M.-M., 1998. From sensation to cognition. *Brain* 121:1013–1052.

MISSON, J.-P., C. AUSTIN, T. TAKAHASHI, C. CEPKO, and V. S. CAVINESS, JR., 1991. The alignment of migrating neural cells in relation to the murine neopallial radial glial fiber system. *Cereb. Cortex* 1:221–229.

MIYAMA, S., T. TAKAHASHI, R. S. NOWAKOWSKI, and V. S. CAVINESS, JR., 1997. A gradient in the duration of the G1 phase in the murine neocortical proliferative epithelium. *Cereb. Cortex* 7:678–689.

MOLNAR, Z., and C. BLAKEMORE, 1995. How do thalamic axons find their way to the cortex? *Trends Neurosci.* 18:389–397.

MORGANE, P., I. GLEZER, and M. JACOBS, 1988. Visual cortex of the dolphin: An image analysis study. *J. Comp. Neurol.* 273:3–25.

MURRAY, A., and T. HUNT, 1993. *The Cell Cycle.* New York: W. H. Freeman.

NAKAYAMA, K., N. ISHIDA, M. SHIRANE, A. INOMATA, T. INOUE, N. SHISHIDO, I. HORII, D. LOH, and K.-I. NAKAYAMA, 1996. Mice lacking p27$^{Kip1}$ display increased body size, multiple organ hyperplasia, retinal dysplasia, and pituitary tumors. *Cell* 85:707–720.

NIJHOUT, H., 1999. When developmental pathways diverge. *Proc. Natl. Acad. Sci. (USA)* 96:5348–5350.

NORTHCUTT, R. G., and J. H. KAAS, 1995. The emergence and evolution of mammalian neocortex. *Trends Neurosci.* 18:373–379.

NOWAKOWSKI, R. S., S. B. LEWIN, and M. W. MILLER, 1989. Bromodeoxyuridine immunohistochemical determination of the lengths of the cell cycle and the DNA-synthetic phase for an anatomically defined population. *J. Neurocytol.* 18:311–318.

OHTSUBO, M., and J. M. ROBERTS, 1993. Cyclin-dependent regulation of G1 in mammalian fibroblasts. *Science* 259:1908–1912.

OHTSUBO, M., A. M. THEODORAS, J. SCHUMACHER, J. M. ROBERTS, and M. PAGANO, 1995. Human cyclin E, a nuclear protein essential to the G1-to-S phase transition. *Mol. Cell. Biol.* 15:2612–2624.

ONO, M., S. JUBIK, and C. D. ABERNATHY, 1990. *Atlas of the Cerebral Sulci.* New York: Thieme Verlag.

PARDEE, A. B., 1989. G1 events and regulation of cell proliferation. *Science* 246:603–608.

PETERS, A., and E. G. JONES, 1984. *Classification of Cortical Neurons.* New York: Plenum Press.

PUELLES, L., and J. RUBENSTEIN, 1993. Expression patterns of homeobox and other putative regulatory genes in the embryonic mouse forebrain suggest a neuromeric organization. *Trends Neurosci.* 16:472–479.

RADEMACHER, J., V. S. CAVINESS, JR., H. STEINMETZ, and A. M. GALABURDA, 1993. Topographical variation of the human primary cortices: Implications for neuroimaging, brain mapping and neurobiology. *Cereb. Cortex* 3:313–329.

RAKIC, P., 1972. Mode of cell migration to the superficial layers of fetal monkey neocortex. *J. Comp. Neurol.* 145:61–84.

RAKIC, P., 1974. Neurons in rhesus monkey visual cortex: Systematic relation between time of origin and eventual disposition. *Science* 183:425–427.

RAKIC, P., 1988. Specification of cerebral cortical areas. *Science* 241:170–176.

RAKIC, P., 1995. Corticogenesis in human and nonhuman primates. In *The Cognitive Neurosciences*, M. S. Gazzaniga, ed. Cambridge, Mass.: MIT Press, pp. 127–145.

RAKIC, P., J.-P. BOURGEOIS, and P. S. GOLDMAN-RAKIC, 1994. Synaptic development of the cerebral cortex: Implications for learning, memory and mental illness. In *The Self-Organizing Brain: From Growth Cones to Functional Networks*, J.

van Pelt, M. A. Corner, H. B. M. Uylings, and F. H. Lopes da Silva, eds. Amsterdam: Elsevier, pp. 227–243.

RHEE, J., R. RABALLO, M. SCHWARTZ, and F. VACCARINO, 1998. Lineage and non-lineage specific effects of fibroblast growth factor (FGF2) on progenitor cells in the developing cerebral cortex. *Soc. Neurosci. Abst.* 24:281.

ROBERTS, J., A. KOFF, K. POLYAK, E. FIRPO, S. COLLINS, M. OHTSUBO, and J. MASSAGUE, 1994. Cyclins, cdks and cyclin kinase inhibitors. *Cold Spring Harbor Symp. Quant. Biol.* 59:31–38.

SAUER, F. C., 1935. Mitosis in the neural tube. *J. Comp. Neurol.* 62:377–405.

SAUER, F. C., 1936. The interkinetic migration of embryonic epithelial nuclei. *J. Morphol.* 60:1–11.

SAUER, F. C., 1937. Some factors in the morphogenesis of vertebrate embryonic epithelia. *J. Morphol.* 61:563–579.

SAUER, M. E., and B. E. WALKER, 1959. Radioautographic study of interkinetic nuclear migration in the neural tube. *Proc. Soc. Ext. Biol. (NY)* 101:557–560.

SCHMIDT-NIELSEN, K., 1984. *Scaling: Why Is Animal Size So Important?* Cambridge: Cambridge University Press.

SHERR, C. J., 1993. Mammalian G1 cyclins. *Cell* 73:1059–1065.

SHERR, C. J., 1994. G1 phase progression: Cycling on cue. *Cell* 79:551–555.

SHERR, C. J., and J. M. ROBERTS, 1995. Inhibitors of mammalian G1 cyclin-dependent kinases. *Genes Dev.* 9:1149–1163.

SHIMAMURA, K., D. HARTIGAN, S. MARTINEZ, L. PUELLES, and J. RUBENSTEIN, 1995. Longitudinal organization of the anterior neural plate and neural tube. *Development* 121:3923–3933.

SIDMAN, R. L., and P. RAKIC, 1973. Neuronal migration, with special reference to developing human brain: A review. *Brain Res.* 62:1–35.

SIDMAN, R. L., and P. RAKIC, 1982. Development of the human central nervous system. In *Histology and Histopathology of the Nervous System*, W. Haymaker and R. D. Adams, eds. Springfield: Charles C Thomas, pp. 3–145.

SMART, I. H. M., and G. M. McSHERRY, 1982. Growth patterns in the lateral wall of the mouse telencephalon. II. Histological changes during and subsequent to the period of isocortical neuron production. *J. Anat.* 131:415–442.

SMART, I. H. M., and M. SMART, 1982. Growth patterns in the lateral wall of the mouse telencephalon. I. Autoradiographic studies of the histogenesis of the iso-cortex and adjacent areas. *J. Anat.* 134:273–298.

SPREAFICO, R., C. FRASSONI, P. ARCELLI, M. SELVAGGIO, and S. DE BIASI, 1995. In situ labeling of apoptotic cell death in the cerebral cortex and thalamus of rats during development. *J. Comp. Neurol.* 363:281–295.

STENSAAS, S. S., D. K. EDDINGTON, and W. H. DOBELLE, 1974. The topography and variability of the primary visual cortex in man. *J. Neurosurg.* 40:747–755.

STEPHAN, H., R. BAUCHOT, and O. ANDY, 1970. Data on the size of the brain and its various brain parts in insectivores and primates. In *The Primate Brain*, C. Noback and W. Montagna, eds. New York: Appleton-Century-Crofts, pp. 289–297.

TAKAHASHI, T., P. BHIDE, T. GOTO, S. MIYAMA, and V. S. CAVINESS, JR., 1999a. Proliferative behavior of the murine cerebral wall in tissue culture: Cell cycle kinetics and checkpoints. *Exp. Neurol.* 156:407–417.

TAKAHASHI, T., T. GOTO, S. MIYAMA, R. S. NOWAKOWSKI, and V. S. CAVINESS, JR., 1999b. Sequence of neuron origin and neocortical laminar fate: Relation to cell cycle of origin in the developing murine cerebral wall. *J. Neurosci.* 19:10357–10371.

Takahashi, T., T. Goto, S. Miyama, R. S. Nowakowski, and V. S. Caviness, Jr., 1996. Intracortical distribution of a cohort of cells arising in the PVE. *Soc. Neurosci. Abst.* 22:284.

Takahashi, T., R. S. Nowakowski, and V. S. Caviness, Jr., 1992. BUdR as an S-phase marker for quantitative studies of cytokinetic behaviour in the murine cerebral ventricular zone. *J. Neurocytol.* 21:185–197.

Takahashi, T., R. S. Nowakowski, and V. S. Caviness, Jr., 1995. The cell cycle of the pseudostratified ventricular epithelium of the murine cerebral wall. *J. Neurosci.* 15:6046–6057.

Takahashi, T., R. S. Nowakowski, and V. S. Caviness, Jr., 1996. The leaving or Q fraction of the murine cerebral proliferative epithelium: A general computational model of neocortical neuronogenesis. *J. Neurosci.* 16:6183–6196.

Takahashi, T., R. S. Nowakowski, and V. S. Caviness, Jr., 1997. The mathematics of neocortical neuronogenesis. *Dev. Neurosci.* 19:17–22.

Takahashi, T., R. S. Nowakowski, and V. S. Caviness, 1999. Cell cycle as operational unit of neocortical neuronogenesis. *Neuroscientist* 5:155–163.

Tan, S.-S., M. Kalloniatis, K. Sturm, P. Tam, and B. Reese, 1998. Separate progenitors for radial and tangential cell dispersion during development of the cerebral cortex. *Neuron* 21:295–304.

Thomaidou, D., M. Mione, J. Cavanagh, and J. Parnavelas, 1997. Apoptosis and its relation to the cell cycle in the developing cerebral cortex. *J. Neurosci.* 17:1075–1085.

Tsai, L.-H., T. Takahashi, V. S. Caviness, Jr., and E. Harlow, 1993. Activity and expression pattern of cyclin-dependent kinase 5 in the embryonic mouse nervous system. *Development* 119:1029–1040.

Vaccarino, F., M. Schwartz, R. Raballo, J. Nilsen, J. Rhee, M. Zhou, T. Doetschman, J. Coffin, J. Wyland, and E. Yu-Ting, 1999. Changes in the size of the cerebral cortex are governed by fibroblast growth factor during embryogenesis. *Nat. Neurosci.* 2:246–253.

Van der Loos H., and J. Dorfl, 1978. Does the skin tell the somatosensory cortex how to construct a map of the periphery? *Neurosci. Lett.* 7:23–30.

Van Essen, D. C., W. T. Newsome, and H. R. Maunsell, 1984. The visual field representation in striate cortex of the macaque monkey: Asymmetries, anisotropies, and individual variability. *Vision Res.* 24:429–448.

Van Essen, D. C., W. T. Newsome, J. H. R. Maunsell, and J. L. Bixby, 1986. The projections from striate cortex (V1) to areas V2 and V3 in the macaque monkey: Asymmetries, areal boundaries, and patchy condensations. *J. Comp. Neurol.* 244:451–480.

Verney, C., T. Takahashi, P. G. Bhide, R. S. Nowakowski, and V. S. Caviness, Jr., 1999. Independent controls for neocortical neuron production and histogenetic cell death. *Dev. Neurosci.* 22:125–138.

Walsh, C., and C. Cepko, 1992a. Generation of widespread cerebral cortical clones. *Soc. Neurosci. Abst.* 18:925.

Walsh, C., and C. Cepko, 1992b. Widespread dispersion of neuronal clones across functional regions of the cerebral cortex. *Science* 255:434–440.

Walsh, C., and C. Cepko, 1993. Clonal dispersion in proliferative layers of developing cerebral cortex. *Nature* 362:632–635.

Welker, W., 1990. Why does cerebral cortex fissure and fold? A review of determinants of gyri and sulci. In *Cerebral Cortex: Comparative Structure and Evolution of Cerebral Cortex, Part II*, E. Jones and A. Peters, eds. New York: Plenum Press, pp. 3–136.

Woolsey, T. A., and H. van der Loos, 1970. The structural organization of layer IV in the somatosensory region (SI) of mouse cerebral cortex. *Brain Res.* 17:205–242.

Zetterberg, A., O. Larsson, and K. Wiman, 1995. What is the restriction point? *Curr. Opin. Cell. Biol.* 7:835–842.

Zilles, K., 1990. Cortex. In *The Human Nervous System*, G. Paxinos, ed. New York: Academic Press, pp. 757–802.

Zilles, K., E. Armstrong, A. Schleicher, and H.-J. Kretschmann, 1988. The human pattern of gyrification in the cerebral cortex. *Anat. Embryol.* 179:173–179.

# 2 Synaptogenesis in the Neocortex of the Newborn: The Ultimate Frontier for Individuation?

J.-P. BOURGEOIS

ABSTRACT  We have identified five distinct phases of synaptogenesis in the cerebral cortex of primates from conception to death. The first two phases, with a low density of synapses, occur during early embryonic life. They are followed by a third phase of very rapid accumulation of synapses around birth. During the fourth phase the density of synapses is maintained at a very high level from the early postnatal period through puberty. This is followed by a true loss of synapses during puberty. The fifth phase begins after sexual maturity and extends into old age. It is characterized by a slow decline in the density of synapses. Experimental observations indicate that the early phases of synaptogenesis are robust neurodevelopmental processes determined by mechanisms intrinsic and common to the whole cortical mantle. The various postnatal phases coincide with final adjustments of many aspects of synaptoarchitectony, depending on normal functional inputs. They overlap with critical periods for diverse cortical functions until puberty. Inside each of these phases, distinct classes of synapses appear in successive waves of synaptogenesis, providing the first examples of a long list of discrete synaptogenetic events we are just beginning to explore.

The development of the neocortex in mammals is a highly orchestrated cascade of histological events including, successively, the generation and differentiation of neurons (Rakic, 1995), the navigation and organization of the axonal projections between ensembles of neurons (Barone et al., 1995), then the formation and maturation of the synaptic contacts that constitute the major final steps of corticogenesis (Bourgeois, Goldman-Rakic, and Rakic, 1994, 2000; Bourgeois and Rakic, 1993; de Felipe et al., 1997; Huttenlocher and Dabholkar, 1997). All these biological events ultimately lead to individuation, the process by which individual mammals become differentiated in their societies.

As reviewed by Zoli and colleagues (1998), intercellular communications in the neocortex can occur either via volume transmission or by wiring transmission. This chapter describes the development of the wiring transmission via synaptic contacts.

J.-P. BOURGEOIS  Laboratoire de Recepteurs et Cognition, Département des Biotechnologies, Institut Pasteur, Paris, France.

The formation of synaptic contacts can be described at two distinct levels. On the one hand, one can describe the assembly of the numerous molecular components building up the pre- and postsynaptic domains of the neuron. On the other hand, one can describe the development of ensembles of synaptic contacts in the cortical neuropil. Putting these two aspects of synaptogenesis in parallel is not trivial because the synaptic contact constitutes a crucial point of articulation between the cellular properties of the single cortical neuron and the neurophysiological functions associated with large ensembles of these cortical neurons, which are under distinct categories of constraints:

1. The constraints related to the multiple intracellular mechanisms control the type, amount, and distribution of presynaptic active zones, as well as postsynaptic densities differentiated on the cell surface of a cortical neuron. Are these constraints all under strict genetic control?

2. The constraints related to intercellular mechanisms are linked to the neurophysiological functions of large ensembles of these cortical neurons and control the development of the topological distribution of the synaptic contacts in the neuropil. Are these constraints all under strict epigenetic control?

The interactions between genetically defined factors and experientially modifying factors are crucial in the development and morphofunctional maturation of the neocortex, in which synaptogenesis is a key event. Knowing the exact timing of synaptogenesis in the cascade of histological events will provide a neuroanatomical basis for the experimental identification of these interactions through the time course of development and maturation. The description of formation of ensembles of synaptic contacts is currently less explored than the description of the mechanisms of assembling of synaptic macromolecules. We tried to re-equilibrate this. The neocortex of the rhesus monkey provides an excellent animal model for the analysis of the developing synaptoarchitectony, plasticity, and physiology of the human neocortex (Teller, 1997). Using quantitative electron microscopy, we first delineated the kinetics of synaptogenesis in several cortical areas of macaque monkeys from conception to death (Bourgeois, Goldman-Rakic, and Rakic, 1994, 2000; Bourgeois and Rakic, 1993).

## Kinetics of synaptogenesis

In the primary visual cortex of the macaque five different phases were identified (figure 2.1):

*Phase 1* is a very early synaptogenesis at low density of synapses, occurring first in the primordial plexiform layer (Marin-Padilla, 1988), then in the marginal zone (MZ, or prospective layer I) and in the subplate (SP), but not in the cortical plate (CP). These synapses are formed by axons of subcortical origin penetrating horizontally within the neuroepithelium (horizontal arrows in figure 2.1). This phase of synaptogenesis begins about 40–60 days after conception (DAC) and coincides with the onset of neurogenesis (Rakic, 1995).

*Phase 2* is an early synaptogenesis at low density of synapses, now within the cortical plate itself, occurring at midgestation between 70 and 100 days after conception, i.e., during the peak of neurogenesis and migration of neuroblasts. These synapses appear first in the infragranular layers, then progressively in the more superficial cortical layers of the CP following the vertical penetration of axonal projections (vertical arrow in figure 2.1) from cortical and subcortical origins (Bourgeois, Goldman-Rakic, and Rakic, 1994). All these "early" synaptic contacts are formed on the dendritic shafts of the neurons (figure 2.2A,B).

*Phase 3* is a phase of very rapid accumulation of synapses. This phase begins 2 months before birth (~100 days after conception) and initially proceeds in the absence of patterned stimulation from the external world. The maximal density of synapses is reached about 2 months after birth. We have shown that the onset of phase 3 is not necessarily linked to the end of neurogenesis (Granger et al., 1995). The most rapid part of phase 3 occurs around birth (in macaque, delivery occurs 165 days after conception), when 40,000 new synapses are formed every second in each striate cortex of the macaque (Rakic, Bourgeois, and Goldman-Rakic, 1994), mainly on the dendritic spines (figure 2.2A,B). This rapid accumulation of synapses coincides with the growth of the dendritic and axonal arbors. However, the onset of phase 3 of synaptogenesis may either precede, as in the primary visual cortex (Bourgeois and Rakic, 1993), or follow, as in the prefrontal cortex (Bourgeois, Goldman-Rakic, and Rakic, 1994), the segregation of the cortical columns.

*Phase 4* is a plateau phase during which the mean density of synapses remains at a very high level, ~600–900 million synapses per cubic millimeter of neuropil (Bourgeois and Rakic, 1993), throughout infancy and adolescence until puberty (in macaque, puberty occurs 3 years after birth).

*Phase 5* is a slow, steady decline in density of synapses from puberty throughout adulthood, resulting mainly from the loss of synapses located on dendritic spines. This decline coincides with another crucial and lengthy phase in the late maturation of cortical functions. Finally, a drop in density of synapses is observed during senescence before death (figure 2.1; Peters, Sethares, and Moss, 1998).

Our observation of these five distinct phases has been confirmed by studies done on macaque using either

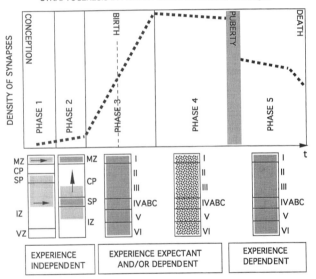

FIGURE 2.1   Changes in the relative density of synapses (discontinuous line in the upper frame) as a function of days after conception expressed on a log scale on the abscissae (*t*) in the primary visual cortex of macaque monkey during normal development. Five different phases of synaptogenesis are identified between conception and death. Each phase is superimposed above the density distribution of synapses in the cortical layers of the neocortex represented in vertical frames in the middle part of the figure. During phase 1 synapses appear first in the marginal zone (MZ), subplate (SP), and intermediate zone (IZ). During phase 2, synapses now appear also in the cortical plate (CP) with a gradient of density represented by a vertical arrow. Roman numerals indicate cortical layers. The proposed effects of experience on cortical development and maturation are represented in horizontal frames in the lower part. (Reproduced from Bourgeois, 1997, with permission from Scandinavian University Press.)

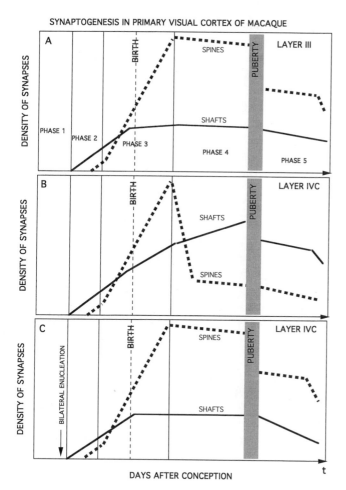

SYNAPTOGENESIS IN PRIMARY VISUAL CORTEX OF MACAQUE

FIGURE 2.2 Distinct classes of synapses appear in distinct waves of synaptogenesis in the primary visual cortex of macaque monkey during normal development. As examples, changes in the relative densities of synaptic contacts located on dendritic shafts (black line) or on dendritic spines (discontinuous line) are represented here as a function of days after conception expressed on a log scale on the abscissae (t) in two cortical layers (layer III in **A** and layer IVC in **B**). The same pattern of synaptogenesis is observed during the first three phases of synaptogenesis in all cortical layers (**A** and **B**), suggesting the existence of highly conserved mechanisms. During phase 2 a first wave of synaptogenesis occurs on dendritic shafts followed two weeks later by a second wave of synaptogenesis now on dendritic spines of the same neurons. During phase 3, before birth, the proportions of these classes of synapses are reversed. During the plateau phase 4 the kinetics of these waves of synaptogenesis differ. A protracted plateau of high density of synapses on dendritic spines is observed in supragranular layer III (**A**), while in granular layer IVC (**B**) we observed a very short wave of synaptogenesis on dendritic spines and a protracted wave of synaptogenesis on dendritic shafts. After an early bilateral enucleation was performed during phase 1 of synaptogenesis (arrow in **C**), the same pattern of synaptogenesis unfolds normally during the first three phases in granular layer IVC (compare **A**, **B**, and **C**). However, during plateau phase 4, the second reversal of densities of synapses on dendritic spines and shafts does not take place (**C**).

brain imaging (Jacobs et al., 1995) or immunocytochemical and histological techniques (Anderson et al., 1995). These phases have also been identified in mouse neocortices (de Felipe et al., 1997) and human brains (Chugani, 1999; Huttenlocher and Dabholkar, 1997). These facts strongly suggest that the mechanisms of corticogenesis and synaptogenesis are highly conserved during the extensive evolution of the neocortex. In human cortex it is easy neither to obtain precise quantitative data on the time course of these phases nor to establish time points equivalent to those described in the macaque. However, from the observations of Zecevic (1998) on the human occipital cortex, we tentatively propose that phase 1 might begin around 6–8 weeks of gestation. Phase 2 would begin near 12–17 weeks of gestation. The onset of phase 3 of rapid synaptogenesis would occur around midgestation (17–24 weeks). On the other hand, data from Huttenlocher and Dabholkar (1997) indicate that, in the primary visual cortex, phase 3 ends somewhere between 8 and 12 months after birth. For phase 4, a plateau of a high density of synaptic contacts, differences appear between cortical areas. In the human primary visual cortex the plateau phase has the same length as that in the macaque (2–3 years; figure 2.3), while in the prefrontal cortex it lasts for a decade, until puberty (figure 2.3; Huttenlocher and Dabholkar, 1997). Both in macaque and human neocortices, phase 5 begins after puberty and proceeds throughout adulthood with almost no decline in densities of synaptic contacts, and is followed by a significant loss of synapses during senescence (figures 2.1 and 2.3).

## Distinct waves of synaptogenesis

The curve presented in figure 2.1 is actually an envelope curve "covering" many distinct waves of synaptogenesis differing in location, timing, or tempo, as revealed by more detailed descriptions (Bourgeois, Goldman-Rakic, and Rakic, 1994; Bourgeois and Rakic, 1993). With respect to location, we observed a wave of synaptogenesis outside the cortical plate during phase 1, and another one inside this plate later on, during phase 2 (figure 2.1). With respect to timing, we observed sequential waves of synaptogenesis first on dendritic shafts, and later on dendritic spines of the same neurons (figure 2.2A,B). As for tempo, in the primary visual cortex we observed a protracted plateau until puberty in supragranular layer III (figure 2.2A), while a short phase 4 of synaptogenesis on dendritic spines was observed postnatally in granular layer IVC (figure 2.2B). In layer III of the prefrontal cortex of the macaque, a protracted plateau of high density of

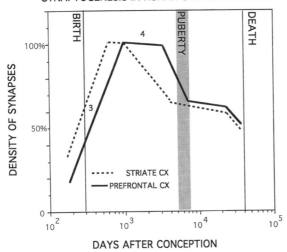

SYNAPTOGENESIS IN HUMAN CEREBRAL CORTEX

FIGURE 2.3 Changes in the relative densities of synapses in the primary visual cortex (discontinuous line) and prefrontal cortex (continuous line) of human brain as a function of days after conception expressed on a log scale on the abscissae. Phases 3 and 4 are indicated with numbers 3 and 4. (This is a schematic representation of data published in Huttenlocher and Dabholkar, 1997, with permission from the authors and John Wiley and Sons, Inc.)

parvalbumin-positive axon cartridges from chandelier cells was observed until puberty, while a short peak of density of dopaminergic varicosities was observed exactly during puberty (Anderson et al., 1995). In the human cerebral cortex, sequential developments of distinct cortical circuits (Burkhalter, Bernardo, and Charles, 1993) most probably correspond to distinct waves of synaptogenesis. These are the first examples of a long list of discrete synaptogenetic events we are just beginning to explore.

All these preliminary studies show that phase 3 is a period of rapid production of all categories of synaptic contacts, even if during the next phases different categories of synapses may display different kinetics in macaque (Anderson et al., 1995; Bourgeois, Goldman-Rakic, and Rakic, 1994; Bourgeois and Rakic, 1993; Zecevic, Bourgeois, and Rakic, 1989; Zecevic and Rakic, 1991), mouse (de Felipe et al., 1997), and human (figure 2.3; Huttenlocher and Dabholkar, 1997) cerebral cortices.

### Phase 3 of synaptogenesis in diverse cortical areas

In diverse cortical fields characterized by different cytoarchitectonies and subserving very different physiological functions, the same phases of synaptogenesis were found at the same developmental stages (Bour-

geois, Goldman-Rakic, and Rakic, 1994, 2000; Bourgeois and Rakic, 1993; Granger et al., 1995; Zecevic, Bourgeois, and Rakic, 1989; Zecevic and Rakic, 1991). The very same early developmental pattern of synaptogenesis—i.e., the ensembles of percentages of different classes of synapses at successive steps of development and maturation—is also observed in all cortical layers (see the example shown in figure 2.2A,B,C) and in all the cortical areas examined.

Unexpectedly, during the perinatal period, we also observed that the rapid phase 3 of synaptogenesis occurs more concurrently than sequentially in the sensory, motor, and associational cortical areas (Bourgeois, Goldman-Rakic, and Rakic, 2000; Rakic et al., 1986; Rakic, Bourgeois, and Goldman-Rakic, 1994). Excitatory and inhibitory synapses also accumulate concurrently during phase 3 in the prefrontal cortex of the macaque monkey (Anderson et al., 1995). These observations are corroborated by brain imaging studies on the cortical mantle of the macaque (Jacobs et al., 1995).

We have defined a "time window" of 41 days encompassing the midpoints of the rapid phase 3 of synaptogenesis in all the cortical areas thus far described in the macaque (Granger et al., 1995). Using available data, we proposed that this is also the case in the human neocortex with a time window of about 3–5 months (figure 2.3; Huttenlocher and Dabholkar, 1997; Rakic, Bourgeois, and Goldman-Rakic, 1994). Although the duration of this time window increases through evolution, it always remains short as compared to the long duration of the succeeding plateau phase 4 (a decade in the human cortex; see figure 2.3), which extends until puberty.

Recent observations reveal that, as in the macaque, phases 2 and 3 of synaptogenesis appear to occur concurrently in the prenatal human cerebral cortex (Zecevic, 1998). Similarly, correspondence analysis of the developmental patterns in several cytoarchitectonically distinct cortical areas also shows a concurrent morphological maturation of the whole cortical mantle in the human postnatal brain (Shankle et al., 1998).

### Modifiability of phase 3 of synaptogenesis

The onset of synaptogenesis long before birth, its tempo, and the concurrent phase 3 in all cortical layers and cortical areas of the macaque strongly suggested to us that these events might be determined by mechanisms intrinsic and common to the whole cortical mantle (Bourgeois, Goldman-Rakic, and Rakic, 2000; Goldman-Rakic, Bourgeois, and Rakic, 1997; Rakic et al., 1986; Rakic, Bourgeois, and Goldman-Rakic, 1994).

We have tested this hypothesis in the following experiments:

1. Using a mild intervention with experimental preterm monkeys (Bourgeois, Jastreboff, and Rakic, 1989), we found that a premature bilaterally equilibrated exposure to visual environment does not accelerate or delay the rate of synaptic accretion during the rapid phase 3 of synaptogenesis in the primary visual cortex. This phase of synaptogenesis proceeds in relation to the time of conception rather than time of delivery, i.e., the onset of visual stimulation.

2. Using a more drastic intervention, we found that an early bilateral enucleation (Bourgeois and Rakic, 1996) does not alter the final mean densities of synapses reached at the end of rapid phase 3 and maintained during the phase 4 plateau in the striate cortex of blind monkeys. Our study also indicates that a few weeks after birth the proportions of synaptic contacts situated on dendritic spines (75%) and shafts (25%) were similar in all cortical layers of normal and enucleated animals. Four months after birth, the localization on dendritic spines or shafts in the thalamorecipient granular layers fails to mature properly in the absence of normal functional input from the periphery (figure 2.2C). These proportions, which normally become reversed during infancy in sublayers IVAB and IVC, were not reversed in the enucleates. The proportions of symmetric (20%) versus asymmetric (80%) synapses located on dendritic spines were within the normal range of variability in both groups of animals. As a result, the granular layers in the striate cortex of early-blind macaques have more excitatory axodendrospines than do normal animals.

This experimental model also provides an additional example of the fact that a perturbation at an early neurodevelopmental stage (before midgestation in the present case) may have a late (late infancy in the present case) and long-lasting effect of disorganization despite an apparently normal intermediary period (latency period for this aspect of synaptoarchitectony).

These experimental observations indicate that early synaptogenesis is a very robust neurodevelopmental process. They reinforce our hypothesis that the onset, time course, magnitude, and rate of cortical synaptogenesis during phase 3 in the primate striate cortex proceed without stimulation from the periphery. They are determined and coordinated by mechanisms intrinsic and common to the whole cortical mantle. The nature of these mechanisms and their interactions (metabolic, trophic, hormonal, genetic, etc.) is under investigation. However, final adjustments of some aspects of the synaptoarchitectony depend on normal functional input.

## Effects of environment on diverse phases of synaptogenesis

The transition from intrinsic to extrinsic control of synaptogenesis in the cerebral cortex most likely involves many steps. Experience, i.e., the presence of patterned evoked activities coming from the world external to the neocortex, has diverse effects on cortical maturation during the different phases of synaptogenesis. As sketched in figure 2.1, we tentatively propose the following interpretations:

1. Phases 1 and 2 of very early synaptogenesis: The early events, such as neurogenesis, neuronal migration, neuritic navigation, individualization of cortical layers, neurochemical differentiation, and early synaptogenesis, are dominated by genetic and epigenetic mechanisms, all of which are intrinsic to the neocortex. These events can be severely disturbed by genetic mutations, viral infections, toxic agents, surgical interventions, and so forth; however, they are not yet influenced by experience coming from the world external to the neocortex. Using Greenough's terminology (Greenough and Alcantara, 1993), these early events are *"experience-independent"* (figure 2.1) and, possibly, are common to all mammals. A spontaneous activity most likely already circulates via the early formed synapses and participates in the wiring of cortical neurons (Maffei and Galli-Resta, 1990; Mooney et al., 1996).

2. Rapid phase 3 of synaptogenesis: This phase is dominated early on by *"experience-expectant,"* and later by *"experience-dependent"* mechanisms (figure 2.1; Greenough and Alcantara, 1993). The intrinsic mechanisms become epigenetically modulated by experience coming to the neocortex from the external world. *Experience-expectant* means that the presence of some visual parameters in the external world (orientation, color, movement, disparity, etc.) are necessary for the proper final adjustment of the cortical circuits being established for their specific processing. This phase 3 coincides with the beginning of critical periods. The mechanisms involved during this phase are assumed to be common to all individuals of a given mammalian species.

Huttenlocher and Dabholkar (1997) claimed that the onset of cortical functions occurs only at the end of phase 3 of synaptogenesis and at different ages in different cortical regions. This is in contradiction with accumulating evidence of very early maturation of anatomical and physiological parameters in the neocortex of primates.

In macaques, many sensory, motor, visceral, and cognitive functions subserved by the neocortex are present very early after birth, when the main aspects of synaptoarchitectony are still being laid down. The patterns of ocular dominance columns are already adult-like in the primary visual cortex of newborn macaques (Horton and Hocking, 1996). Complex receptive field properties, such as face recognition, of inferotemporal neurons are already adult-like, as early as investigators were able to test, i.e., only a few weeks after birth in macaques (Rodman, 1994). The possibility of a cortical circuitry prewired even for highly integrated functions has been invoked (Rodman, 1994). A cardinal cognitive function thought to be subserved by the dorsolateral prefrontal association cortex [i.e., performance on Piaget's A not B task; see this volume, Stiles (chapter 27), Diamond (chapter 29), Luciana (chapter 41)] is present long before the end of the rapid phase 3 of synaptogenesis a few weeks after birth (Bourgeois, Goldman-Rakic, and Rakic, 1994; Diamond and Goldman-Rakic, 1989; Goldman-Rakic, Bourgeois, and Rakic, 1997). Harlow and Harlow (1962) showed that critical periods for social skills of the macaque infants could also begin as early as 2 months after birth. Evoked activity in response to maternal voice seems to be present before birth in human fetuses (Schaal, Lecanuet, and Granier-Deferre, 1999), and newborn human infants most certainly see (Teller, 1997).

Our working hypothesis is that the very rapid and concurrent synaptogenesis in the whole cortical mantle during the rapid phase 3 allows the early coordinated emergence of all these cortical functions (Rakic et al., 1986; Rakic, Bourgeois, and Goldman-Rakic, 1994). This is essential for competitive and selective (Changeux and Danchin, 1976) interactions among the very heterogeneous cortical inputs in each point of the cortex. However, these cortical functions will also require up to 3 years to reach full maturity in the macaque (Goldman-Rakic, Bourgeois, and Rakic, 1997) and more than a decade in human (Huttenlocher and Dabholkar, 1997; Rakic, Bourgeois, and Goldman-Rakic, 1994), i.e., until puberty.

3. Phase 4, *en plateau*: This phase is also dominated by experience-expectant and experience-dependent mechanisms (figure 2.1; Greenough and Alcantara, 1993). This extended period of synaptic plasticity corresponds to a process of continuous reorganization of the intracortical axonal arborizations (Callaway and Katz, 1990; Lowel and Singer, 1992), allowing fine-tuning and maturation of the neuronal circuits during the 3 years after birth until puberty. This topological reorganization of synaptic contacts occurs with a constant mean density of synapses.

Phases 3 and 4 of synaptogenesis coincide with the diverse critical periods extending until puberty in cats (Daw et al., 1992), monkeys (Le Vay, Wiesel, and Hubel, 1980), and humans (Johnson and Newport, 1989). Critical periods for different visual functions subserved by different cortical layers in the primary visual cortex have different timings. Neuronal plasticity lasts longer in the upper and lower cortical layers than in the granular layers. For example, the short postnatal peak of density observed in granular layer IVC in the striate cortex of the macaque (see the section Distinct Waves of Synaptogenesis and figure 2.2B) fits well with the short critical period for orientation selectivity subserved by this layer, while the long-lasting plateau phase 4 observed in supragranular layer III (see the section Distinct Waves of Synaptogenesis and figure 2.2A) coincides with the protracted critical periods described for contrast sensitivity, binocular selectivity, and Vernier hyperacuity, subserved by this layer (Blakemore, Vital-Durand, and Garey, 1981; Harwerth et al., 1986).

4. Phase 5: This phase is dominated by experience-dependent mechanisms (figure 2.1; Greenough and Alcantara, 1993). It corresponds mainly to a very slow decrease in the density of synapses through adulthood. Over several decades of aging the efficacy and the local plastic reorganizations of synaptic contacts are now related only to the experience of each individual (Greenough and Alcantara, 1993), but the main aspects of synaptoarchitectony in the cortical networks remain unchanged.

We observed a true loss of synapses in neocortex of macaque monkey around puberty (Bourgeois, Goldman-Rakic, and Rakic, 1994; Bourgeois and Rakic, 1993). A similar loss of synapses near puberty was also observed, using quantitative synaptology, in the cortices of human brain (Huttenlocher and Dabholkar, 1997) and mouse brains (de Felipe et al., 1997). These observations are confirmed by brain imaging in the macaque (Jacobs et al., 1995) and human cortices (Chugani, 1999).

Although we arbitrarily included this period of rapid loss of synapses during puberty in phase 5, we do not rule out the possibility that it might be a singular phase distinct from the other phases of synaptogenesis, with its own mechanisms and tempo.

One possibility is that the loss of synapses in the prefrontal cortex during puberty might correspond to a "hormonal sanction" on some aspects of neuronal plasticity. The deep hormonal "reorganization" occurring in and near puberty would contribute to the definitive elimination of labile synapses not stabilized during the preceding plateau phase 4. In humans, central visual defects due to cataract become less treatable as puberty approaches (Mitchell and Timney, 1984). At age 12, people stop being able to learn nonmaternal languages without effort and without accents (Johnson and Newport, 1989). And, as frequently reiterated in textbooks, the period around puberty corresponds to a crystallization of personality, marking the end of several basic learning capacities and skills.

## Selectionists versus constructivists hypothesis for synaptogenesis

Studies addressing phases 3 and 4 of synaptogenesis represent foci of contention between selectionist and constructivist hypotheses. Both hypotheses relate the modifications of the synaptoarchitectony during development, maturation, and learning in the neocortex to the evoked activity resulting from individual experience. And both hypotheses recognize that there is an early and rapid accumulation of synapses, the most active of which will ultimately be retained. But the hypotheses differ in the sequence of events invoked.

According to the selective stabilization hypothesis proposed by Changeux and Danchin (1976), connectivity progresses from a larger to a smaller number of connections and synapses. Intrinsic mechanisms control the initial formation of large pools of synaptic contacts, while the subsequent stabilization of the most active synapses, and the elimination of the less active ones, is regulated by evoked activity.

In the constructivist hypothesis proposed by Katz and Shatz (1996), Purves, White, and Riddle (1996), and Quartz and Sejnowski (1997), connectivity matures from a smaller to a larger number of connections and synapses. According to these instructionist models, the spontaneous activity and the patterns of evoked activities cause the formation of synapses, control the extent of their domains, and orient the elaboration of their synaptoarchitectonic organization. Losses of neurons, axons, and synapses, if any, are just epiphenomena.

In the primary visual system of the macaque or cat, the coincidence between the continuous increase in axonodendritic branching, the segregation of ocular dominance columns (Katz and Shatz, 1996; Purves, White, and Riddle, 1996; Quartz and Sejnowski, 1997), and the rapid phase 3 of synaptogenesis (Bourgeois and Rakic, 1993) are taken as support for constructionist hypothesis. However, the fact that the onset of phase 3 of rapid synaptogenesis slightly precedes the loss of a few LGN axonal branches from contralateral ocular dominance columns does not rule out a selective competition between these few axons subserving the two eyes. The massive growth and sprouting of axonal arbors that follow might just as well hide local selectionist competitions between diverse axons now subserving the same eye inside the same dominance column.

During the plateau phase of synaptogenesis, a selective stabilization of synapses might occur during reorganization of the tridimensional distribution of synapses in the neuropil, without any net loss of synapses, because different waves for different classes of synapses occur at different developmental stages (figure 2.2A,B; Bourgeois and Rakic, 1993). All these models include the existence of extensive production, remodeling, and retraction of dendritic and axonal branches and synapses during development of cortex. For example, synapses identified on proximal axon collaterals at a juvenile stage relocate to distal axonal domains at the adult stage on local circuit neurons in cortex (Callaway and Katz, 1990).

The quantitative observations from Greenough and Alcantara (1993) suggest that learning induces formation of new synapses. However, if such an increase in density of synapses occurs everywhere and permanently as primates learn, this density should increase constantly across the life span. This does not fit with the unambiguous loss of diverse classes of synapses, repetitively observed at different moments of phases 4 and 5, in different cortical layers and cortical areas of the macaque (figures 2.1–2.4; Anderson et al., 1995; Bourgeois, Goldman-Rakic, and Rakic, 1994; Bourgeois and Rakic, 1993; Zecevic, Bourgeois, and Rakic, 1989; Zecevic and Rakic, 1991), mouse (de Felipe et al., 1997), or human (Huttenlocher and Dabholkar, 1997) cortices. In addition, Geinisman and colleagues (2000) showed that associative learning does not increase the number of synapses in hippocampus. It is difficult to reconcile all these facts with a strict interpretation of the constructivist models. To go further, one could even hypothesize that these transient bursts of synaptogenesis in the adult neocortex may in fact correspond to a transient phase 4 *within* the phase 5, i.e., transient selectionist episodes of synaptoarchitectonic reorganization.

## Evolution of phase 3 of synaptogenesis in neocortex

Through evolution of neocortex, there is a shift in the onset time of neurogenesis in the primary visual cortex (figure 2.4); it occurs 14 days after conception (DAC) in the rat (Frantz et al., 1994), 30 DAC in the cat (Luskin and Shatz, 1985), 40 DAC in the macaque, and 43 DAC in the human neocortex (Rakic, 1995). With respect to synaptogenesis, the comparison of the tempo of phase 3 in the primary visual cortices of these four mammalian species also reveals two significant modifications, as sketched in figure 2.4:

1. The onset of the rapid phase 3 of synaptogenesis occurs progressively later after conception: from 23

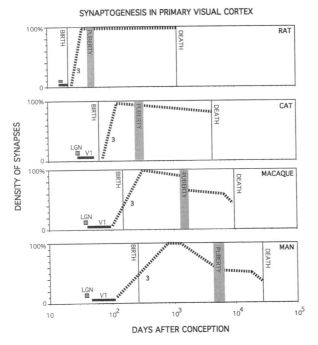

SYNAPTOGENESIS IN PRIMARY VISUAL CORTEX

FIGURE 2.4 Changes in the relative density of synapses (discontinuous lines) in the primary visual cortices of four different mammalian species—rat, cat, macaque, and man—as a function of days after conception expressed on a log scale on the abscissae. Only phases 3, 4, and 5 of synaptogenesis are sketched here. Phase 3 is indicated with the number 3. The striped and the solid black horizontal bars represent the time of neurogenesis in the lateral geniculate nucleus (LGN) and primary visual cortex (V1). (Reproduced from Bourgeois, 1997, with permission from Scandinavian University Press.)

DAC in the rat (Blue and Parnavelas, 1983) to 110 DAC in the human neocortex (table 2.1 and figure 2.4; Huttenlocher and Dabholkar, 1997). Through phylogeny of mammals, this shift is less pronounced than that of the time of delivery (figure 2.4). As a result, the onset of phase 3 of synaptogenesis, a postnatal event in rodents and carnivores, progressively becomes a precocious prenatal event in primates.

2. More importantly, the duration of phase 3 in the primary visual cortex increases significantly from 14 days in the rat (Blue and Parnavelas, 1983) to 30 days in the cat (Cragg, 1975), 136 days in the macaque (Bourgeois and Rakic, 1993), and about 400 days in the human brain (table 2.1 and figure 2.4; Huttenlocher and Dabholkar, 1997). Normalization of the duration of phase 3 of synaptogenesis to the onset time of puberty (table 2.1) shows that it represents a constant proportion of 10–17% of this time in the four species studied, suggesting that phase 3 is a developmental process not apart from others. In an evolutionary perspective this protracted phase 3 postpones the increase in volume of the primate brain well into the late postnatal

period, a crucial parameter which, otherwise, could make delivery problematic.

These observations become even more interesting when one relates them to the evolution of synaptoarchitectony. The final mean density of synapses per unit volume of cortical neuropil in the mature striate cortex (column 5 in table 2.1) is not higher in human than in rat, although it takes about 30 times as many days to produce these synapses in each point of the cortex. Even the mean number of synapses per neuron in the striate cortex remains in the same range from rat to man (column 6 in table 2.1).

As plausible mechanisms for this extension of phase 3 of synaptogenesis, two working hypotheses, which are not mutually exclusive, are now considered:

1. A genetic hypothesis: The time course of phase 3 is controlled by genetic mechanisms, and the number and/or the time needed by the developmental master genes to control phase 3 of synaptogenesis might increase during evolution. This hypothesis leads to one falsifiable experimental prediction: The mutation of these genes or the deregulation of their expression should result in a modification of the onset and/or time course of phase 3 of synaptogenesis.

2. A morphofunctional hypothesis: Morphological and functional heterogeneities of the axonal inputs to the primary visual cortex increase with the addition of extrastriate cortical areas during mammalian evolution, and the increased diversity of synaptic inputs causes the extension of phase 3 of synaptogenesis. During evolution of mammals the neocortex grows more in surface area than in the vertical dimension. From rat to human, the total surface area of the cortical mantle increases by 3 orders of magnitude. Cortical expansion in evolution is achieved largely by addition of radial units, and thus by increases in the number, not the size, of constituent columns (Rakic, 1995). Although the two-dimensional shape of the primary visual cortex appears highly conserved across mammalian species (Duffy, Murphy, and Jones, 1998), its surface increases significantly. The total number of cortical areas also increases significantly (column 7 in table 2.1). More relevant to our purpose, the total number of visual areas increases from 4 in the rat (Coogan and Burkhalter, 1993) to about 25 in the macaque and probably many more in the human brain (column 8 in table 2.1; Van Essen, 1985). Most of these visual areas are directly or indirectly connected to the primary visual cortex (Coogan and Burkhalter, 1993; Salin and Bullier, 1995; Van Essen, 1985), and their inputs are quite heterogeneous. This heterogeneity may be histologically related, for example, to the high diversity of cell adhesion molecules (Alcantara, Pfennin-

TABLE 2.1

*Parameters related to the development of the primary visual cortex of four distinct mammalian species*

| | Gestation | Puberty Onset | Phase 3 Duration (onset–end) | Density of synapses[1] | Synapses per Neuron | Total Number of Cortical Areas | Total Number of Visual Areas |
|---|---|---|---|---|---|---|---|
| Rat | 21 days | 82 DAC (2 months after birth) | 14 days (P2–P16) | 320–946 | 12,500–13,500 | 21 | 4–6 |
| Cat | 65 days | 248 DAC (6 months after birth) | 30 days (P9–P39) | 276–406 | 5800–9300 | 30–50? | 12–17 |
| Macaque | 165 days | 1260 DAC (3 years after birth) | 136 days (E90–P61) | 276–620 | 2000–5600 | 72 | 25 |
| Human | 280 days | 4660 DAC (12 years after birth) | 470 days (E120–P310) | 350 | 6800–10,000 | 200? | 50? |

[1]Density of synapses is expressed in millions per cubic millimeter of cortical tissue.

DAC = days after conception; E = embryonic day; P = postnatal day.

Reproduced from Bourgeois (1997) with permission from Scandinavian University Press.

ger, and Greenough, 1992) and diffusible or signaling molecules (Edlund and Jessel, 1999). This heterogeneity may also be functional: In different cortical areas neurons fire with different temporal patterns (Ferster and Spruston, 1995) and different conduction times (Salin and Bullier, 1995). In the morphofunctional hypothesis all these heterogeneities increase the number and the complexity of cellular interactions between nerve endings during the formation of synapses, their selective stabilization, their elimination, or all these steps. This, along with an increased number of waves of synaptogenesis, might increase the duration of phases 3 and 4 of synaptogenesis.

The morphofunctional hypothesis leads to another falsifiable experimental prediction: The anatomical or functional suppression of a specified number of prestriate cortical areas should shorten the duration of phase 3 of synaptogenesis observed in the primary visual cortex. Conversely, the addition of cortical areas should prolong phase 3.

These two hypothesis are not mutually exclusive: The two classes of mechanisms might be at work at different moments of phase 3 or/and for distinct ensembles of synapses. These mechanisms are expected to be identical in the whole cortical mantle.

## *New perspectives on genetics of synaptogenesis, evolution of epigenesis, and individuation*

In neocortices of nonhuman and human primates, neurogenesis and synaptogenesis are very precocious prenatal developmental events, while complete maturation of cortical functions is protracted until puberty. Although kinetics is not the whole story of synaptogenesis, our identification of distinct phases of synaptogenesis provides a new developmental frame for the description of the establishment and successive adjustments of synaptoarchitectony in neocortex of primates. The density of synapses is the same at birth and after puberty; however, the developmental constraints on synaptogenesis are expected to be totally different. We observed that the onset and time course of phase 3 of synaptogenesis are very robust developmental events, while influences from environment increase thereafter. Among multiple mechanisms, this plasticity is related to the high variability in the density, localization, assembly, and nature of many types of molecules in the pre- and postsynaptic domains of neurons. To cite only a few examples, one should refer to the large diversity and plasticity of the subunits of classical pharmacological receptors (Changeux et al., 1997; Craig 1998; Vannier and Triller, 1997) as well as to new families of molecules such as class I MHC (Corriveau, Huh, and Shatz, 1998) and synaptic cadherins (Hagler and Goda, 1998; Tanaka et al., 2000), which have been observed during formation of synaptic contacts. These numerous structural and signal-transducing molecules assemble and deassemble in highly dynamic pre- and postsynaptic domains of morphologically permanent synaptic contacts.

We hypothesize that, upstream of all these molecular events, new families of genes control the onset and duration of the different phases of synaptogenesis.

Different groups of these genes may be activated, some transiently, some permanently, during distinct waves of synaptogenesis. The identification of the functional interactions between different groups of genes during distinct critical periods of synaptogenesis will constitute an entirely new field of research on corticogenesis. The regulatory genes controlling the onset of phase 3 of synaptogenesis will have to be identified first. The sequencing of the human genome, to be completed within the early years of this century, will allow translation of the cascade of histological events observed during corticogenesis into a cascade of genetic events.

The aim of future projects is to explore the mechanisms of the transitions from strictly intrinsic control (genes) to epigenetic control (environment) of the formation of synaptoarchitectony during cortical development of the normal or pathological individual. Whether these transitions result from a changing overlap of independent mechanisms subserved by distinct ensembles of synaptic circuits, or whether it is a progressive epigenetic transformation from one mechanism into the next in the very same ensembles of synapses, is not yet known.

The recognition of distinct and successive waves of synaptogenesis, along with these studies of genetic controls of synaptogenesis, will also provide new biological approaches to testing diverse neurodevelopmental hypotheses for psychiatric disorders (Bloom, 1993; Feinberg, 1983, 1990; Stefan and Murray, 1997). According to these hypotheses, early perturbations in the development of neuronal circuits remain hidden until some aspects of their late normal maturation reveal the defect.

Synaptogenesis is a crucial part of the phylogenetic and ontogenetic history of the neocortex. However, we do not yet know the sequence of causality, if any, between the extension of phases 3 and 4 of synaptogenesis, the appearance of many new local neuronal circuits, the functional refinement of the multiple receptive fields of the striate cortex, and the increased numbers and plasticity of the neuronal networks, all observed through phylogeny.

According to the heterochronic epigenesis hypothesis (Bourgeois, 1997), the extension of phase 3 of synaptogenesis significantly increases (1) the scale and number of possible epigenetic combinations, (2) the amplitude of the "overshoot" of synapses, (3) the extension of their plasticity well into adulthood, and (4) the morphofunctional interindividual variabilities observed through mammalian phylogeny. This hypothesis also proposes that the extension of phases 3 and 4 of synaptogenesis during evolution of neocortex significantly increases the process of maturation of cognitive and psychosocial competencies, reaching its maximum in the human brain.

All these descriptions, including that of the development of the synaptoarchitectony in the cerebral cortex, participate in the identification of the mechanisms involved in the process of individuation.

ACKNOWLEDGMENTS   I thank Professors Jean-Pierre Changeux, Patricia Goldman-Rakic, and Pasko Rakic for their constant support and numerous discussions about epigenesis. This work was supported at its inception by a Fogarty International Fellowship and constantly by the Centre National de la Recherche Scientifique.

## REFERENCES

ALCANTARA, A. A., K. H. PFENNINGER, and W. T. GREENOUGH, 1992. 5B4-CAM expression parallels neurite outgrowth and synaptogenesis in the developing rat brain. *J. Comp. Neurol.* 319:337–348.

ANDERSON, S. A., J. D. CLASSEY, F. CONDÉ, J. S. LUND, and D. A. LEWIS, 1995. Synchronous development of pyramidal neuron dendritic spines and parvalbumin-immunoreactive chandelier neuron axon terminals in layer III of monkey prefrontal cortex. *Neuroscience* 67(1):7–22.

BARONE, P., C. DEHAY, M. BERLAND, J. BULLIER, and H. KENNEDY, 1995. Developmental remodeling of primate visual cortical pathways. *Cereb. Cortex* 5:22–38.

BLAKEMORE, C., F. VITAL-DURAND, and L. J. GAREY, 1981. Recovery from monocular deprivation in the monkey. I. Reversal of physiological effects in the visual cortex. *Proc. R. Soc. Lond. (B)* 213:399–423.

BLOOM, R. E., 1993. Advancing a neurodevelopmental origin of schizophrenia. *Arch. Gen. Psychiatry* 50:224–227.

BLUE, M. E., and J. G. PARNAVELAS, 1983. The formation and maturation of synapses in the visual cortex of the rat. II. Quantitative analysis. *J. Neurocytol.* 12:697–712.

BOURGEOIS, J.-P., 1997. Synaptogenesis, heterochrony and epigenesis in the mammalian neocortex. *Acta Paediatrica* 422(suppl.):27–33.

BOURGEOIS, J.-P., P. S. GOLDMAN-RAKIC, and P. RAKIC, 1994. Synaptogenesis in the prefrontal cortex of rhesus monkey. *Cereb. Cortex* 4:78–96.

BOURGEOIS, J.-P., P. S. GOLDMAN-RAKIC, and P. RAKIC, 2000. Formation, elimination and stabilization of synapses in the primate cerebral cortex. In *The New Cognitive Neurosciences*, M. Gazzaniga, ed. Cambridge, Mass.: MIT Press, pp. 45–53.

BOURGEOIS, J.-P., P. J. JASTREBOFF, and P. RAKIC, 1989. Synaptogenesis in visual cortex of normal and preterm monkeys: Evidence for intrinsic regulation of synaptic overproduction. *Proc. Natl. Acad. Sci. (USA)* 86:4297–4301.

BOURGEOIS, J.-P., and P. RAKIC, 1993. Changes of synaptic density in the primary visual cortex of the macaque monkey from fetal to adult stage. *J. Neurosci.* 13:2801–2820.

BOURGEOIS, J.-P., and P. RAKIC, 1996. Synaptogenesis in the occipital cortex of macaque monkey devoid of retinal input from early embryonic stages. *Eur. J. Neurosci.* 8:942–950.

BURKHALTER A., K. L. BERNARDO, and V. CHARLES, 1993. Development of local circuits in human visual cortex. *J. Neurosci.* 13:1916–1931.

CALLAWAY, E. M., and L. KATZ, 1990. Emergence and refinement of clustered horizontal connections in cat striate cortex. *J. Neurosci.* 10:1134–1153.

CHANGEUX, J. P., A. BESSIS, J.-P. BOURGEOIS, P. J. CORRINGER, A. DEVILLERS-THIÉRY, J. L. EISELÉ, M. KERSZBERG, C. LÉNA, N. LENOVÈRE, M. PICCIOTO, and M. ZOLI, 1997. Nicotinic receptors and brain plasticity. In *Cold Spring Harbor Symposium on Function and Dysfunction in the Nervous System*, No. 61, pp. 343–362.

CHANGEUX, J. P., and A. DANCHIN, 1976. Selective stabilization of developing synapses as a mechanism for the specification of neural network. *Nature* 264:705–712.

CHUGANI, H. T., 1999. Metabolic imaging: A window on brain development and plasticity. *Neuroscientist* 5:29–40.

COOGAN, T. A., and A. BURKHALTER, 1993. Hierarchical organization of areas in rat visual cortex. *J. Neurosci.* 13(9):3749–3772.

CORRIVEAU, R. A., G. S. HUH, and C. J. SHATZ, 1998. Regulation of class I MHC gene expression in the developing and mature CNS by neural activity. *Neuron* 21:505–520.

CRAGG, B. G., 1975. The development of synapses in the visual system of the cat. *J. Comp. Neurol.* 160:147–166.

CRAIG, A. M., 1998. Activity and synaptic receptor targeting: The long view. *Neuron* 21:459–462.

DAW, N. W., K. FOX, H. SATO, and D. CZEPITA, 1992. Critical period for monocular deprivation in the cat visual cortex. *J. Neurophysiol.* 67:197–202.

DIAMOND, A., and P. S. GOLDMAN-RAKIC, 1989. Comparison of human infants and rhesus monkeys on Piaget's AB task: Evidence for dependence on dorsolateral prefrontal cortex. *Exp. Brain Res.* 74:24–40.

DUFFY, K. R., K. M. MURPHY, and D. R. JONES, 1998. Analysis of the postnatal growth of visual cortex. *Vis. Neurosci.* 15:831–839.

EDLUND, T., and T. M. JESSEL, 1999. Progression from extrinsic to intrinsic signalling in cell fate specification: A view from the nervous system. *Cell* 96:211–224.

FEINBERG, I., 1983. Schizophrenia: Caused by a fault in programmed synaptic elimination during adolescence? *J. Psychiat. Res.* 17:319–334.

FEINBERG, I., 1990. Cortical pruning and the development of schizophrenia. *Schizophrenia Bull.* 16:567–568.

DE FELIPE, J., P. MARCO, A. FAIRÉN, and E. G. JONES, 1997. Inhibitory synaptogenesis in mouse somatosensory cortex. *Cereb. Cortex* 7:619–634.

FERSTER, D., and N. SPRUSTON, 1995. Cracking the neuronal code. *Science* 270:756–757.

FRANTZ, G. D., A. P. BOHNER, R. M. AKERS, and S. K. MC-CONNELL, 1994. Regulation of the POU domain gene SCIP during cerebral cortical development. *J. Neurosci.* 14:472–485.

GEINISMAN, Y., J. F. DISTERHOFT, H. J. G. GUNDERSEN, M. D. MCECHRON, I. S. PERSINA, J. M. POWER, E. A. VAN DER ZEE, and M. J. WEST, 2000. Remodeling of hippocampal synapses after hippocampus-dependent associative learning. *J. Comp. Neurol.* 417:49–59.

GOLDMAN-RAKIC, P. S., J.-P. BOURGEOIS, and P. RAKIC, 1997. Synaptic development of the prefrontal cortex and the emergence of cognitive function. In *Development of the Prefrontal Cortex: Evolution, Neurobiology and Behavior*, N. A. Krasnegor, G. R. Lyon, and P. S. Goldman-Rakic, eds. Baltimore: Paul Brookes, pp. 27–47.

GRANGER, B., F. TEKAIA, A. M. LESOURD, P. RAKIC, and J.-P. BOURGEOIS, 1995. Tempo of neurogenesis and synaptogenesis in the primate cingulate mesocortex: Comparison with the neocortex. *J. Comp. Neurol.* 360:363–376.

GREENOUGH, W. T., and A. A. ALCANTARA, 1993. The roles of experience in different developmental information stage processes. In *Developmental Neurocognition*, B. de Boysson-Bardies, S. de Schonen, P. Jusczyk, P. McNeilage, and J. Morton, eds. Dordrecht: Kluwer Academic Publishers, pp. 3–16.

HAGLER, D. J., and Y. GODA, 1998. Synaptic adhesion: The building blocks of memory? *Neuron* 20:1059–1062.

HARLOW, H. F., and M. K. HARLOW, 1962. Social deprivation in monkeys. *Scientific American* 207:136–146.

HARWERTH, R. S., E. L. SMITH III, G. C. DUNCAN, M. L. J. CRAWFORD, and G. K. VON NOORDEN, 1986. Multiple sensitive periods in the development of the primate visual system. *Science* 232:235–238.

HORTON, J. C., and D. R. HOCKING, 1996. An adult-like pattern of ocular dominance columns in striate cortex of newborn monkeys prior to visual experience. *J. Neurosci.* 16(5):1791–1807.

HUTTENLOCHER, P. R., and A. S. DABHOLKAR, 1997. Regional differences in synaptogenesis in human cerebral cortex. *J. Comp. Neurol.* 387:167–178.

JACOBS, B., H. T. CHUGANI, V. ALLADA, S. CHEN, M. E. PHELPS, D. B. POLLACK, and M. J. RALEIGH, 1995. Developmental changes in brain metabolism in sedated rhesus macaques and vervet monkeys revealed by positron emission tomography. *Cereb. Cortex* 3:222–233.

JOHNSON, J. S., and E. L. NEWPORT, 1989. Critical period effects in second language learning: The influence of maturational state on the acquisition of English as a second language. *Cogn. Psychol.* 21:60–99.

KATZ, L. C., and C. J. SHATZ, 1996. Synaptic activity and the construction of cortical circuits. *Science* 274:1133–1138.

LE VAY, S., T. N. WIESEL, and D. H. HUBEL, 1980. The development of ocular dominance columns in normal and visually deprived monkeys. *J. Comp. Neurol.* 191:1–51.

LOWEL, S., and W. SINGER, 1992. Selection of intrinsic horizontal connections in the visual cortex by correlated neuronal activity. *Science* 255:209–212.

LUSKIN, M. B., and C. J. SHATZ, 1985. Neurogenesis of the cat's primary visual cortex. *J. Comp. Neurol.* 242:611–631.

MAFFEI, L., and L. GALLI-RESTA, 1990. Correlation in the discharges of neighboring rat retinal ganglion cells during prenatal life. *Proc. Natl. Acad. Sci. (USA)* 87:2861–2864.

MARIN-PADILLA, M., 1988. Early ontogenesis of the human cerebral cortex. In *Cerebral Cortex: Development and Maturation of Cerebral Cortex, Vol. 7*, A. Peters and E. G. Jones, eds. New York: Plenum Press, pp. 1–34.

MITCHELL, D. E., and B. TIMNEY, 1984. Postnatal development of function in the mammalian visual system. In *Handbook of Physiology: Sec. I. The Nervous System: Vol. 3. Sensory Processes (part 1)*, I. Darian-Smith, ed. Bethesda, Md.: American Physiological Society, pp. 507–555.

MOONEY, R., A. A. PENN, R. GALLEGO, and C. J. SHATZ, 1996. Thalamic relay of spontaneous retinal activity prior to vision. *Neuron* 17:863–874.

PETERS, A., C. SETHARES, and M. B. MOSS, 1998. The effects of aging on layer 1 in area 46 of prefrontal cortex in the rhesus monkey. *Cereb. Cortex* 8:671–684.

PURVES, D., L. E. WHITE, and D. R. RIDDLE, 1996. Is neural development Darwinian? *Trends Neurosci.* 19:460–464.

QUARTZ, S. R., and T. J. SEJNOWSKI, 1997. The neural basis of cognitive development: A constructivist manifesto. *Behav. Brain Sci.* 20(4):1–60.

RAKIC, P., 1995. A small step for the cell, a giant leap for mankind: A hypothesis of neocortical expansion during evolution. *Trends Neurosci.* 18:383–388.

RAKIC, P., J.-P. BOURGEOIS, M. F. ECKENHOFF, N. ZECEVIC, and P. S. GOLDMAN-RAKIC, 1986. Concurrent overproduction of synapses in diverse regions of the primate cerebral cortex. *Science* 232:232–235.

RAKIC, P., J.-P. BOURGEOIS, and P. S. GOLDMAN-RAKIC, 1994. Synaptic development of the cerebral cortex: Implications for learning, memory, and mental illness. *Prog. Brain Res.* 102:227–243.

RODMAN, H. R., 1994. Development of inferior temporal cortex in the monkey. *Cereb. Cortex* 5:484–498.

SALIN, P. A., and J. BULLIER, 1995. Corticocortical connections in the visual system: Structure and function. *Phys. Rev.* 75:107–154.

SCHAAL B., J. P. LECANUET, and C. GRANIER-DEFERRE, 1999. Sensory and integrative development in the human fetus and perinate: The usefulness of animal models. In *Animal Models of Human Emotion and Cognition*, M. Hang and R. E. Whalen, eds. Washington D.C.: American Psychological Association, pp. 119–142.

SHANKLE, W. R., A. K. ROMNEY, B. H. LANDING, and J. HARA, 1998. Developmental patterns in the cytoarchitecture of the human cerebral cortex from birth to 6 years examined by correspondence analysis. *Proc. Natl. Acad. Sci. (USA)* 95: 4023–4028.

STEFAN, M. D., and R. M. MURRAY, 1997. Schizophrenia: Developmental disturbance of brain and mind? *Acta Paediatrica* 422(suppl.):112–116.

TANAKA H., W. SHAN, G. R. PHILLIPS, K. ARNDT, O. BOZDAGI, L. SHAPIRO, G. W. HUNTLEY, D. L. BENSON, and D. R. COLMAN, 2000. Molecular modification of N-cadherin in response to synaptic activity. *Neuron* 25:93–107.

TELLER, D. Y., 1997. First glances: The vision of infants. *Invest. Ophthalmol. Vis. Sci.* 38(11):2183–2203.

VAN ESSEN, D., 1985. Functional organization of primate visual cortex. In *Cerebral Cortex, Vol. 3*, A. Peters and E. G. Jones, eds. New York: Plenum Press, pp. 259–329.

VANNIER, C., and A. TRILLER, 1997. Biology of the postsynaptic glycin receptor. *Int. Rev. Cytol.* 176:201–244.

ZECEVIC, N., 1998. Synaptogenesis in layer I of the human cerebral cortex in the first half of gestation. *Cereb. Cortex* 8:245–252.

ZECEVIC, N., J.-P. BOURGEOIS, and P. RAKIC, 1989. Synaptic density in motor cortex of rhesus monkey during fetal and postnatal life. *Dev. Brain Res.* 50:11–32.

ZECEVIC, N., and P. RAKIC, 1991. Synaptogenesis in monkey somatosensory cortex. *Cereb. Cortex* 1:510–523.

ZOLI, M., C. TORRI, R. FERRARI, A. JANSSON, I. ZINI, K. FUXE, and L. AGNATI, 1998. The emergence of the volume transmission concept. *Brain Res. Rev.* 26:136–147.

# 3 Myelination in the Developing Human Brain

RICARDO C. SAMPAIO
AND CHARLES L. TRUWIT

ABSTRACT Myelination in the human central nervous system (CNS) is a complex but orderly process, occurring in predictable topographical and chronological sequences. CNS myelination begins as early as 12–14 weeks of gestation in the spinal cord and continues well into the fourth decade of life. The most significant period of CNS myelination, however, occurs between midgestation and the second postnatal year. Myelination can be studied by various methods, including myelin-stained histopathological brain sections and, more recently, magnetic resonance (MR) imaging. The latter constitutes the focus of this chapter.

Myelin is a wrapping of surface membrane of oligodendrocytes (Schwann cells in the peripheral nervous system) around the axons, with little or no cytoplasm in between (Everett, 1971). The process of myelin formation occurs in two, partially overlapping stages. Initially, oligodendrocytes proliferate and differentiate. Subsequently, myelin is synthesized. Although the precise chemical structure has been only partially elucidated (Kinney et al., 1994), myelin, like other membranes, is composed of a lipid bilayer with several large proteins. Proteolipid protein (PLP) and myelin basic protein (MBP) are two such proteins, both of which are necessary for membrane compaction and span the bilayer. The outer layer of the membrane is composed mainly of cholesterol and glycolipids while the inner portion of the lipid bilayer is composed mainly of phospholipids (Braun, 1984).

Myelination in the human central nervous system (CNS) is a complex but orderly process, occurring in predictable topographical and chronological sequences. The sequence of myelination in the human brain has been carefully defined by histochemical (Kinney et al., 1994; Yakovlev and Lecours, 1967) as well as imaging (Barkovich et al., 1988; Bird et al., 1989; Martin et al., 1991; Nakagawa et al., 1998; Staudt et al., 1993; van der Knaap and Valk, 1990) methods. Histochemically, the CNS myelination begins as early as 12–14

weeks of gestation in the spinal cord and continues well into the third and fourth decades of life in the intracortical fibers of the cerebral cortex; but the most important and dramatic changes occur between midgestation and the end of the second postnatal year, with myelination accounting in large part for the large gain in brain weight, which more than triples during this period. The process slows markedly after 2 years of age (Yakovlev and Lecours, 1967).

## General rules of myelination

According to Yakovlev and Lecours (1967), myelination is a synchronized and orderly process of maturation of functionally allied systems of fibers. Several general rules governing the chronological and topographical sequences of the myelination process have been described. No single rule acts alone; rather, the interplay is complex, and one rule may supersede another to dictate the sequence of myelination within or across a particular axonal system.

As summarized by Kinney and colleagues (1994), these general rules are as follows: (1) Proximal pathways myelinate earlier and faster than do distal pathways; (2) sensory pathways myelinate before motor pathways; (3) projection pathways myelinate before associative pathways; (4) central telencephalic sites myelinate before poles; and (5) occipital poles myelinate before frontotemporal poles.

The more proximal the components of the fiber system, the shorter its myelination interval, as exemplified in (a) the visual system, in which the optic tract myelinates faster than the optic radiations which myelinate faster than the subcortical association fibers of the visual cortex; (b) the auditory system, in which the proximal auditory radiation myelinates faster than Heschl's gyrus (thalamic projections into the auditory cortex); and (c) the pyramidal system, in which the posterior limb of the internal capsule myelinates faster than the bulbar pyramid which myelinates faster than the lateral corticospinal tracts.

RICARDO C. SAMPAIO AND CHARLES L. TRUWIT Department of Radiology, University of Minnesota, Minneapolis, Minnesota.

Axonal myelination also proceeds from proximal to distal. Considering trans-synaptic systems, myelination proceeds from the neuron along the direction of impulse conduction. Thus, the proximal components of a fiber system myelinate earlier than do distal components. Moreover, these proximal components myelinate faster. Corollary to this, however, are the principles of central region before pole and occipital before temporal. For example, in the telencephalon, Heschl's gyrus, the distal auditory thalamic projection to the temporal lobe, myelinates after the distal optic radiation to the occipital pole. Proximal motor components also myelinate faster than do distal sensory components. Thus, the posterior limb of the internal capsule, which contains the proximal portion of the pyramidal system, myelinates earlier and faster than Heschl's gyrus, the distal portion of the auditory system (Kinney et al., 1994).

Myelination of fiber systems mediating sensory input to the thalamus and cerebral cortex precedes myelination of those fiber systems carrying output relating to movement, and these latter fibers myelinate before the association fibers. Thus, the fiber systems mediating vestibular and acoustic input myelinate early and rapidly before birth, the optic radiation and the pre- and postcentral cortical thalamic projections myelinate rapidly during the first year after birth, and these sensory systems anticipate the myelination of the pyramidal systems. Postnatally, the visual and auditory systems tend to have shorter myelination intervals than do pyramidal systems (Kinney et al., 1994; Yakovlev and Lecours, 1967).

Primary projection systems begin to myelinate earlier and have shorter myelination intervals than do associative systems. The thalamocorticopyramidal fiber systems have a relatively short cycle of myelination that is completed during the first postnatal year. The nonspecific thalamocorticopontine fiber systems show a long myelination cycle, prolonging into early childhood. In general, the association fibers in the supratentorial brain and the reticular formation in the brainstem continue to myelinate to at least the third decade (Kinney et al., 1994; Yakovlev and Lecours, 1967).

Overall, myelination progresses from caudal to cephalad and from dorsal to ventral. Within any particular region of the brain, the posterior region tends to myelinate first. Myelination in the central white matter of the cerebral hemispheres proceeds from the region around the central sulcus toward the poles, with the occipital pole myelinating before the frontal pole, which in turn myelinates before the temporal pole. In addition, the posterior poles have shorter myelination intervals than the anterior frontotemporal regions. The

posterior limb of the internal capsule myelinates earlier and faster than the anterior limb. The body and splenium of the corpus callosum, interconnecting the posterior frontal and parieto-occipital hemispheres, myelinate earlier and faster than the genu and rostrum, interconnecting the frontal poles.

There are exceptions to these rules, however. In the spinal and cranial nerves, motor roots myelinate earliest and rapidly, and anticipate myelination of the sensory roots. Maturation of myelin occurs in the optic tract before it does in the optic chiasm. Similarly, myelination is completed in the auditory radiation before it is in the brachium of the inferior colliculus. In addition, myelination of the callosal rostrum, genu, body, and splenium occurs before the respective subcortical and central white matter origins (Kinney et al., 1994).

## MR of postnatal brain development

Myelination of the human brain has been studied in vivo by means of magnetic resonance (MR) imaging (Barkovich et al., 1988; Bird et al., 1989; Martin et al., 1991; Nakagawa et al., 1998; Staudt et al., 1993; van der Knaap and Valk, 1990). The fundamental work in this domain was done by Barkovich and colleagues (1988), later complemented by others (Bird et al., 1989; Huppi et al., 1998; Koenig et al., 1990; Martin et al., 1991; Nakagawa et al., 1998; Staudt et al., 1993; Takeda et al., 1997; van der Knaap and Valk, 1990). To better understand the following description, a brief review of MR terminology may be helpful. Most MR images used to assess myelination are based on the concept of T1 or T2 weighting (table 3.1), which reflect differences in tissue water. T1-weighted images are typically more "anatomic," whereas T2-weighted images typically show subtle abnormalities reflected in changes in water, or edema. More importantly, images can be T1- or T2-weighted to optimize tissue characteristics.

T1-weighted images look like "cut brain." Cerebrospinal fluid spaces, such as the ventricles and sulci, are dark on T1-weighted images. Fatty tissues are bright. Myelin, containing phospholipids, is also bright relative to other intracranial structures. Thus, by the process of myelination, brain areas that are myelinated appear bright or hyperintense relative to other areas on the image. Moreover, areas of the brain with very tightly packed fiber bundles, such as the corpus callosum, extrude any free water from their myelin fibers and thus appear even brighter on the image.

T2-weighted images are essentially inverted in their signal characteristics. Hence, myelinated brain, with an abundance of phospholipid, appears hypointense.

TABLE 3.1

*MR milestones of CNS myelination*

| Anatomic Region | Age at Which Myelination Appears | |
|---|---|---|
| | T1-Weighted Images | T1-Weighted Images |
| Inferior cerebellar peduncle | Present at birth | Present at birth |
| Middle cerebellar peduncle | 1 month | 1–2 months |
| Superior cerebellar peduncle | Present at birth | Present at birth |
| Posterior cerebellar peduncle | | |
|   Anterior portion | Present at birth | 4–7 months |
|   Posterior portion | Present at birth | Birth to 2 months |
| Anterior limb internal capsule | 2–3 months | 7–11 months |
| Genu corpus callosum | 4–6 months | 5–8 months |
| Splenium corpus callosum | 3–4 months | 4–6 months |
| Occipital white matter | | |
|   Central | 3–5 months | 9–14 months |
| Peripheral | 4–7 months | 11–15 months |
| Frontal white matter | | |
|   Central | 3–6 months | 11–16 months |
|   Peripheral | 7–11 months | 14–18 months |
| Centrum semiovale | 2–6 months | 7–11 months |

Modified from Barkovich et al., 1988.

Fluid, on the other hand, is ideally imaged on T2-weighted images: The ventricles are bright.

On MR imaging, brain maturation during the first 2 years of life consists primarily of signal changes secondary to the process of myelination and occurs at different rates and at different times on different types of images.

Changes of brain signal due to myelination will appear first on T1-weighted images as increased signal relative to gray matter. Eventually, a corresponding drop of T2 signal will be seen. In general, changes in white matter maturation are best seen on T1-weighted images during the first 6–8 months of life and on the T2-weighted images between the ages of 6 and 18 months (Barkovich et al., 1988). Most recently, a new MR imaging technique, diffusion-weighted imaging, has been used for assessment of brain maturation in humans (Huppi et al., 1998; Takeda et al., 1997). Diffusion-weighted imaging is sensitive to brownian motion of water. Acute injury to the brain, such as edema and/or cytotoxicity, results in restricted brownian motion, and hence altered diffusion, of extracellular water. Similarly, on diffusion-weighted images, it is possible to map brain maturation, as unbound water tends to follow pathways of least resistance. With myelination, water is more likely to follow an axonal bundle than to cross it. This so-called diffusion anisotropy becomes apparent within white matter tracts. In fact, the signal changes on diffusion-weighted images may precede corresponding changes on conventional T1-weighted images. Active myelination from the perinatal period onward can be identified by imaging, and thus the progression of

myelination provides an excellent parameter of brain maturation.

The changes in signal intensity seen on T1- and T2-weighted images closely parallel the known pattern of myelination as determined by histochemical studies. At birth, the dorsal pons, portions of the superior and inferior cerebellar peduncles, the decussation of the superior cerebellar peduncles, the posterior limb of the internal capsule, the central corona radiata, the optic chiasm, the optic tract, the ansa lenticularis, and the fibers originating in the external segment and traversing the internal segment of the globus pallidus are partially myelinated. These are seen as areas of increased signal intensity on the T1-weighted images and as decreased signal intensity on the T2-weighted images of newborns (figures 3.1, 3.2, and 3.3).

On T1-weighted images, unmyelinated white matter is hypointense relative to gray matter. With myelination, phospholipids occupy the space otherwise occupied by interstitial water and the T1 signal increases, from hypointense to hyperintense, relative to gray matter. On T2-weighted images, the reverse picture can be seen, with unmyelinated white matter being hyperintense relative to gray matter. As the white matter matures, its T2 signal decreases from hyperintense to hypointense relative to gray matter, passing through a phase of isointensity to gray matter.

The causes of the T1 shortening (increase in T1 signal intensity) associated with myelination are related to but, at least in part, independent from the causes of T2 shortening (decrease in T2 signal intensity). As already

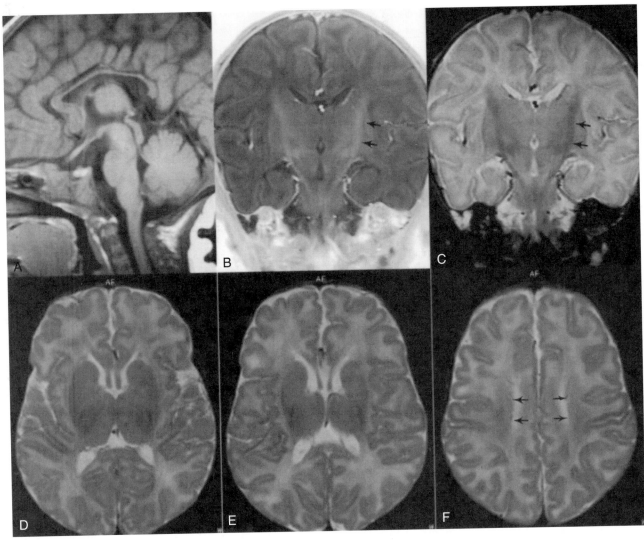

FIGURE 3.1  Sagittal T1-weighted image (**A**) of an 8-week-old boy shows thin, and not yet myelinated corpus callosum. Hyperintense pituitary is normal at this age. Coronal inversion recovery images (**B**, **C**) show myelination of corticospinal tracts (arrows), but the remainder of white matter is still hypointense on the T1-weighted image (**B**) and hyperintense on the T2-weighted image (**C**). Axial T2-weighted images (**D–F**) show subtle myelination of internal capsule and basal ganglia, but the white matter is still hyperintense overall. Note early myelination (mottled hypointensity) of corona radiata (arrows, **F**).

mentioned, brain maturation occurs at different rates and times on T1-weighted and T2-weighted images. The discrepancy is mild in certain areas (2 months in the corpus callosum) but marked in others (6–10 months in the centrum semiovale) (Barkovich et al., 1988). From estimations of T1 and T2 relaxation times, it is evident that a significant and global decrease in T1 and T2 relaxation times occurs during the first few months of life, preceding the myelination of large parts of the brain (van der Knaap and Valk, 1990). This observation is in accord with animal experimental work, which shows that an impressive decrease in water content of the brain occurs just prior to the onset of a wave of

myelination with even a temporary decline in brain weight. It is, however, probable that the changes in T1 and T2 values are due not only to a decreasing water content of the brain, but also to a change in biochemical composition caused by the arrival of precursors of myelin constituents and materials necessary in the process of myelin formation (van der Knaap and Valk, 1990). When myelin is deposited, another important decrease in T1 and T2 values occurs. This decrease is presumed to be related to the degree of myelination. The further T1 shortening correlates temporally with the increase in cholesterol and glycolipids that accompany the formation of myelin from oligodendrocytes

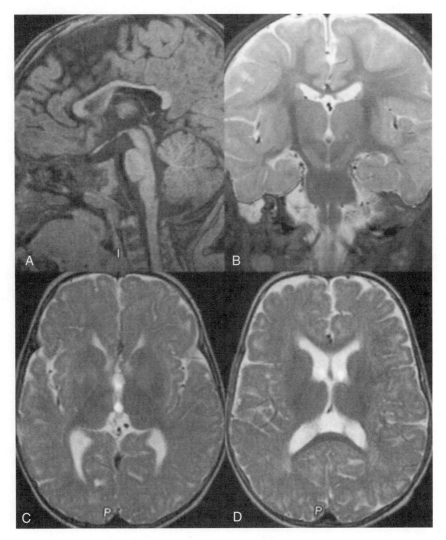

FIGURE 3.2 A sagittal T1-weighted image (**A**) of the same child at 8 months shows normal myelination of corpus callosum (pituitary is normal on adjacent slice, not shown). A coronal inversion recovery image (**B**) shows considerable myelination by virtue of relatively hypointense white matter. Axial T2-weighted images (**C, D**) show that much of the subcortical white matter is not yet myelinated.

and probably reflects shortening of the T1 relaxation time of the water in the white matter resulting from a very large interaction with myelin lipid (Koenig et al., 1990; Nakagawa et al., 1998; Poduslo and Jang, 1984). The further decrease in T2 signal intensity of myelinating white matter correlates temporally with the tightening of the spiral of myelin around the axon, which is accompanied by loss of white matter water content. As myelin matures, it becomes increasingly hydrophobic because of the development of the inner layer of phospholipids. This hydrophobic layer results in the presence of fewer aqueous protons and a diminution in signal intensity on the T2-weighted images secondary to a combination of shortened T2 relaxation time and a decrease in water content. T1-weighted images are a better way of detecting the primary process of myeli-

nation, whereas T2-weighted images seem better suited for evaluating the associated changes in water content (Barkovich et al., 1988). Diffusion-weighted images are able to detect the process of myelination owing to their sensitivity to changes of water diffusion induced by the myelin membranes (Huppi et al., 1998; Takeda et al., 1997). They may be more sensitive than T1-weighted images to white matter myelination, but their use has been limited essentially to experimental work.

Neonatal posterior fossa structures that exhibit high T1 and low T2 signal intensity at birth include the dorsal brainstem and the inferior and superior cerebellar peduncles (Barkovich et al., 1988). An increase in T1 signal intensity denoting early myelination of the deep cerebellar white matter appears near the end of the first month of life and steadily increases, with high signal

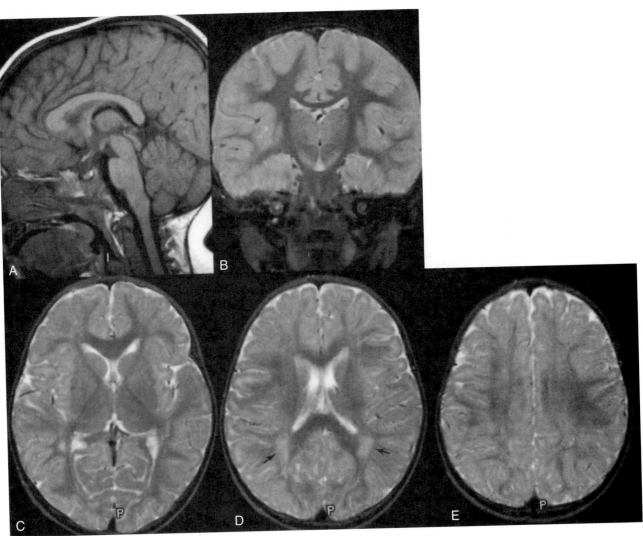

FIGURE 3.3   A sagittal T1-weighted image (**A**) of another child at 13 months shows normal corpus callosum. Coronal inversion recovery image (**B**) shows more advanced myelination of white matter, even at the subcortical level. Axial T2-weighted images (**C, D, E**) show expected myelination of corpus callosum genu and splenium, deep white matter, and internal capsules. Note the still incompletely myelinated subcortical white matter and persistent terminal zones of myelination at peritrigonal level (arrows, **D**).

intensity developing in the subcortical white matter of the cerebellar folia by the third month. At 3 months of age the cerebellum has a T1 appearance similar to that seen in the adult. On T2-weighted images, the middle cerebellar peduncle begin to decrease in signal intensity during the second month of life. Low T2 signal intensity in the subcortical white matter of the cerebellar folia (arborization) begins to develop at approximately the eighth month (5 months later than on T1-weighted images), and the cerebellum reaches an adult appearance at approximately 18 months (15 months later than on T1-weighted images). Signal intensity in the ventral pons increases less rapidly, occurring during the third through the sixth months.

In the supratentorial brain, the decussation of the superior cerebellar peduncles, the ventral lateral region of the thalamus, the dorsal putamen, and the posterior limb of the internal capsule exhibit high T1 signal intensity at birth. To a lesser extent, these structures also demonstrate areas of low T2 signal intensity at birth. The development of T1 and T2 signal changes proceeds rostrally from the pons along the corticospinal tracts into the cerebral peduncles, the posterior limb of the internal capsule, and the central portion of the centrum semiovale. The white matter of the pre- and post-central gyri is of high T1 and low T2 signal intensity, respectively, compared to the surrounding cortex by about 1 month of age. The change to high T1 signal intensity in the subcortical motor tracts is essentially complete by 3 months of age. By age 2 months, patches of low T2 signal intensity are seen in the central centrum semiovale.

In infants less than 1 month old, high T1 signal intensity is present in the optic nerve, optic tracts, and optic radiations. By age 3 months, the occipital white matter surrounding the calcarine fissure is of high T1 signal intensity. Low T2 signal intensity is seen in the optic tracts at age 1 month, the decrease in signal intensity extends posteriorly along the optic radiations during the subsequent 2 months, and by 4 months of age the calcarine fissure shows some low T2 signal intensity. Diffusional anisotropy denoting myelination is present in the optic radiations in infants less than 1 month old.

The posterior limb of the internal capsule is of high T1 signal intensity at birth; high signal intensity does not develop in the anterior limb of the internal capsule until 2–3 months of age. The more anterior portion of the posterior limb of the internal capsule contains a thin strip of T2 hypointensity by approximately 7 months; progressive thickening of the hypointense area continues up to 10 months of age. The anterior limb of the internal capsule is completely T2-hypointense by 11 months in all subjects; T2 hypointensity can be detected as early as 7 months in some subjects but is always preceded by detectability of low signal intensity in the posterior limb.

The splenium of the corpus callosum shows high T1 signal intensity in all infants by 4 months. The increase in signal intensity proceeds rostrally; the genu is always of high signal intensity by age 6 months. Likewise, on T2-weighted images, myelination proceeds in a posterior-to-anterior fashion. The splenium of the corpus callosum shows low T2 signal intensity by age 6 months and the genu by age 8 months. The basal ganglia begin to diminish in T2 signal intensity relative to the subcortical white matter at 7 months of age. The basal ganglia appear essentially isointense with the subcortical white matter by the age of approximately 10 months.

Maturation of the subcortical white matter, other than the visual and motor regions, begins at 3 months on T1-weighted images and at 9–12 months on T2-weighted images. The deep white matter matures in a posterior-to-anterior direction, with the deep occipital white matter maturing first and the frontal and temporal white matter last. On T1-weighted images, peripheral extension and increasing complexity of arborization of the subcortical white matter continue approximately until age 7 months in the occipital white matter and 8–11 months in the frontal and temporal white matter. Only minimal changes are seen on T1-

weighted images after 8 months, consisting of increasing signal intensity in the most peripheral regions of the frontal, temporal, and parietal white matter. On T2-weighted images, peripheral extension of the low signal intensity into the subcortical white matter begins at about 1 year and is essentially complete by 22–24 months.

On T1-weighted images, a brain pattern essentially identical to that seen in adults is seen by approximately 8 months of age. With the exception of the so-called terminal zones (persistent areas of high T2 signal intensity in the white matter dorsal and superior to the trigones of the lateral ventricles), white matter maturation, as assessed by MR imaging, is complete by the end of the second year of life. The terminal zones probably represent the areas of known delayed myelination of fiber tracts involving the association areas of the posterior and inferior parietal and posterior temporal cortex, as described by Yakovlev and Lecours (1967). These areas of high T2 signal intensity are seen throughout the first decade and, in some subjects, into the second decade of life.

It is difficult to distinguish fiber bundles (e.g., medial lemniscus or optic radiation) from surrounding tissue by MR in adults. This is because the white matter surrounding each fiber bundle has the same signal intensity as the fiber bundle. Early in development, fiber bundles can be distinguished from surrounding white matter because myelination of fiber bundles precedes that of surrounding white matter in the neonatal period; later, however, they become indistinguishable owing to the progression of myelination in the surrounding white matter. The time of blurring (when the fiber bundle becomes indistinguishable from surrounding white matter) may be a useful parameter of brain maturation in infancy. Eighteen fiber bundles were analyzed by Nakagawa and colleagues (1998). These authors found that not only do different bundles start to myelinate at different times and myelinate at different rates, but also they blur at different times, with some of the bundles showing no blurring (e.g., posterior limb of internal capsule).

## Sequences of CNS myelination

Historically, in elucidating the factors that determine the topographical and chronological sequences of CNS myelination, the process of myelination has been considered relative to the development of human behavior. This approach resulted in the analysis of the sequence of myelination in terms of relationships among anatomic systems associated with different functions. Yakovlev and Lecours (1967) held that the myelination proceeds along a hierarchy of increasingly complex CNS functions ending in the maturation of association and intracortical fibers critical to the highest intellectual functions, and that myelination represents the anatomic correlate of neurophysiological maturation. Functionally related systems myelinate together, and the timing of myelination reflects the position of the fiber system in the hierarchy of the functional organization of the developing nervous system. They referred to the temporal aspect of myelination in a fiber system, from its onset to completion, as its *myelogenetic cycle* and observed that this cycle may have an early or late onset with a rapid or slow course. Different sites not only begin myelination at different times, but also progress to maturation over different time intervals (Kinney et al., 1994; Yakovlev and Lecours, 1967). The early onset of myelination does not predict early myelin maturation (Kinney et al., 1988; Yakovlev and Lecours, 1967).

Myelin sheaths appear in the *motor root fibers* of the spinal nerves at the end of the fourth fetal month, while the *sensory fibers* begin to myelinate at the end of the fifth month. The motor nerve roots reach their adult pattern of myelination at about term while the sensory nerve rootlets continue to myelinate for several months after birth. Among the cranial nerves, the roots of the eighth pair are the first to show myelinated fibers. At the end of the fifth fetal month, the roots of both divisions of the eighth nerve are myelinated. The oculomotor nerves (III, IV, VI) and the motor division of the trigeminal nerve myelinate next, at about the same time. As in the spinal roots, the cranial motor roots seem to myelinate at a faster pace than the sensory roots. The cycle of myelination of the cranial nerve roots appears to be completed early in the first postnatal year.

Except for the dorsal root fibers in the posterior columns of the spinal cord, there are no myelinated fibers in the CNS before the end of the fifth fetal month. In the brain, the *vestibulocochlear* system of fibers is the first to demonstrate myelination, having not only an early beginning but also a very short cycle of myelination. The fibers of this system in the brainstem complete the cycle of myelination at about the middle of the ninth fetal month, and from the sixth fetal month to term they dominate the myelin-staining preparations of the brainstem.

The cycles of myelination of the inferior, middle, and superior cerebellar peduncles exhibit remarkable differences. The inner, vestibulocerebellar division of the *inferior cerebellar peduncle* begins to myelinate early in the sixth fetal month and attains an adult pattern of myelination by the end of eighth fetal month. The cycle of the inner division is about the same as that of the vestibulocochlear system. In sharp contrast, the outer division, containing spino-, olivo- and reticulocerebellar fibers, shows no myelinated fibers until the eighth fetal month and thereafter continues to myelinate until about the third postnatal month; its cycle is long and comparable to that of the medial lemniscus. Myelination of the *superior cerebellar peduncles* begins in the eighth fetal month, approximately 6 weeks later than the inner division of the inferior peduncle but before myelinated fibers are present in the outer division of this peduncle. In comparison with the superior and inferior peduncles, the *middle cerebellar peduncles* demonstrate the most protracted cycle of myelination. Myelinated fibers in the transverse bundles of the pons appear only during the first postnatal month, and myelination extends into the middle cerebellar peduncles during the second postnatal month. The pontocerebellar fibers continue to gain slowly in intensity of myelination at least until the fourth postnatal year.

In man the *reticular formation* of the brainstem exhibits a very long cycle of myelination and, in this respect, matches the protracted cycle of myelination in the commissural and association fiber systems of the telencephalon.

In the supratentorial brain, no myelinated fibers are encountered before the seventh fetal month. Early in the seventh month the first myelinated fibers appear in the fasciculus habenulointerpeduncularis, which myelinates rapidly and completes its cycle of myelination before term. In the last trimester intense myelination occurs in the subthalamic region, thalamus, and pallidum.

The brachia of the inferior colliculi and the medial geniculate nuclei are among the earliest *extrinsic thalamic afferents* to myelinate. They begin to myelinate in the seventh fetal month, well in advance of the terminal fibers of the medial lemniscus and optic tract, and complete the cycle at about the fourth postnatal month. The contrast between early myelination of the acoustic and late myelination of the optic colliculi is noteworthy. Myelination of the optic nerves and tracts, of the superior colliculi and their brachia, and of the lateral geniculate nuclei begins late in the ninth fetal month. However, the optic system, as a whole, completes the cycle rapidly near the third postnatal month. By the middle of the eighth fetal month, the myelinated fibers of the medial lemniscus reach their thalamic nuclei. Their myelination is complete by the eighth postnatal month. The reticulum and the intrinsic fibers of the thalamus myelinate at a slower pace.

Myelination of *thalamocortical radiations* is related to the thalamic nucleus involved and has been described in terms of so-called "specific" and "nonspecific" thalamic nuclei. Projections from the specific nuclei of the basal complex (or "relay" nuclei) myelinate earlier and exhibit a shorter cycle than do projections from the nonspecific nuclei of the anteromedial and dorsal complex. Among the specific thalamic projections, the optic radiations to the primary visual cortex of the occipital lobe exhibit the shortest cycle of myelination, beginning late in the first postnatal month and reaching maturity about the fourth postnatal month. Myelination of the projections from the ventrobasal complex of the thalamic nuclei to the postcentral cortex appears in the lenticulothalamic region of the posterior limb of the internal capsule at the end of the ninth month and during the tenth month rapidly extends into the core of the postcentral gyrus; but, in contrast to the optic radiations, these projections seem to complete the cycle only at about the first postnatal year. Myelination of the acoustic radiations from the medial geniculate to Heshl's gyrus in the temporal lobe and from the lateroventral complex to the precentral cortex of the frontal lobe exhibits a still longer cycle, which is completed at about 4 years of age. It is also noteworthy that myelination of the cortical end of the acoustic system in the temporal lobe is protracted beyond the first postnatal year, in sharp contrast to the visual system, which myelinates rapidly soon after birth in one short spurt from retina to its end about the calcarine fissure.

The first myelinated fibers in the *internal capsule* appear in the ninth fetal month in the lenticulothalamic sector of the posterior limb. From the ninth fetal month to the fourth postnatal month, the myelination spreads fanwise posteriorly into the retrolenticular sector of the posterior limb and, much more slowly, anteriorly into the anterior limb. The thalamocortical radiations reach the postcentral cortex (somesthetic area) during the first postnatal month, and later appear in the precentral gyrus (propriokinesthetic area). During the first postnatal month there is also a spurt of myelination of the corticofugal fibers from the postcentral and the precentral cortices. Myelination of the fibers in the anterior limb of the internal capsule lags behind that of the posterior limb but accelerates from the fourth postnatal month, and by the eighth month is similar to that of the posterior limb.

Myelination of the *pyramidal tract* is synchronized closely with that of specific thalamocortical projections from the ventrobasal complex of thalamic nuclei. Myelination of the pyramidal tract fibers appears first at the pontine level and spreads cephalad into the cerebral peduncles and internal capsule and caudad into the bulbar pyramids. Below the pons, fibers of the bulbar pyramids complete their myelination cycle at about 1 year. Of all the long descending transcapsular tracts,

the *corticopontine tracts* myelinate latest and longest. The cycle of myelination of the corticopontine tracts appears to be synchronized with the cycle of myelination of the nonspecific thalamocortical projections from the medial dorsal and pulvinar nuclei.

In the white matter of the telencephalon, myelination of the long association and commissural fiber systems is protracted, lasting until at least the end of the first decade of life. The commissural fibers in the splenium of the corpus callosum and forceps major begin to myelinate at about the fourth postnatal month. Myelination spreads gradually and slowly from the splenium toward the genu, the rostrum, and forceps minor of the corpus callosum. From pathologic studies, myelination of commissural fibers in the corpus callosum seems to continue slowly even after the first decade. The intracortical neuropil of the anterolateral convexity of the frontal lobes, of the inferior parietal lobes, and of the basolateral convexity shows even longer myelination cycles.

## Summary

The unique ability of MR imaging to reveal not only gross structural organization of the human brain but also macroscopic changes in intra- and extracellular water (diffusion-weighted MR imaging) enables us to see the in vivo human brain as never before. In this chapter, the process and sequence of brain myelination have been reviewed, as has the correlate appearance on MR images. In tandem with the structural changes that occur with myelination are functional changes of the human central nervous system. Over the past five years, and certainly over the next five years, cognitive neuroscientists and their neuroradiological counterparts have had and will have incredible opportunities to "see" brain function with the relatively new field of functional MR imaging. While fMRI of the pediatric brain remains in its infancy (see Casey, Thomas, and McCandliss, chapter 10), it is anticipated that the field of developmental fMRI will emerge and offer the opportunity to marry anatomic structure with histologic maturation and cognitive development.

REFERENCES

BARKOVICH, A., B. KJOS, D. JACKSON, and D. NORMAN, 1988. Normal maturation of the neonatal and infant brain: MR imaging at 1.5 T. *Radiology* 166:173–180.

BIRD, R., M. HEDBERG, B. DRAYER, P. KELLER, R. FLOM, and J. HODAK, 1989. MR assessment of myelination in infants and children: Usefulness of marker sites. *Am. J. Neuroradiol.* 10:731–740.

Braun, P. E., 1984. Molecular organization of myelin. In *Myelin*, 2d ed., P. Morell, ed. New York: Plenum Press, pp. 97–116.

Everett, N. B., 1971. Histology and cytology of neurons and neuroglia. In *Functional Neuroanatomy*, N. B. Everett, ed. Philadelphia: Lea & Febiger, pp. 16–28.

Huppi, P., S. Maier, S. Peled, G. P. Zientara, P. D. Barnes, F. A. Jolesz, and J. J. Volpe, 1998. Microstructural development of human newborn cerebral white matter assessed in vivo by diffusion tensor magnetic resonance imaging. *Pediatr. Res.* 44:584–590.

Kinney, H., B. Brody, A. Kloman, and F. Gilles, 1988. Sequence of central nervous system myelination in human infancy: Patterns of myelination in autopsied infants. *J. Neuropathol. Exp. Neurol.* 47:217–234.

Kinney, H., J. Karthigasan, N. Borenshteyn, J. Flax, and D. Kirschner, 1994. Myelination in the developing human brain: Biochemical correlates. *Neurochem. Res.* 19:983–996.

Koenig, S., R. Brown, M. Spiller, and N. Lundbom, 1990. Relaxometry of brain: Why white matter appears bright on MRI. *Magn. Reson. Med.* 14:482–495.

Martin, E., S. Krassnitzer, P. Kaelin, and C. Boesch, 1991. MR imaging of the brainstem: Normal postnatal development. *Neuroradiology* 33:391–395.

Nakagawa, H., S. Iawsaki, K. Kichkawa, et al., 1998. Normal myelination of anatomic nerve fiber bundles: MR analysis. *Am. J. Neuroradiol.* 19:1129–1136.

Poduslo, S., and Y. Jang, 1984. Myelin development in infant brain. *Neurochem. Res.* 9:1615–1626.

Staudt, M., C. Schropp, F. Staudt, N. Obletter, K. Bise, and A. Breit, 1993. Myelination of the brain in MRI: A staging system. *Pediatr. Radiol.* 1993:169–176.

Takeda, K., Y. Nomura, H. Sakuma, T. Tagami, T. Okuda, and T. Nakagawa, 1997. MR assessment of normal brain development in neonates and infants: Comparative study of T1- and diffusion-weighted images. *J. Comput. Assist. Tomogr.* 21:1–7.

van der Knaap, M., and J. Valk, 1990. MR imaging of the various stages of normal myelination during the first year of life. *Neuroradiology* 31:459–470.

Yakovlev, P. I., and A. R. Lecours, 1967. The myelogenetic cycles of regional maturation of the brain. In *Regional Development of the Brain in Early Life*, A. Mankowski, ed. Philadelphia: Davis, pp. 3–69.

# 4 Morphological Changes of the Human Hippocampal Formation from Midgestation to Early Childhood

## LÁSZLÓ SERESS

ABSTRACT Cytoarchitectonic layers of the human hippocampal formation are formed by the 24–25th fetal weeks. Consequently, cell formation in the hippocampal ventricular zone is occasional after the 24th week. Cell formation in the hilar region is continuous perinatally, but neuronal cell formation and cell death occur at a very low rate. Cell migration from the proliferative zones lasts until the 32–34th fetal weeks in Ammon's horn. Immature cells accumulate in the hilus of the dentate gyrus throughout the first year, when the subgranular hilar zone appears cell-free, suggesting that immature cells from the hilus migrate to the granule cell layer and differentiate into granule cells. Dendritic development and synapse formation last for several years. Light microscopic changes of dendrites of the hippocampal neurons have been reported until the fifth postnatal year. Although the hippocampal formation of newborn infants has the necessary synaptic connections for memory formation, the number of postnatal morphological changes suggests a significant modification of hippocampal circuits between the neonatal period and adulthood.

The hippocampal formation plays an important role in the mechanisms of memory and learning. Experimental data in rodents and primates as well as clinical data in humans suggest that an individual with an immature or lesioned hippocampus is unable to perform memory and learning tasks as well as a normal adult. Brain development does not stop at birth, and recent data suggest that development may last until adulthood. In harmony with that notion, accumulating data indicate a prolonged development of the human hippocampal formation that includes cell formation, cell migration, and synapse formation. This chapter summarizes the morphological changes that occur from the 24th week of gestation to the period when further changes in the hippocampal formation are not detectable under the light microscope and the structure appears to be adult-like. The 24th week has been chosen, as that week is the approximate time after which most prematurely born infants survive. The aim of this chapter is to provide age-specific morphological data against which behavioral scientists might correlate their relevant behavioral observations. The results of animal experiments are only briefly reviewed.

## Neuronal cell formation in the hippocampal formation

In animal experiments, multiplying neurons can be marked by isotope-labeled thymidine or the uridine analogue bromodeoxyuridine (BrdU). It has been shown, both in rodents and primates, that a majority of neurons in the entorhinal cortex, subicular complex, and Ammon's horn are formed before birth (Angevine, 1975; Rakic and Nowakowski, 1981). In rodents, a few hippocampal neurons continue to form in the last days of pregnancy, but no neurons are formed postnatally (Angevine, 1975). In primates, all neurons are formed in the first half of pregnancy (Rakic and Nowakowski, 1981). There is only one region of the hippocampal formation where postnatal neuronal formation occurs, and that is the dentate gyrus. The major difference between rodents and primates in the formation of granule cells is that in rodents approximately 85% of these neurons are formed postnatally, whereas similar numbers of cells are formed prenatally in primates (Bayer, 1980; Rakic and Nowakowski, 1981). In rodents, the process of granule cell formation lasts for 3 weeks, whereas in monkeys newly formed granule cells have been visualized through the first postnatal month.

In humans, data about neuronal formation are based on the first appearance of stained neurons at their final cytoarchitectonic position; this is because direct labeling of dividing cells is not possible. In the human hippocampus, pyramidal neurons already form distinct cell layers by the 15th gestational week. During the 23–25th gestational weeks the pyramidal cell layer of Ammon's horn and the cytoarchitectonics of the subiculum and

LÁSZLÓ SERESS Central Electron Microscopic Laboratory, Faculty of Medicine, University of Pécs, Pécs, Szigeti, Hungary.

entorhinal cortex are close to what has been observed in adults (Arnold and Trojanowski, 1996a; Humphrey, 1967). The only exception to this general pattern concerns the granule cell layer of the dentate gyrus, which first appears during the 13–14th gestational weeks and continues to grow after birth (Humphrey, 1967; Seress, 1992). However, formation of cell layers includes migration of neurons from the place of final cell division. Therefore, in humans, there are no direct data about the exact time of final cell multiplication in the hippocampal formation.

With recent developments in immunocytochemistry, it is possible to detect cell multiplication in paraffin-embedded postmortem tissue. Ki-67 is a commercially available mouse monoclonal antibody that reacts with an antigen, mainly present in the nucleoli (Verheijen et al., 1989a,b). This monoclonal antibody is widely used in histopathology, and comparison with other cell proliferation markers concluded that Ki-67 is the best proliferation marker in conventional histological preparations (Brown and Gatter, 1990; Rose, Maddox, and Brown, 1994). In our studies we have used the Ki-67 antibody (MIB-1; Immunotech) to detect cell formation in postmortem brains. The human hippocampi have been obtained from autopsy, 6–12 hours after death. In the current study, only those patients who had no history of brain-related disorders and in whom autopsy confirmed the cause of death were included. Our material consists of brains from premature infants (24–35 weeks), newborns (36–40 weeks), infants (1–11.5 months), young children (1–10 years), and adults (table 4.1). The gestational age of premature infants and newborns is based on postovulation time and on somatic measurements at birth, and considered to be accurate by ±1 week. In this chapter, the term "hippocampal formation" refers to the dentate gyrus, Ammon's horn, the subicular complex, and the entorhinal cortex. The terminology suggested by Amaral (1990) has been applied to the subdivisions of each structure.

There is a significant increase in the volume of the hippocampal formation from fetal to postnatal development, but the borders of subdivisions do not change and are distinguishable from the earliest age group demonstrated in this study (figure 4.1). In 24-week-old infants, there are several labeled cells in all parts of the hippocampal formation. Many cells are labeled in the ventricular zone underlying the hippocampal formation (figure 4.2D; see color plate 1) and in the hilar region (figure 4.2A,B; see color plate 1). There are only a few labeled cells inside the pyramidal layer of Ammon's horn (figure 4.2C; see color plate 1). Most labeled cells in the CA1–3 areas are in the subplate zone where immature neurons pass from the ventricular

zone and move toward the developing dentate gyrus (figure 4.2C). There are labeled cells in all layers of the subicular complex and entorhinal cortex (figure 4.3A,B; see color plate 2). Often, the type of labeled cells, based on the morphology of cell nuclei, is unclear; but in several cases, glial and endothelial cells are positively identified among the labeled elements (figure 4.3A). While there are no multiplying cells in the hippocampal ventricular zone, a large mass of cells persists in the subventricular zone underlying the parahippocampal formation and the adjacent neocortex (figure 4.3C; see color plate 2). In that subventricular cell mass at least half of the cells are immunolabeled by Ki-67, suggesting very active cell formation (figure 4.3C). Large numbers of cells are labeled in the temporal cortex, especially in the upper three layers. There are proportionately fewer labeled cells in the hippocampal formation in 28–32-week and 34-week-old infants. In 36–40-week-old newborns practically all labeled cells are glial or endothelial cells in the subicular complex and entorhinal cortex. Similarly, only a few glial elements are labeled in Ammon's horn, but no neurons (figure 4.4C; see color plate 3). The dentate gyrus consists of several labeled cells in the hilar region, both inside the granule cell layer and in the molecular layer (figure 4.4A; see color plate 3). Based on their nuclear morphology, these cells can be neurons, although no cells were immunoreactive for both Ki-67 and neuron-specific enolase (NCL-NSE2; Novocastra) in children born at term who died in a few hours after birth. However, in the very early stage of cellular development, when cell nuclei are labeled by Ki-67, the cytoplasm may not be sufficiently mature to show enolase activity. Most labeled cells are glial cells in the hilus and the molecular layer of the dentate gyrus of newborn infants (figure 4.4B,C; see color plate 3). In the postnatal period, labeled cells are less and less frequent in the dentate gyrus. There are a few immunopositive cells in every section of the hilus in 3- or 3.5-month-old children (figure 4.5B; see color plate 4), but most labeled cells are in the molecular layer (figure 4.5A; see color plate 4). In most cases, cellular morphology of labeled cells indicates that those labeled are glial cells (figure 4.5A,B,C; see color plate 4). In a few cases the labeled nuclei indicate neurons both in the dentate gyrus (figure 4.5F; see color plate 4) and the entorhinal cortex (figure 4.5G; see color plate 4). Double labeling with neuron-specific enolase is unlikely; therefore, our aim is to identify the Ki-67 labeled cell nuclei in the electron microscope, since the nuclear ultrastructures of glial cells and young neurons are distinguishable from each other (Eckenhoff and Rakic, 1988). It is interesting that the number of labeled glial cells is much higher in the

TABLE 4.1

*Summary of personal data, histological stainings, and clinical diagnoses verified by autopsy*

| No. | Case | Age | Diagnosis | Stain |
|---|---|---|---|---|
| 1 | Z. K. | 24 gestational weeks | IRDS | CV, MIB-1 |
| 2 | H. I. | 28 weeks | IRDS | CV, MIB-1 |
| 3 | K. L. | 30 weeks | IRDS | CV |
| 4 | T. R. | 32 weeks | Sepsis, pneumonia, CHD | CV |
| 5 | O. R. | 34 weeks | Pneumonia, IRDS | CV, MIB-1 |
| 6 | K. L. | 36 weeks | IRDS, CHD | CV |
| 7 | J. P. | 36 weeks | Respiratory distress, asphyxia | CV, MIB-1 |
| 8 | T. V. | 38 weeks | CHD, IRDS | CV, MIB-1 |
| 9 | R. M. | 38 weeks | Esophageal atresia, pneumonia | CV |
| 10 | B. B. | 38 weeks | Spina bifida | CV, MIB-1 |
| 11 | B. B. | 39 weeks | Respiratory distress, asphyxia | CV, MIB-1 |
| 12 | SZ. T. | 39 weeks | Pneumonia, asphyxia | CV |
| 13 | K. M. | 40 weeks | Respiratory distress, asphyxia | CV |
| 14 | A. R. | 40 weeks | CHD | CV |
| 15 | L. D. | 1 postnatal week | BPD | CV, MIB-1 |
| 16 | T. T. | 1 week | CHD | CV, MIB-1 |
| 17 | X.Y. | 1 week | SIDS | Rapid-Golgi |
| 18 | K. I. | 1 month | Pneumonia | CV |
| 19 | G. U. | 1 month | SIDS | Rapid-Golgi |
| 20 | B. J. | 2 months | Sepsis | CV |
| 21 | S. P. | 2.5 months | CHD | Rapid-Golgi |
| 22 | T. M. | 3 months | Pneumonia, muscular dystrophy | CV |
| 23 | N. L. | 3 months | CHD | CV, MIB-1 |
| 24 | K. F. | 3 months | CHD | CV, MIB-1 |
| 25 | H.G. | 5 months | Respiratory distress, asphyxia | CV, MIB-1 |
| 26 | J. M. | 7 months | SIDS | Rapid-Golgi |
| 27 | B. K. | 8.5 months | Pneumonia | CV |
| 28 | F. E. | 11.5 months | Muscular atrophy | CV, MIB-1 |
| 29 | S. K. | 11 months | Ileus | CV |
| 30 | T. P. | 15 months | Pneumonia | Rapid-Golgi |
| 31 | M. P. | 3 years | Intestinal neoplasm | Rapid-Golgi |
| 32 | L. H. | 5 years | Drowning | Rapid-Golgi |
| 33 | N. D. | 9 years | CO intoxication | Rapid-Golgi |
| 34 | A. N. | 10 years | Traffic accident | Rapid-Golgi |
| 35 | K. I. | 47 years | Heart attack | CV, Rapid-Golgi |

CV = cresyl-violet staining; MIB-1 = immunostaining with Ki-67 antibody; IRDS = infant respiratory distress syndrome; CHD = congenital heart disease; BPD = bronchopulmonary dysplasia; SIDS = sudden infant death syndrome.

granule cell and molecular layers of the dentate gyrus in the 11.5-month-old child (figure 4.5D,E; see color plate 4) than in either the 3- or the 5-month-old children. The large number of small, round, darkly stained labeled cells in the upper molecular layer suggests an active cell multiplication of oligodendroglia cells that might be related to active myelin formation during this age span. Considering the total number of neurons of the granule cell layer of a newborn child, the labeling index per section is in the range of 1:1000. In later age groups this index is lower. The cerebellum of the same children has always been processed for immunostaining together with the hippocampus. Sparsity of immuno-reactive cells in the hippocampal formation is not a methodological failure: In the external germinal layer of the cerebellum of the 3- and 5-month-old children,

the labeling index is above 35%, while the hippocampal formation shows only a few labeled cells (Ábrahám et al., 1999). There were only a few cases when material could be obtained from children older than 1 year, and those specimens were not suitable for immunostaining. Therefore, we have no direct information about cell formation in children older than 1 year.

*Evidence of cell death*

Cell formation is always accompanied by cell death. Therefore, we have examined the frequency of occurrence of pycnotic nuclei, which indicate that cell death has occurred in the hippocampal formation. In those cases where hypoxic damage was not significant we have found only a few pycnotic nuclei inside the granule cell

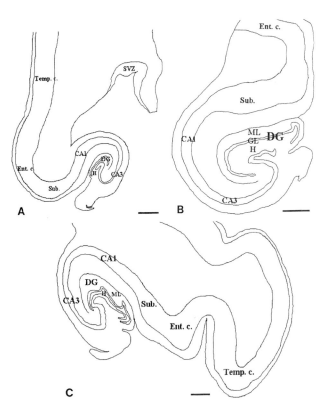

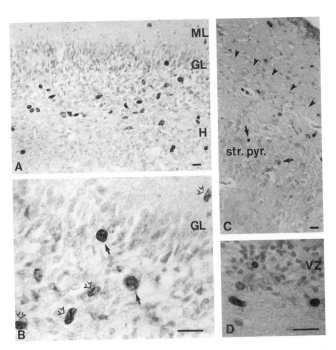

FIGURE 4.1    Camera lucida drawings of the hippocampal formation and the adjacent parahippocampal gyrus in a 24-week-old (**A**), newborn (**B**), and 1-year-old child (**C**). CA1–CA3 = subfields of Ammon's horn; DG = dentate gyrus; GL = granule cell layer; H = hilus of the dentate gyrus; Ent. c. = entorhinal cortex; ML = molecular layer; Sub. = subiculum; SVZ = subventricular zone; Temp. c. = temporal cortex. Calibration bar = 1 mm.

FIGURE 4.2    Photomicrographs of Ki-67 labeled cells in cresyl violet–stained coronal sections of the hippocampal formation of the 24-week-old child. (**A**) Large numbers of labeled cells are in the hilus (H). (**B**) Higher magnification reveals differences in the nuclear structure. Some of the labeled cells appear to be neuronal precursors (arrows), whereas others are glial cells (open arrows). (**C**) There are a few labeled cells inside the pyramidal cell layer (str. pyr. = stratum pyramidale of Ammon's horn) of the CA1 area (arrows). Most labeled cells are in the intermediate and subplate zones, showing a band of probably migrating immature cells (arrowheads). (**D**) There are a few labeled cells in the ventricular zone (VZ) at the hippocampus. Calibration bar = 20 μm.

layer and the hilus of the dentate gyrus. Those are the areas where the frequency of labeled cells is the highest in the hippocampal formation. In order to avoid miscalculation caused by postmortem autolysis or hypoxic damage, we have examined the frequency of pycnotic nuclei in the hippocampi of newborn perfused monkeys. Monkeys have been used to study the postnatal development of hippocampal connections and the maturation of the ultrastructure (Seress and Ribak, 1995a,b). It is known that granule cell formation occurs in the monkey hippocampus until the 32nd postnatal day (Rakic and Nowakowski, 1981). In the perinatal period a large number of young granule cells locate themselves at the hilar border of the granule cell layer. Therefore, we assume that in newborn and 4-day-old monkeys cell death may accompany cell formation. In newborn monkeys, cresyl violet–stained semithin sections reveal the developed granule cells owing to their purple-stained cytoplasm which sharply contrasts with the thin, pale cytoplasmic rim of young cells (figure

4.6A; see color plate 5). The young cells have no cytoplasm and their nuclei are darkly stained (figure 4.6A). Pycnosis has been found rarely in the dentate granular layer and the pycnotic cells are not exclusively at the hilar border, where newly generated cells are supposed to be located, but are distributed in the entire width of the granule cell layer (figure 4.6C; see color plate 5). In a few cases, apoptosis may be assumed based on the nuclear changes of the neurons that were probably granule cells (figure 4.6D; see color plate 5). Such apoptotic cells were evident both at the molecular layer (figure 4.6.D) and hilar borders (figure 4.6B; see color plate 5) of the granule cell layer, suggesting that cell death does not necessarily occur among the newly generated cells. The frequency rate of cell death was extremely low in the monkey dentate gyrus, approximately 2–3 cells per 1000 granule cells.

In conclusion, the overwhelming majority of neurons of the human hippocampal formation are formed in the first half of pregnancy, before the 24th week. There

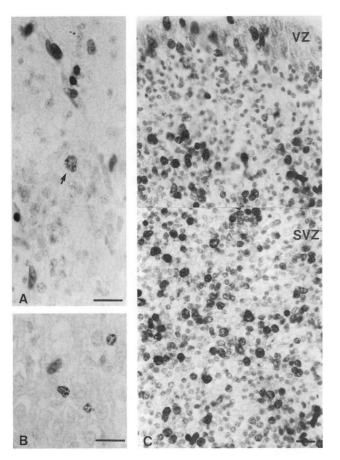

FIGURE 4.3   Photomicrographs of Ki-67–labeled cells in cresyl violet–stained coronal sections of the entorhinal cortex
(**A**), subiculum (**B**), and the subventricular zone under the
temporal cortex (**C**). (**A** and **B**) Some of the labeled cells appear to be neurons (arrow on **A**), whereas the others are glial
cells. (**C**) Large numbers of labeled cells are in the ventricular
zone (VZ) as well as in the subventricular zone (SVZ) at the
temporal neocortex. Calibration bar = 20 μm.

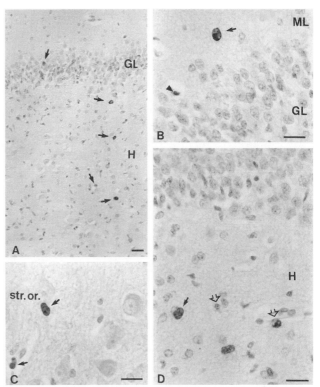

FIGURE 4.4   Photomicrographs of Ki-67–labeled cells in cresyl violet–stained coronal sections of the dentate gyrus (**A**, **B**,
and **D**) and Ammon's horn (**C**) of a newborn child. (**A**) There
are a few labeled cells (arrows) in the hilus (H) and in the
granule cells layer (GL). (**B**) Labeled glial cell (arrowhead)
at the border of the granule cell layer (GL) and another that
could be a nonaligned granule cell (arrow) in the molecular
layer (ML). (**C**) Labeled glial cells (arrows) in the stratum
oriens (str. or.) of the CA1 area of Ammon's horn. (**D**) Some
of the labeled cells in the hilar region (H) of the dentate gyrus
may be neuronal precursors (arrow), whereas others are glial
cells (open arrows). Calibration bar = 20 μm.

is limited cell formation within the dentate gyrus in the
perinatal period, but the number of newly formed cells
is very low relative to the total number of cells. Similarly,
there is no significant cell death in the perinatal period,
neither in the human nor in the monkey hippocampal
formation. This suggests that formation of neuronal
connections is not accompanied by cell death in the
primate hippocampus and that most of the newly generated neurons survive.

## Cell migration in the hippocampal formation

Experimental studies in rodents and primates have
shown that the ventricular zone underlying the hippocampal formation is the source of neurons (Bayer, 1980;
Nowakowski and Rakic, 1981). Migrating neurons in
Ammon's horn, in the subiculum as well as in the en-

torhinal cortex, bypass previously generated neurons
on their way to the superficial limits of the developing
cortical plate (Nowakowski and Rakic, 1981). Therefore, the inside-out migration pattern is similar to that
in the neocortex. The exception is again the dentate
gyrus, where the granule cell layer is formed in an
outside-in pattern (Bayer, 1980; Nowakowski and Rakic,
1981). The dentate gyrus receives neurons both from
the ventricular zone and from the hilar proliferative
zone, which may be a hippocampal equivalent of the
subventricular zone, because the dynamics of cell formation appear to be similar in the subventricular zone
and in the hilus (Bayer, 1980; Seress, 1977). Cell migration to Ammon's horn, the subiculum, and the entorhinal cortex terminates early in pregnancy, whereas
migration of granule cells continues for a long period
of time postnatally. In rodents, granule cell migration

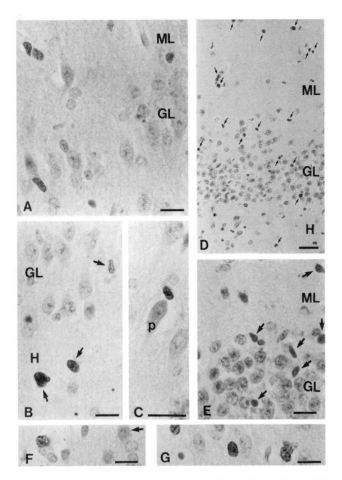

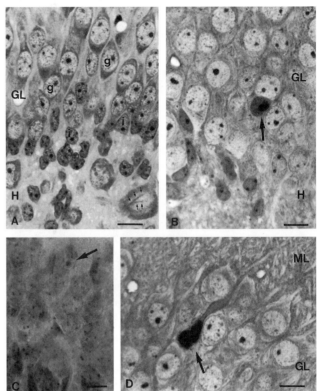

FIGURE 4.5 Photomicrographs of Ki-67–labeled cells in different parts of the hippocampal formation of a 3-month-old (**A**, **B**, **C**, **F**, **G**) and an 11.5-month-old child (**D** and **E**). (**A**) Labeled cells appear to be glial cells in the molecular layer (ML) and granule cell layer (GL). (**B**) Labeled cells (arrows) in the granule cell layer (GL) and hilus (H). (**C**) A labeled astroglia in satellite position to a pyramidal cell (p) in the CA1 area of Ammon's horn. (**D**) Many small, darkly stained labeled cells (arrows) in the different layers of dentate gyrus of the 11.5-month-old child. (**E**) Higher magnification reveals that the Ki-67–labeled cells (arrows) are all glial elements. (**F**) An immunolabeled cell in the hilus of a 3-month-old child. Nuclear morphology of labeled cell suggests that, when compared with an unlabeled neuron (arrow), it may be a neuron. (**G**) Labeled cells in the entorhinal cortex of the 3-month-old child. Calibration bars = 40 μm for **D**, 20 μm for **A**, **B**, **C**, **E**, **F**, **G**.

FIGURE 4.6 Photomicrographs of cresyl violet–stained semi-thin sections of the dentate gyrus of a newborn monkey. (**A**) Inside the granule cell layer (GL), matured granule cells (g) display large pale cell nuclei with a purple cytoplasmic rim, whereas at the hilar (H) border many small dark immature cells (i) accumulate. Some of the large hilar neurons display deep nuclear infoldings (arrows) characteristic of matured GABAergic neurons of the hippocampus. (**B**) An apoptotic cell (arrow) at the hilar border of the granule cell layer. (**C**) A pycnotic cell nucleus (arrow) at the molecular layer border of the granule cell layer. (**D**) An apoptotic granule cell (arrow) at the molecular layer border (ML) of the granule cell layer. Note the shrunken soma and dense cell nucleus as well as the basophilic dendrite of the apoptotic cell. Calibration bar = 10 μm.

lasts only a few days after final cell division occurs, a finding that may be explained by the smaller size of the rodent dentate gyrus. In primates, however, groups of small cells with thin cytoplasm and dark cell nucleus persist in the subgranular zone of the dentate gyrus throughout the first postnatal year (Eckenhoff and Rakic, 1988). Since no neurons were labeled with thymidine after the first month, these cells had to be formed in the perinatal period. Not all of the undiffer-

entiated, immature-looking cells are positive for glial fibrillary acidic protein in the 6-month- and 1.5-year-old monkeys, suggesting that these immature cells are neurons and may differentiate into granule cells later in development (Eckenhoff and Rakic, 1988). Indeed, recent observations suggest that neurogenesis and cell migration occur in the dentate gyrus of adult monkeys (Gould et al., 1999; Kornack and Rakic, 1999). Similar results have previously been described in rats (Bayer, 1982). In cresyl violet–stained preparations the immature neurons display dark, ovoid cell nuclei and very thin cytoplasmic rims that lack organelles (Seress, 1992). The morphology of these immature neurons is very similar to that of those migrating cells described for the developing cerebellum (Rakic, 1971).

The period of time during which immature, migrating cells are detectable in Ammon's horn and the dentate gyrus has been examined. In 24–30-week-old infants, a large number of migrating cells are visible in the subgranular proliferative zone of the hilus as well as in the subplate and intermediate zone between the alveus and pyramidal cell layer (figure 4.2A,C). In the 32-week-old and older infants, Ammon's horn lacks these immature cells (Arnold and Trojanowski, 1996a). However, in the dentate gyrus large numbers of immature cells still persist in the subgranular zone, not only in 32–36-week-olds but also in neonates (figure 4.7A,D; see color plate 6). Cells with small, darkly stained, mostly elongated-ovoid nuclei are dispersed in the hilar region including the subgranular zone (figure 4.7D). In a 5-month-old child, the number of immature cells is much lower (figure 4.7B; see color plate 6); however, clusters of dark, immature cells still occur in the subgranular zone of the 8.5-month-old child (figure 4.7C; see color plate 6). In 1-year-old children the hilar border of the granule cell layer and the deep hilus are free of immature cells (figure 4.7E; see color plate 6) and the general cytoarchitectonic features of the dentate gyrus appear adult-like. It is evident that the cell density of the hilar region is higher in newborn infants than in older children and that the number of granule cells inside the granule cell layer increases after birth (Seress, 1992). It is also known that glial cells are rare inside the granule cell layer. Therefore, it can be assumed that the immature cells of the hilar region migrate to their final position—the granule cell layer—and develop into granule cells. It is likely that another population of cells remains in the hilus, becoming glial cells, because the large neurons of the hilar region are known to form at the same prenatal period when pyramidal cells of Ammon's horn are formed.

Our current results suggest that cell migrations in the human hippocampal formation terminate prenatally in Ammon's horn, the subicular complex, and the entorhinal cortex. In the dentate gyrus, migration of granule cells lasts for approximately 1 year after birth. This is a long period of time considering that active cell formation in the ventricular and intermediate zones terminates in the first half of pregnancy. In the second half of pregnancy, a few cells may still divide in the migratory zone described by Humphrey (1966) or in the subplate and intermediate zone (Arnold and Trojanowski, 1996a; Kostovic et al., 1989), but most of the cells in those zones are migrating, not dividing, neurons. A large number of nondifferentiated granule cells appear to reside in the subgranular zone for a long period of time (1 year or more) before they move to their final positions and begin to proliferate into mature neu-

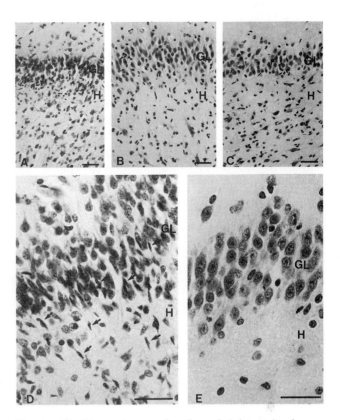

FIGURE 4.7 Photomicrographs of cresyl violet–stained coronal sections of the human dentate gyrus. (**A**) In the newborn infant, the subgranular zone and the deep hilus contain large numbers of darkly stained small cell nuclei. (**D**) Higher magnification reveals the elongated cell nuclei (arrows) of immature neurons that are probably migrating granule cells. In 5-month-old (**B**) and 8.5-month-old (**C**) children, migrating cells are still seen in the hilus (H) and at the hilar border of the granule cell layer (GL). (**E**) In the dentate gyrus of a 1-year-old child, the subgranular zone contains only glial cells (compare **D** with **E**). Calibration bar = 50 μm.

rons. An unknown number of immature cells may persist until adulthood, and those cells may consist of the stem cells for adult neurogenesis (Eriksson et al., 1998). However, immature dividing cells in the adults must be rare, since they are already infrequent in the early postnatal period. The cell number in the granule cell layer does not change significantly after the 30th postnatal day in rats, and no data demonstrate an increase in number of granule cells in the adult primate hippocampus (Seress, 1977, 1987). In monkeys, cell migration may last for 3 months; the last identified granule cells are formed 32 days after birth (Rakic and Nowakowski, 1981) and the migrating neurons disappear from the subgranular zone by the 4th postnatal month. Therefore, the prolonged migration of granule cells is a unique characteristic of the human dentate gyrus, although one must consider that the lifespan of the monkey is three times shorter than that of the human.

Therefore 3–4 months in monkeys may be equivalent to 1 year in the human. Similarly, as in rodents and subhuman primates, it is clear that cell migration in the dentate gyrus lasts as long as the migration of granule cells of the cerebellum, since the external granular layer of the cerebellum disappears between 8.5 and 10 months in human (Rakic, 1971; Ábrahám et al., 1999). There is, however, one important difference between the two regions: The cerebellar external granular layer displays significant cell multiplication as long as the layer persists (Ábrahám et al., 1999), whereas in the hilar region, a similar rate of cell formation is a prenatal event.

## Synapse formation and the development of neuronal connections in the hippocampal formation

Postnatal development of the hippocampal formation and its connections has been described in detail in rats. There are but few available data in primates, and data pertaining to human development are particularly sparse. The lack of empirical study can be partially explained by the difficulties of tissue preservation due to the regulated postmortem delay between the time of death and autopsy. After a few hours' delay, the cellular ultrastructure is obscured in human tissue. In rats, synaptic connections and dendritic development of a few cell types have been described, such as those of the granule cells (Seress and Pokorny, 1981), mossy cells (Ribak, Seress, and Amaral, 1985), and the pyramidal cells of the CA1 area of Ammon's horn (Pokorny and Yamamoto, 1981). Light microscopic changes of the dendrites, such as spine density and spine morphology, correlate with the increasing number of afferent terminals that establish synapses with dendrites of hippocampal neurons. Studies in rats suggest that in the dentate gyrus an increasing number of mossy fiber axon terminals establish connections with the hilar mossy cells and the pyramidal cells of the CA3 area (Amaral and Dent, 1981; Ribak, Seress, and Amaral, 1985). First connections are established with dendritic shafts at birth (Amaral and Dent, 1981). The more complex terminals of mossy fibers induce the development of thorny excrescences on the dendrites of 2-week-old rats (Amaral and Dent, 1981). Maturation of this connection appears to terminate 2–3 weeks after the last granule cells have been formed at the end of the third week. The CA3 pyramidal cells send the Schaffer collaterals to the CA1 pyramidal cells. It is not known when the Schaffer collaterals reach the CA1 cells, nor when this connection is fully mature. However, the CA1 pyramidal cells show a delayed maturation relative to the development of CA3 pyramidal cells; CA1 pyramidal cells show extensive dendritic growth and an increasing synaptic density up to the 90th postnatal day. This correlates with an increasing number of synapses in the stratum radiatum (Pokorny and Trojan, 1986; Pokorny and Yamamoto, 1981).

The circuitries of the hippocampal formation have been known since the time of Ramon y Cajal (1911). Andersen and colleagues (1971) used the term "hippocampal trisynaptic circuit" to refer to the unique unidirectional progression of excitatory pathways that link the subregions of the hippocampal formation (Andersen, Bliss, and Skrede, 1971). Within this circuit the granule cells are the first elements. They connect the dentate gyrus to the CA3 pyramidal neurons of Ammon's horn, which in turn project to the CA1 pyramidal cells. CA1 pyramidal neurons are the sole cortical efferents of the hippocampus (for further discussion, see Johnston and Amaral, 1998).

Granule cells are the last to be formed among the neurons of the trisynaptic circuit. As a consequence, the synaptic connections between the dentate gyrus and Ammon's horn are established late in ontogenesis. This highlights the functional importance of this first link in the trisynaptic circuit, because its morphological maturation correlates with hippocampus-dependent behavioral maturation (Nadel and Willner, 1989).

## Development of principal (pyramidal and granule cells) and nonprincipal (GABAergic) neurons of the primate hippocampus

Granule cells, hilar mossy cells, and CA3 pyramidal cells of monkeys are in an advanced stage of development at birth (Seress and Ribak, 1995a,b). Most granule cells have a complete dendritic arbor, although both spine density and the number of synapses in the molecular layer increase after birth (Seress, Baumgartner, and Ribak, 1995). Mossy cells and CA3 pyramidal cells display thorny excrescences, and terminals of mossy fibers (axons of granule cells) establish multiple synapses with those excrescences (Seress and Ribak, 1995a,b). These features indicate that in monkeys developmental events are mainly prenatal, but the chronological sequence of synaptic development is similar to what occurs in the rat. At present we have no data about the development of CA1 pyramidal cells in monkeys. Our preliminary data indicate a change in spine density and myelin formation up to the postnatal seventh month.

In conclusion, the monkey hippocampal formation displays a fast and dynamic development that terminates several months after birth. In harmony with the advanced stage of development of principal neurons, most GABAergic cells of the hippocampal formation mature very early in monkeys (Berger, Alvarez, and Goldman-Rakic, 1993; Berger, deGrissac, and Alvarez, 1999). This is in contrast to the development of non-principal cells in rats, where GABAergic neurons show a very immature appearance at birth (Seress and Ribak, 1990). Berger, Alvarez, and Goldman-Rakic (1993) assume that functional circuits are forming between the hippocampus and the entorhinal cortex of primates during the first half of gestation. Other data also suggest an early maturation of the human entorhinal cortex (Kostovic, Petanjek, and Judas, 1993; Ulfig, 1993). Light and electron microscopic data are sparse with respect to the developing human hippocampal formation. Nonetheless, the cell types and cytoarchitectonics of the adult hippocampus have been described in several classic reports (Koelliker, 1896; Lorente de No, 1934). Purpura (1975) has included the hippocampus in his description of the human cerebral cortex, but concentrated mainly on the early developmental stages. He observed that a variety of growth processes observed in hippocampal pyramidal neurons in the 20–29-week-old fetus are not prominently displayed in granule cells. In 33-week-old premature infants, many granule cells display dendrites that appear to be mature, except for the total number of spines, whereas other granule cells display immature dendrites. The time period from 20 to 28 weeks of gestation is a phase of maximum dendritic growth for hippocampal pyramidal neurons (Purpura, 1975). Pyramidal neurons of the CA3 area display only a few, small spines (spicules) and filopodia on their dendrites in the 22-week-old fetus. In the 33-week-old fetus, the first thorn-like excrescences appear on the dendrites of pyramidal-type neurons of the hilus and on CA3 pyramidal cells, suggesting that the first connections between granule cells and their postsynaptic targets in the hilus and CA3 area are established by the 33rd gestational week.

In children born at term, the hilus of the dentate gyrus contains large multipolar cells displaying a few complex thorn-like excrescences and a few small, conventional spines (figure 4.8A; see color plate 7). These cells are probably young mossy cells that have already established a few synapses with mossy fiber terminals of granule cells (figure 4.9; see color plate 8). In agreement with the previous observations of Purpura (1975), we have demonstrated that well-developed granule cells frequently appear in the granule cell layer (figure 4.8C; see color plate 7). These granule cells have dendrites that display a large number of spines and an axon that gives rise to several collaterals in the hilus (figure 4.8C). In addition, several granule cells display varicose, stubby, short, and spineless dendrites that terminate in

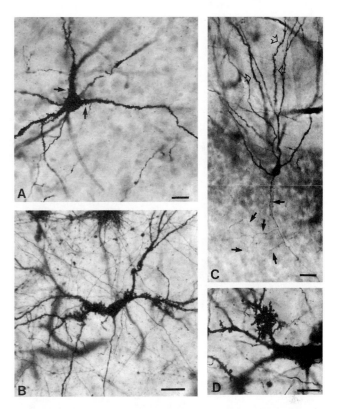

FIGURE 4.8 Photomicrographs of Golgi-impregnated neurons in the human dentate gyrus. (A) Dendrites of the mossy cell in the newborn infant display the conventional simple spines and a few small protrusions that can be thorny excrescences (arrows). (B) Dendrites of mossy cell of the 3-year-old child display large complex spines, the so-called thorny excrescences, that are characteristic for mossy cells of the adult brain (D). (C) Large numbers of granule cells display spiny dendrites (open arrows) and a richly arborizing axon (arrows point to the axon and its collaterals) in the dentate gyrus of the newborn child. Calibration bars = 40 μm for B and 20 μm for A, C, and D.

growth cones (Seress, 1992). These latter granule cells are still growing and may be those that were formed in the perinatal period. Therefore, the diversity in granule cell development seen by Purpura (1975) in the 33-week-old fetus is still observable at birth. It should be noted that a few immature-looking granule cells are still seen in the 15-month-old child (Seress, 1992), suggesting that granule cells exhibit a prolonged period of cell proliferation. The first real thorn-like excrescences appear on mossy cells by the third postnatal month (Seress and Mrzljak, 1992). At seven months thorny excrescences are frequent on mossy cells, but their number and size continue to increase up to the third year, when the first adult-like mossy cells appear (figure 4.8B; see color plate 7). The complex spines or thorny excrescences of the adult human mossy cells (figure 4.8D; see color plate 7) are much larger than those in monkeys

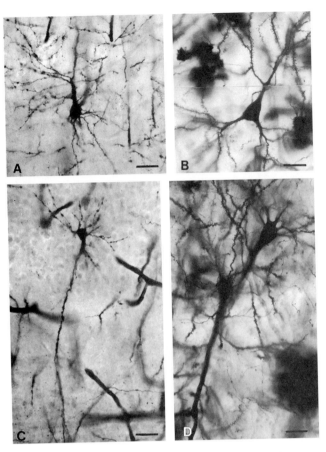

FIGURE 4.9 Photomicrographs of Golgi-impregnated pyramidal cells in the cortex (**A** and **B**) and in Ammon's horn (**C** and **D**) of hippocampal formation in newborn (**A** and **C**) and adult (**B** and **D**) brain. Pyramidal cells in the newborn child display immature, beaded, spine-free short dendrites, whereas in the adult, pyramidal cells have large dendrites fully covered with spines. Calibration bar = 20 μm.

mossy cells (Seress and Ribak, 1995a,b). However, not only the mossy cells but also the pyramidal cells of the CA1 region of Ammon's horn are in an early stage of proliferation at birth. If the CA1 pyramidal cells of adults (figure 4.9D) are visually compared with the pyramidal cells of newborn infants (figure 4.9C), several differences are obvious. The pyramidal cells of newborn infants have few basal dendritic branches and poorly developed side branches of the apical dendrites. A similar pattern has been found in the neocortex, where the pyramidal cells of the newborn child display a few, varicose, short basal dendrites and a few poorly developed side-branches of the apical dendrite (figure 4.9A). There are only a few spines on the pyramidal dendrites of the newborn infant (figure 4.9A), whereas the equivalent pyramidal cell dendrites in the adult cortex are fully packed with spines (figure 4.9B). The postnatal human development of pyramidal cells in Ammon's horn and the neocortex has not been described in detail, but our observations suggest that the morphological development of the principal neurons of those brain areas lasts as long as that in the hilar region.

## Synapse formation in the human hippocampus

Light microscopic studies of the development of dendrites, and the early appearance of first spines, suggest that synapse formation starts early in the human hippocampal formation. It is extremely difficult to achieve adequate preservation of postmortem fetal or child brains for electron microscopy. Data relating to the synaptic development of the human hippocampal formation are rare. In accord with expectations based on studies of monkey brains (Berger, Alvarez, and Goldman-Rakic, 1993), the first synapses have been observed in the marginal zone and in the cortical subplate of Ammon's horn in a 15-week-old fetus (Kostovic et al., 1989). The axodendritic asymmetric synapses in the marginal zone suggest that entorhinal axons have already reached the hippocampus at that age, since those are the sole excitatory afferents in that zone. Recent findings using anterograde and retrograde tracers indicate that reciprocal entorhinal-hippocampal projections may be among the first corticocortical connections to be established in the human brain (Hevner and Kinney, 1996). The perforant pathway projection from the entorhinal cortex to the dentate gyrus develops several weeks later than the connection to Ammon's horn (Hevner and Kinney, 1996). In our electron microscopic preparations of postmortem tissue from neonates (36–40 weeks of gestation), small asymmetric axodendritic and axospinous synapses are frequently found in different layers of the dentate gyrus and Am-

or in rodents (Frotscher et al., 1991). In the 3-year-old child mossy cells still vary with respect to their dendritic spine density and the size of their thorny excrescences. Not until the fifth year do all impregnated mossy cells display similarly large thorny excrescences that are indistinguishable from those seen in adults (Seress and Mrzljak, 1992). The extended morphological development of granule, mossy, and pyramidal cells accords with the prolonged development of cytoskeletal proteins, since an adult pattern of neuronal cytoskeletal protein expression in the hippocampus appears around the second postnatal year (Arnold and Trojanowski, 1996b). There is a similarly extended development of thorny excrescences for CA3 pyramidal neurons, although it appears that CA3 pyramidal cells display more advanced thorns at birth than the mossy cells. Similarly, CA3 pyramidal cells of newborn monkeys appear to show more developed thorn-like excrescences than

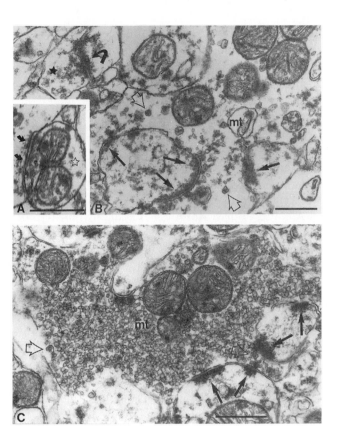

FIGURE 4.10 Electron micrographs of the hilar region of the newborn infant (**A** and **B**) and adult (**C**). (**A**) An axon terminal (open star) that forms a symmetric synapse (arrows) with a dendrite in the hilus of the dentate gyrus of a newborn child. (**B**) A small (star) and a large (mt) terminal in the hilus of the newborn child. Both terminals contain a few vesicles and form asymmetric synapses (arrows and curved arrow) with dendrites. In the mossy terminal (mt) the mitochondria locate away from the synaptic surface and the terminal contains a few dense core vesicles (open arrows). (**C**) A large mossy fiber terminal (mt) in the hilus of the dentate gyrus of an adult human is fully packed with synaptic vesicles and a few of them contain a dense core (open arrows). Mitochondria locate away from the asymmetric synaptic surface (arrow). Calibration bar = 0.5 μm.

mon's horn (figure 4.10B). However, the large complex mossy fibers terminals seen in the adult dentate gyrus (figure 4.10C) cannot be seen. It is highly probable that those terminals are disrupted and the structure destroyed by the postmortem autolysis, but it is also possible that mature mossy fiber terminals are rare in the newborn infant. There are a few large and pale terminals that display a few vesicles close to the synaptic surface and mitochondria that locate away from the synaptic surface (figure 4.10B). These are characteristic of mossy fiber terminals and, as in newborn monkeys, the hilus contains both mature and immature mossy fiber terminals (Seress and Ribak, 1995b). Similarly, as

in monkeys (Berger, Alvarez, and Goldman-Rakic, 1993), nonprincipal GABAergic neurons appear to develop very early in the human hippocampal formation. NADPH-d positive neurons appear at the 15th fetal week and become frequent from the 28th to the 32nd weeks (Yan and Ribak, 1997). In accord with light microscopic data, symmetric synapses were frequent in the different layers of the dentate gyrus (figure 4.10A) and Ammon's horn in newborn children.

In summary, the first afferent fibers to the hippocampus proper arise from the entorhinal cortex and establish synapses with neurons of Ammon's horn early in fetal development (Kostovic et al., 1989). This corresponds to the suggestion of Berger, Alvarez, and Goldman-Rakic (1993) that the remarkably early maturation of the entorhinal cortex during the first half of gestation, together with the early neurochemical development of the hippocampal formation, indicates that functional circuits in primates form during the first half of gestation. Tracing studies also suggest that entorhinal-hippocampal connections are established by midgestation (Hevner and Kinney, 1996). In addition, the presence of the following indirect features suggests that neuronal connections of the inner trisynaptic circuit of the hippocampus, which connect the dentate gyrus with the entorhinal cortex, are also established prenatally: (1) mature-looking granule cells present in the dentate gyrus at birth give rise to richly arborizing axons; (2) small thorny excrescences on dendrites of mossy and CA3 pyramidal cells in newborn children; (3) asymmetric synapses in the dentate gyrus and in the stratum lucidum of Ammon's horn of newborn children; (4) a large number of asymmetric synapses in the strata radiatum and oriens of the CA1 area of Ammon's horn. Therefore, it is reasonable to assume that children born at term have the synaptic connections necessary to establish memory traces (for discussion, see Nelson, 1995). However, the functional capability of those circuits has not been fully examined. One must be extremely cautious when correlating morphology with function, either at the electrophysiological or behavioral level. For instance, Purpura (1975) demonstrated that immature photic-evoked potentials can be recorded in 33-week-old premature infants whose pyramidal cells in the visual cortex have poorly developed basal dendrites and almost no spines. Despite the fact that the adult-like neuronal circuitry needed for information processing was absent, some synaptic connections were nevertheless capable of transmitting visual impulses. It is plausible that similar events occur in the hippocampal formation, and thus the earliest forms of memory formation may not necessarily be related to the adult-like function of the hippocampal formation.

## Conclusion and functional implications

Three major milestones underlie the formation of neuronal circuits: (1) when the participating neurons are formed, (2) when they reach their final position, and (3) when they start to proliferate and establish their first afferent and efferent connections. The neuronal cell formation of the human hippocampus appears to occur within a relatively short period of time, with the exception of the dentate granule cells. The last neurons for Ammon's horn, the subicular complex, and entorhinal cortex may form between the 20th and the 24th gestational weeks, but major cell formation probably ceases around the 15th gestational week. This finding indicates that while pyramidal cells form in the first half of pregnancy, granule cell formation continues until birth, even if the major cell formation of granule cells happens before the 34–36th week of gestation. Cell migration is also rapid in Ammon's horn, the subiculum, and entorhinal cortex; adult-like cytoarchitectonics of those areas are observed at the 24th week (Arnold and Trojanowski, 1996a), whereas the granule cell layer is still growing at birth. At birth, the granule cell layer includes only about 70% of the adult numbers of granule cells and its volume is also about 25–30% less than that in adults (Seress, 1988; unpublished observations). Cell migration lasts for eight months until the last immature-looking cells disappear from the hilus. Such a long period of cell migration explains the presence of proliferating granule cells in the dentate gyrus of the 1.5-year-old child. This observation also suggests that at least 30% of granule cells start to proliferate and establish their afferent and efferent connections postnatally, although only a very small percentage of those cells are formed after the 34th week.

It is very likely that entorhinal afferents are among the first to establish connections with pyramidal cells. There is no ultrastructural evidence concerning the time when entorhinal axons form synapses with granule cells. Indeed, Golgi-impregnated granule cells in the 15-week-old fetus display immature, stubby dendrites without spines. Spine formation on dendrites appears to begin after the 25th week (Seress and Mrzljak, 1987). Afferent circuits develop first in the Ammon's horn–entorhinal complex while the dentate gyrus receives afferents later (Hevner and Kinney, 1996). As a consequence, the intrinsic connections (trisynaptic circuit) of the hippocampal formation start to develop later.

Synaptic elements of the trisynaptic connection are present at birth, but full maturation is not expected to occur before the 5th postnatal year in the human. Four periods can be distinguished by the morphological events during these five years: (1) from the 36th fetal week to the third postnatal month, when cell formation decreases to a minimum but cell migration continues and the first thorny spines appear on the dendrites of hilar mossy cells; (2) from the third month to the first year, when cell migration ceases and the first adult-like large thorny excrescences appear on mossy and CA3 pyramidal cells, suggesting the beginning of a period of excessive synapse formation; (3) from the first year to the third year, when the first mature-looking mossy cells appear; (4) from the third year to the fifth year of life, when most neurons are adult-like both in the hilus and in Ammon's horn. Moreover, it is highly possible that synapse formation continues in the hippocampal formation after the fifth year and results in volumetric and sexual differences (Caviness et al., 1996). However, given currently available morphological methods, these later events cannot be studied. In addition, the number of newly formed granule cells is small after birth; therefore, it is difficult to evaluate the functional importance of granule cell formation in the adult human (Ericsson et al., 1998).

If Ammon's horn develops early and receives its major cortical afferent connection early in gestation, what might be the functional consequence of the late formation of granule cells of the dentate gyrus (and with it the trisynaptic circuit)? Can the dentate gyrus modify the function of the hippocampal formation? Animal experiments demonstrate that it can. In rats there is an important postnatal morphological development of the dentate gyrus during normal development and a corresponding delay in the adult-like hippocampal function of spatial navigation (Nadel and Willner, 1989). Moreover, if the granule cells of the dentate gyrus are removed by irradiation at birth, the normal function of hippocampal formation is never attained in the course of later life (Czurkó et al., 1997). A significant functional reserve capacity of the dentate gyrus is suggested by the fact that if 50% of granule cells remain intact in the dentate gyrus, the effects of a functional lesion are not detectable (Czéh et al., 2001). This finding might explain why not all children who suffer perinatal damage show signs of functional lesions. Previously, we have hypothesized that the development of the hippocampal trisynaptic circuit is under the influence of complex environmental stimuli (Seress and Mrzljak, 1992). After birth, when sensory neocortical information processing increases, it also likely increases the activity of the perforant path from the entorhinal cortex to the hippocampus. As a consequence, higher activity within the perforant path would activate the granule cells, causing them to form additional synapses with those postsynaptic neurons that are their already selected targets. The hippocampal formation is capable of memory formation in the perinatal period when the intrahippo-campal trisynaptic circuit is still forming. This finding may explain why even very young infants show signs of memory formation (Nelson, 1995). The later-forming neuronal connections between granule cells of the dentate gyrus and pyramidal neurons of Ammon's horn may alter the functional circuits of the hippocampus proper. It is therefore proposed that the trisynaptic circuit of the hippocampal formation is critical for the adult-like memory formation. If the morphological development of the hippocampal formation correlates with functional capability, then adult-like memory formation in humans may not be expected earlier than the fifth postnatal year. It is not known how changes of inner and outer environments affect human hippocampal development, a question that brings into focus the need to ensure the welfare of children through early childhood.

ACKNOWLEDGMENTS  The author is grateful to Mária Palleszter, Mária Domján, and Judit Mishley-Loránd for their excellent technical assistance, and thanks Dr. Hajnalka Ábrahám for her participation in the experiments and critical comments to this manuscript. This work was supported by the Hungarian Science Foundation, grant No. T 029214 and by ETT grant No. 80–4/1998.

## REFERENCES

ÁBRAHÁM, H., T. TORNÓCZKY, GY. KOSZTOLÁNYI, and L. SERESS, 1999. Peri- and postnatal cell formation in the human brain. *Soc. Neurosci. Abst.* 25:2267.

AMARAL, D. G., 1990. Hippocampal formation. In *The Human Nervous System*, G. Paxinos, ed. New York: Academic Press, pp. 711–755.

AMARAL, D. G., and J. A. DENT, 1981. Development of mossy fibers of the dentate gyrus: I. A light and electron microscopic study of the mossy fibers and their expansions. *J. Comp. Neurol.* 195:51–86.

ANDERSEN, P., T. V. P. BLISS, and K. SKREDE, 1971. Lamellar organization of hippocampal excitatory pathways. *Exp. Brain Res.* 13:222–238.

ANGEVINE, J. B., 1975. Development of the hippocampal formation. In *The Hippocampus*, R. L. Isaacson and K. H. Pribram, eds. New York: Plenum Press, pp. 61–90.

ARNOLD, S. E., and J. Q. TROJANOWSKI, 1996a. Human fetal hippocampal development: I. Cytoarchitecture, myeloarchitecture, and neuronal morphologic features. *J. Comp. Neurol.* 367:274–292.

ARNOLD, S. E., and J. Q. TROJANOWSKI, 1996b. Human fetal hippocampal development: II. The neuronal cytoskeleton. *J. Comp. Neurol.* 367:293–307.

BAYER, S. A., 1980. The development of the hippocampal region in the rat. I. Neurogenesis examined with $^3$H-thymidine autoradiography. *J. Comp. Neurol.* 190:87–114.

BAYER, S. A., 1982. Changes in the total number of dentate granule cells in juvenile and adult rats: A correlated volumetric and $^3$H-thymidine autoradiographic study. *Exp. Brain Res.* 46:315–323.

BERGER, B., C. ALVAREZ, and P. S. GOLDMAN-RAKIC, 1993. Neurochemical development of the hippocampal region in the fetal rhesus monkey. I. Early appearance of peptides, calcium-binding proteins, DARPP-32 and the monoamine innervation in the entorhinal cortex during the first half of gestation (E47 to E90). *Hippocampus* 3:279–305.

BERGER, B., N. DEGRISSAC, and C. ALVAREZ, 1999. Precocious development of parvalbumin-like immunoreactive interneurons in the hippocampal formation and entorhinal cortex of the fetal Cynamogus monkey. *J. Comp. Neurol.* 403:309–331.

BROWN, D. C., and K. C. GATTER, 1990. Monoclonal antibody Ki-67: Its use in histopathology. *Histopathology* 17:489–503.

CAJAL, S. RAMON Y, 1911. *Histologie du Systeme Nerveux de l'Homme et des Vertebres*, Vol. II. Paris: Maloine.

CAVINESS, V. S. JR., D. N. KENNEDY, C. RICHELME, J. RADEMACHER, and P. A. FILIPEK, 1996. The human brain age 7–11 years: A volumetric analysis based on magnetic resonance images. *Cereb. Cortex* 6:726–736.

CZÉH, B, A. STUCHLIK, M. WESIERSKA, J. M. CIMADEVILLA, J. POKORNY, L. SERESS, and J. BURES, 2001. Effect of dentate gyrus lesion on allothetic and idiothetic spatial behavior. *Neurobiology of Learning and Memory* (in press).

CZURKÓ, A., B. CZÉH, L. SERESS, L. NADEL, and J. BURES, 1997. Severe spatial navigation deficit in the Morris water maze after single high dose of neonatal X-ray irradiation in the rat. *Proc. Natl. Acad. Sci. (USA)* 94:2766–2771.

ECKENHOFF, M. F., and P. RAKIC, 1988. Nature and fate of proliferative cells in the hippocampal dentate gyrus during the life span of the rhesus monkey. *J. Neurosci.* 8:2729–2747.

ERIKSSON, P. S., E. PERFILIEVA, T. BJORK-ERIKSSON, A. M. ALBORN, C. NORDBORG, D. E. PETERSON, and F. H. GAGE, 1998. Neurogenesis in the adult human hippocampus. *Nature Med.* 4:1313–1317.

FROTSCHER, M., L. SERESS, W. K. SCHWERDTFEGLER, and E. BUHL, 1991. The mossy cells of the fascia dentata: A comparative study of their fine structure and synaptic connections in rodents and primates. *J. Comp. Neurol.* 312:145–163.

GOULD, E., A. J. REEVES, M. FALLAH, P. TAPANAT, C. G. GROSS, and E. FUCHS, 1999. Hippocampal neurogenesis in adult Old World primates. *Proc. Natl. Acad. Sci. (USA)* 96:5263–5267.

HEVNER, R. F., and H. C. KINNEY, 1996. Reciprocal entorhinal-hippocampal connections established by human fetal midgestation. *J. Comp. Neurol.* 372:384–394.

HUMPHREY, T., 1966. The development of the human hippocampal formation correlated with some aspects of its phylogenetic history. In *Evolution of Forebrain*, R. Hassler and H. Stephan, eds. New York: Plenum Press, pp. 104–116.

HUMPHREY, T., 1967. The development of the human hippocampal fissure. *J. Anat.* 101:655–676.

JOHNSTON, D., and D. G. AMARAL, 1998. Hippocampus. In *The Synaptic Organization of the Brain*, G. M. Shepherd, ed. New York: Oxford University Press, pp. 418–458.

KOELLIKER, A., 1896. *Handbuch der Gewebelehre des Menschen.* Leipzig: Verlag von Wilhelm Engelmann.

KORNACK, D. R., and P. RAKIC, 1999. Continuation of neurogenesis in the hippocampus of the adult macaque monkey. *Proc. Natl. Acad. Sci. (USA)* 96:5768–5773.

KOSTOVIC, I., Z. PETANJEK, and M. JUDAS, 1993. The early areal differentiation of the human cerebral cortex: Entorhinal area. *Hippocampus* 3:447–458.

Kostovic, I., L. Seress, L. Mrzljak, and M. Judas, 1989. Early onset of synapse formation in the human hippocampus: A correlation with Nissl-Golgi architectonics in 15- and 16.5-week-old fetuses. *Neuroscience* 30:105–116.

Lorente de Nó, R., 1934. Studies on the structure of the cerebral cortex. II. Continuation of the study of the Ammonic system. *J. Psychol. Neurol.* 214:113–177.

Nadel, L., and J. Willner, 1989. Some implications of postnatal maturation of the hippocampus. In *The Hippocampus—New Vistas*, V. Chan-Palay and C. Köhler eds. New York: Alan R. Liss, pp.17–31.

Nelson, C. A., 1995. The ontogeny of human memory: A cognitive neuroscience perspective. *Dev. Psychol.* 31:723–738.

Nowakowski, R. S., and P. Rakic, 1981. The site of origin and route and rate of migration of neurons to the hippocampal region of the rhesus monkey. *J. Comp. Neurol.* 196:129–154.

Pokorny, J., and S. Trojan, 1986. The development of hippocampal structure and how it is influenced by hypoxia. *Acta. Univ. Carol. Med. Monograph.* 113:5–79.

Pokorny, J., and Y. Yamamoto, 1981. Postnatal ontogenesis of hippocampal CA1 are in rats. I. Development of dendritic arborization in pyramidal neurons. *Brain Res. Bull.* 7:113–120.

Purpura, D. S., 1975. Normal and aberrant neuronal development in the cerebral cortex of human fetus and young infant. In *Brain Mechanisms in Mental Retardation, UCLA Forum in Medical Sciences.* New York: Academic Press, pp.141–169.

Rakic, P., 1971. Neuron-glia relationship during granule cell migration in developing cerebellar cortex. A Golgi and electron microscopic study in Macacus rhesus. *J. Comp. Neurol.* 141:283–312.

Rakic, P., and R. S. Nowakowski, 1981. The time of origin of neurons in the hippocampal region of the rhesus monkey. *J. Comp. Neurol.* 196:99–128.

Ribak, C. E., L. Seress, and D. G. Amaral, 1985. The development, ultrastructure and synaptic connections of the mossy cells of the dentate gyrus. *J. Neurocytol.* 14:835–857.

Rose, D. S. C., P. H. Maddox, and D. C. Brown, 1994. Which proliferation markers for routine immunohistology? A comparison of five antibodies. *J. Clin. Pathol.* 47:1010–1014.

Seress, L., 1977. The postnatal development of rat dentate gyrus and the effect of early thyroid hormone treatment. *Anat. Embryol.* 151:335–339.

Seress, L., 1987. Strain differences in granule cell numbers of the hippocampal dentate gyrus are not the result of adult cell formation. In *Ontogenesis of the Brain*, S. Trojan and F. Stastny, eds. Universitas Carolina-Pragensis, pp. 29–32.

Seress, L., 1988. Interspecies comparison of the hippocampal formation shows increased emphasis on the regio superior in the Ammon's horn of the human brain. *J. Hirnforsch.* 29:335–340.

Seress, L., 1992. Morphological variability and developmental aspects of monkey and human granule cells: Differences between the rodent and primate dentate gyrus. *Epilepsy Res.* 7(suppl.):3–28.

Seress, L., B. J. Baumgartner, and C. E. Ribak, 1995. Postnatal development of granule cells and their afferent synapses in the dentate gyrus of Rhesus monkeys. *Soc. Neurosci. Abst.* 21:929.

Seress, L., and L. Mrzljak, 1987. Basal dendrites of granule cells are normal features of the fetal and adult dentate gyrus of both monkey and human hippocampal formation. *Brain Res.* 405:169–174.

Seress, L., and L. Mrzljak, 1992. Postnatal development of mossy cells in the human dentate gyrus: A light microscopic Golgi study. *Hippocampus* 2:127–142.

Seress, L., and J. Pokorny, 1981. Structure of the granular layer of the rat dentate gyrus. A light microscopic and Golgi study. *J. Anat.* 133:181–195.

Seress, L., and C. E. Ribak, 1990. Postnatal development of the light and electron microscopic features of basket cells in the hippocampal dentate gyrus of the rat. *Anat. Embryol.* 181:547–565.

Seress, L., and C. E. Ribak, 1995a. Postnatal development of CA3 pyramidal neurons and their afferents in the Ammon's horn of Rhesus monkey. *Hippocampus* 5:217–231.

Seress, L., and C. E. Ribak, 1995b. Postnatal development and synaptic connections of hilar mossy cells in the hippocampal dentate gyrus of Rhesus monkeys. *J. Comp. Neurol.* 355:93–110.

Ulfig, N., 1993. Ontogeny of the entorhinal cortex. *Hippocampus* 3:27–32.

Verheijen, R., H. J. H. Kuijpers, R. O. Schlingemann, A. L. M. Boehmer, R. van Driel, G. J. Brakenhoff, and F.C.S. Ramaekers, 1989a. Ki-67 detects a nuclear matrix-associated proliferation-related antigen. I. Intracellular localization during interphase. *J. Cell Sci.* 92:123–130.

Verheijen, R., H. J. H. Kuijpers, R. van Driel, J. L. M. Beck, J. H. van Dierendock, G. J. Brakenhoff, and F. C. S. Ramaekers, 1989b. Ki-67 detects a nuclear matrix-associated proliferation-related antigen. II. Localization in mitotic cells and association with chromosomes. *J. Cell Sci.* 92:531–540.

Yan, X. X., and C. E. Ribak, 1997. Prenatal development of nicotinamide adenine dinucleotide phosphate-disphorase activity in the human hippocampal formation. *Hippocampus* 7:215–231.

# 5 Effects of Sex Hormones on Brain Development

JUDY L. CAMERON

ABSTRACT Sex steroid hormones play an important role in regulating plastic changes in neuronal structure and function throughout development and adulthood. There is a diversity of cellular mechanisms by which steroid hormones influence neural function, including metabolism to more active forms, modulation of function through traditional nuclear receptors, binding to membrane receptors, and activation of a variety of second messenger pathways. A wide variety of neural processes are influenced by sex steroid hormones, including neurogenesis, cell migration, growth of the neuronal cell body, dendritic growth, differentiation and synapse formation, synapse elimination, neuronal atrophy and apoptosis, neuropeptide expression, the expression of neurotransmitter receptors, and neuronal excitability. In many cases steroid hormones must be present both developmentally and in adulthood to elicit maximal effects on behavior.

When they have been looked for, differences throughout the brains of males and females have been clearly demonstrated in nearly all species, both with regard to the structural organization of many brain nuclei and neural circuits, and in the functionality and responsiveness of neural systems to internal and external stimuli. Moreover, many of the sex differences in brain structure and function result from differential exposure of males and females to the sex steroid hormones (testosterone in males, estradiol and progesterone in females). Sex steroid hormones play a role early in brain development in the "organization" of neural circuits, and have critical roles throughout adulthood in "activating" specific behaviors. Although some generalizations can be made, the specific neural circuits that are influenced by sex steroid hormones and the time periods of sensitivity to sex steroid hormone influence show dramatic species specificity.

The earliest studies of sex hormone influences on brain structure and function examined the effects of testosterone and estradiol on sexual functions, including reproductive capacity and behavior. In many species, however, it is now clear that there are sex differences in areas of the brain that are not associated with the control of reproductive function, including the hippocampus, striatum, cerebellum, amygdala, and cerebral cortex, and/or are associated with nonreproductive behaviors, such as spatial problem solving abilities, verbal abilities, aggression, defensive behaviors, motor activity, and various aspects of learning and memory.

## Sex steroid receptors within the brain

ESTROGEN RECEPTORS Early studies of the effects of sex steroid hormones on the brain showed that hypothalamic regions, including the preoptic area and ventromedial hypothalamus, played a central role in mediating the action of estrogen on reproductive behaviors and control of the hypothalamic-pituitary-ovarian axis (Madeira and Lieberman, 1995; Pfaff, 1980). Complementary studies identifying regions of the brain with bound labeled estrogens showed that these hypothalamic regions had the highest concentrations of estrogen receptors (ER) in the brain (Pfaff and Keiner, 1973; Stumpf, Sar, and Keefer, 1975). Further localization studies, identifying estrogen receptors by immunocytochemistry or in situ hybridization, confirmed the strong presence of estrogen receptors in the hypothalamus and in brain areas with strong connections to the hypothalamus, including the amygdala, septal nuclei, the bed nucleus of the stria terminalis, the medial part of the nucleus of the solitary tract, and the lateral portion of the parabrachial nucleus. However, these studies showed relatively few estrogen receptors in the hippocampus, cerebellum, or the cerebral cortex (Cintra et al., 1986; DonCarlos, Monroy, and Morrell, 1991; Simerly et al., 1990). No major differences were found in the distribution of estrogen receptors in males versus females (Simerly et al., 1990).

In 1996 a new member of the steroid hormone receptor superfamily, one with a high sequence homology to the classical estrogen receptor (now referred to as ER-α), was isolated from rat prostate; this receptor was named ER-β (Kuiper et al., 1996, 1998). This novel

JUDY L. CAMERON Departments of Psychiatry, Neuroscience, and Cell Biology & Physiology, University of Pittsburgh, Pittsburgh, Pennsylvania; Oregon Regional Primate Research Center, Oregon Health Sciences University, Beaverton, Oregon.

estrogen receptor was shown to bind estradiol and to activate transcription by binding to estrogen response elements (Kuiper et al., 1998). In situ hybridization studies examining the localization of ER-β mRNA have shown that these receptors are present throughout the rostral-caudal extent of the brain, with a high level of expression in the preoptic area, bed nucleus of the stria terminalis, paraventricular and supraoptic nuclei, amygdala, and laminae II–VI of the cerebral cortex, and lower levels of expression in Ammon's horn and the dentate gyrus of the hippocampus (Shughrue, Lane, and Merchenthaler, 1997; Shughrue and Merchenthaler, 2000). Demonstration of ER-β in regions of the brain previously thought to have relatively few estrogen receptors—specifically the cerebral cortex and much of the hippocampus—has provided new insight into how estrogen may modulate neural functions in these brain regions.

PROGESTERONE RECEPTORS In females of a number of species, progesterone can either facilitate or inhibit estrogen-induced sexual behaviors, depending on the timing of the increase in relation to rising estrogen levels during the ovarian cycle (Feder and Marrone, 1977). Specific receptors for progesterone are induced by estrogen in hypothalamic regions of the brain, including the preoptic area, the ventromedial and ventrolateral nuclei, and the infundibular/arcuate nucleus (Bethea et al., 1992; Blaustein et al., 1988; DonCarlos, Greene, and Morrell, 1989). In the monkey, ovariectomy has been shown to decrease, but not eliminate, progesterone receptor levels in much of the hypothalamus, and in the supraoptic nucleus ovariectomy does not decrease progesterone receptor levels, suggesting that there are populations of neurons in which progesterone receptors are constitutively expressed (Bethea et al., 1992). Progesterone has been shown to downregulate its own receptors in many peripheral tissues of the reproductive tract, but it does not appear to have this effect in many regions of the hypothalamus, although progesterone treatment does decrease progesterone receptors in the ventromedial nucleus in the monkey (Bethea, Brown, and Kohama, 1996; Bethea et al., 1992; DonCarlos, Greene, and Morrell, 1989). In contrast, there is evidence that progesterone can act to enhance estrogen induction of some hypothalamic progesterone receptors in the guinea pig (Brown et al., 1990; DonCarlos, Greene, and Morrell, 1989). Thus, there appears to be cellular specificity to the mechanisms regulating progesterone receptor expression in various regions of the hypothalamus.

ANDROGEN RECEPTORS Androgen receptor mapping studies have shown considerable overlap in the distribution of androgen and estrogen receptors throughout the brain (Michael, Clancy, and Zumpe, 1995; Resko and Roselli, 1997; Simerly et al., 1990). The highest density of androgen receptors is found in hypothalamic nuclei known to participate in the control of reproduction and sexual behaviors, including the arcuate nucleus, paraventricular nucleus, medial preoptic nucleus, and ventromedial nucleus, and in brain regions with strong connections to the hypothalamus, including the amygdala, nuclei of the septal region, the bed nucleus of the stria terminalis, the nucleus of the solitary tract, and the lateral division of the parabrachial nucleus. Moderate densities of androgen receptors have been shown in the hippocampus, cerebral cortex, and areas of the telencephalon involved with olfaction and the processing of vestibular and auditory information, as well as in motor nuclei of the brainstem and spinal cord. As with estrogen receptors, no major differences in androgen receptor distribution have been found in males versus females. Androgen receptors are present early in fetal development and increase in number with gestation in both sexes (Resko and Roselli, 1997), a finding that accounts for the fact that developmental treatment of females with exogenous androgens can masculinize numerous behaviors.

## Organizational versus activational effects of sex steroid hormones

The study of sex differences in the brain grew out of our understanding of how gonadal hormones influence sexual differentiation of the body with regard both to primary sexual differences between males and females (the differentiation of the sexual organs) and to the development of secondary sexual differences (body fat distribution, muscle development, breast development, differences in hair distribution). In the case of sexual differentiation of the body, it is clear that exposure of males to various testicular secretory products, including testosterone, during early prenatal development leads to sexual differentiation of the internal and external genitalia. Later activation of the reproductive axis at puberty, with a sustained increase in circulating testosterone, then leads to the development of secondary sexual characteristics. Thus, testosterone has both organizational and activational influences on the sexual differentiation of the body. *Organizational* effects of gonadal hormones are conceptualized as resulting from the early influence of gonadal hormones on structural development that do not require continued hormone exposure to maintain sexual differentiation. *Activational* effects are conceptualized as later stimulation of reversible influences on sexual differentiation that require continued exposure to gonadal hormones to maintain sex differences.

The concept that sex steroid hormones have important and permanent organizational effects on the developing brain was originally postulated on the basis of experimental findings that treatment of developing mice with testosterone produced permanent effects on reproductive capacity (Barraclough and Leathem, 1954), with early treatment with testosterone blocking later activation of ovulation by estradiol. A similar coordination of early and later influences of gonadal steroid hormones on reproductive behavior was first reported by Phoenix and coworkers (1959). These investigators found that exposure of female guinea pigs to testosterone in the prenatal period increased the likelihood of animals' displaying masculine sexual behaviors in adulthood, and simultaneously decreased the likelihood of their displaying feminine sexual behaviors. These observations formed the basis for the hypothesis that, during early brain development, exposure to sex steroids can have long-lasting, organizational effects that will influence CNS neuronal activity and behavior throughout life. Although there are exceptions, it is now recognized that for a multitude of diverse actions of sex steroid hormones on the brain there are specific "critical" periods in early brain development when sex steroid hormone exposure has permanent organizational effects on the regions of the brain mediating these actions (Cooke et al., 1998; MacLusky and Naftolin, 1981).

In general, exposure of males to testicular hormones during prenatal and early postnatal periods leads both to masculinization of some tissues and functions (masculine changes in genital structure, copulatory behavior, and other behaviors characteristic of males) and to defeminization of other tissues and functions (ovulatory competence, feminine sexual behaviors such as lordosis, and other behaviors characteristic of females). Because the various steroid-sensitive tissues of the body and brain have differing critical periods for the organizational effects of testosterone, in some congenital syndromes and under some experimental conditions certain tissues of the body and brain may become masculinized while others do not. Thus, it is often important to consider the degree of masculinization or feminization of specific tissues and functions.

In rodents, the critical period for steroid hormone-mediated organization of brain regions and sexually dimorphic behaviors appears to be postnatal, with most effects occurring during the first 10 days of life. In primates, sexual differentiation of the brain occurs prenatally, over an extended period in midgestation (Phoenix, Goy, and Resko, 1968).

In contrast to the organizational effects of sex steroid hormones on the neural circuits that control behavior, the more common actions of sex steroids on behavior in adulthood are often conceptualized as activational effects. That is, sex steroid treatment causes a temporary and reversible change in neural function and behavior. An example of an activational effect of a sex steroid on behavior is the rapid increase in display of female sexual receptive behavior, lordosis, that occurs in female rats after a brief exposure to elevated estrogen.

Despite the useful conceptual framework of early organizational effects and later activational effects of steroid hormones on neural function, there are clear examples in which effects of steroid hormones in adulthood cause major long-term structural reorganization of the brain. For example, castration of male hamsters and rats in adulthood has been shown to lead to dramatic decreases in neural size and dendritic branching within the medial amygdala, with testosterone treatment in adulthood reversing these changes (Cooke et al., 1998; Gomez and Newman, 1991). Another example of long-term organizational effects of steroid hormones in adulthood is the neurotrophic effects of testosterone on substance P–containing neurons of the medial nucleus of the amygdala and the bed nucleus of the stria terminalis in the rat (Malsbury and McKay, 1994). Male rats have almost twice the area of substance P–containing neurons in these brain regions compared to females, and this sexually dimorphic difference is dependent on the maintenance of adult levels of testosterone. Castrating males in adulthood leads to a dramatic decrease in the area of substance P–containing neurons.

A great many actions of steroid hormones on the brain require both early organizational and later activational effects of the hormones, but this is not true in all cases. The ventromedial hypothalamus (VMH) is a sexually dimorphic nucleus that plays key roles in the control of feminine reproductive behaviors, including maternal behavior and lordosis in rats (Madeira and Lieberman, 1995; Pfaff, 1980). The VMH is significantly larger in males than in females, but individual cell nuclei are larger in females (Dorner and Staudt, 1969). These differences depend on organizational effects of steroid hormones in the first few days of postnatal life, such that castration of males on postnatal day 1, but not postnatal day 7, reduces the volume of the VMH to that of control females (Dorner and Staudt, 1969). In adulthood the VMH is a critical site for the induction of lordosis behavior in response to elevations in estradiol and progesterone (Pfaff, 1980). Estradiol treatment of female rats leads to a number of acute changes in the

VMH, including an increase in protein synthesis and an increase in dendritic spines in VMH neurons, and induction of progesterone receptors and receptors for another reproductive hormone oxytocin (McEwen, 1991). Subsequent progesterone exposure leads to changes in the location of oxytocin receptors and makes the estradiol-primed female sensitive to oxytocin-induced lordosis (McEwen, 1991). Some of these actions depend on both the organizational and activational effects of steroid hormones on VMH neurons. For example, estradiol increases dendritic spines in VMH neurons in the female, but the VMH neurons in the male are refractory to this action of estradiol (Frankfurt et al., 1990; McEwen, 1991). Also, estradiol treatment sensitizes this nucleus to actions of progesterone in females, but not in males (Rainbow, Parsons, and McEwen, 1982). Other actions of estradiol in this nucleus depend only on acute estradiol exposure. For example, estradiol induces oxytocin receptors in the VMH in adulthood in both female and male rats (Coirini, Johnson, and McEwen, 1989). These contrasts highlight the need for specificity when determining the contributions organizational versus activational actions of a sex steroid hormone, both in reference to the particular action of a steroid hormone and the cell type upon which it is acting.

## The role of steroid metabolism in mediating the actions of sex steroids on the brain

AROMATIZATION    In the early 1940s, Frank Beach (1942) showed that castrated male rats receiving exogenous estrogen recovered normal male mating behavior, providing the first evidence that metabolism of androgens to estrogen plays a key role in mediating androgen actions at the level of the central nervous system. Later, experiments in female rodents showed that perinatal estradiol treatment was as effective as testosterone treatment both in suppressing lordosis and in stimulating male-like mounting behavior (Barraclough and Gorski, 1962; Levine and Mullins, 1964; Whalen and Nadler, 1963). A more definitive indication that aromatization of androgen to estrogen (figure 5.1) is necessary for actions of androgens to stimulate sexual behavior was provided by studies showing that treatment of female or castrated male rats with dihydrotestosterone (DHT), a nonaromatizable androgen, was ineffective in stimulating male sexual behavior (Brown-Grant et al., 1971; McDonald et al., 1970). Shortly thereafter, the first direct evidence that neural tissues aromatize androgens to estrogens was provided by Naftolin and colleagues (1971, 1977). Based on this work, the "aromatization hypothesis"—that local conversion

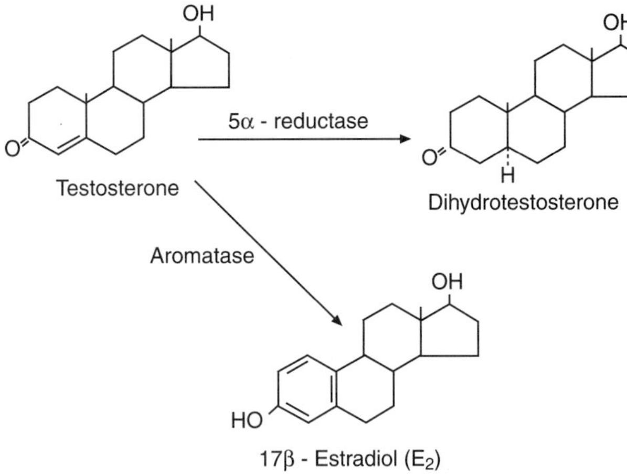

FIGURE 5.1    Pathways for metabolism of testosterone in brain tissue.

of androgens to estrogens in or near brain target cells accounts for actions of androgens on behavior and sexual differentiation—was proposed.

Whereas a great deal of data indicate that many actions of androgens on behavior in rodents are mediated by local conversion to estrogen, a similar role for aromatization in regulating the behavioral effects of androgens on behavior in primate species is more controversial. Early evidence that androgens may not need to be converted to estrogen to influence behavior came from studies in rhesus monkeys showing that prenatal treatment of female monkeys with dihydrotestosterone was effective in masculinizing sexual behavior (Goy and Resko, 1972). Later studies showed that estradiol was not effective in restoring sexual activity in castrated macaques (Michael, Zumpe, and Bonsall, 1990; Phoenix and Chambers, 1982) and that the addition of estradiol to dihydrotestosterone therapy in castrated macaques does not further increase sexual behavior (Michael, Bonsall, and Zumpe, 1987). Such studies further supported the notion that, in the primate, aromatization of androgens to estrogen may not be important in mediating the behavioral effects of androgens. However, aromatase is present in the primate brain (Abdelgadir et al., 1997; Naftolin et al., 1996) and is regulated by androgen exposure (Roselli and Resko, 1989; Resko et al., 1993). Moreover, recent studies have shown that aromatase inhibitors can decrease male sexual behavior in macaques (Zumpe, Bonsall, and Michael, 1993). Thus, aromatization of androgens to estrogens does occur in the brains of primates and apparently plays a role in regulating at least some behavioral effects of androgens; however, aromatization of androgens does not appear to be as critical a step in mediating primate androgen-induced behaviors as it is in rodent species.

The aromatase enzyme complex that catalyzes androgens to estrogens is composed of a specific aromatase, cytochrome P450, P450XIXAI, the product of the CYP19 gene, and NADPH-cytochrome P450 reductase, with a cellular location in the endoplasmic reticulum (Lephart, 1996; Nebert and Gonzales, 1987). Aromatase activity has been localized in specific brain regions by demonstration of enzyme activity and mRNA levels, including many brain nuclei that show sexually dimorphic differences in structure (Abdelgadir et al., 1997; Roselli and Resko, 1987). In the brain, aromatase activity is specific to neurons, glial cells being devoid of the enzyme (Abe-Dohmae, Tanaka, and Harada, 1994). There is an abundance of aromatase activity in neurons of the hypothalamus, preoptic area, and limbic region; but it is present at much lower levels or undetectable in a number of other brain regions including many regions of the cerebral cortex, hippocampus, and cerebellum (Abdelgadir et al., 1997; Lephart, 1996).

In many, but not all, regions of the brain, aromatase activity is regulated by androgen concentrations, as indicated by studies showing that androgen treatment increases aromatase activity while castration decreases aromatase activity, and by the finding that males have higher levels of aromatase activity than females in many brain regions (Roselli and Resko, 1993). Further evidence for androgen regulation of aromatase is provided by data collected in Tfm (testicular feminization mutation) mice, which have a defective structural gene for the androgen receptor. These mice have aromatase levels that are significantly decreased relative to control males (Rosenfeld et al., 1977). A notable exception is the aromatase in areas of the limbic system, including the bed nucleus of the stria terminalis and amygdaloid regions where aromatase enzymatic activity appears to be regulated by an androgen-independent mechanism (Jakab et al., 1993; Roselli and Resko, 1993).

Brain aromatase activity shows a marked developmental pattern of expression, first appearing in the hypothalamus of rats on gestational day 16, peaking at gestational day 19, and declining to low but detectable levels in the perinatal period, then further declining at puberty (figure 5.2; Lephart et al., 1992). However, the factors that regulate the developmental changes in brain aromatase activity are not well understood, and little is known about the developmental pattern of aromatase expression in specific brain nuclei (Lephart, 1996).

5α-REDUCTASE  A second metabolic pathway for androgens that is present in the brain is the 5α-reductase—

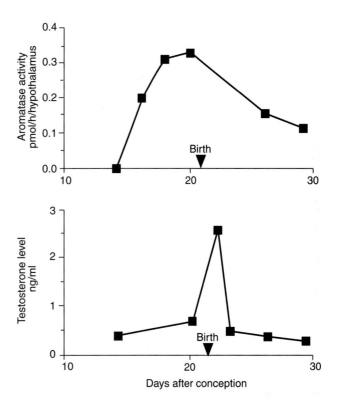

FIGURE 5.2  Developmental time course of hypothalamic aromatase activity (top panel) and testosterone secretion (bottom panel) in the male rat. (Adapted from McEwen, B. S., 1992. Steroid hormones: Effect on brain development and function. *Horm. Res.* 37:1–10.)

3α-hydroxysteroid dehydrogenase pathway (figure 5.1). Transformation of testosterone into dihydrotestosterone (DHT) by 5α-reductase plays a critical role in differentiation of some androgen-dependent structures in the periphery—in particular, the prostate. DHT binds to androgen receptors, but with about four times the affinity of testosterone (Grino, Griffin, and Wilson, 1990). The androgen receptor complex appears to be more stable when DHT is bound, compared to testosterone, and DHT exhibits a much slower dissociation rate from the androgen receptor (Grino, Griffin, and Wilson, 1990). Thus, metabolism of testosterone to DHT within specific cells provides a more potent androgen signal to those cells. There are two forms of 5α-reductase, type 1 and type 2. In the prostate, type 2 enzyme plays a critical role in differentiation.

The brain has both type 1 and type 2 forms of 5α-reductase (Normington and Russell, 1992). There appears to be a preponderance of the type 1 isoform in adult brain, while the type 2 isoform varies with age, being maximal in the perinatal period (Negri-Cesi, Poletti, and Celotti, 1996). Interestingly, the formation of DHT appears to be severalfold higher in white matter structures than in rest of the brain (Celotti, Melcangi, and Martini, 1992). In general, neither in rodents nor primates does the 5α-reductase system appear to be regulated by the presence or absence of sex steroid hormones, and no sexual dimorphism in its distribution has been reported (Negri-Cesi, Poletti, and Celotti, 1996; Sholl, Goy, and Kim, 1989). The role of DHT in guiding sexual differentiation of neural systems in the brain is currently unknown. However, in the rat there appears to be a peak in 5α-reductase activity in the neonatal period (Negri-Cesi, Poletti, and Celotti, 1996); this peak is coincident with the neonatal secretory peak of testosterone that plays a critical role in sexual differentiation of a number of behaviors in the rodent (Weisz and Ward, 1980), suggesting that DHT may be important in this process.

NEUROSTEROIDS  The term "neurosteroid" refers to steroids that are synthesized within the nervous system, either de novo from cholesterol or by metabolism of precursors originating from the circulation (Baulieu, 1991). Enzymes for the production of progesterone and its steroid precursor pregnenolone have been demonstrated in the brain (Guennoun et al., 1995; Mellon, 1994). The Δ5,3β-hydroxysteroid dehydrogenase isomerase enzyme (figure 5.3) that converts pregnenolone to progesterone has been found to be widely distributed in the brain, both in neurons and glial cells, and the production of tritiated progesterone from tritiated pregnenolone has been demonstrated in cultured glial cells (Guennoun et al., 1995). Changes in the concentration of pregnenolone and its derivatives, which vary in concert with behavioral changes, have been found to be correlated with behavioral performance, including performance on memory tests (Baulieu, 1997). Enzymes that can metabolize progesterone, including 5α-reductase and 3α- and 3β-hydroxysteroid oxidoreductases, have been detected in the brain; and these allow production of the 5α-reduced metabolites of progesterone that have been shown to interact with the GABA$_A$ receptor (Baulieu, 1997; Majewska, 1992). Such progesterone metabolites have been reported to have anesthetic, anticonvulsant, hypnotic, anxiolytic, and analgesic activities (Baulieu, 1997).

## Mechanisms by which sex steroids modulate neuronal activity

Over the past few years it has become apparent that sex steroid hormones can modulate neuronal function by acting via a variety of different mechanisms (Alonso and Lopez-Coviella, 1998; McEwen and Alves, 1999; Toran-Allerand, Singh, and Setalo, 1999). The well known intracellular receptors for these hormones (described earlier), once bound by hormone, bind to hormone response elements and act together with other transcription factors to regulate gene expression (Truss and Beato, 1993). Neurons that are targets for this form of steroid hormone modulation must have both receptors for a particular steroid hormone and the appropriate hormone response element. It has been generally believed that actions of steroid hormones mediated via intracellular receptors are relatively slow to occur and are long-lasting. However, more recent evidence indicates that some effects mediated by intracellular steroid hormone receptors can occur quite rapidly (Boyle et al., 1987). There is considerable evidence that intracellular steroid hormone receptors play a role in regulating synthesis of a variety of neuropeptides, neuropeptide and neurotransmitter receptors, and regulatory enzymes for neurotransmitter synthesis (Alonso and Lopez-Coviella, 1998).

Steroid hormones can also act via nongenomic mechanisms. Actions that are mediated this way generally occur quite rapidly, on the order of milliseconds to minutes, and include alterations in neuronal excitability and neuropeptide release (Alonso and Lopez-Coviella, 1998; McEwen and Alves, 1999). Estrogen binding sites have been reported on cell membranes (McEwen and Alves, 1999), but specific membrane-bound estrogen receptors have not yet been cloned. However, recent studies using transient transfection of ERα and ERβ in Chinese hamster ovarian cells have demonstrated that both of these estrogen receptors can be expressed in the cell membrane as well as in the nuclear fraction (Razandi et al., 1999). A-ring–reduced metabolites of progesterone bind to GABA$_A$ receptors on the cell membrane and increase GABA-dependent chloride currents within neurons (Barker et al., 1987; Gee, 1988; McEwen, 1991).

Increasingly, there is evidence that steroid hormones can modulate neuronal activity by acting via intracellular second messenger systems. In the hypothalamus, estrogen-induced depolarization has been reported to activate a cAMP second messenger system, coupled to G proteins (Minami et al., 1990; Nabekura et al., 1986). Estrogen has also been reported to activate MAP kinases, ERK-1 and ERK-2, in cortical neurons (Toran-Allerand, Singh, and Setalo, 1999). Changes in cellular calcium flux constitute a third intracellular messenger system that is affected by estrogen. In rat neostriatal neurons it has been shown that 17β-estradiol rapidly suppresses currents mediated by L-type calcium channels (Mermelstein, Becker, and Surmeier, 1996)—an action that is probably mediated via a membrane receptor. In the hippocampus, however, estradiol has been

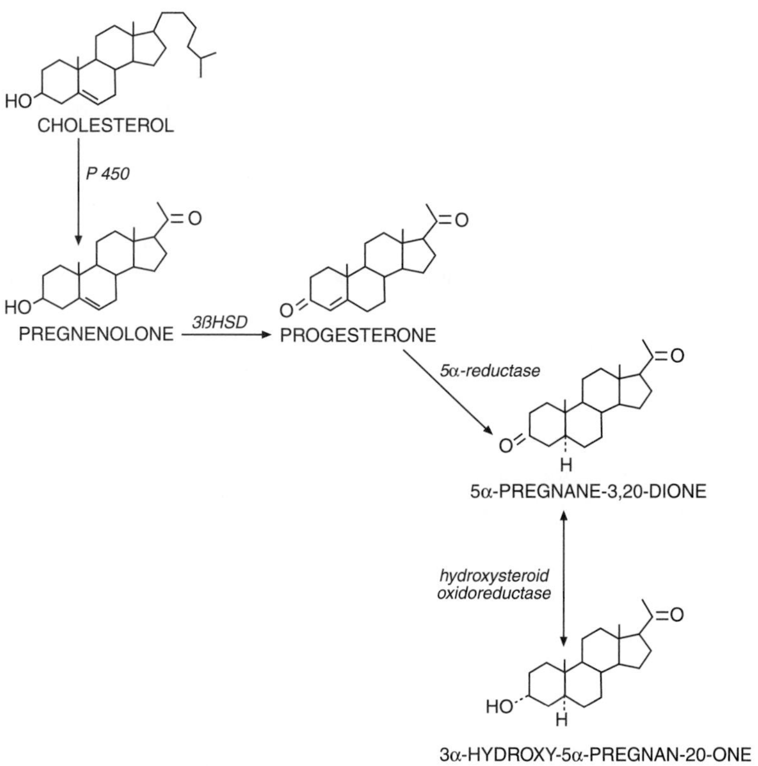

FIGURE 5.3 Biosynthesis of neurosteroids. Enzymes in this pathway include side-chain cleavage cytochrome P450, 3β- hydroxysteroid dehydrogenase (3βHSD), 5α-reductase, and 3α-hydroxysteroid oxidoreductase.

shown to increase both sustained and transient calcium currents—actions that may well be mediated by genomic actions of this steroid hormone (Joels and Karst, 1995).

There is also evidence that estrogen may act as a neural growth factor within the brain, influencing neuronal development, survival, plasticity, and regeneration (Toran-Allerand, Singh, and Setalo, 1999). Neurons in the forebrain coexpress estrogen and neurotrophin receptors, and these neurons are also sites of both estrogen and neurotrophin synthesis. Moreover, estrogen and nerve growth factor can reciprocally regulate the expression of each other's receptors, and accumulating evidence suggests that there is cross-coupling of their signaling pathways (Toran-Allerand, Singh, and Setalo, 1999).

Further evidence of complex interactions between steroid hormones and neural signaling systems comes from studies showing that dopamine can modulate sexual behavior in rodents via a mechanism that requires the presence of intracellular progesterone receptors within hypothalamic neurons (Mani, Blaustein, and O'Malley, 1997). This action of dopamine involves a ligand-independent activation of progesterone receptors (Mani et al., 1994).

## Sexual dimorphisms in the brain

PROCESSES AFFECTED BY SEX STEROIDS  Sex steroid hormones lead to sexual differentiation of behavior by affecting a wide variety of cellular mechanisms within the nervous system (Cooke et al., 1998). Processes that have been shown to be modulated by sex steroid hormones include neurogenesis (Gurney and Konishi, 1979; Jacobson and Gorski, 1981), cell migration (Sengelaub and Arnold, 1986), growth of the neuronal soma (Breedlove and Arnold, 1981), dendritic growth, differentiation and synapse formation (Frankfurt et al., 1990; Goldman and Nottebohm, 1983; Gomez and Newman, 1991; Gould, Woolley, and McEwen, 1990; Juraska, 1991; Raisman and Field, 1973; Woolley and McEwen, 1992), synapse elimination (Leedy, Beattie, and Bresnahan, 1987), neuronal atrophy and apoptosis (Davis, Shryne, and Gorski, 1996; McEwen, 1996; Woolley, Gould, and McEwen, 1990), neuropeptide expression (De Vries, 1990; Malsbury and McKay, 1994), the expression of neurotransmitter receptors (Levesque, Gagnon, and Di Paolo, 1989; McEwen, 1991; Turner and Weaver, 1985), and neuronal excitability (Teyler et al., 1980; Wong and Moss, 1992).

EXAMPLES OF SEXUALLY DIMORPHIC BRAIN REGIONS AND BEHAVIORS   In mammalian species numerous sex differences in brain structure and function have now been documented. Sexual dimorphic brain areas include a number of regions of the hypothalamus, including the medial preoptic area and the ventromedial hypothalamus, the vomeronasal system, amygdala, bed nucleus of the stria terminalis, hippocampus, striatum, cerebellum, and various regions of the cerebral cortex. Behaviors showing documented sex differences include behaviors associated with reproduction (mating and maternal behaviors), aggression, activity, and various cognitive functions including spatial cognition, verbal skills, and various aspects of learning and memory. Examples of sexually dimorphic brain regions and behaviors in nonmammalian species have also proven to be very important for learning about basic mechanisms governing the establishment and maintenance of sexual dimorphisms, including bird and frog song systems. It is beyond the scope of this chapter to review all of these areas and behaviors. Here, we review areas and behaviors that demonstrate especially useful examples of general principles regarding sexual dimorphisms, or are particularly relevant to the topic of developmental cognitive neuroscience.

*The medial preoptic area and sexual behaviors*   One of the first reports of a sexual dimorphism in a brain structure was by Raisman and Field (1973), who examined the rat medial preoptic area (mPOA; a brain area that plays an important role in the regulation of sexual behaviors) by electron microscopy and found that females had more dendritic spine synapses and fewer axosomatic synapses than males. Moreover, they showed that the synapse structure was modulated by the presence of androgen in the neonatal period. Previous reports had shown that the mPOA plays a role in male copulatory behavior in the rat, that implantation of testosterone into the mPOA of castrated males would restore mating behavior, and that similar implants in females would induce male-like mounting and copulatory behaviors (Madeira and Lieberman, 1995). Thus, this was the first report of a structural difference in the brain induced by a gonadal steroid hormone, one that may underlie a known behavioral effect of that hormone.

Later studies by Gorski and colleagues (1978, 1980) identified a more striking sexual dimorphism in the mPOA. They showed a region of densely packed, darkly staining cells in the mPOA that was 2.5–5 times larger in the male rat than in the female rat—a region they designated as the sexually dimorphic nucleus of the medial preoptic area, or SDN-POA. In both male and female rats this region has the highest concentration of

estradiol receptors in the brain (Herbison and Theodosis, 1992), and there is evidence that there are more estradiol receptors in the female than in the male (Brown, Naftolin, and MacLusky, 1992). This area also accumulates androgens to a greater degree in males than in females (Jacobson, Arnold, and Gorski, 1987). The SDN-POA is an excellent example of a nuclear region in which organizational influences of testosterone play a critical role and aromatization of testosterone to estradiol is an important intermediary step. Castration of males in the early neonatal period leads to a permanent decrease in the size of the SDN-POA, whereas treatment of female rats with testosterone in this same time period leads to a permanent increase in size of the SDN-POA (Gorski et al., 1978, 1980). Neonatal treatment with estrogen is even more effective than early androgen treatment in increasing the size of the nucleus, and neonatal treatment of males with an antiestrogen decreases the size of the SDN-POA (Dohler et al., 1984). In this nucleus there is evidence that either androgen or estrogen treatment increases neurogenesis in the early neonatal period (Jacobson and Gorski, 1981), and later prevents programmed cell death (Davis, Shryne, and Gorski, 1996). Despite the abundance of studies on the SDN-POA of the rat, and the profound sexual dimorphism of this nucleus, there is relatively little information about the role of the SDN-POA in mediating behavior. Lesions of the nucleus have been reported to have few behavioral effects (Arendash and Gorski, 1983). Nevertheless, the mPOA has been shown to have significant sexual dimorphism in a wide variety of species (Ayoub, Greenough, and Juraska, 1983; Commins and Yahr, 1985; Hines et al., 1985; Tobet, Zahniser, and Baum, 1986), including humans (Allen et al., 1989; LeVay, 1991; Swaab and Fliers, 1985); thus, there remains a great deal of interest in the possible function of this brain area in mediating sexually dimorphic behaviors.

Other key areas involved in mediating sexual behavior in the rodent are the VMN, the vomeronasal system, and the bed nucleus of the stria terminalis (Cooke et al., 1998). In many cases, these brain areas show sexual dimorphisms in structure. And in many cases gonadal hormones have both organizational and activational activities.

*The bird song system*   Three years after Raisman and Field's report of subtle structural sexual dimorphisms in synapse structure in the mPOA of the rat, Nottebohm and Arnold (1976) published a landmark report showing a much more robust sexual dimorphism in brain structure in songbirds. They found that the nuclei in the vocal control areas of male songbirds (canaries and zebra finches; species in which the male sings but the female does not) were five to six times the size of these same areas in their female counterparts. Later studies showed that species in which both the male and female sing exhibit no sexual dimorphism in these brain areas (Brenowitz, Arnold, and Levin, 1985). Since that time a great deal of research on the bird song system has been performed and there is excellent evidence linking structural differences between sexes with sexual dimorphism of singing behavior (Bottjer and Arnold, 1997).

In zebra finches, both organizational and activational affects of testosterone are apparent, and testosterone works through aromatization to estrogen. When treated with estrogens early in life and then given testosterone or estrogen steroids as adults, female zebra finches will sing in adulthood (Gurney and Konishi, 1979). In the neonatal time period, estrogen treatment increases neuronal number (Gurney and Konishi, 1979). Surprisingly, in zebra finches the converse experiment—castrating males or treating them with anti-estrogens—has not been effective either in preventing structural differentiation of male-like nuclei in vocal control areas or in preventing singing, leading to the proposal that male songbirds may also have a steroid-independent genetic mechanism regulating development of the nuclei in the vocal control areas (Arnold, 1996, 1997).

The neural systems underlying song production in the canary differ from those in the zebra finch in that organizational effects of androgens remain apparent into adulthood. Female canaries treated with androgens in adulthood show structural changes in the nuclei of the vocal control areas, specifically increased dendritic growth, eventually resulting in song production (DeVoogd and Nottebohm, 1981; Goldman and Nottebohm, 1983). This is a good example of steroid hormones in adulthood causing long-term organizational effects in the brain.

*Midbrain dopaminergic systems and motor activity* The striatum is part of the midbrain system that plays a critical role in sensorimotor integration. The striatum receives input fibers from the motor and associated cortical areas, as well as from the substantia nigra. The nigrostriatal projection is dopaminergic, containing more than 90% of the dopamine neurons in the brain. When dopamine activity in this pathway is increased, animals display increased motor activity to sensory stimuli, whereas when dopaminergic activity in this pathway is decreased, animals become hyporesponsive to sensory input (Becker, 1991).

In females, estrogen and progesterone modulate the activity of this dopaminergic pathway (Becker, 1999). Female rats have been shown to have greater behavioral

activity responses when the striatal dopamine system is stimulated on the evening of proestrous, when circulating estradiol levels are high, compared to the day of diestrous, when circulating estradiol levels are much lower (Becker and Cha, 1989). They also show increases in extracellular dopamine concentration within the striatum, amphetamine-stimulated striatal dopamine release, dopamine metabolism, and increased dopamine receptors on estrous compared to diestrous (Becker, 1990, 1999; Di Paolo, Falardeau, and Morisette, 1988; Levesque, Gagnon, and Di Paolo, 1989). With ovariectomy, stimulated activity is decreased (Camp, Becker, and Robinson, 1986), as well as stimulated strial dopamine release and dopamine receptor density (Becker and Ramirez, 1980; Levesque, Gagnon, and Di Paolo, 1989). Estradiol replacement can reverse these changes, although there are differences with acute versus more chronic estradiol treatment (Becker, 1999).

In male rats, estrogen does not affect striatal dopamine release; in addition, castration has little effect on this system (Becker, 1999). Comparison of male and female rats shows that there is sexual dimorphism in striatal dopamine release and dopamine receptors. In castrated male rats, basal extracellular dopamine concentrations in the striatum are twice as high as in ovariectomized female rats (Xiao and Becker, 1994), and amphetamine-induced dopamine release is also higher in males (Becker and Ramirez, 1980). In addition, male rats have more dopamine $D_1$ receptors than do females (Hruska et al., 1982).

It seems likely that these sex differences in activity and ease of activation of the striatal dopamine system play important roles in governing behavior in various circumstances. Becker has postulated, based on studies administering estrogen directly into the striatum, that this system plays a role in pacing the rate of sexual encounters between male and female animals to optimize fertility (Becker, 1999; Xiao and Becker, 1997). One practical implication of these sex differences is that scientists need to be aware that sexual differences in activity may underlie sexual differences that are measured in animal's performances on a variety of laboratory tests, including tests of learning and memory.

*The hippocampus and learning and memory* Clinical studies showing that lesions of the hippocampus lead to severe memory damage indicate that this area of the brain can play a critical role in learning and memory, specifically with regard to deficits in the formation of new memories (anterograde amnesia; Milner, Teuber, and Corkin, 1968). The hippocampus is known to be influenced both by gonadal steroid hormones and by adrenal hormones, specifically glucocorticoids.

Microstructure within the hippocampus has also been shown to be influenced by early experience and rearing environment (Juraska, 1991). Thus, interactions between these two endocrine systems and experiences of an individual during development combine to result in long-term consequences for this brain area, both in structure and function.

The hippocampus is composed of three distinct regions, connected in a circuit—the dentate gyrus, which has granule neurons that send mossy fibers to the pyramidal neurons of the CA3 region of Ammon's horn, which in turn send collaterals to the pyramidal neurons in the CA1 region. In both males and females, cells in the CA1 region of the hippocampus contain ER (Loy, Gerlach, and McEwen, 1988; Simerly et al., 1990), while ER-β receptors are present in Ammon's horn and the dentate gyrus (Shughrue, Lane, and Merchenthaler, 1997; Shughrue and Merchenthaler, 2000). Estradiol administration can alter the morphology of neurons in the CA1 region, increasing the number of spines and the amount of branching in apical dendrites and increasing the density of synapses in the hippocampal CA1 stratum radiatum, whereas the opposite changes occur with ovariectomy (Gould et al., 1990; Juraska, 1991; Woolley and McEwen, 1992). Progesterone administration initially potentiates the effects of estradiol on neurons in this brain region, but later triggers down-regulation of spines on CA1 neurons (Gould et al., 1990; Woolley and McEwen, 1993). Moreover, naturally occurring changes in estradiol and progesterone across the rat estrous cycle have been associated with changes in synaptic density and dendritic morphology in hippocampal CA1 neurons (Woolley and McEwen, 1992, 1993; Woolley et al., 1990). Estrogen effects on CA1 neurons appear to be mediated by an NMDA receptor–mediated mechanism, in that NMDA receptor antagonists block estrogen induction of spines and estrogen induces NMDA receptors in the CA1 region (Woolley and McEwen, 1994). In the adult rat, the effects of estradiol on the hippocampus are sexually dimorphic, with male rats showing fewer effects on hippocampal synapse formation when treated with estrogen (Lewis, McEwen, and Frankfurt, 1995). This appears to result from organizational effects of androgen (converted to estrogen) on the hippocampus, as treatment of neonatal male rats with an aromatase inhibitor can eliminate this sex difference in adulthood (Lewis, McEwen, and Frankfurt, 1995). Developmental changes in estrogen receptors (O'Keefe and Handa, 1990) and aromatase (MacLusky et al., 1987) have been reported in the hippocampus, and these developmental changes may play a critical role in sexual differentiation of this region of the brain.

There are also functional changes in hippocampal neurons associated with experimentally manipulated or naturally occurring fluctuations in estradiol and progesterone in the female rat. In general, there appears to be an increase in neuronal excitability in the hippocampus with elevated estradiol levels. EPSP duration is lengthened following estradiol administration, and population spike amplitude is elevated in response to estradiol (Teyler et al., 1980; Wong and Moss, 1992). Seizure threshold in the dorsal hippocampus is also lower following estrogen administration to ovariectomized female rats or on the day of proestrous in the naturally occurring estrous cycle (Buterbaugh and Hudson, 1991; Teresawa and Timiras, 1968). Long-term potentiation (LTP) in response to standardized stimulus trains has also been shown to be greater in the hippocampus of proestrous rats compared to other times in the estrous cycle (Warren et al., 1995).

Although estradiol receptors do not show sexual dimorphism in their distribution within the hippocampus, there is a sexual dimorphism in glucocorticoid receptors, with female rats having larger numbers of glucocorticoid receptors compared to males (Turner and Weaver, 1985). There is also an interaction between gonadal hormones and the glucocorticoid receptor system such that ovariectomy in females increases glucocorticoid receptors while castration in males has no effects on glucocorticoid receptors (Turner and Weaver, 1985).

Glucocorticoids have significant effects on hippocampal neuronal structure and function. In both the developing and adult rat, adrenalectomy leads to a decrease in size and dendritic arborization of neurons in the dentate gyrus, which can be prevented with adrenal steroid supplementation (Gould, Woolley, and McEwen, 1990; Woolley et al., 1991). In contrast, in the CA3 region of Ammon's horn high levels of glucocorticoids cause atrophy of pyramidal neurons (Woolley, Gould, and McEwen, 1990). Studies by Sapolsky (1990) show that glucocorticoids inhibit glucose uptake by pyramidal neurons, which precipitates atrophy and eventual cell death. These effects of glucocorticoids appear to play a role in the loss of CA3 neurons with aging, in that this loss can be prevented by adrenalectomy (Sapolsky, 1990). Glucocorticoids also lead to atrophy of CA3 neurons in conditions of chronic stress (McEwen, 1996).

In addition to plasticity induced by hormonal signals, environmental conditions during development also have a marked influence on morphology of neurons in the hippocampus, and there are clear sexual dimorphisms in the hippocampal responses to environmental stimuli (Juraska, 1991). For example, granule cells in the dentate gyrus of male rats raised in single cages show relatively few changes in their dendritic morphology as opposed to animals raised in a complex environment containing both toys and other rats. In contrast, these same hippocampal granule cells in female rats show a marked plasticity in response to rearing in a complex environment, with an increase in length of a specific population of dendrites. These sex differences appear to be regulated by organizational influences of testosterone in the neonatal period, in that neonatally castrated males show plasticity equivalent to females (Juraska, 1991).

Numerous reports have indicated sex differences in the processes of learning and memory, particularly learning that involves the use of spatial abilities, a task believed to be strongly dependent on hippocampal function (O'Keefe, 1993). Using a variety of different learning paradigms, including passive avoidance learning, active avoidance learning, and complex maze learning (using the radial-arm maze, T-maze, and Morris water maze), differences have been shown in the performance of male versus female rats (Beatty, 1979; Becker, 1991). In complex maze learning, male rats generally have been found to learn more rapidly and with fewer errors compared to female rats. However, the issue of whether better performance by males results from differences in hippocampal function or from differences in activity, which appear to be governed by other brain systems (as discussed in the previous section; see Midbrain Dopaminergic Systems and Motor Activity), is not clear for some of these tasks. Beatty (1979) argued that females make more errors in many mazes simply because they are more active, and more active motions translate into a greater occurrence of errors. In an attempt to distinguish sex differences in learning from differences in activity, some investigators have focused on the rate of initial learning of a maze compared to that of later maze performance. In one such study, Einon (1980) showed that in a radial-arm maze males were more likely than females to use a successful strategy of visiting adjacent arms. Further studies with this paradigm have shown that males or neonatally androgenized females show faster acquisition of radial-arm maze skill compared to females or neonatally castrated males, but that following skill acquisition the sex difference on this task disappears (Williams, Barnett, and Meck, 1990). It thus appears that there may be minor sex differences in the cognitive strategies that rats utilize to solve spatial learning paradigms, although both sexes show equal mastery of these tasks in the end. Further evidence that there are sex differences in hippocampal function comes from studies showing that bilateral hippocampal lesions in female rats lead to far greater impairment of function in the Morris water maze than do the same lesions in male rats (Therrien, 1982).

In humans, there are also reports of sex differences in spatial problem solving abilities, with males showing greater proficiency (Delgado and Prieto, 1996; Linn and Petersen, 1985; Witkin and Berry, 1975). But these differences are small in magnitude, and apparent only in terms of population statistics; there is considerable overlap in ability among individual males and females. It is also important to remember that spatial problem solving is a higher order cognitive task and that there is evidence that sexual dimorphism in this task reflects not only differences in hippocampal function but also functional differences within other regions of the cortex (De Courten-Myers, 1999; Kimura, 1987; Wisniewski, 1998). There is a small amount of evidence that prenatal androgen exposure may affect spatial problem solving abilities. Resnick and colleagues (1986) reported that females with congenital adrenal hyperplasia (a syndrome involving increased exposure to adrenal androgens in prenatal development) had significantly enhanced performance on tests of spatial ability compared to their unaffected female relatives. However, the effects of sex steroids on this ability do not appear to follow the typical organizational and activational scheme. There is limited evidence that sex steroid hormone levels in adulthood may influence spatial problem solving abilities, with elevated levels of estradiol in females and testosterone in males being associated with lower, rather than higher, performance on tests of spatial ability. Several studies report that women perform worse on tests of spatial problem solving during the midpoint of the menstrual cycle, when estradiol levels are elevated, compared to other times during the menstrual cycle (Broverman et al., 1981; Hampson, 1990a,b; Hampson and Kimura, 1988; Komnenich et al., 1978; Wickham, 1958). Moreover, men with higher testosterone levels have been reported to perform worse on tests of spatial ability than their counterparts with lower testosterone levels (Gouchie and Kimura, 1991; Shute et al., 1983).

*Cerebral cortical areas and higher cognitive functions* We are still in the very early stages of understanding how sex differences in most higher cognitive functions and complex behaviors are linked to sex differences in the brain. In general, research in this area has suffered from inadequate delineation of the behaviors, the anatomical brain regions, and the functional neural systems that have been studied. Another confound in this area of investigation has been that many of these functions can be studied only in humans (e.g., studies of speech), such that invasive experiments are rarely possible and control of factors such as developmental experiences is much more difficult. With the advent of various neural imaging technologies, however, more information is becoming available concerning sexual dimorphisms in the brain, particularly in the cerebral cortex. Moreover, functional magnetic resonance imaging (MRI) is beginning to link differences in cognitive abilities with differences in specific anatomical regions and patterns of neural circuit activation.

Studies of sex differences in verbal abilities provide examples of the considerable difficulty in delineating the neuroanatomical substrates underlying a sexually dimorphic higher order behavior. A number of reports suggest that women perform better on some verbal tasks than do men (Hines, 1991; Hyde and Linn, 1988). There is limited evidence that this sexual dimorphism is related to sex steroid hormones. Several studies have reported that women's performance on verbal tasks is better when estradiol, or estradiol and progesterone, are elevated during the menstrual cycle than when circulating sex steroid hormone levels are very low (Hampson, 1990a,b; Silverman and Zimmer, 1975; Silverman, Zimmer, and Silverman, 1974; Wickham, 1958). It is important to note that such changes in performance over the menstrual cycle are not seen with all verbal tasks. Rather, there appears to be specificity for the type of task that may be influenced by sex steroid hormones (Hampson, 1990a,b).

In most humans, the left side of the brain is primarily responsible for the control of speech (Springer and Deutch, 1998). However, there is evidence that there may be less hemispheric specialization in women than in men, and it is possible that this sexual dimorphism may underlie the differences between the sexes in verbal abilities. Compared to men, for example, women have been reported to have less perceptual asymmetry in dichotic listening tests (McGlone, 1980) and less asymmetry in the size of the cortex, which leads to naming errors in response to electrical stimulus tests performed during surgeries to map out areas of the cortex involved in speech (Mateer, Polen, and Ojemann, 1982). More recently, using functional MRI, men were shown to have left lateralized inferior frontal gyrus activation in phonological tasks, whereas women were shown to have more bilateral activation in this cortical region when they performed the same phonological tasks (Shaywitz et al., 1995). Unilateral damage to the brain has also been reported to have less devastating consequences for performance on tests of verbal abilities in women compared to men (Inglis et al., 1982; McGlone, 1978). Similarly, Lansdell (1961) found that surgical lesions to the left temporal cortex disrupted performance on a verbal proverb test in men, but not

in women. Evidence for organizational effects of prenatal sex steroid hormones on the degree of lateralization of verbal skills was provided by a study by Hines (1982), which found that women whose mothers took diethylstilbesterol (a potent estrogenic compound) in pregnancy to prevent miscarriage had greater lateralization than their nonexposed sisters.

There are also reports of sex differences in the size of cortical regions involved in speech (figure 5.4). Wada and colleagues (1975) reported that the planum temporale (a flat region of the temporal lobe in a language-associated area) is asymmetric, being larger on the left than the right side of the brain, but that this asymmetry was less marked in women than in men. This finding was confirmed in two recent studies (Kulynych et al., 1994; Witelson and Kigar, 1992). More recently, Witelson, Glezer, and Kigar (1995) have reported that women have a greater density of neurons in this cortical region compared to men. In contrast, however, Rabinowicz and colleagues (1999) have found that, compared to females, males have thicker cortex, higher neuronal densities, and more neurons in the left temporal sites involved with language function. In other studies, females have been reported to have larger proportional volumes of gray matter in the dorsolateral prefrontal cortex and superior temporal gyrus compared with males (Schlaepfer et al., 1995), as well as cortex associated with the cingulate sulcus (Paus et al., 1996), and proportionately larger Wernicke and Broca areas (Harasty et al., 1997). At the microscopic level,

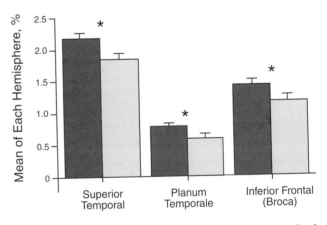

FIGURE 5.4 Sex differences in the proportional cortical volumes in language-related areas of the brain. Data are presented as percentages of brain hemisphere volume occupied by each region. Asterisks indicate a significant differences ($P < 0.05$) between males and females in the regional volume. (Adapted from Harasty, J., K. L. Double, G. M. Halliday, J. J. Kril, and D. A. McRitchie, 1997. Language-associated cortical regions are proportionally larger in the female brain. *Arch. Neurol.* 54:171–176.)

greater dendritic arborizations in Wernicke's area in females compared to males have been reported (Jacobs, Schall, and Scheibel, 1993).

A third sexual dimorphism that has been proposed to underlie the sexual dimorphism in verbal abilities is the size of the corpus callosum. The corpus callosum is a nerve fiber tract that connects the two cerebral hemispheres, allowing transfer of information between the hemispheres for complex cognitive processing, including language (Hines et al., 1992). In 1982, de Lacoste and Holloway hypothesized that the decrease in functional neural asymmetry in women was due to increased interhemispheric exchange via the corpus callosum. Since that time, sexually dimorphic structural asymmetries of the corpus callosum have been reported for its area, shape, and fiber composition (Wisniewski, 1998). However, the issue of whether there is a consistent sexual dimorphism of this fiber tract has been highly controversial. The splenium is the posterior portion of the corpus callosum that contains fibers projecting between the main auditory and visual cortical areas of the two hemispheres. In humans, a number of postmortem studies and MRI investigations provide support for the conclusion that females have a more bulbous splenium, although it is important to control for the overall corpus callosum shape, chronological age of the individuals, cerebral volume, and handedness when making such comparisons (Allen et al., 1991; Burke and Yeo, 1994; Johnson et al., 1996; Wisniewski, 1998). The isthmus of the corpus callosum connects the parietal and temporal lobes, and has been more consistently reported to have a larger area in women compared to men, although for such comparisons it is again important to control for the same factors as in studies of the splenium (Denenberg, Kertesz, and Cowell, 1991; Steinmetz et al., 1992; Witelson, 1989). Sexual dimorphism in the corpus callosum of several rodent species has also been reported (Wisniewski, 1998), and an important finding in these studies is that environmental rearing conditions can have modulatory effects on the sexual dimorphism of corpus callosum (Juraska and Kopcik, 1988). Another interesting finding of these latter studies is that there are sexual dimorphisms in the ultrastructure of the rat corpus callosum, with sex differences in the number and diameter of axons projecting across the corpus callosum (Juraska and Kopcik, 1988; Kopcik et al., 1992).

Despite the great interest in and numerous studies devoted to the neural underpinnings of sexual dimorphisms in verbal abilities, little information is available regarding the role of sex steroid hormones in mediating the development of these functional differences. Although some investigators using rodent models have shown that neonatal exposure to androgens can masculinize some sexually dimorphic neuroanatomical differences found in the cortex, such as cortical thickness (Lewis and Diamond, 1995), little is known about the effects of sex steroid hormones on the morphology of brain areas specifically involved in language processing or the size or shape of the corpus callosum. However, one principle is clear from studies in other parts of the brain, including the hypothalamus and the hippocampus: There is profound cellular and circuit specificity for the actions of sex steroid hormones. Thus, in making conclusions about the role of steroid hormones on cortical functions, it will be important to be very specific with regard to both function and neuroanatomical substrate.

*Effects of sex steroid hormones on behavior over the lifespan*

Most of the data reviewed in this chapter concern effects of sex steroid hormones on adult behavior, resulting either from organizational effects of early hormonal exposure during the fetal or neonatal periods or from activational effects of sex steroid hormones in adulthood. However, sex steroid hormone levels change dramatically both in children as they mature and enter puberty, and in women when the activity of the reproductive axis declines at menopause; thus, one would expect to see accompanying changes in behaviors modulated by sex steroid hormones at these times. One would also predict that sexually dimorphic areas of the brain that are dependent on adult levels of sex steroid hormones for maintenance of the dimorphism would change in morphology over puberty and menopause.

Although we know a good deal about the development of sex-related behaviors at puberty (Baum, 1979), surprisingly few studies have examined pubertal or menopausal changes in other behaviors that appear to be influenced by sex steroid hormones. In part, this paucity may reflect the fact that much of the work examining effects of sex steroid hormones on such behaviors as learning and memory and other cognitive functions is relatively recent. It may also reflect the difficulty in determining what portion of the developmental and aging changes in these behaviors results from changes in sex steroid hormones and what portion is attributable to hormone-independent developmental and aging processes. Finally, methodological problems—poor characterization of the activity of the reproductive axis; the use of widely varying tests of learning, memory, and other cognitive processes; and extreme variation in hormone treatment regimens in postmenopausal studies—also contribute to the lack of clarity in our understanding of how changes in sex steroid hormones across the lifespan influence behavior.

Recent studies have started to document developmental changes within specific neuroanatomical regions of the brain. In a large imaging study of normally developing children between the ages of 4 and 18 years, Giedd and colleagues (1997) found a progressive increase in the volume of the lateral ventricles in boys, with an abrupt increase in volume starting at age 11. Other areas that showed developmental changes in volume included the amygdala in boys and the hippocampus in girls (Giedd et al., 1997). Developmental changes in the density of fiber tracts within the brain have also been reported for the internal capsule and arcuate fasciculus across this same age span, (Paus et al., 1999).

In the past few years, a number of studies have examined how cognitive functions change in women as they enter menopause and how steroid hormone replacement therapy affects cognitive function. Although some protective effects of sex steroid hormones on counteracting age-related changes in cognitive functions have been reported, the majority of recent studies show little or no effect of sex steroid hormones on age-related changes in cognitive functions (Barrett-Connor and Goodman-Gruen, 1999; Haskell, Richardson, and Horwitz, 1997; Hogervorst et al., 1999; Matthews et al., 1999). However, a detailed examination of various tests of cognitive function and different hormone replacement therapies suggests that there may be some subtle effects of specific steroid hormone regimens on specific tests of cognition and memory (Hogervorst et al., 1999). In evaluating these studies, one must keep in mind that general effects of hormone replacement therapy on feelings of well-being may significantly influence performance on these tests, making it very difficult to ascertain effects of hormones on specific cognitive functions.

## General principles of sex steroid actions in the developing brain

As we learn more about how sex steroid hormones influence behavior, some general principles regarding sex steroid actions in the developing brain are emerging. First, it is apparent that the actions of steroid hormones on brain systems are widespread, with steroid hormones acting at multiple sites within the neural circuitry to lead to changes in any one behavior. Second, we now recognize great diversity in the cellular mechanisms by which steroid hormones influence neural function. In some cases, hormones are metabolized to more active forms to exert their actions on neuronal function. Sex steroid hormones can act through traditional nuclear receptors to exert their actions, but they can also bind to membrane receptors and activate a variety of second messenger pathways to influence neuronal activity. Alternatively, some sex steroid hormones appear to modulate function by acting as growth factors. Additionally, novel interactions between steroid hormones and classical neurotransmitters and neuropeptides have become apparent, such as the binding of progesterone to $GABA_A$ receptors and the activation of progesterone receptors by dopamine. Third, a wide variety of neural processes are influenced by sex steroid hormones: neurogenesis, cell migration, growth of the neuronal soma, dendritic growth, differentiation and synapse formation, synapse elimination, neuronal atrophy and apoptosis, neuropeptide expression, the expression of neurotransmitter receptors, and neuronal excitability. Fourth, in many cases steroid hormones must be present both developmentally and in the adult to elicit maximal effects on behavior. Fifth, there is a great deal of plasticity in the developing and adult nervous system, and sex steroid hormones play an important role in regulating plastic changes in neuronal structure and function.

## REFERENCES

ABDELGADIR, S. E., C. E. ROSELLI, J. V. A. CHOATE, and J. A. RESKO, 1997. Distribution of aromatase cytochrome P450 messenger ribonucleic acid in adult rhesus monkey brains. *Biol. Reprod.* 57:772–777.

ABE-DOHMAE, S., R. TANAKA, and N. HARADA, 1994. Cell type- and region-specific expression of aromatase mRNA in cultured brain cells. *Mol. Brain Res.* 24:153–158.

ALLEN, L. S., M. HINES, J. E. SHRYNE, and R. A. GORSKI, 1989. Two sexually dimorphic cell groups in the human brain. *J. Neurosci.* 9:497–506.

ALLEN, L. S., M. F. RICHEY, Y. M. CHAI, and R. A. GORSKI, 1991. Sex differences in the corpus callosum in the living human being. *J. Neurosci.* 11:933–942.

ALONSO, R., and I. LOPEZ-COVIELLA, 1998. Gonadal steroids and neuronal function. *Neurochem. Res.* 23:675–688.

ARENDASH, G. W., and R. A. GORSKI, 1983. Effects of discrete lesions of the sexually dimorphic nucleus of the preoptic area or other medial preoptic regions on the sexual behavior of male rats. *Brain Res. Bull.* 10:147.

ARNOLD, A. P., 1996. Genetically triggered sexual differentiation of brain and behavior. *Horm. Behav.* 30:495–505.

ARNOLD, A. P., 1997. Sexual differentiation of the zebra finch song system: Positive evidence, negative evidence, null hypotheses and a paradigm shift. *J. Neurobiol.* 33:572–584.

AYOUB, D. M., W. T. GREENOUGH, and J. M. JURASKA, 1983. Sex differences in dendritic structure in the preoptic area of the juvenile macaque monkey brain. *Science* 219:197–198.

BARKER, J. L., N. L. HARRISON, G. D. LANGE, and D. G. OWEN, 1987. Potentiation of γ-aminobutyric-acid-activated chloride conductance by a steroid anesthetic in cultured rat spinal neurons. *J. Physiol.* 386:485–501.

BARRACLOUGH, C. A., and R. A. GORSKI, 1962. Studies on mating behaviour in the androgen-sterilized female rat in relation to the hypothalamic regulation of sexual behaviour. *J. Endocrinol.* 25:175–182.

BARRACLOUGH, C., and J. LEATHEM, 1954. Infertility induced in mice by a single injection of testosterone propionate. *Proc. Soc. Exp. Biol. Med.* 85:673–674.

BARRETT-CONNOR, E., and D. GOODMAN-GRUEN, 1999. Cognitive function and endogenous sex hormones in older women. *J. Am. Geriatr. Soc.* 47:1289–1293.

BAULIEU, E. E., 1991. Neurosteroids: A new function in the brain. *Biol. Cell* 71:3–10.

BAULIEU, E. E., 1997. Neurosteroids: Of the nervous system, by the nervous system, for the nervous system. *Rec. Prog. Horm. Res.* 52:1–32.

BAUM, M. J., 1979. Differentiation of coital behavior in mammals: A comparative analysis. *Neurosci. Biobehav. Rev.* 3:265–284.

BEACH, F. A., 1942. Copulatory behavior in prepubertally castrated male rats and its modification by estrogen administration. *Endocrinology* 31:679–683.

BEATTY, W. W., 1979. Gonadal hormones and sex differences in nonreproductive behaviors in rodents: Organizational and activational influences. *Horm. Behav.* 12:112–163.

BECKER, J. B., 1990. Direct effect of 17β-estradiol on striatum: Sex differences in dopamine release. *Synapse* 5:157–164.

BECKER, J. B., 1991. Hormonal influences on extrapyramidal sensorimotor function and hippocampal plasticity. In *Behavioral Endocrinology*, J. B. Becker, M. Breedlove, and D. Crews, eds. Cambridge, Mass.: MIT Press, pp. 325–356.

BECKER, J. B., 1999. Gender differences in dopaminergic function in striatum and nucleus accumbens. *Pharm. Biochem. Behav.* 64:803–812.

BECKER, J. B., and J. CHA, 1989. Estrous cycle-dependent variation in amphetamine-induced behaviors and striatal dopamine release assessed with microdialysis. *Behav. Brain Res.* 35:117–125.

BECKER, J. B., and V. D. RAMIREZ, 1980. Sex differences in amphetamine stimulated release of catecholamines from rat striatal tissue in vitro. *Brain Res.* 204:361–372.

BETHEA, C. L., N. A. BROWN, and S. G. KOHAMA, 1996. Steroid regulation of estrogen and progestin receptor messenger ribonucleic acid in monkey hypothalamus and pituitary. *Endocrinology* 137:4372–4383.

BETHEA, C. L., W. H. FAHRENBACH, S. A. SPRANGERS, and F. FREESH, 1992. Immunocytochemical localization of progestin receptors in monkey hypothalamus: Effect of estrogen and progestin. *Endocrinology* 130:895–905.

BLAUSTEIN, J. D., J. C. KING, D. O. TOFT, and J. TURCOTTE, 1988. Immunocytochemical localization of estrogen-induced progestin receptors in guinea pig brain. *Brain Res.* 474:1–15.

BOTTJER, S. W., and A. P. ARNOLD, 1997. Developmental plasticity in neural circuits for a learned behavior. *Ann. Rev. Neurosci.* 20:459–482.

BOYLE, M., N. MacLusky, F. NAFTOLIN, and L. KACZMAREK, 1987. Hormonal regulation of $K^+$-channel messenger RNA in rat myometrium during oestrus cycle and in pregnancy. *Nature* 330:373–375.

BREEDLOVE, S. M., and A. P. ARNOLD, 1981. Sexually dimorphic motor nucleus in the rat lumbar spinal cord: Response to adult hormone manipulation, absence in androgen-insensitive rats. *Brain Res.* 225:297–307.

BRENOWITZ, E. A., A. P. ARNOLD, and R. N. LEVIN, 1985. Neural correlates of female song in tropical duetting birds. *Brain Res.* 343:104–112.

BROVERMAN, D. M., W. VOGEL, E. L. KLAIBER, D. MAJCHER, D. SHEA, and V. PAUL, 1981. Changes in cognitive task performance across the menstrual cycle. *J. Comp. Physiol. Psychol.* 95:646–654.

BROWN, T. J., N. J. MacLusky, C. LERANTH, M. SHANABROUGH, and F. NAFTOLIN, 1990. Progestin receptor-containing cells in guinea pig hypothalamus: Afferent connections, morphological characteristics, and neurotransmitter content. *Mol. Cell Neurosci.* 1:58–77.

BROWN, T. J., F. NAFTOLIN, and M. J. MacLusky, 1992. Sex differences in estrogen receptor binding in the rat hypothalamus: Effects of subsaturating pulses of estradiol. *Brain Res.* 578:129–134.

BROWN-GRANT, K., A. MUNCK, F. NAFTOLIN, and M. R. SHERWOOD, 1971. The effects of the administration of testosterone propionate alone or with phenobarbitone and of testosterone metabolites to neonatal female rats. *Horm. Behav.* 2:173–182.

BURKE, H. L., and R. A. YEO, 1994. Systematic variations in callosal morphology: The effects of age, gender, hand preference, and anatomic asymmetry. *Neuropsychol.* 8:563–571.

BUTERBAUGH, G. G., and G. M. HUDSON, 1991. Estradiol replacement to female rats facilitates dorsal hippocampal but not ventral hippocampal kindled seizure acquisition. *Exp. Neurol.* 111:55–64.

CAMP, D. M., J. B. BECKER, and T. E. ROBINSON, 1986. Sex differences in the effects of gonadectomy on amphetamine-induced rotational behavior in rats. *Behav. Neural. Biol.* 46:491–495.

CELOTTI, F., R. MELCANGI, and L. MARTINI, 1992. The 5 alpha-reductase in the brain: Molecular aspects and relation to brain function. *Front. Neuroendocrinol.* 13:163–215.

CINTRA, A., K. FUXE, A. HARFSTRAND, L. F. AGNATI, L. S. MILLER, J. L. GREENE, and J.-A. GUSTAFSSON, 1986. On the cellular localization and distribution of estrogen receptors in the rat tel- and diencephalon using monoclonal antibodies to human estrogen receptor. *Neurochem. Int.* 8:587–595.

COIRINI, H., A. JOHNSON, and B. S. McEwen, 1989. Estradiol modulation of oxytocin binding in the ventromedial hypothalamic nucleus of male and female rats. *Neuroendocrinology* 50:193–198.

COOKE, B., C. D. HEGSTROM, L. S. VILLENEUVE, and S. M. BREEDLOVE, 1998. Sexual differentiation of the vertebrate brain: Principles and mechanisms. *Front. Neuroendocrinol.* 19:323–362.

COMMINS, D., and P. YAHR, 1985. Autoradiographic localization of estrogen and androgen receptors in the sexually dimorphic area and other regions of the gerbil brain. *J. Comp. Neurol.* 231:473–489.

DAVIS, E. C., J. E. SHRYNE, and R. A. GORSKI, 1996. Structural sexual dimorphisms in the anteroventral periventricular nucleus of the rat hypothalamus are sensitive to gonadal steroids perinatally, but develop peripubertally. *Neuroendocrinology* 63:142–148.

DE COURTEN-MYERS, G. M., 1999. The human cerebral cortex: Gender differences in structure and function. *J. Neuropath.* 58:217–226.

DE LACOSTE, M. C., and R. L. HOLLOWAY, 1982. Sexual dimorphism in the human corpus callosum. *Science* 216:1431–1432.

DELGADO, A. R., and G. PRIETO, 1996. Sex differences in visuo-spatial ability: Do performance factors play such an important role? *Memory Cog.* 24:404–510.

DENENBERG, V. H., A. KERTESZ, and P. E. COWELL, 1991. A factor analysis of the human's corpus callosum. *Brain Res.* 548:126–132.

DEVOOGD, T. J., and F. NOTTEBOHM, 1981. Gonadal hormones induce dendritic growth in the adult avian brain. *Science* 214:202–204.

DE VRIES, G. J., 1990. Sex differences in neurotransmitter systems. *J. Neuroendocrinol.* 2:1–12.

DI PAOLO, T., P. FALARDEAU, and M. MORISETTE, 1988. Striatal D-2 dopamine agonist binding sites fluctuate during the rat estrous cycle. *Life Sci.* 43:665–672.

DOHLER, K. D., S. S. SRIVASTAVA, J. E. SHRYNE, B. JARZAB, A. SIPOS, and R. A. GORSKI, 1984. Differentiation of the sexually dimorphic nucleus in the preoptic area of the rat brain is inhibited by postnatal treatment with an estrogen antagonist. *Neuroendocrinology* 38:297–301.

DONCARLOS, L. L., G. L. GREENE, and J. I. MORRELL, 1989. Estrogen plus progesterone increases progestin receptor immunoreactivity in the brain of ovariectomized guinea pigs. *Neuroendocrinology* 50:613–623.

DONCARLOS, L. L., E. MONROY, and J. I. MORRELL, 1991. Distribution of estrogen receptor-immunoreactive cells in the forebrain of the female guinea pig. *J. Comp. Neurol.* 305:591–612.

DORNER, G., and J. STAUDT, 1969. Structural changes in the hypothalamic ventromedial nucleus of the male rat, following neonatal castration and androgen treatment. *Neuroendocrinology* 4:278–281.

EINON, D., 1980. Spatial memory and response strategies in rats: Age, sex and rearing differences in performance. *Quart. J. Exp. Psychol.* 32:473–489.

FEDER, H. H., and B. L. MARRONE, 1977. Progesterone: Its role in the central nervous system as a facilitator and inhibitor of sexual behavior and gonadotropin release. *Ann. N.Y. Acad. Sci.* 286:331–354.

FRANKFURT, M., C. GOULD, C. WOOLLEY, and B. S. MCEWEN, 1990. Gonadal steroids modify dendritic spine density in ventromedial hypothalamic neurons: A Golgi study in the adult rat. *Neuroendocrinology* 51:530–535.

GEE, K. W., 1988. Steroid modulation of the GABA/benzodiazepine receptor-linked chloride ionophore. *Mol. Neurobiol.* 2:291–317.

GIEDD, J. N., F. X. CASTELLANOS, J. C. RAJAPAKSE, A. C. VAITUZIS, and J. L. RAPOPORT, 1997. Sexual dimorphism of the developing human brain. *Prog. Neuropsychopharmacol. Biol. Psychiat.* 21:1185–1201.

GOLDMAN, S., and F. NOTTEBOHM, 1983. Neuronal production, migration, and differentiation in a vocal control nucleus of the adult female canary brain. *Proc. Natl. Acad. Sci. (USA)* 80:2390.

GOMEZ, D. M., and S. W. NEWMAN, 1991. Medial nucleus of the amygdala in the adult Syrian hamster. A quantitative Golgi analysis of gonadal hormonal regulation of neuronal morphology. *Anat. Rec.* 231:498–509.

GORSKI, R. A., J. H. GORDON, J. E. SHRYNE, and A. M. SOUTHAM, 1978. Evidence for a morphological sex difference within the medial preoptic area of the rat brain. *Brain Res.* 148:333–346.

GORSKI, R. A., R. E. HARLAN, C. D. JACOBSON, J. E. SHRYNE, and A. M. SOUTHAM, 1980. Evidence for the existence of a sexually dimorphic nucleus in the preoptic area of the rat. *J. Comp. Neurol.* 193:529–539.

GOUCHIE, C. T., and D. KIMURA, 1991. The relationship between testosterone levels and cognitive ability patterns. *Psychoneuroendocrinology* 16:323–334.

GOULD, E., E. WESTLIND-DANIELSSON, M. FRANKFURT, and B. S. MCEWEN, 1990. Sex differences and thyroid hormone sensitivity of hippocampal pyramidal cells. *J. Neurosci.* 10:996–1003.

GOULD, E., C. WOOLLEY, and B. S. MCEWEN, 1990. Short-term glucocorticoid manipulations affect neuronal morphology and survival in the adult dentate gyrus. *Neuroscience* 37:367–375.

GOY, R. W., and J. A. RESKO, 1972. Gonadal hormones and behavior of normal and pseudohermaphroditic nonhuman female primates. *Rec. Prog. Horm. Res.* 28:707–733.

GRINO, P. B., J. E. GRIFFIN, and J. D. WILSON, 1990. Testosterone at high concentration interacts with the human androgen receptor similarly to dihydrotestosterone. *Endocrinology* 126:1165–1172.

GUENNOUN, R., R. J. FIDDES, M. GOUEZOU, M. LOMBES, and E. E. BAULIEU, 1995. A key enzyme in the biosynthesis of neurosteroids, 3β-hydroxysteroid dehydrogenase/Δ5,Δ4-isomerase (3β-HSD) is expressed in rat brain. *Mol. Brain Res.* 30:287–300.

GURNEY, M. E., and M. KONISHI, 1979. Hormone induced sexual differentiation of brain and behavior in zebra finches. *Science* 208:1380–1382.

HAMPSON, E., 1990a. Estrogen-related variations in human spatial and articulatory motor skills. *Psychoneuroendocrinology* 15:97–111.

HAMPSON, E. 1990b. Variations in sex-related cognitive abilities across the menstrual cycle. *Brain Cogn.* 14:26–43.

HAMPSON, E., and D. KIMURA, 1988. Reciprocal effects of hormonal fluctuations on human motor and perceptual-spatial skills. *Behav. Neurosci.* 102:456–459.

HARASTY, J., K. L. DOUBLE, G. M. HALLIDAY, J. J. KRIL, and D. A. MCRITCHIE, 1997. Language-associated cortical regions are proportionally larger in the female brain. *Arch. Neurol.* 54:171–176.

HASKELL, S. G., E. D. RICHARDSON, and R. I. HORWITZ, 1997. The effect of estrogen replacement therapy on cognitive function in women: A critical review of the literature. *J. Clin. Epidemiol.* 11:1249–1264.

HERBISON, A. E., and D. T. THEODOSIS, 1992. Immunocytochemical identification of oestrogen receptors in preoptic neurones containing calcitonin gene-related peptide in the male and female rat. *Neuroendocrinology* 56:761–764.

HINES, M., 1982. Prenatal gonadal hormones and sex differences in human behavior. *Psychol. Bull.* 92:56–80.

HINES, M., 1991. Gonadal hormones and human cognitive development. In *Hormones, Brain and Behavior in Vertebrates*, J. Balthazart, ed. Basel: Karger.

HINES, M., F. C. DAVIS, A. COQUELIN, R. W. GOY, and R. A. GORSKI, 1985. Sexually dimorphic regions in the medial preoptic area and the bed nucleus of the stria terminalis of the guinea pig brain: A description and an investigation of their relationship to gonadal steroids in adulthood. *J. Neurosci.* 5:40–47.

HINES, M., L. A. MCADAMS, L. CHIU, and J. LIPCAMON, 1992. Cognition and the corpus callosum: Verbal fluency, visuospatial ability, and language lateralization related to midsagittal surface areas of callosal subregions. *Behav. Neurosci.* 106:3–14.

HOGERVORST, E., M. BOSHUISEN, W. RIEDEL, C. WILLEKEN, and J. JOLLES, 1999. The effect of hormone replacement therapy on cognitive function in elderly women. *Psychoneuroendocrinology* 24:43–68.

HRUSKA, R. E., L. M. LUDMER, K. T. PITMAN, M. DE RYCK, and E. K. SILBERGELD, 1982. Effects of estrogen on striatal dopamine receptor function in male and female rats. *Pharmacol. Biochem. Behav.* 16:285–291.

HYDE, J. S., and M. C. LINN, 1988. Gender differences in verbal ability: A meta-analysis. *Psychol. Bull.* 104:53–69.

INGLIS, J., M. RUCKMAN, J. S. LAWSON, A. W. MACLEAN, and T. N. MONGA, 1982. Sex differences in the cognitive effects of unilateral brain damage. *Cortex* 18:257–276.

JACOBS, B., M. SCHALL, and A. B. SCHEIBEL, 1993. A quantitative dendritic analysis of Wernicke's area in humans. II. Gender, hemispheric and environmental factors. *J. Comp. Neurol.* 327:97–111.

JACOBSON, C. D., A. P. ARNOLD, and R. A. GORSKI, 1987. Steroid autoradiography of the sexually dimorphic nucleus of the preoptic area. *Brain Res.* 414:349–356.

JACOBSON, C. D., and R. A. GORSKI, 1981. Neurogenesis of the sexually dimorphic nucleus of the preoptic area in the rat. *J. Comp. Neurol.* 196:519–529.

JAKAB, R. L., T. L. HORVATH, C. LERANTH, N. HARADA, and F. NAFTOLIN, 1993. Aromatase immunoreactivity in the rat brain: Gonadectomy-sensitive hypothalamic neurons and an unresponsive 'limbic ring' of the lateral septum-bed nucleus-amygdala complex. *J. Steroid Biochem. Mol. Biol.* 44:481–498.

JOELS, M., and H. KARST, 1995. Effects of estradiol and progesterone on voltage-gated calcium and potassium conductances in rat CA1 hippocampal neurons. *J. Neurosci.* 15:4289–4297.

JOHNSON, S. C., J. B. PINKSTON, E. D. BIGLER, and D. D. BLATTER, 1996. Corpus callosum morphology in normal controls and traumatic brain injury: Sex differences, mechanisms of injury, and neuropsychological correlates. *Neuropsychol.* 10:408–415.

JURASKA, J. M., 1991. Sex differences in "cognitive" regions of the rat brain. *Psychoneuroendocrinology* 16:105–119.

JURASKA, J. M., and J. R. KOPCIK, 1988. Sex and environmental influences on the size and ultrastructure of the rat corpus callosum. *Brain Res.* 450:1–8.

KIMURA, D., 1987. Are men's and women's brains really different? *Can. Psychol.* 28:133–147.

KOMNENICH, P., D. M. LANE, R. P. DICKEY, and S. C. STONE, 1978. Gonadal hormones and cognitive performance. *Physiol. Psychol.* 6:115–120.

KOPCIK, J. R., P. SYMOURE, S. K. SCHNEIDER, J. KIM-HONG, and J. M. JURASKA, 1992. Do callosal projection neurons reflect sex differences in axon number? *Brain Res. Bull.* 29:493–497.

KUIPER, G. G. J. M., E. ENMARK, M. PELTO-HUIKKO, S. NILSSON, and J.-A. GUSTAFSSON, 1996. Cloning of a novel estrogen receptor expressed in rat prostate. *Proc. Natl. Acad. Sci. (USA)* 93:5925–5930.

KUIPER, G. G. J. M., P. J. SHUGHRUE, I. MERCHENTHALER, and J.-A. GUSTAFSSON, 1998. The estrogen receptor β subtype: A novel mediator of estrogen action in neuroendocrine systems. *Front. Neuroendocrinol.* 19:253–286.

KULYNYCH, J. J., K. VLADAR, D. W. JONES, and D. R. WEINBERGER, 1994. Gender differences in the normal lateralization of the supratemporal cortex: MRI surface-rendering mor-

phometry of Heschl's gyrus and the planum temporale. *Cereb. Cortex* 4:107–118.

LANSDELL, H., 1961. The effect of neurosurgery on a test of proverbs. *Am. Psychol.* 16:488.

LEEDY, M. G., M. S. BEATTIE, and J. C. BRESNAHAN, 1987. Testosterone-induced plasticity of synaptic inputs to adult mammalian motoneurons. *Brain Res.* 424:386–390.

LEPHART, E. D., 1996. A review of brain aromatase cytochrome P450. *Brain Res. Rev.* 22:1–26.

LEPHART, E. D., E. R. SIMPSON, M. J. MCPHAUL, M. W. KILGORE, J. D. WILSON, and S. R. OJEDA, 1992. Brain aromatase cytochrome P-450 messenger RNA levels and enzyme activity during prenatal and perinatal development in the rat. *Mol. Brain Res.* 16:187–192.

LEVAY, S., 1991. A difference in hypothalamic structure between heterosexual and homosexual men. *Science* 253:1034–1037.

LEVESQUE, D., S. GAGNON, and T. DI PAOLO, 1989. Striatal D1 dopamine receptor density fluctuates during the rat estrous cycle. *Neurosci. Lett.* 98:345–350.

LEVINE, S., and R. MULLINS, JR., 1964. Estrogen administered neonatally affects adult sexual behavior in male and female rats. *Science* 144:185–187.

LEWIS, C., B. S. MCEWEN, and M. FRANKFURT, 1995. Estrogen-induction of dendritic spines in ventromedial hypothalamus and hippocampus: Effects of neonatal aromatase blockade and adult castration. *Dev. Brain Res.* 87:91–95.

LEWIS, D. W., and M. C. DIAMOND, 1995. The influence of gonadal steroids on the asymmetry of the cerebral cortex. In *Brain Asymmetry*, R. J. Davidson and K. Hugdahl, eds., Cambridge, Mass.: MIT Press, pp. 31–49.

LINN, M. C., and A. C. PETERSEN, 1985. Emergence and characterization of sex differences in spatial ability: A meta-analysis. *Child Devel.* 56:1479–1498.

LOY, R., J. L. GERLACH, and B. S. MCEWEN, 1988. Autoradiographic localization of estradiol-binding neurons in the rat hippocampal formation and entorhinal cortex. *Dev. Brain Res.* 39:245–251.

MACLUSKY, N., A. S. CLARK, F. NAFTOLIN, and P. S. GOLDMAN-RAKIC, 1987. Oestrogen formation in mammalian brain: Possible role of aromatase in sexual differentiation of the hippocampus and neocortex. *Steroids* 50:459–474.

MACLUSKY, N. J., and F. NAFTOLIN, 1981. Sexual differentiation of the central nervous system. *Science* 211:1294–1303.

MADEIRA, M. D., and A. R. LIEBERMAN, 1995. Sexual dimorphisms in the mammalian limbic system. *Prog. Neurobiol.* 45:275–333.

MAJEWSKA, M. D., 1992. Neurosteroids: Endogenous bimodal modulators of the GABA_A receptor. Mechanism of action and physiological significance. *Prog. Neurobiol.* 38:379–395.

MALSBURY, C. W., and K. MCKAY, 1994. Neurotrophic effects of testosterone on the medial nucleus of the amygdala in adult male rats. *J. Neuroendocrinol.* 6:57–69.

MANI, S. K., J. M. C. ALLEN, J. H. CLARK, J. D. BAUSTEIN, and B. W. O'MALLEY, 1994. Convergent pathways for steroid-, hormone- and neurotransmitter-induced rat sexual behavior. *Science* 265:1246–1249.

MANI, S. K., J. D. BLAUSTEIN, and B. W. O'MALLEY, 1997. Progesterone receptor function from a behavioral perspective. *Horm. Behav.* 31:244–255.

MATEER, C. A., S. B. POLEN, and G. A. OJEMANN, 1982. Sexual variation in cortical localization of naming as determined by stimulation mapping. *Behav. Brain Sci.* 5:310–311.

MATTHEWS, K., J. CAULEY, K. YAFFE, and J. M. ZMUDA, 1999. Estrogen replacement therapy and cognitive decline in older community women. *J. Am. Geriatr. Soc.* 47:518–523.

McDONALD, P. G., C. BEYER, F. NEWTON, B. BRIEN, R. BAKER, H. S. TAN, C. SAMPSON, P. KITCHING, R. GREENHILL, and D. PRITCHARD, 1970. Failure of 5α-dihydrotestosterone to initiate sexual behavior in the castrated male rat. *Nature* 227:964–965.

McEWEN, B. S., 1991. Steroids affect neural activity by acting on the membrane and the genome. *Trends Pharmacol.* 12:141–147.

McEWEN, B. S., 1996. Gonadal and adrenal steroids regulate neurochemical and structural plasticity of the hippocampus via cellular mechanisms involving NMDA receptors. *Cell. Mol. Neurobiol.* 16:103–116.

McEWEN, B. S., and S. E. ALVES, 1999. Estrogen actions in the central nervous system. *Endocrinol. Rev.* 20:279–307.

McGLONE, J., 1978. Sex differences in functional brain asymmetry. *Cortex* 14:122–128.

McGLONE, J., 1980. Sex differences in human brain asymmetry: A critical survey. *Behav. Brain Sci.* 3:215–263.

MELLON, S. H., 1994. Neurosteroids: Biochemistry, modes of action, and clinical relevance. *J. Clin. Endocrinol. Metab.* 78:1003–1008.

MERMELSTEIN, P. G., J. B. BECKER, and D. J. SURMEIER, 1996. Estradiol reduces calcium currents in rat neostriatal neurons via a membrane receptor. *J. Neurosci.* 16:595–604.

MICHAEL, R. P., R. W. BONSALL, and D. ZUMPE, 1987. Testosterone and its metabolites in male cynomolgus monkeys (*Macaca fascicularis*): Behavior and biochemistry. *Physiol. Behav.* 40:527–537.

MICHAEL, R. P., A. N. CLANCY, and D. ZUMPE, 1995. Distribution of androgen receptor-like immunoreactivity in the brains of cynomolgus monkeys. *J. Neuroendocrinol.* 7:713–719.

MICHAEL, R. P., D. ZUMPE, and R. W. BONSALL, 1990. Estradiol administration and the sexual activity of castrated male rhesus monkeys (*Macaca mulatta*). *Horm. Behav.* 24:71–88.

MILNER, B., H. L. TEUBER, and S. CORKIN, 1968. Further analysis of the hippocampal amnesic syndrome: 14 year follow up study of H. M. *Neuropsychologia* 6:215–234.

MINAMI, T., Y. OOMURA, J. NABEKURA, and A. FUKUDA, 1990. 17β-Estradiol depolarization of hypothalamic neurons is mediated by cyclic AMP. *Brain Res.* 519:301–307.

NABEKURA, J., Y. OOMURA, T. MINAMI, Y. MIZUNO, and A. FUKUDA, 1986. Mechanism of the rapid effect of 17β-estradiol on medial amygdala neurons. *Science* 233:226–228.

NAFTOLIN, F., T. L. HORVATH, R. L. JAKAB, C. LERANTH, N. HARADA, and J. BALTHAZART, 1996. Aromatase immunoreactivity in axon terminals of the vertebrate brain. *Neuroendocrinology* 63:149–155.

NAFTOLIN, F., K. J. RYAN, and Z. PETRO, 1971. Aromatization of androstenedione by the diencephalon. *J. Clin. Endocrinol. Metab.* 33:368–370.

NAFTOLIN, F., K. J. RYAN, and Z. PETRO, 1977. Aromatization of androstenedione by the anterior hypothalamus of adult male and female rats. *Endocrinology* 90:295–298.

NEBERT, D. W., and F. J. GONZALES, 1987. P450 genes: Structure, evolution, and regulation. *Ann. Rev. Biochem.* 56:945–953.

NEGRI-CESI, P., A. POLETTI, and F. CELOTTI, 1996. Metabolism of steroids in the brain: A new insight into the role of 5α-reductase and aromatase in brain differentiation and functions. *J. Steroid Biochem. Molec. Biol.* 58:455–466.

NORMINGTON, K., and D. W. RUSSELL, 1992. Tissue distribution and kinetic characteristics of rat steroid 5α-reductase isozymes. *J. Biol. Chem.* 267:19548–19554.

NOTTEBOHM, F., and A. ARNOLD, 1976. Sexual dimorphism in vocal control areas of the songbird brain. *Science* 194:211–213.

O'KEEFE, J., 1993. Hippocampus, theta, and spatial memory. *Curr. Opin. Neurobiol.* 3:917–924.

O'KEEFE, J. A., and R. J. HANDA, 1990. Transient elevation of estrogen receptors in the neonatal rat hippocampus. *Dev. Brain Res.* 57:119–127.

PAUS, T., N. OTAKY, Z. CARAMANOS, 1996. In vivo morphometry of the intrasulcal gray matter in the human cingulate, paracingulate, and superior-rostral sulci: Hemispheric asymmetries, gender differences and probability maps. *J. Comp. Neurol.* 376:664–673.

PAUS, T., A. ZIJDENBOS, K. WORSLEY, D. L. COLLINS, J. BLUMENTHAL, J. N. GIEDD, J. L. RAPOPORT, and A. C. EVANS, 1999. Structural maturation of neural pathways in children and adolescents: In vivo study. *Science* 283:1908–1911.

PFAFF, D., 1980. *Estrogens and Brain Function.* New York: Springer-Verlag.

PFAFF, D. W., and M. KEINER, 1973. Atlas of estradiol-concentrating cells in the central nervous system of the female rat. *J. Comp. Neurol.* 151:121–158.

PHOENIX, C. H., and K. C. CHAMBERS, 1982. Sexual behavior in adult gonadectomized female pseudohermaphrodite, female, and male rhesus macaques (*Macaca mulatta*) treated with estradiol benzoate and testosterone propionate. *J. Comp. Physiol. Psychol.* 96:823–833.

PHOENIX, C. H., R. W. GOY, A. A. GERALL, and W. C. YOUNG, 1959. Organizing action of prenatally administered testosterone propionate on the tissues mediating mating behavior in the female guinea pig. *Endocrinology* 65:369–382.

PHOENIX, C. H., R. W. GOY, and J. A. RESKO, 1968. Psychosexual differentiation as a function of androgenic stimulation. In *Perspectives in Reproduction and Sexual Behavior*, M. Diamond, ed. Bloomington, Ind.: Indiana University Press, pp. 33–49.

RABINOWICZ, T., D. E. DEAN, J. M.-C. PETETOT, and G. M. DE COURTEN-MYERS, 1999. Gender differences in the human cerebral cortex: More neurons in males; more processes in females. *J. Child Neurol.* 14:98–107.

RAINBOW, T., B. PARSONS, and B. S. McEWEN, 1982. Sex differences in rat brain oestrogen and progestin receptors. *Nature* 300:648–649.

RAISMAN, G., and P. M. FIELD, 1973. Sexual dimorphism in the neuropil of the preoptic area of the rat and its dependence on neonatal androgen. *Brain Res.* 54:1–29.

RAZANDI, M., A. PEDRAM, G. L. GREENE, and E. R. LEVIN, 1999. Cell membrane and nuclear estrogen receptors (ERs) originate from a single transcript: Studies of ERα and ERβ expressed in Chinese hamster ovary cells. *Mol. Endocrinol.* 13:307–319.

RESKO, J. A., P. B. CONNOLLY, C. E. ROSELLI, S. E. ABDELGADIR, and J. V. A. CHOATE, 1993. Selective activation of androgen receptors in the subcortical brain of male cynomolgus macaques by physiological hormone levels and its relationship to androgen-dependent aromatase activity. *J. Clin. Endocrinol. Metab.* 76:1588–1593.

Resko, J. A., and C. E. Roselli, 1997. Prenatal hormones organize sex differences of the neuroendocrine reproductive system: Observations on guinea pigs and nonhuman primates. *Cell. Mol. Neurobiol.* 17:627–648.

Resnick, S. M., S. A. Berenbaum, I. I. Gottesman, and T. J. Bouchard, 1986. Early hormonal influences on cognitive functioning in congenital adrenal hyperplasia. *Dev. Psychol.* 22:191–198.

Roselli, C. E., and J. A. Resko, 1987. The distribution and regulation of aromatase activity in the central nervous system. *Steroids* 50:495–508.

Roselli, C. E., and J. A. Resko, 1989. Testosterone regulates aromatase activity in discrete brain areas of male rhesus macaques. *Biol. Reprod.* 40:929–934.

Roselli, C. E., and J. A. Resko, 1993. Aromatase activity in the rat brain: Hormonal regulation and sex differences. *J. Steroid Biochem. Mol. Biol.* 44:499–508.

Rosenfeld, J. M., J. D. Daley, S. Ohon, and E. V. Young Lai, 1977. Central aromatization of testosterone in testicular feminized mice. *Experientia* 33:1392–1393.

Sapolsky, R., 1990. Glucocorticoids, hippocampal damage and the glutamatergic synapse. *Prog. Brain Res.* 86:13–23.

Schlaepfer, T. E., G. J. Harris, A. Y. Tien, L. Peng, S. Lee, and G. D. Pearlson, 1995. Structural differences in the cerebral cortex of healthy female and male subjects: A magnetic resonance imaging study. *Psychiatry Res.* 61:129–135.

Sengelaub, D. R., and A. P. Arnold, 1986. Development and loss of early projections in a sexually dimorphic rat spinal nucleus. *J. Neurosci.* 6:1613–1620.

Shaywitz, B., S. E. Shaywitz, K. R. Pugh, R. T. Constable, P. L. Skudlarski, R. K. Fulbright, R. A. Bronen, J. M. Fletcher, D. P. Shankweiler, and L. Katz, 1995. Sex differences in the functional organization of the brain for language. *Nature* 373:607–609.

Sholl, S. A., R. W. Goy, and K. L. Kim, 1989. 5α-Reductase, aromatase, and androgen receptor levels in the monkey brain during fetal development. *Endocrinology* 124:627–634.

Shughrue, P. J., M. V. Lane, and I. Merchenthaler, 1997. The comparative distribution of estrogen receptor-α and β mRNA in the rat central nervous system. *J. Comp. Neurol.* 388:507–525.

Shughrue, P. J., and I. Merchenthaler, 2000. Estrogen is more than just a "sex hormone": Novel sites for estrogen action in the hippocampus and cerebral cortex. *Front. Neuroendocrinol.* 21:95–101.

Shute, V. J., J. W. Pellegrino, L. Hubert, and R. W. Reynolds, 1983. The relationship between androgen levels and human spatial abilities. *Bull. Psychonom. Soc.* 21:465–468.

Silverman, E. M., and C. H. Zimmer, 1975. Speech fluency fluctuations during the menstrual cycle. *J. Speech Hear. Res.* 18:202–206.

Silverman, E. M., C. H. Zimmer, and F. H. Silverman, 1974. Variability of stutterers' speech disfluency during the menstrual cycle. *Percept. Mot. Skills* 38:1037–1038.

Simerly, R. B., C. Chang, M. Muramatsu, and L. W. Swanson, 1990. Distribution of androgen and estrogen receptor mRNA-containing cells in the rat brain: An in situ hybridization study. *J. Comp. Neurol.* 294:76–95.

Springer, S. P., and G. Deutch, 1998. *Left Brain, Right Brain*, 5th ed. New York: W. H. Freeman.

Steinmetz, H., L. Jancke, A. Kleinschmidt, G. Schlaug, J. Volkmann, and Y. Huang, 1992. Sex but no hand difference in the isthmus of the corpus callosum. *Neurology* 42:749–752.

Stumpf, W. E., M. Sar, and D. A. Keefer, 1975. Atlas of estrogen target cells in the rat brain. In *Anatomical Neuroendocrinology*, W. E. Stumpf and L. D. Grant, eds. Basel: Karger, pp. 104–119.

Swaab, D. F., and E. Fliers, 1985. A sexually dimorphic nucleus in the human brain. *Science* 228:1112–1115.

Teresawa, S., and P. S. Timiras, 1968. Electrical activity during the estrous cycle of the rat: Cyclic changes in limbic structures. *Endocrinology* 83:207–216.

Teyler, T. J., R. M. Vardaris, D. Lewis, and A. B. Rawitch, 1980. Gonadal steroids: Effects on excitability of hippocampal pyramidal cells. *Science* 209:1017–1019.

Therrien, B., 1982. *Sex Differences in the Effects of Hippocampal Lesions on Place Navigation*. Doctoral Dissertation. Ann Arbor: Mich.: University of Michigan.

Tobet, S. A., D. J. Zahniser, and M. J. Baum, 1986. Sexual dimorphism in the preoptic/anterior hypothalamic area of ferrets: Effects of adult exposure to sex steroids. *Brain Res.* 364:249–257.

Toran-Allerand, C. D., M. Singh, and G. Setalo, 1999. Novel mechanisms of estrogen action in the brain: New players in an old story. *Front. Neuroendocrinol.* 20:97–121.

Turner, B. B., and D. A. Weaver, 1985. Sexual dimorphism of glucocorticoid binding in rat brain. *Brain Res.* 343:16–23.

Truss, M., and M. Beato, 1993. Steroid hormone receptors: Interaction with deoxyribonucleic acid and transcription factors. *Endocrinol. Rev.* 14:459–479.

Wada, J. A., R. Clarke, and A. Hamm, 1975. Cerebral hemispheric asymmetry in humans. *Arch. Neurol.* 32:239–246.

Warren, S. G., A. G. Humphreys, J. M. Juraska, and W. T. Greenough, 1995. LTP varies across the estrous cycle: Enhanced synaptic plasticity in proestrus rats. *Brain Res.* 703:26–30.

Weisz, J., and I. L. Ward, 1980. Plasma testosterone and progesterone levels of pregnant rats, their male and female fetuses, and neonatal offspring. *Endocrinology* 106:306–316.

Whalen, R. E., and R. D. Nadler, 1963. Suppression of the development of female mating behavior by estrogen administered in infancy. *Science* 141:273–275.

Wickham, M., 1958. The effects of the menstrual cycle on test performance. *Br. J. Psychol.* 49:34–41.

Williams, C. L., A. M. Barnett, and W. H. Meck, 1990. Organizational effects of early gonadal secretions on sexual differentiation in spatial memory. *Behav. Neurosci.* 104:84–97.

Wisniewski, A. B., 1998. Sexually-dimorphic patterns of cortical asymmetry, and the role for sex steroid hormones in determining cortical patterns of lateralization. *Psychoneuroendocrinology* 23:519–547.

Witelson, S. F., 1989. Hand and sex differences in the isthmus and genu of the human corpus callosum. *Brain* 112:799–835.

Witelson, S. F., I. I. Glezer, and D. L. Kigar, 1995. Women have greater density of neurons in posterior temporal cortex. *J. Neurosci.* 15:3418–3428.

Witelson, S. F., and D. L. Kigar, 1992. Sylvian fissure morphology and asymmetry in men and women: Bilateral differences in relation to handedness in men. *J. Comp. Neurol.* 323:326–340.

Witkin, H. A., and J. W. Berry, 1975. Psychological differentiation in cross-cultural perspective. *J. Cross-Cult. Psychol.* 6:4–87.

WONG, M., and R. L. MOSS, 1992. Long-term and short-term electrophysiological effects of estrogen on the synaptic properties of hippocampal CA1 neurons. *J. Neurosci.* 12: 3217–3225.

WOOLLEY, C., E. GOULD, and B. S. McEWEN, 1990. Exposure to excess glucocorticoids alters dendritic morphology of adult hippocampal pyramidal neurons. *Brain Res.* 531:225–231.

WOOLLEY, C., E. GOULD, R. SAKAI, R. L. SPENCER, and B. S. McEWEN, 1991. Effects of aldosterone or RU28362 treatment on adrenalectomy-induced cell death in the dentate gyrus of the adult rat. *Brain Res.* 554:312–315.

WOOLLEY, C. S., and B. S. McEWEN, 1992. Estradiol mediates fluctuation of hippocampal synapse density during the estrous cycle in the adrenalectomized rat. *J. Neurosci.* 12:2549–2554.

WOOLLEY, C. S., and B. S. McEWEN, 1993. Roles of estradiol and progesterone in regulation of hippocampal dendritic spine density during the estrous cycle in the rat. *J. Comp. Neurol.* 336:293–303.

WOOLLEY, C., and B. S. McEWEN, 1994. Estradiol regulates hippocampal dendritic spine density via an NMDA receptor dependent mechanism. *J. Neurosci.* 19:379.

WOOLLEY, C. S., E. GOULD, M. FRANKFURT, and B. S. McEWEN, 1990. Naturally occurring fluctuation in dendritic spine density on adult hippocampal pyramidal neurons. *J. Neurosci.* 10:4035–4039.

XIAO, L., and J. B. BECKER, 1994. Quantitative microdialysis determination of extracellular striatal dopamine concentrations in male and female rats: Effects of estrous cycle and gonadectomy. *Neurosci. Lett.* 180:155–158.

XIAO, L., and J. B. BECKER, 1997. Hormonal activation of the striatum and the nucleus accumbens modulates paced mating behavior in the female rat. *Horm. Behav.* 32:114–124.

ZUMPE, D., R. W. BONSALL, and R. P. MICHAEL, 1993. Effects of the nonsteroidal aromatase inhibitor, Fadrozole, on the sexual behavior of male cynomolgus monkeys (*Macaca fascicularis*). *Horm. Behav.* 27:200–215.

# 6 The Development of Prefrontal Cortex: The Maturation of Neurotransmitter Systems and Their Interactions

FRANCINE M. BENES

ABSTRACT This chapter provides an overview of the development of the prefrontal cortex that begins with the differentiation of its intrinsic projection and local circuit neurons during embryogenesis, but extends well beyond. Despite the early appearance of laminar patterns that reflect those seen in the adult brain, the architecture of synaptic connections and the maturation of intrinsic and extrinsic neurotransmitter systems continue to change in the prefrontal cortex during the postnatal period. It is particularly noteworthy that a variety of studies have demonstrated that the monoaminergic neurons, especially those employing dopamine as a neuromodulator, continue to infiltrate the cortical mantle until the early adult period. More recent evidence, however, even suggests that dopaminergic and serotonergic fibers form appositions with the same projection and local circuit neurons of the prefrontal cortex. Because of this convergence, a disturbance in the development of serotonergic projections in this region is associated with an increase of its dopaminergic innervation. Taken together, these findings suggest that these two monoaminergic systems may compete with each other for the establishment of functional territory on intrinsic neurons of the cortex, although it is not clear whether this interaction is mediated within the cortex itself or possibly at midbrain levels where the respective nuclei are located. Overall, the results described in this chapter suggest that the ontogenesis of the prefrontal cortex is a protracted process in which a marked degree of plasticity, even in the early stages of adulthood, contributes to the establishment of mature patterns of connectivity.

In recent years, it has become apparent that the development of the corticolimbic system continues well beyond the neonatal period, perhaps even as late as the fifth and sixth decades (Benes, 1995, 1997b; Benes et al., 1994). Of particular relevance to our understanding of the maturation of cognitive and emotional behaviors is the development of the prefrontal cortex and the other components of this system with which it is intimately linked. The discussion that follows provides an overview of corticolimbic development at various stages of the life cycle, beginning with gyral development during embryogenesis and extending to the postnatal period. Consideration is given to the maturation of both intrinsic and extrinsic neurons and their respective neurotransmitter systems, and the chapter concludes with a discussion of how the latter interact with one another during postnatal development.

## Gyral development

The development of the cerebral cortex occurs at different rates that, to some extent, reflect phylogeny. For example, at 16–19 weeks of embryogenesis, the cingulate gyrus can be distinguished, but this occurs long before the parahippocampal gyrus and hippocampal formation have become discernible in the medial temporal lobe (Gilles, Shankle, and Dooling, 1983). Cortical regions undergo ontogenesis at varying rates that, to some degree, reflect phylogeny (table 6.1). For example, limbic cortical areas tend to differentiate early in gestation. At 16–19 weeks in humans, the cingulate region can be distinguished as a gyrus, but this is well before the parahippocampal gyrus and the hippocampal formation have begun to take shape in the medial temporal area at weeks 20–23 (Gilles, Shankle, and Dooling, 1983). The superior and medial frontal gyri (prefrontal regions) do not take on a clear gyral configuration until 24–27 weeks of gestational age, and the angular and supramarginal gyri (inferior parietal area) are not distinguished until 28–31 weeks (Gilles, Shankle, and Dooling, 1983). The orbital frontal gyri, which (like the cingulate gyri) are well represented in earlier mammalian forms such as rodents, are among the last

FRANCINE M. BENES   Laboratory for Structural Neuroscience, McLean Hospital, Belmont, Massachusetts; Program in Neuroscience and Department of Psychiatry, Harvard Medical School, Boston, Massachusetts.

TABLE 6.1

*Comparison of the embryonic development of human cortical gyri*

| Gestational Age (weeks) | Gyrus |
|---|---|
| 16–19 | Gyrus rectus, cingulate |
| 20–23 | Parahippocampal, superior temporal |
| 24–27 | Pre- and post-rolandic, middle temporal, superior and middle frontal, occipital, cuneus, lingual |
| 28–31 | Inferior temporal, medial and lateral orbital, callosomarginal, angular, supramarginal, transverse temporal |
| 32–35 | Paracentral |
| 36–39 | Anterior and posterior orbital |

Adapted from Gilles, Shankle, and Dooling (1983)

to appear. It seems likely that perturbations of brain development at various stages of the process might be capable of inducing marked alterations in the formation of normal gyral patterns of human brain.

## Cytoarchitectural maturation of the cortex

The ontogenesis of all cortical regions follows a carefully timed sequence of events (Poliakov, 1965; Sidman and Rakic, 1973). All cortical neurons are generated along the ventricular surface in the so-called marginal zone and migrate toward the surface after undergoing several mitotic divisions. Poliakov (1965) described five stages of cortical development in human brain, beginning with Stage I at approximately the seventh fetal week when postmitotic cells begin to move upward. Stage V, the longest period, occurs between the sixteenth fetal week and the early postnatal period. During Stage V, postmitotic neuronal cells continue migrating and reach their final destination within the cortical plate. As neurons enter the cortical plate, those destined for more superficial layers arrive later than those that occupy deeper layers and show an "inside-out" progression (Rakic, 1974). Studies of motor cortex in humans have shown that by 7 months of gestation, layers V and VI have attained a more advanced degree of development than layers II and III (Marin-Padilla, 1970a; Zilles, Busching, and Schleicher, 1986). The morphological differentiation of neurons in the various layers mirrors this migratory process, such that large pyramidal neurons with a well-developed dendritic arborization and basket cells (inhibitory interneurons) can be distinguished in deeper layers sooner than in superficial layers (Marin-Padilla, 1970b). By 7.5 months in utero, pyramidal neurons in deeper portions of layer III are just beginning to show differentiation of an apical dendrite extending into layer I, while in layers V and

VI, these cells already have elaborate dendritic arborizations. During this same interval, incoming fibers from other regions are present in virtually all layers of the cortex. In the months immediately prior to birth, interneurons begin to appear in the deeper portions of layer III, while in layers II and outer portions of III they are first beginning to form. By birth, both the second and third laminae contain pyramidal neurons; however, basket cells in layer II are largely absent (Marin-Padilla, 1970b). By 2.5 months postnatally, pyramidal neurons continue to mature, showing a dramatic increase in overall size, the amount of dendritic branching, and numbers of dendritic spines (Michel and Garey, 1984). Interestingly, layers VI and I (the marginal zone) are the first laminae to appear and differentiate, while layers II and III are the last to form and the latest to mature (Marin-Padilla, 1970a). At birth, cortical layer II in motor cortex of human brains is still quite immature (Marin-Padilla, 1970b).

Bayer and Altman (1991) have reported that a similar inside-out progression is observed in the medial prefrontal cortex of rodent brain (figure 6.1). Cell migration in this region occurs earlier than it does for the retrosplenial cortex and subicular subdivision of the hippocampal formation (Bayer, 1990). This pattern reflects that described for gyral development, in which the cingulate gyrus differentiates weeks in advance of the parahippocampal gyrus and hippocampal formation; in this instance, however, it follows a dorsal-to-ventral course (see table 6.1). Presumably, the analogous timing of events for the prefrontal cortex of human brain is somewhat different, but its growth and maturation as a gyrus is likely complete by the second year of life. Postnatally, the medial prefrontal cortex of rat shows a progressive expansion of its matrix as the neuropil surrounding neuronal cell bodies increases. As shown in figure 6.2, the increase of neuropil occurs between P10 and P20, an interval that occurs within the preweaning period that is roughly equivalent to preadolescence in humans. The increase of neuropil is probably related to two different events: (1) the ingrowth of fibers from other cortical and subcortical regions, and (2) the collateralization of axons from neurons intrinsic to the cortex. These changes also follow an inside-out progression similar to that seen in relation to cell migration. In the medial prefrontal cortex of rat brain, the thickness is not maximal until P20, which marks the beginning of the postweaning period (Vincent, Pabreza, and Benes, 1995), an interval that is roughly equivalent to adolescence in human development.

Beyond the perinatal period, the packing density of neurons in human cortex decreases dramatically during

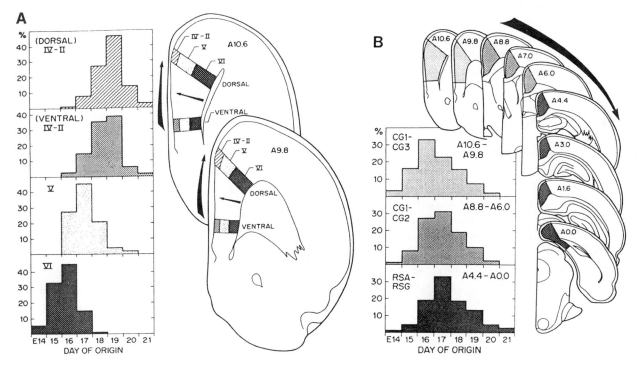

FIGURE 6.1  The time of origin for neurons in the anterior cingulate areas (medial prefrontal cortex) of rat brain. (**A**) Neurons along the ventral-to-dorsal extent are generated earliest in the deeper laminae of the anterior cingulate cortex. The superficial layers, however, show a ventral-to-dorsal gradient for the time of origin of their neurons. (**B**) The time of origin for neurons of medial limbic cortex extending from the anterior cingulate (CG1–CG3) to the posterior (CG1–CG2) and retrosplenial (RSA and RSG) divisions of the region. There is an anterior-to-posterior gradient, such that neurons in the anterior cingulate cortex are generated earlier than those in the retrosplenial area and the subicular portion of the hippocampal formation. (Reprinted with permission from Bayer, S. A., and I. Altman, 1991. *Neocortical Development.* New York: Raven Press, pp. 193–196.)

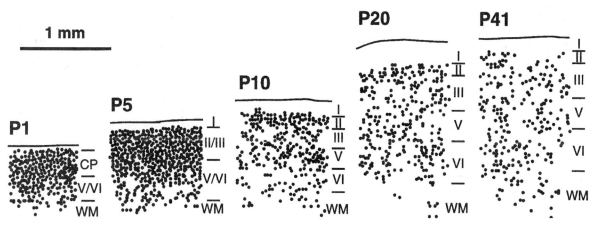

FIGURE 6.2  Light photomicrographs of rat anterior cingulate cortex (medial prefrontal are) at postnatal days P1, P5, P10, P20, and P41. At P1, the immature cortical plate (CP) lies between layer I and deeper layers V and VI. By P5, however, the cortical plate has differentiated into layers II and III, but the density of cells in these superficial laminae is greater than that observed in the deeper layers. Between P10 and P20, the increased thickness of the cortical mantle is primarily related to the expansion of neuropil in layers II and III. Overall, between P1 and P20, there is a gradual increase in the thickness of the cortical mantle as the packing density of neuronal cell bodies decreases. At postweanling day P41, there is no further change in the density of neurons. WM = white matter. (Reprinted with permission from Vincent, S. L., L. Pabreza, and F. M. Benes, 1995. Postnatal maturation of GABA-immunoreactive neurons of rat medial prefrontal cortex. *J. Comp. Neurol.* 355:84.)

the first year of life (Blinkov and Glezer, 1968). In the dorsolateral prefrontal cortex (Brodman areas 9 and 10), neuronal density continues to decrease until 5–7 years of age, although in layer II of some regions, this process may continue until 12–15 years of age (Blinkov and Glezer, 1968).

## The formation of synaptic connections

During embryogenesis, afferent fibers from the thalamus grow toward the cortical mantle and eventually penetrate inward toward layer IV (Wise and Jones, 1978). In rodents, the ingrowth of thalamocortical fibers is not complete until the third postnatal day, while commissural fibers begin to enter the homologous cortex in the contralateral hemisphere by postnatal day 5 and attain a mature pattern of connectivity by postnatal day 7 (Wise and Jones, 1978). The afferent fibers seem to be present before a mature dendritic tree is in evidence and the formation of dendritic spines may be regulated by these afferent inputs (Wise, Fleshman, and Jones, 1979). For rats, the first postnatal week is considered to be similar to the prenatal period of primates and, consistent with this, commissural fibers arising from the principal sulcus of monkey brain have been reported to penetrate into the homologous cortical region of the opposite hemisphere during the late embryonic period (Goldman-Rakic, 1981).

The density of synapses first increases toward peak levels at approximately 5–8 years of age in human cortex, then decreases dramatically through early adolescence (Huttenlocher, 1994; Huttenlocher and Dabholkar, 1997). The latter process, called "pruning," is believed to play a role in the acquisition of mature patterns of connectivity. Presumably, weakly active synapses are eliminated as functionally reinforced ones are maintained.

## Myelination of corticolimbic pathways

A broadly accepted marker for the functional maturation of the central nervous system is the formation of myelin sheaths, the insulating covering that surrounds axon shafts. It has long been known that various neural pathways myelinate at different stages of pre- and postnatal development and, for humans, this process has long been thought to continue well after birth, particularly in the prefrontal cortex (Flechsig, 1920; Yakovlev and Lecours, 1967). There is a general tendency, however, for more cephalad structures to myelinate later than those found at more caudal levels of the neuraxis, and for subcortical pathways to myelinate before cortical associational paths (Yakovlev and Lecours, 1967; see

also Sampaio and Truwit, this volume). For example, the medial longitudinal fasciculus, a pathway that is found along the entire extent of the spinal cord and brainstem, begins myelinating as early as week 20 of the gestational period, while the medial lemniscus, a pathway confined to the brainstem, shows similar changes at gestational week 24 (Gilles et al., 1983). Within the cerebral hemispheres, the posterior limb of the internal capsule begins myelinating at gestational week 32, while the anterior limb does not show evidence of myelin formation until week 38. Interestingly, proximal portions of the cingulum bundle do not begin to myelinate until gestational weeks 38–39 (Gilles et al., 1983). On the other hand, some subcortical relays, such as the fornix and mammilothalamic tract, do not begin to myelinate until gestational weeks 44 and 48, respectively. Some pathways within the corticolimbic system continue to myelinate until much later in the postnatal period (Benes, 1989; Benes et al., 1994). For example, the superior medullary lamina, a fiber bundle found along the surface of the parahippocampal gyrus, shows an increase of myelin-staining not only during the first and second decades of life (Benes, 1989), but even as late as the fifth and sixth decades. It is noteworthy that Yakovlev and Lecours (1967) had postulated that myelin formation might continue to increase in the prefrontal cortex well into the third or, perhaps, even the fourth decade of life. Although empirical evidence for this hypothesis has been lacking, the recent findings just described make this idea seem quite plausible.

## Developmental changes in specific neurotransmitter systems

The maturation of the prefrontal cortex must involve obligatory changes in both the intrinsic and extrinsic neurotransmitter systems that mediate its activity. Although there is a dearth of specific information regarding their development in human brain, the discussion that follows considers data obtained from studies in rodents where developmental changes of cortical neurotransmitters have been extensively characterized. It is true that the specific timing of developmental changes can vary considerably from one species to another; nevertheless, some general principles can be formulated from the studies of rodent and, to a lesser extent, primate brain. In this regard, it is useful to point out that the equivalent of adolescence in rats occurs between postnatal weeks 3 and 8, while the early adult period begins at approximately postnatal day 60. Where available, studies in the developing human brain are also described.

*Glutamate* The amino acid glutamate and the closely related compound aspartate are generally considered to be the transmitters employed by pyramidal neurons projecting to both cortical and subcortical locations (Streit, 1984). The time course for the maturation of various glutamatergic pathways is probably different. For example, the corticocortical projections originating in the visual cortex of rat brain attain adult levels of glutamate before their corticostriatal counterparts projecting to the caudate nucleus (Johnston, 1988). Interestingly, two days after birth, the level of the glutamate reuptake mechanism is 30% of the levels that are eventually seen at P15. In the visual cortex and in the lateral geniculate nucleus, the reuptake mechanism attains adult levels by P15 and P20, respectively (Kvale, Fosse, and Fonnum, 1983). High-affinity glutamate receptors also continue to change postnatally. Between P10 and P15, glutamate receptor binding activity increases by 30% and is 10 times higher than it will eventually be during adulthood (Schliebs, Kullman, and Bigl, 1986). After P15, however, the activity declines substantially through P25 (Schliebs, Kullman, and Bigl, 1986). In rats monocularly deprived of visual input, the overall binding of glutamate is reduced in the lateral geniculate nucleus, but not the visual cortex, and these reductions are maintained into adulthood (Schliebs, Kullman, and Bigl, 1986). In the hippocampus, glutamate receptor binding increases up to P23 (Baudry et al., 1981), possibly reflecting the persistence of long-term potentiation as an important component to both learning and memory (Johnston, 1988).

*γ-Aminobutyric acid (GABA)* This transmitter is thought to be the most important inhibitory neurotransmitter in mammalian brain, particularly in humans. Generally speaking, the activity of the GABA reuptake mechanism seems to increase before the activity of GAD shows appreciable increments (Coyle and Enna, 1976). At birth, the amount of GABA is half that seen in adult, but the latter are not attained until the second postnatal week. The number of GABA-immunoreactive (GABA-IR) neurons present in the medial prefrontal cortex of rat brain reaches a peak density at approximately P5, but thereafter decreases sharply between P10 and P20 as the surrounding neuropil expands (Vincent, Pabreza, and Benes, 1995). As shown in figure 6.3 GABA terminals, however, increase in number between postnatal days 7 and 12 for the deeper layers of this region (figure 6.4), but show an inside-out progression, as they continue to increase in number in superficial laminae until the third postnatal week (Vincent, Pabreza, and Benes,

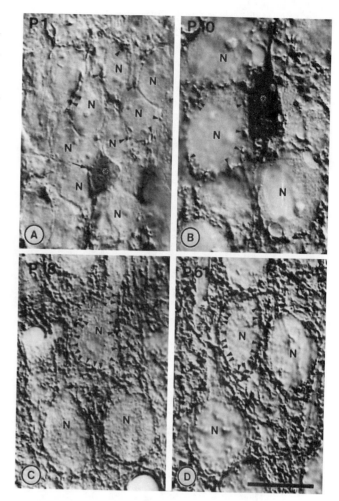

FIGURE 6.3 A set of photomicrographs showing GABA-immunoreactive terminals (arrowheads) in the medial prefrontal cortex of rats at postnatal day 1 (**A**), 10 (**B**), 18 (**C**), and 41 (**D**). At P1, the GABA terminals are sparsely distributed around neuronal cell bodies, while at P10, the number has increased. At P18 and P41, there are numerous axosomatic terminals that form "basket" configurations. Bar = 20 μm. (Reprinted with permission from Vincent, S. L., L. Pabreza, and F. M. Benes, 1995. Postnatal maturation of GABA-immunoreactive neurons of rat medial prefrontal cortex. *J. Comp. Neurol.* 355:84.)

1995). Although GAD levels are negligible at birth, they attain adult levels by the third postnatal week (Johnston and Coyle, 1980).

The amount of GABA and benzodiazepine receptor activity does not begin to increase appreciably until the first postnatal week, but thereafter shows a sharp rise during the second week and an additional 15% increment between the second and seventh postnatal weeks (Candy and Martin, 1979). In contrast, the reuptake mechanism for GABA peaks by the second postnatal week, but later, in the seventh week, it decreases. In human brain, GABA receptor binding activity shows a

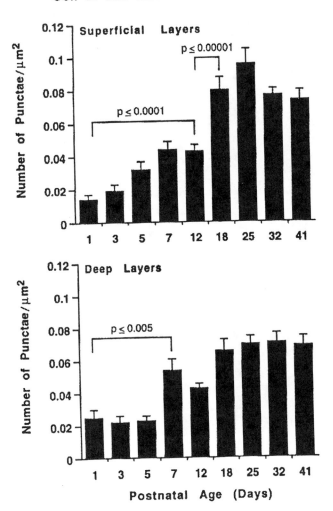

**Average Density of
GABA-Immunoreactive Punctae per
Cell in Rat Medial Prefrontal Cortex**

FIGURE 6.4  A bar graph showing the average density of axo-somatic GABA-immunoreactive terminals in apposition with pyramidal cell bodies in superficial (layers II and III) and deeper (layers V and VI) laminae of rat medial prefrontal cortex. In deeper layers, the density of terminals is close to adult levels by the end of the first postnatal week, while in superficial laminae, the numbers continue to increase until the third postnatal week. (Reprinted with permission from Vincent, S. L., L. Pabreza, and F. M. Benes, 1995. Postnatal maturation of GABA-immunoreactive neurons of rat medial prefrontal cortex. *J. Comp. Neurol.* 355:84.)

fivefold increase during the perinatal period (Brooksbank, Atkinson, and Balasz, 1981; Diebler, Farkas-Bargeton, and Wehrle, 1979) and an additional 100% increase for several weeks thereafter (Brooksbank, Atkinson, and Balasz, 1981). Functional inputs are thought to regulate the maturation of the GABA system. For example, in cat visual cortex, dark-rearing from birth through the sixth postnatal week results in a decrease of normal GAD activity (Fosse, Heggelund, and Fonnu, 1989).

EXTRINSIC NEUROTRANSMITTERS  There are four key extrinsic neurotransmitter systems that project to the prefrontal cortex, and the postnatal development of these four afferent systems are discussed following.

*Acetylcholine*  Most of the acetylcholine (Ach) found in the cortex is derived from the basal forebrain (Johnston, McKinney, and Coyle, 1979) where the nucleus basalis of Meynert gives rise to the principal cholinergic projections (Mesulam, 1983). A small amount of Ach may be synthesized by intrinsic cholinergic neurons (Levey et al., 1984). While the neuronal cell bodies of the cholinergic system are generated early in gestation (Bayer, 1985), they do not begin to accumulate appreciable amounts of choline acetyltransferase (ChAT) until after the first postnatal week, although the activity of this synthetic enzyme continues to increase until the sixth postnatal week (Johnston and Coyle, 1980) and occurs in parallel with increases of muscarinic receptor binding (Coyle and Yamamura, 1976).

The growth of cholinergic fibers into the cortex occurs first in deeper layers and later in the superficial layers and reflects the inside-out progression seen for cortical ontogeny. In humans, cholinergic fibers have been observed to enter the cortex as early as gestational weeks 12–22 (Candy et al., 1985); however, adult levels of ChAT are not attained until approximately 10 years of age (Diebler, Farkas-Bargeton, and Wehrle, 1979). In contrast, muscarinic receptor binding activity in human cortex is highest at birth and diminishes progressively during the second through the sixth decades of life and possibly longer, perhaps as a result of synaptic pruning (Ravikumar and Sastary, 1985). Acetylcholinesterase, the enzyme that degrades Ach, is found principally in interneurons in human cortex during the first postnatal week, but later shows a progressive increase in pyramidal cell bodies of layer III where it reaches peak levels during early adulthood (Kostovic, Skavic, and Strinovic, 1988). Since upper cortical layers are predominantly involved in associative connectivity, these latter changes could reflect maturational changes in cognitive activity.

*Norepinephrine*  Noradrenergic cell bodies found in the locus coeruleus (Levitt and Moore, 1978; Lindvall, Bjorklund, and Divac, 1978) undergo their last mitotic division at gestational days 12–14 in rat brain (Lauder and Bloom, 1974) and at gestational days 27–36 in monkeys (Levitt and Rakic, 1982). By birth, there is a rather extensive network of noradrenergic fibers in rat cortex, and this is considerably more dense than that seen in adult animals (Coyle and Molliver, 1977). Tyrosine hydroxylase (TH), the enzyme involved in the synthesis of norepinephrine and dopamine, increases steadily in rat cortex between the first and seventh postnatal weeks (Johnston and Coyle, 1980). The β-adrenergic receptor increases sharply between the first and second postnatal weeks before plateauing (Harden et al., 1977). Studies in cat have suggested that norepinephrine may play a key role in the plasticity of synaptic connections (Kasamatsu and Pettigrew, 1976). Following monocular visual deprivation, cats depleted of norepinephrine (Kasamatsu and Pettigrew, 1976) or given clonidine, a drug that inhibits the release of this transmitter (Nelson, Schwartz, and Daniels, 1975), fail to convert binocularly driven neurons to a monocularly driven pattern.

*Serotonin*  The timing of developmental changes in the serotonin (5-hydroxytryptamine, or 5-HT) system is similar to that observed for the noradrenergic system (Hamon and Bourgoin, 1977; Hedner and Lundberg, 1980). Serotonin-containing neurons of the raphe nuclei in rat brain (Descarries, Beaudet, and Watkins, 1975) are first visualized between gestational days 13 and 17 when some of their axons have already grown toward the pyriform cortex (Wallace and Lauder, 1983). As seen with other transmitter systems in rat brain (see Dopamine below), 5-HT levels increase steadily between birth and the fourth postnatal week (Johnston, 1988). The synthesizing enzyme for 5-HT, tryptophan hydroxylase, is 10% of adult levels by birth, but rises to adult levels by postnatal day 30 (Deguchi and Barchas, 1972). During the perinatal period, high-affinity 5-HT receptor binding activity is approximately a third of that seen in adults, but does not attain adult levels until the sixth postnatal week (Uphouse and Bondy, 1981). In primates, 5-HT afferent fibers to the cortex appear to have established an adult pattern by postnatal week 6, while the levels of 5-HT continue to increase for an additional 2–3 weeks (Goldman-Rakic and Brown, 1982). In human brain, however, the density of 5-HT$_2$ binding sites shows a linear decline between 17 and 100 years of age; in the hippocampus, a similar, but less striking change in this receptor also occurs (Marcusson et al., 1984).

It has been suggested that timing for the ingrowth of serotonergic fibers may vary according to the degree of maturity for intrinsic circuits within a given region (Lidov and Molliver, 1982). Interestingly, at birth, the serotonin projection to sensory cortex is found preferentially within layers IV and VI, the two laminae predominantly involved in receiving thalamic afferents.

Since the arrival of serotonin fibers precedes that of the thalamocortical afferents (Wise and Jones, 1978), it has been suggested that the serotonergic innervation to cortex may provide a trophic influence on thalamic fibers and/or their target neurons (D'Amato, et al., 1987).

*Dopamine*  Dopamine cells in the ventral tegmental area and substantia nigra of rat brain (Berger et al., 1974; Thierry et al, 1973) begin to differentiate on embryonic day 11 and continue this process through day 15 (Lauder and Bloom, 1974). Afferent dopamine fibers first arrive near the frontal cortex as early as E16 (Verney et al., 1982); however, by birth, these axons begin to penetrate into the cortical mantle and establish an abundant innervation by postnatal week 2 for the frontal area and postnatal week 3 for the cingulate region (Berger and Verney, 1984). As shown in figure 6.5, the density of fibers continues to increase until adulthood. Dopamine afferents to the prefrontal region also follow the typical inside-out progression seen for cholinergic inputs (described earlier), entering the infragranular layers first and the supragranular layers last (Kalsbeek et al., 1988), but a full distribution is not established until adulthood (Kalsbeek et al., 1988; Verney et al., 1982). Dopamine concentrations also rise steadily until adulthood (Johnston, 1988). Dopamine receptors, on the other hand, are expressed in the cortex before birth and continue to increase toward adult levels through postnatal day 31 of rats (Bruinink, Lichtensteiner, and Schlumpf, 1983; Deskin et al., 1981).

## Developmental similarities among transmitter systems

Based on the previous discussion, there are several developmental characteristics that are similar across neurotransmitter systems, and there is no reason to believe that the situation is different for the prefrontal cortex. For example, the progenitor cells responsible for the elaboration of both intrinsic and extrinsic transmitter systems in the cortex become postmitotic long before they show appreciable differentiation of their respective neurotransmitter phenotypes. In addition, virtually all neurotransmitter systems are present in the cortex at birth, but require further maturation. Finally, the postnatal development of most transmitter systems continues beyond the weaning period (similar to early adolescence in humans), during which important changes in gonadal maturity are occurring, and overlaps with the postweaning period (similar to late adolescence when changes in emotional maturity are occurring). Although there is a dearth of information

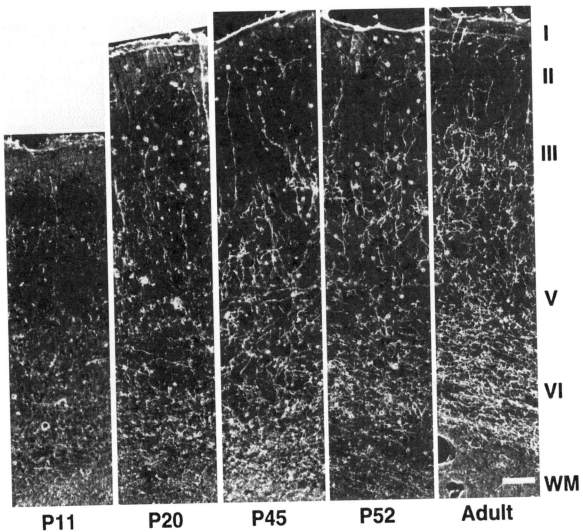

I

II

III

V

VI

WM

**P11**   **P20**   **P45**   **P52**   **Adult**

FIGURE 6.5 Low-power darkfield photomicrographs of dopamine-immunoreactive varicose fibers in medial prefrontal cortex of rats at postnatal days P11, P20, and P45 and during early adulthood. At P11, there are very few fibers in evidence, but the density increases steadily until adulthood, particularly in the deeper layers V and VI. Bar = 100 μm.

(Reprinted with permission from Benes, F. M., S. L. Vincent, R. Molloy, and Y. Khan, 1996. Increased interaction of dopamine-immunoreactive varicosities with GABA neurons of rat medial prefrontal cortex occurs during the postweanling period. *Synapse* 23:237–245.)

regarding human brain, available evidence suggests that postnatal maturation of both the cholinergic and serotonergic systems may continue throughout childhood and adolescence, and may, in some cases, persist throughout the lifespan of the normal individual. Based on observations in rats, however, it seems likely that changes in the dopamine system are also occurring until the early adult period.

*Developmental interactions between intrinsic and extrinsic cortical transmitters*

It is evident from the earlier discussion that the postnatal maturation of both intrinsic and extrinsic neuro-

transmitter systems is extensive. At this juncture, a reasonable question to ask is whether these progressive postnatal changes may involve an increase in the degree to which some or all of these transmitter systems are interacting with one another.

DOPAMINE–GABA INTERACTIONS   As shown in figure 6.6 (see also color plate 9), a recent study has suggested that frequent appositions occur between dopaminergic afferents and both pyramidal neurons and GABAergic interneurons in the medial prefrontal cortex of adult rat (Benes, Vincent, and Molloy, 1993). When the frequency of these contacts was compared for preweanling and postweanling rats, it was found that there is a curvilinear increase in the number of dopamine-

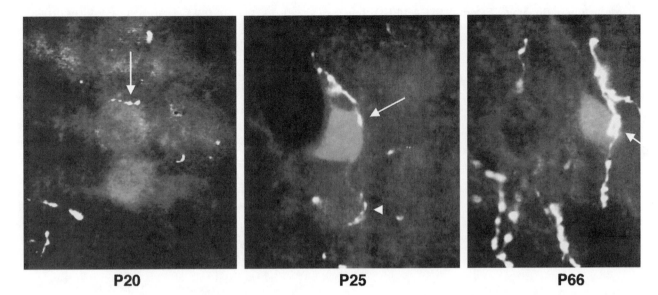

**P20**  **P25**  **P66**

Figure 6.6   A digital confocal photomicrograph of a double-immunofluorescent localization of dopamine fibers (yellow) and GABA cell bodies in layer VI of rat medial prefrontal cortex at postnatal days P20, P25, and P66. By P20, dopamine fibers have already begun to form contacts with GABAergic neurons (arrows). Following weaning, the fibers show a subtle increase, and contacts can be seen both on the cell bodies and on large dendritic branches (arrowhead). By P66, the overall density of fibers is markedly increased and the number of interactions for any given cell is much greater. (Reprinted with permission from Benes, F. M., S. L. Vincent, R. Molloy, and Y. Khan, 1996. Increased interaction of dopamine-immunoreactive varicosities with GABA neurons of rat medial prefrontal cortex occurs during the postweanling period. *Synapse* 23:237–245.)

immunoreactive varicosities found in contact with non-pyramidal neurons in layer VI of rat medial prefrontal cortex (figure 6.7). In layer II of this region, there was a sevenfold increase on nonpyramidal neurons, but no change on pyramidal cells (Benes, 1997b). These findings suggest that (1) postnatal increases in the interaction of one transmitter system with another probably do occur to a significant degree, (2) such changes may vary in magnitude according to cortical layer, and (3) changes of this type may occur differentially for one neuronal cell type versus another within a given cortical layer. In other words, postnatal maturational changes in cortical neurotransmitter systems may be far more complex than heretofore suspected, and to fully understand the implications of postnatal ontogeny, a clear delineation of how changes in neurochemical markers may be reflected in alterations of specific synaptic connectivity is needed.

A variety of studies have demonstrated that both pyramidal and nonpyramidal neurons express receptors that mediate the effect of dopamine. For example, in one study dopamine D1 receptor binding activity has been localized to nonpyramidal cells (Vincent, Khan, and Benes, 1993), while in another it was associated with pyramidal cells (Bergson et al., 1995) in prefrontal cortex. This apparent discrepancy can be explained by methodological and species differences in these two studies, because messenger RNA for both the D1 and D2 subtypes has been localized in both pyramidal and nonpyramidal neurons (Huntley et al., 1992). Consistent with this, a large proportion of interneurons in rat mPFCx have been found to express D1 and D2 binding activities (Vincent, Khan, and Benes, 1992, 1995), and studies in which in vitro microdialysis was employed have demonstrated that agonists for both the D1 and D2 subtypes are associated with a reduction in the release of 3H-GABA (Penit-Soria, Audinat, and Crepel, 1987; Retaux, Besson, and Penit-Soria, 1991a,b). Thus, as suggested by these results, cortical dopamine projections can potentially exert a significant nonsynaptic modulatory influence on GABAergic cells in rat mPFCx.

*Convergence of dopamine and serotonin fibers on prefrontal neurons*

Serotonin fibers are believed to converge on the same pyramidal cells and GABA neurons that receive inputs from catecholaminergic neurons (Gellman and Aghajanian, 1993), and a triple immunofluorescence study was able to confirm that this arrangement occurs in the medial prefrontal cortex of rats to an extensive degree (Taylor and Benes, 1996). It is noteworthy that pyramidal neurons also received inputs to their somata from

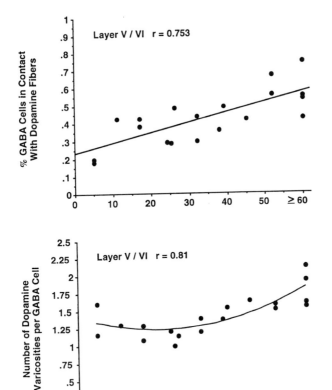

**Interaction of Dopamine Fibers With GABA Neurons In Rat mPFC During Postnatal Development**

FIGURE 6.7 Bivariate plots of the interaction of dopamine-immunoreactive (DA-IR) varicosities with GABA-immunoreactive (GABA-IR) cell bodies at different postnatal ages. In the upper panel, the percentage of GABA-IR cell bodies having appositions with any DA-IR fibers increases in a linear fashion between birth and P60. In the lower panel, the number of DA-IR varicosities forming appositions with any given GABA-IR soma shows very little change during the preweanling period, but then increases in a curvilinear fashion until P60. (Reprinted with permission from Benes, F. M., S. L. Vincent, R. Molloy, and Y. Khan, 1996. Increased interaction of dopamine-immunoreactive varicosities with GABA neurons of rat medial prefrontal cortex occurs during the postweanling period. *Synapse* 23:237–245.)

both TH- and 5-HT-IR fibers. Since these latter cell bodies also received axosomatic inputs from GAD-IR terminals, it was concluded that the principal projection cells of this regions receive a "trivergence" of inputs from the GABA, dopamine, and serotonin systems (Taylor and Benes, 1996; Benes, Taylor, and Cunningham, 2000). With regard to the serotonin system, the 5-HT2 receptor protein has been immunocytochemically lo-

calized to presumptive GABAergic interneurons in layer II of the pyriform cortex (Morilak, Garlow, and Ciaranello, 1993).

It is well established that GABA is an inhibitory neurotransmitter that plays a pivotal role in cortical integration (Jones, 1987). There are many different subtypes of GABAergic interneuron in the cortex, but the most basic dichotomy is between basket cells that exert inhibitory effects on pyramidal neurons (Jones and Hendry, 1984) versus double bouquet cells that are disinhibitory in nature (Somogyi and Cowey, 1984); the latter act by inhibiting other GABAergic cells (for a recent review, see Benes and Berretta, 2001). GABAergic interneurons play a very critical role in discriminative aspects of cortical processing, such as orientation selectivity (Sillito, 1984).

FUNCTIONAL IMPLICATIONS OF CONVERGENCE Physiological studies have demonstrated that SKF38393, a D1 agonist, and RU24926, a D2 agonist, have both been found to inhibit the electrically evoked release of $^3$H-GABA in rat mPFC (Penit-Soria, Retaux, and Maurin, 1989; Retaux, Besson, and Penit-Soria, 1991a,b), although D2 agonists have paradoxically been found to increase the spontaneous release of GABA (Retaux et al., 1991a). This apparent paradox could potentially be explained by an initial depolarization leading to either a presynaptic inhibition or a refractory period in GABA cells (Retaux, Besson, and Penit-Soria, 1991a). Since the D2 receptor is mainly associated with inhibitory mechanisms, the complexity of interactions between dopamine terminals and GABA cells in prefrontal cortex might well mask a similar effect on evoked GABA release (Retaux, Besson, and Penit-Soria, 1991a). Specifically, dopamine binding to D2 receptors on some terminals could produce an inhibition of a GABA neuron (Retaux, Besson, and Penit-Soria, 1991a). It is plausible that dopamine fibers interact with both inhibitory and disinhibitory GABAergic elements, and this could help to explain the paradoxical effects of D2 agonists on spontaneous versus evoked release of dopamine in prefrontal cortex. For the serotonin system, the results of an intracellular recording study have indicated that the effect of this monoamine on GABA cells is blocked by 5-HT2 antagonists (Sheldon and Aghajanian. 1991). Overall, serotonin appears to induce hyperpolarizing postsynaptic potentials in pyramidal neurons, and these are believed to be mediated via the effect of this transmitter on GABAergic interneurons (Sheldon and Aghajanian, 1991).

While it is clear that both dopamine and serotonin can directly influence the activity of cortical interneurons, very little is known regarding any direct interactions between these two systems on individual GABAergic cells. Some investigators believe that serotonin can increase the release of dopamine in nucleus accumbens (Broderick and Phelix, 1997), corpus striatum (Broderick and Phelix, 1997; Gudelsky and Nash, 1996; West and Galloway, 1996) and prefrontal cortex (Iyer and Bradberry, 1996; Gudelsky and Nash, 1996). Contrariwise, others have suggested that serotonin may actually decrease the release of dopamine, since exposure to selective serotonin receptor antagonists has been associated with an increase of extracellular dopamine concentration (Howell, Czoty, and Byrd, 1997; Pehek, 1996). None of these studies has attempted to assess such an interaction at the level of individual neurons. It is important to point out that functional interactions between these two monoaminergic systems may not be mediated solely at the cortical level, but could be mediated, at least in part, at midbrain levels where both the ventral tegmental area and the nucleus raphe dorsalis are located.

## Plasticity of dopamine–serotonin interactions

As noted earlier, the serotonin system has been found to influence the plasticity of the developing neocortex, as it exerts a trophic influence on the ingrowth of thalamocortical fibers (D'Amato et al., 1987). With respect to the current discussion, it is pertinent to ask whether serotonin might also exert a neuroplastic influence on the late ingrowth of dopamine fibers into the medial prefrontal cortex during early adulthood. In order to explore this issue, a series of experiments were conducted using 5,7-dihydroxytryptamine, a specific toxin to serotonergic neurons, to lesion the dorsal raphe nucleus of rat brain during the neonatal period (Taylor, Cunningham, and Benes, 1998). The distribution of TH-IR varicosities was assessed in the ventral tegmental area, where dopaminergic afferents to the cortex originate, and in the medial prefrontal area. The lesioned rats showed a marked reduction in the visualization of 5-HT-IR somata in the ventral periaqueductal gray, while the VTA showed no reduction in staining. In the medial prefrontal area, 5-HT fibers were also markedly reduced, while TH-IR fibers were abundantly present throughout the cortical mantle. When the numerical density of TH-IR varicosities was determined, a significant increase was noted, particularly in layer V where the 5-HT innervation of the cortex is quite dense. These results suggest that there may be a competition between dopamine and 5-HT fiber systems within the prefrontal cortex of rat brain (Benes, Taylor, and Cunningham, 2000).

## Conclusions

It is likely that the ontogenesis of the prefrontal cortex spans not only the embryonic period, but also an extensive postnatal interval that includes the early adult period and possibly even beyond. During embryogenesis, the developmental processes that are operative encompass a broad range of phenomena, including proliferation, migration, and differentiation of neurons—not only those intrinsic to the prefrontal cortex, but also extrinsic ones in a variety of subcortical regions that send significant projections to it. These latter fiber systems include projections from the thalamus, as well as those that originate in the dorsal raphe nucleus, ventral tegmental area, and locus coeruleus. Unlike the "specific" afferent systems from the thalamus, the monoaminergic systems may continue their growth and maturation for a much longer period of time that extends into adulthood. As such, these latter systems may play an important role in modulating the activity of intrinsic circuits within the prefrontal cortex and may ultimately contribute to the acquisition of mature patterns of cognitive behavior that are mediated by this region (Goldman-Rakic, Bourgeois, and Rakic, 1997). The fact that the dopaminergic and serotonin systems converge on intrinsic prefrontal neurons and influence the nature of their activity implies that these two systems may be particularly important to our understanding of how neuronal plasticity contributes to the sculpting of neural circuitry within the adult prefrontal cortex.

### REFERENCES

BAUDRY, M., D. ARST, M. OLIVER, and G. LYNCH, 1981. Development of glutamate binding sites and their regulation by calcium in rat hippocampus. *Dev. Brain Res.* 1:37–38.

BAYER, S. A., 1985. Neurogenesis of the magnocellular basal telencephalic nuclei in the rat. *Int. J. Dev. Neurosci.* 3:229–243.

BAYER, S. A., 1990. Development of the lateral and medial limbic cortices in the rat in relation to cortical phylogeny. *Exp. Neurol.* 107:118–131.

BAYER, S. A., and J. ALTMAN, 1991. Development of the limbic cortical areas. In *Neocortical Development*. New York: Raven Press, pp. 186–200.

BENES, F. M., 1989. Myelination of cortical-hippocampal relays during late adolescence: Anatomical correlates to the onset of schizophrenia. *Schizophrenia Bull.* 15:585–594.

BENES, F. M., 1995. A neurodevelopmental approach to understanding schizophrenia and other mental disorders. In *Developmental Psychopathology*, Vol. I. D. Cicchetti and D. J. Cohen, eds. New York: John Wiley and Sons, pp. 227–253.

BENES, F. M., 1997a. Is there evidence for neuronal loss in schizophrenia? *Int. Rev. Psychiatry* 9:429–436.

BENES, F. M., 1997b. The role of stress and dopamine-GABA interactions in the vulnerability for schizophrenia. *J. Psychiatr. Res.* 31:257–275.

BENES, F. M., and S. BERRETTA, 2001. GABAergic interneurons: Implications for understanding schizophrenia and bipolar disorder. *Neuropsychopharmacology* (in press).

BENES, F. M., J. B. TAYLOR, and M. CUNNINGHAM, 2000. Convergence and plasticity of monoaminergic systems in the medial prefrontal cortex during postnatal period: Implications for the development of psychopathology. *Cerebral Cortex* 10:1014–1027.

BENES, F. M., M. TURTLE, Y. KHAN, and P. FAROL, 1994. Myelination of a key relay zone in the hippocampal formation occurs in human brain during childhood, adolescence and adulthood. *Arch. Gen. Psychiatry* 51:477–484.

BENES, F. M., S. L. VINCENT, and R. MOLLOY, 1993. Dopamine-immunoreactive axon varicosities from non-random contacts with GABA-immunoreactive neurons in rat medial prefrontal cortex. *Synapse* 15:285–295.

BENES, F. M., S. L. VINCENT, R. MOLLOY, and Y. KAHN, 1996. Increased interaction of dopamine-immunoreactive varicosities with GABA neurons of rat medial prefrontal cortex during post-weanling period. *Synapse* 23:237–245.

BERGER, B., J. P. TASSIN, G. BLANK, M. A. MOYNE, and A. M. THIERRY, 1974. Histochemical confirmation for dopaminergic innervation of rat cerebral cortex after the destruction of noradrenergic ascending pathways. *Brain Res.* 81:332–337.

BERGER, B., and C. VERNEY, 1984. Development of the catecholamine innervation in rat neocortex. Morphological features. In *Monoamine Innervation of Cerebral Cortex*, L. Descarries, T. R. Reader, and H. H. Jasper, eds. New York: Allen R. Liss, pp. 95–121.

BERGSON, C., L. MRZLJAK, J. F. SMILEY, M. PAPPY, R. LEVENSON, and P. S. GOLDMAN-RAKIC, 1995. Regional, cellular, and subcellular variations in the distribution of D1 and D5 dopamine receptors in primate brain. *J. Neurosci.* 15(12):7821–7836.

BLINKOV, S. M., and I. I. GLEZER, 1968. *The Human Brain in Figures and Tables. A Quantitative Handbook.* New York: Plenum Press, pp. 123–136.

BRODERICK, P. A., and C. F. PHELIX, 1997. I. Serotonin (5-HT) within dopamine reward circuits signals open-field behavior. II. Basis for 5-HT–DA interaction in cocaine dysfunctional behavior. *Neurosci. Biobehav. Rev.* 21:227–260.

BROOKSBANK, B. W. L., D. J. ATKINSON, and R. BALASZ, 1981. Biochemical development of the human brain. II. Some parameters of the GABAergic system. *Dev. Neurosci.* 1:267–284.

BRUININK, A., W. LICHTENSTEINER, and M. SCHLUMPF, 1983. Pre- and postnatal ontogeny and characterization of dopaminergic D2, serotonergic S2, and spirodecanone binding sites in rat forebrain. *J. Neurochem.* 40:1227–1237.

CANDY, J. M., C. A. BLOXHAM, J. THOMPSON, M. JOHNSON, A. E. OAKLEY, and J. A. EDWARDSON, 1985. Evidence for the early prenatal development of cortical cholinergic afferents from the nucleus of Meynert in the human fetus. *Neurosci. Lett.* 61:91–95.

CANDY, J. M., and I. L. MARTIN, 1979. The postnatal development of the benzodiazepine receptor in the cerebral cortex and cerebellum of the rat. *J. Neurochem.* 32:655–658.

COYLE, J. T., and S. ENNA, 1976. Neurochemical aspects of the ontogenesis of GABAergic neurons in the rat brain. *Brain Res.* 111:119–133.

COYLE, J. T., and M. MOLLIVER, 1977. Major innervation of newborn rat cortex by monoaminergic neurons. *Science* 196:444–447.

COYLE, J. T., and H. I. YAMAMURA, 1976. Neurochemical aspects of the ontogenesis of GABAergic neurons in the rat brain. *Brain Res.* 118:429–440.

D'AMATO, R. J., M. BLUE, B. LARGENT, D. LYNCH, D. LEOBETTER, M. MOLLIVER, and S. SNYDER, 1987. Ontogeny of the serotonergic projection of rat neocortex: Transient expression of a dense innervation of primary sensory areas. *Proc. Natl. Acad. Sci. (USA)* 84:4322–4326.

DEGUCHI, T., and J. BARCHAS, 1972. Regional distribution and developmental change in tryptophan hydroxylase in rat brain. *J. Neurochem.* 19:927–929.

DESCARRIES, L., A. BEAUDET, and K. C. WATKINS, 1975. Serotonin nerve terminals in adult rat neocortex. *Brain Res.* 100:563–588.

DESKIN, R., F. J. SEIDLER, W. L. WHITMORE, and T. A. SLOTKIN, 1981. Development of a noradrenergic and dopaminergic receptor systems depends on maturation of their presynaptic nerve terminals in the rat brain. *J. Neurochem.* 36:1683–1690.

DIEBLER, M. F., E. FARKAS-BARGETON, and R. WEHRLE, 1979. Developmental changes of enzymes associated with energy metabolism and synthesis of some neurotransmitters in discrete areas of human neocortex. *J. Neurochem.* 32:429–435.

FLECHSIG, P., 1920. Anatomie des menschlichen Gehirns und Ruckenmarks auf myelogenetischer Gundlange. Leipzig: G. Thieme.

FOSSE, V. M., P. HEGGELUND, and F. FONNU, 1989. Postnatal development of glutamatergic, GABAergic and cholinergic neurotransmitter phenotypes in the visual cortex, lateral geniculate nucleus pulvinar and superior colliculus in cats. *J. Neurosci.* 9:426–435.

GELLMAN, R. L., and G. K. AGHAJANIAN, 1993. Pyramidal cells in piriform cortex receive a convergence of inputs from monoamine activated GABAergic interneurons. *Brain Res.* 600:63–73.

GILLES, F. H., W. SHANKLE, and E. C. DOOLING, 1983. Myelinated tracts: Growth patterns. In *The Developing Human Brain. Growth and Epidemiologic Neuropathology*, F. H. Gilles, A. Leviton, and E. C. Dooling, eds. Boston: John Wright-PSG, pp. 117–183.

GOLDMAN-RAKIC, P., 1981. Development and plasticity of primate frontal association cortex. In *The Organization of the Cerebral Cortex*, F. O. Smith, eds. Cambridge, Mass.: MIT Press, pp. 69–100.

GOLDMAN-RAKIC, P. S., J.-P. BOURGEOIS, and P. RAKIC, 1997. Synaptic substrate of cognitive development. Life span analysis of synaptogenesis in the prefrontal cortex of nonhuman primate. In *Development of Prefrontal Cortex. Evolution, Neurobiology and Behavior.* Baltimore, Md: Paul H. Brooks Publishing Co.

GOLDMAN-RAKIC, P. S., and R. M. BROWN, 1982. Postnatal development of monoamine content and synthesis in the cerebral cortex of rhesus monkeys. *Dev. Brain Res.* 4:339–349.

GUDELSKY, G. A., and J. F. NASH, 1996. Carrier-mediated release of serotonin by 3,4-methylenedioxymethamphetaine: Implications for serotonin-dopamine interactions. *J. Neurochem.* 66:243–249.

HAMON, M., and S. BOURGOIN, 1977. Biochemical aspects of the maturation of serotonergic neurons in the rat brain. In

*Brain: Fetal and Infant,* S. R. Berenger, ed. The Hague: Nijoff, pp. 239–261.

HARDEN, T. K., B. B. WOLFE, J. R. SPORN, J. P. PERKINS, and P. B. MOLINOFF, 1977. Ontogeny of beta-adrenergic receptors in rat cerebral cortex. *Brain Res.* 125:99–108.

HEDNER, T., and P. LUNDBERG, 1980. Serotonergic development in the postnatal rat brain. *J. Neural Transmission* 49:257–279.

HOWELL, L. L., P. W. CZOTY, and L. D. BYRD, 1997. Pharmacological interactions between serotonin and dopamine on behavior in the squirrel monkey. *Psychopharmacol. (Berlin)* 131:40–48.

HUNTLEY, G. W., J. H. MORRISON, A. PRIKHOZHAN, A., and S. C. SEALFON, 1992. Localization of multiple dopamine receptor subtype mRNAs in human and monkey motor cortex and striatum. *Mol. Brain Res.* 15:181–188.

HUTTENLOCHER, P. R., 1994. Synaptogenesis in human cerebral cortex. In *Human Behavior and the Developing Brain,* G. Dawson and K. W. Fischer, eds. New York: Guilford Press, pp. 137–152.

HUTTENLOCHER, P. R., and A. S. DABHOLKAR, 1997. Developmental anatomy of prefrontal cortex. In *Development of the Prefrontal Cortex,* N. A. Krasnegor, G. R. Lyon, and P. S. Goldman-Rakic, eds. Baltimore: Paul Brookes Publishing, pp. 69–84.

IYER, R. N., and C. W. BRADBERRY, 1996. Serotonin-mediated increase in prefrontal cortex dopamine release: Pharmacological characterization. *J. Pharmacol. Exp. Ther.* 277:40–47.

JOHNSTON, M. V., 1988. Biochemistry of neurotransmitters in cortical development. In *Cerebral Cortex,* Vol. 7, A. Peter and E. G. Jones, eds. New York: Plenum Press, pp. 211–236.

JOHNSTON, M. V., and J. T. COYLE, 1980. Ontogeny of neurochemical markers for noradrenergic, GABAergic and cholinergic neurons in neocortex lesioned with methylazoxymethanol acetate. *J. Neurochem.* 34:1429–1441.

JOHNSTON, M. V., M. MCKINNEY, and J. T. COYLE, 1979. Evidence for a cholinergic projection to neocortex from neurons in basal forebrain. *Proc. Natl. Acad. Sci. (USA)* 76:5392–5396.

JONES, E. G., 1987. GABA-peptide neurons in primate cerebral cortex. *J. Mind Behav.* 8:519–536.

JONES, E. G., and S. H. C. HENDRY, 1984. Basket cells. In *Cerebral Cortex, Vol. 1: Cellular Components of the Cerebral Cortex,* A. Peters and E. G. Jones, eds. New York: Plenum Press, pp. 309–336.

KALSBEEK, A., P. VOORN, R. M. BUIJS, C. W. POOL, and H. B. UYLINGS, 1988. Development of the dopaminergic innervation in the prefrontal cortex of rat. *J. Comp. Neurol.* 269:58–72.

KASAMATSU, T., and J. W. PETTIGREW, 1976. Depletion of brain catecholamines: Failure of monocular dominance shift after monocular conclusion in kittens. *Science* 194:206–209.

KOSTOVIC, I., J. SKAVIC, and D. STRINOVIC, 1988. Acetylcholinesterase in the human frontal associative cortex during the period of cognitive development: Early laminar shifts and late innervation of pyramidal neurons. *Neurosci. Lett.* 90:107–112.

KVALE, I., V. M. FOSSE, and F. FONNUM, 1983. Development of neurotransmitter parameters in lateral geniculate body, superior colliculus and visual cortex of the albino rat. *Dev. Brain Res.* 7:137–145.

LAUDER, J. M., and F. E. BLOOM, 1974. Ontogeny of monoamine neurons in the locus coeruleus, raphe nuclei and substantia nigra of the rat. I. Cell differentiation. *J. Comp. Neurol.* 155:469–482.

LEVEY, A. I., B. H. WAINER, D. B. RAYE, E. J. MUFSON, and M. M. MESULAM, 1984. Choline acetyltransferase immunoreactive neurons intrinsic to rodent cortex and distinction from acetylcholinesterase-positive neurons. *Neuroscience* 13:341–353.

LEVITT, P., and R. Y. MOORE, 1978. Noradrenaline neuron innervation of the neurocortex in the rat. *Brain Res.* 139:219–231.

LEVITT, P., and P. RAKIC, 1982. The time of genesis, embryonic origin and differentiation of brainstem monoamine neurons in the rhesus monkey. *Brain Res.* 4:35–37.

LIDOV, H. G., and M. E. MOLLIVER, 1982. An immunohistochemical study of serotonin neuron development in the rat: Ascending pathways and terminal fields. *Brain Res. Bull.* 8:389–340.

LINDVALL, O., A. BJORKLUND, and I. DIVAC, 1978. Organization of catecholamine neurons projecting to frontal cortex in the rat. *Brain Res.* 142:1–24.

MARCUSSON, J. O., D. G. MORGAN, B. WINBLAD, and C. E. FINCH, 1984. Serotonin-2 binding sites in human frontal cortex and hippocampus: Selective loss of S-2A sites with ages. *Brain Res.* 311:51–56.

MARIN-PADILLA, M., 1970a. Prenatal and early postnatal ontogenesis of the human motor cortex: A Golgi study. I. The sequential development of the cortical layers. *Brain Res.* 23:167–183.

MARIN-PADILLA, M., 1970b. Prenatal and early post-natal ontogenesis of the human motor cortex: A Golgi Study. II. The basket-pyramidal system. *Brain Res.* 23:185–191.

MESULAM, M.-M., 1983. The functional anatomy and hemispheric specialization of directed attention. The role of the parietal lobe and its commentary. *Trends Neurosci.* 6:384–387.

MICHEL, A. E., and L. H. GAREY, 1984. The development of dendritic spines in the human visual cortex. *Human Neurobiol.* 3:223–227.

MORILAK, D. A., S. J. GARLOW, and R. D. CIARANELLO, 1993. Immunocytochemical localization and description of neurons expressing 5-HT-2 receptors in the rat brain. *Neuroscience* 54:701–717.

NELSON, S. B., M. A. SCHWARTZ, and J. D. DANIELS, 1975. Clonidine and cortical plasticity: Possible evidence for noradrenergic involvement. *Dev. Brain Res.* 23:39–50.

PEHEK, E. A., 1996. Local infusion of the serotonin antagonist ritanserin or ICS 205,930 increases in vivo dopamine release in the rat medial prefrontal cortex. *Synapse* 24:12–18.

PENIT-SORIA, J., E. AUDINAT, and F. CREPEL, 1987. Excitation of rat prefrontal cortical neurons by dopamine: An in vitro electrophysiological study. *Brain Res.* 425:363–374.

PENIT-SORIA, J., S. RETAUX, and Y. MAURIN, 1989. Effets de la stimulation des recepteurs D1 et D2 dopaminergiques sur la liberation d'acide y-(3H) aminobutyrique induite electriquement dans le cortex prefrontal du rat. *C.R. Acad. Sci. Paris* 309(III):441–446.

POLIAKOV, G. I., 1965. Development of the cerebral neocortex during the first half of intrauterine life. In *Development of the Child's Brain,* S. A. Sarkisov, ed. Leningrad: Medicina, pp. 22–52.

RAKIC, P., 1974. Neurons in rhesus monkey visual cortex. Systematic relation between time of origin and eventual disposition. *Science* 183:425–427.

RAVIKUMAR, B. V., and P. S. SASTARY, 1985. Muscarinic cholinergic receptors in human fetal brain: Characterization and ontogeny of ($^3$H)quinuclidinyl benzilate bind sites in frontal cortex. *J. Neurochem.* 44:240–246.

RETAUX, S., M. J. BESSON, and J. PENIT-SORIA, 1991a. Opposing effects of dopamine D2 receptor stimulation on the spontaneous and the electrically evoked release of ($^3$H)GABA on rat prefrontal cortex slices. *Neuroscience* 42(1):61–71.

RETAUX, S., M. J. BESSON, and J. PENIT-SORIA, 1991b. Synergism between D1 and D2 dopamine receptors in the inhibition of the evoked release of ($^3$H)GABA in the rat prefrontal cortex. *Neuroscience* 43(2/3):323–329.

SCHLIEBS, R., E. KULLMAN, and V. BIGL, 1986. Development of glutamate binding sites in the visual structures of the rat brain: Effect of visual pattern deprivation. *Biomed. Biophys. Acta* 45:4495–4506.

SHELDON, P. W., and G. K. AGHAJANIAN, 1991. Excitatory responses to serotonin (5-HT) in neurons of the rat piriform cortex: Evidence for mediation by 5-HT1C receptors in pyramidal cells and 5-HT2 receptors in interneurons. *Synapse* 9:208–218.

SIDMAN, R., and P. RAKIC, 1973. Neuronal migration with special reference to developing human brain. *Brain Res.* 62:1–35.

SILLITO, A. M., 1984. Functional considerations of the operation of GABAergic inhibitory processes in the visual cortex. In *Cerebral Cortex. Vol. 2: Functional Properties of Cortical Cells*, E. G. Jones and A. Peters, eds. New York: Plenum Press, pp. 91–118.

SOMOGYI, P., and A. COWEY, 1984. Double bouquet cells. In *Cerebral Cortex, Vol. 1: Cellular Components of Cerebral Cortex*, A. Peters and E. G. Jones, eds. New York: Plenum Press, pp. 337–360.

STREIT, P., 1984. Glutamate and aspartate as transmitter candidates for systems of the cerebral cortex. In *Cerebral Cortex. Vol. 2: Functional Properties of Cortical Cells*, E. G. Jones and A. Peters, eds. New York: Plenum Press, pp. 119–144.

TAYLOR, J., and F. M. BENES, 1996. Colocalization of glutamate decarboxylase, tyrosine hydroxylase and serotonin immunoreactivity in rat medial prefrontal cortex. *NeuroscienceNET* 1:10001.

TAYLOR, J., M. CUNNINGHAM, and F. M. BENES, 1998. Neonatal raphe lesions increase dopamine fibers in prefrontal cortex of adult rats. *NeuroReport* 9:1811–1815.

THIERRY, A. M., G. BLANC, A. SOBEL, L. STINUS, and J. GLOWINSKI, 1973. Dopaminergic terminals in the rat cortex. *Science* 182:499–501.

UPHOUSE, L. L., and S. C. BONDY, 1981. The maturation of cortical serotonergic binding sites. *Dev. Brain Res.* 1:415–417.

VERNEY, C., B. A. J. BERGER, A. VIGNY, and M. GAY, 1982. Development of the dopaminergic innervation of the rat cerebral cortex. A light microscopic immunocytochemical study using anti-tyrosine hydroxylase antibodies. *Dev. Brain Res.* 5:41–52.

VINCENT, S. L., Y. KHAN, and F. M. BENES, 1995. Cellular and co-localization of dopamine with $D_1$ and $D_2$ receptors in rat medial prefrontal cortex. *Synapse.* 19:112–120.

VINCENT, S. L., Y. KHAN, and F. M. BENES, 1993. Cellular distribution of dopamine D1 and D2 receptors in rat medial prefrontal cortex. *J. Neurosci.* 13:2551–2561.

VINCENT, S. L., L. PABREZA, and F. M. BENES, 1995. Postnatal maturation of GABA-immunoreactive neurons of rat medial prefrontal cortex. *J. Comp. Neurol.* 355:81–92.

WALLACE, J. A., and J. M. LAUDER, 1983. Development of the serotonergic system in the rat embryo: An immunocytochemical study. *Brain Res. Bull.* 10:459–479.

WEST, A. R., and M. P. GALLOWAY, 1996. Regulation of serotonin-facilitated dopamine release in vivo: The role of protein kinase A activating transduction mechanisms. *Synapse* 23:20–27.

WISE, S. P., J. W. FLESHMAN, and E. G. JONES, 1979. Maturation of pyramidal cell form in relation to developing afferent and efferent connections of the rat somatic sensory cortex. *J. Neurosci.* 4:1275–1297.

WISE, S. P., and E. G. JONES, 1978. Developmental studies of thalamocortical and commissural connections in the rat somatic sensory cortex. *J. Comp. Neurol.* 178:187–208.

YAKOVLEV, P., and A. LECOURS, 1967. The myelinogenetic cycles of regional maturation of the brain. In *Regional Development of the Brain Early in Life*, A. Minkowski, ed. Blackwell: Oxford, pp. 3–70.

ZILLES, K. W. R., U. BUSCHING, and A. SCHLEICHER, 1986. Ontogenesis of the laminar structure in areas 17 and 18 of the human visual cortex. A quantitative study. *Anat. Embryol.* 174:339–353.

# 7 Adult Neurogenesis in the Hippocampal Formation

PATIMA TANAPAT,
NICHOLAS B. HASTINGS,
AND ELIZABETH GOULD

ABSTRACT   The dentate gyrus of the hippocampal formation continues to produce granule neurons throughout adulthood in many species, including humans. Although the functional significance of adult hippocampal neurogenesis is unknown, its magnitude and conservation across taxa suggest that this process may be fundamental to normal hippocampal function. Previous studies have demonstrated that the production and survival of neurons in the adult hippocampal formation are regulated by both experiential and neuroendocrine factors. Stress reduces the proliferation of granule cell precursors, in part, by increasing circulating levels of adrenal glucocorticoids. Conversely, estrogen increases the proliferation of granule cell precursors and is responsible for a sex difference favoring females in the production of immature granule neurons. Additionally, certain types of learning enhance the number of new neurons in the dentate gyrus of adult rats. Collectively, these findings suggest that adult-generated neurons are a substrate by which experiential and hormonal cues influence normal hippocampal function.

Most neurons in the adult mammalian brain are produced during a discrete part of the embryonic period. However, as indicated by a group of now classic studies, a substantial number of granule cells are produced in the cerebellum, olfactory bulb, and hippocampal formation during the postnatal period (Altman, 1969; Altman and Das, 1966). Furthermore, in the olfactory bulb and dentate gyrus of the hippocampal formation, neurogenesis continues throughout adulthood (Altman and Das, 1965). The concept that structural modifications, such as changes in dendrite length or synapse number, are a normal physiological occurrence in the adult brain was (and remains) fairly controversial. Thus, the observation that new neurons are produced in the mammalian olfactory bulb and dentate gyrus throughout adulthood was surprising, and, in fact, has only recently gained acceptance.

Adult neurogenesis has been demonstrated to occur in the brains of all vertebrate species investigated thus far (Altman and Das, 1965; Goldman and Nottebohm, 1983; Gould et al., 1997, 1998, 1999b; Kornack and Rakic, 1999; Perez-Canellas and Garcia-Verdugo, 1996; Polenov and Chetverukhin, 1993; Zupanc, 1999), including humans (Eriksson et al., 1998), suggesting that it is both a primitive and a highly conserved process. Quantitative estimates indicate that a significant amount of hippocampal neurogenesis even occurs in the adult primate brain (Eriksson et al., 1998; Gould et al., 1998, 1999b). The conservation of adult hippocampal neurogenesis across vertebrate taxa suggests a fundamental biological significance that is only beginning to be explored experimentally. Although the functional significance of this process is not yet known, the discovery of adult neurogenesis in the hippocampal formation has significantly altered the way in which the adult brain is viewed in terms of its potential for structural change. Perhaps of even greater significance is the possibility that adult neurogenesis can be harnessed to improve the clinical prognosis of neurodegenerative disease and traumatic brain injury. However, before this goal can be realized, investigators must first elucidate the role that adult-generated neurons play in normal functional circuitry, as well as the factors that regulate the production, differentiation, survival, and integration of newly generated neurons into the adult neuroanatomic context.

In this chapter, we first consider the key experimental findings that led to the discovery that the adult brain continues to produce hippocampal neurons. In so doing, we discuss techniques important for analyses of neurogenesis in the adult brain. Second, we consider the factors and conditions, including hormones and experience, that regulate neurogenesis in the hippocampal formation. Third, we consider the possible role of late-generated cells in the normal function of this brain region.

PATIMA TANAPAT, NICHOLAS B. HASTINGS, AND ELIZABETH GOULD   Department of Psychology, Princeton University, Princeton, New Jersey.

## The discovery of neurogenesis in the adult mammalian brain

The demonstration and study of neurogenesis depend on methods that can selectively label newly generated cells and identify their phenotype—i.e., glial or neuronal. Early histologists were hampered in this respect by having to rely on methods that, although providing excellent resolution of the fine structural characteristics of brain cells in some cases, were not adequately cell-type selective and were unsuitable for specifically identifying newly generated cells. Thus, the results obtained by such methods, albeit of great value in understanding the morphology of brain cells and the brain in general, were of limited use in studying phenomena such as developmental or adult neurogenesis.

Altman published the first paper that formally presented the possibility that neurogenesis occurs in the olfactory bulb and dentate gyrus of adult rats (Altman and Das, 1965). This seminal work relied upon the development and application of an experimental method called [3]H-thymidine autoradiography. This technique takes advantage of the fact that cells will incorporate [3]H-thymidine during DNA, but not RNA, synthesis. Thus, when injected into an animal, [3]H-thymidine is taken up by cells in the DNA synthetic phase of the cell cycle. [3]H-Thymidine is a heritable marker, meaning that any subsequent progeny of the labeled cell are themselves radioactively labeled. The specificity and stability of thymidine incorporation, combined with the relatively low energy and long half-life of the tritium tag, make this technique ideal for mapping mitotically active cell populations at the single cell level. This degree of resolution also permits the detailed morphological characterization and phenotyping of the labeled cell when sufficiently long survival times are employed, and enabled Altman (Altman and Das, 1965) to determine that [3]H-thymidine-labeled cells in the olfactory bulb and dentate gyrus had morphological characteristics identical to those of resident granule neurons (Altman and Das, 1965).

Although it was clear from Altman's work that new cells are added to the adult rodent olfactory bulb and hippocampal formation, the identity and fate of these cells remained very much in question until recently. Although [3]H-thymidine-labeled cells could be localized to the granule cell layer and resembled neurons morphologically, light microscopic examination was insufficient to identify the labeled cells unequivocally as neurons. Kaplan and Hinds (1977) partially resolved this issue by demonstrating at the ultrastructural level that adult-generated neurons in the dentate gyrus of the rat receive synaptic input on their cell bodies and dendrites.

Because glial cells may, under some circumstances, receive synaptic input (Oppenheim et al., 1978), it was not until immunohistochemical techniques that enable staining for cell-type–specific antigens, and combined thymidine labeling/retrograde axon tracing were developed that definitive evidence of adult-generated neurons in the dentate gyrus was obtained. These studies showed that [3]H-thymidine-labeled cells expressed a marker of mature neurons (Cameron et al., 1993; Okano et al., 1993). [3]H-Thymidine-labeled cells were also shown to incorporate retrograde tracers when injected into the CA3 region (Stanfield and Trice, 1988), indicating that these cells send axons to a major target site of developmentally generated granule cells (figures 7.1 [see color plate 10] and 7.2). Taken together, these studies provided convincing evidence that the adult mammalian dentate gyrus produces cells with neuronal

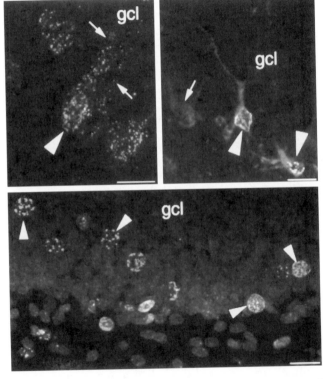

FIGURE 7.1   Confocal laser scanning microscope images of new cells in the rat dentate gyrus. (*Top left*) BrdU-labeled cell (green, arrowhead) in the granule cell layer (gvcl) of an adult rat that is labeled with the retrograde tracer fluororuby. Arrows depict dendrites that are labeled with retrograde tracer. (*Top right*) BrdU-labeled cells (red, arrowheads) in the granule cell layer of an adult rat that are immunoreactive for TOAD-64 (green), a marker of immature neurons. Arrows depict TOAD-64–positive cells that are not labeled with BrdU. (*Bottom*) BrdU-labeled cells (red, arrowheads) in the dentate gyrus of a 3-week-old rat. Granule cells not labeled with BrdU are counterstained with the DNA dye Hoechst 33342 (blue). Scale bar = 10 μm.

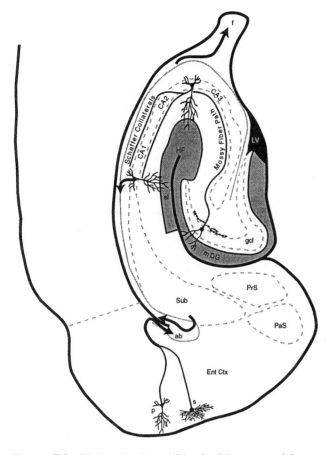

FIGURE 7.2 Major circuitry within the hippocampal formation of the adult rat shown in the horizontal plane. Excitatory cortical inputs to the dentate gyrus and area CA3 arise predominantly from stellate and pyramidal cells in layers 2 and 3, respectively, of the entorhinal cortex. These cortical afferents enter the angular bundle as the perforant path and are distributed to the molecular layer of the dentate gyrus (mDG*n*) and stratum lacunosum moleculare of Ammon's horn (sl; indicated by gray area). Granule cells located in the granule cell layer (gcl) supply a major excitatory afferent to area CA3 via the mossy fiber pathway. From area CA3, information is relayed via the Schaffer collaterals to area CA1. Projections from area CA1 are widespread and include inputs to the subiculum (Sub) proper, as well as to the parasubiculum (PaS) and presubiculum (PrS) and various cortical regions. Evidence suggests that newly generated granule cells become integrated into this circuitry. Cells produced in the dentate gyrus in adulthood extend axons into the CA3 region (Hastings and Gould, 1999; Markakis and Gage, 1999; Stanfield and Trice, 1988). New neurons have been shown to receive synaptic input (Kaplan and Hinds, 1977; Markakis and Gage, 1999) but the origin of these afferents remains unknown. *Abbreviations:* ab = angular bundle; CA1, CA2, and CA3 = regions of Ammon's horn; Ent Ctx = entorhinal cortex; f = fornix; HF = hippocampal fissure; LV = lateral ventricle; p = pyramidal cell of the entorhinal cortex; s = stellate cell of the entorhinal cortex.

characteristics and, moreover, that these cells may become incorporated into a functioning hippocampal circuit.

Although the existence of adult neurogenesis in rodent brains had been firmly established (Gould et al., 1999c), this work did little to encourage study of the phenomenon. This was largely attributable to the inability to demonstrate adult neurogenesis in primates. For example, while [3]H-thymidine-labeled cells could be readily demonstrated in the dentate gyrus of adult macaques, they were few in number and did not have the morphological characteristics of neurons; it was therefore concluded that they were most likely to be glia (Eckenhoff and Rakic, 1988; Rakic, 1985). In addition, the observation that the adult brains of less complex vertebrates, such as fish and amphibians, undergo a remarkable degree of regeneration following injury, whereas the adult mammalian brain does not, seemed incongruous with the concept of continual neurogenesis in the adult mammalian brain. As a result, the phenomenon was discounted as being specific only to certain vertebrate species, and, hence, was considered of relatively little importance.

A NEW METHOD FOR THE DETECTION OF NEWLY GENERATED CELLS PROMOTES THE DISCOVERY OF HIPPOCAMPAL NEUROGENESIS IN ADULT PRIMATES    A significant breakthrough in the study of adult neurogenesis was the replacement of [3]H-thymidine autoradiography with 5-bromo-2'-deoxyuridine (BrdU) labeling. This method provides a more sensitive means by which the number of cells generated in adulthood can be assessed. 5-Bromo-2'-deoxyuridine, a halogenated analog of thymidine, is incorporated into DNA and can be immunohistochemically detected with antibodies raised specifically against its unique structure. The advantages of this technique compared to [3]H-thymidine autoradiography stem from its ability to detect nucleotide incorporation immunohistochemically:

1. Neural tissues are highly permeable to antibodies, allowing cells that have incorporated BrdU to be detected through an entire section. In contrast, because [3]H labels only allow for the detection of labeled cells in the top 1–3 μm of a tissue section, [3]H-thymidine autoradiography underestimates the number of new cells in thicker sections.

2. Because BrdU labeling relies on immunological processes, its sensitivity may be amplified, increasing signal and reducing label dilution in cells that have undergone several divisions.

3. The technique is highly compatible with the immunodetection of cell-type specific antigens used to phenotype cells.

The greater sensitivity and cleaner signal of the BrdU labeling method, combined with unbiased cell counting techniques used in stereological analyses, have led to the first attempts at quantifying neurogenesis in the adult brain. These studies have revealed that several thousand new granule cells are generated daily in the dentate gyrus of adult rats (Gould et al., 1999a; Tanapat et al., 1999). The majority of these adult-generated cells express the immature neuronal markers Turned On After Division 64 kD (TOAD-64) (figure 7.1, top right panel) and the polysialylated form of neural cell adhesion molecule (PSA-NCAM). Moreover, many adult-generated cells ultimately express markers of mature granule cells, including calbindin, neuronal specific enolase (NSE), neuronal nuclei (NeuN) and the NMDA receptor subunit 1 (NR1) (Gould and Tanapat, 1997; Gould et al., 1999a; Tanapat et al., 1999). An additional study using BrdU in conjunction with synapsin immunohistochemistry and fluorescent retrograde tracing methods has suggested that adult-generated neurons receive synaptic input and extend axons into hippocampal area CA3 (Markakis and Gage, 1999). The use of BrdU also allowed researchers to reinvestigate the issue of adult neurogenesis in primates, establishing the occurrence of hippocampal neurogenesis in adult monkeys and humans.

## Development of the dentate gyrus

During the embryonic period, granule neurons arise from progenitor cells located in a discrete part of the neuroepithelium in the wall of the lateral ventricle (figure 7.3). These cells migrate across the hippocampal rudiment to reside in the incipient granule cell layer (Altman and Bayer, 1990). A subpopulation of these progenitor cells does not undergo final division and is maintained in the hilus and subgranular zone of the dentate gyrus. These cells continue to divide and give rise to daughter cells that differentiate into granule neurons and ultimately reside in the granule cell layer.

In the rat, the majority of neurons in the dentate gyrus are produced during the first two postnatal weeks from this secondary proliferative zone as well as from progenitor cells within the developing granule cell layer. By the end of the second postnatal week, cell proliferation and migration decrease significantly and the granule cell layer has been formed. Development of the dentate gyrus in the macaque differs from that of the rat in that the structure of the granule cell layer is formed during the prenatal period (Nowakowski and Rakic, 1981). However, a significant number of new granule neurons continue to be produced within the dentate gyrus well into adulthood in both rodents and

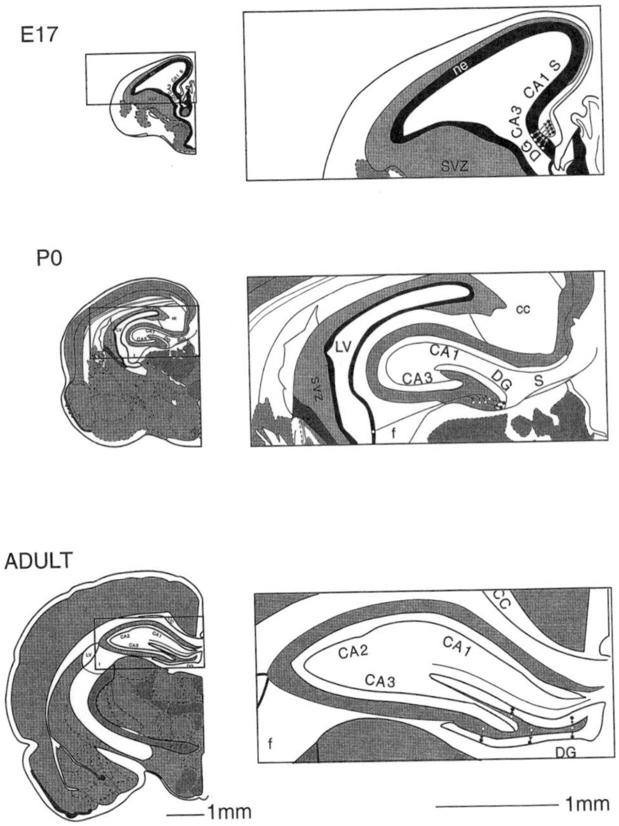

FIGURE 7.3 Coronal representations of the hippocampal formation in the developing and adult rat brain. The diagrams on the right represent a magnified view of the boxed area on the left. *E17:* The production of granule cells begins around embryonic day 17. During this period of development, immature neurons are generated from the mitotic division of precursor cells (white circles) located in the neuroepithelium (black region). These daughter cells then migrate away from the germinal matrix, differentiate and begin to form the granule cell layer (black circles). *P0:* The production of granule cells is maximal during the postnatal period. While dentate gyrus granule neurons continue to be produced from the neuroepithelium, many arise from a secondary germinal matrix formed by precursor cells that have migrated from the embryonic neuroepithelium and reside in the dentate hilar and subgranular zones (white circles). At this point in development, new granule neurons are added predominantly to the growing tip of the ventral blade (black circles). *Adult:* New granule neurons continue to be produced in the dentate gyrus throughout adulthood. Neuronal precursors (white circles) reside in the hilus and subgranular zone. These cells remain mitotically active in the adult mammal, continuously giving rise to new granule cells (black circles). *Abbreviations:* CA1, CA2, and CA3 = regions of Ammon's horn; cc = corpus collosum; DG = dentate gyrus; f = fornix; LV = lateral ventricle; ne = neuroepithelium; S = subicular area; svz = subventricular zone.

primates. These cells are produced from progenitors located in the hilus and subgranular zone, the region between the granule cell layer and hilus. The addition of these new cells to the dentate gyrus in adulthood probably represents a turnover of adult-generated cells as available evidence suggests that many of the new cells eventually die (Cameron et al., 1993; Gould et al., 1999a).

## Postnatal hippocampal neurogenesis is regulated by neuroendocrine factors

The profound influence of steroid hormones on the organization and activation of certain behaviors has been recognized for decades. Numerous studies suggest that these hormones affect the expression of behavior by altering the structural development of the brain. Over the past 15 years, studies have demonstrated that steroid hormones alter the structure of the adult brain as well, by affecting dendrites, synapses, and cell survival (Sapolsky, Krey, and McEwen, 1985; Woolley et al., 1990). More recently, studies have demonstrated a new role for adrenal and ovarian steroids in mediating brain structure by altering the proliferation of granule cell precursors (Cameron and Gould, 1994; Tanapat et al., 1999).

ADRENAL STEROIDS  Several lines of evidence indicate that an inverse relationship exists between adrenal steroid levels and the proliferation of granule cell precursors. First, a naturally occurring negative correlation between levels of circulating adrenal steroids and hippocampal granule neuron production is observed across the lifespan. In the rat, the first two postnatal weeks, a period of time termed the stress hyporesponsive period, are characterized by low levels of circulating adrenal steroids. During this time, granule neuron production is maximal (Sapolsky and Meaney, 1986; Schlessinger, Cowan, and Gottlieb, 1975). Conversely, during adulthood, when levels of circulating adrenal steroids are high, granule neuron production is relatively low. With aging, the production of new cells is significantly diminished in both rats (Kuhn, Dickinson-Anson, and Gage, 1996) and macaques (Gould et al., 1999b) coincident with age-related increases in the levels of circulating glucocorticoids (Sapolsky, 1992; Sapolsky and Altmann, 1991). Consistent with these natural observations, experimental manipulations of glucocorticoids have demonstrated a negative relationship between these adrenal steroids and granule neuron production. For example, experimental increases in glucocorticoids performed in rats during the stress hyporesponsive period diminish the rate of granule cell production in the dentate gyrus (Gould et al., 1991). Likewise, studies examining the effects of glucocorticoid manipulations on cell proliferation in adult rats have demonstrated that the removal of adrenal steroids via adrenalectomy results in an increase in the proliferation of granule cell precursors and, ultimately, in the production of new neurons, whereas treatment with the adrenal glucocorticoid corticosterone results in a decrease (Gould, 1994; Gould et al., 1991). Furthermore, a recent study has demonstrated that removal of circulating glucocorticoids in aged rats stimulates cell proliferation in the dentate gyrus to levels observed in adrenalectomized young adults (Cameron and McKay, 1999). Collectively, these observations suggest that adverse psychological or physical experiences—i.e., stressful experiences, which stimulate the release of adrenal corticosteroids—may act to suppress adult neurogenesis. (We will return later to a discussion of the role of stress in regulating neurogenesis.)

OVARIAN STEROIDS  In contrast to the suppressive action of adrenal steroids on postnatal neuron production, the ovarian steroid hormone estrogen has been shown to stimulate the production of new granule neurons in the dentate gyrus (Tanapat et al., 1999). In the rat, a natural fluctuation in cell proliferation occurs across the estrous cycle; the production of new granule cells is greatest during proestrus, the stage of maximal estrogen levels. Experimental evidence has confirmed that the removal of estrogen via ovariectomy results in a decrease in the proliferation of granule cell precursors, whereas replacement with estrogen rapidly reverses this effect (figure 7.4). In addition to increasing the production of new cells, evidence also suggests that estrogen exerts important survival effects on adult-erated cells in the dentate gyrus (Tanapat et al., 1999). This observation is consistent with evidence from avian systems demonstrating that estrogen enhances the survival of adult-generated cells (Burek, Nordeen, and Nordeen, 1995).

In recent work, it has been demonstrated that female rats produce more new granule cells than do males (Tanapat et al., 1999; figure 7.5). The greater number of cells produced in the dentate gyrus of females appears to be the result of the proestrus-associated peak in cell proliferation. Under standard laboratory conditions, many of these cells degenerate over time such that a sex difference in the number of adult-generated mature granule neurons is eventually undetectable. However, this does not preclude the possibility that estrogen-induced increases in the pool of immature granule neurons exert an important impact on hippocampal function, a possibility that will be examined further.

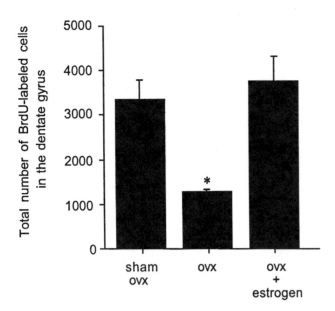

FIGURE 7.4 Stereological estimates of the total numbers of BrdU-labeled cells in the dentate gyrus of adult female rats that were sham-ovariectomized, ovariectomized, or ovariectomized and estrogen replaced. Ovariectomy resulted in a significant decrease in the total numbers of BrdU-labeled cells in the dentate gyrus compared to sham ovariectomy. Estrogen replacement following surgery rapidly reversed this effect. Bars represent mean $\pm$ SEM obtained from 4–5 animals. Asterisk indicates a significant difference, $p < 0.05$.

## Postnatal hippocampal neurogenesis is regulated by experience

Altman originally suggested that the relatively late, postnatal production of granule cells in the dentate gyrus was related to a modulatory role that these "microneurons" might play in shaping immature behavioral processes (Altman, Brunner, and Bayer, 1973; Altman and Das, 1967). Because the majority of neurons in the dentate gyrus are produced postnatally, this brain region has the potential to undergo significant experience-dependent structural changes during both postnatal development and adulthood. Additionally, experiences that regulate the postnatal production of granule neurons may also affect the structure of the hippocampal formation via regulation of processes that are associated with the production of new neurons, such as synaptogenesis, and dendrite and axon formation.

The potential for experience-dependent changes in the structure of the hippocampal formation suggests possible cellular mechanisms that may contribute to the function of this brain region. In the remainder of this chapter, we discuss experiences that are currently known to regulate the postnatal production of new

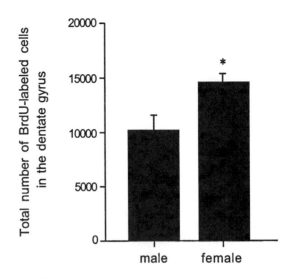

FIGURE 7.5 Stereological estimates of the total numbers of BrdU-labeled cells in the dentate gyrus of adult male and female rats. Two days following a period of 5 daily BrdU injections, females had significantly greater numbers of BrdU-labeled cells in the dentate gyrus compared to males. Bars represent mean $\pm$ SEM obtained from 6 animals. Asterisk indicates a significant difference, $p < 0.05$.

hippocampal granule neurons, and consider the potential functional relevance of adult hippocampal neurogenesis.

STRESS Numerous studies have demonstrated that stressful experiences alter the production of new hippocampal granule cells by affecting the proliferation of precursor cells. During the stress hyporesponsive period, many stressors that normally activate the hypothalamic-pituitary-adrenal (HPA) axis fail to elevate circulating glucocorticoids significantly. During this time, however, exposure to the odors of natural predators is sufficient to increase levels of circulating glucocorticoids in male rat pups (Tanapat, Galea, and Gould, 1998). Given that adrenal steroids are known to suppress the production of new neurons, it is not surprising that exposure to the odors of an unfamiliar adult male rat also suppresses the proliferation of granule cell precursors in male rat pups (Tanapat, Galea, and Gould, 1998). Consistent with this observation, stress-induced suppression of cell proliferation in the dentate gyrus has been shown to occur in adult animals as well. In adult male rats, exposure to trimethylthiazoline, a component of fox feces, results in an activation of the HPA axis accompanied by an inhibition of the proliferation of granule cell precursors (Galea, Tanapat, and Gould, 1996).

Stress-induced suppression of cell proliferation in the dentate gyrus in adulthood appears to be common to many mammalian species. Adult marmosets, when exposed to the social stress of a resident-intruder paradigm, demonstrate significant decreases in the proliferation of granule cell precursors (Gould et al., 1998). Likewise, adult tree shrews demonstrate inhibited cell proliferation following exposure to subordination stress, a condition sufficient to elevate circulating levels of cortisol, the main glucocorticoid of tree shrews (Gould et al., 1997). Experimental evidence indicates that stress-induced suppression of cell proliferation is also capable of exerting an additive effect on the granule cell population. Chronic exposure to subordination stress, a stressor that does not evoke adaptation of the HPA axis with repeated exposure over time, results in continual suppression of cell proliferation (figure 7.6) and a decrease in the volume of the granule cell layer (Fuchs et al., 1997). Collectively, these studies indicate that stress inhibits the proliferation of granule cell precursors during development as well as in adulthood in a variety of mammals. The factors that underlie the effect of stress on cell proliferation remain unknown. However, it is likely that glucocorticoids play a role as these steroids, which are elevated following stress, have an inhibitory effect on the production of new granule cells (Cameron and Gould, 1994).

LEARNING  Previous studies have reported changes in the number of new hippocampal neurons in adult animals living in conditions that are associated with enhanced learning opportunities. For example, a striking relationship between experience and neurogenesis exists in the hippocampal complex of black-capped chickadees (Barnea and Nottebohm, 1994). While significant cell proliferation occurs in the hippocampal complex of adult chickadees throughout the year, the recruitment or maintenance of new neurons is maximal during times of the year when these birds engage in seed storage and retrieval, behaviors that are likely to involve spatial navigation learning and hence the hippocampal complex. Additionally, black-capped chickadees that live in the wild maintain more new hippocampal neurons than do those that live in captivity.

Kempermann and colleagues have shown that mice living in an enriched laboratory environment maintain more new hippocampal granule neurons than do those living in standard laboratory control conditions. In rodents, the influence of environmental complexity on the number of new granule neurons appears to be maintained throughout the lifespan, ranging from juvenile to aged animals (Kempermann, Kuhn, and Gage, 1997, 1998). Although many variables such as stress, social interaction, nutrition, and activity levels differ between living in the wild and living in captivity, and between living in an "enriched" environment compared to living in the relatively deprived conditions of laboratory housing, these findings present the possibility that increased learning opportunities enhance the survival of new neurons.

Recently, we have directly demonstrated that hippocampal-dependent learning enhances the survival of adult-generated neurons in the dentate gyrus of male rats (Gould et al., 1999b). Under standard laboratory conditions, many adult-generated cells degenerate over time, exhibiting a particularly steep decline between one and two weeks following their production. Training on one of two hippocampal-dependent tasks—place learning in a Morris water maze (figure 7.7, p. 100) or classical trace eyeblink conditioning (figure 7.8, p. 101)—during this time period significantly enhances the survival, but not the production (figure 7.9, p. 101), of adult-generated neurons in adult rats. In contrast, training on tasks that do not require the hippocampus, such as cue learning in a Morris water maze or delay eyeblink conditioning, does not alter the number of new neurons (figures 7.6 and 7.10, p. 102).

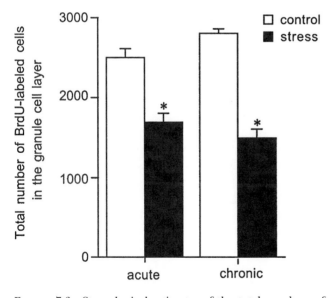

FIGURE 7.6  Stereological estimates of the total numbers of BrdU-labeled cells in the granule cell layer of adult tree shrews. Adult tree shrews demonstrated a significant decrease in the numbers of proliferating cells compared to control animals following exposure to either acute or chronic stress. Bars represent mean ± SEM obtained from 4 animals. Asterisk indicates a significant difference, $p < 0.05$.

**A**

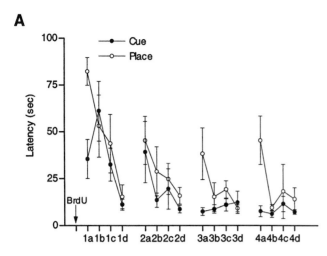

**B**

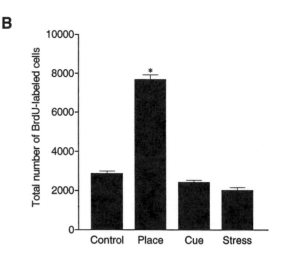

FIGURE 7.7    Place learning in a Morris water maze, a task that is dependent upon the hippocampal formation, enhances the survival of adult-generated cells in the dentate gyrus of adult male rats. (**A**) Acquisition of place and cue learning in the Morris water maze. (**B**) Stereological estimates of the total numbers of BrdU-labeled cells in the dentate gyrus of these animals after training. These animals were injected with BrdU one week prior to training and perfused 24 hours following the last day of training. Bars represent mean ± SEM obtained from 6 animals. Asterisk indicates a significant difference, $p < 0.05$.

It is not clear what specific aspects of these tasks are necessary for the enhanced survival of adult-generated cells. Indeed, electrophysiological studies have shown that both hippocampal-dependent and hippocampal-independent tasks activate the hippocampal formation (Weisz, Clark, and Thompson, 1998). One possible difference between the two sets of tasks is their difficulty. Both place learning and trace eyeblink conditioning are more difficult to acquire than are their hippocampal-independent counterparts (cue learning and delay eyeblink conditioning). However, the observation that place learning (a task that is normally learned in fewer than 10 trials) is sufficient to rescue new cells, whereas delay eyeblink conditioning (a task that typically requires 100–200 trials to reach criterion) suggests that task difficulty is not the only factor. These data clearly demonstrate that certain types of learning are sufficient to enhance the number of new neurons in the dentate gyrus of adult rats and present the possibility that these new cells may play a role in learning.

*Functional significance of adult-generated neurons*

Currently, the functional significance of neurons generated in the dentate gyrus of adult animals is unknown. Given their incorporation into the hippocampal formation, a brain region involved in certain types of learning and memory, and the effect of learning on the survival of these new cells, it seems reasonable to consider a potential role for these new neurons in learning.

Altman was the first to propose that neurons gener-

ated during the postnatal developmental period, such as those in the dentate gyrus, might be important for forming associations during development (Altman, Brunner, and Bayer, 1973; Altman and Das, 1965, 1967), suggesting that microneurons are morphologically well suited for the maturation of learning processes. More recently, Nottebohm suggested that new hippocampal neurons may be a potential cellular substrate for learning in the adult (Nottebohm, 1989). Indeed, a continually rejuvenating population of new neurons seems well suited for the proposed transient role of the hippocampal formation in information storage (Squire, 1992; Squire and Zola, 1998). Although no direct evidence supports the view that adult-generated hippocampal cells are involved in learning, several studies have demonstrated a positive correlation between the number of adult-generated cells and performance on certain types of learning tasks (for review, see Gould et al., 1999c). Moreover, many parallels between the number of new neurons and hippocampal-dependent learning can be observed when considering the neuroendocrine and experiential factors discussed previously.

When considering the functional implications of changes in the postnatal production of new neurons, it is important to bear in mind that new granule cells require time to differentiate and become integrated into functional circuitry. Thus, changes in cell proliferation are not likely to result in immediate functional consequences. However, that does not imply that adult-generated cells are not capable of exerting an impact prior to differentiation into mature granule neurons.

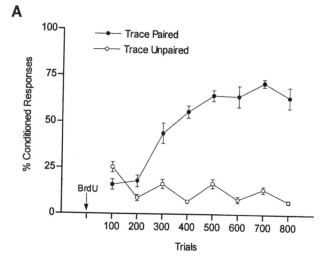

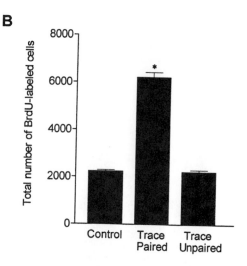

FIGURE 7.8    Conditioning of the trace eyeblink response, a task that is dependent upon the hippocampal formation, enhances the survival of adult-generated cells in the dentate gyrus of adult male rats. (**A**) Acquisition of the trace eyeblink conditioned response (trace paired) and the unpaired condition (trace unpaired). (**B**) Stereological estimates of the total numbers of BrdU-labeled cells in the dentate gyrus of these animals after training. These animals were injected with BrdU one week prior to training and perfused 24 hours following the last day of training. Bars represent mean $\pm$ SEM obtained from 6 animals. Asterisk indicates a significant difference, $p < 0.05$.

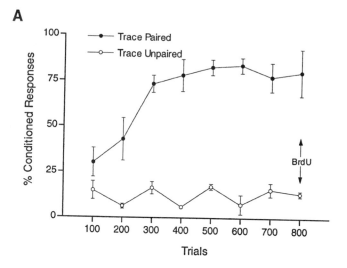

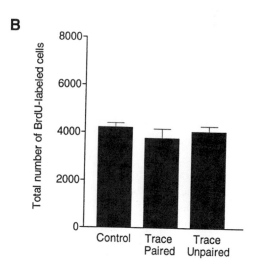

FIGURE 7.9    Conditioning of the trace eyeblink response does not enhance the proliferation of adult-generated cells in the dentate gyrus of adult male rats. (**A**) Acquisition of the trace eyeblink conditioned response (trace paired) and the unpaired condition (trace unpaired) in animals that were injected with BrdU on the last day of training and perfused 24 hours later. (**B**) Stereological estimates of the total numbers of BrdU-labeled cells in the dentate gyrus of these animals after training. Bars represent mean $\pm$ SEM obtained from 5–6 animals. Asterisk indicates a significant difference, $p < 0.05$.

In fact, we have shown that adult-generated neurons extend axons into the CA3 region as early as 4–10 days following mitosis (figure 7.1), considerably prior to the time believed to be required for neuronal maturation (Hastings and Gould, 1999).

In addition, it is important to note that acute changes in cell proliferation and survival may not be of sufficient magnitude to produce an observable functional impact.

Because of this, conditions under which cell proliferation and survival are chronically enhanced or diminished are of particular interest because they are most likely to elucidate the functional consequences of changes in adult neuron production and survival.

In general, chronic increases in the factors that negatively regulate adult granule neuron production are associated with poor performance on hippocampal-

**A**

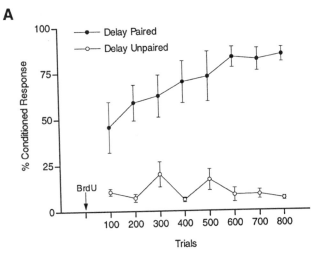

**B**

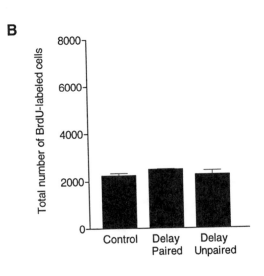

FIGURE 7.10    Training on a task that activates the hippocampal formation but is not hippocampal-dependent does not enhance the survival of adult-generated cells in the dentate gyrus of adult male rats. (**A**) Acquisition of the delay eyeblink conditioned response (delay paired) and the unpaired condition (delay unpaired) (**B**) Stereological estimates of the total numbers of BrdU-labeled cells in the dentate gyrus of these animals after training. These animals were injected with BrdU one week prior to training and perfused 24 hours following the last day of training. Bars represent mean ± SEM obtained from 5–6 animals. Asterisk indicates a significant difference, $p < 0.05$.

dependent tasks, whereas chronic increases in the factors that positively regulate adult granule neuron production are associated with enhanced cognitive function. Several studies have demonstrated that chronic stress results in an impairment of hippocampal-dependent learning. For example, it has been reported that in rats, chronic stress leads to impaired performance on a spatial navigation learning task (Bodnoff et al., 1995; Krugers et al., 1997; Luine et al., 1994, 1996). The stress-induced impairment that is observed is not permanent; animals that were tested on a spatial task at a later time point following the termination of the stress period did not perform significantly differently from unstressed animals (Luine et al., 1994, 1996). The observation that stress-induced impairment of performance on these tasks is not permanent is consistent with a possible role for adult-generated cells. It may be that the impairment persists only as long as the production of these cells has been altered. It should be noted that previous work has reported that brief stress enhances hippocampal-dependent learning (Shors, Weiss, and Thompson, 1992). However, these behavioral changes were observed shortly after stress and are likely to involve other cellular mechanisms, such as changes in synaptic plasticity.

Several studies have demonstrated that estrogen has a positive effect on the acquisition of hippocampal-dependent tasks. Although estrogen treatment has generally been found to enhance learning, some studies report decreases in performance during times of high

levels of circulating estrogen. As in the case of acute stress studies, it is important to recognize that the time frame examined in many studies is one that is likely to be too early to implicate changes in neuron production. Interestingly, in a recent study (Luine et al.,1998), it has been shown that repeated treatment with estrogen for more, but not fewer, than 4 days results in enhanced performance on a hippocampal-dependent task. This finding is consistent with the observation that adult-generated cells do not extend axons prior to 4 days after their production. It is likely that sufficient time for adult-generated cells to extend axons is required for estrogen-induced increases in cell production to have a functional effect.

Consistent with studies that have demonstrated a positive effect of estrogen on the performance of hippocampal-dependent tasks, a recent study has reported a sex difference in rats favoring females in spatial learning in a Morris water maze (Perrot-Sinal et al., 1996). Previous studies of sex differences in spatial navigation learning in rodents on this task have yielded conflicting data (Bucci, Chiba, and Gallagher, 1995; Galea, Kavaliers, and Ossenkopp, 1996). However, the results of this more recent study demonstrate that although male rats initially perform better than female rats on the task, females learn better than males once the animals have been acclimated to the testing apparatus—that is, once stress has been reduced. Thus, a sex difference in reaction to the novelty of this task prevents females from performing well. Once this performance confound is removed, females learn certain aspects of this task better than males. Similarly, another recent study has demonstrated a sex difference favoring females in hippocampal-dependent learning as well. This study reported that females learn trace eyeblink conditioning faster than males (Wood and Shors, 1998). Taken together with the observation that females produce more new hippocampal neurons than males, these data provide additional support for a relationship between new granule neurons and certain types of learning.

Studies have also demonstrated a positive correlation between the number of new granule neurons and performance on hippocampal-dependent learning tasks following enriched environment living (Kempermann, Kuhn, and Gage, 1997, 1998). However, it should be noted that many of the factors and conditions that have been demonstrated to alter the number of new neurons, either by affecting the proliferation of precursor cells or by altering the survival of new neurons, also affect other measures in the hippocampus (e.g., synaptogenesis) as well as other brain regions. Thus, attributing any behavioral change specifically to alterations in the number of new neurons would be ignoring a variety of other, potentially important cellular mechanisms that may underlie changes in hippocampal function.

## Conclusions

It is now clear that new neurons are generated in the hippocampal formation of adult mammals, including humans. The number of new granule neurons produced in adulthood and the variety of species in which this process occurs suggest that these cells are important for normal hippocampal function. Studies performed over the past several years have demonstrated that the production of new hippocampal granule neurons can be modulated by neuroendocrine factors. The production of new neurons can be inhibited by adrenal steroids, which act by suppressing the proliferation of granule cell precursors, and stimulated by estrogens, which act by enhancing this process. Furthermore, experiential cues, such as stress and learning, appear to control the production of new neurons, by affecting either cell proliferation or survival. Collectively, these observations suggest that newly generated granule cells may provide an important cellular substrate by which hormones and experience alter hippocampal function.

Cellular phenomena such as neurogenesis, axon extension, dendritic development, synaptogenesis, and cell death are traditionally viewed as developmental processes. However, the continual addition of new neurons that integrate into hippocampal circuitry as well as their deletion in adulthood indicates that these developmental process continue throughout life in some brain regions.

## REFERENCES

ALTMAN, J., 1969. Autoradiographic and histological studies of postnatal neurogenesis. IV. Cell proliferation and migration in the anterior forebrain, with special reference to persisting neurogenesis in the olfactory bulb. *J. Comp. Neurol.* 137:433–457.

ALTMAN, J., and S. A. BAYER, 1990. Migration and distribution of two populations of hippocampal granule cell precursors during the perinatal and postnatal periods. *J. Comp. Neurol.* 301:365–381.

ALTMAN, J., R. L. BRUNNER, and S. A. BAYER, 1973. The hippocampus and behavioral maturation. *Behav. Biol.* 8:557–596.

ALTMAN, J., and G. D. DAS, 1965. Autoradiographic and histological evidence of postnatal hippocampal neurogenesis in rats. *J. Comp. Neurol.* 124:319–335.

ALTMAN, J., and G. D. DAS, 1966. Autoradiographic and histological studies of postnatal neurogenesis. I. A longitudinal investigation of the kinetics, migration and transformation of cells incorporating tritiated thymidine in neonate rats, with special reference to postnatal neurogenesis in some brain regions. *J. Comp. Neurol.* 126:337–389.

ALTMAN, J., and G. D. DAS, 1967. Postnatal neurogenesis in the guinea-pig. *Nature* 214:1098–1101.

BARNEA, A., and F. NOTTEBOHM, 1994. Seasonal recruitment of hippocampal neurons in adult free-ranging black-capped chickadees. *Proc. Natl. Acad. Sci. (USA)* 91:11217–11221.

BODNOFF, S. R., A. G. HUMPHREYS, J. C. LEHMAN, D. M. DIAMOND, G. M. ROSE, and M. J. MEANEY, 1995. Enduring effects of chronic corticosterone treatment on spatial learning, synaptic plasticity, and hippocampal neuropathology in young and mid-aged rats. *J. Neurosci.* 15:61–69.

BUCCI, D. J., A. A. CHIBA, and M. GALLAGHER, 1995. Spatial learning in male and female Long-Evans rats. *Behav. Neurosci.* 109:180–183.

BUREK, M. J., K. W. NORDEEN, and E. J. NORDEEN, 1995. Estrogen promotes neuron addition to an avian song-control nucleus by regulating post-mitotic events. *Dev. Brain Res.* 85:220–224.

CAMERON, H. A., and E. GOULD, 1994. Adult neurogenesis is regulated by adrenal steroids in the dentate gyrus. *Neuroscience* 61:203–209.

CAMERON, H. A., and R. D. G. McKAY, 1999. Restoring production of hippocampal neurons in old age. *Nat. Neurosci.* 2:894–897.

CAMERON, H. A., C. S. WOOLLEY, B. S. McEWEN, and E. GOULD, 1993. Differentiation of newly born neurons and glia in the dentate gyrus of the adult rat. *Neuroscience* 56:337–344.

ECKENHOFF, M. F., and P. RAKIC, 1988. Nature and fate of proliferative cells in the hippocampal dentate gyrus during the life span of the rhesus monkey. *J. Neurosci.* 8:2729–2747.

ERIKSSON, P. S., E. PERFILIEVA, T. BJORK-ERIKSSON, A. M. ALBORN, C. NORDBORG, D. A. PETERSON, and F. H. GAGE, 1998. Neurogenesis in the adult human hippocampus. *Nat. Med.* 4:1313–1317.

FUCHS, E., G. FLUGGE, B. S. McEWEN, P. TANAPAT, and E. GOULD, 1997. Chronic subordination stress inhibits neurogenesis and decreases the volume of the granule cell layer. *Soc. Neurosci.* 23:317.

GALEA, L. A., M. KAVALIERS, and K. P. OSSENKOPP, 1996. Sexually dimorphic spatial learning in meadow voles *Microtus pennsylvanicus* and deer mice *Peromyscus maniculatus*. *J. Exp. Biol.* 199:195–200.

GALEA, L. A., P. TANAPAT, and E. GOULD, 1996. Exposure to predator odor suppresses cell proliferation in the dentate gyrus of adult rats via a cholinergic mechanism. *Soc. Neurosci. Abstr.* 22.

GOLDMAN, S. A., and F. NOTTEBOHM, 1983. Neuronal production, migration, and differentiation in a vocal control nucleus of the adult female canary brain. *Proc. Natl. Acad. Sci. (USA)* 80:2390–2394.

GOULD, E., 1994. The effects of adrenal steroids and excitatory input on neuronal birth and survival. *Ann. N.Y Acad. Sci.* 743:73–93.

GOULD, E., A. BEYLIN, P. TANAPAT, A. REEVES, and T. J. SHORS, 1999a. Learning enhances adult neurogenesis in the hippocampal formation. *Nat. Neurosci.* 2:260–265.

GOULD, E., H. A. CAMERON, D. C. DANIELS, C. S. WOOLLEY, and B. S. McEWEN, 1992. Adrenal hormones suppress cell division in the adult rat dentate gyrus. *J. Neurosci.* 12:3642–3650.

GOULD, E., B. S. McEWEN, P. TANAPAT, L. A. M. GALEA, and E. FUCHS, 1997. Neurogenesis in the dentate gyrus of the adult tree shrew is regulated by psychosocial stress and NMDA receptor activation. *J. Neurosci.* 17:2492–2498.

GOULD, E., A. J. REEVES, M. FALLAH, P. TANAPAT, C. G. GROSS, and E. FUCHS, 1999b. Hippocampal neurogenesis in adult Old World primates. *Proc. Natl. Acad. Sci. (USA)* 96:5263–5267.

GOULD, E., and P. TANAPAT, 1997. Lesion-induced proliferation of neuronal progenitors in the dentate gyrus of the adult rat. *Neuroscience* 80:427–436.

GOULD, E., P. TANAPAT, B. S. McEWEN, G. FLUGGE, and E. FUCHS, 1998. Proliferation of granule cell precursors in the dentate gyrus of adult monkeys is diminished by stress. *Proc. Natl. Acad. Sci. (USA)* 95:3168–3171.

GOULD, E., C. S. WOOLLEY, H. A. CAMERON, D. C. DANIELS, and B. S. McEWEN, 1991. Adrenal steroids regulate postnatal development of the rat dentate gyrus: II. Effects of glucocorticoids and mineralocorticoids on cell birth. *J. Comp. Neurol.* 313:486–493.

GOULD, E., P. TANAPAT, N. B. HASTINGS, and T. J. SHORS, 1999c. Neurogenesis in adulthood: A possible role in learning. *Trends Cogn. Sci.* 3:186–191.

HASTINGS, N. B., and E. GOULD, 1999. Rapid extension of axons into the CA3 region by adult-generated granule cells. *J. Comp. Neurol.* 413:146–154.

KAPLAN, M. S., and J. W. HINDS, 1977. Neurogenesis in the adult rat: Electron microscopic analysis of light radioautographs. *Science* 197:1092–1094.

KEMPERMANN, G., H. G. KUHN, and F. H. GAGE, 1997. More hippocampal neurons in adult mice living in an enriched environment. *Nature* 386:493–495.

KEMPERMANN, G., H. G. KUHN, and F. H. GAGE, 1998. Experience-induced neurogenesis in the senescent dentate gyrus. *J. Neurosci.* 18:3206–3212.

KORNACK, D. R., and P. RAKIC, 1999. Continuation of neurogenesis in the hippocampus of the adult macaque monkey. *Proc. Natl. Acad. Sci. (USA)* 96:5768–5773.

KRUGERS, H. J., B. R. DOUMA, G. ANDRINGA, B. BOHUS, J. KORF, and P. G. LUITEN, 1997. Exposure to chronic psychosocial stress and corticosterone in the rat: Effects on spatial discrimination learning and hippocampal protein kinase C gamma immunoreactivity. *Hippocampus* 7:427–436.

KUHN, H. G., H. DICKINSON-ANSON, and F. H. GAGE, 1996. Neurogenesis in the dentate gyrus of the adult rat: Age-related decrease of neuronal progenitor proliferation. *J. Neurosci.* 16:2027–2033.

LUINE, V., C. MARTINEZ, M. VILLEGAS, A. M. MAGARINOS, and B. S. McEWEN, 1996. Restraint stress reversibly enhances spatial memory performance. *Physiol. Behav.* 59:27–32.

LUINE, V., M. VILLEGAS, C. MARTINEZ, and B. S. McEWEN, 1994. Repeated stress causes reversible impairments of spatial memory performance. *Brain Res.* 639:167–170.

LUINE, V. N., S. T. RICHARDS, V. Y. WU, and K. D. BECK, 1998. Estradiol enhances learning and memory in a spatial memory task and affects levels of monoaminergic neurotransmitters. *Horm. Behav.* 34:149–162.

MARKAKIS, E. A., and F. H. GAGE, 1999. Adult-generated neurons in the dentate gyrus send axonal projections to field CA3 and are surrounded by synaptic vesicles. *J. Comp. Neurol.* 406:449–460.

NOTTEBOHM, F., 1989. Hormonal regulation of synapses and cell number in the adult canary brain and its relevance to theories of long-term memory storage. In *Neural Control of Reproductive Function*, J. Lakoski, J. R. Perez-Polo, and D. Rossin, eds. New York: Alan R. Liss, pp. 583–601.

NOWAKOWSKI, R. S., and P. RAKIC, 1981. The site of origin and route and rate of migration of neurons to the hippocampal region of the rhesus monkey. *J. Comp. Neurol.* 196:129–154.

OKANO, H. J., D. W. PFAFF, and R. B. GIBBS, 1993. RB and Cdc2 expression in brain: Correlations with $^3$H-thymidine incorporation and neurogenesis. *J. Neurosci.* 13:2930–2938.

OPPENHEIM, R. W., I. W. CHU-WANG, and J. L. MADERDRUT, 1978. Cell death of motoneurons in the chick embryo spinal cord. III. The differentiation of motoneurons prior to their induced degeneration following limb-bud removal. *J. Comp. Neurol.* 177:87–111.

PEREZ-CANELLAS, M. M., and J. M. GARCIA-VERDUGO, 1996. Adult neurogenesis in the telencephalon of a lizard: A [$^3$H]thymidine autoradiographic and bromodeoxyuridine immunocytochemical study. *Dev. Brain Res.* 93:49–61.

PERROT-SINAL, T. S., M. A. KOSTENUIK, K. P. OSSENKOPP, and M. KAVALIERS, 1996. Sex differences in performance in the Morris water maze and the effects of initial nonstationary hidden platform training. *Behav. Neurosci.* 110:1309–1320.

POLENOV, A. L., and V. K. CHETVERUKHIN, 1993. Ultrastructural radioautographic analysis of neurogenesis in the hypothalamus of the adult frog, *Rana temporaria*, with special reference to physiological regeneration of the preoptic nucleus. II. Types of neuronal cells produced. *Cell Tissue Res.* 271:351–362.

RAKIC, P., 1985. Limits of neurogenesis in primates. *Science* 227:1054–1056.

SAPOLSKY, R. M., 1992. Do glucocorticoid concentrations rise with age in the rat? *Neurobiol. Aging* 13:171–174.

SAPOLSKY, R. M., and J. ALTMANN, 1991. Incidence of hypercortisolism and dexamethasone resistance increases with age among wild baboons. *Biol. Psychiatry* 30:1008–1016.

SAPOLSKY, R. M., L. C. KREY, and B. S. McEWEN, 1985. Prolonged glucocorticoid exposure reduces hippocampal neuron number: Implications for aging. *J. Neurosci.* 5:1222–1227.

SAPOLSKY, R. M., and M. J. MEANEY, 1986. Maturation of the adrenocortical stress response: Neuroendocrine control mechanisms and the stress hyporesponsive period. *Brain Res.* 396:64–76.

SCHLESSINGER, A. R., W. M. COWAN, and D. I. GOTTLIEB, 1975. An autoradiographic study of the time of origin and the pattern of granule cell migration in the dentate gyrus of the rat. *J. Comp. Neurol.* 159:149–175.

SHORS, T. J., C. WEISS, and R. F. THOMPSON, 1992. Stress-induced facilitation of classical conditioning. *Science* 257:537–539.

SQUIRE, L. R., 1992. Memory and the hippocampus: A synthesis from findings with rats, monkeys, and humans. *Psychol. Rev.* 99:195–231.

SQUIRE, L. R., and S. M. ZOLA, 1998. Episodic memory, semantic memory, and amnesia. *Hippocampus* 8:205–211.

STANFIELD, B. B., and J. E. TRICE, 1988. Evidence that granule cells generated in the dentate gyrus of adult rats extend axonal projections. *Exp. Brain Res.* 72:399–406.

TANAPAT, P., L. A. GALEA, and E. GOULD, 1998. Stress inhibits the proliferation of granule cell precursors in the developing dentate gyrus. *Int. J. Dev. Neurosci.* 16:235–239.

TANAPAT, P., N. B. HASTINGS, A. J. REEVES, and E. GOULD, 1999. Estrogen stimulates a transient increase in the number of new neurons in the dentate gyrus of the adult female rat. *J. Neurosci.* 19:5792–5801.

WEISZ, D. J., G. A. CLARK, and R. F. THOMPSON, 1984. Increased responsivity of dentate granule cells during nictitating membrane response conditioning in rabbit. *Behav. Brain Res.* 12:145–154.

WOOD, G. E., and T. J. SHORS, 1998. Stress facilitates classical conditioning in males, but impairs classical conditioning in females through activational effects of ovarian hormones. *Proc. Natl. Acad. Sci. (USA)* 95:4066–4071.

WOOLLEY, C. S., E. GOULD, M. FRANKFURT, and B. S. McEWEN, 1990. Naturally occurring fluctuation in dendritic spine density on adult hippocampal pyramidal neurons. *J. Neurosci.* 10:4035–4039.

ZUPANC, G. K., 1999. Neurogenesis, cell death and regeneration in the adult gymnotiform brain. *J. Exp. Biol.* 202(10):1435–1446.

# II

# METHODOLOGICAL

# PARADIGMS

# 8 Inferences about the Functional Development of Neural Systems in Children via the Application of Animal Tests of Cognition

WILLIAM H. OVERMAN
AND JOCELYNE BACHEVALIER

ABSTRACT   The application of animal tests of cognition to children of various ages can provide inferential evidence of the time course of functional maturation of restricted neural substrates. This chapter describes the methods of administering to children various tasks in the Wisconsin General Testing Apparatus, radial-arm maze, and Morris search apparatus. When compared with results from animals, the results from children allow inferences about the functional development of a number of neural systems and structures including orbital prefrontal cortex, entorhinal and perirhinal cortices, hippocampus, and the inferior temporal corticostriatal system.

A primary goal of developmental cognitive neuroscience is to trace the functional maturation of neural systems that underlie various aspects of cognition. Toward this goal, we have tested children on a variety of cognitive tasks that were originally developed for animals. The logic of this approach consists of three steps. First, a number of cognitive tests have been documented to measure the function of specific neural circuits in animals. Second, many of these animal tests can be applied to children with little procedural change. Third, the resulting performance by children of different ages allows us to make logical inferences about the functional development of underlying neural substrates under the assumption that the substrates of animals and humans are similar.

This mixture of animal neuroscience and developmental psychology allows inferences that differ from those generated by the procedures of conventional child development. Traditional tests for children yield

WILLIAM H. OVERMAN   Psychology Department, University of North Carolina at Wilmington, Wilmington, North Carolina.
JOCELYNE BACHEVALIER   Department of Neurobiology and Anatomy, University of Texas Health Science Center, Houston, Texas.

valuable knowledge about age-related sequences of cognitive development, but they provide little information about the functional development of underlying neural circuits.

This chapter describes methodologies of applying animal tests to children, summarizes the results of these tests, discusses inferences about the functional development of restricted brain systems, and presents some of the limitations and caveats inherent in this experimental approach.

## Testing children with tasks developed for monkeys: Use of the Wisconsin General Testing Apparatus

APPARATUS   For more than 40 years, the Wisconsin General Testing Apparatus (WGTA) has been used to administer cognitive tests to animals. The WGTA has been used extensively with nonhuman primates because it takes advantage of reaching and investigative behaviors that occur very early in life (Harlow, 1951, 1958). We have tested children in modified versions of the WGTA on a variety of tasks including object discriminations (Overman, 1990; Overman et al., 1992), trial-unique delayed matching and nonmatching to sample (Overman, 1990; Overman et al., 1992), single pair and concurrent discriminations (Overman et al., 1992), object reversal (Overman et al., 1996b), visual preferential viewing (Overman et al., 1993), trial-unique oddity (Overman et al., 1996a), and landmark discriminations (Coleman and Overman, 1999). Child testing procedures in the WGTA have been changed from animal testing procedures as little as possible; however, a few differences do exist. The human WGTA is of slightly different dimensions from that used for monkeys, and it has a movable tray instead of a stationary tray (figure

8.1). All food trays have recessed food wells. To avoid inadvertent experimenter cues, the experimenter moves the tray at a constant rate to a physical stop device, regardless of the subject's response. When infant and adult humans are tested using the WGTA, there are two experimenters: One sits behind the vertically sliding door facing the subject and manipulates stimuli and rewards; and, on the other side of the apparatus, the other experimenter either holds the infant or sits beside the adult subject. The experimenter operating the WGTA can see neither the second experimenter nor the subject's face or body. The two experimenters exchange roles on alternate days of testing.

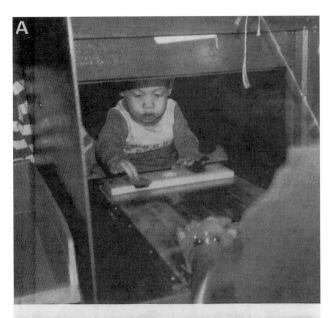

FIGURE 8.1 Testing apparatus for human subjects (**A**) and monkeys (**B**). For these photographs the vertical doors were raised higher than in normal testing, during which the doors were raised only about 10 cm.

For both humans and monkeys, the stimuli are multicolored, three-dimensional objects, small enough to be displaced with one hand. Stimuli used with human subjects are screened in pilot studies so as to be difficult or slow to label verbally as measured by reaction times and rating scales. Stimuli used for human subjects, but not for monkeys, are glued to small black plastic bases that completely cover the food wells. Although the black base is a common feature among all stimuli, its visual impact is considerably reduced because the objects are viewed from the side.

REINFORCEMENT AND LACK OF FOOD RESTRICTION   By necessity, one of the procedural differences between monkeys and humans concerns food restriction. Monkeys are typically food-restricted 24 hours before each test session. Because this is not feasible for human subjects, we attempt to increase their motivational level by using social reinforcers (saying "Good" or "Good job") in addition to food rewards (Cheerios and Froot Loops for infants, M&M's for adults). In order to increase the incentive value of the cereal, infants are tested after their nap and before their afternoon snack. The use of these two reinforcers has proved successful, as shown by the results of testing variously aged subjects on a variety of tasks.

NONVERBAL PROCEDURES ALLOW COMPARISON WITH RESULTS FROM MONKEYS   One of the most important features of testing human subjects in the WGTA is the deliberate absence of verbal instructions. At no time do subjects receive verbal information about the apparatus, stimuli, rewards, demands, or goals of the task. Subjects are pretrained to displace stimuli and retrieve food rewards by nonverbal successive approximations. After pretraining, subjects learn the goals or rules of the various tasks solely from reinforcement contingencies. Only positive reinforcement is used, and incorrect responses are not punished.

This method—the absence of verbal instructions and the use of social and food reinforcement—has been very successful, as even the youngest subjects (12 months of age) have learned some tasks (e.g., object discrimination) extremely rapidly. These results indicate that task and cognitive variables, not motivational states or language abilities, dictate rates of learning and performance (Overman, 1990; Overman et al., 1992, 1996b). The critical role of verbal instructions in the application of animal tests is more thoroughly discussed at the end of this chapter.

REPEATED DAYS OF TESTING ALLOWS COMPARISON OF RESULTS WITH MONKEYS   As is the case for monkeys, children are tested in the WGTA on a limited number of daily trials, usually 15–20, each weekday, week after week, until specific learning criteria are met. Children are tested at their preschool in rooms set aside for this purpose. Learning criterion for each phase of training is almost always 90% correct responses for two consecutive test days. In an attempt to attain this learning criterion, children are tested, in some instances, for more than 100 days (Overman et al., 1996a). Since monkeys are almost always tested for protracted periods of time, long-term testing of children allows us to directly compare learning and performance between monkeys and humans. This critical feature distinguishes our approach from the cross-sectional testing methods widely used in developmental psychology and allows us to make direct cross-species comparisons. Such long-term testing has the obvious benefits of longitudinal within-subject designs as well as the potential confounds of developmental changes that occur during the time span of testing. We have considered and addressed some of these concerns in other writings (Overman, 1990; Overman et al., 1993, 1996b, 1997).

### Testing in the WGTA (1): Inferences about the development of declarative and procedural learning and underlying neural mechanisms

TWO TYPES OF LEARNING AND MEMORY  Data from studies with brain-damaged amnesic humans and monkeys have generated a prevailing view that different forms of learning and memory are subserved by distinct neural systems (Mishkin, Malamut, and Bachevalier, 1984; Overman, Ormsby, and Mishkin, 1990; Phillips et al., 1988; Zola-Morgan and Squire, 1993. For reviews, see Squire, 1987; Salmon and Butters, 1998). There appear to be at least two types of learning and memory, labeled, for the purposes of this chapter, *declarative* and *procedural*. (A number of different nomenclatures have been used. For reviews and discussions, see Schacter and Tulving, 1994; Sherry and Schacter, 1987). Declarative learning and memory (also called *explicit learning* or, simply, *memory*) involves rapid learning, conscious recollection, and explicit declaration of episodes and factual information (Squire, 1987). Procedural learning and memory (also called *habit* or *skill learning*) involves slow learning and unconscious recollection that is expressed through performing specific operations of a task (Graf and Schacter, 1985; Salmon and Butters, 1998).

NEURAL BASIS  Declarative processes appear to be largely dependent upon structures in the medial temporal lobe and midline diencephalon (Mishkin et al.,

1984; Squire, 1987). Previously, the critical neural substrates for declarative memory were thought to be the hippocampus and amygdala in monkeys (Mishkin, 1978; Murray and Mishkin, 1984; Overman, Ormsby, and Mishkin, 1990). Now, however, it appears that the critical medial temporal lobe substrates include the perirhinal and entorhinal cortices, and perhaps their projection targets, medial dorsal thalamus, and orbital frontal cortex (Meunier et al., 1993; Mishkin and Murray, 1998; Mumby and Pinel, 1994; Zola-Morgan et al., 1993). Unlike declarative processes, procedural processes appear to be largely dependent upon the corticostriatal system, which consists of reciprocal connections between the neocortex and basal ganglia (Butters et al., 1985; Knowlton, Mangels, and Squire, 1996; Martone et al., 1984; Salmon and Butters, 1998).

Despite uncertainty about the exact neural substrates for declarative and procedural processes, demonstrations of double dissociations leave little doubt that these processes are cognitively and anatomically distinct (see Squire, 1987, for review). This consequently raises the question of whether the two systems mature at the same rate during ontogeny.

### Delayed nonmatch to sample measures declarative learning and memory while concurrent discrimination measures procedural learning and memory

RESULTS WITH CHILDREN ON DNMS  The delayed nonmatch-to-sample (DNMS) task has been widely used to assess recognition memory, which is thought to be one example of declarative memory (Squire, Zola-Morgan, and Chen, 1988; Mishkin and Delacour, 1975). In the DNMS task, each trial consists of two parts. On the first part of a trial, a to-be-remembered sample object is presented to the subject. When the object is moved, a food reward is revealed and, when humans are participants, a social reinforcer is presented. On the second part, after a delay interval, the sample object and a novel object are presented to the subject. Displacement of the novel object is rewarded. On each subsequent trial, new stimuli are used as the sample and comparison stimuli (trial-unique procedure). At the outset of training, delay intervals are about 8–10 seconds, the approximate minimum obtainable in the WGTA. This is because during the retention interval, the experimenter must lower the vertical door, retrieve the sample stimulus, bait the appropriate food well, place the sample and comparison stimuli on the food tray, and raise the door. Children are given about 15 daily trials and monkeys are given up to 40 daily trials.

In the DNMS task, cognition can be assessed in two ways: The first is by measuring initial learning of the nonmatching rule, and the second is by measuring memory strength. Initial learning is quantified by the number of trials and errors to criterion (two consecutive test days of 90% correct) on the basic 10-second–delay task. After attainment of this criterion, memory strength can be quantified by measuring performance at increasing delays or at increasing numbers of items to be remembered.

We tested children of various ages on 10-second–delay DNMS with procedures that matched those used with monkeys. We found that human and monkey DNMS learning was similar in three respects: (1) rapid learning in adult subjects; (2) gradual but steady learning in infants (18–32 months of age for children and 6–12 months for monkeys); and (3) no learning in younger infants (12–15 months for children and 6 months for monkeys) until they became older, followed by very gradual learning (Overman et al., 1992). After learning criterion was achieved on the basic 10-second–delay task, memory performance on DNMS was challenged for all subjects by increasing retention intervals and by increasing the numbers of items to be remembered. The scores of human subjects on these memory performance tests declined systematically with increasing age of the subject. These human and monkey data correspond quite well when considering a 4:1 ratio of monkey years to human years. The results with both monkeys and children indicate that some cognitive or maturational milestone must be reached before DNMS learning occurs. In humans this minimum appears to be approximately 19 ± 3 months. This milestone appears to be independent of the onset of language for various reasons, including the fact that a similar developmental progression exists in nonverbal monkeys (Overman et al., 1992).

RESULTS WITH CHILDREN ON CONCURRENT DISCRIMINATION  The concurrent discrimination (CD) task has been widely used to measure normal and abnormal procedural (implicit or habit) learning and memory (Bachevalier and Mishkin, 1984; Overman et al., 1992; Squire, Knowlton, and Musen, 1993). In this task, on each test day, the subject is consecutively presented with a number of object pairs at 15-second intervals. One member of each pair is baited with food (positive stimulus) and one is not baited (negative stimulus). The same series of object pairs is presented once each test day (24-hour retention interval). The positive and negative objects within each pair and the serial order of the pairs remain constant across daily sessions, but the left–right positions of the baited and unbaited objects are randomized

daily. Testing continues until the subject attains a criterion of 90% correct choices for two consecutive test days. We found that infant humans required more training than infant monkeys to master the CD task; however, infants of both species mastered this task significantly faster and earlier in life than the DNMS task. For example, 3-month-old monkeys, who would correspond in age to 12-month-old human infants, learned DNMS in an average of 550 errors versus 107 errors for the CD task. Similarly, 12–15-month-old children learned DNMS in an average of 1050 errors versus 238 errors for the CD task.

SUMMARY  It is clear that both infant humans and monkeys solve the CD (procedural) task significantly earlier in life than the DNMS (declarative) task and that learning is very similar between the two species. These behavioral data, together with lesion studies, provide inferential evidence that, in humans, the procedural system (i.e., the corticostriatal system) gains functional maturity earlier in life than the declarative system (i.e., the medial temporal system), as is the case for monkeys (Bachevalier and Mishkin, 1984). In 1992, we argued that the particular medial temporal lobe system in question involved the hippocampus (Overman et al., 1992); however, the actual system may instead involve rhinal cortices and its connections with the orbital prefrontal cortex. This discovery may partially resolve previous controversies concerning the early appearance of simple hippocampally mediated processes such as preferential viewing in humans and monkeys (see Bachevalier, Brickson, and Hagger, 1993; Diamond, 1990; Nelson, 1995; Overman et al., 1993).

*Testing in the WGTA (2): Inferences about the ontogenesis of sex-specific cognition and underlying neural mechanisms*

Two tests developed for monkeys are of particular interest because their use has revealed a double dissociation of cognitive sex differences, which are clearly biologically, and not socially, based. The two tasks are *object reversal learning*, as assessed through an object reversal discrimination task, and *concurrent discrimination learning*.

OBJECT REVERSAL DISCRIMINATION TASK  This task requires that the subject, over a number of days, learn to discriminate between two stimulus objects, one of which conceals a food reward (plus a social reward in the case of children) while the other does not. After reaching criterion performance (90% correct responses for two consecutive days) the subject learns a second discrimination with two new stimuli. These first two discrimination problems serve as control tasks for general learning ability. On the first test session after attaining criterion on the second discrimination problem, the reward contingencies for that problem are reversed without warning. Thus, the previously negative stimulus becomes positive and the previous positive stimulus becomes negative. The subject learns this reversed discrimination to criterion, whereupon the reward contingencies are reversed again, and so on, for as many reversals as the experiment calls for. The subject's score for this task is the number of errors to criterion for each reversal and across all reversals. A high number of errors is interpreted as the failure to inhibit a prepotent response (e.g., the learned response to the initial discrimination) and/or the lack of behavioral flexibility.

CONCURRENT DISCRIMINATION   This task is the same as the concurrent discrimination described in the previous section. Essentially, the subject learns a list of simultaneous object pair discriminations with the serial order of pairs presented once per day.

NEURAL BASIS, GENDER SPECIFICITY, AND THE ROLE OF GONADAL HORMONES   There is a convincing double dissociation on these two tasks showing that two distinct neural systems develop at different rates in infant monkeys and that, consequently, infant males perform better on one of these tasks, object reversal, and infant females perform better on the other, concurrent discrimination. The evidence is as follows:

1. 75-day-old male monkeys are superior to age-matched females on object reversal tasks (Goldman et al., 1974) whereas 90-day-old females are superior to age-matched males on concurrent discrimination tasks (Bachevalier, Hagger, and Bercu, 1989). (It is not known how 75-day-old males and females perform on concurrent discrimination.)

2. Whereas normal infant males outperform infant females on the object reversal task, perinatally androgenized infant females perform as well as normal males and better than normal females (Clark and Goldman-Rakic, 1989).

3. Early ablations of orbital prefrontal cortex impair object reversal performance of normal infant males and androgenized infant females, as do such ablations in both male and female adults; but such lesions do not impair the performance of normal infant females (Clark and Goldman-Rakic, 1989; Goldman, 1971).

4. In contrast, on the concurrent discrimination task, normal infant females outperform infant males (Bachevalier, Hagger, and Bercu, 1989) but orchiectomized infant males perform as well as normal females and better than normal males.

5. Neonatal ablations of area TE in the inferior temporal cortex impair concurrent discrimination performance in normal females but not in infant males (Bachevalier et al., 1990).

6. In males, levels of circulating testosterone are significantly inversely correlated with performance on the concurrent discrimination task (Hagger, Bachevalier, and Bercu, 1987).

In summary, perinatal testosterone in infant males appears to accelerate the functional maturation of orbital prefrontal cortex and slow the functional maturation of area TE in the inferior temporal lobe.

RESULTS WITH CHILDREN ON OBJECT REVERSAL AND CONCURRENT DISCRIMINATION   Our laboratory has replicated in children the behavioral component of the double dissociation found in monkeys. Again, we tested children in the WGTA using almost exactly the same testing procedures as that used with monkeys—a limited number of daily trials for many consecutive days, food and social reward, and no verbal task instructions. The data (Overman et al., 1996b, 1997) were as follows:

1. Male and female children performed equally in initial discrimination learning.

2. Males under the age of 29 months were superior to age-matched females in object reversal learning, following a pattern almost exactly like that found in monkeys. With the addition of more subjects we have recently discovered that the male superiority exists through 34 months of age (Overman and Godin, 1999).

3. In addition to slower learning relative to males, about 20% of the females under 29 months showed hyperemotional behaviors commensurate with the start of reversal training.

4. Females under the age of 36 months were superior to age-matched males in learning a concurrent discrimination task.

5. There were no significant sex differences on either task in older children or adults.

In summary, as shown in figure 8.2, we find that infant male and female humans display significant differences in their learning abilities almost exactly like those displayed by infant monkeys. For infants of both species the direction of the sex differences reverses from one task to the other. When scores for each child are plotted, it is clear that a significant majority of males are superior on object reversal while a significant majority of females are superior on concurrent discrimination (figure 8.2). The distributions of individual performances also show that there are individuals in both

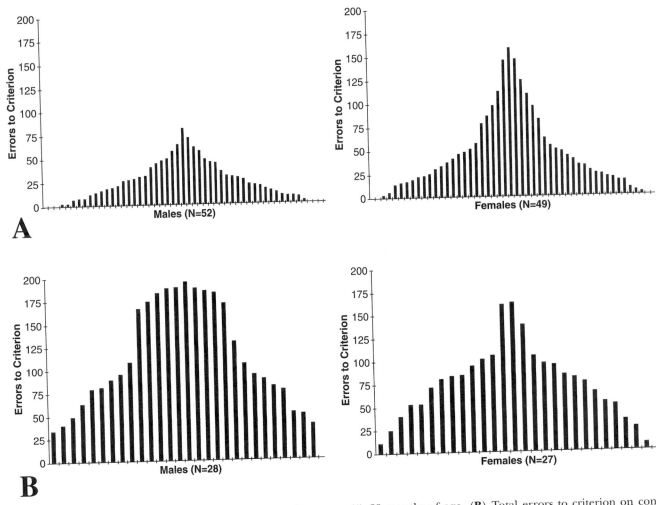

FIGURE 8.2 Scores of individual children plotted as "population" scores on two tasks. Each bar represents the score of a single child. (**A**) Total errors to criterion on object reversals one through three for individual male and female children 15–29 months of age. (**B**) Total errors to criterion on concurrent discrimination task for individual male and female children 13–35 months of age.

groups for whom the population standard does not hold. This would be expected for any sex-biased phenomenon (Halpern, 1992). The extremely close similarity of the tasks, behavioral data, and endocrine functions of infant humans and monkeys provides inferential evidence that, in both species, there is more rapid maturation of orbital prefrontal circuits in males and more rapid maturation of inferior temporal circuits in females. Presumably, this phenomenon is related to the perinatal testosterone surge that occurs in males of both species (Bachevalier, Hagger, and Bercu, 1989; Corbier, Edwards, and Roffi, 1992; Stahl et al., 1978).

This demonstration of cognitive sex differences in children is one of the best examples of the kind of results that can be derived from testing children with tests developed for animals. If our inferences are persistently validated with further experimentation, they may affect not only psychological and social theory but educational practice as well. In our current research we are investigating the implications of individual differences and the fact that, in both species, the sex differences *seem* to disappear in older subjects (over the age of 3 years for children). Preliminary results with cognitively more challenging tests and older subjects suggest that some of these cognitive sex differences, e.g., those that reflect differences in orbital prefrontal functioning, may exist across the lifespan (Reavis et al., 1998). This finding is in agreement with positron emission tomography evidence showing significant differences in several brain areas including the orbital prefrontal cortex and temporal lobes of adult men and women (Andreason et al., 1993; Gur et al., 1995).

CAVEATS OF TESTING IN THE WGTA  Testing children with the WGTA involves several drawbacks. First, two experimenters are required; and, to make the tasks comparable with animal procedures, the experimenters must test children for many days or weeks in a series of short test sessions. Second, the cumbersome nature of the apparatus limits opportunities to test in certain situations—in clinical settings, for example, or in conjunction with neuroimaging techniques. Another limitation is the fact that physical manipulation and baiting of stimuli in the WGTA requires at least 8–10 seconds, rendering shorter interstimulus presentations impossible. The latter point can be critical when conducting memory research (Overman, Ormsby, and Mishkin, 1990; see also Bachevalier, this volume). Nevertheless, the use of a human version of the animal WGTA has provided interesting comparative results.

## Testing children with tasks developed for rodents: Use of the radial-arm maze and Morris search task

PLACE LEARNING  The radial-arm maze (Olton and Samuelson, 1976) and the Morris search task (Morris, 1981) have been widely used to study navigational place learning in rodents. Place learning is defined as learning to move to and remember a particular site in the environment to obtain a reward (Kolb and Whishaw, 1990). There are at least three different processes by which a subject can locate and remember a reward site in the environment: (1) by reference to a specific stimulus that is located at the reward site (e.g., a salient cue at the end of an arm in the maze), (2) by reference to a route to take to the site (e.g., a series of left and right turns from the starting point), and (3) by reference to two or more cues that are some distance from the reward site (e.g., one arm in a maze has a constant location relative to physical cues in the testing environment). We refer to these spatial processes as (1) *cue*, (2) *response*, and (3) *spatial-relational* place learning abilities, although other authors have used somewhat different terms (O'Keefe and Nadel, 1978; Sutherland, 1985). The last process, *spatial-relational*, learning, has captured much attention in the last 30 years because of our increasing knowledge of its brain basis. Both the RAM and Morris search task can be configured to determine if a subject is using cue, response or spatial-relational processes to solve the problem; hence, the role of various neural systems in these processes can be investigated.

NEURAL BASIS OF SPATIAL-RELATIONAL LEARNING IN ANIMALS  There is widespread agreement that the hippocampal system is intimately involved in navigational spatial-relational learning (Cohen and Eichenbaum, 1991; Jarrard, 1993), despite ongoing debates about related issues. For example there is debate about whether the hippocampus is involved in learning and memory for *only spatial* information (Jarrard, 1993; Nadel, 1991; O'Keefe, 1991; Worden, 1992) or whether it is more generally involved in *relational* learning and memory, which may involve both spatial and nonspatial information (Cohen and Eichenbaum, 1991; Olton, Becker, and Handleman, 1979; Squire, 1986; Sutherland and Rudy, 1989; Wallenstein, Eichenbaum, and Hasselmo, 1998).

The involvement of the hippocampal system in spatial relational learning is substantiated by electrophysiological recording studies in animals showing the existence of hippocampal "place" neurons (McNaughton, Barns, and O'Keefe, 1983; O'Keefe, 1976) and neuronal "location ensembles" (Wilson and McNaughton, 1993), by lesion studies showing that the integrity of the hippocampal system is necessary for relational place learning (Jarrard, 1993; Sutherland, Kolb, and Whishaw, 1982; Sutherland and Rudy, 1987), and by developmental studies showing that a complete anatomical maturation of the hippocampal system is necessary for relational place learning (Keith, 1990; Rudy, Stadler-Morris, and Albert, 1987).

RADIAL-ARM MAZE: APPARATUS AND PROCEDURE  Typically, the RAM has a minimum of eight identical runway arms that radiate from a central starting area. Food rewards are hidden in containers at the end of each arm. We constructed a human-size RAM in which to test children's spatial learning abilities (figure 8.3) (Overman et al., 1996c). Each arm had wire "walls," permitting almost unobstructed views of extramaze cues while preventing subjects from falling or crossing from one arm to another without returning to the center. Access to each arm was controlled by swinging doors that could be operated by a system of ropes and pulleys from outside the maze. The maze was located outdoors on the grounds of the subjects' school, and the subjects had visual and physical access to it only during experimental testing.

All subjects were tested for a number of consecutive days without verbal instructions about the task. On the first test day, an experimenter escorted the subject to the center start area and said "This is for you" as she offered a food reward inside a red plastic bucket that was identical to the goal buckets at the end of each arm. Next the experimenter told the subject "You can keep anything you can find." This single prompt was sufficient to start active exploration for every child and adult in the experiment. Two experimenters recorded the subject's search path. Correct responses were

FIGURE 8.3  Human-sized radial arm maze. The 4-year-old subject in the picture is searching for rewards while all eight arms are open. The white table in the foreground is the console from which the entrance doors to each arm could be opened and closed.

reinforced with sweetened cereal for the children and M&M's for the adults and with social rewards (one experimenter said "Good" or "Good job" each time the subject retrieved a food reward.

There were two testing versions in the RAM, free choice and forced choice, either of which could be cued or noncued. The two versions allow measurement of different cognitive processes.

*Free-choice testing*  In this version of the task a subject freely explores the eight open, baited arms of the maze. The optimal strategy is to enter each arm only once. The free-choice task can be solved either by a response-based process or by a spatial-relational process. In the first case, the subject uses an algorithmic solution such as "turn right" after exiting each arm. Here the subject does not have to use spatial memory of which arm has been visited. In contrast, when using a spatial-relational solution, the subject chooses nonadjacent arms; in this case the subject must remember the visited versus the unvisted arms by knowing the arms' positions in relationship to cues inside or outside the maze.

*Forced-choice testing*  The forced-choice RAM procedures prevent the use of algorithmic solutions, thereby ensuring the use of relational cognitive processes. In this procedure, four nonadjacent arms are initially opened for exploration while the remaining four are blocked. On trials 1–4 the subject retrieves rewards from the four open arms. Performance on trials 1–4 provides a measure of working memory. Next, the subject waits in the center for a period of time during which all arms are blocked. During the retention interval, the subjects are free to visually inspect any or all arms of the maze. Then all eight arms are opened and the subject searches for the remaining rewards in the four unvisited arms (trials 5–8). Performance on trials 5–8 yields the critical measure of relational place learning ability, provided there are only extramaze cues.

*Cued versus uncued choice testing*  Both free- and forced-choice versions can be cued or uncued. In the cued version each arm is rendered physically distinct by salient visual stimuli (posters with colorful icons) at the end of the arm. With these proximal cues available, the visited arms can be remembered by simple stimulus–response associations and without reference to extra-maze relational information. In the uncued RAM, visited arms must be remembered by their spatial relationships to distal extramaze cues.

This distinction is critical because rodents with damage to the hippocampal system are impaired in their ability to solve the uncued RAM (i.e., in using spatial-relational cognition), but the same animals are unimpaired in solving cued versions of the task (i.e., in using stimulus–reinforcement cognition) (Barns, 1988; Jarrard, 1993; Nadel and McDonald, 1980; Olton and Papas, 1979; Winocur, 1980).

RESULTS WITH CHILDREN ON RAM    Seventy-seven children and 30 adults served as subjects in RAM testing. The experimentally naive children ranged in age from about 2 to 12 years of age (20–151 months). Children were tested under free-choice and forced-choice conditions for up to 15 consecutive weekdays on either the cued or noncued (relational) version of the RAM. Adult control subjects were college students who were tested under free- and forced-choice conditions on the uncued version of the RAM for four consecutive days. Based on regression analyses of performance during free-choice testing, children were divided into two age groups: a younger group (under 5 year of age) and an older group (over 5 years of age). (The exact youngest and oldest age varied with experiments, but in all cases, there was a statistically significant break in the data at 5 years of age.)

Testing in the RAM yielded six main results:

1. Male and female subjects did not differ on any measure.

2. During free choice, children under the age of 5 years did not use algorithmic solutions in either cued or noncued conditions. About 50% of older children and 50% of adults used algorithmic solutions in both versions of the task.

3. Subjects of all ages exhibited highly accurate performance (90% or better) for four reward locations (trials 1–4) in both the cued and noncued conditions.

4. In both versions of the RAM, children younger than 5 years were impaired relative to older subjects when the task involved eight reward locations (free choice).

5. In the noncued RAM, children younger than 5 years performed at chance levels on the delayed spatial memory task (trials 5–8); older children performed significantly above chance levels but were still inferior to adults.

6. The addition of proximal cues significantly improved the performance of all children on free-choice tests and on trials 5–8 in force-choice testing.

These results clearly show that children under 5 years of age are inferior to older children and adults in place learning when spatial-relational solutions are required, but not when nonrelational solutions are used (i.e., when subjects use cue response associations). In fact, children under the age of 12 years did not perform at the adult level of proficiency on some relational measures, e.g., performance on trials 5–8 in the uncued conditions. Our evidence for late ontogenesis of relational cognition has received confirmation from testing children on spatial working memory tasks (Luciana and Nelson, 1998) as well as from additional relational animal tasks, as described next.

MORRIS SEARCH TASK: APPARATUS AND PROCEDURE
The original Morris apparatus, as developed for rodents, is a swimming pool filled with opaque water (Morris, 1981). A resting platform is located in the water at a site that is fixed relative to extramaze cues. The resting platform can be either visible, slightly above the water, or hidden, slightly under the water's surface. The goal of the task is for a rat to learn the platform location over a series of trials. On each trial, the animal swims from different starting points at the edge of the pool. This procedure eliminates the use of response-based solutions; i.e., the rat cannot learn to swim at a constant heading on each trial. When the platform is visible, the problem can be solved by swimming directly to this visible cue. In this case, the swim task is analogous to the proximally cued radial arm maze. But when the platform is hidden, the solution must be based on the position of the animal relative to the distal cues, i.e., by relational place learning. In this case, the swim task is analogous to the noncued RAM.

*Neural basis in animals*    A number of studies have shown that rats with damage to the hippocampus and related structures are impaired in relational place learning (hidden-platform condition) in the Morris task, but the same rats are not impaired in nonrelational learning (visible-platform task) (Jarrard, 1993; Sutherland and Rudy, 1989). Furthermore, proficient relational place learning in this task closely follows the neuroanatomical maturation of the hippocampus. Rats younger than 19 days are unable to solve the hidden-platform version, yet they easily solve the visible-platform version. In contrast, 21-day-old rats solve the hidden-platform task almost as well as adult rats, although they are still impaired in their 24-hour retention of the task as compared to adults (Keith, 1990; Rudy, Stadler-Morris, and

Albert, 1987). In parallel to this performance change, between postnatal days 19 and 25, the number of granule cells of the fascia dentata of the hippocampus increases dramatically (Bayer, 1980). Thus, the development of relational cognition as assessed in the Morris task parallels specific cellular maturation in the hippocampus.

*Morris task for children* We adapted the Morris task for children by having them search for a candy-filled "treasure chest" buried beneath the surface of a large "pool" (12 feet in diameter) filled with small plastic packing chips (Overman et al., 1996c), as shown in figure 8.4. The treasure chest was located in a constant position in the pool relative to distinctive visual cues mounted on a surrounding curtain. On each trial the subject began searching from a different starting point at the edge of the pool.

A total of 157 children, ranging in age from 3 to 12 years were tested on 16 trials across three consecutive test days. The treasure chest was hidden on all five trials on days 1 and 2, and on the first five trials on day 3; however, it was visible on the sixth trial on day 3. On day 3, the cues were removed from the surrounding curtain. Following the last trial in the large pool, children were taken to a different room and asked to locate the goal site in a scale model of the testing situation (complete with small pool, curtain, cues, and every detail of the larger room). Verbal instructions were used for this task. To increase motivation and to reduce playing, children were told that the faster they found the chest, the more candy they would receive. They earned three pieces, two pieces, and one piece of candy by finding the chest in one, two, or three minutes, respectively. They earned no candy if the chest was not found in three minutes, but were told they would have other chances. Between trials and while the chest was being relocated, the child was outside the surrounding curtain in a play area that contained numerous toys and activities. On each trial the child was told to look at and name each of the salient cues (colorful posters depicting dinosaurs, ice cream cones, stars, and the like) mounted on the surrounding curtain. As the child searched for the chest, two experimenters recorded the latency to find the goal and drew the search path on a scale map of the pool. One group of children ($n = 106$, 3–12 years of age) were tested on the Morris task without being told that the treasure chest was always in the same location from trial to trial. Another group of children ($n = 51$, 3–9 years of age) were told on every trial that the treasure chest was always in the same location

RESULTS WITH CHILDREN IN MORRIS TASK Following are the six main results from the Morris task.

1. Males and females did not differ on any measure.

2. Latency scores were not appropriate for this task because older children were able to walk through the plastic pellets faster than younger subjects. This was demonstrated by the fact that older children found the goal significantly faster than younger children on the first test trial, before learning had occurred. This point is important because it illustrates a situation in which particular animal procedures cannot be used with humans. In addition to path length, the other primary performance measure when testing rats in the Morris task is latency to swim to the goal site. This measure should not be used with children in our version of the Morris task because of the age differences in ability to walk through plastic chips.

3. Based on the distance traversed in reaching the goal, children 6 years of age and younger were inferior to older subjects; however, children of all ages were equally proficient in solving the task when the goal was visible.

4. On the scale model task, children younger than 8 years were inferior to older children in accurately locating the goal site.

5. Informing the subjects that the goal was stationary improved performance for all age groups; nevertheless, children younger than 8 years were inferior to older children.

6. Removal of cues from the surrounding curtain did not impair performance. According to verbal reports from older children, subjects may have been using spatial-relational cues in the larger room beyond the surrounding curtain. Between trials the children played with toys in a designated area outside the curtain but in the same large room as the curtain and pool. Thus, they could have formed a complex mental geometry of the entire large room, including the relationships between all of its elements.

As we did for the results in the RAM, we interpret the findings in the Morris task to indicate that spatial-relational learning has late ontogenesis in humans, perhaps as late as 7–12 years of age. This conclusion was strengthened by a third experiment showing equally late emergence of adult-level spatial-relational performance on an open field task in which both cue-based and response-based solutions were eliminated (Overman et al., 1996c). Since the open field task has no counterpart in the animal literature, it is not described here.

THE QUESTION OF NEURAL MECHANISMS UNDERLYING SPATIAL-RELATIONAL BEHAVIORS IN CHILDREN There are several unresolved issues related to neural mechanisms and relational spatial behavior. Currently two

FIGURE 8.4 Adaptation of the Morris search task for children. A 5-year-old subject is shown searching through plastic chips for a hidden "treasure chest" filled with candy. In some conditions eight large distinctive posters were mounted on the surrounding floor-to-ceiling tarp; however, these are not visible in the photograph.

facts seem clear: (1) In rodents, an intact and anatomically mature hippocampal system is required for relational solutions but not for cue-based solutions in the RAM and Morris task (Jarrard, 1993; Keith, 1990; Rudy et al., 1987; Sutherland, Kolb, and Whishaw, 1982; Sutherland and Rudy, 1989); and (2) performance on spatial-relational tasks does not reach maturity in children until after age 5 and perhaps as late as age 7–15 years.

With these two findings in mind, we speculated in earlier reports (Overman et al., 1996c) that the late maturation of spatial-relational behaviors in children simply reflected late anatomical maturation of the hippocampal and related systems. It is now clear, however, that the true nature of the matter is more complex. First, as shown by Seress (1992, 2001 [chapter 4, this volume]), whereas much of the hippocampal formation development occurs very early in postnatal life of humans, some anatomical details are delayed until at

least the fifth year of life, namely, development of spine structure of mossy cells. This prolonged dendritic development suggests that synaptic connections between granule cells and their postsynaptic targets may last as long as 5 years postnatally. But, paradoxically, some hippocampally mediated behaviors appear very early in life in primates. For example, visual recognition memory as assessed by visual paired comparison procedures (also called preferential viewing for novelty) depends on an intact hippocampus (Zola et al., 2000; Pascalis and Bachevalier, 1999), and this behavior is present at least as early as 1 month of age in monkeys (Bachevalier, 1990) and at birth or earlier (in premature infants) in humans (see Fagan, 1990, for review). Thus, the question is: Why do some hippocampally mediated behaviors (VPC-elicited visual recognition memory) appear early in life while others (spatial-relational behavior) appear much later? There are several possible explanations. In children, perhaps, the infantile hippocampus might be able to support automatic and low-level behaviors such as VPC-elicited recognition memory but is not able to support more complex and effortful behaviors such as spatial-relational learning. (It should be noted that VPC-elicited recognition memory qualifies both as "automatic," because only spontaneous-looking behavior is required, and as "low-level," because it is operationally defined as looking at novel stimuli simply greater than chance levels; see Overman et al., 1993.) Consequently, it may be that the late appearance of spatial-relational behaviors in children depends upon the maturation of either the late developing anatomical details of the hippocampal formation and/or connections between hippocampus and prefrontal cortices which may play a role in strategic search required for adult-level performance. Future comparisons of animals and children on the same tasks may help resolve some of these issues.

## Summary of major inferences from applying animal tests to children

Table 8.1 summarizes the results of applying animal tests to children, including the ages at which various levels of performance occur. Inferences about underlying neural mechanisms are discussed in the relevant sections of text. While these inferences might be considered to be logically strong, there are a number of caveats that should accompany them.

CAVEATS TO THE APPLICATION OF ANIMAL TESTS TO HUMANS   In most instances reported here, the procedures of animal testing can be directly applied to children; however, some procedures and measures do not translate well for use in children. The specific example cited earlier was the use of latency measures for animals in the Morris task. Latency measures cannot be used with children of different ages because motor ability in the Morris apparatus improves with age. It was obvious from the direct search path on the control task (i.e., having the goal visible) that children of all ages were equally motivated and able to seek the goal, yet younger children required more time to move through the filling in the pool. For similar reasons, latency measures would not have been appropriate in the open field task mentioned earlier.

The absence or presence of verbal instructions must be considered very carefully when applying animal tests to children. For some tasks, such as the Morris task, verbal instructions do not appear to confound the results. In fact, it is difficult to imagine how this test might be easily administered without instructions. For other tasks, however, it is absolutely imperative *not* to have verbal instructions if we are to compare the results between children and animals or compare the results between children of different ages. This is especially true of the tasks administered in the WGTA. We discovered a striking example of how verbal instruction changes performance when we administered a trial-unique oddity task to children first without and then with verbal instructions (Overman et al., 1996a). As developed for monkeys, in the oddity problem the subject is presented on every trial with two identical and one odd object simultaneously. New stimuli are used on each trial so that no stimulus is used more than once a month. Subjects are tested for 15 trials per day, 5 days a week until attaining a criterion level of 90% correct choices for two consecutive days.

We tested children (1.5–8.5 years of age) on the oddity problem with no verbal instructions. Children over the age of 7 years learned rapidly with virtually no errors. However, children younger than 7 years displayed extreme difficulty in mastering this task and averaged 76 sessions of training to attain criterion. In fact 5 of

TABLE 8.1
*Results of testing children with cognitive tasks developed for animals*

| Task | Age-Related Findings | Reference |
|---|---|---|
| Delayed nonmatch to sample | High-level performance on concurrent discrimination appears earlier in life (12–18 months of age) than high-level performance on DNMS (after 3 years of age) | Overman, 1990 Overman et al., 1992 |
| Object reversal and concurrent discrimination | Infant male superiority on object reversal vs. infant female superiority on concurrent discrimination up to 3 years of age | Overman et al., 1997 |
| Radial-arm maze and Morris task | Adult-level performance using relational strategy does not appear until approximately 7 years of age | Overman et al., 1996c |
| Oddity task | Slow learning of nonverbal oddity task vs. rapid learning of verbal oddity task through 6 years of age | Overman et al., 1996a |

the 12 children in this group failed to attain criterion in 100 days of training. The children who failed were 32, 43, 42, 49, and 50 months of age. This late developing learning of the oddity problem by children parallels the late emergence of adult performance on this task by monkeys; that is, monkeys do not master the task until they are 3 or 4 years of age (Harlow, 1959; Harlow, Akert, and Schlitz, 1964).

While this parallel between humans and monkeys is an interesting developmental phenomenon, we discovered something even more fascinating regarding the role of verbal instructions on problem solving. After failing the task in 100 nonverbal daily test sessions, five of the children were given verbal instructions of "Pick the toy that doesn't belong," whereupon they all showed instant mastery of the task!

Thus, it would be incorrect to conclude that these children had been incapable of making "same–different" or "oddity" comparisons. Clearly, they were able to *utilize* the oddity rule when it was provided to them. Their difficulty appeared to be that of *evoking* the appropriate rule from the reinforcement contingencies alone. "Evocation" is the ability to choose or invent an appropriate strategy to solve a problem (Flavell, 1971). Furthermore, rule *evocation* is the only ability that can be measured when testing animals, since we cannot verbally convey a rule for *utilization*. Our data show that young children have great difficulty in extracting or evoking the oddity concept from reinforcement contingencies exactly as do monkeys.

Two points emerge from these findings: (1) If cross-species comparisons are to be made, nonverbal operant procedures typically must be used for children as well as for animals on certain tasks; (2) the distinction between rule *evocation* and rule *utilization* must always be kept in mind when testing human subjects. That this distinction even exists underscores our current lack of knowledge about exactly how language systems neuroanatomically interact with other systems in the human brain. And this, in turn, raises the question of exactly how human brains differ from animal brains, which are not capable of language.

As Nelson (1995) and many others have pointed out, linking a particular cognitive function to a particular brain structure is not as straightforward as often implied in a given study. This problem occurs because brain structures are interconnected into complex circuits and interrelated systems. Rather than state that a particular cognitive function is "mediated" by a particular neural system, it is more accurate to state that certain cognitive functions are *heavily* or *largely* dependent upon particular structures.

Finally, conclusions resulting from the application of

animal tests to children are *inferential*. As in all cognitive neuroscience endeavors, validity must be established by converging data from a variety of techniques, including further animal tests, data from brain-damaged humans, humans in special clinical populations, and data from studies using neuroimaging (see Casey, Thomas, and McCandliss, this volume). The last point is particularly important. Nelson (1995) has noted that with traditional testing procedures, it is virtually impossible to know if a monkey, a child, or a human adult is using the same cognitive processes on a given cognitive test; however, cognitive neuroscience can now begin to address such questions for the first time in history. Cross-species studies with functional imaging technologies may disclose if similar brain areas are being used by different subjects on a given task. This, together with knowledge about comparative neuroanatomy and neurochemistry, will begin to answer questions about comparative cognitive processes.

ACKNOWLEDGMENTS We are indebted to the participants in our studies and their parents, as well as to the directors and staff of the following preschools: Creative World Preschool, Winter Park Preschool, Little Friends Preschool, Classy Bears Preschool, Park Avenue Preschool, Early Childhood Learning Center, Total Childhood Learning Center, and Wesley Memorial Preschool, all of which are located in Wilmington, North Carolina.

The research was supported by grants R01-MH50724 from the National Institute of Mental Health and R01-HD35542 from the National Institutes of Child Health and Human Development, and by grants from the Mary Reynolds Babcock Foundation, R.P.M. Incorporated, the Florence Rogers Charitable Trust, the Landmark Organization, and the University of North Carolina at Wilmington Research and Development Fund.

## REFERENCES

ANDREASON, P. J., A. J. ZAMETKIN, A. C. GUO, P. BALDWIN, and R. M. COHEN, 1993. Gender-related differences in regional cerebral glucose metabolism in normal volunteers. *Psychiatr. Res.* 51:175–183.

BACHEVALIER, J., 1990. Ontogenetic development of habit and memory function in primates. In *The Development and Neural Basis of Higher Cognitive Function*, Vol. 608, A. Diamond, ed. New York: New York Academy of Science Press, pp. 457–484.

BACHEVALIER, J., M. BRICKSON, C. HAGGER, 1993. Limbic-dependent recognition memory in moneys develops early in infancy. *NeuroReport* 4:77–80.

BACHEVALIER, J., M. BRICKSON, C. HAGGER, and M. MISHKIN, 1990. Age and sex differences in the effects of selective temporal lobe lesions on the formation of visual discrimination habits in rhesus monkeys (*Macca mulatta*). *Behav. Neurosci.* 104:885–889.

BACHEVALIER, J., C. HAGGER, and B. BERCU, 1989. Gender differences in visual habit formation in 3-month-old rhesus monkeys. *Dev. Psychobiol.* 22:585–599.

BACHEVALIER, J., and M. MISHKIN, 1984. An early and late developing system for learning and retention in infant monkeys. *Behav. Neurosci.* 98:770–778.

BARNS, C. A., 1988. Spatial learning and memory processes: The search for their neurobiological mechanisms in the rat. *Trends Neurosci.* 11:163–269.

BAYER, S. A., 1980. Development of the hippocampal region in the rat: Neurogenesis examined with $^3$H-thymidine autoradiography. *J. Comp. Neurol.* 190:87–114.

BUTTERS, N., J. WOLFE, M. MARTONE, E. GRANHOLM, and L. S. CERMAK, 1985. Memory disorders associated with Huntington's disease: Verbal recall, verbal recognition, and procedural memory. *Neuropsychologia* 6:729–744.

CLARK, A. S., and P. GOLDMAN-RAKIC, 1989. Gonadal hormones influence the emergence of cortical function in nonhuman primates. *Behav. Neurosci.* 103:1287–1295.

COHEN, N. J., and H. EICHENBAUM, 1991. The theory that wouldn't die: A critical look at spatial mapping theory of hippocampal function. *Hippocampus* 1:265–268.

COLEMAN, J. K., and W. H. OVERMAN, 2001. Delayed ontogeny of landmark discrimination in children. In preparation.

CORBIER, P., D. A. EDWARDS, and J. ROFFI, 1992. The neonatal testosterone surge: A comparative study. *Arch. Int. Physiol. Biochem. Biophys.* 100:127–131.

DIAMOND, A., 1990. Rate of maturation of the hippocampus and the developmental progression of children's performance on the delayed non-matching to sample and visual paired comparison tasks. In *The Development and Neural Basis of Higher Cognitive Functions*, Vol. 608, A. Diamond, ed. New York: New York Academy of Sciences Press, pp. 394–433.

FAGAN, J. F., III, 1990. The paired-comparison paradigm and infant intelligence. In *Development and Neural Basis of Higher Cognitive Functions*, A. Diamond, ed. New York: New York Academy of Sciences, pp. 337–364.

FLAVELL, J. H., 1971. Stage-related properties of cognitive development. *Cogn. Psychol.* 2:421–453.

GOLDMAN, P. S., 1971. Functional development of the prefrontal cortex in early life and the problem of neuronal plasticity. *Exp. Neurol.* 32:366–387.

GOLDMAN, P. S., H. T. CRAWFORD, L. P. STOKES, T. GALKIN, and H. E. ROSVOLD, 1974. Sex-dependent behavioral effect of cerebral cortical lesions in the developing rhesus monkey. *Science* 186:540–542.

GRAF, P., and D. L. SCHACTER, 1985. Implicit and explicit memory for new associations in normal and amnesic subjects. *J. Exp. Psychol.: Learn. Mem. Cog.* 11:501–518.

GUR, R. C., L. MOZLEY, P. D. MOZLEY, S. RESNICK, J. KARP, A. ALAVI, S. ARNOLD, and R. E. GUR, 1995. Sex differences in regional cerebral glucose metabolism during a resting state. *Science* 267:528–531.

HAGGER, C., J. BACHEVALIER, and B. B. BERCU, 1987. Sexual dimorphism in the development of habit formation; effects of perinatal steroidal gonadal hormones. *Neuroscience* 22(suppl):S520.

HALPERN, D. F., 1992. *Sex Differences in Cognitive Abilities.* Hillsdale, N.J.: Lawrence Erlbaum Associates.

HARLOW, H. F., 1951. Primate learning. In *Comparative Psychology*, C. P. Stone, ed. New York: Prentice Hall, pp. 183–238.

HARLOW, H. F., 1958. The evolution of learning. In *Behavior and Evolution*, A. Roe and G. C. Simpson, eds. New Haven: Yale University Press, pp. 269–290.

HARLOW, H. F., 1959. The development of learning in the rhesus monkey. *Am. Sci.* 47:459–479.

HARLOW, H. F., K. AKERT, and K. A. SCHILTZ, 1964. The effects of bilateral prefrontal lesions on learned behavior of neonatal, infant, and preadolescent monkeys. In *The Frontal Granular Cortex and Behavior,* J. W. Warren and K. Akert, eds. New York: McGraw Hill, pp. 126–148.

JARRARD, L. E., 1993. On the role of the hippocampus in learning and memory in the rat. *Behav. Neural Biol.* 60:9–26.

KEITH, J., 1990. *Ontogeny of Place Learning and Memory in the Rat.* Unpublished doctoral dissertation. University of Colorado.

KNOWLTON, B. J., J. A. MANGELS, and L. R. SQUIRE, 1996. A neostriatal habit learning system in humans. *Science* 273:1399–1402.

KOLB, B., and I. WHISHAW, 1990. *Fundamentals of Human Neuropsychology.* New York: Freeman.

MARTONE, M., N. BUTTERS, M. PAYNE, J. BECKER, and D. SAX, 1984. Dissociations between skill learning and verbal recognition in amnesia and dementia. *Arch. Neurol.* 41:965–970.

MCNAUGHTON, B. L., C. A. BARNES, and J. O'KEEFE, 1983. The contributions of position, direction, and velocity to single unit activity in the hippocampus of freely moving rats. *Exp. Brain Res.* 53:41–49.

MEUNIER, M., J. BACHEVALIER, M. MISHKIN, and E. A. MURRAY, 1993. Effects on visual recognition of combined and separate ablations of the entorhinal and perirhinal cortex in rhesus monkeys. *J. Neurosci.* 13:5418–5432.

MISHKIN, M., 1978. Memory in monkeys severely impaired by combined but not by separate removal of amygdala and hippocampus. *Nature (Lond.)* 273:297–298.

MISHKIN, M., and J. DELACOUR, 1975. An analysis of short term visual memory. *J. Exp. Psychol: Anim. Behav. Process* 1:297–298.

MISHKIN, M., B. MALAMUT, and J. BACHEVALIER, 1984. Memories and habits: Two neural systems. In *Neurobiology of Learning and Memory*, G. Lynch, J. McGaugh, and N. M. Weinberger, eds. New York: Guilford, pp. 65–77.

MISHKIN, M., and E. A. MURRAY, 1998. Stimulus recognition. In *Findings and Current Opinion in Cognitive Neuroscience*, L. R. Squire and S. M. Kosslyn, eds. Cambridge, Mass: MIT Press, pp. 68–73.

MORRIS, R. G. M., 1981. Spatial localization does not require the presence of local cues. *Learn. Motiv.* 12:239–260.

MUMBY, D. G., and J. P. J. PINEL, 1994. Rhinal cortex lesions and object recognition in rats. *Behav. Neurosci.* 108:1–8.

MURRAY, E. A., and M. MISHKIN, 1984. Severe tactual as well as visual memory deficits follow combined removal of the amygdala and hippocampus in monkeys. *J. Neurosci.* 4:2565–2580.

NADEL, L., 1991. The hippocampus and space revisited. *Hippocampus* 1:221–229.

NADEL, L., and L. McDONALD, 1980. Hippocampus: Cognitive map or working memory? *Behav. Neural Biol.* 29:405–409.

NELSON, C. A., 1995. The ontogeny of human memory: A cognitive neuroscience perspective. *Dev. Psychol.* 31:723–738.

O'KEEFE, J., 1976. Place units in the hippocampus of the freely moving rat. *Exp. Neurol.* 51:78–109.

O'KEEFE, J., 1991. An allocentric spatial model for the hippocampal cognitive map. *Hippocampus* 1:230–235.

O'KEEFE, J., and L. NADEL, 1978. *The Hippocampus as a Cognitive Map.* Oxford, England: Claredon Press.

OLTON, D. S., J. T. BECKER, and G. HANDLEMANN, 1979. Hippocampus, space, and memory. *Behav. Brain Sci.* 2:313–365.

OLTON, D. S., and B. C. PAPAS, 1979. Spatial memory and hippocampal function. *Neuropsychologia* 17:669–682.

OLTON, D. S., and R. J. SAMUELSON, 1976. Remembrance of places passed: Spatial memory in rats. *J. Exp. Psychol.: Anim. Behav. Process* 2:97–116.

OVERMAN, W. H., 1990. Performance on traditional match-to-sample, non-match to sample, and object discrimination tasks by 12–32-month-old children: A developmental progression. In *The Development and Neural Basis of Higher Cognitive Functions,* Vol. 608, A. Diamond, ed. New York: New York Academy of Sciences Press, pp. 365–383.

OVERMAN, W. H., J. BACHEVALIER, M. MILLER, and K. MOORE, 1996a. Children's performance on "animal tests" of oddity: Implications for cognitive processes required for tests of oddity and delayed nonmatch to sample. *J. Exp. Child Psychol.* 62:223–242.

OVERMAN, W. H., J. BACHEVALIER, M. TURNER, and A. PEUSTER, 1992. Object recognition versus object discrimination: Comparison between human infants and infant monkeys. *Behav. Neurosci.* 106:15–29.

OVERMAN, W. H., J. BACHEVALIER, E. SCHUHMANN, and P. RYAN, 1996b. Cognitive gender differences in very young children parallel biologically based cognitive gender differences in monkeys. *Behav. Neurosci.* 110:673–684.

OVERMAN, W. H., J. BACHEVALIER, E. SCHUHMANN, and P. M. RYAN, 1997. Sexually dimorphic brain-behavior development: A comparative perspective. In *Development of the Prefrontal Cortex: Evolution, Neurobiology, and Behavior,* N. A. Krasnegor, G. Reid Lyon, and P. S. Goldman-Rakic, eds. Baltimore: Paul H. Brooks Publishing, pp. 337–357.

OVERMAN, W. H., J. BACHEVALIER, F. SEWELL, and J. DREW, 1993. A comparison of children's performance on two recognition memory tasks: Delayed nonmatch-to-sample vs. visual paired comparison. *Dev. Neurobiol.* 26:345–357.

OVERMAN, W. H., and M. GODIN, 2001. Male superiority on object reversal extends to 34 months of age in children. In preparation.

OVERMAN, W. H., G. ORMSBY, and M. MISHKIN, 1990. Picture recognition vs. picture discrimination learning in monkeys with medial temporal removals. *Exp. Brain Res.* 79:18–24.

OVERMAN, W. H., B. J. PATE, K. MOORE, and A. PEUSTER, 1996c. Ontogeny of place learning in children as measures in the radial arm maze, Morris search task, and open field task. *Behav. Neurosci.* 110:1205–1228.

PASCALIS, O., and J. BACHEVALIER, 1999. Neonatal lesions of the hippocampal formation impair visual recognition memory when assessed by paired-comparison task but not by delayed nonmatching-to-sample task. *Hippocampus* 9:609–616.

PHILLIPS, R. R., B. L. MALAMUT, J. BACHEVALIER, and M. MISHKIN, 1988. Dissociation of the effects of inferior temporal and limbic lesions on object discrimination learning with 24-hour intertrial intervals. *Behav. Brain Res.* 27:99–107.

REAVIS, R., W. H. OVERMAN, S. HENDRIX, W. EXPOSITO, and C. DEZIO-COTTLE, 1998. Possible double dissociation of function between adult males and females in two brain systems. *Soc. Neurosci. Abstr.* 24:1177.

RUDY, J. W., S. STADLER-MORRIS, and P. ALBERT, 1987. Ontogeny of spatial navigation behaviors in the rat: Dissoc-

of "proximal"- and "distal"-cue based behaviors. *Behav. Neurosci.* 101:62–73.

SALMON, D. P., and N. BUTTERS, 1998. Neurobiology of skill and habit learning. In *Findings and Current Opinion in Cognitive Neuroscience,* L. R. Squire and S. M. Kosslyn, eds. Cambridge, Mass.: MIT Press, pp. 91–97.

SCHACTER, D. L., and E. TULVING, 1994. What are the memory systems of 1994? In *Memory Systems,* D. L. Schacter and E. Tulving, eds. Cambridge, Mass.: MIT Press, pp. 1–38.

SERESS, L., 1992. Morphological variability and developmental aspects of monkey and human granule cells: Differences between the rodent and primate dentate gyrus. *Epilepsy Res.* 7(suppl):3–28.

SERESS, L., 2001. Morphological changes of the human hippocampal formation from midgestation to early childhood. In *Handbook of Developmental Cognitive Neuroscience,* C. A. Nelson, and M. Luciana, eds. Cambridge, Mass.: MIT Press, pp. 45–58.

SHERRY, F., and D. L. SCHACTER, 1987. The evolution of multiple memory systems. *Psychol. Rev.* 94:439–454.

SQUIRE, L. R., 1986. Mechanisms of memory. *Science* 232: 1612–1619.

SQUIRE, L. R., 1987. *Memory and Brain.* New York: Oxford University Press.

SQUIRE, L. R., B. KNOWLTON, and G. MUSEN, 1993. The structure and organization of memory. *Ann. Rev. Psychol.* 44:453–495.

SQUIRE, L. R., S. ZOLA-MORGAN, and K. S. CHEN, 1988. Human amnesia and animal models of amnesia: Performance of amnesic patients on tests designed for the monkey. *Behav. Neurosci.* 102:210–221.

STAHL, F., F. GOTZ, I. POPPE, P. AMENDT, and G. DORNER, 1978. Pre- and early postnatal testosterone levels in rat and human. In *Hormones and Brain Development,* G. Dorner and M. Kawakami, eds. New York: Elsevier/North-Holland Biomedical Press, pp. 99–109.

SUTHERLAND, R. J., 1985. The navigating hippocampus: An individual medley of space, memory, and movement. In *Electrical Activity of the Archicortex,* G. Buzaki and C. H. Vanderwolf, eds. Budapest: Akademiai Kiado, pp. 255–279.

SUTHERLAND, R. J., B. KOLB, and I. WHISHAW, 1982. Spatial mapping: Definitive disruption by hippocampal or medial frontal cortical damage in the rat. *Neurosci. Lett.* 32:271–276.

SUTHERLAND, R. J., and J. W. RUDY, 1987. Place learning in the Morris place navigation task is impaired by damage to the hippocampus formation even if temporal demands are reduced. *Psychobiol.* 16:157–163.

SUTHERLAND, R. J., and J. W. RUDY, 1989. Configural association theory: The role of the hippocampal formation in learning, memory, and amnesia. *Psychobiol.* 17:129–144.

WALLENSTEIN, G. V., H. EICHENBAUM, and M. E. HASSELMO, 1998. The hippocampus as an associator of discontiguous events. *Trends Neurosci.* 21:317–323.

WILSON, M. A., and B. MCNAUGHTON, 1993. Dynamics of the hippocampal ensemble code for space. *Science* 261:1055–1058.

WINOCUR, G., 1980. The hippocampus and cue utilization. *Physiol. Psychol.* 8:280–288.

WORDEN, R. P., 1992. Navigation by fragment fitting: A theory of hippocampal function. *Hippocampus* 2:165–187.

ZOLA, S. M., L. R. SQUIRE, E. TENG, L. STEFANACCI, E. A. BUFFALO, and R. E. CLARK, 2000. Impaired recognition memory in monkeys after damage limited to the hippocampal region. *J. Neurosci.* 20:451–463.

ZOLA-MORGAN, S., and L. R. SQUIRE, 1990. The neuropsychology of memory: Parallel findings in humans and nonhuman primates. In *The Development and Neural Basis of Higher Cognitive Functions*, Vol. 608, A. Diamond, ed. New York: New York Academy of Sciences Press, pp. 434–456.

ZOLA-MORGAN, S., and L. R. SQUIRE, 1993. Neuroanatomy of memory. *Annu. Rev. Neurosci.* 16:547–563.

ZOLA-MORGAN, S., L. R. SQUIRE, R. P. CLOWER, and N. L. REMPEL, 1993. Damage to the perirhinal cortex exacerbates memory impairment following lesions to the hippocampal formation. *J. Neurosci.* 13:251–265.

# 9 The Use of Event-Related Potentials in the Study of Cognitive Development

CHARLES A. NELSON
AND CHRISTOPHER S. MONK

ABSTRACT Event-related potentials (ERPs) can be recorded noninvasively at the scalp surface in a matter of minutes and do not require a motor or verbal response; thus, they represent an ideal method by which to study the neural correlates of cognitive function across the entire lifespan. In this chapter we begin by reviewing the physiological basis of ERPs, and then describe the various ERP components that have been used to chart the development of the neural correlates of different cognitive functions. We conclude by describing how ERPs can be used to study brain development across the first 1–2 decades of life.

Our understanding of the behavioral correlates of cognitive development has increased exponentially during the past three decades, and remains a rich vein for mining by the behavioral scientist. Unfortunately, our knowledge of the neurobiological forces that shape—and are shaped by—changes in cognition remains primitive. As has been described elsewhere (Nelson, 1995; Nelson and Bloom, 1997), this paucity of information about the neural bases of cognition can be attributed in part to the fact that developmental psychology and the neurosciences typically seek answers to questions that lie at different points on a knowledge continuum (e.g., physiological basis of attention vs. behavioral description of attention). Furthermore, each science requires different levels of analysis, the tools of the neurosciences being far more reductionistic than those of the behavioral scientist. Gradually, however, the fields of neuroscience and behavioral science have begun to merge. Nowhere is this more evident than in the field of functional brain imaging and cognition. Here we have seen a revolution in our ability to image the living brain at work. Although the majority of research in this area remains confined to the mature organism, increasing effort is being devoted to understanding de-velopment; indeed, this volume is a recognition of this change. We now a have a variety of tools that permit us to study the living brain, although not all are amenable to studying the *developing* brain. This chapter focuses specifically on the use of one such tool, the recording of event-related potentials (ERPs).

Our goal is to provide a tutorial on how ERPs have been used to study the ontogeny of cognition (for other examples using this method, see de Haan, Johnson, and Richards, this volume; Fabiani and Wee, this volume). To accomplish our goal, we begin with an overview of the physiological bases of ERPs. We then move on to review the literature on how particular components of ERPs have been used to study different cognitive phenomena. Because comprehensive reviews of this literature exist elsewhere (see Nelson and Luciana, 1998), we shall provide illustrative examples rather than an exhaustive review.

## The genesis of the ERP signal

In order to measure changes in the brain's electrical activity, scalp electrodes require the summation of large numbers of neurons. Action potentials provide the largest electrical change in the nervous system, but the time course of this change is too brief to permit the necessary summation across neurons. Therefore, excitatory and inhibitory postsynaptic potentials provide the current that is detected by ERPs (Allison, Woods, and McCarthy, 1986). These potentials occur over a relatively long period of time, so that many neurons generating electrical current simultaneously are allowed to summate, then propagate to the scalp surface.

The ERP signal is thought to be primarily derived from pyramidal cells in the cerebral cortex and hippocampus (Allison, 1984). These cells tend to be parallel to one another and many are perpendicular to the scalp. Because many of these cells are aligned in parallel, their synchronous activation leads to the summation of current in the same direction. Therefore, an open field is created (reviewed in Allison, 1984). Open

CHARLES A. NELSON Institute of Child Development and Department of Pediatrics, University of Minnesota, Minneapolis, Minnesota.
CHRISTOPHER S. MONK Institute of Child Development, University of Minnesota, Minneapolis, Minnesota.

fields allow current to be volume-conducted through extracellular space and up to the scalp. In contrast, cells that are in more or less random orientations to one another approximate a closed field, whereby the lack of a uniform signal makes it difficult to detect against the background noise. Furthermore, the perpendicular orientation of pyramidal cells directs the current to the scalp surface, so that their signal is more pronounced relative to cells that are oriented in other directions. Consequently, the tendency for pyramidal cells to be organized in parallel networks allows more current to travel in one particular direction, and the perpendicular orientation to the scalp provides a greater signal for the surface electrode to measure.

The ERP signal is expressed as a series of positive and negative deflections distributed across time. The direction of the deflection depends on the orientation of the *dipole*, which is a separation of charge in a volume conductor. Neurophysiologically, a dipole occurs when either excitatory or inhibitory input from a neighboring cell causes a change in the charge of the postsynaptic cell. In the case of excitatory input, positively charged ions flow into the cell, creating a negative charge in the nearby extracellular space (figure 9.1). The site of this negative current is called the *sink*. The positively charged ions then flow through a segment of the neuron and exit back into the extracellular space. This positively charged area is called the *source*. The terms "sink" and "source" refer to the location where the current flows into and out of the cell, respectively. In the case of an inhibitory synapse (figure 9.2), the inside of the cell is hyperpolarized, leaving the surrounding extracellular space with a positive charge (sink). The negative current flows through an area of the neuron, then returns to the extracellular space (source), establishing a dipole. If one were to place extracellular electrodes at the sink and source, one would find a disparity in electrical charge. In the first example, where the sink is negative and the source is positive, extracellular electrodes would demonstrate that the sink is more negative than the source. When a negative sink is closer to the scalp electrode than the positive source, a negative deflection is measured; and when the positive source is closer to the electrode than the negative sink, a positive deflection is measured. When the source is negative and the sink positive, the reverse is true. That is, when a negative source is located closer to the scalp than a positive sink, a negative deflection is measured from the scalp electrode; and when a positive sink is located closer to the scalp electrode than a negative source, a positive deflection is measured.

To summarize, ERPs predominantly measure the activation patterns of pyramidal cells in the cortex and hippocampus. When a particular neuron is excited or inhibited, positive or negative current flows into the cell. This movement of ions leaves a negative or positive sink in the surrounding extracellular space. In turn, the intracellular ions travel through the neuron, then exit back into the extracellular space, creating a positive or negative source. Therefore, the formation of the sink and source creates a dipole, which is volume-conducted through the extracellular space and can be measured by scalp electrodes. However, while scalp electrodes are able to determine the general orientation of a dipole, it is not possible to know whether the activation leading to this dipole is excitatory or inhibitory. For instance, if a cell's dendrites are located closer to the scalp surface than the axon and the cell is inhibited, a positive sink would be created closer to the surface and a negative source farther from the scalp. The result would be a positive deflection as measured by scalp electrodes. However, if the dendrites are oriented farther from the scalp surface than the axon and the cell is excited, a negative sink would be created farther from the scalp and a positive source would form closer to the scalp. Consequently, this, too, would lead to a positive deflection.

## Recording ERPs and labeling components

Historically, the placement of electrodes generally followed the 10/20 system (Jasper, 1958). In this system, electrodes are placed at relative distances (either 10 or 20%) from one another along the anterior-posterior axis and the lateral axis. The names of electrodes are derived from their proximity to the underlying brain structure as well as its placement in the lateral plane (electrodes on the left are assigned an odd number, those on the right are given an even number, while *z* connotes midline areas). Thus, Fz indicates that the electrode is over the frontal lobe along the midline region, while T3 identifies it as a left temporal lobe lead. However, as described earlier, the brain is a volume conductor; consequently, pronounced activity recorded from T3 does not necessarily indicate that the neural activation occurs in the left temporal lobe.

Recently, the field of ERP research has witnessed the advent of high-density arrays of electrodes. Here 64 or 128 electrodes are placed over the scalp surface by way of a cap or net. Such electrodes obviously do not conform to the 10/20 system, but rather, are designed to provide near-complete coverage of the entire scalp. The closer spacing of these electrodes (on the order of 1 cm interelectrode distances) permits one to perform more accurate interpolations, thereby (potentially) improving the spatial resolution of any given ERP component.

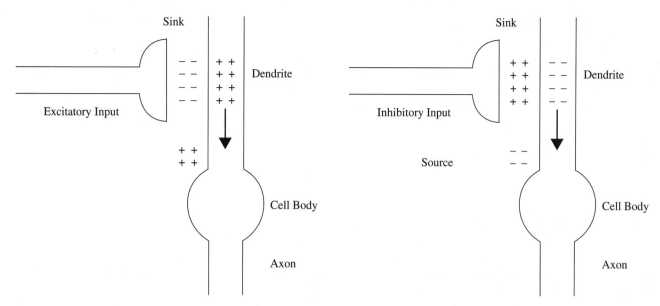

FIGURE 9.1 Excitatory input from a neighboring axon leads to an inflow of positive ions in the cell, leaving more negatively charged ions in the nearby extracellular space (sink). The positive ions then travel down the cell and exit back into the extracellular space (source). This leaves more positive ions in the extracellular space in the lower portion of the figure and more negative ions in the extracellular space of the upper portion of the figure. The result is a dipole in the extracellular space. If the negative ions were closer to the scalp electrode, a negative deflection would be recorded and if the positive ions were closer to the scalp electrode a positive deflection would be recorded.

FIGURE 9.2 Inhibitory input causes negative ions to enter the cell; thus, the neighboring extracellular space is left with a net positive charge (sink). Then, negative ions accumulate in the extracellular space closer to the cell body (source). Consequently, this inhibitory input also creates a dipole in the extracellular space.

## ERP topography and source localization

Because ERPs volume-conduct to the scalp surface, solving the inverse problem—identifying the dipole (or dipoles) responsible for generating a particular ERP component—is not trivial. Nevertheless, a variety of approaches have been adopted that attempt to use ERP topography as a way of inferring information about underlying sources. The simplest and most straightforward is Laplacian analysis, which essentially involves cross-correlating electrodes in order to isolate particular regions of activation. The spatial resolution of Laplacian analysis is rather coarse, however, and is not designed for source localization; it is ideal, though, when only a (relatively) small number of electrodes are used and the investigator wishes to draw some approximate inferences about *potential* sources.

When one benefits from high-density arrays of electrodes (e.g., in which the interelectrode distance is less than 2–3 cm), two more powerful methods can be employed. The first is *independent component analysis*, or ICA. ICA is a formal method for decomposing spatio-temporal data into separate, or independent components. ICA assumes that electrical activity recorded at scalp electrode sites represents a linear combination of concurrent electrical activity of networks of neurons within the brain, and that these networks are spatially fixed and operate independently in time. Each component identified by ICA is described by a waveform representing the time course of activity of the component, with a scalp surface voltage map representing the topography of the component. To the extent that ICA components are thought to reflect underlying brain networks operating independently, differences in components between experimental conditions may reflect differences in neural generators. Thus, ICA may be used to test hypotheses regarding differences in structures (i.e., neural generators) associated with differences in cognitive processes (i.e., between different tasks, or at different times within the same task). ICA may also be useful as a preprocessing step prior to source localization methods, although this use of ICA is still being evaluated.

A second approach is *brain electrical source analysis*, or BESA. Like principal components analysis, BESA utilizes all the information recorded over all electrodes and at all time points. This method permits one to dissect ERPs into constituent source waveforms that reflect the activity of localized brain regions.

## The primary ERP components
## and their development

Based on variations in the task and stimulus, a variety of ERP components have been documented, and the principal components are described in the following sections. In the typical ERP study, brain activity is measured during a brief baseline period (e.g., 100 ms). The stimulus is then presented and the EEG continues to be measured for the next 1500 ms or so. Consequently, deviations in the ERP pattern relative to the baseline period are attributed to the cognitive processing of the stimulus. ERP components usually derive their names from the polarity and latency of the waveform. Components with positive deflections are assigned a P to indicate positive, and waveforms with a negative deflection are given an N for negative. Following the P or N, a number is provided to identify the point in time that this component occurs following the onset of the stimulus. Thus, for example, the label P300 indicates that it is a positive-going deflection that occurs 300 ms following the stimulus onset.

The following section is organized by first discussing the class of negative components, the vast majority of which have been used to index attentional processes, followed by a discussion of positive components, a number of which have been used to index memory processes. Within each class, we suborganize components by latency, such that we begin with the earliest occurring components, moving to progressively later occurring components.

### Negative Components

*Negative difference/Processing negativity* The negative difference (Nd) or processing negativity (PN) component is thought to be related to attention. In the standard paradigm for eliciting this component, visual or auditory stimuli are presented at a rapid rate, and periodically an attribute of the stimulus will vary. In one study, for instance, tones were rapidly presented to both ears and subjects were asked to attend to only one ear (Hillyard et al., 1973). In approximately 10% of the trials, the tone varied in either the attended or the unattended ear. In comparing the ERP responses to the tone deviations for the attended and unattended ear, the attended deviations elicited a larger negative deflection and the difference between these waves was maximal at 100 ms. Thus, the increased level of attention and not the exogenous stimulus leads to the modulation of this negative wave.

Controversy surrounds whether this increased amplitude to the attended stimulus represents a modulation

of the N100 (an early perceptual component appearing as a negative deflection at 100 ms following stimulus onset; Woldorff and Hillyard, 1991) or if this waveform is a separate negative deflection that is derived from separate neural sources from those that give rise to the N100 (Näätänen, 1992; for a discussion of this debate, see Mangun and Hillyard, 1995). Those who suggest that this is a modulation of the N100 call this component the Nd and those who believe that it corresponds to a separate negative deflection call it a PN. At present, this issue has not been resolved, but as will be discussed, a developmental approach may be useful in elucidating whether the Nd/PN is a modulation of the N100 or a separate component.

Little work has been done to examine this component developmentally. This is particularly unfortunate for several reasons. First, attention is a ubiquitous process that is necessary for day-to-day cognitive functioning. By exploring the developmental roots of this component, it is possible to gain a better grasp for how attention develops and how it might influence other forms of cognitive functioning at different ages (for information on attentional development, see Posner and Rothbart, this volume; Richards; and Johnson, this volume). Second, poor attention has long been implicated in psychiatric disorders such as schizophrenia (Bleurer, 1911/1950; McGhie and Chapman, 1961). One study to examine the Nd/PN in children examined subjects between the ages of 8 and 26 years who were at risk for schizophrenia (Schreiber et al., 1992). Relative to matched controls, those at risk for schizophrenia had reduced Nd/PN components. Therefore, this ERP component may provide a marker for later psychopathology. Moreover, the elucidation of the developmental time course of this component in healthy individuals as well as subjects at risk for nervous system disorders might shed light on the epidemiology of certain pathologies. Third, a developmental approach may help indicate whether this ERP component is a modulator of the N100 or if it is a separate component. Specifically, as will be described, the developmental analysis of other ERP components indicates that children manifest waveforms that are often similar to those of adults, but the onset is delayed and the morphology is protracted. If the Nd/PN wave is a separate ERP component from the N100, it is highly possible that the waveform will be delayed relative to the N100, allowing these components to be separated in time.

*Mismatch negativity* The mismatch negativity (MMN) is elicited by presenting an improbable auditory or visual stimulus along with a probable stimulus. This is called an oddball paradigm, because one event is presented frequently (e.g., 80%), while another event is rare or "odd" and is presented infrequently (e.g., 20%). The MMN is derived by subtracting the negative deflection to the frequent event from the negative deflection for the infrequent event, yielding a difference wave with a negative component that peaks at about 200 ms following stimulus onset.

Work by Näätänen and colleagues (Näätänen, Gaillard, and Mantysalo, 1978) indicates that the MMN may occur to both attended and unattended stimuli. Specifically, auditory stimuli were presented to both ears and participants were asked to attend only to one ear. However, when deviant stimuli were presented, an MMN occurred for both the attended and unattended ear. This led to the suggestion that the MMN is an automatic neural response to change that occurs when a deviant event is presented against a backdrop of a repeated, predictable event (reviewed in Näätänen, 1992). However, Woldorff, Hackley, and Hillyard (1991) found that under conditions of highly selective auditory attention, the MMN is modulated. That is, the MMN in the unattended ear was suppressed relative to the MMN in the attended ear. Thus, the MMN may be a neural signature for the detection of an infrequent event, but the neural generators may be at least slightly modified by attention.

Importantly, the MMN has been observed in newborns (Alho et al., 1990) and has even been seen in preterm infants (Cheour-Luhtanen et al., 1996). And, within a few months of life, the MMN looks increasingly similar (although not identical) to the adult MMN (Cheour et al., 1998a,b). Finally, work with children indicates that the MMN may be adult-like at 5–7 years of age (Csépe, 1995).

*NC* Courchesne and colleagues reported a series of studies employing the oddball paradigm with infants and children that described a negative component that peaked between 400 and 800 ms, and that was believed to reflect some aspect of attention (Courchesne, 1977, 1978; Courchesne et al., 1981). A consistent negativity was observed to the rare stimulus that was greater in amplitude than that observed to the frequent stimulus. This basic waveform was subsequently observed by other investigators, with the majority of this work being conducted with infants (Karrer and Ackles, 1987, 1988; Karrer and Monti, 1995; Nelson and Collins, 1991, 1992; for review, see Nelson, 1994, 1996). A major point of departure among these various studies was the extent to which the infrequent (rare) stimulus invoked a larger amplitude NC relative to the frequent stimulus. In studies using the conventional oddball paradigm (Courchesne and colleagues; Karrer and colleagues), rare

events often invoke larger amplitude responses. This is likely attributable to the fact that subjects are drawn to the stimulus that occurs infrequently relative to the background stimulus; thus, this greater NC probably has more to do with simple aspects of attention than with memory. In contrast, Nelson and colleagues typically pre-expose an infant to one stimulus prior to test, and during the test, this (previously exposed) stimulus is presented equally often as a novel stimulus. With one exception, the NC invoked in this paradigm is the same for both events. The exception appears to be when one stimulus is already highly familiar to the infant; thus, for example, de Haan and Nelson (1997) observed that the NC is larger to the infant's mother's face than to a stranger's face. Again, this probably has more to do with the allocation of attentional resources. For this reason, we (see Nelson, 1994, for discussion) have proposed that the NC represents some aspect of obligatory or automatic attention. This argument is bolstered by the fact that the NC in general is typically the most robust of the infant ERP components, and can even be observed on single trials.

*NSW* As described by Karrer and colleagues (e.g., Karrer and Ackles, 1987) and Nelson and colleagues (e.g., Nelson, 1994; de Haan and Nelson, 1997), a long-latency negative slow wave (NSW) is observed to follow the NC in some circumstances. By testing infants under a variety of conditions, we have suggested that this NSW represents the detection of novel events against a background of familiar events. Here, then, what infants appear to be doing is recognizing one stimulus as familiar, then responding to the second stimulus as different than the familiar stimulus. The conditions under which this novelty detection–related NSW occurs are those in which the unfamiliar stimulus has not been encoded into memory. This might happen if, for example, the unfamiliar stimulus is presented too infrequently to be encoded (even partially) or if the infant's memory abilities are too immature to encode an infrequently presented stimulus. As a rule, the NSW has not been observed beyond the infancy period.

*N400* Kutas and Hillyard developed a now classic paradigm to examine the N400 in linguistic processing. Subjects were presented with sentences that ended with semantically appropriate or inappropriate words. For instance, "It was his first day at work" is an example of an appropriate sentence, but "He spread the warm bread with socks" ends with a semantically inappropriate word. Inappropriate words at ends of sentences yield a pronounced N400 component. Based on these data, Kutas and Hillyard (1980) suggested that the N400 may be an index of the "'reprocessing' of semantically anomalous information" (Kutas and Hillyard, 1980, p. 203). The N400 has also been linked to memory processing. In tasks where new and old stimuli are presented, the new stimuli elicit a greater N400 and the amplitude of this component decreases with stimulus repetition (reviewed in Rugg and Doyle, 1994). Taken together, these findings from the language and memory literature led to the speculation that the N400 indexes the facility of integrating the current stimulus into the mental context of the situation (Halgren and Smith, 1987). That is, greater facility is associated with a decreased N400. Thus, the word "socks," being unexpected, may require a greater level of cognitive processing to reconcile it with the current context. Similarly, the repetition of a stimulus may influence the ease with which it is processed, accounting for the damped N400 in repeated presentations relative to novel ones.

*The contingent negative variation (CNV)* The CNV is elicited by establishing a contingency between the presentation of two stimuli across time. For instance, in the first study to establish the existence of the CNV, Walter and colleagues (1964) presented subjects with an auditory click followed by a flash of light after a one-second delay. Subjects were instructed to press a button immediately following the light. Thus, the auditory stimulus alerts the subject to the impending flash of light. This initial auditory click produces a sustained negative deflection that is maximal over the frontal central region and lasts until the subsequent stimulus is presented. This ERP component is thought to index expectation or motor preparation (reviewed in Coles and Rugg, 1995).

The CNV waveform has been segmented into two separate components: the O-wave and the E-wave (Loveless and Sanford, 1974). The O-wave is thought to be a correlate of the subject's orienting to the initial stimulus. In contrast, the E-wave reflects the subject's motor or sensory processing preparation for the subsequent stimulus. Thus, while the O-wave may be manifested in response to a previously displayed stimulus, the E-wave is a response to the anticipation of an event that has yet to occur. Consequently, one of us has suggested that the CNV in general may be an appropriate neurophysiological measure of the status of future-oriented behavior in children and adults (Nelson and Luciana, 1998).

Unfortunately, despite the potential of using the CNV to examine the development of future-oriented behavior, relatively little work has been done to examine the CNV across ages. Segalowitz and colleagues (Segalowitz, Unsal, and Dywan, 1992) found that in 12-year-old chil-

dren the O-wave displayed a sustained positive response to the initial stimulus, while adults exhibited a more pronounced negative deflection following a positive wave. In contrast, no marked differences were found in the E-wave component across ages. These data suggest that while the neural generators for the orienting response of the O-wave are not fully functional at age 12 years, perhaps the neural correlates of anticipation as indexed with the E-wave have reached maturity by this age.

*Miscellaneous negative components* Mills and colleagues presented children with words they understood, words they did not understand, and backward words (Mills, Coffey-Corina, and Neville, 1993). Comprehended words elicited larger N200 and N350 components than did the other stimuli in 20-month-olds. Studying 14- and 16-month-olds, Molfese demonstrated that ERPs discriminate known from unknown words. However, Molfese found that the differences were at 170, 320, and 440 ms in 14-month-olds, and at 270 and 650 ms in 16-month-olds (Molfese, 1989, 1990). Furthermore, the negative components were less negative for the known words than the unknown words, which is contrary to Mills's findings. These contradictory results may be due to differences in the ages of the subjects, methods of analysis, or the procedures. Nevertheless, these studies do indicate that negative components discriminate known from unknown words in infants.

POSITIVE COMPONENTS

*P300* Although the P300 is perhaps the most extensively studied ERP component (Coles and Rugg, 1995), the cognitive processes and neural generators that give rise to it are still unclear. This confusion may be partly due to the apparent fact that the P300 is not a unitary component, but rather represents different components that are manifested under different situations and by distinct neural structures (Knight, 1984, 1996; reviewed in Knight and Scabini, 1998). Specifically, the traditional P300 or P3b is elicited in oddball paradigms (discussed earlier). The infrequently presented stimulus gives rise to a positive wave that peaks between 300 and 900 ms and is maximal over the parietal lobe. The amplitude and latency can be modulated by the specifics of the task. In oddball paradigms, for instance, the less frequently a stimulus is presented, the greater the amplitude of the P3b, and the latency for the P3b increases with increased difficulty of classifying stimuli (reviewed in Coles and Rugg, 1995). In terms of its relation to behavior, the P3b is thought to be involved in context updating or revising the contents of working memory (Donchin, 1981; Rugg, 1995). Thus, items that deviate from the stream of stimuli in some way (e.g., letters in a word are a different size) elicit larger P300s (Fabiani, Karis, and Donchin, 1990; Fabiani et al., 1990; Karis, Fabiani, and Donchin, 1984).

The P3a can be distinguished from the P3b in that it occurs 60–80 ms earlier and the distribution is more frontally oriented (Knight et al., 1989). In addition, while the P3b is manifested by the updating of memory, the P3a is thought to be generated by an automatic response to novel stimuli (Knight et al., 1989). Courchesne and colleagues (1975) found that changes in the task alter the morphology of the P300. Specifically, novel, task-irrelevant stimuli elicit a waveform that fits the description of the P3a. In contrast, task-relevant stimuli are associated with the P3b. Consequently, these two waveforms appear to be recruited in different cognitive tasks and may rely on at least somewhat separate neural generators (see Knight and Scabini, 1998, for a discussion of the neural bases for the P3a and P3b).

Despite the emphasis placed on the P300 in the adult literature, very little work has been conducted to explore the development of this component. One exception to this trend is an early set of studies by Courchesne (Courchesne, 1977, 1978). In these investigations, the P300 to target stimuli (P3b) had a longer latency in children and this latency decreased with age. Furthermore, Courchesne also found that adults displayed a waveform that was comparable to the P3a to nontarget, novel stimuli and "dims" (stimuli presented under low luminance), but this pattern did not exist in young children. Instead, 6–8-year-old and 10–13-year-old children displayed a negative component followed by a positive component to these stimuli. It was not until 14–17 years of age that children began to exhibit a P3a to the novel and dim stimuli.

More recently, Thomas and Nelson (1996) used an oddball task to examine differences in the P300 between adults and 8-year-olds. Confirming Courchesne's findings, the infrequent target stimuli elicited a P300-like component in both groups, but the children's waveforms were broader and the latency was longer. These studies indicate that pronounced development occurs between middle childhood and adulthood and that further investigations using ERPs may help reveal the ways in which the central nervous system organizes and reorganizes itself across development.[1]

*PSW* In Courchesne's early work (1977, 1978), a long-latency positive slow wave (PSW) was observed to infrequently presented stimuli. Again, after conducting a lengthy line of investigation, Nelson and colleagues have speculated that the PSW reflects the updating of working memory for a partially encoded stimulus (see de Haan and Nelson, 1997, and Nelson, 1994, for discussion). Thus, the PSW is typically invoked by stimuli that the infant has only partially encoded. Indeed, as discussed later, an analogy has been drawn to the adult P300, which some investigators (e.g., Donchin, 1981) have interpreted to reflect the updating of working memory, or context updating. Thus, if the infant has been pre-exposed to one stimulus, and then this same stimulus is presented during the test trials but only 50% of the time (versus 80% or more, as is common in oddball paradigms), the infant may not have had enough opportunity to fully encode this stimulus (as a rule, a fully encoded stimulus yields an ERP that returns to baseline following the NC). The updating of memory that occurs each time this stimulus is presented gives rise to the PSW.

SUMMARY   Generally, the NC, NSW and PSW components have been disproportionately observed in infancy (see figure 9.3). The NC has also been observed in children (see Nelson and Nugent, 1990), although its latency of 400 ms may suggest that calling this component the N400 may be more appropriate. Although there is some functional similarity between the infant PSW and the child/adult P300, the morphology, latency, and topography of these components are dramatically different, suggesting that infants do not manifest P300

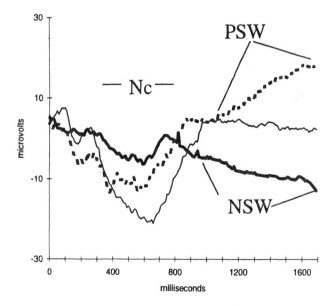

FIGURE 9.3   Nomenclature of components observed in infants, including the NC, PSW, and NSW. (Reprinted with permission from C. A. Nelson, 1996. Electrophysiological correlates of early memory development. In *Thirteenth West Virginia University Conference on Life Span Developmental Psychology: Biological and Neuropsychological Mechanisms*, H. W. Reese and M. D. Franzen, eds. Hillsdale, N.J.: Lawrence Erlbaum, pp. 95–131.)

*qua* P300 responses. The remaining negative components have typically been observed only in children and adults, although the MMN may be an exception; indeed, this component may be the only ERP component to be similar in infancy as in adulthood.

## What develops?

Over and above the glossary of ERP components used to describe different cognitive and/or neural operations, a pressing issue for us to consider is how ERPs can be used to chart changes in brain development.

As described earlier, the NC component is observed very early in life, and appears to evolve into the N400 response by the time children approach preschool age (e.g., 4 years). Importantly, the latency of this component changes over time. As seen in figure 9.4, for example, the latency changes by 100–200 ms between 6 and 12 months. What is responsible for this change is not clear. It may be that additional myelin that has been laid down, for example; or, at a more functional level, it may be that more efficient processing is taking place, which is more dependent on circuit development than on the development of myelin.

Let us now turn to the PSW and P300 responses. In a pilot study currently underway in our laboratory, we have been testing 8-month-old infants, 4-year-old children, and adults under the same task conditions (Wewerka and Luciana, 1999). Across all ages, subjects are presented with images of their own faces and the face of a stranger (the babies and children are also presented with images of their mothers). No instructions are given; rather, children and adults are simply told to watch the pictures.

As the top panel of figure 9.5 illustrates, there is a rather dramatic shift in morphology in the infant ERP; in fact, we typically observe a polarity reversal in the NC from Oz to Pz, and then again a shift to Cz. In contrast, the child (middle panel) and adult (bottom panel) ERP waveforms look fairly similar across the scalp.

In contrast to the infant response, the 4-year-olds show two negative components (N200, N400); the earlier one had been positive at this same latency in the infants, and the later one appears to be like the infant NC. The PSW/"P300" looks more similar to the infant PSW than to the adult P300.

Finally, the adults show the classic waveform of N200 followed by P300; this is very different from the pattern in children and infants.

Now, let us turn to what happens between the age of 4 and adulthood. As described earlier, Thomas and Nelson (1996) reported on a study in which 8-year-olds and

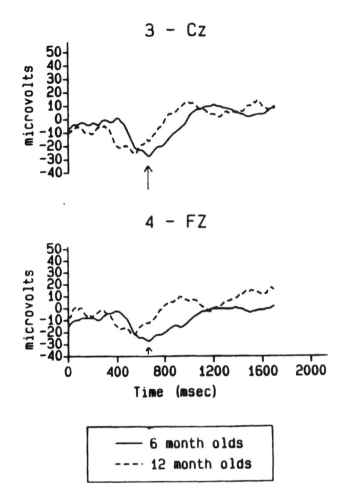

FIGURE 9.4   The NC component observed in 6-month-old infants and 12-month-old infants tested under the same conditions. Note the shift in latency from 6 to 12 months. (Reprinted with permission from C. A. Nelson, 1996. Electrophysiological correlates of early memory development. In *Thirteenth West Virginia University Conference on Life Span Developmental Psychology: Biological and Neuropsychological Mechanisms*, H. W. Reese and M. D. Franzen, eds. Hillsdale, N.J.: Lawrence Erlbaum, pp. 95–131.)

adults were presented with the same task: basically, a standard (ignore) stimulus was presented on 60% of the trials, a target stimulus was presented on 20% of the trials, and trial-unique novel stimuli were presented on the remaining 20% of the trials. As seen in figure 9.6, the waveforms look fairly similar across age groups to the target events, except that the P300 in the children is broader peaked and occurs 150–200 ms later than in the adults; note, though, that the waveforms are very different to the novel stimuli.

Overall, although it is difficult to compare across studies, somewhere between the ages of 4 and 8 years the morphology of the child ERP begins to resemble

# ERP Response to "Self" Face

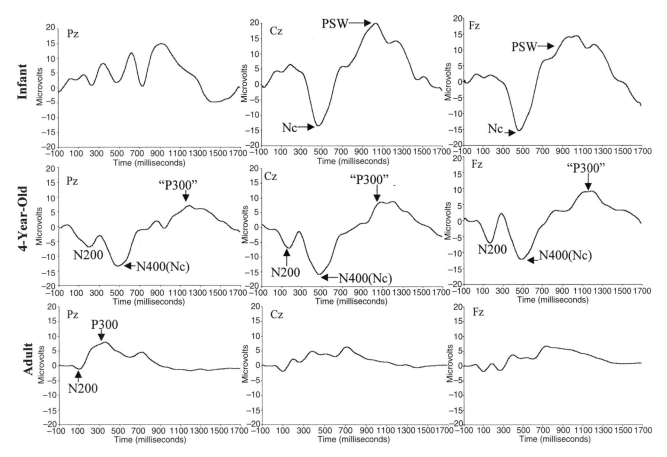

FIGURE 9.5 Pilot study in which 8-month-old infants (*top panel*), 4-year-old children (*middle panel*), and adults (*bottom panel*) were presented with images of their own faces and the face of a stranger.

that of the adult (although undoubtedly task conditions will influence this similarity). Still, at least one late component—the P300—is broader peaked and longer in latency, and the response to novel events is quite different. These observations suggest that much development remains after the age of 8.

## Conclusions

The changes in cognition that occur from infancy to adulthood clearly manifest themselves in different ERP signatures. These electrophysiological "footprints" probably reflect differences in cognitive ability across this span of time, coupled with a host of differences in the neural substrate that underlies cognition (e.g., synaptic connections). In addition, less interesting changes—skull thickness, cell packing density, myeli-

nation, and the like—also contribute to the morphological and topographic differences. Because recording ERPs is completely noninvasive, can be done across the lifespan while employing exactly the same task, and is relatively inexpensive, this method would seem to represent an ideal tool with which to explore a variety of aspects of brain–cognitive relations. Thus far, its use has been confined predominantly to infants and young children, and the majority of studies are cross-sectional in nature. It is our hope that, in the future, long-term longitudinal studies will be launched, and that this method will be cross-registered to other imaging methods that lend themselves to children, such as fMRI. In so doing, the superb temporal resolution of ERPs can be combined with the excellent spatial resolution of fMRI; and when grounded in behavior, considerable more insight will have been gained into brain–behavior relations.

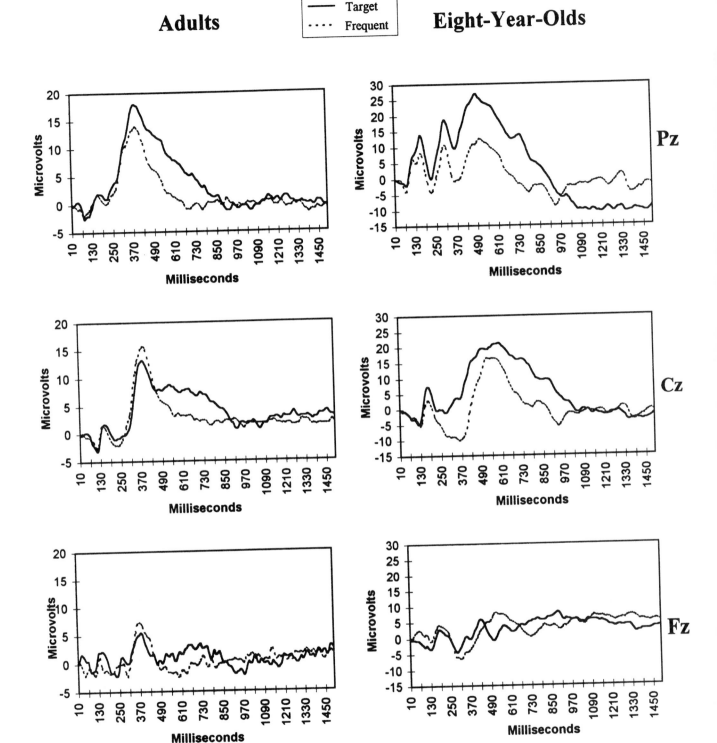

**Adults**

**Eight-Year-Olds**

Target
Frequent

Pz

Cz

Fz

FIGURE 9.6   Thomas and Nelson (1996) study in which 8-year-old children (*right panel*) and adults (*left panel*) were presented with a standard stimulus on 60% of the trials and a target stimulus on a random 20% of the trials; on each of the remaining 20% of the trials a novel stimulus was presented. Data displayed are for the target and standard (frequent) stimulus only, at three midline leads. (Reprinted with permission from K. M. Thomas, and C. A. Nelson, 1996. Age-related changes in the electrophysiological response to stimulus novelty: A topographic approach. *Electroencephalogr. Clin. Neurophysiol.* 98:294–308.)

ACKNOWLEDGMENTS   The writing of this chapter was made possible, in part, by support to C.A.N. from the National Institutes of Health (NS32976) and to C.S.M. from the Institute of Child Development, University of Minnesota.

## NOTE

1. Three studies done with infants have reported adult-like P300 responses (Hoffman and Salapatek, 1981; Hoffman, Salapatek, and Kuskowski, 1981; McIssac and Polich, 1992). In all cases, an auditory oddball paradigm was used, with relatively short (e.g., 600 ms) recording epochs. Thus, it is not clear if the positivity these authors observed was a P300 *qua* P300 or simply a PSW that had not yet resolved to baseline because the recording epoch was truncated.

## REFERENCES

ALHO, K., K. SAINIO, N. SAJANIEMI, K. REINIKAINEN, and R. NÄÄTÄNEN, 1990. Event-related potentials of human newborns to pitch change of an acoustic stimulus. *Electroencephalogr. Clin. Neurophysiol.* 77:151–155.

ALHO, K., N. SAJANIEMI, T. NIJTTYVUOPIO, K. SAINLO, and R. NAATANEN, 1990. ERPs to an auditory stimulus change in preterm and fullterm infants. In *Psychophysiological Brain Research*, C. H. M. Brunia, A. W. K. Gaillard, A. Kok, G. Mulder, and M. N. Verbaten, eds. Tilburg, The Netherlands: Tilburg University Press.

ALLISON, T., 1984. Recording and interpreting event-related potentials. In *Cognitive Psychophysiology: Event-Related Potentials and the Study of Cognition*, E. Donchin, ed. Hillsdale, N.J.: Lawrence Erlbaum.

ALLISON, T., C. C. WOODS, and G. M. MCCARTHY, 1986. The central nervous system. In *Psychophysiology: Systems, Processes, and Applications*, M. G. H. Coles, E. Donchin, and S. W. Porges, eds. New York: Guilford Press.

BLEULER, E., 1911/1950. *Dementia Praecox or the Group of Schizophrenias.* Translated by J. Zinkin. New York: International Universities Press.

CHEOUR, M., K. ALHO, R. CEPONIENE, K. REINIKAINEN, K. SAINIO, M. POHJAVUORI, O. AALTONEN, and R. NÄÄTÄNEN, 1998a. Maturation of mismatch negativity in infants. *Int. J. Psychophysiol.* 29:217–226.

CHEOUR, M., R. CEPONIENE, A. LEHTOKOSKI, A. LUUK, J. ALLIK, K. ALHO, and R. NÄÄTÄNEN, 1998b. Development of language-specific phoneme representations in the infant brain. *Nature Neurosci.* 1:35.

CHEOUR-LUHTANEN, M., K. ALHO, K. SAINIO, T. RINNE, K. REINIKAINEN, M POHJAVUORI, M. RENLUND, O. AALTONEN, O. EEROLA, and R. NÄÄTÄNEN, 1996. The ontogenetically earliest discriminative response of the human brain. *Psychophysiology* 33:478–481.

COLES, M. G. H., and M. D. RUGG, 1995. Event-related potentials: An introduction. In *Electrophysiology of Mind: Event-Related Brain Potentials and Cognition*, M. D. Rugg and M. G. H. Coles, eds. New York: Oxford University Press.

COURCHESNE, E., 1977. Event-related brain potentials: A comparison between children and adults. *Science* 197:589–592.

COURCHESNE, E., 1978. Neurophysiological correlates of cognitive development: Changes in long-latency event-related potentials from childhood to adulthood. *Electroencephalogr. Clin. Neurophysiol.* 45:468–482.

COURCHESNE, E., L. GANZ, and A. M. NORCIA, 1981. Event-related brain potentials to human faces in infants. *Child Dev.* 52:804–811.

COURCHESNE, E., S. A. HILLYARD, and R. GALAMBOS, 1975. Stimulus novelty, task relevance and the visual evoked potential in man. *Electroencephalogr. Clin. Neurophysiol.* 39:131–143.

CSÉPE, V., 1995. On the origin and development of the mismatch negativity. *Ear Hear.* 16:90–103.

DE HAAN, M., and C. A. NELSON, 1997. Recognition of the mother's face by 6-month-old infants: A neurobehavioral study. *Child Dev.* 68:187–210.

DONCHIN, E., 1981. Surprise! . . . Surprise? *Psychophysiology* 18:493–513.

FABIANI, M., G. GRATTON, G. A. CHIARENZA, and E. DONCHIN, 1990. A psychophysiological investigation of the Von Restorff paradigm in children. *J. Psychophysiol.* 4:15–24.

FABIANI, M., D. KARIS, and E. DONCHIN, 1990. Effects of mnemonic strategy manipulation in a Von Restorff paradigm. *Electroencephalogr. Clin. Neurophysiol.* 75:22–35.

FRIEDMAN, D., G. SIMPSON, and M. HAMBERGER, 1993. Age-related changes in scalp topography to novel and target stimuli. *Psychophysiology* 30:383–396.

HALGREN, E., and M. E. SMITH, 1987. Cognitive evoked potentials as modulatory processes in human-memory formation and retrieval. *Human Neurobiol.* 6:129–139.

HILLYARD, S. A., R. F. HINK, V. L. SCHWENT, and T.W. PICTON, 1973. Electrical signals of selective attention in the human brain. *Science* 182:177–180.

HOFMANN, M. J., and P. SALAPATEK, 1981. Young infants' event-related potentials (ERPs) to familiar and unfamiliar visual and auditory events in a recognition memory task. *Electroencephalogr. Clin. Neurophysiol.* 52:405–417.

HOFMANN, M. J., P. SALAPATEK, and M. KUSKOWSKI, 1981. Evidence for visual memory in the averaged and single-trial evoked potentials in human infants. *Infant Behav. Dev.* 4:401–421.

JASPER, H., 1958. The ten/twenty electrode system of the International Federation. *Electroencephalogr. Clin. Neurophysiol.* 10:371–375.

KARIS, D., M. FABIANI, and E. DONCHIN, 1984. P300 and memory: Individual differences in the Von Restorff effect. *Cogn. Psychol.* 16:177–186.

KARRER, R., and P. K. ACKLES, 1987. Visual event-related potentials of infants during a modified oddball procedure. In *Current Trends in Event-Related Potential Research*, R. Johnson, Jr., J. W. Rohrbaugh, and R. Parasuraman, eds. EEG Suppl. 40, pp. 603–608.

KARRER, R., and P. K. ACKLES, 1988. Brain organization and perceptual/cognitive development in normal and Down syndrome infants: A research program. In *The Early Identification of Infants at Risk for Mental Retardation*, P. Vietze and H. G. Vaughan, Jr., eds. Orlando, Fla.: Grune and Stratton, pp. 210–234.

KARRER, R., and L. A. MONTI, 1995. Event-related potentials in 4–7-week-old infants in a visual recognition memory task. *Electroencephalogr. Clin. Neurophysiol.* 94:414–424.

KNIGHT, R. T., 1984. Decreased response to novel stimuli after prefrontal lesions in man. *Electroencephalogr. Clin. Neurophysiol.* 59:9–20.

KNIGHT, R. T., 1996. Contribution of human hippocampal region to novelty detection. *Nature* 383:256–259.

KNIGHT, R. T., and D. SCABINI, 1998. Anatomic bases of event-related potentials and their relationship to novelty detection in humans. *J. Clin. Neurophysiol.* 15:3–13.

KNIGHT, R. T., D. SCABINI, D. L. WOODS, and C. C. CLAYWORTH, 1989. Contribution of the temporal-parietal junction to the auditory P3. *Brain Res.* 502:109–116.

KUTAS, M., and S. A. HILLYARD, 1980. Reading senseless sentences: Brain potentials reflect semantic incongruity. *Science* 207:203–205.

LOVELESS, N. E., and A. J. SANFORD, 1974. Effects of age on the contingent negative variation and preparatory set in a reaction-time task. *J. Gerontol.* 29:52–63.

MANGUN, G. R., and S. A. HILLYARD, 1995. Selective attention: Mechanisms and models. In *Electrophysiology of Mind: Event-Related Brain Potentials and Cognition*, M. D. Rugg and M. G. H. Coles, eds. New York: Oxford University Press.

McGHIE, A., and J. CHAPMAN, 1961. Disorders of attention and perception in early schizophrenia. *Br. J. Med. Psychol.* 34:103–116.

McISSAC, H., and J. POLICH, 1992. Comparison of infant and adult P300 from auditory stimuli. *J. Exp. Child Psychol.* 53:115–128.

MILLS, D. L., S. A. COFFEY-CORINA, and H. J. NEVILLE, 1993. Language acquisition and cerebral specialization in 20-month-old infants. *J. Cogn. Neurosci.* 5:317–334.

MOLFESE, D. L., 1989. Electrophysiological correlates of word meanings in 14-month-old human infants. *Dev. Neuropsychol.* 5:79–103.

MOLFESE, D. L., 1990. Auditory evoked responses recorded from 16-month-old human infants to words they did and did not know. *Brain Lang.* 38:345–363.

NÄÄTÄNEN, R., 1992. *Attention and Brain Function.* Hillsdale, N.J.: Lawrence Erlbaum.

NÄÄTÄNEN, R., A. W. K. GAILLARD, and S. MANTYSALO, 1978. The N1 effect of selective attention reinterpreted. *Acta Psychol.* 42:313–329.

NELSON, C. A., 1994. Neurocorrelates of recognition memory in the first postnatal year of life. In *Human Behavior and the Developing Brain*, G. Dawson and K. Fischer, eds. New York: Guilford Press, pp. 269–313.

NELSON, C. A., 1995. The ontogeny of human memory: A cognitive neuroscience perspective. *Dev. Psychol.* 31:723–738.

NELSON, C. A., 1996. Electrophysiological correlates of early memory development. In *Thirteenth West Virginia University Conference on Life Span Developmental Psychology: Biological and Neuropsychological Mechanisms*, H. W. Reese and M. D. Franzen, eds. Hillsdale, N.J.: Lawrence Erlbaum, pp. 95–131.

NELSON, C. A., and F. E. BLOOM, 1997. Child development and neuroscience. *Child Dev.* 68:970–987.

NELSON, C. A., and P. F. COLLINS, 1991. Event-related potential and looking time analysis of infants' responses to familiar and novel events: Implications for visual recognition memory. *Dev. Psychol.* 27:50–58.

NELSON, C. A., and P. F. COLLINS, 1992. Neural and behavioral correlates of recognition memory in 4- and 8-month-old infants. *Brain Cogn.* 19:105–121.

NELSON, C. A., and M. LUCIANA, 1998. Electrophysiological studies II: Evoked potentials and event-related potentials. In *Textbook of Pediatric Neuropsychiatry*, C. E. Coffey and R. A. Brumback, eds. Washington, D.C.: American Psychiatric Press, pp. 331–356.

NELSON, C. A., and K. NUGENT, 1990. Recognition memory and resource allocation as revealed by children's event-related potential responses to happy and angry faces. *Dev. Psychol.* 26:171–179.

RUGG, M. D., 1995. ERP studies of memory. In *Electrophysiology of Mind: Event-Related Brain Potentials and Cognition*, M. D. Rugg and M. G. H. Coles, eds. New York: Oxford University Press.

RUGG, M. D., and M. C. DOYLE, 1994. Event-related potentials and stimulus repetition in direct and indirect tests of memory. In *Cognitive Electrophysiology*, H. J. Heinze, T. Munte, and G. R. Mangun, eds. Boston: Birkhauser:

SCHREIBER, H., G. STOLZ-BORN, H. H. KORNHUBER, and J. BORN, 1992. Event-related potential correlates of impaired selective attention in children at high risk for schizophrenia. *Biol. Psychiatry* 32:634–651.

SEGALOWITZ, S. J., A. UNSAL, and J. DYWAN, 1992. Cleverness and wisdom in 12-year-olds: Electrophysiological evidence for late maturation of the frontal lobe. *Dev. Neuropsychol.* 8:279–298.

THOMAS, K. M., and C. A. NELSON, 1996. Age-related changes in the electrophysiological response to stimulus novelty: A topographic approach. *Electroencephalogr. Clin. Neurophysiol.* 98:294–308.

WALTER, W. G., R. COOPER, V. J. ALDRIDGE, W. C. McCALLUM, and A. L. WINER, 1964. Contingent negative variation: An electrical sign of sensorimotor association and expectancy in the human brain. *Nature* 230:380–384.

WEWERKA, S., and M. LUCIANA, 1999. Electrophysiological correlates of facial self-recognition memory in adults and children. Poster presented at the 1999 Biennial Meeting of the Society for Research in Child Development, Albuquerque, New Mexico.

WOLDORFF, M. G., S. A. HACKLEY, and S. A. HILLYARD, 1991. The effects of channel-selective attention on the mismatch negativity wave elicited by deviant tones. *Psychophysiology* 28:30–42.

WOLDORFF, M. G., and S. A. HILLYARD, 1991. Modulation of early auditory processing during selective listening to rapidly presented tones. *Electroencephalogr. Clin. Neurophysiol.* 79:170–191.

# 10 Applications of Magnetic Resonance Imaging to the Study of Development

B. J. CASEY, KATHLEEN M. THOMAS,
AND BRUCE McCANDLISS

ABSTRACT   Recent methodological advances in magnetic resonance imaging (MRI) have revolutionized our ability to study the developing human brain. This chapter examines the use and promise of MRI in addressing key developmental questions, including how the healthy normal brain develops and how such development is related to behavior. This methodology can also help us understand the biological substrates of childhood disorders. Examples of studies that examine the biological progression of developmental disorders following treatment and remediation are provided. Used effectively, this methodology could shed light on an array of developmental questions with respect to both healthy and pathological development.

Magnetic resonance imaging (MRI), with its lack of ionizing radiation and capacity to provide exquisite anatomical detail, has revolutionized the study of human brain development. Other imaging modalities, such as conventional radiography, computerized tomography (CT), positron emission tomography (PET), and single photon emission computerized tomography (SPECT), use ionizing radiation. Although these latter techniques may be used with pediatric patient populations when clinically warranted, the ethics of exposing children to radioactive isotopes for the advancement of science are less clear (Casey and Cohen, 1996; Morton, 1996; Zametkin, 1996). The advent of functional MRI (fMRI) has further extended the utility of MRI to explore the developing human brain in ways not previously possible.

This chapter addresses applications of structural and functional MRI to the study of development. Emphasis is placed on the utility of MRI in understanding (1) brain maturation and its relation to behavioral development, (2) the effects of learning on brain development, and (3) the effects of behavioral and pharmacological intervention on brain development (figure 10.1). Examples of behavioral paradigms and details of

B. J. CASEY, KATHLEEN M. THOMAS, AND BRUCE McCANDLISS   Sackler Institute for Developmental Psychobiology, Joan and Sanford I. Weill Medical College of Cornell University, New York, New York.

the neuroimaging methodology will be provided within this context.

## Magnetic resonance imaging

MRI has had a dramatic impact in the diagnosis of a variety of diseases and the in vivo study of the developing brain. This technique provides high spatial resolution images of the brain based on the nuclear magnetic resonance (NMR) properties of water protons and other nuclei found in brain tissue (Young, 1988). NMR consists of applying a radio frequency (RF) pulse (with an excitation frequency coinciding with the natural frequency of the system, known as the Larmor frequency) to the tissue. The RF pulse flips the net magnetization perpendicular to the main field. The MR image is generated by differences in the concentration of nuclei and their nuclear magnetic relaxation times ($T_1$ and $T_2$) in the different tissue environments (Bloch, 1946; Hahn, 1950). $T_1$ relaxation refers to the return of precessing nuclei to alignment with the main field after excitation (i.e., longitudinal relaxation, or spin-lattice). This relaxation is related to surrounding tissue composition in that small water molecules relax faster than larger lipid molecules, thereby providing information on gray and white matter differences. $T_2$ relaxation refers to the fall of the transverse magnetization leading to decay in the signal even though nuclei remain excited. This relaxation time is associated with interactions among nuclear spins and local inhomogeneities in the applied field. This interaction causes nuclei to precess, or spin, at different rates and deviate from the uniform motion of the initial excitation (Bottomley et al., 1984, 1987). The rate of dephasing (loss of uniform motion) depends on resonance within the environment (i.e., spins of neighboring nuclei). For example, $T_2$ in free water is much longer than that in bound water, and so prolonged $T_2$ observed in lesions results from an increase in free/bound water ratio. Localized inhomogeneities in the applied field lead to local differences in the Larmor frequencies, causing a decrease in $T_2$, which is then des-

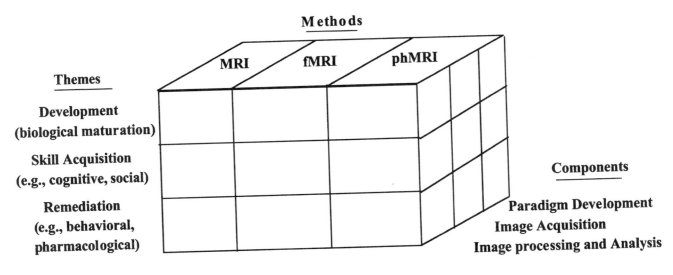

Methods

Themes

Development
(biological maturation)

Skill Acquisition
(e.g., cognitive, social)

Remediation
(e.g., behavioral,
pharmacological)

MRI     fMRI     phMRI

Components

Paradigm Development
Image Acquisition
Image processing and Analysis

FIGURE 10.1   Central themes and methods discussed in this chapter.

ignated $T_2^*$. $T_2^*$-weighted images are important for understanding the basis of functional MRI, as will be described later.

BRAIN DEVELOPMENT   MRI-based anatomical studies have revealed some interesting maturational changes in brain structure. The most informative studies to date are those based on carefully quantified volumetric measures and large sample sizes of 50 or more subjects (e.g., Giedd et al., 1996b,c; Reiss et al., 1996). The most consistent findings across these studies include (1) a lack of any significant change in cerebral volume after 5 years of age (Giedd et al., 1996b,c; Reiss et al., 1996); (2) a significant decrease in cortical gray matter after 12 years (Giedd et al., 1999); and (3) an increase in cerebral white matter throughout childhood and young adulthood (Jernigan et al., 1991; Pfefferbaum et al., 1994; Caviness et al., 1996; Rajapakse et al., 1996; Reiss et al., 1996). Specifically, subcortical gray matter regions (e.g., basal ganglia) decrease in volume during childhood, particularly in males (Giedd et al., 1996b; Rajapakse et al., 1996; Reiss et al., 1996), while cortical gray matter in the frontal and parietal cortices does not appear to decrease until roughly puberty (Giedd et al., 1999). White matter volume appears to increase throughout childhood and well into adulthood (Caviness et al., 1996; Rajapakse et al., 1996). These increases appear to be regional in nature. For example, white matter volume increases in dorsal prefrontal cortex, but not in more ventral prefrontal regions (i.e., orbitofrontal cortex) (Reiss et al., 1996). Total temporal lobe volume appears relatively stable across the age range of 4–18 years, while hippocampal formation volume increases with age for females and amygdala volume in-

creases with age for males (Giedd et al., 1996c). This latter finding may be consistent with the distribution of sex hormone receptors for these structures, with the amygdala having a predominance of androgen receptors (Clark et al., 1988; Sholl and Kim, 1989) and the hippocampus having a predominance of estrogen receptors (Morse et al., 1986).

BEHAVIORAL DEVELOPMENT   One way of linking morphometric changes in the brain with behavior is to correlate MRI-based anatomical measures with behavioral measures. One of the first examples of such a study was reported by Casey and colleagues (1997a). The study examined the role of the anterior cingulate cortex in the development of attention. Attention was assessed with a forced-choice visual discrimination paradigm in 26 normal children between the ages of 5 and 16 years. Performance during attention tasks characterized as predominantly automatic versus effortful was assessed in parallel with MRI-based morphometric measures of the anterior cingulate cortex.

The behavioral paradigm consisted of presenting three stimuli that varied in shape and/or color in a row on a computer screen. The subject's task was to indicate which of the three stimuli was different from the other two in a forced-choice task. Subjects were not informed as to which feature would be salient in making the discriminations. There were two conditions: one requiring predominantly automatic processing and one requiring controlled processing. In the automatic condition the stimuli differed on a single attribute (e.g., color). Forced-choice detection based on a single feature has been suggested to be relatively automatic (Treisman, 1986). In the controlled processing condition, the

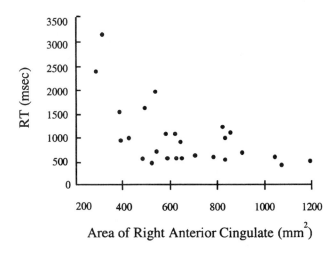

FIGURE 10.2 A plot of the size of the right anterior cingulate region (in square millimeters) as a function of behavioral performance (mean reaction time in milliseconds) on a controlled attention task that involves interfering stimulus information.

unique stimulus attribute changed from trial to trial within a block (e.g., from color to shape). Trials that are inconsistently mapped in this way and require shifts in attentional set have been suggested to require effortful or controlled processing (Shiffrin and Schneider, 1977).

Parasagittal slices from a 3-D volume data set were used to obtain area measurements of the left and right anterior cingulate cortex and cerebrum. Each region of interest was measured twice by an experienced rater who was blind to the subject's age, sex, and behavioral performance. Intrarater reliability for the first and second measures was .94 and .90, respectively.

As would be expected, behavioral performance improved (faster reaction times, higher accuracy) as a function of age. Area measures of the right anterior cingulate cortex increased as a function of age and correlated with estimated IQ and mean reaction time on both tasks. The size of the left anterior cingulate region was not correlated with performance. When age, IQ, and total cerebrum measures were controlled, only a significant correlation between the right anterior cingulate measure and performance during the predominantly controlled attention, but not the automatic, task remained. This result suggests a specific relation between size of the right anterior cingulate region and performance of the controlled attention task (figure 10.2).

REMEDIATION/INTERVENTION    MRI provides the opportunity to examine single case studies as a function of disease and remediation. One methodological con-

cern of repeated scanning designs is error introduced from rescan methodology and rater measurement error. A recent reliability study by Giedd and colleagues (1995) showed that variations in quantitative MRI measures of cerebral structures—whether due to actual changes in structure size (from hormonal or hydration changes), rater measurement error, or rescan methodology—were small when adequately controlled. For volume measures, they observed interclass correlations that ranged between .88 to .99. The error associated with rescanning and remeasuring structures like the caudate nuclei and globus pallidum were just 4% and 6%, respectively. These results are promising, given the importance of longitudinal designs in tracking healthy brain development and the progression of brain changes with the treatment of childhood disorders.

An illustration of how quantitative MRI may be used to track the progression of a childhood disorder was reported by Giedd and colleagues (1996a). They reported the case of a 12-year-old boy with severe worsening of obsessive compulsive disorder following infection with group A β-hemolytic streptococci. Pediatric autoimmune neuropsychiatric disorders associated with streptococcal infections, otherwise known as PANDAS, may arise when antibodies directed against invading bacteria cross-react with tissue in the basal ganglia, resulting in exacerbations of obsessive compulsive disorder or tic disorders (Swedo, 1994; Swedo and Leonard, 1994; Swedo et al., 1994).

Serial MRIs of the brain were obtained to assess the relationship between basal ganglia size, symptom severity, and treatment of the infection with plasmapheresis (plasma exchange). MRIs and ratings of symptom severity were obtained three times during the initial plasmapheresis treatment and again at 5 weeks, 5 months, and 6 months post-treatment during symptom exacerbation and remission. A final MRI was obtained during a second treatment with plasmapheresis. To assess the specificity of volumetric changes, total cerebral volume, as well as anterior frontal, caudate, putamen, and globus pallidum volume, were quantified.

Obsessive compulsive symptoms decreased dramatically during the first plasmapheresis treatment. In parallel, basal ganglia volumes, particularly of the caudate nuclei and globus pallidum, underwent dramatic changes in relation to treatment and severity of symptoms. The volumes were greatest at initial presentation and decreased substantially after plasmapheresis, but remained high relative to unaffected boys of similar age. The magnitude of these changes was 28% for the caudate nuclei and 24% for the globus pallidum. These changes far exceed the error expected from the process of rescanning and remeasuring these structures (4% for

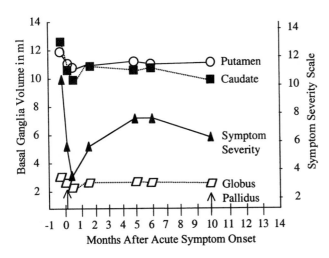

FIGURE 10.3 A plot of the volume of the globus pallidum, caudate nuclei, and putamen as well as symptom severity as a function of the progression of obsessive compulsive symptomology both before and after treatment. (Adapted from Geidd et al., 1996a.)

the caudate nuclei and 6% for the globus pallidum; Giedd et al., 1995). Figure 10.3 presents volume of the basal ganglia with the progression of the disorder before and following treatment in conjunction with symptom severity. It is hypothesized that the early volumetric changes may represent inflammatory changes. Thus, edema from the inflammatory reaction of the cross-reacting antibodies might cause an initial increase in the size of the structure; but with prolonged or repeated episodes of inflammation, a decrease in structure size may result from eventual necrosis (cell death).

## Functional magnetic resonance imaging

Until recently, the use of functional neuroimaging techniques in developmental studies has been limited, largely owing to their reliance on harmful radiation and the vulnerability of developmental populations to such exposure. Over the past decade, a noninvasive neuroimaging technique, fMRI, has been developed to examine brain state changes based on changes in blood oxygenation. Many (Belliveau et al., 1991; Detre et al., 1992; Ogawa et al., 1990, 1992; Rosen, Belliveau, and Chien, 1989; Rosen et al., 1990; Thulborn et al., 1982; Turner et al., 1991, 1992) have contributed to the development of this technique. Most relevant for the study of children are advances in the techniques that do not require the use of injected paramagnetic contrast agents (Kwong et al., 1992; Ogawa et al., 1992; Turner et al., 1991). This work is based on the observation that hemoglobin becomes highly paramagnetic in its deoxygenated state, resulting in a decrease in the MR signal

intensity. In other words, blood oxygenation level can be used as a naturally occurring contrast agent, with highly oxygenated areas producing a larger MR signal than less well oxygenated regions. These changes in signal intensity, related to the oxygenation of hemoglobin, are detectable in $T_2$*-weighted images.

A number of PET studies (e.g., Fox et al., 1988; Fox and Raichle, 1986) have demonstrated that brain areas increase their blood flow disproportionately relative to oxygen metabolism when they become active, resulting in a net increase in the tissue oxygenation. Consequently, the MR signal in those areas increases relative to others, and this contrast can be used to produce MR images of the activated region. Several studies that examined structure–function relationships in the adult brain using this technique have been reviewed (Casey et al., 1996; Shulman et al., 1994).

Perhaps one of the most important aspects of fMRI is its utility in studying human brain development in vivo. We provide a select few of such studies here. (For a summary of fMRI studies of children to date, see Casey et al., 2000.)

BRAIN DEVELOPMENT We have recently completed a number of studies with healthy children using fMRI (Casey et al., 1995, 1997a; Thomas et al., 1999). In one such study, prefrontal activity was examined during the performance of a go/no-go task that was modified for the scanner environment (Casey et al., 1997b). The go/no-go task is a classic neuropsychological task for assessing inhibitory control and frontal lobe function. In this version of the task, subjects were instructed to respond to any letter but X. Letters were presented at a rate of one every 1.5 seconds and 75% of the trials were target trials to build up a compelling tendency to respond. Based on the results from 18 subjects between the ages of 7 and 24 years (9 adults and 9 children), more overall prefrontal activity was observed ($p < .001$) for children (490 mm[3]) relative to adults (182 mm[3]), as illustrated in figure 10.4. This difference in overall prefrontal activity appeared to be specific to the dorsolateral prefrontal cortex, with children activating larger volumes of this region significantly more than adults ($p < .001$). The large volumes of dorsal prefrontal activity in children, but not adults, may suggest an increased selectivity in function of the prefrontal cortex with age. Another interpretation is that prefrontal cortex activation increases with task difficulty. It is the case that the children made twice as many false alarms as the adults; superficially, then, this interpretation seems plausible. However, the subjects with the largest volumes of prefrontal activity were those children with error rates similar to the adults, not the children having

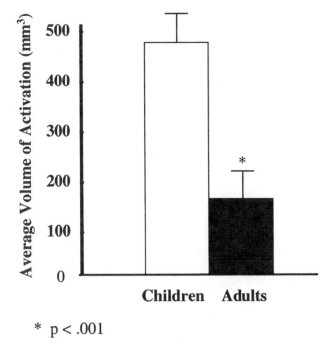

* p < .001

FIGURE 10.4 Overall volume of prefrontal activity observed for children and adults during performance of a go/no-go task using fMRI.

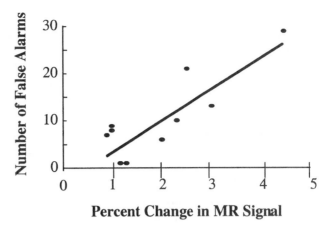

FIGURE 10.5 A plot of the change in MR signal intensity in the region of the anterior cingulate cortex as a function of number of errors (false alarms) during performance of a go/no-go task using fMRI.

the most difficult time performing the task. These results are consistent with the interpretation of increased selectivity of function in prefrontal cortex with age.

BEHAVIORAL DEVELOPMENT   As with structural MRI, fMRI can be used to examine anatomical correlates of behavior. In the case of fMRI, correlations are based on changes in the MR signal of a given region rather than the size or volume of a region. In addition, MR changes and behavioral changes are assessed simultaneously rather than in parallel.

In the preceding section, we described developmental differences in prefrontal activation for children relative to adults during performance of a go/no-go task even when behavioral performance was similar. There were also active brain regions that specifically correlated with task performance, regardless of age. These regions included the anterior cingulate and orbitofrontal cortices ($p < .009$ and $p < .05$, respectively). Specifically, the more difficult the task (i.e., more errors relative to the control task), the greater the magnitude of activity in the anterior cingulate (figure 10.5). In contrast, the greater the volume of activity in the orbitofrontal cortex, the better the performance (i.e., fewer errors). These findings suggest that these two brain regions may be heavily involved in the development of inhibitory control and are consistent with our MRI-

based anatomical study implicating the involvement of the anterior cingulate when there is competition from interfering information.

REMEDIATION/INTERVENTION   Neuroimaging studies of developmental disorders such as dyslexia may provide important insights into the neural bases of such disorders, suggesting fruitful paths for cognitive rehabilitation. Currently, the majority of published fMRI studies of developmental reading disorders have been conducted with adult subjects who demonstrated evidence of dyslexia as children (e.g., Brunswick et al., 1999; Eden and Zeffiro, 1998; Shaywitz et al., 1998). Studies of developmental dyslexia that focus on children at or near the age when these problems first appear will be necessary to separate initial deficits in phonological processing from secondary effects that develop later in life as a consequence of reading failures.

Several studies have demonstrated that adults with a history of developmental phonological dyslexia typically produce less activity in left posterior temporal-parietal areas, relative to controls, during phonologically demanding listening and reading tasks (Brunswick et al., 1999; Flowers et al., 1991; Paulesu et al., 1996; Rumsey et al., 1992; Shaywitz et al., 1998). Furthermore, several of these studies have reported increased activity in occipital and/or frontal regions that may reflect efforts to compensate for impairments in phonological abilities.

Although no fMRI studies of reading difficulties in school-age children have been published to date, such work is currently underway. For example, Pugh and colleagues reported preliminary results showing decreased activity in left temporal-parietal areas of children with reading impairments compared to age-matched controls (Blachman and Pugh, 1999). Furthermore, a number of behavioral intervention studies have reported that mild to severe reading difficulties in children can be successfully remediated through targeted interventions that focus on phonological awareness and letter-sound decoding skills (Foorman et al., 1998; Olson et al., in press; Torgesen, 1997; Vellutino et al., 1996). Combining recent intervention research with fMRI methods for scanning children provides the opportunity to use fMRI to study the specific impact of cognitive interventions on patterns of brain activity.

Several researchers have taken advantage of the fact that fMRI studies can safely be repeated in the same subjects multiple times to track changes in cortical activation patterns associated with learning. For example, Karni and colleagues (1995) examined dynamic changes in cortical representations associated with learning simple hand movements. That study demonstrated rapid learning effects in primary motor areas within a single scanning session, as well as more extended learning effects related to a training intervention that spanned several weeks. Karni and his coworkers provided a new and important use of fMRI, one that holds great potential for studying the development of functional anatomy underlying learned skills and for dynamically tracing the impact of particular interventions at the cortical level.

The prospect of using fMRI to trace learning-related changes in cortical areas holds promise for investigating the impact of intervention programs on cognitive disorders, as in the case of acquired phonological dyslexia. An early example of this approach is illustrated in a case study that used fMRI measures to trace the impact of a specific reading intervention program on cortical reorganization following a stroke (Small, Flores, and Noll, 1998). A patient with a left frontoparietal stroke suffered severe impairments in grapheme-phoneme decoding ability, as evidenced by her inability to read even simple pseudowords. Her ability to read high-frequency words by sight was spared. Whole brain fMRI scans in response to a reading task predominantly demonstrated a strong activation of the left angular gyrus, relatively little activation of left lingual gyrus, and a decreased activation of middle temporal areas relative to a false-font control condition. She then began an intensive remediation program that focused on grapheme-phoneme decoding skills through practice on exemplar words and nonwords, exhibiting dramatic improvement in decoding skills over the course of 24 days. Postintervention scans revealed a decrease in activity of the left angular gyrus regions and an increase in left lingual

gyrus activity during the same reading task used in the pretest scans. These effects were perhaps best characterized as a shift in reading strategy enabled by the grapheme-phoneme decoding intervention. This study was one of the first to directly demonstrate the impact of a specific reading intervention technique on the functional organization of reading skills in adult acquired dyslexia. Furthermore, this study demonstrated that effective interventions can lead to cortical reorganization that can be effectively traced with fMRI.

The approach of combining fMRI with intervention studies to trace changes in cognitive skills and the cortical processes that support them can also be applied to developmental reading disorders. Although such studies are yet to be completed, several are underway (e.g., Blachman and Pugh, 1999; Temple et al., 1999). For example, McCandliss and colleagues (1999a) recently reported preliminary results from a study designed to examine learning-related changes in children with reading disabilities. Behavioral testing with a group of reading-impaired children ($n = 24$) demonstrated gains of 1.4 grade levels in decoding skill after 24 intervention sessions, producing similar gains in phonological awareness measures as well. This rate of skill improvement offers the prospect of using fMRI to examine learning-related changes in cortical areas related to phonological listening and reading skills.

The activation task in this study contrasted responses to blocks of words, pseudowords, and consonant strings in a continuous performance repetition detection task (also known as the one-back task). Each stimulus was presented for 500 ms followed by a 1-second fixation dot presentation. The child's task was to press a button when he/she detected an immediate repetition of any letter string.

Preliminary results from two fMRI case studies suggest that this activation task produced different cortical activation patterns in an 8-year-old child with reading difficulties compared to an age-matched control. Furthermore, the observed differences were roughly consistent with the adult fMRI studies of developmental dyslexia indicating reduced activation in left perisylvian regions for impaired readers. Results from a control subject (8-year-old male with above-average reading ability) revealed robust activation in inferior frontal regions and posterior portions of the superior temporal gyrus for both words and pseudowords relative to consonant strings (figure 10.6; see color plate 11). These data suggest that different processes are being applied to the pronounceable letter strings than to the non-pronounceable pseudowords. McCandliss and colleagues (1999b) also report a case study of an 8-year-old

# Familiar Words    Pseudowords    Consonant Strings

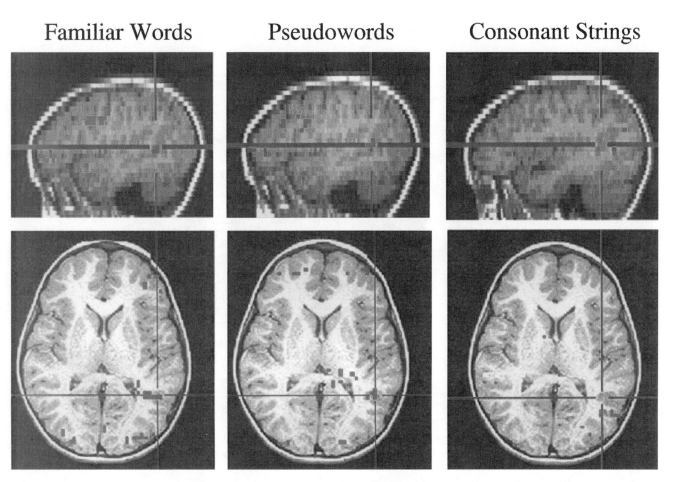

FIGURE 10.6    fMRI results from a single session with an 8-year-old normal reading child performing a repetition detection (one-back) task on familiar words, pseudowords, and consonant strings minus an active fixation monitoring task.

child who commanded a large sight vocabulary (able to read accurately 88% of the 100 most frequent words contained in children's books) yet fell below the 30th percentile for his age in grapheme-phoneme decoding ability as well as in measures of phonological awareness. Further behavioral testing revealed a general inability to read all but the most rudimentary pseudowords. Functional MR images were acquired before and after a 12-week (24 sessions) intervention program that focused on grapheme-phoneme decoding skills via real-word exemplars (McCandliss et al., 1999a). Behavioral testing before and after the intervention revealed a dramatic increase in grapheme-phoneme decoding skills, with gains exceeding 1.5 grade levels in less than a third of a year. Results of the fMRI scans acquired before the intervention demonstrated little activation in the posterior region of the superior temporal gyrus (figure 10.7; see color plate 12). However, following the intervention, significant increases in this target region were reported. This pattern was observed for both the word and pseudoword blocks, yet was absent in consonant

string blocks, suggesting the involvement of phonological processing regions as a result of the cognitive intervention.

Although the conclusions that one can draw from the previously described adult and child case studies are limited until they can be replicated in larger samples, these case studies mark a first step in addressing processes and cortical functions related to the initial acquisition of literacy.

Pediatric fMRI research allows developmental disorders such as developmental dyslexia to be studied within the age range in which they typically first appear, and thus provides opportunities both for early prevention/intervention and dynamic tracking of cortical changes associated with gains in cognitive skills.

## Pharmacologic MRI

Having illustrated how the technique of fMRI has led to a revolution in mapping changes in the human brain

# Before Intervention

# After Intervention

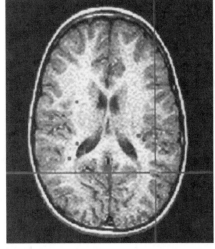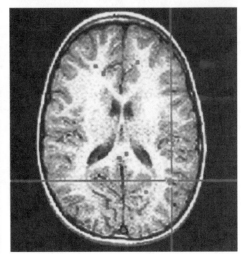

FIGURE 10.7   fMRI results from two separate sessions (before and after intervention) with an 8-year-old child with reading impairments performing a repetition detection (one-back) task on familiar words.

as a function of development and learning, we now turn to an illustration of how we can push the methodology a step further and investigate changes in the human brain in response to pharmacologic probes. A number of recent studies with both humans and animals have shown the detection of neurotransmitter activity using pharmacologic MRI (phMRI) and demonstrated how results from this technique are correlated with PET, microdialysis, and behavioral data (e.g., Chen et al., 1997). These studies have focused largely on animal work, but more recent work illustrates the utility of the method with humans (Braus et al., 1997; Chen et al., 1997; Kleinschmidt et al., 1997; Sell et al.,1997; Vaidya et al. 1998). Ultimately, pharmacologic MRI studies may be sensitive probes in elucidating brain regions involved in developmental disorders. These studies may prove extremely useful in addressing questions relevant to why some individuals are nonresponders to medications and why some medications are less effective in children than in adults.

An illustration of this work with a developmental population was recently reported by Vaidya and col-leagues (1998), who examined patterns of brain activity in children with and without ADHD on ritalin during performance of the go/no-go task (Casey et al., 1997b) described previously. Overall, Vaidya showed improved behavioral performance and an increase in prefrontal activity for healthy children on ritalin and for children with ADHD on ritalin. Significant changes in basal ganglia activity were observed for the ADHD children when on ritalin. Specifically, the pattern of activity in this region for children with ADHD on ritalin was almost identical to the pattern observed in the healthy children off ritalin, suggesting normalization of activity in the basal ganglia with medication.

The previous study reports results that are reminiscent of two classic PET studies (Baxter et al., 1988; Swedo et al., 1989) that demonstrated normalization of brain activity in individuals with obsessive compulsive disorder following pharmacologic treatment. Most interesting for the Baxter et al. study was that normalization in activity occurred with either pharmacological or behavioral intervention. Ultimately, it will be interesting to see whether fMRI studies using behavioral and pharmacologic intervention result in similar brain changes for other childhood disorders and to what extent these changes are lasting.

## Conclusions

This chapter has provided illustrations of the utility and promise of structural and functional MRI and how these techniques can be used to map changes in the human brain as a function of development. For example, a number of regional changes have been reported in the developing human brain, particularly in regions of association cortex that have been linked to higher cognition (language and memory). And, pushing the methodology a step further, we can investigate changes in the human brain associated with learning and intervention. At least three examples of anatomical and functional brain changes associated with behavioral and/or pharmacologic treatment were provided in this chapter. These examples, work on the developmental disorders of ADHD, OCD, and dyslexia, represent but a select sample of disorders investigated with this methodology. Ultimately, phMRI studies may be sensitive probes in further elucidating brain regions involved in these, and other, developmental disorders and may prove extremely useful in addressing developmental neurochemical questions. It is clear that innovative methods such as fMRI, together with MRI-based morphometry and phMRI, will transform our current understanding of human brain development and its disruption in developmental disorders. This methodology promises to shed light on developmental issues as never before.

ACKNOWLEDGMENTS   This work was supported in part by a 5-K01 MH01297 award and funding from the John D. and Catherine T. MacArthur Foundation to B. J. C. The authors thank Clayton H. Eccard for his comments and help in preparation of this manuscript.

## REFERENCES

BAXTER, L. R., JR., J. M. SCHWARTZ, J. C. MAZZIOTTA, M. E. PHELPS, J. J. PAHL, B. H. GUZE, and L. FAIRBANKS, 1988. Cerebral glucose metabolic rates in nondepressed patients with OCD. *Am. J. Psych.* 14:1560–1563.

BELLIVEAU, J. W., D. N. KENNEDY, R. C. MCKINSTRY, B. R. BUCHBINDER, R. M. WEISSKOFF, M. S. COHEN, J. M. VEVEA, T. J. BRADY, and B. R. ROSEN, 1992. Functional mapping of the human visual cortex by magnetic resonance imaging. *Science* 254:716–719.

BLACKMAN, B., and K. PUGH, 1999. Phonologically based tutoring and neuroimaging: What do we hope to learn? Annual Meeting of Society for the Scientific Study of Reading, Montreal, Canada.

BLOCH, F., 1946. Nuclear induction. *Physiol. Rev.* 70:460–474.

BRAUS, D. F., A. KRIER, A. SARTORIUS, G. ENDE, P. HUBRICH-UNGUREANU, and F. A. HENN, 1997. Effects of haloperidol and lorazepam on fMRI data in healthy subjects. *Neuroimage* 5(4):S367.

BOTTEMLEY, P. A., T. H. FOSTER, R. E. ARGERSINGER, and L. M. PFEIFFER, 1984. A review of normal tissue hydrogen NMR relaxation times and relaxation mechanisms from 1–100 MHz. *Med. Phys.* 11:425–460.

BOTTEMLEY, P. A., C. J. HARDY, R. E. ARGERSINGER, and G. ALLEN-MOORE, 1987. A review of hydrogen magnetic resonance relaxation in pathology. *Med. Phys.* 14:1–37.

BRUNSWICK, N., E. MCCRORY, C. J. PRICE, C. D. FRITH, and U. FRITH, 1999. Explicit and implicit processing of words and pseudowords by adult developmental dyslexics: A search for Wernicke's Wortshatz? *Brain* 122:1901–1917.

CASEY, B. J., and J. D. COHEN, 1996. In reply to: C. T. Morton, Is research in normal and ill children involving radiation exposure ethical? *Arch. Gen. Psych.* 53:1059–1060.

CASEY, B. J., J. D. COHEN, P. JEZZARD, R. TURNER, D. C. NOLL, R. J. TRANIOR, J. GIEDD, D. KAYSEN, L. HERTZ-PANNIER, and J. L. RAPOPORT, 1995. Activation of prefrontal cortex in children during a nonspatial working memory task with functional MRI. *Neuroimage* 2:221–229.

CASEY, B. J., J. D. COHEN, D. C. NOLL, W. SCHNEIDER, J. N. GIEDD, and J. L. RAPOPORT, 1996. Functional magnetic resonance imaging. In *Neuroimaging II: Clinical Applications*, E. D. Bigler, ed. New York: Plenum Press, pp. 299–330.

CASEY, B. J., K. M. THOMAS, T. F. WELSH, R. LIVNAT, and C. H. ECCARD, 2000. Cognitive and behavioral probes of developmental landmarks for use in functional neuroimaging. In *The Foundation* and *Future of Functional Neuroimaging in Child Psychiatry*, J. M. Rumsey and M. Ernst, eds. New York: Cambridge University Press, pp. 155–168.

CASEY, B. J., R. TRANIOR, J. GIEDD, Y. VAUSS, C. K. VAITUZIS, S. HAMBURGER, P. KOZUCH, and J. L. RAPOPORT, 1997a. The role of the anterior cingulate in automatic and controlled processes: A developmental neuroanatomical study. *Dev. Psychobiol.* 30:61–69.

CASEY, B. J., R. J. TRANIOR, J. L. ORENDI, A. B. SCHUBERT, L. E. NYSTROM, J. N. GIEDD, F. X. CASTELLANOS, J. V. HAXBY, D. C. NOLL, J. D. COHEN, S. D. FORMAN, R. E. DAHL, and J. L. RAPOPORT, 1997b. A developmental functional MRI study of prefrontal activation during performance of a go-nogo task. *J. Cogn. Neurosci.* 9(6):835–847.

CAVINESS, V. S., JR., D. N. KENNEDY, C. RICHELME, J. RADEMACHER, and P. A. FILIPEK, 1996. The human brain age 7–11 years: A volumetric analysis based on magnetic resonance images. *Cereb. Cortex* 6(5):726–736.

CHEN, Y. C., W. R. GALPERN, A. L. BROWNELL, R. T. MATTHEWS, M. BOGDANOV, O. ISACSON, J. R. KELTNER, M. F. BEAL, B. R. ROSEN, and B. G. JENKINS, 1997. Detection of dopaminergic neurotransmitter activity using pharmacologic MRI: Correlation with PET, microdialysis, and behavioral data. *Magn. Reson. Med.* 38(3):389–398.

CLARK, A. S., N. J. MACLUSKY, and P. S. GOLDMAN-RAKIC, 1988. Androgen binding and metabolism in the cerebral cortex of the developing rhesus monkey. *Endocrinol.* 123(2):932–940.

DETRE, J. A., J. S. LEIGH, D. S. WILLIAMS, and A. P. KORETSKY, 1992. Perfusion imaging. *Magn. Reson. Med.* 23:37–45.

EDEN, G. F., and T. A. ZEFFIRO, 1998. Neural systems affected in developmental dyslexia revealed by functional neuroimaging. *Neuron* 21(2):279–282.

FLOWERS, D. L., F. B. WOOD, and C. E. NAYLOR, 1991. Regional cerebral blood flow correlates of language processes in reading disability. *Arch. Neurol.* 48:637–643.

FOORMAN, B. R., D. J. FRANCIS, J. M. FLETCHER, C. SCHATSCHNEIDER, and P. MEHTA, 1998. The role of instruction in learning to read: Preventing reading failure in at-risk children. *J. Edu. Psychol.* 90:37–55.

FOX, P. T., and M. E. RAICHLE, 1986. Focal physiological uncoupling of cerebral blood flow and oxidative metabolism during somatosensory stimulation in human subjects. *Proc. Natl. Acad. Sci. (USA).* 83:1140–1144.

FOX, P. T., M. E. RAICHLE, M. A. MINTUN, and C. DENCE, 1988. Nonoxidative glucose consumption during focal physiologic neural activity. *Science* 241:1445–1448.

GIEDD, J. N., J. BLUMENTHAL, N. O. JEFFRIES, F. X. CASTELLANOS, H. LUI, A. ZIJDENBOS, T. PAUS, A. C. EVANS, and J. L. RAPOPORT, 1999. Brain development during childhood and adolescence: A longitudinal MRI study. *Nature Neurosci.* 2(10):861–863.

GIEDD, J. N., P. KOZUCH, D. KAYSEN, A. C. VAITUZIA, S. D. HAMBURGER, J. J. BARTKO, and J. L. RAPOPORT, 1995. Reliability of cerebral measures in repeated examinations with magnetic resonance imaging. *Psych. Res.* 61(2)113–119.

GIEDD, J. N., J. L. RAPOPORT, H. L. LEONARD, D. RICHTER, and S. E. SWEDO, 1996a. Case study: Acute basal ganglia enlargement and obsessive-compulsive symptoms in an adolescent boy. *J. Am. Acad. Child Adol. Psych.* 35(7):913–915.

GIEDD, J. N., J. W. SNELL, N. LANGE, J. C. RAJAPAKSE, B. J. CASEY, P. L. KOZUCH, Y. C. VAUSS, S. D. HAMBURGER, D. KAYSEN, and J. L. RAPOPORT, 1996b. Quantitative magnetic resonance imaging of human brain development: Ages 4–18. *Cereb. Cortex* 6:551–560.

GIEDD, J. N., A. C. VAITUZIS, S. D. HAMBURGER, N. LANGE, J. C. RAJAPAKSE, D. KAYSEN, Y. C. VAUSS, and J. L. RAPOPORT, 1996c. Quantitative MRI of the temporal lobe, amygdala, and hippocampus in normal human development: Ages 4–18 years. *J. Comp. Neurol.* 366(2):223–230.

HAHN, E. L., 1950. Spin echoes. *Physiol. Rev.* 80:580–594.

JERNIGAN, T. L., S. ZISOOK, R. K. HEATON, J. T. MORANVILLE, J. R. HESSELINK, and D. L. BRAFF, 1991. Magnetic resonance imaging abnormalities in lenticular nuclei and cerebral cortex in schizophrenia. *Arch. Gen. Psych.* 48:881–890.

KARNI, A., G. MEYER, P. JEZZARD, M. M. ADAMS, R. TURNER, and L. G. UNGERLEIDER, 1995. Functional MRI evidence for adult motor cortex plasticity during motor skill learning. *Nature* 377(6545):155–158.

KLEINSCHMIDT, A., G. KRUGER, K.-D. MERBOLDT, G. STOPPE, and J. FRAHM, 1997. Magnetic resonance neuroimaging of psychotropic drug action: Effects of sedation, stimulation, and placebo on cerebral blood oxygenation. *Neuroimage* 5(4):S366.

KWONG, K. K., J. W. BELLIVEAU, D. A. CHESLER, I. E. GOLDBERG, R. M. WEISSKOFF, B. P. PONCELET, D. N. KENNEDY, B. E. HOPPEL, M. S. COHEN, R. TURNER, H.-M. CHENG, T. J. BRADY, and B. R. ROSEN, 1992. Dynamic magnetic resonance imaging of human brain activity during primary sensory stimulation. *Proc. Natl. Acad. Sci. (USA)* 89:5675.

MCCANDLISS, B., R. SANDAK, I. BECK, W. C. PERFETTI, and W. SCHNEIDER, 1999a. Inroads into reading acquisition failures: Relating alphabetic decoding instructions to changes in behavioral and fMRI measures. Annual Meeting of the Society for the Scientific Study of Reading, June. Montreal, Canada.

MCCANDLISS, B., R. SANDAK, I. BECK, and W. SCHNEIDER, 1999b. Case studies in reading intervention: Behavioral and fMRI results in children. Executive Meeting of the McDonnell Foundation Program in Cognitive Neuroscience, July. San Diego, California.

MERZENICH, M. M., W. M. JENKINS, P. JOHNSTON, C. SCHREINER, S. L. MILLER, and P. TALLAL, 1966. Temporal processing deficits of language-learning impaired children ameliorated by training. *Science* 271(5234):77–81.

MORSE, J. K., S. W. SCHEFF, and S. T. DEKOSKY, 1986. Gonadal steroids influence axon sprouting in the hippocampal dentate gyrus: A sexually dimorphic response. *Exp. Neurol.* 94(3):649–658.

MORTON, C. T., 1966. Is research in normal and ill children involving radiation exposure ethical? *Arch. Gen. Psych.* 53:1060–1061.

OGAWA, S., T. M. LEE, A. R. KAY, and D. W. TANK, 1990. Brain magnetic resonance imaging with contrast dependent on blood oxygenation. *Proc. Natl. Acad. Sci. (USA)* 87:9868–9872.

OGAWA, S., D. W. TANK, R. MENON, J. M. ELLERMANN, S. G. KIM, H. MERKLE, and K. UGURBIL, 1992. Intrinsic signal changes accompanying sensory stimulation: Functional brain mapping using MRI. *Proc. Natl. Acad. Sci. (USA)* 89(13):5951–5955.

OLSON, R. K., B. WISE, J. RING, and M. JOHNSON, 1997. Computer-based remedial training in phoneme awareness and phonological decoding: Effects on the post-training development of word recognition. *Scientific Studies of Reading* 1(3):235–253.

PAULESU, E., U. FRITH, M. SNOWLING, A. GALLAGHER, J. MORTON, R. S. J. FRACKOWIAK, and C. D. FRITH, 1996. Is developmental dyslexia a disconnection syndrome? Evidence from PET scanning. *Brain* 119:143–157.

PFEFFERBAUM, A., D. H. MATHALON, E. V. SULLIVAN, J. M. RAWLES, R. B. ZIPURSKY, and K. O. LIM, 1994. A quantitative magnetic resonance imaging study of changes in brain morphology from infancy to late adulthood. *Arch. Neurol.* 51(9):874–887.

RAJAPAKSE, J. C., M. C. LENANE, K. MCKENNA, L. K. JACOBSEN, C. T. GORDON, A. BREIER, and J. L. RAPOPORT, 1996. Brain magnetic resonance imaging in childhood-onset schizophrenia. *Arch. Gen. Psych.* 53(7):617–624.

REISS, A. L., M. T. ABRAMS, H. S. SINGER, J. L. ROSS, and M. B. DENCKLA, 1996. Brain development, gender and IQ in children: A volumetric imaging study. *Brain* 119:1763–1774.

ROSEN, B. R., J. W. BELLIVEAU, and D. CHIEN, 1989. Perfusion mapping by nuclear magnetic resonance. *Magn. Reson. Quart.* 5:263–281.

ROSEN, B. R., J. W. BELLIVEAU, J. M. VEVEA, and T. J. BRADY, 1990. Perfusion imaging with NMR contrast agents. *Magn. Reson. Med.* 14(2):249–265.

RUMSEY, J. M., P. ANDREASON, A. J. ZAMETKIN, T. AQUINO, A. C. KING, S. D. HAMBURGER, A. PIKUS, J. L. RAPOPORT, and R. M. COHEN, 1992. Failure to activate the left temporoparietal cortex in dyslexia, an H2150 PET study. *Arch. Neurol.* 49:527–534.

SCHULMAN, R. G., D. L. ROTHMAN and A. M. BLAMIRE, 1994. NMR studies of human brain function. *Trends Biochem. Sci.* 19(12):522–526.

SELL, L. A., A. SIMMONS, G. M. LEMMENS, S. C. WILLIAMS, M. BRAMMER, and J. STRANG, 1997. Functional magnetic resonance imaging of the acute effect of intravenous heroin administration on visual activation in long-term heroin addicts: Results from a feasibility study. *Drug Alcohol Depend.* 49(1):55–60.

SHAYWITZ, S. E., B. A. SHAYWITZ, K. R. PUGH, R. K. FULBRIGHT, R. T. CONSTABLE, W. E. MENCL, D. P. SHANKWEILER, A. M. LIBERMAN, P. SKUDLARSKI, J. FLETCHER, L. KATZ, K. E. MARCHIONE, C. LACADIE, C. GATENBY, and J. GORE, 1998. Functional disruption in the organization of the brain for reading in dyslexia. *Proc. Natl. Acad. Sci. (USA)* 95:2636–2641.

SHIFFRIN, R. M., and W. SCHNEIDER, 1977. Controlled and automatic human information processing: II. Perceptual learning, automatic attending, and a general theory. *Psychol. Rev.* 84:127–190.

SHOLL, S. A., and K. L. KIM, 1989. Estrogen receptor in the rhesus monkey brain during fetal development. *Dev. Brain Res.* 50(2):189–196.

SMALL, S. L., D. K. FLORES, and D. C. NOLL, 1998. Different neural circuits subserve reading before and after therapy for acquired dyslexia. *Brain Lang.* 62(2):298–308.

SWEDO, S. E., 1994. Sydenham's chorea: A model for childhood autoimmune neuropsychiatric disorder. *JAMA* 272(22):1788–1791.

SWEDO, S. E., and H. L. LEONARD, 1994. Childhood movement disorders and obsessive compulsive disorder. *J. Clin. Psych.* 55(suppl.):32–37.

SWEDO, S. E., H. L. LEONARD, and L. S. KIESSLING, 1994. Speculations on antineuronal antibody-mediated neuropsychiatric disorders of childhood. *Pediatrics* 93(2):323–326.

SWEDO, S. E., P. PIETRINI, H. L. LEONARD, M. B. SCHAPIRO, D. C. RETTEW, E. L. GOLDBERGER, S. I. RAPOPORT, J. L. RAPOPORT, and C. L. GRADY, 1989. Cerebral glucose metabolism in childhood-onset obsessive-compulsive disorder. *Arch. Gen. Psychol.* 49:690–694.

TALLAL, P., S. L. MILLER, G. BEDI, G. BYMA, X. WANG, S. S. NAGARAJAN, C. SCHREINER, W. M. JENKINS, and M. M. MERZENICH, 1996. Language comprehension in language-learning impaired children improved with acoustically modified speech. *Science* 271(5245)81–84.

TEMPLE, E., R. A. POLDRACK, A. PROTOPAPAS, S. NAGRAJAN, P. TALLAL, M. MERZENICH, and J. D. E. GABRIEL, 1999. Functional organization for rapid auditory processing is disrupted in dyslexia: An fMRI study (abstract). *J. Cogn. Neurosci.* S:95.

THOMAS, K. M., S. W. KING, P. L. FRANZEN, T. F. WELSH, A. L. BERKOWITZ, D. C. NOLL, V. BIRMAHER, and B. J. CASEY, 1999. A developmental fMRI study of spatial working memory. *Neuroimage* 10:327–338.

THULBORN, K. R., J. C. WATERTON, P. M. MATTHEWS, and G. K. RADDA, 1982. Oxygenation dependence of the transverse relaxation time of water protons in whole blood at high field. *Biochem. Biophys. Acta* 714:265–270.

TORGESEN, J. K., 1997. The prevention and remediation of reading disabilities: Evaluating what we know from research. *J. Acad. Lang. Therapy* 1:11–47.

TREISMAN, A., 1988. Features and objects: The fourteenth Bartlett memorial lecture. *Quart. J. Exp. Psychol.* 40:201–237.

TURNER, R., D. LE BIHAN, C. T. W. MOONEN, K. DESPRES, and J. FRANK, 1991. Echo-planar time course MRI of cat brain oxygenation changes. *Magn. Reson. Med.* 22:159–166.

TURNER, R., P. JEZZARD, H. WEN, K. KWONG, D. LE BIHAN, and R. BALABAN, 1992. Functional mapping of the human visual cortex at 4 tesla using deoxygenation contrast EPI. *Society of Magnetic Resonance Medicine, 11th Annual Scientific Meeting and Exhibition*, p. 304.

VAIDYA, C. J., G. AUSTIN, G. KIRKORIAN, H. W. RIDLEHUBER, J. E. DESMOND, G. H. GLOVER, and J. D. GABRIELI, 1998. Selective effects of methylphenidate in attention deficit hyperactivity disorder: A functional magnetic resonance study. *Proc. Natl. Acad. Sci.(USA)* 95(24):14494–14499.

VELLUTINO, F. R., D. M. SCANLON, E. SIPAY, S. SMALL, A. PRATT, R. CHEN, and M. DENCKLA, 1996. Cognitive profiles of difficult-to-remediate and readily remediated poor readers: Early intervention as a vehicle for distinguishing between cognitive and experimental deficits as basic causes of specific reading disability. *J. Edu. Psychol.* 88:601–638.

YOUNG, S. W., 1988. Magnetic Resonance Imaging: Basic Principles. New York: Raven Press.

ZAMETKIN, A. Z., 1996. In reply to: C. T. Morton, Is research in normal and ill children involving radiation exposure ethical? *Arch. Gen. Psych.* 53:1060–1061.

# 11 Genetic Methods

ABSTRACT This chapter reviews how genetic methods are relevant for developmental cognitive neuroscience. Since the brain is the most genetically complex organ in the body, there are important genetic contributions to brain development in terms of both human universals and individual differences. Methods are now available to trace the complex developmental pathway that runs from a DNA sequence in a gene to brain development to aspects of developing behavior. This chapter reviews those methods and considers the implications of results from such methods for fundamental issues in developmental cognitive neuroscience.

Developmental cognitive neuroscience has the ambitious goal of elucidating the neural mechanisms underlying both universals and individual differences in cognitive and behavioral development. In this chapter, we review the way in which genetic methods are relevant, indeed crucial, for achieving that goal. By adding the word *developmental* to the term *cognitive neuroscience*, we are committing ourselves to the proposition that brain–behavior relations in the mature organism cannot be understood without understanding how the brain develops and how the development of the brain mediates the development of cognition and behavior. And once we take development seriously, we must also take genetics seriously.

Here I (1) consider general issues in the relation between genetics and cognitive neuroscience, (2) discuss two broad strategies for studying genetic effects on cognitive development, (3) briefly survey behavioral and molecular genetic methods, and (4) consider the implications of these genetic methods for fundamental issues in developmental cognitive neuroscience.

## Genetics and cognitive neuroscience

On general principles, it should not be surprising that there are genetic influences on cognitive and behavioral development. Of the roughly $10^5$ structural genes in the human genome, approximately 40% are uniquely expressed in the central nervous system (Hahn, van Ness, and Maxwell, 1978), whereas the remaining 60% are expressed both in the central nervous system and elsewhere in the body. We have no reason to suppose

that the genes expressed uniquely in the central nervous system are less polymorphic than other genes. (In this context, being less polymorphic means having fewer alternate forms, or *alleles*, where an allele of a gene is a variant DNA sequence of that gene.) In fact, given the relatively recent evolution of some human behaviors, we have good reasons for supposing they are more polymorphic. Because much of human evolution has involved brain evolution, we should expect the genes expressed in the brain to be more polymorphic than those expressed in evolutionarily older organs. Therefore, we expect individual differences in the alleles of the genes that influence human brain development. Consistent with this theoretical prediction, behavioral geneticists have documented moderate heritability (about 0.50) for most human cognitive and personality traits (Plomin and McClearn, 1993).

Thus, individual differences in cognitive and behavioral development are partly due to allelic differences in polymorphic genes that influence brain development. And because the heritability of these individual differences averages about 0.50, there are also substantial environmental influences on such individual differences.

Unfortunately, most studies of environmental influences on human development confound genetic and environmental influences. Such studies do not use genetically sensitive designs; therefore, their findings of a correlation between an environmental variable and a behavior in the developing child do not necessarily demonstrate an environmental influence on development (Scarr, 1992). Suppose, for instance, we find a correlation between how emotion is regulated in the mother–infant relationship and the child's later emotion regulation in peer relations. It can seem straightforward to conclude that the earlier social experience shaped the later social behavior. However, if the sample consists solely of biological mothers with their infants, the study's design confounds genetic and environmental influences: Such mother–infant pairs share early social experiences, but they also share half their segregating genes (genes that vary across individual humans). Consequently, the observed correlation could be partly, or even totally, mediated by genes. Thus we need genetically sensitive designs not only to study

BRUCE F. PENNINGTON Department of Psychology, University of Denver, Denver, Colorado.

PENNINGTON: GENETIC METHODS 149

genetic influences on development, but also to study environmental influences.

Universals in human development are also a joint product of genes and environments, ones that do *not* vary across human individuals. It is likely that not all genes that influence brain development are polymorphic. Moreover, as Greenough, Black, and Wallace (1987) have discussed, there are very important environmental influences on brain development that do not vary across individuals in a species. As they demonstrate, synaptogenesis cannot proceed normally without these species-typical environmental influences. To understand the etiology of human universals, we need to identify these genes and environments that virtually all humans share. Cross-species studies can help with this identification.

Before proceeding, it is important to address the long history of controversy about genetic studies in psychology. Some of this controversy derived from misleading claims about the implications of such studies, such as the view that the results of behavioral genetic studies support strict genetic determinism or provide a genetic explanation of group differences in behavior, neither of which is true. As Rende and Plomin (1995) point out, it is important to "study nature *and* nurture, rather than nature *versus* nurture." Behavioral development is the emergent product of a complex process of probabilistic epigenesis (Gottlieb, 1991) to which both genes and environments contribute. But neither genes nor environments code for behavior directly. Both sides of the nature–nurture debate share the same erroneous assumption that the instructions for behavior are preexistent either in the genome or the environment and are imposed from without on the developing organism (Oyama, 1985). Instead, genetic and environmental influences are inputs to a developmental process and their impact on behavioral outcome depends on their interactions with all the components of that process. Consequently, it is misleading to speak of the genome as a "blueprint" or to think that genes "code" for a behavior. Genes simply code for protein structure; and variations in the structure of a given protein, in a particular epigenetic context, may push behavioral outcomes in one direction or another. Thus, genetic and environmental factors are best conceptualized as acting as risk (or protective) factors in the development of individual differences in behavior; their effects are probabilistic rather than deterministic.

It is also useful to contrast this view of genetics and development with dominant views both in traditional neuropsychology and in some contemporary cognitive neuroscience. Although the lesion study has been the central paradigm in traditional neuropsychology, a different paradigm is needed in developmental cognitive neuroscience for several reasons. An acquired lesion is rare in childhood, extrinsic to normal development, and essentially an irreproducible natural experiment. Indeed, since no two acquired lesions are exactly alike, some cognitive neuropsychologists have concluded that each single case should be treated separately. In contrast, genetic influences on development are common, are intrinsic to the neurobiological mechanisms underlying cognitive and social development, and are reproducible, thus permitting group studies.

At a deeper, theoretical level the central ideas implicit in the lesion paradigm do not fit well with emerging findings in developmental neurobiology. The lesion paradigm assumes a relatively invariant, modular, species-typical cognitive architecture that can be dissected into independent cognitive components through the method of double dissociation (Shallice, 1988). In contrast, brain development across the lifespan is turning out to be very plastic both within and across individuals (Changeaux, 1985). Moreover, the neural architecture may well be better characterized by recurrent, connectionist networks whose activities are nonlinear and interdependent, than as a set of independent, cognitive modules (Oliver, Johnson, Karmiloff-Smith, and Pennington, 2000; Van Orden, Pennington, and Stone, in press). Therefore, the central ideas of the lesion paradigm are all in question. Although the lesion method has been extremely useful in giving us a "first pass" mapping of structure–function relations, other methods (and metaphors) are needed to tell us how the self-organizing system of the brain puts itself together in both normal and abnormal development.

## Two strategies for relating genes to development

We now turn to a description of genetic designs that are useful for developmental cognitive neuroscience. Such designs may be grouped into two broad categories, representing two different strategies for tracing developmental pathways from genes to brain development to behavior. Genetic studies of cognitive and behavioral development may begin with a known genetic syndrome and work "forward" to understand the impact of the alteration on development; or they may begin with a cognitive or behavioral phenotype and work "backward" to uncover the main genetic and environmental influences on that phenotype.

Both strategies are now being actively pursued, and examples of each are presented both in this volume and in a recent volume on neurodevelopmental disorders (Tager-Flusberg, 1999). Examples of the first strategy are neurodevelopmental studies of Down syndrome, fragile X syndrome, PKU, William's syndrome, and other neurogenetic disorders. Examples of the second strategy are genetic studies of attention deficit hyperactivity disorder (ADHD), autism, dyslexia, developmental speech and language disorders, schizophrenia, Tourette's syndrome, and other psychiatric disorders. Because the details of most of the discoveries using each strategy are described elsewhere, we will not review specific discoveries except in an illustrative way. Instead, this chapter focuses on methods and the general implications of what has already been discovered for developmental cognitive neuroscience.

These two strategies—forward and backward—have somewhat different strengths and weaknesses. The power of the forward strategy, such as tracing the neurodevelopmental consequences of the fragile X or PKU mutations, derives from the fact the genetic alteration is already identified, so groups that are homogeneous with respect to that etiology can be studied. However, this strategy is limited to known syndromes whose prevalence in the population is often a tenth or less of the prevalence of behaviorally defined syndromes. Hence, finding enough subjects at a given age can be difficult. Moreover, multiple aspects of cognition and behavior are usually affected in such syndromes (an instructive fact to which we will return), so they may not be as useful for understanding the neurobiological mechanisms underlying more specific aspects of cognitive development.

The backward strategy, exemplified by recent work on the neuropsychology and genetics of dyslexia and ADHD, usually has the advantage of greater prevalence and larger samples. But given the ubiquitous problems of etiological heterogeneity and phenocopies (the same phenotype is produced by environmental causes), it is almost certain that not all the individuals in these larger samples share the same genetic alteration. Also, they may not share the same specific cognitive phenotype, despite a shared behavioral definition.

It is important to remember that both strategies, when applied only to humans, suffer from some common weaknesses. One of these is the quasi-experimental nature of case-control designs. The genetic alteration is not randomly assigned by the experimenter; hence, we can never be totally sure that the genetic alteration in question is the only factor that differs across groups, no matter how carefully comparison groups are matched. A second shared weakness is that both the genetic and environmental backgrounds of individuals with a given syndrome are obviously free to vary, and this variance may mask the phenotypic effects of the genetic alteration in question.

A solution for both these problems is the use of animal models, in which the genetic alteration is randomly assigned and the genetic and environmental backgrounds are controlled. Complementary studies of humans and animals with the same genetic (or metabolic) alteration offer a powerful strategy, one that has been very usefully applied to PKU (Diamond, this volume) and is now being applied to fragile X (Willems, Reyniers, and Oostra, 1995) and Down syndrome (Crnic and Pennington, 2000). As another important advantage, these animal models permit a clearer test of which brain correlates associated with a syndrome are directly caused by the genetic alteration in question. In contrast, neuroimaging findings from humans with a given syndrome only provide correlates of the syndrome. Such findings could be a product of environmental differences associated with the syndrome rather than a product of its genetic etiology. Thus, establishing a causal relation between a genetic alteration and a brain phenotype is difficult without an animal model.

In what follows, we focus on the methods used in the backward strategy, since those involved in the forward strategy are already well described in other chapters. Then we consider the implications of results from both strategies for fundamental issues in developmental cognitive neuroscience.

## How to go from behavior to genes

Until fairly recently, the main methods available for evaluating genetic influences on individual differences in human behavior were indirect ones that did not examine differences in DNA sequences. Instead, the influence of such differences on the development of individual differences in behavior was inferred through careful quantitative analyses of naturally occurring quasi-experiments, mainly twin births and adoptions. It is important to understand that both direct (molecular) and indirect (quantitative or biometric) genetic methods derive their power from a very strong theoretical constraint: That is, while genotypes exert causal influences on phenotypes, phenotypes do not change genotypes (except in the unusual situation where phenotype leads to a mutation through exposure to ionizing radiation). Our genome can alter our behavior, but our behavior cannot influence our genome (although behavior can influence gene expression). Therefore, if we find a nonartifactual relation between genotype and behavior, it means that there is some causal pathway leading from that genotype to that behavior, no matter how tortuous and no matter how many other causes also act on the behavior. Thus, genetic studies, unlike other nonexperimental studies of human behavior, address causation.

We may organize the genetic analysis of any trait or phenotype into a series of questions, one leading to the next, answering each question by a different method: (1) Is the trait familial? (2) If so, is the familiality due in part to genetic influences? In other words, is the trait heritable? (3) If so, what is the mechanism of genetic transmission? (4) What are the actual gene or genes responsible for that mechanism? Once such genes are discovered, additional questions of key relevance to developmental cognitive neuroscience may be addressed: (5) When and where are these genes expressed in the developing brain, and how do they alter its development? (6) How do those alterations change developing neural networks, thereby changing cognitive and behavioral development? (7) How can the influences of other genes and environmental factors modify these developmental effects?

The four methods used to answer each of the first four questions are (1) family studies, (2) twin and adoption studies, (3) segregation analysis, and (4) linkage and association analysis. Tables 11.1 and 11.2 summarize these methods and some key issues involved in their interpretation. Let us briefly examine these methods and look at some illustrative findings.

The design of family studies is fairly straightforward; the goal is to measure the familiality of a trait, which can be quantified as the correlations among relatives for a continuous trait or as relative risk (the prevalence in relatives divided by the population prevalence) for a categorical trait. These correlations or relative risks are computed separately for different relationships in families and tested for statistical significance. A very useful statistic for genetic studies is the relative risk to full siblings ($\lambda$) because the ease of finding genes that influence a trait is proportional to $\lambda$. For instance, a $\lambda$ of 2 means that the relative risk to full siblings is twice the population risk.

It is now well established that many psychiatric disorders are familial. For instance, the value of $\lambda$ is 9 for schizophrenia, 8 for bipolar disorder, and 3 for major depression (Plomin et al., 1997). Similar values have been found for childhood psychiatric disorders; $\lambda$ values are ~6 for attention deficit hyperactivity disorder (Faraone et al., 1992), ~8 for dyslexia (Gilger, Pennington, and DeFries, 1991), and as high as 100 for autism (Plomin et al., 1997). Although familiality does not prove genetic influence (since familial transmission may be environmentally mediated), data from twin and molecular studies have demonstrated that genetic influences make a large contribution to the familiality of psychiatric disorders.

Segregation analysis is a particular kind of family study, one that formally tests competing models for the mode of transmission of a trait in families. Segregation analysis is a computationally intensive modeling procedure, and the results are limited to the range of modes of transmission that are modeled, which are mainly single-locus, Mendelian modes. The transmission of a complex behavioral phenotype may well involve the interaction of several genes and several environmental risk factors. Obviously, segregation analysis provides only an indirect test of genetic mechanisms. Hence, if a major locus effect is found by segregation analysis, molecular methods are needed to confirm the result and to identify the location of the major locus in the genome.

The most widely used behavioral genetic methods have been twin and adoption studies, which mainly address question 2 concerning heritability. These methods provide a means of testing models of the etiology of a given behavior, or the relation between multiple behaviors, in a population. Such methods take the population variance in a behavioral trait and test which combination of genetic and environmental components best accounts for it. As in all of science, the meaning of the results naturally depends on the choice and validity of

TABLE 11.1
*Biometric (indirect) methods*

| Method | Use | Issues |
|---|---|---|
| Family studies | Estimate familial risk ($\lambda$) | Ascertainment; familiality may be environmentally mediated |
| Twin and adoption studies | Estimate proportions of variance attributable to genes ($h^2$), shared environment ($c^2$), and nonshared environment ($e^2$) | Estimates are both population- and model-dependent |
| Segregation analysis | Model the mode of transmission | Familiality may be environmentally mediated; results are limited to the range of models tested. |

TABLE 11.2

*Molecular methods*

| Method | Use | Issues |
|---|---|---|
| *Linkage* | | |
| Parametric | Find approximate location of a major locus influencing a phenotype | Transmission parameters of complex behavioral phenotypes are often unknown |
| Nonparametric | Find approximate location of genes influencing a phenotype | Less powerful |
| *Association* | | |
| Case-control | Identify an allele that influences a phenotype | Ethnic stratification; multiple mutations of the same gene |
| *Family-Based* | | |
| Transmission disequilibrium test (TDT) | Same | Multiple mutations |
| Haplotype relative risk (HRR) | Same | Multiple mutations |

the models tested and their background assumptions. A good introduction to twin and adoption methods is provided by Plomin and colleagues (1997).

To study the etiology of developmental psychopathology, we need to apply twin and adoption methods to the analysis of extreme variations in behavior rather than the analysis of variance across the whole distribution. Extreme variations may be treated as categories, in which case the appropriate method of analysis is nonparametric and involves comparing the rates of concordance for different degrees of relationship. Twin concordance studies have found genetic influences on most psychiatric disorders (Plomin et al., 1997; Plomin, Owen, and McGuffin, 1994).

However, if the trait in question is quantitative (can be measured using an ordinal or interval scale), treating the trait as categorical does not use all the information contained in the data and is thus less statistically powerful. If we can measure not only whether someone has ADHD or reading disability, but also how severely he or she has it, then our data are quantitative rather than qualitative and can be analyzed with parametric statistics. A particularly powerful twin method for analyzing extreme variation in quantitative traits was developed by DeFries and Fulker (1988) and is now called the DF method in their honor. The DF method is based on the phenomenon of differential regression to the mean, first described by Francis Galton (1869). Let us now examine the logic of the DF method.

Suppose we have an index case or proband who has been selected because he/she is extreme on some dimension; this proband is thus at the low or high end of the distribution for that trait. A relative of this proband will have, on average, a score on this trait distribution that is closer to the mean than the proband's score; this is an example of regression to the mean. If the degree

of this regression in relatives varies as a function of their degree of genetic relation to the proband, we have "differential regression to the mean." A finding of differential regression to the mean indicates that there is genetic influence on the trait, all other things being equal. Thus, in the case of twin pairs selected because at least one twin has an extreme score, comparison of MZ and DZ cotwin means provides a test of whether there is differential regression to the mean. If the DZ cotwin mean is significantly closer to the population mean than the MZ cotwin mean, then there is evidence of genetic influence on the extreme trait.

The degree of genetic influence on the extreme trait is $h_g^2$, where the subscript g refers to the extreme group of probands. So $h_g^2$ measures the heritability of the group deficit (or talent), in contrast to $h^2$, which measures the heritability of variations across the whole distribution. The comparison of $h^2$ and $h_g^2$ provides one test of whether the etiology of normal variations differs from the etiology of extreme ones—a fundamental issue in developmental psychopathology. However, before the advent of the DF method and molecular methods, empirical methods to address this issue were mostly lacking.

The advantage of the DF method is that it provides a statistically powerful method of modeling these components of the etiology of the scores of an extreme group. Another advantage of this method is its flexibility; it can readily be extended to (1) the bivariate case, where we are interested in the etiologic basis of the phenotypic correlation between two extreme traits; (2) an evaluation of differential etiology (of subgroups, such as males and females, or extreme and normal variations); or (3) a test for linkage. Let us briefly examine the bivariate extension.

A phenotypic correlation between two extreme traits might be due to shared genetic, shared environmental influences, or some combination thereof. The bivariate extension of the DF method addresses this question by calculating bivariate $h_g^2$, $c_g^2$, and $e_g^2$, which are, respectively, the degree to which the relation between the two extreme traits is due to shared genes, shared common family environments, or shared nonfamilial environmental influences (shared by the two traits but not shared by siblings within a family). An important application of this bivariate extension is analyzing the etiological basis of comorbidity between two disorders. Since comorbidity is quite common among psychiatric disorders, understanding its etiological basis is an important goal.

To answer the fourth question concerning gene locations, molecular methods are needed (table 11.2). Unlike the methods just discussed, molecular methods can provide direct evidence of genetic influence on a trait or on the relation among traits. All molecular methods test for a relation between DNA sequence variations and phenotypic variations, so they require precise measures in both domains and theoretically sound quantitative methods of relating genetic variation with phenotypic variation. As discussed earlier, it is important to understand that the relation being tested is not simply a correlation; rather, it is the hypothesis that sequence variation in a particular part of the genome causes, at least in part, the phenotypic variation.

We can divide molecular methods into tests of *linkage* and tests of *association*. Generally, we use linkage methods when we lack a hypothesis about which gene influences the trait in question. Tests of association have usually required such a hypothesis, although association methods are now being developed that can be used in a whole genome search.

The initial goal of linkage methods is to find the approximate locations of genes influencing a trait. The phenomenon of linkage depends on the fact that the croupier in the genetic casino, as it were, does not shuffle perfectly. The phenomenon of recombination shuffles genes (cards in this simile) in the process of forming gametes, but genes (cards) that are close together are less likely to be separated in a shuffle owing to this physical proximity: They are "linked." So linkage represents a deviation from Mendel's second law of the independent assortment of genes.

Suppose we are searching the deck for a gene or genes whose location is unknown, say a gene influencing a particular behavioral trait such as dyslexia. The deck in question, the genome, is vast—it contains approximately 100,000 genes in its coding regions and a much larger amount of noncoding DNA. Our job is to find, in this huge deck, sequence variations (particular cards) that influence the trait we are studying. Moreover, the deck contains many, many other sequence variations influencing other traits and many more sequence variations in noncoding regions. A very few of these other sequence variations will happen to lie close enough to the sequence variations we are seeking so as to be linked to them. If we have a map of sequence variations or "markers" across the genome that are roughly evenly spaced and close enough together to detect linkage to most or all of the adjacent genes, we can use these markers to search for the location of sequence variations that influence the trait of interest.

Somewhat more formally, we have a hypothesis that there are sequence variations somewhere in the genome that influence the trait in question. Presumably, this hypothesis is based on studies of the trait with indirect genetic methods, so that we already know that the trait is familial, heritable, and perhaps even subject to major gene influence. If our hypothesis is correct, individuals with more of this trait will have, on average, more of these sequence variations than do individuals with less of the trait. In other words, our hypothesis implies that these particular sequence variations are cotransmitted with levels of the trait across generations (in the case of a single gene and a categorical trait, we would say that they cosegregate). Thus, if our hypothesis is correct, levels of the trait are a proxy for the unknown causative sequence variations. Because of the phenomenon of linkage, nearby sequence variations, some of which are markers in our genomic map, are also cotransmitted within families along with levels of the trait and the unknown sequence variations. Hence, two out of the three cotransmitted things are known to us—levels of the trait and sequence variations in markers—and knowledge of these two things allows us to gain knowledge of the approximate location of the third unknown thing. Thus, a finding of linkage between particular markers and levels of the trait indicates that there is a gene near these markers that influences the trait we are studying.

In sum, cotransmission of genetic markers and a behavioral trait helps us to map the approximate location of genes whose alleles influence that trait.

Linkage methods are broadly divided into those that require specification of the mode of transmission and those that do not. The former, which require specification of these parameters of transmission, are called "parametric" or "model-dependent" and the latter are called "nonparametric" or "model-free." Parametric linkage methods were developed first (Morton, 1955), partly because of the historical emphasis among geneticists on Mendelian traits. For a student of behavior, it is quickly apparent that parametric linkage analysis is testing a very strong hypothesis indeed—namely, that there is a single Mendelian gene that has a major causal influence on the trait in question. If penetrance is modeled at a high value, a finding that only a very few subjects in a family have the relevant marker but not the trait (or the reverse) disconfirms this hypothesis.

For most behavioral traits, however, transmission is unlikely to be Mendelian. Rather, multiple genes and environmental risk factors will influence the trait, and the parameters of transmission will be unknown. Hence, to use parametric linkage methods, we need to make assumptions (specify parameters), which are likely to be incorrect. Parametric linkage methods do have the advantage of statistical power because they are testing such a strong hypothesis—consistent cotransmission in an extended family between a marker and a trait. They can be useful in analyzing data from very large extended families, especially if these are considered one at a time. But since there may be genetic heterogeneity across such families, combining their data may be misleading.

Nonparametric methods require fewer assumptions and are generally preferable in linkage studies of behavioral traits (Pauls, 1993; Rutter, 1994). They also do not require large extended families and often utilize sibling pairs from nuclear families. Sibling pair methods for analyzing quantitative traits utilizing multiple markers have been developed (e.g., Kruglyak and Lander, 1995). However, sibling pair methods are less powerful. The sample size necessary to detect linkage increases considerably as the proportion of families linked to the same single locus goes down. In addition, nuclear families often do not provide enough genetic information to determine which markers are identical by descent in a sibling pair. So, applying model-free methods to extended pedigrees can be a useful compromise.

One sibling pair method, called "interval mapping," is useful for mapping genes that influence extreme, quantitative traits. An extension of the DF method discussed earlier, interval mapping was developed by David Fulker and colleagues at the Institute for Behavioral Genetics in Boulder, Colorado (Cardon and Fulker, 1994; Fulker, Cherny, and Cardon, 1995). Interval mapping is particularly useful in studies of cognitive and behavioral disorders for several reasons: (1) It is appropriate for extreme traits that are measured quantitatively; (2) it is quite powerful statistically; (3) it readily tests whether the same chromosomal region is linked to different levels of the trait, even levels from either end of the distribution; (4) it is quite flexible and can be readily extended to consider dominance, bivariate linkage (which is needed to find genes responsible for comor-

bidities), or interactions with other factors, such as gender. Interval mapping has been used successfully to identify the location of a QTL on the short arm of chromosome 6 that influences dyslexia (Cardon et al., 1994).

We now consider association analysis, which tests for a correlation between a particular allele of a candidate gene and a phenotype. To appreciate the difference between linkage and association analysis (Hodge, 1993), it is important to understand the difference between linkage and linkage disequilibrium. In the case of linkage, the particular allele of a given locus that is linked to a behavioral trait will vary across families because recombination will have sorted different alleles of the marker with the particular causative allele of the linked gene that influences the trait. Say we found linkage between dyslexia and the gene for the ABO blood type. In some families, most or all of the dyslexics would have type A blood, and the nondyslexics would have types B or O. In other families, the dyslexics would have type B blood, and in still others they would have type O blood. So linkage between dyslexia and the ABO gene does *not* mean that all dyslexics have a particular blood type. In this case, the gene that influences dyslexia and the ABO gene are close enough together that recombination (shuffling) between them is reduced but not eliminated. In the thousands of years since the mutation in the dyslexia gene occurred, recombination has shuffled that gene with different alleles of the ABO gene across families. But what if the dyslexia gene and the ABO gene are so close together that little or no reshuffling has occurred over those thousands of years? In this case, we would say the two genes are in linkage disequilibrium and, as a result, virtually all dyslexics across families would have a particular ABO blood type. In that case, there would be an association between dyslexia and the ABO allele that produces that particular blood type.

In sum, if there is allele sharing for a marker gene among individuals with a given trait (e.g., dyslexia) that is found within but not across families, we say there is linkage. If there is allele sharing both within and across families, we say there is association.

There are three possible reasons for a finding of association: (1) There is linkage disequilibrium between the candidate allele and a nearby causal allele; (2) the candidate allele *is* the causal allele (in which case, there would be no recombination); or (3) an artifact produces association but not linkage. One prominent artifact that has been identified in case-control association studies is ethnic stratification. Allele frequencies vary considerably in human populations, even within groups labeled as "Caucasian," "Hispanic," or "African-

American" (Seaman et al., 1999). Therefore, an ethnically matched case-control association study may nonetheless confound allele frequencies with group, producing a spurious association.

To avoid this confound, one can use within-family association methods such as the transmission disequilibrium test (Ewens and Spielman, 1995) and the haplotype relative risk method (Falk and Rubenstein, 1987; Terwilliger and Ott, 1992). Both these methods test whether the candidate allele is more frequently transmitted to affected family members than to nonaffected family members. These methods are now being generalized for use with continuous traits and covariates.

Nonetheless, even within-family association methods will fail to detect a causative gene in which there are multiple mutations across families, each of which produces the disorder. In this case, there would be linkage to markers close to this gene, but not association to a particular allele of the gene.

As stated previously, association analysis is usually appropriate only if one has a hypothesis about which particular gene is influencing a trait. That hypothesis could come from knowledge of the neurobiology of the trait (the trait involves dopamine transmission; therefore, genes for dopamine receptors may be involved in its cause) or from previous linkage studies (there is a gene in this region influencing the trait and one of the known genes in this region has a function that makes it a possible candidate gene).

Obviously, the ultimate goals of both linkage and association methods are to identify the mutations that causally influence the trait in question, and to characterize how these mutations alter the function of their genes in the development of brain and behavior.

Linkage and association methods have begun to unravel part of the etiology of behaviorally defined developmental disorders. Linkage has been found between dyslexia and markers in a 2-centimorgan region of the short arm of chromosome 6 in five samples by three independent laboratories (Cardon et al., 1994; Grigorenko et al., 1997; Gayan et al., 1999; Fisher et al., 1999), although one study (Field and Kaplan, 1998) did not find this linkage. Association between an allele of the gene for dopamine 4 receptor (DRD4) and ADHD has now been found in several studies (e.g., Swanson et al., 1998; Faraone et al., 2000). This association makes theoretical sense because this particular allele causes a blunted response to dopamine.

*Implications for fundamental issues*

What we have already discovered from genetic studies of cognitive development has implications for funda-

mental issues in developmental cognitive neuroscience. We discuss two such issues here: (1) How do conceptions of genetic influences fit with theories of development? (2) What have we already learned from genetic studies about brain mechanisms in atypical development?

With regard to the first issue, one can broadly distinguish two conceptions of development, each of which is compatible with a different view of how genes act in development. Nativism, or neonativism, is compatible with genetic determinism, whereas constructionism is compatible with probabilistic epigenesis (Gottlieb, 1991). As already discussed, it is misleading to think about the actions of genes in a deterministic way. In addition, individual genes frequently affect multiple phenotypes (pleiotropy), and complex behavioral phenotypes are almost undoubtedly affected by multiple genes (polygeny). The combination of these two notions of pleiotropy and polygeny means that the correspondence relations between genes and complex behavioral phenotypes are many-to-many, not one-to-one. Lying between genes and behavioral outcomes are several levels of analysis and an undoubtedly very complicated set of developmental interactions.

So the nativist notion that there might be a gene that affects a very specific aspect of cognition, say a particular aspect of grammar, is very unlikely. Support for this unlikely hypothesis seemed to be provided by an extended family (KE) that appeared to have an autosomal dominantly transmitted deficit in regular inflectional morphology forming regular past tense and plural forms (Gopnik, 1990; Pinker, 1991). Further study revealed that although the KE family had an autosomal dominant disorder, the gene for which was localized to chromosome 7p (Fisher et al., 1998), their speech and language phenotype was actually much broader and included a severe oral facial dyspraxia, about a 20-point deficit in IQ, and deficits on a broad array of language measures (Varga-Khadem et al., 1995). Therefore, instead of having a defective grammar gene, this family has a mutation that broadly disrupts cognitive and motor development but in such a way that speech and language development are more severely affected. This mutation, then, produces a mix of general and specific deficits—a phenomenon characteristic of most genetic syndromes.

In thinking about the genetic contributions to human universals unique to our species (e.g., grammar), one is faced immediately with a severe constraint: The number of genes unique to humans must be quite small, since the genetic homology between humans and chimpanzees is about 99%. Because most of the base pair differences between humans and chimps are in genes that both species share, it is unlikely that very many genes are unique to humans, although the exact number is unknown. Consequently, it is extremely unlikely that there are enough uniquely human genes to allocate each one to a unique human cognitive universal, even if it were biologically plausible for a gene to code for a specific aspect of cognition. A plausible alternative hypothesis is that the genetic basis of human uniqueness is partly due to changes in regulatory genes. Such changes would have increased the number of neurons produced in brain development and lengthened the time to maturity (Changeaux, 1985). These kinds of general changes operating in a particular epigenetic and ecological context may go a long way toward explaining human uniqueness.

The second question concerns what have we already learned about different ways genes alter brain and cognitive development. One can already list three broad classes of genetic effects on brain development: (1) on brain size, by altering the number of neurons or synapses; (2) on neuronal migration, sometimes in a regionally specific fashion; and (3) on neurotransmission, either by changing levels of neurotransmitter or by changing the binding properties of receptor proteins. There will undoubtedly be many other mechanisms; but just with these three, a fairly broad range of individual cognitive differences are being accounted for.

For instance, with regard to the first effect, it is well known that brain size is affected in many genetic syndromes. Thus, there is microcephaly in Down syndrome (Coyle, Oster-Granite, and Gearhart, 1986) and other mental retardation syndromes. In contrast, in about a quarter of individuals with autism (Bailey, Phillips, and Rutter, 1996) and in fragile X syndrome, there is macrocephaly. The mechanism in fragile X appears to be related to a gene that influences synaptic pruning (Willems et al., 1995). Neurocomputational models support the straightforward intuition that having too few or too many neurons or connections in brain networks would affect cognitive development in different ways. Having too few nodes or connections in a neural network would limit its representational capacity. Having too many would lead to a network that fails to generalize (see Oliver et al., 2000).

With regard to the second effect, there are well-studied genetic mutations in both mice and fruit flies that affect neuronal migration (Changeux, 1985), and there is evidence for migrational anomalies in several human syndromes. In the nonhuman cases it has sometimes been demonstrated that the migrational anomalies cause particular behavioral deficits.

The third kind of effect has been demonstrated in PKU, in which an enzyme defect prevents the conversion of phenylalanine to tyrosine, which is the rate-limiting precursor for the synthesis of dopamine. So even the mild elevations of phenylalanine found in treated PKU can produce dopamine depletion in prefrontal cortex (Diamond, this volume).

Another way neurotransmission can be affected is through alterations in the binding properties of receptors for neurotransmitters. These receptors are proteins coded for by genes. Their binding properties depend on their tertiary structure, which is determined by the way they fold up. Base-pair differences in the gene for a receptor can cause differences in its tertiary structure and hence in its binding properties. These changes can, in turn, make a particular neurotransmitter more or less available at the synapse. As discussed earlier, ADHD has been found to be associated with an allele of the DRD4 gene. Evidence of allelic differences in other receptor genes in other psychiatric illnesses is beginning to emerge, so this third kind of effect could account for many psychiatric disorders in which there are known neurotransmitter imbalances.

There are undoubtedly other genetic mechanisms underlying brain development. Work is underway to identify candidate genes that affect brain development (Vicente et al., 1997) and to test whether these genes influence behavioral disorders.

In sum, the complex pathways that run from genes to brain development to behavioral development are beginning to be elucidated. The pace of such discoveries is now beginning to accelerate rapidly owing to the success of the Human Genome Project, the increasing sophistication of the genetic methods applied to the analysis of cognition and behavior, and new methods and findings in other parts of cognitive neuroscience. It is fairly safe to say that these accelerating genetic discoveries will have a widening impact on the field of developmental cognitive neuroscience.

## REFERENCES

BAILEY, A., W. PHILLIPS, and M. RUTTER, 1996. Autism: Towards an integration of clinical, genetic, neuropsychological, and neurobiological perspectives. *J. Child Psychol. Psychiat.* 37:89–126.

CARDON, L. R., S. D. SMITH, D. W. FULKER, W. J. KIMBERLING, B. F. PENNINGTON, and J. C. DEFRIES, 1994. Quantitative trait locus for reading disability on chromosome 6. *Science* 266:276–279.

CARDON, L. R., and D. W. FULKER, 1994. The power of interval mapping of quantitative trait loci, using selected sib pairs. *Am. J. Hum. Genet.* 55:825–833.

CHANGEAUX, J. P., 1985. *Neuronal Man.* New York: Oxford University Press.

COYLE, J. T., M. L. OSTER-GRANITE, and J. D. GEARHART, 1986. The neurobiologic consequences of Down syndrome. *Brain Res. Bull.* 16:773–787.

CRNIC, L. S., and B. F. PENNINGTON, 2000. Down syndrome: Neuropsychology and animal models. In *Progress in Infancy Research*, Vol. 1, C. Rovee-Collier, L. P. Lipsitt, and H. Hayne, eds. Mahwah, N. J.: Lawrence Erlbaum, pp. 69–111.

DEFRIES, J. C., and D. W. FULKER, 1988. Multiple regression analysis of twin data: Etiology of deviant scores versus individual differences. *Acta Genet. Med. Gemel.* 37:205–216.

EWENS, W. J., and R. S. SPIELMAN, 1995. The transmission/disequilibrium test: History, subdivision, and admixture. *Am. J. Hum. Genet.* 98:91–101.

FALK, C. T., and P. RUBENSTEIN, 1987. Haplotype relative risks: An easy reliable way to construct a proper control sample for risk calculations. *Ann. Hum. Gen.* 51:227–233.

FARAONE, J. V., J. BIEDERMAN, W. J. CHEN, B. KRIFCHER, C. MOORE, S. SPRICH, and M. TSUANG, 1992. Segregation analysis of attention deficit hyperactivity disorder. *Psych. Gen.* 2:257–275.

FARAONE, J. V., J. BIEDERMAN, B. WEIFFENBACH, T. KEITH, M. CHU, A. WEAVER, T. J. SPENCER, T. E. WILENS, J. FRAZIER, M. CLEVES, and J. SAKAI, 1999. Dopamine D4 gene 7-repeat allele and attention-deficit hyperactivity disorder. *Am. J. Psychiat.* 156:768–770.

FIELD, L. L., and B. J. KAPLAN, 1998. Absence of linkage of phonological coding dyslexia to chromosome 6p23–p21.3 in a large family data set. *Am. J. Hum. Genet.* 63(5):1448–1456.

FISHER, S. E., A. J. MARLOW, J. M. R. LAMB, D. F. WILLIAMS, A. J. RICHARDSON, and D. E. WEEKS, 1999. A quantitative-trait locus on chromosome 6p influences different aspects of developmental dyslexia. *Am. J. Hum. Gen.* 64:146–156.

FISHER, S. E., F. VARGA-KHADEM, K. E. WATKINS, A. P. MONACO, and M. E. PEMBREY, 1998. Localization of a gene implicated in a severe speech and language disorder. *Nature Genet.* 18:168–170.

FULKER, D. W., S. S. CHERNY, and L. R. CARDON, 1995. Multipoint interval mapping of quantitative trait loci using sib pairs. *Am. J. Hum. Genet.* 56:1224–1233.

GALTON, F., 1869. *Hereditary Genius: An Inquiry into Its Laws and Consequences.* London: Macmillan.

GAYAN, J., S. D. SMITH, S. S. CHERNY, L. R. CARDON, D. W. FULKER, A. M. BROWER, R. K. OLSON, B. F. PENNINGTON, and J. C. DEFRIES, 1999. Quantitative-trait locus for specific language and reading deficits on chromosome 6p. *Am. J. Hum. Gen.* 64:157–164.

GILGER, J. W., B. F. PENNINGTON, and J. C. DEFRIES, 1991. Risk for reading disability as a function of parental history in three family studies. *Read. Writ.* 3:205–217.

GOPNIK, M., 1990. Feature-blind grammar and dysphasia. *Nature* 344(6268):715.

GOTTLIEB, G., 1991. Experiential canalization of behavioral development: Theory. *Dev. Psych.* 27:4–13.

GREENOUGH, W. T., J. E. BLACK, and C. S. WALLACE, 1987. Experience and brain development. *Child Dev.* 58:539–559.

GRIGORENKO, E. L., F. B. WOOD, M. S. MEYER, L. A. HART, W. C. SPEED, A. SHUSTER, and D. L. PAULS, 1997. Susceptibility loci for distinct components of developmental dyslexia on chromosomes 6 and 15. *Am. J. Hum. Gen.* 60:27–39.

HAHN, W., J. VAN NESS, and I. MAXWELL, 1978. Complex population of mRNA sequences in large polyadenylated nuclear RNA molecules. *Proc. Natl. Acad. Sci. (USA)* 75:5544–5547.

HODGE, S. E., 1993. Linkage analysis versus association analysis: Distinguishing between two models that explain disease-marker associations. *Am. J. Hum. Genet.* 53:367–384.

KRUGLYAK, L., and E. S. LANDER, 1995. Complete multipoint sib-pair analysis of qualitative and quantitative traits. *Am. J. Hum. Genet.* 57:439–454.

OLIVER, A., M. H. JOHNSON, A. K. KARMILOFF-SMITH, and B. F. PENNINGTON, 2000. Deviations in the emergence of representations: A neuroconstructivist framework for analyzing developmental disorders. *Dev. Sci.* 3:1–40.

OYAMA, S., 1985. *The Ontogeny of Information.* Cambridge: Cambridge University Press.

MORTON, M. E., 1955. Sequential tests for the detection of linkage. *Am. J. Hum. Genet.* 7:227–318.

PAULS, D. L., 1993. Behavioral disorders: Lessons in linkage. *Nature Genet.* 3:4–5.

PINKER, S., 1991. Rules of language. *Science* 253:530–535.

PLOMIN, R., M. J. OWEN, and P. MCGUFFIN, 1994. The genetic basis of complex human behaviors. *Science* 264:1733–1739.

PLOMIN, R., and G. MCCLEARN, 1993. *Nature, Nurture and Psychology.* Washington, D.C.: American Psychological Association.

PLOMIN, R., G. MCCLEARN, J. C. DEFRIES, and M. RUTTER, 1997. *Behavioral Genetics.* New York: W. H. Freeman.

RENDE, R., and R. PLOMIN, 1995. Nature, nurture, and the development of psychopathology. In *Developmental Psychopathology*, Vol. I, D. Cicchetti and D. J. Cohen, eds. New York: John Wiley and Sons, pp. 291–314.

RUTTER, M., 1994. Psychiatric genetics research challenges and pathways forward. *Am. J. Med. Genet. (Neuropsychiat. Genet.)* 54:185–198.

SCARR, S., 1992. Developmental theories of the 1990s: Development and individual differences. *Child Dev.* 63:1–19.

SEAMAN, M. I., J. B. FISHER, F. M. CHANG, and K. K. KIDD, 1999. Tandem duplication polymorphism upstream of the dopamine D4 receptor gene (DRD4). *Am. J. Med. Genet. (Neurol. Genet).* 88:705–709.

SHALLICE, T., 1988. *From Neuropsychology to Mental Structure.* New York: Cambridge University Press.

SWANSON, J. M., G. A. SUNOHARA, J. L. KENNEDY, R. REGINO, E. FINEBERG, T. WIGAL, M. LERNER, L. WILLIAMS, G. J. LAHOSTE, and S. WIGAL, 1998. Association of the dopamine receptor D4 (DRD4) gene with a refined phenotype of attention deficit hyperactivity disorder (ADHD): A family-based approach. *Mol. Psych.* 3:38–41.

TAGER-FLUSBERG, H., 1999. *Neurodevelopmental Disorders.* Cambridge, Mass.: MIT Press.

TERWILLIGER, J. D., and J. OTT, 1992. A haplotype-based "haplotype relative risk" approach to detecting allelic associations. *Hum. Hered.* 42:337–346.

VAN ORDEN, G. C., B. F. PENNINGTON, and G. STONE, in press. What do double dissociations prove? Modularity yields a degenerating research program. *Cogn. Sci.*

VARGA-KHADEM, F., K. WATKINS, K. ALCOCK, P. FLETCHER, and R. E. PASSINGHAM, 1995. Praxic and nonverbal cognitive deficits in a large family with a genetically transmitted speech and language disorder. *Proc. Natl. Acad. Sci. (USA)* 92:930–933.

VICENTE, A. M., F. MACCIARDI, M. VERGA, A. S. BASSETT, W. E. HONER, G. BEAN, and J. L. KENNEDY, 1997. NCAM and schizophrenia: Genetic studies. *Mol. Psychiat.* 2:65–69.

WILLEMS, P. J., E. REYNIERS, and B. A. OOSTRA, 1995. An animal model for fragile X syndrome. *Mental Retard. Dev. Dis. Res. Rev.* 1:298–302.

# 12 Neural Network Models of Cognitive Development

YUKO MUNAKATA AND
JENNIFER MERVA STEDRON

ABSTRACT This chapter covers neural network modeling (also known as connectionist or parallel distributed processing modeling) as a tool for studying developmental cognitive neuroscience. Neural network models provide a powerful method for exploring the complex relation between brain development and cognitive development. This chapter reviews what neural network models consist of, why modeling is useful, and how models have helped to address fundamental questions about development. Important challenges for this methodology are also discussed, along with productive directions for future work within the neural network modeling framework.

Neural network models provide a powerful tool in the study of developmental cognitive neuroscience. Such models implement neural processes in computer simulations, allowing an exploration of the role of these processes in behavior. The modeling methodology provides an important complement to behavioral methods by building upon findings from behavioral studies and pointing the way toward new studies to advance our understanding of the relation between brain and behavior.

In this chapter, we cover neural network models of cognitive development from the perspective of three critical methodological questions: why, what, and how. More specifically, we explain *why* it is important to use neural network models in the study of developmental cognitive neuroscience, thereby enticing you (we hope) to learn more about *what* the nuts and bolts of neural network models entail. We then describe *how* neural network models have been used to address fundamental developmental questions about the origins of knowledge and how change occurs. We also discuss challenges relevant to each of these issues of the why, what, and how of neural network modeling. This chapter aims both to encourage an appreciation of the potential contributions of neural network models to the advancement of developmental cognitive neuroscience, and to confer the ability to evaluate both the over- and underselling of this methodology.

YUKO MUNAKATA AND JENNIFER MERVA STEDRON Department of Psychology, University of Denver, Denver, Colorado.

## Why

First, we describe some of the benefits of neural network modeling (O'Reilly and Munakata, 2000; see also Elman et al., 1996; Rumelhart and McClelland, 1986; Seidenberg, 1993). All of these benefits are demonstrated by specific models covered later in the *How* section, and support a productive interchange between modeling and behavioral studies. Some of these benefits are arguably conferred to some degree by purely verbal theories; however, implementing a working model of a theory is both more demanding and more powerful than simply stating the theory, and so provides greater benefits.

*Models allow control* Models can be manipulated, tested, and observed much more precisely than the thing being modeled (whether the thing is a single neuron, a small collection of neurons, a human infant, a monkey, and so on). Such control enables a clearer picture of the causal role of different factors.

*Models help us to understand behavior* With such control, we can watch a model in action to get a sense of why behavior unfolds as it does. For example, seemingly unrelated or even contradictory behaviors can be related to one another in nonobvious ways through common neural network mechanisms. Furthermore, neural network models can provide an important bridge between neural and cognitive aspects of behavior. Models can also be lesioned and then tested, providing insight into behavior following specific types of brain damage and, in turn, into normal functioning.

*Models deal with complexity* Complex, emergent phenomena (the brain is more than the sum of its parts) can be captured in models in principled, satisfying ways. Such emergent phenomena arise from the complex interactions of multiple elements of a model, without being obviously present in the behavior of the individual elements. Without the models and the principles, such complexity might otherwise be cheapened by vague, verbal arguments.

*Models are explicit* Creating an implemented model forces you to be explicit about your assumptions. For example, what do children encode about a particular task, and how? How do they subsequently process this information? What kinds of mechanisms support their learning in this task? Explicitness about such assumptions confers many potential benefits, including the generation of novel, empirically testable predictions and the deconstruction of black box constructs.

## What

We will see all of these benefits in action when we consider how models have been used to explore issues in cognitive development, in the next section. First, however, we consider the nuts and bolts of what neural network models are, thus providing the foundation for understanding their contributions. Here, we focus on five critical elements of neural network models: units, and weights, net input, activation functions, and learning algorithms (for more extensive treatments of these and other elements of neural network models, see Elman et al., 1996; O'Reilly and Munakata, 2000; Rumelhart and McClelland, 1986). Each of these elements maps onto neural constructs while capturing important aspects of psychological processing, allowing neural network models to provide an important step in understanding the relation between neural and cognitive development.

UNITS AND WEIGHTS   Neural network models consist of two basic elements: units and weights (figure 12.1a). In models most closely tied to the underlying biology, each unit corresponds to a neuron, the activity of each unit corresponds to the spiking of a neuron, and each weight corresponds to a synapse (the strength of the weight corresponds to the efficacy of the synapse). Models of psychological phenomena are much more scaled down; single units correspond to collections of neurons or even entire brain regions, the activity of each unit corresponds to the overall firing rates of these neurons, and the weights between units represent synapses between the groups of neurons.

Units communicate with one another via their weights. Each unit receives activity from other units via its weights; and if enough such input is received, the unit becomes active. The unit then sends this activity via its weights to other units, influencing the activity of those units in turn.

In most network simulations of behavior, units are organized into layers. An input layer (or layers) receives information that reflects the external world in the form of patterns of activity on the units in the layer. Networks are described as "perceiving" their environments when they receive this input information, with the particular type of perception (seeing, hearing, and so on) depending on the modality that the input layer represents. In the simplistic example shown in figure 12.1b, the network sees the word "dog" when its input units for the letters d, o, and g are activated. An output layer (or layers) produces patterns of activity that are interpreted in terms of some response behavior. For example, the network in figure 12.1b can say either "cat" or "dog" by activating the corresponding output unit. (For much more realistic models of word reading—models that incorporate semantic representations and more complex phonological and orthographic representations—see O'Reilly and Munakata, 2000; Plaut, McClelland, Seidenberg, and Patterson, 1996.) Additionally, some number of hidden layers may sit between the input and the output layers, providing the network with the capability to transform input information in useful ways to support meaningful behavior.

Units can be connected via their weights in a variety of ways (figure 12.1a). Feedforward weights connect units in the input layer(s) to units in the hidden layer(s), and units in the hidden layer(s) to units in the output layer(s). Feedback weights may connect the units in the reverse direction (output to hidden to input). Lateral weights connect units to other units in the same layer. Recurrent weights connect units to themselves. While weights thus vary in direction of connectivity, they may also be excitatory (increasing the input to the receiving unit) or inhibitory (decreasing the input to the receiving unit). Recurrent weights that are excitatory allow units to maintain their activity by continuing to excite themselves. Lateral weights that are inhibitory lead units within a layer to compete with one another for activity, also helping active units to maintain their activity by inhibiting the activity of competing units.

"Knowledge" in the neural network framework takes the form of patterns of activity across the processing units and patterns of connectivity in the weights. Knowledge is thus embodied in the processing machinery [in contrast with the traditional computer metaphor, in which knowledge structures (RAM) are separable from processing (CPU)]. This embodied character of knowledge makes the neural network framework a particularly useful methodology for developmental cognitive neuroscience, given the focus of this field on understanding how knowledge is embodied by the brain and given the parallels between principles of neural communication and relations among units and weights in neural network models.

NET INPUT AND ACTIVATION FUNCTIONS   The process of computing a unit's activity is broken down into two

## A  Network architecture
units and weights

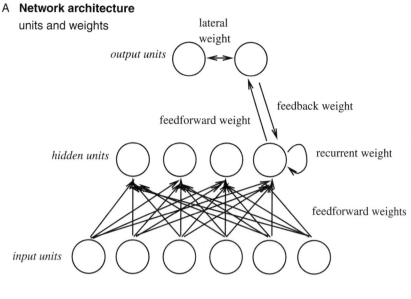

## B  Network processing
net inputs, activations, and learning

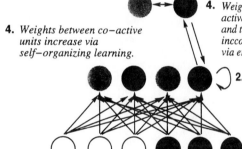

FIGURE 12.1   A diagram of representative neural network architecture (**A**) and processing (**B**). Circles indicate units and their shading indicates activation levels; arrows indicate weights.

steps: computing the net input to the unit, then computing the unit's activity as a function of the net input. The inputs to a unit are weighted by the strength of the connections from the sending units; the stronger the connection, the more the sending unit activity contributes to the net input to the receiving unit. Mathematically, the net input to a unit $j$ ($\eta_j$) is expressed as

$$\eta_j = \sum_i w_{ij} a_i$$

where $w_{ij}$ is a weight from unit $i$ to unit $j$, and $a_i$ is the activity of unit $i$.

The activation function specifies how the units in a network update their activity as a function of this net input. Activation functions are typically S-shaped (fig-ure 12.2), based on a sigmoidal activation function of the following form:

$$a_j = \frac{1}{1 - e^{-\eta_j}}$$

where $a_j$ is the activation of the unit, and $\eta_j$ is its net input. This S-shape reflects two important aspects of neural activity regarding the nonlinear response of neurons in relation to their inputs. First, the unit is not guaranteed to become active just because it is receiving some amount of input. As indicated by the lower left part of the S-shaped curve, this net input must exceed a certain threshold for the unit to become very active. Second, once the unit is active to some degree, it is not guaranteed to become much more active with increasing amounts of input. As indicated by the upper right

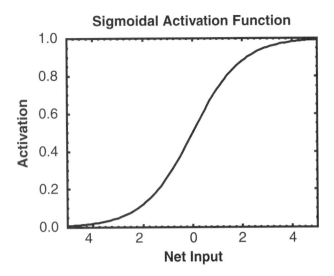

**Sigmoidal Activation Function**

FIGURE 12.2 The sigmoidal activation function, reflecting the nonlinear response of neurons in relation to their inputs.

part of the S-shaped curve, a unit cannot substantially increase its activity level beyond a certain point, even with further net input. This nonlinearity in the activation function allows multiple layers of units to carry out complex computations that are not possible with units using linear activation functions.

LEARNING ALGORITHMS  Learning in neural networks takes the form of changes to the weights, which are viewed as corresponding to changes in the efficacy of synapses. Such changes occur as a result of a network's experience with its environment, and they affect how the network responds to subsequent inputs. Because weights may take a value of zero (which is equivalent to no connection), this learning process allows for the possibility of adding new connections (when a zero weight is increased) and pruning away existing connections (when a weight goes to zero). (See Shultz et al., 1995, for more specialized mechanisms for adding and pruning connections.) Here, we consider two of the primary types of learning algorithms used in neural network models—self-organizing and error-driven.

Self-organizing algorithms are so named because they govern learning without specifying a particular target performance; that is, they lead units to organize their weights themselves based on their local inputs rather than in terms of meeting particular goals. One of the most common self-organizing algorithms is a Hebbian algorithm (Hebb, 1949), whereby units that are simultaneously active increase the weight between them. Mathematically, the basic form of this learning rule is

$$\Delta w_{ij} = \varepsilon \, a_i a_j$$

where $\Delta w_{ij}$ reflects the change in the weight from unit $i$ to unit $j$, and $\varepsilon$ reflects a learning rate parameter. This

form of learning has typically been used by modelers focused on biological plausibility (Miller, Keller, and Stryker, 1989) because the algorithm is grounded in the known biological learning mechanisms of long-term potentiation and long-term depression (Artola, Brocher, and Singer, 1989; Bear and Malenka, 1994). However, the algorithm is not very good at solving complex tasks (while humans are); hence other modelers have turned to more powerful, error-driven algorithms.

Error-driven algorithms are so named because they govern learning based on the discrepancy between a network's performance and its target performance. One of the most common error-driven algorithms is the backpropagation algorithm (Rumelhart, Hinton, and Williams, 1986), whereby the difference between a unit's activity and its target activity is computed and propagated backward through the network, so that the resulting weight changes reduce the unit's error. In this way, the backpropagation algorithm allows networks to learn to solve complex tasks, a necessary criterion for the modeling of human behavior. Mathematically, the backpropagation learning algorithm is

$$\Delta w_{ij} = \varepsilon \delta_j a_i$$

where $\delta_j$ reflects the contribution of a given unit to a network's error. Although the backpropagation algorithm has been criticized for being biologically implausible in the details of its implementation (e.g., in the backward propagation of error terms for which there is no neural evidence), biologically plausible versions have been implemented (Hinton, 1989; Hinton and McClelland, 1988; Movellan, 1990; O'Reilly, 1996). These versions avoid the implausibility problems of backpropagation by indirectly communicating error information through the standard mechanisms of neural communication, the passing of activity signals via weights. Further, these activity signals reflect events in the world and networks' expectations regarding the events, such that error information can be computed based on the discrepancies between expectations and outcomes, without requiring an explicit teacher that provides target signals. Such error-driven algorithms thus allow for the continued exploration of simulating performance on complex tasks. Further still, the existence of such functionally similar algorithms suggests that models using backpropagation, while biologically implausible in their detailed implementation, should not simply be discounted; lessons from them are likely to prove relevant to the biologically plausible, functionally similar implementations.

As shown earlier, learning algorithms can be specified in precise mathematical terms; however, it can be difficult to predict exactly how networks will come to solve tasks and how they will develop, given the complex, nonlinear interactions between network units and the environment. Similarly, even with a precise specification of how synaptic changes occur in the brain, we would not necessarily be able to explain, for example, the complex neural bases of how children learn to read. Understanding changes at the level of the synapse/weight does not translate directly into understanding behavior. Thus, even with a precisely specified learning algorithm, it can be very difficult to predict the behavior of networks of any complexity. We can therefore gain insights into the neural bases of behavior by exploring why networks develop as they do.

## How

Now that we have some sense of *why* we might want to use neural network models as a methodology, and *what* they consist of, we are now in a position to consider *how* they have contributed to the study of developmental cognitive neuroscience. Neural networks have been used to address many different facets of cognitive development, including individual differences and disorders (MacDonald and Christiansen, in press; Oliver et al., in press), U-shaped patterns of development (Munakata, 1998; Plunkett and Sinha, 1991; Rumelhart and McClelland, 1986), constructivism (Shultz et al., 1995), the coordination of separate specialized systems (Jacobs, 1999; Mareschal et al., 1995), and the development of hierarchically organized brain regions (Shrager and Johnson, 1996). Here, we focus on neural network explorations of two fundamental issues in cognitive development: the origins of our knowledge and the mechanisms of change. We aim to convey an overall sense of how neural network models can speak to these developmental issues; but, for brevity's sake, we cover but two examples within each of these areas. Interested readers are directed to the original papers and to other relevant examples, as cited, for fuller treatments of the mechanisms underlying cognitive development in neural network models.

ORIGINS  Where does our knowledge come from? Questions of origins (of knowledge, of life, of the universe, of anything) form the basis for some of our most interesting, challenging, and hotly debated issues. In the context of the origins of our knowledge, the debate has taken the form of nature versus nurture and, more recently, of specifying the nature of the interactions between the two. Neural network models have been used to explore the origins of knowledge in a variety of domains, including language (Elman, 1993; Harm and Seidenberg, 1999; Plaut and Kello, 1999; Plunkett and

Sinha, 1991; Rumelhart and McClelland, 1986), numerical understanding (Dehaene and Changeux, 1993), and problem-solving (McClelland, 1995, 1989; Shultz, Mareschal, and Schmidt, 1994). Here, we focus on models exploring the origins of knowledge of objects, specifically, their continuity and their permanence.

*Object continuity*  Young infants appear to be sensitive to the continuity of object motion—the fact that objects move only on connected paths, never jumping from one place to another without traveling a path in between. For example, infants as young as 2.5 months look longer at events in which objects appear to move discontinuously than at otherwise similar events in which the same objects move continuously (Spelke et al., 1992). Such longer looking times are taken as an indication that infants find the discontinuous events unnatural, and so must possess some understanding of object continuity. What are the origins of such knowledge? Some researchers have concluded that an understanding of object continuity is part of our innate core knowledge, given infants' very early sensitivity to it and the apparent difficulty in learning such information given that objects are rarely continuously visible in our environment (Spelke et al., 1992). However, as many researchers have noted, it is not clear what the label of "innate" really tells us about the nature of the origins of knowledge (Elman et al., 1996; Smith, 1999; Thelen and Smith, 1994). That is, does calling infants' sensitivity to the continuity of object "innate" tell us anything about how infants come to be sensitive to this principle, or about the mechanisms underlying such sensitivity?

In contrast, the neural network approach focuses attention on exactly these kinds of issues—in fact, such mechanisms must actually be implemented in a working model for the account to be considered successful. One such model was devised in the study of imprinting behavior in chicks, and of object recognition more generally (O'Reilly and Johnson, 1994, in press). This model viewed a simplified environment in which objects moved continuously. Based on this experience, the model developed receptive field representations of objects that encoded continuous locations in space, thereby demonstrating a sensitivity to object continuity.

What were the origins of the model's sensitivity to object continuity? First, the network had recurrent excitatory connections and lateral inhibitory connections that allowed active units to remain active; specifically, active units continued to send activation to themselves via the recurrent excitatory connections, and they prevented other competing units from becoming active via the lateral inhibitory connections. Thus, when an object was presented as input to the network, certain hidden units became active, and they tended to stay active even as the object moved around in the input. Second, the network learned according to a Hebbian learning rule, which led the model to associate this hidden unit pattern of activity with the object in different locations in the input. Thus, whenever the object appeared in any of these locations, the network came to activate the same units, or the same object representation. In this way, with exposure to events in the world that conformed to the principle of continuity, the model developed receptive field representations of objects that encoded continuous locations in space, and so learned to "recognize" objects that moved continuously in its environment.

One might argue that this model was innately predisposed to understand the continuity of objects (Spelke and Newport, 1997), given that the network was structured "from birth" with recurrent excitatory and lateral inhibitory connections and a Hebbian learning rule—all it needed was the typical experience of viewing objects moving continuously in its environment. That is, the model required experience only in a generic sense to support an experience-expectant process (Greenough, Black, and Wallace, 1987) that would naturally unfold given the normal environment available throughout our evolutionary history. Again, however, it is not clear what benefits would be conferred by calling the developmental time course of the model "innate." In contrast, the benefits of the model should be clear in providing an explicit, mechanistic account of the potential origins of our sensitivity to object continuity.

*Object permanence* Several models have been proposed to account for infants' apparent sensitivity to the permanence of objects, each having very different assumptions about the origins of object permanence knowledge. At one extreme, such knowledge has been built into a network, with target signals specifying from birth that hidden objects continue to exist when they are hidden (Mareschal et al., 1995). At the other extreme, a model has demonstrated limited sensitivity to the permanence of objects without ever actually developing the ability to represent hidden objects, based on the simple origins of the goal of keeping objects in view (Schlesinger and Barto, 1999). Here, we discuss a model that lies between these two extremes, one in which object permanence knowledge developed without being prespecified (Munakata et al., 1997). The model viewed a simplified environment in which objects disappeared from view behind occluders and reappeared after the occluders were removed. Based on this experience, the model became sensitive to the permanence of objects, continuing to represent objects even after they were hidden.

What were the origins of the model's knowledge of object permanence? As in the object recognition model described earlier, the object permanence model had recurrent excitatory connections that allowed active units to remain active. Unlike the object recognition model, the object permanence model also had a goal of predicting what would happen next in its environment. Through error-driven learning, the network adjusted its weights if its predictions were incorrect, for example, if the network predicted that an occluded object would not reappear when the occluder was removed, and then the object did in fact reappear. So, when a visible object moved out of view, the network gradually learned to use its recurrent connections to maintain a representation of the object, allowing the network to accurately predict its environment (and the reappearance of such hidden objects). In this way, with exposure to events that conformed to the principle of object permanence, the model provided an explicit, mechanistic account of the potential origins of our sensitivity to the permanence of objects.

CHANGE How does change occur? As many researchers have noted (Flavell, 1984; Fischer and Bidell, 1991; Siegler, 1989), this question is one of the most fundamental unanswered questions in the study of cognitive development. In the neural network framework, change can take place at multiple levels—in the activity of units as activations are propagated through the network, in the connection weight changes that occur during learning, and in the emergence of new forms that arise from the complex interactions of elements in the network (as described for the development of representations of object continuity and permanence). Clearly, the issue of change and the issue of origins are not mutually exclusive. Providing an explicit model of origins entails specifying mechanisms of change (unless the model assumes full-fledged knowledge from the start—an assumption that is inconsistent with the neural network framework and with brain development, and at odds with the theories of even the most extreme nativists). So, all of the models described and cited in the previous section also have something to say about change as well as about origins. Here, we focus on models exploring two important issues regarding developmental change: critical periods and stages.

*Critical periods* Humans mature at a slower rate than any other species. Counterintuitively, this slow rate of development may provide the perfect biological environment (and a critical period) for mastering complex domains such as language (Elman, 1993; Newport, 1988, 1990). A neural network model was developed to explore such critical periods in language learning (Elman, 1993). The model "heard" sentences of varying degrees of complexity, with the goal of predicting what word would come next at each point in a sentence. From this experience, the model learned to hold onto words it had heard recently to abstract the grammatical structure of the language input. The model could thus correctly predict grammatically appropriate words within a sentence, even in complex sentences such as "Dogs see boys who cats who Mary feeds chase." The model displayed a critical period: Whereas a "young" network was able to master the language input, an "older" network was unable to do so.

Why did this model display a critical period? The young and older networks differed only in their working memory spans, or how many words they could keep in mind. Children of different ages presumably differ in many more ways, but this single manipulation in the model allowed the potential contribution of working memory to be isolated and evaluated. The young network could keep only three or four words in mind because its working memory was effectively cleared after every three or four words that were heard; this span was increased gradually as the network aged. In contrast, for the older network, no such clearing of working memory occurred, so it could keep more words in mind from the start of learning. Intuitively, one might have expected the older network to be more capable of learning. Instead, by being able to keep more in mind, the older network, bogging down in all of the information it was processing, was unable to abstract the key kernels (of grammatical category, number, and verb argument type) for understanding the structure of its language. (Imagine trying to learn grammar by studying complex sentences like the "Dogs" example—there's quite a bit to get lost in!) In contrast, by being able to keep just a few words in mind, the young network was better able to focus on these key kernels. (Imagine trying to learn grammar by studying simple portions of complex sentences like the "Dogs" example, say "Dogs see boys." That's much less to get lost in.) After abstracting these key kernels, the young network was then able to build on this grammatical knowledge to process more complex sentences as its working memory span increased. Elman (1993) referred to this advantage of limited capacity as "the importance of starting small."

The model thus instantiated an explicit, mechanistic account for the potential causes of critical periods in language learning, leading to the conclusion of the importance of starting small. Interestingly, similar conclusions were reached independently by behavioral

investigations of critical periods in language learning. Newport (1988, 1990) found that persons exposed to American Sign Language or English as a second language early in life subsequently had the best mastery of the language, and these results could not be attributed to total years of experience with the language. These findings led Newport to characterize the advantages of limited processing abilities as "less is more." These two lines of research demonstrate a nice synergy between simulations and behavioral studies. The conclusions from the simulations are bolstered by the similar conclusions from the detailed analyses of the behavioral results, and the conclusions from the behavioral results are bolstered by the working implementation in a neural network model of the somewhat counterintuitive theory.

*Stages* Children appear to pass through qualitatively different stages in solving certain tasks (Case, 1985; Piaget, 1952). For example, in the balance scale task (Inhelder and Piaget, 1958), children view a scale with weights on each side at particular distances from the fulcrum, and they must decide which arm of the scale will fall when supports underneath the scale are released. Children initially answer these problems randomly, using no apparent rule about the physical properties of weight and distance to guide their decisions. They then employ different information to help them solve the task, first displaying behavior characteristic of Rule I (attending only to the information on the amount of weight on each side of the fulcrum), then Rule II (attending to the distance of weights from the fulcrum if weights are equal on each side of the fulcrum), and then Rule III (considering both weight and distance information regardless of whether weights are equal on each side) (Siegler, 1976). Although such stage-like patterns of development might not seem readily addressed in the neural network framework, a neural network model of the balance scale task (McClelland, 1995, 1989) demonstrated how such stage-like progressions can result from small, successive adjustments to connection weights. The model simulated children's performance of progressing from no-rule behavior to Rule I, Rule II, and Rule III behavior.

Why did the model display stage-like behavior? Using error-driven learning, the network's initially random weights were slowly modified with each experience to reduce the discrepancies between the network's predictions about balance scale problems and the actual outcomes. The network first began to develop representations of weight in its hidden layer. In this simulation, the earlier sensitivity to weight over distance arose because the network received greater exposure to problems in which weight predicted the balance scale outcome (reflecting the possibility that children have more experience with the effects of variations in weight than with the effects of variation in distance).[1] For some time while the network was developing representations of weight, its output still reflected random answers because the connections from the hidden layer representations to the output layer were not yet meaningful. As the hidden layer representations of weight became more fully formed, such that units were becoming more distinct in their activation patterns, units could be more readily credited for their contribution to the network's correct performance or blamed for their contribution to its errors. The connections from the hidden units to the output units could then be adjusted appropriately to improve the network's performance, producing a stage-like transition from random answers to Rule I answers based on weight. Sensitivity to the distance cue followed this same pattern of gradual development of hidden unit representations, facilitating credit and blame assignment and the adjustment of connections from the hidden layer to the output layer, leading to a stage-like transition to Rules II and III. In this way, incremental weight adjustments in neural networks can result in small representational changes that then support relatively fast learning, producing stage-like behavior. Similarly, the brain could support stage-like behavior via small synaptic changes that lead to small changes in neural patterns of activity, that then support a quick transition to a new stage as neurons are credited and blamed for their contributions to behavior.

## Challenges to the why, what, and how

As in all active areas of science, each of the aspects of neural network modeling discussed above has been challenged in some way. Here, we focus on one important criticism within each of the areas of why, what, and how (see also discussion in Elman et al., 1996; McClelland and Plaut, 1998; O'Reilly and Munakata, 2000; Seidenberg 1993).

CHALLENGES TO WHY MODELS ARE IMPORTANT   A common criticism of neural network models is that they can do anything, solve any task, and hence their ability to simulate human behavior is uninteresting. That is, so many parameters can be manipulated in a network that it is guaranteed to work eventually. And because getting it to work is guaranteed, the process tells us nothing. Further ammunition for this criticism comes from the fact that several *different* neural network models may succeed in simulating the same human behavior. Each works, but all can't be right. So neural networks are

simply too powerful: Successful simulation proves nothing.

Before countering this criticism using specific examples of neural network models, we first emphasize a general response: *Criticisms about too much power and too many parameters are relevant to any attempts at scientific theorizing, and are not unique to the neural network modeling endeavor.* One could easily level the same criticisms at verbal theories of behavior, for example. Across a range of domains (attention, memory, language, and so on) multiple competing theories can account for the same behavioral data. And, these verbal theories are typically powerful enough to encompass any new piece of behavioral data that comes along, thanks to the vagueness of constructs and the existence of multiple free parameters (in the form of new limitations or capabilities that can be incorporated into the theory). Thus, verbal theories can be constructed to explain anything, and multiple competing theories can account for the same data, so the process of developing theories tells us nothing. Most people probably would not accept this conclusion in the domain of scientific theorizing; nevertheless, many believe it to pose a fundamental problem for neural network models.

We believe that the counterargument to this criticism as applied to neural network models is similar to that applied to scientific theorizing more generally. *Competing theories and models can be evaluated by many other criteria than simply by accounting for a set of data.* People generally know when a theory feels unsatisfying, even if it is able to account for some data. If, for example, a theory needs to add a new component to account for each new piece of data, it will seem more arbitrary than a more unified theory that requires no such adjustments. Or if a theory accounts for data by relying on unspecified constructs, it will seem less compelling than a more fully specified theory. In this way, the plausibility and specificity of underlying assumptions, and the ease with which data can be accounted for and predicted, can be evaluated to compare competing theories. The same holds true for evaluating competing models. The neural network framework may support relatively rapid progress along these lines, because the models require the underlying assumptions to be made explicit and the assumptions are constrained both by bottom-up (biological) and top-down (psychological) information.

Finally, we note that many neural network models have made their contributions by *not* working, that is by not simply simulating the particular behavior they were designed to simulate. For example, neural network models have been lesioned to simulate (and provide insight into) the behavior of patients with brain damage (Cohen et al., 1994; Farah and McClelland

1991; Farah, O'Reilly, and Vecera, 1993; Plaut, 1995; Plaut et al., 1996). Such lesions are performed by removing or damaging units or their connections. In these cases, the models are *not* trained to simulate such atypical performance. Instead, the models are trained to perform correctly, and then they are lesioned; the altered pattern of performance emerges from the basic properties of the models following damage. In other cases, failures of neural network models (e.g., in remembering both specific events and generalizing across multiple events) have provided insight into neural divisions of labor (e.g., between the hippocampus and neocortex) (McClelland, McNaughton, and O'Reilly, 1995).

Thus, neural network models, albeit powerful, can fail and provide insights when they do; and they (like purely verbal theories of behavior) can be evaluated on grounds other than simply accounting for a set of data.

CHALLENGES TO WHAT MODELS COMPRISE   Many challenges have been issued regarding the nuts and bolts described in the *What* section—specifically, with respect to how well the various elements of neural models map onto elements in the brain. Critics argue that the elements of models are simplistic, missing essential aspects of neural communication that render their use misguided at best. We believe that there are no quick and definitive answers to this challenge; rather, we offer some preliminary responses to be further tested and elaborated over the coming years as part of important progress in the neural network framework.

One response is simply, "Simple is good." That is, the simplified elements of neural network models capture the essential aspects of neural communication, thereby providing a critical methodological tool for exploring the complexities of the relation between brain and behavior. We would otherwise bog down in details not particularly relevant to understanding cognition. An analogy may be found in the currently popular technique of creating mosaic images (say, of Princess Diana) from a large collection of smaller images. The details of each of the smaller images (a flower, a landscape, and so on) are not particularly relevant; in fact, one could easily lose sight of the point of the image by focusing on these details. Instead, it is more appropriate to stand back and see the overall image at a simplified level. Neural networks may similarly provide a useful simplification of details, allowing an understanding of neural function and its relevance to cognition. For example, we can understand the efficacy of a synapse in terms of a simplified, single value of a connection weight in much the same way that we understand a collection of small images in terms of the simplified, overall mosaic. Without such a simplification, we might otherwise become mired in all the details of how synaptic efficacies are determined at the biological level (the number of vesicles of neurotransmitter released by the presynaptic neuron, the alignment and proximity of release sites and receptors, the efficacy of channels on the postsynaptic neuron, and so forth). This degree of biological detail might cloud the picture of the brain–behavior relation—a picture that is clarified by the simplifications of the neural network framework.

Of course, the simple-is-good argument assumes that the neural network simplifications do indeed capture the essential computational properties of the biological details. This assumption can be tested by including further details into models and exploring their computational significance. In addition, the appropriateness of the simplifications can be tested by developing models at more than one level of complexity. For example, one simplification in most neural network models is the units' continuous-valued activation term (computed from the net input as described in the *What* section), meant to approximate the rate of firing of discrete spikes. Comparisons of this simplification with more detailed models that actually fire discrete spikes have indicated that the continuous-valued activations do in fact closely approximate the firing rates of the more detailed models (O'Reilly and Munakata, 2000).

Thus, the simplified nature of neural network models may allow for a clearer picture of the brain–behavior relation, and the validity of these simplifications can be tested by developing models at more than one level of complexity and by testing the functional relevance of biological details.

CHALLENGES TO HOW MODELS HAVE CONTRIBUTED TO DEVELOPMENTAL COGNITIVE NEUROSCIENCE   Various aspects of the specific models elaborated above, and their associated claims, have been challenged (Baillargeon and Aguiar, 1998; Marcus, 1998; Smith et al., 1999; Raijmakers, Van, and Molenaar, 1996; Rhode and Plaut, 1999). In general, we believe that many of these challenges will lead to progress in developing better models. Furthermore, the issuing of such challenges points to a strength of the modeling framework: Instantiated models can be subsequently tested on a range of measures, highlighting their potential limitations and suggesting necessary elaborations and revisions, as well as suggesting critical empirical tests to contrast competing models. Here, we focus on one criticism that has been applied to a range of models—namely, their failure to generalize (Marcus, 1998; Pinker and Prince, 1988).

According to this criticism, neural network models may mimic some aspects of human performance, but the bases for human and network behavior differ vastly. Specifically, humans use rules to govern their behavior (e.g., to form the past tense of most words, add "ed") and so they can generalize to new instances (e.g., to know that the past tense of "blicket" must be "blicketed"). In contrast, neural network models use associations to govern their behavior (e.g., "walk" is associated with "walked") and so they cannot generalize to new instances. Therefore, although neural networks may mimic certain aspects of human performance across a range of domains, these models fail to generalize to new instances in these domains in the ways that humans can, indicating a fundamental limitation to the models.

We discuss three responses to this generalization criticism. The first two responses suggest that the discrepancy between human and network generalization has been exaggerated, and the third response highlights important mechanisms for generalization in the neural network framework.

First, it is not clear how much of cognition is driven by rules. Although one might sometimes be able to characterize a person's behavior in terms of rules, this does not mean that those rules are explicitly instantiated in and consulted by the person (McClelland, 1989; McClelland and Plaut, 1999; Munakata et al., 1997; Rumelhart and McClelland, 1986; Thelen and Smith, 1994). This point is particularly relevant for developmental cognitive neuroscience, whose test populations are often preverbal, nonverbal, or limited in their linguistic skills, and hence unable to explicitly indicate whether they are in fact using rules to govern their behavior. Thus, the assumption that rules govern behavior, and that the neural network framework must therefore incorporate rules to be considered valid, is questionable.

Nonetheless, with or without rules, humans are certainly able to generalize their knowledge to new instances, so failures of neural network models to do so would seem damning. However, the claim that neural networks cannot generalize to new instances has been based predominantly on misguided testing methods (Marcus, 1998). In such tests, neural networks are trained on a particular task, but one set of input units is never activated during this training. At test, those units are activated for the first time, and the network is tested on its ability to generalize what it has learned from training (i.e., to respond appropriately to these new instances). This type of test is misguided for two reasons. First, this test assumes that when we are presented with new instances (e.g., the word "blicket"), this activates neurons in our brains that have never fired before. No evidence supports this assumption. Instead, extensive evidence indicates that neural patterns of fir-

ing reflect the similarity of inputs (Desimone and Ungerleider, 1989; Tanaka, 1996), suggesting that generalization to new instances would occur through the overlap between patterns of firing to the new instances and patterns of firing in previous experiences. Second, as described in the *What* section, the basic nuts and bolts of neural network (and neural) processing dictate that units must become active to support learning and meaningful behavior. Therefore, it is not particularly informative to run simulations to test the performance of units that have never become active. In sum, no evidence supports the idea of a pool of never-fired neurons that fire when something new is experienced, and neurons must become active to support learning; yet, tests of network generalization have assumed such never-fired pools and consisted of testing the performance of units that have never become active.

Under more plausible testing conditions, networks can generalize to new instances. For example, networks can be presented with a set of stimuli and then tested on their ability to generalize to new instances that activate novel combinations of previously active units. Neural networks have been shown to generalize to new instances under such circumstances across a range of domains (Hinton, 1986; Munakata et al., 1997; Plaut et al., 1996; O'Reilly, in press; O'Reilly and Johnson, 1994, in press; O'Reilly and Munakata, in press; cf. Marcus, 1998). A key factor in networks' successful generalization (and presumably in humans as well) is the overlap in representations, or the extent to which a new instance is represented in a way that overlaps with previously experienced instances, guiding the response to the new instance. Importantly, this overlap may be present in the input level representation to the network (as one might expect, for example, in the auditory input patterns for the new instance of "blicket" and the familiar instance of "picket") or in higher level re-representations of the input (say, in patterns of activity indicating that a word is a verb). Such higher level representations can function as categories, such that once a new instance is represented appropriately at these higher levels, the network can generalize all of its knowledge about the category (verbs, males, objects, etc.) to the new instance. In this way, the learning mechanisms that build on associations in neural network models support more than simple stimulus–response kinds of learning; higher-level representations allow stimuli to be encoded in more abstract and meaningful ways. Further progress in this area will likely depend upon the exploration of the factors that influence networks' abilities to form systematic representations at appropriate levels of abstraction, which can then be used to support meaningful generalizations across different tasks.

## Conclusions

In this chapter, we have considered why neural network modeling is an important methodology for developmental cognitive neuroscience, what neural network models are, and how neural network models have contributed to addressing two fundamental issues in the study of development—the origins of knowledge and how change occurs. In addition, we have covered criticisms of neural network modeling within each of these areas of why, what, and how. Here, we briefly review how models have offered a unique opportunity to gain insight into cognitive development. We then close with thoughts about the most productive avenues for future work in neural network modeling.

As described in the *Why* section, models provide many potential advantages: (1) allowing control, (2) helping us to understand behavior, (3) dealing with complexity, and (4) being explicit. All of the models cited in this chapter tap each of these advantages; here, we highlight one example for each advantage. First, the ability to control working memory span in a model provided insight into the potential basis for a critical period in language learning (Elman, 1993). This ability to manipulate working memory span in such a controlled manner, and to observe the long-term effects on language learning, is unique to the modeling framework. Second, the ability to watch representations develop in a model provided an understanding of how stage-like progressions might arise based on gradual underlying changes (McClelland, 1989, 1995). This ability to watch learning unfold in networks can help us to understand behavior at a more mechanistic level than would otherwise be possible. Third, the ability to deal with complexity allowed a model to provide a principled account of the potential origins of infants' sensitivity to object continuity (O'Reilly and Johnson, 1994, in press). A purely verbal description of the complex process of developing receptive fields that encode continuous locations in space would probably appear vague; however, the model shows how this process can emerge naturally in a network. Finally, the need to be explicit about various assumptions in implementing a working model led to the deconstruction of the object permanence concept into specific learning mechanisms and resulting representations (Munakata et al., 1997). Without the forcing function of explicitness found in the modeling framework, such constructs often remain only black boxes in purely verbal theoretical accounts.

Of course, all of these advantages of the neural network modeling methodology rely on the existence of careful behavioral studies, which lay out the important phenomena to be addressed and help to test competing models. Models cannot stand alone, and are meant to be put forth as complementary (rather than superior) to behavioral studies, for the reasons elaborated above. While this point may seem obvious, some criticisms of modeling have seemed to assume that the modeling methodology must be held to a higher standard than behavioral work. Specifically, one criticism is that each parameter is not varied and systematically tested in neural network modeling, so that it can be hard to know which parameters are crucial to a network's behavior (Mandler, 1998; McCloskey, 1991). However, the same criticism can be applied to behavioral work. Typically the parameter of interest (e.g., delay in a memory task) is varied and its effects measured. Other parameters (e.g., the size of the testing room) are viewed as less relevant and are not varied. In both the modeling and behavioral methodologies, further progress can be made by subsequently testing such assumptions about which factors are relevant. Such progress has been made more rapidly with behavioral methodologies because the same testing paradigms are often employed by multiple different researchers, helping to isolate which factors are relevant to behavior. As the field of modeling continues to develop, with new models replicating and building on prior models, similar progress in isolating critical factors should result.

This brings us to our final point, which focuses on the most productive way to proceed with neural network modeling as a methodology. We believe it will be most fruitful if researchers appreciate both the strengths and the limitations of neural network models (and recognize that some of the limitations are equally applicable to behavioral work and to verbal theorizing), such that subsequent models can be developed that build on the strengths and begin to address the limitations. Although, again, this point may seem obvious, the field has tended to miss this kind of balance, instead oscillating between zealotry (models should be fully accepted simply because they work) and extreme skepticism (models should be completely rejected simply because someone shows some limitation in them). As a caution against overzealousness, we have emphasized specific contributions from neural network models to our understanding of the processes of cognitive development (not simply touting the fact that a model works), and we have tried to underscore the need to evaluate models (like theories) on a range of criteria other than simply working. As a caution against extreme skepticism, we note that all models involve simplifications and, consequently, limitations, so it is not particularly constructive simply to point out limitations and argue that models should thus be discounted. Rather, it will be most productive if an understanding of limitations can support the development of alternative models, which can then be evaluated on similar grounds. Again, it may be useful to consider the parallels with more traditional behavioral work and verbal theorizing. Researchers rarely critique theories without providing alternatives, or run studies simply to disprove others' theories. Rather, researchers typically put forth alternative theories to account for the data, theories that are on the same playing field as the original theories, equally susceptible to criticism, testing, and so on. We believe that this same process would greatly benefit progress in the modeling endeavor. That is, we will make the most progress by specifying alternative models that build on existing strengths and begin to address limitations. In this way, better models will be developed that tap the unique advantages of this methodology, continuing to advance our understanding of developmental cognitive neuroscience.

ACKNOWLEDGMENTS   Preparation of this chapter was supported by research grants from NIMH (1RO3 MH59066-01), NICHD (1R29 HD37163-01), and NSF (IBN-9873492). We thank Randy O'Reilly, Rob Roberts, Marshall Haith, and the members of the Cognitive Development Center and Developmental Lunch Group for useful comments and discussions.

## NOTE

1. Subsequent simulations demonstrated that the earlier sensitivity to weight could also arise with equal exposure to the two cues, because the weight cue (a single piece of information) is simpler than the distance cue, which requires computing the relation between two pieces of information (McClelland, 1995).

## REFERENCES

ARTOLA, A., S. BROCHER, and W. SINGER, 1989. Different voltage-dependent thresholds for inducing long-term depression and long-term potentiation in slices of rat visual cortex. *Nature* 347:69–72.

BAILLARGEON, R., and A. AGUIAR, 1998. Toward a general model of perseveration in infancy. *Dev. Sci.* 1:190–191.

BEAR, M. F., and R. C. MALENKA, 1994. Synaptic plasticity: LTP and LTD. *Curr. Opin. Neurobiol.* 4:389–399.

CASE, R., 1985. *Intellectual Development: A Systematic Reinterpretation.* New York: Academic Press.

COHEN, J. D., R. D. ROMERO, M. J. FARAH, and D. SERVAN-SCHREIBER, 1994. Mechanisms of spatial attention: The relation of macrostructure to microstructure in parietal neglect. *J. Cogn. Neurosci.* 6(4):377–387.

DEHAENE, S., and J.-P. CHANGEUX, 1993. Development of elementary numerical abilities: A neuronal model. *J. Cogn. Neurosci.* 5:390–407.

DESIMONE, R., and L. G. UNGERLEIDER, 1989. Neural mechanisms of visual processing in monkeys. In *Handbook of Neuropsychology*, Vol. 2, F. Boller and J. Grafman, eds. New York: Elsevier Science, pp. 267–299.

ELMAN, J. L., 1993. Learning and development in neural networks: The importance of starting small. *Cognition* 48(1):71–79.

ELMAN, J., E. BATES, A. KARMILOFF-SMITH, M. JOHNSON, D. PARISI, and K. PLUNKETT, 1996. *Rethinking Innateness: A Connectionist Perspective on Development.* Cambridge, Mass.: MIT Press.

FARAH, M. J., and J. L. MCCLELLAND, 1991. A computational model of semantic memory impairment: Modality specificity and emergent category specificity. *J. Exp. Psychol: General* 120:339–357.

FARAH, M. J., R. C. O'REILLY, and S. P. VECERA, 1993. Dissociated overt and covert recognition as an emergent property of a lesioned neural network. *Psychol. Rev.* 100:571–588.

FISCHER, K. W., and T. BIDELL, 1991. Constraining nativist inferences about cognitive capacities. In *The Epigenesis of Mind*, S. Carey and R. Gelman, eds. Hillsdale, N.J.: Lawrence Erlbaum, pp. 199–236.

FLAVELL, J. H., 1984. Discussion. In *Mechanisms of Cognitive Development*, R. J. Sternberg, ed. New York: Freeman.

GREENOUGH, W. T., J. E. BLACK, and C. S. WALLACE, 1987. Experience and brain development. *Child Dev.* 58:539–559.

HARM, M. W., and M. S. SEIDENBERG, 1999. Phonology, reading acquisition, and dyslexia: Insights from connectionist models. *Psychol. Rev.* 106:491–528.

HEBB, D. O., 1949. *The Organization of Behavior.* New York: John Wiley and Sons.

HINTON, G. E., 1986. Learning distributed representations of concepts. *Proceedings of the 8th Annual Conference of the Cognitive Science Society.* Hillsdale, N.J.: Lawrence Erlbaum, pp. 1–12.

HINTON, G. E., 1989. Deterministic Boltzmann learning performs steepest descent in weight-space. *Neural Comp.* 1:143–150.

HINTON, G. E., and J. L. MCCLELLAND, 1988. Learning representations by recirculation. In *Neural Information Processing Systems, 1987*, D. Z. Anderson, ed. New York: American Institute of Physics, pp. 358–366.

INHELDER, B., and J. PIAGET, 1958. *The Growth of Logical Thinking from Childhood to Adolescence.* New York: Basic Books.

JACOBS, R. A., 1999. Computational studies of the development of functionally specialized neural modules. *Trends Cogn. Sci.* 3:31–38.

MACDONALD, M., and M. CHRISTIANSEN, in press. Reassessing working memory: A reply to Just and Carpenter and Waters and Caplan. *Psychol. Rev.*

MANDLER, J. M., 1998. On theory and modelling. *Dev. Sci.* 2(1):196–197.

MARCUS, G. F., 1998. Rethinking eliminative connectionism. *Cogn. Psychol.* 37:243.

MARESCHAL, D., K. PLUNKETT, and P. HARRIS, 1995. Developing object permanence: A connectionist model. In *Proceedings of the 17th Annual Conference of the Cognitive Science Society.* Hillsdale, N.J.: Lawrence Erlbaum, pp. 170–175.

MCCLELLAND, J. L., 1989. Parallel distributed processing: Implications for cognition and development. In *Parallel Distributed Processing: Implications for Psychology and Neurobiology*, R. G. M. Morris, ed. Oxford University Press, pp. 8–45.

MCCLELLAND, J. L., 1995. A connectionist perspective on knowledge and development. In *Developing Cognitive Competence: New Approaches to Process Modeling*, T. J. Simon and G. S. Halford, eds. Hillsdale, N.J.: Lawrence Erlbaum, pp. 157–204.

McClelland, J. L., B. L. McNaughton, and R. C. O'Reilly, 1995. Why there are complementary learning systems in the hippocampus and neocortex: Insights from the successes and failures of connectionist models of learning and memory. *Psychol. Rev.* 102:419–457.

McClelland, J., and D. Plaut, 1999. Does generalization in infant learning implicate abstract algebra-like rules? *Trends Cogn. Sci.* 283:77–80.

McCloskey, M., 1991. Networks and theories: The place of connectionism in cognitive science. *Psychol. Sci.* 2(6):387–395.

Miller, K. D., J. B. Keller, and M. P. Stryker, 1989. Ocular dominance column development: Analysis and simulation. *Science* 245:605–615.

Movellan, J. R., 1990. Contrastive Hebbian learning in the continuous Hopfield model. In *Proceedings of the 1989 Connectionist Models Summer School*, D. S. Touretzky, G. E. Hinton, and T. J. Sejnowski, eds. San Mateo, Calif.: Morgan Kaufman, pp. 10–17.

Munakata, Y., 1998. Infant perseveration and implications for object permanence theories: A PDP model of the AB task. *Dev. Sci.* 1:161–184.

Munakata, Y., J. L. McClelland, M. H. Johnson, and R. Siegler, 1997. Rethinking infant knowledge: Toward an adaptive process account of successes and failures in object permanence tasks. *Psychol. Rev.* 104(4):686–713.

Newport, E., 1988. Constraints on learning and their role in language acquisition: Studies of the acquisition of American Sign Language. *Lang. Sci.* 10:147–172.

Newport, E. L., 1990. Maturational constraints on language learning. *Cogn. Sci.* 14:11–28.

Oliver, A., M. H. Johnson, A. Karmiloff-Smith, and B. Pennington, 2000. Deviations in the emergence of representations: A neuroconstructivist framework for analysing developmental disorders. *Dev. Sci.* 3:1–40.

O'Reilly, R. C., 1996. Biologically plausible error-driven learning using local activation differences: The generalized recirculation algorithm. *Neural Comp.* 8(5):895–938.

O'Reilly, R. C., in press. Generalization in interactive networks: The benefits of inhibitory competition and Hebbian learning. *Neural Computation.*

O'Reilly, R. C., and M. H. Johnson, 1994. Object recognition and sensitive periods: A computational analysis of visual imprinting. *Neural Comp.* 6(3):357–389.

O'Reilly, R. C., and M. H. Johnson, in press. Object recognition and sensitive periods: A computational analysis of visual imprinting. In *Brain Development and Cognition: A Reader*, 2nd ed., M. H. Johnson, R. O. Gilmore, and Y. Munakata, eds. Oxford: Blackwell.

O'Reilly, R. C., and Y. Munakata, 2000. *Computational Explorations in Cognitive Neuroscience.* Cambridge, Mass.: MIT Press.

Piaget, J., 1952. *The Origins of Intelligence in Childhood.* New York: International Universities Press.

Pinker, S., and A. Prince, 1988. On language and connectionism: Analysis of a parallel distributed processing model of language acquisition. *Cognition* 28:73–193.

Plaut, D. C., 1995. Double dissociation without modularity: Evidence from connectionist neuropsychology. *J. Clin. Exp. Neuropsychol.* 17(2):291–321.

Plaut, D., and C. Kello, 1999. The emergence of phonology from the interplay of speech comprehension and production: A distributed connectionist approach. In *The Emergence of Language*, B. MacWhinney, ed. Mahwah, N.J.: Lawrence Erlbaum, pp. 381–415.

Plaut, D. C., J. L. McClelland, M. S. Seidenberg, and K. E. Patterson, 1996. Understanding normal and impaired word reading: Computational principles in quasi-regular domains. *Psychol. Rev.* 103:56–115.

Plunkett, K., and C. Sinha, 1991. Connectionism and developmental theory. *Psykol. Skrift. Aarhus* 16(1):1–34.

Raijmakers, M. E., K. E. Van, and P. C. Molenaar, 1996. On the validity of simulating stagewise development by means of PDP networks: Application of catastrophe analysis and an experimental test of rule-like network performance. *Cogn. Sci.* 20:101–136.

Rohde, D., and D. Plaut, 1999. Language acquisition in the absence of explicit negative evidence: How important is starting small? *Cognition* 72:67–109.

Rumelhart, D. E., G. E. Hinton, and R. J. Williams, 1986. Learning representations by back-propagating errors. *Nature* 323:533–536.

Rumelhart, D. E., and J. L. McClelland, 1986. PDP models and general issues in cognitive science. In *Parallel Distributed Processing. Vol. 1: Foundations*, D. E. Rumelhart, J. L. McClelland, and PDP Research Group, eds. Cambridge, Mass.: MIT Press, pp. 110–146.

Schlesinger, M., and A. Barto, 1999. Optimal control methods for simulation the perception of causality in young infants. *Proceedings of the 21st Annual Conference of the Cognitive Science Society.* Hillsdale, N.J.: Lawrence Erlbaum.

Seidenberg, M., 1993. Connectionist models and cognitive theory. *Psychol. Sci.* 4(4):228–235.

Shrager, J., and M. H. Johnson, 1996. Dynamic plasticity influences the emergence of function in a simple cortical array. *Neural Networks* 9:1119.

Shultz, T., D. Mareschal, and W. Schmidt, 1994. Modeling cognitive development on balance scale phenomena. *Machine Learning* 16:57–86.

Shultz, T., W. Schmidt, D. Buckingham, and D. Mareschal, 1995. Modeling cognitive development with a generative connectionist algorithm. In *Developing Cognitive Competence: New Approaches to Process Modeling*, T. J. Simon and G. S. Halford, eds. Hillsdale, N.J.: Lawrence Erlbaum, pp. 157–204.

Siegler, R., 1976. Three aspects of cognitive development. *Cogn. Psychol.* 8:481–520.

Siegler, R., 1989. Mechanisms of cognitive development. *Annu. Rev. Psychol.* 40:353–379.

Smith, L. B., 1999. Do infants possess innate knowledge structures? The con side. *Dev. Sci.* 2(2):133–144.

Smith, L. B., E. Thelen, B. Titzer, and D. McLin, 1999. Knowing in the context of acting: The task dynamics of the A-not-B error. *Psychol. Rev.* 106:235–260.

Spelke, E., K. Breinlinger, J. Macomber, and K. Jacobson, 1992. Origins of knowledge. *Psychol. Rev.* 99:605–632.

Spelke, E., and E. Newport, 1997. Nativism, empiricism, and the development of knowledge. In *Theoretical Models of Human Development: Handbook of Child Psychology*, 5th ed., R. M. Lerner, ed. New York: Wiley.

Tanaka, K., 1996. Inferotemporal cortex and object vision. *Annu. Rev. Neurosci.* 19:109–139.

Thelen, E., and L. B. Smith, 1994. *A Dynamic Systems Approach to the Development of Cognition and Action.* Cambridge, Mass.: MIT Press.

# III

# NEURAL PLASTICITY OF DEVELOPMENT

# 13 Early Brain Injury, Plasticity, and Behavior

## BRYAN KOLB AND ROBBIN GIBB

ABSTRACT   Brain development progresses through a series of steps that are genetically programmed but influenced significantly by environmental events, including injury. The morphological and functional effects of brain perturbations during development vary qualitatively with the precise embryological events occurring at the time of injury. Recovery is especially poor if the cortex is injured immediately following the completion of neurogenesis, and is especially good if injury occurs during the time of maximum astrocyte proliferation and synapse formation. The young injured brain is especially sensitive to environmental events, and recovery thus can be enhanced by various forms of stimulation such as tactile stroking in infancy and complex housing as juveniles and adolescents. Recovery is also modulated by gonadal hormones and by neuromodulators (noradrenaline and acetylcholine).

The goal of this chapter is to illustrate some of the general principles underlying how injury to the developing brain, and particularly to the cerebral cortex, can lead to alterations in brain and behavioral development and how such alterations can be modulated. In principle, there are three ways that the brain could show plastic changes that might support recovery during development. First, there could be changes in the organization of the remaining, intact, circuits in the brain. This would likely involve the generation of new synapses in extant pathways. Second, there could be a development of new circuitry that is novel to the injured brain. Third, there could be a generation of neurons and glia to replace at least some lost neurons and glia. In fact, the developing brain makes use of all of these changes, although the details vary with the precise developmental age at the time of injury. Furthermore, each of these outcomes can be influenced by various modulating factors, including especially experience, neuromodulators, and gonadal hormones.

We begin by considering how the normal brain changes in response to experience during development and then consider each of the three types of changes that occur in the developing injured brain. Finally, we consider the way in which the plastic changes, and ul-

BRYAN KOLB AND ROBBIN GIBB   Departments of Psychology and Neuroscience, University of Lethbridge, Lethbridge, Canada.

timately the behavior, are modulated. Because most of what we know about the changes in the normal and injured brain come from studies of the rat brain, our discussion focuses on a consideration of the rat. We are confident, however, that our results will generalize to other mammalian species, and especially to humans.

### Changes in the normal brain

In order to understand how the brain can be changed to support functional restitution, we must first consider how the normal brain can be changed. The general logic is that the nervous system is conservative, and that plastic changes that normally occur during development are likely to be recruited in an attempt to repair the abnormal brain.

NEURONAL CHANGES DURING DEVELOPMENT   There are two aspects of neural development that are especially important in the current context. First, neurons of the neocortex of rats are generated from about embryonic day 12 to 21, birth being on day 22. Thus, the genesis of cortical neurons begins about two-thirds of the way through gestation and is complete at about the time of birth. Neurons and glia arise from neural stem cells that reside in the ventricular zone of the developing brain, as shown in figure 13.1. Neural stem cells can divide symmetrically, to produce two stem cells, or asymmetrically, to produce a stem cell and a progenitor cell. Stem cells can be thought of as multipotent cells that have the potential to reproduce themselves continuously throughout the lifetime of an organism. In contrast, progenitor cells have a limited capacity for reproduction and are destined to produce neurons or glia. Stem cells are located in the subependymal zone and remain active throughout life, although they may have a finite number of divisions before they die. It is believed that progenitor cells that can divide to produce neurons and/or glia can migrate away from the subependymal zone and may lie quiescently in the white or gray matter. While in these locations they can be activated to produce neurons and/or glia. (For a useful

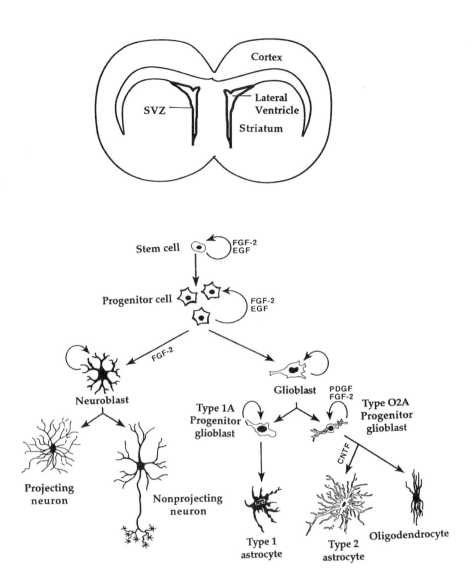

FIGURE 13.1 *Top:* Illustration of the location of the subependymal zone lining the lateral ventricles. *Bottom:* Cartoon illustration of neural cell lineage in the central nervous system. A self-renewing population (circular arrow) of stem cells gives rise to progenitor cells that are also self renewing. The progenitor cells are capable of differentiating into either neural or glial cells in the presence of appropriate neurotrophic factors. (From Ray et al., 1997.)

review, see Weiss et al., 1996.) One challenge with stem and progenitor cells is to find the "switch" to turn on controlled cell production when they are needed after an injury. Considerable evidence now suggests that the mammalian brain, including the primate brain, can generate neurons destined for the olfactory bulb, hippocampal formation, and even the neocortex of the frontal and temporal lobes (Eriksson et al., 1998; Gould et al., 1999; Kempermann and Gage, 1999). The reason for this generation is not at all clear at present, although it may function to enhance brain plasticity, particularly with respect to processes underlying learning and memory. It turns out, however, that although the generation of these neurons occurs continuously in the normal brain, the generation rate is influenced by injury in the developing brain, which, as we shall see, can lead to enhanced cortical regeneration and functional recovery (Kolb et al., 1998).

The second important stage of neural development is the formation of synapses. As neurons migrate to their final destinations, they begin to develop axons and dendrites that will form synapses. Synapses do not form randomly on cortical pyramidal neurons but show important characteristics. One feature is that most excitatory inputs (up to 95%) synapse on spines, which are found on the dendrites but rarely on or near the cell bodies. This means that it is possible to estimate excitatory synaptic numbers by estimating the number of spines, which is typically done by estimating both the length of dendritic material and the density of spines on the dendrites. Both dendrites and spines grow rapidly during development and show remarkable plasticity in adulthood, as dendrites can form spines and axons can form new axon terminations in hours, and possibly even minutes, after some experience (e.g., Greenough and Chang, 1989). This process is most expedient during development and is modified by changes in the developing brain, including experience and injury.

EXPERIENCE-DEPENDENT CHANGES   One of the key principles of behavioral neuroscience is that experience can modify brain structure long after brain development is complete. Indeed, it is generally assumed that structural changes in the brain accompany memory storage (Bailey and Kandel, 1993; Kolb and Whishaw, 1998). We can now identify a large range of neural changes associated with experience. These include increases in brain size, cortical thickness, neuron size, dendritic branching, spine density, synapses per neuron, and glial numbers (Greenough and Chang, 1989). The magnitude of these changes should not be underestimated. For example, in our own studies of the effects of housing rats in enriched environments, we consistently see changes in overall brain weight on the order of 7–10% after 60 days in young animals (Kolb,

1995). This increase in brain weight represents increases in glia, blood vessels, neuron soma size, dendritic elements, and synapses. It would be difficult to estimate the total number of increased synapses, but it is probably on the order of 20% in the cortex, which is an extraordinary change. The magnitude of the effect is easily seen by examining the gross morphology of cortical neurons, which show large and persistent changes in dendritic arborization, as illustrated in figure 13.2.

Most studies of experience-dependent change manipulate experience either by providing special training or experiences or by housing animals in specific types of environments. For example, laboratory animals can be trained to make specific complex movements, such as reaching through a slot for food, or they can be placed in complex environments. In the former case there are changes in the morphology of cells in specific regions, such as primary motor cortex, whereas in the latter case the cellular changes are more global, presumably reflecting the more global activation of cerebral structures. Studies on the effects of experience in the normal developing brain have shown that experience can have very different effects upon the brain at different ages. For example, when rats are placed into complex environments for 3 months, beginning either

## Condo-Housed

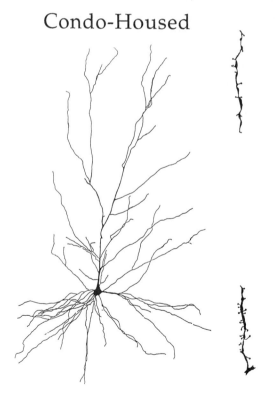

## Lab-Housed

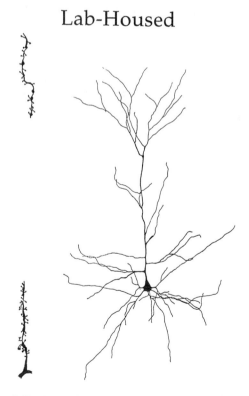

FIGURE 13.2   Representative layer III pyramidal neurons from Zilles's area Par1 in young adult rats that were housed in the condominiums from weaning until about 4 months of age. Cells from the condominium-housed animals showed more dendritic arbor but a reduced spine density relative to cells from lab-housed animals.

at weaning (21 days of age) or young adulthood (4 months of age), there is a qualitative difference. Young adult rats show a large increase in dendritic length in cortical neurons and an associated increase in spine density. In contrast, juvenile rats show a similar increase in dendritic length but a decrease in spine density. That is, the young animals show a qualitatively different change in the distribution of synapses on pyramidal neurons compared to older animals (Kolb, Gibb, and Gorny, 2001). Although infant animals cannot be given the same type of experience, we followed a procedure first used by Schanberg and Field (1987), in which infant rats are given tactile stimulation with a small brush for just 15 min, three times per day for 10 days. We found no change in dendritic length but, paradoxically, a *drop* in spine density that is still present in adulthood. A drop in spine density implies a drop in the number of synapses per neuron—a curious result. [It is not without precedent, however, as young chicks show a similar drop in spine density when they are imprinted on specific environmental stimuli (Wallhausser and Scheich, 1987).] We also hasten to point out that a drop in synapses per neuron does not necessarily mean an overall drop in synapses in the cortex. It is possible that the experience either stimulates the production of more neurons or, more likely, retards the normal programmed loss of neurons during development. In either case, the actual number of synapses in the cortex could be increased rather than decreased with the early experience. This possibility is consistent with our observation that the drop in spine density is not benign, but rather is associated with chronic behavioral changes. For example, tactilely stimulated animals have *enhanced* fine motor and spatial navigation skills in adulthood. This result is remarkable because it shows that two weeks of tactile stroking in infancy significantly enhanced motor learning in adulthood. The mechanism for this enhanced learning is as yet unknown. But what is perhaps even more intriguing is that the early tactile experience is especially effective in stimulating recovery from early brain injury, a result to which we shall return.

In summary, it has long been assumed in the psychological literature that experiences in early childhood have greater effects upon later behavior than do similar experiences in adulthood. Our analysis of behavioral and dendritic effects of experience-dependent changes following exposure to specific experiences during development suggests that there is a structural basis to this differential effect of early experience on behavior. Our results lead us to several conclusions. First, "enriched" experience can have very different effects upon the brain at different ages. Second, experience not only leads to "more," but can also lead to "less." That is,

although it is tempting to presume that experience lead to increased numbers of synapses and probably to increases in glia, it appears that there may be either increases or decreases, the details varying with age and experience. Third, changes in dendritic length and dendritic spine density are clearly dissociable. It is not immediately clear what the differences mean in terms of neuronal function, but it is clear that experience can alter these two measures independently and in different ways at different ages. Finally, because the changes in neural structure that are associated with experience are correlated with more proficient production of a variety of behaviors, it is reasonable to expect that similar functional and morphological changes might be observed in animals with cerebral injuries. Note, however, that there is not a single change to look for in the injured brain, but rather several different types of changes.

## Behavioral sequelae of early brain injury

Perhaps the best-known studies on the effects of early brain injury on behavior were those performed by Margaret Kennard in the late 1930s (Kennard, 1942). She made unilateral motor cortex lesions in infant and adult monkeys. The behavioral impairments in the infant monkeys were milder than those in the adults, leading Kennard to hypothesize that there had been change in cortical organization in the infants and that these changes supported the behavioral recovery. In particular, she hypothesized that if some synapses were removed as a consequence of brain injury, "others would be formed in less usual combinations" and that "it is possible that factors which facilitate cortical organization in the normal young are the same by which reorganization is accomplished in the imperfect cortex after injury" (Kennard, 1942, p. 239). Although Kennard had much to say regarding the limitations of functional recovery after early brain injury (for a review, see Finger and Almli, 1988), her name is usually associated with her demonstration that the consequences of motor cortex lesions in infancy were less severe than similar injury in adulthood; in fact, it is commonly referred to as the Kennard principle.

Kennard was aware that early brain damage might actually produce more severe deficits than expected, but it was Hebb (1947, 1949) who emphasized this possibility. On the basis of his studies of children with frontal lobe injuries, Hebb concluded that an early injury may prevent the development of some intellectual capacities that an equally extensive injury, at maturity, would not have destroyed. Hebb believed that this outcome resulted from a failure of initial organization of the brain, thus making it difficult for the child to develop many behaviors, especially socioaffective behaviors. The difference between the views of Kennard and Hebb is important in the current context, for it provides an important starting point for studies looking for a relationship between synaptic change and behavior. Thus, whereas Kennard hypothesized that recovery from early brain damage was associated with a reorganization into novel neural networks, Hebb postulated that the failure to recover was correlated with a failure of initial organization. Extensive studies of both cats and rats with cortical injuries have shown that both views are partially correct (Kolb, 1995; Villablanca et al., 1993). Thus, studies of both rats and cats with cortical lesions have shown that age at injury is the variable that predicts the Kennard or Hebb outcome.

The relationship between age and behavior is illustrated in the following example. We have removed the frontal cortex of different groups of rats at various ages ranging from embryonic day 18 (the gestation period of a rat is about 22 days) through infancy and adolescence (Kolb, 1987; Kolb and Whishaw, 1989). The behavioral results can be illustrated by the skilled reaching behavior of rats with removal of the frontal cortex on embryonic day 18 (E18), postnatal day 1, 5, 10, or 90 (i.e., adult). Rats are trained to reach through bars to retrieve bits of chicken feed (Whishaw et al., 1991). As shown in figure 13.3, rats with lesions in adulthood or on day 1 show severe deficits relative to control animals, whereas rats with lesions on days 5 or 10 show intermediate deficits and those with E18 lesions show no deficit at all. Functional outcome thus clearly varies with precise age at injury.

On the basis of our studies, we can reach the following conclusion: Damage during the period of neurogenesis, which in the rat cortex is from about E12 to E20, appears to be associated with a good functional outcome; damage in the first week of life, which is a time of neural migration and the initiation of synaptic formation, is associated with a dismal outcome; damage in the second week of life, which is a time of maximal astrocyte generation and synapse development, results in a good functional outcome; and damage after two weeks leads to progressively more severe chronic behavioral loss (figure 13.4). A similar pattern of results can be seen in parallel studies of the effects of cortical lesions in kittens by Villablanca and his colleagues (1993).

A key point here is that birth date is irrelevant. It is the developmental stage of the brain at injury that is critical. Thus, because rats and kittens are born at an embryologically younger age than primates, including humans, the time scale for functional outcome must be adjusted to match the neural events that are underway

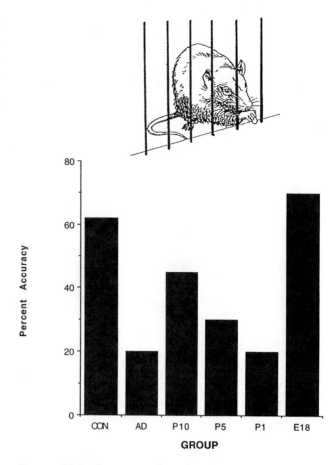

FIGURE 13.3 Summary of performance on the Whishaw reaching task by rats with frontal lesions at different developmental ages. Rats with lesions in adulthood or on postnatal day 1 are severely impaired at the task. Rats with lesions on postnatal days 5 or 10 are progressively better, and rats with lesions of putative frontal cortex on embryonic day 18 perform as well as normal control animals.

at the time of injury (figure 13.5). Because neural generation is most intense during the second trimester in humans and is largely complete by the third trimester, the second trimester is probably most similar to the last week of gestation in the rat. Similarly, because the third trimester in humans is a time of active cell migration and the beginning of differentiation, the third trimester of humans parallels the first week of life in the infant rat. From these observations, we would predict that the worst time for injury in the human brain would likely be the third trimester, whereas there should be relatively good compensation for injuries during the second trimester. It is interesting in this regard that one of the most common causes of epilepsy is now thought to be abnormalities of neural migration, which would occur in the third trimester.

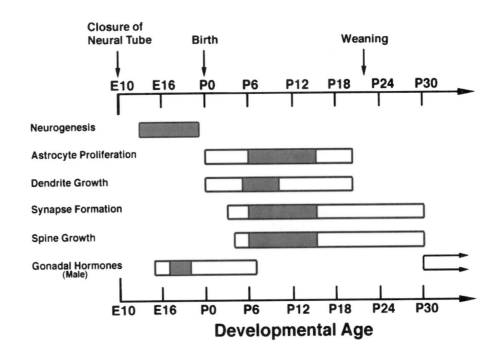

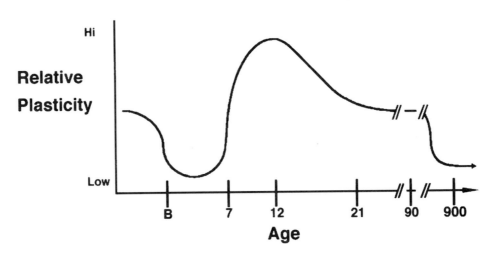

FIGURE 13.4   *Top:* Main cellular events related to cortical plasticity. Bars mark the approximate beginning and ending of different processes. The shaded area illustrates the time of maximum activity. *Bottom:* Summary of the time-dependent differences in cortical plasticity.

## Brain development after early brain injury

In the course of studying the functional effects of early cortical injury in rats, we noticed that brain size in adulthood was directly related to the postnatal age at injury: The earlier the injury, the smaller the brain and the thinner the cortical mantle. Thus, rats with perinatal lesions have very small brains whereas those with lesions at day 10 have larger brains. Curiously, however, the day-10 brains still are markedly smaller than the brains of rats with lesions later in life, such as day 25, even

though the behavioral outcome is far better (Kolb and Whishaw, 1981). Therefore, it must be the *organization* of the brain rather than its *size* that predicts recovery in the day-10 animal. Changes in organization can be inferred from an analysis of synaptic numbers, cortical connectivity, and evidence of neuro- and gliogenesis.

SYNAPTIC SPACE   By staining brains with a Golgi-type stain it is possible to measure and quantify the dendritic structure of neurons. Although dendritic length does not provide a direct measure of synapse number, den-

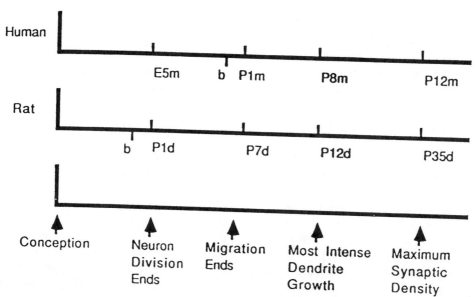

FIGURE 13.5 Schematic of the comparable developmental ages of the brain of the rat and human (E, embryonic day; P, postnatal day; b, day of birth). Note that the day of birth in the rat is much earlier in embryonic development than the day of birth in the human. Rhesus monkeys are born even more developed than humans.

dritic length and spine density can be used as a reasonable estimate of synaptic number. Golgi analyses of cortical neurons of rats with perinatal lesions consistently show a general atrophy of dendritic arborization and a drop in spine density across the cortical mantle (Kolb, Gibb, and van der Kooy, 1994). In contrast, rats with cortical lesions around 10 days of age show an increase in dendritic arbor and an increase in spine density relative to normal control littermates. Thus, animals with the best functional outcome show the greatest synaptic increase whereas animals with the worst functional outcome have a decrease in synapses relative to control animals. Furthermore, factors that act to increase dendritic space also enhance functional outcome whereas those that act to decrease dendritic space act to retard functional outcome.

CHANGES IN CORTICAL CONNECTIVITY   Perhaps the most extensive studies of changes in cortical connectivity are those showing that after unilateral motor cortex lesions in infant rats or cats there is a major expansion of the ipsilateral corticospinal pathway from the undamaged hemisphere, which is correlated with partial recovery of skilled forelimb use (Castro, 1990; Whishaw and Kolb, 1988). The initial studies concluded that these aberrant connections were advantageous and likely provided an explanation for the Kennard effect. It appears, however, that the anomalous corticospinal projections may be formed at a significant cost. For example, when we compared the effects of motor cortex lesions on postnatal days 4, 10, and 90, we found that

although only the youngest animals showed the enhanced ipsilateral connections, the day-10 animals showed the best functional outcome. Furthermore, animals with day-4 lesions showed unexpected deficits on cognitive tasks, such as the acquisition of a spatial navigation task. It thus seems likely that the aberrant corticospinal pathway interfered with the normal functioning of cortical areas that would not ordinarily be involved in motor function. In a parallel set of studies we showed that damage to the medial prefrontal region produced a similar result: Animals with frontal lesions on day 1 showed massive changes in cortical connectivity, but these animals had the worst behavioral outcome (Kolb, Gibb, and van der Kooy, 1994). Furthermore, we showed that the abnormal pathways did not reflect the creation of new connections so much as they reflected a failure of pruning of connections that are normally discarded during development. This was demonstrated by our finding that newborn animals have extensive aberrant pathways that die off during the first week of life. If the cortex is damaged during this time, however, some of these pathways fail to die off, leaving the animal with apparently novel circuitry that is not seen in normally developing animals. Some of this unusual circuitry could prove helpful after an injury; but given that normal animals shed such circuitry, it seems likely that it could prove equally disadvantageous to maintain such circuitry. Indeed, both hypotheses are confirmed. Rats with infant motor cortex lesions do show sparing of some motor skills (Whishaw and Kolb, 1988) but apparently at the price of impairments in other cognitive functions (Kolb, Cioe, and Whishaw, 2000a,b). It therefore seems likely that the presence of abnormal corticofugal pathways after early cortical injury may be as disruptive as it is helpful. This possibility has been termed "crowding" to reflect the idea that the normal functions of a cortical region can be crowded out by the development of abnormal connections (Teuber, 1975).

CHANGES IN NEUROGENESIS   In the course of studies of the effect of restricted lesions of the medial frontal cortex or olfactory bulb, we discovered that, in contrast to lesions elsewhere in the cerebrum, midline telencephalic lesions on postnatal days 7–12 led to spontaneous regeneration of the lost regions, or at least partial regeneration of the lost regions (figure 13.6). Similar injuries either before or after this temporal window did not produce such a result. Analysis of the medial frontal region showed that the area contained newly generated neurons that formed at least some of the normal connections of this region (Kolb et al., 1998). Furthermore, animals with this regrown cortex appeared virtually normal on many, but not all, behavioral measures (Kolb,

Petrie, and Cioe, 1996). Additional studies showed that if we blocked regeneration of the tissue with prenatal injections of the mitotic marker bromodeoxyuridine (BrdU), the lost frontal tissue failed to regrow and there was no recovery of function (Kolb et al., 1999; Kolb, Pedersen, and Gibb, 1999), a result that implies that the regrown tissue was supporting recovery. Parallel studies in which we removed the regrown tissue found complementary results: Removal of the tissue eliminated the functional recovery (Temesvary, Gibb, and Kolb, 1998). Thus, in the absence of the regrown tissue, either because we blocked the growth or because we removed the tissue, function was lost.

One question that arises is whether the regeneration of lost brain during infancy influences later plastic events in the brain. For example, does the generation of so many new cells during infancy compromise the brain's ability to generate cells for the olfactory bulb or hippocampus in adulthood? To test this possibility, we made frontal lesions in mice at P7 and later in adulthood we removed the stem cells from the subventricular zone and placed them in vitro with neurotrophic factors

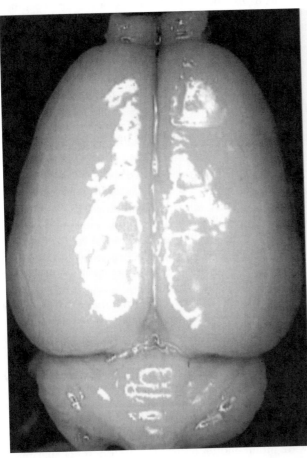 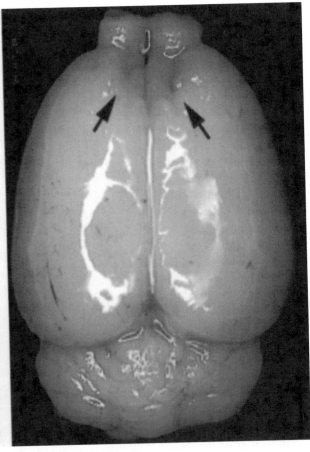

FIGURE 13.6   Photographs of brains of representative control (*left*) and medial frontal lesion (*right*) rat. The lesion cavity has been filled with newly generated neurons in the lesion brain. Arrows point to the lesion scar.

(Kolb et al., 1999). When stem cells are placed in such a medium, they normally divide rapidly, producing large numbers of new stem cells and progenitor cells (Fisher, 1997; Reynolds and Weiss, 1992). In contrast to the cells from control mice, which produced thousands of new cells in vitro, the cells from the brains of the animals with previous P7 lesions produced few new cells. The early brain damage followed by regeneration of the lost tissue appears to have used up the proliferative potential of the subventricular stem cells, leading to an abnormal response in adulthood. We do not yet know what implications this result has for the normal endogenous production of new neurons in adulthood, but it seems likely that it will not be normal. Once again, there appears to be a price to be paid for plastic changes in the infant brain.

In sum, it appears that neurogenesis can be reinitiated after frontal or olfactory bulb lesions on postnatal days 7–12. Why this time and place are special is unclear, but these results show that regeneration of lost tissue is possible. This regeneration may not be without cost to later plastic changes in the brain, however.

In conclusion, studies of laboratory rats with cortical lesions at different developmental ages have shown a variety of morphological changes that follow early cortical injury (table 13.1). These changes include either increases or decreases in synaptic space, alterations in corticofugal connectivity, and the regeneration of cortical tissue. Functional recovery correlates with increases in cortical synaptic space and the generation of new neurons but changes in corticofugal connections may be as disruptive as helpful in stimulating functional recovery.

TABLE 13.1
*Summary of the effects of frontal cortical injury at different ages*

| Age at Injury | Result | Basic Reference |
|---|---|---|
| E18 | Cortex regrows with odd structure<br>Functional recovery | Kolb, Cioe, and Muirhead, 1998 |
| P1–P6 | Small brain, dendritic atrophy<br>Dismal functional outcome | Kolb and Gibb, 1990 |
| P7–P12 | Dendrite and spine growth<br>Cortical regrowth<br>Functional recovery | Kolb and Gibb, 1990; Kolb et al., 1998 |
| P120 | Dendritic atrophy, then growth<br>Partial return of function | Kolb, 1995 |

Abbreviations: E18, embryonic day 18; P*x*, postnatal day *x*.

## Manipulation of endogenous changes

We have seen that if a cerebral injury is followed by an increase in dendritic space, there is a good functional outcome, whereas if an injury leads to an atrophy of dendritic space, there is a poor functional outcome. It follows that if we can potentiate dendritic growth in animals showing poor recovery of function, we should enhance functional recovery. The treatments for the potentiated growth range from behavioral therapy to the application of some sort of pharmacological treatment. The pharmacological treatments could be of various forms, including growth factors (e.g., nerve growth factor), hormones (e.g., sex steroids), or chemicals that influence transmitters, especially the neuromodulators such as acetylcholine and noradrenaline. We focus here on behavioral therapy, neuromodulators, and gonadal hormones.

BEHAVIORAL THERAPY   Although it is generally assumed that behavioral therapies will improve recovery from cerebral injury in humans, there have been few direct studies of how this might work, when the optimal time for therapy might be, or even whether it is actually effective (Kwakkel et al., 1997). Furthermore, as we try to develop animal models of cognitive or motor therapies, we are left with the problem of determining what an appropriate therapy might be. There have been many studies of the effects of various types of experience on functional outcome after cerebral injury in laboratory animals, but the results have been inconsistent and generally disappointing (for reviews, see Shulkin, 1989; Will and Kelche, 1992). One difficulty with these studies is that few actually measured neuronal morphology. Rather, most studies focused primarily on functional outcome with different environmental manipulations. Thus, it may be that treatments fail to potentiate recovery because they are ineffective in stimulating brain plasticity. Our approach has been somewhat different. We chose behavioral manipulations we knew to be capable of changing the brain of intact animals, then exposed our brain-injured animals, especially those with poor functional outcomes, to the same experiences. Here, we illustrate with a few examples from our work with rats with infant lesions. As noted earlier, the developing brain is influenced by tactile stimulation during infancy and the young animal is influenced by housing in enriched environments. Because the animal with a cortical lesion in the first days of life is functionally devastated in adulthood, and because it shows atrophy of cortical neurons, we anticipated that such animals would benefit the most from early experience.

In one series of studies, animals were given frontal or posterior parietal lesions at 4 days of age, following by tactile stimulation (stroking) until weaning. Tactile stimulation for 15 min, three times per day, for just 10 days permanently alters the morphological and neurochemical structure of the cortex of normal animals, but has even bigger effects on the cortex of an injured brain (Kolb and Gibb, 1999). Thus, rats with tactile stimulation show an unexpectedly large attenuation of the behavioral deficits of cerebral injury as a result of this rather brief "therapy." In fact, the rats with frontal lesions on day 4 showed a nearly complete recovery of performance in various motor tasks, such as skilled reaching. This is a stunning reversal of a devastating functional loss normally seen in animals with such injuries at this age. Analysis of the brains showed a reversal of the atrophy of the remaining cortical neurons normally associated with such early lesions. Thus, a treatment that reversed the dendritic atrophy after perinatal lesions also reversed the severe functional disturbance from the early lesion.

In parallel studies, we placed rats that had cortical lesions in the first week of life in complex environments for 3 months, beginning at the time of weaning or in adulthood. The animals placed in the environments as juveniles showed a dramatic reversal of functional impairments that was correlated with increased cortical thickness (Kolb and Elliott, 1987). The dramatic improvement in the animals with the earliest injuries carries an important message, for it suggests that even the young animal with substantial neural atrophy and behavioral dysfunction is capable of considerable neuroplasticity and functional recovery in response to behavioral therapy. When animals with similar injuries were placed into enriched environments as adults, they showed a less impressive reversal of functional losses, although they did show marked reversal of dendritic atrophy (Kolb, Gibb, and Gorny, 2000). The brain thus appears to be capable of considerable environment-mediated modification after early injury, although the timing of the postinjury therapy does appear to make some difference (table 13.2). Perhaps the synaptic organization of the remaining brain can be more easily remodeled if the reorganization occurs while the brain is still developing, whereas it is more difficult to remodel a brain with infant injuries once the synaptic organization has stabilized in adulthood.

One additional question we asked was how experience might modify the cortex of animals with medial frontal removals on postnatal day 7. These animals would normally show significant functional recovery in any event, so one prediction would be that the brain would not show much response to the experience. On the other hand, if we gave the animals experience during the time that they would normally be reorganizing synaptic organization in order to support recovery, we might anticipate a more efficient reorganization and better functional recovery. The results showed that there was a small, but significant added functional benefit of such experience (Kolb, Gibb, and Gorny, 2000). The cortical neurons in the brains of these animals also showed experience-dependent modifications, although these changes were reduced relative to enriched control animals. We expected the anatomical results to be particularly interesting because we knew from our earlier studies that the effects of the lesion and experience would be in opposite directions. That is, rats with frontal lesions on P7 normally show an increase in spine density in response to the lesion, an anatomical adaptation that is presumably related to the functional recovery (Kolb, Stewart, and Sutherland, 1997). In contrast, normal control rats placed in complex environments at weaning normally show a drop in spine density. Thus, rats with P7 lesions would be placed in a situation where one force (the lesion) would stimulate the growth of synapses while the other (complex housing) would stimulate the pruning of synapses. What actually happened was that the lesion animals showed intermediate effects: The complex housing reduced the lesion-induced spine density increase. There was, however, little change in the functional recovery. Thus, the experience did change the cells, but on the behavioral measures we used there were no obvious behavioral consequences. The spine results suggest that the synaptic organization of animals with P7 lesions may be modified in different ways depending upon the experience, whether it be injury or complex housing. It appears, however, that the different modifications are still able to support functional recovery. As with the experiments showing a decrease in spine density (and hence synapses per neuron) after early experiences, the P7 complex-rearing studies leave us with a conundrum: Why do fewer synapses enhance functional outcome? Again, it may be that the early experience encourages the genesis of more neurons and/or glia or that the experience attenuates the normal process of cell death during development. In either case the animals would have more neurons and thus actually have more total synapses. Although really just conjecture at this point, such a result would account for why a decrease in spine density appears functionally advantageous.

One reasonable question we might ask is just how complex or enriched environments for rats relate to environmental stimulation for children. In particular, it seems likely that standard laboratory housing for rats is rather sterile compared to the usual environment of

Table 13.2

*Modification of the effects of early frontal cortical injury*

| Treatment | Result | Basic Reference |
|---|---|---|
| Tactile stimulation after P4 lesion | Functional recovery; reversal of neuronal atrophy | Kolb and Gibb, 1999 |
| Tactile stimulation after P10 lesion | No additional recovery or dendritic growth | Kolb and Gibb, 1999 |
| Complex housing after P1–5 lesion | Functional recovery; dendritic growth | Kolb, Gibb, and Gorny, 2000 |
| Complex housing after P7 lesion | Little additional recovery; small increment in dendritic growth | Kolb, Gibb, and Gorny, 2000 |
| NA depletion before P7 lesion | Blocked recovery; dendritic atrophy; drop in spine density | Kolb and Sutherland, 1992 |
| ACh depletion before P7 lesion | Blocked recovery; anatomical analysis in progress | Kolb, Gibb, Sherren, and Pappas, 2000 |
| High choline diet before and after P4 lesion | Stimulated recovery; enhanced dendritic growth | Tees and Kolb, 1999 |
| GDX before P7 lesion | Reduced recovery; reduced dendritic growth | Kolb and Stewart, 1995 |
| Testosterone to females before P7 lesions | Enhanced recovery; increased spine density | Kolb and Stewart, 1995 |

Abbreviations: P4, P7, P10, postnatal days 4, 7, 10; P1–5, postnatal days 1–5; GDX, castration on day of birth; NA, noradrenaline; ACh, acetylcholine.

feral rats; thus, if we try to generalize to humans, we are left wondering how stimulating an environment would have to be in order to induce functional changes in human infants. One way to answer this question is to consider what animals do in the complex environments. They are provided with novel objects to interact with every few days, they get a lot of activity as they move about the compounds, and they have considerable social experience as they live in groups of 6–8 other animals. The experience is thus perceptually and socially stimulating, motorically demanding, and is continuous for several weeks or months. Although we do not know which aspects of this experience are the most important, our guess is that all contribute because they stimulate different types of brain activity. Thus, our best guess as we generalize to human infants is that therapies would include perceptual stimulation, including novelty, as well as social interaction and motor activities.

NEUROMODULATORS   Both acetylcholine and noradrenaline have been implicated in various forms of cortical plasticity (Bear and Singer, 1986), and as we shall see, both modulate recovery from early cortical injury. We consider each separately.

In the course of doing our experiments on tactile stimulation and recovery, we noticed that tactile stimulation during infancy produced a chronic enhancement of acetylcholinesterase density in the cortex (Kolb and Gibb, 1999). In addition, this increase was significantly greater in the animals with frontal removals than in sham controls. This result led us to speculate that the effect of tactile stimulation might be mediated through increased acetylcholine levels. We reasoned that if this were so, then increasing acetylcholine levels more directly might also enhance recovery. As shown by others, choline-enriched diets could alter cortical plasticity (Pyapali, 1998); therefore, we placed pregnant dams on a choline-enhanced diet during the last two weeks of pregnancy and kept the lactating mothers on the diet until weaning (Tees and Kolb, in preparation). The pups received medial frontal lesions on postnatal day 4 and were assessed on various behavioral tasks in adulthood. Choline treatment significantly ameliorated the expected functional deficits; in addition, there was a significant increase in dendritic branching and spine density in the choline-treated lesion animals. In a follow-up study, we took the opposite approach and depleted the forebrain of cholinergic neurons with intracerebral injections of IgG saporin on postnatal day 4, then gave the animals frontal lesions on P7 (Kolb, Gibb, Sherren, and Pappas, unpublished observations). In this case, we blocked the functional recovery normally seen in P7 operates. Our anatomical analysis of the neurons of these animals is in progress, but we predict that the cholinergic blockade will have the opposite effect of the cholinergic stimulation—namely, an atrophy in dendritic arborization relative to untreated controls.

There are now many studies showing that noradrenaline (NA) is necessary for various forms of experience-dependent cortical plasticity (Kasamatsu, Pettigrew, and Ary, 1979). We therefore depleted newborn rats of forebrain NA, which can be accomplished with subdural doses of the neurotoxin 6-hydroxydopamine in the young animal. This is possible because the forebrain blood–brain barrier is permeable to the toxin in the first few days of life and the noradrenergic terminals are destroyed selectively, leaving dopaminergic terminals and cells undisturbed. Animals then received large frontal lesions at 7 days of age and were later tested in various behavioral tasks before undergoing a Golgi analysis of dendritic and spine morphology (Kolb, Stewart, and Sutherland, 1997; Kolb and Sutherland, 1992; Sutherland et al., 1982). The results showed that in the absence of NA there was no functional recovery, as illustrated in figure 13.7. Analysis of the dendritic and spine changes showed that the NA depletion produced a drop in dendritic morphology in both sham control and lesion animals relative to saline-treated controls. The drop in dendritic length was greater in the lesion animals. The sham NA-depleted animals, who had no obvious behavioral disturbance, apparently compensated for the dendritic loss with an increase in spine density. A similar increase was observed in the lesion animals as well, but these latter animals failed to show recovery, apparently because their synaptic deficit was too great to reverse.

In sum, we have seen that increased cholinergic activity facilitates recovery whereas decreased cholinergic or noradrenergic activity inhibits recovery. We can predict that increasing noradrenergic activity should stimulate recovery. It would be interesting to determine how manipulations of neuromodulators might interact with behavioral treatments such as tactile stimulation or complex rearing.

GONADAL HORMONES   There is accumulating evidence that male and female brains differ in their structure, respond differently to environmental events, and respond differently to injury. For example, we have found that there are hormone-related structural differences in the prefrontal cortex of rats. Cells in the medial prefrontal regions have more dendritic arbor in animals exposed to testosterone, whereas cells in the insular prefrontal regions have more dendritic arbor in animals not exposed to testosterone (Kolb and Stewart, 1991). These differences led us to wonder if early brain injury might influence the pattern of sex-related differences in cortical morphology. It does. As we have seen, rats with medial frontal lesions in postnatal day 7 show marked functional recovery; but, in addition, this recovery is sexually dimorphic (figure 13.8). In particular, males show enhanced recovery of spatial-navigation behaviors whereas females show enhanced recovery of skilled forelimb reaching (Kolb and Cioe, 1996; Kolb, Gibb, and Gorny, 2000; Kolb and Stewart, 1995). These behavioral differences are associated with differences in cortical plasticity: Males with frontal lesions show a

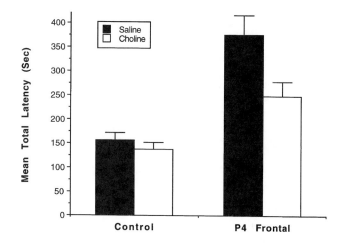

A.   Choline Supplementation

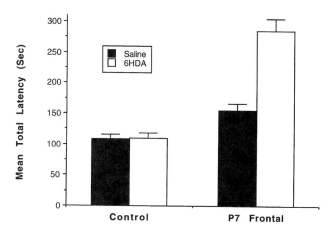

B.   Noradrenaline Depletion

FIGURE 13.7   Summary of the Morris water task performance of rats. (**A**) Rats with frontal lesions on postnatal day 4 and pre- and postnatal choline supplements in their diets. The choline supplements reduced the behavioral deficit (Tees and Kolb, 1999). (**B**) Rats with frontal lesions on postnatal day 7 and prelesion noradrenaline depletion. The noradrenaline depletion blocked the behavioral recovery (Kolb and Sutherland, 1992).

greater increase in spine density whereas females show a larger increase in dendritic arborization (Kolb and Stewart, 1995). Thus, although both sexes show functional recovery, there are differences, and these differences are related to morphological differences. To complicate matters more, there appear to be sex differences in the effect of tactile experience or complex housing on cortical neurons (Kolb, Gibb, and Gorny, 2001). Thus, the question arises as to whether sex, experience, and lesion might all interact. This is an important question if we are to design treatments for children with brain injuries.

## Par 1 Apical Branches

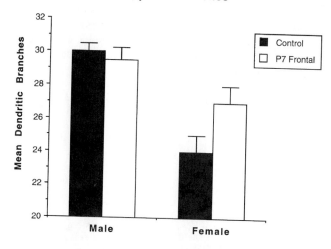

## Par 1 Apical Spine Density

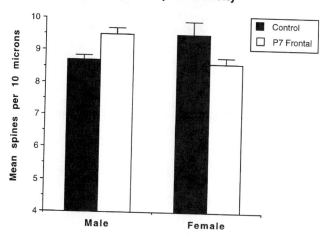

FIGURE 13.8 Summary of sex differences in dendritic changes after frontal lesions on postnatal day 7. There is a sex difference in dendritic branching and spine density in the normal control animals that favors males for branches and females for spines. After the P7 lesions, the female operates show a relative increase in branching, whereas the male operates show an increase in spines. (From Kolb and Stewart, 1995.)

## Summary

One of the most intriguing questions in behavioral neuroscience concerns the manner in which the brain, and especially the neocortex, can modify its structure and ultimately its function throughout one's lifetime. As this chapter has suggested, the cortex can be changed dramatically by events during early development, and especially by early brain damage. Several basic conclusions can be extracted regarding the nature of the relationship between experience, brain plasticity, and behavior.

1. The effects of experience vary both qualitatively and quantitatively at different times in development. For example, "enriched" experiences during the immediate postnatal period have no measurable effect on dendritic length and lead to a chronic decrease in spine density in cortical neurons. Enriched experiences during the juvenile and adolescent period produce chronic increases in dendritic length but decreases in spine density. Similar experiences later in life produce chronic increases in both dendritic length and spine density in cortical pyramidal cells. All of these experiences have behavioral sequelae in adulthood. The age-dependent plastic changes in the cortex presumably reflect the differential sensitivity of the child's brain to experience during development. It is not yet known why there are such differences in response to experience.

2. There are three ways that the brain changes after injury during development: (1) endogenous changes in the organization of the remaining, intact, circuits in the brain; (2) the generation of new circuitry, including circuitry that is novel to the injured brain; and (3) the generation of neurons and glia to replace at least some lost neurons. Details of these changes vary with the precise nature of the developmental events underway at the time of injury.

3. When the cortex is injured during the time of neurogenesis, there is an apparent capacity to replace the lost cells, although cortical organization is not entirely normal. There is an associated sparing of cortical function.

4. Cortical injury in the period immediately following the completion of neurogenesis results in the development of a small brain, thin cortex, and significant reorganization of cortical connectivity. These latter changes are reflected especially in abnormalities in corticofugal connections. In addition, there is an atrophy of dendritic arborization and reduced spine density in cortical neurons. The behavioral outcome is especially poor after injury at this time, as animals show severe and chronic behavioral impairments.

5. Injury to the cortex while astrocytes are maximally developing and cortical neurons are maximally differentiating also produces a somewhat small brain and thin cortex, but there is a compensatory increase in dendritic arborization and an increase in spine density. These changes presumably reflect changes in the intrinsic organization of cortical circuits.

6. Injury-induced changes in cortical structure are modified by experience. Furthermore, brains that show the least change in response to a cortical injury appear to be the most responsive to experience. For instance, animals with neonatal brain injuries show a poor functional outcome and an atrophy of cortical neurons, but

these animals show dramatic functional recovery and marked synaptic growth in response to environmental manipulations. Behavioral manipulations that are initiated in the immediate postinjury period appear to be the most effective in stimulating functional recovery. The response of the developing brain to postinjury manipulations of experience is encouraging, for it suggests that behavioral therapies should be especially helpful in reversing some of the devastating consequences of brain damage in the later periods of prenatal development in human infants.

7. Neuromodulators, including acetylcholine and noradrenaline, influence recovery from early brain injury. Treatments that act to increase the cortical levels of neuromodulators stimulate cortical plasticity and functional recovery, whereas treatments that act to reduce the cortical levels of neuromodulators act to retard recovery.

8. Gonadal hormones influence synaptic organization of the cortex throughout the lifetime of an animal. This is particularly true during development, and the gonadal hormone effects interact with the plastic changes that follow cortical injury, at least at certain stages of development. Perhaps the biggest sex-related difference is that males show larger changes in spine density after cortical injury whereas females are more likely to show changes in dendritic arborization.

9. There are limits to the amount that a brain can change. We still do not know what determines the limits, nor, in most cases, what the limits might be. Nonetheless, it does appear that when the brain changes "spontaneously" after injury, there is a reduction in the plasticity of the affected regions. This implies that behavioral therapies should be initiated early in the postinjury period to ensure that the spontaneous changes can be influenced in such a way as to maximize functional recovery.

ACKNOWLEDGMENTS  This research was supported by Natural Science and Engineering Research Council of Canada and Medical Research Council of Canada grants to BK. The authors thank Grazyna Gorny for her technical help in many of the experiments described here, and Fred Colbourne and Jan Cioe for helpful comments on an earlier version of the manuscript.

## REFERENCES

BAILEY, C. H., and E. R. KANDEL, 1993. Structural changes accompanying memory storage. *Annu. Rev. Physiol.* 55:397–426.

BEAR, M. F., and W. SINGER, 1986. Modulation of visual cortical plasticity by acetylcholine and noradrenaline. *Nature* 320:172–176.

CASTRO, A., 1990. Plasticity in the motor system. In *Cerebral Cortex of the Rat*, B. Kolb and R. Tees, eds. Cambridge, Mass.: MIT Press, pp. 563–588.

ERIKSSON, P. S., E. PERFILIEVA, T. BJORK-ERIKSSON, A. M. ALBORN, C. NORDBORG, D. A. PETERSON, and F. H. GAGE, 1998. Neurogenesis in the adult human hippocampus. *Nature Med.* 4:1313–1317.

FINGER, S., and C. R. ALMLI, 1988. Margaret Kennard and her "principle" in historical perspective. In *Brain Injury and Recovery: Theoretical and Controversial Issues*, S. Finger, T. E. Le Vere, C. R. Almli, and D. G. Stein, eds. New York: Plenum Press, pp. 117–132.

FISHER, L. J., 1997. Neural precursor cells: Applications for the study and repair of the central nervous system. *Neurobiol. Disease* 4:1–22.

GOULD, E., P. TANAPAT, N. B. HASTINGS, and T. J. SHORS, 1999. Neurogenesis in adulthood: A possible role in learning. *Trends Cogn. Sci.* 3:186–191.

GREENOUGH, W. T., J. E. BLACK, and C. S. WALLACE, 1987. Experience and brain development. *Child Dev.* 58:539–559.

GREENOUGH, W. T., and F. F. CHANG, 1989. Plasticity of synapse structure and pattern in the cerebral cortex. In *Cerebral Cortex*, Vol. 7, A. Peters and E. G. Jones, eds. New York: Plenum Press, pp. 391–440.

HEBB, D. O., 1947. The effects of early experience on problem solving at maturity. *Am. Psychol.* 2:737–745.

HEBB, D. O., 1949. *The Organization of Behaviour.* New York: McGraw-Hill.

KASAMATSU, T., J. D. PETTIGREW, and M. ARY, 1979. Restoration of visual cortical plasticity by local microperfusion of norepinephrine. *J. Comp. Neurol.* 185:163–182.

KEMPERMANN, G., and F. H. GAGE, 1999. New nerve cells for the adult brain. *Scientific American* 280:48–53.

KENNARD, M., 1942. Cortical reorganization of motor function. *Arch. Neurol.* 48:227–240.

KOLB, B., 1987. Recovery from early cortical damage in rats. I. Differential behavioral and anatomical effects of frontal lesions at different ages of neural maturation. *Behav. Brain Res.* 25:205–220.

KOLB, B., 1995. *Brain Plasticity and Behavior.* Mahwah, N.J.: Erlbaum.

KOLB, B., and J. CIOE, 1996. Sex-related differences in cortical function after medial frontal lesions in rats. *Behav. Neurosci.* 110:1271–1281.

KOLB, B., J. CIOE, and D. MUIRHEAD, 1998. Cerebral morphology and functional sparing after prenatal frontal cortex lesions in rats. *Behav. Brain Res.* 91:143–155.

KOLB, B., J. CIOE, and I. Q. WHISHAW, 2000a. Is there an optimal age for recovery from unilateral motor cortex lesions? Behavioural and anatomical sequelae of unilateral motor cortex lesions in rats on postnatal days 1, 10, and in adulthood. *Restorative Neurol. Neurosci.* (in press)

KOLB, B., J. CIOE, and I. Q. WHISHAW, 2000b. Is there an optimal age for recovery from motor cortex lesions? Behavioural and anatomical sequelae of bilateral motor cortex lesions in rats on postnatal days 1, 10, and in adulthood. *Brain Res.* 882:62–74.

KOLB, B., and W. ELLIOTT, 1987. Recovery from early cortical damage in rats. II. Effects of experience on anatomy and behavior following frontal lesions at 1 or 5 days of age. *Behav. Brain Res.* 26:47–56.

KOLB B., and R. GIBB, 1990. Anatomical correlates of behavioural change after neonatal prefrontal lesions in rats. *Prog. Brain Res.* 85:241–256.

KOLB, B., and R. GIBB, 1999. Tactile stimulation after cortical injury in infant rats stimulates functional recovery. (in preparation)

KOLB, B., R. GIBB, and G. GORNY, 2000. Therapeutic effects of enriched rearing after frontal lesions in infancy vary with age and sex. *Behav. Brain Res.* (submitted)

KOLB, B., R. GIBB, and G. GORNY, 2001. Experience-dependent changes in dendritic arbor and spine density in neocortex vary with age and sex. *Neurobiology of Learning and Memory.* (in press)

KOLB, B., R. GIBB, G. GORNY, and I. Q. WHISHAW, 1998. Possible brain regrowth after cortical lesions in rats. *Behav. Brain Res.* 91:127–141.

KOLB, B., R. GIBB, and D. VAN DER KOOY, 1994. Neonatal frontal cortical lesions in rats alter cortical structure and connectivity. *Brain Res.* 645:85–97.

KOLB, B., R. GIBB, D. J. MARTENS, B. COLES, and D. VAN DER KOOY, 1999. Proliferation of neural stem cells in vitro and in vivo is reduced by infant frontal cortex lesions or prenatal BrdU. *Soc. Neurosci. Abstr.* 25.

KOLB, B., R. GIBB, N. SHERREN, and B. PAPPAS, 2000. Cholinergic depletion blocks recovery from frontal lesions in infant rats. Unpublished observations.

KOLB, B., B. PEDERSEN, and R. GIBB, 1999. Recovery from frontal cortex lesions in infancy is blocked by embryonic pretreatment with bromodeoxyuridine. *Behav. Neurosci.* (submitted)

KOLB, B., B. PEDERSEN, M. BALLERMAN, R. GIBB, and I. Q. WHISHAW, 1999. Embryonic exposure to BrdU produces chronic changes in brain and behavior in rats. *J. Neurosci.* 19:2337–2346.

KOLB, B., B. PETRIE, and J. CIOE, 1996. Recovery from early cortical damage in rats. VII. Comparison of the behavioural and anatomical effects of medial prefrontal lesions at different ages of neural maturation. *Behav. Brain Res.* 79:1–13.

KOLB, B., and J. STEWART, 1991. Sex-related differences in dendritic branching of cells in the prefrontal cortex of rats. *J. Neuroendocrinol.* 3:95–99.

KOLB, B., and J. STEWART, 1995. Changes in neonatal gonadal hormonal environment prevent behavioral sparing and alter cortical morphogenesis after early frontal cortex lesions in male and female rats. *Behav. Neurosci.* 109:285–294.

KOLB, B., J. STEWART, and R. J. SUTHERLAND, 1997. Recovery of function is associated with increased spine density in cortical pyramidal cells after frontal lesions and/or noradrenaline depletion in neonatal rats. *Behav. Brain Res.* 89:61–70.

KOLB, B., and R. J. SUTHERLAND, 1992. Noradrenaline depletion blocks behavioral sparing and alters cortical morphogenesis after neonatal frontal cortex damage in rats. *J. Neurosci.* 12:2221–2330.

KOLB, B., and I. Q. WHISHAW, 1981. Neonatal frontal lesions in the rat: Sparing of learned but not species-typical behavior in the presence of reduced brain weight and cortical thickness. *J. Comp. Physiol. Psychol.* 95:863–879.

KOLB, B., and I. Q. WHISHAW, 1989. Plasticity in the neocortex: Mechanisms underlying recovery from early brain damage. *Prog. Neurobiol.* 32:235–276.

KOLB, B., and I. Q. WHISHAW, 1998. Brain plasticity and behavior. *Annu. Rev. Psychol.* 49:43–64.

KWAKKEL, G., R. C. WAGENNAR, T. W. KOELMAN, G. J. LANKHORST, and J. KOETSIER, 1997. Effects of intensity of rehabilitation after stroke: A research synthesis. *Stroke* 28:550–1556.

PYAPALI, G. K., D. A. TURNER, C. L. WILLIAMS, W. H. MECK, and H. S. SWARTZWELDER, 1998. Prenatal dietary choline supplementation decreases the threshold for induction of long-term potentiation in young adult rats. *J. Neurophysiol.* 79:1790–1796.

RAY, S., T. D. PALMER, S. SCHONEN, J. TAKAHASHI, and F. H. GAGE, 1997. Neurogenesis in the adult brain: Lessons learned from the studies of progenitor cells from the embryonic and adult central nervous systems. In *Isolation, Characterization and Utilization of CNS Stem Cells*, F. Gage and Y. Christen, eds. Berlin: Springer-Verlag, pp. 129–149.

REYNOLDS, B., and S. WEISS, 1992. Generation of neurons and astrocytes from isolated cells of the adult mammalian central nervous system. *Science* 255:1727–1710.

ROBINSON, T. E., and B. KOLB, 1997. Persistent structural adaptations in nucleus accumbens and prefrontal cortex neurons produced by prior experience with amphetamine. *J. Neurosci.* 17:8491–8498.

SCHANBERG, S. M., and T. M. FIELD, 1987. Sensory deprivation stress and supplemental stimulation in the rat pup and preterm human neonate. *Child Dev.* 58:1431–1447.

SHULKIN, J. (ED.), 1989. *Preoperative Events: Their Effects on Behavior Following Brain Damage.* Hillsdale, N.J.: Erlbaum.

STEWART, J., and B. KOLB, 1988. The effects of neonatal gonadectomy and prenatal stress on cortical thickness and asymmetry in rats. *Behav. Neural Biol.* 49:344–360.

SUTHERLAND, R. J., B. KOLB, J. B. BECKER, and I. Q. WHISHAW, 1982. Cortical noradrenaline depletion eliminates sparing of spatial learning after neonatal frontal cortex damage in the rat. *Neurosci. Lett.* 32:125–130.

TEES, R., and B. KOLB, 1999. Prenatal choline treatment enhances recovery from perinatal frontal injury in rats. (in preparation)

TEMESVARY, A. E., R. GIBB, and B. KOLB, 1998. Recovery of function after neonatal frontal lesions in rats: Function or fiction. *Soc. Neurosci. Abstr.* 24:473.8.

TEUBER, H.-L., 1975. Recovery of function after brain injury in man. In *Outcome of Severe Damage to the Nervous System*, Ciba Foundation Symposium 34. Amsterdam: Elsevier North-Holland.

VILLABLANCA, J. R., D. A. HOVDA, G. F. JACKSON, and C. INFANTE, 1993. Neurological and behavioral effects of a unilateral frontal cortical lesion in fetal kittens: II. Visual system tests, and proposing a 'critical period' for lesion effects. *Behav. Brain Res.* 57:79–92.

WALLHAUSSER, E., and H. SCHEICH, 1987. Auditory imprinting leads to differential 2-deoxyglucose uptake and dendritic spine loss in the chick rostral forebrain. *Dev. Brain Res.* 31:29–44.

WEISS, S., B. A. REYNOLDS, A. L. VESCOVI, C. MORSHEAD, C. G. CRAIG, and D. VAN DER KOOY, 1996. Is there a neural stem cell in the mammalian forebrain? *Trends Neurosci.* 19:387–393.

WHISHAW, I. Q., and B. KOLB, 1988. Sparing of skilled forelimb reaching and corticospinal projections after neonatal motor cortex removal or hemidecortication in the rat: Support for the Kennard doctrine. *Brain Res.* 451:97–114.

WHISHAW, I. Q., S. M. PELLIS, B. P. GORNY, and V. C. PELLIS, 1991. The impairments in reaching and the movements of compensation in rats with motor cortex lesions: An end-point, videorecording, and movement notation analysis. *Behav. Brain Res.* 42:77–91.

WILL, B., and C. KELCHE, 1992. Environmental approaches to recovery of function from brain damage: A review of animal studies (1981 to 1991). In *Recovery from Brain Damage: Reflections and Directions,* F. D. Rose and D. A. Johnson, eds. New York: Plenum Press, pp. 79–104.

# 14 Neural Plasticity and Development

THOMAS ELBERT, SABINE HEIM,
AND BRIGITTE ROCKSTROH

ABSTRACT This chapter illustrates that learning and experience affect the development of perceptual and cognitive abilities through mechanisms of reorganization of functional brain architecture, that is, through neural plasticity on a macroscopic scale. We begin by imparting some fundamentals about the mechanisms that allow the brain to organize and reorganize its functional structure. Then we describe basic aspects of neural plasticity that underlie experience-dependent plasticity, focusing on cortical representational cortex as the best investigated model of macroscopic plasticity. Examples for experience-induced cortical reorganization with its perceptual and cognitive correlates and possible adaptive and maladaptive consequences follows. In reviewing the development of language through the lens of neural plasticity, we point out elements of an emerging new paradigm in developmental cognitive neuroscience.

Traditional concepts suggest that brain development during the prenatal and early postnatal period follows rigid rules whereby phases in development are initiated through a cascade of genetically determined programs. However, the impact of experience is significant. Even in adulthood, the brain has the potential to reorganize the functional organization of its neural networks depending on the particular demands and afferent input. During development, the cortex may alter its functional organization in conjunction with structure in response to experience. Perception and skills will vary with the changes in neural network architecture. On a microscopic scale, structural changes include alterations in synaptic efficacy, synapse formation, synaptic plasticity, spine density, and alterations in dendritic length. As a consequence, supportive tissue elements such as astrocytes and blood vessels are also changed (for review, see Kolb and Whishaw, 1998).

Many insights about aspects of neural plasticity have been gained from studying representational zones. Evidence has been accumulated that the representational maps in the cortex have the ability to alter their functional organization on a macroscopic range. And not only are they highly plastic during development; they also maintain limited ability to respond to alterations in afferent input throughout life. Increasing evidence has

also been assembled showing that the functional maturation of the brain and the development of intellectual and emotional functioning are substantially influenced by social and emotional experiences—learning processes that can occur early in life. Experiences may be beneficial, as is the case with environmental enrichment and (parental) language models; but they may also be disadvantageous, as in cases of parental loss, neglect, lack of care, or even overuse of a certain skill or function. Particularly, early experiences play an important role in the development of social and emotional functions as well as for perceptual, linguistic, and cognitive development. Animal studies (Braun, 1996; Meaney et al., 1996; Meaney et al., 1988; Seckl and Meaney, 1993) have demonstrated that early postnatal experiences, such as brief separation from the mother or the intensity of maternal care (licking and grooming; Chaldji et al., 1998), affect structural, neural, endocrine, and functional brain development. These findings have consequences for various stress responses and learning abilities in later life. Human studies suggest that the impact of experience and learning on later abilities is not confined to very early periods. For instance, Ramey and Ramey (1998; see also Wickelgren, 1999) reported a positive effect of preschool training on school achievement.

Less is known about the influence of early experience on intellectual and cognitive functioning, despite attempts to describe cognitive development in detail (Weinert, 1998; Weinert and Schneider, 1998). In contrast to the prevailing view of the last decades, there is growing evidence that the environment early in life affects intellectual capacity as measured by the intelligence quotient (IQ) (for a brief summary, see Wickelgren, 1999). An impact of early experience on cognitive abilities can also be deduced from animal studies. Meaney and colleagues (1988) observed impaired learning behavior in adult rats that had been briefly separated from their mothers in the preweaning period. Braun (1996) reported that early sensory and social deprivation affect synaptic restructuring of associative networks, thereby preventing normal cognitive, affective, and social development. Reports of delayed intellectual development and cognitive deficits in

THOMAS ELBERT, SABINE HEIM, AND BRIGITTE ROCK-STROH Department of Psychology, University of Konstanz, Konstanz, Germany.

orphans and street children emphasize the relevance of these findings for humans (see Gunnar, this volume).

Therefore, development is a dynamic process, governed by the interplay of experience and developmental stages whereby neural plasticity seems to be one major player. In a seminal paper, Nelson (1999) illustrates this point: Visual input is necessary for the development of stereoscopic vision and ocular dominance columns. By the same token, extensive perceptual learning (over 3–4 years) was found to overcome early visual deprivation in 6–12-year-old children (Grigorieva, 1996). Another example is language: The exposure to particular speech contrasts is necessary for normal speech perception and the networks that facilitate the development of this ability (Pulvermüller, 1999). The ability to distinguish phonemes and syllables, an essential prerequisite for speech perception and language, mainly develops during the first year of life based on environmental experiences. During the first 6 months of life, children adequately discriminate phonemes, which have different meanings in different languages (German, Chinese, English), but they lose this ability if they hear only their native language in the following months. Adaptations to the phoneme categorization in one language may prove maladaptive in another language.

## The brain: A dynamic system

The perception and processing of stimuli depend on the functional organization of the respective neural networks. The structural and functional organization of the brain is shaped in the course of development, but the brain has the potential to reorganize this functional organization and to alter its structure in response to experience. Consequently, development is shaped by a nonlinear dynamic feedback system. Assume, for example, a certain skill, say the finger dexterity that facilitates violin playing. Enhanced dexterity will improve the musician's skill, making positive reinforcement more likely, so that the frequency of musical practice will increase. Thereupon, use-dependent plasticity will reshape such peripheral organs as the muscles and tendons, and will, in particular, adapt the brain's organization (Elbert et al., 1995; Karni et al., 1995) such that dexterity is altered in turn. As will be discussed, this interplay of reorganization and perception/behavior can be either adaptive or maladaptive (Elbert et al., 1998).

Neuronal networks may be particularly plastic during "sensitive" periods in the development of cortical structures, but they maintain the ability to alter their architecture to afferent input throughout life. Sensory information from external/peripheral stimuli is transferred via specific afferent fibers to specific areas in the cortex—the sensory representational zones. The cortical representations of the sensory perception relate in an orderly way to the spatial arrangements of receptors in the periphery. In the case of the somatosensory system, this results in the well known homunculus. The representation of motor responses in the precentral gyrus is similarly organized. Motor and sensory homunculi are not identical; because of different proportional representations of body parts and surface and larger overlap, there is less strict somatotopy of motor representational zones (Gerloff, 1999).

The construction and maintenance of functional brain organization is essentially explained by Hebbian mechanisms (Hebb, 1949). Hebb's rule derives from the fact that synaptic contacts are plastic and are modified as a consequence of simultaneous activation of the pre- and postsynaptic neuron ("cells that fire together, wire together"). Hebb assumed two types of synaptic plasticity: long-term potentiation (LTP) and long-term depression (LTD). Whenever the presynaptic action potential precedes the firing of the postsynaptic cell, the synaptic response will increase (LTP). If the order is reversed, the synaptic response will decrease (LTD). A typical time frame for such synaptic plasticity to occur varies at ~100 ms (Engert and Bonhoeffer, 1999). For pyramidal neurons in neocortical slices, Markram et al. (1997) observed a difference in spike timing of 10 ms to switch the plasticity from LTP to LTD. This means that every spike in a pyramidal cell could potentially affect every excitatory synapse of a cell that is active within 100 ms.

But there are reasons to believe that synaptic plasticity is regulated in different ways. A general form of activity-dependent regulation of synaptic transmission, "synaptic scaling," has been investigated by Turrigiano and colleagues (1998). This type of synaptic plasticity enhances or suppresses all of a neuron's synaptic inputs as a function of activity. The mechanism of multiplicative synaptic strength scaling preserves the relative differences between inputs and also allows the neuron to adjust the total amount of synaptic excitation it receives. Thus, synaptic scaling may help to stabilize firing rates while alterations in connectivity occur. Use- and experience-dependent neural plasticity during development implies synaptic changes and restructuring (pruning, sprouting). Post and Weiss (1997) suggested that LTP and LTD are essential tools not only for sculpting the central nervous system (CNS) in the initial establishment of connections but also for molding behavior based on experience. Neural plasticity for higher order processes will involve larger number of synapses and cell assemblies as "dynamic time-based constructs" (Merzenich et al., 1993, p. 100) formed by coincident temporal activation.

## Basic aspects of neural plasticity

Plasticity has been studied most extensively in the cortical representation of the body surface in primary somatosensory cortex (Brodman area 3b and 1). The organization of the somatotopic maps has been experimentally manipulated by increasing or reducing afferent inputs and by changing the temporal coincidence between inputs. Animal studies by Merzenich and colleagues demonstrated as early as 1984 that *deafferentation* of digits (fingers) results in an altered representation of the hand in cortical area 3b (Merzenich et al., 1984). Pons and colleagues (1991) investigated the organization of the primary somatosensory cortex in owl monkeys that had been deprived of somatosensory input of an upper limb 12 years earlier. They found that neurons in the deafferented area, which usually comprises the representation of the hand, were responsive to the stimulation of neighboring representations, such as the trunk and the face. This large-scale reorganization encompassed more than 10 mm in cortical space in response to the long-term deafferentation. In human amputees, magnetic source imaging disclosed the same type and corresponding magnitude of map alteration (Elbert et al., 1994a). The amount of cortical reorganization is greater if the deafferentation occurs during development. The extent of invasion of the face area into the former hand territory turned out to be strongly correlated with the amount of phantom limb pain (figure 14.1; Flor et al., 1995). Thus, the loss of somatosensory input does not necessarily result in silence and degeneration of the respective cortical neurons, but can be followed by perceptually relevant functional reorganization of the homuncular representation of the body surface in the cortex. Deafferentation-related invasion has also been shown for other modalities, for example, following unilateral hearing loss (Mäkelä et al., 2000).

In addition to deafferentation, increased afferent inputs by intensive use of a digit or limb alter the homunculus, leading to an expansion of the representational cortical zones. This *use-dependent plasticity* was first demonstrated by Jenkins and colleagues (1990), who trained adult monkeys to touch a rotating disk for 15 s with their second and third digit in order to receive a food reward. The disk's irregular surface provided simultaneous stimulation of the receptors of the fingertips, while the food reward made the stimulation behaviorally relevant. After about 600 runs, the repre-

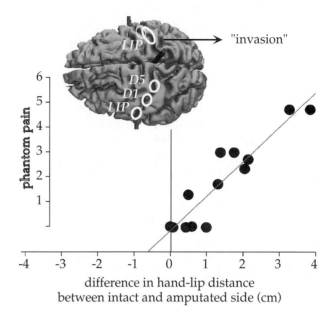

FIGURE 14.1   The amount of reorganization in the primary somatosensory cortex in upper extremity amputees with varying degrees of phantom limb pain was determined noninvasively by the use of neuromagnetic recording techniques. The insert on the upper left illustrates data from a representative subject with intense phantom limb pain. The area of the lip contralateral to the amputated hand (right hemisphere) has shifted from its original position toward the former cortical hand region. The scatterplot depicts the degree of phantom limb pain experienced by the amputees as a function of the magnitude of cortical reorganization (data from Flor et al., 1995).

sentational zones of the stimulated fingers were found to be extended relative to the nonstimulated hand and the nonstimulated fingers. In humans, use-dependent plasticity was first documented by Elbert and colleagues (1995), who found that increased afferent input related to the practice of a musical instrument led to an expansion of the cortical hand region. Deafferentation- and use-related changes of cortical representations can coexist within the same sensory system, as has been demonstrated for upper-limb amputees, in whom the two hemispheres are subject to different stimulation conditions (Elbert et al., 1997).

Use-related alterations of cortical representations depend on the temporal arrangement of the afferent input flow. The representations of neighboring fingers constitute "separate entities," which can, however, be "fused" depending on the stimulation pattern. Wang and coworkers (1995) observed that extensive simultaneous stimulation of the distal or proximal phalanges of digits 2–4 in new world monkeys led to the development of new multidigit receptive fields that were responsive only to the intensively stimulated parts of the hand. Moreover, surgically connecting two digits in monkeys resulted in a fused cortical receptive field for the same digits (Clark et al., 1988; Allard et al., 1991). A similar fusion of cortical representations was found in humans born with webbed fingers (syndactyly), while the surgical separation of the digits led to a separation of the cortical representational zones of the digits (Mogilner et al., 1993). In blind individuals who read Braille with three fingers simultaneously for many hours on a daily basis, Sterr and colleagues (1998a, 1998b) found a topographically disordered cortical representation of the digits. No such derangement was observed in one-finger Braille readers. Thus, extensive simultaneous stimulation of the digits, as well as other types of prolonged sensory input, can produce a use-dependent reorganization in the sense of a smearing of digital receptive fields.

The reorganization can be adaptive or maladaptive. An overlap of the digits' representational zones in blind multifinger Braille readers may be adaptive, enabling decoding of the dot patterns of entire words, that is, favoring fast and efficient reading. But cortical reorganization may also be maladaptive, as in focal hand dystonia. This disorder involves a loss of motor control of one or more digits, often as a consequence of the repetitive, synchronous movements of the digits made by musicians over periods of many years. For the affected hand of dystonic musicians, Elbert and colleagues (1998) reported a smaller distance between the representations of the digits in the somatosensory cortex (indicating fusion of the representational zones) than for the hands of nonmusician control subjects. The data suggest that use-dependent susceptibility to digital representational fusion may be involved in the etiology of focal dystonia. Cortical reorganization is determined by the involvement of neuronal networks in behaviorally relevant perception and performance. Therefore, even "maladaptive" reorganization brought about by unfavorable training and overuse can be reversed by a behaviorally relevant massed practice. Based on these considerations, a treatment for focal hand dystonia has been developed and found to be successful in improving the focal hand dystonia in ten adult (30–70 years of age) professional musicians (Candia et al., 1999).

The *behavioral relevance* of the afferent input is a prerequisite for neuroplastic changes to occur. Recanzone and coworkers (1992) examined the effect of enhanced input on cortical representations, comparing active and passive stimulation conditions in adult owl monkeys. Tactile flutter-vibration stimuli were applied to a small part of the fingertip. One group of monkeys was trained to detect differences in the frequency of a tactile vibration stimulus in order to receive a reward, while a sec-

ond group accomplished an auditory task while the tactile stimuli were applied. Cortical mapping of the somatosensory cortex (area 3b) disclosed an enlarged representation of the stimulated finger for the "active" group, while no expansion of the finger representation was found for the monkeys in the "passive" group. These and similar results confirm that enhanced afferent input must be provided in a behavioral relevant setting to achieve use-dependent adaptation of cortical representations. This behavioral relevance of stimulation and afferent input for cortical reorganization has been found to be essentially mediated by the nucleus basalis. This subcortical structure is uniquely positioned in the brain, as it receives input from limbic and paralimbic structures and projects to the entire brain. In addition, the nucleus basalis is known to be involved in the modulation of learning. Recent evidence indicates that the activation of the nucleus basalis is essential for cortical reorganization and that use-related changes do not occur when activity of the nucleus basalis is blocked (Kilgard and Merzenich, 1998).

*Temporal dynamics* of reorganization have been examined as well in animal studies. Short-term reorganization is highly reversible and may occur within hours to days of somatosensory deafferentation (Kelahan and Doetsch, 1984). It is assumed that such short-term changes of receptive field characteristics reflect the loss of inhibition provided by the fibers before deafferentation (Alloway and Aaron, 1996; Calford and Tweedale, 1988, 1990, 1991). Long-term reorganization can be observed after weeks or months of deafferentation or use-dependent inputs. Alterations of cortical representations are progressive in nature, so that short- and long-term representations most likely depict distinctive stages. Both stages in the reorganizational process are presumably based on neural interactions that are also involved in perceptual learning (Kelahan and Doetsch, 1984; Irvine and Rajan, 1996).

Before introducing examples of developmental plasticity of the sensory cortex, let us note the principles of cortical reorganization:

• Increased use of a limb leads to an expansion of the cortical representation and to a reduction of receptive fields of the respective neurons.
• Deafferentation or disuse causes invasion in the representational zone from sites nearby on the map.
• Synchronous, behaviorally relevant stimulation at nearby sites (e.g., different fingers) results in a fusion of the representations; i.e., temporal coincidence shapes cortical representations.
• Asynchronous stimulation of two different receptor pools tends to segregate the representational zones.

- Cortical reorganization requires a high motivational drive.
- Cortical reorganization emerges in response to a heavy training schedule, i.e., several hours a day, several days in succession (massed practice).
- Cortical reorganization can be evoked in response to a lesion of cortical tissue in closely related cortical regions.

## Developmental plasticity of representational zones: Examples

THE SOMATOSENSORY SYSTEM As illustrated in figure 14.1, an invasion of the hand area by the face area can be found in upper-extremity amputees, this reorganization of the representational map contralateral to the side of the amputation resulting in hemispheric asymmetry of the center of activity of the lip representation. The hemispheric asymmetry of the lip representation in relation to the hand representation has proved a valid and reliable measure of the amount of cortical reorganization in amputees (Elbert et al., 1994a, 1997; Flor et al., 1995). This asymmetry is plotted for adult subjects in figure 14.2 as a function of the age of the amputation (chronicity > 5 years). The significant cor-

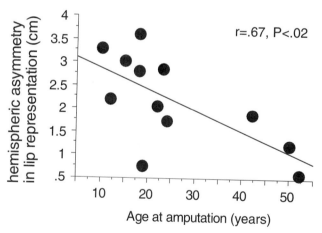

FIGURE 14.2 The center of activity of the lip representation in the hemisphere ipsi- and contralateral to the side of amputation was determined for 12 upper-extremity amputees using magnetic source imaging. The asymmetry of the lip representations between the contra- and the ipsilateral hemisphere was taken as indicator for the shift of the area of lip representation into the hand area contralateral to the side of amputation (ordinate). This asymmetry is plotted against the age of amputation (abscissa). The significant correlation of .67 confirms the more pronounced asymmetry, that is, a more pronounced invasion of the lip into the hand representational zone contralateral to the side of the amputation for individuals who suffered from an amputation at an earlier age.

relation suggests that the capacity for reorganization is greater in children than in adults. In addition, if the alteration in functional organization occurs during development, it may result in abnormal structural organization. Dettmers and colleagues (1999), for instance, demonstrated a lack of the characteristic shape of the central sulcus contralateral to amputation in a 21-year-old patient, who had undergone upper-extremity amputation at the age of seven.

A greater capacity for cortical reorganization during development than during adulthood has been demonstrated not only for injury-related but also for use-dependent alterations. Consider, for example, musicians, who usually practice for hours a day over many years to achieve their specific skills. String instrument players provide a good model for the study of behaviorally relevant use-dependent plasticity. During their practice and performance, the second to the fifth digits (D2–D5) of the left hand are continuously engaged in fingering the strings, while the thumb (D1), which grasps the neck of the instrument, is less active than the fingers. The right-hand task of manipulating the bow involves much less individual finger movement. In musicians, the center of the cortical representational zone of D1 and D5 of the left hand was found to be shifted by 0.5–0.7 cm compared to control subjects who played no instrument, while the strength of the response increased (Elbert et al., 1995). No such group difference was found for the representation of the right hand. A sensitive period of neural plasticity is indicated by the correlation between the age at which the string players began studying their instruments and the magnitude of change in the neural response to D5, as shown in figure 14.3 (top). The representational zone was largest in those subjects who had begun regular practice before the age of 13, that is, before puberty. However, even if regular practice started later in life, the extension of the representational zone of the digits of the left hand still exceeded that of control subjects. The amount of practice in adulthood did not covary with the neuronal response, indicating saturation of the use-dependent changes after years of practice.

THE AUDITORY SYSTEM Playing an instrument involves not only increased sensory input but also increased simultaneous somatosensory and auditory stimulation. Pantev and colleagues (1998) examined skilled musicians with "perfect pitch" hearing skill, musicians without this ability, and subjects who had never played an instrument. Piano tones and sinus tones served as auditory stimuli. All subjects exhibited a tonotopic organization of the auditory cortex, with a more lateral representation of lower frequencies in response.

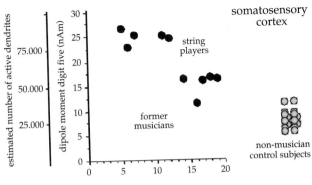

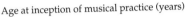

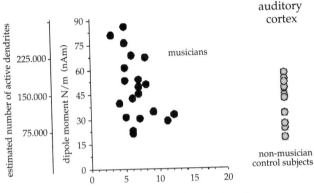

peatedly heard in a behaviorally relevant context—but not for sinus tones, which occur neither in the natural environment nor in musical practice—provides a striking example for *experience*-induced plasticity.

The studies by Elbert and colleagues (1995) and Pantev and colleagues (1998) indicate not only the advantage of juvenile plasticity, but also the maintained neuronal plasticity in adulthood. Similar evidence for the maintenance of juvenile plasticity into adulthood was obtained from animal studies. For example, Knudsen (1998) reported a better adjustment of interaural time differences and the locations of visual receptive fields in young compared to old owls, but also in adult owls who had previously learned abnormal associations between interaural time differences and visual receptive fields as juveniles. Knudsen concludes that learning abnormal associations early in life leaves an enduring trace in the tectal pathway that permits unusual functional connections to be reestablished, as needed, in adulthood, even when the associations represented by these connections have not been used for an extended period of time.

## Developmental plasticity of cognitive functioning: Language

There is compelling evidence that neonates, and even fetuses, are endowed with a remarkable sensitivity to phonetic units used in human speech. For example, DeCasper and Spence (1986) demonstrated that newborns are able to differentiate novel prose passages from those they have heard in the womb during the last 6 prenatal weeks (conceptional age 35–40 weeks). Infants in their first months of life were found to discriminate and categorically perceive consonants in syllables such as /ba/, /da/, and /ga/ (Eimas, 1974) or vowels such as /i/ and /a/ (Kuhl, 1979). This ability is also evident for the phonetic contrasts that infants have never heard (Kuhl et al., 1997b). Although the English phonemic contrast /r/ versus /l/ is not used to distinguish meaning in Japanese language, 6-month-old infants raised in a Japanese home were found to perceive the difference between the syllables /ra/ and /la/. However, by the age of 12 months, the performance resembled that of Japanese adults, who often exhibit great difficulty discriminating words containing these nonnative phonetic segments. Thus, the sensitivity to speech information is tuned to phonemic contrasts that are common to the infant's native language during the first year of life. Incidentally, linguistic experience may also alter speech production. Kuhl and Meltzoff (1996) observed that American infants as young as 5 months imitated specific speech sounds (vowels) after having

FIGURE 14.3  *Top:* Neural activation resulting from tactile stimulation of the fifth digit of the left hand as expressed by the dipole moment is plotted against the age at which subjects began musical practice. Compared to the healthy controls, musicians with early onset of training show the greatest amount of activation, but even those who began playing the instrument later in life showed significantly larger activation than the nonmusician controls. Musicians who ceased to play the instrument (former musicians) show considerably lower activation (data from Elbert et al., 1995). *Bottom:* Mean dipole moment elicited by piano tones as a function of the age at which musical training began in musicians and nonmusician control subjects (data from Pantev et al., 1998).

In nonmusicians, the representations did not differ between piano tones and sinus tones, whereas musicians showed an expanded representation of piano tones, as indicated by a 25% increased dipole strength relative to sinus tones. As reported for the sensory representations in string players, the enlarged representational zone of piano tones in the left auditory cortex correlated significantly with the (younger) age of inception of musical practice; the enlargement was most pronounced in subjects who had started before the age of nine, as shown in figure 14.3 (bottom). The use-dependent change in the auditory representational zones found only for those stimuli (piano tones) that had been re-

been exposed to them in the laboratory for just 15 minutes. Comparing French, North American, Japanese, and Swedish infants in a longitudinal study, de Boysson-Bardies and Vihman (1991) found that the frequency distribution of uttered consonants became more language-specific by the age of 10 months. It is tempting to speculate that this "sensitive" period for experience-based phoneme discrimination may explain, at least in part, why adults have much more trouble learning and speaking a foreign language without accent or speaking their own language without dialect (Flege, 1993). However, the principles of neural plasticity, as outlined previously, suggest that massed practice in a behaviorally relevant setting should allow mastery of these problems. Indeed, Bradlow and colleagues (1997) demonstrated that adult Japanese learned to produce English /r/ and /l/ distinctions after perceptual training. It has also been shown that actors lose their accents in the course of their intensive training in drama school. These results, though, raise the question of why similar training success is rarely observed in everyday life. One might suspect that being a subject in a scientific study—one that might include a financial bonus for participation or a reward for correct performance—would excite a stronger motivation and impetus for learning. The same may hold for actors, with the prospect of ambitious roles. Moreover, learning a second language at school can be satisfying at a lower level of language performance and accent (Schumann, 1997). (A foreign accent preserves part of the cultural identity, thereby rendering the person more interesting to others.)

The neuronal correlates of sound sensitivity to human speech and the transition from a language-universal to a language-specific pattern of speech perception have been elucidated by Cheour and colleagues (Cheour et al., 1998; Cheour-Luhtanen et al., 1996). They determined the mismatch negativity (MMN) from the event-related brain potentials (ERP), a negative deflection that is elicited by infrequent acoustic changes (deviant stimulus) in a train of homogeneous (standard) stimuli even though subjects do not pay attention to the deviant stimuli. The MMN is considered to reflect a neuronal mismatch between a deviant auditory input and a sensory memory trace storing the physical features of the acoustic standard events, as well as temporal information such as verbal and prosodic information (Näätänen, 1992; Näätänen and Winkler, 1999). Similar to adults or children, Finnish preterm infants (conceptional age 30–35 weeks at the time of recording) showed a MMN to a deviant phoneme, the vowel /i/, in the train of standard stimuli, the vowel /y/ (Cheour-Luhtanen et al., 1996). It seems unlikely that the premature infants had learned sound discrimination only

during their first days of life. Rather, the results indicate that neural traces of the basic properties of speech might have originated in the fetal brain. In another study by Cheour and colleagues (1998), Finnish and Estonian infants from monolingual families listened to the frequent standard vowel /e/ (which is shared by Finnish and Estonian languages), which was occasionally replaced either by the Finish vowel /ö/ (which is also used in Estonian) or by the uniquely Estonian vowel /õ/. The difference between the physical acoustic characteristics of the vowels /e/ and /ö/ was smaller than the difference between /e/ and /õ/. In 6-month-old Finns, the MMN was slightly more pronounced for the Estonian /õ/ than for the Finnish /ö/; that is, it was larger for the more pronounced change in acoustic characteristics. At 12 months of age, however, the same Finnish infants responded with the larger MMN to the mother-tongue vowel /ö/, whereas the Estonian 12-month-old children did not exhibit any differences in MMN amplitude for both deviant phonemes. The MMN in 12-month-old Finns and Estonians paralleled those of adult native speakers of these languages (Näätänen et al., 1997). This demonstrates that neural traces of language-dependent phonemes emerge between 6 and 12 months of age.

A study by Kuhl and colleagues (1997a) demonstrates how infants establish phoneme representation. Universally in the world's languages, speech directed toward infants (often called "motherese" or "parentese") is characterized by exaggerated intonation, higher pitch, slower cadence, and simplified sentences. This was confirmed for native-speaking women of American English, Russian, and Swedish, in particular for the vowels /i/, /a/, and /u/, when speaking with their 2- to 5-month-old infants, but not when addressing adults. These vowels form a "vowel triangle" in the acoustic frequency space. A comparison of the representational zone of the vowel triangle for adult- versus infant-directed speech revealed a considerable expansion (figure 14.4). Kuhl and coworkers suggest that such a stretching of the vowel triangle helps infants by enhancing the acoustic distance between vowels, making sound contrasts more distinctive, and by emphasizing the acoustic cues relevant for speech categorization. Because vocal tracts are smaller in infants than in adults, these acoustic cues allow infants to imitate sound units in their own frequency range. Indeed, at 5 months of age, infants' babbling consists of vowel sounds shaping a higher pitched vowel triangle in phonetic space (Kuhl and Meltzoff, 1996). Thus, infants begin life with a sophisticated speech processing capability. During the first year of life the general sensitivity undergoes a change and becomes attuned to those phonetic units needed to distinguish

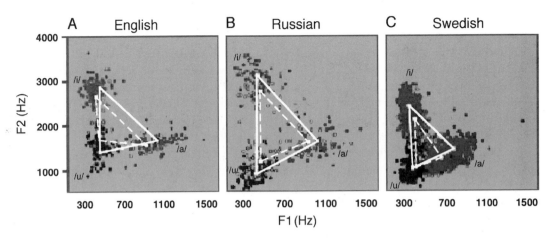

FIGURE 14.4   Vowel triangles formed by the point vowels, /i/, /a/, and /u/, in infant- and adult-directed speech in three languages—English, Russian, and Swedish. Each data point represents the coordinate of the first two formant frequencies of a vowel. A universal stretching of the vowel triangle is observed in infant-directed (solid line) relative to adult-directed (dashed line) speech. (Adapted from Kuhl et al., 1997a.)

meaning in one's native language. This alteration occurs in linguistic experience and provides the basis of rapid and effortless language acquisition. By the time of their first birthday, infants speak several words; by the age of two years, they have a vocabulary of about 50 words and can produce two-word or even multiword combinations (Bates, O'Connell, and Shore, 1987). But if linguistic experience is not forthcoming in an early period of life, speech and language development are hampered. Deaf children who have never been exposed to either spoken or manually coded speech (Goldin-Meadow, 1997) or children who experience severe deprivation of social stimulation by humans (Brown, 1966; Curtiss, 1977) do not acquire language properly. This indicates a "sensitive" period for the development of language ("sensitive" implying the potential to acquire speech discrimination, thus the potential of neural plasticity, in contrast to "critical," which implies invariance; see, for example, Tees and Werker, 1984).

However, even if not suffering from hearing loss or social isolation, some preschool children have great difficulty in acquiring language. In many cases, language disabilities cannot be attributed to mental retardation, psychiatric disorders (e.g., childhood schizophrenia, infantile autism), or neurological causes (e.g., focal brain lesions, seizure disorders). These language-based learning disorders are referred to as specific language impairment (SLI). When they reach school age, children with SLI are at risk for learning problems similar to those seen in dyslexics (Aram, Ekelman, and Nation, 1984; Tallal, Curtiss, and Kaplan, 1988). Conversely, children with developmental dyslexia are typically found to be deficient in some linguistic tasks (see Catts,

1996; Kamhi and Catts, 1989). For many children with SLI and dyslexia, deficient auditory phoneme processing has been confirmed by psychoacoustic studies (Reed, 1989; Stark and Heinz, 1996; Tallal and Piercy, 1974, 1975; Tallal and Stark, 1981; Tallal, Stark, and Mellits, 1985a; for reviews see Farmer and Klein, 1995; Tallal, Miller, and Fitch, 1993). Tallal and colleagues assumed an impaired integration of brief and rapidly changing sounds to be at the basis of SLI, as deficits in stop consonant perception turned out to be correlated with language comprehension scores of SLI children (Tallal, Stark, and Mellits, 1985b). Furthermore, Kraus and colleagues (1996) observed a nearly absent mismatch response to deviant stop consonant-vowel syllables in language- and learning-impaired children. Moreover, the physiological dysfunction was corroborated by the impairment in discriminating these phonemes (viz. /da/ versus /ga/). A relatively attenuated MMN to the phonetic contrast /ba/-/da/ in dyslexic boys was also reported by Schulte-Körne and colleagues (1998). From the explication of the MMN outlined above, it may be concluded that the neural memory traces do not serve as reliable recognition patterns for rapidly changing phonetic contrasts in children with SLI and dyslexia. Determining the sources of the stop consonant-vowel syllables /da/ and /ga/ in the auditory cortex of children with dyslexia from magneto-encephalographic recordings, Heim and colleagues (2000) found that the brain structures generating the magnetic waves at 200 ms were located about 1.5 cm more anterior in children with dyslexia than in normal controls. This difference was also evident relative to the source location of the earlier component at 80 ms, which showed identical topographical distribution in both groups. This finding cannot be attributed to gross anatomical variations, but suggests an abnormal functional organization of auditory cortex in children with dyslexia. Merzenich and Tallal found that impaired processing of rapidly changing sounds could be greatly improved in 5- to 10-year-old children with SLI (Merzenich et al., 1996; Tallal et al., 1996). Considering both the mechanisms of neural plasticity and the inaccurate representation of rapidly changing phonemes in the auditory cortex of SLI children, they designed a computer-based training program. Children were submitted to a training including audiovisual "games" for about 100 min/day extended over four weeks with five training days a week. Rapid transitional speech and nonspeech stimuli were initially disambiguated by prolonging them in time and/or amplifying them (a procedure reminiscent of "parentese"). As training progressed and the children demonstrated success, the modified acoustic stimuli were presented at rates that became closer and closer to those that occur in natural speech. The hypothesis that improper stimulation (e.g., a history of chronic middle ear infection) has originally caused a deficient auditory organization in dyslexic/SLI children is highly speculative. But whatever the cause, there is considerable evidence that training-induced stimulation triggers improvement through processes related to cortical reorganization. Infants who are poor at processing rapidly changing sounds can be identified during the first year of life. Within this sensitive period an intervention employing acoustic perceptual training can be efficient. The deficit in processing acoustic signals might even be corrected before SLI and dyslexia have developed.

In a similar way, cortical reorganization through training-induced stimulation during sensitive periods may affect other cognitive functions such as learning and memory. Since this is the topic of other contributions in this volume, we add only a few concluding remarks. Developmental plasticity of cognitive functions is certainly more difficult to investigate than is developmental plasticity of sensory functions. The organization of cognitive function is more difficult to model than is that of the sensory cortex, and it is more difficult to validate the model through animal studies. It is more difficult to disentangle the function affected by experience and learning from the variety of functions that together constitute "intellect." Perceptual learning leads to the expansion of stimulus representation in the cortex, and associative learning may be viewed as an expansion of the cortical representation of the complex perceptual event (Gaffan, 1996).

However, there is promising evidence that experience improves skills, possibly through cortical reorganization. For instance, animals raised in enriched environments, trained on new and complex motor tasks, or surrounded by information to be learned show an increase of brain volume and thickness and increases in the number of synapses, relative to, for instance, enhanced motor activity without information or learning challenge—changes that regressed when the animals were removed from the enriched environment (Nelson, 1999). Thus the brain is a highly dynamic organ, permanently adapting its functional and structural architecture to environmental needs. According to Heraclitus, "We cannot enter the same river twice." New water always flows by. As for us, we become different with every new experience.

ACKNOWLEDGMENTS This research was supported by the Deutsche Forschungsgemeinschaft and by the Volkswagen-Stiftung.

## REFERENCES

ALLARD, T., S. A. CLARK, W. M. JENKINS, and M. M. MERZENICH, 1991. Reorganization of somatosensory area 3b representations in adult owl monkeys after digital syndactyly. *J. Neurophysiol.* 66:1048–1058.

ALLOWAY, K. D., and G. B. AARON, 1996. Adaptive changes in the somatotopic properties of individual thalamic neurons immediately following microlesions in connected regions of the nucleus cuneatus. *Synapse* 22:1–14.

ARAM, D. M., B. L. EKELMAN, and J. E. NATION, 1984. Preschoolers with language disorders: 10 years later. *J. Speech Hear. Res.* 27:232–244.

BATES, E., B. O'CONNELL, and C. SHORE, 1987. Language and communication in infancy. In *Handbook of Infant Development*, 2nd ed., J. D. Osofsky, ed. New York: John Wiley and Sons, pp. 149–203.

BRADLOW, A. R., D. B. PISONI, R. AKAHANE-YAMADA, and Y. TOHKURA, 1997. Training Japanese listeners to identify English /r/ and /l/: IV. Some effects of perceptual learning on speech production. *J. Acoust. Soc. Am.* 101:2299–2310.

BRAUN, K., 1996. Synaptic reorganization processes accompanying early childhood experiences and learning: Relevance for the etiology of mental disorders. *Zt. Klin. Psychol.* 44:253–266.

BROWN, R., 1966. *Words and Things.* New York: The Free Press.

CHALDJI, C., B. TANNENBAUM, S. SHARMA, D. FRANCIS, P. PLOTSKY, and M. J. MEANEY, 1998. Maternal care during infancy regulates the development of neural systems mediating the expression of fearfulness in the rat. *PNAS* 95:5335–5340.

CALFORD, M. B., and R. TWEEDALE, 1988. Immediate chronic changes in responses of somatosensory cortex in adult flying-fox after digit amputation. *Nature* 332:446–448.

CALFORD, M. B., and R. TWEEDALE, 1990. Interhemispheric transfer of plasticity in the cerebral cortex. *Science* 249:805–807.

CALFORD, M. B., and R. TWEEDALE, 1991. Immediate expansion of receptive fields of neurons in area 3b of macaque monkeys after digit denervation. *Somatosens. Motor Res.* 8:249–260.

CANDIA, V., T. ELBERT, E. ALTENMÜLLER, H. RAU, T. SCHÄFER, and E. TAUB, 1999. A constraint-induced movement therapy for focal hand dystonia in musicians. *Lancet* 353:1–2.

CATTS, H. W., 1996. Defining dyslexia as a developmental language disorder: An expanded view. *Topics Lang. Disorders* 16:14–29.

CHEOUR, M., R. CEPONIENE, A. LEHTOKOSKI, A. LUUK, J. ALLIK, K. ALHO, and R. NÄÄTÄNEN, 1998. Development of language-specific phoneme representations in the infant brain. *Nature Neurosci.* 1:351–353.

CHEOUR-LUHTANEN, M., K. ALHO, K. SAINIO, T. RINNE, K. REINIKAINEN, M. POHJAVUORI, M. RENLUND, O. AALTONEN, O. EEROLA, and R. NÄÄTÄNEN, 1996. The ontogenetically earliest discriminative response of the human brain. *Psychophysiology* 33:478–481.

CLARK, S. A., T. ALLARD, W. M. JENKINS, and M. M. MERZENICH, 1988. Receptive fields in the body-surface map in adult cortex defined by temporally correlated inputs. *Nature* 332:444–445.

CURTISS, S., 1977. *Genie: A Psycholinguistic Study of a Modern-Day "Wild Child."* New York: Academic Press.

DE BOYSSON-BARDIES, B., and M. M. VIHMAN, 1991. Adaptation to language: Evidence from babbling and first words in four languages. *Language* 67:297–319.

DECASPER, A. J., and M. J. SPENCE, 1986. Prenatal maternal speech influences newborns' perception of speech sounds. *Infant Behav. Dev.* 9:133–150.

DETTMERS, C., J. LIEPERT, T. ADLER, R. RZANNY, M. RIJNTES, R. VAN SCHAYCK, W. KAISER, L. BRÜCKNER, and C. WEILLER, 1999. Abnormal motor cortex organization contralateral to early upper limb amputation in humans. *Neurosci. Lett.* 263:41–44.

EIMAS, P. D., 1974. Auditory and linguistic processing of cues for place of articulation by infants. *Percept. Psychophysics* 16:513–521.

ELBERT, T., C. CANDIA, E. ALTENMÜLLER, H. RAU, A. STERR, B. ROCKSTROH, C. PANTEV, and E. TAUB, 1998. Alterations of digital representations in somatosensory cortex in focal hand dystonia. *NeuroReport* 9:3571–3575.

ELBERT, T., H. FLOR, N. BIRBAUMER, S. KNECHT, S. HAMPSON, W. LARBIG, and E. TAUB, 1994a. Extensive reorganization of the somatosensory cortex in adult humans after nervous system injury. *NeuroReport* 5:2593–2597.

ELBERT, T., C. PANTEV, C. WIENBRUCH, B. ROCKSTROH, and E. TAUB, 1995. Increased use of the left hand in string players associated with increased cortical representation of the fingers. *Science* 220:21–23.

ELBERT, T., W. J. RAY, Z. B. J. KOWALIK, J. E. SKINNER, K. E. GRAF, and N. BIRBAUMER, 1994b. Chaos and physiology: Deterministic chaos in excitable cell assemblies. *Physiol. Rev.* 74:1–47.

ELBERT, T., A. STERR, H. FLOR, B. ROCKSTROH, S. KNECHT, C. PANTEV, C. WIENBRUCH, and E. TAUB, 1997. Input-increase and input-decrease types of cortical reorganization after upper extremity amputation. *Exp. Brain Res.* 117:161–164.

ENGERT, F., and T. BONHOEFFER, 1999. Dendritic spine changes associated with hippocampal long-term synaptic plasticity. *Nature* 399:66–70.

FLOR, H., T. ELBERT, S. KNECHT, C. WIENBRUCH, C. PANTEV, N. BIRBAUMER, W. LARBIG, and E. TAUB, 1995. Phantom-

limb pain as a perceptual correlates of cortical reorganization following arm amputation. *Nature* 375:482–484.

FARMER, M. E., and R. M. KLEIN, 1995. The evidence for a temporal processing deficit linked to dyslexia: A review. *Psychonom. Bull. Rev.* 2:460–493.

FLEGE, J. E., 1993. Production and perception of a novel, second-language phonetic contrast. *J. Acoust. Soc. Am.* 93:1589–1608.

GAFFAN, D., 1996. Associative and perceptual learning and the concept of memory systems. *Cogn. Brain Res.* 5:69–80.

GERLOFF, C., 1999. Motorik. In *Biologische Grundlagen der Psychologie, Enzyklopädie der Psychologie*, T. Elbert and N. Birbaumer, eds. Verlag: C. Hogrefe, Göttingen. (in press)

GOLDIN-MEADOW, S., 1997. The resilience of language in humans. In *Social Influences on Vocal Development*, C. T. Snowdon and M. Hausberger, eds. Cambridge: Cambridge University Press, pp. 293–311.

GRIGORIEVA, L. P., 1996. Perceptual learning in overcoming the impacts of visual deprivation in children with low vision. *Human Physiol.* 22:591–596.

HEBB, O. D., 1949. *The organization of behavior: A neurophysiological theory.* New York: Wiley.

HEIM, S., C. EULITZ, J. KAUFMANN, I. FÜCHTER, C. PANTEV, A. LAMPRECHT-DINNESEN, P. MATULAT, P. SCHEER, M. BORSTEL, and T. ELBERT. 2000. Atypical organisation of the auditory cortex in dyslexia as revealed by MEG. *Neuropsychologia* 38:1749–1759.

IRVINE, D. R. F., and R. RAJAN, 1996. Injury- and use-related plasticity in the primary sensory cortex of adult mammals: Possible relationship to perceptual learning. *Clin. Exp. Pharmacol. Physiol.* 23:939–947.

JENKINS, W. M., M. M. MERZENICH, M. T. OCHS, T. ALLARD, and E. GUÍC-ROBLES, 1990. Functional reorganization of primary somatosensory cortex in adult owl monkeys after behaviorally controlled tactile stimulation. *J. Neurophysiol.* 63:82–104.

KAMHI, A., and H. CATTS (EDS.), 1989. *Reading Disabilities: A Developmental Language Perspective.* Boston: Allyn & Bacon.

KARNI, A., G. MEYER, P. JAZZARD, M. M. ADAMS, R. TURNER, and L. G. UNGERLEIDER, 1995. Functional MRI evidence for adult motor plasticity during motor skill learning. *Nature* 377:155–158.

KELAHAN, A. M., and G. S. DOETSCH, 1984. Time-dependent changes in the functional organization of somatosensory cerebral cortex following digit amputation. *Somatosens. Res.* 2:49–81.

KILGARD, M., and M. M. MERZENICH, 1998. Cortical map reorganization enabled by nucleus basalis activity. *Science* 279:1715–1718.

KNUDSEN, E. I., 1998. Capacity for plasticity in the adult owl auditory system expanded by juvenile experience. *Science* 279:1531–1533.

KOLB, B., and I. Q. WHISHAW, 1998. Brain plasticity and behavior. *Annu. Rev. Psychol.* 49:43–64.

KRAUS, N., T. J. MCGEE, T. D. CARRELL, S. G. ZECKER, T. G. NICOL, and D. B. KOCH, 1996. Auditory neurophysiologic responses and discrimination deficits in children with learning problems. *Science* 273:971–973.

KUHL, P. K., 1979. Speech perception in early infancy: Perceptual constancy for spectrally dissimilar vowel categories. *J. Acoust. Soc. Am.* 66:1668–1679.

KUHL, P. K., J. E. ANDRUSKI, I. A. CHISTOVICH, L. A. CHISTOVICH, E. V. KOZHEVNIKOVA, V. L. RYSKINA, E. I. STOLYAROVA,

U. SUNDBERG, and F. LACERDA, 1997a. Cross-language analysis of phonetic units in language addressed to infants. *Science* 277:684–686.

KUHL, P. K., S. KIRITANI, T. DEGUCHI, A. HAYASHI, E. B. STEVENS, C. D. DUGGER, and P. IVERSON, 1997b. Effects of language experience on speech perception: American and Japanese infants' perception of |ral and |lal. *J. Acoust. Soc. Am.* 102:3135–3136.

KUHL, P. K., and A. N. MELTZOFF, 1996. Infant vocalizations in response to speech: Vocal imitation and developmental change. *J. Acoust. Soc. Am.* 100:2425–2438.

MÄKELÄ, J. P, T. ELBERT, R. KAKIGI, L. LOPEZ, T. NAGAMINE, N. NAKASATO, and W. SANNITA, 2000. MEG: Clinical applications. In *Advances in Biomagnetism Research: Biomag96*, C. Aine, Y. Okada, G. Stroink, S. Swithenby, and C. Wood, eds. New York: Springer-Verlag, pp. 980–990.

MARKRAM, H., J. LÜBKE, M. FROTSCHER, and B. SAKMANN, 1997. Regulation of synaptic efficacy by coincidence of postsynaptic APs and EPSPs. *Science,* 275:213–215.

MEANEY, M. J., J. DIORIO, D. FRANCIS, J. WIDDOWSON, P. LAPLANTE, C. CALDJI, S. SHARMA, J. R. SECKL, and P. M. PLOTSKY, 1996. Early environmental regulation of forebrain glucocorticoid receptor gene expression: Implications for adrenocortical responses to stress. *Dev. Neurosci.* 18:49–72.

MEANEY, M., D. AITKEN, C. VAN BERKEL, C. BHATNAGAR, and R. SAPOLSKY, 1988. Effects of neonatal handling on age-related impairments associated with the hippocampus. *Science* 239:766–770.

MERZENICH, M. M., and W. M. JENKINS, 1993. Reorganization of cortical representations of the hand following alterations of skin inputs induced by nerve injury, skin island transfers and experience. *J. Hand Therapy* 6:89–104.

MERZENICH, M. M., W. M. JENKINS, P. JOHNSTON, C. SCHREINER, S. L. MILLER, and P. TALLAL, 1996. Temporal processing deficits of language-learning impaired children ameliorated by training. *Science* 271:77–81.

MERZENICH, M. M., R. J. NELSON, M. P. STRYKER, M. S. CYNADER, A. SCHOPPMANN, and J. M. ZOOK, 1984. Somatosensory cortical map changes following digit amputation in adult monkeys. *J. Comp. Neurol.* 224:591–605.

MOGILNER, A., J. A. I. GROSSMAN, U. RIBARY, M. JOLIOT, J. VOLKMANN, D. RAPAPORT, R. W. BEASLEY, and R. R. LLINAS, 1993. Somatosensory cortical plasticity in adult humans revealed by magnetoencephalography. *Proc. Natl. Acad. Sci. (USA)* 90:3593–3597.

NÄÄTÄNEN, R., 1992. *Attention and Brain Function.* Hillsdale, N.J.: Erlbaum.

NÄÄTÄNEN, R., A. LEHTOKOSKI, M. LENNES, M. CHEOUR, M. HUOTILAINEN, A. IIVONEN, M. VAINIO, P. ALKU, R. J. ILMONIEMI, A. LUUK, J. ALLIK, J. SINKKONEN, and K. ALHO, 1997. Language-specific phoneme representations revealed by electric and magnetic brain responses. *Nature* 385:432–434.

NÄÄTÄNEN, R., and I. WINKLER, 1999. The concept of auditory stimulus representation in cognitive neuroscience. *Psychol. Bull.* 125:826–859.

NELSON, C. A., 1999. Neural plasticity and human development. *Curr. Direct. Psychol. Sci.* 8:42–45.

PANTEV, C., R. OOSTENVELD, A. ENGELIEN, B. ROSS, L. E. ROBERTS, and M. HOKE, 1998. Increased auditory cortical representations in musicians. *Nature* 392:811–814.

PONS, T. P., P. E. GARRAGHTY, A. K. OMMAYA, J. H. KAAS, E. TAUB, and M. MISHKIN, 1991. Massive cortical reorganization after sensory deafferentation in adult macaques. *Science* 252:1857–1860.

POST, R., and S. R. WEISS, 1997. Emergent properties of neural systems: How focal molecular neurobiological alterations can affect behavior. *Dev. Psychopathol.* 9:907–929.

PULVERMÜLLER, F., 1999. Words in the brain's language. *Behav. Brain Sci.* 22:253–279.

RAMEY, C. T., and S. L. RAMEY, 1998. Prevention of intellectual disabilities: Early interventions to improve cognitive development. *Prevent. Med.* 27:224–232.

RECANZONE, G. H., M. M. MERZENICH, W. M. JENKINS, K. A. GRAJSKI, and H. R. DINSE, 1992. Topographic reorganization of the hand representation in cortical area 3b of owl monkeys trained in a frequency-discrimination task. *J. Neurophysiol.* 67:1031–1056.

REED, M. A., 1989. Speech perception and the discrimination of brief auditory cues in reading disabled children. *J. Exp. Child Psychol.* 48:270–292.

SCHULTE-KÖRNE, G., W. DEIMEL, J. BARTLING, and H. REMSCHMIDT, 1998. Auditory processing and dyslexia: Evidence for a specific speech processing deficit. *NeuroReport* 9:337–340.

SCHUMANN, J. H., 1997. *The Neurobiology of Affect in Language.* Malden, Mass.: Blackwell Publishers.

SECKL, J. R., and M. J. MEANEY, 1993. Early life events and later development of ischaemic heart disease. *Lancet* 342:1236.

STARK, R. E., and J. M. HEINZ, 1996. Perception of stop consonants in children with expressive and receptive-expressive language impairments. *J. Speech Hear. Res.* 39:676–686.

STARK, R. E., and P. TALLAL, 1979. Analysis of stop consonant production errors in developmentally dysphasic children. *J. Acoust. Soc. Am.* 66:1703–1712.

STERR, A., M. MÜLLER, T. ELBERT, B. ROCKSTROH, and E. TAUB, 1998a. Changed perceptions in Braille readers. *Nature* 391:134–135.

STERR, A., M. MÜLLER, T. ELBERT, B. ROCKSTROH, and E. TAUB, 1998b. Perceptual correlates of use-dependent changes in cortical representation of the fingers in blind Braille readers. *J. Neurosci.* 18:4417–4423.

TALLAL, P., S. CURTISS, and R. KAPLAN, 1988. The San Diego longitudinal study: Evaluating the outcomes of preschool impairment in language development. In *International Perspectives on Communication Disorders,* S. E. Gerber and G. T. Mencher, eds. Washington, D.C.: Gallaudet University Press, pp. 86–126.

TALLAL, P., S. L. MILLER, G. BEDI, G. BYMA, X. WANG, S. S. NAGARAJAN, C. SCHREINER, W. M. JENKINS, and M. M. MERZENICH, 1996. Language comprehension in language-learning impaired children improved with acoustically modified speech. *Science* 271:81–84.

TALLAL, P., S. MILLER, and R. H. FITCH, 1993. Neurobiological basis of speech: A case for the preeminence of temporal processing. *Ann. N.Y. Acad. Sci.* 682:27–47.

TALLAL, P., and M. PIERCY, 1974. Developmental aphasia: Rate of auditory processing and selective impairment of consonant perception. *Neuropsychologia* 12:83–93.

TALLAL, P., and M. PIERCY, 1975. Developmental aphasia: The perception of brief vowels and extended stop consonants. *Neuropsychologia* 13:69–74.

TALLAL, P., and R. E. STARK, 1981. Speech acoustic-cue discrimination abilities of normally developing and language-impaired children. *J. Acoust. Soc. Am.* 69:568–574.

TALLAL, P., R. E. STARK, and E. D. MELLITS, 1985a. Identification of language-impaired children on the basis of rapid perception and production skills. *Brain Lang.* 25:314–322.

TALLAL, P., R. E. STARK, and E. D. MELLITS, 1985b. The relationship between auditory temporal analysis and receptive language development: Evidence from studies of developmental language disorder. *Neuropsychologia* 23:527–534.

TEES, R. C., and J. F. WERKER, 1984. Perceptual flexibility: Maintenance or recovery of the ability to discriminate nonnative speech sounds. *Can. J. Psychol.* 38:579–590.

TURRIGIANO, G. G., K. R. LESLIE, N. S. DEAI, L. C. RUTHERFORD, and S. B. NELSON, 1998. Activity-dependent scaling of quantal amplitude in neocortical neurons. *Nature* 391:892–896.

WANG, X., M. M. MERZENICH, K. SAMESHIMA, and W. M. JENKINS, 1995. Remodeling of hand representation in adult cortex determined by timing of tactile stimulation. *Nature* 378:71–75.

WEINERT, F. E. (ED.), 1998. *Entwicklung im Kindesalter.* Weinheim: PVU.

WEINERT, F. E., and W. SCHNEIDER (EDS.), 1998. *Individual Development from 3 to 12.* New York: Cambridge University Press.

WICKELGREN, I., 1999. Nurture helps mold able minds. *Science* 283:1832–1834.

# IV
# SENSORY AND
# SENSORIMOTOR
# SYSTEMS

# 15 Development, Plasticity, and Learning in the Auditory System

RICHARD N. ASLIN
AND RUSKIN H. HUNT

ABSTRACT   The human auditory system undergoes dramatic improvement in sensitivity between the onset of function in the last trimester of gestation and the end of the first postnatal year. These early limitations may constrain various aspects of sound discrimination and learning in young infants. Despite these limitations, the newborn is capable of rapid learning of suprathreshold auditory stimuli, rudimentary localization of sound, and elementary processing of complex auditory patterns such as speech. This chapter reviews these basic auditory capacities, examining how various brain mechanisms process both simple and complex sounds, and how these processing mechanisms are elaborated by maturation and experience.

Several weeks before the human newborn is first exposed to visual stimulation, auditory inputs are capable of stimulating hair cells on the basilar membrane, generating neural signals that travel from the auditory nerve to brainstem, thalamic, and cortical areas of the central nervous system, triggering behavioral responses, and establishing rudimentary representations that can affect behavioral preferences several days or weeks later. Newborns also exhibit preferences for certain classes of auditory stimulation and the ability to orient toward sounds, neither of which could have been induced by early experience. Because the apprehension of auditory stimulation does not require an overt attentional response (e.g., turning the eyes to fixate a visual stimulus directly), ambient auditory information is readily available to the developing infant. Given this combination of early maturation and ubiquitous stimulation, the auditory system would seem to be an ideal candidate for studying the sensory and perceptual mechanisms, and their neural correlates, that enable cognitive development.

Why, then, has relatively little attention been paid to the development of the auditory system compared to the visual system? And why do we know relatively little about how auditory information is processed by the developing brain? As we shall see, a variety of technical, methodological, and neuroarchitectural factors have

conspired to constrain access to the functioning of the auditory system. In addition, auditory phenomena only slightly more complex than basic psychoacoustic capacities have not been easily incorporated into a general model of auditory processing.

How can a cognitive neuroscience perspective facilitate progress in understanding the developing auditory system? As Johnson (1997, p. xv) pointed out, "Developmental cognitive neuroscience is specifically concerned with understanding the relation between neural and cognitive phenomena." It is hard to imagine a time when studies of sensory and perceptual development ignored underlying neural substrates. Yet those substrates remain largely inaccessible except in animal studies and recent attempts at various forms of noninvasive neuroimaging. The challenge is to meld together findings from invasive neuroscience, noninvasive neuroimaging, and behavioral studies of human infants and children to provide a coherent account of the mechanisms by which auditory processing develops.

In this chapter we provide a summary of the development of basic auditory capacities in infancy, and we discuss how infants perceive more complex auditory stimuli and how neural specializations for processing both simple and complex auditory signals emerge during development. We also review evidence of functional plasticity in the processing of auditory signals, both during development and in adulthood. Our goal is to provide a selective overview of classic and recent findings on auditory system development that can serve as a guide for future investigations of developmental cognitive neuroscience in the auditory modality.

## Fundamental auditory capacities in infancy

The intricacies of the development of the auditory periphery and the auditory pathways are beyond the scope of the present chapter. Fortunately, the interested reader can consult several recent reviews that cover these issues in great detail (Rubel, Popper, and Fay, 1998; Werner and Marean, 1996; Werner and Rubel,

RICHARD N. ASLIN AND RUSKIN H. HUNT   Department of Brain and Cognitive Sciences, University of Rochester, Rochester, New York.

1992). The goal of studying basic auditory capacities in infancy is not only to document the normative course of auditory development and its underlying neural mechanisms, but also to provide a context or baseline from which higher levels of auditory processing can be evaluated. For example, the speech perception literature (see Werker, this volume) has highlighted the sophisticated discriminative skills of very young infants. However, uncertainty remains as to whether limitations in these skills can be attributed to immaturities in the auditory system or to an underdeveloped speech perception mechanism per se.

THE ONSET OF HEARING   Across a variety of species, birth (or hatching) is a somewhat arbitrary developmental event with respect to the onset of sensory function. Some species, such as chickens and humans, are able to process auditory inputs very early in development. Other species, such as rats and cats, have a more protracted period of postnatal development before the auditory system becomes functional. Interestingly, the onset of hearing is generally correlated with the functional maturation of the auditory periphery (the movement of the ossicles of the middle ear, the mechanics of the basilar membrane, and the responsiveness of the hair cells of the inner ear), even though there are some exceptions to this trend (Saunders, Doan, and Cohen, 1993).

In humans, evidence from the intact fetus and from infants born prematurely suggests that auditory stimuli can elicit changes in heart rate (Lecanuet, Granier-Deferre, and Busnel, 1988), eye blinks (Birnholz and Benacerraf, 1983), gross motor responses (Kisilevsky, Muir, and Low, 1992), and auditory brainstem responses (ABRs; Hecox and Burkard, 1982) as early as the 28th week of gestation. However, behavioral responses to sound are often difficult to elicit in species that are motorically immature, even several weeks after clear evidence of physiological responses in both the peripheral and central auditory system (cats: Clements and Kelly, 1978; humans: Muir and Field, 1979).

ABSOLUTE THRESHOLDS AND INTENSITY DISCRIMINATION   Three techniques have been used to assess sound thresholds in human infants: the conditioned head-turning procedure (CHP; Moore, Thompson, and Thompson, 1975), the observer-based procedure (OBP; Olsho et al., 1987), and the ABR (Hecox, 1975). The latter two techniques have documented significant improvements in absolute thresholds between birth and 6 months of age, and the CHP has documented further improvements between 6 months and 2 years of age. The ABR in newborns is 10–15 dB less sensitive than in

adults (Hecox, 1975), and the OBP in 2-week-olds (Werner and Gillenwater, 1990) is up to 50 dB less sensitive. By 3 months of age, OBP thresholds are 15–30 dB poorer than those in adults (Olsho et al., 1988). The CHP has provided estimates of absolute thresholds in 6- to 18-month-olds for pure-tone and octave-band noise stimuli (Berg and Smith, 1983; Nozza and Wilson, 1984; Schneider, Trehub, and Bull, 1979, 1980; Sinnott, Pisoni, and Aslin, 1983; Trehub, Schneider, and Endman, 1980). Although estimates vary across studies, by 6 months of age absolute thresholds are approximately 10–20 dB poorer than in adults, and these estimates do not differ from those obtained using OBP (Olsho et al., 1988). It is important to note that thresholds obtained free-field with loudspeakers and, more recently, with head- or earphones have yielded very similar results.

These results, together with parallel improvements in ABR and OBP thresholds between 3 and 12 months of age, are consistent with the hypothesis that the fundamental limitation in auditory sensitivity is not due to peripheral auditory immaturities because estimates of peripheral sensitivity are superior to estimates of central sensitivity (Werner, Folsom, and Mancl, 1993, 1994). Unfortunately, more central neural responses are highly variable in infants and do not provide a clear picture of which central auditory areas are primarily responsible for postnatal developmental improvements in absolute thresholds (Stapells et al., 1988). Alternatively, behavioral responses to sound, particularly in younger infants, may be limited by attentional and motivational factors and/or by higher levels of internal noise. Evidence suggesting a role for attentional/motivational factors was provided by Werner and Mancl (1993) who reported that thresholds in 1-month-olds were superior when a reinforcer was used with OBP. In older infants, Bargones, Werner, and Marean (1995) noted that performance rarely reaches 100% correct on any testing procedure, and the slopes of infant psychometric functions (a measure of task sensitivity) are shallower than in adults. However, both Bargones et al. and Nozza (1995) have provided evidence that task variables do not account for the majority of the developmental differences observed between infants and adults, suggesting that these differences are primarily sensory in nature.

Evidence suggesting a role for higher levels of internal noise has not been obtained from newborns, but in 6- to 12-month-olds thresholds in noise are closer to adult values than thresholds in a quiet testing environment (Nozza and Wilson, 1984). The hypothesis that sensory systems in early infancy have higher levels of internal noise has received direct support in the visual system. Skoczenski and Aslin (1995) estimated internal noise by adding external noise to a visual stimulus. They reported that the level of external noise at which performance began to decline was much higher in infants than in adults.

Intensity discrimination has been studied using the CHP in 6-month-olds (Sinnott and Aslin, 1985) and 12-month-olds (Schneider, Bull, and Trehub, 1988). Thresholds to detect an intensity increment improved from 6 dB to 4 dB. Further improvement to 2 dB has been reported for preschoolers (Jensen and Neff, 1993), although this performance does not meet that of adults (less than 1 dB).

In summary, while there are significant postnatal improvements in absolute thresholds, many signals in the natural environment are accessible to young infants (and to the fetus) because they are well above threshold. The most serious limitation in this domain is not sensitivity per se, but the limited distribution of sounds of sufficient intensity to be detected by infants and the distortion introduced by sounds presented at high signal levels. Intensity discrimination is quite good by 6 months of age, but relatively little is known about this important capacity in younger infants.

FREQUENCY DISCRIMINATION, RESOLUTION, AND MASKING  The CHP has provided evidence that 6-month-old infants can discriminate an increment or decrement in frequency of approximately 2% for mid-frequency tones (Olsho, 1984; Olsho et al., 1982; Sinnott and Aslin, 1985). The OBP has confirmed this 2% threshold in 6-month-olds and shown that 3-month-olds have a slightly poorer threshold of 3% (Olsho, Koch, and Halpin, 1987). Interestingly, this developmental difference between 3-month-olds and 6-month-olds was not present at low frequencies (500 Hz). Bargones and Werner (1994) have shown that at least part of this frequency effect stems from an attentional process in which infants do not appear to attend selectively to the frequency range within which signals are presented. This off-frequency listening effect may be relevant to any task that benefits from selective attention to one of several alternative acoustic attributes.

Several studies have used the CHP to assess infants' thresholds for detecting a signal (either an octave-band noise or a pure tone) in the presence of either a narrow or broadband masking noise (Bull, Schneider, and Trehub, 1981; Nozza and Wilson, 1984; Olsho, 1985; Schneider, Morrongiello, and Trehub, 1990; Schneider et al., 1989; Spetner and Olsho, 1990). The masking noise elevated thresholds in infants and adults by the same relative amount, suggesting that frequency resolution is adultlike by 6 months of age. Similar results

have been obtained using the ABR (Abdala and Folsom, 1995; Folsom and Wynne, 1987). The Spetner and Olsho (1990) study used OBP to test 3-month-olds as well as 6-month-olds. While the effects of masking at 500 and 1000 Hz were similar at these two ages, detection at 4000 Hz was affected by a broader range of frequencies in 3-month-olds. Thus, there is evidence that at these higher frequencies young infants are less able to resolve small differences in frequency in the presence of other auditory stimuli. Interestingly, Werner and Bargones (1991) showed that even in 6-month-olds, who have adultlike frequency resolution, it is possible to distract them from the task (and thereby raise their thresholds) by presenting a masker whose frequency is several octaves away from the target frequency. Thus, attentional (distractor) effects can degrade infants' frequency resolution.

Finally, infants are capable of extracting the pitch of a complex configuration of pure tones. In adults, pitch perception is influenced not only by the fundamental (lowest) frequency present in a multicomponent tonal stimulus, but also by the harmonic relations and relative amplitudes of the component tones. As a result, adults perceive the pitch of a tonal complex whose fundamental frequency has been removed to be the same as the pitch when the fundamental frequency is present. Clarkson and Clifton (1985) used the CHP to determine whether infants also perceive the pitch of a tonal complex with a missing fundamental. They reported that 7-month-olds generalize from stimuli with the fundamental frequency to stimuli without the fundamental frequency. Also, like adults, infants have difficulty extracting the pitch of a tonal complex when there is a large frequency gap between the fundamental and the higher harmonics (Clarkson and Rogers, 1995) and when the harmonic relations are altered slightly (Clarkson and Clifton, 1995). Thus, it appears that by 7 months of age infants perceive pitch in a manner similar to adults.

TEMPORAL RESOLUTION  The ability to detect and discriminate rapid spectral changes is an important part of the mechanism that supports speech perception. Duration discrimination is also important for suprasegmental or prosodic aspects of speech, and temporal acuity is important for the processing of binaural cues to sound localization. Morrongiello and Trehub (1987) used the CHP to assess duration discrimination and reported that 6-month olds' thresholds were 25 ms whereas adults' were 10 ms. Werner and colleagues (1992) used OBP to assess gap detection in 3-, 6-, and 12-month-olds. The stimulus consisted of a broadband noise that was interrupted 10 times in rapid succession.

The duration of the interruption (gap) was varied across trials. By altering the low-frequency cutoff of the noise, Werner and colleagues were able to determine which frequencies were used by infants in this gap detection task. Although the data from 12-month-olds were inconsistent, the 3- and 6-month-olds showed gap detection thresholds 4–5 times longer than adults, and their thresholds (like adults') improved when high-frequency information was present. However, Trehub, Schneider, and Henderson (1995), using the CHP, reported that two-tone gap-detection thresholds were only approximately twice as long in 6- and 12-month-olds as in adults.

Several studies (Irwin et al., 1985; Wightman et al., 1989) have shown that gap detection thresholds continue to improve until at least 5 years and perhaps up to 10 years of age. Duration discrimination also continues to improve well into early childhood (Elfenbein, Small, and Davis, 1993; Jensen and Neff, 1993). These results, along with anatomical data on the peripheral to central progression of myelination (Moore, Perazzo, and Braun, 1995; Yakovlev and Lecours, 1967), are consistent with a hypothesis put forward by Tallal, Miller, and Fitch (1993; see also Fitch, Miller, and Tallal, 1997). Tallal and colleagues have proposed that basic deficits in temporal processing may be the primary reason for a variety of childhood speech and language problems. One line of evidence in support of this hypothesis is that the temporal coding of acoustic information loses resolution from the periphery to central auditory cortical areas (Schreiner and Langner, 1988). Aslin (1989) has provided some support for this temporal processing deficit in normal 6- to 9-month-olds using pure tones that were swept in frequency. Using the CHP, Aslin showed that thresholds for discriminating a rising or falling tone from a steady tone were quite good (similar to the 2% thresholds for frequency increments or decrements). However, when these tone-sweeps were rapid (50 ms), thresholds increased by a factor of 2, and when infants were asked to discriminate one rising (or falling) tone from another rising (or falling) tone, their thresholds increased by an additional factor of 3–4.

Another line of evidence supporting Tallal's temporal-deficiency hypothesis comes from her work with Michael Merzenich on the enhancement of children's speech perception skills (Merzenich et al., 1996; Tallal et al., 1996; see Bedi, this volume, for discussion). They reported that preschool children with language impairments were able to enhance their speech perception skills over the course of several weeks of training with speech stimuli whose temporal characteristics were slowed down and made more salient. These provocative studies suggest not only that some children with speech perception problems can benefit from training, but also that short-term training generalizes to speech presented at natural speaking rates, presumably by altering an underlying temporal-processing substrate in auditory cortex.

SUMMARY Fundamental aspects of auditory development undergo substantial improvements in the first few postnatal months. The processing of intensity and frequency information appears to reach values similar to naïve adults by 6 months of age. However, temporal processing appears to have a more protracted development continuing at least into the preschool years. How these basic capacities affect the processing of more complex sounds like speech remains unclear.

## Perception of complex auditory stimuli

Stimuli in the natural environment rarely consist of pure tones or octave-band noise bursts. These types of auditory stimuli are useful for conducting well controlled studies of fundamental auditory capacities, but they are of limited use in characterizing the perception of more complex auditory stimuli, particularly because the perception of complex stimuli cannot be easily predicted from the linear summation of responses to simpler stimuli. In this section we review several key aspects of infants' perception of more complex auditory stimuli.

EARLY LISTENING PREFERENCES The development of two methodological techniques in the 1980s enabled researchers to assess listening preferences in newborns. One was a conditioned sucking technique in which infants initiate a burst of sucks during one of two auditory stimuli (DeCasper and Fifer, 1980), and the other was a variant of the preferential-listening technique used with older infants (Fernald, 1985; see Cooper and Aslin, 1990). The rationale for studying auditory preferences in newborns was twofold. First, any evidence of listening preferences would confirm the newborn's ability to discriminate among two or more classes of sounds (of course, the absence of a preference is uninformative about discriminative capacities). Second, listening preferences in newborns had the potential to reveal the effects of auditory experience (and learning) in the womb, analogous to the effects of auditory experience in prehatchling birds (Gottlieb, 1976).

The plausibility of auditory experience as a significant influence on the human fetus was bolstered by demonstrations that premature infants have a functional auditory system and by hydrophone recordings showing that both internal (maternal) and external sounds of high intensity and low frequency are present in the amniotic fluid surrounding the fetus's ears (Querleu et al., 1988). DeCasper and Fifer (1980) reported that newborns suck differentially to listen to their own mother's voice over the voice of an unfamiliar mother. Thus, not only are maternal sounds available to a functioning auditory system in utero, but also these sounds are apparently encoded during some portion of the prenatal period and retained across a 2–3-day perinatal period to affect the newborn's listening preferences. When given a choice between a low-pass filtered version of their mother's voice (similar to the spectral content available in utero) and an unfiltered version of their mother's voice, newborns prefer the low-pass filtered version (Fifer and Moon, 1985), suggesting that they have learned the proximal characteristics of the most intense and frequent intrauterine sounds.

In addition to a specific preference for the mother's voice, newborns exhibit a general preference for highly familiar auditory materials. DeCasper and Spence (1986) showed that newborns prefer to listen longer to a familiar story, read aloud repeatedly by the mother during the final weeks of pregnancy, than to a novel story. The stories were chosen to have different rhythmic structures, and the newborns' preferences were exhibited despite the presentation of the test stories in a neutral (unfamiliar) female voice. Similarly, Mehler and colleagues (1988) and Moon, Cooper, and Fifer (1993) have shown that newborns prefer their native language to a foreign language. Taken together, these results suggest that newborns have extracted a number of prosodic (rhythmic and intonational) characteristics of auditory input during the last few days or weeks of prenatal development.

During the first postnatal year, infants show a variety of preferences for sounds that have been presented to them in their natural environment. These preferences, presumably induced by passive listening experience, form the basis for a variety of language-specific effects (see Jusczyk, 1997). In addition, across nearly all languages, infants are presented with a pattern of maternal speech called "motherese" or infant-directed (ID) speech. Characterized by a slow speaking rate, a small number of words per utterance, and a highly intoned pitch register, ID speech is preferred over adult-directed (AD) speech by infants as young as newborns (Cooper and Aslin, 1990). Although the voluminous literature on ID speech is beyond the scope of the present chapter (see Cooper, 1997, for a recent review), three facts are relevant to a discussion of the effects of early auditory experience. First, some preferences are clearly the result of exposure to sounds, either pre- or postnatally. Second, there is no evidence that prenatally induced sound preferences are long-lasting in the absence of similar postnatal experience. Third, some preferences in newborns are clearly not induced by prenatal experience. For example, in the absence of prenatal exposure to ID speech (Cooper and Aslin, 1990) or ID singing (Masataka, 1999), newborns show clear preferences for these sounds over AD sounds. Thus, there are some acoustic characteristics of sounds that are intrinsically preferred by infants in the absence of any inducing experience.

MELODY PERCEPTION The mature human auditory system is particularly adept at discriminating and categorizing rapid sequential sound patterns, both in the domain of speech and in the domain of music. Comprehensive coverage of the literature on infants' perception of music is beyond the scope of this chapter. (The interested reader should consult one or more recent reviews, e.g., Dowling, 1999; Trehub, Schellenberg, and Hill, 1997.) In the following, however, we briefly review several aspects of infants' perception of tone sequences that provide an interesting complement to studies of single tones and of sequences of speech sounds.

A fixed sequence of tones that vary in frequency comprise a simple melody. Trehub, Bull, and Thorpe (1984) tested 8- to 10-month-olds with the CHP to examine which aspects of a simple six-tone melody infants can discriminate. They reported that infants discriminated a variety of changes in the frequencies of the individual tones (and the frequency intervals between tones). The easiest discrimination for infants involved changes in the direction of the tone intervals, referred to as a change in *tone contour*. More difficult were changes in tone intervals that preserved the tone-contour or changes involving equal increments (or decrements) in the frequencies of all the tones (a transposition of the melody). These latter two discriminations were eliminated when a 3-s delay was added between the standard melody and the comparison melody. Trehub, Thorpe, and Morrongiello (1985) showed that 6- to 8-month-olds could discriminate a novel six-tone melody when only a single tone frequency violated the tone contour of the standard. Trehub, Thorpe, and Morrongiello (1987) went on to show that tone contour is a salient perceptual dimension even when the component tones are variable. That is, infants generalized their responding to contour-preserving melodies, even though they could clearly discriminate among these contour-preserving exemplars (see also Ferland and Mendelson, 1989).

Trehub and Thorpe (1989) showed that 7- to 9-month-olds discriminated changes in the grouping of tones based on rhythmic cues (e.g., a pause separating two groups of tones), and that these rhythmic cues to grouping were unaffected by the rate of presentation. Similarly, Thorpe and Trehub (1989) showed that the grouping of tones can be based on the common frequency of successive tones. They introduced a pause between groups of tones and reported that the pause was discriminated only when it occurred within a group of similar tones (e.g., hi-hi-pause-hi-lo-lo-lo) and not when the pause occurred between similar tones (e.g., hi-hi-hi-pause-lo-lo-lo). These grouping processes based on rhythmic and similarity cues are similar to those reported for the phrasal structures in music (Jusczyk and Krumhansl, 1993; Krumhansl and Jusczyk, 1990) and speech materials (Jusczyk et al., 1992; Morgan, 1994; Morgan and Saffran, 1995).

Finally, the discrimination of different aspects of simple melodies appears to be lateralized in the two cortical hemispheres. Balaban, Anderson, and Wisniewski (1998) showed that 8-month-olds familiarized to a six-tone melody were better able to discriminate a new melody with the same tone contour when it was presented monaurally to the left ear, whereas infants were better able to discriminate a new melody with a different tone contour when it was presented to the right ear. This is the same pattern of asymmetries observed in adults; that is, a left-ear advantage for processing contour information and a right-ear advantage for processing interval information.

SEQUENCE LEARNING   The ability to categorize the similarities among simple melodies implies that infants can learn to ignore discriminable differences. Remarkably little research has been directed to this process of sequence learning. Several recent studies of sequence learning for streams of speech sounds (Aslin, Saffran, and Newport, 1998; Saffran, Aslin, and Newport, 1996) demonstrated that 8-month-olds can extract the distributional properties of rapid sequences of syllables. That is, after only 2–3 minutes of exposure to syllable sequences containing no acoustic cues to syllable grouping (e.g., duration, rhythm, intonation), infants learned the predictiveness of the syllable ordering embedded in the speech stream.

Saffran and colleagues (1999) extended this line of research to sequences of pure tones. They showed that 8-month-olds can group tones based solely on the distributional properties of the tone sequences. Twelve 333-ms tones drawn from the same octave were organized into four 3-tone units (T1-T2-T3, T4-T5-T6, T7-T8-T9, T10-T11-T12). These 3-tone units were then randomly ordered into a continuous stream of tones and presented to infants for 3 min. After familiariza-

tion, each infant heard 12 test trials during which one of two 3-tone sequences was repeated with a 500-ms interstimulus interval. Six of the test trials consisted of 3-tone sequences that had been grouped in the familiarization stream (e.g., T1-T2-T3 or T7-T8-T9), and six of the test trials were 3-tone sequences from the familiarization stream that spanned two 3-tone groupings (e.g., T3-T7-T8). Infants showed a difference in listening times during these two types of test trials, indicating that they could discriminate between a "good" grouping and a "bad" grouping of the tones. Since the overall frequency of each of the 12 tones was the same across the familiarization stream, infants must have extracted differences in the sequential (co-occurrence) frequencies of tone triplets.

SUMMARY   The foregoing review of infants' perception of maternal speech, music, and tone sequences illustrates the fact that a variety of auditory mechanisms have evolved to process acoustic signals. The next section reviews how some mechanisms are modified by postnatal experience in a species-typical environment.

## Neural specializations and plasticity

The classical view of neocortex is one of functional specialization; that is, separate and discrete regions devoted to different sensory modalities and to the analysis of specialized features of sensory inputs. To some extent, this view is correct, with separate pathways from the sensory periphery to modality-specific regions of primary cortex. However, the interaction among cortical areas is both extensive and far-reaching, suggesting that simple models of neural specialization are at best incomplete and perhaps misleading, particularly models that fail to consider the multitude of direct and indirect inputs to any given cortical area.

A key developmental question in this debate about neural specialization is one of origins. Where do modality-specific and neural processing specializations come from? The two extremes of this question, of course, comprise the nature–nurture debate, in which neural specializations are either an intrinsic property arising from evolutionary processes or an experience-dependent property emerging during ontogeny. Neither of these extremes is likely to be correct, and the debate has shifted to understanding whether neural specializations in the adult can be modified by interventions during development.

AUDITORY LOCALIZATION IN NONHUMANS   Perhaps the best known neural specialization in the auditory system is echolocation in bats (Suga, 1984). Specific brain regions are highly sensitive to the time-of-arrival differences at the two ears that signal sound–source azimuth, and this sensory analysis takes place in a restricted auditory frequency range that is characteristic only of the bat's own vocal productions. Thus, there is a tight coupling between the signal generator and the signal analyzer. However, no such system is present in humans; moreover, relatively little developmental work on echolocation in bats has been conducted. Studies by Rubsamen and colleagues (Rubsamen, 1987; Rubsamen and Schafer, 1990) showed that the specialization for detecting echolocation signals is present as soon as the auditory system becomes functional, suggesting that this specialization is experience-independent. However, other than providing an interesting example of neural specialization, it is not clear how relevant echolocation is for studies of auditory development in humans.

Most mammals that have a well developed visual system combine information from both their visual and auditory systems to localize a sound source. Visual stimuli are essentially two-dimensional projections of the external world onto a sensory surface (the retina), with very high acuity along the line of central sight for some species (e.g., predatory mammals and birds). Auditory stimuli do not have this spatiotopic representation at the sensory periphery (the cochlea), but rather compute sound location from intensity (sound level) and time-of-arrival differences at the two ears. In binaural animals, a sound originating from anywhere other than the midline will strike one ear before the other because the ears are separated on the head, producing an interaural time difference (ITD), which is the main cue for azimuthal localization. In addition, because the head sits between the ears of many binaural creatures, one ear lies in the sound shadow of the head, reducing the intensity of the sound at that ear and resulting in an interaural level difference (ILD). These differences, in combination with monaural influences on sound quality (spectral cues) produced by the shape of the external ears (pinnae) and head, provide the information used in sound localization. Perturbing either the ITD, ILD, or spectral cues (see Parsons et al., 1999) can disrupt the ability to localize a sound source.

The visual and auditory systems form a useful combination of contrasting characteristics: The auditory system detects sound sources regardless of the orientation of the ears, and the visual system provides detailed information about a stimulus and its surrounding environment in the visual field. A major concern is how these two perceptual systems are integrated so that information from one is able to inform the other for stimulus localization. Visual and auditory information come together for the purpose of stimulus localization in the superior colliculus (also known as the optic tectum in birds). The tectum contains separate topographic maps of both visual and auditory space, as well as bimodal neurons that respond to both visual and auditory stimuli (Knudsen and Brainard, 1995). Maps of auditory space are based on the tuning of neurons to auditory localization cues such as ITD and ILD and their correlation with particular regions of space. Although the receptive fields of auditory neurons in the tectum can be quite large, there is typically a region of auditory space for which the neuron fires most strongly, known as the *best area*, and it is these "best areas" that are organized topographically in the tectum. Furthermore, in bimodal neurons there is a close correspondence between the auditory best areas and the visual receptive fields of these maps for locations in external space. Thus, the tectum provides a locus for cross-modal integration of auditory and visual information concerning the location of stimuli in the external world.

In a series of perturbation studies, Knudsen and colleagues altered the correspondence between visual and auditory localization cues by placing prisms in front of the eyes of barn owls. Knudsen (1988) reported that juvenile owls mounted with displacing prisms show an adaptation in localization behavior to auditory stimuli that compensates, in whole or in part, for the visual displacement. However, the extent of adaptation declines with the age at which prisms are first mounted. This period of declining ability to adapt to aberrant visual input is called the *sensitive* period. In contrast, the ability to recalibrate to normal input after prisms are removed is called the *critical* period, and extends well beyond the end of the sensitive period.

Similar evidence for sensitive and critical periods in barn owls comes from studies of monaural occlusion (Knudsen, Esterly, and Knudsen, 1984; Knudsen, Knudsen, and Esterly, 1984). Chronic plugging of one of the animal's ears produces significant alterations in ITDs and ILDs to which juvenile birds are able to adapt but adults are not. Gold and Knudsen (1999) have recently shown that this adaptation is frequency-specific; that is, during the sensitive period juvenile barn owls can adapt to those sound frequencies that carry useful information for localization and ignore unreliable frequencies. The usual end of this sensitive period seems to coincide with the attainment of adult head size, though it is interesting that the period can be extended beyond this point if the ear is occluded soon after adult head size has been obtained but before the animal has had much experience with auditory cues at that head size. As with prism-reared owls, there is also an extended critical period for recalibration to normal auditory cues after the ear plug is removed. Knudsen, Esterly, and Olsen

(1994) suggested that the extension of the critical period beyond the end of the sensitive period may occur because the auditory system has some innate predisposition for what "normal" binaural cues should be and withholds the consolidation of abnormal localization cues for a limited period into adulthood.

Knudsen and Brainard (1991) examined the effects of the correspondence between visual receptive fields and auditory best areas of bimodal cells in the tectum of prism-reared owls. Prisms produce a mismatch between the loci for the visual and auditory receptive fields of bimodal cells in the tectum for a given location in external space. With prolonged prism experience, however, the locations of the auditory best areas realign with the visual receptive fields in the tectum. If the prisms are then removed, yet another misalignment occurs. Knudsen (1988) described a similar realignment of the tectal auditory map following monaural occlusion. Prolonged occlusion altered the location of auditory best areas, including the realignment of the auditory to the visual maps during, but not after, the sensitive period. Additionally, if the plug is removed before the end of the critical period in animals that have adapted, the auditory best areas will once again realign with the visual receptive fields. However, if the plug is removed after the end of the critical period, this realignment is not observed, and a permanent mismatch results. Knudsen and Brainard (1995) noted that it is interesting that the tectal auditory maps adapt to match visual perception, regardless of whether visual or auditory localization cues have been altered. They suggested that visual information tends to override auditory information in forming the tectal maps used for localizing stimuli in space, which does not seem unreasonable given the greater acuity, reliability, and direct topographic representation of vision.

Interestingly, Knudsen (1998) found that owls who had adapted to prisms during the sensitive period and subsequently readapted to normal vision before the close of the critical period, were able as adults to show subsequent shifts in ITD tuning of tectal neurons after the reintroduction of the original prismatic displacement. Similar evidence was not found in control animals that had never experienced prismatic displacement. Although no behavioral results are given, this suggests that there is a trace of the former adaptive experience that remains in the nervous system long after a different set of adaptive parameters has been adopted, and that the neural pathways that were shaped originally by experience during the sensitive period can be resurrected during adulthood.

AUDITORY LOCALIZATION IN HUMAN INFANTS  Auditory localization in human infants has been studied almost exclusively by noting the presence of overt head-turning responses to discrete sound sources (see review by Clifton, 1992). Despite early anecdotal evidence of auditory localization in a newborn (Wertheimer, 1961), Muir and Field (1979) were the first to report definitive evidence that newborns, under special circumstances, could reliably orient their heads toward a sound. Critical factors included supporting the newborn's head to compensate for poor neck muscle strength and using broadband (preferably high-pass) stimuli of at least 1 s in duration (Clarkson, Clifton, and Morrongiello, 1985; Clarkson et al., 1989; Morrongiello and Clifton, 1984).

These localization responses in the newborn are only crudely spatial; that is, the sound source was located 90° to the right or left of the head along the interaural axis and the criterion response was any headturn in the direction of the stimulus. However, the presence of bidirectional headturns in newborns, and even in premature infants at 32 weeks of gestation (Muir, 1985), suggests that this crude localization response is not learned from visual feedback. The subsequent postnatal improvement in the accuracy of headturns (Muir, 1985; Muir, Clifton, and Clarkson, 1989) and their greater accuracy in the light (4°) than in the dark (16°) (Morrongiello and Rocca, 1987a) suggests that visual information serves to improve localization accuracy.

However, poor control of the motor system controlling head orientation could mask superior sensitivity to the cues for auditory localization. Studies of infants' ability to discriminate a change in the spatial location of a sound source (the minimum audible angle, or MAA) reveals a substantial postnatal improvement in the spatial resolution of the auditory system. Studies using both the OBP and CHP have shown that the MAA in the horizontal plane improves from nearly 30° in 2-month-olds to 9° in 11-month-olds (Ashmead et al., 1991; Morrongiello, 1988; Morrongiello, Fenwick, and Chance, 1990). Further improvements to adult levels (1–2°) occur by 5 years of age (Litovsky, 1991). The MAA in the vertical plane, which is much greater in adults than in the horizontal plane because binaural cues are absent along the midline, is approximately the same as the horizontal MAA in 6-month-olds. However, like adults, the MAA in infants relies on the high-frequency spectral information that comes from the shape of the pinnae (Morrongiello, 1987; Morrongiello and Rocca, 1987b). The horizontal MAA in 4- to 7-month-olds improves markedly, but this improvement is not paralleled by improvements in detecting interaural timing differences (Ashmead et al., 1991). The ability to resolve temporal cues is a factor of 2 better than the temporal cues that are present in infant MAAs. Thus, temporal processing is not the limiting factor in the development of the MAA. Rather it appears that these cues must be interpreted before eliciting a localization response, and this interpretation process may be faced with unreliable signals because of internal noise.

Another example of interpretation of localization cues is the suppression of echoes from a sound source. In most enclosed environments, a sound source creates a traveling wavefront that reaches the nearer ear prior to the farther ear and reaches the nearer ear prior to any echoes from nearby surfaces. These echoes must be suppressed or they will be interpreted incorrectly as a second sound source. This suppression is called the precedence effect. Clifton, Morrongiello, and Dowd (1984) showed that the precedence effect is functional in 6-month-olds, but not in newborns or 2-month-olds.

Auditory localization in humans is susceptible to the effects of early deprivation, though detailed occlusion experiments like those conducted with barn owls cannot be performed with human infants. However, Morrongiello (1989) was able to test infants who had unilateral ear infections, both during the infection and after the infection had been successfully treated. As expected, the accuracy of auditory localization was systematically biased while the infant had a hearing loss in one ear. There was no long-term recalibration of auditory localization, presumably because these episodes of unilateral hearing loss were quite brief.

In summary, the spatial resolution and accuracy of auditory localization improve dramatically between birth and 6 months of age. Visual information helps to calibrate auditory cues to the horizontal and vertical location of a sound source, and these temporal and spectral cues must be updated during development to compensate for anatomical changes in the separation of the two ears, the size and shape of the pinnae, and aberrant localization cues.

CORTICAL PLASTICITY IN NONHUMANS    Hyson and Rudy (1987) showed that the same region of cortex can respond to different inputs during development because of changes in the auditory periphery. The basilar membrane (BM) and the outer hair cells undergo a normal developmental process of stiffening and elongation that results in a shift of the best frequency that is represented at a given locus along the BM. As a result, a pure tone of a given frequency will be represented at a different location along the BM as the animal matures. Hyson and Rudy showed that rats conditioned to

a pure tone respond selectively to that tone immediately after training, but they respond selectively to a frequency-shifted tone several days after training. Thus, the cortical representation of the tone is dependent not on its frequency but on the location along the BM from which it originated.

Early in development, the segregation of cortex into modality-specific areas is less discrete than in maturity. In newborn cats, Innocenti, Berbel, and Clarke (1988) found transitory cross-modal projections from cortical auditory areas to the primary visual cortex that were eliminated by the end of the first month of postnatal life. While this early developmental projection from auditory to visual cortex is provocative from the standpoint of developmental selectivity of sensory input, reciprocal projections from visual to auditory cortex were absent in cats, and the pattern of residual cross-modal connectivity in adult cats did not differ from that of cats that were binocularly enucleated at birth. This last point is especially revealing because it suggests that experience plays no role in shaping the developmental loss of these cross-modal connections, at least in this species. However, evidence of this kind leaves open the possibility that inputs to sensory modalities in some animals may not be completely determined by their primary afferents.

A more direct test of whether cortical areas are constrained to receive and process only modality-specific inputs from the sensory periphery was conducted by Sur and colleagues (Sur, Pallas, and Roe, 1990; Roe et al., 1992). They rerouted inputs from the retina of ferrets, which normally terminate in primary visual cortex, and caused them to impinge on thalamic targets that project to primary auditory cortex (normal inputs from the cochlea were also eliminated). This was done by ablating the visual cortex, cutting the ascending auditory fibers to the medial geniculate nucleus (the primary thalamic target of auditory input), and ablating the superior colliculus (SC), which also causes severe atrophy of the lateral geniculate nucleus (these last two structures being the primary targets of retinal output). Under these conditions, retinal afferents that would normally terminate in the lateral geniculate nucleus project to the medial geniculate nucleus, which is no longer connected to its usual source of auditory input. Although the primary auditory cortex of these animals never attained the full function of normal visual cortex, it did become responsive to visual inputs and acquired the retinotopic organization characteristic of primary visual cortex. This is interesting because cortical maps of retinal space are two-dimensional, whereas the normal auditory map found in primary auditory cortex reflects the tonotopic organization of frequency in the cochlea, which is one-dimensional. This suggests that the same area of cortex can support different mappings from the sensory epithelia depending on the source of innervation. Thus, if primary afferents are rerouted during early neural development, they may be able to utilize a region of cortex that would be specialized for processing a different sensory modality under ordinary circumstances.

Currently, the mechanisms enabling this type of reorganization are unknown. It is important to note that the primary experimental manipulation in this preparation is the rerouting of visual afferents to auditory targets in the thalamus, suggesting that much of the adaptation of auditory cortex to resemble the organization and responses of visual cortex may be guided by the innervating thalamic fibers. Sur and colleagues (1990) note that, although a retinotopic map is induced in auditory cortex, this map is elongated along the dimension that would normally correspond to the isofrequency axis of auditory cortex. It is not clear (1) whether this difference in the retinotopic map of experimental animals is due to cellular influences in auditory cortex that are strictly local (either because of intracortical connections or because of the possibility that cells in auditory cortex exert local influences characteristic of auditory cortex simply because it has been their fate to end up in what is normally auditory cortex), (2) whether the state of thalamic projection prior to surgery was sufficient to induce the beginnings of normal auditory cortical topographic organization which continued to show effects after rewiring (although it is unlikely that thalamic afferents had begun to enter the developing cortex at that time), or (3) whether the map in rewired animals reflects a map in the medial geniculate nucleus which is itself elongated in this dimension.

Other researchers have investigated situations in which input from one modality has been cut off without concomitant ablation of structures that process inputs from other modalities. Korte and Rauschecker (1993) demonstrated that cats binocularly deprived (BD) from birth using lid suture have an increased percentage of cells showing auditory azimuthal spatial tuning in the anterior ectosylvian cortex (AE), a multimodal area that is a major source of input to the cat superior colliculus. Furthermore, the median tuning width of spatially tuned cells was narrower for BD cats than for normals. Rauschecker (1995) also found that in BD cats the entire AE visual area was taken over by auditory and somatosensory inputs. Thus, there were at least three effects of binocular deprivation in experimental animals: an increase in cortical area available for process-ing auditory input, an increase in the proportion of cells processing restricted areas of auditory space, and an increase in the sharpness of tuning for those cells that process restricted areas. The BD cats also demonstrated better localization behavior than normal cats. This evidence, in combination with that cited earlier of Sur and colleagues, indicates that under the right conditions the auditory system is capable of remarkable change at the thalamocortical level, the cortical level, and the corticotectal level. However, as is the case with Sur and coworkers (1990), the mechanisms behind the findings of Rauschecker and colleagues are largely unknown (see also Rauschecker, 1999).

These developmental results represent one end of a continuum of plasticity that extends well into adulthood. Robertson and Irvine (1989) showed that the tonotopic map in the primary auditory cortex of adult guinea pigs undergoes reorganization in response to lesions to restricted areas of the cochlea. After the cochlea is lesioned, there is a large initial increase in the threshold to drive cortical cells that previously responded well to frequencies represented at the site of the cochlear lesion. After several weeks, the area that initially contained neurons showing this increase in threshold is found to have cells with normal thresholds that respond to frequencies adjacent to those represented in the lesioned area of the cochlea. This reorganization is similar to that found in the somatosensory cortex following amputation (Calford and Tweedale, 1988; Merzenich et al., 1984).

Recanzone, Schreiner, and Merzenich (1993) investigated changes in the organization of the tonotopic map in primary auditory cortex of adult owl monkeys after extensive frequency-discrimination training. Monkeys were trained on an auditory frequency discrimination task for several weeks and demonstrated an improvement in their performance with training. Compared to untrained controls and passively stimulated monkeys engaged in a tactile discrimination task, electrophysiological recordings in primary auditory cortex of trained monkeys revealed that the number of recording sites as well as the cortical area representing the frequencies used in training were larger than for frequencies not used for training. This increase in cortical area of representation was significantly correlated with behavioral improvement. However, it is unclear whether these changes in cortical organization reflect changes at the cortical level, the subcortical level, or both. The authors also note that there was an increase in the sharpness of frequency tuning near threshold for the behaviorally relevant frequencies of trained monkeys compared to untrained or passively stimulated controls, although this improvement was not correlated with behavioral improvement. Thus it seems that some aspects of the auditory system of some animals remain plastic into adulthood and that changes in behavior based on auditory experience may reflect changes at the neural level.

In summary, there is ample evidence from research with nonhumans that the auditory cortex has considerable plasticity, that some plasticity is present even in adult cortex despite greater plasticity in infancy, and that changes in the inputs from the auditory (and visual) periphery can have significant effects on cortical organization and the representation of sounds.

CORTICAL PLASTICITY IN HUMANS  A number of recent studies using noninvasive neuroimaging have confirmed the presence of cortical plasticity in humans. These studies have approached the question of cortical plasticity by examining subjects who have experienced a variety of sensory deprivations, some beginning at birth and others acquired later in life. Lessard and colleagues (1998) reported evidence of auditory compensation in humans similar to that found in BD cats. They compared the performance of subjects with normal vision, residual peripheral vision, or total blindness on an auditory localization task. In the binaural condition, totally blind subjects were able to localize at least as well as normals, and better than subjects with residual vision. In the monaural condition, the totally blind subjects fell into two different categories: those biased to judge a stimulus presented to the occluded ear as originating from the side of the unoccluded ear (a bias shared by normal subjects and subjects with residual vision), and those not. Biased blind subjects performed similarly to normals, but showed increased variability for stimuli presented to the occluded ear. However, unlike sighted subjects and those with residual peripheral vision, biased blind subjects reported qualitative differences in sounds presented to the occluded ear as compared to those presented to the unoccluded ear. Unbiased blind subjects performed better with stimuli presented to the occluded ear than did both normal subjects and subjects with residual peripheral vision. The fact that unbiased blind subjects outperformed sighted subjects in this condition, and that biased blind subjects reported differences in sound quality even though they did not localize to the correct side, suggests that people blind from birth are able to use monaural cues better than these other two groups in analyzing their auditory environment, perhaps owing to neural changes similar to those Korte and Rauschecker (1993) found in binocularly deprived cats.

Röder and colleagues (1999) combined behavioral and electrophysiological methods to investigate auditory spatial tuning in blind and sighted humans and found better auditory localization in blind subjects, but only in peripheral (lateral) auditory space. In the experiment, speakers were mounted directly ahead and 90° to the side of the subject, with additional speakers displaced by 6°, 12°, and 18°. The task was to detect target sounds in the presence of distractor sounds of different frequency, but to respond only to target sounds from straight ahead (in the attend-center condition) or from 90° (in the attend-periphery condition). False alarms to target sounds at the displaced speakers were used as a measure of auditory spatial tuning. In the attend-center condition, the correct detection rate was greater for sighted subjects, but the sharpness of tuning was not significantly different between the two groups. However, in the attend-periphery condition, both groups demonstrated the same ability to detect sounds at the peripheral target location, but blind subjects showed significantly fewer false alarms to nontarget locations, indicating sharper auditory localization tuning for peripheral auditory space. Normally sighted adults, after a period of recalibration to artificially altered external ears (pinnae), can also adjust their reliance on those spectral cues that are now most reliable for sound localization (Hofman, Van Riswick, and Van Opstal, 1998).

Studies of cortical plasticity in humans lacking normal visual input are mirrored by studies of humans lacking normal auditory input. Bavelier, Corina, and Neville (1998; see also Neville and Bavelier, 2000) recorded functional magnetic resonance (fMRI) images from congenitally deaf subjects who were native signers of American Sign Language (ASL). As these subjects viewed a variety of visual displays, areas of left auditory cortex normally involved in the processing of speech sounds were now activated by visual stimuli that functioned as manual gestures in ASL. Bosworth and Dobkins (1999) showed in perceptual tasks that deaf subjects whose native language was ASL had a left-hemisphere advantage for the processing of motion in the peripheral visual field (a common feature of ASL decoding). Thus, the absence of auditory inputs, or the greater experience with visual inputs, may heighten sensitivity to visual stimuli that are used communicatively or that are located in a part of the visual field where rapid encoding enables greater fluency.

Taken together, these studies of blind and deaf adults suggest that both auditory and visual cortex can adjust to altered sensory input by utilizing regions of cortex that would normally process inputs from a sensory periphery that is now silent. A similar example has been reported for the activation of visual cortex during tactile discrimination tasks by blind subjects (Sadato et al.,

1996). Finally, the normally sparse retinal input from rod photoreceptors to primary visual cortex expands to fill nearly the entire primary visual cortex in subjects who lack all three classes of cone photoreceptors (Baseler and Wandell, personal communication).

## Conclusions

In this chapter, we have provided a selective review of both classic and more recent findings on the development of the auditory system in human infants and in developing animals. Several clear principles emerge from these findings. First, the human auditory system is functional several weeks before birth, and predominant sounds in the uterine environment can have effects on the fetus that last at least a week. Newborn infants are able to localize sounds, but they do so rather crudely. The first six postnatal months are characterized by rapid and significant improvements in nearly all aspects of auditory functioning. Thus, although newborns have rudimentary auditory abilities, their auditory system is quite immature, and these immaturities may constrain their ability to process more complex aspects of auditory stimuli until several months after birth. Although infants' analyses of the spectral characteristics of sounds is relatively adultlike after birth, their analyses of the temporal characteristics of sounds appears to have a protracted period of improvement into early childhood.

With regard to more complex auditory stimuli, human infants exhibit both intrinsic auditory preferences and auditory preferences based on early experience with auditory inputs. These preferences can be modulated by powerful learning mechanisms that are capable of rapidly extracting the distributional information present in complex auditory inputs. The precise neural mechanisms that enable this rapid learning are not well understood and will undoubtedly be a focus of future neuroimaging studies.

Finally, the auditory system, like other sensory modalities, has evolved a variety of neural specializations for processing sounds, and these specializations vary by species. Specialized neural mechanisms emerge during early development and are susceptible to the effects of early experience. For example, in the domain of auditory localization, visual and auditory cues must be calibrated initially and then recalibrated during growth and development. Although the process of calibration occurs during an early sensitive period, some plasticity remains in the adult cortex. Both early and late cortical plasticity enable recovery of function and reallocation of cortical areas when sensory inputs are altered or eliminated. The extent of this reorganization has not received extensive study in humans, largely because noninvasive neuroimaging has not been available until relatively recently.

Taken together, studies of auditory processing during human development continue to provide a fruitful domain, not only for understanding auditory development itself, but also as a window on underlying neural mechanisms that inform us generally about the relationship between sensory processing and higher-level mechanisms of cognitive development.

ACKNOWLEDGMENTS    Preparation of this chapter was made possible, in part, by grants from NIH (HD-37082) and NSF (SBR 98-73477) to RNA. We thank Yale Cohen for helpful comments and discussions during the preparation of this chapter and Charles Nelson and Monica Luciana for editorial and organizational suggestions.

## REFERENCES

ABDALA, C., and R. FOLSOM, 1995. Frequency contribution to the click-evoked ABR in human adults and infants. *J. Acoust. Soc. Am.* 97:2394–2404.

ASHMEAD, D., D. DAVIS, T. WHALEN, and R. ODOM, 1991. Sound localization and sensitivity to interaural time differences in human infants. *Child Dev.* 62:1211–1226.

ASLIN, R. N., 1989. Discrimination of frequency transitions by human infants. *J. Acoust. Soc. Am.* 86:582–590.

ASLIN, R. N., J. R. SAFFRAN, and E. L. NEWPORT, 1998. Computation of conditional probability statistics by 8-month-old infants. *Psychol. Sci.* 9:321–324.

BALABAN, M. T., L. M. ANDERSON, and A. B. WISNIEWSKI, 1998. Lateral asymmetries in infant melody perception. *Dev. Psychol.* 34:39–48.

BARGONES, J. Y., and L. A. WERNER, 1994. Adults listen selectively; infants do not. *Psychol. Sci.* 5:170–174.

BARGONES, J. Y., L. A. WERNER, and G. C. MAREAN, 1995. Infant psychometric functions for detection: Mechanisms of immature sensitivity. *J. Acoust. Soc. Am.* 98:99–111.

BAVELIER, D., C. CORINA, and H. NEVILLE, 1998. Brain and language: A perspective from sign language. *Neuron* 21:275–278.

BERG, K. M., and M. C. SMITH, 1983. Behavioral thresholds for tones during infancy. *J. Exp. Child Psychol.* 35:409–425.

BIRNHOLZ, J. C., and B. R. BENACERRAF, 1983. The development of human fetal hearing. *Science* 222:516–518.

BOSWORTH, R. G., and K. R. DOBKINS, 1999. Left-hemisphere dominance for motion processing in deaf signers. *Psychol. Sci.* 10:256–262.

BULL, D., B. A. SCHNEIDER, and S. E. TREHUB, 1981. The masking of octave-band noise by broad band spectrum noise: A comparison of infant and adult thresholds. *Percept. Psychophysics* 30:101–106.

CALFORD, M. B., and R. TWEEDALE, 1988. Immediate and chronic changes in responses of somatosensory cortex in adult flying-fox after digit amputation. *Nature* 332:446–448.

CLARKSON, M. G., and R. K. CLIFTON, 1985. Infant pitch perception: Evidence for responding to pitch categories and the missing fundamental. *J. Acoust. Soc. Am.* 77:1521–1528.

CLARKSON, M. G., and R. K. CLIFTON, 1995. Infants' pitch perception: Inharmonic tonal complexes. *J. Acoust. Soc. Am.* 98:1372–1379.

CLARKSON, M. G., R. K. CLIFTON, and B. A. MORRONGIELLO, 1985. The effects of sound duration on newborns' head orientation. *J. Exp. Child Psychol.* 39:20–36.

CLARKSON, M. G., R. K. CLIFTON, I. U. SWAIN, and E. E. PERRIS, 1989. Stimulus duration and repetition rate influences newborns' head orientation toward sound. *Dev. Psychol.* 22:683–705.

CLARKSON, M. G., and R. C. ROGERS, 1995. Infants require low-frequency energy to hear the pitch of the missing fundamental. *J. Acoust. Soc. Am.* 98:148–154.

CLEMENTS, M., and J. B. KELLY, 1978. Directional responses by kittens to an auditory stimulus. *Dev. Psychobiol.* 11:505–511.

CLIFTON, R. K., 1992. The development of spatial hearing in human infants. In *Developmental Psychoacoustics*, L. A. Werner and E. W. Rubel, eds. Washington, D.C.: American Psychological Association, pp. 135–157.

CLIFTON, R. K., B. MORRONGIELLO, and J. DOWD, 1984. A developmental look at an auditory illusion: The precedence effect. *Dev. Psychobiol.* 17:519–536.

COOPER, R. P., 1997. An ecological approach to infants' perception of intonation contours as meaningful aspects of speech. In *Evolving Explanations of Development*, C. Dent-Read and P. Zukow-Goldring, eds. Washington, D.C.: American Psychological Association, pp. 55–85.

COOPER, R. P., and R. N. ASLIN, 1990. Preference for infant-directed speech in the first month after birth. *Child Dev.* 61:1584–1595.

DECASPER, A. J., and W. P. FIFER, 1980. Of human bonding: Newborns prefer their mothers' voices. *Science* 208:1174–1176.

DECASPER, A. J., and M. J. SPENCE, 1986. Prenatal maternal speech influences newborns' perception of speech sounds. *Infant Behav. Dev.* 9:133–150.

DOWLING, W. J., 1999. The development of music perception and cognition. In *The Psychology of Music*, D. Deutsch, ed. San Diego, Calif.: Academic Press., pp. 603–625.

ELFENBEIN, J. L., A. M. SMALL, and M. DAVIS, 1993. Developmental patterns of duration discrimination. *J. Speech Hear. Res.* 36:842–849.

FERLAND, M. B., and M. J. MENDELSON, 1989. Infants' categorization of melodic contour. *Infant Behav. Dev.* 12:341–355.

FERNALD, A., 1985. Four-month-old infants prefer to listen to motherese. *Infant Behav. Dev.* 8:181–195.

FIFER, W. P., and C. MOON, 1985. The effects of fetal experience with sound. In *Fetal Behavior: A Psychobiological Perspective*, J. P. Lacanuet, N. A. Krasnegor, W. P. Fifer, and W. P. Smotherman, eds. Hillsdale, N.J.: Erlbaum, pp. 351–366.

FITCH, R. H., S. MILLER, and P. TALLAL, 1997. Neurobiology of speech perception. *Annu. Rev. Neurosci.* 20:331–353.

FOLSOM, R. C., and M. K. WYNNE, 1987. Auditory brain-stem responses from human adults and infants: Wave V tuning curves. *J. Acoust. Soc. Am.* 81:412–417.

GOLD, J. I., and E. I. KNUDSEN, 1999. Hearing impairment induces frequency-specific adjustments in auditory spatial

tuning in the optic tectum of young owls. *J. Neurophysiol.* 82:2197–2209.

GOTTLIEB, G., 1976. Conceptions of prenatal development: Behavioral embryology. *Psychol. Rev.* 83:215–234.

HECOX, K., 1975. Electrophysiological correlates of human auditory development. In *Infant Perception: From Sensation to Cognition*, L. B. Cohen and P. Salapatek, eds. New York: Academic Press, pp. 151–191.

HECOX, K., and R. BURKARD, 1982. Developmental dependencies of the human auditory evoked response. *Ann. N.Y. Acad. Sci.* 388:538–556.

HOFMAN, P. M., J. G. A. VAN RISWICK, and A. J. VAN OPSTAL, 1998. Relearning sound localization with new ears. *Nature Neurosci.* 1:417–421.

HYSON, R. L., and J. W. RUDY, 1987. Ontogenetic change in the analysis of sound frequency in the infant rat. *Dev. Psychobiol.* 20:189–207.

INNOCENTI, G. M., P. BERBEL, and S. CLARKE, 1988. Development of projections from auditory to visual areas in the cat. *J. Comp. Neurol.* 272:242–259.

IRWIN, R. J., A. K. R. BALL, N. KAY, J. A. STILLMAN, and J. ROSSER, 1985. The development of temporal acuity in children. *Child Dev.* 56:614–620.

JENSEN, J. K., and D. L. NEFF, 1993. Development of basic auditory discrimination in preschool children. *Psychol. Sci.* 4:104–107.

JOHNSON, M. H., 1997. *Developmental Cognitive Neuroscience.* Cambridge, Mass.: Blackwell.

JUSCZYK, P. W., 1997. *The Discovery of Spoken Language.* Cambridge, Mass.: MIT Press.

JUSCZYK, P. W., K. HIRSH-PASEK, D. G. KEMLER NELSON, L. KENNEDY, A. WOODWARD, and J. PIWOZ, 1992. Perception of acoustic correlates of major phrasal units by young infants. *Cogn. Psychol.* 24:252–293.

JUSCZYK, P. W., and C. L. KRUMHANSL, 1993. Pitch and rhythmic patterns affecting infants' sensitivity to musical phrase structure. *J. Exp. Psychol.: Hum. Percept. Perform.* 19:627–640.

KISILEVSKY, B. S., D. W. MUIR, and J. A. LOW, 1992. Maturation of human fetal responses to vibroacoustic stimulation. *Child Dev.* 63:1497–1508.

KNUDSEN, E. I., 1988. Sensitive and critical periods in the development of sound localization. In *Message to Mind: Directions in Developmental Neurobiology*, S. S. Easter, K. F. Barald, and B. M. Carlson, eds. Sunderland, Mass.: Sinauer Associates.

KNUDSEN, E. I., 1998. Capacity for plasticity in the adult owl auditory system expanded by juvenile experience. *Science* 279:1531–1533.

KNUDSEN, E. I., and M. S. BRAINARD, 1991. Visual instruction of the neural map of auditory space in the developing optic tectum. *Science* 253:85–87.

KNUDSEN, E. I., and M. S. BRAINARD, 1995. Creating a unified representation of visual and auditory space in the brain. *Annu. Rev. Neurosci.* 18:19–43.

KNUDSEN, E. I., S. D. ESTERLY, and P. F. KNUDSEN, 1984. Monaural occlusion alters sound localization during a sensitive period in the barn owl. *J. Neurosci.* 4:1001–1011.

KNUDSEN, E. I., S. D. ESTERLY, and J. F. OLSEN, 1994. Adaptive plasticity of the auditory space map in the optic tectum of adult and baby barn owls in response to external ear modification. *J. Neurophysiol.* 71:79–94.

KNUDSEN, E. I., P. F. KNUDSEN, and S. D. ESTERLY, 1984. A critical period for the recovery of sound localization accuracy following monaural occlusion in the barn owl. *J. Neurosci.* 4:1012–1020.

KORTE, M., and J. P. RAUSCHECKER, 1993. Auditory spatial tuning of cortical neurons is sharpened in cats with early blindness. *J. Neurophysiol.* 70:1717–1721.

KRUMHANSL, C. L., and P. W. JUSCZYK, 1990. Infants' perception of phrase structure in music. *Psychol. Sci.* 1:70–73.

LECANUET, J. P., C. GRANIER-DEFERRE, and M. C. BUSNEL, 1988. Fetal cardiac and motor responses to octave-band noises as a function of central frequency, intensity and heart rate variability. *Early Human Dev.* 18:81–93.

LESSARD, N., M. PARE, F. LEPORE, and M. LASSONDE, 1998. Early-blind human subjects localize sound sources better than sighted subjects. *Nature* 395:278–280.

LITOVSKY, R., 1991. *Developmental Changes in Sound Localization Precision under Conditions of the Precedence Effect.* Unpublished doctoral dissertation, University of Massachusetts, Amherst, Mass.

MASATAKA, N., 1999. Preference for infant-directed singing in 2-day-old hearing infants of deaf parents. *Dev. Psychol.* 35:1001–1005.

MEHLER, J., P. W. JUSCZYK, G. LAMBERTZ, N. HALSTED, J. BERTONCINI, and C. AMIEL-TISON, 1988. A precursor of language acquisition in young infants. *Cognition* 29:144–178.

MERZENICH, M. M., J. K. JENKINS, P. JOHNSTON, C. SCHREINER, S. L. MILLER, and P. TALLAL, 1996. Temporal processing deficits of language-learning impaired children are ameliorated by training. *Science* 271:77–81.

MERZENICH, M. M., R. J. NELSON, M. P. STRYKER, M. S. CYNADER, A. SCHOPPMANN, and J. M. ZOOK, 1984. Somatosensory cortical map changes following digit amputation in adult monkeys. *J. Comp. Neurol.* 224:591–605.

MOON, C., R. P. COOPER, and W. P. FIFER, 1993. Two-day-old infants prefer their native language. *Infant Behav. Dev.* 16:495–500.

MOORE, J. K., L. M. PERAZZO, and A. BRAUN, 1995. Time course of axonal myelination in the human brainstem auditory pathway. *Hear. Res.* 87:21–31.

MOORE, J. M., G. THOMPSON, and M. THOMPSON, 1975. Auditory localization of infants as a function of reinforcement conditions. *J. Speech Hear. Disorders* 40:29–34.

MORGAN, J. L., 1994. Converging measures of speech segmentation in preverbal infants. *Infant Behav. Dev.* 17:389–403.

MORGAN, J. L., and J. R. SAFFRAN, 1995. Emerging integration of sequential and suprasegmental information in preverbal speech segmentation. *Child Dev.* 66:911–936.

MORRONGIELLO, B. A., 1987. Infants' localization of sounds in the medial sagittal plane: Effects of signal frequency. *J. Acoust. Soc. Am.* 82:900–905.

MORRONGIELLO, B. A., 1988. Infants' localization of sounds in the horizontal plane: Estimates of minimum audible angle. *Dev. Psychol.* 24:8–13.

MORRONGIELLO, B. A., 1989. Infants' monaural localization of sounds: Effects of unilateral ear infections. *J. Acoust. Soc. Am.* 86:597–602.

MORRONGIELLO, B. A., and R. K. CLIFTON, 1984. Effects of sound frequency on behavioral and cardiac orienting in newborn and five-month-old infants. *J. Exp. Child Psychol.* 38:429–446.

MORRONGIELLO, B. A., K. FENWICK, and G. CHANCE, 1990. Sound localization acuity in very young infants: An observer-based testing procedure. *Dev. Psychol.* 26:75–84.

MORRONGIELLO, B. A., and P. T. ROCCA, 1987a. Infants' localization of sounds in the horizontal plane: Effects of auditory and visual cues. *Child Dev.* 58:918–927.

MORRONGIELLO, B. A., and P. T. ROCCA, 1987b. Infants' localization of sounds in the median vertical plane: Estimates of minimum audible angle. *J. Exp. Child Psychol.* 43:181–193.

MORRONGIELLO, B. A., and S. E. TREHUB, 1987. Age-related changes in auditory temporal perception. *J. Exp. Child Psychol.* 44:413–426.

MUIR, D., 1985. The development of infants' auditory spatial sensitivity. In *Auditory Development in Infancy,* S. E. Trehub and B. A. Schneider, eds. New York: Plenum Press, pp. 51–84.

MUIR, D., R. K. CLIFTON, and M. G. CLARKSON, 1989. The development of human auditory localization response: A U-shaped function. *Can. J. Psychol.* 43:199–216.

MUIR, D., and T. FIELD, 1979. Newborn infants orient to sounds. *Child Dev.* 50:431–436.

NEVILLE, H. J., and D. BAVELIER, 2000. Specificity and plasticity in neurocognitive development in humans. In *The Cognitive Neurosciences,* M. Gazzaniga, ed. Cambridge, Mass.: MIT Press, pp. 83–98.

NOZZA, R. J., 1995. Estimating the contribution of nonsensory factors to infant-adult differences in behavioral thresholds. *Hear. Res.* 91:72–77.

NOZZA, R. J., and W. R. WILSON, 1984. Masked and unmasked pure tone thresholds of infants and adults: Development of auditory frequency selectivity and sensitivity. *J. Speech Hear. Res.* 27:613–622.

OLSHO, L. W., 1984. Infant frequency discrimination as a function of frequency. *Infant Behav. Dev.* 7:27–35.

OLSHO, L. W., 1985. Infant auditory perception: Tonal masking. *Infant Behav. Dev.* 8:371–384.

OLSHO, L. W., E. G. KOCH, and C. F. HALPIN, 1987. Level and age effects in infant frequency discrimination. *J. Acoust. Soc. Am.* 82:454–464.

OLSHO, L. W., E. G. KOCH, E. A. CARTER, C. F. HALPIN, and N. B. SPETNER, 1988. Pure-tone sensitivity of human infants. *J. Acoust. Soc. Am.* 84:1316–1324.

OLSHO, L. W., E. G. KOCH, C. F. HALPIN, and E. A. CARTER, 1987. An observer-based psychoacoustic procedure for use with young infants. *Dev. Psychol.* 23:627–640.

OLSHO, L. W., C. SCHOON, R. SAKAI, V. SPERDUTO, and R. TURPIN, 1982. Auditory frequency discrimination in infancy. *Dev. Psychol.* 18:721–726.

PARSONS, C. H., R. G. LANYON, J. W. H. SCHNUPP, and A. J. KING, 1999. Effects of altering spectral cues in infancy on horizontal and vertical sound localization by adult ferrets. *J. Neurophysiol.* 82:2294–2309.

QUERLEU, D., X. RENARD, F. VERSYP, L. PARIS-DELURE, and G. CREPIN, 1988. Fetal hearing. *Eur. J. Obstet. Gynecol. Reproduct. Biol.* 29:191–212.

RAUSCHECKER, J. P., 1995. Compensatory plasticity and sensory substitution in the cerebral cortex. *Trends Neurosci.* 18:36–43.

RAUSCHECKER, J. P., 1999. Auditory cortical plasticity: A comparison with other sensory systems. *Trends Neurosci.* 22:74–80.

RECANZONE, G. H., C. E. SCHREINER, and M. M. MERZENICH, 1993. Plasticity in the frequency representation of primary auditory cortex following discrimination training in adult owl monkeys. *J. Neurosci.* 13:87–103.

ROBERSTON, D., and D. R. F. IRVINE, 1989. Plasticity of frequency organization in auditory cortex of guinea pigs with partial unilateral deafness. *J. Comp. Neurol.* 282:456–471.

RÖDER, B., W. TEDER-SALEJARVL, A. STERR, F. ROSLER, S. A. HILLYARD, and H. J. NEVILLE, 1999. Improved auditory spatial tuning in blind humans. *Nature* 400:162–166.

ROE, A. W., S. L. PALLAS, Y. H. KWON, and M. SUR, 1992. Visual projections routed to the auditory pathway in ferrets: Receptive fields of visual neurons in primary auditory cortex. *J. Neurosci.* 12:3651–3664.

RUBEL, E. W., A. N. POPPER, and R. R. FAY (EDS.), 1998. *Development of the Auditory System.* New York: Springer.

RUBSAMEN, R., 1987. Ontogenesis of the echolocation system in the rufous horseshoe bat, *Rhinolophus rouxi* (audition and vocalization in early postnatal development). *J. Comp. Physiol. [A] Sens. Neural Behav. Physiol.* 161:899–904.

RUBSAMEN, R., and M. SCHAFER, 1990. Ontogenesis of auditory fovea representation in the inferior colliculus of the Sri Lankan rufous horseshoe bat, *Rhinolophus rouxi. J. Comp. Physiol. [A] Sens. Neural Behav. Physiol.* 167:757–769.

SADATO, N., A. PASCUAL-LEONE, J. GRAFMAN, V. IBANEZ, M.-P. DEIBER, G. DOLD, and M. HALLETT, 1996. Activation of the primary visual cortex by Braille reading in blind subjects. *Nature* 380:526–528.

SAFFRAN, J. R., R. N. ASLIN, and E. L. NEWPORT, 1996. Statistical learning by 8-month-old infants. *Science* 274:1926–1928.

SAFFRAN, J. R., E. K. JOHNSON, R. N. ASLIN, and E. L. NEWPORT, 1999. Statistical learning of tone sequences by adults and infants. *Cognition* 70:27–52.

SAUNDERS, J. C., D. E. DOAN, and Y. E. COHEN, 1993. The contribution of middle-ear sound conduction to auditory development. *J. Comp. Biochem. Physiol.* 106:7–13.

SCHNEIDER, B. A., D. BULL, and S. E. TREHUB, 1988. Binaural unmasking in infants. *J. Acoust. Soc. Am.* 83:1124–1132.

SCHNEIDER, B. A., B. A. MORRONGIELLO, and S. E. TREHUB, 1990. The size of the critical band in infants, children, and adults. *J. Exp. Psychol.: Hum. Percept. Perform.* 16:642–652.

SCHNEIDER, B. A., S. E. TREHUB, and D. BULL, 1979. The development of basic auditory processes in infants. *Can. J. Psychol.* 33:306–319.

SCHNEIDER, B. A., S. E. TREHUB, and D. BULL, 1980. High-frequency sensitivity in infants. *Science* 207:1003–1004.

SCHNEIDER, B. A., S. E. TREHUB, B. A. MORRONGIELLO, and L. A. THORPE, 1989. Developmental changes in masked thresholds. *J. Acoust. Soc. Am.* 86:1733–1742.

SCHREINER, C. E., and G. LANGNER, 1988. Coding of temporal patterns in the central auditory nervous system. In *Functions of the Auditory System: Neurobiological Bases of Hearing,* G. M. Edelman, W. E. Gall, and W. M Cowan, eds. New York: Wiley, pp. 337–361.

SINNOTT, J. M., and R. N. ASLIN, 1985. Frequency and intensity discrimination in human infants and adults. *J. Acoust. Soc. Am.* 78:1986–1992.

SINNOTT, J. M., D. B. PISONI, and R. N. ASLIN, 1983. A comparison of pure-tone auditory thresholds in human infants and adults. *Infant Behav. Dev.* 6:3–17.

SKOCZENSKI, A. M., and R. N. ASLIN, 1995. Assessment of vernier acuity development using the "equivalent intrinsic blur" paradigm. *Vis. Res.* 35:1879–1888.

SPETNER, N. B., and L. W. OLSHO, 1990. Auditory frequency resolution in human infancy. *Child Dev.* 61:632–652.

STAPELLS, D. R., R. GALAMBOS, J. A. COSTELLO, and S. MAKEIG, 1988. Inconsistency of auditory middle latency and steady-state responses in infants. *Electroencephalogr. Clin. Neurophysiol.* 71:289–295.

SUGA, N., 1984. Neural mechanisms of complex-sound processing for echolocation. *Trends Neurosci.* 7:20–27.

SUR, M., S. L. PALLAS, and A. W. ROE, 1990. Cross-modal plasticity in cortical development: Differentiation and specification of sensory neocortex. *Trends Neurosci.* 13:227–233.

TALLAL, P., S. L. MILLER, G. BEDI, G. BYMA, X. WANG, S. S. NAGARAJAN, C. SCHREINER, W. M. JENKINS, and M. M. MERZENICH, 1996. Language comprehension in language-learning impaired children improved with acoustically modified speech. *Science* 271:81–84.

TALLAL, P., S. MILLER, and R. H. FITCH, 1993. Neurobiological basis of speech: A case for the preeminence of temporal processing. *Ann. N.Y. Acad. Sci.* 682:27–47

THORPE, L. A., and S. E. TREHUB, 1989. Duration illusion and auditory grouping in infancy. *Dev. Psychol.* 24:484–491.

TREHUB, S. E., D. BULL, and L. A. THORPE, 1984. Infants' per9ception of melodies: The role of melodic contour. *Child Dev.* 55:821–830.

TREHUB, S. E., G. SCHELLENBERG, and D. HILL, 1997. The origins of music perception and cognition: A developmental perspective. In *Perception and Cognition of Music,* I. Deliège and J. Sloboda, eds. East Sussex, UK: Psychology Press, pp. 103–128.

TREHUB, S. E., B. A. SCHNEIDER, and M. ENDMAN, 1980. Developmental changes in infants' sensitivity to octave-band noises. *J. Exp. Child Psychol.* 29:282–293.

TREHUB, S. E., B. A. SCHNEIDER, and J. L. HENDERSON, 1995. Gap detection in infants, children, and adults. *J. Acoust. Soc. Am.* 98:2532–2541.

TREHUB, S. E., and L. A. THORPE, 1989. Infants' perception of rhythm: Categorization of auditory sequences by temporal structure. *Can. J. Psychol.* 43:217–229.

TREHUB, S. E., L. A. THORPE, and B. A. MORRONGIELLO, 1985. Infants' perception of melodies: Changes in a single tone. *Infant Behav. Dev.* 8:213–223.

TREHUB, S. E., L. A. THORPE, and B. MORRONGIELLO, 1987. Organizational processes in infants' perception of auditory patterns. *Child Dev.* 58:741–749.

WERNER, L. A., and J. Y. BARGONES, 1991. Sources of auditory masking in infants: Distraction effects. *Percept. Psychophysics* 50:405–412.

WERNER, L. A., R. C. FOLSOM, and L. R. MANCL, 1993. The relationship between auditory brainstem response and behavioral thresholds in normal hearing infants and adults. *Hear. Res.* 68:131–141.

WERNER, L. A., R. C. FOLSOM, and L. R. MANCL, 1994. The relationship between auditory brainstem response latency and behavioral thresholds in normal hearing infants and adults. *Hear. Res.* 77:88–98.

WERNER, L. A., and J. M. GILLENWATER, 1990. Pure-tone sensitivity of 2- to 5-week-old infants. *Infant Behav. Dev.* 13:355–375.

WERNER, L. A., and L. R. MANCL, 1993. Pure-tone thresholds of 1-month-old human infants. *J. Acoust. Soc. Am.* 93:2367.

WERNER, L. A., and G. C. MAREAN, 1996. *Human Auditory Development.* Boulder, Colo.: Westview Press.

WERNER, L. A., G. C. MAREAN, C. F. HALPIN, N. B. SPETNER, and J. M. GILLENWATER, 1992. Infant auditory temporal acuity: Gap detection. *Child Dev.* 63:260–272.

WERNER, L. A., and E. W. RUBEL, 1992. *Developmental Psychoacoustics.* Washington, D.C.: American Psychological Association.

WERTHEIMER, M., 1961. Psychomotor coordination of auditory and visual space at birth. *Science* 134:1692.

WIGHTMAN, F., P. ALLEN, T. DOLAN, D. KISTLER, and D. JAMIESON, 1989. Temporal resolution in children. *Child Dev.* 60:611–624.

YAKOVLEV, P. I., and A. R. LECOURS, 1967. The myelogenetic cycles of regional maturation of the brain. In *Regional Development of the Brain in Early Life,* A. Minkowski, ed. Oxford: Blackwell, pp. 3–70.

# 16 Brain–Behavior Relationships in Early Visual Development

JAMES L. DANNEMILLER

ABSTRACT  Anatomical, physiological, and functional data on early visual development are reviewed by discussing models of brain–behavior relationships during this period. Models have been formulated at the retinal, subcortical, and cortical levels. Constraints based on front-end (optical and photoreceptoral) limitations have been reasonably successful in explaining the data on the development of spatial contrast vision. Cortically based models have relied on putative differences in the rates of maturation of various subpathways within the visual system to explain the order of emergence of various visual functions. These cortically based models are inherently more difficult to evaluate because of the complexities associated with brain–behavior relationships at this level of the visual system. Formulating developmental versions of these cortical brain–behavior relationships adds another level of subtlety to the problem when subpathways within the visual system develop "on-line" postnatally.

Models of brain–behavior relationships in early visual development have focused on several levels within the visual pathway. These models address development at the retinal (Banks and Bennett, 1988, 1991; Candy, Crowell, and Banks, 1998; Fulton et al., 1999; Hansen and Fulton, 1999), subcortical (Bronson, 1974), or cortical levels (Atkinson, 1984, 1992; Banton and Bertenthal, 1997; Johnson, 1990; Johnson and Vecera, 1996) and have attempted to link observed data on visual function, whether behavioral or evoked electrical activity, to properties of the underlying neural substrate. Such models of brain–behavior relationships in early visual development typically make inferences either from the known anatomy or physiology to observed behavior or from observed behavior to the anatomy and physiology. In the former case, data on the states of various neural elements within the visual system of human or primate infants are used to explain observed behavioral data (e.g., acuity or contrast sensitivity). In the latter case, observed behavioral data are used to make inferences about the presence and functioning of various subpopulations of feature-selective neurons within the visual pathway (e.g., orientation or direction selectivity). These models are developmental examples of

JAMES L. DANNEMILLER  Department of Psychology, University of Wisconsin at Madison, Madison, Wisconsin.

what Teller (1984) referred to as *linking propositions* in visual science—formal statements that attempt to link aspects of visual anatomy and physiology with observed visual capacities or behaviors.

A common theme that emerges from these models is the idea that different pathways within the visual system may develop at different rates (Atkinson, 1998; Banton and Bertenthal, 1997; Johnson, 1990). For example, Atkinson (1998) proposed that the magnocellular pathway may lag slightly behind the parvocellular pathway early in postnatal development. Johnson (1990) and Banton and Bertenthal (1997) based their models on data showing that different layers within primary visual cortex develop at different rates. On a simpler level, it has been proposed primarily on the basis of behavioral data that the short-wavelength sensitive (sws) cones may lag slightly in development over the first several weeks of postnatal life behind the medium- and long-wavelength sensitive (mws and lws) cones (Banks and Bennett, 1988). It is important to realize that these models, especially the cortical level ones, are arguing that vision in the early postnatal human infant is not simply a scaled version of vision in the mature adult. It is not simply that there is more noise in the young visual system or that the signals are generally weaker, but rather that the kinds of information available to the infant for purposes of object recognition and action may differ in kind from that available to normal human adults.

The purpose of this chapter is to review the available data on the early postnatal development of the visual system. I focus on the theme just noted—that different parts of the visual pathways develop at different rates. To organize this review, I discuss these various extant models of early visual development, then review the anatomical and physiological data from human and non-human primate visual development in the context of discussing these models. I do not review the extensive literature on plasticity and deprivation in early visual development (Daw, 1998; Pizzorusso and Maffei, 1996). The interested reader may consult the chapter by Maurer in this volume for a discussion of visual system plasticity.

## Retinal development

The absorption of photons of light by the photoreceptors is the first step in the visual cascade that eventually leads to seeing. Why is it important to focus on this first stage of information transmission in the visual pathway? There is a simple answer to this question. Information in the optical image that is lost at this first stage of processing can never be recovered. The only thing that subsequent stages in the visual pathway can do is to operate on the information that leaves the retina; they cannot recreate information (spatiotemporal contrast) that has been lost at this level. If the anatomical data on which the models are based are accurate and representative, and if their assumptions are valid, then these models tell us, importantly, that vision can be no better than what has been calculated; it can only be equal to or worse than this. It pays, therefore, to understand these models because they tell us what spatial information is available to the remainder of the infant's visual system for important tasks like object recognition and the perception of spatial layout.

Before discussing these retinal models in detail, we must understand their limitations. First, the actual anatomical data base upon which these models are built is actually quite sparse. This raises questions about the accuracy and representativeness of the models. Second, these models consider only the constraints on spatial but not on temporal processing imposed by the front-end characteristics. Undoubtedly, temporal contrast is important for many visual tasks (e.g., motion processing), so these models tell us nothing about what to expect when temporal contrast variation is added to the picture. The reason for neglecting temporal processing in these retinally inspired models is a simple one: Temporal contrast processing at the retinal level is determined by more than the morphological characteristics of the photoreceptors. It is difficult to construct ideal observer analyses like those favored by Banks and colleagues once temporal contrast variation is permitted because to incorporate such effects it is necessary to make assumptions about temporal integration, and such assumptions move us further from the "ideal" observers possible with purely spatial contrast information. An "ideal observer" makes optimal use of all available information for doing some task (e.g., detection or discrimination); as such, it serves as a useful benchmark against which real performance can be compared.

Fortunately, two factors make it possible to construct reasonably rigorous, quantitative developmental models at the retinal level. First, the contributions of various structures in the eye to the amount of information in the pattern of photoreceptor absorptions are fairly well understood. For example, the diameter and length of photoreceptor inner and outer segments determine what proportion of the incident photons are likely to be absorbed by the photopigment. This is a purely physical/optical calculation, like calculating the optical aperture of a telescope. Second, anatomical data exist on the characteristics of these optical and retinal structures, so it is possible to use these data to calculate estimates of information transmission to, and including, the point at which photons are actually absorbed by the photopigment.

Examples of the models that have been proposed at this level are ones covering scotopic (night) vision (Brown, Dobson, and Maier, 1987; Hansen and Fulton, 1999) and photopic (day) vision (Banks and Bennett, 1988; Banks and Crowell, 1993; Brown, 1993; Brown, Dobson, and Maier, 1987; Candy, Crowell, and Banks, 1998; Wilson, 1988, 1993). The Hansen and Fulton model is somewhat simpler because it is meant to explain only the large differences that exist between the absolute thresholds of infants and adults in the detection of light. Absolute threshold is simply a measure of the minimum amount of light that can be detected reliably under a set of fixed viewing conditions. I will turn next to the Hansen and Fulton (1999) model because it illustrates how anatomical measurements can be used to make reasonably accurate predictions of the development of visual sensitivity.

Absolute thresholds are significantly higher in young infants than in adults (see Brown, 1990, for a review). Why is this true? It would be possible to answer this question in many ways. The answer to this simple question illustrates one of the primary virtues of these models. One could point to the weaker attentional capacities of young infants or to their lack of motivation for behaving like practiced psychophysical observers as explanations for why their thresholds are higher. Instead, these models choose to answer this question by using known anatomical data to constrain best or "ideal" visual performance. In other words, if one is going to explain improvements in absolute threshold, perhaps the place to start is at the very beginning, in the photoreceptors themselves. Only after estimates have been derived using these anatomical data should one proceed to attribute any remaining infant/adult differences to higher level attentional or motivational processes. These models have the virtue of simplicity; more complex, psychological processes should only be invoked as explanations for some observed behavior after simpler, more peripheral explanations have been ruled out as being complete.

With postmortem anatomical measurements, Fulton and colleagues (1999) showed that the amount of rhodopsin—the photosensitive pigment in rods—is much less in preterm and term infant eyes than it is in adult eyes, and that it increases rapidly during infancy. At birth, rhodopsin content is approximately 35% of its adult value, and it reaches 50% of its adult value by 5 weeks postnatally. It appears to reach its adult value sometime near 40 weeks of age. These increases in rhodopsin are likely to reflect the increases in the lengths of the rod outer segments (OS) in which the rhodopsin is held (Hendrickson, 1994).

Hansen and Fulton (1999) noted that rod outer segment lengths at a peripheral retinal site in adults are approximately 2.3 times longer than they are in 5-day-old infants. Given that the amount of rhodopsin should be directly proportional to the length of the rod OS (assuming equal densities), this would predict a threshold increase for infants relative to adults of 0.4 log units. In their study of the development of absolute thresholds, Hansen and Fulton (1999) reported that the thresholds for 10-week-old infants were approximately 0.58 log units higher than they were in adults. At a more parafoveal retinal site, rod OS lengths in adults are approximately 9 times as long as they are in 5-day-old human infants. This would predict a difference of approximately 1 log unit. The 10-week-old absolute threshold at this parafoveal site was approximately 1.06 log units higher than the adult threshold. Finally, at 11 months of age, infant rod OS lengths are approximately 68% of the adult value, leading to the prediction that infant thresholds at this age should be only 0.16 log units higher than adult thresholds. Hansen and Fulton (1999) noted that no infant in their study who was 6 months of age or older had an absolute threshold that was more than 0.1 log units above the median adult threshold. These data show quite simply how increases in rod OS length, and by inference in the amounts of photon-catching rhodopsin (Fulton et al., 1999), go a long way toward explaining the differences between young infants and adults in their absolute thresholds and how those differences narrow over the course of postnatal development (see also Nusinowitz, Birch, and Birch, 1998).

Others have used the same strategy to model the development of visual acuity and contrast sensitivity (Banks and Bennett, 1988; Banks and Crowell, 1993; Brown, 1993; Brown, Dobson, and Maier, 1987; Candy, Crowell, and Banks, 1998; Wilson, 1988, 1993). These models also include the spatial distribution of the cone photoreceptors, because this distribution differs significantly across the retina in adults, and it has strong implications for photon capture and spatial contrast

transfer from the retina. I will concentrate here on the models proposed by Banks and colleagues, because Banks and Crowell (1993) showed that many of the conclusions offered by these alternative models regarding front-end constraints on vision in early infancy are very similar.

These models start with the optics of the eye. Prior to being absorbed by the photoreceptors, photons must pass through the optics of the eye. Several factors contribute to the optical quality of retinal images. For the purposes of this chapter, it is sufficient to note two things. First, Candy and colleagues (1998) and Banks and Bennett (1988) both assume that the optical transfer function of the neonatal eye is similar to that of the adult eye. The optical transfer function represents the extent to which contrast is attenuated as it passes through the optics of the eye (cornea, lens, and ocular media) as a function of spatial frequency. Optical systems generally attenuate contrast more at high spatial frequencies than at low spatial frequencies. The second factor that is important for the purposes of this chapter is that the length of the infant's eye is shorter than the length of the adult's eye. This has two consequences: (1) the retinal image is spread over a smaller area in the infant's eye; (2) the number of photons falling on a small patch of retina (photons/deg$^2$) would be higher in the infant's eye if pupil sizes did not differ. The latter intensity effect is offset by the smaller pupil size of the infant's eye, so that the actual number of incident photons per patch of retina is probably not that different between infants and adults, except for small differences resulting from the slightly higher media transmittance in the neonate (Candy, Crowell, and Banks, 1998). Candy and colleagues (1998) estimated that the image of a small, distant object would be approximately two-thirds as large on the neonatal retina as on the adult retina. If photoreceptor packing densities were the same at these two ages, and they most certainly are not, then this difference in eye size alone would spread the image over fewer photoreceptors in the neonate's eye, leading to a less detailed initial encoding.

Once the optical properties of the cornea, lens, and media have been factored into the model, the most important remaining factors are (1) the morphologies of individual cone photoreceptors and (2) their spatial arrangements (packing densities). Data on the development of these properties and their mature, adult values are available from several sources (Abramov et al., 1982; Curcio, 1987; Curcio et al., 1990; Hendrickson, 1994; Hendrickson and Drucker, 1992; Yuodelis and Hendrickson, 1986). It should be noted, however, that these anatomical data used to model spatial contrast vision during early infancy come from one 5-day-old human infant (Yuodelis and Hendrickson, 1986), so the issue of the representativeness of this example must always be kept in mind (Candy, Crowell, and Banks, 1998). It is known that in adults there is considerable individual variability in some of the anatomical parameters used in these models (Curcio et al., 1990).

The morphologies of individual cones in the neonatal retina are markedly different from those of adults (Yuodelis and Hendrickson, 1986). As was true of rods, the outer segments of the cones are much shorter in the neonate than in the adult. Banks and Bennett (1988) modeled this difference as a factor of approximately 16:1 for foveal cones. Of course, this length difference implies that the amount of photosensitive material for capturing incident photons is that much less in the neonate assuming equal densities. Additionally, the effective apertures of these cones through which photons must be funneled to be absorbed was estimated by Banks and Bennett (1988) to differ by a factor of approximately 1.88 $[(0.48/0.35)^2]$ in favor of infants. The slightly larger aperture of the neonate's cones means that slightly more photons will be absorbed per infant cone given the same flux, but it also means that higher spatial frequency information will be degraded more because of greater spatial averaging over the cone's aperture.

The cones are also packed much less densely in the newborn's fovea. This packing density is important because it determines, to a large extent, the highest spatial frequency that can be reliably signaled from the photoreceptor catches across a small region of the retina. Sampling the image very finely permits information about high spatial frequencies (fine detail) to be transmitted well, while sampling the image very coarsely attenuates this high spatial frequency information significantly.[1] Additionally, lower packing densities also imply fewer photon absorptions given a fixed nodal distance because more of the photons pass through the retinal space not occupied by photoreceptors. When all of these factors were taken into account, Banks and Bennett (1988) estimated that if identical patches of light were to be presented to newborn and adult central retina, approximately 350 photons would be absorbed by the adult cone lattice for every one photon absorbed by the newborn's cones.

It is hard to overstate the significance of this factor for newborn vision. Fewer photon absorptions means much noisier signals because the emission of light is an inherently random process. Because the variance in the number of photons emitted from a source or reflected from a surface is proportional to the mean number of photons emitted or reflected (Poisson process), the sig-

nal:noise ratio expressed as the ratio of the mean to the standard deviation will increase with the square root of the mean. In other words, the availability of more photons ideally leads to an improvement in sensitivity that is proportional to the square root of the mean. The 350:1 ratio of absorbed photons for adults compared to infants means that the signal:noise ratio for infants would be at best 1/18 (square root behavior) as strong in newborns as in adults. Imagine trying to estimate a mean with a set of observations that was 18 times as variable as another set. Any visual task (e.g., intensity discrimination at an edge) that depends on pooling and averaging the responses from these isomerizations will surely suffer tremendously by having such impoverished information on which to base performance. Is it any wonder that contrast sensitivity is quite poor early in postnatal life? A good demonstration of what it might be like to see through the eyes of infants at various ages from birth to 6 months is shown in figure 16.1 (see color plate 13; Teller, 1997).

The most interesting conclusion from these models is that the front-end retinal limitations just described are insufficient to explain the poor contrast sensitivities and reduced acuities observed during this period (Banks and Crowell, 1993; Candy, Crowell, and Banks, 1998; but see also Wilson, 1988, 1993). In other words, observed values for these visual measures are *worse* than would be predicted from a visual system with the optical and retinal characteristics included in these models. It should be noted that these front-end limitations do explain a large proportion of the difference between infant and adult spatial contrast vision, but they do not explain *all* of it. This is an important conclusion for two reasons. First, it tells us that there must be additional, postreceptoral sites in the visual pathways at which significant information loss occurs in the infant's system. Second, it points to the possibility that some of the visual capabilities observed during early infancy may be constrained by the state of other structures within the visual pathways. One obvious structure is the visual cortex. I turn next to models that have examined the development of brain–behavior relationships at the cortical level.

## A selective look at cortical development

There are several differences between the developmental models involving cortical characteristics and those involving retinal characteristics. First, the retinal models make quantitative predictions. The predicted measures in such models tend to be continuous: absolute threshold, visual resolution acuity, and contrast sensitiv-

FIGURE 16.1 Simulated views of the same scene as viewed at birth (**A**), 3 months (**B**), 6 months (**C**), and adult (**D**). (Reprinted with permission from Tony Young.)

ity. In contrast, models involving cortical function tend to make qualitative predictions. These models are concerned with predicting the presence or absence of some perceptual capacity thought to depend on cortical processing (e.g., orientation sensitivity). Second, the anatomical data on which the retinal models are based are generally easier to relate to visual performance than are the corresponding cortical data. It is easier to make predictions based on the lengths of cone outer segments than it is to make predictions based on the complexity of synaptic connectivity.

One exception to this statement that should be noted is the attempt by Wilson (1993) to relate cortical synaptic density, as reported by Huttenlocher and colleagues (1983; see also Huttenlocher and de Courten, 1987), to the development of various functions most likely to be mediated cortically (e.g., orientation selectivity, binocular rivalry, and stereopsis). Figure 16.2 shows that there is a time-lagged but close correlation between stereopsis development and the increase in synaptic density over the first year of life. Of course, this correlation cannot be interpreted causally, mainly because it is difficult, if not impossible, at this point in our understanding of cortical circuitry to relate quantitatively a measure like synaptic density to a measure like stereoacuity. Figure 16.3 shows Conel's (1939, 1951) renderings of sections of visual cortex from a newborn human infant (left) and a 6-month-old human infant (right). Although the postnatal increase in dendritic complexity is evident even to the naked eye, it is another matter to try to relate this increase quantitatively to some aspect of visual performance. All that one can do at this point is to agree with Wilson (1993) that until adequate models of functions like stereopsis are available, it is best to be content with the apparent correlation between the brain and behavioral measures.

Several investigators have proposed models of early visual development that involve cortical brain–behavior relationships (Atkinson, 1984, 1992, 1998; Banton and Bertenthal, 1997; Bronson, 1974; Johnson, 1990). One theme common to these models is that early visual development may be characterized by differential rates of maturation both within subpathways and between subpathways in the visual system. The most common example of this type of model involves earlier maturation of subcortical function than of cortical function (e.g.,

Atkinson, 1984; Bronson, 1974). This theme is also evident in Atkinson's (1992, 1998) proposals that the parvocellular pathway may lead the magnocellular pathway in maturation during early postnatal development, thereby leading to the earlier emergence of certain visual functions typically attributed to the parvocellular pathway. Finally, Johnson (1990) and Banton and Bertenthal (1997) have used anatomical data showing differential maturation of the laminae in primary visual cortex to argue for the differential emergence of certain aspects of visual attention and motion processing. Before reviewing these models and the evidence on which they are based, it is probably best to review briefly the major visual pathways that are important to these models.

Figure 16.4 is a schematic of several subcortical and cortical visual pathways, although this is certainly not an exhaustive diagram of such pathways. The major subcortical pathway involves direct projections from the retina to the superior colliculus (SC). The axons of retinal ganglion cells terminate primarily in the superficial layers of the superior colliculus (Kaas and Huerta, 1988). The major cortical pathway runs from the retina to the lateral geniculate nucleus (LGN) to area V1 of visual cortex (VC). There are also numerous descending pathways from VC to subcortical structures (e.g., LGN, SC, pulvinar) that are not shown here. I will discuss selective aspects of these pathways as they are relevant to the models listed above. A good general discussion of these pathways as they exist in mature primates can be found in Rodiek (1998).

The retinocortical pathway is thought to consist of two parallel and quasi-independent streams of processing: parvocellular and magnocellular (Livingstone and Hubel, 1988; Maunsell and Newsome, 1987; Van Essen, Anderson, and Felleman, 1992). These streams are evident in distinct classes of ganglion cells in the retina, are segregated in layers within the LGN (four parvocellular and two magnocellular layers), and project to distinct layers with the recipient zone of layer 4C of primary visual cortex. The parvocellular stream, postulated to subserve mainly color and form vision and comprising 80% of all ganglion cells in the primate retina, projects mainly to layer 4Cβ, while the magnocellular stream projects to layer 4Cα. This division is important because, as noted earlier, several of the models argue that differential maturation of cortical layers implies corresponding differences in certain aspects of visual performance.

The division of this pathway into magnocellular and parvocellular streams persists to some extent into other cortical areas. The magnocellular or parietal-directed stream is associated with areas V3, MT, MST, and pos-

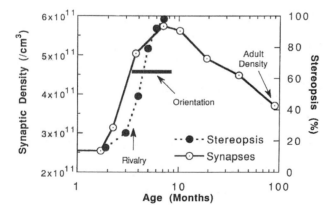

FIGURE 16.2 Cortical synaptic density (left y-axis) and the percentage of infants displaying stereopsis (right y-axis) plotted against postnatal age (x-axis). Synaptic density is plotted with open symbols and stereopsis is plotted with closed symbols. There is a close, time-lagged correlation between this anatomical measure and this functional measure. (Reprinted with permission from Wilson, 1993.)

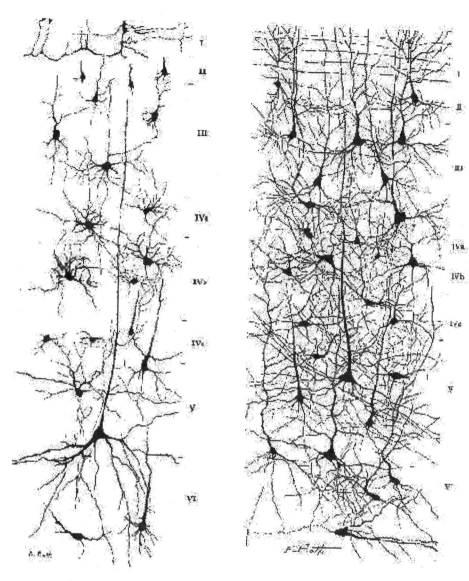

FIGURE 16.3  Striate cortex from a newborn (left) and a 6-month-old (right) human infant. (Reprinted with permission from Conel, 1939 [left], and Conel, 1951 [right].)

terior parietal areas. The parvocellular or temporal-directed stream is associated with areas V4 and inferotemporal cortex. It is important to keep in mind that this division into two primary streams does not imply complete independence between the processing of information within these streams. As is evident below, even in area V1 there is evidence for crosstalk between these two streams.

Given this brief review of the visual pathways, I now turn to the developmental models based on subcortical and cortical processing. Bronson (1974) first proposed that early in postnatal life much of the visual capacity of the neonate could be explained by supposing that the subcortical pathway from retina to superior colliculus matured or was functional earlier than the cortical

pathway from retina to visual cortex. Atkinson (1984) echoed this proposal that much of the observed visual behavior in the first month is controlled subcortically and added the additional postulate that the descending pathways from visual cortex to superior colliculus matures later, leading to changes around 2 months in certain visual capacities (e.g., attentional switching, binocular convergence).

Using resting positron emission tomography (PET), Chugani and Phelps (1986) concluded that prior to 3 months various subcortical areas (e.g., thalamus, midbrain-brainstem) were probably more functionally mature than various cortical areas (e.g., occipital, parietal, and temporal). Different cortical areas also mature earlier than others (e.g., temporal prior to frontal;

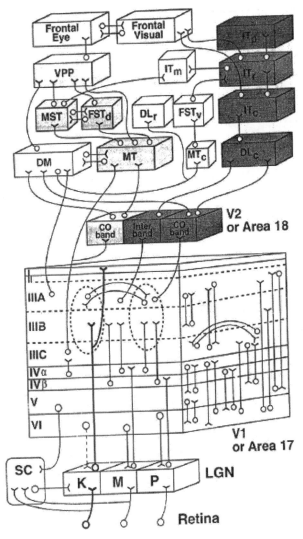

FIGURE 16.4 Various subcortical and cortical visual pathways. M = magnocellular and P = parvocellular. Notice the retinal projections both to the superior colliculus and to the LGN. There are also extensive reciprocal connections between various extrastriate cortical areas and the pulvinar not shown here. The K (koniocellular) pathway is not discussed in this chapter. (Reprinted with permission from Casagrande, 1994.)

out the operation of visual cortex. What visual capacities might we expect to be present when only subcortical structures are mediating vision or when vision is mediated by pathways other than the ones through primary visual cortex? Several reports exist that are relevant to this question (see Stoerig and Cowey, 1997, for a review). For example, color vision is typically thought to involve cortical processing within the parvocellular stream, although the substrate for this is surely set up initially within the color opponent ganglion cells of the retina. Despite this cortical involvement, Stoerig and Cowey (1992) and Barbur and colleagues (1998) reported color discrimination in individuals with significant primary cortical lesions or without primary visual cortices.

Additionally, Braddick and colleagues (1992) have reported on several visual capacities present in unilaterally decorticate human infants. This report is important because absence of striate visual cortex does not necessarily imply that all visual function is then mediated subcortically; it is possible that projections to extrastriate visual cortex could also be involved. In these two cases reported by Braddick and colleagues (1992), however, both striate and extrastriate cortex were missing, so subcortical pathways must have mediated the remaining visual capacities. These infants could visually orient to a conspicuous target presented to the contralesioned visual field, as would be expected if such a function were subserved by the superior colliculus. Somewhat unexpectedly, however, binocularly symmetric OKN, previously thought to be mediated by crossed subcortical pathways, was found to be asymmetric in both of these infants. This implies that, contrary to earlier ideas that cortical involvement need not be invoked to explain symmetric binocular OKN, such cortical involvement may indeed be necessary. This is significant because, even in the newborn infant, OKN is binocularly symmetric.

One other recent report is relevant to the question of what vision might be like in the absence of striate visual cortex. Shewmon, Holmes, and Byrne (1999) reported clinical observations on multiple functions in four congenitally decorticate children. Of particular relevance are their reports that some of these children could actively track, albeit not very smoothly, moving objects such as faces, visually orient to objects moved into the peripheral visual field, and (in one case) fixate steadily. Additionally, several of these children were said to be able to recognize familiar adults, although this probably occurred through other sensory modalities. All of these children were assumed to be cortically blind. Shewmon and colleagues (1999) proposed the interesting idea that some of these visual capacities

Erickson et al., 1998). Aspects of visual behavior such as orienting probably depend heavily on the superior colliculus, so it is natural to suppose that the visual orienting in newborns, however sluggish, reflects the function of this structure. Additionally, early postnatal asymmetries in optokinetic nystagmus (OKN), a reflexive visual tracking of large moving fields, and the disappearance of these asymmetries later in the first half year of life imply that the superior colliculus alone may mediate much of the visual behavior observed in the neonatal period.

However, when examining these models it is important to determine just what vision is like with and with-

might represent "vertical" plasticity in subcortical structures. It is generally accepted that "horizontal" plasticity between different cortical areas may take place when tissue in one area is disrupted and its function is taken over or usurped by remaining cortical tissue (Baseler, Morland, and Wandell, 1999; Chugani, Muller, and Chugani, 1996; Cohen et al., 1997; Sadato et al., 1996). What Shewmon and colleagues (1999) propose is that subcortical structures may be vertically plastic and organize prenatally or reorganize to take over supposed cortical functions in the absence of target occipital cortex (see also Kalil and Behan, 1987). Until more systematic visual tests are done on such children, it is difficult to say precisely how good these remaining visual capacities are. Nevertheless, observations such as these are valuable in giving some insight into what vision is like without cortical pathways.

The remaining models of visual development have all proposed differential maturation of specific subpathways in the visual system as explanations for the emergence of various visual capacities. Atkinson (1992, 1998) has proposed that the parvocellular pathway is more mature early in postnatal development than the magnocellular pathway. The behavioral evidence that is meant to be explained by this model is primarily pattern vision (e.g., orientation sensitivity). Johnson's (1990) model is meant to explain primarily orienting and attentional behavior based on anatomical data from Conel (1939, 1951) that the primary visual cortex matures from deeper (levels 5 and 6) to more superficial layers (layers 1–3). Additionally, Johnson proposed that descending pathways from striate and extrastriate cortex to superior colliculus mature at different rates. Finally, Banton and Bertenthal (1997) also proposed that differential postnatal maturation of the laminar structure of striate cortex from deeper to more superficial layers may explain various aspects of the development of motion processing.

I will use Atkinson's (1992, 1998) model to illustrate the theme of explaining early visual development by pointing to differential maturation of subpathways. This model is a good example of using behavioral evidence to infer the state of various cortical areas. As such, it relies heavily on modern visual neurophysiology with its major division of visual processing into parvocellular and magnocellular streams. This model affords a good opportunity to review the behavioral evidence on early visual development as well as the anatomical and neurophysiological evidence on the maturation of various areas in visual cortex.

Atkinson's model (1992, 1998) relies heavily on the idea that certain aspects of visual processing are the province of the parvocellular (ventral) stream while others are the province of the magnocellular (dorsal) stream. Additionally, development in this model consists of integration across these streams (the binding problem) so that the infant eventually comes to have a complete representation of objects in the world and of their spatial positions. This representation serves the purposes of object recognition and action. Atkinson argues that the ability of very young infants in the first few weeks of life to discriminate the orientations of grating patterns (Atkinson et al., 1988) and the temporal-frequency dependency shown by evoked responses to orientation changes are evidence of the early maturation of the parvocellular pathway (Braddick, Wattam-Bell, and Atkinson, 1986) because this function is subserved primarily by parvocellular neurons in adults (but see also Levitt, Lund, and Yoshioka, 1996).

In contrast, motion processing that is selective for direction is supposed to be handled primarily by the magnocellular pathway. Excluding OKN, true evidence of direction selective responding does not emerge until after 6–8 weeks of age, and it is evident at slow velocities before it is at faster ones (Wattam-Bell, 1991). Thus, unlike orientation discrimination which is evident well before 6–8 postnatal weeks, this magnocellular characteristic—directional selectivity—is not evident until near the end of the second month. Atkinson (1998) concludes that magnocellular function lags parvocellular function early in development.

Disparity sensitivity and binocular correlation detection do not emerge until approximately 3–4 months postnatally (Birch, Gwiazda, and Held, 1982; Fox et al., 1980). Depth processing is thought to be handled by the magnocellular pathway. In contrast, 8-week-olds (Hamer, Alexander, and Teller, 1982; Packer, Hartmann, and Teller, 1984) and possibly even neonates and 4-week-olds (Adams, Maurer, and Davis, 1986; Maurer and Adams, 1987) can detect pattern differences based on color alone, and color is thought to be processed primarily by the parvocellular pathway (although see Barbur et al., 1998). Once again, functions attributed mainly to the magnocellular stream (disparity, depth) appear to emerge slightly later than ones attributed to the parvocellular stream (color).

What do we know about the differential emergence of these two processing streams from anatomical and neurophysiological studies on humans or closely related species? The retinal ganglion cells that make up these two streams diverge early in embryonic development in the primate visual system, and they project to the appropriate lamina in the developing LGN well before any visual experience (Meissirel et al., 1997). The projections from relay neurons in LGN arrive at their targets in layer 4C in striate cortex prenatally, and the axons terminate in appropriate sublaminae within 4C, again before any visual experience (Mates and Lund, 1983). Initially, it appears that LGN neurons may also project to layer 6 of striate cortex before birth (Rakic, 1976, 1977). Intrinsic retinal activity during prenatal development may play a role in organizing the laminar characteristics, feature maps (e.g., orientation preferences, ocular dominance columns), and appropriate projections in the retinogeniculocortical pathway prior to extrinsic visual experience (Hubener, 1998; Godecke and Bonhoeffer, 1996; Katz and Shatz, 1996; Shatz, 1996). Indeed, the laminar structure of visual cortex and its reciprocal connections with LGN even develop when slices of future visual cortex and LGN are cocultured in vitro (Toyama et al., 1991).[2]

Anatomical data on the development of visual cortical areas from humans and closely related primates present a mixed picture on whether or not one of the two processing streams is ahead of the other in terms of its state at birth and its postnatal maturation. One of the problems in using the anatomical data to make inferences about the presence of a particular function is that it is not clear exactly which characteristics should be used to infer effective function. One could examine myelination as a marker for effective function, or one could examine synaptic connectivity and morphology for clues to when a particular region appears to be functional. As others have noted (e.g., Banton and Bertenthal, 1997), Conel (1939) pointed out that axons in the deeper laminae (5 and 6) of striate cortex appear to myelinate earlier than those in more superficial laminae. Thus, extrastriate areas receiving projections from neurons in striate laminae 5 and 6 (e.g., area MT) might be expected to support effective function before those receiving projections for more superficial laminae. This is the basis for Banton and Bertenthal's (1997) proposal that newborns may be expected to respond to translatory motion.

If one examines other markers of anatomical development in striate cortex, differential gradients of maturation are either not as clear or are conflicting. For example, Lund and Holbach (1991) showed that the development of type I dendritic spines, which are associated with synaptic contacts, reaches a peak in macaque monkeys approximately 5 weeks postnatally for neurons in lamina 4Cα (magnocellular) whereas a similar peak is not reached for neurons in lamina 4Cβ until 8 weeks postnatally (see also LeVay, Wiesel, and Hubel, 1980; Lund, Holbach, and Chung, 1991). The same was also true of type II inhibitory synapses in layer 4C, with those in the magnocellular recipient layer developing slightly ahead of those in the parvocellular layer (Lund and Harper, 1991). It is also interesting that these pre-sumed inhibitory synapses in layer 4C lag the development of excitatory synapses in the same laminae (Lund and Harper, 1991). Becker and colleagues (1984) showed that in humans, dendritic branching was more advanced in layer 5 than in layer 3 in visual cortex prenatally and during early postnatal development, a trend consistent with the myelination from deeper to more superficial laminae. Neuronal densities in human striate visual cortex also appear to follow the gradient noted above, with deeper layers preceding more superficial layers until densities stabilize several months after birth (Leuba and Garey, 1987).

Finally, Lund, Boothe, and Lund (1977) concluded that in macaque monkeys, maturation of the morphology of visual cortical neurons occurs at the same rate in all laminae, with perhaps some advantage based on the size of the neuron; large pyramidal neurons in layer 5 tended to mature earlier than smaller neurons in other laminae. From this brief review, it is evident that whether or not there is a noticeable advance in the maturation of magnocellular versus parvocellular neurons or neurons in one layer or another depends on what aspect of cortical or neuronal morphology is being considered, although one has to agree with Banton and Bertenthal (1997) that, on many of these characteristics, magnocellular neurons appear to be slightly ahead of parvocellular neurons.

## Subtleties of the differential maturation hypothesis

Most of the models based on cortical development argue that the order of emergence of certain visual functions in early postnatal development reflects the differential maturation of subpathways in the visual system. I will conclude with several subtleties and implicit assumptions that should be noted with this basic hypothesis.

1. *The degree of independence of the subpathways involved in these models may not be as great as postulated.* For example, Dobkins and Albright (1994) showed that neurons in area MT of the macaque, thought to be the paradigm case for magnocellular processing, are capable of using color differences to signal the directions of motion. Maunsell, Nealey, and DePriest (1990) had reported similar results earlier showing that both magnocellular and parvocellular influences can be detected in the responses of area MT neurons. Color processing by a strict division of labor would be expected to fall to the parvocellular system, so this result indicates less independence of these subpathways than may be indicated in some of the models discussed previously. Gegenfurtner and Kiper (1996) showed that as early as cortical area V2, neurons were multiply selective for

form, color, and motion and argued that there is no functional segregation of these stimulus features at this level of the visual pathway. These neurophysiological studies are supported by anatomical studies showing interneurons as early as cortical areas V1 and V2 that merge the parvocellular and magnocellular streams (Levitt, Lund, and Yoshioka, 1996; Levitt, Yoshioka, and Lund, 1994; Lund, 1987; Lund and Yoshioka, 1991; Yoshioka, Levitt, and Lund, 1994).

2. *A particular visual function that is ascribed to one subsystem in the mature adult may not necessarily be mediated by that subsystem when it first emerges in development.* For example, Dobkins, Lia, and Teller (1997) and Dobkins, Anderson, and Lia (1999) have argued from psychophysical tests of chromatic and luminance temporal contrast sensitivity that the magnocellular pathway may mediate detection of both luminance and chromatic spatiotemporal contrast. If this were true, it would differ substantially from the case later in development in which chromatic contrast sensitivity is signaled primarily by a temporally low-pass parvocellular channel and luminance contrast is signaled by a temporally bandpass magnocellular channel. Dobkins and Teller (1996) concluded that for 3-month-old infants, patterns defined by color contrast alone or patterns defined by luminance contrast are both detected by mechanisms sensitive to the direction of motion. This contrasts strongly with the case in adults in which mechanisms sensitive to luminance contrast are selective for direction of motion, but those mediating detection of color contrast are not.

Morton and Johnson (1991) have proposed that face processing, a function typically attributed to the ventral/temporal cortical pathway, may first emerge during the newborn period mediated by subcortical structures. In all of these cases, a visual function typically attributed to one level or subpathway within the mature visual system may emerge first in development being mediated by a different subsystem. If the hypothesis of differential rates of maturation of subpathways is taken seriously, it should not be surprising that the most sensitive pathway for mediating detection of some stimulus feature early in development may not necessarily be the same pathway that mediates detection of that feature later in childhood or in adulthood (see also Banton and Bertenthal, 1997, for a similar suggestion).

A corollary to this point is that infants and adults almost certainly differ in the effort required to execute visual tasks. Differences in effort or automaticity have been shown in adults to be related to differential activation of cortical versus subcortical areas (Alexander et al., 1999; Schneider, Pimm-Smith, and Worden, 1994). Thus, the extent of cortical versus subcortical mediation

for a given task early in development may differ substantially from that seen in mature adults.

3. *Even if subpathways are quasi-independent in mature adults, when they first emerge there may be considerable overlap in how they process visual information.* For example, Hawken, Blakemore, and Morley (1997) showed that in the monkey LGN, spatial contrast sensitivity functions of magnocellular and parvocellular neurons overlap quite substantially at birth. Only later in the first year do the contrast sensitivities of the magnocellular neurons improve substantially enough to separate them from the parvocellular neurons that showed little improvements in peak luminance contrast sensitivity over 8 months. It may prove very difficult to attribute processing early in development to one subsystem or another simply because the subsystems may not show the degree of stimulus separation early in life characteristic of the mature visual system.

This is similar to Johnson and Vecera's (1996) "cortical parcellation" hypothesis in which the segregation of visual information processing into subsystems only occurs postnatally, with many of these subsystems operating initially after birth unsegregated. A corollary to this point is that early in postnatal development there may be transient connections between cortical regions that disappear later in development (Huntley et al., 1988; Rodman and Consuelos, 1994). There is even evidence from the other end of the lifespan that the two major processing streams may become less distinct with age (Grady et al., 1992).

4. *There may be significant temporal lags between the emergence of a given function at the single-unit level and behavioral evidence for that function.* This makes it very difficult to try to link the anatomical and neurophysiological data and the behavioral data. For example, Chino and colleagues (1997) demonstrated that binocular, disparity-sensitive neurons exist at or near birth in macaque area V1, although it is not for several weeks that stereopsis can be demonstrated behaviorally.

5. *"Bottleneck" developmental theories (e.g., Banton and Bertenthal, 1997; Johnson, 1990) which propose that gradients of maturation within striate cortical laminae are responsible for the order of emergence of various behavioral functions may overlook the extensive alternative pathways to extrastriate cortex that do not go through striate cortex.* For example, Benson, Guo, and Blakemore (1998) showed that many of the motion perception functions typically associated with cortical area MT (direction discrimination, perception of moving plaid direction, and coherent motion in random dot displays) remain after loss of primary (V1) visual cortex and its subsequent input to area MT. Benson and colleagues (1998) suggested that a subcortical pathway from superior colliculus through the in-

ferior pulvinar to area MT may mediate such capacities in the absence of input/output from primary visual cortex. A similar suggestion was made by Baseler, Morland, and Wandell (1999). Differential maturation of laminae within primary visual cortex early in postnatal development would only be expected to impose an order on the emergence of visual capacities if these alternative routes from subcortex to extrastriate cortex were immature or if these extrastriate areas themselves were also immature.

## Conclusions

An immature and developing visual system is not necessarily an adult visual system that has been scaled down in terms of its spatial and temporal processing; nor is it necessarily like an adult visual system in which some subpathways have simply been deleted. It is entirely possible that prior to the point at which these subpathways are segregated and subsequently integrated in a mature fashion they may interact and process information in ways that are not characteristic of the adult visual system. Thus, the magnocellular pathway early in postnatal development may signal chromatic contrast to a much greater extent than in the adult, or scanning eye movements may produce enough spatiotemporal contrast to allow the magnocellular stream to process chromatic boundaries to the point at which discrimination is possible (Teller, 1998). Epelbaum and Teller (1995) showed that asymmetries in OKN in 2-month-olds are reversed, *not* eliminated, when isoluminant chromatic stimuli are used to drive the eye movements—a result that is not found in adults. Unlike models based on photoreceptor morphology and geometry in which the brain–behavior relationships can be modeled based on well-understood physical and optical principles, our lack of understanding of complex cortical circuitry and of how various visual functions arise from such circuits makes it inherently more difficult to link brain and behavior when the brain side of the link is visual cortex. Nevertheless, much of the interesting development that occurs postnatally in the visual system undoubtedly involves striate and extrastriate cortical areas and inhibitory interactions within and between these areas. Our modeling should respect the additional, specifically developmental subtleties likely to arise when multiple subsystems develop "on-line" during the postnatal period.

ACKNOWLEDGMENTS This research was supported by NICHD R01 HD32927 to JLD. I thank Jackie Roessler for her help in securing most of the references for this chapter and Pat Klitzke for her help in preparing the manuscript. I also thank Fred Wightman for help in scanning the figures.

## NOTES

1. I will not discuss the phenomenon of aliasing that occurs in undersampled systems. The interested reader can consult Thibos, Walsh, and Cheney (1987) for an example and a discussion of spatial aliasing in vision.
2. One note of caution is in order. Horton and Hocking (1996) reported the presence of clearly defined ocular dominance columns in newborn macaque monkeys, although Horton and Hedley-Whyte (1984) did not observe these columns in newborns, but only in a 6-month-old human. Possible species differences should always be kept in mind when generalizing from monkeys to humans.

## REFERENCES

ABRAMOV, I., J. GORDON, A. HENDRICKSON, L. HAINLINE, V. DOBSON, and E. LABOSSIERE, 1982. The retina of the newborn human infant. *Science* 217:265–267.

ADAMS, R., D. MAURER, and M. DAVIS, 1986. Newborns' discrimination of chromatic from achromatic stimuli. *J. Exp. Child Psychol.* 41:267–281.

ALEXANDER, G. E., M. J. MENTIS, J. D. VAN HORN, C. L. GRADY, K. F. BERMAN, M. L. FUREY, P. PIETRINI, S. I. RAPOPORT, M. B. SCHAPIRO, and J. R. MOELLER, 1999. Individual differences in PET activation of object perception and attention systems predict face matching accuracy. *NeuroReport* 10:1965–1971.

ATKINSON, J., 1984. Human visual development over the first 6 months of life: A review and a hypothesis. *Hum. Neurobiol.* 3:61–74.

ATKINSON, J., 1992. Early visual development: Differential functioning of parvocellular and magnocellular pathways. *Eye* 6:129–135.

ATKINSON, J., 1998. The 'where and what' or 'who and how' of visual development. In *The Development of Sensory, Motor and Cognitive Capacities in Early Infancy*, F. Simion and G. Butterworth, eds. East Sussex: Psychology Press, pp. 3–24.

ATKINSON, J., B. HOOD, J. WATTAM-BELL, S. ANKER, and J. TRICKLEBANK, 1988. Development of orientation discrimination in infancy. *Perception* 17:587–595.

BANKS, M. S., and P. J. BENNETT, 1988. Optical and photoreceptor immaturities limit the spatial and chromatic vision of human neonates. *J. Optical Soc. Am. [A]* 5:2059–2079.

BANKS, M. S., and P. J. BENNETT, 1991. Anatomical and physiological constraints on neonatal visual sensitivity and determinants of fixation behavior. In *Newborn Attention: Biological Constraints and the Influence of Experience*, M. J. S. Weiss and P. R. Zelazo, eds. Norwood, N.J.: Ablex Publishing, pp. 177–217.

BANKS, M. S., and J. A. CROWELL, 1993. Front-end limitations to infant spatial vision: Examination of two analyses. In *Early Visual Development, Normal and Abnormal*, K. Simons, ed. New York: Oxford University Press, pp. 91–116.

BANTON, T., and B. I. BERTENTHAL, 1997. Multiple developmental pathways for motion processing. *Optometry Vis. Sci.* 74:751–760.

BARBUR, J. L., A. SAHRAIE, A. SIMMONS, L. WEISKRANTZ, and S. C. R. WILLIAMS, 1998. Residual processing of chromatic signals in the absence of a geniculostriate projection. *Vis. Res.* 38:3447–3453.

BASELER, H. A., A. B. MORLAND, and B. A. WANDELL, 1999. Topographic organization of human visual areas in the absence of input from primary cortex. *J. Neurosci.* 19:2619–2627.

BECKER, L. E., D. L. ARMSTRONG, F. CHAN, and M. M. WOOD, 1984. Dendritic development in human occipital cortical neurons. *Dev. Brain Res.* 13:117–124.

BENSON, P. J., K. GUO, and C. BLAKEMORE, 1998. Direction discrimination of moving gratings and plaids and coherence in dot displays without primary visual cortex (V1). *Eur. J. Neurosci.* 10:3767–3772.

BIRCH, E. E., J. GWIAZDA, and R. HELD, 1982. Stereoacuity development for crossed and uncrossed disparities in human infants. *Vis. Res.* 22:507–513.

BRADDICK, O., J. ATKINSON, B. HOOD, W. HARKNESS, G. JACKSON, and F. VARGHA-KHADEM, 1992. Possible blindsight in infants lacking one cerebral hemisphere. *Nature* 360:461–463.

BRADDICK, O. J., J. WATTAM-BELL, and J. ATKINSON, 1986. Orientation-specific cortical responses develop in early infancy. *Nature* 320:617–619.

BRONSON, G., 1974. The postnatal growth of visual capacity. *Child Dev.* 45:873–890.

BROWN, A. M., 1990. Development of visual sensitivity to light and color vision in human infants: A critical review. *Vis. Res.* 30:1159–1188.

BROWN, A. M., 1993. Intrinsic noise and infant visual performance. In *Early Visual Development, Normal and Abnormal*, K. Simons, ed. Oxford: Oxford University Press, pp. 178–196.

BROWN, A. M., V. DOBSON, and J. MAIER, 1987. Visual acuity of human infants at scotopic, mesopic and photopic luminances. *Vis. Res.* 27:1845–1858.

CANDY, T. R., J. A. CROWELL, and M. S. BANKS, 1998. Optical, receptoral, and retinal constraints on foveal and peripheral vision in the human neonate. *Vis. Res.* 38:3857–3870.

CASAGRANDE, V. A., 1994. A third parallel visual pathway to primate area V1. *Trends Neurosci.* 17:305–310.

CHINO, Y. M., E. L. SMITH, S. HATTA, and H. CHENG, 1997. Postnatal development of binocular disparity sensitivity in neurons of the primate visual cortex. *J. Neurosci.* 17:296–307.

CHUGANI, H. T., R. A. MULLER, and D. C. CHUGANI, 1996. Functional brain reorganization in children. *Brain Dev.* 18:347–356.

CHUGANI, H. T., and M. E. PHELPS, 1986. Maturational changes in cerebral function in infants determined by 18FDG positron emission tomography. *Science* 231:840–843.

COHEN, L. G., P. CELNIK, A. PASCUAL-LEONE, B. CORWELL, L. FAIZ, J. DAMBROSIA, M. HONDA, N. SADATO, C. GERLOFF, M. D. CATALA, and M. HALLETT, 1997. Functional relevance of cross-modal plasticity in blind humans. *Nature* 389:180–183.

CONEL, J. L., 1939. *The Postnatal Development of the Human Cerebral Cortex*, Cambridge, Mass.: Harvard University Press.

CONEL, J. L., 1951. *The Postnatal Development of the Human Cerebral Cortex*, 4th ed. Cambridge, Mass.: Harvard University Press.

CURCIO, C. A., 1987. Diameters of presumed cone apertures in human retina. In *Annual Meeting of the Optical Society of America*, pp. 1–11.

CURCIO, C. A., K. R. SLOAN, R. E. KALINA, and A. E. HENDRICKSON, 1990. Human photoreceptor topography. *J. Comp. Neurol.* 292:497–523.

DAW, N. W., 1998. Critical periods and amblyopia. *Arch. Ophthalmol.* 116:502–505.

DOBKINS, K. R., and T. D. ALBRIGHT, 1994. What happens if it changes color when it moves? The nature of chromatic input to macaque visual area MT. *J. Neurosci.* 14:4854–4870.

DOBKINS, K. R., C. M. ANDERSON, and B. LIA, 1999. Infant temporal contrast sensitivity functions (tCSFs) mature earlier for luminance than for chromatic stimuli: Evidence for precocious magnocellular development? *Vis. Res.* 39:3223–3239.

DOBKINS, K. R., B. LIA, and D. Y. TELLER, 1997. Infant color vision: Temporal contrast sensitivity functions for chromatic (red/green) stimuli in 3-month-olds [review]. *Vis. Res.* 37:2699–2716.

DOBKINS, K. R., and D. Y. TELLER, 1996. Infant motion: detection (M:D) ratios for chromatically defined and luminance-defined moving stimuli. *Vis. Res.* 36:3293–3310.

EPELBAUM, M., and D. Y. TELLER, 1995. Infant eye movement asymmetries: Temporal-nasal asymmetry is reversed at isoluminance in 2-month-olds. *Vis. Res.* 35:1889–1895.

ERICKSON, S. L., M. AKIL, A. I. LEVEY, and D. A. LEWIS, 1998. Postnatal development of tyrosine hydroxylase- and dopamine transporter-immunoreactive axons in monkey rostral entorhinal cortex. *Cereb. Cortex* 8:415–427.

FOX, R., R. N. ASLIN, S. L. SHEA, and S. T. DUMAIS, 1980. Stereopsis in human infants. *Science* 207:323–324.

FULTON, A. B., J. DODGE, R. M. HANSEN, and T. P. WILLIAMS, 1999. The rhodopsin content of human eyes. *Invest. Ophthalmol. Vis. Sci.* 40:1878–1883.

GEGENFURTNER, K. R., and D. C. KIPER, 1996. Processing of color, form, and motion in macaque area V2. *Vis. Neurosci.* 13:161–172.

GODECKE, I., and T. BONHOEFFER, 1996. Development of identical orientation maps for two eyes without common visual experience. *Nature* 379:251–254.

GRADY, C. L., J. V. HAXBY, B. HORWITZ, M. B. SHAPIRO, S. I. RAPOPORT, L. G. UNGERLEIDER, M. MISHKIN, R. E. CARSON, and P. HERSCOVITCH, 1992. Dissociation of object and spatial vision in human extrastriate cortex: Age-related changes in activation of regional cerebral blood flow measured with [15O]water and positron emission tomography. *J. Cogn. Neurosci.* 4:23–34.

HAMER, R. D., K. ALEXANDER, and D. Y. TELLER, 1982. Rayleigh discriminations in human infants. *Vis. Res.* 22:575–587.

HANSEN, R. M., and A. B. FULTON, 1999. The course of maturation of rod-mediated visual thresholds in infants. *Invest. Ophthalmol. Vis. Sci.* 40:1883–1886.

HAWKEN, M. J., C. BLAKEMORE, and J. W. MORLEY, 1997. Development of contrast sensitivity and temporal-frequency selectivity in primate lateral geniculate nucleus. *Exp. Brain Res.* 114:86–98.

HENDRICKSON, A. E., 1994. The morphologic development of human and monkey retina. In *Principles and Practice of Ophthalmology: Basic Sciences*, D. M. Albert and F. A. Jakobiec, eds. Philadelphia: W.B. Saunders, pp. 561–577.

HENDRICKSON, A. E., and D. DRUCKER, 1992. The development of parafoveal and mid-peripheral human retina. *Behav. Brain Res.* 49:21–31.

HORTON, J. C., and E. T. HEDLEY-WHYTE, 1984. Mapping of cytochrome oxidase patches and ocular dominance columns in human visual cortex. *Phil. Trans. R. Soc. Lond. [B]* 304:255–272.

HORTON, J. C., and D. R. HOCKING, 1996. An adult-like pattern of ocular dominance columns in striate cortex of newborn monkeys prior to visual experience. *J. Neurosci.* 16:1791–1807.

HUBENER, M., 1998. Making maps in the dark. *Curr. Biol.* 8:R342–R345.

HUNTLEY, G. W., S. H. C. HENDRY, H. P. KILLACKEY, L. M. CHALUPA, and E. G. JONES, 1988. Temporal sequence of neurotransmitter expression by developing neurons of fetal monkey visual cortex. *Dev. Brain Res.* 43:69–96.

HUTTENLOCHER, P. R., and C. DE COURTEN, 1987. The development of synapses in striate cortex of man. *Hum. Neurobiol.* 6:1–9.

HUTTENLOCHER, P. R., C. DE COURTEN, L. J. GAREY, and H. VAN DER LOOS, 1983. Synaptogenesis in human visual cortex—evidence for synapse elimination during normal development. *Neurosci. Lett.* 33:247–252.

JOHNSON, M. H., 1990. Cortical maturation and the development of visual attention in early infancy. *J. Cogn. Neurosci.* 2:81–95.

JOHNSON, M. H., and S. P. VECERA, 1996. Cortical differentiation and neurocognitive development—the parcellation conjecture. *Behav. Proc.* 36:195–212.

KAAS, J. H., and M. F. HUERTA, 1988. The subcortical visual system of primates. In *Comparative Primate Biology,* Vol. 4, H. D. Steklis and J. Erwin, eds. New York: Alan R. Liss, pp. 327–391.

KALIL, R. E., and M. BEHAN, 1987. Synaptic reorganization in the dorsal lateral geniculate nucleus following damage to visual cortex in newborn or adult cats. *J. Comp. Neurol.* 257:216–236.

KATZ, L. C., and C. J. SHATZ, 1996. Synaptic activity and the construction of cortical circuits. *Science* 274:1133–1138.

LEUBA, G., and L. J. GAREY, 1987. Evolution of neuronal numerical density in the developing and aging human visual cortex. *Hum. Neurobiol.* 6:11–18.

LEVAY, S., T. N. WIESEL, and D. H. HUBEL, 1980. The development of ocular dominance columns in normal and visually deprived monkeys. *J. Comp. Neurol.* 191:1–51.

LEVITT, J. B., J. S. LUND, and T. YOSHIOKA, 1996. Anatomical substrates for early stages in cortical processing of visual information in the macaque monkey. *Behav. Brain Res.* 76:5–19.

LEVITT, J. B., T. YOSHIOKA, and J. S. LUND, 1994. Intrinsic cortical connections in macaque visual area V2: Evidence for interaction between different functional streams. *J. Comp. Neurol.* 342:551–570.

LIVINGSTONE, M., and D. HUBEL, 1988. Segregation of form, color, movement, and depth: Anatomy, physiology, and perception. *Science* 240:740–749.

LUND, J. S., 1987. Local circuit neurons of macaque monkey striate cortex: I. Neurons of laminae 4C and 5A. *J. Comp. Neurol.* 257:60–92.

LUND, J. S., R. G. BOOTHE, and R. D. LUND, 1977. Development of neurons in the visual cortex (area 17) of the monkey (*Macaca nemestrina*): A Golgi study from fetal day 127 to postnatal maturity. *J. Comp. Neurol.* 176:149–188.

LUND, J. S., and T. R. HARPER, 1991. Postnatal development of thalamic recipient neurons in the monkey striate cortex: III. Somatic inhibitory synapse acquisition by spiny stellate neurons of layer 4C. *J. Comp. Neurol.* 309:141–149.

LUND, J. S., and S. M. HOLBACH, 1991. Postnatal development of thalamic recipient neurons in the monkey striate cortex: I. Comparison of spine acquisition and dendritic growth of layer 4C alpha and beta spiny stellate neurons. *J. Comp. Neurol.* 309:115–128.

LUND, J. S., S. M. HOLBACH, and W.-W. CHUNG, 1991. Postnatal development of thalamic recipient neurons in the monkey striate cortex: II. Influence of afferent driving on spine acquisition and dendritic growth of layer 4C spiny stellate neurons. *J. Comp. Neurol.* 309:129–140.

LUND, J. S., and T. YOSHIOKA, 1991. Local circuit neurons of macaque monkey striate cortex: III. Neurons of laminae 4B, 4A, and 3B. *J. Comp. Neurol.* 311:234–258.

MATES, S. L., and J. S. LUND, 1983. Neuronal composition and development in lamina 4C of monkey striate cortex. *J. Comp. Neurol.* 221:60–90.

MAUNSELL, J., T. NEALEY, and D. DePRIEST, 1990. Magnocellular and parvocellular contributions to responses in the middle temporal visual area (MT) of the macaque monkey. *J. Neurosci.* 10:3233–3334.

MAUNSELL, J. H. R., and W. T. NEWSOME, 1987. Visual processing in monkey extrastriate cortex. *Annu. Rev. Neurosci.* 10:363–401.

MAURER, D., and R. ADAMS, 1987. Emergence of the ability to discriminate blue from gray at one month of age. *J. Exp. Child Psychol.* 44:147–156.

MEISSIREL, C., K. C. WIKLER, L. M. CHALUPA, and P. RAKIC, 1997. Early divergence of magnocellular and parvocellular functional subsytems in the embryonic visual system. *Proc. Natl. Acad. Sci. (USA)* 94:5900–5905.

MORTON, J., and M. H. JOHNSON, 1991. CONSPEC and CONLERN: A two-process theory of infant face recognition. *Psychol. Rev.* 98:164–181.

NUSINOWITZ, S., D. G. BIRCH, and E. E. BIRCH, 1998. Rod photoresponses in 6-week- and 4-month-old human infants. *Vis. Res.* 38:627–635.

PACKER, O., E. E. HARTMANN, and D. Y. TELLER, 1984. Infant color vision: The effect of test field size on Rayleigh discriminations. *Vis. Res.* 24:1247–1260.

PIZZORUSSO, T., and L. MAFFEI, 1996. Plasticity in the developing visual system. *Curr. Opin. Neurol.* 9:122–125.

RAKIC, P., 1976. Prenatal genesis of connections subserving ocular dominance in the rhesus monkey. *Nature* 261:467–471.

RAKIC, P., 1977. Prenatal development of the visual system in rhesus monkey. *Phil. Trans. R. Soc. Lond. [B]* 278:245–260.

RODIEK, R. W., 1998. *The First Steps in Seeing.* Sunderland, Mass.: Sinauer.

RODMAN, H. R., and M. J. CONSUELOS, 1994. Cortical projections to anterior inferior temporal cortex in infant macaque monkeys. *Vis. Neurosci.* 11:119–133.

SADATO, N., A. PASCUAL-LEONE, J. GRAFMAN, V. IBANEZ, M.-P. DEIBER, G. DOLD, and M. HALLETT, 1996. Activation of the primary visual cortex of Braille reading in blind subjects. *Nature* 380:526–528.

Schneider, W., M. Pimm-Smith, and W. Worden, 1994. Neurobiology of attention and automaticity. *Curr. Opin. Neurobiol.* 4:177–182.

Shatz, C. J., 1996. Emergence of order in visual system development. *Proc. Natl. Acad. Sci. (USA)* 93:602–608.

Shewmon, D. A., G. L. Holmes, and P. A. Byrne, 1999. Consciousness in congenitally decorticate children: Developmental vegetative state as self-fulfilling prophecy. *Dev. Med. Child Neurol.* 41:364–374.

Stoerig, P., and A. Cowey, 1992. Wavelength discrimination in blindsight. *Brain* 115:425–444.

Stoerig, P., and A. Cowey, 1997. Blindsight in man and monkey. *Brain* 120:535–559.

Teller, D. Y., 1984. Linking propositions. *Vis. Res.* 24:1233–1246.

Teller, D. Y., 1997. First glances: The vision of infants. The Friedenwald lecture. *Invest. Ophthalmol. Vis. Sci.* 38:2183–2203.

Teller, D. Y., 1998. Spatial and temporal aspects of infant color vision. *Vis. Res.* 38:3275–3282.

Thibos, L. N., D. J. Walsh, and F. E. Cheney, 1987. Vision beyond the resolution limit: Aliasing in the periphery. *Vis. Res.* 27:2193–2197.

Toyama, K., Y. Komatsu, N. Yamamoto, T. Kurotani, and K. Yamada, 1991. In vitro approach to visual cortical development and plasticity. *Neurosci. Res.* 12:57–71.

Van Essen, D. C., C. H. Anderson, and D. J. Felleman, 1992. Information processing in the primate visual system: An integrated systems perspective. *Science* 225:419–423.

Wattam-Bell, J., 1991. Development of motion-specific cortical responses in infancy. *Vis. Res.* 31:287–297.

Wilson, H. R., 1988. Development of spatiotemporal mechanisms in infant vision. *Vis. Res.* 28:611–628.

Wilson, H. R., 1993. Theories of infant visual development. In *Early Visual Development, Normal and Abnormal*, K. Simons, ed. New York: Oxford University Press, pp. 560–572.

Yoshioka, T., J. B. Levitt, and J. S. Lund, 1994. Independence and merger of thalamocortical channels within macaque monkey primary visual cortex: Anatomy of interlaminar projections. *Vis. Neurosci.* 11:467–489.

Yuodelis, C., and A. Hendrickson, 1986. A qualitative and quantitative analysis of the human fovea during development. *Vis. Res.* 26:847–855.

# 17 Visual Acuity and Spatial Contrast Sensitivity: Normal Development and Underlying Mechanisms

DAPHNE MAURER
AND TERRI L. LEWIS

ABSTRACT This chapter considers the role of experience and of competitive interactions between the eyes in the development of spatial vision. We first describe the postnatal development of grating acuity and spatial contrast sensitivity in normal infants and the neural changes underlying that development. We then evaluate the role of visual input in driving postnatal development by drawing on evidence from children deprived of patterned visual experience by dense and central cataracts. Animal models allow us to deduce the impact of visual input on different levels of the nervous system. We conclude that experience and competitive interactions between the eyes for cortical connections play a prominent role in the development of spatial vision.

No matter how it is measured, the spatial vision of the newborn is poor. For example, the smallest high-contrast elements to which a newborn responds are 30–60 times larger than the smallest that are visible to an adult with normal vision. In the first half of this chapter, we describe the postnatal development of two aspects of spatial vision—grating acuity and spatial contrast sensitivity—and the neural changes underlying that development. In the second half, we evaluate the role of visual input in driving the postnatal development of spatial vision and draw inferences from animal models about the impact of visual input on different levels of the nervous system. Although various methods have been used to assess spatial vision during infancy, we concentrate on measurements using preferential looking, using results from other methods only to help unravel the neural basis of the observed developmental changes.

DAPHNE MAURER Department of Psychology, McMaster University, Hamilton, Ontario; Department of Ophthalmology, The Hospital for Sick Children, Toronto, Canada.
TERRI L. LEWIS Department of Psychology, McMaster University, Hamilton, Ontario; Department of Ophthalmology, The Hospital for Sick Children, Toronto, Ontario; Department of Ophthalmology, University of Toronto, Toronto, Canada.

## Normal development

GRATING ACUITY Preferential looking takes advantage of the fact that young infants look longer at a patterned stimulus than at a plain gray field (Fantz, Ordy, and Udelf, 1962). To measure grating acuity, black-and-white stripes are usually paired with a plain gray stimulus, and the size of stripe is varied across trials, with the stripes appearing randomly on the right or left side of the field. Early versions of the test usually took 20–30 minutes per measure of acuity. They involved psychophysical rules to determine thresholds and cumbersome equipment to reinforce correct responses once the natural preference for patterns waned after early infancy (Birch et al., 1983; Lewis and Maurer, 1986; Mayer and Dobson, 1980, 1982; van Hof-van Duin and Mohn, 1986). A more subjective and portable version of the test, commonly called the Acuity Card Procedure, dispenses with psychophysical rules and typically yields a measurement of grating acuity in less than 5 minutes (McDonald et al., 1985; Teller et al., 1986). On each trial, a tester guesses whether the stripes are on the right or on the left side of the card, based on any reliable cues provided by the child (direction of first look, direction of longest look, etc.). To minimize bias, the tester is kept unaware of the actual location of the stripes. The child's grating acuity is defined as the smallest stripe size that the tester can locate correctly.

Figure 17.1 shows typical changes in grating acuity between birth and 48 months of age as measured by preferential looking. The size of the smallest stripes to which subjects respond at each age is given in cycles per degree of visual angle (c/deg), where one cycle represents one black and one white stripe. The greater the number of cycles per degree, the higher the spatial frequency and the narrower the stripes. Although grating acuity is poor at birth—typically about 40 times worse than that of a normal adult (Brown and Yamamoto,

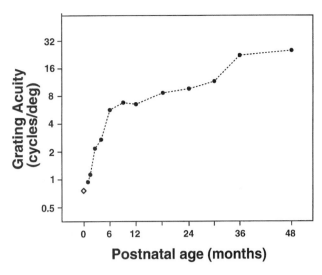

FIGURE 17.1 Typical changes in grating acuity between birth and 48 months. The *y*-axis shows the size of the smallest stripes to which subjects respond, plotted in cycles per degree of visual angle, where one cycle represents one black and one white stripe. Thus, the larger the number, the better the grating acuity. Filled circles represent the mean acuity of 1- to 48-month-olds tested monocularly by Mayer and colleagues (1995). The open symbol represents the log mean grating acuity of newborns tested binocularly (Brown and Yamamoto, 1986; Courage and Adams, 1990; Dobson et al., 1987; Mayer and Dobson, 1982; Miranda, 1970; van Hof-van Duin and Mohn, 1986). Monocular and binocular acuities do not differ prior to 6 months of age (Birch, 1985). Grating acuity is adult-like somewhere between 4 and 6 years of age, depending on the testing conditions.

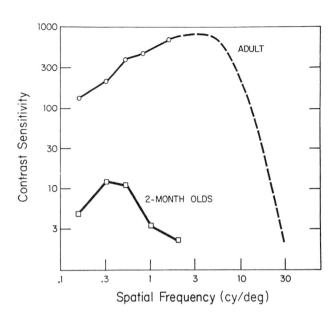

FIGURE 17.2 Typical contrast sensitivity functions for adults (upper curve) and 2-month-olds (lower curve). The *y*-axis plots contrast sensitivity (the inverse of the minimum contrast necessary to resolve the pattern) so that larger numbers represent greater sensitivity to contrast. The *x*-axis plots spatial frequency in cycles per degree of visual angle, where one cycle represents one black and one white stripe. Two-month-olds are about 20 times less sensitive than adults up to about 2–3 c/deg and show no evidence of seeing narrower stripes at even very high contrast. (Reprinted with permission from M. S. Banks and P. Salapatek, 1981. Infant pattern vision: A new approach based on the contrast sensitivity function. *J. Exp. Child Psychol.* 31, Figure 4.)

1986; Courage and Adams, 1990; Dobson et al., 1987; Mayer and Dobson, 1982; Miranda, 1970; van Hof-van Duin and Mohn, 1986), it improves rapidly over the first few months of life, so that by 6 months of age it is only about 8 times worse than that of a normal adult. Thereafter, grating acuity improves more gradually and reaches adult values by 4–6 years of age (Courage and Adams, 1990; Mayer and Dobson, 1982; van Hof-van Duin and Mohn, 1986).

CONTRAST SENSITIVITY Grating acuity provides a measure of the smallest visible stripe size. However, spatial vision is limited not only by size, but also by the difference in luminance between objects and their background. High contrast objects are more easily detected than are lower contrast objects, and the minimum amount of contrast necessary to resolve an object varies with the size of the object. The contrast sensitivity function plots contrast sensitivity (the inverse of the minimum contrast necessary to resolve the pattern) for stripes of various sizes (or, more accurately, for sine waves of different spatial frequency). A typical function

for normal adults is shown by the upper curve in figure 17.2. Contrast sensitivity peaks at 3–5 c/deg, drops off gradually for lower spatial frequencies (wider stripes), and declines sharply for higher spatial frequencies (narrower stripes).

Several groups of investigators have used preferential looking to measure contrast sensitivity in young infants (Adams et al., 1992; Atkinson, Braddick, and Moar, 1977; Banks and Salapatek, 1978, 1981; Gwiazda et al., 1997; Peterzell, Werner, and Kaplan, 1995). As with grating acuity, stripes of a particular spatial frequency and contrast are paired with a plain gray stimulus, and the tester looks for evidence that the baby has detected the stripes (e.g., that the baby looks first or most toward the side where the stripes appear). Over trials, contrast is varied to determine the minimum contrast for which babies show a preference for stripes of that spatial frequency. The process is then repeated at different spatial frequencies to derive the contrast sensitivity function.

All investigators agree that contrast sensitivity is very immature during early infancy. The lower curve in figure 17.2 shows typical results from 2-month-olds. Although the function has the same overall shape as that of adults, it is shifted markedly downward and to the left: 2-month-olds are about 20 times less sensitive than adults up to about 2–3 c/deg and show no evidence of seeing narrower stripes even at very high contrast. One-month-olds (the youngest age tested with behavioral techniques) perform even more poorly and produce a function with a different shape, without the low-frequency fall-off typical of adults and older infants (Adams et al., 1992; Atkinson, Braddick, and Moar, 1977; Banks and Salapatek, 1978). After 2 months of age, contrast sensitivity continues to improve, but it is still very immature throughout the first year of life (Adams et al., 1992). In fact, studies of older children using variants of preferential looking or psychophysical techniques designed for adults indicate that contrast sensitivity is not adult-like until middle childhood, with estimates of when it reaches adult levels ranging from 6 years to sometime after 15 years of age (Arundale, 1978; Bradley and Freeman, 1982; Derefeldt, Lennerstrand, and Lundh, 1979; Ellemberg et al., 1999a; Gwiazda et al., 1997; Mantyjarvi et al., 1989; Mayer, 1977).

## Mechanisms underlying normal development

What factors might contribute to poor spatial vision at birth and to its subsequent improvement? Nonvisual factors such as changes in motivation or attention are unlikely causes of the rapid postnatal improvement: During early infancy, measurements of contrast sensitivity derived from visually evoked potentials, which presumably are influenced little by motivation or attention, yield values similar to those obtained from preferential looking, provided that stimulus conditions are matched across the two procedures (Atkinson and Braddick, 1989; Harris, Atkinson, and Braddick, 1976; Pirchio et al., 1978). Rather, the important factors seem to be changes with age in the retinal mosaic and in postretinal factors, with perhaps some contribution from changes in the optics of the eye.

The contribution from changes in the optics of the eye appears to be minimal. First, growth of the eyeball cannot be the main explanation because its rate of growth does not correspond to the rate of improvement in spatial vision (Courage and Adams, 1990; Larsen, 1971; Mayer and Dobson, 1982; Mayer et al., 1995; van Hof-van Duin and Mohn, 1986). Second, changes with age in pupil diameter, in the amount of diffraction, or in the amount of spherical and chromatic aberration probably have negligible effects on spatial vision (reviewed in Banks and Bennett, 1988). Moreover, transmittance through the ocular media is *better* in newborns

than in adults, especially at short wavelengths (reviewed in Banks and Bennett, 1988). Finally, inaccurate accommodation does not appear to impose an important limitation because, even at birth, acuity does not vary with viewing distance (Cornell and McDonnell, 1986; Salapatek, Bechtold, and Bushnell, 1976). Taken together, the evidence suggests that postnatal changes in the optical properties of the eye make little contribution to the postnatal changes in spatial vision.

In contrast, retinal development appears to play a major role. Compared to the adult's fovea, in the newborn's fovea, the length of the outer segments of cones is 16-fold shorter and cone-packing density is 4-fold lower (Banks and Bennett, 1988; Hendrickson and Youdelis, 1984; Youdelis and Hendrickson, 1986). Short outer segments of newborns' foveal cones make the cones less efficient in producing isomerization for a given quantum of light. This characteristic limits acuity and spatial contrast sensitivity, both of which decrease as luminance decreases (Allen, Bennett, and Banks, 1992; Brown, Dobson, and Mayer, 1987; Pasternak and Merigan, 1981). Reduced cone packing density causes a reduction in spatial sampling, which limits acuity (Banks and Bennett, 1988; Wilson, 1988, 1993). Immaturities in the newborn's peripheral retina, although less marked, may be a more important limitation during early infancy because normal infants and infants with no anatomical fovea (because of oculocutaneous albinism) have similar grating acuity (Mayer, Fulton, and Hansen, 1985). Although the newborn's peripheral retina beyond about 5 degrees is more mature than the central retina, even in the peripheral retina, the outer segments of cones are much shorter in young infants than in adults (Abramov et al., 1982; Drucker and Hendrickson, 1989; Hendrickson and Kupfer, 1976).

During later infancy, measurements of grating acuity by preferential looking exceed the resolution limits of the peripheral retina and so must be dominated by the central retina and its projections. Although considerable foveal maturation occurs between birth and early childhood, measurements from a 45-month-old indicate that, even at this age, foveal cone packing density is still only half the adult value and the length of the outer segments of foveal cones is still 30–50% shorter than in adults (Youdelis and Hendrickson, 1986). Together, these retinal immaturities can account for at least some of the limitations in acuity and contrast sensitivity at birth and the fact that neither aspect of spatial vision is mature at 4 years of age (Banks and Bennett, 1988; Wilson, 1988, 1993).

However, retinal immaturities probably do not tell the whole story (Candy and Banks, 1999; Kiorpes and Movshon, 1998). Studies of infant monkeys indicate that the inputs both from the retina to the LGN and from the LGN to the visual cortex are immature (Blakemore, 1990; Blakemore and Vital-Durand, 1986a; Kiorpes and Movshon, 1998; Movshon and Kiorpes, 1993). These immature connections may account, at least in part, for findings that cortical contrast sensitivity and acuity, as measured by visually evoked potentials, mature no faster than the contrast sensitivity and acuity measured by the electroretinogram (Fiorentini, Pirchio, and Sandini, 1984; Fiorentini, Pirchio, and Spinelli, 1983). Moreover, in humans, many aspects of the geniculostriate pathway are immature until well past infancy. LGN neurons do not reach their adult size until 2 years of age (Hickey, 1977). Within the primary visual cortex, synaptic density increases dramatically, then decreases, and is not adult-like until approximately 11 years of age (Garey and De Courten, 1983; Huttenlocher, 1984; Huttenlocher et al., 1982). This pruning may be related to the reduction in the size of cortical neurons' receptive fields and to the increase in the fine tuning of their selectivity for spatial frequency, all of which have been documented in developing monkeys (Blakemore, 1990). These cortical changes may contribute to the increase in acuity and contrast sensitivity that occurs during childhood (until sensitivity reaches the Nyquist limit set by the retina).

Thus it appears that the development of spatial vision is limited primarily by slow retinal and postretinal development. In the monkey, improvements in behavioral acuity with age closely parallel improvements in the sensitivity of cells in the LGN (Blakemore, 1990); therefore, the main post-retinal limit probably lies in the LGN itself and/or the connections between the retina and the LGN (Blakemore, 1990; Blakemore and Vital-Durand, 1986a; Ellemberg et al., 1999a; Movshon and Kiorpes, 1993). Such limits at the level of the LGN would, of course, restrict the information that reaches the visual cortex and higher levels of the visual system.

## The role of visual input

In the rest of this chapter, we consider the role of visual input in driving the postnatal improvements in visual acuity and spatial contrast sensitivity. The data come from children who had dense central cataracts in one or both eyes. A cataract is an opacity in the lens of the eye which, in the children we selected for study, was sufficiently dense to block visual input to the retina and prevent fixation and following. The cataractous lens was removed surgically and the eye given an optical correction, usually a contact lens, to provide nearly normal visual input. This cohort allows us to evaluate the effect of a period of visual deprivation on the development of visual function, and hence to infer the role that visual input plays in normal visual development. By measuring deficits in children treated for congenital cataracts, we can infer the importance of visual input immediately after birth. By measuring deficits in children treated for developmental cataracts, in whom the visual deprivation followed a period of normal visual input, we can infer the importance of visual input during later periods of development and deduce the sensitive period for these visual functions.

Studies of children treated for bilateral cataracts allow inferences about the effects of visual deprivation per se. Comparisons to children treated for unilateral cataract allow additional inferences about the effects of uneven competition between the eyes for cortical connections. For example, worse outcomes after monocular than after binocular deprivation of the same duration after birth provide evidence that the two eyes compete for cortical connections. Because of this competition, parents of children treated for unilateral congenital cataract were instructed to patch the nondeprived eye to force usage of the previously deprived eye, but the amount of patching varied across patients. Better outcomes when there was more patching of the nondeprived eye provide additional evidence for competitive interactions during normal development.

ACUITY IMMEDIATELY AFTER THE END OF VISUAL DEPRIVATION FROM CONGENITAL CATARACT   To assess the importance of patterned visual input for the postnatal development of acuity, we measured the grating acuity of 28 infants immediately after the end of deprivation, that is, just after the ophthalmologist inserted contact lens(es) about 1 week after the removal of dense, central congenital cataracts from one ($n = 16$) or both ($n = 12$) eyes (Maurer et al., 1999). Whether the deprivation had been monocular or binocular, grating acuity was, on average, like that of normal newborns, despite variation in the duration of deprivation ranging from 1 week to 9 months. As a result, the acuity of deprived eyes fell farther below normal, the later during the first year they were treated. In contrast, the acuity of the nondeprived eyes of unilateral cases was normal and higher, the later during the first year it was tested.

The results indicate that visual acuity does not improve postnatally in the absence of patterned visual input. For deprivation lasting up to 9 months after birth, acuity remains near the newborn level. Even when the deprivation had been monocular so that muted signals from the deprived eye coexisted with signals from a normally developing eye, the acuity of the deprived eye was not degraded below newborn levels. In kittens, spontaneous retinal activity has been shown to influence the organization of the visual cortex even before eye opening (reviewed in Katz and Shatz, 1996). It is possible that such spontaneous retinal activity provides sufficient cortical stimulation during early deprivation in humans to maintain the connections that were formed prenatally—at least when the deprivation begins at birth and lasts no longer than 9 months.

## DEVELOPMENT OF ACUITY AFTER TREATMENT FOR CONGENITAL CATARACT

*After 1 hour of visual input* To determine the effect of the onset of patterned visual input, we retested the acuity of the 28 patients after 1 hour of such input, 1 week later, and 1 month later (Maurer et al., 1999). Whether the eye had been treated for monocular or binocular deprivation, there were significant improvements in acuity after the first hour of visual input, with a mean improvement of about 0.4 octaves (an octave is a halving or a doubling of a value). To verify that the improvement was the result of visual input, we conducted a second experiment following the same protocol for the immediate and 1-hour tests except that one treated eye of each of 17 patients was patched after the first test so that it did not receive the hour of patterned visual input. There was no significant improvement in the 17 patched eyes (eight from bilateral cases and nine from unilateral cases). In the six bilateral cases in which we were able to measure changes in acuity for both the eye that had been patched and in the fellow eye that had received 1 hour of visual input, there was significantly more improvement in the experienced eyes than in the patched eyes. Figure 17.3 shows the mean improvement in the 28 patients in the first experiment who received visual input between the immediate and 1-hour tests compared to age-matched normals and the 17 patched eyes in the second experiment.

The results indicate that the onset of patterned visual input initiates rapid functional development in humans, as it does in kittens (Mitchell and Gingras, 1998). The improvement may be caused by cortical changes similar to those observed in kittens immediately after deprivation. For example, in kittens reared in darkness from birth (Beaver, Mitchell, and Robertson, 1993) or for 1 week beginning at 5 weeks of age (Kaplan, Guo, and Mower, 1996; Mower, 1994), there is expression of Fos, the protein produced by the immediate early genes *c-fos*, in all layers of the visual cortex after as little as 1 hour of binocular visual input. Because the expression of Fos appears to reflect a step in long-term physiological changes rather than current neuronal activity, at least in the cat (Beaver, Mitchell, and Robertson, 1993; Kaplan, Guo, and Mower, 1996, but see Kaczmarek,

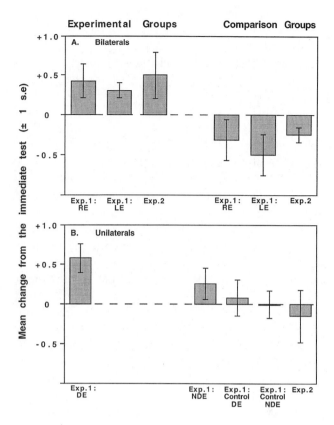

FIGURE 17.3 Mean change in acuity ($\pm 1$ SE) between the immediate and 1-hour tests. The *y*-axis plots the amount of change in octaves, where one octave is a doubling or a halving of a value. Values above zero represent an improvement from the immediate test; values below zero represent a decline. The left half of each panel shows the results for experimental groups, all of which received their first hour of patterned visual input between the immediate and 1-hour tests. The right half of each panel shows the results for comparison groups, none of which received their first hour of patterned visual experience between the immediate and 1-hour tests either because they were age-matched normals with prior visual experience or because the deprived eye was patched between the two tests. (**A**) The results for bilateral cases and their comparison groups; (**B**) the results for unilateral cases and their comparison groups. In panel A, the three experimental means are, respectively from left to right, from the right eye of bilateral cases in Experiment 1, the left eye of bilateral cases in Experiment 1, and the unpatched eye of bilateral cases in Experiment 2. The three comparison means are from the right eye of age-matched normals for Experiment 1, the left eye of age-matched normals for Experiment 1, and the patched eye of bilateral cases in Experiment 2. In panel B, the experimental mean is from the treated eyes of unilateral cases in Experiment 1. The four comparison means are from, respectively, the nondeprived eye of unilateral cases in Experiment 1, the normal eyes matched to the treated eyes of unilateral cases in Experiment 1, the normal eyes matched to the nondeprived eyes of unilateral cases in Experiment 1, and the patched eyes of unilateral cases tested in Experiment 2. In every comparison, eyes in the experimental groups improved more between the immediate and 1-hour test than did eyes in the comparison groups, a result that indicates that the improvement resulted from receiving patterned visual input for the first time.

Zangenehpour, and Chaudhuri, 1999), these results imply that 1 hour of visual input after dark-rearing is sufficient to induce cortical changes. Similarly, after 5 weeks of monocular deprivation, the kitten's visual cortex shows only small patches of Fos-immunoreactive neurons related to the deprived eye, but those patches are already slightly larger 1 day after the opening of the deprived eye and the suturing shut of the fellow eye (Mitchell, Beaver, and Ritchie, 1995).

*One month later* By 1 month after treatment, we found significant additional improvement in the visual acuity of the 28 patients such that the deficit was reduced to a mean of about 1 octave compared to normals (Maurer et al., 1999). The amount of improvement was not related to the age of first patterned visual input. Nor, in unilateral cases, was the improvement over the first month related to the amount of patching of the nondeprived eye, which varied from 0 to 7.7 hours/day ($M = 4.6$ hours/day). The improvement is unlikely to be merely a practice effect because there was no significant improvement over the month in the fellow nondeprived eyes of infants treated for unilateral congenital cataract nor in any of the groups of age-matched controls.

Surprisingly, there was no difference between unilateral and bilateral cases in the amount of recovery either over the first hour or during the first month, and no beneficial effect of patching over that month (Maurer et al., 1999). Unlike the later results (described following), the initial improvements in acuity appear to be determined by visual activity, with no deleterious effects of uneven competition. Mitchell and Gingras (1998) reached a similar conclusion in a study of recovery from monocular deprivation in kittens: The initial recovery was similar whether or not the nondeprived eye was sutured shut (reverse-sutured) to reduce the competitive disadvantage of the previously deprived eye. Mitchell and Gingras concluded that the initial recovery of acuity after monocular deprivation is driven solely by visually evoked cortical activity and that only much later, after a scaffold of connections from the deprived eye has been established in the visual cortex, does uneven competition between the eyes limit the amount of recovery. The implication is that normal development during infancy may also be driven solely or mainly by visual activity and that only later, after a number of robust cortical connections have been established from both eyes, do competitive interactions influence subsequent refinements of acuity.

The recovery after the end of deprivation from congenital cataract might reflect mainly the relative sparing of neurons representing the peripheral visual field.

That possibility is suggested by the aforementioned evidence that preferential looking measurements of acuity during the first year of life may be dominated by input from the peripheral retina. It is consistent with evidence that the primary visual cortex of monocularly deprived kittens exhibits a substantial loss of NMDA receptors, which have been shown to be involved in cortical plasticity, only in areas representing the central visual field (Duffy and Murphy, 1999). It also fits with evidence that both the light sensitivity and spatial contrast sensitivity of older children with a history of early monocular deprivation are degraded less in the periphery than in the central visual field (Bowering, 1992; Maurer and Lewis, 1993). Measurements during infancy with techniques that appear to be influenced more by central vision than is preferential looking—optokinetic nystagmus (Lewis, Maurer, and Brent, 1995) and visually evoked potentials (McCulloch and Skarf, 1994)—indicate much less recovery during the first months following treatment for congenital cataract.

*At 1 year of age* By 1 year of age, the acuity of most eyes treated for congenital cataract has improved such that it falls within normal limits (Birch and Stager, 1988; Birch, Stager, and Wright, 1986; Birch et al., 1993; Catalano et al., 1987; Jacobson, Mohindra, and Held, 1983; Lewis, Maurer, and Brent, 1995; Lloyd et al., 1995; Mayer, Moore, and Robb, 1989). By implication, acuity in previously deprived eyes must improve at a rate faster than normal between the time of treatment and the first birthday. Our own data provide information on the largest cohort tested at 1 year of age (Lewis, Maurer, and Brent, 1995). Using inclusion criteria identical to those in the study of acuity immediately after treatment, we measured the preferential looking acuity of the deprived eye of 42 children treated at various ages during the first year of life for unilateral congenital cataract and 88 eyes from 51 patients treated at similar ages for bilateral congenital cataracts. Most (79% of unilaterally deprived eyes and 85% of bilaterally deprived eyes) fell within normal limits. Nevertheless, the mean acuity was below the normal mean and below the mean of the nondeprived eyes of the unilateral cases. In bilateral cases, there was an effect of the duration of deprivation: Acuity at 1 year of age was better the earlier the eye was treated ($r = .43$ based on one eye of each of the 51 patients, $p < .01$). In other words, during the first year, acuity had improved the most in eyes that had had the most visual input.

In unilateral cases, acuity at 1 year of age was not related significantly to the duration of deprivation after birth, even though it varied from as little as 1 month to as much as 12 months, with a mean of 4.2 months

(Lewis, Maurer, and Brent, 1995). Rather, it was related to the number of hours per day that the nondeprived eye had been patched after treatment: The more hours of patching, the better the acuity ($r = .36$, $p < .05$). In fact, children who had patched the nondeprived eye for less than 3 hours/day had acuity in the deprived eye that was significantly worse than the acuity of children treated for binocular deprivation of comparable duration. Similarly, Mayer and colleagues (1989) found that the difference in acuity between the deprived and nondeprived eyes at 1 year of age was correlated negatively with the amount of patching but, with patching held constant, unrelated to the child's age at surgery. These results imply that by 1 year of age, competitive interactions have begun to influence recovery from deprivation. After monocular deprivation, they have become a stronger influence than the duration of the initial deprivation or the amount of visual activity after deprivation. Thus, the initial recovery appears to be driven by visual activity, perhaps taking advantage of the normal postnatal exuberant proliferation of synapses in the visual cortex (Huttenlocher and de Courten, 1987; Huttenlocher et al., 1982). And once that activity has induced functional changes, presumably by strengthening cortical responses driven by the previously deprived eye, competitive interactions emerge and quickly become the strongest determinant of visual outcome.

*At 3 years of age* After 1 year of age, the acuity of most patients treated for congenital cataract continues to improve, but does so at a below-normal rate so that most eyes fall outside normal limits after about 2 years of age (Birch and Stager, 1988; Birch, Stager, and Wright, 1986; Lewis, Maurer, and Brent, 1995; Mayer, Maurer, and Robb, 1989; but see Birch et al., 1993; Lloyd et al., 1995). For example, in the cohort we followed longitudinally from 1 year of age, 85% of the 26 eyes treated for unilateral congenital cataract and 74% of the 78 eyes treated for bilateral congenital cataract had preferential looking acuity below normal limits at 3 years of age, with mean deficits of 1.2 octaves in unilateral cases and 1.1 octaves in bilateral cases. These data imply that early visual deprivation caused changes in the nervous system that diminished its ability to profit from visual input during later infancy and early childhood. In children treated for bilateral congenital cataracts, those effects are related to the duration of the deprivation after birth: The longer the deprivation, the worse the acuity at 2.5–3 years of age ($r = .51$ based on one eye from each of 51 patients treated for bilateral congenital cataract, $p = .0001$). The deficits at 3 years of age may reflect damage to neurons with receptive fields involving central vision that dominate measurements of prefential looking acuity at 3 years, but not at 1 year of age (Lewis, Maurer, and Brent, 1995). Alternatively, they may reflect damage to the processes by which cortical synapses are pruned, processes that are especially evident in the visual cortex from 9 to 18 months of age and in higher visual areas after 2 years of age (Huttenlocher, 1979; Huttenlocher and Dabholkar, 1997; Huttenlocher and de Courten, 1987).

As at 1 year of age, we found that the duration of monocular deprivation from birth is not related to the acuity of the affected eyes at 3 years of age (Lewis, Maurer, and Brent, 1995). Rather, as at 1 year of age, the outcome at 2.5–3 years was related significantly to the number of hours per day that the nondeprived eye had been patched since treatment: In the 36 treated eyes that we tested at 2.5–3 years, there was a correlation of .53 between patching and acuity ($p = .001$). Moreover, when the nondeprived eye had been patched for less than 3 hours/day, 3-year acuity was significantly worse than that of children treated for bilateral congenital cataracts. Like the results at 1 year, these findings imply that once visual activity has allowed the previously deprived eye to nearly catch up to the nondeprived eye, competitive interactions between the eyes become paramount. Similarly, Mayer and colleagues (1989) found that interocular differences in acuity at 3 years of age were related to how much the nondeprived eye had been patched and not the age at which the deprived eye was treated. However, there might be a nonlinear relationship between the duration of deprivation, patching, and acuity at 3 years. Consistent with that possibility, Birch and colleagues (1993) found that among children treated for unilateral congenital cataract, all of whom had patched the nondeprived eye for 6–8 hours/day, measured acuity was better at most ages if the affected eye had been treated before 6 weeks of age rather than after 2 months of age.

*After 5 years of age* By 5 years of age, the grating acuity of normal children has reached (Mayer and Dobson, 1982), or nearly reached (Ellemberg et al., 1999a), the adult level of more than 30 c/deg. Patients treated for congenital cataract almost never achieve such high levels of acuity. For example, in our study of 13 patients treated for bilateral congenital cataract, grating acuity after age 5 ranged from 4.5 to 17.5 c/deg or, on average, 1.5 octaves below normal (Ellemberg et al., 1999b). As in previous studies of patients treated for bilateral congenital cataract (Birch et al., 1998; Mioche and Perenin, 1986; Tytla et al., 1988), these patients showed losses in spatial contrast sensitivity that increased monotonically with spatial frequency, with losses exceeding half a log unit in every eye. Within our small sample, there was no effect of the duration of the binocular deprivation on the size of the deficit in grating acuity or in contrast sensitivity at 5 c/deg, even though the duration of deprivation had varied from 1.5 to 9 months. This result resembles a similar finding in binocularly deprived monkeys (Harwerth et al., 1991) and previous findings that the duration of binocular deprivation from cataracts does not affect the size of the ultimate deficit in linear letter acuity (Birch et al., 1998; Maurer and Lewis, 1993; but see Kugelberg, 1992). Thus, binocular deprivation for as little as the first 1.5 months of life—a period during which normal infants can see only low spatial frequencies—prevents the later development of normal sensitivity to high spatial frequencies, and causes deficits as large as binocular deprivation lasting far longer into the first year of life. However, there is evidence that after *extremely* early treatment—before 10 days of age—some, but not all, children are able to achieve a linear letter acuity of 20/20 (Kugelberg, 1992).

The deficits are greater in children treated for unilateral congenital cataract unless treatment was early *and* followed by aggressive patching of the nondeprived eye (Birch et al., 1993, 1998; Ellemberg et al., 2000; Mayer, Moore, and Robb, 1989; Tytla et al., 1988). When treatment was very early (before 6 weeks) and followed by aggressive patching (at least 75% of waking time), a few treated eyes achieve a linear letter acuity of 20/20 and normal contrast sensitivity at all spatial frequencies (Birch et al., 1993). When treatment is delayed and followed by little patching, there are profound losses in grating acuity and in contrast sensitivity at all spatial frequencies (Ellemberg et al., 2000). For example, in two children with monocular deprivation lasting more than 8 months followed by little patching of the nondeprived eye (<3 hours/day), we found deficits in grating acuity of about 1.5 log units (5–6 octaves) and losses of about 1 log unit in spatial contrast sensitivity even at 0.5 c/deg, losses that were much larger than those seen in a child treated for binocular deprivation of the same duration (Ellemberg et al., 1999b). As at earlier test points (Birch et al., 1993), among good patchers, there appears to be a nonlinear relationship between outcome and the duration of the monocular deprivation: The outcome is better if treatment occurred anytime during the first 6 weeks of life than if it occurred later, with no effect of the duration of deprivation during the first 6 weeks (Birch and Stager, 1996). Only when treatment occurred after 6 weeks of age (and was followed by aggressive patching) is there a linear relationship, such that the outcome is worse the longer the deprivation lasted. [When there was little patching, the outcome is poor, regardless of how long the monocular deprivation lasted (Maurer and Lewis, 1993).] The emergent influence of the duration of monocular deprivation after 6 weeks of age may be related to the increasing cortical influence over infants' visual behavior beginning at about 2 months of age (Birch and Stager, 1996; Braddick, Atkinson, and Hood, 1996; Johnson, 1990).

NONDEPRIVED EYE OF CHILDREN TREATED FOR UNILATERAL CONGENITAL CATARACT    As in our previous study (Lewis et al., 1992), we found small losses in the grating acuity of nondeprived eyes, even though the eyes appeared normal on repeated ophthalmological examinations. The losses ranged from 0.3 to 0.8 octaves and were unrelated to the amount of patching (Ellemberg et al., 2000). Similarly, most nondeprived eyes show small losses in contrast sensitivity, but only at high spatial frequencies (Ellemberg et al., 2000; Lewis et al., 1992). These findings complement previous reports of a shift in the distribution of letter acuities in the nondeprived eye toward values that are slightly lower than normal (Lewis et al., 1992; Thompson et al., 1996) and of abnormalities in some aspects of the nondeprived eye's VEP response to small checks (McCulloch and Skarf, 1994). [Birch and colleagues (1993) may not have observed these deficits because they tested the nondeprived eyes at age 5, an age at which sensitivity to high spatial frequencies is not yet adult-like on their test and/or because their test of recognition acuity did not include the 20/15 line, which many normal children, but few patients, are able to read.] The subtle deficits in the nondeprived eye—which we observed even in patients who did little patching of the nondeprived eye—suggest that uneven competition between the eyes adversely affects the development of connections from both the previously deprived and the "normal" eye. Interestingly, when the "normal" eye is paired with an eye that does not transmit visually driven signals (e.g., when a serious uniocular disorder like a dense cataract or optic atrophy remains untreated), there is no evidence of such deficits (Thompson et al., 1996).

SENSITIVE PERIOD    Like the improvements in acuity during infancy, studies of children treated for cataract indicate that the later refinements in acuity also depend on visual input. Evidence comes from children who were born with apparently normal eyes but who subsequently developed cataracts that blocked all patterned visual input in one or both eyes until the cataracts were removed surgically and the eyes given contact lenses or glasses to focus input on the retina. When the cataract was caused by an eye injury, we can be confident about when the blockage began and hence the age of onset and duration of complete patterned deprivation. We cannot be so confident when the cataract was caused by a metabolic or genetic disorder, because such cataracts usually develop gradually and block more and more visual input as they become larger. Nevertheless, permanent deficits in visual acuity after treatment for developmental or traumatic cataracts signal the importance of patterned visual input after early infancy.

The *y*-axis in figure 17.4 shows the asymptotic linear letter acuity achieved by the deprived eyes of 29 children treated for unilateral developmental or traumatic cataract and, for comparison, 31 children treated for unilateral congenital cataract. Each dot is plotted at the age when we estimate that the cataract was sufficiently dense to block all patterned visual input. Filled circles indicate that the child had had the nondeprived eye patched for at least 3 hours/day from the time of treatment until 5 years of age. The figure indicates that no child whose deprivation began before about 8 years of age developed normal or nearly normal letter acuity, even though the good eye had, in some cases, been patched aggressively. Figure 17.5 shows similar results for 33 children treated for bilateral congenital cataract and 40 children treated for bilateral developmental cataract. It illustrates the asymptotic linear letter acuity for one eye per child, in panel A for the eye with the better

prognosis based on eye alignment and in panel B for the eye with the worse prognosis. With later onset of deprivation, the asymptotic acuity is generally better but it does not reach nearly normal levels unless the deprivation began after about 7–9 years of age. Thus, visual input is necessary throughout the 5–6 years that it takes letter acuity to reach adult levels. It is also necessary to consolidate connections for several years after the age at which normal development is complete.

MECHANISMS UNDERLYING THE PERMANENT DEFICITS
The deficits in patients treated for congenital cataract are not likely to arise from optical factors because they are not observed in patients with similar optics after treatment for cataracts with onset in adulthood (Ellemberg et al., 1999b). Nor are they likely to arise from the nystagmus or strabismus commonly associated with congenital cataracts because the same pattern of deficits is

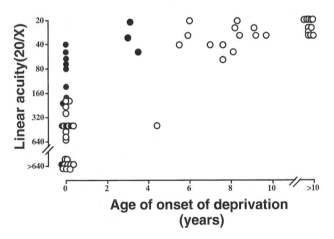

FIGURE 17.4 Asymptotic linear letter acuity as a function of age of onset of monocular deprivation. The *y*-axis plots the denominator of the Snellen fraction such that 20 represents 20/20 vision, which is normal. Larger numbers represent increasingly poor letter acuity. Each dot represents the result for one deprived eye. Data are for the deprived eyes of children treated for unilateral cataract whose deprivation began at birth or who had a normal early visual history and then developed a dense cataract in one eye sometime after 3 months of age. Filled circles are for children who had patched the nondeprived eye more than 3 hours/day from the time of treatment until 5 years of age.

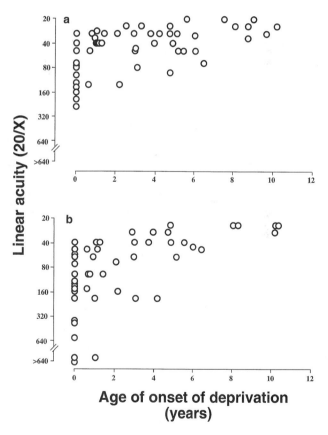

FIGURE 17.5 Asymptotic linear letter acuity as a function of age of onset of binocular deprivation. Data are from children treated for bilateral cataracts whose deprivation began at birth or who had a normal early visual history and then developed dense cataracts sometime after 7 months of age. (a) Results from the better eye of each patient, determined on the basis of the history of eye alignment; (b) results from the worse eye. Other details as in figure 17.4.

observed in patients without these associated conditions (Ellemberg et al., 1999b, 2000; Lewis, Maurer, and Brent, 1995; Maurer and Lewis, 1993). Rather they are likely to reflect neural damage caused by the visual deprivation.

Studies of monkeys that were deprived of visual input by lid suture allow inferences about the likely site of the neural damage. As in the children treated for cataract, the later acuity and contrast sensitivity of such monkeys are degraded, with the deficit worse after monocular than after binocular deprivation unless the monocular deprivation was short and followed by extensive occlusion of the fellow eye (Harwerth et al., 1983a,b, 1989, 1991). In monkeys, visual deprivation during infancy causes damage to the primary visual cortex, but not to earlier levels of the geniculostriate pathway. There are no changes in the topography of photoreceptors (Clark, Hendrickson, and Curcio, 1988; Hendrickson and Boothe, 1976) or in the electroretinogram (Crawford et al., 1975). Unless the deprivation extended from birth past 2 years of age (which is probably comparable to more than 8 years of deprivation in humans), the morphology of retinal ganglion cells is normal (reviewed in Boothe, Dobson, and Teller, 1985). (Very long-term deprivation may cause retinal damage in humans: The electroretinogram for the deprived eye was abnormal in a patient with 13 years of monocular deprivation from birth; see Levi and Manny, 1982.) Cells in the monkey's lateral geniculate nucleus are smaller than normal but nevertheless have normal physiological properties, even after 5 years of monocular deprivation from birth (Blakemore and Vital-Durand, 1986b; Levitt et al., 1989). Thus, LGN cells presumably send normal signals to the primary visual cortex.

There are marked abnormalities in the primary visual cortex of monkeys after early visual deprivation. After early binocular deprivation, a few cells respond normally, but most respond more sluggishly than normal, have receptive fields that are abnormally large, and are poorly tuned to orientation and spatial frequency (Blakemore, 1990; Blakemore and Vital-Durand, 1983; Crawford et al., 1975, 1991). Across the population of cells, there is a large reduction in sensitivity to higher spatial frequencies and low contrast (Blakemore, 1990; Blakemore and Vital-Durand, 1983). Thus, reductions in acuity and spatial contrast sensitivity after early binocular deprivation probably reflect abnormalities in neurons in the primary visual cortex and their projections, abnormalities that can be induced even by short periods of binocular deprivation. That interpretation is strengthened by evidence that in monkeys (Miller, Pasik, and Pasik, 1980)—unlike cats (Lehmkuhle, Kratz,

and Sherman, 1982)—lesions to the primary visual cortex drastically reduce contrast sensitivity for all spatial frequencies. Similarly, humans with damage to the primary visual cortex show marked losses of grating acuity in the affected regions of the visual field (Weiskrantz, 1986). After early binocular deprivation in humans, the visual abilities that develop normally may be mediated by the few remaining normal cells in the primary visual cortex, by the many visual cortical cells that respond abnormally, or by cells in extrageniculostriate pathways that appear to play a greater role than normal in mediating some visual functions after binocular deprivation—at least in cats (Zablocka and Zernicki, 1996; Zablocka, Zernicki, and Kosmal, 1976, 1980).

After early monocular deprivation in monkeys, abnormalities in the primary visual cortex are even more marked. Although the periodicity of the areas dominated by each eye (the "ocular dominance columns") is unchanged (Crawford, 1998), the width of columns driven by the deprived eye is decreased and the width of those driven by the nondeprived eye is correspondingly increased (Horton and Hocking, 1997; Hubel, Wiesel, and LeVay, 1977; LeVay, Wiesel, and Hubel, 1980), with larger changes, the earlier the deprivation started (Horton and Hocking, 1997). The changes are greater in layers that receive input from parvocellular cells of the LGN (which are known to mediate sensitivity to high spatial frequencies) than in layers that receive input from magnocellular cells (Horton and Hocking, 1997). Even after very short periods of monocular deprivation, the deprived eye can drive very few cells in the primary visual cortex (Crawford, 1988; Crawford et al, 1991; Hubel, Wiesel, and LeVay, 1977; LeVay, Wiesel, and Hubel, 1980). The cells that can be driven by the deprived eye exhibit sensitivity to spatial frequency and contrast similar to (or even worse than) cells in the primary visual cortex of a newborn monkey (Blakemore, 1988). Reverse suture—closing the fellow eye at the same time that the originally deprived eye is opened—increases the proportion of cells in the primary visual cortex that can be driven by the originally deprived eye (Blakemore, Garey, and Vital-Durand, 1978; Crawford et al., 1989; LeVay, Wiesel, and Hubel, 1980; Swindale, Vital-Durand, and Blakemore, 1981). These changes in the primary visual cortex may explain the greater deficits in grating acuity and spatial contrast sensitivity after monocular than binocular deprivation in humans, unless there was aggressive patching of the nondeprived eye. The mild deficits even in the nondeprived eye may be related to an absence of functional connections in the zones into which its axons have expanded (Horton and Hocking, 1997).

Studies of monocularly deprived kittens have begun to elucidate the mechanisms underlying competitive interactions between a deprived and nondeprived eye. Some results support a model of spatial competition governed by competition for a scarce resource, such as neurotrophins, that play a role in the stabilization of developing axons and the supply of which is limited and activity-dependent (Cabelli, Hohn, and Shatz, 1995). Supplying more of that scarce resource appears to mitigate the effects of monocular deprivation. Thus, infusion of neurotrophins into the visual cortex during monocular deprivation prevents shrinkage of LGN cells and leaves the deprived eye still able to drive a nearly normal number of cortical cells (Carmignoto et al., 1993; Galuske et al., 1996). It also preserves normal acuity (Carmignoto et al., 1993; Fiorentini, Berardi, and Maffei, 1995). However, evidence that cells near the site where the neurotrophin was infused lack normal orientation tuning and cannot be driven in normal numbers by the *nondeprived* eye (Galuske et al., 1996) suggests that the mechanism of monocular deprivation extends beyond competition between geniculocortical afferents for neurotrophic support.

Other results indicate that competition might be better thought of as temporal competition between patterns of activity (Blais, Shouval, and Cooper, 1999; Hata and Stryker, 1994). These models subsume Hebb's original postulate that cortical connections are strengthened by use that leads to correlation between pre- and postsynaptic activity (Hebb, 1949). They go beyond Hebb in postulating that monocular deprivation alters the cortex not because of the absence of input from the deprived eye but because of an actual mismatch of pre- and postsynaptic activity. The mismatch arises when spontaneous activity in the deprived eye drives presynaptic activity out of synchrony with the postsynaptic activity driven by the nondeprived eye. The mismatch leads to long-term synaptic depression, which is normally observed as a shift in ocular dominance, that is, a reduction in the proportion of cells that can be driven by the previously deprived eye. The mismatch may continue even after the monocular deprivation has ended if visual signals from the previously deprived eye are transmitted more slowly than signals from the nondeprived eye, as they appear to be (Kasamatsu et al., 1998; McCulloch and Skarf, 1994). The strongest evidence for this model comes from demonstrations that manipulations that reduce the mismatch between pre- and postsynaptic activity reduce the effects of monocular deprivation. For example, 2 days of monocular deprivation around 7 weeks of age are sufficient to induce a shift in ocular dominance toward the nonde-

prived eye. However, using tetrodotoxin (TTX) to block retinal activity in the deprived eye during the 2 days of monocular deprivation prevents the shift in ocular dominance, presumably because it prevented any signals from the deprived eye from reaching the cortex and hence any mismatch between pre- and postsynaptic activity (Rittenhouse et al., 1999). There are similarly paradoxical findings when monocular deprivation of 2–4 weeks beginning around 4 weeks of age is accompanied by injections of muscimol, which binds selectively to GABA receptors on postsynaptic sites and blocks their activity (Hata and Stryker, 1994; Hata, Tsumoto, and Stryker, 1999). Near the site of infusion, the deprived eye is able to drive more than the normal number of cells and its normal-looking axons cover an expanded area. Axons serving the nondeprived eye are shorter and less elaborate than normal and look worse even than axons serving the deprived eye in untreated cortex (Hata, Tsumoto, and Stryker, 1999). The shrinkage of axons serving the nondeprived eye presumably reflects the frequent mismatch between presynaptic activity induced by visual stimulation and the inhibited postsynaptic activity. Axons serving the deprived eye would have been spared by the infrequency of its spontaneous activity. The likelihood of a mismatch is also affected by the modification threshold of the postsynaptic neuron, which varies with the overall level of cortical activity (Kind, 1999). Binocular deprivation may have weaker cortical effects than monocular deprivation because it lowers the overall level of cortical activity and hence lowers both the modification threshold of the postsynaptic neuron and the probability of a mismatch between pre- and postsynaptic activity (Blais, Shouval, and Cooper, 1999; Kind, 1999; Rittenhouse et al., 1999).

The competitive interactions underlying the deleterious effects of monocular deprivation are likely to vary with the timing and duration of the deprivation. For example, a short period of monocular deprivation at the height of the sensitive period in kittens causes a radical shift in ocular dominance toward the nondeprived eye, such that the deprived eye stimulates few visual cortical cells when it is stimulated monocularly. It also causes a shrinkage of geniculocortical axons serving the deprived eye (Antonini and Stryker, 1996). Nevertheless, for most cells, input from the deprived eye alters the cortical response during binocular (dichoptic) stimulation, both suppressing and enhancing the response stimulated by the nondeprived eye on its own, depending on the relative phase of input to the two eyes (Freeman and Ohzawa, 1988). These results imply that the deprived eye, although unable to drive most cortical cells when stimulated monocularly, nevertheless remains sufficiently connected to influence them during binocular viewing. A similar conclusion arises from evidence of responses to stimulation of the deprived eye after removal of the nondeprived eye or injections of $GABA_A$-receptor antagonist (reviewed in Kasamatsu et al., 1998). After very long monocular deprivation (more than 11 months beginning at 3 weeks), evidence of such residual connections is virtually absent (Freeman and Ohzawa, 1988). After such long periods of monocular deprivation, the deprived eye appears to be disconnected.

## Conclusions

In summary, spatial vision improves rapidly during early infancy but takes many years to reach adult levels. Much of this improvement can be explained by the postnatal development of the retina and primary visual pathway. However, the improvement depends on patterned visual input, the onset of which alters the nervous system rapidly and sufficiently to support better acuity as early as 1 hour later. The initial improvements in acuity appear to be determined solely by visually evoked cortical activity, and only later, after sufficient numbers of cortical connections have been established from both eyes, do competitive interactions influence subsequent refinements of spatial vision. Permanent deficits in visual acuity after treatment for developmental or traumatic cataracts signal the importance of patterned visual input for consolidating connections, even after the age at which spatial vision is normally mature.

The permanent deficits in spatial vision after early deprivation probably reflect abnormalities in and beyond the primary visual cortex, deficits that are larger after monocular than after binocular deprivation, unless the competitive disadvantage of the previously deprived eye was ameliorated by reverse suture or occlusion. Binocular deprivation may have weaker effects because it lowers the overall level of cortical activity and hence lowers the probability of a mismatch between pre- and postsynaptic activity. Whatever the underlying mechanisms, it is clear that experience and competitive interactions play a prominent role in the development of spatial vision.

ACKNOWLEDGMENTS We thank Dr. Alex Levin and Dr. Henry Brent for providing the opportunity to test the patients treated for cataracts. We also thank The Hospital for Sick Children in Toronto for providing space for the studies of patients, K. Harrison and Bausch and Lomb (Toronto, Canada) for donating the contact lenses necessary for the tests of some patients, R. Barclay for clinical assistance, S. Geldart for technical assistance, the children and their families for participation, and the Medical Research Council of Canada (grant MOP 36430) for support during the writing of this chapter.

## REFERENCES

ABRAMOV, I., J. GORDON, A. HENDRICKSON, L. HAINLINE, V. DOBSON, and E. LaBOSSIER, 1982. The retina of the newborn human infant. *Science* 217:265–267.

ADAMS, R. J., M. E. MERCER, M. L. COURAGE, and J. van HOF-van DUIN, 1992. A new technique to measure contrast sensitivity in human infants. *Optom. Vis. Sci.* 69:440–446.

ALLEN, D., P. J. BENNETT, and M. S. BANKS, 1992. The effects of luminance of FPL and VEP acuity in human infants. *Vis. Res.* 32:2005–2012.

ANTONINI, A., and M. STRYKER, 1996. Plasticity of geniculocortical afferents following brief or prolonged monocular occlusion in the cat. *J. Comp. Neurol.* 369:64–82.

ATKINSON, J., and O. BRADDICK, 1989. Newborn contrast sensitivity measures: do VEP, OKN, and FPL reveal differential development of cortical and subcortical streams? *Invest. Ophthalmol. Vis. Sci. Suppl.* 30:311.

ATKINSON, J., O. BRADDICK, and K. MOAR, 1977. Contrast sensitivity of the human infant for moving and static patterns. *Vis. Res.* 17:1045–1047.

ARUNDALE, K., 1978. An Investigation into the variation of human contrast sensitivity with age and ocular pathology. *Br. J. Ophthalmol.* 62:213–215.

BANKS, M. S., and P. J. BENNETT, 1988. Optical and photoreceptor immaturities limit the spatial and chromatic vision of human neonates. *J. Opt. Soc. Am. [A]* 5:2059–2079.

BANKS, M. S., and P. SALAPATEK, 1978. Acuity and contrast sensitivity in 1-, 2-, and 3-month-old human infants. *Invest. Ophthalmol. Vis. Sci.* 17:361–365.

BANKS, M. S., and P. SALAPATEK, 1981. Infant pattern vision: A new approach based on the contrast sensitivity function. *J. Exp. Child Psychol.* 31:1–45.

BEAVER, C. J., E. E. MITCHELL, and H. A. ROBERTSON, 1993. Immunohistochemical study of the pattern of rapid expression of c-fos protein in the visual cortex of dark-reared kittens following initial exposure to light. *J. Comp. Neurol.* 333:469–484.

BIRCH, E. E., 1985. Infant interocular acuity differences and binocular vision. *Vis. Res.* 25:571–576.

BIRCH, E. E., J. GWIAZDA, J. A. BAUER, J. NAEGELE, and R. HELD, 1983. Visual acuity and its meridional variations in children aged 7–60 months. *Vis. Res.* 23:1019–1024.

BIRCH, E. E., and D. R. STAGER, 1988. Prevalence of good visual acuity following surgery for congenital unilateral cataract. *Arch. Ophthalmol.* 106:40–43.

BIRCH, E. E., and D. R. STAGER, 1996. The critical period for surgical treatment of dense congenital unilateral cataract. *Invest. Ophthalmol. Vis. Sci.* 37:1532–1538.

BIRCH, E. E., D. STAGER, J. LEFFLER, and D. WEAKLEY, 1998. Early treatment of congenital unilateral cataract minimizes unequal competition. *Invest. Ophthalmol. Vis. Sci.* 39:1560–1566.

BIRCH, E. E., D. R. STAGER, and W. W. WRIGHT, 1986. Grating acuity development after early surgery for congenital unilateral cataract. *Arch. Ophthalmol.* 104:1783–1787.

BIRCH, E. E., W. H. SWANSON, D. STAGER, M. WOODY, and M. EVERETT, 1993. Outcome after very early treatment of dense congenital unilateral cataract. *Invest. Ophthalmol. Vis. Sci.* 34:3687–3699.

BLAIS, B., H. SHOUVAL, and L. COOPER, 1999. The role of presynaptic activity in monocular deprivation: comparison of homosynaptic and heterosynaptic mechanisms. *Proc. Natl. Acad. Sci. (USA)* 96:1083–1087.

BLAKEMORE, C., 1988. The sensitive periods of the monkey visual cortex. In *Strabismus and Amblyopia: Experimental Basis for Advances in Clinical Management,* G. Lennerstrand, G. K. von Noorden, and E. C. Campos, eds. New York: Plenum Press, pp. 219–234.

BLAKEMORE, C., 1990. Vision: coding and efficiency. In *Maturation of Mechanisms for Efficient Spatial Vision,* C. Blakemore, ed. Cambridge: Cambridge University Press.

BLAKEMORE, C., L. GAREY, and F. VITAL-DURAND, 1978. The physiological effects of monocular deprivation and their reversal in the monkey's cortex. *J. Physiol.* 237:195–216.

BLAKEMORE, C., and F. VITAL-DURAND, 1983. Visual deprivation prevents the postnatal maturation of spatial contrast sensitivity neurons of the monkey's striate cortex. *J. Physiol.* 345:40P.

BLAKEMORE, C. and F. VITAL-DURAND, 1986a. Organization and postnatal development of the monkey's lateral geniculate nucleus. *J. Physiol.* 380:453–491.

BLAKEMORE, C. and F. VITAL-DURAND, 1986b. Effects of visual deprivation on the development of the monkey's lateral geniculate nucleus. *J. Physiol.* 380:493–511.

BOOTHE, R. G., V. DOBSON, and D. Y. TELLER, 1985. Postnatal development of vision in human and nonhuman primates. *Annu. Rev. Neurosci.* 8:495–545.

BOWERING, M. E. R., 1992. *The Peripheral Vision of Normal Children and of Children Treated for Cataracts.* (Doctoral dissertation, McMaster University). Dissertation Abstracts International.

BRADDICK, O., J. ATKINSON, and B. HOOD, 1996. Striate cortex, extrastriate cortex, and colliculus: some new approaches. In *Infant Vision,* F. Vital-Durand, J. Atkinson, and O. J. Braddick, eds. Oxford, UK: Oxford University Press, pp. 203–220.

BRADLEY, A., and R. D. FREEMAN, 1982. Contrast sensitivity in children. *Vis. Res.* 22:953–959.

BROWN, A. M., V. DOBSON, and J. MAYER, 1987. Visual acuity of human infants at scotopic, mesopic, and photopic luminances. *Vis. Res.* 27:1845–1858.

BROWN, A., and M. YAMAMOTO, 1986. Visual acuity in newborn and preterm infants measured with grating acuity cards. *Am. J. Ophthalmol.* 102:245–253.

CABELLI, R. J., A. HOHN, and C. J. SHATZ, 1995. Inhibition of ocular dominance column formation by infusion of NT-4/5 or BDNF. *Science* 267:1662–1666.

CANDY, R. T., and M. S. BANKS, 1999. Use of an early nonlinearity to measure optical and receptor resolution in the human infant. *Vis. Res.* 39:3386–3398.

CARMIGNOTO, G., R. CANELLA, P. CANDEO, M. COMELLI, and L. MAFFEI, 1993. Effects of nerve growth factor on neuronal plasticity of the kitten visual cortex. *J. Physiol.* 464:343–360.

CATALANO, R. A., J. W. SIMON, P. L. JENKINS, and G. L. KADEL, 1987. Preferential looking as a guide for amblyopia therapy in monocular infantile cataracts. *J. Ped. Ophthalmol. Strab.* 24:56–63.

CLARK, D., A. HENDRICKSON, and C. CURCIO, 1988. Photoreceptor topography in lid-sutured *Macaca Fascicularis. Invest. Ophthalmol. Vis. Sci. Suppl.* 35:33.

CORNELL, E. H., and P. M. MCDONNELL, 1986. Infants' acuity at twenty feet. *Invest. Ophthalmol. Visual Sci.* 27:1417–1420.

COURAGE, M. and R. ADAMS, 1990. Visual acuity assessment from birth to three years using the acuity card procedure: cross-sectional and longitudinal samples. *Optom. Vis. Sci.* 67:713–718.

CRAWFORD, J., 1988. Electrophysiology of cortical neurons under different conditions of visual deprivation. In *Strabismus and Amblyopia: Experimental Basis for Advances in Clinical Management.* G. Lennerstrand, G. K. von Noorden, and C. C. Campos, eds. New York: Plenum Press, pp. 207–218.

CRAWFORD, J., 1998. Column spacing in normal and visually deprived monkeys. *Exp. Brain Res.* 123:282–288.

CRAWFORD, J., R. BLAKE, S. COOL, and G. VON NOORDEN, 1975. Physiological consequences of unilateral and bilateral eye closure in macaque: Some further observations. *Brain Res.* 85:150–154.

CRAWFORD, M. J. L., J.-T. DE FABER, R. S. HARWERTH, E. L. SMITH, and G. K. VON NOORDEN, 1989. The effects of reverse monocular deprivation in monkeys II. Electrophysiological and anatomical studies. *Exp. Brain Res.* 74:338–347.

CRAWFORD, M. L. J., T. W. PESCH, G. K. VON NOORDEN, R. S. HARWERTH, and E. L. SMITH, 1991. Bilateral form deprivation in monkeys. *Invest. Ophthalmol. Vis. Sci.* 32:2328–2336.

DEREFELDT, G., G. LENNERSTRAND, and B. LUNDH, 1979. Age variations in normal human contrast sensitivity. *Acta Ophthalmol.* 57:679–690.

DOBSON, V., T. L. SCHWARTZ, D. J. SANDSTROM, and L. MICHEL, 1987. Binocular visual acuity of neonates: the acuity card procedure. *Dev. Med. Child Neurol.* 29:199–206.

DRUCKER, D. N., and A. E. HENDRICKSON, 1989. The morphological development of extrafoveal human retina. *Invest. Ophthalmol. Vis. Sci. Suppl.* 30:226.

DUFFY, K. R., and K. M. MURPHY, 1999. Monocular deprivation promotes a visuo-topic specific loss of the NMDAR1 subunit in the visual cortex. *Soc. Neurosci. Abstr.* 25:1315.

ELLEMBERG, D., T. L. LEWIS, C. H. LIU, and D. MAURER, 1999a. The development of spatial and temporal vision during childhood. *Vis. Res.* 39:2325–2333.

ELLEMBERG, D., T. L. LEWIS, D. MAURER, and H. P. BRENT, 2000. Influence of monocular deprivation during infancy on the later development of spatial and temporal vision. *Vis. Res.* 40:3283–3295.

ELLEMBERG, D., T. L. LEWIS, D. MAURER, C. H. LIU, and H. P. BRENT, 1999b. Spatial and temporal vision in patients treated for bilateral congenital cataracts. *Vis. Res.* 39:3480–3489.

FANTZ, R., J. ORDY, and M. UDELF, 1962. Maturation of pattern vision in infants during the first six months. *J. Comp. Physiol. Psychol.* 55:907–917.

FIORENTINI, A., N. BERARDI, and L. MAFFEI, 1995. Nerve growth factor preserves behavioral visual acuity in monocularly deprived kittens. *Vis. Neurosci.* 12:51–55.

FIORENTINI, A., M. PIRCHIO, and G. SANDINI, 1984. Development of retinal acuity in infants evaluated with pattern electroretinogram. *Hum. Neurobiol.* 3:93–95.

FIORENTINI, A., M. PIRCHIO, and D. SPINELLI, 1983. Development of retinal and cortical responses to pattern reversal in infants: A selective review. *Behav. Brain Res.* 10:99–106.

FREEMAN, R. D., and OHZAWA, I., 1988. Monocularly deprived cats: binocular tests of cortical cells reveal functional connections from the deprived eye. *J. Neurosci.* 8:2491–2506.

GALUSKE, R. A., D.-S. KIM, E. CASTREN, H. THOENEN, and W. SINGER, 1996. Brain-derived neurotrophic factor reverses experience-dependent synaptic modification in kitten visual cortex. *Eur. J. Neurosci.* 8:1554–1559.

GAREY, L. J., and C. DE COURTEN, 1983. Structural development of the lateral geniculate nucleus and visual cortex in monkey and man. *Behav. Brain Res.* 10:3–13.

GWIAZDA, J., J. BAUER, F. THORN, and R. HELD, 1997. Development of spatial contrast sensitivity from infancy to adulthood: Psychophysical data. *Optom. Vis. Sci.* 74:785–789.

HARRIS, L., J. ATKINSON, and O. BRADDICK, 1976. Visual contrast sensitivity of a 6-month-old infant measured by the evoked potential. *Nature* 264:570–571.

HARWERTH, R. S., E. L. SMITH, M. L. J. BOLTZ, M. L. J. CRAWFORD, and G. K. VON NOORDEN, 1983a. Behavioral studies on the effect of abnormal early visual experience in monkeys: spatial modulation sensitivity. *Vis. Res.* 23:1501–1510.

HARWERTH, R. S., E. L. SMITH, M. L. J. BOLTZ, M. L. J. CRAWFORD, and G. K. VON NOORDEN, 1983b. Behavioral studies on the effect of abnormal early visual experience in monkeys: temporal modulation sensitivity. *Vis. Res.* 23:1511–1517.

HARWERTH, R. S., E. L. SMITH, M. L. J. CRAWFORD, and G. K. VON NOORDEN, 1989. The effects of reverse monocular deprivation in monkeys I. Psychophysical experiments. *Exp. Brain Res.* 74:327–337.

HARWERTH, R. S., E. L. SMITH, A. D. PAUL, M. L. J. CRAWFORD, and G. K. VON NOORDEN, 1991. Functional effects of bilateral form deprivation in monkeys. *Invest. Ophthalmol. Vis. Sci.* 32:2311–2327.

HATA, Y., and M. P. STRYKER, 1994. Control of thalamocortical afferent rearrangement by postsynaptic activity in developing visual cortex. *Science* 265:1732–1735.

HATA, Y., T. TSUMOTO, and M. STRYKER, 1999. Selective pruning of more active afferents when cat visual cortex is pharmacologically inhibited. *Neuron* 22:375–381.

HEBB, D. O., 1949. *The Organization of Behavior.* New York: Wiley.

HENDRICKSON, A., and R. BOOTHE, 1976. Morphology of the retinal and dorsal lateral geniculate nucleus in dark-reared monkeys (*Maccaca nemestrina*). *Vis. Res.* 16:517–521.

HENDRICKSON, A., and C. KUPFER, 1976. The histogenesis of the fovea in the macaque monkey. *Invest. Ophthalmol.* 15:746–756.

HENDRICKSON, A., and C. YOUDELIS, 1984. The morphological development of the human fovea. *Ophthalmol.* 91:603–612.

HICKEY, T. L., 1977. Postnatal development of the human lateral geniculate nucleus: Relationship to a critical period for the visual system. *Science* 198:836–838.

HORTON, J., and D. HOCKING, 1997. Timing of the critical period for plasticity of ocular dominance columns in macaque striate cortex. *J. Neurosci.* 17:3684–3709.

HUBEL, D. H., T. N. WIESEL, and S. LEVAY, 1977. Plasticity of ocular dominance columns in monkey striate cortex. *Phil. Trans. R. Soc. Lond. [B]* 278:377–409.

HUTTENLOCHER, P. R., 1979. Synaptic density in human frontal cortex—Developmental changes and effects of aging. *Brain Res.* 163:195–205.

HUTTENLOCHER, P. R., 1984. Synapse elimination and plasticity in developing human cerebral cortex. *Am. J. Med. Deficiency* 88:488–496.

HUTTENLOCHER, P. R., and A. S. DABHOLKAR, 1997. Regional differences in synaptogenesis in human cerebral cortex. *J. Comp. Neurol.* 387:167–178.

HUTTENLOCHER, P. R., and C. DE COURTEN, 1987. The development of synapses in striate cortex of man. *Hum. Neurobiol.* 6:1–9.

HUTTENLOCHER, P. R., C. DE COURTEN, L. J. GAREY, and H. VAN DER LOOS, 1982. Synaptogenesis in human visual cortex—evidence for synaptic elimination during normal development. *Neurosci. Lett.* 33:247–252.

JACOBSON, S. G., I. MOHINDRA, and R. HELD, 1983. Binocular vision from deprivation in human infants. *Doc. Ophthalmol.* 55:237–249.

JOHNSON, M., 1990. Cortical maturation and the development of visual attention in early infancy. *J. Cogn. Neurosci.* 2:81–95.

KACZMAREK, L., S. ZANGENEHPOUR, and A. CHAUDHURI, 1999. Sensory regulation of immediate-early genes *c-fos* and *zif268* in monkey visual cortex at birth and throughout the critical period. *Cereb. Cortex* 9:179–187.

KAPLAN, I., Y. GUO, and G. MOWER, 1996. Immediate early gene expression cat visual cortex during and after the critical period: differences between EGR-1 and Fos proteins. *Mol. Brain Res.* 36:12–22.

KASAMATSU, T., M. KITANO, E. E. SUTTER, and A. M. NORCIA, 1998. Lack of lateral inhibitory interactions in visual cortex of monocularly deprived cats. *Vis. Res.* 38:1–12.

KATZ, L. C., and C. J. SHATZ, 1996. Synaptic activity and the construction of cortical circuits. *Science* 274:1132–1138.

KIND, P., 1999. Cortical plasticity: Is it time for a change? *Curr. Biol.*, 9:R640–643.

KIORPES, L., and J. A. MOVSHON, 1998. Peripheral and central factors limiting the development of contrast sensitivity in Macaque monkeys. *Vis. Res.* 38:61–70.

KUGELBERG, U., 1992. Visual acuity following treatment of bilateral congenital cataracts. *Doc. Ophthalmol.* 82:211–215.

LARSEN, J. S., 1971. The sagittal growth of the eye. *Acta Ophthalmol.* 49:873–886.

LEHMKUHLE, S., K. E. KRATZ, and S. M. SHERMAN, 1982. Spatial and temporal sensitivity of normal and amblyopic cats. *J. Neurophysiol.* 48:372–387.

LEVAY, S., T. N. WIESEL, and D. H. HUBEL, 1980. The development of ocular dominance columns in normal and visually deprived monkeys. *J. Comp. Neurol.* 191:1–51.

LEVI, D., and R. MANNY, 1982. The pathophysiology of amblyopia: Electrophysiological studies. *Ann. N.Y. Acad. Sci.* 388:243–263.

LEVITT, J. B., J. A. MOVSHON, S. M. SHERMAN, and P. D. SPEAR, 1989. Effects of monocular deprivation on macaque LGN. *Invest. Ophthalmol. Vis. Sci. Suppl.* 30:296.

LEWIS, T. L., and D. MAURER, 1986. Preferential looking as a measure of visual resolution in infants and toddlers: A comparison of psychophysical methods. *Child Dev.* 57:1062–1075.

LEWIS, T. L., D. MAURER, and H. P. BRENT, 1995. Development of grating acuity in children treated for unilateral or bilateral congenital cataract. *Invest. Ophthalmol. Vis. Sci.* 36:2080–2095.

LEWIS, T. L., D. MAURER, M. E. TYTLA, E. R. BOWERING, and H. P. BRENT, 1992. Vision in the 'good' eye of children treated for unilateral congenital cataract. *Ophthalmol* 99:1013–1017.

LLOYD, I. C., J. G. DOWLER, A. KRISS, L. SPEEDWELL, D. A. THOMPSON, I. RUSSELL-EGGITT, and D. TAYLOR, 1995. Modulation of amblyopia therapy following early surgery for unilateral congenital cataracts. *Br. J. Ophthalmol.* 79:802–806.

MANTYJARVI, M. I., M. H. AUTERE, A. M. SILVENNOINEN, and T. MYOHANEN, 1989. Observations on the use of three different contrast sensitivity tests in children and young adults. *J. Ped. Ophthalmol. Strab.* 26:113–119.

MAURER, D., and T. L. LEWIS, 1993. Visual outcomes after infantile cataract. In *Early Visual Development: Normal and Abnormal.* K. Simons, ed. Committee on Vision. Commission on Behavioral and Social Sciences and Education. National Research Council. New York: Oxford University Press, pp. 454–484.

MAURER, D., T. L. LEWIS, H. P. BRENT, and A. V. LEVIN, 1999. Rapid improvement in the acuity of infants after visual input. *Science* 286:108–110.

MAYER, M., 1977. Development of anisotropy in late childhood. *Vis. Res.* 17:703–710.

MAYER, D. L., A. S. BEISER, A. F. WARNER, E. M. PRATT, K. N. RAYE, and J. M. LANG, 1995. Monocular acuity norms for the Teller acuity cards between ages one month and four years. *Invest. Ophthalmol. Vis. Sci.* 36:671–685.

MAYER, D. L., and V. DOBSON, 1980. Assessment of vision in young children: a new operant approach yields estimates of acuity. *Invest. Ophthalmol. Vis. Sci.* 19:566–570.

MAYER, D. L., and V. DOBSON, 1982. Visual acuity development in infants and young children, as assessed by operant preferential looking. *Vis. Res.* 22:1141–1151.

MAYER, D. L., A. B. FULTON, and R. M. HANSEN, 1985. Visual acuity of infants and children with retinal degeneration. *Ophthalmol. Paed. Gen.* 5:51–56.

MAYER, D. L., B. MOORE, and R. M. ROBB, 1989. Assessment of vision and amblyopia by preferential looking tests after early surgery for unilateral congenital cataracts. *J. Ped. Ophthalmol. Strab.* 26:61–68.

McCULLOCH, D., and B. SKARF, 1994. Pattern reversal visual evoked potentials following early treatment of unilateral, congenital cataract. *Arch. Ophthalmol.* 112:510–518.

McDONALD, M., V. DOBSON, S. L. SERBIS, L. BAITCH, D. VARNER, and D. Y. TELLER, 1985. The acuity card procedure: a rapid test of infant acuity. *Invest. Ophthalmol. Vis. Sci.* 26:1158–1162.

MILLER, M., P. PASIK, and T. PASIK, 1980. Extrageniculostriate vision in the monkey. VII. Contrast sensitivity functions. *J. Neurophysiol.* 43:1510–1526.

MIOCHE, L., and M. PERENIN, 1986. Central and peripheral residual vision in humans with bilateral deprivation amblyopia. *Exp. Brain Res.* 62:259–272.

MIRANDA, S. B., 1970. Visual abilities and pattern preferences of premature and fullterm neonates. *J. Exp. Child Psychol.* 10:189–205.

MITCHELL, D., C. BEAVER, and P. RITCHIE, 1995. A method to study changes in eye-related columns in the visual cortex of kittens during and following early periods of monocular deprivation. *Can. J. Physiol. Pharmacol.* 73:1352–1363.

MITCHELL, D., and G. GINGRAS, 1998. Visual recovery after monocular deprivation is driven by absolute, rather than relative, visually evoked activity levels. *Curr. Biol.* 8:1179–1182 (Erratum: R897).

MOVSHON, J. A., and L. KIORPES, 1993. Biological limits of visual development in primates. In *Early Visual Development: Normal and Abnormal,* K. Simons, ed. Committee on Vision. Commission on Behavioral and Social Sciences and Education. National Research Council. New York: Oxford University Press, pp. 296–304.

MOWER, G., 1994. Differences in the induction of Fos protein in cat visual cortex during and after the critical period. *Mol. Brain Res.* 21:47–54.

PASTERNAK, T., and W. H. MERIGAN, 1981. The luminance dependence of spatial vision in cats. *Vis. Res.* 21:1333–1339.

PETERZELL, D. H., J. S. WERNER, and P. S. KAPLAN, 1995. Individual differences in contrast sensitivity functions: Longitudinal study of 4-, 6-, and 8-month-old human infants. *Vis. Res.* 35:961–979.

PIRCHIO, M., D. SPINELLI, A. FIORENTINI, and L. MAFFEI, 1978. Infant contrast sensitivity evaluated by evoked potentials. *Brain Res.* 141:179–184.

RITTENHOUSE, C. D., H. Z. SHOUVAL, M. A. PARADISO, and M. F. BEAR, 1999. Monocular deprivation induces homosynaptic long-term depression in visual cortex. *Nature* 397:347–350.

SALAPATEK, P., A. G. BECHTOLD, and E. W. BUSHNELL, 1976. Infant visual acuity as a function of viewing distance. *Child Dev.* 47:860–863.

SWINDALE, N. V., F. VITAL-DURAND, and C. BLAKEMORE, 1981. Recovery from monocular deprivation in the monkey. III. Reversal of anatomical effects in the visual cortex. *Proc. R. Soc. Lond. [B]* 213:435–450.

TELLER, D. Y., M. A. McDONALD, K. PRESTON, S. L. SEBRIS, and V. DOBSON, 1986. Assessment of visual acuity in infants and children: the acuity card procedure. *Dev. Med. Child Neurol.* 28:779–789.

THOMPSON, D. A., H. MØLLER, J. RUSSELL-EGGITT, and A. KRISS, 1996. Visual acuity in unilateral cataract. *Br. J. Ophthalmol.* 80:794–798.

TYTLA, M. E., D. MAURER, T. L. LEWIS, and H. P. BRENT, 1988. Contrast sensitivity in children treated for congenital cataract. *Clin. Vis. Sci.* 2:251–264.

VAN HOF-VAN DUIN, J., and G. MOHN, 1986. The development of visual acuity in normal fullterm and preterm infants. *Vis. Res.* 26:909–916.

WEISKRANTZ, L., 1986. *Blindsight.* Oxford: Clarenden Press.

WILSON, H. R., 1988. Development of spatiotemporal mechanisms in infant vision. *Vis. Res.* 28:611–628.

WILSON, H. R., 1993. Theories of infant visual development. In *Early Visual Development: Normal and Abnormal,* K. Simons, ed. Committee on Vision. Commission on Behavioral and Social Sciences and Education. National Research Council. New York: Oxford University Press, pp. 560–572.

YOUDELIS, C., and A. HENDRICKSON, 1986. A quantitative and qualitative analysis of the human fovea during development. *Vis. Res.* 26:847–855.

ZABLOCKA, T., and B. ZERNICKI, 1996. Discrimination learning of grating orientation in visually deprived cats and the role of the superior colliculi. *Behav. Neurosci.* 110:621–625.

ZABLOCKA, T., B. ZERNICKI, and A. KOSMAL, 1976. Visual cortex role in object discrimination in cats deprived of pattern vision from birth. *Acta Neurobiol. Exp.* 36:157–168.

ZABLOCKA, T., B. ZERNICKI, and A. KOSMAL, 1980. Loss of object discrimination after ablation of the superior collicula-pretectum in binocularly deprived cats. *Behav. Brain Res.* 1:521–531.

# 18 Stability and Flexibility in the Acquisition of Skilled Movement

MELISSA W. CLEARFIELD
AND ESTHER THELEN

ABSTRACT  The process by which new motor skills emerge has been a fundamental question in developmental psychology. One issue that must be faced when learning a new skill is the requirement that skilled movements be both stable and flexible. In this chapter, we explore how infants resolve the inherent tension between newly emerging stability and flexible adaptation. We illustrate these dual themes by examining how infants learn to reach out and grab objects. We show that infants begin learning to reach with flexibility in the neuromotor system, as well as constraints on coordination patterns. This combination allows for multiple solutions while still limiting the nearly endless possibilities. Furthermore, we show that stability and flexibility can be thought of as part of the same dynamic system, reflecting the interconnectedness and redundancy of the neuromotor system.

During their first year of life, human infants experience a dramatic transformation in their abilities to control their bodies. Newborn infants are prisoners of the forces of gravity, unable even to raise their heads. Yet after just one year, they are able to sit, reach for and manipulate objects, crawl, stand, walk, climb, gesture, and sometimes even speak a few words. These new skills mark changes across all the systems of the body. Moreover, these abilities completely reorganize infants' relationships with their physical and social worlds. The ability to control the head enables babies to choose what to look at. The ability to sit erect frees the hands for exploring and manipulating objects. The ability to gesture and speak allows full communication with others.

There is more than a century of scientific study of these orderly developmental milestones. The recurrent theme of these descriptive and experimental studies has been to document the emergence and improvements in motor skills and the processes that underlie these changes (for reviews of motor development, see Berthenthal and Clifton, 1999; Catell, 1939; Fentress and McLeod, 1986; Jouen and Lepecq, 1990; Kirkpatrick, 1899; Schmidt and Fitzpatrick, 1996; Zelazo, 1998). Thus, the concern has been not only when and how

new forms of movements arise, but also how movements become more accurate, faster, more graceful, and more finely tuned to the environment (Adolph, 1997; Adolph, Eppler, and Gibson, 1993; von Hofsten, 1979; Thelen et al., 1993).

In this chapter, we focus on a related aspect of motor skill: the dual requirements that skilled behavior be both *stable* and *flexible*. Consider for a moment the achievements of baseball legend Mark McGuire, who broke the Major League record for home runs in a single season. To break that record, McGuire had to be consistent in the timing, placement, and force of the swing of the bat. His skills were stable and repeatable. But no two pitches are exactly the same. So McGuire also had to be flexible in order to adjust his swing to hit balls pitched at different angles and different speeds. Most remarkably, the adaptation of the swing must be done largely "on-line," only after the ball leaves the pitcher's hand with a specific combination of speed and direction. Estimates are that a batter has but 200 milliseconds or so to adjust his swing to the oncoming ball. But despite such a small window of opportunity, McGuire was repeatedly able to make the necessary adjustments to his swing to contact the ball with enough force to hit it out of the ballpark.

Most tasks in everyday life do not require the speed and precision seen in professional athletes, but the dual qualities of stability and flexibility still apply. How are movements controlled such that they show these two qualities? How did they get that way during early development? In this chapter, we consider the seemingly simple, everyday skill of reaching for objects, the development of that skill in infancy, and its neural foundations. We make the following points:

1. In adults, reaching is both highly repeatable and very flexible.

2. These dual qualities develop gradually during the first year of life.

3. Infants' first task is to acquire a measure of stability, that is, a general category of successful movements.

MELISSA W. CLEARFIELD AND ESTHER THELEN   Department of Psychology, Indiana University, Bloomington, Indiana.

4. Aspects of on-line flexibility are apparent only after a few months of reaching practice.

5. Under some circumstances, infants do not seem able to adapt flexibly, but get "stuck" in an old movement pattern.

6. Both "stuckness" and flexibility are part of the same dynamic system and reflect the distributed control of movement in the brain.

## Skilled reaching in adults

Adults reach out and grasp objects hundreds of times over the course of one day and have been doing so for many years. Reaching is a highly practiced, highly skilled movement. Adult reaches can be extraordinarily stable and repeatable. Figure 18.1 shows the hand trajectories and velocity curves of an adult reaching to a target for many trials. As has been described in many studies, adults tend to move their arms smoothly and along a straight path (Flash and Hogan, 1985; Morasso, 1981). The velocity curves are smooth and bell-shaped (figure 18.1); moreover, such movements are characterized by fairly constant durations, regardless of the distance and direction of the reach (Morasso, 1981). Underlying these kinematic properties are stable patterns of muscle activation, as also illustrated in figure 18.1.

Along with this stability comes a remarkable ability to adjust movements to changes in the task context. Adults skillfully adapt their reaches to changes in both the visual and biomechanical environment (e.g., Held and Schlank, 1959; see Jeannerod, 1988, for a review). These adaptations can be "on-line," much like Mark McGwire's adjustments of his swing to the airborne ball. For instance, in the classic "two-step" paradigm, researchers switched the target location after the participants had initiated a reach. If the target switch was within 100 ms of the reach initiation, participants seamlessly adjusted their movements to the new target, often without conscious awareness that the target had been moved a short distance away (Castiello, Paulignon, and Jeannerod, 1991; Goodale, Pelisson, and Prablanc, 1986; Paulignon et al., 1991). Likewise, adults can rapidly adapt their movements to unexpected mechanical perturbations to their limbs. In these classic experiments, researchers used torque motors to displace the limb briefly during the reaching movement. Despite these unexpected tugs, participants always attained the intended targets (Bizzi et al., 1978; Kelso and Holt, 1980).

When a visual target is suddenly moved or when the limb is unaccountably pulled off course, participants must flexibly use different patterns of forces and different patterns of muscle contractions in order to maintain stability in their goal—to reach for the target. This principle of recruiting flexible solutions to achieve a stable goal is also illustrated in adult experiments that require adaptations of movements over a longer time scale. Several important and elegant experiments illustrate this long-term perceptual–motor adaptation. These experiments provide participants with novel circumstances and track their abilities to find stable solutions. The well-known prism studies are a good example. Hamilton and Bossom (1964), for example, fitted participants with prism goggles that shifted the visual scene 20° from center. At first, participants reached incorrectly and missed the target. After 15 minutes of practice, however, participants learned to adjust their reaches and accurately hit the target. Upon removal of the prism goggles, participants had to readjust their movements to the normal visual world.

People can make similar adjustments to changes in the "feel" of their arms. Dizio and Lackner (1995), for example, subjected participants to a novel rotational force while they attempted to reach for targets. At first, participants were inaccurate and variable. They were unaccustomed to the feel of their arms in the rotational field. However, after 70 practice trials, participants could readily compensate for the unusual forces and became highly accurate in their reaches. Again, this learned adaptation persisted for some time after the rotational forces were discontinued.

How can the motor system attain the benefits of stability yet retain flexibility to adapt to changing circumstances? It is clear from these and many other studies that the neuromotor system is blessed with abundant redundancy. By this, we mean that the system can recruit many different ways of achieving a particular goal for action. The redundancy lies not only in the mechanical degrees of freedom afforded by the linked system of joints and flexible spine and elastic muscles, but also in the neurological degrees of freedom. A large portion of the brain is devoted to the control of movement (Schwartz, 1994; Georgoupolous, 1995). Moreover, the dense interconnectedness between cortical areas and cortical–subcortical areas means that there are multiple ways to achieve the same behavior (see Passingham, 1993).

## The development of control: Learning to reach

For the developing infant, these degrees of freedom pose both a challenge and an opportunity (Bernstein, 1967). On the one hand, redundancy means that there may be an unconstrained number of solutions to

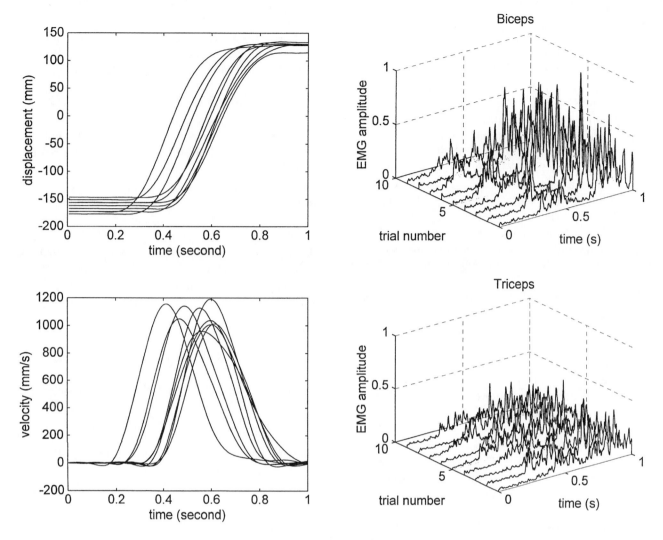

FIGURE 18.1   Example of typical adult reaches. The left panels show the hand displacement and velocity curves of an adult reaching for a target for many trials. The right panels show the accompanying muscle activation in the biceps and triceps.

a particular task. Indeed, there are seemingly limitless ways of organizing the combinations of muscles and joints to bring a hand to a target. What solutions are chosen and how are these solutions retained? On the other hand, redundancy provides the substrate for flexibility. Without alternative solutions, behavior would be rigid and inflexible.

This issue raises the question of how infants resolve the inherent tension between control (stability) and adaptation (flexibility). We examine these dual themes of stability and flexibility by looking closely at how infants learn to reach out and grab objects.

Infants first reach for and grab things when they are about 4 months old. Until then, they may bring their hands to their mouths, grasp objects placed in their hands, and wave and wiggle their arms and hands; but they cannot, for instance, obtain a toy placed at arm's length in front of them. The developmental question has been to examine from what ongoing structures and processes this new behavior arises. For many years, following Piaget (1952) and White, Castle, and Held (1964), developmentalists believed that the primary issue was infants' abilities to match the sight and feel of their hands to the sight of the target. It is now doubtful that infants' vision of their own hands is the sole critical element (Clifton et al., 1994), but clearly infants must learn some sort of match between the properties of their limbs and the visual properties of a target in space (Berthier, 1996).

FROM WIGGLING TO REACHING: SELECTING A STABLE PATTERN   We have looked at the transition to reaching in a different way, by tracking changes from the precursor movements—wavings and wigglings—to the first instances of infants' actually attaining a small toy dangled in front of them. What does reaching out and grasping a toy require? Are reaches fashioned from the nonreaching movements of wiggling? And if so, how? Are there processes or mechanisms that reduce the rampant degrees of freedom? What changes and what stays the same?

Although the precise matching of the hand to the target is a critical element in successful reaching, other elements of limb control must come first. In particular, infants must control their arms sufficiently to get the arms within the "ballpark" of the target so that the visual adjustments of the hand can be made. This requires infants' learning the relationship between the direction and strength of the forces they generate by activating their muscles and the consequent movements of their arms. They must also be able to hold their arms in an extended position so that they can make these visual adjustments. These abilities develop, we believe, both as a consequence of infants' self-generated movements and as a result of other changes occurring in the neuromotor system.

It was our detailed longitudinal study of infants' learning to reach that highlighted the importance of these early movements. In particular, we noticed that, even from the first weeks of life, infants had very different styles of moving their arms. For instance, in the four infants in our initial study, we saw two extremes of movement frequency and vigor. The infant Gabriel was extremely active, wiggling and moving his arms frequently. His movements were large and vigorous, with the kinematic and kinetic analyses revealing large excursions, high velocities, large torques (forces moving the arm), and large bursts of electromyographic (EMG) activity, reflecting much muscle activation. The infant Hannah, in stark contrast, moved much less, and when she did move, her movements were quiet, small, of low velocity and torque, and with weaker EMG patterns (Thelen et al., 1993).

What is the significance of these movement differences? At first, neither infant's movements were appropriate for reaching and grabbing an object. Gabriel, while moving actively, had no control over the spatial trajectory of his arms: his movements were too fast and imprecise. Hannah's movements were too small and slow and her arms remained flexed and close to her body. Both infants had to change the patterns of forces, but in different directions. Gabriel had to damp down his exuberant movements, while Hannah had to learn to extend and straighten her arms. Indeed, in the weeks before their first reaches, we observed these changes: Gabriel moved more slowly and less forcefully, while Hannah moved faster and with more extended arm postures.

Although their problems were different, both infants learned to modulate their ongoing movements to fit the task of reaching out and grabbing a toy placed in front of them. Thelen and colleagues (1993) suggested that the infants discovered these adjustments through their spontaneous, prereaching movements. That is, through these movements, the infants were exploring a range of patterns of force and muscle activation and selecting those patterns that occasionally moved their hands into the vicinity of the desired toy. The movement parameters that accompanied more successful movements were selectively retained and strengthened over the parameters leading to the less successful movements. Thus, infants progressively narrowed the large number of possible movements into a smaller repertoire of more goal-adapted movements (Sporns and Edelman, 1993). In this sense, a more stable category of movement patterns emerged from an initially larger set of movements, most of which were not successful for obtaining an object.

A STABLE CONSTRAINT ON THE SELECTION OF REACHING PATTERNS   This initial selection of ballpark parameters in the prereaching period is the first step in learning to reach, and it sets the stage for further improvements in hand–eye coordination and more precise control. How do infants do it? Recall that the possible combinations of joints and muscles used for moving the arms are nearly limitless. How can infants, in just a few months, select adaptive patterns from all these possibilities?

Zaal and colleagues (1999) discovered a set of constraints in the infants' neuromotor organization that helps reduce the initial degrees of freedom and likely aids in the selection of functional movements. The so-called "linear synergy" was first described in adults by Gottlieb and colleagues (1996). Adult movements are extremely flexible and generative. Adults have no problem intentionally moving their arms by rotating only one joint, say flexing and extending the forearm around the elbow or lifting and lowering the upper arm around the shoulder. Thus, depending on the task, adults can control joints independently. In most movements, however, multiple joints must move together. In these instances, control is coordinated. In particular, when adults are asked to perform natural reaching movements to targets in front of them, they exhibit a linear, proportional relationship between the torques that rotate the shoulder and the torques that rotate the elbow. This means that the control problem is greatly simplified as the torques are distributed proportionally. Not all movements that adults can do show the linear synergy, but it is characteristic of reaching movements within a "comfortable" reaching space.

The developmental question about linear synergy was whether this coordination pattern is a consequence of learning to reach well or whether it predates successful reaching and is a more foundational property of the neuromotor system. Indeed, the latter possibility proved to be the case. Zaal and colleagues (1999) looked at the torque patterns of infants before they learned to reach and as reaching improved over the first year. They found that the linear synergy was universal throughout the year, whether infants were reaching for toys or just waving their arms around. Figure 18.2 illustrates the hand trajectories, joint excursions, and torque patterns of a single infant during the prereaching period, soon after reach onset, and late in the first year. Note that despite increasingly smooth hand trajectories, joint rotations, and joint torques, the synergy between the shoulder and elbow joint torques remains strongly linear throughout. Movements that violated the linear synergy were simply not seen, and presumably, were not performed by the babies.

This constraint, available from the first weeks of life, means that infants are not using all of the possible, independent configurations of their joints in multijoint movements. The constraint makes the appropriate parameters for reaching easier to discover by limiting the possibilities within what, for adults, appears to be a comfortable reaching space. Adults can reach across the midline to scratch their opposite ears (babies do not!),

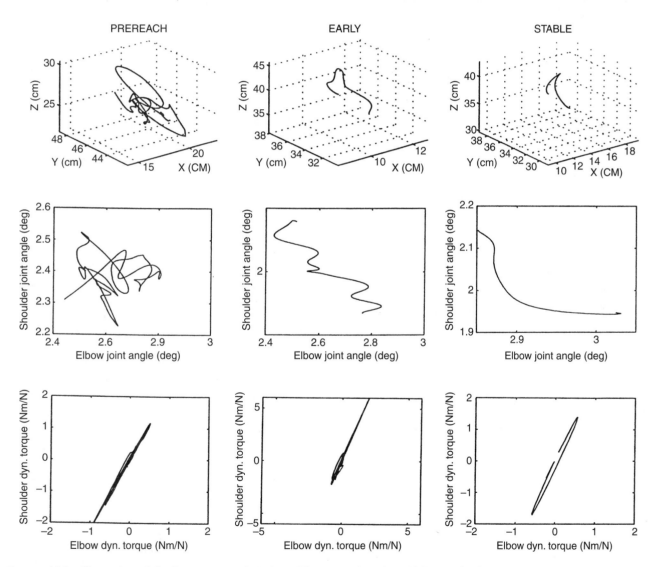

FIGURE 18.2   Illustration of the linear synergy in infants. The three panels show the same infant sampled in the prereach period, in the first month of reaching, and in the stable last quarter of the first year. The top panels are the 3-D hand paths. The middle panels plot the elbow joint angle versus the shoulder joint angle. The bottom panel is the shoulder and elbow torques (calculated as in Gottlieb et al., 1996). (Reprinted with permission from Thelen, in press.)

a movement that violates the linear synergy, but our data suggest they must subsequently learn to do this. It is not available in the initial movement repertoire. Thus, the linear synergy provides a stable constraint within which infants must discover the appropriate reaching parameters.

MUSCLE PATTERNS CHANGE AT THE ONSET OF REACHING   While the linear synergy constraint remains constant, other contributions to the onset of reaching are changing. One important discontinuity in the transition to reaching is the pattern of muscle activation used to move the arms. Spencer and Thelen (2000) looked at how four muscle groups that move the arm work together during the periods before and after infants learned to reach. They described the patterns of co-activity by first applying an algorithm to the EMG signal of the biceps, triceps, anterior deltoid, and trapezius muscles that determined whether at each sampling instant (at 750 Hz) a particular muscle was ON or OFF. The next step was to consider all four muscles at that instant: With four muscles, there are 16 possible states of ON or OFF. After the combination state was determined for each EMG sample, Spencer and Thelen cumulated the percentages of each state at each age in the prereach and postreach period. Figure 18.3 is a summary of that analysis.

Spencer and Thelen found a sharp discontinuity in the co-activity of the arm muscles. As seen in figure 18.3, before infants could successfully attain the objects in front of them, the predominant muscles used were the biceps and triceps working alone: the biceps to flex the arm at the elbow and bring the hand to the mouth, the triceps to extend the arm. After reach onset, other muscle patterns were predominant. In particular, infants used the deltoid muscle to lift and extend the arm, the trapezius muscle to stabilize the shoulder, neck, and head, and all muscles activated together; this served to stiffen the arm in the extended position, enabling the stability needed to make visual adjustments.

It is known from studies of adults that patterns of muscle activity shift as a function of the location of the hand in three-dimensional space (Flanders, 1991; Flanders, Pelligrini, and Soechting, 1994). It is reasonable to ask, therefore, whether the changes in patterns seen as infants learn to reach might not simply reflect that they were moving in different places in space. Spencer and Thelen (2000) found this not to be the case. They compared infants' muscle state patterns to their concurrent hand locations during reaching and nonreaching movements. Infants actually used different predominant muscle patterns while moving through the same areas in space. This is illustrated in figure 18.4, which shows the proportion of muscle activation states that involved the deltoid as a function of the location of the hand. At each location, more deltoid was used after reach onset than in movements completed before that milestone.

What is the role of these muscle pattern shifts in the emergence of reaching? Do infants' repeated attempts to reach actually strengthen the neck and shoulder muscles? Or does increased strength and control in these muscles facilitate reaching?

At present, we have no definitive answers to these questions. However, there are some indications that it may be infants' early improvements in *posture* that provide the neuromotor basis for reaching. Spencer and colleagues (2000) looked at infants' changes in preferred postures and movements week-by-week while the babies were interacting with parents in a natural "play" situation. One postural milestone that always preceded reach onset was the ability of the infants to control their heads and, in particular, to maintain a centered, midline position (see also Butterworth and Hicks, 1977; Rochat, 1992). This ability requires increased strength and control, especially in the trapezius muscles. In addition, infants always were able to lift their heads and torsos while prone before they could reach, perhaps again reflecting strength and control of the extensor muscles of the back to stabilize the torso and keep the head steady.

These processes—controlling the head, gaining in extensor strength—are not specific to reaching, but are part of infants' postural development as they gain over-

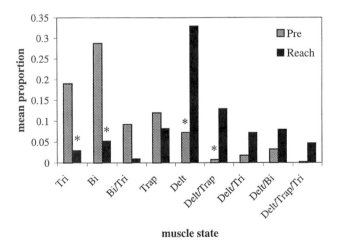

FIGURE 18.3   Mean proportion of time nine muscle states occurred relative to the total amount of nonzero state activity for the prereach and reach periods. Asterisks indicate significant differences in mean proportions across the two periods. (Reprinted with permission from Spencer and Thelen, 2000.)

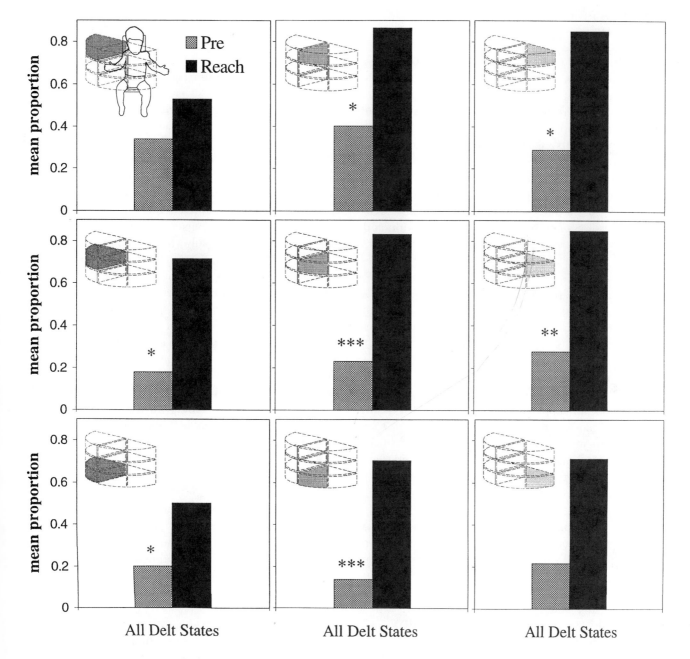

FIGURE 18.4 Mean proportion of time deltoid-related activity occurred within the side (left column), 45° (center column), and front (right column) regions across the prereach and reach periods. The inset in each graph indicates from which spatial region the data originate. Asterisks indicate significant differences in mean proportions across the prereach and reach periods: * t(3) < −3.25, p < .05; ** t(3) < −6.25, p < .01; *** t(3) < −9.1, p <. 005). (Reprinted with permission from Spencer and Thelen, 2000.)

all antigravity strength to roll, sit, and stand. Nonetheless, the same muscles that are used to attain these postural milestones also provide the stability needed to reach successfully. If the head and trunk are not held steady when the arm is lifted, the forces generated by the arm may, in turn, move the head and trunk. This is especially critical for the head, because a steady head position is necessary for a stable visual image. Moreover, the increasing strength and control of torso, shoulder, and neck muscles allows infants to activate differentially those muscles needed for the movement of the arm and those needed to provide stability in posture.

## Developmental changes in reaching:
## More stable, more flexible

We have described the onset of reaching as a process in which infants learn a reliable repetoire of directionally specific muscle patterns and forces to get their hands to objects they desire. Moreover, these changes co-occur with changes in other motor skills, most notably posture. At first, infants' reaches are poorly controlled. In contrast to the adult movements seen in figure 18.1, infants do not reach directly to the target, but often move their hands in a wandering and jerky path. The velocity of the movements is not smooth and bell-shaped, but shows multiple phases of acceleration and deceleration. Most importantly, these reach parameters are highly variable, even when the reaching task remains the same (Thelen, Corbetta, and Spencer, 1996). Although infants are often successful in attaining objects, they are not skilled: They may bat at an object and miss, for instance, or need to make numerous adjustments to reach it.

It is only after the middle of the first year—around 7 months or later—that infants' reaches become less variable. They no longer wildly swat and miss, but consistently use an appropriate and successful hand speed—not too fast and not too slow (Thelen, Corbetta, and Spencer, 1996). Reaches are more likely to be initiated from a quiet position than from an ongoing flapping movement.

We have some evidence that with this increased consistency, indicating better control, infants also become more flexible. In particular, they become able to adjust movements to more challenging contexts, including reaching for small objects and making corrections in their movements while they are performing them. For instance, Zaal and Thelen (2000) found that at 7 months, infants slowed down their movements when reaching for very small objects (little buttons), especially when close to the targets. This is about the same age at which infants will first reach to small objects at all, and before they have perfected a precision grip. Similarly, Berthier and Robin (1998) discovered that 9-month-old infants could correct their hand trajectories to targets that moved after the infants' had begun to move. This on-line correction took 400 ms, however—more than twice the time it takes adults to do a similar task.

PERSEVERATIVE REACHING    The increased stability and control in reaching seen around 7 months has another, perhaps surprising, consequence: location perseveration. When faced with the seemingly simple task of reaching for one of two identical targets, infants of 8–10 months often make perseverative reaching errors. In a typical task, after being cued to one target (location A) several times and reaching for it, infants continue to reach for A even when the experimenter clearly signals location B, several centimeters away from A. Routinely, infants first look at the B target during the cue, and although they have the ability to reach for it, they return their glances to A and then reach perseveratively to the original location. This location perseveration, traditionally known as the A-not-B error, has usually involved hiding objects under the two reaching targets for infants to search and find (Diamond, 1985). However, recent studies have eliminated the hidden object and reported equal rates of perseveration when the two target objects are continually visible (Smith et al., 1999; Diedrich, Thelen, Smith, and Corbetta, 2000; Munakata, 1997; Thelen et al., in press). Thus, the location perseveration seems to be a property of reaching itself.

Here, we propose that perseverative reaching emerges at around 8 months of age because that is when infants' reaches are just stable enough to get "stuck" in a motor habit, but not yet skilled enough to adapt flexibly to slight changes in location. Thus, the A-not-B task demonstrates the changing relationship between stability and flexibility in reaching. In the first months, infants are learning a stable motor pattern. However, stability may also temporarily limit flexibility. There are several lines of evidence to support our proposal.

THE EFFECT OF REPETITION    We suggest that the A-not-B task is a consequence of a particular stage of reaching development and, in particular, of the newly emerged ability to form a stable movement habit from repeating the same movement several times. The first issue is whether the particular task actually promotes a habit: Does repeating the reach to the A location several times lead to perseveration?

This issue has been frequently debated over the last 20 years (for reviews, see Marcovitch and Zelazo, 2000; Wellman, Cross, and Bartsch, 1986). The most recent evidence, however, is compelling in support of the formation of a location habit (Marcovitch and Zelazo, 2000; Smith et al., 1999). For example, Smith and colleagues (1999) tested 8- and 10-month-old infants in three versions of the A-not-B task. In one, infants received four training trials to the A location to teach them to uncover a hidden toy. This was followed by two test trials to A, with the toy hidden, and then two test trials to B. In the second condition, infants received only the two test trials to A and then the two switch trials to B, with no training. In the third condition, infants were trained to a third location, C, which was centered, and then tested at A and B. Thus, the conditions differed in the number of reaches to the A side before the test trials and whether the infants were trained to uncover the toy at the same or a different place. Seventy percent of the infants who received the training trials to A perseverated; they had previously reached 6 times to the A side. Infants in the two other conditions, who reached only twice to A, did not reliably perseverate. They reached back to A only 30% of the time. It did not matter whether infants had been taught to uncover the toy in the center. What mattered was the number of reaches to the same location; repeating the same movement to the same location in space increased the likelihood of perseveration to that location.

In another experiment, Smith and colleagues (1999) cued the B location after 1, 3, or 5 spontaneous reaches to A. In this version of the task, no toy was hidden. When the experimenter cued the B side after only 1 reach to A, 55% of the infants switched sides and reached correctly. When the experimenter picked up the B lid after 3 reaches to A, 50% of the infants reached correctly to B. In contrast, when the experimenter picked up the B lid after 5 reaches to A, only 16% of the infants reached to B.

In sum, with each reach to the A location, the likelihood of repeating a movement in the same direction increases. In a simple Hebbian fashion, each movement strengthens the neural pathways associated with that reach such that after many repetitions, the response becomes stable. Indeed, in the A-not-B situation, the location response becomes so stable that the new cue cannot compete with the built-up memory (Thelen et al., in press). We can elicit the perseverative response in 8- to 10-month-old infants because of the particular, transitional, developmental stage of their reaching skill and the special nature of the two-target task. In the next section, we provide further evidence for this view.

HAND TRAJECTORIES AND PERSEVERATIVE REACHING
We have suggested that, at this point of emerging control, we may have a window on how motor patterns become both stable and flexible. The A-not-B-type task provides a unique, and somewhat difficult, situation for infants. Normally, babies reach out for single, well-defined objects that remain in view. Across all variations of the experimental task, infants must reach for one of two identical targets. This situation may indeed constrain reaches considerably, making it more likely that infants would use a similar movement trial after trial, and thus develop a movement habit.

Remarkably, we can see such a process at work by looking at the actual hand paths of infants as they reach for either one or two targets, and we can compare the changes in hand paths as a function of perseveration.

Diedrich and colleagues (in press) attached infrared diodes to infants' arms while they reached during an A-not-B task without hidden objects to examine the kinematics (time–space trajectories) and speed of their movements. Recall that infants of this age do not make smooth and direct movements. Thus, each reach has a particular kinematic signature of direction and speed changes. It was found that these signature trajectories became more similar for infants who perseverated in the two-target task. That is, over time, and with the presumed build-up of the motor habit, infants repeated the same time–space configuration. Figure 18.5 demonstrates this in two ways for one infant. First, the displacement graph shows that the infant replicated nearly the same reach over and over because the path of the hand through space was nearly identical for six of the eight trials. Second, this infant demonstrated highly similar speed profiles for five trials, speeding up and slowing down twice.

In contrast, the reaches of those infants who did not perseverate did not converge. Figure 18.6 depicts the displacement and speed profile of an infant who did not perseverate. Note that this infant showed no consistent pattern of moving his hand through space. Each trial looked completely different. He showed a similar lack of pattern in his speed profile, where the number of direction changes is not the same from one trial to another. Infants reaching to a single target also did not show patterns of trajectory convergence.

THE DEVELOPMENT OF PERSEVERATION   If perseveration indeed emerges at this transition to more controlled reaching, then a clear developmental prediction is that younger infants, whose reaches are not well controlled, ought to perseverate *less* than older ones. This prediction is counter to the more intuitive idea that perseveration is the more immature behavior.

This prediction would be difficult to test using the conventional hidden toy task because infants below the ages of 7 or 8 months will not uncover a hidden toy despite training. However, with the discovery that perseveration is equally robust with fully visible targets, it was possible to test infants as young as 5 months of age in the two-target task. This is a time when all could easily reach and grab a single visible object. Clearfield, Thelen, and Smith (2000) found that, as predicted, the youngest infants who reached in the task did not reliably perseverate and instead were reliably correct (see figure 18.7). They reached correctly on the A trials, and then flexibly shifted to reach to B when the B location was cued. The 6- and 7-month-olds reached incorrectly on the A trials (they reached to B even when the A lid was cued) and randomly on the B trials. Only at 8

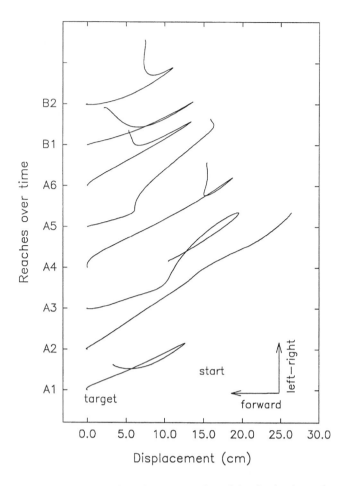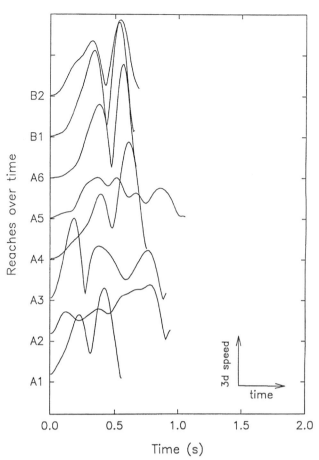

FIGURE 18.5  Reach trajectory, as viewed in the horizontal plane (left) and the corresponding three-dimensional speeds (right) of an infant who perseverated on both B trials. (Reprinted with permission from Diedrich et al., 2000.)

months of age did the infants actually perseverate, reaching correctly on the A trials and incorrectly on the B trial.

THE THEMES OF STABILITY AND FLEXIBILITY REVISITED
These results, together with the kinematic results of Diedrich and colleagues (2000), confirm a shifting developmental pattern between stability and flexibility of reaching. The first task for infants in learning to reach is to select, from the many possibilities, a pattern of movements that moves their hands into the vicinity of the target. This represents an increase of stability over the more random movements of the first months. Between 4 and 7 or 8 months, this selective pattern is refined as variability is decreased and accuracy increases. As described by Thelen and colleagues (1996), at 7 or 8 months infants seem to discover a quite stable pattern of speed and smoothness. It is at this time that perseveration becomes predominant in the two-target task (and infants also are able to reach for small objects

and adjust on-line). Making fine adjustments requires better trajectory control, but better control could also lead to the development of a motor habit under the special circumstances of the A-not-B task.

At about 1 year of age, infants do not perseverate at the typical delays and circumstances of the A-not-B task. As their reaching improves with continued practice, they become flexible enough to follow the new cue and reach to the second location. Where does this increased flexibility come from? At this point, we can only speculate. One possibility is that infants become better able to distinguish between the two identical targets so that they seem less novel and confusing. Another possibility is that increased practice in reaching provides more available motor patterns and thus less possibility of getting stuck in the pattern of what infants have just done. Alternatively, infants may retain a stronger memory of the actual cue to the location and thus overcome the tendency to repeat the previous action (Thelen et al., in press).

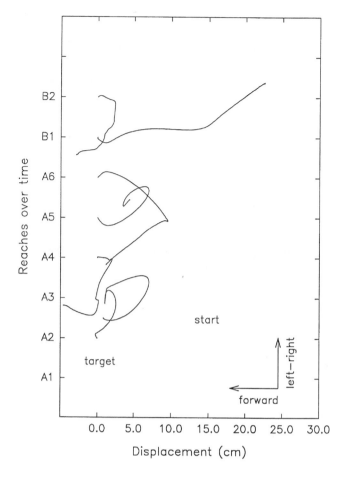

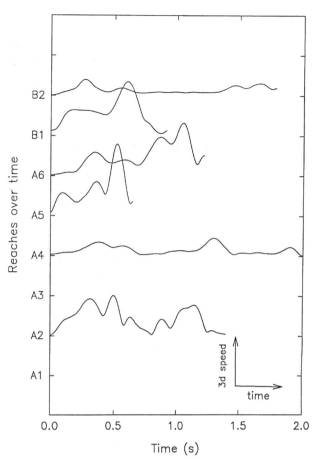

FIGURE 18.6   Reach trajectory, as viewed in the horizontal plane (left) and the corresponding three-dimensional speeds (right) of an infant who reached to B on both B trials. (Reprinted with permission from Diedrich et al., 2000.)

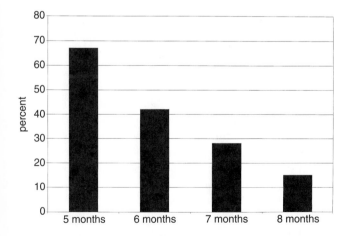

FIGURE 18.7   Percentage of infants who reached correctly on the first B trial, of the infants who reached at all in the two-target task ($n$ = 6 for 5 months, 13 for 6 months, 14 for 7 months, and 13 for 8 months).

## The neural basis of motor skill acquisition in the first year

We have described a contingent and nonlinear path in reaching development, marked by periods of rapid change and plateaus, in which improved control can lead to seemingly worse performance. What are the neural correlates of these behavioral changes? In reality, little is known about the actual changes in the brain that accompany the acquisition of new motor skills. Perhaps most attention has been devoted to the dorsolateral prefrontal cortex in relation to performance in the classic A-not-B task. According to Diamond (1985), perseveration at 8–10 months is a result of immature prefrontal cortex, and hence poor abilities both to remember the location of the hidden toy over a delay and to inhibit the previous motor response. Monkeys with lesioned prefrontal cortices do, indeed, behave like 8-month old babies when tested in similar tasks. Moreover, EEG studies in infants offer evidence of changes in prefrontal activity associated with behavior on the A-not-B task (Bell and Fox, 1992). Infants who tolerated longer and longer delays during the A-not-B task showed increased EEG activity over regions of the frontal lobe, whereas infants who were less successful showed little frontal EEG activity.

However, if the A-not-B task is viewed as part of the whole developmental process of reaching (and not so much as a hidden-object task), the neural basis for these changes is not very clear, and probably much more complex. We have virtually no data from human infants, so we are limited to speculations about the brain mechanisms involved based on detailed and elegant studies in primates. What is particularly clear from both single-cell and population studies of reaching tasks done over the last decade is that the control of visually guided reaching is widely distributed in the brain, and that the final behavior results from the cooperative activity of these multiple areas.

Even the seemingly simple action of reaching for a target involves many processes: attention to the stimulus, motivation to reach, visual processing, planning the appropriate response, setting the needed movement parameters, initiating the muscle contractions, and remembering the consequences of action. Many of these processes occur in parallel, suggesting that many densely interconnected areas of the brain must be involved. For instance, at least eight distinct motor fields have been identified in primate frontal cortex—each field receiving varying input from frontal and parietal visuospatial cortical regions and having, as well, multiple connections from basal ganglia and cerebellum, all of which are critically implicated in motor sequencing, timing, planning, memory, and learning (Jeannerod, 1997; Schwartz, 1994).

Studies of awake, behaving monkeys reaching for targets, sometimes with delays imposed, have shown this interconnectivity in two ways. First, many areas are active during a single aspect of a task. For example, activity related to the visual cue can be detected not only in classic visual association areas like parietal cortex, but also in those involved in motor planning and execution—the motor, premotor, and prefrontal cortex. Likewise, neurons coding for reach direction are found in parietal cortex as well as traditional motor areas. At the same time, single neurons in a specific area may respond to both visual and motor aspects of a task. Cells in the motor cortex respond to the visual stimulus and hold a cue over the delay as well as coding for movement direction (summarized in Thelen et al., in press). What is clear is that the distinction between what is visual input, planning, memory, and motor output is increasingly blurred (Anderson et al., 1997).

What are the implications of this wide distribution and multiple representations of reaching to visual targets? First, such responses are possible only if all areas of the brain are multiple and densely interconnected. Second, given what is now known about the plasticity of the brain, it is likely that infants' experiences of learning to reach have a profound and wide-ranging impact on brain development. One important issue concerns the relation between construction and selection. Is dense interconnectivity a feature of the brain from the start, with experience selecting and sculpting relevant pathways (Edelman, 1987)? Or are the connections constructed through experience, with the individual areas more isolated at first and only becoming coordinated through action (Quartz and Sejnowski, 1997)? At present, we do not know.

A third implication of the distributed neural basis of the motor skill of reaching is that we can now see how both stability and flexibility can be inherent in the same system. One important property of complex, heterogeneous dynamic systems such as the brain is the self-organization of stable patterns (Kelso, 1995). As reaching develops, we can speculate, repetition creates patterns that become increasingly stable and repeatable, recruiting these multiple areas. At the same time, the distributed nature of control allows for great context flexibility.

## Conclusions

Stability and flexibility can be thought of as part of the same dynamic system, reflecting the interconnectedness and redundancy of the neuromotor system. We have proposed that infants begin learning to reach with flexibility in the neuromotor system and stable constraints on coordination patterns. This combination then guides infants through their exploration of possible solutions, eventually enabling them to make the transition from unskilled and wild flapping movements to skilled, stable reaches.

Although we have focused on a single behavior—reaching—we believe that the same dynamic principles must be at work in the acquisition of all skills, from the simplest eye movements to highly complex skills requiring memory, categorization, and decision making. Stability and flexibility are hallmarks of skilled persons in every domain, from those tasks requiring physical dexterity to those requiring mental agility or social skill. People must have a large and stable store of experiences in order to recognize a situation and compare it to others encountered in the past. But because no two situations are exactly alike, people must also be able to adjust their responses to the particulars of that situation. Indeed, one characterization of maladjusted behavior is getting stuck in an old habitual response when confronted with a new circumstance. For example, people who respond to their spouses with emotional habits formed with their parents often end up in divorce court.

Likewise, we believe that this ability to be both stable and flexible in all activities is a result of the distributed and dynamic nature of the developing system. In more purely mental as well as motor activities, no skill is learned in isolation. All the system components are critical. This means that changes in a target behavior may be the result of concomitant changes in other, less obvious components. (Reaching improved as a result of more general postural changes, for instance.) As development is a continuing cascade, each step builds on the framework of the previous accomplishment. We can think of the current state, then, as providing some constraints on the search space for the acquisition of the new skill, setting up boundaries so that the exploration is focused. In this formulation, we need not make a distinction, therefore, as to whether the constraints are "innate" or learned. The interesting issues are to describe the current state and to understand the processes of change.

Finally, we believe that because development is this dynamic cascade, with each new step a system-wide modulation of the previous state, the dichotomy between what is purely "conceptual" and what is sensorimotor is misleading. The act of reaching is a simple "motor" act; but it requires considerable mental agility to plan, decide, and remember how to fit the action to the task. The abstraction of a category of appropriate reaching acts to a category of targets is, in principle, no different from any other "mental" category and is thus a pure "cognitive" act as well. What changes in the developmental cascade is not a separation of the mental from the sensorimotor, but the child's ability to correct behavior "on-line" more flexibly and to execute part of their behavior "off-line." That is, what improves is the ability to detect and categorize the meaningful part of the present task, remember previous similar situations, rapidly compare the present one to the stored knowledge, decide and execute the action, and make adjustments even while the behavior is in progress. The two skills, "off-line" and "on-line," are not separate, but part of the same single dynamic system that we illustrated in the case of learning to reach.

ACKNOWLEDGMENTS  This research was funded by NIH RO1 HD22830 and by a Research Scientist Award from NIMH to E. Thelen. We are grateful to Daniela Corbetta, Kristin Daigle, Fred Diedrich, Dexter Gormley, Linda Smith, John Spencer, and Frank Zaal for invaluable contributions to the research reported here. We thank Cole Galloway for helpful comments on earlier versions of this manuscript.

## REFERENCES

ADOLPH, K. E., 1997. Learning in the development of infant locomotion. *Monographs of the Society for Research in Child Development*, Vol. 62, No. 3.

ADOLPH, K. E., M. A. EPPLER, and E. J. GIBSON, 1993. Development of perception of affordances. In *Advances in Infancy Research*, Vol. 8, C. Rovee-Collier and L. P. Lipsitt, eds. Norwood: Ablex, pp. 52–98.

ANDERSON, R. A., L. H. SNYDER, D. C. BRADLEY, and J. XING, 1997. Multimodal representation of space in the posterior parietal cortex and its use in planning movements. *Annu. Rev. Neurosci.* 20:303–330.

BELL, M. A., and N. A. FOX, 1992. The relations between frontal brain electrical activity and cognitive development during infancy. *Child Dev.* 63:1142–1163.

BERNSTEIN, N. A., 1967. *Coordination and Regulation of Movements.* New York: Pergamon Press.

BERTENTHAL, B. I., and R. K. CLIFTON, 1999. Perception and action. In *Handbook of Child Psychology. Vol. 2: Cognition, Perception, and Language,* D. Kuhn and R. Siegler, eds. New York: Wiley.

BERTHIER, N. E., 1996. Learning to reach: A mathematical model. *Dev. Psychol.* 32:811–823.

BERTHIER, N. E., and D. J. ROBIN, 1998. Midreach correction in 7-month-olds. *J. Motor Behav.* 30(4):290–300.

BIZZI, E., P. DEV, P. MORASSO, and A. POLIT, 1978. Effect of load disturbances during centrally initiated movements. *J. Neurophysiol.* 41:542–556.

BUTTERWORTH, G., and L. HICKS, 1977. Visual proprioception and postural stability in infancy: A developmental study. *Perception* 6(3):255–262.

CASTIELLO, U., Y. PAULIGNON, and M. JEANNEROD, 1991. Temporal dissociation of motor responses and subjective awareness. A study in normal subjects. *Brain* 114:2639–2655.

CATELL, P., 1939. The development of motor functions and mental abilities in infancy. *Rev. Edu. Res.* 9:5–17.

CLEARFIELD, M. W., E. THELEN, and L. B. SMITH, 2000. The development of perseverative reaching errors. (in preparation).

CLIFTON, R. K., R. PHILIPPE, D. J. ROBIN, and N. E. BERTHIER, 1994. Multimodal perception in the control of infant reaching. *J. Exp. Psychol.: Hum. Percept. Perform.* 20(4):876–886.

DIAMOND, A., 1985. Development of the ability to use recall to guide action, as indicated by infants' performance on A‾B. *Child Dev.* 56:868–883.

DIEDRICH, F. J., E. THELEN, L. B. SMITH, and D. CORBETTA, 2000. Motor memory is a factor in infant perseverative errors. *Dev. Sci.* 3:479–494.

DIZIO, P., and J. R. LACKNER, 1995. Motor adaptation to coriolis force perturbations of reaching movements: Endpoint but not trajectory adaptation transfers to the nonexposed arm. *J. Neurophysiol.* 74(4):1787–1792.

EDELMAN, G. M., 1987. *Neural Darwinism: The Theory of Neuronal Group Selection.* New York: Basic Books.

FENTRESS, J. C., and P. J. McLEOD, 1986. Motor patterns in development. In *Handbook of Behavioral Neurobiology. Vol. 8:*

*Developmental Psychobiology and Developmental Neurobiology,* E. M. Blass, ed. New York: Plenum Press, pp. 35–97.

FLANDERS, M., 1991. Temporal patterns of muscle activation for arm movements in three-dimensional space. *J. Neurosci.* 11:2680–2693.

FLANDERS, M., J. J. PELLEGRINI, and J. F. SOECHTING, 1994. Spatial/temporal characteristics of a motor pattern for reaching. *J. Neurophysiol.* 71:811–813.

FLASH, T., and N. HOGAN, 1985. The coordination of arm movements: An experimentally confirmed mathematical model. *J. Neurosci.* 5:1688–1703.

GEORGOPOULOS, A. P., 1995. Motor cortex and cognitive processing. In *The Cognitive Neurosciences,* M. Gazzaniga, ed. Cambridge, Mass.: MIT Press.

GOODALE, M. A., D. PELISSON, and C. PRABLANC, 1986. Large adjustments in visually guided reaching do not depend on vision of the hand or perception of target displacement. *Nature* 320:748–750.

GOTTLIEB, G. L., Q. SONG, D. HONG, and D. CORCOS, 1996. Coordinating two degrees of freedom during human arm movement: Load and speed invariance of relative joint torques. *J. Neurophysiol.* 76:3196–3206.

HAMILTON, C. R., and J. BOSSOM, 1964. Decay of prism after-effects. *J. Exp. Psychol.* 67(2):148–150.

HELD, R., and M. SCHLANK, 1959. Adaptation to disarranged eye-hand coordination in the distance-dimension. *Am. J. Psychol.* 72:603–605

JEANNEROD, M., 1988. The neural and behavioural organization of goal-directed movements. Oxford: Oxford University Press.

JEANNEROD, M., 1997. *The Cognitive Neuroscience of Action.* Cambridge: Blackwell Publishers.

JOUEN, F., and J. C. LEPECQ, 1990. Early perceptuo-motor development: Posture and locomotion. In *Developmental Psychology: Cognitive, Perceptuo-motor and Neurophysiological Perspectives. Advances in Psychology,* Vol. 64, C. Hauert, ed. Amsterdam: North Holland, pp. 61–83.

KELSO, J. A. S., 1995. *Dynamic Patterns: The Self-Organization of Brain and Behavior.* Cambridge, Mass.: MIT Press.

KELSO, J. A. S., and J. G. HOLT, 1980. Exploring a vibratory systems analysis of human movement production. *J. Neurophysiol.* 34:908–919.

KIRKPATRICK, E. A., 1899. The development of voluntary movement. *Psychol. Rev.* 6(3):275–281.

MARCOVITCH, S., and P. D. ZELAZO, 2000. The A-not-B error: Results from a logistic meta-analysis. *Child Dev.* 70(6):1297–1313.

MORASSO, P., 1981. Spatial control of arm movements. *Exp. Brain Res.* 42:223–227.

MUNAKATA, Y., 1997. Perseverative reaching in infancy: The roles of hidden toys and motor history in the AB task. *Infant Behav. Dev.* 20(3):405–416.

PASSINGHAM, R. E., 1993. *The Frontal Lobes and Voluntary Action.* Oxford: Oxford University Press.

PAULIGNON, Y., C. MACKENZIE, C. MARTENIUK, and M. JEANNEROD, 1991. Selective perturbation of visual input during prehension movements. I. The effects of changing object position. *Exp. Brain Res.* 83:502–512.

PIAGET, J., 1952. *The Origins of Intelligence in Children.* New York: International Universities Press.

QUARTZ, S., and T. J. SEJNOWSKI, 1997. The neural basis of cognitive development: A constructivist manifesto. *Behav. Brain Sci.* 20(4):537–596.

ROCHAT, P., 1992. Self-sitting and reaching in 5- to 8-month-old infants: The impact of posture and its development on early eye-hand coordination. *J. Motor Behav.* 24(2):210–220.

SCHMIDT, R. C., and P. FITZPATRICK, 1996. Dynamical perspective on motor learning. In *Advances in Motor Learning and Control,* H. N. Zelaznik, ed. Champaign, Ill.: Human Kinetics, pp. 195–223.

SCHWARTZ, A. B., 1994. Neuronal substrate for volitional movement. *Adv. Psychol.* 105:59–83.

SMITH, L. B., E. THELEN, R. TITZER, and D. MCLIN, 1999. Knowing in the context of acting: The task dynamics of the A-not-B error. *Psychol. Rev.* 106(2):235–260.

SPENCER, J. P., and E. THELEN, 2000. Spatially-specific changes in infants' muscle co-activity as they learn to reach. *Infancy* 1:275–302.

SPENCER, J. P., B. VEREIJKEN, F. J. DIEDRICH, and E. THELEN, 2000. Posture and the emergence of manual skills. *Dev. Sci.* 3:216–233.

SPORNS, O., and G. M. EDLEMAN, 1993. Solving Bernstein's problem: A proposal for the development of coordinated movement by selection. *Child Dev.* 64:960–981.

THELEN, E., in press. Dynamic mechanisms of change in early perceptual-motor development. In *Mechanisms of Cognitive Development: Behavioral* and *Neural Perspective,* J. McClelland and R. Siegler, eds. Mahwah, N.J.: Laurence Earlbaum.

THELEN, E., D. CORBETTA, K. KAMM, J. P. SPENCER, K. SCHNEIDER, and R. F. ZERNICKE, 1993. The transition to reaching: Mapping intention and intrinsic dynamics. *Child Dev.* 64:1058–1098.

THELEN, E., D. CORBETTA, and J. P. SPENCER, 1996. The development of reaching during the first year: The role of movement speed. *J. Exp. Psychol.: Hum. Percept. Perform.* 22:1059–1076.

THELEN, E., G. SCHÖNER, C. SCHEIER, and L. B. SMITH, in press. The dynamics of embodiment: A field theory of infant perseverative reaching. *Behav. Brain Sci.*

VON HOFSTEN, C., 1979. Development of visually directed reaching: The approach phase. *J. Hum. Movement Studies* 5:160–178.

WELLMAN, H. M., D. CROSS, and K. BARTSCH, 1986. Infant search and object permanence: A meta-analysis of the A-not-B error. *Monographs of the Society for Research in Child Development,* Vol. 51(3, Serial No. 214).

WHITE, B. L., P. CASTLE, and R. HELD, 1964. Observations on the development of visually-directed reaching. *Child Dev.* 35(2):349–364.

ZAAL, F. T. M. J., K. DAIGLE, G. L. GOTTLIEB, and E. THELEN, 1999. An unlearned principle for controlling natural movements. *J. Neurophysiol.* 82:255–259.

ZAAL, F. T. M. J., and E. THELEN, 2000. The speed-accuracy trade-off in infants' reaching movements (submitted).

ZELAZO, P. R., 1998. McGraw and the development of unaided walking. *Dev. Rev.* 18(4):449–471.

# V

# LANGUAGE

# 19 Speech and Language Processing in Infancy: A Neurocognitive Approach

JANET F. WERKER AND
ATHENA VOULOUMANOS

ABSTRACT  Behavioral studies have revealed much about the development of speech perception and early word learning during infancy. In recent years, emerging neuroimaging and magneto- and electrophysiological techniques have provided a new window through which to examine neural correlates of language processing. In this chapter, we integrate findings from the behavioral and neurophysiological literatures to explore the brain's initial organization for language processing and the role of experience in modifying or maintaining this initial organization. We focus on three content areas in which our lab has participated. At the most fundamental level we ask whether speech is perceived differently from nonspeech. Within the realm of speech perception, we focus on the perception of speech segments. Finally, we explore how speech perception might intersect with language acquisition by reviewing recent research on the use of phonetic detail in early word learning. The pattern of findings across these three content areas provides converging evidence for preferred detection of some kinds of change over others in the young infant, and increasing neurocognitive specialization as a function of age and experience.

To most adults, linguistic processing seems unremarkable. We talk a "mile a minute" and speak "without thinking." We process speech information effortlessly, instantaneously calibrating for differences in gender, age, accent, and speaking rate. We readily distinguish minimal differences in phonemes, parsing the words, phrases, and sentences of our native language with the greatest of ease. These abilities are so effortless and rapid that they suggest specialized mental processes and dedicated neural mechanisms. Not surprisingly, research has identified areas in the brain that respond preferentially to language (Geschwind, 1970; Lenneberg, 1967), whether it be spoken or signed (Neville et al., 1998).

At the same time, as any world traveler can confirm, we encounter difficulties in processing unfamiliar languages. This "foreign listening syndrome" is pervasive (Mehler, Pallier, and Christophe, 1998). A relative insensitivity to rhythmic structures that are unlike those used in our native language makes it difficult for us to segment words, phrases, and sentences in nonnative speech (Cutler et al., 1989). Our failure to distinguishing many nonnative phonemic contrasts (Werker, 1995) may lead us to confuse similar sounding foreign words. The difficulties we experience in processing unfamiliar or even second languages suggest that experience plays a role in the establishment or maintenance of specialized linguistic processing substrates.

Decades of behavioral studies have unraveled many mysteries of the development of speech and language processing. In recent years, neuroimaging and electrophysiological techniques have given us exciting new tools to examine language processing. As a result, we now have the opportunity to sharpen our understanding, and perhaps even begin to resolve some of the theoretical controversies that have defined the field. In this chapter, we bring together some of the findings from the behavioral and neural processing literatures to explore how a developmental cognitive neuroscience approach can be used to address old controversies and move the field on to addressing new questions. In particular, we explore the brain's initial organization for language processing and the role experience plays in modifying or maintaining this initial organization. We focus on three content areas to which our lab has contributed: the processing of speech versus nonspeech, phonetic perception, and early word learning. We touch on the broad array of research in each of these areas, but direct our discussion to the specific questions that have been approached from both behavioral and neuroscience perspectives.

## Processing of speech and nonspeech: A window into linguistic foundations

Do dedicated neuroanatomical modules compute particular kinds of perceptual information, or can information processing be explained by general sensory and learning mechanisms? This controversy has found expression in a number of arenas, but was first explored in the domain of language. From the early debates between Piaget and Chomsky (Piaget, 1980) to Fodor's *The Modularity of Mind* (1983) and its more recent connectionist challenges (e.g., Elman, 1993), theorists and experimentalists have debated the foundations of language processing. One way to address this question is to ask whether or not there are specialized neurocognitive systems dedicated to processing speech.

Such investigations are inherently complicated by the indeterminate nature of the speech stimulus: Speech is a complex auditory stimulus that shares each of its properties with other acoustic stimuli, and the properties that convey unique "speech" information are unknown. These difficulties aside, a developmental perspective prompts three types of questions: (1) Do young infants show the brain specialization for linguistic processing that is evident in adults? (2) If neural specialization for language is not immediately observable in newborn infants, when and how does this specialization emerge during development? (3) Do young infants make functional use of a specialization for language to preferentially attend to linguistic stimuli (speech) over others (nonspeech)?

Anatomical studies reveal that infants' brains display some of the same kinds of structural hemispheric asymmetries seen in adults (Wada, Clarke, and Hamm, 1975). However, behavioral and electrophysiological studies have been somewhat inconclusive in demonstrating a functional hemispheric specialization for speech processing in infants. Some dichotic listening tasks indicate that newborn infants (Bertoncini et al., 1989) and 2-month-olds (Glanville, Best, and Levenson, 1977) show a right ear/left hemisphere (LH) advantage for detecting a change in phonetic detail compared to a left ear/right hemisphere (RH) advantage for detecting changes in music, but this result does not hold across all studies (Best, Hofman, and Glanville, 1982). ERP studies suggest that this inconsistency might result from a gradual organization of neural systems for speech processing. Novak and colleagues (1989) compared electrophysiological recordings to a syllable (/da/) and its three isolated formants in infants of three ages: newborn, 3 months and 6 months. (Speech can be described in terms of a complex waveform consisting of the *fundamental frequency*, which corresponds roughly to pitch, and several higher frequency broadband resonances termed *formants*.) In newborns, both 3-formant speech and individual formants elicited similar bilateral brain potentials with a comparable topography. By 3–6 months, however, full syllables elicited highly asymmetric (RH advantage) brain responses. This hemispheric asymmetry, albeit attenuated, was also observed for the second and third isolated formants,

whereas responses to the first formant were fully bilateral. Inasmuch as electrophysiological recordings reflect changes in underlying neural activity, the hemispheric asymmetry that becomes apparent by 3–6 months to full speech and to higher formants (putative carriers of consonant information) could reflect a gradual specialization of the neural structures involved in speech processing.

Although this series of studies demonstrates an apparent emergence of hemispheric specialization during development, studies on place of articulation contrasts and vowel discrimination suggest that asymmetric processing is already present at birth, and perhaps even in preterm infants. For example, ERPs are larger in amplitude over the LH than over the RH in syllable discrimination tasks in which the initial consonants vary in their places of articulation (Dehaene-Lambertz and Baillet, 1998; Dehaene-Lambertz and Dehaene, 1994; Molfese and Molfese, 1979b, 1980, 1985). The results for voice onset time discrimination in newborns are inconsistent and suggest either bilateral (Novak et al., 1989) or greater RH involvement (Molfese and Molfese, 1979a). An early lateralization has also been observed in the few studies investigating vowel discrimination. Using the mismatch negativity (MMN) as an index of sensory processing, Cheour and colleagues (Cheour et al., 1997, 1998; Cheour-Luhtanen et al., 1996) traced infants' ERP responses to a vowel discrimination (/y/ and /i/) and found that, although generated by both left and right auditory cortices, a greater MMN is seen in the RH in all ages studied, from preterm infants (6–8 weeks premature; Cheour et al., 1998) to 3-month-old full-term infants (Cheour et al., 1997).

While investigations of hemispheric asymmetries can be revealing, a literal interpretation can also be misleading. In adults, we typically find left hemispheric specialization for the processing of speech. But studies by Neville, Mills, Bates, and others reveal that, during early development, the primary hemisphere involved, and even the specific location within the hemisphere, can change (Bates et al., 1997; Mills, Coffey-Corina, and Neville, 1994). Beyond investigating specialization for speech processing at the hemispheric level, electrophysiological studies have been designed to observe more local specialization for processing speech (and other auditory stimuli) through differences in the topography, latency, or amplitude of responses. In one study, Dehaene-Lambertz (2000) showed that whereas discrimination of both syllables and 5-harmonic complex tones elicits higher activation in the LH than the RH in 4-month-olds, responses to the two kinds of stimuli are topographically different. Central and occipital site activation is evident for tones, while speech produces more frontal and temporal site activation, suggesting that processing of speech and nonspeech originates within different regions of the temporal lobe. In another study, Mills and Neville (1997) showed that by 6 months of age, brain potentials to normal words and words presented backward begin to diverge by about 150–200 ms after stimulus onset, with backward words characterized by an attenuation in response. In these studies, the counterparts to speech share some of its properties: The complex tones used by Dehaene-Lambertz have energy in the same area of the spectrum as speech sounds, and the backward words used by Neville and Mills maintain the acoustic complexity of forward speech and preserve many of its characteristics. Thus the evidence for differential processing suggests that by 4 or 6 months of age, the brain encodes speech-specific properties faithfully enough to differentiate speech from other highly similar acoustic signals.

Evidence for specialized processing of speech also comes from studies showing that infants listen differently to speech than to nonspeech stimuli. For example, newborn infants are better able to discriminate equally dissimilar sounds in a well-formed syllable ("tap" vs. "pat") than in a nonspeech form ("tsp" vs. "pst") (Bertoncini and Mehler, 1981). Infants as young as 4 months of age show a preference for listening to speech over other sounds such as white noise (Colombo and Bundy, 1981) or music (Glenn, Cunningham, and Joyce, 1981), suggesting a potential initial processing bias that could facilitate attention to specific properties of speech. This idea can be addressed more directly by comparing infants' behavioral responses to speech and nonspeech stimuli that are matched both in spectral complexity and timing.

To explore this idea more carefully, we tested infants on their preference for one-syllable infant-directed nonsense words ("lif" and "neem") over their 3-formant sine wave counterparts. (The sine wave stimuli were created by extracting the fundamental and the first three formants of the speech tokens, then replacing the center frequencies of each with simple sinusoidal waves.) By 4 months of age, infants show a robust preference for speech over these highly matched nonspeech counterparts (Vouloumanos et al., 1999). However, in our ongoing work there is, as yet, no evidence of a preference for speech over the matched nonspeech stimuli in newborn infants (Vouloumanos, Werker, Bhatnager, and Burns, in preparation).

The similarity of our nonspeech stimuli to speech sounds makes it difficult to conclude whether or not there is a specialized speech processor in the newborn. Such a specialization might emerge only through ex-

perience. However, on the basis of the current evidence, it is also possible that such a mechanism exists but that the 3-formant sine wave stimuli are sufficiently similar to engage it early in life. The robust preference for our nonsense words in infants 4 and 6 months of age, however, together with the neurophysiological evidence just reviewed, shows that, irrespective of the organization at birth, by 4 months the system is sufficiently well tuned to the properties of speech to respond quite selectively.

*Speech perception: Listening to the sounds of language*

From very early in life, human infants can categorically discriminate information at various levels in speech. The categorical processing of linguistically relevant information is remarkable for two reasons: (1) It provides a kernel of evidence for arguments in favor of biological preparedness for language processing; (2) It readies infants for ultimately breaking into language. This doesn't intimate that language is innate or special for newborns, but it does provide evidence of evolutionarily selected capabilities that can be exploited later for specific functional purposes (see Gottlieb, 1991). Our perceptual systems are set up to notice change, not constancies, in the input. But if the system responded equally to any and all change that occurred, it would be virtually impossible to leave the starting gate into acquiring language. Fortunately, it appears that our perceptual systems are designed to maximally detect just those changes that are critical to the infant for the task at hand. Thus, one would predict age-related differences in just which changes a listener detects.

And this is consistent with the pattern of findings. Newborns have been shown to distinguish their own languages from other rhythmically distinct languages (Mehler et al., 1988; Mehler and Christophe, 1994; Nazzi, Bertoncini, and Mehler, 1998), prefer their mother's voice to those of other women (DeCasper and Fifer, 1980), differentiate one syllable type (Eimas et al., 1971) or number (Bijeljac-Babic, Bertoncini, and Mehler, 1993) from another, and differentiate grammatical words from lexical words (Shi, Werker, and Morgan, 1999).

For an older infant who is facing the challenge of constructing a phonological system in her or his native language, native-language distinctions are most important (Werker and Tees, 1984a). Accordingly, the broad-based sensitivities to speech shown by the newborn infant prior to significant listening experience are rapidly molded by the input to which the infant is exposed, unleashing a barrage of abilities. Within the first days and weeks of life, infants show both discrimination (Mehler et al., 1988; Nazzi et al., 1998) and preference (Moon, Cooper, and Fifer, 1993) for native over unfamiliar languages. Between 4 and 7 months, infants become sensitive to the cues that signal native phrase and clause boundaries (Hirsh-Pasek et al., 1987). By 6 months of age, their perception of vowels is beginning to show the influence of native language input (Kuhl et al., 1992; Polka and Werker, 1994). By 10 months, infants no longer easily discriminate nonnative consonant distinctions (Best, 1995; Best et al., 1995; Pegg and Werker, 1997; Werker and Tees, 1984a; Werker and Lalonde, 1988). English-learning infants of this age prefer the most common phonotactic sequences used in their native languages (Jusczyk et al., 1993: Friederici and Wessels, 1993) and show a preference for the dominant strong–weak stress pattern used in English (Jusczyk, Cutler, and Redanz, 1993). Indeed, by 9–10 months of age, infants know enough about their native language to properly segment words (Myers et al., 1996) and to detect the insertion of an unacceptable form in the place of a function word in ongoing speech (Shafer et al., 1998). By attending to changes most relevant to the task at hand, our mental machinery reveals one of the ways in which experience can interact with initial biases.

## Phonetic perception: Tuning to the native language

A prime example of infants' perceptual sensitivities to relevant changes in the input is in the perception of phonetic contrasts. In 1971 in a now classic study, infants of 1 and 4 months of age were shown to have, like adults, "categorical" perception of speech stimuli varying along a voicing continuum. Young infants can discriminate stimuli from two sides of an adult phonemic category boundary (e.g., /ba/ from /pa/), but not two equally distinct stimuli from within the /ba/ or the /pa/ categories (Eimas et al., 1971). However, unlike adults, young infants readily discriminate even those fine phonetic differences not used to distinguish meaning in their native language. For example, Kikuyu-learning infants of 4 months are able to discriminate an English voiced–voiceless contrast (ba vs. pa) even though this contrast is not used in the Kikuyu language (Streeter, 1976). Similar results showing broad-based phonetic discrimination abilities have been obtained from a number of cross-linguistic consonant discrimination studies with infants 6 months of age and younger (Aslin, Pisoni, and Hennessy, 1981; Best, McRoberts, and Sithole, 1988; Eimas, 1975; Lasky, Syrdal-Lasky, and

Klein, 1975; Trehub, 1976; Werker et al., 1981; Werker and Tees, 1984a).

The change from language-general to language-specific phonetic perception occurs within the first year of life. In an early study, Werker and Tees (1984a) showed that English-learning infants of 6–8, but not 10–12, months can discriminate the Hindi retroflex /Da/ versus dental /da/ and the Thompson glottalized velar /k'i/ versus uvular /q'i/. Similar findings have been reported in several other studies (Best, McRoberts, and Sithole, 1988; Best et al., 1995; Polka and Werker, 1994; Werker and Lalonde, 1988). This same pattern of findings was replicated in an ERP study with infants aged 6 and 12 months. At 6 months, Finnish infants show a discriminative ERP response to both a native and a nonnative (Estonian) vowel change, but by 12 months, only to a native vowel change (Cheour et al., 1998). In contrast, infants of this age maintain the ability to discriminate Zulu clicks they have never previously heard. Because the clicks do not map onto English phonology, infants may be able to listen to them outside of a linguistic context and deploy their general auditory sensitivities in the task (Best, McRoberts, and Sithole, 1988). These findings suggest that it is not just a lack of experience that accounts for the age-related change in discrimination ability. Instead, it appears that it is the reliance on an emerging phonological system that predicts discrimination performance (see also Pegg and Werker, 1997).

Adults also show remarkable discrimination abilities for phonetic differences that are used in their native language, and some remaining sensitivity for nonnative contrasts. Native-language phonetic perception in adults is categorical—shown both in behavioral (Liberman et al., 1967; Repp, 1984) and ERP (Näätänen et al., 1997) experiments—and may be computed by specialized architecture in the LH (Phillips, Pellathy, and Marantz, 1999; Studdert-Kennedy and Shankweiler, 1970). In comparison to the language-general sensitivities shown by young infants, adults have difficulty discriminating minimal phonetic differences that are not used to contrast meaning in their native language. Japanese adults, who have only a single phoneme intermediate between the English /r/ and /l/, have difficulty discriminating the difference between /ra/ and /la/ (Strange and Jenkins, 1978). English adults have difficulty discriminating the Hindi retroflex /Da/ from the Hindi dental /da/ (Werker et al., 1981; Werker and Lalonde, 1988), the Thompson /k'i/–/q'i/ contrast (Werker and Tees, 1984b), and a non-English Czech /za/–/ra/ distinction (Trehub, 1976). The circumstances under which adults are able to discriminate nonnative phonetic contrasts are also revealing. A shortened interstimulus interval (Werker and Logan, 1985) or repeated training (Tees and Werker, 1984; Werker and Tees, 1984b) allows English listeners to discriminate the Hindi /Da/–/da/ distinction. Similarly, with training, Japanese listeners improve on their ability to discriminate the English /r/–/l/ (McClelland, personal communication; Pisoni et al., 1982; Strange and Dittman, 1984). Another condition under which nonnative discrimination is possible is when the nonnative distinctions are not heard as "speech-like." For example, English speakers can be tricked into discriminating two truncated Thompson syllables when told they are drops of water (Werker and Tees, 1984b). Moreover, like 10–12-month-old infants, English adults can discriminate acoustically similar Zulu clicks (Best et al., 1989).

We have alluded to Best's hypothesis (1995) accounting for the continued ability to make these discriminations: Discrimination is maintained because Zulu clicks, or truncated Thompson syllables, do not engage a native language phonological processing system. This hypothesis was recently confirmed in two types of studies. In a dichotic listening task, both English and Zulu/Xhosa speakers were able to discriminate the Zulu clicks (as reported by Best, McRoberts, and Sithole, 1988), but only the Zulu/Xhosa speakers showed a right ear advantage (Best and Avery, 1999). And in an fMRI study, speakers of click languages, such as Zulu and Xhosa, showed greater activation in the LH than the RH in response to the clicks, whereas English listeners showed bilateral activation (Best et al., 1999). These findings provide striking evidence in support of organized neural systems for processing the native language.

Together, infant and adult studies support the idea that experience helps hone specialized neurocognitive systems for processing speech. A number of neurophysiological studies examine this more directly by assessing the neural systems involved in native and nonnative speech discrimination in adults. Sharma and Dorman (1999) conducted an ERP study of a Hindi voicing continuum which spans the Hindi /ba/–/pa/ category boundary but stays within the English /ba/ category. Their results suggest that the neural signature reflects only native language phonemic processing. Similarly, in a magnetoencephalography (MEG) study, Marantz and colleagues (1996) tested English and Japanese listeners on a contrast that is used in both languages (/d/–/t/) and one that is used only in English (/r/–/l/). The English subjects showed a significantly enhanced MMF (mismatched field) in response to deviant trials in both the /d/–/t/ and /r/–/l/ comparisons, whereas the Japanese listeners showed it only in response to the /d/–/t/ contrast. Finally, Näätänen and colleagues

(1997) examined the MMN (mismatched negativity) response to a continuum of vowels sounds spanning the /e/–/ö/–/o/ phoneme categories in Finnish and the /e/–/ö/–/õ/–/o/ categories in Estonian. Although MMN amplitude typically increases with increased acoustic difference between stimuli, Näätänen and colleagues found that for these vowels, the size of the MMN response varied more as a function of phonemic category difference than absolute acoustic difference. The magneto- and electrophysiological studies are consistent with the behavioral studies, and point to the existence of specialized processing systems for the native language. Moreover, neurophysiological studies, like the behavioral studies, can also reveal the impact of training on nonnative discrimination (Tremblay et al., 1997).

One group of neurophysiological studies has investigated adult processing of native and nonnative phonetic contrasts using the same stimuli set, first developed for testing infant speech perception in the Werker and Lalonde (1988) study. These studies compared adult brain potentials to three place of articulation contrasts: (1) a native bilabial/alveolar /ba/–/da/ contrast that spans different phonetic categories (native AC), (2) a nonnative Hindi retroflex/dental /Da/–/da/ contrast also spanning different phonetic categories (nonnative AC), and (3) an acoustic contrast within the same phonetic category /$da_1$/–/$da_2$/ (WC). Using these three contrasts, Dehaene-Lambertz (1997) conducted an ERP study with French-speaking adults and found significant early (within 200 ms) negative responses to the native AC change, primarily in the temporal lobe of the LH. There was no differential evoked response to the nonnative AC change, and only a small, bilateral late positive response to the WC change. More recently, Rivera-Gaxiola and colleagues (2000) tested (British) English speakers on the same three contrasts and obtained slightly different results. The ERPs again revealed a pronounced response to the native AC change and some sensitivity to the WC change. However, unlike the Dehaene-Lambertz study, the nonnative AC change also elicited a response, which differed both in latency and topography from the native AC change. It is not clear whether differences in participants' linguistic background (French vs. British English) or differences in methodology can account for the inconsistent results obtained in these studies.

As a whole, these neurophysiological studies suggest that when language processing is invoked, the brain responds only to native language phonemic categories. Indeed, so far the neurophysiological and behavioral studies are equally insensitive in revealing nonnative discrimination. Of the studies reviewed here, only the

ERP study of Rivera-Gaxiola and colleagues (2000) and the fMRI study of Best and colleagues (1999) revealed a neural signature to nonnative phoneme discrimination. What mechanisms are involved in the continuing sensitivity to nonnative contrasts? One possibility is that linguistic experience is necessary for consolidating specialized processing systems. If this were the case, one would expect a specialized (perhaps lateralized) system to function in native speech perception and a more general (perhaps bilateral) involvement in nonnative perception. A second possibility is that there are two specialized neurocognitive systems, one for native contrasts and another for processing nonnative variation. A final possibility is that all linguistic signals (both native and nonnative) are processed by a single specialized neural system, which, through differential exposure, has a lower threshold of responsiveness to native contrasts. To date, neurophysiological techniques have not answered this question. However, the data are unambiguous in confirming that native phonetic contrasts are processed by dedicated neural systems.

## Word learning: The role of speech perception in mapping sound onto meaning

At the same time that infants are becoming tuned to the properties of the native language, and perhaps as part of that same process, they are also developing a set of skills that prepares them for mapping sound onto meaning and learning words. As early as 4 months of age, infants can detect their own name in fluent speech (Mandel, Jusczyk, and Pisoni, 1995), and by 7½ months, they can segment single syllable or SW (strong–weak) bisyllabic words (e.g., "DOCtor") from fluent speech (Jusczyk and Aslin, 1995). By engaging their sensitivities to native language stress (Jusczyk, Cutler, and Redanz, 1993) and phonotactic patterns (Jusczyk, Luce, and Charles-Luce, 1994), 10-month-old infants can even segment WS words (e.g., "guiTAR") from the speech stream (Myers et al., 1996; see Jusczyk, 1999, for a review of segmentation). Although infants clearly recognize known words by (or before) 12 months of age (Golinkoff et al., 1987), word recognition becomes much more rapid and automatic between 15 and 20 months of age (Fernald et al., 1998). At 12 months, infants best learn new words that are presented in sentence final position in infant-directed speech (cited in Fernald et al., 1998), but a few months later, they can easily learn new words in a number of different experimental settings (Schafer and Plunkett, 1998; Werker et al., 1998; Woodward, Markman, and Fitzsimmons, 1994; see Hollich, Hirsh-Pasek, and Golinkoff, 2000, for a review of studies showing age-related changes in successful word-learning conditions).

We have seen that infants of 10–12 months are sensitive only to phonetic details that are used to distinguish meaning in their native languages. This phonetic sensitivity, coupled with their nascent recognition of possible words, should prepare infants to use their language-specific perceptual sensitivities to segment, encode, and represent the new words they are learning. Do infants detect and represent fine phonetic detail when they are first learning to comprehend words? Theory and research by child phonologists supports the notion that with only a small vocabulary, children will not represent and/or access all the fine phonetic detail of words (Ferguson and Farwell, 1979; Garnica, 1973; Kay-Raining Bird, and Chapman, 1998). Using more a sensitive procedure, however, Jusczyk and Aslin (1995) showed that 7½-month-old infants do show quite detailed phonetic representations. Infants were tested using a Headturn Preference Procedure (HPP) in tasks requiring them to respond preferentially to words (or passages containing words) to which they had previously been familiarized. When previously familiarized with words (or nonwords) such as "dog" or "tup," infants of 7½ months showed a preference for listening to those words, but did not show a preference for listening to phonetically similar words such as "bog" and "cup."

In a very similar study with slightly older French-learning infants, Hallé and de Boysson-Bardies (1996) obtained very different results. Unlike the English-learning infants of 7½ months tested by Aslin and Jusczyk, the French-learning infants of 11–12 months confused unfamiliar words with similar sounding familiar words. Hallé and de Boysson-Bardies (1996) proposed that the older infants, in contrast to 7½-month-old infants, listen to words as potential sources of semantic content, and that this listening strategy may predispose them to adopt a more holistic, less analytic processing strategy.

Using a procedure we developed for teaching infants to associate new words with objects (Werker et al., 1998), we assessed whether or not infants access or store less phonetic detail when they are listening to words as potential sources of meaning than when they are just listening to words as sounds. In the explicit word-learning form of this procedure, infants are familiarized to two word–object pairings, then tested on their ability to detect a switch in the pairing. For example, they are familiarized to Word A with moving Object a and Word B with moving Object b, then tested on a same trial (Aa or Bb) and a switch trial (Ab or Ba). By 14 months—but not at 8, 10, or 12 months—infants can learn the association between two words and two moving objects when the objects are physically dissimilar and the words are phonetically dissimilar (e.g., "lif" and "neem"). If familiarized to only one word–object pairing (e.g., Aa), infants as young as 8 months (and probably younger) can discriminate a change to a new word (e.g., Ba) or a new object (Ab), showing that they can pick up the details of both the word and the object in a discrimination task (Werker et al., 1998). However, the failure of the younger infants in the two-word/two-object switch task shows that they lack the ability to pair novel words with novel objects in this testing situation.

In a follow-up series of studies, Stager and Werker (1997) used the switch and discrimination procedures to test infants aged 8–14 months on their ability to learn the association between phonetically similar words (e.g., "bih" vs. "dih") and objects. Whereas infants of 8 months (who cannot be tested in the switch task) easily discriminate the phonetically similar "bih" from "dih" in the discrimination task, infants of 14 months fail in both the switch and discrimination tasks.

We interpret these results to suggest that 8-month-olds and 14-month-olds use different processing strategies in these tasks: Inasmuch as the 8-month-olds approach the discrimination task as one of discrimination, they are able to discriminate "bih" from "dih"; but 14-month-olds, in treating the discrimination task as one of word-learning, fail to detect the fine phonetic difference between "bih" and "dih." To provide a strong test of this hypothesis, we tested 14-month-olds in a virtually identical task but used a stationary unbounded nonobject visual stimulus (see Spelke, 1990) that was unlikely to encourage word learning. When the word "bih" (or "dih") was presented together with a stationary checkerboard that filled the screen, following familiarization, infants of 14 months easily detected a change to the contrasting word. These results confirm that infants of 14 months are able to detect the phonetic difference between "bih" and "dih." The difficulty comes when they attempt to attach meaning to the word. When first engaging in a computationally more complex task such as word-learning, infants may have to temporarily drop detail—either in the encoding and representation phase or in the access and use phase.

The potential contributions of cognitive neuroscience techniques to understanding behavior are well illustrated in subsequent studies designed to explain the "failure" of 14-month-olds and to predict when infants would again have access to fine phonetic detail in word-learning. In previous work, Mills, Coffey-Corina, and Neville (1993, 1997) observed that infants show different ERP responses to known and unknown words. At 13–17 months, this difference is detected in both hemi-

spheres and shows up at frontal, temporal, and parietal scalp electrode sites. By 20 months, it is restricted to the LH over the temporal and parietal lobes, suggesting the emergence of specialized brain systems for processing words by that age. In their work, Mills and colleagues (1993) reported that 17-month-old infants who were post-vocabulary spurt (>150 words) showed the localized LH response, whereas infants with smaller vocabularies (<50 words) showed the more distributed response, indicating that the increasingly local nature of the differential ERP signature seen in older infants reflects greater sophistication in word knowledge. Mills and colleagues interpreted these results as indicating that the word spurt comes about as a result of the establishment of specialized neural systems for word-learning (see also Schafer and Mills, 1997).

In collaboration with the labs of Helen Neville (University of Oregon) and Debbie Mills (University of California at San Diego), we used the ERP technique to examine the phonetic representation of words in novice and experienced word learners. We tested infants of 14 and 20 months in the same ERP procedure used by Mills, Coffey-Corina, and Neville (1993). This time, however, in addition to presenting the infants with 10 known and 10 unknown words, we included 10 unknown words that are phonetically similar to the known words. For example, we would present the word "dog," which is known to infants of this age, the phonetically similar unknown word "bog," and the dissimilar unknown word "lif."

The results to date with 9 subjects at each age are unequivocal. Infants of both 14 and 20 months show precisely the same pattern for the known (e.g., "dog") and unknown (e.g., "lif") words as reported previously by Mills and colleagues. However, the response to the phonetically similar unknown words (e.g., "bog") was quite different for the two ages. For the 14-month-olds, the ERP responses to the phonetically similar unknown words looked just like those to the known words. In other words, the infants of 14 months confused the phonetically similar words, and treated a word like "bog" as one that they knew. For the infants of 20 months, the ERP responses to the phonetically similar words patterned just like those to the unknown words. By 20 months, these now more proficient word-learning infants were no longer confusing the phonetically similar unknown words with known words (Prat et al., 1999).

These findings were useful for two reasons. First, they provided confirmation that infants of 14 months do indeed have difficulty distinguishing similar sounding words. On the basis of our behavioral work using the switch design, we had to draw this conclusion by comparing a series of positive findings to the failures of the

14-month-old infants. In the ERP task, the infants of 14 months did not fail anything. Instead, they showed a special "I know that one!" ERP signature to the phonetically similar words. Second, the ERP study made a strong prediction that by 20 months of age infants should no longer confuse phonetically similar words in a word-learning switch design. When we tested this hypothesis with 20-month-old infants, we found that, as predicted, infants in this age range do detect a switch between "bih" and "dih" in our word-learning procedure (Werker, Corcoran, Fennelli, and Stager, under review). We have also found that 17-month-old infants, and even 14-month-olds with particularly large receptive vocabularies, can easily discriminate similar sounding words (Werker et al., under review). Swingley and Aslin (2000) have reported similar findings for infants of 17 and 20 months in their responses to known words in comparison to minimally different words (e.g., "baby" vs. "vaby"; Swingley and Aslin, 2000.)

Finally, in a novel twist, Schafer and Mareschal (2000) have recently modeled these data on a neural network and found that a simple learning algorithm can account for the failure to distinguish phonetically similar words with more "experience." Moreover, in ongoing work, Schafer, Werker, and Pulleyblank (in preparation) have found that the vocabulary size and its phonological characteristics as well as total language exposure and extent of habituation contribute to discrimination ability. This work represents an initial exploration into using neural networks to model and predict infant performance in lexical representation tasks.

This approach, combining behavioral, electrophysiological, and computational modeling techniques, illustrates the exciting investigative potential of developmental cognitive neuroscience, and provides a rich interface for better understanding language learning.

## Summary: From linguistic foundations to first words

In this chapter, we have explored three different aspects of language processing. Using both behavioral and neurophysiological data, we have attempted to describe what is known about initial brain organization and to illustrate ways in which experience can reorganize neural processing systems. At the most fundamental level, we asked whether there is a basic difference in the processing of speech versus nonspeech. Within the realm of speech perception itself, we focused on neural and behavioral processing of phonetic detail. Finally, in an attempt to begin to address how speech perception might intersect with language acquisition, we reviewed

recent research on the use of phonetic detail in early word learning. The pattern of findings across these three different content areas provides converging evidence for increasing neurocognitive specialization with development (cf. Neville, 1995; Nelson, 1999).

How early is this specialization evident? In our review, we found that very young infants do respond to speech differently than to some nonspeech sounds (white noise, music), and do show a different topography in the ERP response to phonetic contrasts versus tone differences (Dehaene-Lambertz, 2000); however, newborn infants fail to prefer speech over spectrally similar nonspeech sine waves and show ERP responses to full syllables similar to those of their constituent formants (Novak et al., 1989). Thus far, it is difficult to conclude whether the differences shown by neonates in speech processing and phonetic discrimination, compared with nonspeech and acoustic processing, reflect the functioning of a specialized speech processor. The brain might initially be responding to components in speech common to other auditory signals, and grant special status to speech as a product of experience. On the other hand, the fact that newborn infants respond to speech and other highly similar signals differently than to nonspeech keeps open the possibility that a specialized processor operates at birth, but only gradually becomes tuned to the precise characteristics of speech. The increasing specificity of infants' response to speech is consistent with both possibilities.

Irrespective of the extent to which a speech-specific mechanism operates from birth, it is still essential to understand the role of experience. Indeed, in the perception of any acoustic signal (including spoken language), the study of the neonate does not necessarily illuminate the "initial state," as the fetus has the opportunity to experience stimulation of the auditory system for close to 3 months prior to birth (Eisenberg, 1976). In previous writings we have suggested that epigenetic processes (Gottlieb, 1991; Werker and Tees, 1992) early in life may play a critical role in setting initial sensitivities to speech by organizing the connections within the auditory cortex. We have hypothesized that "experience-expectant" processes (Greenough and Juraska, 1986), universal and species-specific, consolidate a permanent foundation for processing speech. These may mediate the early appearing preference for speech over nonspeech, and discrimination of language-general phonetic distinctions (Werker and Tees, 1992, 1999). Attunement to the properties of the native language and the eventual use of these sensitivities in word processing may rely on more plastic "experience-dependent" processes, responding to the unique experiences of each individual.

It is in the use of phonetic detail in word learning and lexical representation that we see the least evidence for initial specialization and the clearest evidence of experiential influences on the establishment of a distinct neural system. Here, the behavioral and electrophysiological work both point to the emergence, at around 18–20 months of age, of rapid and efficient word learning. Accompanying the achievement of this language explosion milestone appears to be a specialized neural system for word learning (Mills, Coffey-Corina, and Neville, 1993, in press; Schafer and Mills, 1997), and with the establishment of this system, attention to fine phonetic detail is again possible (Prat et al., 1999; Werker, Corcoran, and Stager, 1999; Werker et al., under review). The consistency in the brain areas involved from individual to individual suggests that, even in word learning, some areas in the brain are more suited for, and more likely to take on this task, than others (Neville et al., 1998).

In summary, we have focused on infants' sensitivity to change as a critical first entry into the construction of a functional language processing system. At birth, the system appears to be set up to notice some rather than other changes in the environment, which, with experience, become more specific and attuned to, for example, speech over nonspeech, and the characteristics of the native language. This attunement may help maintain and extend functionally relevant sensitivities while others regress. It also may provide a perceptual foundation, which, together with the emergence of specialized word-learning systems, allows the child to rapidly learn words in the native language.

ACKNOWLEDGMENTS We thank the Natural Sciences and Engineering Research Council of Canada (NSERC) for research grant support to J. Werker (1103–95), and an NSERC graduate fellowship to A. Vouloumanos. Special thanks to M. Fung and E. Job for their assistance throughout.

## REFERENCES

ASLIN, R. N., D. R. PISONI, and B. L. HENNESSY, 1981. Discrimination of voice onset time by human infants: New findings and implications for the effects of early experience. *Child Dev.* 52:1135–1145.

BATES, E., D. THAL, D. TRAUNER, J. FENSON, D. ARAM, J. EISELE, and R. MASS, 1997. From first words to grammar in children with focal brain injury. *Developmental Neuropsychology* 13:275–343.

BERTONCINI, J., and J. MEHLER, 1981. Syllables as units in infant speech perception. *Infant Behav. Dev.* 4:247–260.

BERTONCINI, J., J. MORAIS, R. BIJELJAC-BABIC, S. MCADAMS, I. PERETZ, and J. MEHLER, 1989. Dichotic perception and laterality in neonates. *Brain Lang.* 37:591–605.

BEST, C. T., 1995. Learning to perceive the sound pattern of

English. In *Advances in Infancy Research*, Vol. 9, C. Rovee-Collier and L. P. Lipsitt, eds. Greenwich, Conn.: Ablex, pp. 217–230.

BEST, C. T., and R. A. AVERY, 1999. Left-hemisphere advantage for click consonants is determined by linguistic significance and experience. *Psychol. Sci.* 10(1):65–70.

BEST, C. T., H. HOFFMAN, and B. B. GLANVILLE, 1982. Development of infant ear asymmetries for speech and music. *Percept. Psychophysics* 31:75–85.

BEST, C. T., G. D. MCROBERTS, R. LAFLEUR, and J. SILVER-ISENSTADT, 1995. Divergent developmental patterns for infants perception of two nonnative consonant contrasts. *Infant Behav. Dev.* 18:339–350.

BEST, C. T., G. W. MCROBERTS, and N. M. SITHOLE, 1988. Examination of perceptual reorganization for nonnative speech contrasts: Zulu click discrimination by English-speaking adults and infants. *J. Exp. Psychol.: Hum. Percept. Perform.* 14:345–360.

BEST, C. T., E. MENCL, K. PUGH, T. CONSTABLE, R. FULBRIGHT, J. GORE, C. LACADIE, P. SKUDLARSKI, A. FABER, and D. HARRISON, 1999. *Native-language phonetic and phonological constraints on perception of non-native speech contrast.* Paper presented at the March Meeting of Acoustical Society of America, Berlin, Germany.

BEST, C. T., M. STUDDERT-KENNEDY, S. MANUEL, and J. RUBIN-SPITZ, 1989. Discovering phonetic coherence in acoustic patterns. *Percept. Psychophysics* 45(3):237–250.

BIJELJAC-BABIC, R., J. BERTONCINI, and J. MEHLER, 1993. How do 4-day-old infants categorize multisyllabic utterances? *Dev. Psychol.* 29(4):711–721.

CHEOUR, M., K. ALHO, R. CEPONIENE, K. REINIKAINEN, K. SAINIO, M. POHJAVUORI, O. AALTONEN, and R. NÄÄTÄNEN, 1998. Maturation of mismatch negativity in infants. *Int. J. Psychophysiol.* 29:217–226.

CHEOUR, M., K. ALHO, K. SAINIO, K. REINIKAINEN, M. RENLUND, O. AALTONEN, O. EEROLA, and R. NÄÄTÄNEN, 1997. The mismatch negativity to changes in speech sounds at the age of three months. *Dev. Neuropsychol.* 13(2):167–174.

CHEOUR-LUHTANEN, M., K. ALHO, K. SAINIO, T. RINNE, K. REINIKAINEN, M. POHJAVUORI, M. RENLUND, O. AALTONEN, O. EEROLA, and R. NÄÄTÄNEN, 1996. The ontogenetically earliest discriminative response of the human brain. *Psychophysiology* 33:478–481.

COLOMBO, J., and R. S. BUNDY, 1981. A method for the measurement of infant auditory selectivity. *Infant Behav. Dev.* 4:219–223.

CUTLER, A., J. MEHLER, D. NORRIS, and J. SEGUI, 1989. Limits on bilingualism. *Nature* 340(6230):229–230.

DECASPER, A. J., and W. P. FIFER, 1980. Of human bonding: Newborns prefer their mother's voices. *Science* 208:1174–1176.

DEHAENE-LAMBERTZ, G., 1997. Electrophysiological correlates of categorical phoneme perception in adults. *NeuroReport* 8(4):919–924.

DEHAENE-LAMBERTZ, G., 2000. Cerebral specialization for speech and non-speech stimuli in infants. *J. Cogn. Neurosci.* 12(3):449–460.

DEHAENE-LAMBERTZ, G., and S. BAILLET, 1998. A phonological representation in the infant brain. *NeuroReport* 9(8):1885–1888.

DEHAENE-LAMBERTZ, G., and S. DEHAENE, 1994. Speed and cerebral correlates of syllable discrimination in infants. *Nature* 370:292–295.

EIMAS, P. D., 1975. Auditory and phonetic coding of the cues for speech: Discrimination of the r–l distinction by young infants. *Percept. Psychophysics* 18:341–347.

EIMAS, P. D., E. R. SIQUELAND, P. W. JUSCZYK, and J. VIGORITO, 1971. Speech perception in infants. *Science* 171:303–306.

EISENBERG, R., 1976. *Auditory Competence in Early Life.* Baltimore: University Park Press.

ELMAN, J. L., 1993. Learning and development in neural networks: The importance of starting small. *Cognition* 48(1): 71–99.

FERGUSON, C. A., and C. B. FARWELL, 1979. Words and sounds in early language acquisition. *Language* 51:419–439.

FERNALD, A., J. P. PINTO, D. SWINGLEY, A. WEINBERG, and G. W. MCROBERTS, 1998. Rapid gains in speed of verbal processing by infants in the 2nd year. *Psychological Sci.* 9(3):228–231.

FODOR, J. A., 1983. *The Modularity of Mind: An Essay on Faculty Psychology.* Cambridge, Mass.: MIT Press.

FRIEDERICI, A. D., and J. M. L. WESSELS, 1993. Phonotactic knowledge of word boundaries and its use in infant speech perception. *Percept. Psychophysics* 54(3):287–295.

GARNICA, O. K., 1973. The development of phonemic speech perception. In *Cognitive Development and the Acquisition of Language,* T. E. Moore, ed. New York: Academic Press, pp. 215–222.

GESCHWIND, N., 1970. The organization of language and the brain. *Science* 170:940–944.

GLANVILLE, B. B., C. T. BEST, and R. LEVENSON, 1977. A cardiac measure of cerebral asymmetries in infant auditory perception. *Dev. Psychol.,* 13:54–59.

GLENN, S. M., C. C. CUNNINGHAM, and P. F. JOYCE, 1981. A study of auditory preference in nonhandicapped infants and infants with Down's syndrome. *Child Dev.* 52:1303–1307.

GOLINKOFF, R. M., K. HIRSH-PASEK, K. M. CAULEY, and L. GORDON, 1987. The eyes have it: Lexical and syntactic comprehension in a new paradigm. *J. Child Lang.* 14(1):23–45.

GOTTLIEB, G., 1991. Experimental canalization of behavioral development: Theory. *Dev. Psychol.* 27(1):4–13.

GREENOUGH, W. T., and J. M. JURASKA, 1986. *Developmental Neuropsychobiology.* Orlando, Fla.: Academic Press.

HALLÉ, P. A., and B. DE BOYSSON-BARDIES, 1996. The format of representation of recognized words in infants' early receptive lexicon. *Infant Behav. Dev.* 19:463–481.

HIRSH-PASEK, K., D. G. K. NELSON, P. W. JUSCZYK, K. W. CASSIDY, B. DRUSS, and L. KENNEDY, 1987. Clauses are perceptual units for young infants. *Cognition* 26:269–286.

HOLLICH, G., K. HIRSH-PASEK, and R. M. GOLINKOFF, 2000. Breaking the language barrier: An emergentist coalition model of word learning. *Monographs of the Society for Research in Child Development, 65 (3, Serial No.262).*

JUSCZYK, P. W., 1999. How infants begin to extract words from speech. *Trends Cog. Sci.* 3:323–328.

JUSCZYK, P. W., and A. N. ASLIN, 1995. Infants' detection of the sound patterns of words in fluent speech. *Cogn. Psychol.* 29:1–23.

JUSCZYK, P. W., A. CUTLER, and N. J. REDANZ, 1993. Infants' preference for the predominant stress patterns of English words. *Child Dev.* 64:675–687.

JUSCZYK, P. W., A. D. FRIEDERICI, J. N. WESSELS, V. Y. SVENKERUD, and A. JUSCZYK, 1993. Infants' sensitivity to the sound pattern of native language words. *J. Memory Lang.* 32:402–420.

JUSCZYK, P. W, P. A. LUCE, and J. CHARLES-LUCE, 1994. Infants' sensitivity to phonotactic patterns in the native language. *J. Memory and Lang.* 33:630–645.

KAY-RAINING BIRD, E., and R. S. CHAPMAN, 1998. Partial representations and phonological selectivity in the comprehension of 13- to 16-month olds. *First Language.* 18(52):105–127.

KUHL, P. K., K. A. WILLIAMS, F. LACERDA, K. N. STEVENS, and B. LINDBLOM, 1992. Linguistic experience alters phonetic perception in infants by 6 months of age. *Science* 255:606–608.

LASKY, R. E., A. SYRDAL-LASKY, and R. E. KLEIN, 1975. VOT discrimination by four to six month old infants from Spanish environments. *J. Exp. Child Psychol.* 20:215–225.

LENNEBERG, E., 1967. *Biological Foundations of Language.* New York: Wiley.

LIBERMAN, A. M., F. S. COOPER, D. P. SHANKWEILER, and M. STUDDERT-KENNEDY, 1967. Perception of the speech code. *Psychol. Rev.* 74:431–461.

MANDEL, D. R., P. W. JUSCZYK, and D. B. PISONI, 1995. Infants' recognition of the sound patterns of their own names. *Psychological Sci.* 6(5):315–318.

MARANTZ, A., C. PHILLIPS, M. MCGINNIS, E. YELLIN, S. MANUEL, K. WEXLER, D. POEPPEL, T. ROBERTS, H. ROWLEY, M. SUGISHITA, S. SEKIMOTO, and K. YONEDA, 1996. *A cross-linguistic perspective on phoneme perception using magnetic mismatch fields.* Paper presented at the 3rd Annual Cognitive Neuroscience Society Meeting, San Francisco, California.

MEHLER, J., and A. CHRISTOPHE, 1994. Language in the infant's mind. *Phil. Trans. R. Soc. Lond. [B]* 346(1315):13–20.

MEHLER, J., P. W. JUSCZYK, G. DEHAENE-LAMBERTZ, G. HALSTED, J. BERTONCINI, and C. AMIEL-TISON, 1988. A precursor of language acquisition in young infants. *Cognition* 29:143–178.

MEHLER, J., C. PALLIER, and A. CHRISTOPHE, 1998. Language and cognition. In *Advances in Psychological Science. Vol. 2: Biological and Cognitive Aspects,* M. Sabourin, F. Craik, and M. Robert, eds. East Sussex, UK: Psychology Press, pp. 381–398.

MILLS, D. L., S. A. COFFEY-CORINA, and H. J. NEVILLE, 1993. Language acquisition and cerebral specialization in 20-month-old infants. *J. Cogn. Neurosci.* 5:317–334.

MILLS, D. L., S. A. COFFEY-CORINA, and H. J. NEVILLE, 1994. Variability in cerebral organization. In *Human Behavior and the Developing Brain,* G. Dawson, and K. W. Fischer, eds. New York: The Guildford Press, pp. 427–455.

MILLS, D. L., S. A. COFFEY-CORINA, and H. J. NEVILLE, 1997. Language comprehension and cerebral specialization from 13–20 months. *Dev. Neuropsychol.* 13(3):397–445.

MILLS, D. L., and H. J. NEVILLE, 1997. Electrophysiological studies of language and language impairment. *Sem. Ped. Neurol.* 4(2):125–134.

MOLFESE, D. L., and V. J. MOLFESE, 1979a. Hemisphere and stimulus differences as reflected in the cortical responses of newborn infants to speech stimuli. *Dev. Psychol.* 15:505–511.

MOLFESE, D. L., and V. J. MOLFESE, 1979b. Infant speech perception: Learned or innate? In *Advances in Neurolinguistics,* Vol. 4, H. A. Whitaker and H. Whitaker, eds. New York: Academic Press.

MOLFESE, D. L., and V. J. MOLFESE, 1980. Cortical responses of preterm infants to phonetic and nonphonetic speech stimuli. *Dev. Psychol.* 16:574–581.

MOLFESE, D. L., and V. J. MOLFESE, 1985. Electrophysiological indices of auditory discrimination in newborn infants: The bases for predicting later language development? *Infant Behav. Dev.* 8:197–211.

MOON, C., R. COOPER, and W. FIFER, 1993. Two-day-olds prefer their native language. *Infant Behav. Dev.* 16:495–500.

MYERS, J., P. W. JUSCZYK, D. G. KEMLER-NELSON, J. CHARLES-LUCE, A. WOODWARD, and K. HIRSH-PASEK, 1996. Infants' sensitivity to word boundaries in fluent speech. *J. Child Lang.* 23:1–30.

NÄÄTÄNEN, R., A. LEHTOKOSKI, M. LENNES, M. CHEOUR, M. HUOTILAINEN, A. IIVONEN, M. VAINIO, P. ALKU, R. J. ILMONIEMI, A. LUUK, J. ALLIK, J. SINKKONEN, and K. ALHO, 1997. Language-specific phoneme representations revealed by electric and magnetic brain responses. *Nature* 385:432–434.

NAZZI, T., J. BERTONCINI, and J. MEHLER, 1998. Language discrimination by newborns: Towards an understanding of the role of rhythm. *J. Exp. Psychol.: Hum. Percept. Perform.* 24(3):756–766.

NELSON, C. A., 1999. Neural plasticity and human development. *Curr. Direct. Psychol. Sci.* 8(2):42–45.

NEVILLE, H. J., 1995. Developmental specificity in neurocognitive development in humans. In *The Cognitive Neurosciences*, M. S. Gazzaniga, ed. Cambridge, Mass.: MIT Press, pp. 219–231.

NEVILLE, H. J., D. BAVELIER, D. CORINA, J. RAUSCHECKER, A. KARNI, A. LALWANI, A. BRAUN, V. CLARK, P. JEZZARD, and R. TURNER, 1998. Cerebral organization for language in deaf and hearing subjects: Biological constraints and effects of experience. *Proc. Natl. Acad. Sci.* 95:922–929.

NOVAK, G. P., D. KURTZBERG, J. A. KREUZER, and H. G. VAUGHAN JR., 1989. Cortical responses to speech sounds and their formants in normal infants: Maturational sequence and spatiotemporal analysis. *Electroencephalogr. Clin. Neurophysiol.* 73:295–305.

PEGG, J. E., and J. F. WERKER, 1997. Adult and infant perception of two English phonemes. *J. Acoust. Soc. Am.* 102(6):3742–3753.

PHILLIPS, C., T. PELLATHY, and A. MARANTZ, 1999. *Magnetic mismatch field elicited by phonological feature contrast.* Paper presented at the 6th Annual Cognitive Neuroscience Society Meeting, Washington, D.C.

PIAGET, J., 1980. Language and cognition. In *Language and Learning: The Debate between Jean Piaget and Noam Chomsky*, M. Piattelli-Palmarini, ed. Cambridge, Mass.: Harvard University Press.

PISONI, D. B., R. N. ASLIN, A. J. PEREY, and B. L. HENNESSY, 1982. Some effects of laboratory training on identification and discrimination of voicing contrast in stop consonants. *J. Exp. Psychol.: Hum. Percept. Perform.* 8(2):297–314.

POLKA, L., and J. F. WERKER, 1994. Developmental changes in perception of non-native vowel contrasts. *J. Exp. Psychol.: Hum. Percept. Perform.* 20:421–435.

PRAT, C. S., C. L. STAGER, T. V. MITCHELL, A. M. ADAMSON, and L. D. SANDERS, 1999. *Semantic processing of phonetically similar words in infants: Indications from event-related potentials.* Poster presented at the Society for Research in Child Development, Albuquerque, New Mexico.

REPP, B. H., 1984. Categorical perception: Issues methods findings. In *Speech and Language: Advances in Basic Rresearch and Practice*, Vol. 10, N. J. Lass, ed. New York: Academic Press, pp. 243–335.

RIVERA-GAXIOLA, M., G. CSIBRA, M. H. JOHNSON, and A. KARMILOFF-SMITH, 2000. Electrophysiological correlates of cross-linguistic speech perception in native English speakers. *Behav. Brain Res.* 111(1–2):13–23.

SCHAFER, G., and D. MARESCHAL, in press. Can functional re-organization be data driven? Stage-like behavior in a simple associative network. *Infancy*.

SCHAFER, G., and D. MILLS, 1997. *Early Word Learning: From Cerebral Specialisation to Underlying Mechanism.* Paper presented at the Society for Research in Child Development, Washington, D.C.

SCHAFER, G., and K. PLUNKETT, 1998. Rapid word learning by fifteen-month-olds under tightly controlled conditions. *Child Devel.* 69(2):309–320.

SHAFER, V. L., D. W. SHUCARD, J. L. SHUCARD, and L. GERKEN, 1998. An electrophysiological study of infants sensitivity to the sound patterns of English speech. *J. Speech Lang. Hear. Res.* 41:874–886.

SHARMA, A., and M. DORMAN, 1999. Neurophysiologic correlates of cross-language perception of phonetic categories. *J. Acoust. Soc. Am.* 105(2):1096.

SHI, R., J. F. WERKER, and J. L. MORGAN, 1999. Newborn infants sensitivity to perceptual cues to lexical and grammatical words. *Cognition.* 72(2):B11–B21.

SPELKE, E., 1990. Principles of object perception. *Cogn. Sci.* 14(1):29–56.

STAGER, C. L., and J. F. WERKER, 1997. Infants listen for more phonetic detail in speech perception than in word-learning tasks. *Nature* 388:381–382.

STRANGE, W., and S. DITTMANN, 1984. Effects of discrimination training on the perception of /r–l/ by Japanese adults learning English. *Percept. Psychophysics* 36:131–145.

STRANGE, W., and J. J. JENKINS, 1978. Role of linguistic experience in the perception of speech. In *Perception and Experience*, R. D. Walk and H. J. Pick, eds. New York: Plenum Press, pp. 125–169.

STREETER, L. A., 1976. Kikuyu labial and apical stop discrimination. *J. Phonetics* 4:43–49.

STUDDERT-KENNEDY, M., and D. SHANKWEILER, 1970. Hemispheric specialization for speech perception. *J. Acoust. Soc. Am.* 48:599–602.

SWINGLEY, D., and R. N. ASLIN, 2000. Spoken word recognition and lexical representation in very young children. *Cognition* 76:147–166.

TEES, R. C., and J. F. WERKER, 1984. Perceptual flexibility: Maintenance or recovery of the ability to discriminate non-native speech sounds. *Can. J. Psychol.* 38(4):579–590.

TREHUB, S. E., 1976. The discrimination of foreign speech contrasts by infants and adults. *Child Dev.* 47:466–472.

TREMBLAY, K., N. KRAUS, T. D. CARRELL, and T. MCGEE, 1997. Central auditory system plasticity: Generalization to novel stimuli following listening training. *J. Acous. Soc. Am.* 102(6):3762–3773.

VOULOUMANOS, A., M. D. BHATNAGAR, D. E. GIASCHI, and J. F. WERKER, 1999. *Do infants prefer speech over spectrally similar non-speech sounds?* Paper presented at the 29th annual meeting of the Society for Neuroscience, Miami, Florida.

WADA, J. A., R. CLARKE, and A. HAMM, 1975. Cerebral hemispheric asymmetry in humans: Cortical speech zones in 100 adult and 100 infant brains. *Arch. Neurol.* 32(4):239–246.

WERKER, J. F., 1995. Exploring developmental changes in cross-language speech perception. In *An Invitation to Cognitive Science, 2nd ed. Language: Vol. 1*, D. N. Osherson, L. R. Gleitman, and M. Liberman, eds. Cambridge, Mass.: MIT Press, pp. 87–106.

WERKER, J. F., L. B. COHEN, V. L. LLOYD, M. CASASOLA, and C. L. STAGER, 1998. Acquisition of word-object associations by 14-month-old infants. *Dev. Psychol.* 34(6):1289–1309.

WERKER, J. F., K. M. CORCORAN, C. T. FENNELL, and C. L. STAGER (under review). Infants' ability to learn phonetically similar words: Effects of age and vocabulary size.

WERKER, J. F., J. H. V. GILBERT, K. HUMPHREY, and R. C. TEES, 1981. Developmental aspects of cross-language speech perception. *Child Dev.* 52:349–355.

WERKER, J. F., and C. E. LALONDE, 1988. Cross-language speech perception: Initial capabilities and developmental change. *Dev. Psychol.* 24(5):672–683.

WERKER, J. F., and J. S. LOGAN, 1985. Cross-language evidence for three factors in speech perception. *Percept. Psychophysics* 37(1):135–144.

WERKER, J. F., and R. C. TEES, 1984a. Cross-language speech perception: Evidence for perceptual reorganization during the first year of life. *Infant Behav. Dev.* 7:49–63.

WERKER, J. F., and R. C. TEES, 1984b. Phonemic and phonetic factors in adult cross-language speech perception. *J. Acoust. Soc. Am.* 75:1866–1878.

WERKER, J. F., and R. C. TEES, 1992. The organization and reorganization of human speech perception. *Annu. Rev. Neurosci.* 15:377–402.

WERKER, J. F., and R. C. TEES, 1999. Influences on infant speech processing: Toward a new synthesis. *Annu. Rev. Psychol.* 5:509–535.

WOODWARD, A. L., E. M. MARKMAN, and C. M. FITZSIMMONS, 1994. Rapid word-learning in 13 and 18-month-olds. *Developmental Psych.* 30(4):553–566.

# 20 Language Development in Children with Unilateral Brain Injury

ELIZABETH BATES
AND KATHERINE ROE

ABSTRACT Aphasia (defined as the loss or impairment of language abilities following acquired brain injury) is strongly associated with damage to the left hemisphere in adults. This well-known finding has led to the hypothesis that the left hemisphere is innately specialized for language, and may be the site of a specific "language organ." However, we have known for more than a century that young children with left-hemisphere damage (LHD) do not suffer from aphasia, and in most studies do not differ significantly from children with right-hemisphere damage (RHD). This result provides strong evidence for plasticity—brain reorganization in response to experience—and constitutes a serious challenge to the language organ hypothesis. This chapter reviews the history of research on language outcomes in children versus adults with unilateral brain injury. In that review we address some of the discrepancies in the literature to date, including the methodological confounds that may be responsible for those discrepancies. We also review recent prospective studies of children with unilateral injury as they pass through the first stages of language development. Prospective studies have demonstrated specific correlations between lesion site and profiles of language delay, but they look quite different from lesion–symptom correlations in adults, and gradually disappear across the course of language development. The classic pattern of brain organization for language observed in normal adults may be the product rather than the cause of language learning, emerging out of regional biases in information processing that are relevant for language, but only indirectly related to language itself. If those regions are damaged early in life, other parts of the brain can emerge to solve the language-learning problem.

Aphasia, the loss of language abilities following brain injury, has been studied systematically in adults for more than a century, and its existence has been documented since the first Egyptian surgical papyrus more than 4000 years ago (Goodglass, 1993; O'Neill, 1980). There is now a large body of research on adult aphasia, and although there is still substantial controversy regarding its nature and causes, consensus has emerged on at least two points: (1) Injuries to the left hemisphere are overwhelmingly more likely to cause aphasia

ELIZABETH BATES AND KATHERINE ROE Center for Research in Language, University of California at San Diego, La Jolla, California.

than injuries to the right, suggesting in turn that (2) the left hemisphere plays a privileged role in language processing by normal adults. The second conclusion has been independently confirmed in the 20th century by methods ranging from sodium amytal (WADA) tests and/or point-to-point electrical stimulation in adult candidates for neurosurgery (Ojemann, 1991) to neural imaging studies of normals, including positron emission tomography (PET), functional magnetic resonance imaging (fMRI), magnetoencephalography (MEG), and event-related brain potentials (ERP). (For reviews, see Brown and Hagoort, 1999; Xiong et al., 1998.)

The privileged status of the left hemisphere for language processing is now beyond dispute (with estimates averaging from 95% to 98% of normal adults, independent of handedness), but the origins and development of this specialization are still poorly understood. There must be something about the left hemisphere that makes it especially suited for language—but what is that "something"? Is it present at birth, or does it develop gradually? Is it possible to develop normal language in the absence of a normal left hemisphere? And if an intact left hemisphere is not required for language development, then when, how, and why does it *become* necessary for language use in adults? Finally, if alternative forms of brain organization for language can emerge in the presence of early left-hemisphere damage, is there some critical period in which this must occur?

The sparse but growing body of evidence on language development in children with left- versus right-hemisphere damage is relevant to all these points, and it has yielded two very puzzling results: (1) Most children with early left-hemisphere damage go on to acquire language abilities within the normal range (although performance is often at the low end of the normal range), and (2) most studies fail to find any significant differences in language outcomes when direct comparisons are made between children with left- versus right-hemisphere damage. These unexpected findings in children are hard to reconcile with one of the most popular ideas in neuropsychology: that the left hemisphere of the human brain contains an innate and highly specialized organ for language (Fodor, 1983; Gopnik, 1990; Gopnik and Crago, 1991; Newmeyer, 1997; Pinker, 1994; Rice, 1996). The language-organ hypothesis is appealing on many grounds. Aside from its value in explaining left-hemisphere specialization, the existence of a specialized language organ might help to explain why all normal adults are virtuosi in this domain. For example, adult speakers of English produce an average of 150 words per minute, each rapidly selected from a pool of 20–40 thousand lexical options. As quickly as these words are spoken (often blurred together, without well-marked boundaries), the average listener can parse these unbroken streams of sound into words and phrases, accessing the meaning of each word (from that same large pool) while simultaneously processing all the complex grammatical cues necessary for comprehension. This is an ability no other species on the planet appears to have, and one that today's largest and fastest computers have yet to master.

Perhaps even more phenomenal than the speed and ease with which we produce and perceive speech is the speed and ease with which we learn how to do it. Most 4-year-olds cannot tie their own shoes, but they can easily ask someone else to help them. In fact, most 4-year-olds have a vocabulary of 6000 words or more, and produce well-formed sentences as grammatically complex as those observed in any adult (Bates, in press; Bates et al., in press; Fletcher and MacWhinney, 1995). Children master their native language (or *languages,* for that matter) without formal instruction, without explicit corrections, and seemingly, without effort. Perhaps we are the only animals on earth that can manage this feat because we have an innate language organ. But the organ metaphor carries a number of assumptions that are contradicted by research on language development in children with early brain injury: (1) The brain in general and the left hemisphere in particular are specialized for language at birth; (2) this specialization involves compact and well-defined regions of the left hemisphere that are dedicated to language (and language alone); (3) this specialization is irreversible, so that normal levels of language are precluded if the language organ is severely damaged at birth; (4) even if some degree of language learning does take place (presumably through compensatory mechanisms), children with early left-hemisphere injuries should display persistent deficits that are not observed with early injuries to homologous areas on the right side of the brain.

All of these assumptions are in peril. Although these issues are not yet settled to everyone's satisfaction, one fact is clear: In the absence of other confounding factors (e.g., severe and intractable seizures), the language deficits observed in children with early left-hemisphere injury are (if they exist at all) far less pronounced than the aphasic syndromes seen in adults (Bates, 1999; Bates, Vicari, and Trauner, 1999; Eisele and Aram, 1995; Vargha-Khadem, Isaacs, and Muter, 1994; Vargha-Khadem et al., 1992). Other conclusions are still controversial, regarding the time course of recovery, the nature of the mechanisms that support it, and whether there are ultimately any significant differences (i.e., mild deficits) between children with left- versus right-hemisphere damage.

Our ability to answer these questions is limited by a number of factors. First, focal lesions in young children are very rare, so that generalizations are sometimes based on samples too small to support them. Second, results across studies are often in direct conflict, due to methodological variations including sample size, etiology (e.g., stroke, tumor, trauma, and conditions that might predispose children to any of these injuries), age of lesion onset, age of testing, the developmental sensitivity (or insensitivity) of the instruments used to evaluate language, and the kinds of statistical comparisons that were made (e.g., whether children with LHD and RHD are compared directly, versus indirect comparisons in which each clinical group is evaluated against a separate set of normal controls).

Due in part to these troubling methodological factors, research on language outcomes following early brain injury has swung back and forth between two extreme views: *equipotentiality* (site or side of injury does not matter at all in young children, because both sides of the brain are equivalent at birth) and *irreversible determinism* (the left hemisphere is innately and irreversibly specialized for language, precluding the possibility of complete and normal language development if it is severely damaged). We argue that the bulk of the evidence supports a compromise view between these two extremes, in which the two hemispheres are characterized at birth by innate but "soft" biases in information processing that are relevant to language but not specific to language, permitting both neural and behavioral reorganization across the course of language development (see also Satz, Strauss, and Whitaker, 1990). On this argument (which we will call *the emergentist view*), we would expect to see left/right-hemisphere differences early in life, but these differences will decrease with time and may eventually disappear.

We will review the evidence in three partially overlapping phases in the history of this field: an equipotentiality phase, an irreversible determinism phase, and (after a brief stop to consider the contribution of methodological factors) the current move toward an emergentist view. A summary of evidence involving measures of verbal and nonverbal IQ is presented in table 20.1. Evidence based on more specific measures of language is summarized in table 20.2.

## Phase I: Equipotentiality

Not long after the first 19th-century studies linking aphasia to left-hemisphere damage in adults, studies appeared suggesting that children with the same kinds of damage have little or no difficulty with language (Cotard, 1868; Clarus, 1874; both cited in Woods and Teuber, 1978), or that they show temporary deficits that quickly disappear (Bernhardt, 1897).

In this century, Basser (1962) reported on 34 children with severe epilepsy who underwent a radical process called hemispherectomy (removal of the damaged side of the brain) to control intractable seizures. Results were consistent with those from the century before: all but one of these children developed speech abilities in the normal range (see also Rasmussen and Milner, 1977). It was Basser's study that led Lenneberg (1967) to his controversial notion that the brain is "equipotential" at birth, with lateralization determined gradually across the course of development. As a corollary, Lenneberg also argued that this period of equipotentiality and plasticity is brought to an end at puberty, providing the first systematic argument in favor of a "critical period" for language. Lenneberg's views were quite compatible with an earlier proposal by Lashley (1950), who interpreted lesion studies of animals to indicate that loss of learning is predicted by the size of the lesion rather than its location (see also Irle, 1990). Lenneberg's critical period proposal was compatible not only with the evidence on recovery from unilateral damage (i.e., the difference between children and adults with comparable injuries), but also with (1) the difficulty that adults display in acquiring a second language without an accent and (2) some influential "wild child" studies, especially the famous case of Genie (Curtiss, 1977), which seemed to suggest that acquisition of a first language is also precluded if normal input is delayed until late childhood or puberty.

However, Lenneberg's equipotentiality hypothesis did not sit well with some of his contemporaries, who were persuaded by the research of Sperry, Gazzaniga, Geschwind, and others that the two hemispheres are too different to support a complete change of roles even early in life (Gazzaniga and Sperry, 1967; Geschwind and Kaplan, 1962; Levy, Nebes, and Sperry, 1971). Equipotentiality was also difficult to reconcile with Noam Chomsky's theory of generative grammar, with all its claims regarding the autonomy, innateness and "unlearnability" of language (Botha, 1989; Newmeyer, 1980). Another round of studies of children with early brain injury rapidly ensued, leading to an entirely different view.

## Phase II: Irreversible determinism

In response to Lashley and Lenneberg's controversial ideas about equipotentiality, a number of studies appeared between 1960 and 1980 suggesting that early brain injury does lead to subtle but persistent language impairments, deficits that are more likely following left-hemisphere damage (LHD) than right-hemisphere damage (RHD). For example, Woods and colleagues (Woods, 1980; Woods and Carey, 1979; Woods and Teuber 1973, 1978) concluded that LHD in children does lead to speech and language problems, especially if lesion onset occurs *after* one year of age, and they attributed earlier evidence for equipotentiality to limitations in medical knowledge at that time (Woods and Teuber, 1978). In the same vein, Dennis and colleagues (Dennis, 1980; Dennis and Kohn, 1975; Dennis and Whitaker, 1976, 1977; Dennis, Lovett, and Wiegel-Crump, 1981) reported that left-hemispherectomized children are more likely to have phonological and grammatical problems than children with right hemispherectomies (although the reported deficits were quite subtle).

Although these studies were influential (and are cited in many textbooks), most of them do not include direct statistical comparisons of children with LHD and children with RHD (see tables 20.1 and 20.2). Some looked exclusively at LHD children and controls, while others compared each group to its own set of age-matched controls (a practice followed in many of the studies reviewed below). The latter practice is common, but it is also problematic: Authors infer that effects of LHD are quantitatively and perhaps qualitatively different than the effects of RHD, but this supposed difference in patterning assumes an untested statistical interaction (i.e., that the difference between LHD and their controls is statistically greater than the difference between RHD and their controls). As we shall see, studies that have looked for such statistical interactions (or compared LHD and RHD directly) have generally failed to find the predicted effects.

As evidence accumulated, the picture became more complex, and more confusing. For example, Alajouanine and Lhermitte (1965) reported that children with LHD do have initial difficulty with some aspects of language, especially expressive language, but these difficulties were far less pronounced than those seen in adults and disappeared within 6 months to 2 years after

*(text continues on page 296)*

TABLE 20.1

Summary of IQ data from studies of children with focal brain injury

| Authors | Site | Neuro-imaging | Age of Onset | Patients: Age at Testing | Seizures | RHD vs. LHD | Results |
|---|---|---|---|---|---|---|---|
| Woods and Teuber (1973) | 19 RHD 17 LHD | No | PN–15 years | NR | NR | Yes | FIQ: LHD < controls / RHD < controls / LHD = RHD  PIQ: LHD < controls / RHD < controls  VIQ: LHD < controls / RHD = controls |
| Woods (1980) | 23 RHD 27 LHD | No | Early (<1 yr): 10 RHD = RE 11 LHD = LE  Late (>1 yr): 13 RHD = LR $X_O = 6; 4$ 6 LHD = LL $X_O = 5; 7$ | RE: $X_T = 14; 10$ LE: $X_T = 17; 2$ RL: $X_T = 10; 3$ LL: $X_T = 8; 6$ | RE: 5(−S); 5(+S) LE: 8(−S); 3(+S) RL: 11(−S); 2(+S) LL: 13(−S); 3(+S)  Comparisons between +S and −S not made | No | VIQ: RE < population mean & controls / LE < population mean & controls / RL = population mean & controls / LL < population mean & controls  PIQ: RE < population mean & controls / LE < population mean & controls / RL < population mean & controls / LL < population mean & controls |
| Vargha-Khadem, O'Gorman, and Watters (1985) | 28 RHD 25 LHD | Some | 33 Prenatal (<2 mos.) (16 RHD, 18 LHD)  11 Early postnatal (2 mos. to 5 yrs.) (5 RHD, 6 LHD)  9 Late postnatal (5–14 yrs.) (5 RHD, 4 LHD) | NSR  At least >2 yrs. post-onset | NR | No | Prenatal RHD: VIQ = PIQ / Prenatal LHD: VIQ < PIQ  Early postnatal RHD: VIQ = PIQ / Early postnatal LHD: VIQ < PIQ  Late postnatal RHD: VIQ = PIQ / Late postnatal LHD: VIQ = PIQ |

| Study | Sample | | Lesion onset | Lesion at testing | | | Results |
|---|---|---|---|---|---|---|---|
| Aram et al. (1985) | 8 RHD<br>8 LHD | Yes | RHD:<br>$X_O = 1; 4$<br>(2 mos. to 9; 0 yrs.)<br><br>LHD:<br>$X_O = 1; 6$<br>(1 mo. to 6; 2 yrs.) | RHD:<br>$X_T = 3; 10$<br>(1; 8–5; 10)<br><br>LHD:<br>$X_T = 4; 6$<br>(2 mos. to 8; 2 yrs.) | None | No | FIQ:<br>LHD < controls<br>RHD < controls<br><br>PIQ:<br>LHD < controls<br>RHD < controls<br><br>VIQ:<br>LHD = controls<br>RHD < controls |
| Riva and Cazzaniga (1986) | 26 RHD<br>22 LHD | Some | Early (<1 yr):<br>13 RHD = RE<br>10 LHD = LE<br><br>Late (>1 yr):<br>13 RHD = LR<br>12 LHD = LL<br>$X_O = 6; 6$ | Early (<1 yr):<br>$X_T = 8; 5$<br><br>Late (>1 yr):<br>$X_T = 11; 8$ | None | No | FIQ:<br>LE = controls<br>LL = controls<br>RE < controls<br>RL < controls<br><br>PIQ:<br>LE < controls<br>LL = controls<br>RE < controls<br>RL < controls<br><br>VIQ:<br>LE < controls<br>LL = controls<br>RE = controls<br>RL = controls |
| Riva et al. (1986) | 8 RHD<br>8 LHD | Yes | RHD:<br>$X_O = 4; 6$<br>(1; 8–8; 3)<br><br>LHD:<br>$X_O = 6; 4$<br>(0; 8–12; 8) | RHD: $X_T = 10; 7$<br><br>LHD: $X_T = 11; 1$ | 5 RHD(−S)<br>3 RHD(+S)<br><br>5 LHD(−S)<br>3 LHD(+S)<br>Comparisons between +S and −S not made | No | PIQ:<br>LHD < controls<br>RHD < controls<br><br>VIQ:<br>LHD < controls<br>RHD = controls |
| Nass, Peterson, and Koch (1989) | 12 RHD<br>14 LHD | Yes | Pre- or perinatal | RHD: $X_T = 8; 6$<br><br>LHD: $X_T = 6; 8$ | | Yes | FIQ: LHD > RHD<br>PIQ: LHD = RHD<br>VIQ: LHD > RHD<br><br>LHD: PIQ < VIQ<br>RHD: PIQ = VIQ |

(continued)

TABLE 20.1 (*Continued*)

Summary of IQ data from studies of children with focal brain injury

| Authors | Patients | | | | | RHD vs. LHD | Results |
|---|---|---|---|---|---|---|---|
| | Site | Neuro-imaging | Age of Onset | Age at Testing | Seizures | | |
| Vargha-Khadem et al. (1992) | 40 RHD 42 LHD | Yes | Pre- or perinatal | RHD(−S): $X_T = 11; 3$ RHD(+S): $X_T = 11; 6$ LHD(−S): $X_T = 12; 9$ LHD(+S): $X_T = 11; 8$ | 24 RHD(−S) 16 RHD(+S) 28 RHD(−S) 14 RHD(+S) | Yes | FIQ: RHD = LHD +S < controls −S < controls +S < −S  PIQ: RHD = LHD +S < controls −S < controls +S < −S  VIQ: RHD = LHD +S < controls −S controls +S ≤ −S |
| Eisele and Aram (1993) | 12 RHD 21 LHD | Yes | RHD: $X_O = 1; 06$ (PN–9; 08) LHD: $X_O = 2; 03$ (PN–11; 07) | RHD: $X_T = 5; 8$ (2; 06–14; 7) LHD: $X_T = 7; 5$ (2; 07–14; 2) | None | Yes | VIQ: LHD = LHD PIQ:  LHD = controls RHD < LHD = controls RHD < controls |
| Ballantyne, Scarvie, and Trauner (1994) | 9 RHD 8 LHD | Yes | Pre- or perinatal | RHD: $X_T = 11; 2$ (4; 11–20; 1) LHD: $X_T = 9$ (4; 1–16; 5) | NR | No | FIQ: LHD < controls RHD < controls  PIQ: LHD < controls RHD < controls  VIQ: LHD < controls RHD < controls  LHD: PIQ = VIQ RHD: PIQ < VIQ |

| Study | Sample | Seizures | Lesion onset | Age | Subgroups | | Results |
|---|---|---|---|---|---|---|---|
| Muter, Taylor, and Vargha-Khadem (1997) | 18 RHD 23 LHD | Some | Pre- or perinatal | $X_T$ = 4; 11 (3; 6–6; 8) | 11 RHD (−S) 4 RHD (+S) 15 LHD (−S) 8 LHD (+S) | Yes | Two testing periods (t1, t2) 1 yr apart: FIQ: RHD = LHD (t1 & t2) +S < controls (t1 & t2) −S < controls (t1 & t2) +S < −S (t1 & t2) PIQ: RHD = LHD +S < controls (t1 & t2) −S = controls (t1) −S < controls (t2) +S < −S VIQ: RHD = LHD (t1 & t2) +S < controls (t1 & t2) −S = controls (t1 & t2) +S < −S |
| Bates, Vicari, and Trauner (1999) | 15 RHD 28 LHD | Yes | < 6 mos. | 3–9 yrs. | 8 RHD (−S) 7 RHD (+S) 16 LHD (−S) 11 LHD (+S) | Yes | PIQ: LHD < controls RHD < controls LHD = RHD VIQ: LHD < controls RHD < controls LHD = RHD |
| | 27 RHD 46 LHD | Yes | < 6 mos. | 3–14 yrs. | 20 RHD (−S) 7 RHD (+S) 35 LHD (−S) 11 LHD (+S) | Yes | FIQ: LHD < controls RHD < controls LHD = RHD |

RHD, right-hemisphere damage; LHD, left-hemisphere damage; PN, prenatal; +S patients suffering seizures; −S, patients with no seizure activity; NR, not reported; N/A, not applicable; $X_O$, mean age of onset (years; months); $X_T$, mean age of testing (years; months).

Note: < indicates worse performance regardless of the specific measure used; = indicates that groups did not differ significantly.

TABLE 20.2

*Summary of data from studies of children with focal brain injury using various language assessment measures*

| Authors | Site | Patients | | | | | Tests Used | Results |
|---|---|---|---|---|---|---|---|---|
| | | Neuro-imaging | Age of Onset | Age at Testing | Seizures | RHD vs. LHD | | |
| McFie (1961) | 24 RHD 14 LHD | No | 35 infantile (before 1 yr.) (19 RHD, 11 LHD) | NR | NR | NR | Clinical/observational | 7 RH infantile with clinical dysphasia |
| | | | | | | | | 1 RH juvenile with clinical dysphasia |
| | | | 8 juvenile (after 1 yr.) (5 RH, 3 LH); range of onset 15 mos. to 5 yrs. | | | | | 4 LH infantile with clinical dysphasia |
| | | | | | | | | 4 LH juvenile with clinical dysphasia |
| | | | | | | | Weigl Sorting test Sentence Learning test Memory for Designs test | LHD: Impaired on Weigl Sorting and Sentence Learning, but not on Memory for Designs |
| | | | | | | | | RHD: Impaired on Weigl Sorting and Sentence Learning, but not on Memory for Designs |
| Basser (1962) | 48 LHD 54 RHD | No | 72 prespeech onset (34L, 38R) | NR | NSR | No | Clinical/observational | None of the RHD or LHD had dysphasia |
| | | | 30 postspeech (14 L, 16 R) | | | | | 8/48 LHD had stuttering or articulation problems |
| | | | | | | | | 8/48 LHD had reduced or nonexistent speech |
| | | | | | | | | 7/54 RHD had stuttering or articulation problems |
| | | | | | | | | 11/54 RHD had reduced or nonexistent speech |
| | | | | | | | | 34 prespeech onset LHD had delayed first word production |
| | | | | | | | | 38 prespeech onset RHD had delayed first word production |

| Study | Subjects | Handedness | Age | | | | Measure | Results |
|---|---|---|---|---|---|---|---|---|
| Alajouanine and Lhermitte (1965) | 32 LHD patients only | No | 6–15 yrs. | NR | NR | N/A | Clinical/observational | 32/32 had impaired expression (written, spoken, gestural)<br>7/32 exhibited paraphasias<br>10/32 had impaired comprehension<br>18/32 had alexia |
| Woods and Teuber (1978) | 31 RHD<br>34 LHD | No | LHD:<br>$X_O$ = 6;3 (1; 4–15; 2)<br>RHD:<br>$X_O$ = 7;2 (1; 9–14; 4) | NR | NR | No | Clinical/observational | 25/34 LHD had language disturbances post-onset<br>4/31 RHD had language disturbances post-onset (3 were premorbid left-handers) |
| Woods and Carey (1979) | 27 LHD patients only | No | Early LHD (before 1 yr.), $N$ = 11<br>Late LHD (after 1 yr.), $N$ = 16<br>$X_O$ = 5; 7 yrs. (1; 2–15; 1) | Early LHD:<br>$X_T$ = 17; 8 yrs.<br>Late LHD:<br>$X_T$ = 15; 8 yrs. | Early LHD:<br>2(−S), 9(+S)<br>Late LHD:<br>15(−S), 1(+S)<br>Comparison between +S and −S groups not made | N/A | Oldfield-Wingfield Picture Naming<br><br>Spelling<br><br>Rhymes (complete 6 nursery rhymes)<br><br>Sentence Completion (from the BDAE)<br><br>Relations Task (possible/not)<br><br>That-Clause syntax<br><br>Ask–Tell distinction<br><br>Token Test | Early LHD = controls<br>Late LHD < controls<br><br>Early LHD < controls<br>Late LHD < controls<br><br>Early LHD = controls<br>Late LHD = controls<br><br>Early LHD = controls<br>Late LHD < controls<br><br>Early LHD = controls<br>Late LHD < controls<br><br>Early LHD = controls<br>Late LHD < controls<br><br>Early LHD = controls<br>Late LHD = controls<br><br>Early LHD < controls<br>Late LHD < controls |
| Vargha-Khadem, O'Gorman, and Watters (1985) | 28 LHD<br>25 RHD | Some | 33 prenatal (< 2 mos) (16 RHD, 18 LHD)<br>11 early postnatal (2 mos. to 5 yrs.) (5 RHD, 6 LHD)<br>9 late postnatal (5–14 yrs.) (5 RHD, 4 LHD) | NR | At least < 2 yrs. post-onset | Yes | Token Test | RHD > LHD<br>All 3 RHD groups = controls<br>All 3 LHD groups < controls<br>Late postnatal LHD < prenatal and late RHD |

(continued)

TABLE 20.2 (Continued)

*Summary of data from studies of children with focal brain injury using various language assessment measures*

| Authors | Site | Neuro-imaging | Patients — Age of Onset | Patients — Age at Testing | Seizures | RHD vs. LHD | Tests Used | Results |
|---|---|---|---|---|---|---|---|---|
| Vargha-Khadem (cont.) | | | | | | | Oldfield-Wingfield Picture Naming | RHD > LHD<br>Prenatal RHD groups = controls<br>Early postnatal RHD = controls<br>Late postnatal RHD = controls<br>All 3 LHD groups < controls<br>Late postnatal LHD < all other groups |
| Aram et al. (1985) | 8 RHD<br>8 LHD | Yes | RHD:<br>$X_O$ = 1; 4 (2 mos. to 9; 0 yrs.)<br>LHD:<br>$X_O$ = 1; 6 (1 mo. to 6; 2 yrs.) | RHD:<br>$X_T$ = 3; 10 (1; 8–5; 10)<br>LHD:<br>$X_T$ = 4; 6 (2 mos. to 8; 2 yrs.) | None | No | PPVT<br>EOWPVT<br>Northwestern Syntax Screening Test (NSST)<br>Photo Articulation Test<br>Free speech: Mean length of utterance (MLU) in morphemes<br>Free speech: Developmental sentence scoring (DSS) | LHD < controls<br>RHD < controls<br>LHD < controls<br>RHD = controls<br>LHD < controls<br>RHD = controls<br>LHD = controls<br>RHD = controls<br>LHD < controls<br>RHD = controls<br>LHD < controls<br>RHD = controls |
| Aram, Ekelman, and Whitaker (1986) | 8 RHD<br>8 LHD | Yes | RHD:<br>$X_O$ = 1; 4 (2 mos. to 9; 0 yrs.)<br>LHD:<br>$X_O$ = 1; 6 (1 mo. to 6; 2 yrs.) | RHD:<br>$X_T$ = 3; 10 (1; 8–5; 10)<br>LHD:<br>$X_T$ = 4; s (2 mos. to 8; 2 yrs.) | None | No | Free speech: Mean length of utterance (MLU) in morphemes<br>Free speech: Developmental sentence scoring (DSS)<br>% of correctly produced sentences | LHD < controls<br>RHD = controls<br>LHD < controls<br>RHD < controls<br>LHD < controls<br>RHD < controls |

| Study | Subjects | | | | | | Test | Results |
|---|---|---|---|---|---|---|---|---|
| Riva et al. (1986) | 8 RHD<br>8 LHD | Yes | RHD:<br>$X_O$ = 4; 6<br>(1; 8–8; 3)<br><br>LHD:<br>$X_O$ = 6; 4<br>(0; 8–12; 8) | RHD:<br>$X_T$ = 10; 7<br><br>LHD:<br>$X_T$ = 11; 1 | No | 5 RHD(−S)<br>3 RHD(+S)<br><br>5 RHD(−S)<br>3 RHD(+S)<br><br>Comparison between<br>+S and −S<br>groups not made | PPVT | LHD < controls<br>RHD < controls |
| | | | | | | | Benton Sequence Repetition test | LHD < controls<br>RHD = controls |
| | | | | | | | Token Test | LHD < controls<br>RHD < controls |
| Aram et al. (1987) | 13 RHD<br>19 LHD | Yes | RHD:<br>$X_O$ = 2; 2<br>(PN−5; 4)<br><br>LHD:<br>$X_O$ = 5; 2<br>(PN−15; 11) | RHD:<br>$X_T$ = 7; 5<br>(5; 4–17; 3)<br><br>LHD:<br>$X_T$ = 10; 4<br>(6; 2–16; 5) | No | None | Word-Finding Test:<br>Requires child to access the name of the word in 3 cued conditions | |
| | | | | | | | Visual (from a line drawing) | Latency:<br>LH < controls<br>RH = controls<br><br>% Error<br>LH = controls<br>RH = controls |
| | | | | | | | Semantic (from a verbal description) | Latency:<br>LH < controls<br>RH = controls<br><br>% Error<br>LH = controls<br>RH = controls |
| | | | | | | | Rhyming (given a category and a rhyming word) | Latency:<br>LH = controls<br>RH < controls<br><br>% Error<br>LH < controls<br>RH = controls |
| | | | | | | | Rapid Automatized Naming Test:<br>Repeatedly name visually presented exemplars in 4 categories (objects, number, letters, colors) | LHD:<br>Objects < numbers & letters<br>Colors < number<br>RHD:<br>Objects < numbers & letters<br>Colors < number |

(continued)

TABLE 20.2 (*Continued*)

*Summary of data from studies of children with focal brain injury using various language assessment measures*

| Authors | Site | Patients — Neuro-imaging | Patients — Age of Onset | Patients — Age at Testing | Patients — Seizures | RHD vs. LHD | Tests Used | Results |
|---|---|---|---|---|---|---|---|---|
| Aram, Meyers, and Ekelman (1990) | 13 RHD 20 LHD | Yes | RHD: $X_O = 2; 2$ (PN–5; 3) LHD: $X_O = 4; 8$ (PN–15; 11) | RHD: $X_T = 7; 0$ (4; 7–17; 3) LHD: $X_T = 9; 10$ (3; 10–16; 5) | None | No | Free speech analysis of: Normal-type nonfluencies (whole-word & phrase repetitions, revisions/incomplete phrases, interjections, unfilled pauses, parenthetical remarks) | LHD = controls RHD = controls |
| | | | | | | | Stuttering-type nonfluencies (part-word repetitions, prolongations, tense pauses) | LHD < controls RHD = controls |
| | | | | | | | Speech rate (syllables/sec) | LHD < controls RHD = controls |
| Eisele and Aram (1993) | 12 RHD 21 LHD | Yes | RHD: $X_O = 1; 06$ (PN–9; 08) LHD: $X_O = 2; 03$ (PN–11; 07) | RHD: $X_T = 5; 08$ (2; 06–14; 07) LHD: $X_T = 7; 05$ (2; 07–14; 02) | None | Yes | PPVT | LHD < controls RHD < controls RHD < LHD |
| | | | | | | | EOWPVT | No significant differences between groups |
| Eisele and Aram (1994) | 9 RHD 16 LHD | Yes | RHD: $X_O = 2; 08$ (PN–9; 08) LHD: $X_O = 4; 05$ (PN–15; 11) | RHD: $X_T = 12; 11$ (9; 01–23; 01) LHD: $X_T = 14; 2$ (7; 02–22; 4) | None | No | Imitation of: Coordinate sentences Passive sentences Relative sentences | LHD < controls RHD < controls LHD: coordinates < passives < relatives RHD: passives < coordinates < relatives |
| | | | | | | | Comprehension of: Coordinate sentences Passive sentences Relative sentences | LHD = controls RHD = controls LHD: coordinates < passives = relatives RHD: passives < coordinates = relatives |

| Study | N | | Time post onset | Age | | Narrative | Measures | Results |
|---|---|---|---|---|---|---|---|---|
| Eisele and Aram (1994) (cont.) | | | | | | | | LHD: comprehension > production |
| | | | | | | | | RHD: comprehension = production |
| | | | | | | | | 7/16 LHD < controls on imitation only |
| | | | | | | | | 2/16 LHD of these were also < controls on both imitation and comprehension |
| | | | | | | | | 2/9 RHD < controls on comprehension only |
| | | | | | | | | 1/9 RHD < controls on imitation only |
| | | | | | | | | 1/9 RHD < controls on both imitation and comprehension |
| Reilly, Bates, and Marchman (1998) | 13 RHD 18 LHD | Yes | ≤ 6 mos. | RHD: $X_T = 6;6$ (4;1–9;1) LHD: $X_T = 6;4$ (3;7–9;4) Younger (<5 yrs.) (7 LHD, 4 RHD) Older (≥5 yrs.) (11 LHD, 9 RHD) | 1 (+S) | Yes | Narrative speech sample analyzed: Propositional length | RHD = LHD R/LHD < controls Older = younger |
| | | | | | | | Total word token/types | RHD = LHD R/LHD < controls Older = younger |
| | | | | | | | Type/token ration | RHD = LHD R/LHD = controls Older = younger |
| | | | | | | | Use of mental verbs or terms for mental state/motivation | RHD = LHD R/LHD = controls Older > younger |
| | | | | | | | Forms of reference (noun/pronoun ratio) | RHD = LHD R/LHD = controls Older = younger |
| | | | | | | | Use of complex, complete referring expressions (noun and antecedent within a sentence) | RHD = LHD R/LHD = controls Older > younger |
| | | | | | | | Proportion of morphological errors | RHD = LHD RHD < controls LHD controls Older > younger Younger + Temp < − Temp |

(continued)

TABLE 20.2 (Continued)

Summary of data from studies of children with focal brain injury using various language assessment measures

| Authors | Patients | | | | | RHD vs. LHD | Tests Used | Results |
|---------|----------|--|--|--|--|-------------|-----------|---------|
| | Site | Neuro-imaging | Age of Onset | Age at Testing | Seizures | | | |
| Reilly, Bates, and Marchman (1998) (cont.) | | | | | | | Proportion of syntactic complexity (coordinates, passives, relative clauses, sentences with adverbial clauses and/or verb complements) | Older > younger<br>RHD > LHD<br>Younger RHD > younger LHD<br>Younger RHD = controls<br>Younger LHD < controls<br>Older RHD = older LHD<br>Older LHD, RHD < controls |
| | | | | | | | Syntactic diversity | Older > younger<br>RHD > LHD<br>Younger RHD > younger LHD<br>Younger RHD = controls<br>Younger LHD = controls<br>Older RHD = older LHD<br>Older LHD, RHD < controls |
| | | | | | | | Proportion of pragmatic connectors | RHD = LHD<br>R/LHD = controls<br>Older = younger |
| | | | | | | | Inclusion of major story components (8) | RHD = LHD<br>R/LHD < controls<br>Older > younger |
| | | | | | | | If/how often theme of narrative is mentioned | RHD = LHD<br>R/LHD < controls<br>Older > younger |
| Bates et al. (1997) | 10 RHD 16 LHD | Yes | Under 6 mos. | 10–17 mos. | 7 RHD(−S)<br>3 RHD(+S)<br>14 LHD(−S)<br>2 LHD(+S) | Yes | MacArthur CDI word comprehension | LHD = RHD<br>LHD = controls<br>RHD < controls<br>R/LHD < controls |
| | 9 RHD 11 LHD | Yes | Under 6 mos. | 10–17 mos. | NSR | Yes | MacArthur CDI gesture | LHD > RHD<br>R/LHD < controls |
| | 10 RHD 16 LHD | Yes | Under 6 mos. | 10–17 mos. | 7 RHD(−S)<br>3 RHD(+S)<br>14 LHD(−S)<br>2 LHD(+S) | Yes | MacArthur CDI % of receptive vocabulary produced | LHD = RHD<br>R/LHD < controls<br>+LTemp < LTemp |

| | | | | | | | | |
|---|---|---|---|---|---|---|---|---|
| 12 RHD<br>17 LHD | Yes | Under 6 mos. | Yes | 19–31 mos. | 9 RHD(−S)<br>3 RHD(+S)<br>15 LHD(−S)<br>2 LHD(+S) | MacArthur CDI word production | Yes | LHD = RHD<br>R/LHD < controls<br>+LTemp < −LTemp<br>+Frontal < −Frontal |
| | | | | | | MacArthur CDI expressive grammar | | LHD = RHD<br>R/LHD < controls<br>+LTemp < −LTemp<br>+Frontal < −Frontal |
| 8 RHD<br>8 LHD | Yes | Under 6 mos. | Yes | 19–31 mos. | NSR | MacArthur CDI % function words | Yes | LHD < RHD<br>LHD = controls<br>RHD > controls |
| 6 RHD<br>24 LHD | Yes | Under 6 mos. | Yes | 20–44 mos. | 2 RHD(−S)<br>4 RHD(+S)<br>21 LHD(−S)<br>3 LHD(+S) | Free speech: Mean length of utterance in morphemes | Yes | LHD = RHD<br>R/LHD < controls<br>+LTemp < −LTemp |
| Bates, Vicari, and Trauner (1999) | | | | | | | | |
| 12 RHD<br>18 LHD | Yes | Under 6 mos. | Yes | 3–13 yrs. | None | Peabody Picture Vocabulary Test | Yes | R/LHD < controls<br>(R/LHD = controls with mental age controlled) |
| 12 RHD<br>10 LHD | Yes | Under 6 mos. | Yes | 3–13 yrs. | None | Boston Naming Test | Yes | R/LHD < controls<br>(R/LHD < controls with mental age controlled) |
| 15 RHD<br>19 LHD | Yes | Under 6 mos. | Yes | 3–13 yrs. | None | Semantic Fluency | Yes | R/LHD < controls<br>(R/LHD = controls with mental age controlled) |
| 8 RHD<br>9 LHD | Yes | Under 6 mos. | Yes | 5–13 yrs. | None | Token Test | Yes | R/LHD < controls<br>(R/LHD = controls with mental age controlled) |
| 5 RHD<br>9 LHD | Yes | Under 6 mos. | Yes | 4–8 yrs. | None | Test for Receptive Grammar (TROG) | Yes | LHD = RHD = controls |

RHD, right-hemisphere damage; LHD, left-hemisphere damage; PN, prenatal; +S patients suffering seizures; −S, patients with no seizure activity; +Temp, injury includes damage to the temporal lobe; −Temp, injury spares the temporal lobe; +Frontal, injury includes damage to the frontal lobe; −Frontal, injury spares the frontal lobe; NR, not reported; N/A, not applicable; $X_O$, mean age of onset (years; months); $X_T$, mean age of testing (years; months).

*Note:* < indicates worse performance regardless of the specific measure used; = indicates that groups did not differ significantly.

lesion onset. Note that Alajouanine and Lhermitte did not study RHD patients. Riva and colleagues (1986) found that while left-hemispherectomized children performed more poorly than right-hemispherectomized children on some grammatical comprehension tests, LHD and RHD children were equally impaired on mea~~sures of~~ vocabulary production and comprehension. Similar findings have been reported in a series of studies by Aram and colleagues (Aram et al., 1985; Aram, Ekelman, and Whitaker, 1986; Aram, Meyers, and Ekelman, 1990) and Eisele (Eisele and Aram, 1993, 1994, 1995). While Aram and colleagues (1985) and Eisele and Aram (1993) found that on measures of lexical competence, RHD and LHD children were both impaired relative to age-matched controls, it appeared that children with LHD performed worse than their normal controls on a number of other language measures, including tests of both grammatical comprehension and production, phonological discrimination tests, and tests of lexical fluency. By contrast, children with RHD showed no statistical difference from their own controls on nearly all such measures. However, later studies by the same research team reached a different conclusion. For example, Eisele and Aram (1994) reported no differences between LHD and RHD on a test on syntax comprehension, although several children from both groups performed at chance. Based on a detailed qualitative examination of lesion data (albeit without a statistical test), the authors concluded that subcortical involvement to either hemisphere may be the most important determiner of failure on this syntax task (Eisele and Aram, 1995).

A similar history can be traced in research by Vargha-Khadem and colleagues. For example, Vargha-Khadem, O'Gorman, and Watters (1985) reported that performance on grammatical comprehension tests was more impaired in children with LHD. However, as they added more cases to their sample, this difference disappeared (Vargha-Khadem, Isaacs, and Muter, 1994). It now appears from studies by this research group that seizure history is the most important predictor of language impairments in brain-injured children, regardless of side or size of injury or of the age at which the lesion was acquired.

Variations in the tests used to assess language (see tables 20.1 and 20.2) may be responsible for some of the discrepancies seen between studies. However, even when standardized tests of IQ are used, studies differ in factors like age of onset, subcortical involvement, and presence or absence of seizures. When IQ scores are broken down into verbal and nonverbal (performance) quotients, adult LHD patients typically have higher PIQ scores compared to their VIQ scores, whereas RHD

patients typically show the opposite pattern. The extent to which findings for children fit this pattern varies from study to study, due in part to methodological confounds.

In one study, Woods (1980) found that results for VIQ and PIQ depended both on side of lesion and on the age at which the lesion was acquired. He found that (1) children with LHD scored significantly below normal on both VIQ and PIQ, regardless of the age at which the lesion was acquired; (2) children with RHD also scored below normal on both subscales, but only if their lesions were acquired before one year of age; (3) if children with RHD acquired their lesions after the first year, they scored in the normal range for language but below normal on performance IQ. This complex nest of findings led Woods, Teuber, and colleagues to propose the "crowding" hypothesis: In an effort to salvage language in the presence of LHD, language functions are moved to the right hemisphere, where they interfere with the spatial tasks normally conducted in those areas of the brain.

Riva and colleagues (1986) also reported differential effects of age of onset and lesion side, but their results were virtually the opposite of Woods (1980). Children with early LHD were significantly lower than controls on both VIQ and PIQ, but only if their lesions occurred *before* one year of age; children with later lesions did not differ significantly from normal controls on either subscale. Children with RHD scored reliably below normal controls on PIQ, but *not* on VIQ, regardless of the age at which damage occurred. More recently, Ballantyne, Scarvie, and Trauner (1994) found that brain-injured children as a group performed below controls on all IQ subscales; VIQ was no worse than PIQ for LHD children, but VIQ was better than PIQ for RHD children. Note that none of these studies (Woods, 1980; Riva et al., 1986; Ballantyne et al., 1994) reports a direct statistical comparison of LHD and RHD.

Nass, Peterson, and Koch (1989) did conduct direct comparisons of children with congenital LHD and RHD, with surprising results: Children with LHD actually did *better* on VIQ than PIQ, and they also performed better than children with RHD on the verbal scale. Eisele and Aram (1993) also compared groups of brain-injured children directly. They found the adult pattern for PIQ (with RHD performing worse than both LHD and controls), but there were no effects of lesion side on VIQ (where LHD and RHD were both indistinguishable from controls). Vargha-Khadem (Vargha-Khadem et al., 1992) and Muter (Muter, Taylor, and Vargha-Khadem, 1997) found no differences between RHD and LHD groups on either VIQ or PIQ, although children with seizures were more impaired on both scales than children without seizures.

As we move out of the 1990s and into the next millennium, some of the confusion that has characterized research in this area has begun to lift. Most investigators now embrace a "third view" midway between equipotentiality and irreversible determinism, a bidirectional relationship between brain and behavioral development in which initial biases and subsequent reorganization are both acknowledged. This consensus is due in no small measure to methodological improvements, including the availability of imaging techniques to clarify the relationship between lesion type and language outcomes. But improved neural imaging is not the only relevant factor. Before reviewing a final set of studies in support of this emergentist view, let us consider several crucial methodological factors and their theoretical consequences: timing of lesion onset, lesion type (both site and size), lesion etiology, sample size, and the importance of prospective studies that employ developmentally sensitive measures.

*Intermezzo: Methodological confounds*

TIME OF LESION ONSET AND ITS IMPLICATIONS FOR PLASTICITY   There is now a large body of evidence demonstrating that the brains of young animals (especially mammals) are quite plastic, and that many aspects of cortical specialization are activity dependent. That is, cortical specialization is determined not by endogenous growth plans under direct genetic control but by the input that cortical areas receive from the animal's own body (before and after birth) and from the outside world (for reviews, see Kolb and Gibb, this volume; Elbert, Heim, and Rockstroh, this volume; see also Deacon, 1997; Elman et al., 1996; Johnson, 1997; Quartz and Sejnowski, 1994, 1997). It has been shown, for example, that if the cortex of a fetal ferret is rewired so that input from the eye is fed to auditory cortex, then auditory cortex takes on retinotopic maps (Pallas and Sur, 1993). And if slabs of fetal tissue are transplanted from visual to somatosensory areas (and vice versa), the transplanted cortex takes on representations appropriate to the input received in its new home, as opposed to the representations typically seen in their regions of origin (O'Leary and Stanfield, 1985, 1989; Stanfield and O'Leary, 1985). Lesion studies of animals also provide striking evidence for plastic reorganization. For example, Payne (1999) has shown that cats with early bilateral removal of primary visual cortex are virtually indistinguishable from normal on visual tasks, whereas mature cats with the same operation are functionally blind. Webster, Bachevalier, and Ungerleider (1995)

have shown that infant monkeys with bilateral removal of area TE (the ventral temporal areas that are the final way station of the "what is it?" visual system in mature animals) perform only slightly below unoperated controls on a task that measures memory for new visual objects, whereas mature animals with the same lesions display severe visual amnesia. The accumulated evidence strongly suggests that cortical specialization is (at least in part) driven by cortical input, and that new forms of organization can emerge following early brain injury. Based on this evidence, we should expect to find that early injuries in humans are followed by substantial reorganization, for language and other cognitive functions as well (Stiles et al., 1998).

This well-attested finding leads to a prediction that seems, at first glance, to be quite obvious: If plasticity is greater in the young brain, we ought to find a monotonic relationship between cognitive outcomes and age of lesion onset. Although the shape of this function might vary in a number of theoretically interesting ways (dropping sharply at some point in a nonlinear pattern, or decreasing gradually from birth to puberty), later lesions ought to produce worse outcomes than early ones under any scenario. In fact, the shape of the function governing loss of plasticity in humans is still entirely unknown, and it may not even be monotonic (i.e., plasticity may fall, and then rise again). Many of the studies summarized in tables 20.1 and 20.2 have conflated cases of congenital injury with lesions that were acquired at points later in childhood. Other studies have divided age of lesion onset into broad epochs, with mixed and often contradictory results. For example, Woods and Teuber (1978) concluded that injuries in the first year of life are actually more dangerous than injuries acquired after age 1, a finding that seems to fly in the face of accumulated evidence for early plasticity in animal models.

Even more puzzling findings come from Goodman and Yude (1996) and from unpublished data by Vargha-Khadem and colleagues (personal communication, July 1996, cited in Bates, Vicari, and Trauner, 1999). The latter two studies employed relatively large samples (by the standards of this field), and both revealed a result that would not be predicted either by the theory of equipotentiality or the theory of irreversible determinism: In the absence of severe seizures (which seem to preclude recovery to normal levels of language in most cases), the best outcomes in both verbal and nonverbal IQ are seen either with congenital lesions (pre- or perinatal) or with lesions that occur between 4 and 12 years of age! It is possible, of course, that this U-shaped function is an artifact of other methodological factors, including etiology (e.g., the medical conditions that lead to unilateral injury, including stroke, may be quite different in infants, preschool children, and children in the elementary school years) and the developmental status of the child when testing occurs (e.g., grade school children may have more sophisticated behavioral strategies at their disposal, permitting them to perform better on standardized tests in the short run, and to exploit their residual plasticity and recover to higher levels in the long run). It is also possible that this result would not replicate with even larger samples (e.g., according to Vargha-Khadem, personal communication June 1999, the significant U-shaped function reported for her unpublished data by Bates, Vicari, and Trauner, 1999, dropped below significance when the same was expanded to include more than 300 cases). For present purposes, we can only conclude that the limits of plasticity and capacity for recovery in young children are still unknown, and that there is ample reason for families of children with unilateral injury to be hopeful about their children's chances for recovery.

LESION TYPE: SITE AND SIZE    Earlier studies (including most of the studies reviewed in tables 20.1 and 20.2) were restricted to a global distinction between left- and right-hemisphere damage, often established via external neurological signs such as hemiparesis. More recent studies have taken advantage of structural brain imaging, and have begun to qualify the crude distinction between LHD and RHD with further distinctions revolving around lesion size, the presence/absence of subcortical damage, and the lobes of the damaged hemisphere that are involved. Nevertheless, the term "focal brain injury" is still defined quite broadly in most studies, referring to a single (contiguous) lesion restricted to one half of the brain, of any size, cortical and/or subcortical.

Variations in lesion size merit consideration, although evidence on the contribution of lesion size to language outcomes is still mixed. Lashley's *principle of mass action* (the complement of equipotentiality) predicts that larger lesions will have greater behavioral repercussions, with less chance for functional recovery. His experiments with adult rats supported this idea. However, when Irle (1990) carried out a meta-analysis of more than 200 lesion studies in monkeys, she found that while lesion size did affect skill reacquisition, the function was curvilinear: Midsized lesions were significantly more likely to cause permanent damage than were small or large lesions, the latter including lesions of up to 60% of total brain tissue. At first glance, this result is counterintuitive. But Irle suggests a compelling explanation, which she calls the "fresh-start" hypothesis: Small lesions have little effect because they are small;

midsize lesions are large enough to lead to permanent behavioral impairments, but not quite large enough to precipitate/cause the brain to reorganize; large lesions result in a better outcome because the animal makes a "fresh start," abandoning the inefficient strategies that an animal with a midsized lesion still struggles to apply. Preliminary evidence by Thal and colleagues appeared to provide support for the fresh-start hypothesis, reflected in a significant U-shaped effect of lesion size on early language outcomes (i.e., small lesions or very large lesions were both associated with better language abilities than those observed in children with lesions in the middle range). However, this U-shaped function dropped below significance when the sample size was doubled (Bates et al., 1997); hence the fresh-start hypothesis still awaits confirmation, and our understanding of the effects of lesion size on language outcomes is still very tenuous.

LESION ETIOLOGY AND ITS NEUROLOGICAL CORRELATES    The prospective studies reviewed below have concentrated entirely on children with congenital injuries (before 6 months postnatal age) that are usually due to pre- or perinatal stroke (although it is not always possible to make a definitive diagnosis of the cause or timing of congenital injuries). We should not be surprised to find that these studies yield different results from those that have included children with trauma or tumor (Anderson et al., 1999). Results may also differ from studies of children who suffered postnatal strokes secondary to cardiac catheterization (which is often associated with a lifetime of inadequate oxygen intake), and from studies of outcomes following hemispherectomy in children who have suffered for many years from intractable seizures. In fact, as Vargha-Khadem and her colleagues have recently reported (see also Ballantyne and Trauner, 1999), seizures are the single greatest risk factor for language and cognitive outcomes in children with unilateral brain injury. We also need to consider when the seizure condition appeared and its subsequent course. For example, Thal, Bates, and others found no effects of seizure history were found in prospective studies of early language development. However, such studies necessarily conflate relatively benign neonatal seizure conditions with more severe and persistent forms of epilepsy that may not appear for months or even years after birth.

SAMPLE SIZE    Sample size is a banal but potentially powerful factor to consider when evaluating studies with discrepant results. There are massive individual differences in the rate and nature of language development in perfectly normal children (Bates, Dale, and

Thal, 1995). Unilateral injuries are superimposed upon this landscape of variation, which means that single-case studies or small-sample studies must be interpreted with caution. Consider a recent report by Stark and McGregor (1997) on two cases of childhood hemispherectomy, one to the left and the other to the right hemisphere. These authors report an "adult-like" pattern: Selectively greater deficits for language in the case of LHD, compared with a more even profile of delay in the case of RHD, results interpreted to support a mild variant of innate/irreversible determinism. However, these two cases contrast sharply with Vargha-Khadem's case study of Alex, a child with severe LHD and intractable seizures who was virtually mute when he underwent hemispherectomy at 8 years of age (Vargha-Khadem et al., 1997). After an initial delay, Alex went on to attain fluent control over language (with no articulatory problems or specific delays in grammar) commensurate with his mental age. Although case studies can be quite informative in showing us the range of outcomes that are *possible* following various forms of unilateral injury, they should not be used as the basis for generalizations about the correlation between various forms of injury and their linguistic sequelae.

DEVELOPMENTAL SENSITIVITY AND TIMING OF LANGUAGE TESTING   Two related factors are at issue here. First, the amount of time that has elapsed since lesion onset may influence how "recovered" a child appears during testing. That is, when children are tested in the middle school years or beyond, those who suffered their lesions earlier in life have also had more time to reorganize and recover. Second, there may be specific effects of lesion type that are evident only in particular phases of development, when children start to come to terms with the demands of a new language task. For both these reasons, studies that focus on the early stages of language may yield qualitative information about the initial state of the system, and about the processes involved in plastic reorganization of language and other cognitive functions.

Most of the studies summarized in tables 20.1 and 20.2 have been *retrospective* in nature, testing children well after the period in which language is usually acquired and (we presume) after much of the recovery for which this population is so famous has already occurred. For the remainder of this chapter, we will concentrate on developmental studies of children with focal brain injury that take the children's level of development into account, tracking change over time using age- and stage-appropriate language outcome measures. In particular, we will focus on *prospective studies* of children with congenital injuries to one side of the

brain, relying primarily on studies by the San Diego group and their collaborators.

## Phase III: The emergentist view

All of the studies considered here involve children with congenital injuries (prior to 6 months of postnatal age), producing a single contiguous lesion (though often very large) confined to one side of the brain. These lesions are due primarily to pre- or perinatal stroke and have, in all cases, been confirmed by CT or MRI. Children were excluded if the lesion was due to tumor, trauma, arteriovenal malformation, or any form of diffuse or multifocal brain damage, or if they suffered from any serious medical conditions (other than seizures subsequent to the lesion itself). All children come from families in which the predominant language is English, and although they represent a broad socioeconomic spectrum, children of middle-class parents tend to predominate (as they do in much of the behavioral literature in developmental psychology).

The San Diego group and their collaborators have conducted cross-sectional and longitudinal studies of this clinical group for approximately 15 years, focusing on many aspects of development including visual-spatial cognition, attention and hemispatial neglect, and perception and production of facial and vocal affect. We will concentrate here on studies of speech and language. (For reviews of development in other domains, see Stiles, this volume; also see Stiles, 1995; Stiles et al., 1998. For more detailed reviews of language development in this population, see Bates et al., in press; Bates, Vicari, and Trauner, 1999; Broman and Fletcher, 1999; Elman et al., 1996.)

We will start with results of cross-sectional studies that focus on development after 5 years of age, which largely confirm results of other large-sample studies of language outcomes in this population. Then we will end with studies that have examined the acquisition of language in this population, starting in the first year of life. These studies demonstrate that side- and site-specific biases are present early in life; although the lesion–symptom correlations observed in these studies do not map directly onto the patterns observed in adults, different lesions have different effects on early language learning that must be overcome. The fact that they are overcome (disappearing entirely by 5–7 years of age in the domain of language) provides powerful evidence for the plastic and experience-dependent nature of brain and behavioral development. Furthermore, the evidence suggests that language learning itself is the catalyst for this reorganization.

Starting with studies of language outcomes at later stages of development, Bates, Vicari, and Trauner (1999) summarize performance by 43 English-speaking children from the San Diego sample (28 LHD and 15 RHD) and 33 Italian-speaking children (18 LHD and 15 RHD) from Rome, tested cross-sectionally between 3 and 14 years of age. Mean full-scale IQs were in the low-normal range (94–97), although the range was quite broad (from 40 to 140). There were also more cases in the below-80 range (which some investigators use as a cut-off for mild mental retardation) than we would expect if we were drawing randomly from the normal population. However, there were absolutely no differences between LHD and RHD children in full-scale, verbal or nonverbal IQ. For the Italian sample, Bates and colleagues also summarize performance on several language tests, including lexical comprehension (an Italian version of the Peabody Picture Vocabulary Test), lexical production (an Italian adaptation of the Boston Naming Test), grammatical comprehension (the Token Test and an Italian version of the Test of Receptive Grammar), and semantic category fluency. Again, although brain-injured children performed significantly below normal controls on all language measures except the TROG, there was no evidence for a difference between LHD and RHD on any measure. Furthermore, when mental age was controlled in analyses of covariance, the difference between brain-injured children and normal controls disappeared for every measure except the Boston Naming Test.

These cross-sectional results suggest that the plastic reorganization for which this population is known takes place prior to 5–7 years of age. As a result, children with early focal brain injury recover far better (relative to age-matched controls) than do adults with comparable injuries. Although this conclusion has been around for quite a while, and there is a large body of evidence on plasticity from animal research to support it, adults and children have rarely been compared directly on a common set of measures. More direct comparisons would be helpful in assessing the nature and magnitude of this presumed plasticity. We are aware of just three studies (all by the San Diego group and their collaborators) that have compared school-age children and adults directly on the same measures (other than verbal and nonverbal IQ), using z-scores based on data from age-matched controls.

The first study in this series, by Kempler and colleagues (1999), compared adults with RHD and LHD to a sample of 6–12-year-old children who had suffered comparable injuries (also due to cerebrovascular accidents, or CVA) during the pre/perinatal period. Child and adult patients with LHD versus RHD were com-pared directly in an age-by-side-of-lesion design, using age-based z-scores derived from relatively large samples of age-matched controls on the van Lancker and Kempler Familiar Phrases Test. As can be seen in figure 20.1, RHD and LHD adult patients display a double dissociation on this task. LHD patients have more difficulty on familiar phrases, whereas patients with RHD are significantly worse on idioms or familiar phrases matched for length and complexity. As figure 20.1 also shows, child patients displayed absolutely no evidence for a double dissociation: Children with LHD versus RHD both performed significantly below normal controls as a group, but did not differ significantly from each other. Even more important, the child patients performed within the low-normal range on both measures, while the adult patients performed many standard deviations below their age-matched controls on their weakest measure (i.e., novel phrases for patients with LHD; familiar phrases for patients with RHD). In other words, the children were not significantly impaired (i.e., their performance did not reach criteria required to establish the existence of a language deficit) following either right- or left-hemisphere damage, and no selective effects of lesion side were detected.

The second study, by Dick and colleagues (1999), compared performance by children and adults with unilateral brain injury and their age-matched controls in an on-line auditory sentence comprehension test that contrasts syntactically simple sentences (active and subject clefts that follow canonical word order) with syntactically complex sentences (passives and object clefts that violate canonical word order). All sentences were fully grammatical, and semantically reversible. All groups (including normal controls) displayed the same basic profile of lower accuracy on noncanonical sen-

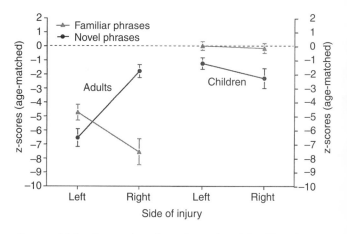

FIGURE 20.1   Comprehension of novel and familiar phrases by children and adults with left versus right hemisphere injury.

tences (object clefts and passives). Among the children, group by sentence type interactions were obtained indicating that (1) the youngest normal children were at a greater disadvantage than older children on the more difficult noncanonical sentence types; (2) as a group, brain-injured children showed a greater disadvantage on the difficult sentences than their age-matched controls; however, (3) the brain-injured children were still within the normal range for their age; and, most important for our purposes here, (4) there were no significant differences between children with LHD and children with RHD on any of the sentence types. In contrast with these findings for children, adults with unilateral brain injury were severely impaired, especially on the noncanonical sentences. Direct comparisons of adults and children with LHD clearly demonstrate that LHD is associated with receptive agrammatism in adults but not in children.

The third study in this series focused on language production instead of comprehension, based on samples of free speech (Bates et al., 1999) collected within the framework of a biographical interview tailored to reflect the different interests of children and adults. Participants included 38 brain-injured children (24 LHD, 14 RHD) between 5 and 8 years of age, 38 normal controls matched for age and gender, 14 adults with LHD (including 3 Broca's aphasics, 3 Wernicke's aphasics, 5 anomic aphasics, and 3 nonaphasic patients), 7 adults with RHD, and 12 adult controls in the same range of age and education. The structured interviews were videotaped and transcribed following conventions of the Child Language Data Exchange System, and coded into various categories assessing amount of speech (number of word types, word tokens, morphemes, and utterances), length (mean length of utterance in morphemes, or MLU), grammatical complexity (number of complex syntactic structures, in both types and tokens), and errors (word omissions, morphological errors, lexical errors). Although it was generally true that children talk far less than adults (including adult aphasics), when proportion scores were used to correct for overall amount of output, results were exceedingly clear: (1) There were absolutely no differences between children with LHD versus RHD on any measure. (2) In this open-ended free-speech task, there were also very few differences between brain-injured children (combining LHD and RHD) and their controls (the exceptions were small but significant disadvantages for FL children as a group in number of word omission errors and in number of word types). (3) In striking contrast to the child data, there were huge differences between adults with LHD versus RHD on virtually every measure, in the predicted directions. (4) LHD adults also showed

qualitative variations in their symptoms, reflecting different aphasia subtypes (e.g., more morphological and omission errors in Broca's aphasics, more lexical errors in Wernicke's aphasics). One small illustration of these results can be seen in figure 20.2a, which plots the total number of errors per proposition in children versus adults within each lesion group, and figure 20.2b, which plots the same data for LHD and RHD children and adults in z-scores based on performance by age-appropriate controls. Figure 20.2a shows that error rates are certainly higher for children than adults (as we have known for many years), but figure 20.2b shows that LHD and RHD children are very close to normal (with z-scores close to zero) while the worst aphasics produce error rates that are orders of magnitude higher than normal controls (whose error rate is extremely small, leading to very small standard deviations). Although these results are not surprising, in view of the accumulated evidence for plasticity following early brain injury in humans and in other species, they document this phenomenon with exceptional clarity.

This brings us to a summary of evidence by the same research group looking at the first stages of language development, prior to 5–7 years of age.

In a study focusing on the earliest stages of language development, Thal and colleagues (1991) describe results for 27 congenitally brain-damaged infants between 12 and 35 months of age, using an early version of the MacArthur Communicative Development Inventories, or CDI (Fenson et al., 1993), a parent-report instrument for the assessment of early lexical and grammatical development. Delays in word comprehension in the very first stages of development were actually more common in children with RHD. Delays in first word production occurred for almost all the brain-injured children, regardless of lesion side or site, but tended to be more severe in children with left posterior damage—an apparent reversal of the expected association between comprehension deficits and damage to Wernicke's area.

Bates and colleagues (1997) followed up on Thal and colleagues (1991) with a larger sample, using a combination of CDI data and free speech to assess early language development in 53 children between 10 and 40 months of age (36 LHD, 17 RHD), including 18 of the 27 cases from Thal's study. The study was divided into three cross-sectional epochs (although many of the children participated in more than one): a period focusing on the dawn of word comprehension, word production, and gesture (26 children from 10 to 17 months); a second substudy focusing on word production and the emergence of grammar (29 children from 19 to 31 months); and an analysis of grammatical development

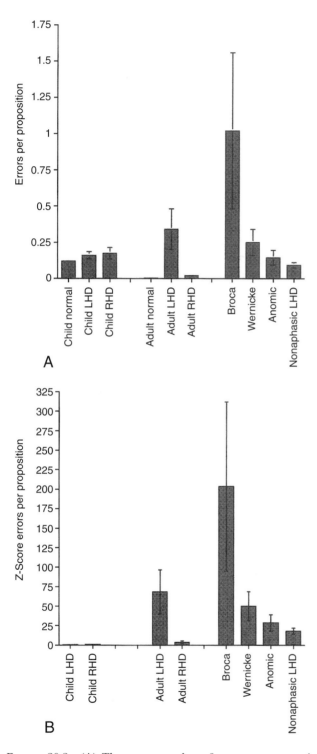

A

B

FIGURE 20.2 (**A**) The mean number of errors per proposition for normally developing children, adult controls, and children and adults with right or left hemisphere damage. LHD patients are further subdivided by aphasia type. (**B**) Z-score error rates per proposition for children versus adults with right or left hemisphere damage. LHD patients are further subdivided by aphasia type.

from free-speech samples (30 children from 20 to 44 months). Performance at these various stages of development was evaluated in comparisons based on lesion side, size, and site (i.e., whether or not the frontal lobes or temporal lobes were involved). There were no effects of lesion size in any of these analyses (including a failure to replicate the U-shaped effect of lesion size described by Thal and colleagues). Interesting effects of lesion side and intrahemispheric lesion site did emerge, but in complex patterns that are surprising from the point of view of the adult aphasia literature.

Between 10 and 17 months, delays in receptive language were particularly evident in children with RHD (i.e., more RHD cases than we would expect by chance fell into bottom tenth percentile for word comprehension). By contrast, the LHD children performed within the normal range on word comprehension, even if their lesions involved the temporal lobe (the presumed site of Wernicke's area, which is implicated in moderate to severe forms of receptive aphasia in adults). However, there was no significant difference between LHD and RHD on direct statistical comparisons, so the RHD disadvantage is not robust and should be investigated further. There was also a significant RHD disadvantage in the development of communicative and symbolic gesture, and this time the RHD disadvantage did reach significance in a direct LHD/RHD comparison. This result is also surprising, since deficits in the production of symbolic gestures are atypically associated with left-hemisphere damage when they occur in adults (Goodglass, 1993). Finally, Bates and colleagues do report a selective delay in expressive vocabulary for children with LHD. However, in line with the earlier report by Thal and colleagues, this disadvantage was only evident in children whose lesions involved the temporal lobe.

The second substudy followed children's language development between 19 and 31 months, when the so-called vocabulary burst is said to occur (e.g., an intense period of development for vocabulary/lexical production) and when children's comprehension is often so vast it is difficult to measure. This is also the period in which children typically start to combine words, followed by the emergence of grammatical inflections and function words. For the 29 children whose scores on this scale were obtained, a selective disadvantage for children with LHD appeared both for expressive vocabulary and the emergence of grammar (with no evidence whatsoever for a dissociation between grammatical and lexical production). However, this LHD disadvantage was due once again to children with left temporal involvement, in contrast with the typical adult pattern in which expressive deficits (especially nonfluent aphasia) are usually associated with left frontal involvement (i.e.,

Broca's area and adjacent cortical and subcortical regions). Similar delays in expressive vocabulary and grammar appeared when children with frontal lobe involvement were compared with children whose lesions spared the frontal lobe. However, in contrast with the asymmetric left temporal disadvantage that we have just discussed, this frontal effect was perfectly symmetric: Delays were equally severe with left frontal or right frontal lesions.

Curiously, an abnormal proportion of the children with RHD were also producing a higher than normal number of function words for their vocabulary size. As described in some detail by Bates, Bretherton, and Snyder (1988) and by Bates and colleagues (1994), such overuse of function words for children in the early stages of vocabulary development (i.e., under 400 words) is definitely *not* a sign of precocious grammar. In fact, children who overuse pronouns and other function words in the early stages tend to be relatively slow in grammatical development later on. For these children, function words tend to appear in frozen or rote expressions like "I wan dat," a style of early expressive language that has been called "pronominal style," or "holistic style." At the opposite end of the continuum are children who avoid function words in their first word combinations, producing telegraphic utterances like "Adam truck" or "Mommy sock". This style of early expressive language has been referred to as "nominal style" or "analytic style." Given the terms "holistic" and "analytic," which are often attributed to right- versus left-hemisphere processing, respectively, one might have predicted that holistic style would be more common in children with LHD (who are presumably relying more on holistic right-hemisphere processes to acquire language). This prediction is roundly contradicted by the Bates study, in which holistic style was robustly associated with RHD (indicating that the overproduction of function words in early speech reflects reliance on the intact left hemisphere). Bates and colleagues (1997) suggest that children with RHD are relying heavily on the more precise acoustic analysis and/or greater acoustic memory available in the left hemisphere, storing up frozen expressions that they are unable to segment or understand beyond a relatively superficial level of analysis (rather like an American who says "Gesundheit" when someone sneezes, with no idea regarding the structure or meaning of that word in German). This would mean, in turn, that right-hemisphere processes are very important in the early stages of language learning for the breakdown of acoustic material and its integration into a larger cognitive system. However, once the material has been analyzed, understood, and integrated into a larger framework, the contribution of the right hemisphere may be much less important, so that control may shift (in the undamaged brain) to rapid, automatic processes mediated primarily by the left hemisphere.

In the third and final subgroup of children, Bates and colleagues (1997) collected free-speech samples between 21 and 44 months of age. As their CDI scores predicted, the MLU scores of children with damage that encompassed the left temporal region of their brain were significantly lower than normal, and significantly lower than scores for brain-injured children whose lesions spared this region (including all children with RHD and the subset of LHD children with no temporal involvement). Children with right or left frontal damage also still looked delayed, but this difference was not statistically significant in the 21–44-month subsample.

Vicari and colleagues (in press) attempted a partial replication of the Bates results for early lexical development, administering an Italian version of the MacArthur CDI to the parents of 43 children between 13 and 46 months of age. Their study differed from the methods used by Bates in two crucial respects: Children beyond the age range covered by the MacArthur CDI were included in the study (which means that they could not use age-based percentile scores), and parents were given the Infant or the Toddler version of the MacArthur based not on age but on their child's current level of linguistic ability (children who were still in the one-word stage were assigned the Infant form, but children who were starting to combine words were assigned the Toddler form). For these reasons, the studies are not entirely comparable, but results replicate and extend Bates's findings in some interesting directions. First, Vicari and colleagues also report a massive across-the-board delay in early vocabulary development for brain-injured children as a group. Hence, even though the long-term prospects for these children are relatively good, it is obviously hard to get language off the ground when significant damage has occurred to either hemisphere. Second, Vicari and colleagues report a large and significant interaction between side of lesion (LHD versus RHD) and stage of language development (single word versus multiword). Among children who were still in the one-word stage, LHD were significantly slower in vocabulary development than RHD (because 10 out of 12 of the one-word-stage children with LHD had temporal lobe involvement, a specific replication of Bates's left temporal findings was not possible). By contrast, among children who were now in the multiword stage, the LHD disadvantage had disappeared entirely. In fact, LHD children in the multiword group had a numerical advantage over their RHD counterparts. This advantage was not statistically significant, but it contributed to the robust interaction between language stage and lesion side. Vicari and colleagues suggest that recovery from this initial delay may begin very early for some children, and may be forced in part by the delay itself. That is, children who are particularly disadvantaged in the first stages of language acquisition (e.g., LHD cases) may be forced to abandon a failing strategy in favor of some alternative approach, leading to earlier and (ultimately) more successful language learning.

Reilly, Bates, and Marchman (1998) conducted a cross-sectional study of 15 RHD and 15 LHD children, between 3 and 12 years of age, using a story-telling format (the well-known Frog Story narratives—Berman and Slobin, 1994) to assess lexical, grammatical, and discourse development. For children between 3 and 6 years of age, the now-familiar left temporal disadvantage was observed in syntactic complexity and in persistence of morphological errors. However, this effect of lesion site was not observed in children between 6 and 12 years of age. Among the older children, there were still significant differences between focal lesion children (LHD and RHD combined) and their age-matched controls on a number of measures, but the focal lesion children were nevertheless performing within the normal or low-normal range. Hence the Reilly results for grammar suggest a later variant of the recovery pattern that Vicari's group observed within the lexical domain.

Because the Reilly and Vicari studies are both cross-sectional, it would be very useful to replicate these results with longitudinal samples. Although their results are still preliminary, based on a relatively small sample, Reilly and colleagues (Losh, Reilly, and Bates, 1996) have tested a longitudinal subgroup across the 5–7-year age range, which seemed to be a watershed in their cross-sectional study. They report that children with left temporal involvement do indeed move sharply upward in syntax and morphology across this age range, scoring numerically above children with RHD at the later time point. The general picture seems to be one in which children with LHD display sharper or "steeper" growth functions, while children with RHD show a flatter profile of growth in the language domain.

*Conclusions*

Putting these lines of evidence together, we may conclude (or perhaps hypothesize) that the infant brain contains strong biases that, in the absence of early brain damage, guarantee the eventual emergence of left-hemisphere specialization for language. Although (if anything) the right hemisphere seems to play a more important (or at least equally important) role in the emergence of word comprehension and communicative gesture, progress in expressive language (both lexical and grammatical) seems to be delayed with frontal damage (to either side of the brain) and with temporal damage (but in this case, temporal damage restricted to the left hemisphere). In other words, there is an early bias that predisposes the left hemisphere to "take over" rapid and efficient production of words and sentences, a development that may also result in the emergence of left-hemisphere specialization for many aspects of receptive language as well. In the absence of evidence to the contrary, one might have assumed that this early left-hemisphere advantage for speech/language production (but not reception) has a motor base. And yet several studies by the San Diego group suggest that the source of this left-hemisphere bias lies primarily within the temporal lobe, a region that is supposed to be specialized for perception rather than production.

In this regard, Bates and colleagues note that some children with severe otitis media (i.e., middle-ear infections) also show selective delays in the emergence of expressive (but not receptive) language. Why would middle-ear impedance have greater effects on language production than on comprehension? The answer may lie in a simple fact: Language learning is not the same thing as fluent language use. When a child is trying to break into the language system for the first time, the amount of perceptual analysis required to produce her own versions of a new word is greater than the amount of perceptual analysis that she needs to recognize the word (especially if she is asked to recognize that word in a richly supportive social and physical context, which can be integrated with the acoustic signal to achieve comprehension). If these assumptions are correct, we can put the story together as follows: Left temporal regions may be particularly well suited (perhaps at or before birth) for the extraction of perceptual detail. Indeed, there is ample evidence from visual-spatial processing in adults to support this view; hence the hypothesized "perceptual detail advantage" would not be specific to language, or even to audition. However, such a bias would be particularly relevant in the first stages of language learning, leading (in the absence of injury) to the establishment of left-hemisphere dominance. What these prospective studies do clearly show is that this bias is "soft," and can be overcome. Indeed, by 5–7 years of age the initial disadvantages associated with left-hemisphere damage seem to have disappeared, or at least fallen below the levels detectable with the measures that we have developed so far.

Finally, it appears from these studies that the emergence of organization for language (in the undamaged brain) and reorganization for language (in the damaged brain struggling to overcome initial biases) both occur within the period in which language is acquired, i.e., somewhere between birth and 5 years of age. We may speculate that this correlation between brain and behavioral development is no accident. In fact, we propose that learning itself plays a major role in organizing the brain for efficient language use, as children struggle to find an optimal solution to the challenges associated with language and communication.

## REFERENCES

ALAJOUANINE, T., and F. LHERMITTE, 1965. Acquired aphasia in children. *Brain* 88:653–662.

ANDERSON, S. W., A. BECHARA, H. DAMASIO, D. TRANEL, and A. R. DAMASIO, 1999. Impairment of social and moral behavior related to early damage to human prefrontal cortex. *Nature Neurosci.* 2:1032–1037.

ARAM, D. M., B. EKELMAN, D. ROSE, and H. WHITAKER, 1985. Verbal and cognitive sequelae following unilateral lesions acquired in early childhood. *J. Clin. Exp. Neuropsychol.* 7:55–78.

ARAM, D., B. EKELMAN, and H. WHITAKER, 1986. Spoken syntax in children with acquired unilateral hemisphere lesions. *Brain Lang.* 27:75–100.

ARAM, D. M., B. EKELMAN, and H. WHITAKER, 1987. Lexical retrieval in left and right brain-lesioned children. *Brain Lang.* 31:67–87.

ARAM, D. M., S. C. MEYERS, and B. L. EKELMAN, 1990. Fluency of conversational speech in children with unilateral brain lesions. *Brain Lang.* 38:105–121.

BALLANTYNE, A. O., K. M. SCARVIE, and D. TRAUNER, 1994. Verbal and performance IQ patterns in children after perinatal stroke. *Dev. Psychol.* 10:39–50.

BALLANTYNE, A. O., and D. A. TRAUNER, 1999. Neuropsychological profiles of infants and children with early focal brain damage. *JINS* 5:145.

BASSER, L., 1962. Hemiplegia of early onset and the faculty of speech with special reference to the effects of hemispherectomy. *Brain* 85:427–460.

BATES, E., 1999. Plasticity, localization and language development. In *The Changing Nervous System: Neurobehavioral Consequences of Early Brain Disorders,* S. Broman and J. M. Fletcher, eds. New York: Oxford University Press, pp. 214–253.

BATES, E., in press. On the nature and nurture of language. In *Frontiere della Biologia [Frontiers of Biology]. The brain of homo sapiens,* R. Levi-Montalcini, D. Baltimore, R. Dulbecco, and F. Jacob, series eds.; E. Bizzi, P. Calissano, and V. Volterra, vol. eds. Rome: Giovanni Trecanni.

BATES, E., I. BRETHERTON, and L. SNYDER, 1988. *From First Words to Grammar: Individual Differences and Dissociable Mechanisms.* New York: Cambridge University Press.

BATES, E., P. S. DALE, and D. THAL, 1995. Individual differences and their implications for theories of language development. In *Handbook of Child Language,* P. Fletcher and B. MacWhinney, eds. Oxford, UK: Basil Blackwell, pp. 96–151.

BATES, E., V. MARCHMAN, D. THAL, L. FENSON, P. S. DALE, J. S. REZNICK, J. REILLY, and J. HARTUNG, 1994. Developmental and stylistic variation in the composition of early vocabulary. *J. Child Lang.* 21:85–123.

BATES, E., D. THAL, B. L. FINLAY, and B. CLANCY, in press. Early language development and its neural correlates. In *Handbook of Neuropsychology, Vol. 7: Child Neurology,* 2nd ed., F. Boller and J. Grafman, series eds.; I. Rapin and S. Segalowitz, vol. eds. Amsterdam: Elsevier.

BATES, E., D. THAL, D. TRAUNER, J. FENSON, D. ARAM, J. EISELE, and R. NASS, 1997. From first words to grammar in children with focal brain injury. *Dev. Neuropsychol.* 13:447–476.

BATES, E., S. VICARI, and D. TRAUNER, 1999. Neural mediation of language development: Perspectives from lesion studies of infants and children. In *Neurodevelopmental Disorders,* H. Tager-Flusberg, ed. Cambridge, Mass.: MIT Press, pp. 533–581.

BATES, E., B. WULFECK, M. OPIE, J. FENSON, S. KRIZ, J. REILLY, N. DRONKERS, L. MILLER, R. JEFFRIES, and K. HERBST, 1999. Comparing free speech in children and adults with left- vs. right-hemisphere injury (Abstract). *Brain Lang.* 69:377–379.

BERMAN, R. A., and D. I. SLOBIN, 1994. *Relating Events in Narrative: A Cross-linguistic Developmental Study* [in collaboration with Ayhan Aksu-Koc et al.]. Hillsdale, N.J.: Erlbaum.

BERNHARDT, M., 1897. Die Erkrankungen der peripherischen Nerven [Peripheral nerve diseases]. In *Spezielle Pathologie und Therapie 9* [Specific Pathology and Therapy 9], H. Nothnagel, ed. Vienna: Alfred Holder.

BOTHA, R. P., 1989. *Challenging Chomsky: The Generative Garden Game.* Oxford, UK: Basil Blackwell.

BROMAN, S., and J. M. FLETCHER, eds., 1999. *The Changing Nervous System: Neurobehavioral Consequences of Early Brain Disorders.* New York: Oxford University Press.

BROWN, C. M., and P. HAGOORT, eds., 1999. *The Neurocognition of Language.* New York: Oxford University Press.

CLARUS, A., 1874. Ueber Aphasie bei Kindern [Aphasia in children]. *Jahresb. Kinderheilkd.* 7:369–400.

COTARD, J., 1868. *Etude sur l'atrophie partielle du cerveau.* Thèse de Paris.

CURTISS, S., 1977. *Genie: A Psycholinguistic Study of a Modern-Day Wild Child.* New York: Academic Press.

DEACON, T., 1997. *The Symbolic Species: The Co-evolution of Language and the Brain.* New York: Norton.

DENNIS, M., 1980. Capacity and strategy for syntactic comprehension after left or right hemidecortication. *Brain Lang.* 10:287–317.

DENNIS, M., and B. KOHN, 1975. Comprehension of syntax in infantile hemiplegics after cerebral hemidecortication. *Brain Lang.* 2:472–482.

DENNIS, M., M. LOVETT, and C. A. WIEGEL-CRUMP, 1981. Written language acquisition after left or right hemidecortication in infancy. *Brain Lang.* 12:54–91.

DENNIS, M., and H. A. WHITAKER, 1976. Language acquisition following hemidecortication: Linguistic superiority of the left over the right hemisphere. *Brain Lang.* 3:404–433.

DENNIS, M., and H. WHITAKER, 1977. Hemispheric equipotentiality and language acquisition. In *Language Development and Neurological theory,* S. J. Segalowitz and F. A. Gruber, eds. New York: Academic Press, pp. 93–106.

DICK, F., B. WULFECK, E. BATES, D. SALTZMAN, N. NAUCLER, and N. DRONKERS, 1999. Interpretation of complex syntax in aphasic adults and children with focal lesions or specific language impairment (Abstract). *Brain Lang.* 69:335–336.

EISELE, J., and D. ARAM, 1993. Differential effects of early hemisphere damage on lexical comprehension and production. *Aphasiology* 7:513–523.

EISELE, J., and D. ARAM, 1994. Comprehension and imitation of syntax following early hemisphere damage. *Brain Lang.* 46:212–231.

EISELE, J., and D. ARAM, 1995. Lexical and grammatical development in children with early hemisphere damage: A cross-sectional view from birth to adolescence. In *The Handbook of Child Language*, P. Fletcher and B. MacWhinney, eds. Oxford, UK: Basil Blackwell, pp. 664–689.

ELMAN, J. L., E. BATES, M. JOHNSON, A. KARMILOFF-SMITH, D. PARISI, and K. PLUNKETT, 1996. *Rethinking Innateness: A Connectionist Perspective on Development.* Cambridge, Mass.: MIT Press.

FENSON, L., P. S. DALE, J. S. REZNICK, D. THAL, E. BATES, J. HARTUNG, S. PETHICK, and J. REILLY, 1993. *The MacArthur Communicative Development Inventories: User's Guide and Technical Manual.* San Diego: Singular Publishing Group.

FLETCHER, P., and B. MACWHINNEY, eds., 1995. *Handbook of Child Language.* Oxford, UK: Basil Blackwell.

FODOR, J. A., 1983. *The Modularity of Mind: An Essay on Faculty Psychology.* Cambridge, Mass.: MIT Press.

GAZZANIGA, M. S., and R. W. SPERRY, 1967. Language after section of the cerebral commissures. *Brain* 90:131–148.

GESCHWIND, N., and E. KAPLAN, 1962. A human cerebral deconnection syndrome. *Neurology* 12:675–685.

GOODGLASS, H., 1993. *Understanding Aphasia.* San Diego: Academic Press.

GOODMAN, R., and C. YUDE, 1996. IQ and its predictors in childhood hemiplegia. *Dev. Med. Child Neurol.* 38:881–890.

GOPNIK, M., 1990. Feature-blind grammar and dysphasia. *Nature* 344(6268):715.

GOPNIK, M., and M. B. CRAGO, 1991. Familial aggregation of a developmental language disorder. *Cognition* 39:1–50.

IRLE, E., 1990. An analysis of the correlation of lesion size, localization and behavioral effects in 283 published studies of cortical and subcortical lesions in old-world monkeys. *Brain Res. Rev.* 15:181–213.

JOHNSON, M. H., 1997. *Developmental Cognitive Neuroscience: An Introduction.* Cambridge, Mass.: Blackwell Publishers.

KEMPLER, D., D. VAN LANCKER, V. MARCHMAN, and E. BATES, 1999. Idiom comprehension in children and adults with unilateral brain damage. *Dev. Neuropsychol.* 15:327–349.

LASHLEY, K. S., 1950. In search of the engram. In *Symposia of the Society for Experimental Biology. No. 4: Physiological Mechanisms and Animal Behaviour.* New York: Academic Press, pp. 454–482.

LENNEBERG, E. H., 1967. *Biological Foundations of Language.* New York: Wiley.

LEVY, J., R. D. NEBES, and R. W. SPERRY, 1971. Expressive language in the surgically separated minor hemisphere. *Cortex* 7:49–58.

LOSH, M., J. S. REILLY, and E. BATES, 1996. *Language development: Neural plasticity in children with early focal brain injury.* Poster session presented at the 8th Annual Meeting of the American Psychological Association, San Francisco.

MCFIE, J., 1961. Intellectual impairment in children with localized post-infantile cerebral lesions. *J. Neurol. Neurosurg. Psychiatry* 24:361–365.

MUTER, V., S. TAYLOR, and F. VARGHA-KHADEM, 1997. A longitudinal study of early intellectual development in hemiplegic children. *Neuropsychologia* 35:289–298.

NASS, R., H. PETERSON, and D. KOCH, 1989. Differential effects of congenital left and right brain injury on intelligence. *Brain Cogn.* 9:258–266.

NEWMEYER, F. J., 1980. *Linguistic Theory in America.* New York: Academic Press.

NEWMEYER, F. J., 1997. Genetic dysphasia and linguistic theory. *J. Neurolinguistics* 10:47–73.

OJEMANN, G. A., 1991. Cortical organization of language. *J. Neurosci.* 11:2281–2287.

O'LEARY, D. D., and B. B. STANFIELD, 1985. Occipital cortical neurons with transient pyramidal tract axons extend and maintain collaterals to subcortical but not intracortical targets. *Brain Res.* 336:326–333.

O'LEARY, D. D., and B. B. STANFIELD, 1989. Selective elimination of extended by developing cortical neurons is dependent on regional locale: Experiments utilizing fetal cortical transplants. *J. Neurosci.* 9:2230–2246.

O'NEILL, Y. V., 1980. *Speech and Speech Disorders in Western Thought Before 1600.* Westport, Conn.: Greenwood Press.

PALLAS, S. L., and M. SUR, 1993. Visual projections induced into the auditory pathway of ferrets: II. Corticocortical connections of primary auditory cortex. *J. Comp. Neurol.* 337:317–333.

PAYNE, B. R., 1999. Immature visual cortex lesions: Global rewiring, neural adaptations, and behavioral sparing. In *The Changing Nervous System: Neurobehavioral Consequences of Early Brain Disorders*, S. Broman and J. M. Fletcher, eds. New York: Oxford University Press, pp. 114–145.

PINKER, S., 1994. *The Language Instinct: How the Mind Creates Language.* New York: William Morrow.

QUARTZ, S. R., and T. J. SEJNOWSKI, 1994. Beyond modularity: Neural evidence for constructivist principles in development. *Behav. Brain Sci.* 17:725–726.

QUARTZ, S. R., and T. J. SEJNOWSKI, 1997. The neural basis of cognitive development: A constructivist manifesto. *Behav. Brain Sci.* 20:537.

RASMUSSEN, T., and B. MILNER, 1977. The role of early left brain injury in determining lateralization of cerebral speech functions. *Ann. N.Y. Acad. Sci.* 229:355–369.

REILLY, J., E. BATES, and V. MARCHMAN, 1998. Narrative discourse in children with early focal brain injury. *Brain Lang.* 61:335–375.

RICE, M., ED., 1996. *Toward a Genetics of Language.* Mahwah, N.J.: Erlbaum.

RIVA, D., and L. CAZZANIGA, 1986. Late effects of unilateral brain lesions before and after the first year of life. *Neuropsychologia* 24:423–428.

RIVA, D., L. CAZZANIGA, C. PANTALEONI, N. MILANI, and E. FEDRIZZI, 1986. Acute hemiplegia in childhood: The neuropsychological prognosis. *J. Ped. Neurosci.* 2:239–250.

SATZ, P., E. STRAUSS, and H. WHITAKER, 1990. The ontogeny of hemispheric specialization: Some old hypotheses revisited. *Brain Lang.* 38:596–614.

STANFIELD, B. B., and D. D. O'LEARY, 1985. Fetal occipital cortical neurones transplanted to the rostral cortex can extend and maintain a pyramidal tract axon. *Nature* 313(5998):135–137.

STARK, R. E., and K. K. MCGREGOR, 1997. Follow-up study of a right- and left-hemispherectomized child: Implications for localization and impairment of language in children. *Brain Lang.* 60: 222–242.

STILES, J., 1995. Plasticity and development: Evidence from children with early focal brain injury. In *Maturational Windows and Adult Cortical Plasticity: Is There Reason for an Optimistic View? Proceedings of the Santa Fe Institute Studies in the Sciences of Complexity, Vol. 23,* B. Julesz and I. Kovacs, eds. Reading, Mass.: Addison-Wesley, pp. 217–237.

STILES, J., E. BATES, D. THAL, D. TRAUNER, and J. REILLY, 1998. Linguistic, cognitive and affective development in children with pre- and perinatal focal brain injury: A ten-year overview from the San Diego Longitudinal Project. In *Advances in Infancy Research*. C. Rovee-Collier, L. Lipsitt, and H. Hayne, eds. Norwood, N.J.: Ablex, pp. 131–163.

THAL, D., V. MARCHMAN, J. STILES, D. ARAM, D. TRAUNER, R. NASS, and E. BATES, 1991. Early lexical development in children with focal brain injury. *Brain Lang.* 40:491–527.

VARGHA-KHADEM, F., L. CARR, E. ISAACS, E. BRETT, C. ADAMS, and M. MISHKIN, 1997. Onset of speech after left hemispherectomy in a nine-year-old boy. *Brain* 120:59–182.

VARGHA-KHADEM, F., E. ISAACS, S. VAN DER WERF, S. ROBB, and J. WILSON, 1992. Development of intelligence and memory in children with hemiplegic cerebral palsy: The deleterious consequences of early seizures. *Brain* 115:315–329.

VARGHA-KHADEM, F., E. ISAACS, and V. MUTER, 1994. A review of cognitive outcome after unilateral lesions sustained during childhood. *J. Child Neurol.* 9(suppl.):2S67–2S73.

VARGHA-KHADEM, F., A. O'GORMAN, and G. WATTERS, 1985. Aphasia and handedness in relation to hemispheric side, age at injury and severity of cerebral lesion during childhood. *Brain* 108:677–696.

VICARI, S., A. ALBERTONI, A. CHILOSI, P. CIPRIANI, G. CIONI, and E. BATES, 2000. Plasticity and reorganization during early language learning in children with congenital brain injury. *Cortex* 36:31–46.

WEBSTER, M. J., J. BACHEVALIER, and L. G. UNGERLEIDER, 1995. Development and plasticity of visual memory circuits. In *Maturational Windows and Adult Cortical Plasticity: Is There Reason for an Optimistic View? Proceedings of the Santa Fe Institute Studies in the Sciences of Complexity, Vol. 23*, B. Julesz and I. Kovacs, eds. Reading, Mass.: Addison-Wesley, pp. 73–86.

WOODS, B. T., 1980. The restricted effects of right-hemisphere lesions after age one: Wechsler test data. *Neuropsychologia* 18:65–70.

WOODS, B. T., 1983. Is the left hemisphere specialized for language at birth? *Trends Neurosci.* 6:115–117.

WOODS, B. T., and S. CAREY, 1979. Language deficits after apparent clinical recovery from childhood aphasia. *Ann. Neurol.* 6:405–409.

WOODS, B. T., and H. L. TEUBER, 1973. Early onset of complementary specialisation of the cerebral hemispheres in man. *Trans. Am. Neurol. Assoc.* 98:113–117.

WOODS, B. T., and H. L. TEUBER, 1978. Changing patterns of childhood aphasia. *Ann. Neurol.* 3:272–280.

XIONG, J., S. RAO, J.-H. GAO, M. WOLDORFF, and P. T. FOX, 1998. Evaluation of hemispheric dominance for language using functional MRI: A comparison with positron emission tomography. *Hum. Brain Mapp.* 6:42–58.

# 21 Experience-Dependent Plasticity and the Treatment of Children with Specific Language Impairment or Dyslexia

GAIL C. BEDI

ABSTRACT  The temporal processing theory of speech and language processing suggests that accurate perception of rapid acoustic cues (auditory temporal processing) is critical to speech perception. It has been hypothesized that both specific language impairment (SLI) and dyslexia are characterized by impaired auditory temporal processing. Training programs that use methods aimed at remediating these developmental disorders by promoting experience-dependent neural plasticity have been effective in developing auditory temporal processing and have resulted in improved auditory processing and language comprehension. In these programs, neural plasticity was facilitated by training until a behavioral asymptote or criterion was achieved, as well as by maintaining attention to training. Application of these training principles holds promise for increasing the effectiveness of cognitive remediation and rehabilitation of both children and adults.

Recently, research findings in neuroscience, psychology, and speech and language have been integrated to develop new treatments for developmental language and language-based disorders. The fact that speech and language processing is dependent upon the ability to perceive rapid acoustic cues (auditory temporal processing) and that many children with language-based disorders exhibit impaired auditory temporal processing has been extensively studied. Within this context, training programs have been developed that are aimed at improving auditory temporal processing and thus remediating language-based disorders of development. What makes these programs unique is their use of methods that neuroscience research has shown to be effective in inducing experience-related changes in the brain. This chapter reviews the temporal processing theory of speech and language and research suggesting that both specific language impairment and dyslexia are characterized by impaired temporal processing. This review is followed by a discussion of the neural basis of experience-dependent plasticity and experience-dependent plasticity of speech perception, including a summary of principles drawn from this work and their application to training programs for children with specific language impairment or dyslexia. Finally, the implications of this research and direction for future research are addressed.

*Temporal processing theory of speech*

A considerable body of research has examined the theory that the brain relies upon temporal cues to code or process speech (for review, see Kraus, McGee, and Koch, 1998; Steinschneider, Arezzo, and Vaughan, 1990). According to temporal processing theory, speech perception is dependent upon accurate perception of very short duration acoustic cues and/or the perception of rapidly sequenced acoustic stimuli (Tallal, Miller, and Fitch, 1993). Certain sounds in English incorporate rapidly changing or rapidly occurring acoustic cues. For example, during the production of stop consonants (b, d, g, p, t, k) a rapid rise and/or fall in frequency occurs within approximately 40 ms. Precisely timed transitional elements characterize not only certain consonant sounds but also voice onset time and place of articulation. It has been further theorized that the hemisphere dominant for processing and production of speech and language (most commonly, the left hemisphere) is specialized for processing these rapid acoustic cues, not speech and language per se (Nussbaum et al., 1999; Tallal, Miller, and Fitch, 1993).

GAIL C. BEDI  Director, Manhattan Neuropsychology; Assistant Clinical Professor, The Mount Sinai School of Medicine, New York, New York.

## Language-based developmental disorders: Specific language impairment and dyslexia

Children who have at least average intelligence but do not acquire communication skills with the facility exhibited by their age mates are said to have specific language impairment (SLI). Their communication deficit(s) can be specific or global, ranging from a primary deficit in expressive functions to a combination of deficits in both receptive and expressive functions. For a diagnosis of SLI, these difficulties cannot be attributed to neurological disorder or injury (e.g., seizure disorder or closed head injury) or to hearing impairment, nor can they be attributed to behavioral or emotional disorders (i.e., pervasive developmental disorder).

Dyslexia describes children whose reading achievement is below average though they have at least average intellectual ability. This lack of achievement cannot be attributed to visual or auditory acuity deficits, neurological, emotional, or behavioral disorders, or lack of school attendance.

Although dyslexia is defined by reading impairment, a history of SLI is strongly predictive of delayed achievement in reading. In the United States, studies that prospectively followed children with SLI from preschool to first, second, or third grade (roughly, ages 3 or 4 to 8 years) found a significant positive correlation between language problems and impaired reading (Bishop and Adams, 1990; Levi et al., 1982; Share and Silva, 1987). Furthermore, the same relationship between language problems and later reading impairment has been found in children who were identified as having language difficulties at as young as 2½ years of age (Scarborough, 1990).

There is also a considerable body of literature documenting a strong relationship between impaired phonological awareness skills[1] and dyslexia (Bradley and Bryant, 1983; Bryant and Bradley, 1983; Calfee, Lindamood, and Lindamood, 1973; Liberman et al., 1974; Wagner, Torgesen, and Rashotte, 1994). The findings of longitudinal studies (Bradley and Bryant, 1983; Mann, 1991; Wagner, Torgesen, and Rashotte, 1994) and of a treatment study in which reading achievement of children with dyslexia improved following training in phonological awareness skills (Warrick, Rubin, and Rowe-Walsh, 1993) provide additional support for the theory that phonological awareness deficits impede reading achievement.

The relationship between phonological awareness deficits and achievement in single word reading has also been examined in children with SLI. Catts (1993) administered phonological synthesis and analysis tasks to a group of kindergarten students with SLI and chronological age-matched normal readers. During first and second grade (ages 6–8 years), achievement in single word reading and pseudoword reading[2] was measured. In addition, during second grade, achievement in decoding speed and accuracy during paragraph reading was assessed. The children with SLI performed significantly below normal readers on all tests of reading achievement at both the first and second grade (ages 6 and 7 years). Further, there was a significant positive correlation between phonological awareness and reading achievement for both real and pseudowords, as well as between phonological awareness skills and decoding speed and accuracy when reading paragraphs.

## Temporal processing deficits in SLI and dyslexia

Tallal and Piercy (1973) investigated the ability of children with SLI and controls to perform an auditory discrimination task and an auditory temporal order judgment task. Presented with two tones in various sequences (1–1, 2–1, 1–2, 2–2), the children were required to determine if the tones were the same or different (discrimination) or to reproduce the sequence by pressing the correct panels in the correct order (temporal order judgment). On both the discrimination test and the temporal order judgment test, the interstimulus interval (ISI) was manipulated; ISI ranged from 4062 ms to 8 ms. The children with SLI were impaired, relative to normal controls, on both tasks only when the ISIs were brief, demonstrating that impaired temporal order judgment was secondary to impaired discrimination of rapidly presented stimuli. That is, because children with SLI were unable to discriminate between two rapidly presented stimuli, they were unable to reproduce the order in which the stimuli were presented (Tallal, 1980a).

Tallal (1980b) extended the findings of Tallal and Piercy (1973) to children with dyslexia by assessing their performance on the same auditory temporal processing tests. Similar to the children with SLI, the children with dyslexia showed impaired discrimination and temporal order judgment, compared to matched controls, when nonverbal stimuli were presented rapidly. These results were interpreted as suggesting that some children with dyslexia have deficits in discriminating rapidly presented auditory stimuli and that these deficits are qualitatively similar to those documented in children with SLI. In an attempt to determine the relationship between auditory processing and reading, Tallal administered a test of pseudoword reading to the children with dyslexia. There was a highly significant correlation

($r$ = .81) between errors on the auditory temporal processing tests and errors in reading pseudowords.

Some findings to the contrary notwithstanding (Johannes et al., 1996; Mody, Studdert-Kennedy, and Brady, 1997; Smith, Early, and Grogan, 1986), impaired temporal processing has been well documented in children with dyslexia (Bedi and Halperin, 1995; Eden et al., 1995; Lovegrove, Martin, and Slaghuis, 1986; Reed, 1989; Slaghuis and Lovegrove, 1985; Tallal 1980b; Wright et al., 1997). Auditory temporal processing deficits in stimulus individuation (Wright et al., 1997), discrimination (Elliott et al., 1990; Reed, 1989), and temporal order judgment of nonverbal (Bedi and Halperin, 1995) and verbal stimuli (Reed, 1989) have been documented.

In summary, there is empirical evidence that children with SLI and children with dyslexia have many characteristics in common. Although dyslexia is defined by impairment in reading, children with SLI are at very high risk for reading impairment. In both children with SLI and children with dyslexia (without a previous diagnosis of SLI), a positive relationship between reading impairment and impaired phonological awareness skills has been found. Most children with SLI and many children with dyslexia are impaired in their ability to process rapidly presented auditory stimuli (Bedi and Halperin, 1995; Reed, 1989; Tallal, 1980b). Both the receptive language of children with SLI and the ability of children with dyslexia to perform phonological awareness tasks are highly correlated with deficits in discriminating stimuli that incorporate rapidly changing acoustic cues (Tallal, 1980b).

## Does a common mechanism underlie impaired phonological awareness and reading impairment?

SLI and dyslexia may have a cognitive process in common, which could, if impaired, affect phonological awareness, language, and reading. It has been theorized that the ability to discriminate between speech sounds is critical to the ability to develop sound–symbol relationships (Goswami, 1990; Tallal, 1980b). SLI and dyslexia have been shown to be related to a deficit in discriminating rapidly presented acoustic information, specifically within the time window essential for processing brief, rapidly changing components of speech (Reed, 1989; Tallal 1980b), and herein may lie the common mechanism. Impaired phonological awareness may be related to a neural timing deficit which constrains the processing of stimuli that incorporate short-duration, rapidly sequenced, or rapidly changing acoustic components (Stark and Tallal, 1988). According to this hypothesis, a temporal processing deficit

would interfere with the development of a clear neural representation of each phoneme of the child's native language, making speech discrimination problematic. Then poor speech discrimination would compromise the development of language and phonological awareness, which would, in turn, impede progress in learning to read phonetically. Reading impairment may indeed develop due to impaired phonological awareness skills (Liberman et al., 1974; Stanovich, 1986), but impaired phonological awareness itself may develop due to impaired speech discrimination subsequent to impaired auditory temporal processing.

### Experience-driven or training-induced plasticity

Training is considered effective if its implementation results in improvement or decrement of a target behavior. It is assumed that the behavior changes measured following training are the result of experience-driven brain plasticity or changes in brain chemistry, morphology, and/or physiology that correlate with the specific training or experience.

Indeed, within the audiovocal and other sensory systems, experience-induced plasticity has been demonstrated in human and nonhuman primates through measurement of changes in topographical representation of cortical functions (Recanzone, Merzenich, and Schreiner, 1992; Recanzone, Schreiner, and Merzenich, 1993). More specifically, improved auditory discrimination, tactile discrimination, and performance of motor tasks have been shown to be correlated with changes in neural representation in sensory relevant or related motor areas (Cansino and Williamson, 1997; Karni et al., 1998; Recanzone, Merzenich, and Schreiner, 1992; Recanzone, Schreiner, and Merzenich, 1993; Xerri et al., 1996).

It is theorized that a distributed series of Hebb-like synapses and dynamic cortical cell assemblies underlie experience-induced plasticity (Merzenich and Sameshima, 1993; Rose, 1992a; Rosenzweig and Bennett, 1996; Rosenzweig et al., 1992). Hebb (1949) hypothesized that an association could be formed between neurons such that a neuron induced to discharge following specific neuronal input would have increased synaptic effectiveness if this association was repeated successively. Repeated or successive coincidental input and discharge between the two neurons would result in metabolic and structural changes in one or both neurons. These changes would account for the neuron's higher likelihood of discharge to future inputs.

During training, neurons that fire in response to specific environmental stimuli will become more responsive with repeated exposure to the same environmental stimuli. Training induces the neurons to discharge to newly effective inputs, thus inducing the molecular steps associated with short-term, intermediate-term, and long-term memory (Rose, 1992a,b). Therefore, training produces a linear sequence of processes in a small ensemble of neurons that results in a lasting modification of synaptic connectivity within the ensemble. This lasting modification of synaptic connectivity within an ensemble of neurons is presumed to be the brain's representation of behavioral training (Rose, 1992a,b). Thus, an experience-dependent cell assembly is formed.

## Characteristics of training necessary to induce experience-dependent plasticity

Hebb's model of associative learning implies that repeated or successive coincidental input and discharge between neurons is not only necessary but sufficient to induce experience-dependent plasticity. However, it has been argued that to induce experience-dependent plasticity, training must have behavioral relevance (Ahissar et al., 1992). Ahissar and colleagues (1992) isolated pairs of primate auditory cortical neurons that exhibited correlated activity. One neuron in each pair was designated the "conditioned-stimulus" neuron while the other was designated the "conditioned-response" neuron. The primate was then presented with an auditory discrimination task in which the stimuli varied from broadband noises to pure tones or they were two pure tones of different frequencies. The firing pattern of the neuron pairs was examined under three conditions. (1) The auditory stimulus changed shortly (2–4 ms) after the conditioned-stimulus neuron fired, and the animal was rewarded for producing a target behavior in response to the change in auditory stimulus. (2) The auditory stimulus changed shortly after the conditioned-stimulus neuron fired, but no behavior was required and no reinforcement was delivered. (3) The auditory stimulus changed, but this change was not contingent upon the firing of the conditioned-stimulus neuron. The strongest increase in the average firing rate between a pair of neurons was consistently obtained during the first condition. When auditory stimulus change was almost coincident with firing of the conditioned-stimulus neuron and the animal was rewarded for making a correct behavioral response, there was the strongest increase in conditional-stimulus/conditioned-response neuron firing. These results suggest that in order to drive change in the brain, attended and rewarded behaviors are a necessary part of the experience.

The importance of attended and reinforced behavior in driving experience-induced changes in brain organization was highlighted further by Recanzone and colleagues (Recanzone, Merzenich, and Schreiner, 1992; Recanzone, Schreiner, and Schreiner, 1993). Training on a tactile frequency discrimination task was followed by reorganization of primate somatosensory cortex when correct responses were reinforced during training. However, reorganization of primate somatosensory cortex was not found when the same tactile stimulation was presented during training on an auditory discrimination task (Recanzone, Merzenich, and Schreiner, 1992). Similarly, reorganization of primate auditory cortex subsequent to training on an auditory frequency discrimination task in which correct responses were reinforced was found, but not when the same auditory stimuli were presented coincident with tactile discrimination training in which correct responses were reinforced (Recanzone, Schreiner, and Schreiner, 1993).

Rose (1992b) hypothesized that in order for neuronal morphological changes to occur, training must be associated with strongly aversive or rewarding experiences. Certainly, results of studies examining experience-induced plasticity have established that the stimuli must have behavioral importance and that reinforcement can increase the behavioral relevance of a stimulus. However, reinforcement in and of itself does not appear to be a necessary component of training aimed at inducing experience-dependent plasticity (McCandliss et al., 1999). Within this context, the results of Ahissar and colleagues (1992) and Recanzone and colleagues (1992, 1993) suggest that attention during task performance confers behavioral relevance and thus enhances training-induced plasticity, while reinforcement is a training method that can be employed to facilitate maintaining attention during task performance.

The duration or intensity of training also appears to be an important feature of training aimed at inducing changes in the brain. In several studies that documented change in neural representation following behavioral training, training was continued either until the task was executed with a high degree of accuracy or until a behavioral asymptote was achieved (Karni et al., 1988; Recanzone, Merzenich, and Schreiner, 1992; Recanzone, Schreiner, and Merzenich, 1993; Xerri et al., 1996). Accordingly, it has been suggested that training-induced plasticity is a slowly evolving, incremental process (Merzenich and Sameshima, 1993). Indeed, while improved motor performance with correlated changes in neuronal organization have been demonstrated to occur rapidly after only limited training, this fast learning effect quickly saturates and is followed by the slow incremental emergence of a large performance gain (Karni et al., 1998). This larger performance gain is triggered by continued training (Karni et al., 1998). However, it is important to note that overtraining can result in a reduction of task-specific responding in the cortex (Aizawa et al., 1990). Merzenich and Sameshima (1993) suggested that this reduction in task-specific cortical response is a function of decreased attention secondary to training that was conducted well past task mastery. Thus, training until a task has been mastered or until change in behavior has reached a plateau seems to be an important feature of training aimed at inducing experience-driven neural plasticity. However, training well past task acquisition may negatively affect experience-driven neural plasticity, most likely because the experience becomes routine or boring and, in consequence, results in decreased attention during training.

## Experience-dependent plasticity following speech perception training

Speech discrimination training has been shown to improve speech perception and has been shown, using mismatched negativity (MMN), to alter the physiology of central auditory cortex. Mismatched negativity is a passively elicited evoked auditory response that is recorded when a deviant or "oddball" stimulus is presented within the context of several hundred identical (standard) stimuli (for review, see Näätänen, 1995). A "difference wave" is obtained by subtracting the response elicited by the standard stimuli from the response elicited by the deviant stimuli (Näätänen, 1995). The difference wave shows a negativity at the 100–200 ms latency range that is dependent upon the magnitude of the deviation between the standard and oddball stimuli (Näätänen, 1995). It reflects specific processes in the primary and association auditory cortex (Näätänen, Gaillard, and Mantysalo, 1978) and preattentive discrimination of acoustic input (Näätänen et al., 1978; Tremblay et al., 1997). Thus, it is a neurophysiological response that indicates auditory discrimination without the participant's having to pay attention.

Normal adults were trained to discriminate two speech contrasts which, prior to training, would not have been recognized as distinct from each other or would infrequently have been recognized as being distinct from each other (Kraus et al., 1995a; Tremblay et al., 1997; Tremblay, Kraus, and McGee, 1998). In this series of studies, training resulted in significant improvement in discriminating between the two stimuli

and changes in central auditory cortex neurophysiology as measured by changes in MMN evoked potentials. Specifically, following speech perception training, an increased magnitude of MMN responses was demonstrated (Kraus et al., 1995a; Tremblay et al., 1997; Tremblay, Kraus, and McGee, 1998). Furthermore, this change in neurophysiology preceded or occurred coincidentally with behavioral changes (Tremblay, Kraus, and McGee, 1998). These results indicated that the training changed the neural representation of speech sounds and that behavioral changes followed these neurophysiological changes. Both the behavioral and neurophysiological changes associated with speech sound discrimination training generalized to novel or untrained stimuli (Tremblay et al., 1997).

Native speakers of Japanese cannot discriminate between the /r/ and /l/ sounds that occur in American English. Instead, they identify both sounds as the /r/ sound in Japanese. Using an adaptive training procedure based upon a Hebbian experience-induced model of plasticity, native speakers of Japanese were trained to discriminate between the /r/ and /l/ phonemes that occur in American English but not in Japanese (McCandliss et al., 1999). Participants were presented with words that began with one of these phonemes (e.g., load, road) and were required to respond whether the word began with an /r/ or /l/. No feedback about response accuracy was provided. Two conditions were studied: One group heard natural speech samples; the other group was trained using a continuum of stimuli that progressed from a signal that was modified to enhance discrimination to natural speech. This second type of training involved an adaptive training approach. Specifically, after eight consecutive correct responses, stimuli from the next step along the continuum were presented. After three 20-minute training sessions, significant improvement in the ability to discriminate between /r/ and /l/ was seen in the training group that heard the modified speech but not in the natural speech group.

In summary, adaptive training modeled upon the principles of Hebbian experience-driven plasticity results in improved speech discrimination in normal adults. Speech discrimination training in normal adults results in experience-driven plasticity as demonstrated by changes in neurophysiology that correlate with training. Next, research investigating the effectiveness of training that incorporates features aimed at facilitating experience-driven plasticity to train speech perception deficits associated with the developmental disorders of SLI and dyslexia will be reviewed.

## Training modeled upon principles of experience-induced plasticity for children with SLI

Tallal and colleagues (1996) and Merzenich and colleagues (1996) developed and implemented a training program to modify the speech discrimination and receptive language abilities of children with SLI. The training involved two simultaneously occurring components: (1) Language and phonology training using ongoing, natural speech that was acoustically modified, via a computer algorithm, to extend in duration and increase in amplitude (20 dB) the rapidly changing acoustic components of speech; (2) computer-based training aimed at improving the children's auditory temporal processing. Thus, children received language and phonology training using acoustically modified speech, which they could more accurately perceive (Tallal and Piercy, 1974, 1975), simultaneously with computer-based training aimed at improving their auditory temporal processing.

This training program incorporated many of the features determined to be important for promoting experience-driven plasticity. Training was conducted for 3½ hours per day, 5 days a week, for 4 consecutive weeks. Further, it was adaptive to each individual child. Specifically, the computer games were designed to drive the child toward improved temporal processing by adjusting the task difficulty level according to each child's ability level. As a child achieved greater accuracy, the task gradually became more difficult by manipulating stimulus parameters. For speech stimuli, the duration of rapid acoustic components in the speech stimuli (i.e., the amount of stretching of the natural speech via the computer algorithm) or the amplitude amplification was decreased as the child met performance criteria. For nonspeech stimuli, stimulus duration and/or the duration of the interstimulus interval (ISI) was decreased as the child progressed through the game. Although a mastery criterion was not employed to determine the length of training (i.e., training would continue until the child reached a given level of accuracy on a target behavior), the training was individualized, intensive, and long enough in duration to presume that a behavioral asymptote had been achieved.

To ensure and maintain attention to the task, performance feedback was continually provided during training and participation was rewarded. During language training exercises, an item was presented to the child, eliciting a response, whereupon the trainer followed that response with feedback about its accuracy. Then, regardless of the accuracy of the child's response, the item was repeated while the trainer demonstrated the correct response. Thus, after each response the child was presented with the item again with preknowledge of the correct response. During the computer activities, a correct response was greeted with a chime while an incorrect response evoked a "bonk" noise. In addition, a token economy was employed in which participation in all activities was rewarded with points. These points were redeemed for prizes on a weekly basis.

In two independent studies that employed this training with language-impaired school-aged children, the results indicated that auditory temporal processing, speech discrimination, and receptive language were significantly improved (Merzenich et al., 1996; Tallal et al., 1996). In the second of these studies, this specialized treatment proved significantly more effective than language and phonology training that was conducted in natural speech and paired with computer training which was not aimed at improving auditory rate processing. Children who received this specialized training achieved significantly more growth in their receptive language and auditory processing skills than did children who received similar training presented in natural speech paired with computer games which were not aimed at improving auditory processing rate. Children were better able to hear the difference between sounds in words. It was presumed that the training promoted neural reorganization and distinct representations for sounds within English.

## Training modeled upon principles of experience-induced plasticity for children with dyslexia

Two studies conducted by Hurford (1990) and Hurford and Sanders (1990) showed that an intense, individually adaptive training program aimed at improving auditory rate processing was effective in remediating deficits in speech discrimination exhibited by children with dyslexia. These researchers further demonstrated that such training was effective in remediating impaired phonological awareness.

Hurford (1990) theorized that if children with dyslexia have difficulty processing the rapid frequency changes characteristic of stop consonants, they should benefit from adaptive temporal processing training. Hurford employed a systematic progression from stable stimuli (steady-state vowels) to stimuli with briefer formant transitions (CV syllables beginning with liquid consonants) and finally to stimuli with very brief formant transitions (CV syllables beginning with stop consonants). Two pairs of each syllable type were presented with an interstimulus interval (ISI) interposed between syllables in each pair. The child had to determine if the second pair was the same as or different from the first pair. Each of these three types of syllable pairs was trained using an eight-step progression from long (400 ms) to short (10 ms) ISIs

This program also reflected training aimed at promoting experience-induced plasticity in that behavior was trained until a criterion was achieved and reinforcement was employed to maintain attention. For each child, training was conducted until each child achieved eight consecutive correct responses at the shortest ISI for each syllable type. The training was individually adaptive such that each child started training for a particular syllable type at the longest ISI. He or she was required to achieve a criterion of eight consecutive correct responses before the next shorter ISI was presented. If this criterion was not met within 24 trials, syllable pairs with an ISI halfway between the last ISI passed and the failed ISI were presented. This iterative procedure was applied in an ascending or descending sequence until the initially failed ISI was passed or stimuli with an ISI within 5 ms of the initially failed ISI were passed. The children required 3–4 days of 30–45-minute sessions to complete the training sequence. To maintain attention, immediate feedback was provided and correct responses were rewarded; the child was presented with a smiling face for each correct response.

After determining that a group of second and fourth graders with dyslexia were indeed impaired in making same/different judgments for pairs of stop consonant–vowel syllables relative to grade-matched average readers, Hurford (1990) randomly assigned the children with dyslexia to one of two treatment groups. One group received the discrimination training just described while the other group received "training" that was not aimed at remediating discrimination. Following training, discrimination for pairs of syllables was reassessed using novel pairs of stop consonant–vowel syllables. The performance of the children with dyslexia who received discrimination training was significantly improved, to the point that they were no longer significantly different from average readers. However, the performance of the children with dyslexia who did not receive discrimination training did not differ significantly from that at pretraining levels, remaining significantly below that of the average readers.

In another treatment study, Hurford and Sanders (1990) identified a group of second- and fourth-grade children with dyslexia who had deficits in phonemic segmentation relative to grade-matched average readers. These children were then randomly divided into two groups, with one group receiving the same discrimination training that was employed by Hurford (1990) and the other group receiving the training control intervention. Upon completion of training, post-testing

was conducted to assess phonemic segmentation. All of the children with dyslexia who had received discrimination training showed significant improvement in phonemic segmentation skills while the performance of the untrained children with dyslexia was not significantly different from their pretraining levels.

## Discussion

The results from the training programs for children with SLI and dyslexia suggest that, once an underlying cognitive deficit for a disorder has been determined, training that incorporates characteristics important to promoting experience-induced plasticity can effectively remediate the disorder. Important training features for facilitating experience-driven plasticity are (1) intense training that is maintained until a mastery criterion or behavior asymptote is achieved and (2) maintaining attention during task performance.

It is presumed that these training programs obtained their results because the training produced neural reorganization. However, it is important to document that this training does indeed promote reorganization of the brain or experience-induced plasticity. Although fMRI and PET have been used to assess cortical activation during cognitive tasks and could presumably be used to assess change in cortical activation as a function of training, there can be limitations to employing these two methods with children as participants (but see Casey, Thomas, and McCandliss, this volume). PET is too invasive to employ with children. Functional MRI has been successfully employed to study cortical activation in children 6 years of age and older. However, it can be difficult to keep children quiet/still during the length of time needed to conduct many fMRI procedures. Thus, imaging artifacts that are secondary to movement may complicate data interpretation. Therefore, consideration should be given to also employing alternative methods to determine whether change in neurophysiology occurs following these specific training programs for SLI and dyslexia. The Mismatched Negativity technique appears to be a viable option (Kraus et al., 1995a,b; Näätänen, 1995).

Discussions of neural plasticity encompass the commonly held view that a young nervous system is more capable of recovery of function following brain damage than is an older nervous system (Lenneberg, 1967). This view is supported by findings of normal language development in prepubescent children following focal, unilateral brain injury unaccompanied by seizure disorder (Dall'Oglio et al., 1994; Muter, Taylor, and Vargha-Khadem, 1997), or following hemispherectomy (Vargha-Khadem et al., 1991). In contrast, adults with receive and/or expressive aphasia following focal brain injury demonstrate significantly less complete recovery of language (for review, see Stiles, 1995). It has therefore been concluded that the young brain is more plastic than the adult brain; the young brain has a greater capacity for reorganization (Bates et al., 1997).

Neuroscience research has indicated that even in adult primate brains, learned behavior can drive cortical change—that the *adult* brain is indeed plastic. Furthermore, it has been suggested that the emergence of learning-related changes in adult cortex follows principles that are identical to those underlying plasticity that occurs as a function of development (Karni, 1996). Just as experience can promote change in the young brain, experience can drive change in adult brains. It therefore seems reasonable to assume that the adult brain is plastic enough to demonstrate recovery of function following brain damage.

The application of training aimed at producing experience-induced plasticity to promote recovery of function following brain damage has been previously addressed (Xerri et al., 1996). However, employing a temporal processing training program similar to that employed to train children with SLI specifically to promote recovery of function following acquired receptive aphasia should be considered. There is empirical evidence for the following: (1) Adults with receptive aphasia show deficits in perceiving rapidly changing acoustic cues within speech, such as stop consonants (b, d, g, p, t, k), that are similar to those found in children with SLI (Robin, Tranel, and Damasio, 1990; Tallal and Newcombe, 1978). (2) There is a very strong relationship between impaired speech discrimination and impaired receptive language in adults with receptive aphasia (Varney, 1984a). (3) Recovery of receptive language functions in adults with aphasia is strongly correlated with intact auditory discrimination (Varney, 1984a,b). (4) Speech perception in normal adults can be modified and the emergence of improved perception correlates with changes in neurophysiology (Kraus et al., 1995a; McCandliss et al., 1999; Tremblay et al., 1997, Tremblay, Kraus, and McGee, 1998). Taken together, these findings suggest that receptive language and speech discrimination deficits in adults with receptive aphasia may be related to impaired discrimination of rapidly changing acoustic components in speech, and that intensive, individually adaptive training aimed at remediating this deficit will restore receptive language and speech discrimination function.

The integration of neuroscience, psychology, and speech and language research findings, as exemplified by the new treatments for SLI and dyslexia reviewed in this chapter, offers exciting possibilities for increasing the effectiveness of cognitive remediation and cognitive rehabilitation of both children and adults. The training programs reviewed here were presumed to be more effective than more traditional training because the training promoted enduring reorganization of the brain. Application of this approach to cognitive remediation or rehabilitation of other disorders first requires considerable research to determine the core deficits underlying cognitive impairments. However, even without this determination, it appears that training that promotes experienced-driven neural plasticity has the potential to increase the effectiveness of remediation for other developmental and acquired cognitive disorders. Therefore, attention should be immediately focused upon increasing training efficacy by increasing the intensity of training, by training until a behavioral asymptote or criterion has been achieved, and by maintaining attention to the target behavior during training.

## NOTES

1. Wagner and Torgesen (1987) define phonological awareness as the awareness of and access to the sounds of one's language. It has been theorized that phonological awareness is critical to the development of sound–symbol associations; if the reader is not aware of phonemes as the basic units of spoken words, then he/she will be unable to associate individual sounds with individual letters (Liberman et al., 1974; Stanovich, 1986). Within this theoretical framework, weak phonological awareness causes impaired acquisition of single word reading because phonetic decoding is dependent upon accurate learning of sound–symbol or phoneme–grapheme associations.
2. In order to read a pseudoword, the child must minimally be able to convert graphemes to phonemes. Therefore, accuracy in reading pseudowords requires phonological awareness skills (Stanovich, 1986).

## REFERENCES

AHISSAR, E., E. VAADIA, M. AHISSAR, H. BERGMAN, A. ARIELI, and M. ABELES, 1992. Dependence of cortical plasticity on correlated activity of single neurons and on behavioral context. *Science* 257:1412–1415.

AIZAWA, H., M. INASE, H. MUSHIAKE, K. SHIMA, and J. TANJI, 1990. Reorganization of activity in the supplementary motor area associated with motor learning and functional recovery. *Exp. Brain Res.* 84:668–671.

BATES, E., D. THAL, D. TRAUNER, J. FENSON, D. ARAM, J. EISELE, and R. NASS, 1997. From first words to grammar in children with focal brain injury. *Dev. Neuropsychol.* 13(3):275–343.

BEDI, G. C., and J. M. HALPERIN, 1995. Auditory and visual temporal order deficits in dyslexic children. *J. Intl. Neuropsychol. Soc.* 1(2):155.

BISHOP, D., and C. ADAMS, 1990. A prospective study of the relationship between specific language impairment, phonological disorders and reading retardation. *J. Child Psychol. Psychiatry* 31:1027–1050.

BRADLEY, L., and P. BRYANT, 1983. Categorizing sounds and learning to read: A causal connection. *Nature* 301:419–421.

BRYANT, P. E., and L. BRADLEY, 1983. Auditory organization and backwardness in reading. In *Developmental Neuropsychiatry*, M. Rutter, ed. New York: Guilford Press, pp. 489–497.

CALFEE, R. C., P. LINDAMOOD, and C. LINDAMOOD, 1973. Acoustic-phonetic skill and reading, kindergarten through 12th grade. *J. Ed. Psychol.* 64:293–298.

CANSINO, S., and S. J. WILLIAMSON, 1997. Neuromagnetic fields reveal cortical plasticity when learning an auditory discrimination task. *Brain Res.* 764:53–66.

CATTS, H. W., 1993. The relationship between speech-language impairments and reading disabilities. *J. Speech Hear. Res.* 36:948–958.

DALL'OGLIO, A. M., E. BATES, V. VOLTERRA, M. DICAPUA, and G. PEZZINI, 1994. Early cognition, communication and language in children with focal brain injury. *Dev. Med. Child Neurol.* 36(12):1076–1098.

EDEN, G. F., H. M. STEIN, H. M. WOOD, and F. B. WOOD, 1995. Temporal and spatial processing in reading-disabled and normal children. *Cortex* 31:451–468.

ELLIOTT, L. L., M. E. SCHOLL, J. O. GRANT, and M. A. HAMMER, 1990. Perception of gated, highly familiar spoken monosyllabic nouns by children with and without learning disabilities. *J. Learn. Dis.* 23(4):249–252, 259.

GOSWAMI, U., 1990. A special link between rhyming skill and the use of orthographic analogies by beginning readers. *J. Child Psychol. Psychiatry* 31:301–311.

HEBB, D. O., 1949. *The Organization of Behavior: A Neuropsychological Theory.* New York: Wiley.

HURFORD, D. P., 1990. Training phonemic segmentation ability with a phonemic discrimination intervention in second- and third-grade children with reading disabilities. *J. Learn. Dis.* 23(9):564–569.

HURFORD, D. P., and R. F. SANDERS, 1990. Assessment and remediation of a phonemic discrimination deficit in reading-disabled second and fourth graders. *J. Exp. Child Psychol.* 50:396–415.

JOHANNES, S., C. L. KUSSMAUL, T. F. MUNTE, and G. R. MANGUN, 1996. Developmental dyslexia: Passive visual stimulation provides no evidence for a magnocellular processing deficit. *Neuropsychologia.* 34(11):1123–1127.

KARNI, A., 1996. The acquisition of perceptual and motor skills: A memory system in the adult human cortex. *Cogn. Brain Res.* 5:39–48.

KARNI, A., G. MEYER, C. REY-HIPOLITO, P. JEZZARD, M. M. ADAMS, R. TURNER, and L. G. UNGERLEIDER, 1998. The acquisition of skilled motor performance: Fast and slow experience-driven changes in primary motor cortex. *Proc. Natl. Acad. Sci. USA* 95:861–868.

KRAUS, N., T. MCGEE, T. D. CARRELL, C. KING, K. TREMBLAY, and T. NICOL, 1995a. Central auditory system plasticity associated with speech discrimination training. *J. Cogn. Neurosci.* 7(1):25–32.

KRAUS, H., T. MCGEE, T. D. CARRELL, and A. SHARMA, 1995b. Neurophysiologic bases of speech discrimination. *Ear Hearing* 16(1):19–37.

KRAUS, N., T. J. MCGEE, and D. B. KOCH, 1998. Speech sound representation, perception and plasticity: A neurophysiologic perspective. *Audiol. Neurootol.* 3:168–182.

LENNEBERG, E. H., 1967. *Biological Foundations of Language.* New York: John Wiley and Sons.

LEVI, G., F. CAPOZZI, A. FABRIZI, and E. SECHI, 1982. Language disorders and prognosis for reading disabilities in developmental age. *Percept. Motor Skills* 54:1119–1122.

LIBERMAN, I. Y., D. SHANKWEILER, F. W. FISCHER, and B. CATER, 1974. Explicit syllable and phoneme segmentation in the young child. *J. Exp. Child Psychol.* 18:201–212.

LOVEGROVE, W. J., R. MARTIN, and W. SLAGHUIS, 1986. A theoretical and experimental case for a visual deficit in specific reading disability. *Cogn. Neuropsychol.* 3(2):225–267.

MANN, V. A., 1991. Phonological abilities: Effective predictors of future reading ability. In *Learning to Read*, L. Rieben and C. A. Perfetti, eds. Hillsdale, N.J.: Lawrence Erlbaum, pp. 121–133.

MCCANDLISS, B. D., J. A. FIEZ, M. CONWAY, and J. L. MCCLELLAND, 1999. Eliciting adult plasticity for Japanese adults struggling to identify English /r/ and /l/: Insights from a Hebbian model and a new training procedure. Cogn. Neurosci. Soc. Ann. Meeting Prog., *J. Cogn. Neurosci.* (suppl.)

MERZENICH, M. M., W. M. JENKINS, P. JOHNSTON, C. SCHREINER, S. L. MILLER, and P. TALLAL, 1996. Temporal processing deficits of language-learning impaired children ameliorated by training. *Science* 271:77–81.

MERZENICH, M. M., and K. SAMESHIMA, 1993. Cortical plasticity and memory. *Cogn. Neurosci.* 3:187–196.

MODY, M., M. STUDDERT-KENNEDY, and S. BRADY, 1997. Speech perception deficits in poor readers: Auditory processing or phonological coding? *J. Exp. Child Psychol.* 64(2):199–231.

MUTER, V., S. TAYLOR, and F. VARGHA-KHADEM, 1997. A longitudinal study of early intellectual development in hemiplegic children. *Neuropsychologia* 35(3):289–298.

NÄÄTÄNEN, R., 1995. The mismatch negativity: A powerful tool for cognitive neuroscience. *Ear Hearing* 16(1):6–18.

NÄÄTÄNEN, R., A. GAILLARD, and S. MANTYSALOA, 1978. Early selective attention effect on evoked potential reinterpreted. *Acta. Psychol.* 42:313–329.

NUSSBAUM, A. O., C. Y. TANG, G. C. BEDI, E. S. DORSETT, M. BUCHSBAUM, and S. W. ATLAS, 1998. Functional MRI during rapid auditory processing in normal adults: Correlation to task performance and implication for the study of dyslexia. *Proceedings of the 84th Sci. Assembly Ann. Meeting Radiol. Soc. N. Amer.*

RECANZONE, G. H., M. M. MERZENICH, M and C. E. SCHREINER, 1992. Changes in the distributed temporal response properties of SI cortical neurons reflect improvements in performance of a temporally based tactile discrimination task. *J. Neurophysiol.* 67(5):1071–1091.

RECANZONE, G. H., C. E. SCHREINER, and M. M. MERZENICH, 1993. Plasticity in the frequency representation of primary auditory cortex following discrimination training in adult owl monkeys. *J. Neurosci.* 13(1):87–103.

REED, M. A., 1989. Speech perception and the discrimination of brief auditory cues in reading-disabled children. *J. Exp. Child Psychol.* 48:270–292.

ROBIN, D. A., D. TRANEL, and H. DAMASIO, 1990. Auditory perception of temporal and spectral events in patients with focal left and right cerebral lesions. *Brain Lang.* 39:539–555.

ROSE, S. P. R., 1992a. Synaptic plasticity, learning and memory. In *Synaptic Plasticity: Molecular, Cellular and Functional Aspects*, M. Baudry, R. F. Thompson, and J. L. Davis, eds. Cambridge, Mass.: MIT Press, pp. 209–229.

ROSE, S. P. R., 1992b. On chicks and rosetta stones. In *Neuropsychology of Memory*, 2nd ed., L. R. Squire and N. Butters, eds. New York: Guilford Press, pp. 547–574.

ROSENZWEIG, M. R., and E. L. BENNETT, 1996. Psychobiology of plasticity: Effects of training and experience on brain and behavior. *Behav. Brain Res.* 78:57–65.

ROSENZWEIG, M. R., E. L. BENNETT, J. L. MARTINEZ, P. J. COLOMBO, D. W. LEE, and P. A. SERRANO, 1992. Studying stages of memory formation with chicks. In *Neuropsychology of Memory*, 2nd ed., L. R. Squire and N. Butters, eds. New York: Guilford Press, pp. 533–546.

SCARBOROUGH, H. S., 1990. Very early language deficits in dyslexic children. *Child Dev.* 61:1728–1743.

SHARE, D. L., and P. A. SILVA, 1987. Language deficits and specific reading retardation: Cause or effect? *Br. J. Dis. Comm.* 22:219–226.

SLAGHUIS, W. L., and W. J. LOVEGROVE, 1985. Spatial-frequency-dependent visible persistence and specific reading disability. *Brain Cogn.* 4:219–240.

SMITH, A. T., F. EARLY, and S. C. GROGAN, 1986. Flicker masking and developmental dyslexia. *Perception* 15:473–482.

STANOVICH, K. E., 1986. Cognitive processes and the reading problems of learning-disabled children: Evaluation of the assumption of specificity. In *Psychological and Educational Perspectives on Learning Disabilities*, J. K. Torgesen and B. Y. L. Wong, eds. New York: Academic Press, pp. 87–131.

STARK, R., and P. TALLAL, 1988. *Language, Speech, and Reading Disorders in Children: Neuropsychological Studies.* Boston: Little, Brown.

STEINSCHNEIDER, M., J. C. AREZZO, and H. G. VAUGHAN, 1990. Tonotopic features of speech-evoked activity in primate auditory cortex. *Brain Res.* 519:158–168.

STILES, J., 1995. Plasticity and development: Evidence from children with early focal brain injury. In *Maturational Windows and Cortical Plasticity in Human Development: Is There Reason for an Optimistic View?* B. Julesz and I. Kovacs, eds. Reading, Mass.: Addison-Wesley, pp. 217–237.

TALLAL, P., 1980a. Language and reading: Some perceptual prerequisites. *Bull. Orton Soc.* 30:170–178.

TALLAL, P., 1980b. Auditory temporal perception, phonics and reading disabilities in children. *Brain Lang.* 9:182–198.

TALLAL, P., S. L. MILLER, G. BEDI, G. BYMA, X. WANG, S. S. NAGARAJAN, C. SCHREINER, W. M. JENKINS, and M. MERZENICH, 1996. Language comprehension in language-learning impaired children improved with acoustically speech. *Science* 271:81–84.

TALLAL, P., S. MILLER, and R. H. FITCH, 1993. Neurobiological basis of speech: A case for the preeminence of temporal processing. In *Temporal Information Processing in the Nervous System: Special Reference to Dyslexia and Dysphasia*, P. Tallal, A. M. Galaburda, R. R. Llinas, and C. von Euler, eds. New York: New York Academy of Sciences, pp. 27–47.

TALLAL, P., and F. NEWCOMBE, 1978. Impairment of auditory perception and language comprehension in dysphasia. *Brain Lang.* 5:13–24.

TALLAL, P., and M. PIERCY, 1973. Defects of non-verbal auditory perception in children with developmental aphasia. *Nature* 241:468–469.

TALLAL, P., and M. PIERCY, 1974. Developmental aphasia: Rate of auditory processing and selective impairment of consonant perception. *Neuropsychologia* 12:83–93.

TALLAL, P., and M. PIERCY, 1975. Developmental aphasia: The perception of brief vowels and extended stop consonants. *Neuropsychologia* 13:69–75.

TREMBLAY, K., N. KRAUS, T. D. CARRELL, and T. MCGEE, 1997. Central auditory system plasticity: Generalization to novel stimuli following listening training. *J. Acoust. Soc. Am.* 102(6):3762–3773.

TREMBLAY, K., N. KRAUS, and T. MCGEE, 1998. The time course of auditory perceptual learning: Neurophysiological changes during speech-sound training. *NeuroReport* 9:3557–3560.

VARNEY, N. R., 1984a. Phonemic imperception in aphasia. *Brain Lang.* 1:85–94.

VARNEY, N. R., 1984b. The prognostic significance of sound recognition in receptive aphasia. *Arch. Neurol.* 41:181–182.

WAGNER, R. K., and J. K. TORGESEN, 1987. The nature of phonological processing and its causal role in the acquisition of reading skills. *Psychol. Bull.* 101(2):192–212.

WAGNER, R., J. TORGESEN, and C. RASHOTTE, 1994. Development of reading-related phonological processing abilities: New evidence of bidirectional causality from a latent variable longitudinal study. *Dev. Psychol.* 30(1):73–87.

WARRICK, N., H. RUBIN, and S. ROWE-WALSH, 1993. Phoneme awareness in language-delayed children: Comparative studies and intervention. *Ann. Dyslexia* 43:153–173.

WRIGHT, B. A., L. J. LOMBARDINO, W. M. KING, C. S. PURANIK, C. M. LEONARD, and M. M. MERZENICH, 1997. Deficits in auditory temporal and spectral resolution in language-impaired children. *Nature* 387:176–178.

XERRI, C., J. O. COQ, M. M. MERZENICH, and W. M. JENKINS, 1996. Experience-induced plasticity of cutaneous maps in the primary somatosensory cortex of adult monkeys and rats. *J. Physiol. (Paris)* 90:277–287.

# VI

# COGNITION

# 22 Attention in Young Infants: A Developmental Psychophysiological Perspective

## JOHN E. RICHARDS

ABSTRACT   This chapter reviews the development of attention in young infants, emphasizing heart rate changes in psychophysiological experiments as a measure of an arousal brain system. The neural systems affecting attention that may be indexed by psychophysiological measures are briefly reviewed. Heart rate, electroencephalogram (EEG), event-related potentials (ERP), and other physiological measures are reviewed that have been used for the study of attention development in young infants. The developmental changes in infant attention are related to changes occurring in the neural systems underlying attention. Several studies are reviewed that show how heart rate may be used as a measure of a general arousal system in young infants.

Attention, generally defined, shows dramatic development over the period of infancy. At birth infants attend primarily to salient physical characteristics of their environment or attend with nonspecific orienting (Berg and Richards, 1997). Between birth and two years the development of alert, vigilant sustained attention occurs. At the end of the first two years, infants' executive attention system is beginning to function (Ruff and Rothbart, 1996; also see Rothbart and Posner, this volume). These dramatic changes in infants are commonly thought to be based predominantly on age-related changes in brain structures responsible for attention control.

This chapter has three objectives. First, brain systems that may be involved in attention and show development in infancy are reviewed. These systems include a general arousal system that affects many cognitive functions as well as specific attention systems that are limited in their effect on cognition and attention. Second, psychophysiological measures that have been useful in the study of brain–attention relations in infants are presented. The use of heart rate as a measure of the general arousal system is emphasized. Finally, several studies are examined that used these psychophysiological methods to study the development of infant attention. This re-

JOHN E. RICHARDS   Department of Psychology, University of South Carolina, Columbia, South Carolina.

view is limited to the use of heart rate as an index of the development of sustained attention, which is a general arousal system affecting a wide number of behavioral and cognitive functions controlled by the brain. These experiments are related to changes occurring in the neural systems underlying attention.

### Brain systems involved in attention

AROUSAL ATTENTION SYSTEM   One emphasis in the cognitive neuroscience of attention has been on the arousal associated with energized cognitive activity (Posner, 1995). The arousal emphasis has focused upon the increased behavioral performance that occurs when attention is engaged. This increased behavioral performance is associated with shortening of reaction times in detection tasks, increased focus of performance on specific tasks, and the sustaining of performance over extended periods of time. The arousal emphasis is nonspecific, affecting multiple modalities, cognitive systems, and cognitive processes. This arousal emphasis characterizes attention's energizing effect on cognitive and behavioral performance. Attention also may have a selective effect on specific cognitive processes or behavior without arousal properties. In fact, selective attention may serve in some situations to inhibit behavior if such inhibition is appropriate for the goal of the task.

Specific locations or systems in the brain control the arousal aspect of attention. The brain systems underlying the arousal aspect of attention have been detailed in the theoretical and empirical research literature for a number of years. An example of this arousal emphasis is a model of neuroanatomical connections between the mesencephalic reticular activating system and the cortex (Heilman et al., 1987; Mesulam, 1983). This model (diagrammed in figure 22.1) presumes that there are centers broadly scattered throughout the mesencephalic reticular activating system that are activated by sensory stimulation. In turn, the mesencephalic

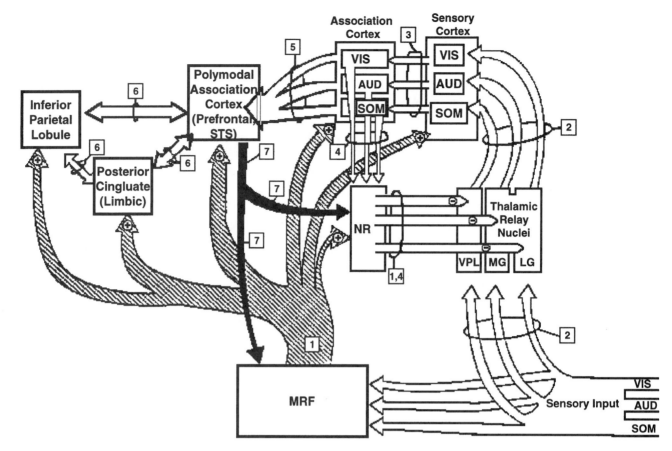

FIGURE 22.1　The arousal system of the brain. (1) Polysynaptic reticulocortical pathways; (2) sensory transmission; (3) associative cortex projections; (4) unimodal projections to reticular nucleus of the thalamus (NR); (5) sensory convergence to polymodal cortex; (6) supramodal cortex (inferior parietal lobule); (7) cortical arousal through mesencephalic reticular formation (MRF) and NR. STS, superior temporal sulcus; VIS, visual; AUD, auditory; SOM, somatosensory; VPL, ventralis posterolateralis; MG, medial geniculate; LG, lateral geniculate. (Copyright 1981, American Medical Association. Reprinted with permission from Watson, R. T., E. Valenstein, and K. M. Heilman 1981. Thalamic neglect: Possible role of the medial thalamus and nucleus reticularis in behavior. *Arch. Neurol.* 38:501–506.)

reticular activating system directly influences the limbic system, thalamus, and cortex. The cingulate cortex receives information from areas of the limbic system such as the basolateral nucleus of the amygdala and the subicular portion of the hippocampus. The cingulate cortex is a major afferent relay center that projects to parietal area PG, visual association cortical areas, and other cerebral cortex centers involved in complex cognitive functions. This neuroanatomical system acts in synchrony to "energize" primary sensory areas in the cortex and increase the efficiency of responding in those areas. This system also influences association areas and other attention systems, such as the posterior attention system described by Posner (Posner, 1995; Posner and Petersen, 1990). The nonspecificity of this system is implied by its interconnections with multiple areas that influence cognitive processing. This arousal system "invigorates" or "energizes" cognitive processes, leading to increased processing efficiency, shorter re-

action times, better detection, and sustaining of cognitive performance for extended periods of time.

Another perspective on the arousal aspect of attention is a model based on the neurochemical systems involved in arousal. Robbins and Everitt (1995) distinguish four neurochemical systems that form the basis for the arousal functions of attention: noradrenergic, cholinergic, dopaminergic, and serotoninergic. Figure 22.2 (see color plate 14) shows the projections from midbrain nuclei for these four brain systems. The nuclei that give rise to these four neurochemical systems are located in brain regions adjacent to the mesencephalic reticular activating system. Robbins and Everitt (1995) review the evidence linking these neurochemical projection systems to attention and arousal. The noradrenergic and cholinergic systems are thought to be the neurochemical systems that are most closely involved in cortical arousal as it is related to attention. The dopaminergic system affects the motivational and energetic

# Cholinergic

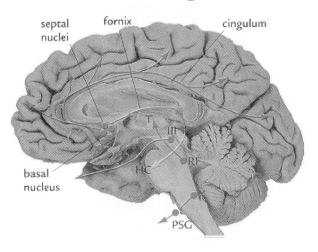

# Noradrenergic

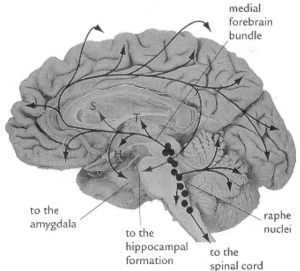

# Dopaminanergic

# Serotininergic

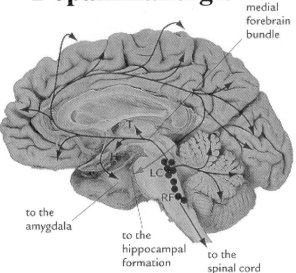

FIGURE 22.2 The neurochemical systems involved in attention and arousal. *Abbreviations:* III, oculomotor nucleus; T, thalamus; HC, hippocampal formation; RF, reticular formation; PSG, parasympathetic ganglion cell; X, dorsal motor nucleus of the vagus; H, hypothalamus; LC, locus ceruleus; C, caudate nucleus; P, putamen; S, septal nuclei; V, ventral striatum. (Reprinted with permission from Nolte, J., and J. B. Angevine, 1995. *The Human Brain.* St. Louis, MO: Mosby.)

aspects of cognitive processing and the serotonin system affects the overall control of state. These four neurochemical systems are closely linked so that more than one is likely to be operating during an aroused state.

SELECTIVE ATTENTION The second manner in which the brain affects the development of attention in infants is found in brain systems specific to selected functions. These brain areas show enhanced functioning under attention but affect only a single (or few) cognitive func-

tions. Therefore, these systems have only a narrow and selective impact on attention-based cognitive functioning. Two of these are worth mentioning in this respect. The enhancement of visual receptive fields during attention to visual stimuli has been widely studied in invasive preparations (Desimone and Duncan, 1995; Maunsell and Ferrera, 1995). This type of attention is selective for particular objects, particular spatial locations, or particular tasks. For example, the responses of visual receptive fields are enhanced in tasks requiring focused allocation of attention to that specific visual field or to objects occurring in that visual field. Objects occurring outside of that receptive field have unaffected responses when the field is irrelevant to the task, or may have attenuated responses if the object occurring in that location interferes with task performance in the specific visual field. For neurons (or neural areas) that respond in this manner, this type of attentional modulation is specific to a limited number of cognitive aspects (e.g., a specific stimulus, modality, or task) and typically occurs in a very restricted portion of the brain (e.g., individual neurons or restricted brain areas).

There are single brain systems that are distributed over large areas but whose component neural subsystems operate in a functionally dedicated or specific manner. For example, the "posterior attention system" described by Posner (Posner, 1995; Posner and Petersen, 1990; see also Rothbart and Posner, this volume) involves the parietal cortex, pulvinar, superior colliculus, and perhaps, the frontal eye fields. This attentional network has a specific purpose—that of moving attention (visual attention?) around in space and localizing receptors (eyes?) to targets at specific locations. This attention system is not sensitive to specific targets, is unrelated to attention in stimulus modalities or cognitive functions that do not involve spatial localization, and does not enhance or attenuate other cognitive systems when it operates.

These specific brain systems show development in the period of infancy and are related to behavioral indices of infant attention that show development in the same time period. Such considerations may be found in the chapters by Johnson and by Rothbart and Posner in this volume and in other sources (e.g., see Johnson's eye movement–attention model; Johnson, 1990, 1995; Johnson, Gilmore, and Csibra, 1998; Johnson, Posner, and Rothbart, 1991). These specific attention systems are not covered extensively in this chapter.

*Psychophysiological measures of infant attention*

Psychophysiological measures are useful in the study of infant attention and infant brain development. Psychophysiology, which studies psychological processes using physiological measures, is focused on the psychological processes themselves as well as their relation to the processes affecting the physiological measures (Andreassi, 1989). The physiological measures used in psychophysiology are noninvasive and thus may be used with human participants such as infants. Additionally, most of these physiological measures are practical in psychological experiments. Recording equipment and sensors are nonintrusive and the sensors do not disrupt the infant's

normal behavior patterns. The use of heart rate and EEG/ERP as psychophysiological measures of attention is reviewed briefly, exemplifying this approach.

HEART RATE  Heart rate is the most common measure used by psychophysiologists who study young infants. The electrocardiogram (ECG) is measured with surface electrodes placed on the infant's chest, back, arms, or legs. Heart rate is derived from the ECG by measuring the interval between two "R-waves" of the ECG and is defined as the "inter-beat interval" (IBI; R–R Interval), or as the inverse of the IBI, heart rate (beats per minute, bpm). The infant's heart rate may be measured in response to psychological manipulations as a measure of attention .The infant's heart rate also may form the basis for determining if the infant is attending to a stimulus, and psychological manipulations are then made on the basis of the heart rate change (e.g., Richards, 1987). Heart rate may be used to distinguish general and specific forms of attention.

Richards (Berg and Richards, 1997; Richards, 1995; Richards and Casey, 1992; Richards and Hunter, 1998) has presented a model in which infants' heart rate changes during stimulus presentation are used to distinguish four attention phases: the automatic interrupt, the orienting response, sustained attention, and attention termination. Heart rate and attention level vary during these phases. Figure 22.3 schematically depicts the heart rate changes occurring during these phases of attention. This figure represents heart rate changes of infants from 3 to 6 months of age presented with a visual stimulus (Richards and Casey, 1991). The figure also has labeled a "preattention" phase and "preatten-

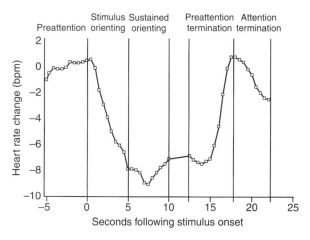

FIGURE 22.3  Average heart rate change as a function of stimulus following stimulus onset for the heart rate defined attention phases for infants from 3 to 6 months of age. (From Richards and Casey, 1991.)

tion termination" phase. These periods are simply the period of time before the presentation of the stimulus (preattention) and before heart rate returns to its prestimulus level but after sustained attention has occurred (preattention termination).

Sustained attention and attention termination affect a wide range of cognitive functions in infants. The heart rate slows down and remains below prestimulus levels during sustained attention. Cognitively, this phase of attention involves subject-controlled processing of stimulus information. Sustained attention is accompanied behaviorally by maintaining fixation on a focal stimulus in the presence of a peripheral distracting stimulus (Hicks and Richards, 1998; Hunter and Richards, 1997; Lansink and Richards, 1997; Richards, 1987, 1997a), acquiring stimulus information (Richards, 1997b) and exhibiting recognition memory (Richards and Casey, 1990), and enhancement of responses in a selected stimulus modality and inhibition of responses in a non-selected stimulus modality (Richards, 1998, 2000a). Alternatively, at the end of sustained attention the heart rate returns to its prestimulus level and the phase of attention termination occurs. Attention termination is accompanied by inattentiveness toward the stimulus in the presence of continued fixation on the stimulus, i.e., heightened levels of distractibility, lack of acquisition of stimulus information, and lack of selective modality effects.

The arousal system of the brain controls the heart rate changes that occur during sustained attention. The neural control of this heart rate change originates from cardioinhibitory centers in the orbitofrontal cortex. This area has reciprocal connections with the limbic system and through these connections is involved in modulating activity within the mesencephalic reticular formation arousal system (Heilman et al., 1987; Mesulam, 1983) and probably the dopaminergic and cholinergic neurotransmitter systems (Robbins and Everitt, 1995). The cardioinhibitory centers act through the parasympathetic nervous system to slow heart rate when the arousal system is engaged. This slowing of heart rate occurs as "vagus nerve" (10th cranial nerve) activity increases, leading to a slowing of the cardiac pacemaker firing, increases in interbeat intervals, and heart rate slowing. The "arousal" system does not result in more activity in heart rate, but inhibited activity. Similarly, some other peripheral physiological processes (e.g., body movement) are inhibited during conditions of attentive arousal. Thus, the arousal brain system when operating in this arousal-attention manner selectively enhances some brain systems and functions while inhibiting others.

The phases of sustained attention and attention termination are markers of the nonspecific arousal system of the brain (Richards and Casey, 1992; Richards and Hunter, 1998). This nonspecific arousal system sustains attention and maintains a vigilant state. The heart rate changes occurring during sustained attention (sustained heart rate slowing) index the onset and continuing presence of this arousal. The heart rate changes during attention termination (return of heart rate to its prestimulus level) index the lack of activation of this arousal system. These two phases of attention therefore reflect the nonspecific arousal that may affect a number of sensory and brain systems. Incidentally, these phases and the "automatic interrupt" and "stimulus orienting" attention phases also may be used to measure specific attentional systems in the young infant (e.g., Balaban, 1996; Berg and Richards, 1997; Richards, 1998, 2000a).

The heart rate changes occurring during attention and their indexing of arousal brain systems are important for developmental cognitive neuroscience because these heart rate changes show important developmental changes in the first six months of infancy. A consistent pattern of developmental changes has been shown to occur in the sustained attention phase. The level of the heart rate deceleration during sustained attention increases from 14 to 26 weeks of age (3 to 6 months) (Casey and Richards, 1988; Richards, 1985, 1987, 1989a,b, 1994). The level of heart rate during sustained attention is thought to reflect the depth of the arousal. Thus, the changes in the evoked heart rate response during sustained attention imply that the arousal controlled by the brain is increasing over this age range.

The age change in heart rate during sustained attention parallels some of the behavioral manifestations of attention. This includes an increasing ability of infants to acquire familiarity with stimulus characteristics in a fixed period of time (Frick and Richards, 2001; Richards, 1997b), enhanced tracking of moving stimuli (Richards and Holley, 1999), and the selective modality enhancement effect found in selective attention (Richards, 1998, 2000a). The behavioral and heart rate indices of attention are not as well synchronized at younger ages (e.g., 8 weeks) as they are at older ages (Hicks and Richards, 1998; Hunter and Richards, 1999, 2000; Richards, 1989b). The age-related changes in heart rate during sustained attention, and these age changes in the tasks corresponding to sustained attention, imply that this general arousal system develops in the first few months of infancy and that it increasingly affects infants' cognitive behavior.

OTHER PSYCHOPHYSIOLOGICAL MEASURES   There are other psychophysiological measures that have been used in the study of infant attention and its development. Although not reviewed extensively in this chapter, two in particular are worth mentioning: the electroencephalogram (EEG) and scalp-recorded event-related-potentials (ERPs). Spontaneous electrical activity of very small magnitude may be recorded from the human scalp. This activity is termed the "electroencephalogram" (EEG). Scalp EEG consists of continuous voltage changes that are caused by action potentials summed over large numbers of neurons, synapses, or neural pathways. This activity in the brain comes primarily from activity in the cerebral cortex and thalamocortical connections and so measures activity in the cerebral cortex. The EEG has been used in adults as a measure of nonspecific arousal (e.g., Ray, 1990) and occasionally in infants as a measure of arousal during task performance (e.g., see Bell, 1998). This measure could be useful for a relatively direct measure of cortical activity (though it cannot be easily linked to specific cortical areas). However, EEG has not been used frequently in the context of infant attention development. This chapter does not review the developmental changes occurring in EEG, but the reader may refer to other sources (e.g., Bell, 1998, 1999; Bell and Fox, 1992, 1994; Berg and Berg, 1987).

Scalp-recorded event-related-potentials (ERPs) are derived from the EEG recording. The EEG may be time-locked to specific experimental events and averaged over multiple trials, resulting in averaged ERPs. The ERP has varying positive and negative electrical waves that are referred to as "components." These components are hypothesized to be caused by specific cortical events, which are, in turn, hypothesized to be closely related to psychological processes. These components include those such as the P1 (or P100), N1, P2, N2, P3 (or P300), and various slow waves (for a discussion of these components in infants, see Nelson, 1994; Nelson and Dukette, 1998; or de Haan and Nelson, 1997; for a discussion of these components in adults, see Hillyard et al., 1995, or Swick, Kutas, and Neville, 1994).

The ERP is thought to reflect specific cognitive processes, and also may provide a noninvasive and direct measure of functioning within specific brain areas (see Hillyard et al., 1995). For example, specific components of the ERP change in response to familiar and unfamiliar visual stimuli (Nelson and Collins, 1991, 1992). These authors demonstrated changes in the amplitudes and latencies of specific ERP components in response to visually presented novel stimuli. Likewise, the ERP may be used to index specific attentional responses. One such measure is the Nc (negative central) component (Courchesne, 1977, 1978) which is thought to represent a relatively automatic alerting response to the presence of a visual stimulus, especially a novel stimulus (cf. heart-rate–defined "stimulus orienting," Richards and Casey, 1992; see also Recognition of Briefly Presented Visual Stimuli). The ERP has been used extensively in infant participants, and many reviews of this measure are available (Berg and Berg, 1987; Nelson, 1994; Nelson and Dukette, 1998; see also Nelson and Monk, this volume; Johnson, Mareschal, and Csibra, this volume).

PSYCHOPHYSIOLOGICAL MEASURES AS "MARKER TASKS"
Some comments should be made on the nature of the psychophysiological measures as direct or indirect measures of brain activity. Many psychophysiological measures are indirect measures of brain activity. Heart rate as an index of a general arousal system in the brain should be considered an indirect measure. The connections between the mesencephalic reticular activating system, its associated attention-arousal system (Heilman et al., 1987; Mesulam, 1983), and heart rate control are well known. Also, the connection between the neurochemical arousal systems (Robbins and Everitt, 1995) and cardiac control are known. But the measurement of such brain systems is indirect when using heart rate as a psychophysiological measure of infant attention. The EEG is an indirect measure of such a brain system when used to measure arousal.

The indirect measure of brain activity with psychophysiological measures is similar to the "marker task" concept detailed by Johnson (1997). Marker tasks are behavioral tasks that have been studied in animal or invasive preparations and are controlled by specific brain areas or systems. Johnson (1997) proposes that such tasks may be used in infants and children with the understanding that developmental changes in these tasks should reflect developmental changes in the brain areas that control their functioning. In the case of behavioral marker tasks or psychophysiological measures, a solid theoretical or empirical basis for relating the measure to a brain system or controlling brain functions is necessary. The study of attention further requires that these brain systems be related to common attention functions (arousal, selection). Finally, the psychophysiological measures, or the behavioral tasks, should be used in experimental situations in which relevant psychological processes affect the physiological system (or behavioral marker task). The indirect psychophysiological measures (and behavioral marker tasks) allow inferences to be made about brain development and help to inform a developmental cognitive neuroscience approach to attention.

Some psychophysiological indices reflect brain activity more directly. The EEG and ERP are direct measures of brain function in some contexts. For example, auditory brainstem-evoked potentials are derived from highly filtered, event-averaged EEG. These brainstem-evoked potentials are generated at specific points in the neural pathway from the peripheral auditory apparatus through the auditory nerves to the brainstem. They measure functioning of these pathways in a direct sense. Similarly, some cortical ERP measures may be similarly interpreted using high-density recording (Tucker, 1993; Tucker et al., 1994), and cortical sources may be hypothesized and compared with the scalp distribution of the ERP components (Nunez, 1990; Scherg, 1990; Scherg and Picton, 1991). Functioning of the cortical areas may be inferred from these cortical source localization procedures in a direct fashion. The use of the ERP and cortical source localization procedures as a direct measure in the study of attention is only beginning with infant participants. Such use of the EEG and ERP should lead to a higher quality of information about the relation between the brain and attention in infant psychological development.

In the rest of the chapter we review studies that show the developmental changes that occur in the arousal form of attention. The first section reviews two studies (Richards, 1998, 2000a) that use modification of the blink reflex with selective attention. These studies show how a specific attention system interacts with the development of the general arousal system. Next we review a study (Richards and Holley, 1999) showing the effect of the developing arousal system on eye movements that themselves show development over the first six months in infancy. The final section of the reviews presents some studies that show developmental changes in sustained attention that are related to a "higher cognitive function," infants' recognition of briefly presented visual stimuli (Frick and Richards, 2001; Richards, 1997b, 2000b; Richards and Casey, 1990). These studies show that familiarization of patterns presented for only a few seconds during sustained attention results in recognition memory (Frick and Richards, 2001; Richards, 1997b). This section also presents some new, as yet unpublished data which show that during attentive states infants will recognize stimuli very quickly, exhibiting appropriate EEG and ERP changes associated with recognition memory (Richards, 2000b). These studies should be considered examples of how developmental psychophysiology may contribute to developmental cognitive neuroscience of attention.

### Selective attentional modification of blink reflexes

Here we review studies showing the effect of selective attention on the blink reflex and examine how the de-velopment of the arousal attention system in young infants modulates this selective attention effect. The startle reflex is a response to high-intensity short-duration stimuli, and includes widespread flexor jerk and whole body startle. One aspect of the startle reflex is the startle blink reflex. The blink reflex occurs in response to visual, auditory, tactile, and other stimuli. The acoustic startle blink reflex and the visual startle blink reflex are based upon short-latency reflex pathways involving first-order neurons in the sensory pathways and the brainstem cranial nerves that move the muscles for the blink (Balaban, 1996; Davis, 1997; Hackley and Boelhouwer, 1997). The blink reflex represents an "automatic interrupt" system that interrupts ongoing information processing and shifts the organism's goals for other activities (Graham, 1979, 1992).

One characteristic of the blink reflex that has been of interest to cognitive psychophysiologists is its modifiability by selective attention. Directing attention to one stimulus modality enhances the blink reflex to a stimulus of that modality and attenuates the blink reflex to stimuli in other modalities (Anthony, 1991; Anthony and Graham, 1983, 1985; Balaban, Anthony, and Graham, 1989; Hackley and Graham, 1983; Haerich, 1994; Richards, 1998, 2000a). This attentional modulation shows that a higher-order cognitive process, selective attention to a specific modality, may modify reflexes controlled by simple reflex arcs in the central nervous system. This attenuation/modification of the blink reflex also may be used as an index of the amount of higher-order selective attention. The modality-selective effect of attention on the blink reflex has been shown in young infants (Anthony and Graham, 1983; Balaban, Anthony, and Graham, 1989; Richards, 1998, 2000a).

Two recent studies used heart rate changes associated with the arousal aspect of attention to show developmental changes in the selective modality effect on the blink reflex (Richards, 1998, 2000a). In these studies, infants at 8, 14, 20, or 26 weeks of age were presented in the foreground with interesting visual or auditory stimuli (Richards, 1998) or a multimodal auditory-visual stimulus (Richards, 2000a). The infant's heart rate was recorded and delays were defined according to heart rate changes associated with phases of attention. For example, "sustained attention" was defined as a significant heart rate deceleration beyond the prestimulus level, and "attention termination" was defined as a return of heart rate to its prestimulus level following a period of sustained attention. When it was thought that sustained attention was engaged, or attention was unengaged, an auditory or visual stimulus that elicits a blink reflex was presented. The amplitude of the blink reflex was measured and compared in the attentive (aroused) and inattentive (unaroused) conditions.

There were three results relevant to the present chapter. As expected from previous studies with adults and young infants, there was a selective modality effect on the blink reflex. Figure 22.4 (Richards, 1998) shows the blink reflex magnitude for attentive and inattentive conditions as a function of the match between the foreground stimulus and the blink reflex stimulus. During sustained attention the blink magnitude was larger when the foreground and blink reflex stimulus were in the same modality, and the blink magnitude was smaller when the modalities did not match. Alternatively, during attention termination this selective modality effect was not found. These effects were very similar when single modality foreground stimuli were used (Richards, 1998) or multimodal foreground stimuli were used (Richards, 2000a).

There was a developmental change in the level of the selective modality effect from 8 to 26 weeks of age in this study. Figure 22.5 (Richards, 1998) shows the difference between a prestimulus condition in which attention was not engaged and the modality-match and modality-mismatch conditions during sustained attention. Over these ages there was a clear increase in the enhancement of the blink reflex for the modality-match conditions and an increase in the attenuation of the blink reflex for the modality-mismatch conditions. This implies that the selective modality effect occurs primarily when the infants were highly aroused (sustained attention) but does not occur during lack of arousal or inattentiveness (attention termination).

There were no selective modality effects on heart rate itself, and the heart rate changes worked similarly in their enhancement/attenuation effects for auditory, visual, and multimodal auditory-visual stimuli. For example, the heart rate changes in response to the visual and auditory blink stimuli were the same regardless of the foreground stimulus to which attention was directed. This implies that the heart rate changes were indexing a general arousal system rather than one tied to a specific sensory modality or a specific attention system. This is consistent with the idea that the heart rate changes during sustained attention reflect the general arousal systems of the brain.

These studies show how a specific attention system interacts with the developing general arousal system of the brain. The heart rate changes that indicated sustained attention or attention termination are hypothesized to be an index of the general arousal system of the brain (Heilman et al., 1987; Mesulam, 1983; Robbins and Everitt, 1995). This general arousal system shows development over this period of infancy (i.e., 2–6 months). The blink reflex represents simple preatten-

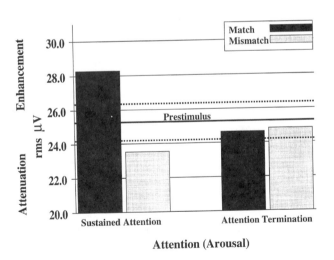

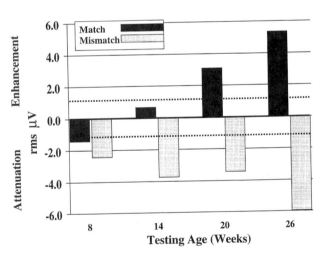

FIGURE 22.4  Blink reflex magnitude (rms, μV) as a function of the sustained attention or attention termination and the match/mismatch between the foreground and the blink stimulus. The solid black bars represent trials on which the foreground and the blink reflex stimuli were in the same modality, and the light bars represent trials on which the foreground and blink reflex stimuli were in different modalities. Also shown is the average blink magnitude on prestimulus trials with no foreground stimulus (solid line; SE ranges as dashed line). (Adapted from Richards, 1998.)

FIGURE 22.5  Blink reflex magnitude (rms, μV) difference from the prestimulus to the sustained attention conditions and the match/mismatch between the foreground and the blink stimulus, separately for the four testing ages. The solid black bars represent trials on which the foreground and the blink reflex stimuli were in the same modality, and the light bars represent trials on which the foreground and blink reflex stimuli were in different modalities. The SE for the prestimulus trials is shown as a dashed line around the 0 rms μV point. (Adapted from Richards, 1998.)

tive cognitive processes (e.g., "automatic interrupt"; see Graham, 1979, 1992) and is controlled by subcortical pathways and brain mechanisms. The spinal motor neurons controlling the blink muscles and the brainstem afferent pathways involved in the blink reflexes are relatively mature at birth (Balaban, 1996). Thus, the reflex itself shows little developmental change over the testing ages such as those used in this study. The development of sustained attention over this age range thus influences the extent to which selective attention will affect this low-level cognitive process. Over this age range there is an increasing influence of the general arousal system over this very specific attention system, both controlled by brain processes.

## Visual smooth pursuit eye movements and attention

This section reviews the relation between the development of the arousal attention system in young infants and three eye movement control systems that show development in the same period of time. There are three types of eye movements that may be made when tracking visual stimuli. Each eye movement type is controlled by separate areas of the brain. *Reflexive saccadic* eye movements occur in response to the sudden onset of a peripheral stimulus. These eye movements are controlled by a brain pathway involving the retina, lateral geniculate nucleus, superior colliculus, and perhaps the primary visual area (Schiller, 1985, 1998). *Voluntary saccadic* eye movements occur under voluntary or planned control. These eye movements often involve attention-directed targeted eye movements. The voluntary saccadic eye movements are controlled by a brain pathway involving several parts of the cortex, visual areas 1, 2, and 4, the parietal cortex area PG, and the frontal eye fields (Schiller, 1985, 1998). *Smooth pursuit* eye movements represent a third type of eye movements used in tracking visual stimuli. These eye movements occur only in the presence of smoothly moving visual stimuli, and smoothly track visual stimuli over a wide range of visual space. Smooth pursuit eye movements also are controlled by brain pathways involving the cortex, including areas MT (medial temporal) and MST (middle superior temporal), and perhaps the parietal cortex (Schiller, 1985, 1998). The voluntary saccadic and smooth pursuit eye movements are affected by attention whereas reflexive saccadic eye movements are relatively independent of attention control.

Unlike the blink reflex, the brain areas involved in the control of these three eye movement systems undergo developmental changes in the first six months. There have been several models of the brain changes

affecting eye movement development, including models by Bronson (1974, 1997), Maurer and Lewis (1979, 1991, 1998), Johnson and colleagues (Johnson, 1990, 1995; Johnson, Gilmore, and Csibra, 1991; Johnson, Posner, and Rothbart, 1998), Hood (Hood, 1995; Hood, Atkinson, and Braddick, 1998), and Richards (Richards and Casey, 1992; Richards and Hunter, 1998). A model proposed by Johnson (1990, 1995; Johnson, Gilmore, and Csibra, 1991; Johnson, Posner, and Rothbart, 1998) describes the developmental changes in these three eye movement systems. This model hypothesizes that layers of the primary visual area develop at different rates and become mature at different ages. The primary visual area layers containing brain pathways that control reflexive eye movement are relatively mature at birth, hence reflexive saccadic eye movements dominate the infant's behavior in the first 2 postnatal months. The primary visual area layers that contain brain pathways which control voluntary saccadic eye movements develop rapidly from the first to the sixth postnatal months. In conjunction with this development, attention-directed voluntary saccades show developmental changes over the first six months. Finally, the primary visual area layers that contain brain pathways which control smooth pursuit eye movements develop more slowly than the other layers. Several parts of the brain pathways that control smooth pursuit eye movements show protracted developmental changes over the first two years (Richards and Hunter, 1998). Thus, smooth pursuit eye movements are the latest to begin development and show changes over a longer period than just the first six months of infancy. Figure 22.6 (Richards and Hunter, 1998) shows a hypothetical developmental trend for these three eye movement systems.

Richards and Holley (1999) examined infants' tracking behavior over this age range under conditions of attention and inattention. Their study shows how the development of the general arousal system affects the exhibition of eye movements in the first six months of infancy. Infants at 8, 14, 20, and 26 weeks of age were presented with stimuli that moved at varying speeds (8–24 deg/s) on a television monitor. The infants' heart rate was recorded and periods of visual tracking were separated into attentive and inattentive states using the heart-rate–defined attention phases described earlier. The infants' eye movements were tracked with an electrooculogram (EOG) by recording electrical potential changes due to shifts in the eyes. The eye movements were separated into smooth pursuit and saccadic eye movements and related to the attentiveness of the infant.

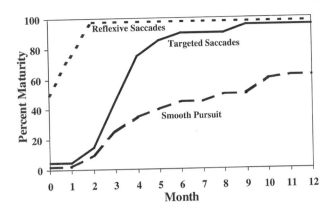

FIGURE 22.6 Development of three visual systems involved in visual tracking. The percent maturity shown as a function of months, from birth through 12 months. There are three lines, corresponding to the reflexive saccadic eye movements (Reflexive Saccades), voluntary saccadic eye movements (Targeted Saccades), and smooth pursuit eye movements (Smooth Pursuit). (From Richards and Hunter, 1998.)

There were several results from that study. As expected, there was an increase in tracking ability over this age range, smooth pursuit eye movements improved, and the infants' use of saccades to track the stimuli complemented their use of smooth pursuit eye movements. Two findings in that study are most relevant to the present chapter. As expected from the Johnson model and the age changes in the three eye movement systems described by that model, there were developmental changes in the voluntary saccadic and smooth pursuit eye movement systems but not in the reflexive saccadic eye movements. Figure 22.7 shows the smooth pursuit and saccadic eye movement results under conditions of attention and inattention. In figure 22.7, the youngest two ages (8 and 14 weeks) and the oldest two ages (20 and 26 weeks) were combined (although these results actually were graded over all four ages). The lower right part of figure 22.7 shows the saccade frequency occurring during the inattentive periods. These would be most similar to the reflexive saccadic eye movements. The younger and older infants show approximately equal numbers of these eye movements. Alternatively, in the upper panels it can be seen that saccade frequency and smooth pursuit gain showed a difference in the youngest and oldest infants. These two systems correspond to voluntary saccadic and smooth pursuit eye movements. These findings show the expected age changes for these three eye movement systems as might be predicted from figure 22.6.

A second finding from that study is also related to our current concerns. The tracking stimulus was presented at speeds ranging from "very slow" to "very fast"

for the capabilities of infants' smooth pursuit (Richards and Holley, 1999). The reflexive saccadic eye movements were unresponsive to the stimulus speed (figure 22.7, lower right panel), whereas smooth pursuit tracking and saccadic tracking during attention were responsive to stimulus speed (figure 22.7, upper panels). Additionally, at the two older ages it took faster speeds before there was a significant drop in tracking gain. The complementary nature of the smooth pursuit and saccadic eye movement systems also was shown during attention. When the older infants (4.5 and 6 months of age) were attentive to the stimulus display, the infants shifted from smooth pursuit tracking to saccadic tracking as the speed of the tracking stimulus became too fast for smooth pursuit eye movements to follow (figure 22.7, cf. left and right panels). Thus during aroused attentive states the oldest infants used the smooth pursuit and voluntary saccadic eye movements to track the visual stimulus and adjusted the parameters of the eye movements according to the speed of the tracking stimulus.

The results from this study suggest at least two roles that sustained attention may play in behavior. First, the arousal system of the brain acts to energize specific brain systems involved in cognitive activities. In this study the general level of increased performance during sustained attention reflects this arousal. The simultaneous development of the eye movement systems (smooth pursuit, voluntary saccadic) and arousal system (sustained attention) resulted in a synchrony between attention and eye movement control. Second, sustained attention does more than just energize involved systems. Tracking behavior during sustained attention was preserved over increases in tracking speeds by shifting from smooth pursuit tracking to saccadic tracking when smooth tracking failed. The attention-arousal system also acts to select the appropriate behavior, given the feedback being received from the stimulus display and whatever goals the infant has in the situation.

*Recognition of briefly presented visual stimuli*

This section reviews studies showing the effect of sustained attention on infant recognition memory. Infant recognition memory is often studied with the paired-comparison procedure (Fagan, 1974). In this procedure infants are familiarized with a single stimulus (*familiar stimulus*) during a familiarization phase. Then, during the recognition memory test phase the familiar stimulus is paired with a stimulus not previous seen (*novel stimulus*). Recognition memory for the familiar stimulus is inferred if the infants show a novelty pref-

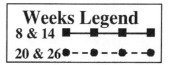

## Sustained HR Deceleration

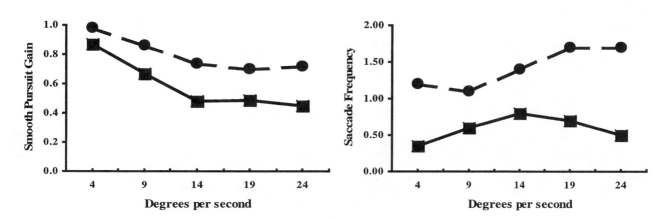

## Return of HR to Prestimulus Level

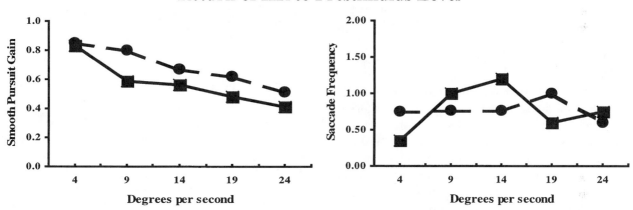

FIGURE 22.7  The smooth pursuit EOG gain and saccade frequency (saccades per second) as a function of stimulus tracking speed and testing age (8 and 14 weeks combined, 20 and 26 weeks combined). The top two plots were taken from the period when sustained heart rate deceleration was occurring, and the bottom two plots were taken from the period after heart rate had returned to its prestimulus level. (Adapted from Richards and Holley, 1999; Richards and Hunter, 1998.)

erence, i.e., look longer at the novel stimulus than the familiar stimulus during the paired-comparison test phase.

Two studies using heart-rate–defined attention phases have shown that exposure to the familiar stimulus during sustained attention results in recognition memory for stimuli presented for just 5 or 6 seconds (Frick and Richards, 2001; Richards, 1997b). In these studies infants at 14, 20, or 26 weeks of age were presented with a Sesame Street movie, "Follow That Bird," on a television monitor. This movie is very interesting to young infants and reliably elicits the full range of

heart rate changes that are related to the attention phases. On separate trials, at a delay defined by the deceleration of heart rate, a delay defined by the return of heart rate to its prestimulus level, or time-defined delays, a familiarization stimulus was presented for 5 or 6 seconds. One condition with the Sesame Street movie alone was provided (no familiarization stimulus, i.e., no-exposure control) and one condition with a 20-second exposure to the familiar stimulus was presented. Following each familiar stimulus presentation, a paired-comparison recogniton memory test was done. The infants' duration of fixation on the novel and the familiar stimulus during the first 10 seconds of the test phase were recorded.

Several results showed that the infants recognized the familiar stimulus and preferred to look at the novel stimulus in the test phase, with only 5 seconds of familiar stimulus exposure. For example, when compared to the no-exposure control trial, infants looked longer at the novel stimulus than at the familiar stimulus. Furthermore, infants looked at the novel stimulus in the test phase for the brief exposure trials (5 or 6 s) as long as they did during the traditional 20-second accumulated fixation exposure trial.

The most interesting result from these studies is illustrated in figure 22.8 (Richards, 1997b). This figure shows the duration of the exposure to the familiar stimulus during the familiarization phase, but for different lengths of exposure during the sustained heart rate deceleration. That is, for some trials the infants' sustained attention overlapped the familiar stimulus exposure for only a brief period of time (e.g., <1 s), and on other trials the overlap was much greater (e.g., >5 s). This exposure is shown for different trials, and the percent fixation on the novel stimulus in the recognition memory test phase is plotted. A very brief overlap of sustained attention and the familiar stimulus resulted in novelty preference scores at or below the no-exposure control condition. As the amount of familiar stimulus exposure during sustained attention increased, there was a corresponding increase in the novelty preference. This positive correlation between familiar exposure during sustained attention and later recognition memory level (novelty preference level) implies that incorporation of stimulus information is accomplished when the infant is in a highly aroused (attentive) state.

We also have shown that the distributions of the fixations on the novel and familiar stimulus in the test phase of the paired-comparison recognition memory procedure are affected by the infants' attention state (Richards and Casey, 1990). In that study heart rate was recorded and the heart-rate–defined attention phases were evaluated during the test phase of the recognition memory procedure. The infants showed novelty preference, indicating recognition memory, primarily during sustained attention. For example, on the average in these 3–6-month-old infants, there was about 11.8 s of sustained attention on the recognition memory test phase. Of this, about 7.3 s was spent looking at the novel stimulus and 4.5 s was spent looking at the familiar stimulus. Alternatively, during attention termination (or inattentiveness) the infants spent equal amounts of time looking at the novel and familiar stimulus. And on no-familiar-stimulus trials (no-exposure control) there were equal amounts of looking at the novel and familiar

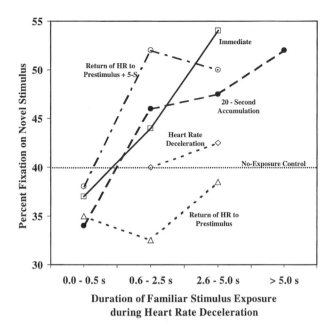

FIGURE 22.8  The duration of familiar exposure occurring during heart rate deceleration (sustained attention) and the percent fixation on the novel stimulus in the recognition memory test phase. The no-exposure control time (40%) should be considered the baseline percent fixation with no exposure to the familiar stimulus. (Adapted from Richards, 1997.)

stimulus during each phase. These results show that the exhibition of recognition memory generally takes place during sustained attention, when heart rate is below baseline. That is, the infants recognize the familiar stimulus and move fixation to the novel stimulus. This move to the novel stimulus most likely is to acquire new stimulus information. Thus the exhibition of recognition memory during this paired-comparison procedure, shown as novelty preference, is precisely the infant's attempt to acquire new information from the previously unseen stimulus during sustained attention!

We are now conducting a study to examine the effect of attention on individual cognitive processes that may occur in the brain upon exposure to familiar and novel stimuli (preliminary data presented in Richards, 2000b). Nelson and colleagues (Nelson and Collins, 1991, 1992; Nelson and deRegnier, 1992; Nelson and Salapatek, 1986; also see reviews by Nelson, 1994; Nelson and Dukette, 1998; Nelson and Monk, this volume) and others (Karrer and Ackles, 1987, 1988; Karrer and Monti, 1997; Courchesne, 1977, 1978; Courchesne, Ganz, and Norcia, 1981) have examined infant recognition memory recording ERPs during stimulus presentations of very brief duration (~150 ms). These studies use the "oddball" paradigm in which one stimulus is presented relatively frequently and a second stimulus is presented infrequently. These studies report a large negative ERP component occurring about 400–800 ms after stimulus onset located primarily in the frontal and central EEG leads. This has been labeled the Nc (negative central) component (Courchesne, 1977, 1978). In most studies the Nc component is larger to the infrequently presented stimuli and is thought to represent a general attentive state or alerting to the presence of a novel stimulus. If the frequently presented and infrequently presented stimuli are already familiar to the infant, the Nc component does not differ (Nelson and Collins, 1991, 1992). This distinction does not occur in 4-month-old infants (Karrer and Ackles, 1987; Nelson and Collins, 1991, 1992) but does occur in infants 6 months old and older.

These oddball procedure studies also report later components in the ERP. These components are slowly changing positive or negative potential shifts from about 800 to 1500 ms following stimulus presentation. Nelson and Collins (1991) reported that in 6-month-old infants there are three distinctions that may be made. First, a familiar stimulus that was presented infrequently (infrequent familiar, IF) resulted in an increased slow-wave positivity in this later period relative to the ERP observed when the familiar stimulus was presented frequently (frequent familiar, FF). Second, a series of stimuli that were never previously presented to the infant and were presented infrequently (infrequent novel, IN) were presented. These stimuli resulted in a negative slow wave component in this later interval. Thus, these novel stimuli show that infants were sensitive to novelty per se (IN versus IF) as well as the relative probability of stimulus occurrence (IF versus FF). As with the Nc component, at 4 months of age there was no difference between the later occurring slow waves, whereas by 6 months of age (Nelson and Collins, 1991) or 8 or 12 months (Nelson and Collins, 1992; Nelson and deRegnier, 1992) these three stimulus presentation procedures resulted in differing ERP potential shifts.

We are currently conducting a study using this procedure, measuring ERPs, and presenting the FF, IF, and IN stimuli in different phases of attention (Richards, 2000b). As with the other studies of infant recognition memory (Frick and Richards, 2001; Richards, 1997b) 1the infant's attention is elicited with a Sesame Street movie, "Follow That Bird," that elicits the heart-rate–defined attention phases. Then, during stimulus orienting, sustained attention, or attention termination, the brief visual stimuli are presented overlaying (replacing) the attention-eliciting stimulus. These briefly presented stimuli consist of static computer-generated patterns that are easily discriminable by infants at these

ages (e.g., checkerboard pattern, circles, squares). We have data from 6-month-old infants and are currently testing 4.5- and 7.5-month-old infants to extend these findings to other ages and to test developmental changes occurring in these memory processes.

Figure 22.9 shows ERP changes from the central (Cz) and parietal (Pz) leads in 6-month-old infants in response to the visual stimuli. The top two graphs show the ERP changes for the first stimulus on each trial (stimulus orienting), during sustained attention, and during inattentiveness. The ERP changes in these two graphs show a significantly larger Nc component (negative component about 400–700 ms) for the "attentive" phases (stimulus orienting, sustained attention, dashed lines) compared to the "inattentive" phase (attention termination, solid line). This confirms the idea that the Nc component represents an "attention-alerting" mechanism that occurs in response to any visual stimulus. The bottom two graphs of figure 22.9 show the ERP changes for the three presentation procedures (FF, IF, and IN) only for the presentations occurring during sustained attention. The Nc is not different for these three procedures, but the slow wave portion of the graphs (750–1500 ms) shows a large positive slow wave for the infrequent familiar presentation and a smaller negative slow wave for the infrequent novel stimulus. The stimulus presentations occurring during inattention did not show the slow wave differences between the three presentation procedures (not shown in figure 22.9).

Figure 22.10 (see color plate 15) shows topographical maps of the Nc and a later slow wave for the IF and FF stimuli during sustained attention. These show the Nc component as a widespread negativity in the central area of the scalp occurring for the frequent and infrequent familiar stimuli, but the later slow wave component occurred primarily in the frontal-central regions only for the infrequently presented stimuli.

The relation between sustained attention and infants' recognition of briefly presented visual stimuli shows that the arousal form of attention is related to complex infant cognition. Recognition memory is accomplished by several brain areas and cognitive functions. It requires the acquisition of stimulus information and memory storage over some period of time. The measurement of recognition memory also requires performance on a task exhibiting the existence of the stored memory. The results of these studies show that the arousal aspect of attention may "invigorate" each of these cognitive processes. This enhances familiarization when information acquisition is occurring, may facilitate memory consolidation during the waiting period, and enhances the processes involved in the exhibition

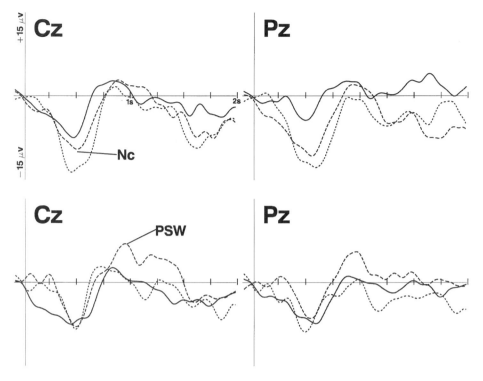

FIGURE 22.9   The ERP in response to the frequent familiar, infrequent familiar, and infrequent novel presentations for 6-month-old infants. These recordings are from the Pz (parietal scalp area) and Cz (central scalp area) leads. The top two plots represent the ERP for the first stimulus in a trial (stimulus orienting, small dashes), when sustained heart rate deceleration was occurring (sustained attention, long dashes), and when heart rate had returned to its prestimulus level (atten- tion termination, solid line). The Nc component is identified on the Cz recording. The bottom two plots represent the ERP occurring during sustained attention for the frequent familiar (solid line), infrequent familiar (long dashes), and infrequent novel (short dashes) presentations. The positive slow wave (PSW) is identified for the ERP to the infrequent familiar stimulus.

of recognition memory. The effect on recognition memory is true for the overall responses to the stimulus in the paired-comparison recognition-memory test phase (Richards and Casey, 1990) and for the individual cognitive processes occurring for transient responses to the stimulus (Richards, 2000b).

*Conclusions*

Attention shows dramatic development in the early pe- riod of infancy, from birth to 12 months. This chapter has emphasized an attention system that represents a general arousal of cognitive functions. The system in the brain controlling this arousal develops in the first few months of life, and this brain development is re- sponsible for the behavioral/attentional development seen in young infants. This chapter reviewed several studies that showed the effect of this arousal system, indexed by heart rate changes showing sustained atten- tion. There were developmental changes in infant sus- tained attention that were reflected in developmental

changes in specific attentional systems or that corre- sponded to developments occurring in other brain- based attention-directed infant behavior.

There are three ways in which future research and progress in the study of the development of attention- arousal in infants could progress. First, this review was limited to studies using heart rate as a measure of the general arousal system in the brain. There are other measures that may be useful in this regard. For exam- ple, continuous levels of EEG activity are thought to be influenced by general arousal mechanisms in the brain. Since the EEG represents the summed activity of large groups of neurons, one might expect that the brain ar- eas controlling arousal or the neurochemical systems should have an influence on overall neural activity (ex- tent, duration, and localization). Thus, measures of EEG such as spectral power and coherence may give information about arousal. Such measures also may show relatively localized CNS arousal.

A second area in which research on the development of the brain systems controlling arousal may benefit is

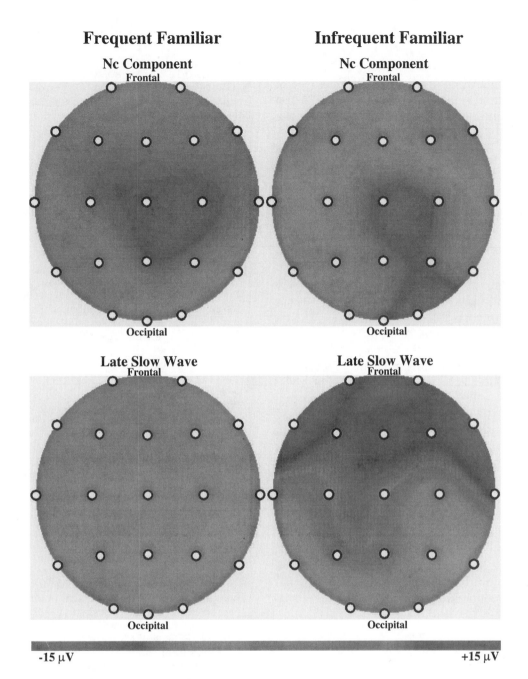

**Frequent Familiar**

**Nc Component**
Frontal

Occipital

**Infrequent Familiar**

**Nc Component**
Frontal

Occipital

**Late Slow Wave**
Frontal

Occipital

**Late Slow Wave**
Frontal

Occipital

-15 µV                                    +15 µV

FIGURE 22.10   A topographical mapping of the ERP components occurring during sustained attention. The ERP components were the Nc (400–700 ms; top figures) and the later slow wave component (700–1500 ms; bottom figures) taken during the presentation of the frequent familiar (left figures) and the infrequent familiar (right figures) stimuli. The data in each figure represent an 80-ms average of the ERP for the Nc (centered at 560 ms) and the slow wave (centered at 1120 ms) components for the 20 recording electrodes. The data are plotted with a cubic spline interpolation algorithm, with an averaged electrode reference, and represents absolute amplitude of the ERP for the recorded data rather than difference ERPs.

direct measures of the brain. Such measures in animal models have included invasive chemical manipulations and measurement as well as destruction of the areas controlling arousal through lesions or neurochemical inhibitors. These measures cannot be applied in infant participants because of ethical considerations. However, noninvasive measurements from psychophysiological measures that are tuned to specific neurochemical systems might be found. Perhaps one type of quantitative activity in the EEG may be linked to a specific neurochemical system and another type linked to another system. The simple recording of EEG, ERP, or heart rate cannot be used to distinguish the four arousal systems detailed in Robbins and Everitt (1995). The EEG and heart rate would be expected to respond to any manipulation of an underlying arousal system. Some type of quantitative activity in the EEG would have to be linked to the underlying neurochemical system in order to use psychophysiological measures for this direct evaluation of the brain systems controlling this arousal form of attention.

Finally, the measurement of brain function for specific attentional systems may have the brightest future for studies of infant attention. Techniques such as high-density EEG and ERP recording should lead to the identification of specific cortical areas involved in attention in infants. High-density ERP recording allows the use of cortical localization techniques in which the locations on the cortex thought to generate the ERP activity are identified. The increased resolution of 64 or 128 electrodes allows the localization of such sources with increased accuracy relative to the 19 electrodes used in the traditional 10–20 recording montage. Johnson and colleagues (Csibra, Tucker, and Johnson, 1998, 2001; Johnson, Gilmore, and Csibra, 1998; also see Johnson, Mareschal, and Csibra, volume) and I (Richards, 2000c, 2001) have been using such high-density EEG recording techniques in the study of attention-linked saccadic eye movements. These techniques could be expanded to study several brain areas involved in infant attention. This work is still in its infancy, but the use of these techniques should be profitably applied to an understanding of the developmental changes in brain areas that are involved in the development of infant attention. Such techniques will lead to a more informed developmental cognitive neuroscience approach to the development of attention in young infants.

ACKNOWLEDGMENT   The writing of this chapter was supported by a grant from the National Institute of Child Health and Human Development, R01-HD19842.

REFERENCES

ANDREASSI, J. L., 1989. *Psychophysiology.* Hillsdale, N.J.: Lawrence Erlbaum.
ANTHONY, B. J., 1991. Mechanisms of selective processing in development: Evidence from studies of reflex modification. In *Handbook of Cognitive Psychophysiology,* J. R. Jennings and M.G.H. Coles, eds. New York: Wiley, pp. 657–683.
ANTHONY, B. J., and F. K. GRAHAM, 1983. Evidence for sensory-selective set in young infants. *Science* 220:742–744.
ANTHONY, B. J., and F. K. GRAHAM, 1985. Blink reflex modification by selective attention: Evidence for the modulation of "automatic" processing. *Biol. Psychol.* 21:43–59.
BALABAN, M. T., 1996. Probing basic mechanisms of sensory, attentional, and emotional development: Modulation of the infant blink response. In *Advances in Infancy Research,* Vol. 10, C. Rovee-Collier and L. P. Lipsitt, eds. Norwood, N.J.: Ablex, pp. 219–256.
BALABAN, M. T., B. J. ANTHONY, and F. K. GRAHAM, 1989. Prestimulation effects on blink and cardiac reflexes of 15-month human infants. *Dev. Psychobiol.* 22:115–127.
BELL, M. A., 1998. Frontal lobe function during infancy: Implications for the development of cognition and attention. In *Cognitive Neuroscience of Attention: A Developmental Perspective,* J. E. Richards, ed. Hillsdale, N.J.: Lawrence Erlbaum, pp. 287–316.
BELL, M. A., 1999. The ontogeny of the EEG during infancy and childhood: Implications for cognitive development. In *Neuroimaging in Childhood Psychiatric Disorders,* B. Garreay, ed. Paris: Springer-Verlag.
BELL, M. A., and N. A. FOX, 1992. The relations between frontal brain electrical activity and cognitive development during infancy. *Child Dev.* 63:1142–1163.
BELL, M. A., and N. A. FOX, 1994. Brain development over the first year of life: Relations between electroencephalographic frequency and coherence and cognitive and affective behaviors. In *Human Behavior and the Developing Brain,* G. Dawson and K. W. Fischer, eds. New York: Guilford, pp. 314–345.
BERG, W. K., and K. M. BERG, 1987. Psychophysiological development in infancy: State, startle and attention. In *Handbook of Infant Development,* Vol. 2, J. Osofsky, ed. New York: Wiley, pp. 238–317.
BERG, W. K., and J. E. RICHARDS, 1997. Attention across time in infant development. In *Attention and Orienting: Sensory and Motivational Processes,* P. J. Lang, R. F. Simons, and M. T. Balaban, eds. Mahwah, N.J.: Erlbaum, pp. 347–368.
BRONSON, G. W., 1974. The postnatal growth of visual capacity. *Child Dev.* 45:873–890.
BRONSON, G. W., 1997. The growth of visual capacity: Evidence from infant scanning patterns. In *Advances in Infancy Research,* Vol. 11, C. Rovee-Collier and L. P. Lipsitt, eds. Greenwich, Conn.: Ablex, pp. 109–141.
CASEY, B. J., and J. E. RICHARDS, 1988. Sustained visual attention in young infants measured with an adapted version of the visual preference paradigm. *Child Dev.* 59:1515–1521.
COURCHESNE, E., 1977. Event-related brain potentials: Comparison between children and adults. *Science* 197:589–592.
COURCHESNE, E., 1978. Neurophysiological correlates of cognitive development: Changes in long-latency event-related potentials from childhood to adulthood. *Electroencephalogr. Clin. Neurophysiol.* 45:468–482.
COURCHESNE, E., L. GANZ, and A. M. NORCIA, 1981. Event-related brain potentials to human faces in infants. *Child Dev.* 52:804–811.
CSIBRA, G., L. A. TUCKER, and M. H. JOHNSON, 1998. Neural correlates of saccade planning in infants: A high-density ERP study. *Intl. J. Psychophysiol.* 29:201–215.
CSIBRA, G., L. A. TUCKER, and M. H. JOHNSON, 2001. Anticipatory and reactive saccades in infants: A high-density ERP study. *Infancy* 2 (in press).
DAVIS, M., 1997. The neurophysiological basis of acoustic startle modulation: Research on fear motivation and sensory gating. In *Attention and Orienting: Sensory and Motivational Processes,* P. J. Lang, R. F. Simons, and M. T. Balaban, eds. Mahway, N.J.: Erlbaum, pp. 69–96.
DE HAAN, M., and C. A. NELSON, 1997. Recognition of the mother's face by six-month-old infants: A neurobehavioral study. *Child Dev.* 68:187–210.

DESIMONE, R., and J. DUNCAN, 1995. Neural mechanisms of selective visual attention. *Annu. Rev. Neurosci.* 18:193–222

FAGAN, J. F., 1974. Infant recognition memory: The effects of length of familiarization and type of discrimination task. *Child Dev.* 59:1198–1210.

FRICK, J., and J. E. RICHARDS, 2001. Individual differences in recognition of briefly presented visual stimuli. *Infancy* 2 (in press).

GRAHAM, F. K., 1979. Distinguishing among orienting, defense, and startle reflexes. In *The Orienting Reflex in Humans,* H. D. Kimmel, E. H. van Olst, and J. F. Orlebeke, eds. Hillsdale, N.J.: Lawrence Erlbaum, pp. 137–167.

GRAHAM, F. K., 1992. Attention: The heartbeat, the blink, and the brain. In *Attention and Information Processing in Infants and Adults: Perspectives from Human and Animal Research,* B. A. Campbell, H. Hayne, and R. Richardson, eds. Hillsdale, N.J.: Lawrence Erlbaum, pp. 3–29.

HACKLEY, S. A., and F. K. GRAHAM, 1983. Early selective attention effects on cutaneous and acoustic blink reflexes. *Physiol. Psychol.* 11:235–242.

HACKLEY, S. A., and A. J. W. BOELHOUWER, 1997. The more or less startling effects of weak prestimulation—revisited: Prepulse modulation of multicomponent blink reflexes. In *Attention and Orienting: Sensory and Motivational Processes,* P. J. Lang, R. F. Simons, and M. T. Balaban, eds. Mahway, N.J.: Erlbaum, pp. 205–228.

HAERICH, P., 1994. Startle reflex modification: Effects of attention vary with emotional valence. *Psychol. Sci.* 5:407–410.

HEILMAN, K. M., R. T. WATSON, E. VALENSTEIN, and M. E. GOLDBERG, 1987. Attention: Behavior and neural mechanisms. In *Handbook of Physiology,* V. B. Mountcastle, F. Plum, and S. R. Geiger, eds. Bethesda, Md.: American Physiological Society, pp. 461–481.

HICKS, J. M., and J. E. RICHARDS, 1998. The effects of stimulus movement and attention on peripheral stimulus localization by 8- to 26-week-old infants. *Infant Behav. Dev.* 21:571–589.

HILLYARD, S. A., G. R. MANGUN, M. G. WOLDROFF, and S. J. LUCK, 1995. Neural systems mediating selective attention. In *The Cognitive Neurosciences,* M. S. Gazzaniga, ed. Cambridge, Mass.: MIT Press, pp. 665–682.

HOOD, B. M., 1995. Shifts of visual attention in the human infant: A neuroscientific approach. *Adv. Infancy Res.* 10:163–216.

HOOD, B. M., J. ATKINSON, and O. J. BRADDICK, 1998. Selection-for-action and the development of orienting and visual attention. In *Cognitive Neuroscience of Attention: A Developmental Perspective,* J. E. Richards, ed. Hillsdale, N.J.: Lawrence Erlbaum, pp. 219–250.

HUNTER, S. K, and J. E. RICHARDS, 1999. Peripheral stimulus localization by 5- to 14-week-old infants during phases of attention. (submitted).

HUNTER, S. K, and J. E. RICHARDS, 2000. Postural and stimulus effects on eye movement in young infants. (submitted).

JOHNSON, M. H., 1990. Cortical maturation and the development of visual attention in early infancy. *J. Cogn. Neurosci.* 2:81–95.

JOHNSON, M. H., 1995. The development of visual attention: A cognitive neuroscience perspective. In *The Cognitive Neurosciences,* M. S. Gazzaniga, ed. Cambridge, Mass.: MIT Press, pp. 735–747.

JOHNSON, M. H., 1997. *Developmental Cognitive Neuroscience.* London: Blackwell.

JOHNSON, M. H., R. O. GILMORE, and G. CSIBRA, 1998. Toward a computational model of the development of saccade planning. In *Cognitive Neuroscience of Attention: A Developmental Perspective,* J. E. Richards, ed. Hillsdale, N.J.: Lawrence Erlbaum, pp. 103–130.

JOHNSON, M. H., M. I. POSNER, and M. K. ROTHBART, 1991. Components of visual orienting in early infancy: Contingency learning, anticipatory looking and disengaging. *J. Cogn. Neurosci.* 3:335–344.

KARRER, R., and P. K. ACKLES, 1987. Visual event-related potentials of infants during a modified oddball procedure. In *Current Trends in Event-Related Potential Research,* R. Johnson, J. W. Rohrbaugh, and R. Parasuraman, eds. Amsterdam: Elsevier Science, pp. 603–608.

KARRER, R., and P. K. ACKLES, 1988. Brain organization and perceptual/cognitive development in normal and Down syndrome infants: A research program. In *The Early Identification of Infants with Developmental Disabilities,* P. Vietze and H. G. Vaughan, Jr., eds. Philadelphia: Grune & Stratton.

KARRER, R., and L. A. MONTI, 1995. Event-related potentials of 4–7-week-old infants in a visual recognition memory task. *Electroencephalogr. Clin. Neurophysiol.* 94:414–424.

LANSINK, J. M., and J. E. RICHARDS, 1997. Heart rate and behavioral measures of attention in six-, nine-, and twelve-month-old infants during object exploration. *Child Dev.* 68:610–620.

MAUNSELL, J. H. R., and V. B. FERRERA, 1995. Attentional mechanisms in visual cortex. In *The Cognitive Neurosciences,* M. S. Gazzaniga, ed. Cambridge, Mass.: MIT Press, pp. 451–461.

MAURER, D., and T. L. LEWIS, 1979. A physiological explanation of infants' early visual development. *Can. J. Psychol.* 33:232–252.

MAURER, D., and T. L. LEWIS, 1991. The development of peripheral vision and its physiological underpinnings. In *Newborn Attention: Biological Constraints and the Influence of Experience,* M. J. S. Weiss and P. R. Zelazo, eds. Norwood, N.J.: Ablex, pp. 218–255.

MAURER, D., and T. L. LEWIS, 1998. Overt orienting toward peripheral stimuli: Normal development and underlying mechanisms. In *Cognitive Neuroscience of Attention: A Developmental Perspective,* J. E. Richards, ed. Hillsdale, N.J.: Lawrence Erlbaum, pp. 51–102.

MESULAM, M. M., 1983. The functional anatomy and hemispheric specialization for directed attention. *Trends Neurosci.* 6:384–387.

NELSON, C. A., 1994. Neural correlates of recognition memory in the first postnatal year. In *Human Behavior and the Developing Brain,* G. Dawson and K. W. Fischer, eds. New York: Guilford Press, pp. 269–313.

NELSON, C. A., and P. F. COLLINS, 1991. Event-related potential and looking-time analysis of infants' responses to familiar and novel events: Implications for visual recognition memory. *Dev. Psychol.* 27:50–58.

NELSON, C. A., and P. F. COLLINS, 1992. Neural and behavioral correlates of visual recognition memory in 4- and 8-month-old infants. *Brain Cogn.* 19:105–121.

NELSON, C. A., and D. DUKETTE, 1998. In *Cognitive Neuroscience of Attention: A Developmental Perspective,* J. E. Richards, ed. Hillsdale, N.J.: Lawrence Erlbaum, pp. 327–362.

NELSON, C. A., and R. A. deREGNIER, 1992. Neural correlates of attention and memory in the first year of life. *Dev. Neuropsychol.* 8:119–134.

NELSON, C. A., and P. SALAPATEK, 1986. Electrophysiological correlates of infant recognition memory. *Child Dev.* 57:1483–1497.

NUNEZ, P. L., 1990. Localization of brain activity with electro-encephalography. *Adv. Neurol.* 54:39–65.

POSNER, M. I., 1995. Attention in cognitive neuroscience: An overview. In *The Cognitive Neurosciences,* M. S. Gazzaniga, ed. Cambridge, Mass.: MIT Press, pp. 615–624.

POSNER, M. I., and S. E. PETERSEN, 1990. The attention system of the human brain. *Annu. Rev. Neurosci.* 13:25–42.

RAY, W. J., 1990. Electrical activity of the brain. In *Principles of Psychophysiology: Physical, Social, and Inferential Elements,* J. T. Cacioppo and L. G. Tassinary, eds. Cambridge, England: Cambridge University Press, pp. 385–412.

RICHARDS, J. E., 1985. The development of sustained visual attention in infants from 14 to 26 weeks of age. *Psychophysiology* 22:409–416.

RICHARDS, J. E., 1987. Infant visual sustained attention and respiratory sinus arrhythmia. *Child Dev.* 58:488–496.

RICHARDS, J. E., 1989a. Development and stability in visual sustained attention in 14, 20, and 26 week old infants. *Psychophysiology* 26:422–430.

RICHARDS, J. E., 1989b. Sustained visual attention in 8-week-old infants. *Infant Behav. Dev.* 12:425–436.

RICHARDS, J. E., 1994. Baseline respiratory sinus arrhythmia and heart rate responses during sustained visual attention in preterm infants from 3 to 6 months of age. *Psychophysiology* 31:235–243.

RICHARDS, J. E., 1995. Infant cognitive psychophysiology: Normal development and implications for abnormal developmental outcomes. In *Advances in Clinical Child Psychology,* Vol. 17, T. H. Ollendick and R. J. Prinz, eds. New York: Plenum Press, pp. 77–107.

RICHARDS, J. E., 1997a. Peripheral stimulus localization by infants: Attention, age and individual differences in heart rate variability. *J. Exp. Psychol.: Hum. Percept. Perform.* 23:667–680.

RICHARDS, J. E., 1997b. Effects of attention on infants' preference for briefly exposed visual stimuli in the paired-comparison recognition-memory paradigm. *Dev. Psychol.* 33:22–31.

RICHARDS, J. E., 1998. Development of selective attention in young infants. *Dev. Sci.* 1:45–51.

RICHARDS, J. E., 2000a. Development of multimodal attention in young infants: Modification of the startle reflex by attention. *Psychophysiology* 37:1–11.

RICHARDS, J. E., 2000b. The effect of attention on the recognition of brief visual stimuli: An ERP study. Paper presented at the International Conference on Infancy Studies, Brighton, England, July, 2000.

RICHARDS, J. E., 2000c. Localizing the development of covert attention in infants using scalp event-related-potentials. *Dev. Psychol.* 36:91–108.

RICHARDS, J. E., 2001. Cortical indices of saccade planning following covert orienting in 20-week-old infants. *Infancy* 2.

RICHARDS, J. E., and B. J. CASEY, 1990. Infant visual recognition memory performance as a function of heart rate defined phases of attention. *Infant Behav. Dev.* 13:585.

RICHARDS, J. E., and B. J. CASEY, 1991. Heart rate variability during attention phases in young infants. *Psychophysiology* 28:43–53.

RICHARDS, J. E., and B. J. CASEY, 1992. Development of sustained visual attention in the human infant. In *Attention and Information Processing in Infants and Adults,* B.A. Campbell, H. Hayne, and R. Richardson, eds. Mahway, N.J.: Erlbaum, pp. 30–60.

RICHARDS, J. E., and F. B. HOLLEY, 1999. Infant attention and the development of smooth pursuit tracking. *Dev. Psychol.* 35:856–867.

RICHARDS, J. E., and S. K. HUNTER, 1997. Peripheral stimulus localization by infants with eye and head movements during visual attention. *Vision Res.* 37:3021–3035.

RICHARDS, J. E., and S. K. HUNTER, 1998. Attention and eye movement in young infants: Neural control and development. In *Cognitive Neuroscience of Attention: A Developmental Perspective,* J. E. Richards, ed. Mahway, N.J.: Erlbaum, pp. 131–162.

ROBBINS, T. W., and B. J. EVERITT, 1995. Arousal systems and attention. In *The Cognitive Neurosciences,* M. S. Gazzaniga, ed. Cambridge, Mass.: MIT Press, pp. 703–720.

RUFF, H. A., and M. K. ROTHBART, 1996. *Attention in Early Development.* New York: Oxford University Press.

SCHERG, M., 1990. Fundamentals of dipole source potential analysis. In *Auditory Evoked Magnetic Fields and Potentials,* F. Grandori, M. Hoke, and G. L. Romani, eds. Basel: Karger, pp. 40–69.

SCHERG, M., and T. W. PICTON, 1991. Separation and identification of event-related potential components by brain electrical source analysis. In *Event-Related Brain Research,* C. H. M. Brunia, G. Mulder, and M. N. Verbaten, eds. Amsterdam: Elsevier Science, pp. 24–37.

SCHILLER, P. H., 1985. A model for the generation of visually guided saccadic eye movements. In *Models of the Visual Cortex,* D. Rose and V. G. Dobson, eds. New York: John Wiley, pp. 62–70.

SCHILLER, P. H., 1998. The neural control of visually guided eye movements. In *Cognitive Neuroscience of Attention: A Developmental Perspective,* J. E. Richards, ed. Mahway, N.J.: Erlbaum, pp. 3–50.

SWICK, D., M. KUTAS, and H. J. NEVILLE, 1994. Localizing the neural generators of event-related brain potentials. In *Localization and Neuroimaging in Neuropsychology. Foundations of Neuropsychology,* A. Kertesz, ed. San Diego: Academic Press, pp. 73–121.

TUCKER, D. M., 1993. Spatial sampling of head electrical fields: The geodesic sensor net. *Electroencephalogr. Clin. Neurophysiol.* 87:154–163.

TUCKER, D. M., M. LIOTTI, G. F. POTTS, G. S. RUSSELL, and M. I. POSNER, 1994. Spatiotemporal analysis of brain electrical fields. *Human Brain Mapp.* 1:134–152.

# 23 The Functional Development and Integration of the Dorsal and Ventral Visual Pathways: A Neurocomputational Approach

MARK H. JOHNSON, DENIS MARESCHAL, AND GERGELY CSIBRA

ABSTRACT In this chapter we discuss evidence from computational, brain imaging, and behavioral studies relating to the development of the dorsal and ventral visual pathways. This evidence indicates that (1) for both pathways some aspects of function are delayed in development relative to others and (2) the two pathways may be less integrated during infancy than in later life. We discuss some of the factors that contribute to these differential timetables of development and some of the possible consequences thereof.

In the emerging field of developmental cognitive neuroscience, we approach our understanding of the functional development of the human brain by integrating evidence from neural development with that from cognitive and behavioral studies. Whereas it is relatively straightforward to *correlate* changes at the neural level with changes in behavior, it is challenging to *integrate* information from these sources into a single, cohesive account of developmental change. We believe that recent advances in two areas, one theoretical and one technological, will allow more rapid progress in integrating neural and behavioral evidence in development. First, the advent of neural network and connectionist modeling will provide the appropriate level of theoretical framework in which evidence from neural development and behavior can be modeled simultaneously (see Munakata and Stedron, this volume). Second, recent advances in neuroimaging now allow the noninvasive measurement of brain activity in healthy infants with reasonable spatial and temporal accuracy. In this chapter we discuss evidence gathered through both of these new techniques in an attempt to advance our knowledge of the functional development of the two main cortical visual pathways in the human brain.

There is now a substantive body of evidence that visual information processing in the primate cortex is divided into two relatively distinct streams (see Stiles, this volume). However, only recently has the dual route visual processing paradigm been applied to the study of infant perceptual and cognitive development (Atkinson, 1998; Berthenthal, 1996; Mareschal, Plunkett, and Harris, 1999), and many fundamental questions remain. One question is whether it is the dorsal or the ventral route that functionally develops first during infancy, while another concerns whether there is increasing separation, or increasing integration, between the two pathways with development. In this chapter we review evidence from neuroimaging, computational modeling, and behavior, indicating that these questions are unlikely to have simple answers. Although there is some evidence that dorsal stream eye movement control is relatively delayed, other aspects of dorsal route function (such as reaching) may be more precocial. Computational and behavioral evidence indicates that even when the dorsal route is functioning, there may be an initial lack of integration between the two pathways resulting in specific patterns of behavioral deficits. We conclude with speculations as to the causes and consequences of different developmental timetables in the dorsal and ventral cortical streams.

## The dorsal and ventral routes of visual processing

In this section we briefly review the neurocomputational properties of the dorsal and ventral routes (for a more detailed review, see Milner and Goodale, 1995). The data used to identify anatomically distinct pathways

MARK H. JOHNSON, DENIS MARESCHAL, AND GERGELY CSIBRA Centre for Brain and Cognitive Development, Department of Psychology, Birkbeck College, University of London, London, England.

are based largely on primates other than humans. However, analogous structures do exist in humans, and lesion studies suggest that these structures also function in a similar way in humans. The connectivity of these cortical routes is very complex (see van Essen, Anderson, and Felleman, 1992). Although two pathways can be identified, there is a degree of crosstalk between the two pathways at many different points along the pathway, and information can arrive at several points from subcortical routes. One pathway (the ventral route) extends from the primary visual cortex through to portions of the temporal cortex. The other pathway (the dorsal route) extends from the primary visual cortex to the parietal cortex. The exact point at which the routes separate is still debated. The ventral route is sometimes called the "what" or "perception" pathway while the dorsal route is often called the "where" or "action" pathway (Milner and Goodale 1995; Ungerleider and Mishkin, 1982). These names reflect the differing processing objectives attributed to each route by different authors.

Ungerleider and Mishkin (1982) initially proposed that the ventral and dorsal stream were completely separate from the retina to the temporal or parietal cortex, and that the ventral stream played a crucial role in object identification whereas the dorsal stream was critical in localizing the object in the visual field. Livingstone and Hubel (1988) went much further. They suggested that the dorsal stream is concerned with the global spatial organization of objects. That is, it segments and defines individual objects in a scene as well as keeping track of their relative locations in space. In contrast, the ventral stream analyzes the scene in much more detail and at a more leisurely rate. It is sensitive to color, shape, and other surface properties of objects.

Some evidence indicates that the dissociation in processing is not as complete as suggested by Livingston and Hubel (Milner and Goodale, 1995). In particular, there appear to be cells in either pathway that respond to properties that are characteristic of the other pathway. Moreover, both the ventral and dorsal routes seem to receive some input from both the magnocellular and parvocellular populations, although most of the input in the dorsal stream is magnocellular in origin (Ferrera, Nealey, and Maunsell, 1992; Livingstone and Hubel, 1984; Milner and Goodale, 1995). However, the fact that anatomical segregation is not complete does not preclude the possibility of functional dissociation. On reflection, it is not entirely surprising that the ventral route should receive both types of input information. Spatial-temporal cues can also be used to identify an object. However, features such as color cannot help to determine an object's spatial or temporal properties. Hence the dorsal route has no need for this type of information, or for any other more detailed surface features. As far as we know, color is not processed in the dorsal stream at all.

PROCESSING IN THE DORSAL PATHWAY   There is evidence of multiple (and parallel) spatial processing systems within the dorsal route. Some cells in the parietal cortex anticipate the retinal consequences of saccadic eye movements, and update the cortical (body-centered) representation of visual space to provide continuously accurate coding of the location of objects in space. Other cells have gaze-dependent responses. That is, they mark where the animal is looking with respect to eye-centered or body-centered coordinate systems. These representations are useful only over very short periods of time since the coordinates have to be recomputed every time the animal moves.

In many real-world settings, target objects are moving. It is necessary to anticipate an object's movement in order to act on it effectively. Some cells in the parietal cortex appear to be involved in the tracking of moving objects. Moreover, many of these cells continue to respond during occluded pursuit after the stimulus has disappeared (Newsome, Wurtz, and Komatsu, 1988). In addition, there is selectivity in other parts of the dorsal stream for relative motion and size changes due to looming. Many cells are also driven by large-scale optical flow fields, suggesting that self-motion is being computed. Cells in the dorsal pathway also code size, shape, and orientation—information that is necessary for the proper reaching and grasping of an object (Jeannerod, 1988).

There is also some evidence suggesting that the different spatial-temporal systems are partially segregated into different regions and routes within the dorsal pathway. Thus the dorsal stream could be viewed as a pathway with many parallel computations of different spatial-temporal properties occurring at once. Different streams compute different spatial-temporal analyses in different coordinate systems, possibly with different effector systems as outputs. This is illustrated by the links between the parietal and frontal lobes. Milner and Goodale (1995) argue that the cells of the parietal cortex are neither sensory nor motor, but rather sensorimotor cells. They are involved in transforming retinal information (sensory) into motor coordinates (motor), and provide an adaptive medium for transducing perceptual input into motor actions.

Note, finally, that some cells in the parietal cortex do not respond differentially to objects that differ in surface features and in affect. Rolls and colleagues (1979) showed that visual fixation and reaching cells fired independently of whether the target object was a desired object. These authors conditioned monkeys to respond with a reach for a desired object and not to respond for an undesired object. They found that the cells in the parietal cortex fired (i.e., computed the appropriate spatial-temporal properties) even if the object was an undesired object and the monkey did not reach. Hence, processing in this channel appears to be independent of superficial feature recognition and any of the responses associated with the target object.

PROCESSING IN THE VENTRAL PATHWAY The properties of cells in the ventral stream seem to complement those in the dorsal stream. There appears to be some kind of hierarchical representation in the ventral stream. As one progresses down the stream, cells respond to more and more complex clusters of features. At the higher levels, the complex cells show remarkable selectivity in their firing (e.g., face recognition cells). These neurons are all selective to the figural and surface properties of objects, and have very large receptive fields on the retina. Although they can process feature information, they lose much of their spatial resolution on the retina. In effect, these cells develop spatially invariant representations of objects by responding to the presence of a consistent feature cluster independently of its position. Some cells seem to respond maximally to a preferred object orientation (independently of position), thereby computing a "view-centered representation." Other cells respond equally to an object in any orientation. These cells have developed a transformation-invariant representation. Transformation-invariant representations could provide the basic raw material for recognition memory and other long-term representations of the visual world. There is evidence that the responsiveness of cells in the ventral stream can be modulated by the prior occurrence of a stimulus. Moreover, there is evidence indicating that some cells continue to fire for several seconds after the object has disappeared (Ungerleider, 1985), suggesting that some kind of memory trace remains.

In this chapter, we are less concerned with whether these pathways are called "what" and "where" (Ungerleider and Mishkin, 1982) or "perception" and "action" (Milner and Goodale, 1995) and more concerned with the fact that they process different types of object information, carry out different computations, and develop different object representations with distinct properties. Nevertheless, one can speculate as to the computational reasons for why two streams of processing may have evolved. If we agree with Milner and Goodale (1995) that the representations in the dorsal stream are closely linked to the functions of the motor system, it is not surprising that spatial-temporal infor-

mation is at a premium down this pathway. Motor actions involve localizing targets within a three-dimensional spatial temporal world. In contrast, recognition or identification of objects requires that spatial-temporal variability be minimized. Early work in machine vision found that view-invariant recognition (i.e., the ability to recognize an object as the same independently of orientation and location) was a very difficult computational problem (Boden, 1989). One of the most efficient ways of achieving view-invariant recognition is to factor out spatial variability. However, removing spatial information from the object representation is completely at odds with the requirements of the motor system. Hence the need for two distinct classes of object representations.

Finally, Jeannerod (1999) has argued that recent neuroimaging evidence indicates that the dissociation between the two pathways is less clear than presented by Milner and Goodale (1995). Specifically, structures on the dorsal pathway are often activated following the presentation of objects, without manual response being required. Leaving aside the question of whether eye movements are elicited or planned in these passive viewing paradigms, it is hard to rule out the possibility that reaching actions are automatically planned, even if not executed, on the presentation of graspable objects. Our view is that the coactivation of the two pathways is entirely consistent with two streams of information processing in which the type of processing that occurs within each pathway is incompatible.

## The development of the dorsal and ventral streams

Identifying the presence of two visual processing streams begs the question of how these streams develop and how they interact with each other during development. Over the past few years there have been some speculations about the developmental sequence of the two pathways. For example, Atkinson (1998) has argued, on the basis that infants and children are delayed on their judgments of motion coherence compared to their thresholds for perceiving coherent forms, that the dorsal pathway develops later than the ventral. In contrast, studies of developmental neuroanatomy in 1-week-old macaque monkeys led Webster and colleagues (1995) to the view that the patterns of connectivity of temporal lobe structures on the ventral pathway were still relatively immature, while the connectivity of the parietal lobe (on the dorsal route) was already adult-like. Evidence from developmental neuroanatomy in human infants is not compelling in this regard. For example, in resting PET studies of glucose uptake, virtually identical overall patterns of developmental change are seen in the temporal and parietal cortices (Chugani, Phelps, and Mazziotta, 1987). However, resting blood flow measurements and structural neuroanatomy studies cannot inform us directly about function. In one active PET paradigm, 2-month-old infants showed activity in structures of the ventral pathway, but the task was one in which dorsal pathway activation would have been unlikely even in adults (passive viewing of faces) (de Schonen, Mancini, and Leigeois, 1998). In nonhuman primates, there is evidence of ventral pathway functioning from as young as 6 weeks of age. Rodman and colleagues (Rodman, Gross, and Scalaidhe, 1993) established that neurons within the superior temporal sulcus were activated by complex visual stimuli, including faces, from the earliest age at which they could record—6 weeks. Unfortunately, equivalent data are not available for dorsal pathway functions, and so no comparison is possible. This paucity of data about the dorsal pathway may be due to the great technical difficulty in recording from neurons in young monkeys. Thus, there is currently very little evidence that directly speaks to the question of the relative development of the dorsal and ventral pathways during postnatal life.

In the next two sections we explore evidence from neuroimaging and behavioral studies suggesting that aspects of dorsal pathway function develop later than the majority of ventral stream functions. The ERP evidence focuses on markers for the two pathways, face processing and saccade planning. The behavioral evidences focuses on infant abilities to form perceptual compounds from features processed preferentially by one cortical stream or the other, and infant responses to temporarily occluded objects.

EVIDENCE FROM HIGH-DENSITY ERP STUDIES OF THE DORSAL AND VENTRAL PATHWAYS   One of the functions most clearly associated with the ventral pathway is the processing of the surface features of objects. Face processing is commonly regarded as a special class of object processing. Specifically, in adults PET, fMRI, ERP, and cellular recording experiments have all implicated regions of the inferior temporal cortex as being important for face processing. For example, Bentin and colleagues (1996) identified a component of the scalp-recorded ERP which occurs around 170 ms after the presentation of a face and which, by using procedures for estimating the likely underlying brain source that gives rise to scalp surface voltage changes, is localizable to parts of the inferior temporal cortex. In many, but not all, adults the specificity of this region for face processing is lateralized, with the right side being more face-specific than the left, a finding confirmed with other brain imaging methods (Kanwisher, McDermott,

and Chun, 1997). De Haan, Oliver, and Johnson (1998; see also de Haan, this volume) conducted a study in which they showed both adults and 6-month-old infants pictures of upright and inverted faces while recording ERPs from the infants' heads. Adult participants showed a pattern consistent with several previous studies, indicating face-sensitive cortical processing from structures on the ventral visual pathway. Like adults, the infants also showed a face-sensitive response over temporal leads, albeit at a later time after stimulus presentation (see figures 26.1 and 26.2 in chapter 26 of this volume). This finding indicates some degree of cortical specialization for face processing from this pathway by 6 months of age. However, infants' responses also differed in two other ways, indicating that at this age ventral processing may be less specialized for face processing than in adults. First, the response in infants shows less hemispheric specialization than in adults, possibly indicating less localization to the right ventral pathway in infants than in adults. Second, the response is less selective in infants. The latter point was established by showing that while monkey faces elicit similar responses to human faces in infants, in adults the response is human face–selective (Johnson and de Haan, in press; de Haan, Olivier, and Johnson, submitted).

In sum, these lines of evidence indicate clear functionality in the ventral pathways by 6 months, even though further tuning is required in order to reach adult levels of competence. In the rest of this section we examine whether a similar or different pattern of development emerges from studies of dorsal route processing.

One function attributed to the dorsal visual pathway is the planning of target-directed saccades via the parietal eye movement centers. The functioning of these cortical regions can be measured by event-related potentials (ERPs) time-locked to the initiation of the eye movement (Balaban and Weinstein, 1985; Csibra, Johnson, and Tucker, 1997). These experiments reveal characteristic presaccadic components recorded over the parietal cortex prior to the execution of saccades. The clearest of these components is the presaccadic spike potential (SP), a sharp positive-going deflection that precedes the saccade by 8–20 ms (Csibra, Johnson, and Tucker, 1997). The spike potential is observed in most saccade tasks in adults, and is therefore thought to represent an important stage of cortical processing required to generate a saccade.

We investigated whether there are presaccadic potentials recordable over parietal leads in 6-month old infants (Csibra, Tucker, and Johnson, 1998). Given the prevailing view that by this age infants have essentially the same pathways active for saccade planning as adults (e.g., Johnson, 1990), we were surprised to find no evidence of these components (figure 23.1) in our infant subjects (see also Kurtzberg and Vaughan, 1981; Richards, in press). This finding suggests that the target-driven saccades performed by 6-month-olds in our study were controlled solely by subcortical routes for visually guided responses mediated by the superior colliculus.

Because this result was surprising, we conducted two follow-up studies. In one, we tested 12-month-olds with the same procedure. Preliminary results from this experiment indicate that these older infants do show a spike potential like that observed in adults, though smaller in amplitude (figure 23.2). The other study explored whether the dorsal pathway could be activated in very young infants through a more demanding saccade task. Specifically, we compared ERPs before reactive (target-elicited) and anticipatory (endogenous) saccades in 4-month-old infants (Csibra, Tucker, and Johnson, in press). We were not able to record any reliable posterior activity prior to either reactive or anticipatory eye movements. Thus, even when the saccade is generated by cortical computation of the likely location of the next stimulus, as in the case of anticipatory eye movements, the dorsal pathway does not seem to be involved in the planning of this action.

As an aside, we should note that the lack of evidence for parietal (dorsal pathway) control over eye movements in our experiments with 6-month-olds does not lead us to conclude that there is no cortical influence over saccades at this age. In all our studies with this age group we have observed effects recorded over frontal leads consistent with frontal eye field disinhibition of subcortical (collicular) circuits when a central foveated stimulus is removed (Csibra, Tucker, and Johnson, 1998; in press). In brief, we interpret these findings in terms of the frontal eye fields maintaining fixation onto foveated stimuli by inhibiting collicular circuits (see Johnson, 1990). However, when saccades to peripheral stimuli are made, we believe these are largely initiated by collicular circuits, sometimes as a consequence of inhibition being released by the frontal eye fields.

In the saccadic ERP data from 6-month-olds there was strong evidence for a postsaccadic component known as the lambda wave. The lambda wave is a sharp potential appearing over visual cortical areas that is generated when a peripheral target stimulus is foveated (Kurtzberg and Vaughan, 1977). While lambda waves can be observed in adults, they were markedly enhanced in our infant subjects. One conclusion from this work is that while dorsal pathway control of eye movements is not evident at 6 months, early visual cortical responses to foveal stimuli, believed to originate from structures at the gateway to the ventral pathway (V2 and V4), are present. Thus, within a single ERP trace, there is evidence for the relatively delayed development of the dorsal pathway with respect to the ventral pathway. But why should the lambda wave be enhanced in infants relative to adults? One possibility may lie in the fact that in order to successfully integrate visual input with eye movements, adults "forward-map" the expected visual input at the end of their saccade (see Johnson et al., 1998). If infants are unable to integrate information about visual input and eye movements due to a lack of

**A**

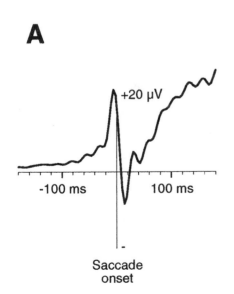

**B**

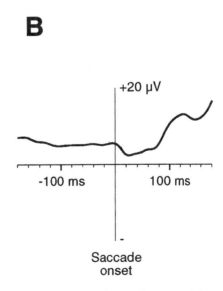

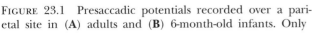
FIGURE 23.1 Presaccadic potentials recorded over a parietal site in (**A**) adults and (**B**) 6-month-old infants. Only the adults (**A**) show a clear spike potential.

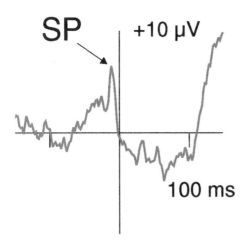

FIGURE 23.2   Presaccadic potentials in a single 12-month-old infant.

development of the dorsal pathway, then a peripheral target stimulus entering the fovea will be "unexpected" and thus elicit a bigger response. We are currently examining this hypothesis in more detail in a series of behavioral experiments.

A related aspect of dorsal pathway function involves the use of "body-centered" frames of reference for action, including eye movements. In single unit recording studies in monkeys, Anderson and colleagues (1993) have found cells in the posterior parietal cortex that appear to integrate visual information with proprioceptive information about eye and body position in order to generate accurate saccades to targets. In a series of experiments, Gilmore and Johnson (1997, 1998) investigated the development of these abilities in infants. In one of these experiments, we examined the patterns of saccade sequences made by 3- and 7-month-old infants performing a two-dimensional version of the double step task (figure 23.3). When we examined the second saccade made by the infants in response to the two sequentially presented visual targets, we found that the younger infants tended to make this saccade to a "retinocentric" location. That is, they acted as if they were unable to integrate the visual information about where the target is, with information about their own (changed) eye and head position. In contrast, the 7-month-olds made around two-thirds of their second saccades to the "correct" spatial location, suggesting that they were able to take into account the eye movement that had already taken place to the first target. The combined results from several such studies support the hypothesis that the representations for planning saccades shift from retinocentric to cranio- or egocentric in accordance with the graded experience-dependent development of cortical, especially parietal, centers where

these higher order representations are instantiated. This behavioral evidence reinforces the conclusion of the ERP studies of saccade planning by indicating that the development of dorsal pathway control over saccades occurs relatively late in infant development.

Taken together, the results from the ERP studies described indicate that while the ventral pathway can be activated at 6 months (albeit with some further specialization to take place), the dorsal pathway is still not influencing eye movement control at that age, suggesting that at least this aspect of dorsal pathway function is somewhat slower to develop than the ventral pathway.

BEHAVIORAL EVIDENCE OF DORSAL AND VENTRAL DISSOCIATION IN INFANTS   The second hypothesis we wish to explore—that there is a dissociation between processing in the two pathways during infancy—requires us to consider behavioral evidence. Specifically, indirect evidence of the independent processing of surface-feature (a predominantly ventral function) and spatial-temporal (a predominantly dorsal function) properties of objects can be found in the literature addressing infant cognition (largely dealing with infants' responses to hidden objects) as well as infant perception (dealing with infants' responses to visible objects). The perceptual evidence is presented first and the cognitive evidence is presented second.

A number of studies relying on preferential looking and dishabituation techniques also provide evidence for a feature/spatial-temporal dissociation. These studies focus on infant abilities to form perceptual compounds involving a surface feature (e.g., color) with a spatial-temporal feature (e.g., motion). The role of movement in object perception is complex and has been investigated in great detail (see Burnham, 1987, for a review). Movement can have a number of roles in object perception. Movement can (1) act as a suppresser of feature perception, (2) act as a facilitator of feature perception, (3) be incidental to objects, and (4) act as a feature of objects. Contrary to Bower's initial claims (Bower and Patterson, 1973), it is now well established that by 2.5 months infants can process the features of a moving object and relate those features to the features of a stationary object (Day and Burnham, 1981; Hartlep, 1983; Hartlep and Forsythe, 1977). Some studies also suggest that infants can selectively attend to either surface-feature or spatial-temporal information independently of the other dimension, suggesting that surface features and spatial-temporal object information can be processed independently. Burnham and Kyriacos (cited in Burnham, 1987) looked at 4- and 6-month-olds' abilities to develop feature representations over different motion transformations and infants' abil-

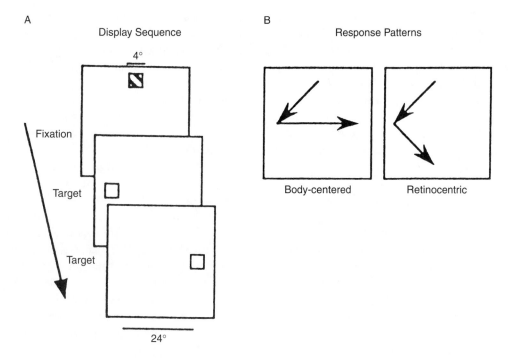

A
Display Sequence

4°

Fixation

Target

Target

24°

B
Response Patterns

Body-centered          Retinocentric

FIGURE 23.3   The two-dimensional version of the double-step saccade task. (From Gilmore and Johnson, 1997.)

ities to develop a motion representation over different feature transformations. In one experiment, these authors habituated infants to an object moving in different ways. They then tested the infant with either the same object moving in a novel way, or a novel object moving in the same novel way. They found that infants looked reliably longer at the novel object. The implication is that the infants had encoded the shapes of the objects and based their responses on the novel shape rather than the novel movement: Infants could encode shape independently of movement. In a second experiment, the authors habituated infants to different objects moving in the same way. They then tested the infants with a novel object moving either the same way or in a novel way. They found that infants looked reliably longer at the novel movement. The implication is that the infants had encoded the movements of the objects independently of shape and based their responses on the novel movement rather than the novel shape: Infants could encode movement independently of shape.

Further behavioral evidence comes from studies of infant responses to temporarily occluded objects. Early competence in preferential looking tasks that claimed to show the coordination of position and feature information in reasoning about hidden objects (e.g., Baillargeon, 1993) have—on close scrutiny—provided evidence only for the use of positional information in

conjunction with size or volume information (Mareschal, 1997). Both size and volume are spatial dimensions that are likely to be encoded by the dorsal route. Thus, these tasks only provide evidence of dorsal route processing.

Further data supporting the suggestion of a dissociation between ventral and dorsal processing have recently become available. Infants fail to use surface-feature information to individuate and enumerate objects that move behind and out from a screen (Leslie et al., 1998; Simon, Hespos, and Rochat, 1995; Xu and Carey, 1996). In these studies, infants watched two different objects move in and out (one at a time) from behind an occluder. The screen was subsequently removed to reveal either one or two objects. Young infants consistently ignored surface-feature information and relied on spatial-temporal cues when assessing the number of objects behind the occluder as indexed by fixation time. Using a paradigm similar to that of Xu and Carey (1996), Wilcox (1999) systematically varied (one at a time) the features by which pairs of objects differed when they appeared from behind the occluding screen. She found that at 4.5 months, infants will use shape and size information to individuate objects, but only at 7.5 months will they use surface texture information, and not until 11.5 months do they use color to individuate objects. Note that shape is not a cortically separable object feature as it is processed in both the dorsal and ventral routes. Thus, an infant relying on the dorsal representation only can still access both shape and position information simultaneously. The age at which surface information (e.g., texture and color) is used in *conjunction* with spatial-temporal information to monitor the number of hidden objects behind an occluder corresponds to the age at which infants begin to succeed at manual retrieval tasks (i.e., 7.5–9.5 months).

Taken together, these studies suggest that infants can process surface-feature information independently from spatial-temporal information and, at times, are unable to process both surface features and spatial-temporal information in conjunction. When viewed in the light of the fact that surface features are processed by the ventral route and that spatial-temporal information is processed (predominantly) by the dorsal route, these findings argue for a dissociation between dorsal and ventral route processing in early infancy.

TOWARD A COMPUTATIONAL MODEL OF DORSAL AND VENTRAL ROUTE OBJECT PROCESSING    In this section we review a recent attempt to develop a model of the interaction between dorsal and ventral route processing during development. Figure 23.4 shows a schematic outline of the dual-route processing model described by Mareschal, Plunkett, and Harris (1999). This model was initially developed to account for a developmental lag in infant object-directed behaviors (Baillargeon, 1993). When tested on their memory of hidden objects with perceptual, surprise-based techniques, infants show a precocious understanding of hidden objects. However, it is not until much later that they are able to retrieve a hidden object even though they possess the motor ability to do so. In short, there appears to be a lag between infants' knowledge of hidden objects and their abilities to demonstrate that lag in an active retrieval task. The model uses the dual-route processing hypothesis to account for this lag.

The model has a modular architecture. Each functional module is enclosed by a dashed line. Some units are shared by two modules (e.g., the 75 hidden units are shared by the response integration and trajectory prediction networks) and serve as a gateway for information between the modules. In accordance with the evidence reviewed above, spatial-temporal information about objects in the world is processed independently of feature information. Information enters the network through a two-dimensional retina homogeneously covered by feature detectors. It is then concurrently funneled into one pathway that learns to process the spatial-temporal history of the object and another pathway that develops a spatially invariant feature representation of the object.

The *object recognition module* generates a spatially invariant representation of the object by using a modified version of the unsupervised learning algorithm developed by Foldiak (1996), and is intended to characterize properties of the ventral visual pathway. The Foldiak algorithm belongs to the family of competitive learning algorithms. Initially, a bank of five complex cells is fully and randomly connected to all feature detectors. The algorithm exploits the fact that an object tends to be contiguous with it at successive temporal intervals.

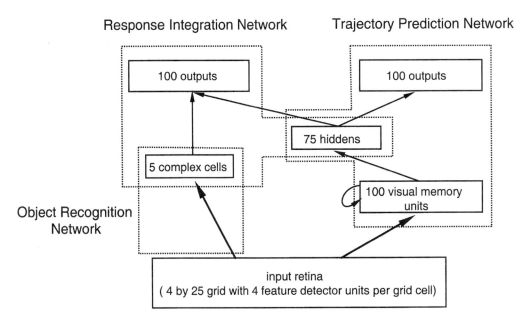

FIGURE 23.4   Schema of object processing model. (From Mareschal, Plunkett, and Harris, 1999.)

Thus, two successive images will probably be derived from the same object. At the end of learning each complex cell becomes associated with a particular feature combination wherever it appears on the retina.

The *trajectory prediction module* uses a partially recurrent, feed-forward network trained with the backpropagation learning algorithm. This network learns to predict the next instantaneous, retinal position of the object, and is designed to capture properties associated with the dorsal route of visual processing. The internal representations it develops are constrained both by the computational properties of the associative mechanisms in the network and by the spatial-temporal prediction task it is engaged in.

All units in the visual memory layer have a self-recurrent connection. The resulting spatial distribution of activation across the visual memory layer takes the form of a comet with a tail that tapers off in the direction from which the object has come. The length and distinctiveness of this tail depend on the velocity of the object. The information in this layer is then forced through a bottleneck of 75 hidden units to generate a more compact, internal rerepresentation of the object's spatial-temporal history. As there are no direct connections from the input to the output, the network's ability to predict the next position is a direct measure of the reliability of its internal object representation. We interpret the response of the trajectory prediction network as a measure of its sensitivity to spatial-temporal information about the object.

The output of the *response integration network* corresponds to the infant's ability to coordinate and use the information it has about object position and object identity. This network integrates the internal representations generated by other modules (i.e., the feature representation at the complex cell level and spatial-temporal representation in the hidden unit layer) as required by a retrieval response task. It consists of a single layered perception whose task is to output the same next position as the prediction network for two of the objects, and to inhibit any response (all units set to 0.0) for the other two objects. This reflects the fact that infants do not retrieve (e.g., reach for) all objects. In general, infants are not asked or rewarded for search. The experimental set-up relies on spontaneous search by the infant. Some objects are desired (e.g., sweet) whereas others are not desired (e.g., sour). Heightening the desirability of an object (e.g., by providing the infant with a prior opportunity to play with the object) has been shown to elicit more search in manual retrieval tasks (Harris, 1986). Any voluntary retrieval response will necessarily require the processing of feature information (to identify the object as a desired one) as

well as trajectory information (to localize the object). Related arguments about the need to coordinate "what" and "where" information in object-directed tasks have been presented elsewhere (e.g., Leslie et al., 1998; Prazdny, 1980).

The model embodies the basic architectural constraints on visual cortical pathways revealed by contemporary neuroscience: an object-recognition network that develops spatially invariant feature representations of objects, a trajectory-prediction network that is blind to surface features and computes appropriate spatial-temporal properties even if no actions are undertaken toward the object, and a response module that integrates information from the two latter networks for use in voluntary actions. In this model surprise is caused by a mismatch between the information stored in an internal representation and the new information arriving from the external world. More specifically, in the trajectory-prediction module, surprise occurs when there is a discrepancy between the predicted reappearance of an object from behind an occluder and its actual reappearance on the retina. In the object-recognition module, surprise occurs when there is a discrepancy between the feature representation stored across the complex units and the new representation produced by the new image.

The model learns to track both visible and occluded objects. Each pathway develops specific task-appropriate representations that persist beyond direct perception. It is successful in demonstrating how the requirement to integrate information across two object representations in a voluntary retrieval task can lead to a development lag relative to performance on surprise tasks that only require access to either spatial-temporal information concerning an occluded object or surface-feature information accessed separately. Moreover, this lag appears only when the network is required to deal with hidden objects, as is the case with infants.

Note that early surprise responses can arise from feature violations, from spatial-temporal violations, and even from both types of violation arising concurrently and independently, but not from a violation involving the *integration* of feature and spatial-temporal information concerning an occluded object. The model predicts that infants will show a developmental lag not just on manual search tasks but also on surprise tasks that involve such integration. Conversely, the model suggests that infants will show early mastery of response tasks that do not require the integration of information across cortical representations.

As noted earlier, the developmental lag in the model is not caused simply by the need to integrate spatial-temporal and featural information. The same integration demands are present when the network is required to respond to a desired, visible object. However, no lag is observed in this condition. Consistent with the model, infants reach accurately for moving visible objects as young as 4.5 months of age. In such cases, information is directly available in the perceptual array.

The developmental lag for occluded objects arises as a natural consequence of the associative learning process. Internal object representations developed over the complex cells and the hidden units persist when the object passes behind the screen, but decay with time. Hence, activation levels drop when the object is occluded. The learning algorithm updates network weights in proportion to the *sending unit's* activation level. For an identical error signal, the weight updates are smaller when the object is hidden, given the lower activation of the sending units. Consequently, it will take longer to arrive at an equivalent level of learning for hidden as compared to visible objects. This outcome is not unique to the learning algorithm used in the current model; it will arise in any learning mechanism that updates weights in proportion to the sending unit activation, providing a clear example of how developmental behaviors are constrained by microlevel mechanisms.

Finally, the model also shows different rates of development for the surface-feature and spatial-temporal modules. The spatial-temporal module is the slower of the two modules to develop. However, the precision of the anticipatory localization response is crucial in determining the slow rate of development. Identifying the exact next position of a moving object takes a long time. A corollary of this finding is that tasks that require less spatial-temporal accuracy would not be as delayed. This requirement of precision may account for why dorsal control of saccades is not evident at 6 months whereas dorsally controlled (but less accurate) reaching is evident by 6 months. Indeed, when accurate or detour reaching is required, infants continue to make errors until they are much older (Diamond, in press). Insofar as the dorsal stream consists of multiple parallel systems closely coupled to motor output systems (Milner and Goodale, 1995), we may expect to find some systems operational by 6 months (e.g., those associated with a less accurate reaching response) while others will not be (e.g., those associated with accurate saccadic responses).

In summary, the computational model illustrates possible causes and consequences of a lack of integration between the pathways in early infancy, and demonstrates that the degree of integration could be task-dependent (i.e., tasks with hidden objects versus tasks with visible objects).

Finally, the close match between the performance of this model and adult neuropsychological data is worth noting. There are documented cases of patients with ventral stream damage but an intact dorsal stream who suffer from a kind of visual form agnosia (they are unable to recognize objects based on shape information alone) and yet are able to reach accurately and even catch objects (Goodale et al., 1991; Milner and Goodale, 1995). After training, the feature recognition module of the model could be damaged in a way that does not affect its ability to respond with a targeted reach (Mareschal, 1997). As discussed, shape (or form) can be encoded down both pathways so damage of the ventral stream shape processing does not interfere with shape processing in the dorsal stream.

## Discussion and future directions

We have explored evidence and modeling pertaining to hypotheses about the development of the dorsal and ventral streams of visual processing. With regard to differential timetables of development in the two pathways, while ERP evidence provided support for the contention that the dorsal pathway is delayed relative to the ventral, behavioral evidence indicates that infants 6 months and younger are capable of fairly well directed reaching to visible objects, a function attributed to the dorsal pathway. Thus, we conclude that different aspects of dorsal pathway function may emerge at different ages. Similarly, with regard to the ventral pathway, behavioral evidence from Wilcox (1999) indicates that while at 4.5 months infants can individuate objects on the basis of shape and size information, only at 7.5 months can they use surface texture, and at 11.5 months color. We are thus wary of general claims about the differential maturation of the two steams of visual processing, and suggest that more detailed analyses of different streams and structures within the dorsal and ventral pathways will be required. However, we suggest that there are a number of causes and consequences of differential development timetables in cortical visual processing.

It is commonly accepted that the later developing a brain system is, the more scope there is for postnatal environmental influence. This may be particularly important for components of the dorsal pathway that have to integrate information from sensory systems with proprioceptive feedback to generate "body-centered" representations for action. As the body of the infant is developing physically, important factors such as length and weight of limbs continue to change. Thus, it may be more important to retain plasticity in the dorsal pathway than in the ventral (see Gilmore and Johnson,

1998). Furthermore, as the infant becomes more mobile toward the end of the first year of life, the nature of his or her experience of the world changes. From his or her initial stance as a relatively passive viewer of the world, the infant becomes able to explore objects and spatial environments manually. This new "infant-generated" experience no doubt helps shape appropriate dorsal pathway cortical circuitry.

Why might there be a dissociation within the dorsal pathway between eye movement control and reaching? It is established that there is an effective subcortical (collicular) route for eye movement control. As we suggested earlier, this route may be adequate for many situations in which saccades are required, and is sufficient to produce an adaptive response in most circumstances. It is only when more challenging saccade paradigms are tried, such as the double-step paradigm, that maladaptive behavior is revealed. Thus, while there are clearly benefits to dorsal pathway control over eye movements, the gains to be made may be less than those for the cortical control of reaching.

By delaying aspects of the development of the dorsal pathway, plasticity can be retained for longer periods of time. However, there is a potential cost to this in that later developing systems tend to be more vulnerable to disruptions in development (see Johnson, 1997). Thus, we anticipate that the dorsal visual stream should show more evidence of plastic changes following differences in experience in otherwise healthy children, but that the dorsal pathway will also show more evidence of deficits in some developmental disorders. There is evidence consistent with both of these predictions.

In a series of experiments involving comparisons between congenitally deaf and hearing subjects, Neville and colleagues have found results indicating that the dorsal stream may be more modifiable in response to alterations in afferent input than the ventral pathway (Neville, 1995). For example, while visual responses recorded at the scalp to peripheral and transient signals are greatly enhanced in the congenitally deaf as compared to hearing, there are no differences between these groups in measured responses to foveal stimuli. In a parallel series of studies, Maurer and colleagues have investigated the effect of early visual deprivation on subsequent visual acuity (Bowering et al., 1996). Children who had cataracts earlier in life subsequently showed deficits in their sensitivity to peripheral visual stimuli several years later. Even children who had had unilateral cataracts subsequently showed prolonged deficits in their sensitivity to peripheral visual stimuli, leading the authors to conclude that cortical systems subserving peripheral vision appear to be more sensitive to experience early in life.

We have presented some elements of a future research program into the development of the dorsal and ventral visual pathways. In these future studies we anticipate a tighter integration between neuroimaging, modeling, and behavior, which will lead us to a more cohesive account of the development of visually guided behavior during infancy.

ACKNOWLEDGMENTS We acknowledge financial support from MRC Programme grant G97 15587, EU Biomed grant BMH4-CT97–2032, and Birkbeck College.

## REFERENCES

ANDERSON, R. A., L. H. SYNDER, C. S. LI, and B. STRICANNE, 1993. Coordinate transformations in the representation of spatial information. *Curr. Opin. Neurobiol.* 3:171–176.

ATKINSON, J., 1998. The 'where and what' or 'who and how' of visual development. In *The Development of Sensory, Motor and Cognitive Capacities in Early Infancy: From Perception to Cognition,* F. Simion and G. Butterworth, eds. Hove, East Sussex: Psychology Press, pp. 3–20.

BAILLARGEON, R., 1993. The object concept revisited: New directions in the investigation of infant's physical knowledge. In *Visual Perception and Cognition in Infancy,* C. E. Granrud, ed. Hillsdale, N.J.: Lawrence Erlbaum, pp. 265–315.

BALABAN, C. D., and J. M. WEINSTEIN, 1985. The human presaccadic spike potential: Influences of a visual target, saccade direction, electrode laterality and instruction to perform saccades. *Brain Res.* 347:49–57.

BENTIN, S., T. ALLISON, A. PUCE, E. PEREZ, and G. MCCARTHY, 1996. Electrophysiological studies of face perception in humans. *J. Cogn. Neurosci.* 8(6):551–565.

BERTENHAL, B. I., 1996. Origins and early development of perception, action and representation. *Annu. Rev. Psychol.* 47:431–459.

BODEN, M. A., 1989. *Computer Models of Mind.* Cambridge: Cambridge University Press.

BOWER, T. G. R., and J. G. PATTERSON, 1973. The separation of place, movement and object in the world of the infant. *J. Exp. Child Psychol.* 15:161–168.

BOWERING, E., D. MAURER, T. L. LEWIS, H. P. BRENT, and P. RIEDEL, 1996. The visual field in childhood: Normal development and the influence of deprivation. Developmental Cognitive Neuroscience Technical Report No. 96.1.

BURNHAM, D. F., 1987. The role of movement in object perception by infants. In *Perceptual Development in Early Infancy: Problems and Issues,* B. McKennie, and R. H. Day, eds. Hillsdale, N.J.: Lawrence Erlbaum.

CHUGANI, H. T., M. E. PHELPS, and J. C. MAZZIOTTA, 1987. Positron emission tomography study of human brain functional development. *Ann. Neurol.* 22:487–497.

CSIBRA, G., M. H. JOHNSON, and L. TUCKER, 1997. Attention and oculomotor control: A high density ERP study of the gap effect. *Neuropsychologia* 35:855–865.

CSIBRA, G., L. A. TUCKER, and M. H. JOHNSON, 1998. Neural correlates of saccade planning in infants: A high-density ERP study. *Intl. J. Psychophysiol.* 29:201–215.

CSIBRA, G., L. A. TUCKER, and M. H. JOHNSON, in press. Anticipatory and reactive saccades in infants: A high-density ERP study. *Infancy.*

DAY, R. H., and D. K. BURNHAM, 1981. Infants' perception of shape and colour in laterally moving patterns. *Infant Behav. Dev.* 4:341–357.

DE HAAN, M., A. OLIVIER, and M. H. JOHNSON, 1998. Electrophysiological correlates of face processing by adults and 6-month-old infants. *J. Cogn. Neurosci.* 36(suppl.).

DE HAAN, M., A. OLIVER, and M. H. JOHNSON, submitted. Spatial and temporal characteristics of cortical activation in adults and infants viewing faces.

DE SCHONEN, S., J. MANCINI, and F. LEIGEOIS, 1998. About functional cortical specialisation The development of face recognition. In *The Development of Sensory, Motor and Cognitive Capacities in Early Infancy: From Perception to Cognition,* F. Simion and G. Butterworth, eds. Hove, East Sussex, UK: Psychology Press, pp. 103–120.

DIAMOND, A., in press. Inability of 5-month-old infants to retrieve a contiguous object: A failure of conceptual understanding or of control of action? *Child Dev.*

FERRERA, V. P., T. A. NEALEY, and J. H. R. MAUNSELL, 1992. Mixed parvocellular and magnocellular geniculate signals in visual area V4. *Nature* 358:756–758.

FOLDIAK, P., 1996. Learning constancies for object perception. In *Visual Constancies: Why Things Look as They Do,* V. Walsh and J. Kulikovski, eds. Cambridge, UK: Cambridge University Press.

GILMORE, R. O., and M. H. JOHNSON, 1997. Body-centred representations for visually-guided action emerge during early infancy. *Cognition* 65:B1–B9.

GILMORE, R. O., and M. H. JOHNSON, 1998. Learning what is where: Oculomotor contributions to the development of spatial cognition. In *The Development of Sensory, Motor and Cognitive Capacities in Early Infancy: From Sensation to Cognition,* F. Simion and G. Butterworth, eds. Hove, East Sussex, UK: Psychology Press, pp. 25–47.

GOODALE, M. A., A. D. MILNER, L. S. JAKOBSON, and D. P. CAREY, 1991. A neurological dissociation between perceiving objects and grasping them. *Nature* 349:154–156.

HARRIS, P. L., 1986. The development of search. In *Handbook of Infant Perception,* P. Salapatek and L. B. Cohen, eds. New York: Academic Press.

HARTLEP, K., 1983. Simultaneous presentation of moving objects in an infant tracking task. *Infant Behav. Dev.* 6:79–84.

HARTLEP, K., and G. A. FORSYTHE, 1977. Infants' discrimination of moving and stationery objects. *Percept. Motor Skills* 45:27–33.

JEANNEROD, M., 1988. The neural and behavioural organization of goal-directed movements. Oxford, UK: Oxford University Press.

JEANNEROD, M., 1999. A dichotomous visual brain? *Psyche* 5(25). http://psyche.cs.monash.edu.au/v5/psyche-5-25-jeannerod.html.

JOHNSON, M. H., 1990. Cortical maturation and the development of visual attention in early infancy. *J. Cogn. Neurosci.* 2(2):81–95.

JOHNSON, M. H., 1997. The neural basis of cognitive development. In *Handbook of Child Psychology,* W. Damon, D. Kuhn, and R. S. Siegler, eds. New York: John Wiley, pp. 1–49.

JOHNSON, M. H., and M. DE HAAN, in press. Developing cortical specialisation for visual-cognitive function: The case of face recognition. In *Mechanisms of Cognitive Development: Behavioural and Neural Perspectives,* Hillsdale, N.J.: Lawrence Erlbaum Associates.

JOHNSON, M. H., R. O. GILMORE, and G. C. CSIBRA, 1998. Toward a computational model of the development of saccade planning. In *The Cognitive Neuroscience of Attention,* J. Richards, ed. Hillsdale, N.J.: Lawrence Erlbaum, pp. 103–130.

JOHNSON, M. H., L. A. TUCKER, J. STILES, and D. TRAUNER, 1998. Visual attention in infants with perinatal brain damage: Evidence of the importance of anterior lesions. *Dev. Sci.* 1:53–58.

KANWISHER, N., J. MCDERMOTT, and M. M. CHUN, 1997. The fusiform face area: A module in human extrastriate cortex specialized for face perception. *J. Neurosci.* 17(11):4302–4311.

KURTZBERG, D., and H. G. VAUGHAN, 1977. Electrophysiological observation on the visuomotor system and visual neurosensorium. In *Visual Evoked Potentials in Man: New Developments,* J. E. Desmedt, ed. Oxford: Clarendon Press, pp. 314–331.

KURTZBERG, D., and H. G. VAUGHAN, 1981. Topographic analysis of human cortical potentials preceding self-initiated and visually triggered saccades. *Brain Res.* 243:1–9.

LESLIE, A. M., F. XU, P. D. TREMOULET, and B. J. SCHOLL, 1998. Indexing and the object concept: Developing 'what' and 'where' systems. *Trends Cogn. Sci.* 2:10–18.

LIVINGSTONE, M., and D. HUBEL, 1984. Anatomy and physiology of a color system in the primate visual cortex. *J. Neurosci.* 4:309–356.

LIVINGSTONE, M., and D. HUBEL, 1988. Segregation of form, color, movement and depth: Anatomy, physiology and perception. *Science* 240(4853):740–749.

MARESCHAL, D., 1997. *Visual Tracking and the Development of Object Permanence: A Connectionist Enquiry.* Unpublished doctoral dissertation, Oxford University, Oxford, UK.

MARESCHAL, D., K. PLUNKETT, and P. HARRIS, 1999. A computational and neuropsychological account of object-oriented behaviours in infancy. *Dev. Sci.* 2:306–317.

MILNER, A. D., and M. A. GOODALE, 1995. *The Visual Brain in Action.* Oxford: Oxford University Press.

NEVILLE, H. J., 1995. Developmental specificity in neurocognitive development in humans. In *The Cognitive Neurosciences,* M. S. Gazzaniga, ed. Cambridge, Mass.: MIT Press, pp. 219–231.

NEWSOME, W. T., R. H. WURTZ, and H. KOMATSU, 1988. Relation of cortical area MT and MST to pursuit eye movements. II: Differentiation of retinal to extraretinal inputs. *J. Neurophysiol.* 60:604–624.

PRAZDNY, S., 1980. A computational study of a period of infant object-concept development. *Perception* 9:125–150.

RICHARDS, J. E., in press. Cortical indices of saccade planning following covert orienting in 20-week-old infants. *Infancy.*

RODMAN, H. R., C. G. GROSS, and S. P. SCALAIDHE, 1993. Development of brain substrates for pattern recognition in primates: Physiological and connectional studies of inferior temporal cortex in infant monkeys. In *Developmental Neurocognition: Speech and Face Processing in the First Year of Life,* B. de Boysson-Bardies, S. de Schonen, P. Jusczyk, P. MacNeilage, and J. Morton, eds. Dordrecht: Kluwer Academic Press, pp. 63–75.

ROLLS, E. T., D. PERRET, S. J. THORPE, A. PUERTO, A. ROPERHALL, and S. MADDISON, 1979. Response of neurons in area 7 of the parietal cortex to objects of different significance. *Brain Res.* 169:194–198.

SIMON, T. J., S. J. HESPOS, and P. ROCHAT, 1995. Do infants understand simple arithmetic? A replication of Wynn (1992). *Cogn. Dev.* 10:253–269.

UNGERLEIDER, L. G., and M. MISHKIN, 1982. Two cortical visual systems: Separation of appearance and location of objects. In *Analysis of Visual Behavior*, D. L. Ingle, M. A. Goodale, and R. J. Mansfield, eds. Cambridge, Mass.: MIT Press.

UNGERLEIDER, L. G., 1985. The cortical pathways for object recognition and spatial perception. In *Pattern Recognition Mechanisms*, C. Changas and C. Gross, eds. Berlin: Springer-Verlag, pp. 21–37.

VAN ESSEN, D. C., C. H. ANDERSON, and D. J. FELLEMAN, 1992. Information processing in the primate visual system: An integrated system perspective. *Science* 255:419–422.

WEBSTER, M. J., J. BACHEVALIER, and L. G. UNGERLEIDER, 1995. Development and plasticity of visual memory circuits. In *Maturational Windows and Adult Cortical Plasticity*, B. Julesz and I. Kovacs, eds. Reading, Mass.: Addison-Wesley, pp. 73–86.

WILCOX, T., 1999. Object individuation: Infants' use of shape, size, pattern and colour. *Cognition* 72:125–166.

XU, F., and S. CAREY, 1996. Infants' metaphysics: The case of numerical identity. *Cogn. Psychol.* 30:11–153.

# 24 Mechanism and Variation in the Development of Attentional Networks

MARY K. ROTHBART
AND MICHAEL I. POSNER

ABSTRACT   Two major approaches to understanding development are the delineation of common mechanisms of emotion and cognition and the study of individual differences among these mechanisms. In this chapter we attempt to integrate these two approaches within the domain of attentional reactivity and self-regulation. We examine brain networks involved in orienting and executive control and discuss how they relate to temperamental differences in attention. We believe consideration of individual variations in how common mechanisms of attention function can greatly enlarge our understanding of normal and pathological development.

This chapter describes efforts to develop a common framework for studies arising from two quite different traditions within psychology. The first involves the development of attention as a mechanism common to all humans and related to regulation of other types of cognitive and emotional behavior (Posner and Petersen, 1990; Posner and Rothbart, 1998). We argue that attention operates through a series of networks to allow people to regulate selection of sensory input, motor output, and emotions in the service of internal goals. The second tradition involves the study of individual differences in the ability to orient attention and to regulate activity through effort (Rothbart, Ahadi, and Evans, 2000). The temperamental dimensions of orienting and effortful control summarize differences among people in their orienting reactivity and in their ability to exercise attentional regulation.

We begin by developing the theme that attention can be considered a vehicle for self-regulation. This is not a common view, so we focus on how this perspective arose. We then briefly outline what is known from research on attention networks and their development. Because there are extensive reviews of this material (e.g., Richards, 1998; Ruff and Rothbart, 1996), we emphasize only those aspects that deal with our general theme. We then discuss how temperament is defined and measured and what is currently known about dimensions of attentional focusing and shifting and effortful control. Finally, we briefly consider the role of temperament in empathy and conscience.

## Attention and self-regulation

In 1958, Donald Broadbent summarized British work in the field of attention in his volume *Perception and Communication*. He proposed the existence of a filter that held back signals from an unattended sensory channel to keep them from interfering with selected input. His beautiful studies, summarized in nearly every textbook in psychology, provided a basis for studying how individuals select relevant information from masses of potential input. The studies reviewed in Broadbent's book were conducted largely in Britain during and immediately following World War II. The viewpoint expressed in this body of work is that attention is a high-level skill devoted to the selection of relevant information. Most attention research has been carried out within a cognitive framework following the Broadbent model. It has involved adult subjects, who are instructed to carry out a specific task. Attempts have been made to develop models of information flow within the nervous system that could be generalized across all subjects.

An important link between studies of attention in human cognition and those using the methods of neurophysiology was provided by Y. N. Sokolov (1963). Sokolov's description of the orienting reflex provided a physical basis for filtering sensory input and presaged the intense interest within neurophysiology in how attention might modulate activity within sensory specific areas (Hillyard and Anllo-Vento, 1998). Luria (1973) recognized the importance of orienting and distinguished between an early developing (largely involuntary), biological attention system and a later developing (more voluntary) social attention system. We believe that Luria was roughly correct in making a distinction between voluntary and involuntary attention systems,

MARY K. ROTHBART   Department of Psychology, University of Oregon, Eugene, Oregon.
MICHAEL I. POSNER   Sackler Institute for Developmental Psychobiology, Weill Medical College of Cornell University, New York, New York.

but that contrary to his original belief, current work shows more clearly how both systems are shaped by a complex interaction between biology and experience that together determine their regulatory properties.

The concept of orienting was readily adapted to the study of preverbal infants who could not be instructed on where to attend by experimenters (see review by Ruff and Rothbart, 1996). Ruff and Rothbart (1996) identified landmark periods in the first year of life with regard to orienting to objects and control of distress, and in the second year and beyond in children's ability to plan and regulate cognitive skills. It was a relatively easy step to link the behavioral development of the child's ability to self-regulate with the neurodevelopment of brain areas devoted to selective attention in adults.

This linkage has a powerful consequence. It allows us to apply knowledge that has accumulated on the anatomy and circuitry of attentional networks (Posner and Raichle, 1994) to what is currently known about the behavioral development of orienting and attention regulation in infants and adults (Posner and Rothbart, 1998). Neuroimaging studies of attention show that attention can modify the neuronal activity within sensory, motor, or emotional networks (Posner and Raichle, 1994). This finding suggests that attention regulates a wide variety of brain networks dynamically and sets the basis for studying self-regulation from an attentional perspective.

The view of attention as a property of the brain that develops under the control of genetics and of the environment fits well with an individual differences approach. Following Rothbart and Bates (1998), we use the term *temperament* to refer to individual differences in motor and emotional reactivity and in attentional self-regulation. Temperament researchers originally believed that temperament systems would be in place very early in development and change little over time (Buss and Plomin, 1975), but we have since learned that temperament systems follow a developmental course (Rothbart, 1989; Rothbart and Bates, 1998). It appears that children's reactive tendencies to experience and express emotions such as fear, frustration, and positive affect, as well as their orienting responses to events in the environment, can be observed early in life; but their self-regulatory executive attention develops relatively late and continues to develop throughout the early school years.

## Networks of attention

Attention is currently being examined in terms of three major functions: orienting to sensory stimuli, maintaining the alert state, and executive functions (Posner and Raichle, 1994). Although knowledge of the precise neural mechanisms responsible for these operations is still incomplete, some of the brain areas and networks involved have been identified. Posner and Raichle (1994) summarized the attentional network approach, and based the localization of the different networks on the brain-imaging literature. Each attentional function is not localized in a single brain area, but involves a network of interconnected brain areas. The organization of these networks is shown in figure 24.1.

Let us briefly describe the networks subserving each of the three major functions of attention.

ORIENTING NETWORK A network for covert orienting to sensory, particularly visual, signals has been discussed in some detail previously (Posner and Dehaene, 1994). Neuroimaging evidence has shown that covert shifts of visual attention strongly activate the posterior parietal lobe. Frontal areas related to the oculomotor system are also activated (Corbetta, 1998). There is strong evidence that attending to a spatial location increases blood flow and electrical activity in the extrastriate cortical regions involved in the processing of color, form, and motion (Corbetta et al., 1990; Heinze et al., 1994). In conditions of cluttered visual fields, or when integration of contours over distances is required, there is evidence of activity in primary visual cortex (Posner and Gilbert, 1999).

ALERTING In order to sustain attention, a second network is involved in maintaining the alert state. Alerting is carried out by a network of brain areas lateralized in the right frontal lobe (superior region of Brodmann area 6), the right parietal lobe, and the locus coeruleus (Posner and Petersen, 1990; Posner and Raichle, 1994). This network is involved in establishing a vigilant state and maintaining readiness to react. Studies of alert monkeys have shown clearly that the readiness induced by warning signals can be blocked by drugs that reduce norepinephrine (Marrocco and Davidson, 1998). In addition, patients with right parietal lesions show difficulty in sustaining attention and in the use of warning signals to improve alertness (Robertson et al., 1997).

EXECUTIVE CONTROL NETWORK This network has been related to the control of goal-directed behavior, target detection, error detection, conflict resolution, and inhibition of automatic responses (Norman and Shallice, 1986). Baddeley (1992) has argued that the executive function in his model of working memory is the same as the system discussed in attentional research. The executive control network includes midline frontal areas including the anterior cingulate gyrus, supple-

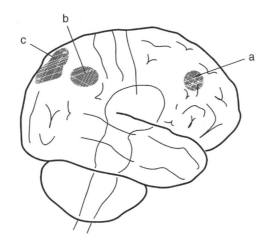

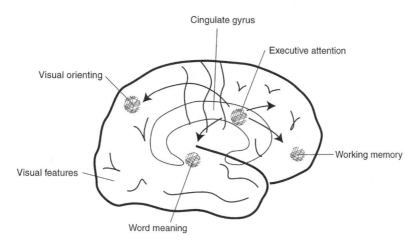

FIGURE 24.1 Alerting and orienting networks. The upper panel indicates the frontal and parietal areas involved in alerting (a, b) and the superior parietal areas shown to be active during attention shifts (c). The lower panel indicates the role of the anterior cingulate in interacting with cortical areas involved in a wide variety of cognitive processes.

mentary motor area (SMA), and portions of the basal ganglia. Neuroimaging studies have shown activity in these areas during tasks that require mental effort, such as in dealing with conflict (Posner and DiGirolamo, 1998). It has also been argued that tasks involving both cognitive and emotional controls, both of which require the selection of relevant information, produce activation in separate areas of the anterior cingulate (Bush et al., 1998; Bush, Luu, and Posner, 2000). Figure 24.2 indicates the separation between areas activated during emotional control tasks and those activated during cognitive tasks involving neutral valence.

Accumulating evidence suggests involvement of the basal ganglia, and more specifically the caudate nucleus, in cognitive functioning (Hayes et al., 1998). The caudate and the prefrontal cortex showed similar patterns of activation when recorded with depth electrodes during tasks such as lexical decisions and semantic categorizations that were not due to motor or premotor programming (Abdullaev, Bechtereva, and Melnichuk, 1998). Many studies have shown behavioral deficits on these tasks in animals following experimental lesions of the anterior dorsolateral frontal cortex and the caudate.

The basal ganglia have been considered to be particularly important in mediating the connection between executive attention and other attentional networks (LaBerge, 1995). Lateral areas of the frontal cortex have also often been identified with executive attention. However, there is also much literature suggesting that these areas involve representation of specific kinds of spatial, verbal, or form information

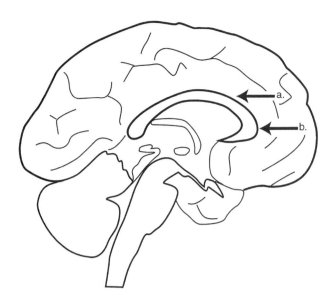

FIGURE 24.2  The more dorsal area (a) of the anterior cingulate is involved in cognitive processes as in figure 24.1, while the more anterior and ventral area (b) is involved with emotional processing. (From Bush et al., 1998.)

related to general attentional operations (Smith and Jonides, 1995).

SUMMARY  We have outlined some evidence favoring three distinct attention networks. These networks interact with various cognitive and emotional brain areas and provide the substrate for allocating task priority among thoughts, feelings, and actions.

### Development

While much of the nervous system develops prior to birth, a long period of postnatal development is needed to complete the basic formation of the brain in primates and humans. During this period, infants gain control of their behavior and mental state so that as older children and adults, they can exercise a degree of central control over their emotions, thoughts, and actions. Despite the immature state of infant sensory systems, the ability to select interesting aspects of the environment and to learn where important stimuli are located begins surprisingly early. It is possible to use this development to trace the mechanisms that will eventually produce voluntary control.

ORIENTING  When infants examine objects, they orient their heads and eyes toward those objects. Eye movements have long been considered a key indicator of the direction of infant attention (Bronson, 1974; Haith, 1980). Although we know from adult work that

attention and eye location can be dissociated (Posner, 1980), their anatomical control systems overlap considerably (Corbetta, 1998), and shifts in eye position are closely associated with attentional shifts. The degree of association between attention and duration of fixation is less clear (Richards and Hunter, 1998). Eye movements are present even before birth, and infants can follow the movement of objects at birth (Haith, 1980). In infancy, acuity is limited and the ability to discriminate objects is rather poor. It is also difficult to attract eye movements toward peripheral objects because the extent of the infant's visual field is limited. However, orienting in order to attend to peripheral objects undergoes a very rapid development between 2 and 4 months.

According to Haith (1980), infants' eyes are initially attracted to stimuli that have many contours and edges. This tendency makes sense for the infant's learning about the visual world, because such features mark the boundaries of objects and provide strong activation of cells in the primary visual cortex. If adults orient to a high-frequency pattern like a checkerboard, they might find it slightly distressing because of its regular pattern. If infants of 1–3 months orient toward the checkerboard pattern, their eyes appear to be caught by it, and they may remain fixated for long periods of time. The checkerboard has a very strong stimulating effect on the infant's visual system, and this effect may cause the infant to become distressed. This tendency for the infant's eyes to become fixated and "stuck" on some stimuli is sometimes called "obligatory looking."

At the end of the first postnatal month of human life, a brain pathway from the basal ganglia to the superior colliculus develops that may support obligatory looking (Johnson, 1990). Obligatory looking seems to occur between the time when this pathway develops until maturation of the parietal lobe provides the infant with an improved ability to disengage from a visual stimulus. During the period of obligatory looking, infants also gaze into the caregivers' eyes, laying a basis for the strong bonds with them (Robson and Moss, 1970). Because the caregiver is likely to use this opportunity to provide pleasurable stimuli to the infant, the infant may react with a more positive behavioral response than to the checkerboard, which elicits a negative reaction. Nonetheless, the internal mechanisms underlying the initial orienting to positive or to negative stimuli at this age appear to be the same.

In one method used to test orienting in infants (Johnson, Posner, and Rothbart, 1991), infants' attention is brought to a powerful central attractor that either looms or spirals on a computer screen. At 2 months, even strong peripheral stimuli are not sufficient to cause the infant to disengage from fixation to this central attractor and shift to these new objects. This pattern changes very dramatically in the period between 2 and 4 months of age, when infants will disengage from fixation and orient to newly presented peripheral stimuli, a finding that might partly reflect the improved visual acuity that co-occurs during this period (Gwiazda, Bauer and Held, 1989). However, infants of 4 months are also able to learn to use central cues to reorient attention. When distinct attractors were used to cue right-sided and left-sided targets, respectively, 4-month-olds learned to anticipate the target by moving their eyes in the direction indicated by each cue. This ability to direct the eyes toward a target based on an arbitrary association was present at 4 months, but not at 2 months (Johnson, Posner, and Rothbart, 1991).

By 4 months, it has been demonstrated that the shift of attention can be entirely covert, that is, without any eye movement. In one such study, a brief flash was presented at a peripheral location where it captured the infant's attention but did not cause an eye movement. Covert orienting was confirmed when infants demonstrated a high probability and a reduced latency in moving their eyes to a subsequent strong target at the previously cued location, rather than to a location at a similar distance on the opposite side (Hood, 1993). Hence, like adults, infants at 4 months of age can have attention captured by a cue without actually executing an eye movement.

The similar development of the control of eye movement and covert orienting by peripheral and central cues seems to reflect the common parietal mechanisms that have been shown to be involved in such attention shifts in adults by both lesion (Posner and Dehaene, 1994) and PET studies (Corbetta et al., 1993). Between 2 and 4 months, just at the time PET studies suggest a strong increase in metabolic processes in the parietal lobe (Chugani, 1994), we find improvement in the infant's ability to shift attention to a peripheral target even when strong attractors are present on the fovea.

NOVELTY One principle of visual system development is that subcortical visual mechanisms tend to develop prior to cortical mechanisms (Bronson, 1974). In adults, orienting away from a just-attended location reduces the probability of returning attention to that location. This phenomenon, called inhibition of return (IOR), was first demonstrated in reaction time studies with normal adults. It seems to reflect one of many inherent responses that favor novelty. In vision, IOR favors searching in new locations rather than ones already examined.

Studies with patient populations showed that lesions of a midbrain eye movement structure, the superior colliculus, but not of various cortical structures, interfered with this tendency to visually explore a novel location. Since inhibition of return appears to depend upon a collicular mechanism, we expected inhibition of return to be present at the youngest ages we studied (Posner et al., 1985). There is now widespread agreement that inhibition of return is found in 4-month-old infants, but not infants of 2–3 months (Richards and Hunter, 1998). However, studies show that inhibition of return can be present in newborn infants, presumably reflecting the midbrain mechanisms that are dominant at birth (Valenza, Simion, and Umilta, 1994). It is not unusual to find functions that are present very early in infancy, based on a subcortical system, that seem to disappear for a period, only to return later with cortical maturation. For example, infants at birth favor a real face over a scrambled face (Johnson and Morton, 1991). This difference in responding to real versus scrambled faces is thought to be based on a primitive midbrain mechanism, but the preference disappears for a few months, only to return at 4 months, but now with more adult-like properties.

Much infant research has used duration of looking as a measure of interest or attention (Fantz, 1961). During the first 6 months of life, the average time that an infant looks at an object declines markedly (Colombo, 1995). There is evidence that during sustained fixation, there are periods of close attention, but also periods in which interest, as measured, for example, by heart rate or latency to disengage, declines (Richards, 1998; Richards and Hunter, 1998). Infants with long fixation duration also tend to be slow to disengage (Frick, Colombo, and Saxon, 1999).

Infants exhibit a strong preference for novel objects over familiar ones (Fantz, 1961; Rose et al., 1982). This is particularly true when familiar objects have been exposed many times (habituation) or when infants have a long period of exposure before being given a choice between objects (Rose et al., 1982). There has been some dispute as to whether newborns favor novel stimuli over familiar ones, although some evidence suggests that they, as well as older children, may look longer at familiar objects under some circumstances (Barille, Armstrong, and Bower, 1999; Ruff and Rothbart, 1996).

In adults, mechanisms underlying preference for location versus object novelty seem to be based on quite different systems (Egly, Driver, and Rafal, 1994). We compared the same forty 6-month-old infants in single trial novelty preference studies for locations and for objects (Posner et al., 1998), finding both forms of novelty preference in these infants. Because of the number of infants involved in this study, it was possible to ask whether the two forms of novelty preference were correlated. The data were clear in showing that they were not. This finding is congruent with the interpretation that the measures involve two independent forms of novelty preference. The independence of novelty preference for objects and locations fits well with the view emerging from adult data that the processing of these different stimulus types involves different mechanisms (Egly, Driver, and Rafal, 1994).

SUMMARY  In this section we have briefly reviewed infant studies designed to examine the development of orienting in the first year of life. All of these results support an approach to the development of orienting based upon the maturation of specific brain networks. We have found that orienting arises in close correspondence with the eye movement system, and elements of orienting are present from birth. The course of behavioral development appears to reflect the general maturation of cortical visual systems during the first year of life (Johnson, 1990). However, evidence on the exact developmental time course of relevant neural structures and pathways is by no means definitive. Inhibition of return is present at birth, but only later does the ability to voluntarily disengage from fixation show strong development. The development seen between 2 and 4 months fits with the evidence on maturation of parietal metabolism (Chugani, 1994). The novelty preference for objects appears to develop strongly from 4 to 6 months and is probably driven by maturation of the parts of the visual system involved in object identification. Orienting from exogenous and endogenous cues appear to develop together, supporting the lesion and PET evidence of strong involvement of the parietal lobe in both forms of orienting. The ability of 4-month-old infants to use centrally presented cues to direct anticipatory eye movements toward an upcoming target suggests that a form of implicit learning is exhibited by the eye movement system at this age.

We now turn to a discussion of how these emerging attentional skills relate to the development of self-regulation and soothing abilities in young infants.

SOOTHING  The maturation of visual attention in the early months of infancy has important consequences for aspects of the infants' behavior that might appear far removed from vision as normally defined. The early life of the infant is concerned with the regulation of a variety of internal states, including distress (Sander, 1962). During the first year of life, attention may be critically important in the individual infant's development of this form of regulatory control. The behavior

of caregivers provides clues as to how attention is used, within the infant–caregiver dyad, to regulate the infant's behavioral state. Before infants reach 3 months of age, caregivers usually report that they use holding and rocking as the primary means of quieting them. However, when infants reach 3 months of age, many caregivers, particularly in Western cultures, alter their means of soothing and attempt to distract their infants by bringing the infants' attention to other stimuli. As infants attend to external cues, they are often quieted, and their distress appears to diminish (Blass, 1992; Wolff, 1987). Notably, this is the same period of time (roughly 3 months of age) when infants first begin to demonstrate the ability to disengage fixation from central objects and shift their attention to peripheral cues.

To investigate this apparent association further, we conducted a systematic study of attention and soothing in 3–6-month-old infants (Harman, Rothbart, and Posner, 1997). Infants first became distressed to overstimulation from lights and sounds, but then strongly oriented to interesting visual and auditory events when these were presented. While the infants oriented, facial and vocal signs of distress disappeared. However, as soon as the orienting stopped (e.g., when the new object was removed), the infants' distress returned to almost exactly the levels shown prior to presentation of the object.

Apparently the loss of overt signs of distress is not always accompanied by a genuine internal loss of distress. Instead, we speculated that some internal system which we termed "the distress keeper" appears to transiently inhibit the initial level of distress, which returns if the infants' orientation to the novel event is interrupted. In later studies (Harman, Rothbart, and Posner, 1997), infants were quieted by distraction for as long as one minute without changing the eventual level of distress reached once orienting was ended. The effectiveness of a repeated stimulus in achieving sustained orienting in the infants also appeared to be reduced at 6 months over its influence at 3 and 4 months.

There may be related phenomena present in the adult. Adults who report themselves as having a good ability to focus and shift attention also report that they experience less negative affect (Derryberry and Rothbart, 1988). Moreover, adults who perform well on a spatial-conflict task of executive attention tend to report lower levels of anxiety and higher levels of self-reported attentional control (Derryberry and Reed, 1999). Thus, attention may serve to control levels of distress in adults in a somewhat similar way to that found early in infancy. Indeed, many of the ideas of modern cognitive therapy are based upon presumed inverse associations between attention and negative ideation (Wells and Matthews, 1994).

For infants, the control of orienting is partially determined by the extent to which caregivers present relevant information. However, infants are not entirely helpless, and they are clearly also capable of soliciting attention from adults (Stern, 1985). During the first years of life, more direct control of attention is transferred from caregivers to their children. It seems possible, then, that the coping mechanisms underlying emotional self-regulation in early development extend to encompass the control of cognition during later infancy and childhood.

LEARNING As described previously, there is considerable evidence that 3–4-month-old infants can learn to anticipate the locations of visual stimuli by moving their eyes to them in advance of their presentation (Canfield et al., 1997; Haith, Hazan, and Goodman, 1988; Johnson, Posner, and Rothbart, 1991). In our studies (Clohessy, Posner, and Rothbart, in press), 4-month-olds learned a sequence of three successive spatial locations arranged in a triangle; presentation of a stimulus at one location predicted unambiguously the stimulus presentation at the next location and so on. This skill may depend upon maturation of basal ganglia and/or parietal structures, both of which are involved in the implicit learning of sequences by adults (Grafton, Hazeltine, and Ivry, 1995). Like infants, adults can learn sequences of spatial locations implicitly when each location is invariably associated with another location (e.g., locations 13241324). This learning occurs even when the adult is distracted with a secondary task known to occupy focal attention (Curran and Keele, 1993). In adults, the implicit form of skill learning seems also to rely mainly upon subcortical structures.

Children at about 18 months of age, but not earlier, also show the ability to learn context-sensitive sequences (Clohessy, Posner, and Rothbart, in press). Context-sensitive sequences (e.g., 1213) are ones in which an association (e.g., where to go after location 1), is ambiguous unless one considers information other than the immediately preceding item. In adults, when all the associations are ambiguous (e.g., 123213), learning appears to require access to the kind of higher level "executive" attention that is needed to resolve conflict (Curran and Keele, 1993). Although adults can learn unambiguous sequences in the presence of distractors, adults are not similarly able to learn context-sensitive sequences (e.g., locations 123213), in which each association is ambiguous in that a given location predicts more than one subsequent location, in the presence of distractors. Consistent with the increased difficulty that adults have in learning context-sensitive sequences, individual children showed wide differences

in their learning abilities, and we found that the ability to learn context-sensitive cues was positively related to caregivers' reports of their children's vocabulary development and to other aspects of executive control (discussed following). Hence, we believe that this type of context-dependent learning reflects functioning within higher level attentional networks involved in executive control.

EXECUTIVE CONTROL Many psychologists agree with Denckla (1996) that "the difference between the child and adult resides in the unfolding of executive functions." In an early study of cognitive control, Diamond (1991) found evidence that 9–12-month-old children proceed through a series of stages in resolving conflict between reaching directly and reaching along the line of sight in order to retrieve an object in a box. At 9 months of age, the line of sight completely dominates the nature of the child's response. Even if the child's hand touches the toy through the open side of the box, if it is not in line with the side where the child is looking, the infant will withdraw the hand and reach along the line of sight, striking the closed side. Three months later, infants are able to look at a closed side but reach through the open end to retrieve the toy (see Diamond, this volume).

However, being able to reach for a target independent of the line of sight is a very limited form of conflict resolution. Gerstadt, Hong, and Diamond (1994) studied verbal conflict using a modification of the Stroop paradigm in children as young as 3½ years. Two cards were prepared to suggest day and night to the children. Children in the conflict condition were instructed to say "day" to the moon and "night" to the sun card. Children in the control condition said either day or night to a checkerboard or ribbon card. At every age, accuracy scores were significantly lower for children in the conflict versus control conditions. Other efforts have been made (for example, using the Wisconsin Card Sort task; Zelazo, Reznick, and Pinon, 1995) to study children as young as 31 months on inhibitory control tasks; little evidence of successful inhibitory control before 3 years of age has been found.

According to this analysis, a more direct measure of the development of executive attention might be reflected in the ability to resolve conflict between simultaneous stimulus events as in the Stroop effect. Since 2- and 3-year-old children do not read, we reasoned that the use of basic visual dimensions of location and identity might be the most appropriate way to study the early resolution of conflict. The variant of the Stroop effect we designed to be appropriate for ages 2–3 years involved presenting a picture depicting a simple object on one side of a screen in front of the child and requiring the child to respond with a key that matched the stimulus they were shown (Gerardi-Caulton, 2000) The appropriate key could be either on the side of the stimulus (compatible trial) or on the side opposite the stimulus (incompatible trial). The child's prepotent response was to press the key on the side of the target irrespective of its identity. However, the task required the child to inhibit the prepotent response and to respond instead based on identity. The ability to resolve this conflict was measured by the accuracy and speed of key press responses. Results of the study strongly suggested that executive attention undergoes a dramatic change during the third year of life. Performance by toddlers at the very beginning of this period was dominated by a tendency to repeat the previous response. Perseveration is associated with frontal dysfunction (Luria, 1973), so the finding of perseveration in toddlers is consistent with the idea that executive attention is still very immature at 24 months. However, even at this young age, toddlers already showed a significant accuracy difference between compatible and incompatible trials. Toddlers during the last half of the third and beginning of the fourth year showed a strikingly different pattern of responses. These children performed with high accuracy for both compatible and incompatible conditions, showing the expected slowing for incompatible relative to compatible trials. The transition in the development of this skill appeared to occur at about 30 months.

It was also possible to examine the relationship of our laboratory measures of conflict resolution to performance on a battery of tasks requiring the child to exercise inhibitory control over behavior. Substantial correlations were found between these two sets of measures. Even more impressive, elements of the laboratory task were significantly positively correlated with aspects of parent-reported temperamental effortful control and negatively correlated with negative affect. Children who were less slowed by conflict were described as showing lower negative affect. It appears that the cognitive measure of conflict resolution has a substantial relation to the natural aspects of the child's self control that parents can report (Gerardi-Caulton, 2000).

## Individuality

Although we have described general trends in the early development of attentional networks, there are wide individual variations in the ability to focus, shift, and sustain attention. Particularly in light of new discoveries in genetics that undoubtedly underlie these individual differences, it is important to describe the variations in

attention that may serve as the appropriate phenotypes for analysis of both genetic and environmental influences on attentional development.

ORIENTING  Attentional processes show considerable development from infancy through the early school years (Ruff and Rothbart, 1996). Orienting, one type of attentional process, is an expression of the infant's connection to his or her sensory world. The automatic nature of orienting makes it a part of the reactive temperament of the infant. Infants demonstrate reactive orienting that, when sustained, appears to be related to interest in an object. This orienting system is subject to habituation when repeated events no longer evoke as strong a reaction, but it also supports learning, when an event indicates where something interesting or important will appear next (Posner and Raichle, 1994). The posterior orienting network, including cortical, midbrain, and thalamic areas, underlies early orienting (Posner and Raichle, 1994). Our work with adults has clearly distinguished the processes involved in orienting to a novel object and those underlying sustained attention to the object's location. Combined studies of the habituation of orienting and of sustained attention in infants and young children may clarify the origins of their processing mechanisms.

Children differ in both their latency to orient and in their duration of orienting to novelty (Ruff and Rothbart, 1996). In caregiver reports, individual differences in infant duration of interest are related to smiling and laughter and vocal activity (Rothbart, Derryberry, and Hershey, 2000). However, we have not found a predictive relationship between laboratory orienting in early infancy and later developing aspects of executive attention. This correlational structure fits with the hypothesized hierarchical relation between the two networks derived from experimental studies with adults (Posner and Raichle, 1994). We think that the later developing control systems described below provide the more important source of individual variation once they have developed.

EFFORTFUL CONTROL DURING CHILDHOOD  The temperamental variable related to the development of executive attention is called effortful control, representing the ability to inhibit a dominant response in order to perform a subdominant response. Effortful control is extremely important in understanding the influence of temperament on behavior. Until recently, almost all of the major theories of temperament have focused on temperament's more reactive aspects as related to positive and negative affect, reward, punishment, and arousal to stimulation (Eysenck, 1967; Gray,

1982; Strelau, 1983). According to many of these theorists, individuals were at the mercy of their dispositions to approach or avoid a situation or stimulus, given reward or punishment cues. More extraverted individuals were expected to be sensitive to reward and to show tendencies to rapid approach; more fearful or introverted individuals, sensitive to punishment, were expected to show inhibition or withdrawal from excitement (Gray, 1987).

These frameworks may neglect important moderators of approach and avoidance behaviors. For example, systems of effortful control allow approach to situations in the face of immediate cues for punishment, and avoidance of situations in the face of immediate cues for reward. In this sense, the programming of effortful control is critical to socialization, which often demands that behavior proceed in a manner that is counter to reactive tendencies. Indeed, the ability to rise above prepotent emotional drives may underlie human conscientiousness and empathy. Consistent with this hypothesis, the laboratory work of Kochanska and her associates indicates that the development of conscience is related to temperamental individual differences in effortful control (Kochanska, Murray, and Coy, 1997; Kochanska, Murray, and Harlan, 1999). Other research suggests some stability of executive attention during childhood. In Mischel's work, for example, the number of seconds delayed by preschool children while waiting for physically present rewards predicted parent-reported attentiveness and ability to concentrate as well as regulation of negative affect when the children were adolescents (Mischel, 1983; Shoda, Mischel, and Peake, 1990).

Questionnaire studies of 6- and 7-year-olds have found an effortful control factor to be defined in terms of scales measuring attentional focusing, inhibitory control, low-intensity pleasure, and perceptual sensitivity (Rothbart et al., submitted). Effortful control is consistently negatively related to a negative affectivity temperament factor. This negative relation is in keeping with the notion that attentional skill may help attenuate negative affect. An interesting example involves the negative relation between effortful control and aggression. Aggression relates positively to surgency and to negative affectivity, especially anger (Rothbart, Ahadi, and Hershey, 1994). Effortful control is negatively related to aggression, but it makes no unique contribution to it, and effortful control may regulate aggression indirectly by controlling reactive tendencies underlying surgency and negative affectivity. For example, children high in effortful control may be able to direct attention away from the rewarding aspects of aggression, or to decrease the influence of negative affectivity by shifting attention away from the negative cues related to anger.

Empathy is also strongly related to effortful control, with children high in effortful control showing greater empathy (Rothbart, Ahadi, and Hershey, 1994). Effortful control may support empathy by allowing the individual to attend to the thoughts and feelings of another without becoming overwhelmed by their own distress. Similarly, guilt/shame in 6- and 7-year-olds is positively related to effortful control and negative affectivity (Rothbart, Ahadi, and Hershey, 1994). Negative affectivity may contribute to guilt by providing the individual with strong internal cues of discomfort, thereby increasing the probability that the cause of these feelings is attributed to an internal rather than external cause (Dienstbier, 1984). Effortful control may contribute further by allowing the flexibility needed to relate these negative feelings of responsibility to one's own specific actions and to negative consequences for another person (Derryberry and Reed, 1994, 1996).

CONCLUSIONS   To summarize, the neural system related to effortful control shows an important development between 2 and 4 years, but it continues to develop during childhood and into adolescence, allowing more sophisticated forms of self-regulation based on verbal information, representations of the self, and projections concerning the future. These findings suggest the importance of effortful control to the child's emotional, cognitive, and social development. Without underestimating environmental influences, underlying temperament systems may serve a central role in the self-organization of personality (Derryberry and Reed, 1994, 1996). This is particularly evident in the functions of attention, which serve to select and coordinate the most important information, contribute to the storage of this information in memory, and provide an important regulatory function.

ACKNOWLEDGMENT   This research was supported by NIMH Grant RO1-43361 to the University of Oregon.

## REFERENCES

ABDULLAEV, Y. G., N. P. BECHTEREVA, and K. V. MELNICHUK, 1998. Neuronal activity of caudate nucleus and prefrontal cortex in cognitive tasks. *Behav. Brain Res.* 97:159–177.

BADDELEY, A., 1992. Is working memory working? The fifteenth Bartlett lecture. *Quart. J. Exp. Psychol.* 44A:1–31.

BARILLE, M., E. S. ARMSTRONG, and T. G. R. BOWER, 1999. Novelty and frequency as determinants of newborn preference. *Dev. Sci.* 2:47–52.

BLASS, E., 1992. Linking developmental and psychobiological research. *SRCD Newsletter.* Chicago: University of Chicago Press.

BROADBENT, D. E., 1958. *Perception and Communication*. London: Pergamon.

BRONSON, G., 1974. The postnatal growth of visual capacity. *Child Dev.* 45:873–890.

BUSH, G., P. LUU, and M. I. POSNER, 2000. Cognitive and emotional influences in the anterior cingulate cortex. *Trends Cogn. Sci.* 4(6):215–222.

BUSH, G., P. J. WHALEN, B. R. ROSE, M. A. JENIKE, S. C. MCINERNEY, and S. L. RAUCH, 1998. The counting Stroop: An interference task specialized for functional neuroimaging—validation study with functional MRI. *Hum. Brain Mapp.* 6:270–282.

BUSS, A. H., and R. PLOMIN, 1975. *A Temperament Theory of Personality Development*. New York: Wiley.

CANFIELD, R. L., E. G. SMITH, M. P. BREZSNYAK, and K. L. SNOW, 1997. Information processing through the first year of life: A longitudinal study using the visual expectation paradigm. *Monographs of the Society for Research in Child Development*, Vol. 62, Serial No. 250.

CHUGANI, H. T., 1994. Development of regional brain glucose metabolism in relation to behavior and plasticity. In *Human Behavior and the Developing Brain*, G. Dawson and K. W. Fisher, eds. New York: Guilford, pp. 153–175.

CLOHESSY, A. B., M. I. POSNER, and M. K. ROTHBART, in press. Development of the functional visual field. *Acta Psychologica*.

COLOMBO, J., 1995. On the neural mechanisms underlying development and individual differences in visual fixation in infancy: Two hypotheses. *Dev. Rev.* 15:97–135.

CORBETTA, M., 1998. Frontoparietal cortical networks for directing attention and the eye to visual locations: Identical, independent, or overlapping neural systems. *Proc. Natl. Acad. Sci. USA* 95:831–838.

CORBETTA, M., F. M. MIEZIN, S. DOBMEYER, G. S. SHULMAN, and S. E. PETERSEN, 1990. Attentional modulation of neural processing of shape, color, and velocity in humans. *Science* 248:1556–1559.

CORBETTA, M., F. M. MIEZIN, G. L. SHULMAN, and S. E. PETERSEN, 1993. A PET study of visuospatial attention. *J. Neurosci.* 13:1202–1226.

CURRAN, T., and S. W. KEELE, 1993. Attentional and nonattentional forms of sequence learning. *J. Exp. Psychol.: Learn. Mem. Cogn.* 19:189–202.

DENCKLA, M. B., 1996. A theory and model of executive function: A neuropsychological perspective. In *Attention, Memory and Executive Function*, G. R. Lyon and N. A. Krasnegor, eds. Baltimore: Paul H. Brookes Publishing, pp. 263–278.

DERRYBERRY, D., and M. A. REED, 1994. Temperament and the self-organization of personality. *Dev. Psychopathol.* 6:653–676.

DERRYBERRY, D., and M. A. REED, 1996. Regulatory processes and the development of cognitive representations. *Dev. Psychopathol.* 8:215–234.

DERRYBERRY, D., and M. A. REED, 1999. Individual differences in attentional control: Adaptive regulation of response interference. Submitted.

DERRYBERRY, D., and M. K. ROTHBART, 1988. Arousal, affect and attention as components of temperament. *J. Personality Soc. Psychol.* 55:958–966.

DIAMOND, A., 1991. Neuropsychological insights into the meaning of object concept development. In *The Epigenesis of Mind: Essays on Biology and Cognition*, S. Carey and R. Gelman, eds. Hillsdale, N.J.: Lawrence Erlbaum, pp. 67–110.

DIENSTBIER, R. A., 1984. The role of emotion in moral socialization. In *Emotions, Cognition, and Behavior*, C. E. Izard, J. Kagan, and R. B. Zajonc, eds. Cambridge: Cambridge University Press, pp. 484–514.

EGLY, R., J. DRIVER, and R. D. RAFAL, 1994. Shifting attention between objects and location. *J. Exp. Psychol.* 123:161–177.

EYSENCK, H. J., 1967. *The Biological Basis of Personality*. Springfield, Ill: Charles C. Thomas.

FANTZ, J. F., 1961. The origins of form perception. *Sci. Amer.* 204:66–72.

FRICK, J. E., J. COLOMBO, and T. F. SAXON, 1999. Individual and developmental differences in disengagement of fixation in early infancy. *Child Dev.* 3:537–548.

GERARDI-CAULTON, G., 2000. Sensitivity to spatial conflict and the development of self-regulation in children 24–36 months of age. *Dev. Sci.* 3:397–404.

GERSTADT, C. L., Y. J. HONG, and A. DIAMOND, 1994. The relationship between cognition and action: Performance of children 3½–7 years old on a Stroop-like day-night test. *Cognition* 53:129–153.

GRAFTON, S. T., E. HAZELTINE, and R. IVRY, 1995. Functional mapping of sequence learning in normal humans. *J. Cogn. Neurosci.* 7:497–510.

GRAY, J. A., 1982. *The Neuropsychology of Anxiety*. Oxford: Oxford University Press.

GRAY, J. A., 1987. Perspectives on anxiety and impulsivity: A commentary. *J. Res. Personality* 21:493–509.

GWIAZDA, J., J. BAUER, and R. HELD, 1989. From visual acuity to hyperacuity: Ten year update. *Can. J. Psychol.* 43:109–120.

HAITH, M. M., 1980. *Rules That Babies Look By*. Hillsdale, N.J.: Erlbaum.

HAITH, M. M., C. HAZAN, and G. S. GOODMAN, 1988. Expectation and anticipation of dynamic visual events by 3.5-month-old babies. *Child Dev.* 59:467–479.

HARMAN, C., M. K. ROTHBART, and M. I. POSNER, 1997. Distress and attention interactions in early infancy. *Motiv. Emot.* 21:27–43.

HAYES, A. E, M. C. DAVIDSON, S. W. KEELE, and R. D. RAFAL, 1998. Toward a functional analysis of the basal ganglia. *J. Cogn. Neurosci.* 10:178–198.

HEINZE, H. J., G. R. MANGUN, W. BURCHERT, H. HINRICHS, M. SCHOLZ, T. F. MÜNTE, A. GOS, M. SCHERG, S. JOHANNES, H. HUNDESHAGEN, M. S. GAZZANIGA, and S. A. HILLYARD, 1994. Combined spatial and temporal imaging of brain activity during visual selective attention in humans. *Nature* 372:543–546.

HILLYARD, S. A., and L. ANLLO-VENTO, 1998. Event-related potentials in the study of visual selection attention. *Proc. Natl. Acad. Sci. USA* 9:781–787.

HOOD, B. M., 1993. Inhibition of return produced by covert shifts of visual attention in 6-month old infants. *Infant Behav. Dev.* 16:245–254.

JOHNSON, M. H., 1990. Cortical maturation and the development of visual attention in early infancy. *J. Cogn. Neurosci.* 2:81–95.

JOHNSON, M. H., and J. MORTON, 1991. *Biology and Cognitive Development*. Cambridge, Mass.: Basil Blackwell.

JOHNSON, M. H., M. I. POSNER, and M. K. ROTHBART, 1991. Components of visual orienting in early infancy: Contingency learning, anticipatory looking and disengaging. *J. Cogn. Neurosci.* 3(4):335–344.

KOCHANSKA, G., K. T. MURRAY, and K. COY, 1997. Inhibitory control as a contributor to conscience in childhood: From toddler to early school age. *Child Dev.* 68:263–267.

362    COGNITION

KOCHANSKA, G., K. T. MURRAY, and E. HARLAN, 2000. Effortful control in early childhood: Continuity and change, antecedents, and implications for social development. *Dev. Psychol.* 36:220–232.

LABERGE, D. H., 1995. *Attentional Processing.* Cambridge Mass.: Harvard University Press.

LURIA, A. R., 1973. *The Working Brain.* New York: Basic Books.

MARROCCO, R. T., and M. C. DAVIDSON, 1998. Neurochemistry of attention. In *The Attentive Brain*, R. Parasuraman, ed. Cambridge, Mass.: MIT Press, pp. 35–50.

MISCHEL, W., 1983. Delay of gratification as process and as person variable in development. In *Human Development: An Interactional Perspective*, D. Magnusson and V. P. Allen, eds. New York: Academic Press, pp. 149–165.

NORMAN, D. A., and T. SHALLICE, 1986. Attention to action: Willed and automatic control of behavior. In *Consciousness and Self-Regulation*, R. J. Davidson, G. E. Schwartz, and D. Shapiro, eds. New York: Plenum Press, pp. 1–18.

POSNER, M. I., 1980. Orienting of attention. The 7th Sir F. C. Bartlett Lecture. *Quart. J. Exp. Psychol.* 32:3–25.

POSNER, M. I., and S. DEHAENE, 1994. Attentional Networks. *Trends Neurosci.* 7:75–79.

POSNER, M. I., and G. J. DIGIROLAMO, 1998. Executive attention: Conflict, target detection and cognitive control. In *The Attentive Brain*, R. Parasuraman, ed. Cambridge: MIT Press, pp. 401–423.

POSNER, M. I., and C. D. GILBERT, 1999. Attention and primary visual cortex. *Proc. Natl. Acad. Sci. USA* 96(6):2585–2587.

POSNER, M. I., and S. E. PETERSEN, 1990. The attention system of the human brain. *Annu. Rev. Neurosci.* 13:25–42.

POSNER, M. I., R. D. RAFAL, L. CHOATE, and J. VAUGHAN, 1985. Inhibition of return: Neural mechanisms and function. *Cogn. Neuropsychol.* 2:211–228.

POSNER, M. I., and M. E. RAICHLE, 1994. *Images of Mind.* New York: Scientific American Library.

POSNER, M. I., and M. K. ROTHBART, 1998. Attention, self-regulation and consciousness. *Phil. Trans. R. Soc. Lond. [B]* 353:1915–1927.

POSNER, M. I., M. K. ROTHBART, L. THOMAS-THRAPP, and G. GERARDI, 1998. Development of orienting to locations and objects. In *Visual Attention*, R. Wright, ed. New York: Oxford University Press, pp. 269–288.

RICHARDS, J. E. (ED.), 1998. *Cognitive Neuroscience of Attention: A Development Perspective.* Mahway, N.J.: Erlbaum.

RICHARDS, J. E., and S. K. HUNTER, 1998. Attention and eye movements in young infants: Neural control and development. In *Cognitive Neuroscience of Attention: A Developmental Perspective*, J. E. Richards, ed. Mahway, N.J.: Erlbaum, pp. 131–162.

ROBERTSON, I. H., M. JEHKONEN, L. PIZZAMIGLIO, A. SHIEL, and E. WEBER, 1977. Auditory sustained attention is a marker of unilateral spatial neglect. *Neuropsychologia* 35:1527–1532.

ROBSON, K. S., and H. A. MOSS, 1970. Patterns and determinants of maternal attachment. *J. Pediatr.* 77:976–985.

ROSE, S. A., A. W. GOTTFRIED, P. MELLY-CARMINAR, and W. H. BRIDGER, 1982. Familiarity and novelty preferences in infant recognition memory: Implications for information processing. *Dev. Psychol.* 18:704–713.

ROTHBART, M. K., 1989. Temperament and development. In *Temperament in Childhood*, G. A. Kohnstamm, J. E. Bates, and M. K. Rothbart, eds. New York: John Wiley and Sons, pp. 187–247.

ROTHBART, M. K., S. A. AHADI, and D. E. EVANS, 2000. Temperament and personality: Origins and outcomes. *J. Personality Soc. Psychol.* 78:122–135.

ROTHBART, M. K., S. A. AHADI, and K. L. HERSHEY, 1994. Temperament and social behavior in childhood. *Merrill-Palmer Quart.* 40:21–39.

ROTHBART, M. K., S. A. AHADI, K. L. HERSHEY, and P. FISHER, submitted. Investigations of temperament at 3–7 Years: The Children's Behavior Questionnaire.

ROTHBART, M. K., and J. E. BATES, 1998. Temperament. In *Handbook of Child Psychology*, Vol. 3, W. S. E. Damon and N. V. E. Eisenberg, eds. *Social, Emotional and Personality Development*, 5th ed. New York: Wiley, pp. 105–176.

ROTHBART, M. K., D. DERRYBERRY, and K. HERSHEY, 2000. Stability of temperament in childhood: Laboratory infant assessment to parent report at seven years. In *Temperament and Personality Development Across the Life Span*, V. J. Molfese and D. L. Molfese, eds. Mahwah, N. J.: Lawrence Erlbaum, pp. 85–119.

RUFF, H. A., and M. K. ROTHBART, 1996. *Attention in Early Development: Themes and Variations.* New York: Oxford University Press.

SANDER, L. W., 1962. Issues in early mother-child interaction. *J. Amer. Acad. Child Psychiatry* 1:141–166.

SHODA, Y., W. MISCHEL, and P. K. PEAKE, 1990. Predicting adolescent cognitive and self-regulatory competencies from preschool delay of gratification: Identifying diagnostic conditions. *Dev. Psychol.* 26:978–986.

SMITH, E. E., and J. JONIDES, 1995. Working memory in humans: Neuropsychological evidence. In *The Cognitive Neurosciences*, M. S. Gazzaniga, ed. Cambridge, Mass.: MIT Press, pp. 1009–1020.

SOKOLOV, Y. N., 1963. *Perception and the Conditioned Reflex.* New York: Macmillan.

STERN, D. N., 1985. *The Interpersonal World of the Infant.* New York: Basic Books.

STRELAU, J., 1983. *Temperament, Personality, Activity.* New York: Academic Press.

VALENZA, E., F. SIMION, and C. UMILTA, 1994. Inhibition of return in newborn infants. *Infant Behav. Dev.* 17:293–302.

WELLS, A., and G. MATTHEWS, 1994. *Attention and Emotion: A Clinical Perspective.* Hillsdale, N.J.: Erlbaum.

WOLFF, P. H., 1987. *The Development of Behavioral States and the Expressions of Emotion in Early Infancy.* Chicago: University of Chicago Press.

ZELAZO, P. D., J. S. REZNICK, and D. E. PINON, 1995. Response control and the execution of verbal rules. *Dev. Psychol.* 31:508–517.

# 25 Neural Bases of Memory Development: Insights from Neuropsychological Studies in Primates

JOCELYNE BACHEVALIER

ABSTRACT Despite considerable information on the capacity of infants to learn and remember under a variety of conditions, little is known about the neural basis of memory processes early in life. This chapter reviews studies in nonhuman primates demonstrating that memory comprises multiple systems that are subserved by different neural circuits developing at different time points in early infancy. The procedural memory system mediated by the striatum and cerebellum is present at birth and reaches functional maturity in the first postnatal months in monkeys. In contrast, the declarative memory system, mediated by the hippocampal formation, and the working memory system, mediated by the dorsolateral prefrontal cortex, have a more protracted development, reaching functional maturity around one year of age for the former and three years of age for the latter. Given the many similarities in the developmental time course of memory processes and neural systems in humans and monkeys, the experimental findings have important implication for our understanding of the development of memory functions and their neural substrates in humans.

Studies aimed at investigating the neural bases of infant memory have burgeoned during the last two decades and several excellent reviews have recently appeared in the literature (Cowan, 1997; Herschkowitz, Kagan, and Zilles, 1997; Nelson, 1995, 1997; Rovee-Collier, 1997). This chapter focus on studies of nonhuman primates that have provided insights into the neurobiological bases of early memory development. Two areas of memory have been more investigated by developmental neurobehavioral studies in primates. One relates to the development of long-term memory, involving procedural and declarative memory processes, and the other is the development of short-term memory, involving working memory processes.

Our current understanding of the organization of memory has gradually evolved from reports of clinical cases with circumscribed lesions and from psychological testing, neurorecording, and neuroimaging of normal and diseased brains. Together with neurobiological experiments in nonhuman primates, these studies have led to the notion that memory can be divided into broad categories.

The distinction between procedural and declarative memory emerged from the study of patients with damage to the medial temporal region (Squire, 1992). This damage yields deficits in retention at long delays but not at short ones. In addition, the long-term memory loss affects the ability to recollect past events or knowledge, generally labeled declarative memory, while an array of learning and retention abilities, labeled procedural memory, remain intact (Squire and Knowlton, 1995). A similar dissociation was found through lesion studies in nonhuman primates. That is, damage to the medial temporal lobe produces a selective loss in recognizing objects when long, but not short, delays are tested, while the acquisition and retention of visual discrimination skills even for relatively long periods of 24 hours are spared (Mishkin and Appenzeller, 1987). Thus, long-term memory appears to include two independent systems mediated by different neural substrates. The declarative (Squire, 1992) or propositional (Tulving, 1995) memory systems permit the acquisition of facts and specific events and are indexed by memory tests, such as recognition and recall, that require explicit recollection. These memory systems are dependent on the medial temporal lobe/diencephalic structures and their interactions with cortical areas. In contrast, the procedural memory system mediates the acquisition and retention of skilled performance indexed by tasks in which memory is expressed implicitly

JOCELYNE BACHEVALIER   Department of Neurobiology and Anatomy, University of Texas Health Science Center, Houston, Texas.

by changes in performance as a result of prior experience. The procedural memory system is independent of the medial temporal lobe structures, and involves different brain circuits, such as the striatum for motor skills learning and the cerebellum for classical conditioning (for review, see Squire and Knowlton, 1995).

In addition to the procedural and declarative memory systems that mediate the formation of long-term memory, there is another memory system that allows retention of information for shorter periods of time while this information is being actively processed and updated. This memory system is generally labeled "working memory" and has been shown to be mediated by the prefrontal cortex in both human and nonhuman primates (for review, see Goldman-Rakic, 1990).

Critical questions immediately emerge from this categorization of memory systems in adults: When do these memory systems emerge during development, and how do the brain systems that mediate them mature during ontogeny? These questions are important not only for providing information on the different types of memory systems and neural processes available at different time points during maturation, but also to further our understanding of how adult memory is achieved. Undeniably, this developmental approach of the study of memory is likely to provide information on how the different components of memory are assembled to result, finally, in adult memory functions (for a full discussion, see Nelson, 1997).

To answer these questions, neuropsychological studies in nonhuman primates have taken three different approaches. The first is to determine when adult proficiency on behavioral tasks known to be critical for a type of memory in the adult monkey emerges in infancy. This approach provides information on the developmental time course of the different memory systems. In addition, given the current knowledge of the neural substrate mediating each of these systems in adults, one could make inferences about the specific neural substrate that becomes available to an infant at different time points during maturation. However, this is an indirect approach to the development of the neurobiological bases of memory that can generally be substantiated by two other sets of studies. The first set of studies employs more direct neuroanatomical, neurobiological, and electrophysiological techniques to assess the maturation of specific neural structures in infancy and correlates the time course of the neural maturation with the time course of emergence of the memory abilities mediated by a specific brain area. A final approach is to determine whether brain lesions that are done in early infancy and that affect a specific memory system in adult monkeys will preclude the emergence of this

system during ontogeny. The basic assumption behind this last approach is that the behavioral deficit will occur only when the lesion is made at a time when the area has reached a certain level of functional maturity (Goldman, 1971).

The neuropsychological studies of memory development in primates have begun only recently, but the data are notable and promising. The main objective of this chapter is to review the most relevant findings, emphasize the numerous gaps in our knowledge, and suggest important areas for future investigations.

## Development of procedural memory

Procedural memory entails an array of diverse learning and memory processes indexed by tasks measuring the acquisition and retention of conditioned responses, skills or habits, as well as perceptual responses (Squire and Knowlton, 1995). One important characteristic of these memory tasks is that the abilities required to solve them necessitate practice (or trial and error) and do not require the integrity of the structures in the medial temporal lobe. In an attempt to establish a primate model of human temporal lobe amnesia, several behavioral paradigms have been used to demonstrate the spared learning abilities of monkeys with bilateral damage to the medial temporal lobe. For instance, it was shown that monkeys with medial temporal lobe lesions can normally learn motor skills and pattern discrimination tasks (Zola-Morgan and Squire, 1984) as well as concurrent discrimination tasks (Malamut, Saunders, and Mishkin, 1984). The question then to be addressed is how this form of learning and memory emerges during infancy. The development of procedural memory in monkeys has almost exclusively been studied with visual discrimination tasks (Bachevalier and Mishkin, 1984; Harlow, 1959; Mahut and Zola, 1977; Zimmerman, 1961), although one study (Harlow, 1959) has used classical conditioning responses.

EMERGENCE OF ADULT PROCEDURAL MEMORY ABILITIES Classical conditioning in infant monkeys was studied by Harlow (1959). During the first postnatal week, infant monkeys can rapidly learn a conditioned response when an auditory stimulus is paired with a brief and mild electric shock. At this early age, monkeys also learn to associate visual cues to the delivery of food, indicating that acquisition of conditioned responses is present almost immediately after birth.

In the simplest version of the discrimination task, the animal is presented with two visual cues (or objects) and must select the cue that is consistently associated with a food reward. These two visual cues are presented successively over several trials until the animal selects the rewarded cue on almost every trial. Monkeys 9–15 days old rapidly master black/white and left/right discriminations (Harlow, 1959) and at 15–25 days can discriminate between two patterns or forms (Harlow, 1959; Harlow, Harlow, Rueping, and Mason, 1960; Zimmerman, 1961; Zimmerman and Torrey, 1965). Furthermore, the ability to solve more complex discrimination tasks in which the animal has to learn a series of object-discriminations presented concurrently also emerges relatively early in life. Thus, by 3–4 months of age (the earliest age tested), infant monkeys can learn, as efficiently as adult monkeys, a short list of object pairs with short intertrial intervals (Mahut and Zola, 1977) and even long lists of object pairs with extremely long intertrial intervals (Bachevalier and Mishkin, 1984). These data suggest that the ability to acquire and retain perceptual-motor associative responses, and hence to form some types of procedural memory, is present in the first few postnatal months in monkeys. Consequently, some of the neural components of this memory system are clearly functional early in life to enable adult performance on procedural memory tasks.

MATURATION OF NEURAL CIRCUITS MEDIATING PROCEDURAL MEMORY   The ability to acquire conditioned responses has been shown to involve the cerebellum and associated brainstem structures (for a review, see Woodruff-Pak and Thompson, 1988). In contrast, the neural circuitry and structures that mediate visual discrimination learning are still a matter of intense debate. The evidence gathered to date suggests that perceptual-motor learning (underlying discrimination tasks) requires the interactions between sensory and motor cortical areas, with the participation of the striatum and cerebellum (Gaffan, 1996; Mishkin, Malamut, and Bachevalier, 1984; Ungerleider, 1995; Wise, 1996). Thus, impairment in visual discrimination tasks follows damage to the inferior temporal cortex, where object features are processed (Buffalo et al., 1999; Mishkin, 1954; Phillips et al., 1988); some of the striatal regions, to which this visual cortex projects (Buerger, Gross, and Rocha-Miranda, 1974; Divac, Rosvold, and Szwarcbart, 1967; Wang, Aigner, and Mishkin, 1990); or the white matter of the temporal stem, which presumably interrupts connections between the visual cortical areas and the striatum (Horel, 1978; Zola-Morgan, Squire, and Mishkin, 1982).

Both metabolic (Bachevalier, Hagger, and Mishkin, 1991) and electrophysiological (Rodman, 1994) studies have indicated that functional maturity of the ventral visual cortical areas, which provide visual inputs to motor cortical areas and to the striatum, proceeds progressively from the occipital areas to the most anterior temporal areas and appears to be completed around 3–6 months postnatally in monkeys.

In the neostriatum, the cellular components are in place in early gestation (165 days in monkeys), and by the end of gestation, cortical inputs begin to invade the neostriatum (Brand and Rakic, 1979; Goldman-Rakic, 1981). In the caudate nucleus and putamen, synaptic density continues to increase until the end of the first postnatal month (Brand and Rakic, 1984) and changes in neuronal and neuropil morphology are observed until 2–4 months postnatally (Cano, Pasik, and Pasik, 1989; Difiglia, Pasik, and Pasik, 1980). Refinement within the striatum proceeds until the end of the first postnatal year when the striatal neurochemical mosaic attains an adult pattern (Martin, Spicer, and Cork, 1992). Furthermore, histoanatomical studies indicate that motor cortical areas are predominantly connected with subcortical structures at birth, and thereafter, intercortical connections progressively develop between the motor cortex and other cortical areas (Kemper, Caveness, and Yakovlev, 1973). In fact, the corticospinal projections in the macaque monkey mature gradually over a period of at least 11 months, long after simple measures of dexterity show functional maturity. This result suggests that the later changes may contribute to the improved speed and coordination of skilled motor tasks (Armand et al., 1994; Flament, Hall, and Lemon, 1992; Galea and Darian-Smith, 1995; Olivier et al., 1997).

Finally, in the cerebellum, neurogenesis in the cortex and deep nuclei occurs early during gestation and neuron differentiation continues through midgestation (Kornguth, Anderson, and Scott, 1967). At birth, the morphology of the Purkinje cells and their axodendritic synapses is similar in structure to the adult pattern (Kornguth, Anderson, and Scott, 1967). Migration of granule cells continues during the first few postnatal months (Rakic, 1971). Synapses from the Purkinje cells are already present prenatally on the soma and axons of deep nuclear neurons, and synapses from climbing fibers of the inferior olive onto Purkinje cells and those from mossy fibers onto granule cells occur approximately at midgestation (Kornguth, Anderson, and Scott, 1968). Finally, at birth, all Purkinje cells have received synaptic contacts (Levitt et al., 1984). Neurochemically, abundant NGF receptors are present on Purkinje cells, granule cells, and neurons of the deep nuclei in fetal cerebellum, but they decrease in the neonatal period (Schatteman et al., 1988). Similarly, many cells in the cerebellum are immunoreactive to neuropeptides early in gestation, but this immunoreactivity decreases significantly during the first postnatal months

(Yamashita et al., 1990). In addition, while glutamate acid decarboxylase (GAD) and tyrosine hydroxylase (TH) activities show a gradual increase until adulthood, choline acetyltransferase (ChAT) activity has already reached adult levels at birth (Hayashi, 1987).

Thus, all neural components necessary to support classical conditioning and visual discriminations appear to be in place, and at almost complete maturity, relatively soon after birth. However, no studies have assessed the effects of early damage to either the cerebellum or the striatum on classical conditioning and discrimination learning in monkeys. The only information currently available concerns the effects of damage to the higher-order associative cortical areas in the ventral visual stream. Thus, damage to inferior temporal cortical area TE in adult monkeys retards the acquisition of concurrent visual discriminations but does not totally abolish this learning ability. The same lesions in infant monkeys during the first month after birth result in a mild, transient retardation in learning concurrent discriminations at 3 months of age (Bachevalier et al., 1990) and no impairment when the same operated animals were retested as adults (Málková, Mishkin, and Bachevalier, 1995). The relative preservation of the ability to learn visual discriminations after early area TE damage suggests that this area is not yet fully functional in infancy and that this ability can be served effectively by visual tissue other than area TE. Indeed, we know that visual inputs to the ventral striatum do not originate uniquely from area TE but also from visual cortical areas located earlier in the ventral visual stream. Thus, in the absence of area TE, these sensory processing outputs from occipitotemporal visual areas to the ventral striatum (caudate nucleus and putamen) could support visual discrimination abilities. In addition, since the early lesions yield greater functional sparing than do lesions in adulthood, these occipito-temporo-striatal connections may make a greater contribution to discrimination learning in infants than in adults.

To summarize, although much remains to be known about the maturation of the neural structures subserving procedural memory processes, all evidence obtained thus far indicates that the neural circuitry mediating this type of memory appears to reach maturity during the first few postnatal months in monkeys, corresponding to roughly the first year of life in humans.

### Development of declarative memory

Declarative memory is thought to support the learning and retention of facts and the recollection of prior events and is indexed by memory tests, such as recall and recognition tasks, requiring the explicit remembering of specific episodes. One important characteristic of this type of memory is that, unlike procedural memory, it is very often formed after a single exposure to a situation and is dependent on the integrity of the structures in the medial temporal lobe and medial diencephalon. Recently, considerable emphasis has been placed on identifying the specific role played by different structures within the medial temporal region on declarative memory processes in monkeys. Although some investigators argue that the medial temporal lobe structures operate as a single functional system to support this type of memory (Squire and Zola, 1996, 1998; Zola-Morgan, Squire, and Ramus, 1994), others have proposed that each structure contributes to declarative memory in a very specific way (Mishkin et al., 1997; Mishkin, Vargha-Khadem, and Gadian, 1998; Murray, 1999). According to this latter view, the entorhinal (Brodmann's area 28) and perirhinal (Brodmann's areas 35 and 36) cortical areas are specialized for memorizing information about objects, whereas the hippocampus is more important for memorizing information about events and places. For example, damage to the perirhinal cortex yields profound object recognition memory impairment whereas damage to the hippocampus results in severe deficits in spatial and relational learning (for review, see Murray, 1999). When does this memory system emerge in ontogeny? The development of declarative memory in monkeys has most often been studied using recognition memory tasks and more recently with relational memory tasks.

EMERGENCE OF ADULT RECOGNITION MEMORY ABILITIES Studies of the development of recognition memory in monkeys have yielded disparate results, depending on the recognition tasks used to assess this memory process.

The visual paired comparison (VPC) task measures the distribution of time spent looking at recently presented stimuli as compared to novel ones (for additional details, see Overman and Bachevalier, this volume). Recognition memory in this task is inferred when the subjects spend a longer period of time looking at new stimuli than at old ones (Fagan, 1970). The VPC task thus measures a spontaneous tendency to respond to novelty and no rules need to be learned by the subjects. Using this task, several studies (Bachevalier, Brickson, and Hagger, 1993; Gunderson and Sackett, 1984; Gunderson and Swartz, 1986) have demonstrated that strong novelty preference is present within the first postnatal month in monkeys. Thus, recognition memory appears to be an early developing memory process even when long retention intervals of 24 hours are used

(Gunderson and Swartz, 1985). Furthermore, preference for novelty is abolished in monkeys that have received early or late lesions to either the medial temporal lobe, including the amygdala, hippocampus, and adjacent cortical areas (Bachevalier, Brickson, and Hagger, 1993) or to the hippocampal formation (Clark et al., 1996; Alvarado and Bachevalier, 2000; Pascalis and Bachevalier, 1999). These data imply not only that recognition memory is an early developing process, but also that the hippocampal formation is functional early in life to support this ability.

The other behavioral task that has been used to assess recognition memory in infant monkeys is a problem-solving task, the delayed nonmatching-to-sample (DNMS) task. In the DNMS task, the animal must first learn that the rule is to choose on every trial a novel object paired with another object seen just a few seconds earlier (for additional details, see Overman and Bachevalier, this volume). After learning the DNMS rule with a single object and a short delay, the animal is given a memory test in which its recognition ability is assessed further with longer delays and also with longer lists of to-be-remembered objects. The results indicate that it is not before 4 months of age that monkeys begin to learn the DNMS rule, and it is not before 2 years of age that they learn it with adult proficiency. In addition, as compared to adult monkeys, immature monkeys are deficient in performing the memory test with extended delays and lists (Bachevalier and Mishkin, 1984). Because recognition memory is an early developing process, it is apparent that the difficulty young normal infant monkeys show in learning DNMS cannot be due to an absence of the adult preference for novelty or even to a deficiency in recognizing stimuli, which the DNMS task exploits. Instead, the results suggest that the difficulty is due to a deficiency in rule learning, and particularly a difficulty in associating the reward in the well with the abstract quality (e.g., novelty) of the object (Bachevalier, 1990; Bachevalier, Brickson, and Hagger, 1993; Diamond, 1990a; Málková et al., in press; see also Overman and Bachevalier, this volume). Because performance on the DNMS task is not impaired by neonatal or late damage to the hippocampal formation (Bachevalier, Beauregard, and Alvarado, 1999; Murray and Mishkin, 1998), the data indicate that the difficulty in DNMS rule learning is due to immaturity within structures of a neural circuit lying outside of the hippocampus.

MATURATION OF NEURAL CIRCUITS MEDIATING RECOGNITION MEMORY   Taken together, the findings with the visual recognition tasks indicate that recognition memory taxed by the VPC and mediated by the hip-

pocampal formation emerges very early in life. These findings are supported by anatomical studies indicating that almost all anatomical components of the hippocampal formation appear to be present at birth in monkeys. Thus, neurogenesis in the monkey hippocampus begins early in gestation (Rakic and Nowakowski, 1981; Seress and Ribak, 1995a,b), and at birth, all pyramidal cells of the Ammon fields and almost all granule cells of the dentate gyrus have completed their migration. Despite this early maturation, refinement of hippocampal circuitry continues well into postnatal life. Thus, the adult-like ultrastructural features of the pyramidal cells is not achieved until the end of the third postnatal month in the monkey, and the dentate cells continue to establish synaptic contacts until the end of the first postnatal year (Seress and Ribak, 1995a,b). Although there have been no metabolic or electrophysiological studies to assess the functional status of the hippocampal formation in early infancy, the anatomical findings suggest that at birth the hippocampus has reached a state of functional maturation sufficient to support spontaneous recognition memory processes. However, this state of functional maturity may not be sufficient to support adult-level visual recognition performance. The hippocampus needs to receive visual information about objects, which, in the adult, is provided by higher-order visual temporal cortical areas. Anatomical connections between area TE, the cortical areas on the parahippocampal gyrus, and the hippocampus do indeed exist in the first week of life in monkeys (Webster, Ungerleider, and Bachevalier, 1991a). However, area TE is not fully functional before the fourth postnatal month (Bachevalier, Hagger, and Mishkin, 1991; Rodman, 1994) and neurogenesis in this cortical area proceeds well into adulthood (Gould et al., 1999). Hence, to support visual recognition, the hippocampus must interact with visual areas other than area TE. One possible pathway that could support visual recognition processes at birth is a pathway linking visual cortical areas located earlier in the ventral visual pathway with the hippocampal formation. The existence of such transient connections has already been demonstrated, and these connections are known to retract progressively between the third and sixth postnatal months (Webster, Ungerleider, and Bachevalier, 1991a,b). An alternative possibility is that early visual recognition processes are mediated by subcortical visual systems. Based on data gathered in humans, it has been proposed that the newborn visual system, unlike the adult visual system, is largely controlled by subcortical neural structures, and that the visual cortical areas begin to play a more important role in visual functions after the third postnatal month (Atkinson, 1979; Bronson, 1974; Held, 1985;

Johnson, 1993; Rovee-Collier, Hankins, and Bhatt, 1992). This shift of functions from subcortical to cortical systems in early development has already been suggested for cognitive memory processes mediated by the prefrontal cortex (Goldman, 1971). Thus, interactions between visual subcortical systems and the hippocampal formation may be able to support visual recognition memory in early infancy. Further studies are clearly needed to further our understanding of the visual pathways that could support visual recognition memory at birth.

In contrast to VPC, the cognitive processes (novelty–reward associations) taxed by the DNMS develop progressively during the first two years of life and appear to be mediated in part by a neural circuit involving the interactions between the inferior temporal and prefrontal cortical areas. This view has emerged from findings in adult monkeys showing that the ability to perform on the DNMS task does not require the participation of the hippocampal formation (for review, see Mishkin and Murray, 1996). Rather, it requires the interactions between the visual temporal cortical areas (perirhinal cortex and area TE) and the inferior prefrontal cortex (inferior convexity and orbitofrontal cortex). Thus, performance on the DNMS task is severely affected by damage to cortical areas on the medial temporal lobe, such as perirhinal cortex (Alvarez, Zola-Morgan, and Squire, 1995; Eacott, Gaffan, and Murray, 1994; George, Horel, and Cirillo, 1989; Horel et al., 1987; Meunier et al., 1993; Murray, 1992; Suzuki et al., 1993; Zola-Morgan et al., 1989, 1993) and area TE (Buffalo et al., 1999; Mishkin, 1982). It is also impaired by damage to the inferior convexity (Kowalska, Bachevalier, and Mishkin, 1991; Weinstein, Saunders, and Mishkin, 1988) and orbital regions (Meunier, Bachevalier, and Mishkin, 1997) in the prefrontal cortex. In contrast, DNMS performance is relatively spared after selective neurotoxin lesions to the hippocampal formation (Murray and Mishkin, 1998).

Thus, immaturity of the temporo-prefrontal cortical areas, but not that of the hippocampus, could be one of the limiting factors for the slow development of performance on the DNMS task. This notion first received support from lesion studies comparing the effects of neonatal damage to three different stations in the neural pathway underlying visual recognition memory in the adult, i.e., the entorhinal and perirhinal cortices, the visual temporal cortical area TE, and the inferior convexity and orbital prefrontal cortex (Bachevalier and Mishkin, 1994; Málková et al., 1998, in press; Málková, Mishkin, and Bachevalier, 1995; Pixley et al., 1997). The results showed that neonatal rhinal cortical damage resulted in a behavioral pattern strikingly similar to that found after late rhinal cortical damage (Mish-

kin, 1978; Málková et al., 1998). That is, like such lesions in adulthood, those in infancy resulted in a severe impairment in both acquisition of the DNMS rule and performance on the memory test. This deficit was present in the first year of life and persisted into adulthood. Unlike area TE and inferior prefrontal convexity lesions in adulthood, which also produce severe deficit in visual recognition memory (Buffalo et al., 1998; Kowalska, Bachevalier, and Mishkin, 1991; Mishkin, 1982; Mishkin and Phillips, 1990), the same lesions in infancy led to substantial and permanent sparing of visual recognition ability. This sparing of DNMS performance after early lesions of the temporoprefrontal cortical circuit suggests instead that it is these cortical areas that are not fully functional at birth. Therefore, it is this circuit's functional immaturity that is one of the limiting factors in the young animal's ability to achieve adult proficiency on the DNMS task. Indeed, as reported above, the visual inferior temporal areas are functionally immature in early infancy and do not reach adult functional levels before 4–6 postnatal months of age in monkeys (Bachevalier, Hagger, and Mishkin, 1991; Bachevalier et al., 1986; Rodman, 1994; Rodman, Skelly, and Gross, 1991; Webster, Bachevalier, and Ungerleider, 1995). The maturation of the inferior portion of the prefrontal cortex has not received extensive study, but it is likely that, as for other prefrontal cortical areas (Goldman-Rakic et al., 1983), the inferior convexity prefrontal cortex will attain functional maturity in the first few months postnatally. This age range corresponds to the first two years in human infants.

EMERGENCE OF ADULT RELATIONAL MEMORY ABILITIES
Relational memory has been measured in monkeys with several behavioral tasks. In the biconditional discrimination task (Saunders and Weiskrantz, 1989), the animal first learns to discriminate four object pairs (AB, AC, CD, and BD), in which only two of the pairs are rewarded (e.g., AC and BD). The transverse patterning task (Spence, 1952) requires the animal to concurrently learn three object pairs (A+ versus B−, B+ versus C−, C+ versus A−). For the oddity task (Harlow, 1959), on every trial the animal is presented with three objects. Two are identical objects and one is a different object (AAB, CCD, EEF, etc.). The animal must select the odd object of the triad to unveil the reward. Finally, in spatial memory tasks the animal must use spatial relationships between cues to solve spatial memory tasks, such as the radial arm maze and Morris search task (for details, see Overman and Bachevalier, this volume).

Interestingly, unlike recognition memory, relational learning appears to mature progressively during the first two years of life in monkeys. Thus, both 6-month-old and 1-year-old monkeys are impaired on biconditional discrimination learning as compared to adults (Killiany and Mahut, 1990). Furthermore, the ability to learn transverse patterning emerges around 1 year of age, although complete adult proficiency is not reached before 2 years of age (Málková et al., 1999). Finally, adult-like performance on the oddity task is not attained before 3–4 years of age (Harlow, 1959). There have been no studies that have investigated the development of spatial relational memory abilities in monkeys.

MATURATION OF THE NEURAL CIRCUIT MEDIATING RELATIONAL LEARNING   Very little is known about the neural circuitry subserving relational learning. One neural structure that seems crucial for this learning process is the hippocampal formation. Thus, selective damage to the hippocampal region in adult monkeys is known to impair performance on the transverse patterning (Alvarado, Bachevalier, and Mishkin, 1998) and spatial memory tasks (Mahut, 1972; Mahut and Zola, 1973; Murray, Baxter, and Gaffan, 1998; Parkinson, Murray, and Mishkin, 1988). Although there are, as yet, no data on the effects of hippocampal lesions on biconditional discrimination or oddity tasks in monkeys, the findings indicate a critical role of the hippocampal formation for normal performance on relational tasks. In contrast, lesions of the ventrolateral portions of the prefrontal cortex (i.e., inferior convexity and orbitofrontal cortex), which produce a severe deficit in recognition memory, do not affect relational learning (Alvarado et al., 1997). These data from lesion studies, together with the evidence regarding the protracted development of relational learning in monkeys, imply that the hippocampal formation is not fully functional during approximately the first year of age in monkeys to efficiently support this form of memory. This conclusion seems to contradict the early functional maturation of the hippocampus to support recognition memory. One possibility is that mediation of relational learning may require the participation of the hippocampus and its interactions with higher-association cortical areas, such as the temporal and prefrontal cortical areas. There is already evidence indicating that the maturation of the hippocampus progresses until adolescence in monkeys. Thus, although neurogenesis within the hippocampus is almost complete in all the Ammon fields at birth (Rakic and Nowakowski, 1981), the ultrastructural features of the neurons do not achieve the adult-like pattern until the end of the first 3 postnatal months of life (Seress and Ribak, 1995a,b). In addition, neurogenesis in the dentate gyrus continues well into postnatal life and tapers off between 4 and 6 months of age in the monkey (Eckenhoff and Rakic, 1988; Rakic and Nowakowski, 1981). Finally, synaptogenesis in the hippocampal formation increases, and a remodeling of the synaptic contacts continues, until the end of the first year of life (for review, see Alvarado and Bachevalier, 2000; Seress and Ribak, 1995a,b). This remodeling and refinement of synaptic interactions within the hippocampal formation also implies that the functional crosstalk between the hippocampal formation and other neocortical areas may not reach functional maturity until the end of the first postnatal year in the monkey, corresponding to the fourth year in humans.

Given all the evidence gathered to date, it is likely that while interactions between the hippocampal formation and subcortical and allocortical areas (perirhinal and entorhinal cortex) may be functional early in life to support some form of recognition memory, the interactions between the hippocampal formation and the neocortical areas on the inferior temporal cortex and prefrontal cortex may develop more progressively during the first year postnatally to account for the protracted appearance of adult proficiency on the relational memory tasks (Alvarado and Bachevalier, 2000; see also Nelson, 1995, 1997). To summarize, as for procedural memory, the development of declarative memory appears to comprise several subsystems (see Mishkin, Vargha-Khadem, and Gadian, 1998 for a similar conclusion), some of which emerge earlier than others during ontogenesis.

## Development of working memory

The active maintenance of short-term memories is commonly termed "working memory" (Baddeley, 1987; Goldman-Rakic, 1987). This form of memory has typically been studied in monkeys with the use of delayed response (DR) or delayed alternation (DA) tasks (Jacobsen, 1936). In both tasks, the monkey is required to maintain a sensory cue in memory for a short delay, then use it to guide a behavioral response. In the classic DR task, two lateral wells of a test tray are covered with identical plaques, and the experimenter shows the monkey that a reward is being hidden under one of the plaques. After a delay of a few seconds, the animal must select the plaque under which the reward has been hidden. In the DA task, the reward alternates from trial to trial from the right well to left well, both covered with identical plaques. On any given trial, the monkey must remember under which plaque the reward was hidden during the previous trial in order to subsequently select the correct one.

The role of the dorsolateral prefrontal cortex in the mediation of working memory is now well established by numerous approaches (for review, see Goldman-Rakic, 1987). Damage to the dorsolateral prefrontal cortex in adult monkeys severely impairs performance on working memory tasks, even with a very short delay of a few seconds (Goldman and Rosvold, 1970; Goldman et al., 1971). In contrast, lesions of the hippocampal formation (including adjacent cortical areas) impair performance only when the delays are longer than 30 s (Diamond, Zola-Morgan, and Squire, 1989). In addition, reversible inactivation of the dorsolateral prefrontal cortex by cooling, electrical stimulation, or dopamine depletion also results in impairment in DR tasks (Brozovski et al., 1979; Fuster and Alexander, 1971; Stamm and Rosen, 1969; Weiskrantz, Mihailovic, and Gross, 1962). Also, using the 2-deoxyglucose metabolic mapping technique, Bugbee and Goldman-Rakic (1981) have demonstrated that local glucose utilization is elevated in dorsolateral prefrontal cortex during performance of DR, while other areas (such as motor cortex) show no changes relative to baseline during DR performance. Finally, many electrophysiological recording studies in awake monkeys trained in DR tasks (Fuster and Alexander, 1971; Kubota and Niki, 1971) have shown that prefrontal neurons respond to the initial cue and maintain their activity at some level throughout the delay period (for review, see Fuster, 1995). Thus, by maintaining the activity of cells that represent the cue, the memory of the cue appears to endure. Cells with such properties have been found in other cortical areas, i.e., inferior temporal cortex for visual patterns or for color cues, posterior parietal cortex for visuospatial cues, premotor cortex for cues for particular responses (for review, see Desimone, 1996; Ungerleider, 1995). Nevertheless, prefrontal neurons respond to all types of cues, and the degree to which they maintain their activity during the delay is typically greater than that in the inferior temporal cortex. Also, unlike activity in the temporal cortex, the prefrontal activity is not disrupted when the monkey processes other visual inputs during the delay period (Wilson, O'Scalaidhe, and Goldman-Rakic, 1993). These results suggest that prefrontal cells may be the major originators of the delay activity and may activate sensory representations in posterior processing areas during the delay via feedback projections to those areas (Goldman-Rakic and Chafee, 1994; Ungerleider, 1995). Thus, the role of the dorsolateral prefrontal cortex in working memory is well recognized.

EMERGENCE OF ADULT LEVEL OF PROFICIENCY   A significant amount of information exists on the development of working memory in monkeys. In the first experiment investigating the development of DR performance in monkeys, Harlow (1959) showed that this ability improves progressively from 2 months to 8 months. Thus, performance at a 5-s delay reached 70% in 5-month-old monkeys, 80% in 7-month-old monkeys, and 90% in 8-month-old monkeys (Harlow et al., 1960). Similarly, Diamond and Goldman-Rakic (1986) showed that while 1.5–2.5-month-old infant monkeys failed the DR task at delays of 2–5 s, 4-month-old monkeys succeeded on the task at delays over 10 s. A working memory task similar to the DR task is the object permanence task, generally labeled A–not B (Piaget, 1954). This task has been extensively used to study cognitive development in human infants (for review, see Diamond, this volume; Stiles, this volume). Performance on this task is severely impaired by dorsolateral prefrontal lesions in adult monkeys (Diamond and Goldman-Rakic, 1989). This task was used to study the development of working memory in normal infant monkeys (Wise, Wise, and Zimmermann, 1973; for review, see Diamond, 1990b). Like human infants, infant monkeys showed a clear progression in performance on this task. Thus, AB errors occurred at 53 days of age for 2-s delays, at 74 days of age for 5-s delays, and at 113 days of age for 10-s delays. This progression in performance on the A–not B task indicates that while working memory is present in the second month postnatally in monkeys, this process becomes progressively more efficient with maturation.

Although no systematic developmental study has been done on the DA task, Goldman and Rosvold (1970) showed that, with a 5-s delay, 1-year-old monkeys required 513 trials to learn the task, whereas 2–3-year-old monkeys took only 170 trials. Thus, even with a relatively short delay, performance on this working memory task continues to improve until adulthood, and adult proficiency on this task appears to be achieved much later than that of the DR and A–not B tasks.

Other working memory tasks have recently been administered to monkeys with dorsolateral prefrontal lesions. One is the search task developed by Passingham (1985) and the other is the self-ordered working memory task developed by Petrides (1995). In the former task, a tray containing 25 wells is used and each well is covered with identical plaques and contains a reward. The animal's task is to retrieve the reward from each well without returning to a well that had already been visited. In the latter task, the monkey is presented with three objects covering a row of three wells. At the beginning of a trial, all three objects are baited and the monkey is allowed to displace only one object to retrieve the reward. On the next trial, the position of the objects on the tray is changed and only the two objects that were not selected on the previous trial are rewarded. Thus, to make a correct choice, the animal has to remember which object he had picked on the previous trial and avoid it in favor of the other two objects. There have been no developmental studies to assess the maturation of abilities to solve these two working memory tasks in monkeys, although there are studies in human populations (Luciana and Nelson, 1998). However, in a similar task, the Hamilton Perseverance Test, Harlow (1959) showed a protracted maturation in monkeys. In the Hamilton Perseverance Test, the animal is presented on each trial with four identical boxes mounted with a spring-loaded lid that automatically closes as soon as the lid is opened. Only one of the four boxes, aligned in a row in front of the monkey, contains the food reward. The rewarded box changes in a random manner from trial to trial, with the provision that the same box is never rewarded twice in succession. On each trial, the monkey is allowed four responses to find the reward, and an error is defined as any return to an unrewarded box after it had been visited once. Thus, in this task too, the monkey needs to keep track of the boxes visited during a given trial to avoid making unrewarded choices. Adult monkeys 4–5 years old rapidly develop a strategy to avoid making unrewarded choices during the task. However, 1- and 2.5-year-old monkeys make many more errors on this task and do not appear to use a strategy. Although the effects of lesions of the dorsolateral prefrontal cortex on that task have never been investigated, the protracted maturation on this task suggests that adult performance for some working memory tasks (search task, self-ordered, and Hamilton Perseverance tasks) may emerge later in life than others (delayed response and A–not B), a finding similar to that found for the development of hippocampal-dependent memory functions.

MATURATION OF DORSOLATERAL PREFRONTAL CORTEX
Neurogenesis of pyramidal neurons in the prefrontal cortex occurs prenatally in the monkey, and, by the end of gestation, all neurons in the prefrontal cortex have reached their final laminar distribution (Schwartz, Rakic, and Goldman-Rakic, 1991). However, new neurons reach this cortical area even in adulthood (Gould et al., 1999). Local circuitry GABA neurons are also generated before birth; but subsets of GABAergic neurons become functionally mature at different times during development, and for some of them, maturation continues during the first few months after birth (for review, see Lewis, 1997). Afferent projection systems also arrive prenatally in the prefrontal cortex, although callosal fibers reach a peak at birth and are eliminated during the first 3 postnatal months (LaMantia and Rakic, 1990; Schwartz and Goldman-Rakic, 1984). Furthermore synaptogenesis within the prefrontal cortex

reaches a maximum rate of accumulation around birth and is maintained at a constant level between 2 months to 3 years of age (Bourgeois, Goldman-Rakic, and Rakic, 1994). Finally, synapses are eliminated until 20 years of age, a process referred to as "synaptic pruning." Interestingly, during synaptic pruning most of the dendrites eliminated are from the dendritic spines of the pyramidal neurons and not those of the dendritic shafts. Similarly, dopamine receptors appear to reach a peak around 2–4 months of age and then decline to reach adult levels by 3 years of age (Lidow, Goldman-Rakic, Rakic, 1991; Lidow and Rakic, 1992). Thus, although the gross morphological development of the prefrontal cortex progresses rapidly prenatally and postnatally, substantial changes in synaptic connectivity can be observed well into adolescence (for review, see Lewis, 1997). Similar findings were obtained with electrophysiological recordings of prefrontal neurons in infant monkeys. Thus, the percentage of prefrontal neurons that exhibit delay period activity doubles between 12 and 36 months of age, suggesting that developmental changes in prefrontal circuitry facilitate the recruitment of these neurons to support working memory (Alexander, 1982).

This progressive maturation of the prefrontal cortex has also been demonstrated by studying the effects of early damage to this cortical area. Longitudinal studies investigating the consequences of early damage to the prefrontal cortex (for review, see Goldman-Rakic et al., 1983) indicated that DR performance of monkeys operated on around 1.5–2.5 months of age did not differ from that of control animals when tested at 1 year of age, but was significantly worse when the same monkeys were retested at 2.5 years. These findings indicate that the dorsolateral prefrontal cortex is not functionally committed to DR performance before 2–3 years of age in the monkey. Comparable results were found with reversible cooling of the prefrontal cortex (Alexander and Goldman, 1978). Cooling of the dorsolateral prefrontal cortex at a temperature that causes 21–25% decrements in DR performance in monkeys of 3 years of age, produces a decrement of only 7–8% in monkeys of 2 years of age and no detectable changes in monkeys of 1 year of age.

For the DA task, performance was reduced by local hypothermia as early as 8.5 months of age, but the reduction in performance was maximal only when hypothermia was induced at 3 years of age (Alexander and Goldman, 1978). These findings suggest that DR and DA have a different developmental time course and that performance of prepubertal monkeys on the DR task before complete maturation of the dorsolateral prefrontal cortex could be mediated by other subcortical systems, such as the caudate nucleus (Goldman and Rosvold, 1972), thalamus (Alexander and Goldman, 1978; Goldman, 1974), and orbitofrontal cortex (Goldman, 1971; Miller, Goldman, and Rosvold, 1973).

For the A–not B task (Diamond, 1990b), two infant monkeys that had learned the task between 1.5 and 2.5 months of age received damage to the dorsolateral prefrontal cortex around 4 months of age. Upon retesting immediately after surgery on the A–not B task, these two operated monkeys failed A–not B trials at all delays tested (2–10 s), whereas the normal control progressed through the delays at a rapid rate. Thus, dorsolateral prefrontal cortex appears to be committed to A–not B performance even earlier than for DR and DA performance. Interestingly, although in many ways, A–not B trials are very similar to delayed alternation (DA) in that the subject must update his/her memory from trial to trial, it appears that performance on the A–not B task matures earlier than that on the DA task. This dissociation in the two working memory tasks is reminiscent of that described for the two visual recognition tasks, and suggests that, although the two tasks are quite similar, they may be solved by different strategies. Thus, there is a specific rule to guide knowledge of where the reward will be represented in future trials in the DA task, but not in the A–not B task. The use of such a rule may require a further maturation of the dorsolateral prefrontal cortex.

The data thus suggest that for working memory processes subserved by the dorsolateral prefrontal cortex, an adult level of proficiency emerges during the third to fourth months postnatally for some tasks, but much later (2–3 years of age) for other tasks. Therefore, as already proposed by others (Lewis, 1997), the improvement in performance on working memory tasks with increasing age may reflect both the maturation of the functional architecture of the dorsolateral prefrontal cortex and its progressive, integrated participation with other neural circuits that mediate these memory processes.

## Concluding remarks

The developmental data reviewed here demonstrate that memory involves different processes subserved by different neural systems. In addition, these multiple memory processes appear to have a specific developmental time course. For example, the ability to solve procedural memory tasks is present at birth in monkeys and reaches adult proficiency in the first postnatal months, suggesting an early maturation of the neural system (striatum and cerebellum) mediating this form of memory. The abilities to solve declarative memory

tasks are also present at birth for some forms of recognition tasks, but do not reach adult proficiency before the end of the first year for relational learning tasks. These data indicate that the progressive maturation of hippocampal-dependent memory functions during development may reflect both the maturation of the functional architecture of the hippocampus and its progressive, integrated participation in the neural circuits that mediate declarative memory. A similar developmental time course is also present for working memory, suggesting that the participation of dorsolateral prefrontal cortex in working memory processes increases progressively with age.

Despite the significant progress made in our understanding of the neural bases of memory development in monkeys, much remains to be learned. For example, the maturation of the neural structures mediating procedural and declarative memory systems has only been studied with anatomical techniques. Although informative, these procedures do not provide knowledge on the functional state of a structure very early in life. Therefore, further analysis of the functional maturation of the striatum, cerebellum, and hippocampal formation using electrophysiological or metabolic studies is clearly needed. Such developmental studies are critical since they have important implications for our understanding of the development of memory processes in human infants.

As summarized in other chapters (Diamond, this volume; Overman and Bachevalier, this volume; Stiles, this volume), the development of procedural, declarative, and working memory appears to show a comparable developmental time course in monkeys and humans (see table 25.1). Such similarities in the emergence of these multiple memory systems in infant monkeys and human infants imply that basic neural systems are likely to follow similar development sequences in both species. If so, additional studies in infant monkeys on the development of these multiple neural systems are likely to provide invaluable information on the maturation of neural basis of memory functions in humans.

In addition, the fact that infants might use different neural circuits, and consequently different strategies, than adults to acquire and retain information dictates caution when making inferences on the type of memory processes measured by specific tasks, insofar as the memory processes measured in infancy may not necessarily correspond to the memory processes measured in adulthood. Finally, the findings indicate the need for a much more extensive analysis of which memory processes become available to monkey and human infants at different points in their maturation and which neural systems are the limiting factor at each point. What are

#### TABLE 25.1
*Functional development of multiple memory systems in monkeys and humans*

| Memory Systems/Tasks | Monkeys | Humans |
|---|---|---|
| *Procedural Memory* | | |
| Conditioned responses | 1 week | 1–2 days[a] |
| Visual discrimination tasks: | | |
|   Two pairs | 2–3 weeks | |
|   Concurrent multiple pairs | 3–4 months | 1–1.5 years[a,b] |
| *Declarative Memory* | | |
| Recognition tasks: | | |
|   Visual paired—Comparison | 2 weeks | 3 days[a] |
|   Delayed nonmatching | 2 years | 4–5 years[a,b] |
| Relational tasks: | | |
|   Biconditional discrimination | 2–3 years | |
|   Transverse patterning | 2–3 years | 4–5 years[c] |
|   Oddity | 3–4 years | 7 years[b] |
| *Working Memory* | | |
| A-not-B | 2–4 months | 8–12 months[a] |
| Spatial delayed response | 2–4 months | 8–12 months[a] |
| Spatial delayed alternation | 1–2 years | |

*Note:* For visual functions 1 week of development in monkeys corresponds roughly to 1 month of development in humans.

[a]Nelson, 1995; [b]Overman, this volume; [c]Rudy, Keith, and Georgen, 1993.

the similarities or differences between the early and the adult memory systems? Does the early memory system change progressively with age, is it maintained while other processes develop, or does it disappear to be replaced by new ones? Answers to these questions will not only guide our search for neurobiological correlates underlying memory processes early in infancy, but will also shed light on the neurobiological correlates underlying adult memory processes.

ACKNOWLEDGMENTS The work discussed here was supported by NIMH grants (MH-54167 and MH-58846).

## REFERENCES

ALEXANDER, G. E., 1982. Functional development of frontal association cortex in monkeys: Behavioral and electrophysiological studies. *Neurosci. Res. Prog. Bull.* 20:471–479.

ALEXANDER, G. E., and P. S. GOLDMAN, 1978. Functional development of the dorsolateral prefrontal cortex: An analysis utilizing reversible cryogenic depression. *Brain Res.* 143:233–249.

ALVAREZ, P., S. ZOLA-MORGAN, and L. R., SQUIRE, 1995. Damage limited to the hippocampal region produces long-lasting memory impairment in monkeys. *J. Neurosci.* 15:3796–3807.

ALVARADO, M. C., and J. BACHEVALIER, 2000. A protracted maturation of hippocampal memory functions in primates. *Learning Memory* 7:244–256.

ALVARADO, M. C., J. BACHEVALIER, and M. MISHKIN, 1998. Neurotoxic lesions of the hippocampal formation impair monkeys' acquisition of the transverse patterning problem. *Soc. Neurosci. Abstr.* 24:928.

ALVARADO, M. C., L. MÁLKOVÁ, C. K. LEX, M. MISHKIN, and J. BACHEVALIER, 1997. Effects of early lesions of the inferior convexity and orbital prefrontal cortices on relational memory in rhesus monkeys. *Soc. Neurosci. Abstr.* 23:498.

ARMAND, J., S. A. EDGLEY, R. N. LEMON, and E. OLIVIER, 1994. Protracted postnatal development of corticospinal projections from the primary motor cortex to hand motoneurones in the macaque monkey. *Exp. Brain Res.* 101:178–182.

ATKINSON, J., 1979. Development of optokinetic nystagmus in the human infant and monkey infant: An analog to development in kittens. In *NATO Advanced Study Institute Series*, R. D. Freeman, ed. New York: Plenum Press.

BACHEVALIER, J., 1990. Ontogenetic development of habit and memory formation in primates. *Ann. N.Y. Acad. Sci.* 608:457–477.

BACHEVALIER, J., M. BEAUREGARD, and M. C. ALVARADO, 1999. Long-term effects of neonatal damage to the hippocampal formation and amygdaloid complex on object discrimination and object recognition in rhesus monkeys (*Macaca mulatta*). *Behav. Neurosci.* 113:1–25.

BACHEVALIER, J., M. BRICKSON, and C. HAGGER, 1993. Limbic-dependent recognition memory in monkeys develops early in infancy. *NeuroReport* 4:77–80.

BACHEVALIER, J., M. BRICKSON, C. HAGGER, and M. MISHKIN, 1990. Age and sex differences in the effects of selective temporal lobe lesion on the formation of visual discrimination habits in rhesus monkeys. *Behav. Neurosci.* 104:885–899.

BACHEVALIER, J., C. HAGGER, and M. MISHKIN, 1991. Functional maturation of the occipitotemporal pathway in infant rhesus monkeys. In *Alfred Benzon Symposium No. 31: Brain Work and Mental Activity, Quantitative studies with radioactive tracers*, N. A. Lassen, D. H. Ingvar, M. E. Raichle, and L. Friberg, eds. Copenhagen, Munksgaard, pp. 231–240.

BACHEVALIER, J., and M. MISHKIN, 1984. An early and late developing systems for learning and retention in infant monkeys. *Behav. Neurosci.* 98:770–778.

BACHEVALIER, J., and M. MISHKIN, 1994. Effects of selective neonatal temporal lobe lesions on visual recognition memory in rhesus monkeys. *J. Neurosci.* 14:2128–2139.

BACHEVALIER, J., L. G. UNGERLEIDER, B. O'NEILL, and D. P. FRIEDMAN, 1986. Regional distribution of [3H]naloxone binding in the brain of a newborn rhesus monkey. *Dev. Brain Res.* 25:302–308.

BADDELEY, A., 1987. *Working Memory*, Oxford, England: Clarendon Press.

BOURGEOIS, J. P., P. S. GOLDMAN-RAKIC, and P. RAKIC, 1994. Synaptogenesis in the prefrontal cortex of rhesus monkeys. *Cereb. Cortex* 4:78–96.

BRAND, S., and P. RAKIC, 1979. Genesis of the primate neostriatum: [3H]Thymidine autoradiographic analysis of the time of neuron origin in the rhesus monkey. *Neuroscience* 4:767–778.

BRAND, S., and P. RAKIC, 1984. Cytodifferentiation and synaptogenesis in the neostriatum of fetal and neonatal rhesus monkeys. *Anat. Embryol.* 169:21–34.

BRONSON, G., 1974. The postnatal growth of visual capacity. *Child Dev.* 45:873–890.

BROZOVSKI, T., R. M. BROWN, H. E. ROSVOLD, and P. S. GOLDMAN, 1979. Cognitive deficit caused by regional depletion of dopamine in prefrontal cortex of rhesus monkey. *Science* 205:929–932.

BUERGER, A. A., C. G. GROSS, and C. E. ROCHA-MIRANDA, 1974. Effects of ventral putamen lesions on discrimination learning in monkeys. *J. Comp. Physiol. Psychol.* 86:440–446.

BUFFALO, E. A., S. J. RAMUS, R. E. CLARK, E. TENG, L. R. SQUIRE, and S. M. ZOLA, 1999. Dissociation between the effects of damage to perirhinal cortex and area TE. *Learn. Mem.* 6:572–599.

BUFFALO, E. A., L. STEFANACCI, L. R. SQUIRE, and S. ZOLA, 1998. A reexamination of the concurrent discrimination learning task: The importance of anterior inferotemporal cortex, area TE. *Behav. Neurosci.* 112:3–14.

BUGBEE, N. M., and P. S. GOLDMAN-RAKIC, 1981. Functional 2-deoxyglucose mapping in association cortex: Prefrontal activation in monkeys performing a cognitive task. *Soc. Neurosci. Abstr.* 6:822.

CANO, J., P. PASIK, and T. PASIK, 1989. Early postnatal development of the monkey globus pallidus: A golgi and electron microscopic study. *J. Comp. Neurol.* 279:353–367.

CLARK, R. E., E. TENG, L. R. SQUIRE, and S. ZOLA, 1996. The visual paired-comparison task and the medial temporal lobe memory system. *Soc. Neurosci. Abstr.* 22:281.

COWAN, N., 1997. *The Development of Memory in Childhood.* Hove East Sussex, UK: Psychology Press.

DESIMONE, R. 1996. Neural mechanisms for visual memory and their role in attention. *Proc. Natl. Acad. Sci. USA* 93:13494–13499.

DIAMOND, A., 1990a. Rate of maturation of the hippocampus and the developmental progression of children's performance on the delayed nonmatching-to-sample and visual paired comparison tasks. *Ann. N.Y. Acad. Sci.* 608:394–426.

DIAMOND, A., 1990b. The development and neural bases of memory functions as indexed by the AB and delayed response task in human infants and infant monkeys. *Ann. N.Y. Acad. Sci.* 608:267–303.

DIAMOND, A., and P. S. GOLDMAN-RAKIC, 1986. Comparative development in human infants and infant rhesus monkeys of cognitive functions that depend on prefrontal cortex. *Soc. Neurosci. Abstr.* 12:742.

DIAMOND, A., and P. S. GOLDMAN-RAKIC, 1989. Comparison of human infants and rhesus monkeys on Piaget's A-not-B task: Evidence of dependence on dorsolateral prefrontal cortex. *Exp. Brain Res.* 74:24–40.

DIAMOND, A., S. ZOLA-MORGAN, and L. R., SQUIRE, 1989. Successful performance by monkey with lesion of the hippocampal formation on A-not-B and object retrieval, two tasks that mark developmental changes in human infants. *Behav. Neurosci.* 103:526–537.

DIFIGLIA, M., P. PASIK, and T. PASIK. 1980. Early postnatal development of the monkey neostriatum: A golgi and ultrastructural study. *J. Comp. Neurol.* 190:303–331.

DIVAC, I., H. E. ROSVOLD, and M. K. SZWARCBART, 1967. Behavioral effects of selective ablation of the caudate nucleus. *J. Comp. Physiol. Psychol.* 63:184–190.

EACOTT, M. J., D. GAFFAN, and E. A. MURRAY, 1994. Preserved recognition memory for small sets, and impaired stimulus identification for large sets, following rhinal cortex ablations in monkeys. *Eur. J. Neurosci.* 6:1466–1478.

ECKENHOFF, M. F., and P. RAKIC, 1988. Nature and fate of proliferative cells in the hippocampal dentate gyrus during the life span of the rhesus monkey. *J. Neurosci.* 223:1–21.

FAGAN, J. F., 1970. Memory in the infant. *J. Exp. Child Psychol.* 9:217–226.

FLAMENT, D., E. J. HALL, and R. N. LEMON, 1992. The development of cortico-motoneuronal projections investigated using magnetic brain stimulation in the infant macaque. *J. Physiol. Lond.* 447:755–768.

FUSTER, J. M., 1995. *Memory in the Cerebral Cortex: An Empirical Approach to Neural Networks in the Human and Nonhuman Primate,* Cambridge, Mass.: MIT Press.

FUSTER, J. M., and G. E. ALEXANDER, 1971. Neuron activity related to short-term memory. *Science* 173:652–654.

GAFFAN, D., 1996. Memory, action, and the corpus striatum: Current developments in the memory-habit distinction. *Sem. Neurosci.* 8:33–38.

GALEA, M. P., and I. DARIAN-SMITH, 1995. Postnatal maturation of the direct corticospinal projections in the macaque monkey. *Cereb. Cortex* 5:518–540.

GEORGE, P. J., J. A. HOREL, and R. A. CIRILLO, 1989. Reversible cold lesions of the parahippocampal gyrus in monkeys results in deficits of the delayed matching-to-sample an other visual tasks. *Behav. Brain Res.* 34:163–178.

GOLDMAN, P. S., 1971. Functional development of the prefrontal cortex in early life and the problem of neuronal plasticity. *Exp. Neurol.* 32:366–387.

GOLDMAN, P. S., 1974. An alternative to developmental plasticity: Heterology of CNS structures in infants and adults. In *CNS Plasticity and Recovery of Function,* D. J. Stein, J. Rosen, and N. Butters, eds. New York, Academic Press, pp.149–174.

GOLDMAN, P. S., and H. E. ROSVOLD, 1970. Localization of function within the dorso-lateral prefrontal cortex of the rhesus monkey. *Exp. Neurol.* 27:291–304.

GOLDMAN, P. S., and H. E. ROSVOLD, 1972. The effects of selective caudate lesions in infant and juvenile rhesus monkeys. *Brain Res.* 43:53–66.

GOLDMAN, P. S., H. E. ROSVOLD, B. VEST, and T. W. GALKIN, 1971. Analysis of the delayed alternation deficit produced by dorsolateral prefrontal lesions in the rhesus monkey. *J. Comp. Physiol. Psychol.* 77:212–220.

GOLDMAN-RAKIC, P., 1981. Prenatal formation of cortical input and development of cytoarchitectonic compartments in the neostriatum of the rhesus monkey. *J. Neurosci.* 1:721–735.

GOLDMAN-RAKIC, P., 1987. Cellular and circuit basis of working memory in prefrontal cortex of nonhuman primates. *Prog. Brain Res.* 85:325–336.

GOLDMAN-RAKIC, P., 1990. Cellular and circuit basis of working memory in prefrontal cortex of nonhuman primates. *Prog. Brain Res.* 85:373–417.

GOLDMAN-RAKIC, P. S., and M. CHAFEE, 1994. Feedback processing in prefronto-parietal circuits during memory-guided saccades. *Soc. Neurosci. Abstr.* 20:808.

GOLDMAN-RAKIC, P. S., A. ISSEROFF, M. L. SCHWARTZ, and N. M. BUGBEE, 1983. The neurobiology of cognitive development. In *Handbook of Child Psychology: Biology and Infancy Development,* Vol. 2, P. Mussen, ed. New York: Wiley, pp. 281–344.

GOULD, E., A. J. REEVES, M. S. GRAZIANO, and C. G. GROSS, 1999. Neurogenesis in the neocortex of adult primates. *Science* 286:548–552.

GUNDERSON, V. M., and G. P. SACKETT, 1984. Development of pattern recognition in infant pigtailed macaques (*Macaca nemestrina*). *Dev. Psychol.* 20:418–426.

GUNDERSON, V. M., and K. B. SWARTZ, 1985. Visual recognition in infant pigtailed macaques after 24-hour delay. *Am. J. Primat.* 8:259–264.

GUNDERSON, V. M., and K. B. SWARTZ, 1986. Effects of familiarization time on visual recognition memory in infant pigtailed macaques (*Macaca nemestrina*). *Dev. Psychol.* 22:477–480.

HARLOW, H. F., 1959. The development of learning in the rhesus monkey. *Am. Scientist* Winter:459–479.

HARLOW, H. F., M. K. HARLOW, R. R. RUEPING, and W. A. MASON, 1960. Performance of infant rhesus monkeys on discrimination learning, delayed response, and discrimination learning set. *J. Comp. Physiol. Psychol.* 53:113–121.

HAYASHI, M., 1987. Ontogeny of glutamic acid decarboxylase, tyrosine hydroxylase, choline acetyltransferase, somatostatin and substance P in monkey cerebellum. *Dev. Brain Res.* 32:181–186.

HELD, R., 1985. Binocular vision: Behavioral and neuronal development. In *Neonates Cognition: Beyond the Booming, Buzzing, Confusion,* J. Mehler and R. Fox, eds. Hillsdale, N.J.: Lawrence Erlbaum, pp. 37–44.

HERSCHKOWITZ, N., J. KAGAN, and K. ZILLES, 1997. Neurobiological bases of behavioral development in the first year. *Neuropediatrics* 28:296–306.

HOREL, J. A., 1978. The neuroanatomy of amnesia: A critique of the hippocampal memory hypothesis. *Brain* 101:403–445.

HOREL, J. A., D. E. PYTKO-JOYNER, M. L. VOYTKO, and K. SALSBURY, 1987. The performance of visual tasks while segments of the inferotemporal cortex are suppressed by cold. *Behav. Brain Res.* 23:29–42.

JACOBSEN, C. F., 1936. Studies of cerebral function in primates. *Comp. Psychol. Monogr.* 13:1–68.

JOHNSON, M. H., 1993. Cortical maturation and perceptual development of visual attention in early infancy. In *Brain Development and Cognition: A Reader,* M. H. Johnson, ed. Cambridge, Mass.: Blackwell, pp. 167–194.

KEMPER, T. L., W. F. CAVENESS, and P. I. YAKOVLEV, 1973. The neuronographic and metric study of the dendritic arbours of neurons in the motor cortex of *Macaca mulatta* at birth and at 24 months of age. *Brain* 96:765–782.

KILLIANY, R., and H. MAHUT, 1990. Hippocampectomy in infant monkeys facilitates object reward association learning but not for conditional object-object associations. *Soc. Neurosci. Abstr.* 16:847.

KORNGUTH, S. E., J. W. ANDERSON, and G. SCOTT, 1967. Observations on the ultrastructure of the developing cerebellum of the *Macaca mulatta. J. Comp. Neurol.* 130:1–24.

KORNGUTH, S. E., J. W. ANDERSON, and G. SCOTT, 1968. The development of synaptic contacts in the cerebellum of *Macaca mulatta. J. Comp. Neurol.* 132:531–546.

KOWALSKA, D., J. BACHEVALIER, and M. MISHKIN, 1991. The role of the inferior prefrontal convexity in performance of delayed nonmatching-to-sample. *Neuropsychologia* 29:583–600.

KUBOTA, K., and H. NIKI, 1971. Prefrontal cortical activity and delayed alternation performance in monkeys. *J. Neurophysiol.* 34:337–347.

LAMANTIA, A. S., and P. RAKIC, 1990. Axon overproduction and elimination in the corpus callosum of the developing rhesus monkey. *J. Neurosci.* 10:2156–2175.

LEVITT, P., P. RAKIC, P. DE CAMILLI, and P. GREENGARD, 1984. Emergence of cyclic guanosine 3′:5′-monophosphate-dependent protein kinase immunoreactivity in developing rhesus monkey cerebellum: Correlative immunocytochemical and electron microscopic analysis. *J. Neurosci.* 4:2553–2564.

LEWIS, D. A., 1997. Development of the primate prefrontal cortex. In *Neurodevelopment and Adult Psychopathology,* M. S. Keshavan and R. M. Murray, eds. Cambridge, UK: Cambridge University Press, pp. 12–30.

LIDOW, M. S., P. S. GOLDMAN-RAKIC, and P. RAKIC, 1991. Synchronized overproduction of neurotransmitter receptors in diverse regions of the primate cerebral cortex. *Proc. Natl. Acad. Sci. USA* 88:10218–10221.

LIDOW, M. S., and P. RAKIC, 1992. Scheduling of monoaminergic neurotransmitter receptor expression in the primate neocortex during postnatal development. *Cereb. Cortex* 2:401–416.

LUCIANA, M., and C. A. NELSON, 1998. The functional emergence of prefrontally-guided working memory systems in four- to eight-year-old children. *Neuropsychologia* 36:273–293.

MAHUT, H., 1972. A selective spatial deficit in monkeys after transection of the fornix. *Neuropsychologia* 10:65–74.

MAHUT, H., and S. ZOLA, 1973. A non-modality specific impairment in spatial learning after fornix lesions in monkeys. *Neuropsychologia* 11:255–269.

MAHUT, H., and S. ZOLA, 1977. Ontogenetic time-table for the development of three functions in infant macaques and the effect of early hippocampal damage upon them. *Soc. Neurosci. Abstr.* 3:428.

MALAMUT, B. L., R. C. SAUNDERS, and M. MISHKIN, 1984. Monkeys with combined amygdalo-hippocampal lesions succeed in object discrimination learning despite 24-hour intertrial intervals. *Behav. Neurosci.* 98:759–769.

MÁLKOVÁ, L., M. C. ALVARADO, E. L. PIXLEY, A. M. BELCHER, M. MISHKIN, and J. BACHEVALIER, 1999. Maturation of relational memory processes in monkeys. *Soc. Neurosci. Abstr.* 25:88.

MÁLKOVÁ, L., J. BACHEVALIER, M. WEBSTER, and M. MISHKIN, in press. Effects of neonatal inferior prefrontal and medial temporal lesions on learning the rule for delayed nonmatching-to-sample. *Dev. Neuropsychol.*

MÁLKOVÁ, L., M. MISHKIN, and J. BACHEVALIER, 1995. Long-term effects of selective neonatal temporal lobe lesions on learning and memory in monkeys. *Behav. Neurosci.* 109:212–226.

MÁLKOVÁ, L., G. I. PIXLEY, M. J. WEBSTER, M. MISHKIN, and J. BACHEVALIER, 1998. The effects of early rhinal lesions on visual recognition memory in rhesus monkeys. *Soc. Neurosci. Abstr.* 24:1906, 1998.

MARTIN, L. J., D. M. SPICER, and L. C. CORK, 1992. Postnatal development of the striatal mosaic in rhesus monkey. *Soc. Neurosci. Abstr.* 18:957.

MEUNIER, M., J. BACHEVALIER, and M. MISHKIN, 1997. Effects of orbital frontal and anterior cingulate lesions on object and spatial memory in rhesus monkeys. *Neuropsychologia* 35:999–1015.

MEUNIER, M., J. BACHEVALIER, M. MISHKIN, and E. A. MURRAY, 1993. Effects on visual recognition of combined and separate ablations of the entorhinal and perirhinal cortex in rhesus monkeys. *J. Neurosci.* 13:5418–5432.

MILLER, E. A., P. S. GOLDMAN, and H. E. ROSVOLD, 1973. Delayed recovery of function following orbital lesions in infant monkeys. *Science* 182:304–306.

MISHKIN, M., 1954. Visual discrimination performance following partial ablations of the temporal lobe: II. Ventral surface vs. hippocampus. *J. Comp. Physiol. Psychol.* 47:187–193.

MISHKIN, M., 1978. Memory in monkeys severely impaired by combined but not by separate removal of amygdala and hippocampus. *Nature* 273:297–298.

MISHKIN, M., 1982. A memory system in the monkey. *Phil. Trans. R. Soc. Lond.* B298:85–95.

MISHKIN, M., and T. APPENZELLER, 1987. The anatomy of memory. *Scientific American* 256:80–89.

MISHKIN, M., B. MALAMUT, and J. BACHEVALIER, 1984. Memories and habits: Two neural systems. In *Neurobiology of Learning and Memory*, G. Lynch, J. L. McGaugh, N. M. Weinberger, eds. New York: Guilford Press, pp. 287–296.

MISHKIN, M., and E. A. MURRAY, 1996. Stimulus recognition. *Curr. Opin. Neurobiol.* 4:200–206.

MISHKIN, M., and R. R. PHILLIPS, 1990. A corticolimbic path revealed through its disconnection. In *Brain Circuits and Functions of the Mind. Essays in Honor of Roger W. Sperry*, C. Trevarthen, ed., Cambridge: Cambridge University Press, pp. 196–210.

MISHKIN, M., W. A. SUZUKI, D. G. GADIAN, and F. VARGHA-KHADEM, 1997. Hierarchical organization of cognitive memory. *Phil. Trans. R. Soc. Lond.* B 352:1461–1467.

MISHKIN, M., F. VARGHA-KHADEM, and D. G. GADIAN, 1998. Amnesia and the organization of the hippocampal system. *Hippocampus* 8:212–216.

MURRAY, E. A., 1992. Medial temporal lobe structures contributing to recognition memory: the amygdaloid complex versus the rhinal cortex. In *The Amygdala: Neurobiological Aspects of Emotion, Memory, and Mental Dysfunction*, J. P. Aggleton, ed. New York: Wiley, pp. 453–470.

MURRAY, E. A., 1999. Memory for objects in nonhuman primates. In *The Cognitive Neurosciences*, 2nd ed., M. Gazzaniga, ed., Cambridge, Mass.: MIT Press, pp. 753–763.

MURRAY, E. A., M. G. BAXTER, and D. GAFFAN, 1998. Monkeys with rhinal cortex damage or neurotoxic hippocampal lesions are impaired on spatial scene learning and object reversals. *Behav. Neurosci.* 112:1291–1303.

MURRAY, E. A., and M. MISHKIN, 1998. Object recognition and location memory in monkeys with excitotoxic lesions of the amygdala and hippocampus. *J. Neurosci.* 18:6568–6582.

NELSON, C. A., 1995. The ontogeny of human memory: A cognitive neuroscience perspective. *Dev. Psychol.* 31:723–738.

NELSON, C. A., 1997. The neurobiological basis of early memory development. In *The Development of Memory in Childhood*, N. Cowan, ed. Hove East Sussex, UK: Psychology Press, pp. 41–82.

OLIVIER, E., S. A. EDGLEY, J. ARMAND, and R. N. LEMON, 1997. An electrophysiological study of the postnatal development of the corticospinal system in the macaque monkey. *J. Neurosci.* 17:267–276.

PARKINSON, J. K., E. A. MURRAY, and M. MISHKIN, 1988. A selective mnemonic role of the hippocampus in monkeys: Memory for the location of objects. *J. Neurosci.* 8:4159–4167.

PASCALIS, O., and J. BACHEVALIER, 1999. Neonatal aspiration lesions of the hippocampal formation impair visual recognition memory when assessed by paired-comparison task but not by delayed nonmatching-to-sample task. *Hippocampus* 9:609–616.

PASSINGHAM, R. E., 1985. Memory of monkeys (*Macaca mulatta*) with lesions in prefrontal cortex. *Behav. Neurosci.* 99:3–21.

PETRIDES, M., 1995. Impairments on nonspatial self-ordered and externally ordered working memory tasks after lesions of the mid-dorsal part of the lateral frontal cortex in the monkey. *J. Neurosci.* 15:359–375.

PHILLIPS, R. R., B. L. MALAMUT, J. BACHEVALIER, and M. MISHKIN, 1988. Dissociation of the effects of inferior temporal and limbic lesions on object discrimination learning with 24-hr intertrial intervals. *Behav. Brain Res.* 27:99–107.

PIAGET, J., 1954. *The Construction of Reality in the Child*. New York: Basic Books [Original French version, 1936].

PIXLEY, G. L., L. MÁLKOVÁ, M. J. WEBSTER, M. MISHKIN, and J. BACHEVALIER, 1997. Early damage to both inferior convexity and orbital prefrontal cortices impairs DNMS learning in infant monkeys. *Soc. Neurosci. Abstr.* 23:499.

RAKIC, P., 1971. Neuron-glia relationship during granule cell migration in developing cerebellar cortex. A golgi and electromicroscopic study in macaque rhesus. *J. Comp. Neurol.* 141:283–312.

RAKIC, P., and R. S. NOWAKOWSKI, 1981. The time of origin of neurons in the hippocampal region of the rhesus monkey. *J. Comp. Neurol.* 196:99–128.

RODMAN, H. R., 1994. Development of inferior temporal cortex in the monkey. *Cereb. Cortex* 5:484–498.

RODMAN, H. R., J. P. SKELLY, and C. G. GROSS, 1991. Stimulus selectivity and state dependence of activity in inferior temporal cortex of infant monkeys. *Proc. Natl. Acad. Sci. USA* 88:7572–7575.

ROVEE-COLLIER, C., 1997. Dissociations in infant memory: Rethinking the development of implicit and explicit memory. *Psychol. Rev.* 104:467–498.

ROVEE-COLLIER, C., E. HANKINS, and R. BHATT, 1992. Textrons, visual pop-out effects, and object recognition in infancy. *J. Exp. Psychol. Gen.* 121:435–445.

SAUNDERS, R. C., and L. WEISKRANTZ, 1989. The effects of fornix transection and combined fornix transection, mammillary body lesions and hippocampal ablation on object-pair association memory in the rhesus monkey. *Behav. Brain Res.* 35:85–94.

RUDY, J. W., J. R. KEITH, and K. GEORGEN, 1993. The effect of age on children's learning of problems that require a configural association solution. *Dev. Psychobiol.* 26:171–184.

SCHATTEMAN, G. C., L. GIBBS, A. A. LANAHAN, P. CLAUDE, and M. BOTHWELL, 1988. Expression of NGF receptor in the developing and adult primate central nervous system. *J. Neurosci.* 8:860–873.

SCHWARTZ, M. L., and P. S. GOLDMAN-RAKIC, 1984. Callosal and intrahemispheric connectivity of the prefrontal association cortex in rhesus monkey: Relation between intraparietal and principal sulcus cortex. *J. Comp. Neurol.* 226:403–420.

SCHWARTZ, M. L., P. RAKIC, and P. S. GOLDMAN-RAKIC, 1991. Early phenotype expression of cortical neurons: Evidence that a subclass of migrating neurons have callosal axons. *Proc. Natl. Acad. Sci. USA* 88:1354–1358.

SERESS, L., and C. E. RIBAK, 1995a. Postnatal development of CA3 pyramidal neurons and their afferents in the Ammon's horn of rhesus monkeys. *Hippocampus* 5:217–231.

SERESS, L., and C. E. RIBAK, 1995b. Postnatal development and synaptic connections of hilar mossy cells in the hippocampal dentate gyrus of rhesus monkeys. *J. Comp. Neurol.* 355:93–110.

Spence, K. W., 1952. The nature of response in discrimination learning. *Psychol. Rev.* 59:89–93.

Squire, L. R., 1992. Declarative and nondeclarative memory: Multiple brain systems supporting learning and memory. *J. Cogn. Neurosci.* 4:232–243.

Squire, L. R., and B. J. Knowlton, 1995. Memory, hippocampus, and brain systems. In *The Cognitive Neurosciences*, M. Gazzaniga, ed. Cambridge, Mass.: MIT Press, pp. 825–837.

Squire, L. R., and S. M. Zola, 1996. Structure and function of declarative and nondeclarative memory systems. *Proc. Natl. Acad. Sci. USA* 93:13515–13522.

Squire, L. R., and S. M. Zola, 1998. Episodic memory, semantic memory, and amnesia. *Hippocampus* 8:205–211.

Stamm, J. S., and S. C. Rosen, 1969. Electrical stimulation and steady potential shifts in prefrontal cortex during delayed response performance by monkeys. *Acta Biol. Exp.* 29:385–399.

Suzuki, W. A., S. Zola-Morgan, L. R. Squire, and D. G. Amaral, 1993. Lesions of the perirhinal and parahippocampal cortices in the monkey produce long lasting memory impairments in the visual and tactual modalities. *J. Neurosci.* 13:2430–2451.

Tulving, E., 1995. Organization of memory: Quo vadis? In *The Cognitive Neurosciences*, M. S. Gazzaniga, ed. Cambridge, Mass.: MIT Press, pp. 839–847.

Ungerleider, L. G., 1995. Functional brain imaging studies of cortical mechanisms for memory. *Science* 270:769–775.

Wang, J., T. Aigner, and M. Mishkin, 1990. Effects of neostriatal lesions on visual habit formation in rhesus monkeys. *Soc. Neurosci. Abstr.* 16:617.

Webster, M. J., L. G. Ungerleider, and J. Bachevalier, 1991a. Connections of inferior temporal areas TE and TEO with medial temporal-lobe structures in infant and adult monkeys. *J. Neurosci.* 11:1095–1116.

Webster, M. J., L. G. Ungerleider, and J. Bachevalier, 1991b. Lesions of inferior temporal area TE in infant monkeys alter cortico-amygdalar projections, *NeuroReport* 2:769–772.

Webster, M. J., J. Bachevalier, and L. G. Ungerleider, 1995. Development and plasticity of visual memory circuits. In *Maturational Windows and Adult Cortical Plasticity*, B. Julesz and I. Kovacs, eds. Redwood City, Calif.: Addison-Wesley, pp. 73–86.

Weinstein, J., R. C. Saunders, and M. Mishkin, 1988. Temporo-prefrontal interaction in rule learning by macaques. *Soc. Neurosci. Abstr.* 14:1230.

Weiskrantz, L., L. Mihailovic, and C. G. Gross, 1962. Effects of stimulation of frontal cortex and hippocampus on behavior in the monkey. *Brain* 85:487–504.

Wilson, F. A. W., S. P. O'Scalaidhe, and P. S. Goldman-Rakic, 1993. Dissociation of object and spatial processing domains in primate prefrontal cortex. *Science* 260:1955–1957.

Wise, K. L., L. A. Wise, and R. R. Zimmermann, 1973. Piagetian object permanence in the infant rhesus monkey. *Dev. Psychol.* 3:429–437.

Wise, S. P., 1996. The role of the basal ganglia in procedural memory. *Sem. Neurosci.* 8:39–46.

Woodruff-Pak, D. S., and R. F. Thompson, 1988. Cerebellar correlates of classical conditioning across the life span. In *Life-Span Development and Behavior*, P. B. Baltes, R. M. Lerner, and D. M. Featherman, eds. Hillsdale, N.J.: Erlbaum, pp. 1–37.

Yamashita, A., M. Hayashi, K. Shimizu, and K. Oshima, 1990. Neuropeptide-immunoreactive cells and fibers in the developing primate cerebellum. *Dev. Brain Res.* 51:19–25.

Zimmerman, R. R., 1961. Analysis of discrimination learning capacities in the infant rhesus monkey. *J. Comp. Physiol. Psychol.* 54:1–10.

Zimmerman, R. R., and C. C. Torrey, 1965. Ontogeny of learning. In *Behavior of Nonhuman Primates: Modern Research Trends*, Vol. 2, A. M. Schrier, H. F. Harlow, and F. Stollnitz, eds. New York: Academic Press, pp. 405–447.

Zola-Morgan, S., and L. R. Squire, 1984. Preserved learning in monkeys with medial temporal lesions: Sparing of motor and cognitive skills. *J. Neurosci.* 4:1072–1085.

Zola-Morgan, S., L. R. Squire, D. G. Amaral, and W. A. Suzuki, 1989. Lesions of the perirhinal and parahippocampal cortex that spare the amygdala and hippocampal formation produce severe memory impairment. *J. Neurosci.* 9:4355–4370.

Zola-Morgan, S., L. R. Squire, R. P. Clower, and N. L. Rempel, 1993. Damage to the perirhinal cortex exacerbates memory impairment following lesions of the hippocampal formation. *J. Neurosci.* 13:251–265.

Zola-Morgan, S., L. R. Squire, and M. Mishkin, 1982. The neuroanatomy of amnesia: Amygdala-hippocampus versus temporal stem. *Science* 218:1337–1339.

Zola-Morgan, S., L. Squire, and S. J. Ramus, 1994. Severity of memory impairment in monkeys as a function of locus and extent of damage within the medial temporal lobe memory system. *Hippocampus* 4:483–495.

# 26 The Neuropsychology of Face Processing during Infancy and Childhood

MICHELLE DE HAAN

ABSTRACT The human face is typically one of babies' first sights following birth, and from this time they show an interest in orienting to facelike patterns. Yet in spite of this impressive early competency, face processing follows a protracted developmental course before becoming adultlike. This chapter describes the development of face processing abilities and outlines theories of the neural and cognitive mechanisms underlying developmental change. It is concluded that the cortical specialization for face processing observed in adults is achieved through a gradual specialization of an initially more general-purpose processing system.

The human face holds special significance as a powerful visual source of social information. Normally, adults can, with seemingly little effort, quickly and accurately perceive the complex array of characteristics encoded in the face, such as identity, emotion, and direction of gaze. Even newborns appear to know something about the structure of the face; shortly after birth, they will move their eyes further to keep a moving pattern in sight if its elements are positioned in a facelike arrangement (Johnson et al., 1991). These impressive abilities make it easy to forget both the highly sophisticated mechanisms underlying adults' face processing abilities and the protracted developmental pathway by which the basic abilities of the newborn are transformed into the mature state. Studying this developmental process can provide a unique perspective on debates that are central to the study of face processing, such as the domain-specificity of the neural and cognitive mechanisms mediating face processing and the relative contributions of innate cortical organization and visual experience in the development of face processing. Moreover, as these questions regarding cortical specialization are not unique to the topic of face processing, this line of study also has implications more

MICHELLE DE HAAN Cognitive Neuroscience Unit, Institute of Child Health and Great Ormond Street Hospital, University College London Medical School, The Wolfson Centre, London, England.

generally for understanding brain and behavioral development.

This chapter provides a description of developmental changes in face processing together with a critical evaluation of hypotheses regarding the neural and cognitive mechanisms underlying these changes. It is divided into three sections, the first addressing general issues in the study of face processing, the second providing an overview of normative development during infancy and childhood, and the third considering atypical development of face processing.

## What's special about face recognition?

A fundamental question in the study of face processing is whether, within the ventral visual object-processing pathway, there is further division into face and object processing pathways. In other words, is the cortical face processing system different, in terms of (1) anatomical localization and/or (2) perceptual-cognitive specialization, from the cortical object processing system? It is no exaggeration to say that the majority of studies of face processing in adults address this question, either directly or indirectly. More studies than not have found differences between face and object processing on various neural and perceptual-cognitive measures (reviewed in Farah et al., 1998; Nachson, 1995). Some investigators accept these results as evidence in favor of cortical localization and specialization of face processing, while others argue that the differences can be attributed to confounding factors (e.g., differences in level of categorization for face and object tasks; see Damasio, Tranel, and Damasio, 1990; Gauthier et al., 1999). It is beyond the scope of this chapter to provide a comprehensive review of the adult literature on this point; the purpose here is simply to briefly review aspects of face processing by adults that are proposed to be unique in order to provide a general background and to show how developmental studies can address these issues.

CORTICAL FACE AREAS HYPOTHESIS According to this hypothesis, there are cortical areas that are devoted solely to processing of faces. The main lines of evidence in support of this view are as follows:

1. *Face-responsive neurons in monkeys:* Certain neurons in the monkey temporal and frontal lobes are face-sensitive in that they fire more to faces than to a variety of nonface stimuli (reviewed in Gauthier and Logothetis, in press).

2. *Double dissociation of face and object processing:* Neuropsychological studies show that some patients with damage to the brain show impaired face recognition but intact object recognition (prosopagnosia) while others show the reverse pattern. This type of double dissociation of impairments in two abilities is classically interpreted as evidence that the two abilities rely on different neural substrates (De Renzi et al., 1994).

3. *Face-responsive brain activation in humans:* The results of numerous neuroimaging studies using a variety of techniques such as positron emission tomography (PET; Sergent, Ohta, and MacDonald, 1992), functional magnetic resonance imaging (fMRI; Kanwisher, McDermott, and Chun, 1997), magnetoencephalography (MEG; Sams et al., 1997), and event-related potentials (ERPs; Bentin et al., 1996) show that certain occipitotemporal cortical areas, particularly parts of the fusiform gyrus, are activated only by faces or are activated more by faces than other objects.

RELATIONAL / CONFIGURAL / HOLISTIC ENCODING HYPOTHESIS In this hypothesis, the type of information that is encoded and remembered for faces differs from that encoded and remembered for objects. The difference in the nature of processing has been described in various ways (see Diamond and Carey, 1986; Farah, 1990; Rhodes et al., 1998 for different definitions), but the essence of these ideas is that objects are represented in terms of isolated features or parts whereas faces are represented in terms of a global pattern or relations among the parts. The main line of evidence in support of this view is the *face inversion effect:* the fact that stimulus inversion disproportionately impairs face compared to object processing (Diamond and Carey, 1986). In this view, inversion impairs face more than object processing because inversion disrupts relational more than parts-based encoding.

RIGHT HEMISPHERE HYPOTHESIS According to this hypothesis, the right hemisphere is faster and more efficient than the left at processing some aspects of facial information such as facial identity and facial emotion.

The major lines of evidence in support of this view are as follows:

1. *Divided visual field studies:* When a face is presented first to the right hemisphere (by presenting it very briefly in the left visual field), it is recognized more quickly and more accurately than when a face is presented only to the left hemisphere (Ellis and Shepherd, 1975).

2. *Lesion sites in prosopagnosics:* Studies examining the sites of cortical lesions in prosopagnosia indicate that damage limited to the right hemisphere is sufficient to cause impairments in face processing, indicating that this area is necessary for normal face processing (De Renzi et al., 1994).

3. *Greater right than left activation to faces in neuroimaging studies.* Some studies using neuroimaging techniques show greater activation over right than left hemisphere areas during face processing tasks (e.g., Gauthier et al., 1999; Kanwisher, McDermott, and Chun, 1997).

There are two main cognitive explanations for the greater right than left hemisphere involvement in face processing. One explanation is that the hemispheric difference occurs because relational encoding is mediated primarily by the right hemisphere and feature-based encoding is mediated by the left (Farah, 1990). A second explanation is that the hemisphere difference occurs because processing of social/emotional information is mediated primarily by the right hemisphere (Cicone, Wapner, and Gardner, 1980).

Collectively these three hypotheses—cortical face areas, relational/configural/holistic encoding, and right hemisphere—suggest that the adult face processing system is unique in that certain occipitotemporal cortical areas, particularly those in the right hemisphere, are necessary for normal face (but not object) processing, at least in part because they mediate configural processing. A developmental approach is helpful in evaluating these ideas because it allows one to assess associations or dissociations in the developmental emergence of the various components of visual recognition. For example, evidence that face and object processing abilities emerge at different times or develop at different rates would support the hypothesis that the two abilities rely on different neurocognitive mechanisms. In addition, the developmental approach allows for the potential study of components of the recognition system in isolation in a way that is not possible in adults. For example, if the face recognition system develops before the object recognition system, then it would be possible to study the face recognition system in isolation and examine its unique characteristics in a way that is not possible in adults. Finally, the developmental approach can provide information regarding the role of experience in the emergence of the cortical face processing system. For example, is a distinction between face and object processing present at birth, or does it only develop following extensive visual experience with faces? This information is critical not only for understanding normative development of face processing skills but also for identifying the factors underlying developmental impairments in face processing skills.

## Normative development of face processing

THE NEWBORN  Studying the newborn's ability to perceive and remember faces is of considerable interest because it allows one to assess the representational biases the infant is born with that might guide subsequent learning/experience. Since visual experience begins at birth, these biases are innate in the sense that they rely on little or no visual experience with faces to emerge.

*Facedness*  Newborn babies move their eyes, and sometimes their heads, longer to keep a moving facelike pattern in view than several other comparison patterns (Johnson et al., 1991). It seems that all that is needed to elicit a response is a very schematic version of the face: Just a triangular arrangement with three blobs for eyes and a mouth is sufficient (Johnson and Morton, 1991). Some authors have argued that these data can be explained by a sensory hypothesis. In this hypothesis, there is no aspect of the system that is responding specifically to faces; instead, the preferential orienting of the newborn to faces is just a consequence of more general mechanisms guiding visual attention. For example, in the linear systems model of infant visual attention, visual preferences in the first months of life are based on the amplitude spectra of the stimuli (the amount of energy in a pattern, defined by the amplitudes and orientations of the component spatial frequencies; Banks and Ginsburg, 1985; Banks and Salapatek, 1981). Thus, it is argued that infants will prefer facelike patterns because they tend to have more energy at the spatial frequencies to which they are more sensitive. In contrast, others explain newborns' preferential orienting to faces with a social hypothesis. In this view, infants have an innate preference for facelike stimuli that is based not only on the visibility of the stimuli but on a more specific knowledge of the configuration of the face. For example, in the Conspec/Conlern hypothesis, an innate, subcortical mechanism, Conspec, causes newborns to orient to patterns with elements in a facelike arrangement (Morton and Johnson, 1991). Recent studies demonstrating that babies will still prefer a facelike pattern even to one that is more (Valenza et al.,

1996) or equally (Kleiner and Banks, 1987; Mondloch et al., 1999) visible support the social hypothesis and cannot be explained by the sensory hypothesis. Since infants show this preferential orienting as little as hours after birth, it is either a very quickly learned or a congenital representational bias.

What are the neural bases of infants' preferential orienting to facelike stimuli in the visual environment? One hypothesis is that it is mediated by a subcortical retinotectal pathway (Morton and Johnson, 1991). For example, newborns only show the preference in conditions to which the subcortical systems are sensitive (when stimuli are moving and are in the peripheral visual field but not when they are in the central visual field). Further experimental evidence in support of this view is that infants orient more toward facelike patterns than inverted face patterns in the temporal, but not the nasal, visual field (Simion et al., 1998). Since the retinotectal (subcortical) pathway is thought to have greater input from the temporal hemifield and less input from the nasal hemifield than the geniculostriate (cortical) pathway, this asymmetry in the preferential orienting to faces is consistent with subcortical, but not cortical, involvement. The lack of preferential orienting to faces in the nasal field is not simply due to a general lack of sensitivity, since in this same visual field there is increased responding to an optimal spatial frequency nonface stimulus over another nonface stimulus (Simion et al., 1998). This evidence is consistent with the hypothesis that the preferential orienting to faces is mediated by a subcortical mechanism; however, as the visual cortex of the newborn is at least partially functional (Maurer and Lewis, 1979), it might also contribute to the response.

*Identity*  Not only do newborns preferentially orient to faces, but they also process information about facial identity. Newborns look longer at the mother's face than a stranger's face just hours to days after birth (even when cues from her smell and her voice are eliminated; Bushnell et al., 1989; Field et al., 1984; Pascalis et al., 1995). This observation represents a difficulty both for the sensory and for the social hypothesis, since it demonstrates that from the beginning of life there is a mechanism involved in face processing that is sensitive to experience with individual faces. Both views must postulate the existence of an additional mechanism capable of learning about individual faces based on experience. This early learning may be mediated by the hippocampal complex (Johnson and de Haan, in press; Nelson, 1995), since this area is known be involved in memory, to functionally mature early relative to memory-related neocortical areas, and to mediate memory in visual paired comparison tasks in infant monkeys (the same type of task used to assess memory in human infants; Webster, Ungerleider, and Bachevalier, 1995; reviewed in Nelson, 1995). This system is likely a general-purpose mechanism and not a face-specific one as newborns are also able to recognize nonface stimuli to which they have been habituated (Slater, Morison, and Rose, 1983).

While newborns are able to learn to recognize individual faces, their representations of facial identity differ from adults'. This was demonstrated in a study showing that newborns look longer at the mother's face than a stranger's face when her full face is presented but not when only her internal facial features are presented. These results suggest that newborns' recognition may be based on the external features of the face, such as the contour and headline, rather than the internal features, such as the eyes and mouth (Pascalis et al., 1995). This pattern is opposite to that of adults, for whom the internal facial features are more important than the external contour for recognition of familiar faces (Ellis, Shepherd, and Davies, 1979). It may be that the external regions of the face attract the baby's attention because they are high-contrast regions which are more visible to the newborn than are the internal facial features. In support of this view, newborns tend to scan the external contour, rather than the inner features, of a static face (Maurer and Salapatek, 1976). In any case, this "externality effect" is not specific to faces as it has been reported in other studies that before 2 months of age infants tend not to notice a pattern or shape within a larger frame (Maurer, 1983; Milewski, 1976). However, infants may show increased sensitivity to internal features made more salient by high contrast or movement (Bushnell, 1979). In real-life learning situations, it is possible that infants do in fact encode internal facial features because they are made more salient through such factors as the motion that occurs while a person speaks or expresses emotion.

*Emotion* The results of two studies suggest that newborns are also able to process information about facial expression (Field et al., 1982, 1983). In these studies, 36-hour-old infants were presented with a happy, sad, or surprised expression posed by a live female model until they looked for less than 2 seconds, and then saw the other two expressions presented in the same way. Infants' looking times increased when the expression changed, suggesting that they could discriminate between them. While this study suffers from some methodological problems (e.g., there was no comparison group tested with the same procedure without changing the expressions to see if the increased looking was due

to the change in expression or just movement of the face), if replicated with a better controlled procedure it would suggest that, at least from live faces, some information from the internal features is encoded. Perhaps even more impressive is the fact that infants not only showed visual discrimination between expressions but also imitated the expression posed by the adult.

*Conclusions* Newborns can preferentially orient to faces, recognize the mother and other familiar faces, and imitate facial expressions. Yet there are clear limitations to the newborn's face processing skills. The newborn will orient more to three blobs arranged as eyes and nose than to a nonface pattern. But if this were the only mechanism biasing the infant to attend to faces, one would have to question its effectiveness in real life given that (1) there is no evidence that the newborn shows special interest in the face once it is fixated in central vision, (2) the infant has competing biases for attention that can have greater influence than the facedness dimension (Johnson and Morton, 1991), and (3) it has never been shown that the infant visually follows a real human face further than other stimuli. The newborn will look longer at the mother's face than a stranger's face, but whether this is "face" recognition is doubtful in that it appears to involve only the external contour rather than the internal features of the face. Newborns will imitate facial expressions; however, they also "imitate" other nonsocial stimulation with similar responses (e.g., a looming and retracting pencil is "imitated" with tongue protrusion; Jones, 1996).

These responses of the newborn to facial stimuli can perhaps best be viewed as parts of a collection of tendencies (together with preferences for motion, for orienting to auditory stimuli such as voice, for orienting to mother's voice and smell, etc.) that orient young infants toward faces and make faces one of the first and most frequent things babies see. These abilities are quite different from the sophisticated mechanisms involved in adult face processing, and none of these tendencies alone should necessarily be viewed as the direct "precursor" of the adult cortical face processing system. Instead, these responses might serve the purpose of providing input into developing cortical circuits that will at some later time functionally emerge to mediate face processing (Johnson, 1997).

INFANCY

*Facedness* A marked change in infants' visual attention to faces occurs at approximately 8 weeks of age: At this time, infants' preferential following of peripheral moving faces declines (Johnson et al., 1991), and a preference emerges for fixating faces compared to other patterns presented in the central visual field (Maurer and Barrera, 1981). This behavioral change is thought to be due to the functional development of visual cortical pathways that inhibit the preferential following response and mediate the new preferential fixation response (Johnson and Morton, 1991).

Although 2-month-old infants do look longer at centrally presented faces than at other patterns, there are factors other than facedness that can be equally or more salient in attracting their attention, such as stimulus complexity. For example, in one series of studies (Haaf, 1974, 1977) the looking times of infants 1–5-months old were measured to a set of four stimuli that varied independently in complexity (number of elements) and facedness (number of facial features in the proper place). The looking of infants 1–2 months old was determined solely by the complexity of the pattern (they looked longer at more complex patterns), while older infants' looking was affected both by the complexity and the facedness of the pattern.

Moreover, at this young age infants' representation of facedness appears quite different from that of adults in that it is based primarily on the eyes rather than on the entire constellation of facial features. For example, when 2-month-olds are shown schematic faces paired with faces that are scrambled or are missing various parts, they will look equally long at the full face and a face with only eyes present (nose and mouth missing), and will look at both of these longer than at a face with only nose and mouth present (eyes missing; Maurer, 1985). Furthermore, the position of the eyes in the face does not make a difference to the infants' preference, although they are able to discriminate among faces with eyes in varying positions following habituation (Maurer, 1985). Thus, at 2 months of age the eyes are a more salient feature of the face than the nose or mouth, but where the eyes are located is immaterial to the babies' preference for facelike drawings. The importance of the eyes is also noticeable in infants' social interactions: Hains, Muir, and Franke (1994) found that 3–5-month-olds' smiling decreased during a social interaction when their adult partner's eyes were averted and recovered when mutual gaze was reestablished. It may not be until 4–6 months of age that infants begin to have a more adultlike representation of facedness and respond to faces independently of complexity and with a greater appreciation of facial features in addition to the eyes (see Maurer, 1985).

Even by 6 months of age, babies' mental representation of facedness may differ from that of adults in being broader and less tuned to the human face. For example, studies using event-related potentials (ERPs)[1] to exam-ine the neural correlates of face processing have shown that face-responsive ERP components are more specific to human faces in adults than in infants (de Haan, Johnson, and Oliver, 1998; de Haan et al., 1999). In adults, the N170, a negative deflection over occipitotemporal electrodes that peaks approximately 120–200 ms after stimulus onset, is thought to reflect the initial stage of the structural encoding of the face (Bentin et al., 1996). It is of larger amplitude and longer latency for inverted than for upright faces (Bentin et al., 1996; de Haan, Johnson, and Oliver, 1998; see figure 26.1), a pattern that parallels behavioral studies showing that adults are slower at recognizing inverted than upright faces (Carey and Diamond, 1994). In adults the effect of stimulus inversion on the N170 is specific for human faces and does not occur for monkey faces or sheep faces (de Haan et al., 1999; see figure 26.1; see color plate 16). In 6-month-old infants, the P400, a positive deflection over occipitotemporal electrodes that peaks approximately 350–450 ms after stimulus onset, is, like the N170, affected by stimulus inversion. However, the infant P400 differs from the adult N170 on a number of parameters. First, the effect of stimulus inversion is evident in the ERPs approximately 200 ms later for 6-month-olds than for adults (see figure 26.2; see color plate 17). This difference in timing is not necessarily due to an overall slower rate of information processing in infants since the P1 component, reflecting earlier stages of visual processing, occurs only slightly later for infants than for adults. This suggests that the inversion effect may occur at a different and later stage in face processing for infants than adults (Johnson and de Haan, in press). Second, infants, like adults, show an inversion effect bilaterally for human faces but, unlike adults, they also show an inversion effect over left hemisphere electrodes for monkey faces. The fact that the inversion effect was specific to human faces in adults but was not in infants suggests that at 6 months of age the infant's face processing system is more broadly responsive to the category of faces than is the adult's. The fact that the inversion effect for monkey faces occurred only over the left-hemisphere, and not the right-hemisphere electrodes, might be because the right hemisphere develops specificity to human face processing earlier than does the left.

In adults, the N170 is thought to reflect activation of the fusiform gyrus and/or cortical regions lateral to it, as these areas have been identified as face-responsive in studies using fMRI (Bentin et al., 1996; Kanwisher, McDermott, and Chun, 1997) and intracranial recordings (Allison et al., 1999). It is not known whether the infant P400 also reflects activation of these areas. In adults, there is evidence to show that fusiform involvement in visual processing is related to visual expertise.

## Adults

### Upright Human Face      Inverted Human Face

140 ms

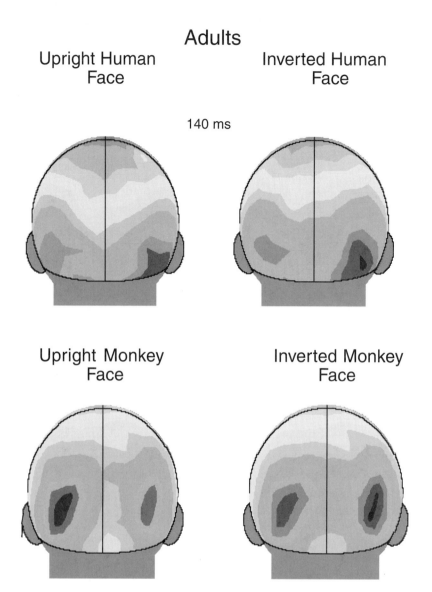

### Upright Monkey Face      Inverted Monkey Face

FIGURE 26.1 Amplitude distributions of activity at the peak of the N170 created using spherical spline interpolation. The view is looking straight on from the back of the head. The peak of the negativity of the N170 is seen in blue. The white/light areas indicate positivities. The black/dark areas indicate negativities.

For example, "face-selective" areas of the fusiform gyrus are also activated when individuals are tested with categories of visual stimuli in which they are either naturally experts or are trained to be experts (Gauthier et al., 2000). This suggests the possibility that the process of acquiring visual expertise in adulthood parallels the development of face processing, and that both involve recruitment of fusiform areas. However, there is some indication that the two processes may not be completely similar. One indication is that the developmental process appears to be characterized by a narrowing, or limiting, of the specialized processing (e.g., from all faces to just human faces), while the adult's learning process is characterized by an "expanding" of the use of the fusiform area to other object categories (e.g., from activation only to faces to activation in addition to other expert categories). One factor that may contribute to this difference is that, during development, the infant must handle both the task of discovering the category itself ("facedness") and the task of discovering mechanisms to encode individual examples within the category; in contrast, when adults acquire expertise with a visual category, either the structure of the experimental situation or their own previous knowledge means that they are faced with only the second of these two tasks. Further studies using ERPs (which are easily measurable in both infant and adults) to compare the development of face processing with the development of visual expertise in adults would be of interest in this context.

# Infants

### Upright Human Face

### Inverted Human Face

376 ms

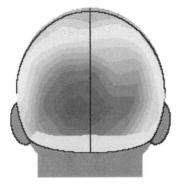

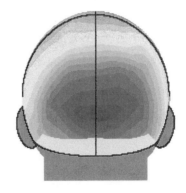

### Upright Monkey Face

### Inverted Monkey Face

FIGURE 26.2   Amplitude distributions of activity at the peak of the P400 created using spherical spline interpolation. The view is looking straight on from the back of the head. The peak of the positivity of the P400 is seen in red. The white/light areas indicate positivities. The black/dark areas indicate negativities.

*Identity*   At approximately 2 months of age several changes in infants' visual processing occur that affect their processing of facial identity. One such change is that infants become more sensitive to the internal facial features of static faces. For example, 2–3-month-old infants are able to remember faces from only the internal features both after a 2- and a 24-hour delay (Pascalis et al., 1998), they show preferential looking to the mother even if only her internal facial features are showing (Morton, 1993), and they can recognize a familiar face from a novel viewpoint based on only internal features (Pascalis et al., 1998). Studies of infants' scanning patterns show that at this age there is an increase in scanning of the internal features of faces, particularly the eyes (Maurer and Salapatek, 1976). Several prominent theories of adult face processing postulate that adults encode facial identity using information about the spatial relations among the features of the face (e.g., Diamond and Carey, 1986; Rhodes et al., 1998). This enhanced sensitivity to internal facial features might allow infants to encode faces in a manner more similar to how adults encode faces. However, this increased sensitivity to internal features is not specific to faces and also occurs for other nonface patterns.

A second change in face processing that occurs at approximately 2–3 months of age is that infants begin to relate information between individual faces. For adults, one important aspect of encoding facial identity is thought to be information about how an individual face differs from a prototypic or average representation (Rhodes, 1993; Rhodes, Brake, and Atkinson, 1993).[2] A recent study tested infants' abilities to recognize individual faces and "average" faces made by a computer averaging of a set of faces. The results indicated that following a familiarization to four individual faces, 3-month-olds are able to recognize both the individual faces and an average of the four, while 1-month-olds can recognize only the individual faces (de Haan et al., 1999; see also Rubenstein, Kalakanis, and Langlois, 1999, for similar results with older infants). According to one hypothesis, the change between 1 and 3 months may reflect functional development of temporal cortical areas and their connections with the hippocampus (Johnson and de Haan, in press). The memory of the 1-month-old may reflect a "pure" form of hippocampal encoding in which input is relatively uninfluenced by preprocessing of visual input from the still underdeveloped cortex. This may allow the infant to learn about faces individually but without processing information such as relations between faces and their commonalities. With gradual experience over the first months of life, the neocortical circuits of the ventral visual pathway may gradually extract invariances from the array of faces to which the infants have been exposed and discover the structure of this class of stimuli, and change the nature of input to the hippocampus. However, this change in the nature of processing may not be specific to faces, as by 3 months of age infants are able to form perceptual categories not only of faces but also of a variety of other complex, natural or artificial categories (see Quinn, 1998, for review).

By 4–9 months of age, hemispheric differences in face processing emerge. One procedure used to demonstrate this effect is the divided visual field procedure.[3] Infants of 4–9 months move their eyes more quickly to the mother's face than a stranger's face presented in the left visual field (LVF) but not to the same stimuli presented in the right visual field (RVF) (de Schonen, Gil de Diaz, and Mathivet, 1986; de Schonen and Mathivet, 1989), and they show the same pattern of hemispheric asymmetry in responding to a familiarized compared to a novel face (de Schonen, Gil de Diaz, and Mathivet, 1986). In contrast, simple geometric shapes are discriminated equally well in either visual field (if anything, better in the RVF; de Schonen, Gil de Diaz, and Mathivet, 1986). This hemispheric asymmetry in face processing is also found in ERP studies of infant face processing, which show that at 6 months of age ERP activity related to recognition of the mother's face is more prominent over the right- than left-sided elec-

trodes while ERP activity related to recognition of familiar toys is bilateral (de Haan and Nelson, 1997, 1999). Together these results suggest that by 4–9 months of age the right hemisphere may be more proficient than the left in recognizing faces.

This hemispheric difference in face processing may be related to a difference in the nature of encoding of faces compared to other stimuli. This is demonstrated by studies using the divided visual field procedure. These studies showed that infants are better able to detect a spatial change (eye size or eye tilt) in the face in the LVF than in the RVF, while, in contrast, for detection of a feature change (a different eye) there is a tendency for the opposite pattern of visual field advantage (Deruelle and de Schonen, 1998). However, this pattern is not necessarily unique to faces, but is consistent with findings from other studies using stimuli such as geometric patterns showing that in infants of this age the right hemisphere generally tends to be better at detecting changes in spatial positions of features while the left generally tends to be better at detecting changes in the nature of the features (Deruelle and de Schonen, 1991, 1995).

*Emotion* Infants are capable of discriminating among a number of different facial expressions of emotion early in life. For example, 3-month-olds tested with a habituation–dishabituation procedure show evidence of being able to discriminate happy from surprised faces (Young-Browne, Rosenfeld, and Horowitz, 1977) and smiling from frowning faces (Barrera and Maurer, 1981). However, they do have difficulty making some discriminations (e.g., sad with surprise or happy; Young-Browne, Rosenfeld, and Horowitz, 1977); and it appears that not until 7 months of age do they begin to recognize an expression as the same in spite of changes in intensity, identity of the model, and the like (reviewed in de Haan and Nelson, 1998). It is possible that limitations in infants' perceptual concept of facedness before this age make some pairs of expressions more difficult to discriminate than others and also makes it difficult for them to reliably detect the common emotion-relevant features across such changes.

Recent evidence suggests that by 7 months infants, like adults, show categorical perception of facial expressions. Categorical perception is defined as the discontinuity of discrimination at the category boundary of a physical continuum, with greater difficulties in discriminating member pairs of the same category than members of different categories even though the amount of physical difference between both pairs is the same (Harnad, 1987). For example, individuals are superior at discriminating pairs of colors that cross a color category than pairs that are equally physically different but are both within the same category. In the domain of speech and color perception, the categorical perception paradigm has been extensively used to argue for basic perception categories (Repp, 1984). To study categorical perception of emotional expressions, realistic drawings (Etcoff and Magee, 1992) and/or photographs were changed in equal steps so that a face showing one expression gradually transformed into another (de Gelder, Teunisse, and Benson, 1997; Young et al., 1997). With these types of stimuli, adults show the classic pattern of categorical perception, with enhanced discrimination of faces that cross an emotion category compared to pairs that are equally physically different but are both within the same emotion category. A recent study using looking times measures showed that by 7 months of age infants also show categorical perception of a happy–fear continuum (Kotsoni, de Haan, and Johnson, 1999). Whether this categorical perception represents a broad positive–negative dimension or more specific emotion categories remains to be determined. However, the results support the idea that infants perceive at least some emotions categorically from very early in life, and this ability may, like other cases of categorical perception such as color vision, have a hardwired basis.

Recent studies with adults suggest that perception of different types of emotional expressions may have different neural bases. For example, the amygdala appears to be involved during processing of fearful and sad faces but not of angry faces (Blair et al., 1999). Moreover, even within a category of expression there may be different, parallel pathways of processing. For example, in one neuroimaging study it was found that the right amygdala, pulvinar, and superior colliculus were activated only in response to masked ("unseen") fear-related stimuli but not those that were seen, while the left amygdala was activated to both seen and unseen fearful stimuli (Morris, Ohman, and Dolan, 1999). These results were interpreted to suggest that there is a subcortical pathway involving the right amygdala via midbrain and thalamus that processes unseen fearful stimuli in parallel to the cortical pathway for conscious identification. At present, very little is known about the development of these neural pathways mediating face recognition during infancy (reviewed in Nelson and de Haan, 1997). There is some evidence that the amygdala may be involved in processing of facial expressions during infancy (Balaban, 1995), but it is not clear whether processing of different expressions is subserved by different pathways or whether there are parallel pathways in processing of expressions during infancy.

*Conclusions* The evidence suggests that by at least 3–6 months of age cortical areas are involved in face processing. This is evident in some characteristics of cortical processing of faces that are quite adultlike by 6 months: (1) the hemispheric difference in the nature of information encoded from the face, (2) the right hemisphere bias for recognizing facial identity, and (3) the effect of inversion on electrocortical measures of processing faces. However, for the infant these characteristics may not be unique to faces. For example, there is also a hemispheric difference in the nature of information encoded from geometric patterns; the right hemisphere is also activated during object processing; and the inversion effect is not specific to human faces (and possibly not specific to faces at all, as this has yet to be tested). Moreover, important changes that occur in facial identity and emotion processing, such as increased processing of internal features and the relation of individual examples of faces and ability to form categories, appear to be more general cognitive changes that affect not only processing of faces but also processing of other visual stimuli. Thus, it may be that the cortical mechanisms involved in face processing are not yet highly unique to faces themselves.

In spite of this, it should be noted that the abilities of the young infant are sufficient to allow them to respond to faces in social situations. By 3–6 months, infants appear to have some expectations regarding the nature of social interactions in the presence of a person's face (Ellsworth, Muir, and Hains, 1993; Tronick et al., 1978). They appear to be particularly attentive to the emotional aspects of the face, and show this in their own emotional reactions by becoming distressed when their adult partner ceases interacting normally and smiling less if their partner is a puppet or an upside-down human rather than a normal upright human (D'Entremont, 1994; Ellsworth, Muir, and Hains, 1993; Gusella, Muir, and Tronick, 1988; Muir and Rach-Longman, 1989).

## CHILDHOOD

*Facedness* There is evidence to suggest that even beyond infancy the child's mental representation of facedness differs from that of the adult. One way this has been demonstrated is by studies of the development of the "other race" and "other species" effects. These effects refer to the fact that adults are worse at recognizing the faces of individuals of another race or species than those of their own race and species. This presumably occurs because the latter are seen most frequently and can thus more easily and effectively be related to the prototype formed from faces seen most frequently in their daily experience (Rhodes et al., 1989). In other words, the effects are thought to occur because adults' prototype of the face is highly specific to the species and race of faces that they commonly see. In contrast, children do not show the same pattern: Caucasian 6-year-olds are equally adept at recognizing Caucasian and Asian faces, while older Caucasian children and adults are better at recognizing Caucasian than Asian faces (Chance, Turner, and Goldstein, 1982). These results might indicate that 6-year-olds' representations of facedness are broader and less specific to their own race.

A second way that children's mental representation of facedness has been studied is by assessing the development of distinctiveness effects on face recognition. Adults find distinctive, unusual faces easier to remember than typical faces (Light, Kayra-Stuart, and Hollander, 1979; Valentine and Bruce, 1986). This is thought to occur because typical faces cluster around the prototype and thus are more easily confused with one another. Ellis (1992; Johnston and Ellis, 1995) found that 6- and 7-year-olds, unlike adults, do not recognize atypical faces better than typical faces. These results suggest that either children's mental representation differs from that of adults (e.g., perhaps due to their more limited experience with faces) and/or they simply do not use the prototype to encode information about individual faces in the same way as adults (see Johnston and Ellis, 1995, for further discussion).

Electrophysiological indices of face processing also show changes in face-responsive ERP components during childhood (Taylor et al., 1999). The N170 component is observable in children as young as 5 years, but its latency decreases with age and its amplitude over right-sided electrodes increases with age. Moreover, a face-sensitive positivity that in adults occurs over frontal-central electrodes at the same time as the N170 is absent in children under 12 years of age. The functional correlates of this electrophysiological change are not known, but it is possible that the age of 10–12 years reflects a period of transition in face processing mechanisms. For example, researchers have noted that sex differences in face processing emerge at this time (Chance et al., 1982), and that the steady improvement in face recognition from 5 years onward plateaus at this time (Carey, Diamond, and Woods, 1980; Grusser, Selke, and Zynda, 1985).

*Identity* It is undisputed that memory for facial identity improves over childhood (e.g., Diamond and Carey, 1977; Grusser, Selke, and Zynda, 1985). Recognition of familiar, well-known faces (e.g., family, classmates)

reaches adult levels relatively early, by approximately 4 years, but recognition of unfamiliar faces only recently learned does not reach adult levels until much later into childhood. What remains uncertain is the mechanism underlying these developmental changes. Here, we discuss four hypotheses that have been put forth to account for the changes: the encoding switch hypothesis, the norm-based encoding hypothesis, the depth of processing hypothesis, and the right hemisphere hypothesis.

According to the *encoding switch* hypothesis, younger children tend to encode faces in terms of isolated features, while older children tend to encode faces in terms of relational information. One line of evidence in favor of this view is that early studies indicated that the inversion effect only appears by 10 years of age. For example, Carey and Diamond (1977; Diamond and Carey, 1977) found that inversion impaired performance on faces more than on houses for 10-year-olds, but not for younger children. According to these investigators, inversion did not affect younger children's performance because they encoded the faces in terms of isolated features. In contrast, the older children's performance with faces was influenced by inversion because they used relational information to encode the upright faces. These changes in children's performance were attributed specifically to changes in the way upright faces were processed, and not to changes in information processing in general, because there were no age-related changes in encoding of houses or encoding of upside-down faces.

The encoding switch hypothesis in this original form cannot account for subsequent findings that effects of inversion on face processing are detectable even in infancy (de Haan and Nelson, 1998; Kestenbaum and Nelson, 1990) and that the absence of an inversion effect in younger children in the initial studies may have been caused by floor effects (Flin, 1985). Part of the confusion may be due to a failure to define configural encoding independently of the inversion effect. The effects of inversion on face recognition are not necessarily due solely to disruption of configural encoding. This was demonstrated by a study that assessed configural encoding using the composite face paradigm (Carey and Diamond, 1994). In this study, 6-year-olds, 10-year-olds, and adults were asked to identify faces of classmates that were "composites" created by putting the top half-face of one person with the bottom half-face of another and "noncomposites." If children are encoding configural information, composites should be more difficult to identify than noncomposites, because the new configuration created by the two different half-faces makes it more difficult to identify the person in the top half-face.

All ages tested showed a composite effect: composites were recognized less well than noncomposites, suggesting that configural encoding was used at all ages. However, adults and 10-year-old children did show an additional inversion effect in that upright faces were generally recognized more quickly than inverted ones; in contrast, 6-year-olds responded equally quickly to the two (Carey and Diamond, 1994).

In order to account for this pattern of findings, the authors argued that there is more than one type of configural encoding: (1) a type of configural encoding that is measured by the composite/noncomposite effect, that causes an inversion effect, and that is presented at least from 6 years; (2) a type of configural encoding that causes an age-dependent increase in the inversion effect. They argue that this second type of encoding that "switches" with development is *norm-based encoding* (i.e., encoding relative to a prototype or common face space) and causes age-related changes in face processing and inversion effects during childhood. This two-process explanation also can account for the results of infancy studies: The type of configural encoding assessed in the composite effect might be the form that is present and causes inversion effects and right hemisphere bias in infant face processing.

A different account of developmental changes in face processing during childhood is the *depth of processing* hypothesis. Adults' memory for faces is better if during learning they make a "deep" judgment regarding a personality trait (e.g., honesty) of a face than if they make a more "shallow" judgment based on a physical characteristic (e.g., hair color, gender; Coin and Tiberghien, 1997; McKelvie, 1985; Mueller and Wherry, 1980; Yoshikawa, 1995). This deep encoding does not necessarily lead to superior memory than that observed after normally employed strategies, suggesting that adults normally spontaneously engage in deep rather than shallow types of face processing (Sporer, 1991). The exact reason for the benefit from deep encoding is not known, but it has been proposed to be due to encoding of a semantic representation of the face (McKelvie, 1985) and/or to an increased likelihood of encoding distinctive features (Winograd, 1981). It is possible that children, unlike adults, only gradually come to automatically use a deep or optimal strategy for encoding new faces, and therefore their recognition of unfamiliar faces gradually improves throughout childhood. These changes might be linked to functional development of left frontal cortical areas as left prefrontal cortex is activated during encoding of faces by adults (Haxby et al., 1994, 1995) and during deep encoding (Kapur et al., 1994). Since children do show superior memory for deeply versus shallowly encoded items (Schultz, 1983),

it may be that developmental changes in recognizing unfamiliar faces are due to their increased employment of this strategy.

Yet another account of the mechanism underlying developmental changes in face recognition during childhood is the *right hemisphere development* hypothesis. Carey and Diamond (1977) hypothesized that developmental changes in face recognition are due to development of the right hemisphere. In support of their argument, they pointed out that young children's performance on face processing tasks was similar to that observed in adult patients with right hemisphere brain damage. However, studies using the divided visual field technique in children have yielded mixed results. Some studies report that a left visual field advantage in face processing emerges only after age 8 (Reynolds and Jeeves, 1978) while others report that even at age 7 there is a left visual field advantage and the degree of advantage does not change with further development (Young and Bion, 1981).

*Conclusions* During childhood a major change in face processing may occur that relates to emergence of norm-based encoding of faces. As the child's prototype of the face becomes more adultlike, it may become more tuned to the types of faces that the child most often sees, and with this may emerge the distinctiveness effects and other-race and other-species effects seen in adult face processing. Since norm-based encoding is thought to reflect development of visual expertise with a category (Rhodes, 1993), it may be that it is this type of processing that is related to fusiform face-area activation, as recent studies suggest that activation of this area is related to expertise with a particular category of visual stimulus (Gauthier et al., 1999). The fusiform gyrus may mediate this expert processing itself or it may select the input to channel into a special type of processing. Neurally, changes in children's face processing might be due in part to functional development of the fusiform areas and left frontal areas known to be involved in adults' memories for faces, and these changes may be in part driven by experience due to increased exposure to faces and the number and type of features children can or do attend to and encode. In addition, children may tend to automatically process faces deeply as they grow older, resulting in better face recognition.

## Developmental disorders of face processing

Specific developmental disorders of face processing are relatively rare. However, studying these cases can be of interest because it can allow one to determine whether there exists already early in life a domain-specific face processing system that can be specifically damaged. For example, if the areas involved in face processing in adults are damaged in infancy, can normal face processing develop? In addition, understanding the development of face recognition in these atypical circumstances can reveal the degree of plasticity of the early-developing system. For example, are developmental disorders of face processing best characterized as normal development halted at an immature stage or does an alternate organization of the face processing system develop?

DEVELOPMENTAL PROSOPAGNOSIA  A small number of reports of prosopagnosia occurring in children or attributed to childhood lesions in adults suggests that specific deficits in face processing can occur after early brain damage. However, in four cases the authors concluded that the face processing deficits were due to more general visual processing deficits or agnosia (Ariel and Sadeh, 1996; de Haan and Campbell, 1991; Temple, 1992; Young and Ellis, 1989). Moreover, in three of these cases the face processing deficits themselves were quite general, including identity, emotion, and other aspects of face processing. This is in contrast to adult prosopagnosics, who often show a more selective deficit in a particular aspect of face processing (Campbell et al., 1996). However, there are a few reported cases that appear to have more selective deficits that are more similar to those reported in adult prosopagnosia (Bentin, Deouell, and Soroker, 1999; Farah et al., 2000). This would suggest that specific deficits following early damage, though rare, are possible, and that there may be some degree of specialization and localization of face processing early in life. The factors that determine the degree of and limits to plasticity of this early system are not yet known. One caution in interpreting these cases is that in such retrospective cases it is difficult to determine exactly when the damage relevant to the prosopagnosia occurred, and age of injury might be an important factor for determining whether specific deficits emerge.

PERINATAL LESIONS OF FACE PROCESSING AREAS  In adults, impairments in face recognition can occur following brain damage, even if basic visual processing and object recognition are unaffected (Damasio, Tranel, and Damasio, 1990). If the face processing system is domain-specific and anatomically localized from very early in life, then damage to all or parts of it should results in major impairments of face processing. Using a prospective approach, Mancini and colleagues (1999) have studied the effects of perinatal unilateral lesions on later face processing abilities. Their data show that

when the children are 5–14 years of age the effects of the lesions are mild, with less than half of the children showing impaired performance relative to controls on tests of face or object identity recognition. Furthermore, (1) face processing deficits were no more common than object processing deficits following a right hemisphere lesion; (2) face processing deficits were no more common after right- than left-sided damage; and (3) a face processing deficit never occurred in absence of an object processing deficit. The main consistent effect of site of lesion was that deficit in recognition occurred only with early posterior damage and not with anterior damage. This general pattern of results is similar to that reported in other studies (Ballantyne and Trauner, 1999; Mancini et al., 1994) and suggests that the infant's system may be more plastic following damage than is the adult's system.

AUTISM  According to Hobson (1993), people with autism are impaired in the primary representations that are relevant for socioemotional interpersonal relations. Thus, autism may be one condition in which processing of faces is uniquely affected relative to processing of nonface (nonsocial) objects. Numerous reports indeed suggest that there are abnormalities of face processing associated with autism (Capps, Yirmiya, and Sigman, 1992; Celani, Battacchi, and Arcidiacono, 1999; de Gelder, Vroomen, and van der Heide, 1991; Hobson, 1986a,b; Ozonoff, Pennington, and Rogers, 1990). Impairments of recognition of facial expression of emotion are most consistently observed, while impairments in recognition of identity are only sometimes observed (Braverman et al., 1989; Ozonoff, Pennington, and Rogers, 1990). However the extent to which these impairments are specific to face processing is not clear, with some studies finding intact processing of nonsocial objects and patterns (Tantam et al., 1989) and some finding impairments (Davies et al., 1994).

One explanation for the abnormalities in face processing is that children with autism have atypical perceptual processes that in turn cause deficits in face recognition. Several aspects of face perception by children with autism do appear to be atypical: Children with autism tend to attend selectively to different aspects of the face than do children without autism (Langdell, 1978; Weeks and Hobson, 1987), they are less affected by face inversion than are children without autism (Hobson, Ouston, and Lee, 1988; Langdell, 1978; Tantam et al., 1989), they fail to show evidence of categorical perception of facial expressions (Teunisse and de Gelder, in press), and they are impaired on matching faces with voices on the basis of identity (Boucher, Lewis, and Collis, 1998) or emotion (de

Gelder, Vroomen, and van der Heide, 1991). Together, these results suggest that children with autism might normally spontaneously process different aspects of facial information than do children without autism and that they have difficulty in perceiving cross-modal information.

The fact that many characteristics of face processing that normally begin to emerge already in the first half-year of life (e.g., inversion effects, categorical perception) are atypical in children with autism suggests that these abnormalities begin at an early age. However there is also evidence that children can develop strategies that compensate for these abnormalities. For example, the absence of categorical perception of facial expression in children with autism occurs at all IQ levels, even though only those with a lower IQ show an impairment in expression recognition. The fact that individuals with the same perceptual deficit could yet show different levels of ability in expression recognition suggests that some individuals are able to use compensatory strategies. Thus there appears to be a degree of plasticity in the developing system that allows for development of alternative strategies/mechanisms in face processing.

## Conclusions: How does face processing develop?

Infants are born with many tendencies that work together to make the human face a frequent focus of infant visual attention. However impressive, these tendencies are only the beginning step in a long developmental process. They may best be considered not as the immediate precursors to the adult face processing system, but as more general orienting tendencies that serve a number of developmental purposes. One might be that they cause faces to be a frequent input to the developing face processing system; another, that they assist the relatively helpless infant to elicit care from their caretakers, and so on.

The evidence suggests that by at least 3–6 months, when electrocortical responses to familiar faces and hemisphere differences in recognition of faces are seen, cortical areas are involved in face processing. However, in spite of the fact that several adultlike characteristics of face processing are present by this time, such as inversion effects and the right hemisphere bias, these characteristics are not unique to face processing. In this way, the infant's face processing system appears to be much broader in nature than the adult's. To a certain extent, this may be true even into childhood. The idea that during development the face processing system is less specialized is consistent with results of studies of early cortical lesions, which suggest that specific impairments in face processing following unilateral focal cortical lesions are uncommon.

What factors underlie this slow developmental specialization of face processing? In adults this specialization is thought to reflect in part extensive experience in encoding faces and, more specifically, even in encoding particular types of faces. Thus, part of the developmental process may be driven by increases in the number of faces seen during development together with general increases in speed and capacity of processing that allow children to process and remember greater numbers of faces. If such experience does play a role, it might be particularly interesting to study changes in face processing at times when the exposure to faces and demands on the system naturally increase (e.g., when children first enter school or large playgroups) because these might be times at which transitions in the mechanisms of face processing can be observed. These changes in input may themselves play a role in reorganization of the cerebral mechanisms underlying face processing at different ages.

With respect to brain mechanisms, one view is that there may be special "windows of opportunity" during which neural systems "expect" a particular input or experience to shape their normal development. The neural system remains open to this input only for a limited amount of time, and if it is absent or atypical, development will follow an abnormal trajectory. In this "experience-expectant" view (Greenough and Black, 1992), structure within the environment that is typically common to all members of the species (e.g., seeing patterned light, seeing faces, seeing emotional expressions) is allowed to shape development so that not all aspects have to be prespecified. It has been proposed that, at a more microscopic level, these windows of opportunity are reflected by the period of synaptic overproduction and subsequent "pruning" of synapses to adult levels in the cerebral cortex (Greenough and Black, 1992). In this view, development of specialization for face processing may not be the same as development of expertise in adulthood because the "neural environment" may differ at the two ages. The visual recognition system may have a window of opportunity when environmental inputs can "tune" the system to be maximally efficient at processing the types of stimuli typically seen in the visual environment. For the developing infant, faces will provide a frequent input so some aspects of the system may become specially tuned to the types of processing most useful for encoding faces; however, faces are not the only input, so other aspects of the system may be driven by other, nonface inputs. Later in life these systems in their "steady state" may still be best tuned to the input received during development, but may still be suitable, and recruited for, other purposes (e.g., the face processing system may be recruited when learning other forms of visual expertise).

Clearly, neural systems remain open to experience in some way throughout life in that new learning about faces and development of visual expertise in other domains is possible through adulthood. While the experience-expectant learning period is meant to be open to experiences common to all individuals, many aspects of learning are unique to an individual. This type of mechanism may be that which characterizes acquisition of visual expertise in adulthood, and may also underlie some aspects of development of face processing that are unique to individual circumstances (e.g., norm-based encoding, other-race effects). Thus, normative development of face processing may involve both experience-expectant and experience-dependent mechanisms.

In spite of the relatively large body of literature on the development of face processing, relatively little is known about the cognitive and neural mechanisms that mediate normal and abnormal development in this domain. For one thing, it is only recently that many neuroimaging techniques have been applied to problems of cognitive development. In the future, developments in neuroimaging techniques that render them more suitable for use with normally developing infants will help to further this line of investigation. Another important direction for the future is for research to move toward more integrative studies that include multiple age groups (e.g., to span the current gap in knowledge of face processing between early infancy and childhood) and multiple aspects of face processing (e.g., to assess whether expression and identity are independently processed). In the future, increased collaboration among researchers studying development at different stages and with different populations will help to create a more integrated and comprehensive account of the development of face processing and its neural underpinnings.

ACKNOWLEDGMENTS    I thank Mark H. Johnson, Charles A. Nelson, Olivier Pascalis, and Mortimer Mishkin for helpful discussions that have assisted in the writing of this chapter.

## NOTES

1. Event-related potentials are transient changes in brain activity that occur in response to a discrete event, such as presentation of a face on a computer screen. They are believed to reflect primarily the activity of groups of cortical neurons that fire in synchrony in response to the event.

2. The cognitive representation of faces in adults can be described in terms of this prototype-based model, but can equally well be described in terms of an exemplar-based model in which each individual face is represented as a point in a multidimensional "face space." The relative merits of these different models are discussed by Rhodes and colleagues (1998) and Valentine (1991). This chapter focuses on the prototype model, but the developmental pattern could equally well be accounted for in terms of the exemplar-based model (see Johnston and Ellis, 1995, for discussion).

3. In this procedure, stimuli are presented to the right or left of the center of gaze. Because of the nature of the neural projections from the retina to the primary visual cortex, information about stimuli presented to the left of the center of gaze (left visual field; LVF) will reach the right before the left hemisphere, and information presented to the right of the center of gaze (right visual field; RVF) will reach the left before the right hemisphere. Using this method, differences in the way the two hemispheres process information can be assessed. For example, if a stimulus is detected more quickly and accurately in the LVF than in the RVF, then the LVF/right hemisphere can be said to have an "advantage" for processing that type of stimulus. This procedure can be used with infants if latency to eye movements to the peripherally presented patterns, rather than error rates or reaction times, is used as the dependent measure.

## REFERENCES

ALLISON, T., A. PUCE, D. D. SPENCER, and G. McCARTHY, 1999. Electrophysiological studies of human face perception. I. Potentials generated in the occipitotemporal cortex by face and non-face stimuli. *Cereb. Cortex* 9:415–430.

ARIEL, R., and M. SADEH, 1996. Congenital visual agnosia and prosopagnosia in a child: A case report. *Cortex* 32:221–240.

BALABAN, M., 1995. Affective influences on startle in five-month-old infants: Reactions to facial expressions of emotion. *Child Dev.* 66:28–36.

BALLANTYNE, A. O., and D. A. TRAUNER, 1999. Facial recognition in children after perinatal stroke. *Neuropsychiatry Neuropsychol. Behav. Neurol.* 12:82–87.

BANKS, M., and A. P. GINSBURG, 1985. Infant visual preferences: A review and new theoretical treatment. *Adv. Child Dev. Behav.* 19:207–246.

BANKS, M., and P. SALAPATEK, 1981. Infant pattern vision: A new approach based on the contrast sensitivity function. *J. Exp. Child Psychol.* 31:1–45.

BARRERA, M., and D. MAURER, 1981. The perception of facial expression by the three-month-old. *Child Dev.* 52:203–206.

BENTIN, S., T. ALLISON, A. PUCE, E. PEREZ, and G. McCARTHY, 1996. Electrophyisological studies of face perception in humans. *J. Cogn. Neurosci.* 8:551–565.

BENTIN, S., L. Y. DEOUELL, and N. SOROKER, 1999. Selective visual streaming in face recognition: Evidence from developmental prosopagnosia. *NeuroReport* 10:823–827.

BLAIR, R. J., S. MORRIS, C. D. FRITH, D. I. PERRETT, and R. J. DOLAN, 1999. Dissociable neural responses to facial expressions of sadness and anger. *Brain* 122:883–893.

BOUCHER, J., V. LEWIS, and G. COLLIS, 1998. Familiar face and voice matching and recognition in children with autism. *J. Child Psychol. Psychiatry* 39:171–181.

BRAVERMAN, M., D. FEIN, D. LUCCI, and L. WATERHOUSE, 1989. Affect comprehension in children with pervasive developmental disorders. *J. Autism Dev. Disorders* 19:301–315.

BUSHNELL, I. W., 1979. Modification of the externality effect in young infants. *J. Exp. Child Psychol.* 28:211–229.

BUSHNELL, I. W. R., F. SAI, and J. T. MULLIN, 1989. Neonatal recognition of the mother's face. *Br. J. Dev. Psychol.* 7:3–15.

CAMPBELL, R., B. BROOKS, E. DE HAAN, and T. ROBERTS, 1996. Dissociating face processing skills: Decision about lip-read speech, emotion and identity. *Quart. J. Exp. Psychol.* A49:295–314.

CAMPBELL, R., and M. TUCK, 1995. Recognition of parts of famous-face photographs by children: An experimental note. *Perception* 24:451–456.

CAPPS, L., N. YIRMIYA, and M. D. SIGMAN, 1992. Understanding of simple and complex emotions in non-retarded children with autism. *J. Child Psychol. Psychiatry* 33:1169–1182.

CAREY, S., and R. DIAMOND, 1977. From piecemeal to configurational representation of faces. *Science* 195:312–314.

CAREY, S., and R. DIAMOND, 1994. Are faces perceived as configurations more by adults than by children? *Vis. Cogn.* 1:253–274.

CAREY, S., R. DIAMOND, and B. WOODS, 1980. Development of face recognition—A maturational component? *Dev. Psychol.* 16:257–269.

CARON, A., R. CARON, C. MUSTELIN, and J. ROBERTS, 1992. Infant responding to aberrant social stimuli. *Infant Behav. Dev.* 15:335.

CELANI, G., M. W. BATTACCHI, and L. ARCIDIACONO, 1999. The understanding of emotional meaning of facial expressions in people with autism. *J. Autism Dev. Disorders* 29:57–66.

CHANCE, J. E., A. L. TURNER, and A. G. GOLDSTEIN, 1982. Development of differential recognition for own- and other-race faces. *J. Psychol.* 112:29–37.

CICONE, M., W. WAPNER, and H. GARDNER, 1980. Sensitivity to emotional expressions and situations in organic patients. *Cortex* 16:145–158.

COIN, C., and G. TIBERGHIEN, 1997. Encoding activity and face recognition. *Memory* 5:545–568.

DAMASIO, A. R., D. TRANEL, and H. DAMASIO, 1990. Face agnosia and the neural substrates of memory. *Annu. Rev. Neurosci.* 13:89–109.

DAVIES, S., D. BISHOP, A. MANSTEAD, and D. TANATAM, 1994. Face perception in autistic children. *J. Child Psychol. Psychiatry* 35:1033–1058.

DE GELDER, B., J.-P. TEUNISSE, and P. J. BENSON, 1997. Perception of facial expressions: Categories and their internal structure. *Cogn. Emotion.* 11:1–23.

DE GELDER, B., J. VROOMEN, and L. VAN DER HEIDE, 1991. Face recognition and lipreading in autism. *Eur. J. Cogn. Psychol.* 3:69–86.

DE HAAN, E., and R. CAMPBELL, 1991. A fifteen-year follow-up of a case of developmental prosopagnoia. *Cortex* 27:489–509.

DE HAAN, M., M. H. JOHNSON, and A. OLIVER, 1998. A high-density ERP study of infant and adult face processing. Technical Report of the Human Frontiers Scientific Foundation Developmental Cognitive Neuroscience Team.

DE HAAN, M., M. H. JOHNSON, H. A. HATZAKIS, and O. PASCALIS, 1999. Does cerebral specialization for face processing develop? A high-density ERP study. Poster presented at the European Developmental Psychology Conference, Spetses, Greece.

DE HAAN, M., M. H. JOHNSON, D. MAURER, and D. PERRETT, 1999. Recognition of individual faces and average face prototypes by 1- and 3-month-old infants. Submitted

DE HAAN, M., and C. A. NELSON, 1997. Recognition of the mother's face by six-month-old infants: A neurobehavioral study. *Child Dev.* 68:187–210.

DE HAAN, M., and C. A. NELSON, 1998. Discrimination and categorisation of facial expressions of emotion during infancy. In *Perceptual Development*, A. Slater, ed. Hove, UK: Psychology Press, pp. 287–309.

DE HAAN, M., and C. A. NELSON, 1999. Brain activity differentiates face and object processing in 6-month-old infants. *Dev. Psychol.* 35:1113–1121.

D'ENTREMONT, B., 1994. Young infants' responding to static and dynamic happy and sad expressions during a social interaction. *Infant Behav. Dev.* 17:600.

DE RENZI, E., D. PERANI, G. A. CARLESIMO, M. C. SILVERI, and F. FAZIO, 1994. Prosopagnosia can be associated with damage confined to the right hemisphere—An MRI and PET study and a review of the literature. *Neuropsychologia* 32:893–902.

DERUELLE, C., and S. DE SCHONEN, 1991. Hemispheric asymmetries in visual pattern processing in infancy. *Brain Cognition* 16:151–179.

DERUELLE, C., and S. DE SCHONEN, 1995. Pattern processing in infancy: Hemispheric differences in the processing of shape and location of visual components. *Infant Behav. Dev.* 18:123–132.

DE SCHONEN, S., M. GIL DE DIAZ, and E. MATHIVET, 1986. Hemispheric asymmetry in face processing in infancy. In *Aspects of Face Processing*, H. D. Ellis, M. A. Jeeves, F. Newcombe, and A. Young, eds. Dordrecht: Martinus Nijhoff Publishers, pp. 199–209.

DE SCHONEN, S., and E. MATHIVET, 1989. First come, first served: A scenario about the development of hemispheric specialization in face recognition during infancy. *Eur. Bull. Cogn. Psychol.* 9:3–44.

DIAMOND, R., and S. CAREY, 1977. Developmental changes in the representation of faces. *J. Exp. Child Psychol.* 23:1–22.

DIAMOND, R., and S. CAREY, 1986. Why faces are and are not special: An effect of expertise. *J. Exp. Psychol. Gen.* 115:107–117.

ELLIS, H. D., 1992. The development of face processing skills. *Philos. Trans. R. Soc. London B. Biol. Sci.* 335:105–111.

ELLIS, H. D., and J. W. SHEPHERD, 1975. Recognition of upright and inverted faces presented in the left and right visual fields. *Cortex* 11:3–7.

ELLIS, H. D., J. W. SHEPHERD, and G. M. DAVIES, 1979. Identification of familiar and unfamiliar faces from internal and external features: Some implications for theories of face recognition. *Perception* 8:431–439.

ELLSWORTH, C., D. W. MUIR, and S. HAINS, 1993. Social competence and person-object differentiation: An analysis of the still-face effect. *Dev. Psychol.* 29:63–73.

ETCOFF, N., and J. J. MAGEE, 1992. Categorical perception of facial expressions. *Cognition* 44:227–240.

FARAH, M. J., 1990. *Visual Agnosia.* Cambridge, Mass.: MIT Press.

FARAH, M. J., C. RABINOWITZ, G. E. QUINN, and G. T. LIU, 2000. Early commitment of neural substrates for face recognition. *Cogn. Neuropsychol.* 17:117–124.

FARAH, M. J., K. D. WILSON, M. DRAIN, and J. N. TANAKA, 1998. What is 'special' about face perception? *Psychol. Rev.* 105:482–498.

FIELD, T., D. COHEN, R. GARCIA, and R. COLLINS, 1983. Discrimination and imitation of facial expressions by term and preterm neonates. *Infant Behav. Dev.* 6:485–489.

FIELD, T. M., D. COHEN, R. GARCIA, and R. GREENBURG, 1984. Mother-stranger face discrimination by the newborn. *Infant Behav. Dev.* 7:19–25.

FIELD, T., R. W. WOODSON, R. GREENBERG, and C. COHEN, 1982. Discrimination and imitation of facial expressions by neonates. *Science* 218:179–181.

FLIN, R. H., 1985. Development of face recognition: An encoding switch? *Br. J. Psychol.* 76:123–134.

GAUTHIER, I., P. SKUDLARSKI, J. C. GORE, and A. W. ANDERSON, 2000. Expertise for cars and birds recruits brain areas involved in face recognition. *Nature Neurosci.* 3:191–197.

GAUTHIER, I., M. J. TARR, A. W. ANDERSON, P. SKUDLARSKI, and J. C. GORE, 1999. Activation of the middle fusiform 'face area' increases with expertise in recognizing novel objects. *Nature Neurosci.* 2:568–573.

GREENOUGH, W. T., and J. E. BLACK, 1992. Induction of brain structure by experience: Substrates for cognitive development. In *The Minnesota Symposia on Child Psychology, Vol. 24, Developmental Behavioral Neuroscience*, M. Gunnar and C. A. Nelson, eds. Hillsdale, N.J.: Erlbaum, pp. 155–200.

GRUSSER, O. J., T. SELKE, and B. ZYNDA, 1985. A developmental study of face recognition in children and adolescents. *Hum. Neurobiol.* 4:33–39.

GUSELLA, J., D. MUIR, and E. TRONICK, 1988. The effect of manipulating maternal behavior during an interaction on three- and six-month-olds' affect and attention. *Child Dev.* 59:1111–1124.

HAAF, R., 1974. Complexity and facial resemblance as determinants of response to facelike stimuli by 5- and 10-week-old infants. *J. Exp. Child Psychol.* 18:480–487.

HAAF, R., 1977. Visual response to complex facelike patterns by 15- and 20-week-old infants. *Dev. Psychol.* 13:77–78.

HAINS, S. M. J., D. W. MUIR, and D. FRANKE, 1994. Eye contact modulates infant affect during infant-adult interactions. *Infant Behav. Dev.* 17:678.

HARNAD, S., 1987. *Categorical Perception: The Groundwork of Cognition.* Cambridge: Cambridge University Press.

HAXBY, J. V., L. G. UNGERLEIDER, B. HORWITZ, J. M. MAISOG, and C. L. GRADY, 1994. Neural systems for encoding and retrieving new long-term visual memories: A PET rCBF study. *Invest. Ophthalmol. Vis. Sci.* 35:1813.

HAXBY, J. V., L. G. UNGERLEIDER, B. HORWITZ, S. I. RAPOPORT, and C. L. GRADY, 1995. Hemispheric differences in the neural systems for face working memory: A PET rCBF study. *Hum. Brain Mapp.* 3:68–82.

HOBSON, R. P., 1993. *Autism and the Development of Mind.* London: Lawrence Erlbaum Associates.

HOBSON, R. P., 1986a. The autistic child's appraisal of expressions of emotion. *J. Child Psychol. Psychiatry* 27:321–342.

HOBSON, R. P., 1986b. The autistic child's appraisal of expressions of emotion: A further study. *J. Child Psychol. Psychiatry* 27:671–680.

HOBSON, R. P., J. OUSTON, and A. LEE, 1988. What's in a face? The case of autism. *Br. J. Psychol.* 79:601–623.

JOHNSON, M. H., 1997. The neural basis of cognitive development. In *Handbook of Child Psychology Vol. 2: Cognition, Perception and Language,* 5th ed., W. Damon, D. Kuhn, and R. Siegler, eds. New York: John Wiley, pp. 1–49.

JOHNSON, M. H., and M. DE HAAN, in press. Developing cortical specialization for visual-cognitive function: The case of face recognition.

JOHNSON, M. H., S. DZIURAWIEC, H. ELLIS, and J. MORTON, 1991. Newborns' preferential tracking of face-like stimuli and its subsequent decline. *Cognition* 40:1–19.

JOHNSON, M. H., and J. MORTON, 1991. *Biology and Cognitive Development. The Case of Face Recognition.* Oxford, UK: Blackwell.

JOHNSTON, R. A., and H. D. ELLIS, 1995. Age effects in the processing of typical and distinctive faces. *Quart. J. Exp. Psychol.* 48:447–465.

JONES, S. S., 1996. Imitation or exploration? Young infants' matching of adult's oral gestures. *Child Dev.* 67:1952–1969.

KANWISHER, N., J. McDERMOTT, and M. M. CHUN, 1997. The fusiform face area: A module in human extrastriate cortex specialized for face perception. *J. Neurosci.* 17:4302–4311.

KAPUR, S., F. I. CRAIK, E. TULVING, A. A. WILSON, S. HOULE, and G. M. BROWN, 1994. Neuroanatomical correlates of encoding in episodic memory: Levels of processing effect. *Proc. Natl. Acad. Sci. USA* 91:2008–2011.

KESTENBAUM, R., and C. A. NELSON, 1990. The recognition and categorization of upright and inverted emotional expressions. *Infant Behav. Dev.* 13:497–511.

KLEINER, K. A., and M. S. BANKS, 1987. Stimulus energy does not account for 2-month-olds' preferences. *J. Exp. Psychol.: Hum. Percept. Perform.* 13:594–600.

KOTSONI, E., M. DE HAAN, and M. JOHNSON, 1999. Categorical perception of facial expressions by 7-month-old infants. Poster presented at the European Developmental Psychology Conference, Spetses, Greece.

LANGDELL, T., 1978. Recognition of faces: An approach to the study of autism. *J. Child Psychol. Psychiatry* 19:255–268.

LIGHT, L., F. KAYRA-STUART, and S. HOLLANDER, 1979. Recognition memory for typical and unusual faces. *J. Exp. Psychol.: Hum. Learn. Mem.* 5:212–228.

MANCINI, J., C. CASSE-PERROT, B. GIUSIANO, N. GIRARD, R. CAMPS, C. DERUELLE, and S. DE SCHONEN, 1999. Face processing development after perinatal unilateral brain lesion. Submitted

MANCINI, J., S. DE SCHONEN, C. DERUELLE, and A. MASSOULIER, 1994. Face recognition in children with early left or right brain damage. *Dev. Med. Child Neurol.* 36:156–166.

MAURER, D., 1983. The scanning of compound figures by young infants. *J. Exp. Child Psychol.* 35:437–448.

MAURER, D., 1985. Infants' perception of facedness. In *Social Perception in Infants,* T. M. Field and N. Fox, eds. Norwood, N.J.: Ablex, pp. 73–100.

MAURER, D., and M. BARRERA, 1981. Infants' perception of natural and distorted arrangements of a schematic face. *Child Dev.* 52:196–202.

MAURER, D., and T. L. LEWIS, 1979. A physiological explanation of infant's early visual development. *Can. J. Psychol.* 33:232–252.

MAURER, D., and P. SALAPATEK, 1976. Developmental changes in the scanning of faces by young infants. *Child Dev.* 47:523–527.

McKELVIE, S. J., 1985. Effects of depth of processing on recognition memory for normal and inverted faces. *Percept. Motor Skills* 60:503–508.

MILEWSKI, A. E., 1976. Infants' discrimination of internal and external pattern elements. *J. Exp. Child Psychol.* 22:229–246.

MONDLOCH, C. J., T. L. LEWIS, D. R. BUDREAU, D. MAURER, J. L. DANNEMILLER, B. R. STEPHENS, and K. A. KLEINER-GATHERCOAL, 1999. Face perception during early infancy. *Psychol. Sci.* 10:419–422.

MORRIS, J. S., C. D. FRITH, D. I. PERRETT, D. ROWLAND, A. W. YOUNG, A. J. CALDER, and R. J. DOLAN, 1996. A differential neural response in the human amygdala to fearful and happy facial expressions. *Nature* 383:812–815.

MORRIS, J. S., A. OHMAN, and R. J. DOLAN, 1999. A subcortical pathway to the right amygdala mediating 'unseen' fear. *Proc. Natl. Acad. Sci. USA* 96:1680–1685.

MORTON, J., 1993. Mechanisms of infant face processing. In *Developmental Neurocognition: Speech and Face Processing in the First Year of Life*, B. S. de Boysson-Bardies, S. de Schonen, P. Jusczyk, P. McNeilage, and J. Morton, eds. London: Kluwer Academic Publishers, pp. 93–102.

MORTON, J., and M. JOHNSON, 1991. CONSPEC and CONLERN: A two-process theory of infant face recognition. *Psychol. Rev.* 2:164–181.

MUELLER, J. H., and K. L. WHERRY, 1980. Orienting strategies at study and test in facial recognition. *Am. J. Psychol.* 93:107–117.

MUIR, D. W., S. M. J. HAINS, and L. A. SYMONS, 1994. Baby and me: Infants need minds to read! *Eur. Bull. Cogn. Psychol.* 13:669–682.

MUIR, D. W., and K. RACH-LONGMAN, 1989. Once more with expression: On de Schonen and Mathivet's (1989) model for the development of face perception in human infants. *Eur. Bull. Cogn. Psychol.* 9:103–109.

NACHSON, I., 1995. On the modularity of face recognition: The riddle of domain specificity. *J. Clin. Exp. Neuropsychol.* 17:256–275.

NELSON, C. A., 1995. The ontogeny of human memory: A cognitive neuroscience perspective. *Dev. Psychol.* 31:723–738.

NELSON, C. A., and M. DE HAAN, 1997. A neurobehavioral approach to the recognition of facial expressions in infancy. In *The Psychology of Facial Expression*, J. A. Russell and J. M. Fernandez-Dols, eds. Cambridge, Mass.: Cambridge University Press, pp. 176–204.

OZONOFF, S., B. F. PENNINGTON, and S. J. ROGERS, 1990. Are there emotional perception deficits in young autistic children? *J. Child Psychol. Psychiatry* 31:343–361.

PASCALIS, O., M. DE HAAN, C. A. NELSON, and S. DE SCHONEN, 1998. Long-term recognition memory for faces assessed by visual paired comparison in 3- and 6-month-old infants. *J. Exp. Psychol.: Learn. Mem. Cogn.* 24:249–260.

PASCALIS, O., S. DE SCHONEN, J. MORTON, C. DERUELLE, and M. FABRE-GRENET, 1995. Mother's face recognition in neonates: A replication and an extension. *Infant Behav. Dev.* 18:79–86.

QUINN, P. C., 1998. Object and spatial categorisation in young infants. In *Perceptual Development*, A. Slater, ed. Hove, UK: Psychology Press, pp. 131–165.

REPP, B. H., 1984. Categorical perception: Issues, methods, findings. *Speech Lang.* 10:243–335.

REYNOLDS, D. M., and M. A. JEEVES, 1978. A developmental study of hemisphere specialization for recognition of faces in normal subjects. *Cortex* 14:511–520.

RHODES, G., 1993. Configural coding, expertise, and the right hemisphere advantage for face recognition. *Brain Cogn.* 22:19–41.

RHODES, G., S. BRAKE, and A. P. ATKINSON, 1993. What's lost in inverted faces? *Cognition* 47:25–57.

RHODES, G., S. CAREY, G. BYATT, and F. PROFFITT, 1998. Coding spatial variations in faces and simple shapes: A test of two models. *Vis. Res.* 38:2307–2321.

RHODES, G., S. TAN, S. BRAKE, and K. TAYLOR, 1989. Race sensitivity in face recognition: An effect of different encoding processes. In *Cognition in Individual and Social Contexts*, A. F. Bennett and K. M. McConkey, eds. Amsterdam: Elsevier, pp. 83–90.

RUBENSTEIN, A. J., L. KALAKANIS, and J. H. LANGLOIS, 1999. Infant preferences for attractive faces: A cognitive explanation. *Dev. Psych.* 35:848–855.

SAMS, M., J. K. HIETANEN, R. HARI, R. J. ILMONIEMI, and O. V. LOUNASMAA, 1997. Face-specific response from the human inferior occipito-temporal cortex. *Neuroscience* 77:49–55.

SCHULTZ, E. E., JR., 1983. Depth of processing by mentally retarded and MA-matched nonretarded individuals. *Am. J. Mental Deficiency* 88:307–313.

SERGENT, J., S. OHTA, and B. MACDONALD, 1992. Functional neuroanatomy of face and object processing: A positron emission tomography study. *Brain* 115:15–36.

SIMION, F., E. VALENZA, C. UMILTA, and B. DALLA BARBA, 1998. Preferential orienting to faces in newborns: A temporal-nasal asymmetry. *J. Exp. Psychol.: Hum. Percept. Perform.* 24:1399–1405.

SLATER, A., V. MORISON, and D. ROSE, 1983. The perception of shape by the new-born baby. *Br. J. Psychol.* 1:135–142.

SPORER, S. L., 1991. Deep—deeper—deepest? Encoding strategies and the recognition of human faces. *J. Exp. Child Psychol.: Learn. Mem. Cogn.* 17:323–333.

TANTAM, D., L. MONAGHAN, H. NICHOLSON, and J. STIRLING, 1989. Autistic children's ability to interpret faces: A research note. *J. Child Psychol. Psychiatry* 30:623–630.

TAYLOR, M. J., G. MCCARTHY, E. SALIBA, and E. DEGIOVANNI, 1999. ERP evidence of developmental changes in processing of faces. *Clin. Neurophysiol.* 110:910–915.

TEMPLE, C. M., 1992. Developmental memory impairment: Faces and patterns. In *Mental Lives*, R. Campbell, ed. Oxford: Blackwell.

TEUNISSE, J.-P., and B. DE GELDER, in press. Impaired categorical perception of facial expressions in high-functioning adolescents with autism. *Child Neuropsychol.*

TRONICK, E., H. ALS, L. ADAMSON, S. WISE, and T. B. BRAZELTON, 1978. The infant's response to entrapment between contradictory messages in face-to-face interaction. *J. Am. Acad. Child Psychiatry* 17:1–13.

VALENTINE, T., 1991. A unified account of the effects of distinctiveness, inversion and race in face recognition. *Quart. J. Exp. Psych.* 43(A):161–204.

VALENTINE, T., and V. BRUCE, 1986. The effects of distinctiveness in recognising and classifying faces. *Perception* 15:525–535.

VALENZA, E., F. SIMION, V. M. CASSIA, and C. UMILTA, 1996. Face preference at birth. *J. Exp. Psychol.: Hum. Percept. Perform.* 22:892–903.

WEBSTER, M. J., L. G. UNGERLEIDER, and J. BACHEVALIER, 1995. Development and plasticity of the neural circuitry underlying visual recognition memory. *Can. J. Physiol. Pharmacol.* 73:1364–1371.

WEEKS, S. H., and R. P. HOBSON, 1987. The salience of facial expression for autistic children. *J. Child Psychol. Psychiatry* 28:137–152.

WINOGRAD, E., 1981. Elaboration and distinctiveness in memory for faces. *J. Exp. Psych.: Hum. Learn.* 7:181–190.

YOSHIKAWA, S., 1995. Two types of facial impression judgements and recognition memory for faces. *Shinrigaku Kenkyu* 66:191–198.

YOUNG, A. W., and P. H. BION, 1981. Accuracy of naming laterally presented known faces by children and adults. *Cortex* 17:97–106.

YOUNG, A. W., and H. D. ELLIS, 1989. Child prosopagnosia. *Brain Cogn.* 9:16–47.

YOUNG, A. W., D. ROWLAND, A. J. CALDER, N. L. ECTOFF, A. SETH, and D. I. PERRETT, 1997. Facial expression megamix: Tests of dimensional and category accounts of facial expression recognition. *Cognition* 63:271–313.

YOUNG-BROWNE, G., H. M. ROSENFELD, and F. D. HOROWITZ, 1977. Infant discrimination of facial expressions. *Child Dev.* 48:555–562.

# 27 Spatial Cognitive Development

## JOAN STILES

ABSTRACT   This chapter focuses on the development of the behavioral and cortical systems that mediate basic spatial cognitive functions. The review of spatial development is organized around the convenient neuroanatomical dissociation between functions associated with the dorsal and ventral visuospatial streams. The first part of the chapter considers the development of spatial processes associated with the dorsal, or "where," system, focusing principally on spatial localization and spatial attention. The second part considers the ventral, or "what," system and focuses on the analysis of spatial patterns. The discussion of each spatial cognitive function begins with an overview of the adult profile of cognitive-neural mediation. Patterns of development and change in both the behavioral profiles and in the neural substrate are then considered in light of the adult model.

The term *spatial cognition* refers to a wide variety of abilities and skills, which include tracking a moving object, localizing and attending to an object or event in the spatial array, and understanding how the parts or features of an object combine to form an organized whole. Although spatial cognitive functions are not limited to the visual domain, much of the work on spatial processing has focused on the visuospatial processing system. Neuropsychological studies of visual system architecture have identified dozens of interrelated visual areas in the posterior cortices, each of which contributes to some aspect of visuospatial processing (e.g., Van Essen, Anderson, and Felleman, 1992). In the early 1980s, Ungerleider and Mishkin (1982) outlined a useful scheme for understanding the organization of this complex set of cortical areas and functions. Their description of a dual visuospatial processing system derived from the growing body of evidence from both human and animal studies suggesting distinct functional dissociations within striate and extrastriate visual areas. According to their proposal, the cortical visual system can be functionally and anatomically subdivided into two principal processing streams—a dorsal pathway and a ventral pathway (figure 27.1; see color plate 18). The dorsal stream mediates spatial processing associated with attention to movement and location, while the ventral stream is primarily involved in processing information about patterns and objects. Their

JOAN STILES   Department of Cognitive Science, University of California at San Diego, La Jolla, California.

proposal introduced an alternative to earlier accounts in which attention to location and movement was associated principally with the tectal visual system while form processing was linked to the genicostriate system (Schneider, 1967; Trevarthen, 1968). Ungerleider and Mishkin's account did not deny the role of the tectal system in, particularly, the oculomotor aspects of spatial processing. Rather, it provided a more complete account of the organization and functioning of higher cortical systems, and of spatial cognitive processing more generally.

The dorsal visual pathway begins at the retina and projects via the lateral geniculate nucleus (LGN) of the thalamus to primary visual cortex, area V1. From there the pathway proceeds to areas V2 and V3, then projects dorsally to the medial (MT/V5) and medial superior (MST) regions of the temporal lobe, and then to the ventral inferior-parietal lobe (IP). Input to the dorsal pathway is derived principally, though not exclusively, from the large M-type retinal ganglion cells that project to the magnocellular layers of LGN and then to layer $4C(\alpha)$ of V1. Cells in this pathway are maximally sensitive to movement and direction, and less responsive to color or form. The dorsal stream processes information about optic flow and other aspects of motion, processes information about spatial location, and plays an important role in allocation of spatial attention. It has thus been described as the "where" pathway (for discussions of the role of the inferior parietal lobe in visual control of motor output, see Anderson et al., 1997; Goodale and Milner, 1992).

The ventral visual pathway also begins at the retina and projects via the LGN of the thalamus to primary visual cortex, area V1. From there, the pathway proceeds to areas V2 and V4, then projects ventrally to the posterior (PIT) and anterior (AIT) regions of the inferior temporal lobe. Input to the ventral pathway is derived principally, though not exclusively, from P-type retinal ganglion cells that project to the parvocellular layers of the LGN and then to layer $4C(\beta)$ of V1. Parvocellular input to V1 organizes into distinct areas called the blob and interblob regions (Livingstone and Hubel, 1984; Wong-Riley, 1979). Cells in the blob regions are maximally sensitive to form, while cells in the interblob regions respond principally to color. The ventral stream, which has been described as the "what"

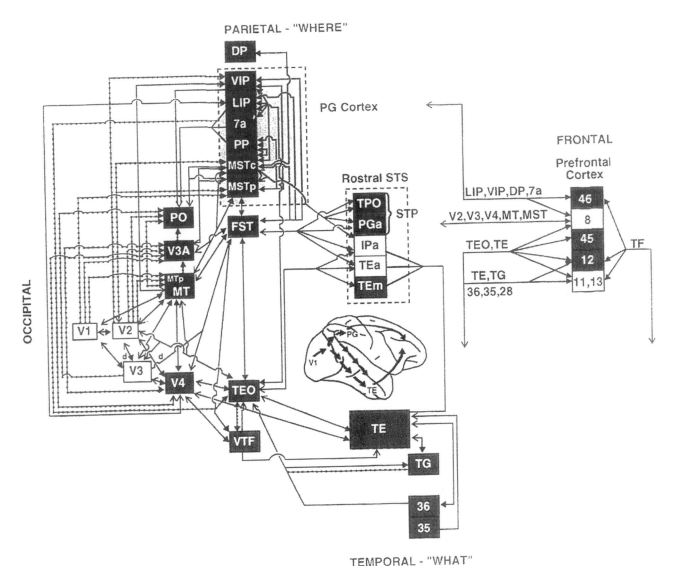

PARIETAL - "WHERE"

PG Cortex

FRONTAL

Prefrontal
Cortex

Rostral STS

STP

OCCIPITAL

TEMPORAL - "WHAT"

FIGURE 27.1 Visual processing pathways in monkeys. Solid lines indicate connections arising from both central and peripheral visual field representations; dotted lines indicate connections restricted to peripheral field representations. Red boxes indicate ventral stream areas related primarily to object vision; green boxes indicate dorsal stream areas related primarily to spatial vision; white boxes indicate areas not clearly allied with either stream. The shaded region on the lateral view of the brain represents the extent of the cortex included in the diagram. Abbreviations are as follows: DP, dorsal prelunate area; FST, fundus of superior temporal area; HIPP, hippocampus; LIP, lateral intraparietal area; MSTc, medial superior temporal area, central visual field representation; MSTp, medial superior temporal area, peripheral visual field representation; MT, middle temporal area; MTp, middle temporal area, peripheral visual field representation; PO, parieto-

occipital area; PP, posterior parietal sulcal zone; STP, superior temporal polysensory area; V1, primary visual cortex; V2, visual area 2; V3, visual area 3; V3A, visual area 3, part A; V4, visual area 4; and VIP, ventral intraparietal area. Inferior parietal area 7a; prefrontal areas 8, 11 to 13, 45, and 46, perirhinal areas 35 and 36; and entorhinal area 28 are from Brodmann (Brodmann, 1909). Inferior temporal areas TEO and TE, parahippocampal area TF, temporal pole area TG, and inferior parietal area PG are from von Bonin and Bailey (von Bonin and Bailey, 1947). Rostral superior temporal sulcal (STS) areas are from Seltzer and Pandya (Seltzer and Pandya, 1978) and VTF is the visually responsive portion of area TF (Boussaoud, Desimone, and Ungerleider, 1991). (Figure and caption reprinted with permission from Ungerleider, L. G., 1995. Functional brain imaging studies of cortical mechanisms for memory. *Science* 270:770.)

pathway, processes information about visual properties of objects and patterns.

The dorsal and ventral pathways project rostrally, each going to both common and adjacent areas of the prefrontal cortex. Finally, there is substantial evidence that the two pathways are richly interconnected and at least partially overlapping both in the mature (e.g., Dobkins and Albright, 1994, 1995, 1998; Marangolo et al., 1998; Merigan and Maunsell, 1993) and the developing visual system (Dobkins and Teller, 1996a,b).

The anatomical division of function into the dorsal and ventral streams provides a convenient organizational structure for discussing the functional organization and development of spatial cognitive processes. Accordingly, the next two sections of this chapter reflect this anatomical division. The first section focuses on processes associated with the dorsal stream and concentrates on the complementary issues of the development of spatial localization and of spatial attention. The second section takes up issues related to processes associated with the ventral stream and is centered on the development of pattern processing.

It should be noted that although a great deal is known about the neuropsychology of each of these processes in adult human and animal populations, the study of the *development* of the neuropsychological underpinnings of spatial cognitive processing is, itself, in its infancy . . . or at least its childhood. To date, there have been very few developmental studies that provide *direct* evidence mapping specific behavioral changes in spatial processing to specific change in the neural substrate. Nonetheless, important basic information about the postnatal development of the visuospatial processing system is available. This kind of information, coupled with very specific measures of behavioral change, makes it possible to begin to make inferences about associations between change in the neural substrate and change in behavior.

### The development of spatial processes associated with the dorsal stream: Location and attention to space

A variety of spatial processes have been associated with activation of the dorsal visual pathway. Two of the most basic are considered in this section: (1) processing of information about spatial location and (2) spatial attention. The division into two distinct processes is somewhat artificial in that, for example, localization of an object may also require a shift in spatial attention. Nonetheless, there is substantial evidence for functional and anatomical independence of key features of each process.

SPATIAL LOCATION   Neuroimaging studies of adults suggest that spatial location tasks activate widely distributed brain areas. Haxby has used functional MRI to examine brain activation profiles in normal adult subjects on tasks requiring them to compare the location of objects in two visually presented arrays (Haxby et al., 1991, 1994). Activation was observed in several areas along the dorsal pathway. In the most posterior brain regions, areas of extrastriate cortex were activated bilaterally; these included the calcarine, medial, and lateral areas of the occipital lobe. These areas are presumed to be involved in early visual processing and are typically activated on a wide array of visual processing tasks. In addition, the dorsolateral occipital (area 19) and the posterior superior parietal areas, extending rostrally to the intraparietal sulcus (area 7), were also activated bilaterally. These areas are considered to be critical to processing of location information. Finally, the dorsolateral prefrontal cortex (area 6) was activated unilaterally on the right. This activation may be related to spatial memory demands or to eye movement. Very similar patterns of activation were observed in studies of spatial working memory (Jonides et al., 1993; Smith, Jonides, and Koeppe, 1996; Smith et al., 1995; for discussion of imaging studies of spatial memory with children, see also Casey et al., 1998; Nelson et al., 2000). Overall, subjects showed greater right lateralization and, importantly, much more extensive frontal activation, including right dorsolateral prefrontal cortex (areas 46 and 47), and the anterior cingulate.

There is also strong evidence that the dorsal frontoparietal system plays a major role in control of visually guided motor behavior, including both eye movement and reach (Johnson et al., 1996; Wise et al., 1997). The task of looking or reaching to a location in space involves a complex network of neural areas within the dorsal system pathway. Prefrontal motor areas mediate planning and preparation for motor action; activation of these areas typically precedes the actual motor event. There is considerable evidence for superior parietal input to dorsal premotor and motor cortices. Patterns of activity in linked frontal and superior parietal areas are concordant, suggesting a network of spatial-motor control. In addition, recent studies have shown that inferior parietal areas connect to frontal premotor areas and play an important modulatory role in spatial-motor activity (Anderson et al., 1997). Cells in this region respond to modification or correction of motor actions. Further, different cells are selective for movement type such that different groups of cells respond to eye movement and reach. Consistent with these findings, Goodale and Milner (1992) have reported the case of a woman with bilateral parietal lesions who showed specific difficulty in accurately reaching for objects. These data suggest that the "where" system may also serve as a "how" system to mediate action in the spatial world.

These data from the adult neuropsychological literature suggest that the seemingly simple task of spatial localization involves a complex network of brain and cognitive systems. Neural activation varies systematically with small task variations, suggesting that a specific task may recruit different parts of the system in differing degrees. Thus, frontal activation is observed on a perceptual localization task, but greatly enhanced on tasks that impose a memory load. Given these data, it is perhaps not surprising that one of the largest, and perhaps most controversial, bodies of data on the early visuospatial processing comes from a simple, spatial hiding task, originally introduced by Jean Piaget (1952). In the most basic version of this task, the child watches as an object is hidden under one of two similar, closely positioned screens; then the child is encouraged to retrieve the object. At about 8–10 months, children begin to make an intriguing error when presented with a series of search trials. In a typical test sequence, the object is first hidden under the same screen (screen A) for two to three consecutive trials; and on these trials 7-month-old children easily retrieve the hidden object (but see also Smith et al., 1999). However, when, on the next trial, the object is hidden—in full view of the child— under the second screen (screen B), children typically search under screen A, the location of the object on earlier trials. This error has been termed the A-not-B error (or, for brevity, the $\overline{AB}$ error). The $\overline{AB}$ error is easily elicited, and its prevalence is not a matter of dispute. However, the interpretation of this behavior has been the source of controversy for several decades (for reviews of this literature see Harris, 1987; Smith et al., 1999; Wellman et al., 1987).

The typical age at which the $\overline{AB}$ error is observed on the standard task is approximately 8–12 months. However, children's experience outside the task setting can influence the likelihood of making the error (for discussion, see Hauser, 1999). A number of studies have shown that the experience of self-locomotion, either naturally occurring or introduced by the use of an infant walker, significantly reduces the likelihood of $\overline{AB}$ error (Bertenthal and Campos, 1990; Horobin and Acredolo, 1986; Kermoian and Campos, 1988). Furthermore, healthy preterm infants show a systematic advantage on the AB search task over their full-term peers when the groups are matched for conceptional age (Matthews, Ellis, and Nelson, 1996). Apparently the extra experience in the world offers the healthy preterms a developmental advantage.

Altering task demands also has a dramatic effect on AB search performance. Some factors enhance performance. The use of salient nearby landmarks or distinctive screens and increasing the distance between the screens all improve infant performance on the task (Butterworth, Jarret, and Hicks, 1982; Wellman et al., 1987). Similarly, tasks that require only a look to the hiding location, rather than an actual reach, reduce the frequency of $\overline{AB}$ error (Ahmed and Ruffman, 1998; Baillargeon and Graber, 1988; Hofstadter and Reznick, 1996), even among children as young as 4 months (Baillargeon and DeVos, 1991). Furthermore, a simple change in the infant's posture from sitting during A trials to standing during the B hiding trials greatly reduces the frequency of $\overline{AB}$ error (Smith et al., 1999).[1] On the other hand, increasing memory demands makes the standard reaching task more difficult. Diamond (1985) has shown that imposition of a delay between hiding and retrieval increases the frequency of the error in children who have mastered the standard, no-delay task. Indeed, she has shown that the length of delay required to induce the $\overline{AB}$ error increases systematically with age, such that even 12-months-olds make the error with delays of 10 seconds or more. Similarly, creating very difficult task conditions elicits the $\overline{AB}$ error in children well beyond the age at which it is usually seen. Spencer, Smith, and Thelen (1997) showed that 2–3-year-old children make the $\overline{AB}$ error when tested on an array consisting of a large uniform field (a sandbox) with no visual cues and relatively small separation between the hiding locations. The variability in task performance introduced by widely different task and subject factors suggests that what appears to be a simple spatial location task is indeed much more complex.

Although data from neuropsychological studies of performance on the AB search task are very limited, they provide some evidence about the neural systems critical for successful search performance. Adult rhesus monkeys can be readily trained to ceiling performance on the standard AB search task and perform well with delays as long as 15 seconds (Diamond, 1991; Diamond, Werker, and Lalonde, 1994). However, bilateral lesions of dorsolateral prefrontal cortex severely disrupt performance in the memory load conditions. With no delay between hiding and retrieval, the performance of monkeys with prefrontal lesions is comparable to that of unoperated monkeys. However, under conditions of even short delays (2–5 s), performance declines and the frequency of $\overline{AB}$ errors rises dramatically. By contrast, bilateral lesions to parietal cortex (Diamond, 1991; Diamond, Werker, and Lalonde, 1994) or to the hippocampal formation (Diamond, Zola-Morgan, and

Squire, 1989) have little effect on AB search performance.

Infant rhesus monkeys show a developmental pattern on the AB search task that is very similar to that of human children. At 1.5–2.5 months, the frequency of $\overline{AB}$ error is high, mirroring the performance of 7.5–8.5-month-old human infants. Between 2.5 and 4 months, performance improves and is affected by increasingly longer delays, such that by 4 months, 12-second delays do not significantly increase the frequency of the $\overline{AB}$ error. At 4.5 months, bilateral lesions of dorsolateral prefrontal cortex produce effects very similar to comparable lesions in adult monkeys.

Diamond suggests that the dorsolateral prefrontal lesion data implicate two important functions necessary for the successful performance of the AB search task: explicit spatial memory and inhibitory control. It has been well documented that prefrontal lesions impair spatial memory (Goldman-Rakic, 1987). Studies of rats have shown that lesions to dorsomedial prefrontal cortex specifically impair memory for temporal order of spatial location (Chiba, Kesner, and Gibson, 1997). The AB search task explicitly requires memory for the most recent hiding location in a series of trials. Furthermore, the effects of lesions to dorsolateral prefrontal cortex are consistent with the human adult activation studies reported earlier. Although dorsolateral prefrontal activation was observed in both the perception and memory for location tasks, it was enhanced, particularly in the right hemisphere, under conditions of memory load. Frontal lesions have also been associated with failure of inhibitory control (Welsh and Pennington, 1988). The AB search task requires children to inhibit a prepotent response (reach to A) in order to make the new, correct response (reach to B). Diamond (1991; Diamond, Werker, and Lalonde, 1994) compared performance on the AB search task and an object retrieval task that required inhibition of a prepotent response but had no memory component, and found that children showed similar patterns of developmental change on both.

The results of the lesion studies led Diamond to conclude that "maturational change in the frontal cortices underlies improved performance on AB [search] . . . and object retrieval between 7.5 and 12 months in human infants and 1.50–2.5 months in infant monkeys" (Diamond, 1991, p. 167). She cites two sources of evidence specifically linking the timing of markers of maturational change in frontal cortex to developmental change on the behavioral tasks (Diamond, Werker, and Lalonde, 1994). First, Chugani's studies of regional change in brain metabolic activation over the first year of life in human children indicate that increases in fron-

tal metabolic activity begin at about 8 months of age, a time that coincides with improved performance on the AB search task (Chugani, Phelps, and Mazziotta, 1987; but see also Jacobs et al., 1995, for data from infant rhesus monkeys). Second, Fox and Bell (1990) reported systematic increases in EEG spectral power over frontal brain regions over a time period that corresponded to developmental improvement in the AB search task; such increases were not observed in parietal or occipital regions. It should be noted, however, that Fox and Bell also reported that no such association was observed for the object retrieval task. Thus, the two marker tasks indexing frontal lobe maturation yielded different profiles of association on this important brain index.

Diamond's studies point to the importance of developmental change in prefrontal brain systems for successful performance on the $\overline{AB}$ error task, and it is clear that important changes do take place in frontal systems during this period. However, other data suggest that the developmental story may be somewhat more complex. For example, in addition to their work on frontal EEG spectral power, Bell and Fox (1992) have also examined patterns of long-range EEG coherence. They reported that a systematic increase in anterior-posterior coherence was associated with improved performance on the $\overline{AB}$ error task. These data suggest that another important factor involved in neural mediation of AB task performance is the stabilization of long-range axonal connections within the dorsal stream. As discussed earlier, these pathways may be critical for control of spatial reaching. Baillargeon and DeVos (1991) have reported that the frequency of $\overline{AB}$ error among 4-month-old infants is greatly reduced when the requirement to reach for the hidden object is eliminated. Thus, while related to frontal lobe development, the coherence data suggest more widespread change in the dorsal system that may well affect different aspects of performance on this task. The complexity of the developmental story is also evident in the behavioral studies reported earlier. Data from a wide range of studies suggest that performance on the $\overline{AB}$ error task can be affected by a wide variety of factors. Under some conditions, children much younger than 8 months can solve the task easily, while under other conditions even toddlers fail the task. Some of the factors that affect performance are task-related and include such things as landmark information or increasing the spacing between hiding locations. Others, such as reports of enhanced performance among healthy preterms or among infants who begin to self-locomote early, are related specifically to the child's experience. The simple case of frontal lobe maturation alone cannot account for all of these data.[2]

In order to understand the dynamics of neural and cognitive development for spatial processing, it is important to consider a construct Johnson has termed as partial cortical functioning (see Johnson, Mareschal, and Csibra, this volume). Partial cortical functioning refers to the idea that the state of a cortical system need *not* be construed as either "on" or "off." Rather, early in development, a given cortical region may play a more limited role in system function, and that role may change gradually with development. It is clear that cortical development does not proceed uniformly. A wide variety of physiological markers suggest that frontal cortices lag behind other regions, but this lag is observed not over weeks or months, but over years. Important developments during the second half of the first year (in humans) may well contribute to the increasing stability and robustness of performance on tasks like the $\overline{AB}$ error task. But the data also show that successful performance does not depend on those changes. Thus, while any single finding about the cognitive or neural system is important and contributes to our knowledge of development, it cannot tell the whole developmental story. Immature frontal lobes and limited self-locomotor experience can each constrain development, and *either* of those constraints may effect the development of *both* the neural system and behavior.

SPATIAL ATTENTION  A closely related line of investigation focuses on the neural systems associated with attention to different locations in space. In contrast to the work examining profiles of brain activity when subjects are required to directly perceive or remember the location of an object in space, spatial attention tasks investigate the brain systems activated when subjects are asked to shift their attention to different locations in the spatial array. The ability to shift attention to different spatial locations is one part of the larger attentional system involving widely distributed brain areas. Review of the full literature on attention is well beyond the scope of this chapter. This section focuses more narrowly on those aspects of the attention system involved in shifting of attention in space.

There is considerable clinical and experimental evidence that the posterior parietal lobes play a crucial role in the ability to shift attention to different spatial locations (Heilman and Valenstein, 1993; Hillyard and Anllo-Vento, 1998; Ivry and Robertson, 1998; Posner, 1980; Posner et al., 1984; Rafal and Robertson, 1995; Robertson, 1992). Posner (1980; Posner and Petersen, 1990) has presented one influential model of the attention system that involves an interconnected network of structures that modulate and control different aspects of attention. According to Posner, the posterior parietal network plays an essential role in disengaging attention from one location and allowing a shift of attention to another location.

In the standard task used to test covert shifts of attention (Posner and Cohen, 1980), subjects are seated in front of a computer and instructed to fixate, continuously, on a point located centrally between two identical, flanking squares. After a fixed period, a visual cue is presented either centrally (e.g., an arrow pointing right or left) or peripherally (e.g., one box brightens briefly), and soon thereafter a target appears briefly in one box. The subject responds as soon as the target is detected. The critical variable is the validity of the cue. On most trials (75–80%) the cue is "valid" and the target appears in the cued box. On the remaining trials, the cue is "invalid," and the target appears in the opposite box. If cuing serves to covertly shift attention, it should take less time to detect the target when the cue is valid than when it is invalid. One additional, well-established finding concerns response differences associated with the length of the interval between the valid cue and the target, or stimulus onset asychrony (SOA). With short SOAs (<200 ms), the classic facilitation of response time is observed. However, at longer SOAs (300–1300 ms) responses to the cued target are slowed (Posner et al., 1985). This phenomenon, which has been called inhibition of return (IOR), is thought to reflect an evolutionarily important suppression of a response to an already attended location.

In order to examine patterns of brain activation associated with shifting attention, Corbetta used a variant of the attentional cuing task (Corbetta, 1998; Corbetta et al., 1993). The results of this study confirmed earlier reports from both human and animal work on the role of the parietal lobes in shifting spatial attention. Significant foci of brain activation were observed in both left and right superior parietal regions. However, the patterns of activation to stimuli presented to the right visual field (RVF) and left visual field (LVF) were not symmetrical across the hemispheres. Presentation of targets to the LVF produced significantly more activation in the RH than the LH, while presentation of targets to the RVF produced significant levels of activation in both the RH and LH. Furthermore, distinct activation sites for RVF and LVF targets were identified within the right superior parietal region, thus suggesting that different brain regions within the RH are responsible for processing information from the two sides of space.

Adult patient data are consistent with these findings. Patients with injury to posterior parietal areas, including the cortex, superior colliculus, and pulvinar, have difficulty with shifting attention. Specifically, patients with injury to the parietal cortex show exaggerated slowing of RT following presentation of invalid cues (Posner et al., 1984). By contrast, patients with supranuclear palsy, a disorder associated with damage to the superior colliculus, fail to show IOR responses. Finally, patients with thalamic damage are slow to detect targets presented anywhere in the visual field.

There is a small, but growing, literature on infant ability to shift attention in the visual field. A number of infant studies have used procedures that allow for examination of both cue facilitation and IOR. These studies show that by at least 6 months, infants show both facilitation and IOR (Clohessy et al., 1991; Harman et al., 1994; Hood, 1993; Johnson, Posner, and Rothbart, 1994; Johnson and Tucker, 1996). Attempts to evoke these responses from younger children have been mixed. However, control of factors, such as SOA duration and cue/target eccentricity, appear to be critical to elicitation of the responses. Using 200 and 700 SOAs, Johnson and Tucker (1996) demonstrated reliable facilitation and IOR among 4-month-old children but did not show facilitation among 6-month-olds. However, when a 133-ms SOA was introduced, 6-months-olds showed strong facilitation. This finding suggests that while the basic attentional responses may be robust as early as 4 months, the timing parameters that elicit the response may change with development. Similarly, Harman and colleagues found no IOR response among 3-month-old children when stimuli were presented at 30° eccentricity but found a strong response when presented at 10°. Thus, distribution of attention across the visual field may also change with development. Few studies have examined facilitation and IOR in children 2 months and younger. Johnson reported only weak facilitation effects and no IOR effects among 2-month-old infants. However, Valenza's study of newborns suggests that IOR may be present in the first days of life (Valenza, Simion, and Umilta, 1994).

Studies of children with early brain injury provide some insight into the neural mechanisms that mediate these basic attentional processes in development. Craft and White (1994) examined attention shift in a group of 33 children with perinatal brain injury, using the shift attention standard task with 100- and 800-ms SOAs. Children were grouped by site of lesion: anterior ($n = 6$), posterior ($n = 10$), diffuse ($n = 8$), and no apparent lesion ($n = 9$). In contrast to adult patients, children with posterior lesions did not show any of the specific deficits noted for patients with injury to the parietal complex. However, children with anterior lesions failed to show the facilitation effect to valid cues presented in the right, but not the left, visual field, suggesting an effect of left anterior injury not observed among adult patients. Johnson reported a similar finding for infants with unilateral left anterior perinatal focal brain injury (Johnson et al., 1998). These data suggest that the systems crucial to the control of attentional processes may change with development, such that early on, frontal regions, and in particular left frontal regions, may be crucial to efficient allocation of attention across the spatial field.

NEGLECT Hemispatial neglect is an attentional disorder frequently observed in adults following unilateral parietal injury. In severe cases, hemispatial neglect patients appear to be unaware of objects and events in the visual hemispace contralateral to their lesion (Heilman and Valenstein, 1993). They may eat only half the food on their plates, fail to comb half their hair, and on simple paper-and-pencil copying tasks, fail to reproduce half of the model form. Impairments associated with neglect cannot be accounted for by sensory deficits. Indeed, the disruption experienced by neglect patients may be more devastating than those experienced by patients with visual sensory deficits (McFie, Piercy, and Zangwill, 1950). There is evidence that the attentional disorder may extend beyond the immediate, perceptually available environment and may include the patient's representation of space (e.g., Bisiach and Luzzatti, 1978). In many patients, a milder form of hemispatial inattention known as extinction is evident. These patients appear to be able to attend to the contralesional field if there are no distractors in the ipsilesional field. For example, a patient may be able identify an object presented singly to either the right or left visual field; but when two objects are presented simultaneously, one to each field, the patient fails to identify the object in the contralesional field.

The literature on neglect in child populations is very limited (see Temple, 1997, for a summary). There are several reports of documented neglect in cases of pathology acquired after the age of 5 (Fero, Martins, and Tavora, 1984; Heller and Levine, 1989). Fero and colleagues (1984) provided three case studies of documented neglect in children with acute RH pathology; in all three cases, the neglect resolved after a period of treatment and recovery. Heller and Levine (1989) examined children with brain injury occurring either before or after age 6. Although children with LH or RH injury acquired after age 6 showed evidence of contralesional neglect, no evidence of neglect was found among children with earlier acquired RH lesions, nor among children with LH injury.

More recently, Thompson reported a case of a child who suffered right posterior traumatic brain injury at 3 years, 8 months (Thompson et al., 1991). The child showed a transient period of contralesional neglect and recovery within one year of injury. Hugdahl and Carlsson (1994) used dichotic listening tasks with a group of children with either right or left congenital hemiplegia. In this study both groups of children showed patterns of responsiveness consistent with hemi-inattention to the contralesional side. In this study, stimuli were presented to both ears simultaneously, and on successive blocks of trials the children were required to attend to information in one ear and to ignore information in the other ear. Similar to evidence of subtle neglect reported for patients in extinction studies, these data suggest that early unilateral brain injury may result in subtle forms of hemi-inattention. Finally, Trauner and Ballantyne (submitted) used cancellation and tactile exploration tasks to study hemi-inattention in children with congenital focal brain injury. They report subtle, but persistent, evidence for neglect in both patient groups. However, the pattern of deficit differed somewhat from that reported for adults patients. Like their adult counterparts, children with RH lesions showed evidence for neglect of the contralateral hemispace. However, children with LH lesions, unlike adults with comparable lesions, showed evidence of subtle bilateral neglect.

In summary, while the body of data on early neglect is still small, there is growing evidence that neglect may represent a subtle, but significant, clinical risk for children with early brain injury. Combined with the data from the studies of the early development of infant attention, these studies suggest that the brain systems that mediate the ability to allocate attention across the visual field develop early and are vulnerable to early neural insult.

### Development of spatial processes associated with the ventral stream: Understanding parts and wholes and how they go together

A major function of the ventral visual stream is the analysis of pattern information. Behaviorally, spatial analysis is defined as the ability to specify the parts and the overall configuration of a visually presented pattern, and to understand how the parts are related to form an organized whole (Delis, Kiefner, and Fridlund, 1988; Delis, Robertson, and Efron, 1986; Palmer, 1977, 1980; Palmer and Bucher, 1981; Robertson and Delis, 1986; Smith and Kemler, 1977; Vurpillot, 1976). It thus involves the ability both to segment a pattern into a set of constituent parts (local level processing) and to integrate those parts into a coherent whole (global level processing). Spatial analysis, then, refers to processing of the spatial relations among the parts of spatial patterns or objects. Studies of spatial analytic processing

within the ventral stream have shown systematic differences in the distribution of global and local level processing across the cerebral hemispheres. Specifically, right posterior temporal regions have been associated with global level processing, and left posterior temporal regions with local level processing.

Studies of adult patients have shown that left posterior (LP) or right posterior (RP) focal brain injury results in dissociable disorders of spatial analytic functioning (Arena and Gainotti, 1978; Delis, Kiefner, and Fridlund, 1988; Delis, Robertson, and Efron, 1986; Gainotti and Tiacci, 1970; Ivry and Robertson, 1998; Lamb, Robertson, and Knight, 1989, 1990; McFie and Zangwill, 1960; Robertson and Delis, 1986; Robertson, Lamb, and Knight, 1988; Swindell et al., 1988). LP injury disrupts local processing and results in disorders involving difficulty defining the parts of a spatial array. In drawing, for example, patients tend to oversimplify spatial patterns and omit details, and on perceptual judgment tasks, they rely upon overall configural cues and ignore specific elements. By contrast, patients with RP lesions have difficulty with global processing; RP injury disrupts the configural aspects of spatial analysis. In drawing, they include details but fail to maintain a coherent organization among the elements. In perceptual judgment tasks, they focus on the parts of the pattern without attending to the overall form.

A large number of reaction time (RT) studies with normal adults have confirmed the lateralization of local level processing to the LH and global level processing to the RH (Martin, 1979; Martinez et al., 1997; Sergent, 1982). Sergent has suggested that hemispheres differ in terms of higher-order perceptual processes that differentially emphasize processing of lower spatial frequencies in the RH and higher spatial frequencies in the LH. In accordance with this view, experiments using sinusoidal gratings containing a single spatial frequency and appearing in the RVF or LVF have shown that low spatial frequencies are responded to faster in the RVF-LH than in the LVF-RH and high spatial frequencies are responded to faster in the LVF-RH than in the RVF-LH (Kitterle, Christman, and Hellige, 1990; Kitterle, Hellige, and Christman, 1992; Kitterle and Selig, 1991). This pattern of hemispheric lateralization as a function of attention to spatial frequency has also been confirmed electrophysiologically (Martinez, Anllo-Vento, and Hillyard, 1997).

Lateralized differences in inferior temporal lobe activation during global and local processing have been examined using functional magnetic resonance imaging (fMRI). In her study of lateralized differences in brain activation during global and local processing tasks, Martinez (Martinez et al., 1997) focused on inferior temporal lobes (including inferior-temporal and fusiform gyri). These areas have been identified in animal (Desimone, Albright, and Gross, 1984; Tanaka et al., 1991) and in human neuroimaging studies (Haxby et al., 1991; Malach et al., 1995) as crucial for identifying object shape and features. Martinez used both RT and measures of functional brain activation to investigate profiles of neural mediation when subjects were asked to attend to either the global or the local level of a pattern. In both tasks, subjects were shown a series of hierarchical forms (i.e., large patterns made of smaller patterns, such as a large square made of small circles) and, on separate blocks of trials, were asked to identify targets at either the global or the local level. In the RT study, stimuli were presented centrally, or to the right or left visual half-fields (RVF, LVF), and the subject's task was to detect when a target was present at the attended level. In the fMRI study, the subject's task was to count the number of predesignated targets in a rapid series of centrally presented hierarchical stimuli. For both RT and fMRI measures, a clear advantage for global targets was associated with RH processing. Global targets presented to the LVF-RH were processed faster than local targets, and attention to global targets produced markedly greater levels of brain activation than attention to local targets. The opposite pattern of dissociation between global and local targets was evident, but much less pronounced, in the LH. RTs to global and local targets were comparable. Both areas of activation and intensity were marginally greater to the local than global targets in the LH.

Studies of normally developing children have shown that even young infants are capable of spatial analysis. Cohen and Younger (1984) have shown evidence of systematic change in the complexity of infants' ability to process pattern information that reflects both global and local level processing. Deruelle and de Schonen (1991, 1995) have shown that infants as young as 4 months show a profile of lateralized processing differences on global and local processing tasks that is similar to those described in the adult imaging study reported by Martinez and colleagues (1997). Change in the complexity and sophistication of spatial analytic processing has been documented across the preschool and school age period (Akshoomoff and Stiles, 1995a,b; Feeney and Stiles, 1996; Stiles and Stern, in press; Tada and Stiles, 1996). Data from a large series of studies using different measures and testing children ranging in age from 3 to 12 years show that, initially, children segment out well-formed, independent units and use simple combinatorial rules to integrate the parts into an overall configuration. With development, change is observed in both the nature of the parts and the relations

children use to organize the parts. Furthermore, pattern complexity affects how children approach the problem of analysis. In studies using both the Rey-Osterrieth complex form and simplified variants, it has been shown that simplification of the pattern induced more advanced reproduction strategies (Akshoomoff and Stiles 1995a,b).

Imaging studies of normal children provide evidence for protracted development of the neural systems associated with spatial analytic processing. In a developmental study (Stiles et al., 1999), 15 healthy children between 11 and 15 years were tested using RT and fMRI protocols identical to those used by Martinez and colleagues (1997) with adult subjects. There were two major findings of this study. First, the pattern of RT data obtained from children across the age span tested in this study did not match that of adults. Across all age groups, children were faster with global than with local targets; however, within task, the same general patterns of laterality as those observed with adults were obtained. Second, in the fMRI, children's profiles of activation differed from the patterns observed among adults. For both the attend global and attend local tasks, children showed statistically greater activation in the RH than in the LH (figure 27.2; see color plate 19). However, overall activation among children was greater than for adults, and children showed considerably more bilateral activation, particularly on the local processing tasks, than did adults. These studies suggest that, at least for these perceptually demanding tasks, children show both a global processing advantage and overall RH dominance.

An extensive series of studies of children with pre- and perinatal focal brain injury has provided detailed profiles of deficit and recovery for spatial functioning associated with early lateralized brain injury (Stiles et al., 1997, 1998; Stiles-Davis et al., 1988; Vicari et al., 1998). These studies have shown that on construction and perception tasks, children with RH injury have difficulty with spatial integration. While they are able to segment a spatial form into its elements, they have difficulty organizing those elements to form a coherent whole. A strikingly different profile of deficit is associated with early LH injury. Children with LH injury oversimplify complex spatial forms and fail to encode the details or elements of these forms. These two profiles are consistent with patterns of deficit reported for adults with injury to comparable brain regions, and suggest that the basic lateralized dissociation for global and local processing is robust from very early in development.

But while the basic adultlike patterns of deficit are evident even among very young children, the severity

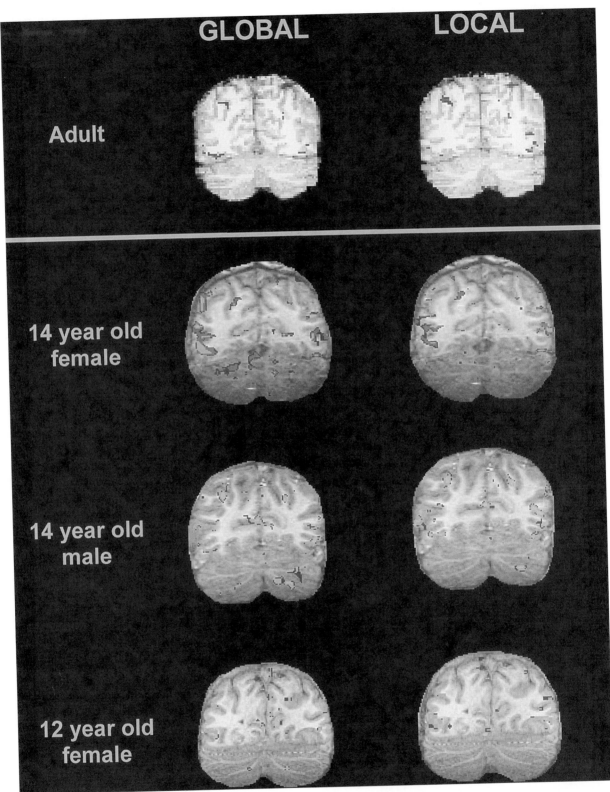

FIGURE 27.2    Brain activation patterns from a functional MRI study of global–local processing. The top panel shows representative activation patterns for adult subjects. During the attend global condition, activation is greater on the right than on the left; during the attend local condition, activation is greater on the left. The bottom three panels show activation profiles from three representative children. Unlike adults, children show greater right than left activation for both the attend global and attend local condition.

of deficit is greatly attenuated among children, and children appear to compensate in ways that adults cannot. In addition to data documenting patterns of specific deficit, longitudinal studies of children with early focal brain injury also provide evidence of functional recovery. Longitudinal studies indicate that, with development, children with both LH and RH injury show considerable behavioral improvement, eventually achieving ceiling level performance on most spatial construction tasks. However, the time course over which this improvement occurs is protracted, and several studies suggest that although the output of various spatial processing tasks appears comparable to that of normal peers, the processing strategies of children with early lesions continue to reflect persistent deficit. Two studies illustrate this point.

A block construction study with 3–6-year-olds (Stiles et al., 1996) demonstrated impairment among children with both RH and LH injury. In this task children were presented with simple block models (e.g., a line of blocks or a double arch) and asked to reproduce them with the model present. Children with LH injury initially showed delay, producing simplified constructions. By the time they were 4 years old, they showed an interesting dissociation in performance. Most of the children were able to produce accurate copies of the target constructions; however, the procedures they used in copying the forms were greatly simplified. This dissociation between product and process, which is not observed among normally developing children, persisted at least through age 6. Children with RH injury were also initially delayed on this task, producing only simplified constructions. At about age 4, they produced more complex, but disordered and poorly configured constructions. At this time the procedures used to generate these ill-formed constructions were comparable to those of age-matched controls. By age 6, the performance profile for this group of children changed. They were able to accurately copy the target constructions, but, like their LH injured peers, they used simple procedures. This study suggests that there is impairment in spatial processing following early injury, and there is compensation with development. However, close examination of how spatial constructions are generated suggest persistent deficits. These findings have been replicated in a study of Italian children with localized brain injury (Vicari et al., 1998). In addition, that study showed that the profiles of deficit were evident among children with isolated subcortical injury, as well as in children with injury involving both cortical and subcortical areas.

A parallel set of findings was observed among older children using a more difficult construction task, the Rey-Osterrieth Complex Figure (ROCF). The ROCF is a complex geometric pattern that has been used for many years to evaluate spatial planning in adult neurological patients. This figure is organized around a central rectangle that is symmetrically divided by vertical, horizontal, and diagonal bisecting lines; additional pattern details are positioned both within and surrounding the core rectangle. The most efficient and advanced strategy for copying the ROCF is to begin with the core rectangle and bisectors, then add pattern details. However, this strategy also places great demands on spatial analytic processing. Akshoomoff and Stiles (1995a,b) have shown that typically developing children do not regularly use this advanced copying strategy until quite late in development. Younger children parse the figure into smaller units and the size of the unit increases with age: 6–7-year-olds typically use a very piecemeal strategy, drawing each small subdivision separately, while older children use progressively larger subunits (quadrants, halves) until, finally, by about 10–12 years, their organization strategy centers around the core rectangle.

Akshoomoff and Stiles (Akshoomoff and Stiles, in press; Akshoomoff, Feroleto, Doyle, and Stiles, submitted) examined data collected longitudinally in 18 children with pre- or perinatal focal brain injury from the time when they were 6 to 13 years of age. Two versions of the task were administered—a copy task, in which the children were asked to reproduce the figure with the model present, and an immediate memory task. On the copying task, the children with both RH and LH injury performed worse than normal age-matched controls. Deficits were particularly evident among the youngest children (age 6–7) in the lesion groups, in that their drawings were sparser and less accurate than normal controls. However, there were no striking differences between LH and RH injury groups. With development, performance improved considerably, such that by 9–10 years of age, these children were able to produce reasonably accurate copies of the ROCF. However, analysis of how they generated the figure indicated continuing subtle deficit. Specifically, at 10–12 years of age, the children in the lesion groups continued to use the most immature and piecemeal approach to generating the figure. As was the case with the block construction task, the children's products improved, but continuing deficit was evident in their construction procedures. The failure to find differences between the RH and LH injury groups on the ROCF task could reflect underlying task demands that place equal emphasis on the segmentation and integrative processes, and thus equally disrupt performance on the task.

Interestingly, while the copy task data failed to differentiate the lesion groups, the memory task data did.

Copy and memory data from ten children with LH injury and nine children with RH injury were examined at a single data point (age 11–14). There were no significant group differences on the copy data; however, the memory task data, which were collected immediately after the copy task data, were strikingly different. Nine of the ten LH children organized their memory reproductions around the core rectangle and then continued to produce figures with relatively few additional details. Only two children in the LH injury group had organized their drawings around the core rectangle during the copy task. By contrast, only one of the nine children with RH injury organized the copy and memory reproductions around the core rectangle. Furthermore, the memory reproductions from the RH injury group were strikingly similar to their original copies in terms of both the piecemeal nature of their organizational strategy and the richness of pattern details represented.

In summary, the profiles of spatial deficit for children with LH and RH injury are quite distinct, consistent with profiles of deficit observed among adults, and evident very early in development. Longitudinal data indicate that with development, children with both LH and RH injury show considerable behavioral improvement, eventually achieving ceiling level performance on most spatial construction tasks. However, the time course over which this improvement occurs is protracted, and in cases where we have been able to examine the underlying processes associated with recovery, anomalous processing profiles have emerged (Stiles et al., 1998).

## Conclusion

This chapter reviewed findings from a large number of studies, all focused on some aspect of spatial cognitive development. The specific goal was to examine patterns of association between behavioral and neural development. The review was not intended to be a comprehensive survey of all facets of spatial information processing. Rather, it was designed to focus on several major spatial processing systems within both the dorsal and ventral visual pathways, and to use data on the anatomical organization and behavioral functioning of those systems at different points in development to try to understand how basic neural systems come to mediate specific functions. Several general points emerge from these data.

First, the basic neural systems mediating spatial functions appear to be specified quite early in development. Infants are able to track and retrieve hidden objects by at least the middle of the first year of life. Basic markers for control of spatial attention can be documented by

4 months of age and may be available earlier, and early brain injury results in at least subtle forms of neglect. Dissociable patterns of spatial analytic deficit can be documented in children with pre- or perinatal brain injury. All of these data are indicative of neural systems that are specified for processing certain types of information. However, the nature of that specification, and its degree, appears to be constrained. It is these constraints that lead to discussion of the remaining points.

Early specification of the neural system does not imply a fully or optimally functioning system early in development. The idea of partial cortical functioning is a crucial one here, and it should be coupled with the idea of partial behavioral functioning (see also Haith and Benson, 1998). Data from the spatial localization tasks make it clear that the neural and behavioral systems for spatial localization are *not* discretely absent or present at a given point in early development. For example, children who fail the standard hiding task solve it easily when a landmark is provided. Thus, at some level, the behavioral and neural systems for a spatial localization system must be available, but they are not functioning effectively enough to support the demands of the full range of task variation. A second example of limited functioning comes from the data on the early development of spatial attention. Data from normal infants suggest that, while the basic behavioral abilities to shift attention may be available early on, they are detectable only under certain temporal and spatial conditions, and those conditions change with development. Furthermore, data from the early lesion population suggest that neural mediation of apparently adultlike attentional processes may be mediated by different neural systems. Thus, the key to the notion of partial behavioral and neural mediation is to understand what the specific task demands are, and how they interact with and engage the available neural processing resources.

Finally, early specification may not determine final organization. There are large animal and human literatures on the concept of early brain plasticity (e.g., Nelson, 1999; Stiles, 1998, in press) that demonstrate quite clearly that (1) normal profiles of brain development require specific kinds of input, (2) variation in input can affect the pattern of neural organization, and (3) injury to the neural substrate can induce alternative patterns of neural organization. Within the spatial domain, it is clear that early injury results in persistent deficits. Findings from both the spatial attention and spatial analysis studies demonstrate that years after insult, specific deficits can be detected in a population of children with pre- and perinatal brain injury. However, the deficits are subtler than those observed in adults with comparable injury. These findings are consistent with a view of early brain development in which both early specification and plastic adaptation play prominent roles. Early injury constitutes a perturbation of normal development. Specific neural resources are lost, and there should be consequent impairment of the system, and that is precisely what is observed. However, it is also a developing system, and therefore a system with an exuberance of resources, the fate of which is determined in large measure by input. Thus, the magnitude and duration of the initial impairment may well depend on a range of factors such as the timing of insult, extent and location of injury, and specificity of the neural substrate.

ACKNOWLEDGEMENTS   This work was supported by the National Institute of Child Health and Human Development Grant R01-HD25077, National Institute of Neurological Disorders and Stroke Grant #P50-NS22343, and National Institute of Deafness and Communicative Disorders Grant #P50-DC01289. The author thanks the parents and children for their participation in the studies presented in this article.

## NOTES

1. It is possible that the effects of the postural manipulation are not effective across a wide age range. All of the infants in the reported study were 10 months of age at time of testing. Perhaps such manipulation would not be effective with younger children. That is an empirical question. In any case, maturation of frontal cortices alone cannot explain these findings.
2. One could argue that early or even delayed experience affects the onset of frontal lobe development, and that could be true. Bell and Fox (1996) have shown an association between self-locomotion and anterior-posterior EEG coherence. These findings are consistent with a large body of evidence documenting experience-expectant or learning-dependent change in other aspects of neural development (e.g., Greenough, Black, and Wallace, 1987). However, this kind of dynamic interaction is different from a simple maturation account. If experience induces development in frontal regions, what are the consequences of this kind of early or late induction for the rest of the developing cognitive or neural system?

## REFERENCES

AHMED, A., and T. RUFFMAN, 1998. Why do infants make A not B errors in a search task, yet show memory for the location of hidden objects in a nonsearch task? *Dev. Psychol.* 34(3):441–453.

AKSHOOMOFF, N. A., and J. STILES, 1995a. Developmental trends in visuospatial analysis and planning: I. Copying a complex figure. *Neuropsychology* 9(3):364–377.

AKSHOOMOFF, N. A., and J. STILES, 1995b. Developmental trends in visuospatial analysis and planning: II. Memory for a complex figure. *Neuropsychology* 9(3):378–389.

AKSHOOMOFF, N. A., and J. STILES, in press. Children's performance on the Rey-Osterrieth Complex Figure and the development of spatial analysis. In *The Handbook of Rey-Osterrieth Complex Figure Usage: Clinical and Research Applications*, J. Knight and E. Kaplan, eds.

AKSHOOMOFF, N. A., C. C. FEROLETO, R. E. DOYLE, AND J. STILES, submitted. The impact of early unilateral brain injury on perceptual organization and visual memory.

ANDERSON, R. A., L. H. SNYDER, D. C. BRADLEY, and J. XING, 1997. Multimodal representation of space in the posterior parietal cortex and its use in planning movements. *Annu. Rev. Neurosci.* 20:303–330.

ARENA, R., and G. GAINOTTI, 1978. Constructional apraxia and visuoperceptive disabilities in relation to laterality of cerebral lesions. *Cortex* 14:463–473.

BAILLARGEON, R., and J. DEVOS, 1991. Object permanence in young infants: Further evidence. *Child Dev.* 62:1227–1246.

BAILLARGEON, R., and M. GRABER, 1988. Evidence of location memory in 8-month-old infants in a nonsearch AB task. *Dev. Psychol.* 24(4):502–511.

BELL, M. A., and N. A. FOX, 1992. The relations between frontal brain electrical activity and cognitive development during infancy. *Child Dev.* 63:1142–1163.

BELL, M. A., and N. A. FOX, 1996. Crawling experience is related to changes in cortical organization during infancy: Evidence from EEG coherence. *Dev. Psychol.* 29(7):551–561.

BERTENTHAL, B. I., and J. J. CAMPOS, 1990. A systems approach to the organizing effects of self-produced locomotion during infancy. In *Advances in Infancy Research*, C. Rovee-Collier and L. P. Lipsitt, eds. Norwood, N.J.: Ablex, pp. 1–60.

BISIACH, E., and C. LUZZATTI, 1978. Unilateral neglect of representational space. *Cortex* 14(1):129–133.

BOUSSAOUD, D., R. DESIMONE, and L. G. UNGERLEIDER, 1991. Visual topography of area TEO in the macaque. *J. Comp. Neurol.* 306(4):554–575.

BRODMANN, K., 1909. *Vergleichende Lokalisationslehre der Grosshimrinde.* Leipzig: J. A. Barth.

BUTTERWORTH, G. E., N. JARRET, and L. HICKS, 1982. Spatio-temporal identity in infancy: Perceptual competence or conceptual deficit? *Dev. Psychol.* 18:435–449.

CASEY, B. J., J. D. COHEN, K. O. CRAVEN, R. DAVIDSON, C. A. NELSON, D. C. NOLL, X. HU, M. LOWE, B. ROSEN, C. TRUWIT, and P. TURSKI, 1998. Reproducibility of fMRI results across four institutions using a spatial working memory task. *Neuroimage* 8:249–261.

CHIBA, A. A., R. P. KESNER, and C. J. GIBSON, 1997. Memory for temporal order of new and familiar spatial location sequences: Role of the medial prefrontal cortex. *Learn. Mem.* 4:311–317.

CHUGANI, H. T., M. E. PHELPS, and J. C. MAZZIOTTA, 1987. Positron emission tomography study of human brain functional development. *Ann. Neurol.* 22(4):487–497.

CLOHESSY, A. B., M. I. POSNER, M. K. ROTHBART, and S. P. VECERA, 1991. The development of inhibition of return in early infancy. *J. Cogn. Neurosci.* 3(4):345–350.

COHEN, L. B., and B. A. YOUNGER, 1984. Infant perception of angular relations. *Infant Behav. Dev.* 7(1):37–47.

CORBETTA, M., 1998. Frontoparietal cortical networks for directing attention and the eye to visual locations: Identical, independent, or overlapping neural systems? *Proc. Natl. Acad. Sci. USA* 95(3):831–838.

CORBETTA, M., F. M. MIEZIN, G. L. SHULMAN, and S. E. PETERSEN, 1993. A PET study of visuospatial attention. *J. Neurosci.* 13(3):1202–1226.

CRAFT, S., and D. A. WHITE, 1994. Visual attention in children with perinatal brain injury: Asymmetric effects of bilateral lesions. *J. Cogn. Neurosci.* 6(2):165–173.

DELIS, D. C., M. G. KIEFNER, and A. J. FRIDLUND, 1988. Visuospatial dysfunction following unilateral brain damage: Dissociations in hierarchical hemispatial analysis. *J. Clin. Exp. Neuropsychol.* 10(4):421–431.

DELIS, D. C., L. C. ROBERTSON, and R. EFRON, 1986. Hemispheric specialization of memory for visual hierarchical stimuli. *Neuropsychologia* 24(2):205–214.

DERUELLE, C., and S. DE SCHONEN, 1991. Hemispheric asymmetries in visual pattern processing in infancy. *Brain Cogn.* 16:151–179.

DERUELLE, C., and S. DE SCHONEN, 1995. Pattern processing in infancy: Hemispheric differences in the processing of shape and location of visual components. *Infant Behav. Dev.* 18:123–132.

DESIMONE, R., T. ALBRIGHT, and C. GROSS, 1984. Stimulus selective properties of inferior temporal neurons in the macaque. *J. Neurosci.* 4:2051–2062.

DIAMOND, A., 1985. Development of the ability to use recall to guide action, as indicated by infants' performance on AB. *Child Dev.* 56:868–883.

DIAMOND, A., 1991. Frontal lobe involvement in cognitive changes during the first year of life. In *Maturation and Cognitive Development: Comparative and Cross-Cultural Perspectives*, K. R. Gibson and A. C. Petersen, eds. New York: De Gruyter, pp. 127–180.

DIAMOND, A., J. F. WERKER, and C. LALONDE, 1994. Toward understanding commonalities in the development of object search, detour navigation, categorization, and speech perception. In *Human Behavior and the Developing Brain*, G. Dawson and K. W. Fischer, eds. New York: Guilford Press, pp. 380–426.

DIAMOND, A., S. ZOLA-MORGAN, and L. R. SQUIRE, 1989. Successful performance by monkeys with lesions of the hippocampal formation of AB and object retrieval, two tasks that mark developmental changes in human infants. *Behav. Neurosci.* 103(3):526–537.

DOBKINS, K. R., and A. D. ALBRIGHT, 1994. What happens if it changes color when it moves? The nature of chromatic input to macaque visual area MT. *J. Neurosci.* 14(8):4854–4870.

DOBKINS, K. R., and T. D. ALBRIGHT, 1995. Behavioral and neural effects of chromatic isoluminance in the primate visual motion system. *Vis. Neurosci.* 12:321–332.

DOBKINS, K. R., and T. D. ALBRIGHT, 1998. The influence of chromatic information on visual motion processing in the primate visual system. In *High-Level Motion Processing: Computational, Neurobiological, and Psychophysical Perspectives*, T. Watanabe, ed. Cambridge, Mass.: MIT Press, pp. 53–94.

DOBKINS, K. R., and D. Y. TELLER, 1996a. Infant contrast detectors are selective for direction of motion. *Vis. Res.* 36(2):281–294.

DOBKINS, K. R., and D. Y. TELLER, 1996b. Infant motion: Detection (M:D) ratios for chromatically defined and luminance-defined moving stimuli. *Vis. Res.* 36(20):3293–3310.

FEENEY, S. M., and J. STILES, 1996. Spatial analysis: An examination of preschoolers' perception and construction of geometric patterns. *Dev. Psychol.* 32(5):933–941.

FERO, J. M., I. P. MARTINS, and L. TAVORA, 1984. Neglect in children. *Ann. Neurol.* 15(3):281–284.

FOX, N. A., and M. A. BELL, 1990. Electrophysiological indices of frontal lobe development: Relations to cognitive and affective behavior in human infants over the first year of life. *Ann. N.Y. Acad. Sci.* 608:677–704.

GAINOTTI, G., and C. TIACCI, 1970. Patterns of drawing disability in right and left hemispheric patients. *Neuropsychologia* 8(3):379–384.

GOLDMAN-RAKIC, P. S., 1987. Development of cortical circuitry and cognitive function. *Child Dev.* 58:601–622.

GOODALE, M. A., and A. D. MILNER, 1992. Separate visual pathways for perception and action. *Trends Neurosci.* 15(1):20–25.

GREENOUGH, W. T., J. E. BLACK, and C. S. WALLACE, 1987. Experience and brain development. *Child Dev.* 58:539–559.

HAITH, M. M., and J. B. BENSON, 1998. Infant cognition. In *Handbook of Child Psychology: Vol. 2. Cognition, Perception and Language*, 5th ed., D. Kuhn and R. Siegler, eds. New York: Wiley, pp. 199–254.

HARMAN, C., M. I. POSNER, M. K. ROTHBART, and L. THOMAS-THRAPP, 1994. Development orienting to locations and objects in human infants. *Can. J. Exp. Psychol.* 48(2):301–318.

HARRIS, P. L., 1987. Bringing order to the A-not-B error. *Monogr. Soc. Res. Child Dev.* 51(3):52–61.

HAUSER, M. D, 1999. Perseveration, inhibition and the prefrontal cortex: A new look. *Curr. Opin. Neurobiol.* 9:214–222.

HAXBY, J. V., C. L. GRADY, B. HORWITZ, L. G. UNGERLEIDER, M. MISHKIN, R. E. CARSON, P. HERSCOVITCH, M. B. SCHAPIRO, and S. I. RAPOPORT, 1991. Dissociation of object and spatial visual processing pathways in human extrastriate cortex. *Proc. Natl. Acad. Sci. USA* 88:1621–1625.

HAXBY, J. V., B. HORWITZ, L. G. UNGERLEIDER, J. M. MAISOG, P. PIETRINI, and C. L. GRADY, 1994. The functional organization of human extrastriate cortex: A PET-rCBF study of selective attention to faces and locations. *J. Neurosci.* 14(11):6336–6353.

HEILMAN, K. M., and E. VALENSTEIN, 1993. *Clinical Neuropsychology.* New York: Oxford University Press.

HELLER, W., and S. C. LEVINE, 1989. Unilateral neglect after early brain damage. *J. Clin. Exp. Neuropsychol.* 11:79.

HILLYARD, S. A., and L. ANLLO-VENTO, 1998. Event-related brain potentials in the study of visual selective attention. *Proc. Natl. Acad. Sci. USA* 95(3):781–787.

HOFSTADTER, M., and S. REZNICK, 1996. Response modality affects human infant delayed-response performance. *Child Dev.* 67:646–658.

HOOD, B. M., 1993. Inhibition of return produced by covert shifts of visual attention in 6-month-old infants. *Infant Behav. Dev.* 16:245–254.

HOROBIN, K., and L. ACREDOLO, 1986. The role of attentiveness, mobility history, and separation of hiding sites on Stage IV search behavior. *J. Exp. Child Psychol.* 41(1):114–127.

HUGDAHL, K., and G. CARLSSON, 1994. Dichotic listening and focused attention in children with hemiplegic cerebral palsy. *J. Clin. Exp. Neuropsychol.* 16(1):84–92.

IVRY, R. B., and L. C. ROBERTSON, 1998. *The Two Sides of Perception.* Cambridge, Mass.: MIT Press.

JACOBS, B., H. T. CHUGANI, A. VIVEKANAND, S. CHEN, M. E. PHELPS, D. B. POLLACK, and M. J. RALEIGH, 1995. Developmental changes in brain metabolism in sedated rhesus macaques and vervet monkeys revealed by positron emission tomography. *Cereb. Cortex* 3:222–233.

JOHNSON, M. H., M. I. POSNER, and M. K. ROTHBART, 1994. Facilitation of saccades toward a covertly attended location in early infancy. *Psychol. Sci.* 5(2):90–93.

JOHNSON, M. H., and L. A. TUCKER, 1996. The development and temporal dynamics of spatial orienting in infants. *J. Exp. Child Psychol.* 63:171–188.

JOHNSON, M. H., L. A. TUCKER, J. STILES, and D. TRAUNER, 1998. Visual attention in infants with perinatal brain damage: Evidence of the importance of anterior lesions. *Dev. Sci.* 1(1):53–58.

JOHNSON, P. B., S. FERRAINA, L. BIANCHI, and R. CAMINITI, 1996. Cortical networks for visual reaching: Physiological and anatomical organization of frontal and parietal lobe arm regions. *Cereb. Cortex* 6(2):102–119.

JONIDES, J., E. E. SMITH, R. A. KOEPPE, E. AWH, S. MINOSHIMA, and M. A. MINTUN, 1993. Spatial working memory in humans as revealed by PET. *Nature* 363:623–625.

KERMOIAN, R., and J. J. CAMPOS, 1988. Locomotor experience: A facilitator of spatial cognitive development. *Child Dev.* 59(4):908–917.

KITTERLE, F. L., S. CHRISTMAN, and J. HELLIGE, 1990. Hemispheric differences are found in the identification, but not detection of low versus high spatial frequencies. *Percept. Psychophysics* 48:297–306.

KITTERLE, F. L., J. B. HELLIGE, and S. CHRISTMAN, 1992. Visual hemispheric asymmetries depend on which spatial frequencies are task relevant. *Brain Cogn.* 20:308–314.

KITTERLE, F. L., and L. M. SELIG, 1991. Visual field effects in the discrimination of sine wave gratings. *Percept. Psychophysics* 50:15–18.

LAMB, M. R., L. C. ROBERTSON, and R. T. KNIGHT, 1989. Attention and interference in the processing of global and local information: Effects of unilateral temporal-parietal junction lesions. *Neuropsychologia* 27(4):471–483.

LAMB, M. R., L. C. ROBERTSON, and R. T. KNIGHT, 1990. Component mechanisms underlying the processing of hierarchically organized patterns: Inferences from patients with unilateral cortical lesions. *J. Exp. Psychol.: Learn. Mem. Cogn.* 16:471–483.

LIVINGSTONE, M. S., and D. H. HUBEL, 1984. Anatomy and physiology of a color system in primate visual cortex. *J. Neurosci.* 4:309–356.

MALACH, R., J. B. REPPAS, K. K. KWONG, H. JIANG, W. A. KENNEDY, P. J. LEDDEN, T. J. BRADY, B. R. ROSEN, and R. B. TOOTELL, 1995. Object-related activity revealed by functional magnetic resonance imaging in human occipital cortex. *Proc. Natl. Acad. Sci. USA* 92(18):8135–8139.

MARANGOLO, P., E. DI PACE, R. RAFAL, and D. SCABINI, 1998. Effects of parietal lesions on humans on color and location priming. *J. Cogn. Neurosci.* 10(6):704–716.

MARTIN, M., 1979. Hemispheric specialization for local and global processing. *Neuropsychologia* 17:33–40.

MARTINEZ, A., L. ANLLO-VENTO, and S. A. HILLYARD, 1997. Brain electrical activity during selective attention to spatial frequency. *Soc. Neurosci. Abstr.*

MARTINEZ, A., P. MOSES, L. FRANK, R. BUXTON, E. WONG, and J. STILES, 1997. Hemispheric asymmetries in global and local processing: Evidence from fMRI. *NeuroReport* 8:1685–1689.

MATTHEWS, A., A. E. ELLIS, and C. A. NELSON, 1996. Development of preterm and full-term infant ability on AB, recall memory, transparent barrier detour, and means-end tasks. *Child Dev.* 67:2658–2676.

McFIE, J., M. F. PIERCY, and O. L. ZANGWILL, 1950. Visual-spatial agnosia associated with lesions of the right cerebral hemisphere. *Brain* 73:167–190.

McFIE, J., and O. L. ZANGWILL, 1960. Visual-constructive disabilities associated with lesions of the left cerebral hemisphere. *Brain* 83:243–259.

MERIGAN, W. H., and J. MAUNSELL, 1993. How parallel are the primate visual pathways? *Annu. Rev. Neurosci.* 16:369–402.

NELSON, C. A., 1999. Neural plasticity and human development. *Curr. Direct. Psychol. Sci.* 8(2):42–45.

NELSON, C. A., J. LIN, L. J. CARVER, C. S. MONK, K. M. THOMAS, and C. L. TRUWIT, 2000. Functional neuroanatomy of spatial working memory in children. *Dev. Psychol.* 36:109–116.

PALMER, S. E., 1977. Hierarchical structure in perceptual representation. *Cogn. Psychol.* 9(4):441–474.

PALMER, S. E., 1980. What makes triangles point: Local and global effects in configurations of ambiguous triangles. *Cogn. Psychol.* 12(3):285–305.

PALMER, S. E., and N. M. BUCHER, 1981. Configural effects in perceived pointing of ambiguous triangles. *J. Exp. Psychol.: Hum. Percept. Perform.* 7(1):88–114.

PIAGET, J., 1952. The origins of intelligence in children. New York: International Universities Press.

POSNER, M. I., 1980. Orienting of attention. *Quart. J. Exp. Psychol.* 32:3–25.

POSNER, M. I., and Y. COHEN, 1980. Attention and the control of movements. In *Tutorials in Motor Behavior,* G. E. Stelmach and J. Requin, eds. Amsterdam: North Holland Publishing, pp. 243–258.

POSNER, M. I., and S. E. PETERSEN, 1990. The attention system of the human brain. *Annu. Rev. Neurosci.* 13:25–42.

POSNER, M. I., R. D. RAFAL, L. S. CHOATE, and J. VAUGHN, 1985. Inhibition of return: Neural basis and function. *Cogn. Neuropsychol.* 2(3):211–228.

POSNER, M. I., J. A. WALKER, F. J. FRIEDRICH, and R. D. RAFAL, 1984. Effects of parietal injury on covert orienting of attention. *J. Neurosci.* 4(7):1863–1874.

RAFAL, R. D., 1994. Neglect. *Curr. Opin. Neurobiol.* 4:231–236.

RAFAL, R. D., and L. ROBERTSON, 1995. In *The Neurology of Visual Attention,* M. S. Gazzaniga, ed. Cambridge, Mass.: MIT Press.

ROBERTSON, L. C., 1992. Perceptual organization and attentional search in cognitive deficits. In *Cognitive Neuropsychology in Clinical Practice,* D. I. Margolin, ed. New York: Oxford University Press,

ROBERTSON, L. C., and D. C. DELIS, 1986. "Part-whole" processing in unilateral brain damaged patients: Dysfunction of hierarchical organization. *Neuropsychologia* 24(3):363–370.

ROBERTSON, L. C., M. R. LAMB, and R. T. KNIGHT, 1988. Effects of lesions of temporal-parietal junction on perceptual and attentional processing in humans. *J. Neurosci.* 8:3757–3769.

SCHNEIDER, G. E., 1967. Contrasting visuomotor functions of tectum and cortex in the golden hamster. *Psychol. Forsch.* 31(1):52–62.

SELTZER, B., and D. N. PANDYA, 1978. Afferent cortical connections and architectonics of the superior temporal sulcus and surrounding cortex in the rhesus monkey. *Brain Res.* 149(1):1–24.

SERGENT, J., 1982. The cerebral balance of power: Confrontation or cooperation? *J. Exp. Psychol.: Hum. Percept. Perform.* 8:253–272.

Smith, E. E., J. Jonides, and R. A. Koeppe, 1996. Dissociating verbal and spatial working memory using PET. *Cereb. Cortex* 6:11–20.

Smith, E. E., J. Jonides, R. A. Koeppe, E. Awh, E. H. Schumacher, and S. Minoshima, 1995. Spatial versus object working memory: PET investigations. *J. Cogn. Neurosci.* 7(3):337–356.

Smith, L. B., and D. Kemler, 1977. Developmental trends in free classification: Evidence for a new conceptualization of perceptual development. *J. Exp. Child Psychol.* 24:279–298.

Smith, L. B., E. Thelen, R. Titzer, and D. McLin, 1999. Knowing in the context of acting: The task dynamics of the A-not-B error. *Psychol. Rev.* 106(2):235–260.

Spencer, J., L. B. Smith, and E. Thelen, 1997. Tests of a dynamic systems account of the A-not-B error: Perseverative reaching by 2- to 3-year olds. Unpublished manuscript.

Stiles, J., 1998. The effects of early focal brain injury on lateralization of cognitive function. *Curr. Direct. Psychol. Sci.* 7(1):21–26.

Stiles, J., in press. Neural plasticity and cognitive development.

Stiles, J., E. A. Bates, D. Thal, D. Trauner, and J. Reilly, 1998. Linguistic, cognitive, and affective development in children with pre- and perinatal focal brain injury: A ten-year overview from the San Diego Longitudinal Project. In *Advances in Infancy Research,* C. Rovee-Collier, L. P. Lipsitt, and H. Hayne, eds. Stamford, Conn.: Ablex, pp. 131–163.

Stiles, J., P. Moses, K. Roe, E. Wong, and R. Buxton, 1999. Developmental change in lateralization of global-local processing: Evidence from hemifield and fMRI studies. Paper presented at the Symposium on Developmental Applications of fMRI, Society for Research in Child Development, Albuquerque, New Mexico, April 17, 1999.

Stiles, J., and C. Stern, in press. Developmental change in spatial cognitive processing: Complexity effects and block construction performance in preschool children. *J. Cogn. Devel.*

Stiles, J., C. Stern, D. Trauner, and R. Nass, 1996. Developmental change in spatial grouping activity among children with early focal brain injury: Evidence from a modeling task. *Brain Cogn.* 31:46–62.

Stiles, J., D. Trauner, M. Engel, and R. Nass, 1997. The development of drawing in children with congenital focal brain injury: Evidence for limited functional recovery. *Neuropsychologia* 35(3):299–312.

Stiles-Davis, J., J. Janowsky, M. Engel, and R. D. Nass, 1988. Drawing ability in four young children with congenital unilateral brain lesions. *Neuropsychologia* 26(3):359–371.

Swindell, C. S., A. L. Holland, D. Fromm, and J. B. Greenhouse, 1988. Characteristics of recovery of drawing ability in left and right brain-damaged patients. *Brain Cogn.* 7(1):16–30.

Tada, W. L., and J. Stiles, 1996. Developmental change in children's analysis of spatial patterns. *Dev. Psychol.* 32(5):951–970.

Tanaka, K., H. Saito, Y. Fukuda, and M. Moriya, 1991. Coding visual images of objects in the inferotemporal cortex of the macaque monkey. *J. Neurophysiol.* 66:170–189.

Temple, C., 1997. *Developmental Cognitive Neuropsychology.* East Sussex, UK: Psychology Press.

Thompson, N. M., L. Ewing-Cobb, J. M. Fletcher, M. E. Miner, and H. S. Levin, 1991. Left unilateral neglect in a preschool child. *Dev. Med. Child Neurol.* 33:636–644.

Trauner, D. A., and A. Ballantyne, submitted. Hemispatial neglect after perinatal stroke.

Trevarthen, C. B., 1968. Two mechanisms of vision in primates. *Psychol. Forsch.* 31(4):299–348.

Ungerleider, L. G., and M. Mishkin, 1982. Two cortical visual systems. In *Analysis of Visual Behavior,* D. J. Ingle, M. A. Goodale, and R. J. W. Mansfield, eds. Cambridge, Mass.: MIT Press.

Valenza, E., F. Simion, and C. Umilta, 1994. Inhibition of return in newborn infants. *Infant Behav. Dev.* 17:293–302.

Van Essen, D. C., C. H. Anderson, and D. J. Felleman, 1992. Information processing in the primate visual system: An integrated systems perspective. *Science* 255:419–423.

Vicari, S., J. Stiles, C. Stern, and A. Resca, 1998. Spatial grouping activity in children with early cortical and subcortical lesions. *Dev. Med. Child Neurol.* 40:90–94.

von Bonin, G., and P. Bailey, 1947. *The Neocortex of Macaca mulatta.* Urbana, Ill.: University of Illinois Press.

Vurpillot, E., 1976. *The Visual World of the Child.* New York: International Universities Press.

Wellman, H. M., M. Henry, D. Cross, and K. Bartsch, 1987. Infant search and object permanence: A meta-analysis of the A-not-B error. *Monogr. Soc. Res. Child Dev.* 51(3):1–51.

Welsh, M. C., and B. F. Pennington, 1988. Assessing frontal lobe functioning in children: Views from developmental psychology. *Dev. Neuropsychol.* 4(3):199–230.

Wise, S. P., D. Boussaoud, P. B. Johnson, and R. Caminiti, 1997. Premotor and parietal cortex: Corticocortical connectivity and combinatorial computations. *Annu. Rev. Neurosci.* 20:25–42.

Wong-Riley, M. T. T., 1979. Changes in the visual system of monocularly sutured or enucleated cats demonstrable with cytochrome oxidase histochemistry. *Brain Res.* 171:11–28.

# 28 Bridging the Gap between Cognition and Developmental Neuroscience: The Example of Number Representation

SUSAN CAREY

ABSTRACT  Developmental cognitive neuroscience necessarily begins with a characterization of the developing mind. One cannot discover the neural underpinnings of cognition without detailed understanding of the representational capacities that underlie thought. Characterizing the developing mind involves specifying the evolutionarily given building blocks from which human conceptual abilities are constructed, describing what develops, and discovering the computational mechanisms that underlie the process of change. Here, I present the current state of the art with respect to one example of conceptual understanding: the representation of number. Lessons for developmental cognitive neuroscience are drawn at two levels of analysis: first, structural analogy between developmental processes described at the neural level and at the cognitive level, and second, challenges posed at the level of systems neuroscience.

## Bridging biology and psychology

The past 20 years have witnessed stunning advances in our understanding of how the brain develops (for reviews aimed at drawing implications for cognitive neuroscience, see Gazzaniga, 1995, 1999; Johnson, 1997; Quartz and Sejnowski, 1997). Similarly, new techniques for experimental work with human infants have yielded a wealth of evidence concerning the unfolding of early perceptual, conceptual, and linguistic capacities (for illustrative studies, see Baillargeon, 1993; Carey and Spelke, 1994; Kuhl, 1999; Leslie, 1994; Mandler, 2000; Marcus et al., 1999; Saffran, Aslin, and Newport, 1996; Spelke et al., 1992; Teller, 1999). In spite of the advances on each of these fronts, Rakic's comment in his introduction to the Neural and Psychological Development section of the 1995 version of *The Cognitive Neurosciences* (Rakic, 1995) still stands: "Yet the connections

SUSAN CAREY  Department of Psychology, New York University, New York, New York.

between neuroanatomy, neurochemistry, and neurodevelopment, on the one hand, and the behavioral research in cognition, on the other, are rather tenuous." (See Nelson and Bloom, 1997, for a similar lament.) What is needed to bridge the gap, to forge less tenuous connections?

SEEKING STRUCTURAL PARALLELS; STRUCTURAL ANALOGY  Developmental neurobiology aims to understand the mechanisms underlying cell differentiation, cell formation, cell migration, axon migration, synapse formation, dendrite growth, and so forth. Developmental psychology (of humans) aims to understand the formation of the functional architecture of the mind (how memory, emotion, attention, executive function, etc., come into being) as well as the origins of concepts, language, and the computational capacities that constitute human reason.

Biology and psychology provide different levels of analysis, but practitioners of the two disciplines share fundamental intellectual goals. Both seek to understand the role of the genetic code in structuring the developing brain and mind, and both seek to specify the huge variety of processes that determine the path to the adult state. Both assume that the functional architecture of the brain, its connectivity and patterns of neural activity, provide the underpinnings of the mind, and both assume that a functional account of what the brain does (i.e., an understanding of the mind) is a necessary guide to our understanding of how the brain works. Therefore, detailed understanding of mechanism at one level of analysis is, at the very least, a source of structural analogy for mechanism at the other.

We appeal to a *structural analogy* whenever we see a process at one level as similar to a process at the other, in the absence of any claim that we have reduced one to the other or that we have actually discovered the neural underpinnings of some cognitive ability or some developmental change. For example, we make a structural analogy when we see the similarity between the processes of overproduction and subsequent selection in synaptic development (e.g., Rakic et al., 1986; Rakic, Bourgeois, and Goldman-Rakic, 1994) and the processes of selection in phonological development (Kuhl et al., 1992; Werker and Lalonde, 1988) or parameter setting in syntactic development. In these examples, going beyond structural analogy would require discovering what processes of neural selection (if any) subserve losing access to previously available phonological distinctions or choosing among previously specified syntactic parameters. Similarly, we make a structural analogy when we see the similarity between neural activity–driven mechanisms of axon or dendrite growth and evidence-driven formation of new representational resources (Quartz and Sejnowski, 1997). Going beyond this structural analogy would require discovering actual cases of axon or dendritic growth that underlie any actual case of perceptual or cognitive development.

Structural analogies are useful, for they force us to think of mechanisms at a very abstract level. But we must not be fooled into thinking that they go very far in closing the gap. Going beyond structural analogy will require discovering the neural mechanisms underlying actual cases of representational change. Because structural analogies hold at an abstract level, they are fruitful as each discipline looks to the other for broad insights into how to think about development, such as how to separate the role of genetically specified constraints from the role of experientially derived information on development, the relative roles of selective and constructive processes in development, continuity versus discontinuity in development, and so on. For example, developmental psychologists who worry about whether sense can be made of the claim that representational and computational capacities, even knowledge itself, may be innate should study neurobiology. On the assumption that patterns of neural connectivity underlie representational and computational capacities, studies of genetic constraints on the growth of neural connectivity provide a relevant existence proof for genetic specification of such capacities, albeit only at the level of structural analogy. There is an explosion of knowledge concerning the genetic mechanisms subserving brain development. For instance, Levitt (1999) described the establishment of the earliest rough map of the nervous system—the hierarchy of molecular interactions that determine cell differentiation and the production of axon guidance proteins. Rakic (1999) described the mechanisms by which the total size of the cerebral cortex is determined, as well as ways in which the six cortical layers are formed. Similarly, much is known about the regionalization of the cerebral cortex, and the great variety of mechanisms by which its final cytoarchitectonic structure is determined.

Besides the intrinsic fascination of this elegant work, there are many lessons for developmental psychologists. First (and most obviously), stimulus-driven activity cannot modulate brain connectivity until there is enough connected to support the activity. Even the earliest patterns of connections are highly organized, and largely under genetic control. Second, this work shows that it is possible to disentangle genetic and (chemical) environmental factors in determining the precise course of neural development, and to further disentangle these two together from the role of both intrinsically and extrinsically driven neural activity. Progress in establishing the role of genes in determining the details of neural development lends hope that there can be comparable progress in establishing the respects in which genetic factors contribute to the development of cognitive architecture and conceptual representations of the world.

Conversely, behavioral work establishes early emerging representational capacities (providing evidence relevant to *possible* evidentiary sources of the relevant knowledge). For example, evidence that neonates prefer face to nonface stimuli (cf. Morton, Johnson, and Maurer, 1990) suggests innate face representations that must not have needed extended exposures to faces for their construction, and looking time experiments that show that 2-month-olds represent objects as spatiotemporally continuous, even under conditions of occlusion, and subject to solidity constraints (e.g., Spelke et al., 1992) shows that experience manipulating objects is not necessary for these developments. In addition, formal work (e.g., learnability proofs; see Gold, 1967, Osherson, Stob, and Weinstein, 1986, Wexler and Culicover, 1980; connectionist modeling; see Elman et al., 1996) explores how different models of the learning process, different ideas about the initial state, and different ideas about the final state constrain each other. Such work also contributes to conceptual clarity with regard to distinguishing nature from nurture and studying their interactions.

Still, one must not oversell what can be learned from structural analogy. Structural analogy is important *because* of the gap between what is known about conceptual development from behavioral and computational work, on the one hand, and developmental neurobiology, on the other. It's because we don't yet know how *any* conceptual knowledge, language, or reasoning is represented in the nervous system (at the level of neural connections and activity) that we must appeal to structural analogy in our thinking about how the developing brain underlies and in turn is shaped by the developing mind.

CLOSING THE GAP—THE LEVEL OF SYSTEMS NEUROSCIENCE, DIAGNOSTIC MARKERS  Besides seeking structural parallels between mechanisms of developmental change specified at different levels, there are many more direct methods of building bridges between the two disciplines, as the chapters in the present volume attest. The most obvious derives from a premise that articulates much of the discipline of cognitive neuroscience: Large regions of the brain participate in specialized neural circuits, the functions of which may be studied through a combination of research methods—behavioral, imaging, computational, and lesion (experimentally produced in animal studies, neuropsychological studies with humans). One descriptive goal of developmental cognitive neuroscience is to discover when functions known to be subserved by specific brain regions come on-line. In some cases, young children fail tasks on which failure is a *diagnostic marker* of specific brain damage in adults. Such a finding is a source of hypothesis—perhaps the child's failure is due to immaturity of the neural structure required for adult performance. Of course, there are always alternative explanations for the young child's failure. It may be, for instance, that the child simply has not yet mastered the knowledge required to perform the task. Such alternatives may be empirically tested. Notice that such research only partially fills the gap—and that, only insofar as the neural substrate of the computations carried out by the circuit is fully understood, as well as the neurobiological mechanisms underlying the development of the circuit. These conditions, I submit, have not yet been met in any domain of perceptual, conceptual, or linguistic representation.

Goldman-Rakic (Goldman, 1971) provided a paradigmatic example of diagnostic marker research. She noted that young rhesus monkeys (less than 2 months of age) performed as did adult monkeys with lesions in dorsolateral prefrontal cortex on the marker task of delayed response. Shown food hidden in one of two or more wells, distracted, and then allowed to search, adult monkeys with prefrontal lesions (and young infant monkeys) often fail to retrieve the food, especially with repeated trials and with delays of more than a few seconds. Rather, a variety of perseverative patterns of response emerge. The infant performance develops to adult levels by 4 months of age. Infant monkeys lesioned in dorsolateral prefrontal cortex do not undergo normal development; their performance never improves,

bolstering the inference that normal development involves dorsolateral prefrontal maturation.

This particular case is of great interest to developmental psychologists because of the observation that the delayed response task is almost identical to Piaget's object permanence task (Piaget, 1955). Diamond and Goldman-Rakic (1989; see also Diamond, 1991) established that infant monkey development on the A/not B object permanence task between ages 2 and 4 months matches, in parametric detail, human infant development between 7 and 11 months, implicating frontal development in the human case as well. Confirmatory evidence is provided by development of other marker tasks for frontal development, such as detour reaching, that are conceptually unrelated to object permanence. Thus, this work provides an alternative explanation to Piaget's for young infants' failures on object permanence tasks. Rather than reflecting different representations of objects, as Piaget believed, the failures reflect immature executive function (means/ends planning, inhibition of competing responses, deployment of working memory).

We do not yet know the nature of the maturational change involving prefrontal dorsolateral cortex between 2 and 4 months in rhesus and between 7 and 11 months in humans, specified at the level of the neurobiological mechanisms. The method of diagnostic markers does not completely close the gap; it establishes phenomena related to developing brain function for which neurobiological underpinnings are yet to be worked out.

OTHER PARTIAL STEPS  The method of diagnostic markers depends upon studies of brain-damaged human beings and lesion studies in animals. Studies of brain-damaged children (whether due to lesions or genetic abnormalities) add relevant data concerning dissociations of function and plasticity during development. Noninvasive imaging techniques add new methods to the arsenal of tools for bridging the disciplines at the level of systems neuroscience (for a discussion of how imaging techniques might serve this purpose, see Nelson and Bloom, 1997). These tools are by nature interdisciplinary; they require precise psychological task analysis to provide interpretable data concerning the functions of the brain regions implicated in any given lesion or imaging study.

A common thread runs through my remarks so far—the importance of understanding the mind to understanding the brain. Before turning to an extended developmental example, I explicitly defend this assumption.

## Starting from an understanding of the mind

It is obvious to any psychologist, rightly or wrongly, that any functional/computational understanding of the brain must begin with a functional/computational understanding of the mind—of perception, action, language, cognition, and reasoning. Consider those cases in which satisfying work bridging the gap has been accomplished. Much is known, for example, about how neural computations subserve color vision, from retinal processes on (e.g., Cornsweet, 1970; Wald, 1950). But *how* the brain codes for color vision was understood, at least in broad outlines, for decades before anything about the neural implementation was discovered— from straightforward psychophysical studies of color mixture, color contrast, and from studies of abnormal color vision (color blindness). Research that stemmed from Helmholz (1910) and from Hering (1920) guided the search for neural underpinnings. How could it be otherwise, given the bewildering complexity of the brain?

Generalizing this point to the topic at hand, it is equally obvious that *developmental cognitive neuroscience* must begin with a functional/computational understanding of the developing mind. This requires empirical study of the initial representations of the world available to infants, including a specification of their representational format, and detailing the computations performed over them. It also requires characterizing *development*, specifying the ways in which these initial representations become enriched over time and specifying the learning and maturational mechanisms involved.

The study of the development of numerical representations bears on two fundamental debates couched at the level of structural analogy. One concerns the relative importance of selection mechanisms and constructive mechanisms in both neural development and cognitive development (for a summary of this controversy and a defense of the importance of constructivism, see Quartz and Sejnowski, 1997). The two parallel selection/constructivism debates (within psychology and within neurobiology) are merely structural analogies. For example, at present there is no way to bridge the gap between parameter-setting models of language acquisition, or the narrowing of phonological representations (selection processes), and mechanisms of pruning of synaptic connections (also a selection process). These are *far* analogies; it is quite possible that the mechanisms that underlie parameter setting or the narrowing of phonological space are not neural selection processes of the sort that prune synaptic connections. At the level of cognitive development, a related debate concerns continuity of representational resources. Does cognitive development involve, at least in part, the construction of genuinely new representational resources, or is the strong continuity hypothesis of theorists such as Fodor (1975), Macnamara (1982, 1987), and Pinker (1984) true? If constructivism is correct, through what mechanisms are new representational resources created? These questions must be answered at psychological and computational levels before any search for neurological underpinnings may even begin.

In the rest of this chapter, I shall argue on the developmental discontinuity and constructivist side of the debates, at least in the case of number representations. The point of this example is to show what sort of understanding of the developing mind is necessary to begin to bridge the gap. I shall argue that the level of detail concerning representational format that is need to inform current debates at the level of structural analogy is also needed to guide the search for neural underpinnings at the level of systems neuroscience.

## An extended example—The development of number representations

PRELINGUISTIC REPRESENTATIONS OF NUMBER Data from many different paradigms provide convergent evidence that preverbal infants represent individual tokens of various types (events, syllables, objects) and keep track of the number of individuals in an array, in at least some contexts. Habituation experiments provide one sort of evidence. In these, babies are presented with arrays containing a fixed number of individuals until they decrease their attention to the arrays, and their sensitivity to numerosity is inferred from their recovery of interest to new arrays containing a new, but not the old, number of individuals. Successful discrimination of 1 vs. 2 or 2 vs. 3 individuals has been shown for syllables (Bijeljac-Babic, Bertoncini, and Mehler, 1991); for successive actions (Wynn, 1996); for dots varying in position (Antell and Keating, 1983, Starkey and Cooper, 1980), for pictures of objects varying in shape, size, and position (Strauss and Curtis, 1981; Starkey, Spelke, and Gelman, 1983); and for moving forms undergoing occlusion (Van Loosbroek and Smitsman, 1990), at ages varying from birth to 6 months. In contrast, infants often fail to discriminate 3 from 4 elements (Strauss and Curtis, 1981) and they consistently fail to discriminate 4 from 5, 4 from 6, or 8 from 12 elements (Strauss and Curtis, 1981; Starkey and Cooper, 1980; Xu and Spelke, 2000). In one study, however, 6-month-old infants were found to discriminate 8 from 16 dots (Xu and Spelke, 2000). As we shall see, not all of these studies adequately controlled for *nonnumerical* bases of discrimination, but others (e.g., Wynn, 1996; Xu and Spelke, 2000) did. Insofar as the controls are adequate, these studies reveal representation of number in the sense of discrimination on the basis of numerical differences. But confidence in these representations as *number* representations requires more; it is important that computations defined over them have at least some of the conceptual role of number representations. This condition is met: Infants use their representations of number to compute more/less and carry out simple addition and subtraction.

Some of the evidence for number-relevant computations derives from experiments using the violation of expectancy looking time method. Wynn's (1992a) classic addition/subtraction studies, now replicated in many laboratories (Koechlin, Dehaene, and Mehler, 1997; Simon, Hespos, and Rochat, 1995; Uller et al., 1999) suggest that babies represent the numerical relations among small sets of objects. In a typical experiment, an object is placed on an empty stage while the baby watches; then a screen is raised that covers the object, a second object is introduced behind the screen, and the screen is lowered to reveal either one object or two. In this $1 + 1 = 2$ vs. 1 event, infants of ages ranging from 4 to 10 months look longer at the impossible outcome of 1 than at the possible outcome of 2. That infants expect precisely 2 objects is shown by the fact that they also look longer at the impossible outcome of 3 in a $1 + 1 = 2$ vs. 3 event (Wynn, 1992a). Infants also succeed at $2 - 1 = 2$ vs. 1. Success with larger numbers such as $3 - 1$ and $2 + 1$ is less robust (Baillargeon, Miller, and Constantino, 1993; Uller and Leslie, 2000).

Preliminary data from a third paradigm, developed by Hauser, Carey, and Hauser (2000) to study spontaneous representation of number by free-ranging rhesus macaques, suggests that prelinguistic infants represent the ordinal relations among small sets of different numbers of objects. Each infant gets only one trial; these are totally spontaneous number representations. Ten- and 12-month-old infants watched as an experimenter put a number of small cookies successively into one opaque container and a different number into a different opaque container, whereupon they were allowed to crawl to the container of their choice. Infants of both ages approached a container with 2 cookies over a container with just 1 cookie, and a container of 3 cookies over one with just 2 cookies. Infants of both ages failed at choices involving 3 vs. 4, as well as at choices involving 3 vs. 6; see figure 28.1 (Feigenson et al., 2000).

As in Wynn's paradigm, infants must compute $1 + 1$ or $1 + 1 + 1$. In addition, this is the first demonstration of ordinal comparison of two sets represented in mem-

ory in prelinguistic infants. In sum, the violation of expectancy studies and the choice studies suggest that preverbal infants discriminate among sets on the basis of numerosity and represent numerical relations among sets, such as $1 + 1 = 2$ and $2 > 1$. Numerical representations predate language learning, and thus the mechanisms by which they are formed do not involve mastering the culturally constructed, explicit, integer-list representations of natural language. Indeed, these demonstrations open the question of continuity. Is the integer-list representation ("one, two, three, four, five, . . .") and the counting algorithm merely an explicit form of the representational system underlying these infant capacities? Or is the integer-list representation discontinuous with those that underlie the infant's behavior? To begin to answer this question, we must consider the format of infants' representation of number.

GELMAN AND GALLISTEL'S CONTINUITY HYPOTHESIS
Gelman and Gallistel (1978) suggested that infants establish numerical representations through a nonverbal counting procedure: Babies represent a list of symbols, or "numerons," such as &, ^, #, $, @. Entities to be counted are put in 1:1 correspondence with items on this list, always proceeding through it in the same order. The number of items in the set being counted is represented by the last item on the list reached, and its numerical value is determined by the ordinal position of that item in the list. For example, in the list &, ^, #, $, @, the symbol ^ represents 2, because ^ is the second item in the list.

Gelman and Gallistel's proposal for the nonlinguistic representation of number is a paradigm example of a continuity hypothesis, for this is exactly how languages with explicit integer lists represent the positive integers. On their hypothesis, the child learning "one, two, three, four, five, . . ." need only solve a mapping problem: identify the list in their language that expresses the antecedently available numeron list. Originally learning to count in Russian should be no more difficult than learning to count in Russian once one knows how to count in English.

WYNN'S EASE OF LEARNING ARGUMENT AGAINST THE GELMAN/GALLISTEL CONTINUITY PROPOSAL Between the ages of 2 and 4 years, most children learn to count; and contrary to the predictions of a numeron-list theory, learning to count is not a trivial matter (Fuson, 1988; Wynn, 1990, 1992b). Of course, this fact in itself does not defeat the continuity hypothesis, for we do not know in advance how difficult it is to learn an arbitrary list of words or to discover that one such list (e.g., "one,

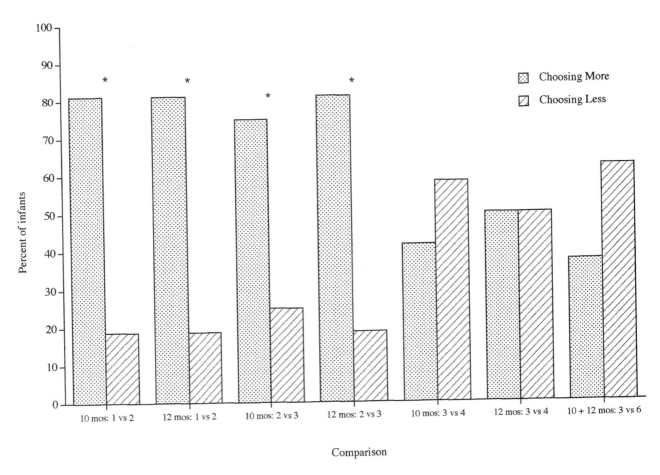

FIGURE 28.1   Percent choice of container with greater number of crackers.

two, three, . . ." rather than "a, b, c, . . ." or "Monday, Tuesday, Wednesday, . . .") is the list in English that represents number. However, Wynn's (1990, 1992b) studies show that children have difficulty discovering the meanings of specific number words even after they have solved these two problems. The sequence in which children learn the meanings of the number words therefore is at odds with that predicted by the continuity thesis.

Wynn began by confirming that young children do not know the numerical meanings of the words in the count sequence. First, she identified children who could count at least to six when asked "how many" objects there were in an array of toys. These 2–3-year-old children honored 1:1 correspondence in their counts, and used a consistently ordered list, although sometimes a nonstandard one such as "one, two, four, six, seven, . . ." She then showed that if such a child were given a pile of objects and asked to give the adult "two" or "three" or any other number the child could use in the game of counting, most 2- and 3-year-old children failed. Instead, young children grabbed a random num-

ber of objects (always more than one) and handed them to the experimenter. Also, shown two cards depicting, for example, 2 vs. 3 balloons and asked to indicate which card had 2 balloons on it, young children responded at chance. Analyses of within-child consistency between the "give $n$" and "which card has $n$" tasks bolstered the conclusion that young children count for more than a year before they learn what the words in the count sequence mean: i.e., before they learn how "one, two, three, four, five, . . ." represents number.

There is one more observation of Wynn's that is important to the evaluation of the Gelman/Gallistel continuity hypothesis. Wynn (1990, 1992b) showed that from the beginning of learning to count, children know what "one" means. They can pick one object from a pile when asked, and they correctly distinguish a card with "one fish" from a card with "three fish." Furthermore, they know that the other words in the count sequence contrast with one. They always grab a random number of objects greater than one when asked to hand over "two, three, four, . . ." objects, and they also successfully point to a card with three fish when it is contrasted with a card with one, even though their choices are random when "three" is contrasted with "two." Thus, Wynn's studies provide evidence that toddlers learn the English count list and identify the list as relevant to number very early on (younger than age 2½): They know what "one" means, they use "two, three, four, etc.," in contrast with "one," and they only use the number words above one when presented with sets greater than one. They are in this state of knowledge for a full year before they work out the principle that allows them to determine which number each numeral refers to. This state of affairs is impossible on the numeron-list continuity hypothesis, whereby the English count list need only be identified and mapped onto the preexisting nonlinguistic numeron list that the infant already uses to represent number.

Wynn's work is important for another reason, because her data constrain our hypotheses about the process through which children construct the integer-list representation. Her studies show that children learn the meanings of the number words as follows: First, they learn what "one" means, as indicated above, with other number words contrasting with "one"; then they learn what "two" means, with other words contrasting with "two" and referring to numbers bigger than 2. Wynn's longitudinal data established that some children are in this state for several months. Then they learn what "three" means; some children induce the meaning of all the number words in the list at this point; others know what "three" means, and take the other words to contrast with "three" and refer indiscriminately to higher numbers. Wynn found no children who knew what "four" meant who had not worked out how the whole list represents number.

In spite of the evidence that prelinguistic infants represent number, it seems that the child is still in the process of constructing an integer-list representation of number in the years 2–4. How then do infants represent number, and how do their representations differ from the integer-list representation?

Two Possible Prelinguistic Representational Systems for Number  Two quite different nonlinguistic systems of number representation have been proposed to underlie infants' abilities to discriminate, compare, and compute over representations of number: analog-magnitude representations and object-file representations. I characterize each in turn, considering the evidence for and against the hypothesis that each one may underlie the behaviors in which infants display knowledge of number.

*Analog-magnitude representations*  Both human adults and animals deploy analog-magnitude representations

of number (for reviews, see Gallistel, 1990; Dehaene, 1997). Rather than being represented by a list of discrete symbols, in such systems number is represented by a physical magnitude that is proportional to the number of individuals in the set being enumerated. An external analog-magnitude representational system could represent one as ——, two as ———, three as ————, and so on. In such systems, numerical comparisons are made by processes that operate over these analog magnitudes, in the same way that length or time comparisons are made by processes that operate over representations of these physical magnitudes. For this reason, number comparisons are subject to Weber's law (1 and 2 are more discriminable than are 7 and 8). Sensitivity to Weber's law is one of the main sources of evidence that both animals and human adults prevented from verbal counting deploy analog-magnitude representations of number (for reviews of other sources of evidence, see Dehaene, 1997; Gallistel, 1990).

There are many different ways that analog-magnitude representations of number might be constructed. One proposal is the accumulator model of Meck and Church (1983). The idea is simple: Suppose the nervous system has the equivalent of a pulse generator that generates activity at a constant rate, and a gate that can open to allow energy through to an accumulator that registers how much has been let through. When the animal is in a counting mode, the gate is opened for a fixed amount of time (say 200 ms) for each individual to be counted. The total energy accumulated then serves as an analog representation of number. Meck and Church's model seems best suited for sequentially presented individuals, such as bar presses, tones, light flashes, or jumps of a puppet. Gallistel (1990) proposed, however, that this mechanism functions as well in the sequential enumeration of simultaneously present individuals. Others (e.g., Dehaene and Changeux, 1989; Church and Broadbent, 1990) have proposed computational models that create analog-magnitude representations without implementing any iterative process. Furthermore, there is unequivocal evidence that in at least some circumstances, number representations are created by noniterative processes. For example, the time that subjects require to discriminate two numerosities depends on the ratio difference between the numerosities, not on their absolute value (Barth, Kanwisher, and Spelke, under review). In contrast, time should increase monotonically with $N$ for any iterative counting process. Moreover, subjects are able to discriminate visually presented numerosities under conditions of stimulus size and eccentricity in which they are not able to attend to individual elements in sequence (Intrilligator, 1997). Their numerosity discrimination therefore could not depend on a process of counting each entity in turn, even very rapidly.

Analog-magnitude representations are numerical in four senses. First, and most importantly, each analog magnitude stands for a numerical value, albeit imprecisely. Second, the processes for constructing such representations are subject to no upper bound beyond those imposed by perceptual thresholds such as the discriminability of interelement distances (e.g., individual tones or dots may fail to be resolved if they are too crowded) and the ultimate capacity of the system. Third, distinct analog magnitudes provide a natural and explicit representation of more/less relationships between distinct numerosities, with the larger magnitude representing the more numerous set. Fourth, analog magnitudes provide a medium for computations of addition and multiplication, at least in principle (see Gallistel and Gelman, 1992), although it is an empirical question whether they are used for this purpose in practice. Studies of neurological patients with dyscalculia and of bilingual students performing arithmetic suggest that analog magnitudes are used to estimate sums but not products, at least in these populations (Dehaene, 1997; Dehaene et al., 1999; Spelke and Tsivkin, 1999). Studies of patients with dyscalculia also suggest that analog-magnitude representations are recruited during single digit subtraction and in computations of "between" (what is between 6 and 8, 3 and 5, etc.; Dehaene, 1997).

Analog-magnitude representations differ from other numerical representations (in particular, from any representation of the natural numbers, including integer-list representations) in some crucial respects. Because such representations are inexact and subject to Weber fraction considerations, they fail to capture small numerical differences between large sets of objects. The distinction between seven and eight, for example, cannot be captured by the analog-magnitude representations found in adults. Also, noniterative processes for constructing analog-magnitude representations, such as those proposed by Dehaene and Changeux (1989) and Church and Broadbent (1990), include nothing that corresponds to the successor function, the operation of "adding one," and they do not capture the fact that 1 and 2, 7 and 8, and 69 and 70 differ by the same amount. Analog-magnitude representations therefore are not powerful enough to represent the natural numbers and their key property of discrete infinity, and they do not support any computations of addition or multiplication that build on the successor function.

Can analog-magnitude representations underlie human infants' sensitivity to number? Such representations could underlie infants' discrimination of 2 individuals from 3 individuals, including syllables and jumps of a puppet. In analog-magnitude representations, these small sets would differ as ——— differs from ————. In contrast, noniterative analog magnitude processes could not easily represent the numbers in Wynn's addition and subtraction tasks, because they do not implement the successor function. Similarly, the ordinal comparison tasks in which one food object is placed into one closed container and two are placed into another, one at a time (or two vs. three, each set being constructed by successive placings), require that the infant represent "one" and succession. Because they lack any representation of "adding one," noniterative analog-magnitude representations provide a cumbersome procedure for representing the addition event itself in these studies: Infants would have to represent occluded as well as visible objects and perform density and extent measurements on the set of all the objects in an array, visible and occluded.

Further results provide other difficulties for this class of models. Analog-magnitude representations cannot account for the finding that infants discriminate 2 from 3 dots but not 4 from 6 dots (Starkey and Cooper, 1980) or 8 from 12 dots (Xu and Spelke, 2000). Because these pairs of numerosities differ by a constant ratio, they should be equally discriminable by any process whose sensitivity follows Weber's law. Similarly, analog-magnitude representations also cannot account for the finding that infants succeed at addition tasks such as 1 + 1 = 2 or 1, but fail at 5 + 5 = 10 or 5 (Chiang and Wynn, 2000). Nor can analog-magnitude representations account for the finding in the choice experiments (see figure 28.1) that infants can compare 1 vs. 2 and 2 vs. 3, but not 3 vs. 6. Infants' performance in these cases, as well, departs from Weber's law.

One set of findings, however, strongly supports the thesis that infants construct analog-magnitude representations of number. Xu and Spelke (2000) found that, when overall surface area, brightness, and density of dots was controlled across presentations, infants could discriminate 8 from 16 dots and failed to discriminate 8 from 12 dots under the same presentation conditions. Presented with simultaneously visible arrays of 4 or more individuals, infants' number representations appear to accord with Weber's law. Moreover, details of Xu and Spelke's (2000) data suggest that a noniterative process supports performance in this task. Infants took no longer to habituate to 16-dot arrays than to 8-dot arrays, suggesting that they formed representations of the different numerosities with equivalent speed, contrary to the predictions from any iterative process.

Thus, I conclude that infants *do* have available analog-magnitude representations of number, but that they are unlikely to underlie performance on many of the tasks involving small set sizes.

*Object-file representations* A wealth of studies provide evidence that human adults can attend to small numbers of objects simultaneously, keeping track of each object by following it as it moves continuously and accumulating information about its properties (Kahneman, Treisman, and Gibbs, 1992; Pylyshyn and Storm, 1988). Adults are able to perform this task even when distinct objects have no distinguishing properties other than their location, and when a single object maintains no common properties over time as it moves. Conversely, when two objects with distinct properties share a common location (for example, a small circle is embedded in a large one), or when a single object moves discontinuously, adults sometimes fail to represent the two objects' distinctness or the single object's identity (Scholl and Pylyshyn, 1999; Trick and Pylyshyn, 1994). All these phenomena testify to the existence of a spatiotemporal system for representing objects—up to about four of them at once—in visual scenes. Such object representations have been proposed to underlie adults' rapid apprehension of numerosity in arrays of simultaneously visible elements, when each element occupies a distinct location and the total number of elements does not exceed about 4 (Trick and Pylyshyn, 1994). Such representations also have been proposed to underlie adults' rapid apprehension of the identity of individual visible objects through time and their accumulation of information about the properties of each object. These representations have been called by different names, and different theorists do not exactly agree as to their nature or properties. Here, I abstract over these differences and, following Kahneman and colleagues (1992), refer to such representations as "object files."

Object-file representations are numerical in four senses. First, the opening of new object files requires principles of individuation and numerical identity; models must keep track of whether this object, seen now, is the same *one* as that object seen before. Spatiotemporal information must be recruited for this purpose, because the objects in many experiments are physically indistinguishable from each other and because, in any case, property/kind changes within an object are not sufficient to cause the opening of a new object file (for reviews, see Carey and Xu, in press; Pylyshyn, in press). Second, the opening of a new object file in the presence of other active files provides a natural representation for the process of adding one to an array of objects. Third, object-file representations provide implicit representations of sets of objects; the object files that are active at any given time as a perceiver

explores an array determines a set of attended objects. If the perceiver can establish a 1:1 correspondence between objects and active files, therefore, the computations over object-file representations provide a process for establishing numerical equivalence. Fourth, object files represent numerosity exactly for set sizes up to about 4 and are not subject to Weber's law.

Object-file representations differ from integer-list representation in three ways. Most importantly, they contain no symbols for cardinal values. The only symbols in such models represent the individual objects themselves. Second, object-file models have an upper bound (of about 4; see Pylyshyn and Storm, 1988; Trick and Pylyshyn, 1994). Third, object-file representations serve only to represent individuals that obey the spatiotemporal constraints on objects; they do not serve to enumerate events or other entities. Of course, the existence of object-file representations does not preclude similar representational systems for other types of individuals (event-file representations, syllable-file representations).

Many have suggested that infants construct mental models of the objects in number discrimination and addition experiments, deploying the object tracking capacities studied in the adult object-based attention literature to update these representations as objects are added and subtracted from the arrays (Carey and Xu, in press; Leslie and Scholl, 1999; Simon, 1997; Uller et al., 1999). That is, infants may be constructing a representation consisting of one object file for each object in a given array. Object-file representations could underlie infants' discrimination of two individuals from three individuals; in these representations, the small sets of objects differ as 0 0 differs from 0 0 0. Object-file representations also provide a natural account for performance in the infant addition experiments. During the setup of a 1 + 1 = 2 or 1 experiment, for example, the infant would open an object file for the first object introduced on the stage and a second object file for the second object introduced behind the screen, yielding the representation 0 0. Then when the outcome array is revealed, the infant again creates object file representations, 0 0 for the expected outcome of two objects and 0 for the impossible outcome of 1 object. The model of the setup array and the model of the outcome array are compared on the basis of 1:1 correspondence, and a mismatch draws the infant's attention. Evidence in favor of this account comes from the finding that infants do not use property/kind information (e.g., the information that distinguishes a cat from a dog) to open new object files in addition experiments (Simon, Hespos, and Rochat, 1995; Xu and

Carey, 1996), just as adults fail to use such information in object tracking experiments (Pylyshyn, in press).

The pattern of success in the choice experiment (see figure 28.1) is the set-size signature of object-file representations. That the limit of performance in the choice experiments is 2 vs. 3, in the face of failure at 3 vs. 6, suggests that object-file representations underlie performance on this task. If so, these studies show that the child can create *two* models in short-term memory, each with a limit of 2 or 3, and compare them on the basis of 1:1 correspondence or overall spatial extent. Such representations also can explain limits in Wynn's addition/subtraction paradigm, such as their evident failure to recognize that $5 + 5 = 10$ not 5.

Finally, compelling evidence in favor of object-file representations comes from studies comparing infants' ability to add objects to their ability to add other perceptible entities that violate the conditions on objects: piles of sand (Huntley-Fenner, Carey, and Solimando, under review) and piles of blocks (Chiang and Wynn, 2000). For example, Huntley-Fenner and colleagues presented 8-month-old infants with a $1 + 1 = 2$ vs. 1 addition problem either with two solid objects of the shape, color, and texture of sand piles or with two real sand piles. Although these displays were closely matched on perceptual grounds, babies succeeded at the addition task with the solid objects and failed with the sand piles. This pattern strongly suggests that a process for individuating and tracking objects is central to performance in such addition experiments.

In further support of the hypothesis that object-file representations underlie performance on the infant addition/subtraction tasks, Uller and colleagues (1999) showed that manipulations that would affect the robustness of object-file representations held in short-term memory, but that should not affect analog-magnitude representations, have a large influence on infant success in these experiments. For example, suppose a symbolic representation of the number of a set of 2 objects is created by incrementing an accumulator twice. It should not matter whether the infant actually sees the first object on the stage floor before a screen is raised and the second object is added to the array (object first) or whether the screen is raised first and then the objects are added one at a time (screen first). However, if the child is creating and storing a mental model of the objects in the event, seeing the first object and requiring only one update in imagery might well have a huge effect. The latter result is obtained: Infants succeed in object-first $1 + 1 = 2$ or 1 experiments by 4–5 months of age, but not in screen-first $1 + 1 = 2$ or 1 experiments until 10 months of age (Uller et al., 1999).

Finally, recent findings from Clearfield and Mix (1999) and from Feigenson and colleagues (in press) strongly suggest that analog-magnitude representations of *number* do not underlie the habituation findings with small sets. These authors point out that no previous study of small number discrimination successfully controlled for the possibility that a continuous quantity correlated with number—such as the total spatial extent of the array—might be driving infants' responses in these studies. Attempted controls (e.g., Starkey and Cooper, 1980) failed—even when stimulus size is randomly varied across trials, the average spatial extent of the habituation series will be a closer match to that of the familiar number test items than to that of the novel number test items. When Clearfield and Mix (1999) and Feigenson and colleagues (in press) corrected this design flaw, no evidence for sensitivity to numerical differences between sets below 4 was found in 6- and 7-month-old infants. Rather, infants were sensitive to changes in total spatial extent of the arrays (total contour length in Clearfield and Mix; total front surface area in Feigenson et al.). Although the evidence from other paradigms that infants represent number stands, these results provide no evidence that infants represent number at all for very small sets when tested with a numerosity discrimination paradigm. In contrast, one experiment using the same type of discrimination paradigm and including proper controls for spatial extent and other continuous variables provides evidence for discrimination of numerosity (Xu and Spelke, 2000). It is noteworthy that in this study infant discrimination cannot be based on object files, for the numbers discriminated (8 vs. 16) are too large. The findings of Clearfield and Mix and of Feigenson and colleagues, however, are consistent with object-file representations, in which models of objects are compared with respect to the total spatial extent of the arrays.

THE FORMAT OF INFANT REPRESENTATION OF NUMBER
As the preceding discussion indicates, the issue of which nonlinguistic system of representation underlies performance in the infant number experiments is currently a matter of debate, and no single system of representation appears adequate to account for all the findings. Object-file representations appear to underlie performance in some tasks, but not all of them. It seems likely that prelinguistic infants, like nonhuman primates and human adults, have access both to object-file representations and to analog-magnitude representations. When infants are presented with small numbers of material objects in addition and subtraction experiments, they appear to keep track of those objects by means of object files. When they are presented with

large sets of objects in discrimination experiments, they appear to represent those sets with analog-magnitude representations. When they are presented with small sets of objects in discrimination experiments, they may not represent numerosity at all. Finally, it is not clear whether infants keep track of small numbers of events by means of analog-magnitude representations or by an entirely different system of parallel individuation. The hypothesis that human infants are endowed both with analog magnitude and object-file representations of number is not implausible, because a wide variety of species, including rats, parrots, chickens, pigeons, and primates, command both systems of representations (for reviews, see Gallistel, 1990; Dehaene, 1997).

WHY THE INTEGER-LIST REPRESENTATION IS A GENUINELY NEW REPRESENTATIONAL RESOURCE The integer-list representation differs deeply from both object-file and analog-magnitude representations of number, and it transcends each of them singly and together. Object-file representations are sharply limited to small sets by constraints on parallel individuation and short-term memory for distinct items, whereas integer-list representations contain no such limit. There is no intrinsic upper bound on the lists that one can commit to long-term memory (think of the alphabet). Once an integer list embodies a recursive component for generating symbols in the list, there is no upper limit at all (think of the base-10 system). Moreover, object-file representations contain no symbol for any integer value and no counting algorithm, even implicitly, whereas integer-list representations are constituted by lists of explicit symbols for numerosities. Nonetheless, object-file representations have two important properties in common with integer-list representations. First, principles of individuation and numerical identity, plus the capacity to compare models on the basis of 1:1 correspondence, enable sets of 1, 2, and 3 individuals ($1 + 1 = 2, 2 > 1$, etc.) to be *precisely*, if *implicitly*, represented. Second, object files provide a natural representation of the successor function, for *adding one* corresponds to the opening of a new object file. In integer-list representations, the successor relation ($+1$) between adjacent numbers similarly enables the numerical relations among sets of individuals to be *precisely* encoded.

Analog-magnitude representations, like integer-list representations, have no intrinsic upper limit and contain a distinct symbol for each integer value represented (e.g., — — — represents 2). Discriminability of these symbols, however, is limited by Weber's law, such that one cannot represent the precise relation between 14 and 15, although one may be able to represent that 15 is greater than 12. Integer-list representations, in con-

trast, capture all relations among whole numbers, no matter how close (14, 15, 114, 115, 116, etc.). Moreover, analog-magnitude representations, especially those produced by a noniterative process, obscure the arithmetic successor relation ($+1$) between successive states in two ways. First, there is no operation within the process that constructs these representations that corresponds to the operation of *adding one*. Second, Weber fraction considerations make the difference between the states that represent 1 and 2 appear larger than the difference between 2 and 3, or 29 and 30.

Even if the infant is endowed with both analog magnitude and object file systems of representation, therefore, the infant's capacity to represent number will be markedly weaker than that of the child who commands the integer-list representation. Neither object files nor analog magnitudes can serve to represent large exact numerosities: Object files fail to capture number concepts such as "seven" because they exceed the capacity limit of four, and analog-magnitude representations fail to capture such concepts because they exceed the limits on their precision. Children endowed with both these representations therefore lack the representational resources provided by the integer-list system.

In sum, a consideration of the format of infant number representation reinforces the conclusions from Wynn's ease of learning argument. The integer-list representation is discontinuous with its developmental precursors; acquiring it requires the construction of a new representational resource. How do children build an explicit, integer-list, representation of the natural numbers?

*Constructing the integer-list representation of number*

The problem of how the child builds an integer-list representation decomposes into the related subproblems of learning the ordered list itself ("one, two, three, four, five, six, . . ."), learning the meaning of each symbol on the list (e.g., "three" means *three*), and learning *how* the list itself represents number such that the child can infer the meaning of a newly mastered integer symbol (e.g., "eleven") from its position in the integer list. On Gelman and Gallistel's (1978) continuity proposal, the second and third questions collapse into the first—the child identifies a natural language list such as "one, two three four, five six, . . ." as an integer list that corresponds to the mental numeron list, and in doing so knows the meanings of all its symbols at once. Empirical considerations against this proposal were presented earlier.

BOOTSTRAPPING MECHANISMS Presenting a full answer to the question of the mechanisms underlying the construction of the integer-list representation (a new representational resource) is beyond the scope of this chapter. Carey (in preparation) and Carey and Spelke (in press) provide an account of bootstrapping mechanisms in general, and sketch four different bootstrapping processes that might underlie this achievement. Bootstrapping processes have several properties. They often involve integrating previously distinct representational systems through processes that are not merely combinatorial; they are nonalgorithmic, involving such optional operations as creating analogical mappings between different representations and making inductive leaps. And they involve initial stages of learning in which concepts are acquired directly in relation to each other before being grounded in the meanings they will initially attain, a process quite unlike abstraction. The four bootstrapping processes suggested by Carey and Spelke (in press) differ in the representations the child starts with, and thus in the analogies drawn and particular inductive leaps made. All four proposals assume, following Wynn (1990) and Fuson (1988), that the child first learns "one, two, three, four, five, . . ." as a list of meaningless lexical items. There is no doubt that children have this capacity—they learn sequences such as "eeny, meeny, miney, mo," the alphabet, the days of the week, and so on. As Terrace (1984) has shown, non-human primates (rhesus macaques) also have the capacity to learn to order arbitrary lists of visual symbols; they can be taught to touch 4 pictures (e.g., dog, house, tree, cup), displayed in successive trials in randomly determined positions on a video screen, in a fixed order. (For a fascinating application of this ability in monkeys to the exploration of monkey number representation, see Brannon and Terrace, 1998).This step is a paradigmatic example of one aspect of bootstrapping processes: The meanings of the counting words are exhausted, initially, by their interrelations—their relative order in the list.

All four proposals also capture the fact that the meanings of small number words are learned first. The proposals differ in the learning processes proposed to underlie working out the meaning of these number words, of the larger number words, and of the counting algorithm. All agree that the learning process involves combining antecedently available representations. Bootstrapping learning processes begin in representations already grounded, as well as in representations that derive meaning from their interrelations. The proposals differ in which numerical system(s) available to infants—the analog magnitude system and the object-file system—play a role in the learning process, as well as to what additional representational resources are recruited.

A SKETCH OF ONE PROPOSAL Many authors (e.g., Hurford, 1987) have offered versions of the proposal that the integer-list system is built from object-file representations and the meaningless ordered list of words. For reasons too complex for present purposes, Spelke and I do not favor this proposal; but here I offer it as an illustration of how bootstrapping processes might create new representational resources.

First, infants spontaneously represent small numbers of objects deploying the object-file model: 0, 0 0, and 0 0 0 are the representations of 1, 2, and 3 objects respectively. Further, infants compare models on the basis of 1:1 correspondence, represent ordinal relations among sets of 1, 2, and 3 objects, and know that (0) plus another object yields (0 0), and that (0 0) plus another object yields (0 0 0). (Empirical support for these propositions was provided in an earlier section.) Second, the child learns the integer list as a meaningless ordered list of words and the counting routine as a number-irrelevant game like patty-cake. In the course of playing the counting game, the child learns first that "one" applies to arrays in which just one object file is open (0), next that "two" applies to arrays in which two object files are open (0 0), and next that "three" applies to arrays in which three object files are open (0 0 0).

The stage is set, now, for the crucial induction, which begins by the recognition of an analogy. The child notices an analogy between two different "follows" relations—the relation of (+0) between (0), (0 0), and (0, 0, 0), instantiated by the opening of a new object file, and the relation of *follows* in the count list. This analogy licenses the crucial induction: if *x* is followed by *y* in the counting sequence, opening a new object file in what is called an *x* array results in what is called a *y* array. This proposal does not yet embody the arithmetic successor function, but one additional step is all that is needed. Since the child has already mapped single object files onto "one," opening a new object file is equivalent to *adding one*.

## Lessons from the study of the development of number representations: Structural analogy

I began with evidence that prelinguistic infants represent number, that they can carry out computations that establish numerical equivalence, establish ordinal relations between the numerosity of two sets, and compute the outcome of adding or subtracting one from small sets. These data fall on the side of positions that posit rich initial representations as the building blocks of cognition. But before such behavioral data can inform debates at the level of structural analogy between cognitive and neurobiological mechanisms, it is important to discover the nature of the representational systems that subserve behavior on these tasks.

Infants most probably deploy two distinct systems in tasks that require representation of number—object-file and analog-magnitude representations. Further, I sketched some respects in which each is very different from, and weaker than, the explicit integer-list representation of number that is mastered in the child's fourth year of life. The acquisition of the integer-list representation of number thus constitutes an example of a developmental discontinuity. I concluded with a speculative sketch of bootstrapping mechanisms, illustrating with an example of a bootstrapping process that might achieve the new representational resource. These latter arguments fall on the side of constructivist accounts of the creation of new representational resources during development.

At the level of structural analogy, then, I have argued that constructive processes, rather than selective ones, underlie the acquisition of the integer-list representation of number, and that this process involves the creation of a representational resource with more power than those from which it is built. As far as I am aware, there are no known neural developmental processes analogous to the bootstrapping mechanisms sketched above. For example, the activity-driven processes that are involved in dendrite growth that Quartz and Sejnowski (1997) offer as an example of constructive processes provide only a very distant analogy to those that are involved in the case of cognitive development detailed here. How might we go further in closing the gap in this case?

## Closing the gap: Integrating cognitive development with systems neuroscience

Detailed models of representational format play two roles in the argument I am developing here. Heretofore, my main point has been that it is only by examining the initial representational systems in detail that we can say in what ways they are continuous and in what ways discontinuous with later representational systems, and only then can we motivate possible learning mechanisms that take the initial systems as input and output representational systems that transcend them. Here, I wish to emphasize a second point: It is the same level of detail (at least) that is needed to begin to close the gap between characterizations of the developing mind and characterizations of the developing brain.

I have provided evidence for two systems of numerically relevant representations (object-file representations, analog-magnitude representations) that become integrated, during development, in the creation of a third system—the explicit integer-list representation that supports counting. This work motivates several questions at the level of systems neuroscience. Are there distinct neural circuits for these computationally distinct representational systems? Do they continue to articulate mathematical reasoning into adulthood? Existing evidence suggests an affirmative answer on both counts (for reviews, see Dehaene, 1997; Butterworth, 1997).

The object-file system was originally studied in the context of object-based attention, and it clearly continues to articulate midlevel vision in adulthood. Data from studies of patients with neuropsychological damage and from imaging studies converge on the conclusion that parietal cortex, especially inferior parietal cortex, is part of the neural circuit underlying midlevel object-based attention. For example, Culham, Brandt, Cavanagh, Kanwisher, Dale, and Tootell (1998) found that activity levels in this area were correlated with the number of objects being simultaneously being tracked in the Pylyshyn multiple object tracking task (other areas, including regions of frontal cortex, also showed this relation). Parietal damage is also implicated in object-based neglect (e.g., Behrman and Tipper, 1994) and the even more striking Balint syndrome (for a review, see Rafel, 1997). Patients with Balint syndrome exhibit simultanagnosia, the incapacity to perceive two objects at once, in the face of normal sensory processing. They cannot do simple tasks such as telling which of two lines is longer, and do not report seeing two simultaneously presented disks, although if the disks are joined by a bar, making a dumbbell, they report seeing the whole dumbbell (Luria, 1959). It seems likely that these syndromes reflect damage to the midlevel object-file/object indexing attentional systems (for development of this point, see Scholl, in press).

The object-file system, with its capacity to simultaneously index and track up to 4 objects, is not a dedicated number representational system. Number is merely implicitly represented here; the objects indexed constitute a set number that is represented by one object-file for each object in the set. The analog-magnitude representational systems, in contrast, represent specifically *number*. There are analog-magnitude representations for other physical quantities, of course, such as distance, size, and time; but the computations that establish representations of number in a model such as Meck and Church's create an analog symbol for number alone. Dehaene (1997) has summarized the evidence that analog-magnitude representations of number are implicated when adults compare numerical quantities and carry out some arithmetical operations (addition and subtraction). Furthermore, there is very strong evidence that the inferior parietal cortex is also a crucial part of the circuit that subserves the mental representation of approximate numerical quantities.

As Dehaene reviews, extensive neuropsychological data indicate that damage to the inferior parietal cortex of the dominant hemisphere impairs comprehending, producing, and calculating with numbers; and damage to these areas early in development results in Gerstmann's syndrome, a permanent disability in calculation. Sometimes the damage is selective for calculation, sparing reading, writing, spoken recognition, and production of Arabic digits and numerals. Dehaene (1997) argues that the core deficit is due to the disorganization of the analog-magnitude representation of numerical quantities, rather than calculation per se. He presents a case, Mr. Mar, who makes 75% errors on single-digit subtraction (e.g., 3 − 1), and 16% errors judging which of two numbers is larger. Most tellingly, Mr. Mar makes 77% errors in saying what number comes between two other (e.g., 7, 9), in spite of being flawless at saying which letter comes between two (b, d), which day comes between two (Tuesday, Thursday), and which month comes between two (March, May). In both PET and fMRI studies, the same area is active during simple calculation, and activity during number comparison tasks reflects difficulty as reflected in the Weber fraction (Dehaene, 1997).

In this chapter I have stressed the functional differences between the small number, object-file, system and the analog-magnitude system. As just reviewed, parietal regions are centrally involved in both. Within-subject studies are needed to establish whether different parietal areas are differentially implicated in the two sorts of tasks.

Dehaene (1997) makes it clear that at least three separate representations of number are involved in adult number processing. In addition to the circuit that includes parietal number sense, there is a separate system that represents visual Arabic numerals and involves the ventral occipitotemporal section of both hemispheres, and also a system that represents the verbally coded integer list, which, like any verbal representation, crucially implicates left inferior temporal cortex. Dehaene points out that each of these different systems supports different calculations; the analog-magnitude representations are automatically recruited in number comparisons and in simple calculation, and in calculations involving approximate representations, whereas verbal systems support multiplication and exact calculation that draw on memorized number facts.

This merest sketch allows us to explore how to begin to close the gap between the description of the acquisition of number representations culled from cognitive studies and developmental neuroscience. It seems likely that the infant's numerical competence is subserved by the circuits that include parietal cortex, those that play a role both in object-file representations and analog-magnitude representations. And it certainly is the case that the integer-list representation of number constructed during the preschool years is subserved by the circuits that include inferior temporal cortex. Presumably, the initial representation of the list of words as a meaningless ordered list also recruits these areas. So how are we to think, in neurological terms, about the processes that construct *numerical* meaning for that verbally represented list? At the very least, we would want to know how the brain constructs mappings between different representational systems. As argued above, in this case the mapping process is not merely a process of association. This is the principal challenge that understanding of the development of number representations at the behavioral and computational levels puts to developmental cognitive neuroscience.

One test that meaningful connections between the neural and cognitive/computational levels of description are being forged is that data about the developing brain can be brought to bear on controversies formulated at the more abstract level of description. An example alluded to earlier was the Diamond and Goldman-Rakic work suggesting that A/not B errors on Piagetian object permanence tasks reflect frontal lobe immaturity rather than lack of object representations. I conclude my case study of number representation with an illustration of how developmental cognitive neuroscience studies might resolve an important question concerning the development of number representations.

As Dehaene (1997) summarizes, there is no doubt that in the adult state the analog-magnitude representations of number are integrated with both the verbal integer list and the written Arabic numeral representations, and are activated automatically during number comparison tasks and certain arithmetic calculations. In some real sense, then, these evolutionarily ancient and early developing nonverbal representations ground number understanding throughout the lifetime. But are they the ontogenetic roots of explicit number representation? Do they ground the initial forming of the integer-list representation? The bootstrapping proposal presented above had no role for analog-magnitude representations of number in the process through which toddlers build the integer-list representation of number. If that proposal is on the right track, two very important questions become *when* and *how* does the integer-list representation become integrated with analog-magnitude representations? Although purely behavioral data will bear on these questions, imaging studies with preschool-aged children, should the techniques become available, also will provide invaluable information.

## Final conclusions

We are far from being able to say anything about the growth of the patterns of neural connectivity that underlie the development of number representations described in this chapter. I have argued that characterizing the details of representational format and the computations defined over those representations, as well as characterizing development at these levels, is a necessary prerequisite for such understanding. As always, an understanding of the mind must guide the search for its neural underpinnings.

### REFERENCES

ANTELL, S., and D. KEATING, 1983. Perception of numerical invariance in neonates. *Child Dev.* 54:695–701.

BAILLARGEON, R., 1993. The object concept revisited: New directions in the investigation of infants' physical knowledge. In *Visual Perception and Cognition in Infancy*, C. E. Granud, ed. Hillsdale, N.J.: Erlbaum, pp. 265–315.

BAILLARGEON, R., K. MILLER, and J. CONSTANTINO, 1993. Ten-month-old infants' intuitions about addition. Unpublished manuscript, University of Illinois at Urbana-Champaign.

BARTH, H., KANWISHER, N., and SPELKE, E., under review. Constructing representations of large numbers of entities.

BEHRMAN, M., and S. P. TIPPER, 1994. Object-based visual attention: Evidence from unilateral neglect. In C. Umilta & M. Moscovitch, eds. *Attention and performance XIV: Conscious and nonconscious processing and cognitive functioning.* Cambridge, Mass.: MIT Press.

BIJELJAC-BABIC, R., J. BERTONCINI, and J. MEHLER, 1991. How do four-day-old infants categorize multi-syllabic utterances? *Dev. Psychol.* 29:711–721.

BRANNON, E. M., and H. S. TERRACE, 1998. Ordering of the numerosities 1–9 by monkeys. *Science* 282:746–749.

BUTTERWORTH, B., 1999. *What Counts: How Every Brain is Hardwired for Math.* New York: Simon & Shuster, The Free Press.

CAREY, S., in preparation. *The Origin of Concepts: Evolution vs. Culture.* Cambridge, Mass.: MIT Press.

CAREY, S., and E. SPELKE, 1994. Domain specific knowledge and conceptual change. In L. Hirschfeld and S. Gelman, eds. *Mapping the Mind: Domain Specificity in Cognition and Culture.* Cambridge: Cambridge University Press, 169–200.

CAREY, S., and E. SPELKE, in press. On the very possibility of conceptual change: The integer-list representation of number. In *Conceptual Development—A Reappraisal*, L. Bonati, J. Mehler, and S. Carey, eds. Cambridge, Mass.: MIT Press.

CAREY, S., and F. XU, in press. Beyond object-files and object tracking: Infant representations of objects. *Cognition.*

CLEARFIELD, M. W., and K. S. MIX, 1999. Number vs. contour length in infants' discrimination of small visual sets. *Psychological Science,* 10:408–411.

CHIANG, W.-C., and K. WYNN, 2000. Infants' representation and tracking of objects: Implications from collections. *Cognition.* 77:169–195.

CHURCH, R. M., and H. A. BROADBENT, 1990. Alternative representations of time, number and rate. *Cognition* 33:63–109.

CORNSWEET, T. M. 1970. *Visual Perception.* New York: Academic Press.

CULHAM, J., S. BRANDT, P. CAVANAGH, N. KANWISHER, A. L. DALE, AND R. TOOTELL, 1998. Cortical fMRI activation produced by attentive tracking of moving targets. *Journal of Neurophysiology,* 80:2657.

DEHAENE, S., 1997. *The Number Sense.* Oxford: Oxford University Press.

DEHAENE, S., and J. P. CHANGEUX, 1989. Neuronal models of cognitive function. *Cognition* 33:63–109.

DEHAENE, S., E. SPELKE, P. PINEL, R. STANESCU, and S. TSIVKIN, 1999. Sources of mathematical thinking: Behavioral and brain-imaging evidence. *Science,* 284: 970–974.

DIAMOND, A., 1991. Neuropsychological insights into the meaning of object concept development. In *The Epigenesis of Mind: Studies in Biology and Cognition*, S. Carey and R. Gelman, eds. Hillsdale, N.J.: Erlbaum, pp. 67–110.

DIAMOND, A., and P. S. GOLDMAN-RAKIC, 1989. Comparison of human infants and rhesus monkeys on Piaget's AB task: Evidence for dependence on dorsolateral prefrontal cortex. *Exp. Brain Res.* 74:24–40.

ELMAN, J. L., E. A. BATES, M. H. JOHNSON, A. KARMILOFF-SMITH, D. PARISI, and K. PLUNKETT, 1996. *Rethinking Innateness: A Connectionist Perspective on Development.* Cambridge, Mass.: MIT Press.

FEIGENSON, L., S. CAREY, and E. SPELKE, in press. Infants' Discrimination of Number vs. Continuous Extent. *Cognitive Psychology.*

FEIGENSON, L., S. CAREY, and M. HAUSER, 2000. Spontaneous ordinal judgments by preverbal infants. Poster presented at the 12th Biennial International Conference on Infant Studies, Brighton, UK.

FODOR, J., 1975. *The Language of Thought.* New York: Crowell.

FUSON, K. C., 1988. *Children's Counting and Concepts of Number.* New York: Springer-Verlag.

GALLISTEL, C. R., 1990. *The Organization of Learning.* Cambridge, Mass.: MIT Press.

GALLISTEL, C. R., and R. GELMAN, 1992. Preverbal and verbal counting and computation. *Cognition* 44:43–74.

GAZZANIGA, M. S., 1995. *The Cognitive Neurosciences.* Cambridge, Mass.: MIT Press.

GELMAN, R., and C. R. GALLISTEL, 1978. *The Child's Understanding of Number.* Cambridge, Mass.: Harvard University Press.

GOLD, E. M., 1967. Language identification in the limit. *Informat. Control* 10:447–474.

GOLDMAN, P. S., 1971. Functional development of the prefrontal cortex in early life and the problem of neuronal plasticity. *Exp. Neurol.* 32:366–387.

HAUSER, M. D., S. CAREY, and L. B. HAUSER, 2000. Spontaneous number representation in semi-free-ranging rhesus monkeys. *Proc. R. Soc. Lond. B. Biol. Sci.* 267(1445):829–833.

HELMHOLZ, H., 1910. *Treatise on physiological optics.* Translated and ed. From the 3rd German ed. Southall, J. P. Rochester, NY. Optical Society of America.

HERING, 1920. *Outline of a theory of the light sense.* L. M. Hurvich and D. Jameson, eds. Cambridge, Mass.: Harvard University Press.

HUNTLEY-FENNER, G., S. CAREY, and A. SOLIMANDO, in press. Objects are individuals but stuff doesn't count: Perceived rigidity and cohesiveness influence infants' representations of small groups of discrete entities. *Cognition.*

HURFORD, J. R., 1987. *Language and Number.* Oxford: Basil Blackwell.

INTRILLIGATOR, J. M., 1997. *The Spatial Resolution of Attention.* Unpublished Ph.D., Harvard, Cambridge, Mass.

JOHNSON, M., 1997. *Developmental Cognitive Neuroscience: An Introduction.* Oxford: Blackwell.

KAHNEMAN, D., A. TREISMAN, and B. GIBBS, 1992. The reviewing of object files: Object specific integration of information. *Cogn. Psychol.* 24:175–219.

KOECHLIN, E., S. DEHAENE, and J. MEHLER, 1998. Numerical transformations in five month old infants. *Math. Cogn.* 3:89–104.

KUHL, P. K., K. A. WILLIAMS, F. LACERDA, K. N. STEVENS, and B. LINDBLOM, 1992. Linguistic experiences after phonetic perception in infants by 6 months of age. *Science* 255:606–608.

KUHL, P. K., 1999. Language, mind, and brain: Experience alters perception. In *The New Cognitive Neurosciences,* M. S. Gazzaniga, ed. Cambridge, Mass.: MIT Press, pp. 99–115.

LESLIE, A. M., 1994. ToMM, ToBy, and agency: Core architecture and domain specificity. In *Mapping the Mind: Domain Specificity in Cognition and Cultural,* L. Hirschfeld and S. Gelman, eds. New York: Cambridge University Press, pp. 119–148.

LEVITT, P., 1999. Molecular determinants of regionalization of the forebrain and cerebral cortex. In *The Cognitive Neurosciences,* M. S. Gazzaniga, ed. Cambridge, Mass.: MIT Press, pp. 23–32.

MACNAMARA, J., 1982. *Names for Things.* Cambridge, Mass.: MIT press.

MACNAMARA, J., 1987. *A Border Dispute: The Place of Logic in Psychology.* Cambridge, Mass.: MIT Press.

MANDLER, J. M., 2000. Perceptual and conceptual processes in infancy. *J. Cogn. Dev.* 1:3–36.

MARCUS, G. F., S. VIJAYAN, S. BANDI RAO, and P. M. VISHTON, 1999. Rule-learning in seven-month-old infants. *Science* 283:77–80.

MECK, W. H., and R. M. CHURCH, 1983. A mode control model of counting and timing processes. *J. Exp. Psychol.: Animal Behav. Proc.* 9:320–334.

MORTON, J., M. H. JOHNSON, and D. MAURER, 1990. On the reasons for newborns' responses to faces. *Infant Behav. Dev.* 13:99–103.

NELSON, C. A., and F. E. BLOOM, 1997. *Child Dev. Neurosci.* 68(5):970–987.

OSHERSON, D. N., M. STOB, and S. WEINSTEIN, 1986. *Systems That Learn.* Cambridge, Mass.: MIT Press.

PIAGET, J., 1955. *The Child's Construction of Reality.* London: Routledge and Kegan Paul.

PINKER, S., 1984. *Language Learnability and Language Development.* Cambridge, Mass.: Harvard University Press.

PYLYSHYN, Z. W., in press. Visual indexes, preconceptual objects and situated vision. *Cognition.*

PYLYSHYN, Z. W., and R. W. STORM, 1988. Tracking of multiple independent targets: Evidence for a parallel tracking mechanism. *Spatial Vis.* 3(3):1–19.

QUARTZ, S. R., and T. J. SEJNOWSKI, 1997. The neural basis of cognitive development: A constructivist manifesto. *Behav. Brain Sci.* 20:537–596.

RAFEL, R. D., 1997. Balint syndrome. In *Behavioral Neurology and Neuropsychology,* T. E. Feinberg and M. J. Farah, eds. New York: McGraw-Hill, pp. 337–356.

RAKIC, P., 1995. Corticogenesis in human and nonhuman primates. In *The Cognitive Neurosciences,* M. S. Gazzaniga, ed. Cambridge, Mass.: MIT Press, pp. 127–145.

RAKIC, P., 1999. Setting the stage for cognition: Genesis of the primate cerebral cortex. In *The New Cognitive Neurosciences,* M. S. Gazzaniga, ed. Cambridge, Mass.: MIT Press, pp. 7–21.

RAKIC, P., J.-P. BOURGEOIS, M. F. ECKENHOFF, N. ZECEVIC, and P. S. GOLDMAN-RAKIC, 1986. Concurrent overproduction of synapses in diverse regions of the primate cerebral cortex. *Science* 232:232–235.

RAKIC, P., J.-P. BOURGEOIS, and P. S. GOLDMAN-RAKIC, 1994. Synaptic development of the cerebral cortex: Implications for learning, memory, and mental illness. *Prog. Brain Res.* 102:227–243.

SAFFRAN, J. R., R. N. ASLIN, and E. L. NEWPORT, 1996. Statistical learning by 8-month-old infants. *Science* 274:1926–1928.

SCHOLL, B. J., in press. Objects and attention: The state of the art. *Cognition.*

SCHOLL, B. J., and Z. W. PYLYSHYN, 1999. Tracking multiple items through occlusion: Clues to visual objecthood. *Cogn. Psychol.* 38(2):259–290.

SIMON, T. J., 1997. Reconceptualizing the origins of number knowledge: A "non-numerical" account. *Cogn. Dev.* 12:349–372.

SIMON, T., S. HESPOS, and P. ROCHAT, 1995. Do infants understand simple arithmetic? A replication of Wynn (1992). *Cogn. Dev.* 10:253–269.

SPELKE, E. S., K. BREINLINGER, J. MACOMBER, and K. JACOBSON, 1992. Origins of knowledge. *Psychol. Rev.* 99:605–632.

STARKEY, P., E. S. SPELKE, and R. GELMAN, 1983. Detection of intermodal numerical correspondences by human infants. *Science* 222:179–181.

STARKEY, P., and R. COOPER, 1980. Perception of numbers by human infants. *Science* 210:1033–1035.

STRAUSS, M., and L. CURTIS, 1981. Infant perception of numerosity. *Child Dev.* 52:1146–1152.

TELLER, D. Y., 1999. Visual development: Psychophysics, neural substrates, and casual stories. In *The New Cognitive Neurosciences,* M. S. Gazzaniga, ed. Cambridge, Mass.: MIT Press, pp. 73–81.

TERRACE, H. S., 1984. Simultaneous chaining: The problem it poses for traditional chaining theory. In *Quantitative Analysis of Behavior: Discrimination Process,* M. L. Commons, R. J. Herrnstein, and A. R. Wagner, eds. Cambridge, Mass.: Ballinger, pp. 115–138.

TRICK, L. M., and Z. W. PYLYSHYN, 1994. Why are small and large numbers enumerated differently? A limited capacity preattentive stage in vision. *Psychol. Rev.* 10(1):1–23.

ULLER, C., G. HUNTLEY-FENNER, S. CAREY, and L. KLATT, 1999. What representations might underlie infant numerical knowledge? *Cogn. Dev.* 14:1–36.

VAN LOOSBROEK, E., and A. SMITSMAN, 1990. Visual perception of numerosity in infancy. *Dev. Psychol.* 26:916–922.

WALD, G. 1950. Eye and camera. *Scientific American,* 183:32–41.

WERKER, J. F., and C. E. LALONDE, 1998. Cross-language speech perception: In capabilities and developmental change. *Dev. Psychol.* 24(5):672–683.

WEXLER, K., and P. CULICOVER, 1980. *Formal Principles of Language Acquisition.* Cambridge, Mass.: MIT Press.

WYNN, K., 1990. Children's understanding of counting. *Cognition* 36:155–193.

WYNN, K., 1992a. Addition and subtraction by human infants. *Nature* 358:749–750.

WYNN, K., 1992b. Children's acquisition of the number words and the counting system. *Cogn. Psychol.* 24:220–251.

WYNN, K., 1996. Infants' individuation and enumeration of physical actions. *Psychol. Sci.* 7:164–169.

XU, F., and S. CAREY, 1996. Infants' metaphysics: The case of numerical identity. *Cogn. Psychol.* 30(2):111–153.

XU, F., and S. SPELKE, 2000. Large number discrimination in 6-month-old infants. *Cognition* 74:B1–B11.

# 29    A Model System for Studying the Role of Dopamine in the Prefrontal Cortex during Early Development in Humans: Early and Continuously Treated Phenylketonuria

ADELE DIAMOND

ABSTRACT    After a brief overview of the anatomy of dorso-lateral prefrontal cortex (DL-PFC) and of its anatomical connections with other brain regions, findings are summarized that DL-PFC subserves working memory and inhibitory control abilities even during infancy. Evidence suggests that one change in the prefrontal neural circuit helping to make possible some of the cognitive advances seen in infants between 6 and 12 months of age might be changes in the dopaminergic innervation of prefrontal cortex. The period of 3–6 years is then examined as a period when there is particularly marked improvement in the working memory and inhibitory control abilities thought to depend upon DL-PFC. Perhaps that improvement is made possible, in part, by maturational changes in DL-PFC, perhaps even in its dopamine projection, although that remains to be demonstrated. (To propose that changes in the dopamine innervation of prefrontal cortex play a role in making possible some cognitive advances is not to negate the role of experience nor the role of other maturational changes in the prefrontal neural system.)

As an initial way to begin looking at the role of dopamine in prefrontal cortex function in human beings during infancy and early childhood, we studied a group of children who, there was reason to believe, have reduced levels of dopamine in prefrontal cortex but otherwise normal brains. These are children treated early and continuously for phenylketonuria (PKU), whose phenylalanine levels are 3–5 times normal and whose tyrosine (Tyr) levels are below normal. The rationale for studying these children and the results obtained in those studies are summarized, as are the results from our work with an animal model of early, and continuously, treated PKU. Evidence on dissociations among tasks that require DL-PFC but are differentially sensitive to the dopamine content of DL-PFC is discussed. The evidence shows that not all cognitive tasks dependent on DL-PFC are dependent on dopamine in DL-PFC. It is my hope that this review will offer some insight into cognitive development, into the role of prefrontal cortex in cognitive development, and into the role of dopamine in prefrontal cortex function.

Dorsolateral prefrontal cortex (DL-PFC) undergoes an extremely protracted period of maturation and is not fully mature until adulthood (Huttenlocher, 1979, 1984, 1990; Huttenlocher et al., 1982; Orzhekhovskaya, 1981; Rosenberg and Lewis, 1994; Sowell et al., 1999; Thatcher, Walker, and Giudice, 1987; Yakovlev and Lecours, 1967). Growing evidence indicates, however, that some of the cognitive advances seen as early as the first year of life (6–12 months) are made possible, in part, by early changes in DL-PFC (e.g., Bell and Fox, 1992, 1997; Diamond, 1991a,b; Fox and Bell, 1990). One maturational change in DL-PFC that might help make possible these early cognitive advances is increasing levels of the neurotransmitter dopamine in DL-PFC.

Prefrontal cortex is richer in dopamine than any other region of the cerebral cortex (Bjorklund, Divac, and Lindvall, 1978; Brown, Crane, and Goldman, 1979; Gaspar et al., 1989; Levitt, Rakic, and Goldman-Rakic, 1984; Lewis et al., 1988, 1998; Williams and Goldman-Rakic, 1993, 1995). Not surprisingly, given its high concentration in prefrontal cortex, dopamine plays an important role in DL-PFC function in adult human and nonhuman primates (Akil et al., 1999; Brozoski et al., 1979; Luciana et al., 1992; Sawaguchi, Matsumura, and Kubota, 1988; Sawaguchi and Goldman-Rakic, 1991; Watanabe, Kodama, and Hikosaka, 1997).

We know that during the period that infant rhesus macaques are improving on tasks dependent on DL-PFC (the A-not-B, delayed response, and object retrieval

ADELE DIAMOND    Director, Center for Developmental Cognitive Neuroscience, Eunice Kennedy Shriver Center, Professor, Department of Psychiatry, University of Massachusetts School of Medicine, Waltham, Massachusetts.

tasks) the level of dopamine is increasing in their brains (Brown, Crane, and Goldman, 1976; Brown and Goldman, 1977), the density of dopamine receptors in their prefrontal cortex is increasing (Lidow and Rakic, 1992), and the distribution within their DL-PFC (Brodmann area 9) of axons containing the rate-limiting enzyme for the production of dopamine (tyrosine hydroxylase) is markedly changing (Lewis and Harris, 1991; Rosenberg and Lewis, 1995). Moreover, in adult rhesus macaques, the cognitive abilities that depend on DL-PFC (as indexed by tasks such as delayed response) rely critically on the dopaminergic projection to prefrontal cortex (Brozoski et al., 1979; Sawaguchi and Goldman-Rakic, 1991; Sawaguchi, Matsumura, and Kubota, 1990; Taylor et al., 1990a,b).

Evidence such as that summarized here makes it plausible that one change in the prefrontal neural circuit helping to make possible some of the cognitive advances that occur in infants between 6 and 12 months of age might be changes in the dopaminergic innervation of prefrontal cortex. Maturational changes in the prefrontal dopamine system are protracted, and therefore it is conceivable that later maturational changes in that system might help make possible subsequent improvements in the cognitive abilities dependent on prefrontal cortex as well. (To propose that changes in the dopamine innervation of prefrontal cortex play a role in making possible some of the cognitive advances during development is not to negate the role of experience nor the role of other maturational changes in the prefrontal neural system, such as in the communication between prefrontal cortex and other neural regions.)

To begin to look at the role of the dopamine projection to DL-PFC in helping to subserve cognitive functions early in life in humans, we have been studying children who, the evidence suggests, have reduced levels of dopamine in prefrontal cortex but otherwise remarkably normal brains. These are children treated early and continuously for the genetic disorder phenylketonuria (PKU) in whose bloodstreams the levels of the amino acid phenylalanine (Phe) are 3–5 times normal (6–10 mg/dL).

## Where is DL-PFC?

The cerebral cortex is distinguished from subcortex by generally having six different layers of cells (subcortical regions have fewer layers) and by being the outer mantle of the brain (closer to the surface), whereas subcortical structures are buried deep inside the brain below the cortex. In general, cortical regions are phylogenetically newer regions of the brain than subcortical regions, mature later during development, and receive more highly processed information that has already passed through subcortical structures. During primate evolution, the cerebral cortex changed from being smooth to having marked "hills" (gyri) and "valleys" (sulci). This infolding permitted an extraordinary expansion in cerebral cortex size despite a much less marked expansion in cranium size—an adaptive solution that increased surface area in a limited space.

The central sulcus divides the front of the brain from the back. All of the cerebral cortex in front of the central sulcus is frontal cortex (see figure 29.1). The most posterior region of frontal cortex, directly in front of the central sulcus, is primary motor cortex (Brodmann's area 4). The anterior boundary of motor cortex is the precentral sulcus. In front of that is premotor cortex and the supplementary motor area (SMA), two distinct subregions of Brodmann's area 6. All of the cortex in front of that is prefrontal cortex (areas 8, 9, 10, 12, 44, 45, 46, 47, and 9/46). Prefrontal cortex is not only the most anterior region of frontal cortex, but the only region of frontal cortex with a granule cell layer.

While the brain as a whole has increased in size during evolution, the proportion of the brain devoted to prefrontal cortex has increased much more dramatically, especially in humans (Brodmann, 1912). For example, prefrontal cortex makes up 25% of the cortex in the human brain, but only 15% in chimpanzees, 7% in dogs, and 4% in cats. Prefrontal cortex is an association area; its functions are primarily integrative, neither exclusively sensory nor motor. In accord with its late maturational timetable and massive expansion during primate evolution, prefrontal cortex is credited with underlying the most sophisticated cognitive abilities, often called "executive processes," such as reasoning, planning, problem-solving, and coordinating the performance of multiple tasks (Goldman-Rakic, 1987; Pennington and Ozonoff, 1996; Postle, Berger, and D'Esposito, 1999; Shallice, 1988; Warren and Akert, 1964).

Within prefrontal cortex, the mid-dorsolateral subregion (areas 9, 46, and 9/46) has increased disproportionately in size during evolution even compared to the other regions of prefrontal cortex. Mid-DL-PFC consists of the middle section of the superior and middle frontal gyri, extending from behind the frontal pole (area 10) to area 8 (see figure 29.1; Petrides and Pandya, 1999). DL-PFC has historically been defined by its reciprocal connections with the parvocellular subdivision of the mediodorsal nucleus of the thalamus (Akert, 1964; Goldman-Rakic and Porrino, 1985; Jacobson, Butters, and Tovsky, 1978; Kievit and Kuypers, 1977; McLardy, 1950; Rose and Woolsey, 1948; Siwek and Pandya, 1991; Tobias, 1975; Walker, 1940). The size of the parvocel-

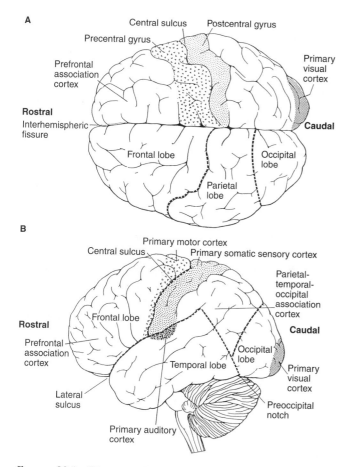

A

- Central sulcus
- Postcentral gyrus
- Precentral gyrus
- Prefrontal association cortex
- Primary visual cortex
- **Rostral**
- Interhemispheric fissure
- **Caudal**
- Frontal lobe
- Occipital lobe
- Parietal lobe

B

- Primary motor cortex
- Central sulcus
- Primary somatic sensory cortex
- Parietal-temporal-occipital association cortex
- **Rostral**
- Frontal lobe
- **Caudal**
- Prefrontal association cortex
- Occipital lobe
- Temporal lobe
- Primary visual cortex
- Lateral sulcus
- Preoccipital notch
- Primary auditory cortex

FIGURE 29.1    Diagram of the human brain, indicating the location of dorsolateral prefrontal cortex. (Reprinted with permission from Kandel, E. R., J. H. Schwartz, and T. M. Jessell, eds., 1991. *Principles of Neural Science*, 3rd ed. New York: McGraw Hill.)

lular portion of the mediodorsal nucleus has increased phylogenetically in proportion to the increase in size of DL-PFC and disproportionately compared even to other regions of the mediodorsal nucleus (Clark, 1930; Khokhryakova, 1979; Pines, 1927).

No area of the brain acts in isolation. A neural region functions as part of system of functionally and anatomically interrelated structures. Through its reciprocal connections with the *superior temporal cortex* (Petrides and Pandya, 1988; Seltzer and Pandya, 1989), *posterior parietal cortex* (area 7a; Cavada and Goldman-Rakic, 1989; Goldman-Rakic and Schwartz, 1982; Johnson et al., 1989; Petrides and Pandya, 1984; Schwartz and Goldman-Rakic, 1984; Selemon and Goldman-Rakic, 1988), *anterior and posterior cingulate* (Vogt and Pandya, 1987; Vogt, Rosene, and Pandya, 1979), *premotor cortex* (Barbas and Mesulam, 1985, 1987; Künzle, 1978), SMA (McGuire, Bates, and Goldman-Rakic, 1991; Wiesendanger, 1981), *retrosplenial cortex* (Morris, Pandya, and Petrides, 1999; Morris, Petrides, and Pandya, 1999; see

also Petrides and Pandya, 1999, concerning all of these interconnections), and the *neocerebellum* (Diamond, 2000; Leiner, Leiner, and Dow, 1989; Middleton and Strick, 1994, 1997; Sasaki et al., 1979; Schmahmann and Pandya, 1995; Yamamoto et al., 1992), mid-DL-PFC can modulate the activity of those regions, as well as receive information from, and be modulated by, these regions. In addition, mid-DL-PFC sends a strong projection to the caudate nucleus (Arikuni and Kubota, 1986; Goldman and Nauta, 1977; Kemp and Powell, 1970; Selemon and Goldman-Rakic, 1985). The projections from DL-PFC, posterior parietal cortex, and the superior temporal cortex are intricately interdigitated throughout the brain, including in the caudate nucleus, providing multiple opportunities for these neural regions to communicate with, and influence, one another (Goldman-Rakic and Schwartz, 1982; Johnson et al., 1989; Schwartz and Goldman-Rakic, 1984; Selemon and Goldman-Rakic, 1985, 1988).

## Evidence that DL-PFC subserves cognitive abilities even during infancy

The A-not-B task has been used in scores of laboratories throughout the world to study cognitive development in infants since it was first introduced by Piaget in 1936 (see Piaget, 1954). Under the name "delayed response," an almost-identical task has been the classic paradigm for studying the functions of DL-PFC in macaques since it was first introduced for that purpose by Jacobsen (1935, 1936). In the A-not-B/delayed response task, the participant watches as a desired object is hidden in one of two hiding places that differ only in their left–right location, and then a few seconds later is allowed to reach to find that object. The participant must hold in mind over those few seconds where the object was hidden. Over trials, the participant must update his or her mental record to reflect where the reward was hidden last. When the participant reaches correctly, he or she is rewarded by being allowed to retrieve the desired object. In this manner, the behavior of reaching to that hiding location is reinforced, and hence the tendency to emit that response is strengthened. When the reward is then hidden at the other location, the participant must inhibit the natural tendency to repeat the rewarded response and instead respond according to the representation held in mind of where the reward was just hidden. Thus, the A-not-B task requires holding information in mind (where the reward was last hidden) and inhibition of a prepotent response tendency. By roughly 7½–8 months of age, infants reach correctly to the first hiding location with delays as long as 3 s. When the reward is then hidden at the other hiding place, however, infants err by going back to the first location (called the "A-not-B error"). As infants get older, they are able to succeed at longer and longer delays. Thus, for example, one sees the A-not-B error (correct at the first location, but incorrectly repeating that response on the reversal trials) at delays of 5 s in infants of 9 months and at delays of 7–8 s in infants of 10 months (Diamond, 1985; Diamond and Doar, 1989).

In the object retrieval task (Diamond, 1981, 1988, 1990a), nothing is hidden and there is no delay. A toy is placed within easy reach in a small, clear box, open on one side. Difficulties arise when the infant sees the toy through one of the closed sides of the box. Here, the infant must integrate seeing the toy through one side of the box with reaching through a different side. There is a strong pull to try to reach straight for the toy; that prepotent response must be inhibited when a detour reach is required. The following variables are manipulated: (1) which side of the box is open (top, front, left, or right), (2) distance of the toy from the box opening, (3) position of the box on the testing surface (e.g., near the front edge of table or far), (4) box size, and (5) box transparency. The experimental variables jointly determine through which side of the box the toy is seen. Initially, infants reach only at the side through which they are looking. They must look through the opening, and continue to do so to reach in and retrieve the toy. As they get older, the memory of having looked through the opening is enough; infants can look through the opening, sit up, and reach in while looking through a closed side. Still older infants do not need to look along the line of reach at all. Infants progress through a well-demarcated series of 5 stages of performance on this task between 6 and 12 months of age (Diamond, 1981, 1988, 1990a).

Although the A-not-B/delayed response task and the object retrieval task appear to share few surface similarities, human infants improve on these tasks during the same age period (6–12 months; Diamond, 1988, 1991a,b) and so do infant rhesus macaque (1½–4 months; Diamond, 1988, 1991a,b; Diamond and Goldman-Rakic, 1986). Indeed, although there is considerable individual variation in the rate at which different infants improve on any of these tasks, the age at which a given infant reaches "phase 1B" on the object retrieval task is remarkably close to the age at which that same infant can first uncover a hidden object in the A-not-B/delayed response paradigm (Diamond, 1991a,b). Developmental improvements on both in human infants are related to the same changes in the EEG pattern over frontal leads and in frontal-parietal EEG coherence (re: A-not-B: Bell and Fox, 1992, 1997; Fox and Bell, 1990; re: object retrieval: Fox, personal communication). Both the A-not-B/delayed response task and the object retrieval task depend on DL-PFC and are sensitive to the level of dopamine there.

There is no behavioral task more firmly linked to DL-PFC than the A-not-B/delayed response task. Lesions that destroy DL-PFC disrupt performance of A-not-B and delayed response in adult macaques (Butters et al., 1969; Diamond and Goldman-Rakic, 1989; Goldman and Rosvold, 1970) and infant macaques (Diamond, 1990b; Diamond and Goldman-Rakic, 1986; Goldman, Rosvold, and Mishkin, 1970), while performance of other tasks such as delayed nonmatching to sample (Bachevalier and Mishkin, 1986) and visual discrimination (Goldman, Rosvold, and Mishkin, 1970) is unimpaired. Lesions of other brain regions do not affect A-not-B or delayed response performance at the same brief delays (e.g., medial temporal lobe [Diamond, Zola-Morgan, and Squire, 1989]; posterior parietal cortex [Bauer and Fuster, 1976; Diamond and Goldman-Rakic, 1989; Harlow et al., 1952]). Successful delayed response performance has been linked to dorsolateral PFC by techniques as varied as *reversible cooling* (where function is only temporarily disrupted, and an animal can serve as his own control; e.g., Bauer and Fuster, 1976; Fuster and Alexander, 1970), *single unit recording* (where the functions of individual neurons are studied in the intact brain; e.g., Fuster, 1973; Fuster and Alexander, 1971; Niki, 1974), and *2-deoxyglucose metabolic labeling* (where the functions of diverse neural regions are studied in the intact brain; Bugbee and Goldman-Rakic, 1981). Blocking dopamine receptors in DL-PFC produces deficits on the delayed response task as severe as when DL-PFC is removed altogether (Brozoski et al., 1979). Indeed, there is a precise dose-dependent relation between how large a dose of the dopamine antagonist is injected and performance on the delayed response task (Sawaguchi and Goldman-Rakic, 1991). Disruption of the prefrontal dopamine system by injections of MPTP (1-methyl-4-phenyl-1,2,3,6-tetrahydropyridine) also impairs performance on the task (Schneider and Kovelowski, 1990). Destruction of the dopamine neurons in the ventral tegmental area (VTA) that project to prefrontal cortex impairs performance on the task as well (Simon, Scatton, and LeMoal, 1980). Pharmacological activation of $D_2$ dopamine receptors in normal human adults has been found to facilitate performance on the task (Luciana et al., 1992).

DL-PFC lesions in the macaque also disrupt performance on the object retrieval task (Diamond, 1990b; Diamond and Goldman-Rakic, 1985), while lesions of the medial temporal lobe (Diamond, Zola-Morgan, and Squire, 1989) or of posterior parietal cortex (Diamond and Goldman-Rakic, 1989) do not. MPTP injections, which reduce the level of dopamine in prefrontal cortex, also produce deficits on the task (e.g., Saint-Cyr et al., 1988; Schneider and Roeltgen, 1993; Taylor et al., 1990a,b). (MPTP also affects the level of dopamine in the striatum, but lesions of the striatum do not impair performance on the object retrieval task [Crofts et al., 1999].) Cumulative doses of 15–75 mg of MPTP do not produce Parkinsonian-type motor deficits in rhesus macaques, although larger doses do. At the lower doses of MPTP (15–75 mg), monkeys are impaired on the object retrieval and A-not-B/delayed response tasks (Schneider and Kovelowski, 1990; Taylor et al., 1990a,b), although they perform normally on other tasks such as visual discrimination.

Importantly, human infants, infant rhesus macaques, and infant and adult rhesus macaques with lesions of DL-PFC fail the A-not-B/delayed response task under the same conditions and in the same ways. The same is true for the object retrieval task. Thus, for example, on A-not-B, macaques with lesions of DL-PFC and human infants of 7½–9 months succeed when there is no delay (*macaques:* Bättig, Rosvold, and Mishkin, 1960; Goldman, Rosvold, and Mishkin, 1970; Harlow et al., 1952; *infants:* Gratch et al., 1974; Harris, 1973), succeed when allowed to circumvent the memory requirements by continuing to stare at or strain toward the correct well during the delay (*macaques:* Bättig, Rosvold, and Mishkin, 1960; Miles and Blomquist, 1960; Pinsker and French, 1967; *infants:* Cornell, 1979; Fox, Kagan, and Weiskopf, 1979), succeed if a landmark reliably indicates where the reward is located (*macaques:* Pohl, 1973; *infants:* Butterworth, Jarrett, and Hicks, 1982), fail even at brief delays of only 2–5 s (*macaques:* Diamond and Goldman-Rakic, 1989; Goldman and Rosvold, 1970; *infants:* Diamond, 1985; Diamond and Doar, 1989; Fox, Kagan, and Weiskopf, 1979; Gratch and Landers, 1971), and fail if the hiding places differ either in left–right or up–down location (*macaques:* Fuster, 1980; Goldman, Rosvold, and Mishkin, 1970; *infants:* Butterworth, 1976; Gratch and Landers, 1971). See figure 29.2 for details.

Note that most of these manipulations indicate that the presence of the delay is critical, since even very young infants and prefrontally-lesioned macaques perform well when there is no delay or when the requirements of the delay can be circumvented. This suggests that the ability to hold in mind the information on where the reward was last hidden (this might be termed "sustained attention" or the information-maintenance component of "working memory" [Baddeley, 1992]) is critical to success on this task. The information that must be held in mind is relational (Was the reward hidden on the right or the left most recently? "Left" is only left in relation to right and, similarly, "recent" implies a before-and-after relation.) There is also a character-

istic pattern to the errors made by infants and by pre-frontally-lesioned macaques on the A-not-B task: Their errors tend to be confined to the reversal trials and to the trials immediately following a reversal error when the reward continues to be hidden at the new location (Diamond, 1985, 1990a, 1991a,b). If the only source of error on the task were failure to keep the critical information in mind, one would expect errors to be random; but they are not (Diamond, Cruttenden, and Neiderman, 1994). The nonrandom pattern of errors, and the fact that participants occasionally look at the correct location (as if they remember that the reward is there) while at the same time reaching back to the previously correct location (Diamond, 1990a, 1991a; see also Hofstadter and Reznick, 1996), suggests that success on the task also requires resisting, or inhibiting, the tendency to repeat the previous response. (I have suggested that there is a predisposition to repeat the previous response because it had been rewarded. Smith and colleagues [1999] suggest that there is a predisposition to repeat the previous response simply because the response was made before [not because of reinforcement], just as it is easier for neurons in visual cortex to process a visual stimulus if they have previously processed that visual stimulus. Either account of the source of the predisposition works equally well for my theoretical position. The important point is that there is a tendency to repeat the previous response; the source of that predisposition is unimportant for my argument.)

A few errors can be elicited simply by taxing how long information must be held in mind even when no inhibition is required, such as by using a long delay at the first hiding location (Sophian and Wellman, 1983). Similarly, a few errors can be elicited simply by taxing inhibitory control even when the participant does not have to remember where the reward was hidden; for example, a few infants err on the reversal trial even when the covers are transparent (Butterworth, 1977; Willatts, 1985). However, the overwhelming majority of errors occur when participants must both hold information in mind and also exercise inhibitory control (i.e., on reversal trials when the covers are opaque and a delay is imposed).[1]

Similar close parallels in the parameters determining success or failure, and in the characteristics of performance, hold for the object retrieval task (*infants:* Diamond, 1981; 1990b, 1991a; *macaques with lesions of DL-PFC:* Diamond, 1990b; 1991a; Diamond and Goldman-Rakic, 1985; *MPTP-treated macaques:* Saint-Cyr et al., 1988; Schneider and Roeltgen, 1993; Taylor et al., 1990a,b). Human infants of 7½–9 months, rhesus macaques with lesions of DL-PFC, and macaques treated with MPTP all succeed on the object retrieval task when

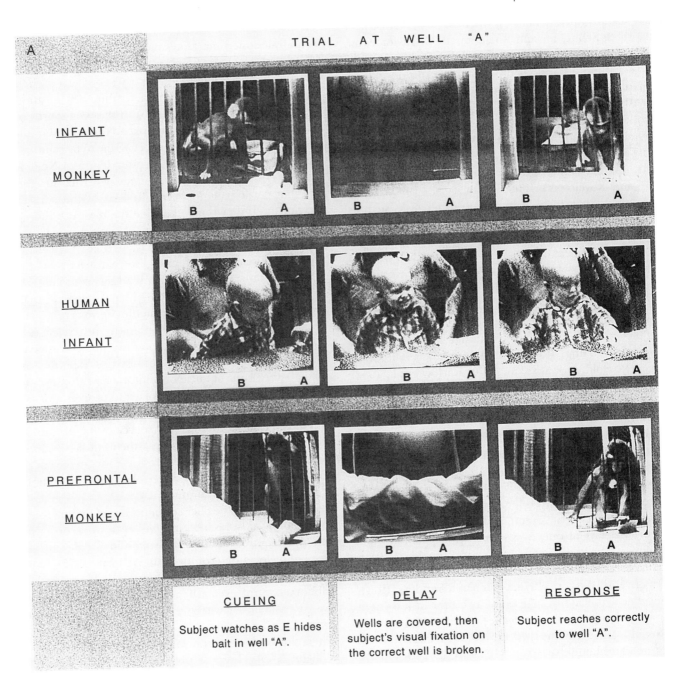

INFANT

MONKEY

HUMAN

INFANT

PREFRONTAL

MONKEY

**CUEING**

Subject watches as E hides
bait in well "A".

**DELAY**

Wells are covered, then
subject's visual fixation on
the correct well is broken.

**RESPONSE**

Subject reaches correctly
to well "A".

FIGURE 29.2 Illustration of a 1½-month-old infant rhesus macaque, 8-month-old human infant, and an adult rhesus macaque in whom dorsolateral prefrontal cortex had been removed bilaterally performing the A-not-B/delayed response task. All are correct at the first hiding place (**A**).

*(continued)*

they are looking through the open side of the box. They fail when they are looking through a closed side, and they fail by trying to reach straight through the transparent barrier instead of detouring around it. Human infants of 7½–9 months, rhesus macaques with lesions of DL-PFC, and macaques treated with MPTP perform better when the box is opaque than when the box is transparent. They lean over to look in the box opening when the left or right side of the box is open and recruit the contralateral hand to reach in the opening (see figure 29.3) and show that "awkward reach" on both the left and right sides of the box.

This pattern of performance highlights the importance, for success on the object retrieval task, of being able to inhibit the strong tendency to reach straight in the side of the box through which one is looking. Behaviors such as the "awkward reach" also highlight the importance of holding the location of the box opening

TRIAL AT WELL "B"

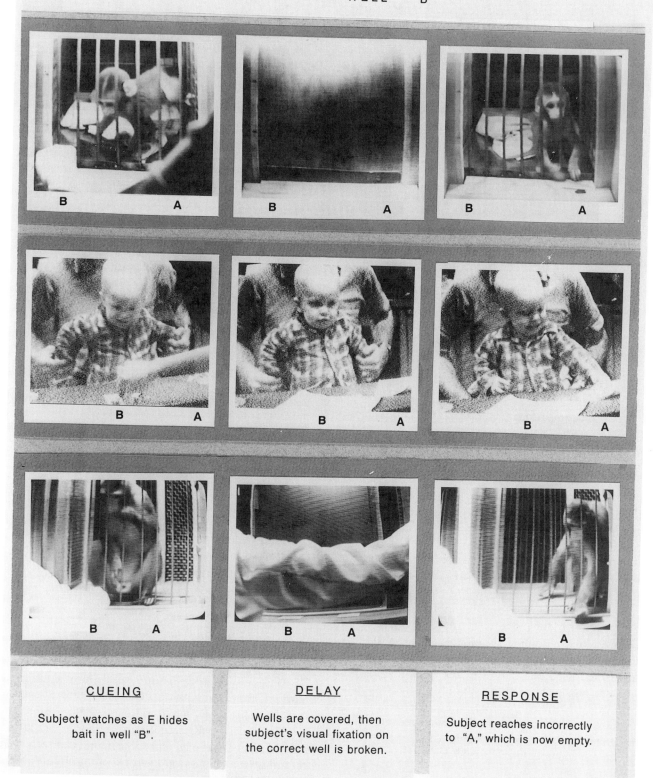

| CUEING | DELAY | RESPONSE |
|---|---|---|
| Subject watches as E hides bait in well "B". | Wells are covered, then subject's visual fixation on the correct well is broken. | Subject reaches incorrectly to "A," which is now empty. |

FIGURE 29.2 *(Continued)*. After 2 trials, there is a switch and the reward is hidden at the second hiding place (**B**). Although they all watch the hiding at B, and although the delay at B is no longer than at A, they all err by reaching back to A. This error is called the A-not-B error because they are correct on the A trials, but not on the B trials; they reach to A, not B. (Reprinted with permission from Diamond, 1990a,b.)

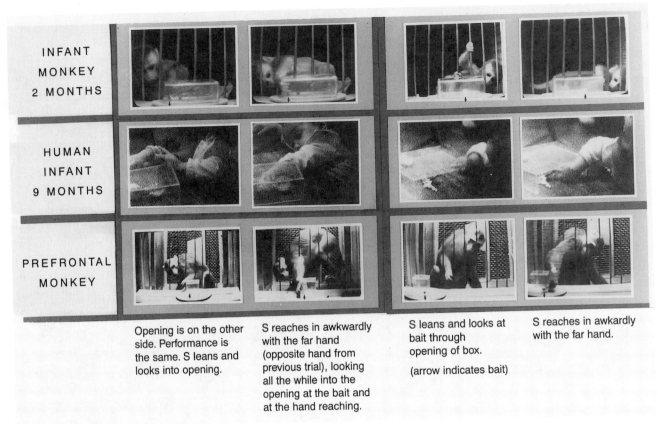

| INFANT MONKEY 2 MONTHS | | | |
| HUMAN INFANT 9 MONTHS | | | |
| PREFRONTAL MONKEY | | | |

Opening is on the other side. Performance is the same. S leans and looks into opening.

S reaches in awkwardly with the far hand (opposite hand from previous trial), looking all the while into the opening at the bait and at the hand reaching.

S leans and looks at bait through opening of box.

(arrow indicates bait)

S reaches in awkwardly with the far hand.

FIGURE 29.3  Illustration of a 2-month-old infant rhesus macaque, 9-month-old human infant, and an adult rhesus macaque in whom dorsolateral prefrontal cortex had been removed bilaterally performing the object retrieval task. They lean and look in the side opening of the transparent box, and then while continuing to look through the opening, recruit the contralateral hand to reach in and retrieve the reward. This is seen on both sides of the box and does not reflect a hand preference. Because of its appearance, the recruitment of the contralateral arm is dubbed the "awkward reach. (Reprinted with permission from Diamond, 1990a,b.)"

in mind when looking at the reward and holding the location of the reward in mind when looking at the box opening, and of integrating the two pieces of information. Focusing exclusively on the reward or the box will not work for this task; both must be taken into account. Reaching through the opening when looking through a closed side requires integrating in one's mind looking at the reward along one route with reaching for the reward along a completely different route. Infants of 8½–9 months and prefrontally-lesioned macaques are only able to succeed when the left or right side of the transparent box is open by simplifying the task. They lean over to look in the opening, hence lining up the opening and the reward so that they can see both at once and so that their line of sight is the same as the line along which they will reach.

In sum, human infants of 7½–9 months, infant macaques of 1½–2½ months, adult macaques with bilateral removals of DL-PFC, infant macaques of 5 months in whom DL-PFC was removed at 4 months, and adult macaques who have received MPTP injections to disrupt the prefrontal dopamine system fail the A-not-B/delayed response and object retrieval tasks under the same conditions and in the same ways (table 29.1). This does not prove that maturational changes in DL-PFC during infancy contribute to the emergence of success on these tasks during infancy, but this body of work makes that hypothesis plausible.

*Evidence of improvement in the cognitive abilities that depend on DL-PFC during early childhood*

DL-PFC continues to mature until early adulthood. Marked improvements on tasks that require working memory plus inhibition (tasks thought to require the functions of DL-PFC) are seen in children between 3 and 6 years of age. At 3 years of age, one can see errors reminiscent of the A-not-B error seen in infants and in prefrontally-lesioned macaques, but with a slightly more difficult task. On this task, children who are 3 years old can sort cards correctly by the first criterion they are given (either color or shape; Kirkham, Cruess, and

TABLE 29.1

*Performance of human infants, infant rhesus monkeys, and adult rhesus monkeys with selective ablations on the same three tasks*

|  | A-not-B | Delayed Response | Object Retrieval |
|---|---|---|---|
| Human infants show a clear developmental progression from 7½ to 12 months | Diamond, 1985 | Diamond and Doar, 1989 | Diamond, 1988 |
| Adult monkeys with lesions of prefrontal cortex fail | Diamond and Goldman-Rakic, 1989 | Diamond and Goldman-Rakic, 1989 | Diamond and Goldman-Rakic, 1985 |
| Adult monkeys with lesions of parietal cortex succeed | Diamond and Goldman-Rakic, 1989 | Diamond and Goldman-Rakic, 1989 | Diamond and Goldman-Rakic, 1985 |
| Adult monkeys with lesions of the hippocampal formation succeed | Diamond, Zola-Morgan, and Squire, 1989 | Squire and Zola-Morgan, 1983 | Diamond, Zola-Morgan, and Squire, 1989 |
| Infant monkeys show a clear developmental progression from 1½ to 4 months | Diamond and Goldman-Rakic, 1986 | Diamond and Goldman-Rakic, 1986 | Diamond and Goldman-Rakic, 1986 |
| 5-month-old infant monkeys who received lesions of prefrontal cortex at 4 months fail | Diamond and Goldman-Rakic, 1986 | Diamond and Goldman-Rakic, 1986 | |
| Disruption of the prefrontal dopamine system impairs performance in monkeys | | Taylor et al., 1990a,b; Schneider and Roeltgen, 1993 | Schneider and Kovelowski, 1990; Sawaguchi and Goldman-Rakic, 1991 |

Diamond, submitted; Zelazo, Frye, and Rapus, 1996; Zelazo and Reznick, 1991; Zelazo, Reznick, and Piñon, 1995), just as infants of 7½–9 months and prefrontally-lesioned macaques are correct at the first hiding place, and just as adults with prefrontal cortex damage are correct at sorting cards according to the first criterion (Wisconsin Card Sort test: Drewe, 1974; Milner, 1963, 1964). Three-year-old children err when correct performance demands switching to a new criterion, i.e., when cards previously sorted by color (or shape) must now be sorted according to the other criterion (shape or color), just as infants of 7½–9 months and prefrontally lesioned macaques err when required to switch and search for the reward at the other location, and just as adults with prefrontal cortex damage err when required to switch to a new sorting criterion.

Although 3-year-old children fail to sort by the new sorting criterion (sticking steadfastly to the previously correct criterion), they can correctly state the new sorting criterion (Kirkham et al., submitted; Zelazo, Frye, and Rapus, 1996). Similarly, infants of 7½–9 months can sometimes tell you with their eyes that they know the reward is in the new hiding place even as they persist in reaching back to the previously correct location (Diamond, 1990a, 1991a,b; Hofstadter and Reznick, 1996), and patients with prefrontal cortex damage can sometimes tell you correctly the new sorting criterion even as they persist in sorting by the previously correct criterion (Luria and Homskaya, 1964; Milner, 1963, 1964). When there are only two sorting criteria (color and

shape) and only two values for each criterion (e.g., red/blue, truck/star) children are able to succeed at the card sorting task by 4–5 years of age. If the task is made more complicated, by, for example, adding a third sorting dimension, then children cannot succeed until they are 5–6 years old. The problem for the children appears to be in relating two or more dimensions to a single stimulus (thinking of a stimulus as either red or blue and also thinking about the same stimulus as either a truck or a star) and in inhibiting the tendency to repeat their previously correct way of categorizing the stimulus.

Similarly, children 3 years old have great difficulty with "appearance–reality" tasks (Flavell, 1986, 1993) where, for example, they are presented with a sponge that looks like a rock. Three-year-olds typically report, for example, that it looks like a rock and really is a rock, whereas a child of 4–5 years correctly answers that it looks like a rock but really is a sponge. The problem for the younger children is in relating two conflicting identities to the same object (Rice et al., 1997) and in inhibiting the response that matches their perception (thus manipulations that reduce the perceptual salience, by removing the object during questioning, find significantly better performance by children of 3–4 years [e.g., Heberle, Clune, and Kelly, 1999]). "Theory of mind" and "false belief" tasks are other tasks that require holding two things in mind about the same situation (the true state of affairs and the false belief of another person) and inhibiting the impulse to give the

DIAMOND: THE ROLE OF DOPAMINE IN THE PREFRONTAL CORTEX    441 veridical answer. For example, the child must keep in mind where the hidden object is now and where another person saw it placed before, and the child must inhibit the inclination to say where the object really is and instead say where the other person would think it is, even though the child knows that answer to be "wrong" because the object is not there now. Here, as well, manipulations that reduce the perceptual salience of the true state of affairs aid children of 3–4 years (Fritz, 1991; Zaitchik, 1991). Carlson, Moses, and Hix (1998) reasoned that pointing veridically to true locations and identities is likely to be a well-practiced and reinforced response in young children, and that children of 3–4 years have trouble inhibiting that tendency when they should point to the false location, as is required on false belief tasks. Carlson, Moses, and Hix (1998) found that when they gave children a novel response by which to indicate the false location, children of 3–4 years performed much better on the false belief task.

Many of the advances of Piaget's "preoperational" child of 5–7 years over a child of 3–4 years, who is in the stage of "concrete operations," similarly reflect the development of the ability to hold more than one thing in mind and to inhibit the strongest response tendency of the moment. Evidence that children 3 or 4 years old have difficulty keeping two things in mind at the same time, or that they tend to focus on only one aspect of a problem, can be seen in (1) their failure on tests of liquid conservation (they fail to attend to both height and width, attending only to height), (2) their difficulty on tests of perspective-taking where they must mentally manipulate a scene to say what it would look like from another perspective and must inhibit the strong tendency to give the most salient response (i.e., their current perspective), (3) their difficulty in comparing an old idea with a new one and hence seeing the contradiction, and (4) their difficulty in working through a two-step problem without losing track of what they are doing. By 5 or 6 years of age, children are capable of doing all of these things. Certainly, part of the difficulty posed by Piaget's liquid conservation task (Piaget and Inhelder, 1941) is the salience of the visual perception that the tall, thin container appears to have more liquid in it. Thus, if an opaque screen is placed between the child and the containers before the child answers, younger children are much more likely to answer correctly (Bruner, 1964).

Many investigators have similarly found evidence of improved ability to exercise inhibitory control over one's behavior between 3 and 6 years of age, especially when children must hold two things in mind and relate them to one another. For example, in the delay of grat-

ification paradigm, when faced with the choice of a smaller, immediate reward or a later, larger reward, children of 3–4 years are unable to inhibit going for the immediate reward although they would prefer the larger one. By 5–6 years of age, children are much better at waiting for the bigger reward (Mischel and Mischel, 1983). Similarly, on the windows task, where children are rewarded for pointing to a box that is visibly empty, and are not rewarded for pointing to a box in which they can see candy, 3-year-olds fail to inhibit the tendency to point to the baited box (Russell et al., 1991). Children 3–4 years of age also tend to fail go/no-go tasks because they cannot inhibit responding. They appear to understand and remember the task instructions (e.g., they can verbalize the instructions), but cannot get themselves to act accordingly. By 5–6 years, they succeed on these tasks (Bell and Livesey, 1985; Livesey and Morgan, 1991).

Difficulty in holding two things in mind can also be seen in persons with frontal cortex damage. For example, they can have difficulty when asked to do two things (such as clean the windshield and change the oil). They are inclined to focus on only one aspect of a story, instead of on the story as a whole. Indeed, Goldstein (1936, 1944) considered the fundamental disorder caused by damage to the frontal lobe to be an "inability to grasp the entirety of a complex situation." Patients with frontal cortex damage also have a well-documented difficulty inhibiting a strong response tendency. For example, they are impaired on the Stroop task, which requires inhibiting the normal tendency to say the word when one is reading; one is instructed instead to say the color of the ink in which the word is printed (Perret, 1974; Richer et al., 1993). They fail a perspective-taking task much like Piaget's, and make the same error as do the younger children (they give as their answer their current perspective, when the current answer is the scene as viewed from a different perspective; Price et al., 1990).

We have followed the developmental improvement in these abilities between 3½ and 7 years of age using three tasks, the "day–night Stroop-like" task (Gerstadt, Hong, and Diamond, 1994), the tapping task (Diamond and Taylor, 1996), and the three pegs task (Diamond et al., 1997). These three tasks were also used in our research on the role of dopamine in prefrontal cortex function early in life in treated PKU children and so will be described briefly here.

For the day–night task, children must hold two rules in mind ("Say 'night' when you see a white card with a picture of the sun, and say 'day' when you see a black card with a picture of the moon and stars") and must inhibit the tendency to say what the stimuli really represent; instead they must say the opposite. Children of 3½–4½ years find the task terribly difficult; by 6–7 years of age, the task is trivially easy. Children younger than 6 years of age err often, whereas children of 6–7 years are correct on roughly 90% of the trials (see figure 29.4). Children of 3½ and 4 years show long response latencies on the task (roughly 2 s); older children take roughly half as long (1 s). The age-related increase in the percentage of correct responses is relatively continuous from 3½ to 7 years of age, but the decrease in speed of responding occurs primarily between 3½ and 4½ years. Passler, Isaac, and Hynd (1985) tested children on a similar, though slightly easier, variant of this task, which required children to recognize the correct answer, whereas our task requires that they recall the correct answer. They found that children of 6 years were performing at ceiling on their task, which is consistent with the excellent performance that we found at 6–7 years of age.

To test whether the requirement to remember two rules alone is sufficient to cause the younger children difficulty, we tested a version of our day–night test where each card contained one of two abstract designs (Gerstadt, Hong, and Diamond, 1994). Children were instructed to say "day" to one design and "night" to the other. Here the children were still required to hold two rules in mind, but they did not also have to inhibit the tendency to say what the stimuli really represented because the stimuli were abstract designs. Even the youngest children performed superbly here. Thus, the requirement to learn and remember two rules is not in itself sufficient to account for the poor performance of the younger children on the day–night task.

Moreover, children's difficulty with the task depends critically on the correct responses being semantically related to the responses that must be inhibited. When we used the same white/sun and black/moon cards, but instructed the children to say "dog" to one and "pig" to the other, even the youngest children again performed well (Diamond, Kirkham, and Amso, submitted). The task of holding two rules in mind and inhibiting one's natural inclination is sufficiently hard for the younger children that they need a long time to formulate their answers in order to respond correctly. Although we gave children unlimited time, they tended to speed up their responses over the 16 test trials, and the accuracy of the youngest children correspondingly fell. When we made the children wait to respond, by singing a brief ditty to them on each trial after the stimulus was presented, the younger children were able to perform well, even though the period before their response was filled with potentially interfering verbal stimulation (Diamond et al., submitted). It is not simply that slowing down the testing helped because when the children were made to wait before the start of each trial, they performed poorly. The day–night task is sufficiently difficult for young children that it takes them several seconds to compute the answer. Often they do not take the needed time; when forced to take extra time they can perform well.

Luria's tapping test (Luria, 1966) also requires (1) remembering two rules and (2) inhibiting the response you were inclined to make, making the opposite response instead. Here, one needs to remember the rules, "Tap once when the experimenter taps twice, and tap twice when the experimenter taps once," and one needs to inhibit the tendency to mimic what the experimenter does. Children improve on this task over the same age period as they do on the day–night task (see figure 29.4). Over the period of 3½–7 years, children improve in both speed and accuracy on the tapping task, with most of the improvement occurring by the age of 6 (Becker, Isaac, and Hynd, 1987; Diamond and Taylor, 1996; Passler, Isaac, and Hynd, 1985).

Adults with large frontal lobe lesions fail this same tapping task (Luria, 1966). They have similar problems when instructed to raise a finger in response to the experimenter's making a fist and to make a fist in response to the experimenter's raising a finger (Luria, 1966). The most common error by young children is always tapping once, or always tapping twice, regardless of what the experimenter does. It may be that the young children are able to keep in mind only one of the two rules. Or, it may be that they lack the ability to switch

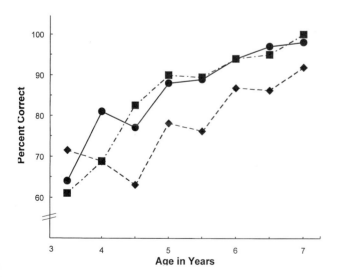

FIGURE 29.4 Performance of children, 3½ through 7 years of age, on the day–night, tapping, and three pegs task. Note the close parallels in performance on all three tasks throughout this age range.

flexibly between the two rules, although they remember both. (It cannot be because they do not understand what they should do, because no child is tested who does not demonstrate understanding during training of what he or she should do when the experimenter taps once or twice.) This error is reminiscent of a characteristic error Luria (1966) observed in his patients. For example, when asked to draw, alternately, a circle and a cross, patients with extensive frontal lobe damage start out performing correctly (as do even the youngest children), but the patients soon deteriorate into following only one of the rules (i.e., drawing only circles or only crosses).

Other errors by the children seem more clearly to reflect inadequate inhibitory control. One common error among the younger children is to be unable to resist tapping many times, instead of just once or twice. Again, this error is reminiscent of behavior Luria noted in patients with excessive damage to the frontal lobe: "[When asked] to tap three times or to squeeze the doctor's hand three times . . . although the patient retains the verbal instruction and repeats it correctly, he taps many times or squeezes the doctor's hand five, six, or more times instead of three" (Luria, 1966: p. 252). Another error made by the younger children is to match what the experimenter does, instead of doing the reverse. Luria (1966; Luria and Homskaya, 1964) has extensively described such "echopractic" errors in frontal lobe patients. Indeed, on the tapping task itself, Luria found that although the patients could correctly comply with the instructions for a short while (like the younger children), they very soon began to imitate the experimenter's movements. Luria also found that the frontal patients could verbalize the rules even as they failed to act in accord with them.

Since Luria introduced the tapping test more than 30 years ago, it has been widely used in neurological assessments of frontal lobe damage in patients. However, much of the work with this test comes from old studies with patients with massive damage. It is not clear from such studies which regions within frontal cortex are critical for the task, or even whether the cortex, rather than the basal ganglia, is the critical site.

For the three pegs task (Balamore and Wozniak, 1984) a child is shown a pegboard containing three pegs arranged in the order red, yellow, green. The child is asked to tap the pegs in the order red, green, yellow. This task requires remembering a three-item sequence and inhibiting the tendency to tap the pegs in their spatial order. The tapping and day–night tasks are more similar to each other than is the three pegs task, but it, too, requires acting counter to one's initial tendency on the basis of information held in mind. Children show

developmental improvements on the three pegs task during the same age period that they are improving on the tapping and day–night tasks (see figure 29.4; Diamond et al., 1997), and performance on the three tasks is correlated (tapping and three pegs: $r[144] = .53$, $p = .0001$; tapping and day–night: $r[144] = .35$, $p = .0001$; day–night and three pegs: $r[151] = .20$, $p = .01$; Diamond et al., 1997).

Clearly, improvement in the performance of tasks requiring memory plus inhibition occurs between 3 and 6 years of age. Perhaps that improvement is made possible, in part, by maturational changes in DL-PFC, although that remains to be demonstrated. Perhaps one of those maturational changes in DL-PFC is in its dopamine system, although little is known about what is happening in the dopamine system in prefrontal cortex during this period. To begin to look at the role of the dopamine innervation of DL-PFC in helping to subserve cognitive functions during infancy and early childhood, we have been studying children who, we had good reason to believe, have reduced levels of dopamine in prefrontal cortex but otherwise remarkably normal brains—children treated early and continuously for phenylketonuria (PKU), whose phenylalanine (Phe) levels are 3–5 times normal (6–10 mg/dL [360–600 mmol/L]).

At the time we began this work, there were almost no data on the role of dopamine in prefrontal function in humans, and no data on the role of dopamine in aiding prefrontal function early in development in any species. As an initial way of beginning to look at the role of dopamine in prefrontal cortex function in humans early in development, we conducted a large, longitudinal study of children treated early and continuously for PKU (Diamond et al., 1997). We complemented that with work with an animal model of early-and-continuously-treated PKU, where we could investigate the underlying biological mechanism (Diamond et al., 1994). Additionally, we sought to obtain converging evidence from a study of visual contrast sensitivity in children treated early and continuously for PKU (Diamond and Herzberg, 1996), where we postulated that the same underlying mechanism was at work.

## The reasoning and evidence leading to the hypothesis of a selective deficit in dopamine in prefrontal cortex in children treated early and continuously for PKU

PHENYLKETONURIA (PKU) DEFINED   The core problem in PKU is a mutation of the gene on chromosome 12 (12q22–12q24.1) that codes for the enzyme phenylalanine hydroxylase. Phenylalanine hydroxylase is essential for hydroxylating (i.e., converting) the amino acid phenylalanine (Phe) into the amino acid tyrosine (Tyr) (DiLella et al., 1986; Lidsky et al., 1985; Woo et al., 1983; see figure 29.5). In the roughly 1 in every 10,000 people born with PKU, phenylalanine hydroxylase activity is either absent or markedly reduced. Hence, PKU is a member of the class of disorders called "inborn [i.e., genetic] errors of metabolism." In the case of PKU, the error is in the metabolism of Phe.

Since little, if any, Phe is metabolized, Phe levels in the bloodstream reach dangerously high levels. Indeed, when PKU is untreated, levels of Phe in the bloodstream rise to well over 10 times normal (>20 mg/dL [>1200 mmol/L]). Since little or no Tyr is produced from Phe, the level of Tyr in the bloodstream is low (Nord, McCabe, and McCabe, 1988). (Tyr levels would be still lower were it not for the availability of Tyr directly through the foods we eat.) This imbalance in blood levels of Phe and Tyr, if not corrected early, causes widespread brain damage and severe mental retardation (Cowie, 1971; Hsia, 1967; Koch et al., 1982; Krause et al., 1985; Tourian and Sidbury, 1978). Indeed, PKU is the most common biochemical cause of mental retardation. The primary cause of the widespread brain dam-

age is thought to be the toxic effects of grossly elevated levels of Phe in the brain.

THE TREATMENT FOR PKU: A DIET LOW IN PHENYLALANINE    The treatment for PKU consists of a diet low in Phe. Since Phe is a constituent of protein, the low-Phe diet severely restricts the intake of milk and milk products (such as ice cream, butter, and cheese), and all meat and fish. When PKU is treated early and continuously by a diet low in Phe, gross brain damage and severe mental retardation are averted (Bickel, Hudson, and Woolf, 1971; Holtzman et al., 1986). Note that here is an example of how a behavioral change (changing what you eat) can profoundly affect your biochemistry and your brain.

*Limitations of the diet: Why problems might still exist when PKU is treated*    The low-Phe diet rarely results in fully normal levels of Phe or Tyr. This is because the need to minimize Phe intake must be balanced with the need for protein. Eliminating all Phe from the diet would require eliminating all protein. Outside of protein, Phe is not present in any naturally occurring food. The human body needs to ingest protein; moreover, the body

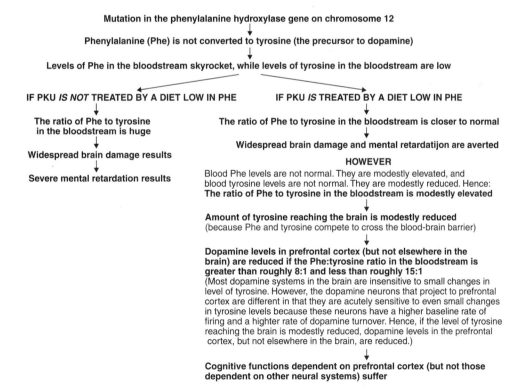

FIGURE 29.5    Diagram illustrating the reasoning leading to the hypothesis that children treated early and continuously for PKU, whose blood Phe levels are 6–10 mg/dL, would have a selective decrease of dopamine in prefrontal cortex and a selective deficit in the cognitive abilities dependent on prefrontal cortex.

needs a small quantity of Phe to produce its own protein. Hence, because persons with PKU need protein, blood Phe levels remain somewhat elevated in a person with PKU, even with conscientious adherence to the recommended diet, as an inevitable consequence of consuming even a small amount of protein. The advice of the U.S. National Collaborative Study of Treated PKU has been that as long as Phe levels in the bloodstream do not exceed 5 times normal (10 mg/dL [600 mmol/L]), persons with PKU are considered to be under adequate control (Koch and Wenz, 1987; Williamson et al., 1981). The diet has historically done little to correct the reduction in Tyr, although recently the companies that manufacture the "formula" that persons with PKU drink instead of milk have added additional Tyr to their formulas. Still, Tyr levels are below normal in most children treated for PKU.

*Even with a low-Phe diet, there are moderate elevations in the Phe:Tyr ratio in the bloodstream and deficits in certain cognitive abilities* For PKU children, following a dietary regimen of reduced Phe intake and mild Tyr supplementation results in moderately elevated levels of Phe and moderately reduced levels of Tyr in their bloodstreams. (Were they not following this dietary regimen, the elevation in their Phe:Tyr ratio be huge, rather than moderate, and they would likely incur brain damage and become severely cognitively impaired.)

Given that the low-Phe diet does not return Phe and Tyr levels to normal, one can see how the possibility for problems could still exist. Indeed, a number of studies have found significant cognitive deficits in PKU children on the low-Phe diet (Dobson et al., 1976; Faust, Libon, and Pueschel, 1986; Pennington et al., 1985; Smith and Beasley, 1989; Williamson et al., 1981). For example, the IQs of these children are often significantly lower than the IQs of their siblings. Children with PKU, even when they have been on the special diet since shortly after birth, typically have IQs in the 80s or 90s—lower than the mean score of 100 of their same-age peers, though still within the normal range (Berry et al., 1979; Dobson et al., 1976; Williamson et al, 1981).

In the 1980s, studies reported problems in holding information in mind, problem-solving, and "executive functions" in children with PKU on the low-Phe diet (Brunner, Berch, and Berry, 1987; Faust, Libon, and Pueschel, 1986; Krause et al., 1985; Pennington et al., 1985; Smith and Beasley, 1989). These problems are reminiscent of the deficits seen after damage to prefrontal cortex, and that similarity did not escape the notice of others (see, especially, Welsh et al., 1990). Indeed, damage to prefrontal cortex typically results in IQs lowered to the 80s or 90s (Stuss and Benson, 1986,

1987)—the same range one sees in children treated for PKU. The impact of these findings was muted, however, because people were not sure how to make sense of them. No one had suggested a mechanism whereby the cognitive functions dependent on prefrontal cortex might be impaired in treated PKU children, while other cognitive functions appeared normal. Actually, the facts needed for understanding the underlying mechanism were already available. However, the neuroscientists working on the prefrontal dopamine system in the rat and the cognitive neuropsychologists and pediatricians working with PKU children did not know of one another's work, so no one had put the facts together.

PROPOSED MECHANISM: HOW A MODEST IMBALANCE IN THE LEVELS OF PHE AND TYR IN THE BLOODSTREAM MIGHT PRODUCE DEFICITS SPECIFIC TO THE COGNITIVE ABILITIES DEPENDENT ON PREFRONTAL CORTEX  Children treated early and continuously for PKU have a moderate increase in the ratio of one amino acid (Phe) to another (Tyr) in their bloodstreams (Tyr is the precursor of dopamine.) We predicted that when the imbalance is moderate it would selectively affect the dopamine projection to prefrontal cortex.

Why should a modest imbalance in the levels of Phe and tyrosine in the bloodstream produce deficits in the cognitive abilities dependent on DL-PFC? And why should deficits be confined to that neural system and not extend to other functions of the brain?

*Modest reduction in the level of Tyr reaching the brain* The modest elevation in Phe relative to Tyr in the bloodstream results in a modest reduction in the level of Tyr reaching the brain. This is because Phe and Tyr compete for the same limited supply of proteins to transport them across the blood–brain barrier (Chirigos, Greengard, and Udenfriend, 1960; Oldendorf, 1973; Pardridge, 1977). Indeed, those transport proteins have a higher binding affinity for Phe than for Tyr (Miller et al., 1985; Pardridge and Oldendorf 1977). Thus, elevations in blood levels of Phe relative to Tyr place Tyr at a competitive disadvantage in finding transport into the brain. Because the ratio of Phe to Tyr in the bloodstream is only modestly increased in those on dietary treatment for PKU, the decrease in the amount of Tyr reaching the brain is correspondingly modest. In this way, the moderate plasma imbalance in Phe:Tyr results in modestly reduced Tyr levels in the brain.

*The dopamine neurons that project to prefrontal cortex are unusually sensitive to modest reductions* The special properties of the dopamine projection to prefrontal cortex make prefrontal cortex more sensitive to small changes in the level of Tyr than other brain regions. The brain needs Tyr to make dopamine (see figure 29.6). Indeed, the hydroxylation of Tyr is the rate-limiting step in the synthesis of dopamine. Most dopamine systems in the brain are unaffected by small decreases in the amount of available Tyr. Not so prefrontal cortex. The dopamine neurons that project to prefrontal cortex are unusual in that they have a higher firing rate and higher rate of dopamine turnover than other dopamine neurons (Bannon, Bunney, and Roth, 1981; Roth, 1984; Thierry et al., 1977). These unusual properties of the prefrontally projecting dopamine neurons in the ventral tegmental area (VTA) make prefrontal cortex acutely sensitive to even a modest change in the supply of Tyr (Tam et al., 1990; Wurtman et al., 1974). Reductions in the availability of Tyr too small to have much effect on other dopamine systems in other neural regions (such as the striatum) have been shown to profoundly reduce dopamine levels in prefrontal cortex (Bradberry et al., 1989).

*Reducing the level of dopamine in prefrontal cortex produces deficits in the cognitive abilities dependent on prefrontal cortex*

As mentioned earlier, selectively depleting DL-PFC of dopamine can produce cognitive deficits as severe as those found when DL-PFC is removed altogether (Brozoski et al., 1979). Local injection of dopamine antagonists into DL-PFC impairs performance in a precise, dose-dependent manner (Sawaguchi and Goldman-Rakic, 1991). Destruction of the dopamine neurons in the VTA that project to prefrontal cortex also impairs performance on tasks dependent on DL-

PFC (Simon, Scatton, and LeMoal, 1980). Similarly, injections of MPTP that disrupt the dopamine projection to prefrontal cortex, but are of sufficiently low dose that motor deficits are avoided, impair performance on the A-not-B/delayed response and object retrieval tasks (Schneider and Kovelowski, 1990; Taylor et al., 1990a,b).

SUMMARY OF THE REASONING LEADING TO THE PREFRONTAL DOPAMINE HYPOTHESIS IN TREATED PKU   For these reasons it seemed plausible that the moderate imbalance in the Phe:Tyr ratio in the bloodstreams of children treated early and continuously for PKU might well result in deficits in the cognitive abilities dependent on prefrontal cortex (because of the unusual vulnerability of the dopamine projection to prefrontal cortex to a moderate reduction in the amount of available tyrosine) without significantly affecting other brain regions or other cognitive abilities. Hence, we hypothesized that here was a mechanism by which the modest elevation in the Phe:Tyr ratio in the bloodstream of some children treated for PKU, which results in moderate reductions in the level of Tyr reaching the brain, might selectively affect prefrontal cortex (by modestly decreasing the level of Tyr reaching the brain).

*A 4-year longitudinal study of children treated early and continuously for PKU*

To investigate our prediction that children treated early and continuously for PKU have selective deficits in the cognitive functions dependent on prefrontal cortex, we

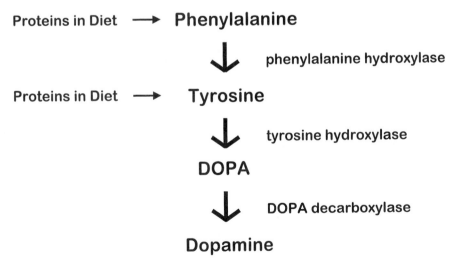

FIGURE 29.6   Diagram illustrating the mechanism by which the neurotransmitter dopamine is produced in the body. Persons with PKU either lack the enzyme phenylalanine hydroxylase or have it in an inactive form. Note that the body acquires tyrosine via two routes, the hydroxylation of Phe and directly through diet. The hydroxylation of tyrosine is the rate-limiting step in the production of dopamine.

tested 148 children longitudinally and 364 children cross-sectionally (Diamond et al., 1997). Included were children treated early and continuously for PKU, siblings of the PKU children, matched controls, and children from the general population. Children from the general population were tested cross-sectionally; all other groups were tested longitudinally.

If a PKU child starts dietary treatment too late or discontinues it, the very high plasma Phe levels during those off-treatment periods can cause permanent, widespread brain damage. Therefore, we were careful to include in this study only those PKU children who started dietary treatment soon after birth (80% began the low-Phe diet within 14 days of age; all had been placed on a low-Phe diet within 1 month of birth) and who had been continuously maintained on the diet thereafter (i.e., children with early- and continuously-treated PKU).

Because no control group is perfect, we included three different control groups. Siblings provide a partial control for family background and genetic make-up. However, they are an imperfect control group because, except for twins, they are not matched on age or birth order, and often not on gender or health status. Therefore, we also studied children who, though unrelated to our PKU participants, matched them on a host of background and health variables—gender, gestational age at birth, birthweight, ethnic background, religion, age at beginning of testing, community of residence, childcare arrangements, number of siblings, and birth order, as well as the age, level of education, and occupational status of each parent. Selecting control subjects by matching on a list of variables is imperfect as well, however, because the children thus selected may not match on other critical variables that one had not considered. Therefore, we complemented the inclusion of siblings and matched controls with a normative sample of children from the general population. With this last group we attempted to get an estimate of the "normal" developmental progression on each of our tasks.

All children studied had normal birthweights, IQs within the normal range, and no known learning disabilities or serious medical problems. Almost all were full-term (100% of the children tested cross-sectionally; 96% tested longitudinally). PKU is found primarily among Caucasians, so almost all of our participants were Caucasian (95% of the children tested cross-sectionally; 93% tested longitudinally). Because of the large age range studied (6 months to 7 years), three different batteries of cognitive neuropsychological measures were used—one for infants (6–12 months), one for toddlers (15–30 months), and one for young children (3½–7 years). A total of 19 cognitive neuropsychological measures were administered (see table 29.2). Infants were tested every month, toddlers every 3 months, and young children every 6 months. At each age, each child was tested on multiple tasks linked to prefrontal cortex and on multiple control tasks not linked to prefrontal cortex.

FINDINGS

*Deficits in the working memory and inhibitory control abilities dependent on DL-PFC in children treated early and continuously for PKU* We found that PKU children, who had been on a low-Phe diet since the first month of life but who had moderately elevated blood Phe levels (levels roughly 3–5 times normal [6–10 mg/dL; 360–600 µmol/L]) were impaired on all six tests that require both holding information in mind and overriding or resisting a dominant response, i.e., tasks dependent on DL-PFC. These six tasks were the A-not-B and the object retrieval tasks for infants; A-not-B with invisible displacement for toddlers; the day–night Stroop-like test, the tapping test, and the three pegs test for young children (see figure 29.7). The fact that even *infants* showed these impairments suggests that the dopaminergic innervation to prefrontal cortex is critical for the proper expression of these abilities even during the first year of life.

These deficits in the working memory and inhibitory control abilities dependent on DL-PFC were evident in all age groups (infants, toddlers, and young children), and remained significant even controlling for IQ, gender, health variables, and background characteristics. The deficits were clear whether the PKU children with blood Phe levels 3–5 times normal were compared to (1) other PKU children with lower Phe levels, (2) their own siblings, (3) matched controls, or (4) children from the general population.

One way to summarize the many comparisons across the three age groups and 19 tasks is to look at the results on one dependent measure for every task. For each task (the control tasks as well as those requiring working memory plus inhibitory control) we selected the dependent measure that yielded the strongest between-group differences on that particular task. This gave each task the best possible opportunity to yield a difference between groups, whether we had predicted a group difference or not. Of the 24 comparisons between PKU children with blood Phe levels 3–5 times above normal and the four other groups of children (PKU children with Phe levels closer to normal [<3× normal], siblings of PKU children, matched controls, and children from the general population) on the six

TABLE 29.2
*List of tasks*

| | Tasks Used with Infants (ages 6–12 months) |
|---|---|
| | *Tests of working memory + inhibitory control, dependent on DL-PFC* |
| A-not-B | A hiding task requiring working memory and inhibition of a previously rewarded response. Subject sees a reward hidden to left or right (2 identical hiding wells); after a delay, subject is allowed to search one well. Linked to DL-PFC by work with rhesus monkeys (Diamond and Goldman-Rakic, 1989). |
| Object retrieval | A transparent barrier detour task. Subject can see the reward through all sides of a transparent box, but can reach through only the one open side (Diamond, 1981, 1990a,b). Linked to DL-PFC by work with rhesus monkeys (Diamond and Goldman-Rakic, 1985). |
| | *Tests that do not require working memory + inhibitory control* |
| Spatial discrimination | An associative rule-learning and memory task. Hiding done unseen; subject must learn and remember that reward is always hidden to left or right (2 identical hiding places); after delay between trials, subject is allowed to reach. *Not* impaired by lesions to prefrontal cortex (Goldman and Rosvold, 1970). |
| Visual paired comparison | A recognition memory task in which a sample is presented, a delay imposed, and then subject is given a choice of that stimulus or something new. Linked to medial temporal lobe (Bachevalier, Brickson, and Hagger, 1993; McKee and Squire, 1992). |
| | Tasks Used with Toddlers (ages 15–30 months) |
| | *Tests of working memory + inhibitory control, dependent on DL-PFC* |
| A-not-B with invisible displacement | A hiding task requiring memory of where the container-with-reward was last moved and inhibition of a previously rewarded response. Similar to A-not-B for infants, but not independently, directly linked to prefrontal cortex. |
| | *Tests that do not require working memory + inhibitory control* |
| Three boxes (boxes scrambled after each reach) | A memory task in which subjects are to try to open all boxes without repeating a choice; a delay is imposed between reaches. S must remember color/shape of the boxes; spatial location is irrelevant. Linked to DL-PFC by work with rhesus monkeys (Petrides, 1995b). |
| Three boxes (stationary) | Here, uncovering the boxes in spatial order will suffice. Similar to a condition *not* impaired by damage to DL-PFC (Petrides and Milner, 1982). |
| Delayed nonmatching to sample | A recognition memory task in which one is rewarded for reaching to the stimulus not matching the sample that was presented shortly before. Linked to the medial temporal lobe by work with rhesus monkeys and amnesic patients (Meunier, Bachevalier, Mishkin, and Murray, 1993; Squire, Zola-Morgan, and Chen, 1988; Zola-Morgan, Squire, and Amaral, 1989). |
| Global-local (preferential looking procedure) | A visual-spatial attention task. Assesses attention to the global and local features of composite stimuli (e.g., and H made up of S's). Similar to task linked to parietal cortex by work with brain-damaged patients (Lamb, Robertson, and Knight, 1989; Robertson, Lamb, and Knight, 1988) and to a task linked to parietal cortex through functional magnetic imaging (fMRI) of neural activity in normal adults. |
| | Tasks Used with Young Children (ages 3½–7 years) |
| | *Tests of working memory + inhibitory control, dependent on DL-PFC* |
| Day–night Stroop-like test | Requires holding 2 rules in mind and exercising inhibitory control. S must say "night" when shown a white-sun card, and say "day" when shown a black-moon card. Hypothesized to require the functions of DL-PFC, but has yet to be studied in relation to brain function. |
| Tapping | A conflict test requiring memory of 2 rules and inhibitory control. When E taps once, S must tap 2 times; when E taps twice, S must tap twice. Linked to prefrontal cortex by work with brain-damaged patients (Luria, 1966). |
| Three pegs | S is shown a board containing 3 colored pegs arranged in the order red, yellow, green. S is instructed to tap the pegs in the order red, *green,* yellow. This requires remembering the instructed sequence and inhibiting the tendency to tap the pegs in their spatial order. It has yet to be studied in relation to brain function. |

*(continued)*

TABLE 29.2

*List of tasks (continued)*

| | *Tests that do not require working memory + inhibitory control* |
|---|---|
| Corsi–Milner test of temporal order memory | Subject is shown a series of stimuli one at a time, and is periodically shown 2 previously presented stimuli and asked, "Which of these two pictures did you see last?" Linked to prefrontal cortex by work with brain-damaged human adults (Milner, Corsi, and Leonard, 1991). |
| Six boxes (boxes scrambled after each reach) | A memory task in which subject must try to open all boxes without repeating a choice; a delay is imposed between reaches. Similar to tasks linked to prefrontal cortex in rhesus monkeys (Petrides, 1995a,b) and in brain-damaged human adults (Petrides and Milner, 1982). |
| Stroop control condition | Requires learning and remembering 2 rules (as does the Stroop task above), but requires no inhibition (unlike the Stroop task above)—2 arbitrary patterns used; to one, subject must say "day"; to the other, subject must say "night." |
| Corsi–Milner test of recognition memory | S is shown a series of pictures and periodically asked, "Among the pictures I've shown you, which of these two have you already seen?" Linked to medial temporal lobe by work with brain-damaged patients (Milner, 1982; Milner, Corsi, and Leonard, 1991). |
| Six boxes (stationary) | Here, uncovering the boxes in spatial order will suffice. Similar to a condition *not* impaired by damage to DL-PFC (Petrides and Milner, 1982). |
| Global-local (forced choice procedure) | A visual-spatial attention task. Assesses attention to the global and local features of composite stimuli (e.g., an H made up of S's). Linked to parietal cortex by work with brain-damaged patients (Lamb et al., 1989; Robertson, Lamb, and Knight, 1988) and by fMRI with normal adults. |
| Line bisection | A spatial perception task. Subject is asked to indicate the middle of each line. Linked to parietal cortex by work with brain-damaged patients (Benton, 1969). |

tasks requiring working memory plus inhibitory control (6 tasks × 4 comparisons per task), PKU children with higher Phe levels performed significantly worse than the comparison groups on 79% of these comparisons using the stringent criterion of $p \le .005$ for each test to correct for multiple comparisons (see table 29.3). This pattern of 19 out of 24 comparisons in the predicted direction would be very unlikely to occur by chance ($p < .004$ [binomial distribution]). In short, the impairment of the PKU children, whose blood Phe levels were 3–5 times above normal, on the tasks that require the working memory and inhibitory control functions dependent on DL-PFC was clear and consistent.

This finding of deficits in the working memory and inhibitory control abilities dependent on DL-PFC in PKU children whose blood Phe levels are mildly elevated (3–5× normal) is consistent with the results of a number of other studies. The most relevant are those by Welsh and colleagues (1990) and Smith and colleagues (1996), as these investigators used cognitive tasks tailored to the functions of DL-PFC.

The cognitive deficits documented in many studies of children treated for PKU could be explained away by saying that (1) the blood Phe levels of many of the children were outside the "safe" range (i.e., >5× normal); (2) even if current Phe levels were not excessively elevated, earlier Phe levels had been (during the years the children had been off diet); and/or (3) the low-Phe diet had been started too late to avert early brain damage. Those disclaimers are not applicable to the study done by Diamond and colleagues (1997).

*A linear relationship between Phe level and performance* The higher a PKU child's current Phe level (the higher a child's Phe:Tyr ratio), the worse that child's performance on the tasks that required the working memory and inhibitory control functions dependent on DL-PFC. PKU children whose blood Phe levels had been maintained at 2–6 mg/dL performed comparably to all control groups on our tasks. Thus, at least in this subgroup of PKU children, deficits in the ability to exercise working memory and inhibitory control simultaneously did not appear to be a necessary, unavoidable consequence of being born with PKU. The effect of elevated Phe levels appeared to be acute rather than chronic: Performance on these tasks was most strongly and consistently related to *current* blood Phe levels, not mean Phe levels over a wide age range during the first year of life or during the first month of life. As current Phe levels varied, so too, inversely, did behavioral performance on five of the six tasks that required acting counter to one's initial tendency on the basis of information held in mind (the exception being A-not-B with invisible displacement). Indeed, over time, changes in blood Phe levels *within the same child* were accompanied by concomitant, inverse changes in performance on these cognitive tasks.

The findings that performance is most closely tied to current blood Phe levels (rather than to Phe levels earlier in life) and that performance covaries with a child's current blood Phe levels is consistent with the aforementioned biological mechanism concerning the cause of the cognitive deficits. That is, these findings are con-

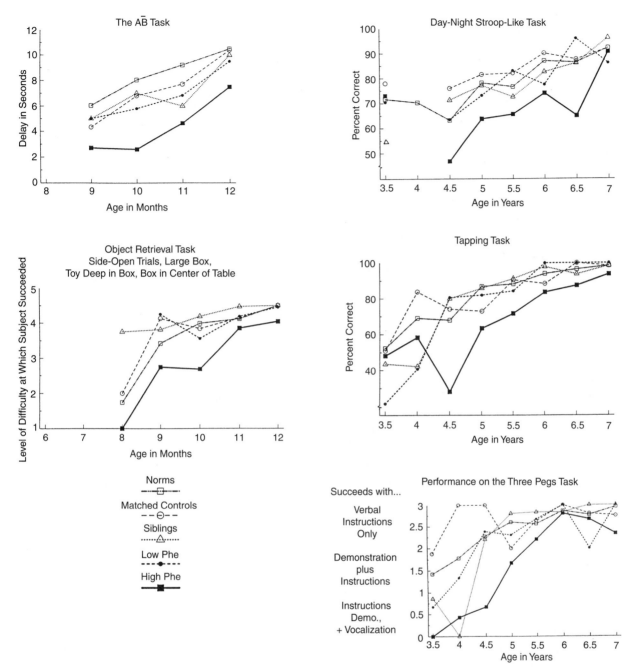

FIGURE 29.7    Performance of PKU children whose blood Phe levels are 6–10 mg/dL (3–5 times normal) on tasks requiring both working memory and inhibitory control. Note that they are significantly impaired compared to each comparison group: other PKU children with Phe levels closer to normal, siblings of the PKU children, control children matched to the PKU children on a large number of variables, and children from the general population. Note also that they are significantly impaired in the youngest age range investigated (as infants they are impaired on the A-not-B/delayed response and object retrieval tasks) and in the oldest age range investigated (as young children on the day–night, tapping, and three-pegs tasks). (Reprinted with permission from Diamond et al., 1997.)

sistent with an effect of reduced dopamine on prefrontal cortex function, which would vary directly with changes in the Phe:Tyr ratio in the bloodstream, as opposed to structural, neuroanatomical changes, which might be more fixed.

Like us, Welsh and colleagues (1990) and Smith and colleagues (1996) found that performance on measures of DL-PFC function was significantly and negatively correlated with concurrent Phe levels and less so with lifetime Phe levels. Brunner, Jordan, and Berry (1983)

**TABLE 29.3**

*Pairwise comparisons between subject groups significant at p ≤ .005\**

| | The 6 tasks that required the working memory and inhibitory control abilities dependent on DL-PFC | The 10 control tasks that are not dependent on PFC |
|---|---|---|
| PKU children whose plasma Phe levels were 3–5× normal performed significantly worse than the other groups of children on . . . | 19 out of 24 comparisons (79%) | 4 out of 40 comparisons (10%) |
| The other groups of children performed significantly different from one another on . . . | 2 out of 36 comparisons (5%) | 3 out of 60 comparisons (5%) |

\*The .005 significance level was chosen to correct for multiple comparisons. This is similar to what a Bonferroni correction would do.

found that cognitive neuropsychological performance was significantly correlated with concurrent Phe levels but not with Phe levels during infancy. Using IQ and school achievement as the outcome measures, Dobson and colleagues (1976) also found a significant, negative correlation with concurrent blood Phe levels, and a much weaker association with Phe levels earlier in life. Like us, Stemerdink and colleagues (1995) found that when blood Phe levels were kept below 3× normal from birth to the present, PKU children showed no cognitive deficits. The only contrary finding is the report of Sonneville and colleagues (1990), who found that Phe levels during the 2 years preceding cognitive testing were a better predictor of speed of responding on a continuous performance test than were concurrent Phe levels.

The relationship found between blood Phe level and performance in three studies (Diamond et al., 1997; Smith and Beasley, 1989; Welsh et al., 1990) is particularly impressive considering the truncated range of Phe levels; all PKU children in those studies were on a dietary regimen and their Phe levels were generally within the "acceptable" range. Because participants in the study by Diamond and colleagues (1997) were followed longitudinally, we are able to present evidence for the first time that performance on tasks requiring the working memory and inhibitory control functions of DL-PFC covaried inversely with Phe levels in the same child over time. Because of the evidence of cognitive deficits in PKU children whose blood Phe levels are 6–10 mg/dL, the national guidelines for the treatment of PKU have been changed in the United Kingdom, the Netherlands, and Denmark: Phe levels higher than 6 mg/dL are no longer considered acceptable. In addition, several clinics in the United States have similarly revised their guidelines.

*A developmental delay or absolute, lasting deficits?* Are the cognitive deficits in treated PKU children indicative of a developmental delay or of lasting deficits? On the one hand, all children, even PKU children with Phe levels 3–5 times above normal, improved over time on our tasks. On the other hand, the impression that PKU children may "catch up" to other children is probably misleading. In almost all cases this "catch up" was due to ceiling effects: The same tasks were administered over a wide age range, and these tasks were often too easy for children at the upper end of an age range. We have repeatedly found that the between-group differences reappeared on the next battery of tasks for the next age group. The impairment of the PKU children with higher Phe levels in simultaneously holding information in mind and inhibiting a prepotent response was as evident in our oldest age range (3½–7 years) as it was in our youngest age range (6–12 months). The deficit showed no evidence of subsiding within the age range we studied (6 months to 7 years).

The oldest children tested by Diamond and colleagues (1997) were 7 years old. One cannot tell from our study whether some time after 7 years PKU children whose Phe levels remain only moderately elevated might no longer show the kinds of cognitive deficits we have documented. Many studies of elementary school–age PKU children on the low-Phe diet have found cognitive deficits (Smith and Beasley, 1989; Weglage et al., 1995; Welsh et al., 1990). Recent studies by Ris and colleagues (1994) and Smith and colleagues (1996) report deficits in the cognitive abilities dependent on prefrontal cortex in young adults with PKU. However, dietary compliance tends to become progressively more lax after children enter school, so that these studies have included participants whose blood Phe levels were higher than 10 mg/dL. What would happen if blood Phe levels were maintained at 3–5 times normal: Would the cognitive deficits eventually disappear? The data to answer that question do not currently exist. Amino acid uptake across the blood–brain barrier changes during development, offering more protection against blood Phe elevations as children get older (Greengard and Brass, 1984; Lajtha, Sershen, and Dunlop, 1987). Thus, it is quite possible that the blood Phe levels we found to be detrimental during infancy and early childhood might be more benign in later childhood or adolescence.

Early cognitive deficits or developmental delays—especially when they extend over a long period (such as the 6-year period we have documented)—are likely to have profound and enduring effects, even if the cognitive deficits themselves are subsequently resolved. They affect children's perceptions of, and expectations for, themselves and the perceptions and expectations of others for the children. Such perceptions and expectations can be inordinately difficult to change and can have major effects in shaping development and behavior.

*Selective, rather than global, cognitive deficits* The same children who were impaired on all six working memory plus inhibitory control tasks performed well on the ten control tasks, which required other cognitive abilities dependent on other neural systems such as parietal cortex or the medial temporal lobe. Performance on the control tasks, moreover, was not related to current blood Phe levels. For each of the ten control tasks, we compared the performance of PKU children with higher blood Phe levels (6–10 mg/dL; 3–5× normal) to that of the four comparison groups: other PKU children with lower blood Phe levels, siblings of the PKU children, matched controls, and children from the general population. This yielded a total of 40 pairwise comparisons (10 tasks × 4 comparisons per task). PKU children with higher Phe levels performed worse on only 10% of these comparisons (see table 29.3). This pattern of 36 out of 40 comparisons in the predicted direction would be extremely unlikely to occur by chance ($p < .001$ [z distribution]). The consistency of the deficits of the PKU children with Phe levels 3–5 times normal on the working memory plus inhibitory control tasks and the paucity of deficits on the control tasks is quite striking: 55 out of 64 comparisons in the predicted direction (86%), $p < .0001$, z distribution.

Thus, for children treated early and continuously for PKU whose blood Phe levels are 3–5 times normal, the cognitive deficits appear to be selective. The functions of parietal cortex and of the medial temporal lobe appear to be spared, even if the children's Phe levels go up to 6–10 mg/dL. This is consistent with reports by Welsh and colleagues (1990) and Smith and colleagues (1996) who found (1) greater impairments on tasks dependent on prefrontal cortex than on tasks dependent on parietal cortex or the medial temporal lobe in those treated early and continuously for PKU, and (2) an inverse relationship between Phe levels and performance on tasks dependent on prefrontal cortex function but no such relationship for tasks dependent on parietal cortex or the medial temporal lobe. This is an example of a very specific, selective effect resulting from a global insult (a moderate elevation in Phe and a moderate reduction in Tyr in the bloodstream that feeds the entire body, and moderately too little Tyr in the entire brain). The reason for the specificity is the differential, unique sensitivity of prefrontally projecting dopamine neurons to a mild reduction in the dopamine precursor, tyrosine.

This finding of a deficit in the working memory and inhibitory control functions of DL-PFC, but not in the cognitive functions dependent on other neural systems, is consistent with the mechanism I have hypothesized as the cause of the cognitive deficits: A moderate imbalance in the Phe:Tyr ratio in blood (as when Phe levels are 3–5 times normal in PKU children) adversely affects the dopamine concentration in prefrontal cortex but not other dopamine systems in the brain because of the special properties of the prefrontally projecting dopamine neurons, which makes them unusually vulnerable to modest reductions in the level of Tyr reaching the brain. The specificity of the deficits suggests that the cause of those deficits is probably too little Tyr reaching the brain, rather than too much Phe reaching the brain, because all neural regions would be equally vulnerable to the negative effects of too much Phe; the functions of DL-PFC would not be disproportionately affected. That is, if the cause of the cognitive deficits were too much Phe in the brain, the cognitive deficits should be global, rather than limited to the prefrontal neural system.

*Findings we had not predicted: Preserved performance on self-ordered pointing and temporal order memory tasks* The mechanism I have proposed to explain the cause of the cognitive deficits in children treated early and continuously for PKU, whose Phe levels are 3–5 times normal, rests on the special properties of the dopamine neurons that project to prefrontal cortex. I had not hypothesized that only certain cognitive functions dependent on DL-PFC would be affected. I was surprised, therefore, when we found that PKU children with Phe levels 3–5 times normal performed normally on three tasks dependent on DL-PFC: the three- and six-boxes tasks (boxes scrambled after each reach), which are adaptations of the Petrides and Milner self-ordered pointing task; and the Corsi–Milner test of temporal order memory. These tasks require working memory (remembering what choices one has already made or remembering the order in which stimuli have been presented) but not inhibitory control. Thus, the treated PKU children with moderately elevated Phe levels were only impaired on the subclass of prefrontal cortex tasks that required *both* working memory and resisting a prepotent action tendency.

These findings were puzzling since nothing in my hypothesis would lead one to predict that certain cognitive functions dependent on dorsolateral PFC should be affected but not others. Although I have emphasized the conjunction of working memory plus inhibitory control as the hallmark of tasks dependent on DL-PFC, I had no explanation at the time for why performance on only certain cognitive tasks that require the functions of prefrontal cortex should be affected in PKU children. The evidence linking self-ordered pointing and temporal order memory to DL-PFC is strong, with converging evidence from lesion studies in rhesus macaques, human adult patients with damage to DL-PFC, and neuroimaging studies in normal human adults (Milner, Corsi, and Leonard, 1991; Petrides, 1995a; Petrides and Milner, 1982; Petrides, Alivatos, Meyer, and Evans, 1993). It was extremely unlikely that the failure to find a deficit on these tasks was due to their not requiring DL-PFC.

An excellent recent study by Collins and colleagues (1998) begins to make sense of what we found. They compared the effect of lesioning prefrontal cortex to the effect of depleting prefrontal cortex of dopamine. Their anatomical lesions were excitotoxic, which is a technique that destroys the cell bodies in the target region, but not the fibers of passage, so that one can have more confidence than with traditional lesioning methods that the observed effect is due to damage to the target region specifically. They depleted prefrontal cortex of dopamine by injecting it with 6-hydroxydopamine (6-OHDA). The concentrations of norepinephrine and serotonin in prefrontal cortex were not similarly reduced because the investigators pre-injected prefrontal cortex with a norepinephrine antagonist (talsupram) and a serotonin antagonist (citalopram). Although their work is in the marmoset, they replicated the findings of others in the rhesus macaque; plus, they added one important new finding.

Replicating the work of others (Butters et al., 1969; Diamond and Goldman-Rakic, 1989; Goldman and Rosvold, 1970), Collins and colleagues (1998) found that their lesions of prefrontal cortex impaired perfor-

mance on the delayed response task. Similarly, like others (Petrides, 1995a; Petrides and Milner, 1982), they found that their lesions of prefrontal cortex impaired performance on the self-ordered pointing task, and to the same degree as the same lesions impaired performance on delayed response. Finally, as others had reported (Sawaguchi and Goldman-Rakic, 1991), they found that depleting prefrontal cortex of dopamine impaired performance on delayed response. No one before had looked at the effect of dopamine depletion on self-ordered pointing, however. Collins and colleagues (1998) found that, when they depleted the same region of prefrontal cortex of dopamine, performance on the self-ordered pointing task was *not* impaired. (See table 29.4 for a summary of this set of results.)

Thus, even though prefrontal cortex is necessary for successful performance on self-ordered pointing (as can be seen from the lesion results), the dopamine innervation of prefrontal cortex is not necessary for successful performance of the task. Luciana and Collins (1997) found a dissociation that is perhaps similar in that performance on one of their working memory tasks appeared to rely critically on dopamine while performance of the other working memory task did not. They found that a dopamine agonist (bromocriptine) improved performance on delayed response and a dopamine antagonist (haloperidol) impaired performance on delayed response, but neither affected performance on a nonspatial working memory task. Unfortunately, though, there is no evidence that Luciana and Collins' nonspatial working memory task requires DL-PFC.

The effects we documented in children treated with PKU whose blood Phe levels were 6–10 mg/dL are (we contend) due to reduced dopamine in prefrontal cortex. Consistent with the results that Collins and colleagues (1998) obtained after our study was completed, we found that these treated PKU children were impaired on our delayed response task (A-not-B) but not on our self-ordered pointing tasks (three- and six-boxes [boxes scrambled after each reach]). The results that had seemed puzzling at the time end up providing additional support for our hypothesis. It appears that the dopamine content of prefrontal cortex is critical for certain cognitive functions dependent on prefrontal cortex (working memory plus inhibition) but not for others (when working memory is taxed alone). We still do not understand, however, *why* that is the case. Luciana and Collins (1997) suggested that dopamine might be critical when the information that must be held in mind is spatial. Such an explanation cannot account for our results, however: Although the prefrontal tasks on which we found sparing were nonspatial, we also found

**TABLE 29.4**
*Summary of the results of the 1998 study by Collins, Roberts, Dias, Everitt, and Robbins*

| | Behavioral Task | |
| --- | --- | --- |
| Type of lesion to frontal cortex | Delayed response (requires working memory + inhibition) | Self-ordered pointing (requires working memory |
| Excitotoxic (cell bodies destroyed) | Performance impaired | Performance impaired |
| 6-OHDA (dopamine depleted) | Performance impaired | Performance *spared* |

impairments on the day–night and tapping tasks, which are also nonspatial.

## An animal model of mild, chronic plasma Phe elevations

With children it was possible only to measure blood levels of Phe and Tyr and cognitive performance. To investigate the biological mechanism underlying the cognitive deficits of children treated for PKU more directly, we developed and characterized the first animal model of treated PKU (Diamond et al., 1994) and subsequently worked with the genetic mouse model of PKU (Zagreda et al., 1999). The animal model enabled us to study the effect of moderate, chronic plasma Phe elevations on neurotransmitter and metabolite levels in specific brain regions. Thus, we could directly investigate our hypothesis that the cognitive deficits associated with moderately elevated plasma Phe levels are produced by a selective reduction in dopamine synthesis in prefrontal cortex.

Building on work modeling the untreated PKU condition (Brass and Greengard, 1982; Greengard, Yoss, and Del Valle, 1976), Diamond and colleagues (1994) administered a phenylalanine hydroxylase inhibitor (α-methylphenylalanine) plus a small supplement of Phe to mildly and chronically elevate the blood Phe levels in rat pups. (The Phe supplement was needed because α-methylphenylalanine does not inhibit phenylalanine hydroxylase completely.) There were two experimental groups: (1) pups whose blood Phe levels were elevated postnatally, and (2) pups whose blood Phe levels were elevated pre- and postnatally. Control animals came from the same litters as the first group and received daily control injections of saline.

All were tested on delayed alternation, a task sensitive to prefrontal cortex dysfunction (Bättig, Rosvold, and Mishkin, 1960; Bubser and Schmidt, 1990; Kubota and Niki, 1971; Larsen and Divac, 1978; Wikmark, Divac, and Weiss, 1973). Testers were blind to the group assignment of their animals. Each of the testers was assigned four animals in each group and the order of

testing was randomized across experimental condition. Blood samples were collected at multiple time points to determine the animals' Phe levels. High-performance liquid chromatographic (HPLC) analyses of the brain tissue assessed the distributions and concentrations of dopamine, serotonin, norepinephrine, and their metabolites in various brain regions (prefrontal cortex, caudate-putamen, and nucleus accumbens).[2]

The most dramatic neurochemical effects of the moderate elevation in blood Phe levels were the reduction in dopamine and in the dopamine metabolite HVA in prefrontal cortex in each of the PKU-model animals. There was almost no overlap between HVA levels in the prefrontal cortex of controls and either PKU-model group: All control animals but one had higher HVA levels in prefrontal cortex than *any* animal in either experimental group. In contrast, as predicted, the levels of dopamine and dopamine metabolites were not reduced elsewhere in the brain, and norepinephrine levels were not reduced elsewhere in the brain or in prefrontal cortex. We had predicted that norepinephrine levels would be unaffected (even though norepinephrine is made from dopamine) because previous work had shown that norepinephrine levels are relatively insensitive to alterations in precursor availability (Irie and Wurtman, 1987).

The PKU-model animals were impaired on delayed alternation in the same ways and under the same conditions as are animals with prefrontal cortex lesions. On the delayed alternation task, the animal is rewarded only for alternating goal arms (i.e., for selecting the goal arm *not* selected on the previous trial). Thus, the animal must remember which goal arm was last entered over the delay between trials and must inhibit repeating that response. The hallmark of performance after prefrontal cortex is removed is that subjects fail when a delay is imposed between trials, although they are unimpaired at learning the alternation rule or in performing the task when no delay is imposed (*in rats:* Bubser and Schmidt, 1990; Larsen and Divac, 1978; Wikmark, Divac, and Weiss, 1973; *in monkeys:* Bättig, Rosvold, and Mishkin, 1960; Jacobsen and Nissen, 1937; Kubota and

Niki, 1971). We found that the animals with moderately elevated plasma Phe levels learned the delayed alternation task normally and performed well when there was no delay, but failed when a delay was imposed between trials (see figure 29.8), just as do prefrontally lesioned animals.

Moreover, we found that the lower an animal's prefrontal dopamine levels, the worse that animal performed on the delayed alternation task. The neurochemical variable most strongly and consistently related to performance on delayed alternation was the level of HVA in prefrontal cortex. This is consistent with previous work, which has demonstrated that delayed alternation performance is highly dependent on the level of dopamine in prefrontal cortex, and is uncorrelated with serotonin or norepinephrine levels (Brozoski et al., 1979; Sahakian et al., 1985; Simon, Scatton, and LeMoal, 1980) or with dopamine elsewhere in the brain (Sahakian et al., 1985; Simon, Scatton, and LeMoal, 1980).

Thus, Diamond and colleagues (1994) found the neurochemical changes (reduced levels dopamine and the dopamine metabolite HVA in prefrontal cortex) and the cognitive deficits (impaired performance on a behavioral task dependent on prefrontal cortex [delayed alternation]) predicted by our model in both groups of PKU-model animals with moderately elevated blood Phe levels. The only result that deviated from those predicted was an effect on the serotoninergic system in PKU-model animals. The lack of complete specificity may have been because blood Phe levels were a bit more elevated than intended (6.5× normal, rather than ≤ 5× normal) or because the neurochemical effects of moderately elevated blood Phe levels are not quite as localized as I have hypothesized. We are investigating this further with the genetic mouse model of PKU created by McDonald and colleagues (McDonald et al., 1990; Shedlovsky et al., 1993).

## *What we thought was independent, confirming evidence from visual psychophysics for the proposed causal mechanism*

If it is the special properties of the dopamine neurons projecting to prefrontal cortex that make the functions of prefrontal cortex particularly vulnerable to moderate increases in the Phe:Tyr ratio in the bloodstream, then any other dopamine neurons that share those special properties should also be affected by moderately elevated blood Phe:Tyr ratios. It so happens that the dopamine neurons in the retina share all those same unusual properties. They, too, have unusually rapid fir-

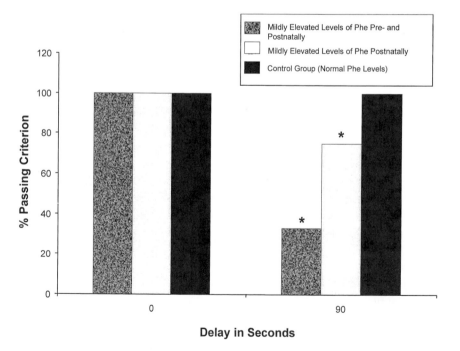

**Delay in Seconds**

FIGURE 29.8  Rats with chronic, mild elevations in their blood Phe levels, to create an animal model of early and continuously treated PKU, show the same pattern of performance on the delayed alternation task, as do monkeys whose dorsolateral prefrontal cortex has been lesioned and rats whose homolog to dorsolateral prefrontal cortex has been lesioned. That is, they can learn the delayed alternation rule and perform well when there is no delay, but are impaired when a delay is introduced.

ing and dopamine turnover rates (Fernstrom, Volk, and Fernstrom, 1986; Iuvone et al., 1978, 1989). Moreover, the competition between Phe and Tyr at the blood–retinal barrier is fully comparable to their competitive uptake at the blood–brain barrier (Fernstrom, Volk, and Fernstrom, 1986; Hjelle et al., 1978; Rapoport, 1976; Tornquist and Alm, 1986). Indeed, it has been shown that a small reduction in the level of Tyr reaching the retina dramatically reduces retinal dopamine synthesis (Fernstrom and Fernstrom, 1988; Fernstrom, Volk, and Fernstrom, 1986), mirroring the effect on dopamine synthesis in prefrontal cortex. Therefore, to be consistent, we had to predict that retinal function should also be affected in PKU children who have been on a low-Phe diet since the first month of life, but who have moderately elevated blood Phe levels (levels roughly 3–5 times normal [6–10 mg/dL; 360–600 μmol/L]), even though no visual deficit had been reported in these children before.

The aspect of retinal function most firmly linked to the level of dopamine in the retina is contrast sensitivity. Contrast sensitivity refers to the ability to detect differences in luminance (brightness) of adjacent regions in a pattern. Your contrast sensitivity threshold is the limit of how faint items printed in gray can become before you fail to perceive them at all. People with good contrast sensitivity can perceive fainter lines than those who require a greater luminance difference between foreground and background. Patients with Parkinson's disease, who have greatly reduced levels of dopamine, have impaired contrast sensitivity (Bodis-Wollner, 1990; Bodis-Wollner et al., 1987; Kupersmith et al., 1982; Regan and Neima, 1984; Skrandies and Gottlob, 1986). It is thought that this occurs because dopamine is important for the center-surround organization of retinal receptive fields (Bodis-Wollner, 1990; Bodis-Wollner and Piccolino, 1988).

To investigate contrast sensitivity, we (Diamond and Herzberg, 1996) tested children between the ages of 5.4 and 9.8 years on the Vistech test (Gilmore and Levy, 1991; Ginsberg, 1984; Lederer and Bosse, 1992; Mäntyjärvi et al., 1989; Rogers, Bremer, and Leguire, 1987; Tweten, Wall, and Schwartz, 1990). We found that children treated early and continuously for PKU, whose blood Phe levels were 6–10 mg/dL (3–5× normal), were impaired in their sensitivity to contrast at each of the five spatial frequencies tested (1.5–18.0 cycles per degree; see figure 29.9). Even though all children had been tested under conditions of 20/20 acuity, the PKU children were significantly less sensitive to visual contrast than their same-aged peers across the entire range of spatial frequencies. These group differences remained robust even when the two PKU children whose

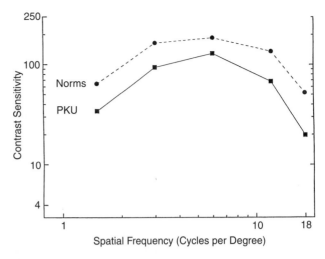

FIGURE 29.9  PKU children whose blood Phe levels are 6–10 mg/dL were found to be significantly impaired in contrast sensitivity compared to children of the same age at every spatial frequency investigated.

IQs were below 90 were omitted from the analyses. Indeed, at the next to the highest spatial frequency (12 cycles per degree), the "group" variable accounted for 70% of the variance, controlling for acuity, gender, age, and test site. At no spatial frequency was the contrast sensitivity of any PKU child better than that of his or her own sibling. Standard eye exams had never detected a problem in this population because acuity is normally tested under conditions of high contrast; an impairment in contrast sensitivity was not revealed before because no one had tested for it.

At the time, we interpreted these results as providing converging evidence in support of the biological mechanism I had proposed. I had predicted the contrast sensitivity deficit for the same reason I had predicted DL-PFC cognitive deficit. Both predictions had been based on the special sensitivity of dopamine neurons that fire rapidly and turn over dopamine rapidly to moderate reductions in the level of available tyrosine. We had found two superficially unrelated behavioral effects, a selective deficit in cognitive functions dependent on DL-PFC and a selective visual defect in contrast sensitivity, both of which had been predicted based on the same underlying hypothesis.

However, I was troubled by one lack of convergence. In the Diamond and Herzberg study (1996), we found that contrast sensitivity performance did not correlate with children's current blood Phe levels, but rather with their Phe levels during the first month of life. In another study (Diamond et al., 1997), however, we had found that, on the cognitive tasks that required the working memory and inhibitory control functions dependent on DL-PFC, performance had correlated with children's current blood Phe levels, not their Phe levels during the first month of life.

If contrast sensitivity was poor because the retina was low on "fuel" (i.e., low in dopamine), then contrast sensitivity performance should have covaried with current blood Phe levels. The failure to find such a relationship might have been due simply to the truncated range of concurrent Phe levels in the contrast sensitivity study. Only PKU children whose current Phe levels were 6–10 mg/dL had been included in that study, whereas the cognitive study had included PKU children with lower Phe levels as well as those with Phe levels of 6–10 mg/dL. On the other hand, the range in Phe levels during the first month of life was great and so included sufficient variability to find a relationship with contrast sensitivity performance. The possibility also existed, however, that long-lasting structural damage might occur to the visual system during the first weeks of life, when the visual system is maturing rapidly, and when the Phe levels of PKU infants are dramatically elevated. PKU infants in the United States are generally not placed on the low-Phe diet until they are about 2 weeks old; thus, for the first 2 weeks of life, their Phe levels can easily reach 20–30 mg/dL. Might those extremely high Phe levels, at a time of very rapid maturation of the visual system, cause irreparable damage to the visual system? (In utero, the fetus's levels of Phe and Tyr depend upon the mother's levels, so it is believed that the detrimental effects of PKU begin postnatally.)

One way to test for the latter possibility is to study pairs of siblings, both of whom have PKU. Since more than 150 different mutations of the phenylalanine hydroxylase gene can cause PKU, amniocentesis testing for PKU is extremely expensive. Therefore, fetuses are not usually tested for PKU unless there is already one child with PKU in the family. In the United States, the older sibling with PKU (in whom it was detected postnatally) usually starts the low-Phe diet at about 1½–2 weeks of age, while the younger sibling (in whom PKU was detected prenatally) usually starts on the diet by 2 or 3 days of age. Thus, for this study we have been flying in pairs of PKU siblings from all over the USA and UK (Diamond et al., 1999a). Within each of these families, the earlier-born child (mean age at testing 13 years, range 9–16 years) was exposed to extremely high levels of Phe for a mean of 11 days (range 8–14 days before initiation of diet), while the later born sibling (mean age at testing 10 years, range 6–14 years) was exposed to extremely high levels of Phe for a mean of only 3 days (range 1–5 days). All of the children began the low-Phe diet within the first month of life and have remained on it continuously ever since.

Our preliminary results indicate that earlier-born PKU siblings show worse contrast sensitivity (as measured by the Regan low contrast letter acuity charts [Regan and Neima, 1983]) than their later born siblings under conditions of low contrast (4% contrast; see figure 29.10). This is striking because contrast sensitivity usually improves with age. For example, among siblings pairs without PKU, older siblings performed signifi-

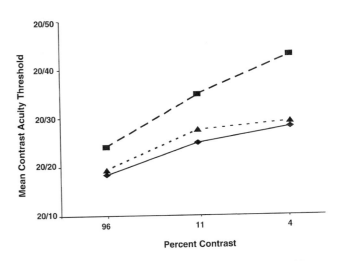

FIGURE 29.10 *Top,* Partial schematic representation of Regan Low Contrast Acuity Charts. The panel on the left represents high contrast (96%) and the panel on the right represents low contrast (11%). *Bottom,* Discrimination performance for the PKU sibling pairs and a normal comparison group are shown for the three Regan Low Contrast Acuity Charts, each chart was presented at a different level of contrast (96%, 11%, and 4%). Thresholds were calculated using the least squares error method to apply a linear curve fit to the obtained data and selecting the 75% correct discrimination value as the threshold. Earlier-born PKU children, who started on dietary treatment at roughly 11 days of age, showed impaired acuities compared to the other children, as can be seen by their elevated line on the graph. Since the charts differed only in contrast, the sharper drop-off in performance of the earlier-born PKU children when tested at lower contrast, indicates that these children have a deficit in contrast sensitivity.

Earlier-born PKU siblings (13 years) (began diet at 11 days) — ■ —; later-born PKU siblings (10 years) (began diet at 3 days) -▲-; children from the general population (mean age = 11 years) —◆—.

cantly *better* than their younger siblings, the reverse of the pattern seen in the PKU sibling pairs. The earlier born PKU siblings (who started the diet at 1½–2 weeks of age) also showed worse contrast sensitivity than their same-age peers.

These results suggest that extremely high Phe levels during the first weeks of life, even if subsequently lowered and maintained at lower levels, may cause long-lasting damage to the visual system. Evidently, a short-term exposure to high concentrations of Phe of only a couple of weeks during the sensitive neonatal period can have long-lasting effects on contrast sensitivity, evident 9–16 years later. This is significant because it suggests that the current practice of allowing up to 2 weeks to pass before beginning treatment for an infant born with PKU may be ill-advised. Since the blood sample to test for PKU is taken at birth, it would be feasible to start the diet earlier. These results also suggest that although we obtained the results I had predicted for contrast sensitivity in the Diamond and Herzberg (1996) study, we may have obtained those results for reasons *other* than the ones predicted. The deficits in the working memory and inhibitory control abilities dependent on DL-PFC do indeed appear to occur for the reason hypothesized (because of reduced levels of dopamine in DL-PFC due to elevated blood Phe:Tyr ratios). Those deficits covary with concurrent levels of Phe in the bloodstream. However, the retinal deficit in contrast sensitivity appears to be caused, at least in part, by the inordinately high levels of Phe in the first weeks of life, does not covary with current levels of Phe, and appears to be structural.

## Conclusions

DL-PFC begins subserving cognitive functions even during the first year of life. Even as infants, we are thinking problem-solvers. Prefrontal cortex continues to mature over the next 15–20 years of a child's life, just as the child's cognitive development, while remarkable by 1 year, continues to unfold over the next 15–20 years. Tasks that require simply holding one piece of information in mind (such as delayed nonmatching to sample) are too simple to require DL-PFC (Bachevalier and Mishkin, 1986). I have emphasized that DL-PFC is recruited when one must both hold information in mind and inhibit a prepotent response. Other investigators have characterized the functions of DL-PFC more broadly, proposing that when one must both hold information in mind and manipulate or process that information, then DL-PFC becomes critical (D'Esposito, 1995; D'Esposito et al., 1999; Owen et al., 1996, 1999; Petrides, 1994, 1995b; Postle, Berger, and D'Esposito,

1999; Smith and Jonides, 1999; Smith et al., 1998). Under such conceptualizations, holding information in mind plus inhibiting a dominant response becomes part of a subset of "holding information in mind plus another cognitive operation." I am in complete accord with such formulations. In general, tasks that require DL-PFC are more difficult than tasks that do not. However, if one increases how much information must be held in mind so that the task is as difficult as one that requires both holding information in mind plus either inhibition (Diamond, O'Craven, and Savoy, 1998) or alphabetizing the information held in mind (Postle, Berger, and D'Esposito, 1999; Rypma and D'Esposito, 1999), then that task, too, will activate DL-PFC.

There may be differential developmental trajectories for the working memory and inhibitory control abilities dependent on DL-PFC. Between 7½–12 months of age there is evidence of clear age-related improvements in inhibitory control (from results with the object retrieval task) and in how long infants can hold information in mind (from results with the A-not-B task) (Diamond, 1988, 1991). For example, infants make the A-not-B error at delays under 2 s at 7½–8 months and at delays of 10 s or more at 12 months, an average improvement of about 2 s per month in their ability to hold information in mind (see figure 29.11). On the other hand, between 4 and 22 years of age there are marked improvements in inhibitory control but little improvement in the ability to hold information in mind, which appears to be quite robust even by the age of 4 (see figures 29.12 and

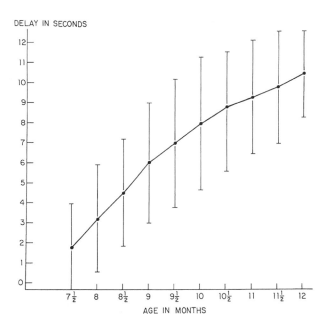

FIGURE 29.11 The delay at which 25 infants studied longitudinally made the A-not-B error during the first year of life. (Reprinted with permission from Diamond, 1985.)

29.13). The periods of 7½–12 months and 3–6 years appear to be times of particularly dramatic improvement in the abilities dependent on DL-PFC.

Dopamine is a particularly important neurotransmitter in prefrontal cortex. The level of dopamine increases in the brains of rhesus macaques during the period when infant rhesus macaques are improving on the A-not-B/delayed response and object retrieval tasks, tasks linked to DL-PFC. To begin to look at the role of dopamine in prefrontal cortex function early in life in humans, we studied children treated early and continuously for PKU because we predicted that they would have lower levels of dopamine in prefrontal cortex but otherwise normal brains, a prediction we were able to confirm in an animal model. We predicted this because the children have moderately elevated levels of Phe (3–5 times normal [6–10 mg/dL]) and moderately reduced levels of Tyr in their bloodstreams. Since Phe and Tyr compete to cross from blood to brain, and since the transporter proteins have a higher affinity for Phe than for Tyr, the upshot of a moderate increase in the Phe:Tyr ratio in the bloodstream is a moderate reduction in the amount of Tyr reaching the brain. Most dopamine systems in the brain are insensitive to modest

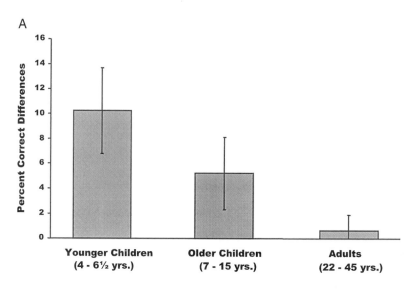

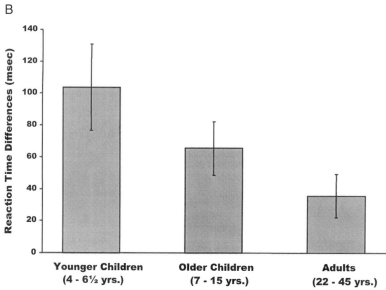

FIGURE 29.12   Performance on our directional Stroop task when inhibitory control was *not* required minus when it was required. Trials that required inhibitory control were trials where participants had to resist the tendency to respond with the hand on the same side as the stimulus ("spatial incompatibility"). The addition of an inhibitory requirement lowered the accuracy (panel A) and increased the reaction times (panel B) of younger children more than older children and older children more than adults.

A

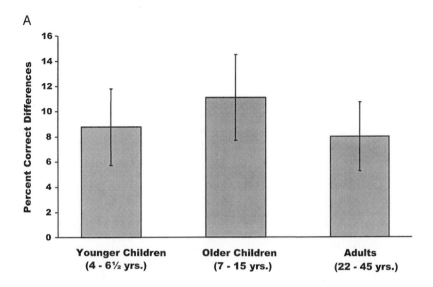

B

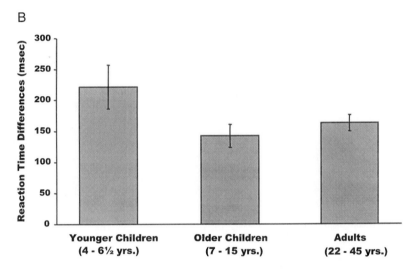

FIGURE 29.13 Performance on our directional Stroop task when memory load was greater minus when it was less. Memory load was greater when the rules for 6 abstract shapes had to be remembered than when the rules for only 2 abstract shapes had to be remembered. The condition where memory load was greater was harder for all participants, but it was not differentially harder for any age group. Hence, the effect on the accuracy (panel A) and on reaction times (panel B) of younger children, older children, and adults were comparable.

decreases in the amount of precursor (i.e., Tyr). However, the dopamine neurons that project to prefrontal cortex are different. They fire faster and turn over dopamine faster, and are acutely sensitive to even a modest change in the level of Tyr. Because of the special properties of this dopamine projection, we predicted and found a specific, localized effect (prefrontal cortex affected but not other regions of the brain) even though the insult is global (a mildly increased Phe:Tyr ratio throughout the bloodstream and mildly reduced Tyr levels throughout the brain).

The dopamine neurons in the retina share the same special properties as the dopamine neurons that project to prefrontal cortex. We predicted, therefore, that reti-

nal function would also be affected in early and continuously treated PKU children whose Phe levels are 3–5 times normal. Indeed, we found the predicted impairment in contrast sensitivity. However, this effect appears to be due to the exceedingly high Phe levels during the first two weeks of life, when most children with PKU have not yet begun treatment.

Cognitive deficits in children treated early and continuously for PKU whose blood Phe levels are 3–5 times normal went officially unrecognized for years, despite the protestations of parents and teachers that something was wrong, in part because the children performed within the normal range on IQ tests. Their IQ scores were in the 80s and the 90s, just as are the IQ scores of patients in whom prefrontal cortex has been damaged or removed. IQ tests, or any general tests of intellectual functioning, can easily miss specific deficits. The global cognitive measures that had been in use in clinics were too imprecise to detect the children's deficits. Global measures, such as overall IQ score, are poor indices of *specific* cognitive functions and poor indicators of what particular neural system might be affected if there is a problem. Developmental cognitive neuroscientists now have precise measures of specific cognitive functions, sensitive to the functions of particular neural subsystems. These measures can help in the study and treatment of diverse developmental disorders.

The other reason for the lack of official recognition of the cognitive deficits in children treated early and continuously for PKU was the lack of any hypothesized causal mechanism whereby a global insult might produce a selective effect on the functions of only one neural system (prefrontal cortex). The information on such a causal mechanism already existed in neuropharmacology through the work of Anne-Marie Thierry, Robert Roth, Michael Bannon, and colleagues, but the clinicians working on PKU and the neuroscientists working on the properties of the dopamine projection to prefrontal cortex did not know of one another's work.

To study DL-PFC function in children treated early and continuously for PKU, we used tasks linked to DL-PFC by work in macaques (by methods that disrupt the functioning of, or destroy, a specific neural region, then look at what deficits the animals show; and by methods that look at functioning in the intact brain, such as single cell recording) and by work with brain-damaged adults. It is not a foregone conclusion, however, that a task that requires a particular neural system in one species (say, macaques) will be solved in the same way, and require the same neural system, in a different species (say, humans). Nor is it a foregone conclusion that a task that requires a particular neural system in adults will be solved in the same way, and require the same neural system, in children. In addition, there are a number of reasons why inferring what functions a neural region might subserve from what functions are disrupted when that region is damaged, inactivated, or functioning improperly might lead to erroneous conclusions about structure–function relations.

Thus, it is critical to obtain evidence in *children*, looking at functioning in the *intact brain*. To begin to do this, we have developed a directional Stroop task that is appropriate for children as young as 4 years as well as adults (and even adults are not at ceiling in their performance). The task permits demands on working memory and inhibitory control to be varied indepen-

dently (see table 29.5), and can be used in the magnetic resonance (MR) scanner. Thus, the neural systems activated under the various conditions of the task can be studied noninvasively in the intact brain using fMRI [functional magnetic resonance imaging] (Diamond, O'Craven, and Savoy, 1998; Diamond et al., 1999b; Savoy et al., 1999). Participants are given a response box with two buttons—one for the left hand and one for the right. In the "dots-side" variant, when a large gray dot appears to the left or right, the child (or adult) is to press the button on the same side as the dot. When a large black-and-white striped dot appears to the left or right, the child (or adult) is to press the button on the side opposite the stimulus (see figure 29.14a). In the "mixed" condition of dots-side, the two kinds of dots are randomly intermixed over trials, requiring the participant to remember two rules and to inhibit the tendency to respond on the same side as the stimulus when the dot is striped. (The tendency to respond on the same side as a stimulus has been well-documented. People are slower and less accurate when required to respond on the side opposite a stimulus than when required to respond on the same side. This is called "spatial incompatibility" or the "Simon effect" (Craft and Simon, 1970; Fitts and Seeger, 1953; Simon and Berbaum, 1990). In the "arrows-side" variant, when an arrow pointing straight down appears to the left or right, the participant is to press the button on the same side as the arrow. When the arrow points diagonally toward the opposite side, the participant is to press the button on the side opposite the stimulus (see figure 29.14b). This still requires inhibiting the tendency to respond on the same side as the stimulus when a diagonal arrow appears, but it requires little or no working memory, as the arrow points directly to the correct response button on all trials. In a third variant of the directional Stroop task, "abstract-center-six," the partic-

TABLE 29.5

*Inhibitory demand and memory load are independently varied in different conditions of the directional Stroop task*

| Memory Load | Inhibition | |
| --- | --- | --- |
| | *Low* | *High* |
| *Low* | Arrows-center | Arrows-side |
| *Medium* | Abstract-two-center | Abstract-two-side |
| *High* | Abstract-six-center | Dots-side-mixed |

# A

## Dot Variant (Congruent Condition)

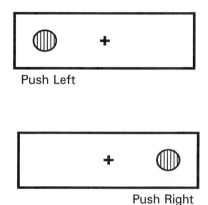

Push Left

Push Right

## Dot Variant (Opposite Condition)

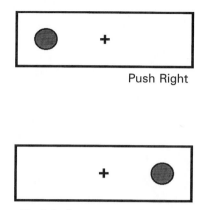

Push Right

Push Left

FIGURE 29.14   (**A**) Figure illustrating the stimuli in the "dots-side" variant of the directional Stroop task. Here, half the participants were instructed to press the response button on the same side as the dot if the dot is striped and on the opposite side if the dot is gray. (Half the participants were given the opposite instructions. Participants were given a two-button response box: one button for their right thumb and one for their left.)

*(continued on following page)*

ipant sees one of six abstract figures at the midline, and needs to remember the rule associated with each figure ("press right" or "press left"; see figure 29.14c). The abstract-center-six variant taxes working memory heavily (participants must hold six rules in mind), but it requires little or no inhibition (as the stimuli appear at the center of the screen and do not preferentially activate the right or left hand). It is work with this task that produced the results on the age-related improvements between 4 and 22 years in inhibitory control, but not in the amount of information that could be held in mind, as illustrated in figures 29.12 and 29.13.

Because inhibitory control undergoes such a protracted development, young children often fail to inhibit the prepotent response, despite their best intentions and despite knowing what they should do. It would be a shame to mistakenly label such a young child as "bad," "stupid," or "willful." It is not enough to know something or remember it; one must get that knowledge into one's behavior. Infants and young children, in whom prefrontal cortex is not yet mature, sometimes do the wrong thing even though they know what they should do and are trying to do it. Their attention is sometimes so captured by the desired goal object that they either cannot inhibit responding (as in delay of gratification or Go-NoGo paradigms) or cannot override the strong tendency to go straight to that goal when an indirect route is required (as in the object retrieval and windows tasks). To sustain the focused concentration required for hearing someone in a noisy room or for a difficult task, one needs to be able to resist distraction; to relate multiple ideas to one another, one needs to resist focusing exclusively on only one idea; when visual perception is misleading, one needs to be able to resist acting in accord with what one sees; and to act in new ways, one needs to resist falling back into one's usual way of acting or thinking. That is, one needs inhibitory control, dependent upon prefrontal cortex. The ability to exercise inhibitory control, which prefrontal cortex makes possible, frees us to act according to what we choose to do rather than being simply creatures of habit or immediate perception. The ability to hold information in mind, which also depends upon prefrontal cortex, enables us to remember what we are supposed to do, to consider alternatives, to remember the past and consider the future, and to use what we know—not just what we see—to help guide our actions and choices. These abilities make it possible for us to solve new, undreamed-of challenges, permitting us to exercise free will and self-determination. Not that it's easy, of course; but prefrontal cortex helps make it possible.

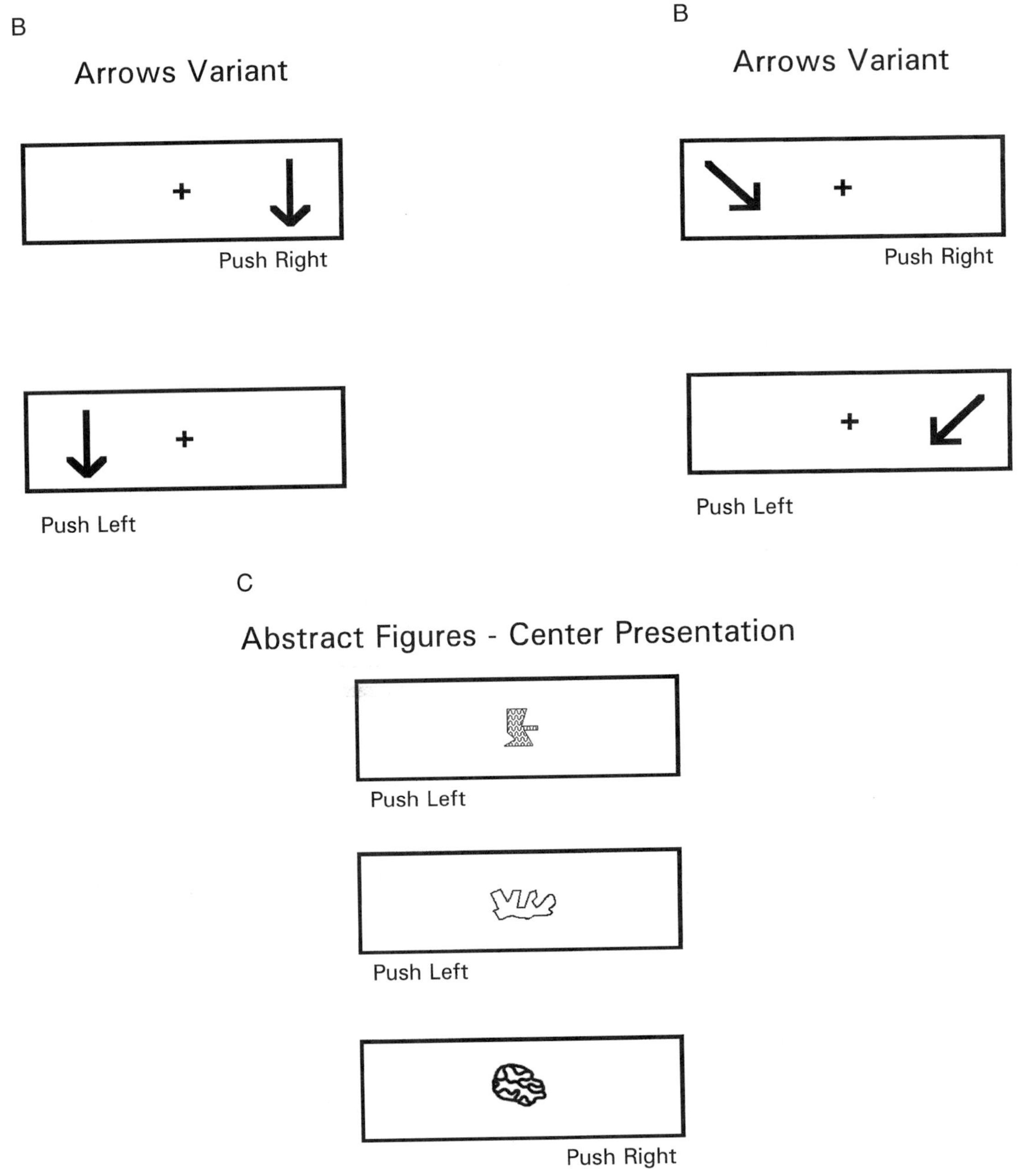

B

Arrows Variant

Push Right

Push Left

B

Arrows Variant

Push Right

Push Left

C

Abstract Figures - Center Presentation

Push Left

Push Left

Push Right

FIGURE 29.14 *(Continued)*. **(B)** Figure illustrating the stimuli in the "arrows-side" variant of the directional Stroop task. Here, participants were instructed to press the response button to which the arrow was pointing. If the arrow pointed straight down, they were to press the button on the same side as the arrow; and if the arrow pointed diagonally to the opposite side, they were to press the button on the side opposite the arrow. **(C)** Figure illustrating some of the stimuli in the "abstract-center-six" variant of the directional Stroop task. Participants were taught a rule for each of six abstract shapes ("press right" or "press left"). The stimuli were presented at the midline, not peripherally as in the dots-side and arrows-side variants.

## NOTES

1. At the core of my hypothesis about the cause of the A-not-B error has always been the notion of a competition or battle between the information held in mind (i.e., where the toy was last hidden) and the prepotent tendency (a type of procedural or implicit memory) formed by the experience of previous trials. The key element is conflict: What is required is not simply holding in mind the newest information, but that stored information has to win against a competitor (a conditioned tendency), which is probably subcortical in origin, since even extremely simple organisms can show conditioned tendencies.

2. We had intended to include two regions of frontal cortex (prefrontal cortex and the anterior cingulate). However, it turned out the brain sections we sampled to assess the anterior cingulate were actually from prefrontal cortex.

ACKNOWLEDGMENTS  The work summarized here was supported by grants from NIMH (R01-#MH41842, R01-#MH09007, R01-#MH00298, & R01-#MH38456), NICHD (R01-#HD35453, R01-#HD34346, R01-#HD10094, P30-#HD26979, P30-#HD04147), BRSG (S07-#RR07054-22, S07-#RR07083-23, & S07-#RR07083-26), March of Dimes (#12-253 & #12-0554), NSF (Doctoral Dissertation Grant #BNS8013447), the Sloan Foundation, and the Arc Foundation. I would like to thank Natasha Kirkham and Kristin Shutts for their astute comments on an earlier draft.

## REFERENCES

AKERT, K., 1964. Comparative anatomy of frontal cortex and thalamofrontal connections. In *The Frontal Granular Cortex and Behavior,* J. M. Warren and K. Akert, eds. New York: McGraw-Hill, pp. 372–376.

AKIL, M., J. N. PIERRI, R. E. WHITEHEAD, C. L. EDGAR, C. MOHILA, A. R. SAMPSON, and D. A. LEWIS, 1999. Lamina-specific alterations in the dopamine innervation of the prefrontal cortex in schizophrenic subjects. *Am. J. Psychiatry* 156:1580–1589.

ARIKUNI, T., and K. KUBOTA, 1986. The organization of pre-frontocaudate projections and their laminar origin in the macaque monkey: A retrograde study using HRP-gel. *J. Comp. Neurol.* 244:492–510.

BACHEVALIER, J., M. BRICKSON, and C. HAGGER, 1993. Limbic-dependent recognition memory in monkeys develops early in infancy. *NeuroReport* 4:77–80.

BACHEVALIER, J., and M. MISHKIN, 1986. Visual recognition impairment follows ventromedial but not dorsolateral pre-frontal lesions in monkeys. *Behav. Brain Res.* 20:249–261.

BADDELEY, A., 1992. Working memory. *Science* 255:556–559.

BALAMORE, U., and R. H. WOZNIAK, 1984. Speech-action co-ordination in young children. *Dev. Psychol.* 20:850–858.

BARBAS, H., and M. M. MESULAM, 1985. Cortical afferent input to the principalis region of the rhesus monkey. *Neuroscience* 15:619–637.

BANNON, M. J., E. B. BUNNEY, and R. H. ROTH, 1981. Meso-cortical dopamine neurons: Rapid transmitter turnover compared to other brain catecholamine systems. *Brain Res.* 218:376–382.

BÄTTIG, K., H. E. ROSVOLD, and M. MISHKIN, 1960. Comparison of the effects of frontal and caudate lesions on delayed response and alternation in monkeys. *J. Comp. Physiol.* 53:400–404.

BAUER, R. H., and J. M. FUSTER, 1976. Delayed-matching and delayed-response deficit from cooling dorsolateral prefrontal cortex in monkeys. *J. Comp. Physiol. Psychol.* 90:293–302.

BECKER, M. G., W. ISAAC, and G. W. HYND, 1987. Neuropsychological development of nonverbal behaviors attributed to "frontal lobe" functioning. *Dev. Neuropsychol.* 3:275–298.

BELL, J. A., and P. J. LIVESEY, 1985. Cue significance and response regulation in 3- to 6-year-old children's learning of multiple choice discrimination tasks. *Dev. Psychobiol.* 18:229–245.

BELL, M. A., and N. A. FOX, 1992. The relations between frontal brain electrical activity and cognitive development during infancy. *Child Dev.* 63:1142–1163.

BELL, M. A., and N. A. FOX, 1997. Individual difference in object permanence performance at 8 months: Locomotor experience and brain electrical activity. *Dev. Psychobiol.* 31:287–297.

BENTON, A. L., 1969. Disorders of spatial orientation. In P. Vincken and G. Bruyn, eds., *Handbook of Clinical Neurology,* Vol. 3. Amsterdam: North-Holland Publishing.

BERRY, H. K., D. J. O'GRADY, L. J. PERLMUTTER, and M. K. BOFINGER, 1979. Intellectual development and achievement of children treated early for phenylketonuria. *Dev. Med. Child Neurol.* 21:311–320.

BICKEL, H., F. P. HUDSON, and L. I. WOOLF, 1971. *Phenylketonuria and Some Other Inborn Errors of Metabolism.* Stuttgart: Georg Thiese Verlag.

BJORKLUND, A., I. DIVAC, and O. LINDVALL, 1978. Regional distribution of catecholamines in monkey cerebral cortex, evidence for a dopaminergic innervation of the primate prefrontal cortex. *Neurosci. Lett.* 7:115–119.

BODIS-WOLLNER, I., 1990. Visual deficits related to dopamine deficiency in experimental animals and Parkinson's disease patients. *Trends Neural Sci.* 13:296–302.

BRADBERRY, C. W., D. H. KARASIC, A. Y. DEUTSCH, and R. H. ROTH, 1989. Regionally-specific alterations in mesotelencephalic dopamine synthesis in diabetic rats: Associations with precursor tyrosine. *J. Neural Transmission* 78:221–229.

BRASS, C. A., and O. GREENGARD, 1982. Modulation of cerebral catecholamine concentrations during hyperphenylalaninaemia. *Biochem. J.* 208:765–771.

BRODMANN, K., 1912. Neue ergebnisse über die vergleichende histologische lokalisation der grosshirnrinde mit besonderer berücksichtigung des stirnhirns. *Anat. Anz.* 41(suppl.):157–216.

BROWN, R. M., A. M. CRANE, and P. S. GOLDMAN, 1976. Catecholamines in neocortex of rhesus monkeys: Regional distribution and ontogenetic development. *Brain Res.* 124:576–580.

BROWN, R. M., A. M. CRANE, and P. S. GOLDMAN, 1979. Regional distribution of monoamines in the cerebral cortex and subcortical structures of the rhesus monkey: Concentrations and in vivo synthesis rates. *Brain Res.* 168:133–150.

BROWN, R. M., and P. S. GOLDMAN, 1977. Catecholamines in neocortex of rhesus monkeys: Regional distribution and ontogenetic development. *Brain Res.* 127:576–580.

BROZOSKI, T. J., R. M. BROWN, H. E. ROSVOLD, and P. S. GOLDMAN, 1979. Cognitive deficit caused by regional depletion of dopamine in prefrontal cortex of rhesus monkey. *Science* 205:929–932.

BRUNER, J. S., 1964. The course of cognitive growth. *Amer. Psychologist* 19:1–15.

BRUNNER, R. L., D. B. BERCH, and H. BERRY, 1987. Phenylketonuria and complex spatial visualization: An analysis of information processing. *Dev. Med. Child Neurol.* 29:460–468.

BRUNNER, R. L., M. K. JORDAN, and H. K. BERRY, 1983. Early-treated phenylketonuria: Neuropsychologic consequences. *J. Pediatr.* 102:831–835.

BUBSER, M., and W. J. SCHMIDT, 1990. 6-Hydroxydopamine lesion of the rat prefrontal cortex increases locomotor activity, impairs acquisition of delayed alternation tasks, but does not affect uninterrupted tasks in the radial maze. *Behav. Brain Res.* 37:157–168.

BUGBEE, N. M., and P. S. GOLDMAN-RAKIC, 1981. Functional 2-deoxyglucose mapping in association cortex: Prefrontal activation in monkeys performing a cognitive task. *Soc. Neurosci. Abstr.* 7:239.

BUTTERS, N., D. PANDYA, K. SANDERS, and P. DYE, 1969. Behavioral deficits in monkeys after selective lesions within the middle third of sulcus principalis. *J. Comp. Physiol. Psychol.* 76:8–14.

BUTTERWORTH, G., 1976. Asymmetrical search errors in infancy. *Child Dev.* 47:864–867.

BUTTERWORTH, G., 1977. Object disappearance and error in Piaget's stage IV task. *J. Exp. Child Psychol.* 23:391–401.

BUTTERWORTH, G., 1982. Structure of the mind in human infancy. In *Advances in Infancy Research*, L. P. Lipsitt and C. K. Rovee-Collier, eds. Norwood, N.J.: Ablex.

BUTTERWORTH, G., N. JARRETT, and L. HICKS, 1982. Spatiotemporal identity in infancy: Perceptual competence or conceptual deficit? *Dev. Psychol.* 18:435–449.

CARLSON, S. M., L. J. MOSES, and H. R. HIX, 1998. The role of inhibitory processes in young children's difficulties with deception and false belief. *Child Dev.* 69:672–691.

CAVADA, C., and P. S. GOLDMAN-RAKIC, 1989. Posterior parietal cortex in rhesus monkey: II. Evidence for segregated corticocortical networks linking sensory and limbic areas with frontal lobe. *J. Comp. Neurol.* 287:422–445.

CHIRIGOS, M., P. GREENGARD, and S. UDENFRIEND, 1960. Uptake of tyrosine by rat brain in vivo. *J. Biol. Chem.* 235:2075–2079.

COLLINS, P., A. C. ROBERTS, R. DIAS, B. J. EVERITT, and T. W. ROBBINS, 1998. Perseveration and strategy in a novel spatial self-ordered task for nonhuman primates: Effect of excitotoxic lesions and dopamine depletions of the prefrontal cortex. *J. Cogn. Neurosci.* 10:332–354.

CORNELL, E. H., 1979. The effects of cue reliability on infants' manual search. *J. Exp. Child Psychol.* 28:81–91.

COWIE, V. A., 1971. Neurological and psychiatric aspects of phenylketonuria. In *Phenylketonuria and Some Other Inborn Errors of Amino Acid Metabolism*, H. Bickel, F. P. Hudson, and L. I. Woolf, eds. Stuttgart: Georg Thiese Verlag.

CRAFT, J. L., and J. R. SIMON, 1970. Processing symbolic information from a visual display: interference from an irrelevant directional cue. *J. Exp. Psychol.* 83:415–420.

CROFTS, H. S., M. T. HERRERO, A. DEL VECCHIO, J. D. WALLIS, P. COLLINS, B. J. EVERITT, T. W. ROBBINS, and A. C. ROBERTS, 1999. Excitotoxic lesions of the caudate nucleus in the marmoset: Comparison with prefrontal lesions on discrimination learning, object retrieval and spatial delayed response. *Soc. Neurosci. Abstr.* 25:891.

D'ESPOSITO, M., 1995. The neural basis of the central executive system of working memory. *Nature* 378:279–281.

D'ESPOSITO, M., E. ZARAHN, G. K. AGUIRRE, and B. RYPMA, 1999. The effect of normal aging on the coupling of neural activity to the bold hemodynamic response. *Neuroimage* 10:6–14.

DIAMOND, A., 1981. Retrieval of an object from an open box: The development of visual-tactile control of reaching in the first year of life. *Soc. Res. Child Dev. Abstr.* 3:78.

DIAMOND, A., 1985. Development of the ability to use recall to guide action, as indicated by infants' performance on A not B. *Child Dev.* 56:868–883.

DIAMOND, A., 1988. Differences between adult and infant cognition: Is the crucial variable presence or absence of language? In *Thought without Language*, L. Weiskrantz, ed. Oxford: Oxford University Press, pp. 337–370.

DIAMOND, A., 1990a. Developmental time course in human infants and infant monkeys, and the neural bases, of inhibitory control in reaching. *Ann. N.Y. Acad. Sci.* 608:637–676.

DIAMOND, A., 1990b. The development and neural bases of memory functions as indexed by the AB and delayed response tasks in human infants and infant monkeys. *Ann. N.Y. Acad. Sci.* 608:637–676.

DIAMOND, A., 1991a. Neuropsychological insights into the meaning of object concept development. In *The Epigenesis of Mind: Essays on Biology and Cognition*, S. Carey and R. Gelman, eds. Hillsdale, N.J.: Lawrence Erlbaum Associates, pp. 67–110.

DIAMOND, A., 1991b. Frontal lobe involvement in cognitive changes during the first year of life. In *Brain Maturation and Cognitive Development: Comparative and Cross-Cultural Perspectives*, K. R. Gibson and A. C. Petersen, eds. New York: Aldine de Gruyter, pp. 127–180.

DIAMOND, A., 2000. Close interrelation of motor development and cognitive development and of the cerebellum and prefrontal cortex. *Child Dev.* 71:44–56.

DIAMOND, A., V. CIARAMITARO, E. DONNER, S. DJALI, and M. ROBINSON, 1994. An animal model of early-treated PKU. *J. Neurosci.* 14:3072–3082.

DIAMOND, A., L. CRUTTENDEN, and D. NEIDERMAN, 1994. A-not-B with multiple wells: I. Why multiple wells are sometimes easier than two wells. II. Memory or memory + inhibition? *Dev. Psychol.* 30:192–205.

DIAMOND, A., M. DAVIDSON, L. CRUESS, S. BADALI, D. AMSO, and S. OROSS, 1999a. Long-lasting, selective visual deficits from short-term exposure to high neonatal phenylalanine levels in humans. *Soc. Neurosci. Abstr.* 25:501.

DIAMOND, A., and B. DOAR, 1989. The performance of human infants on a measure of frontal cortex function, the delayed response task. *Dev. Psychobiol.* 22(3):271–294.

DIAMOND, A., and P. S. GOLDMAN-RAKIC, 1985. Evidence for involvement of prefrontal cortex in cognitive changes during the first year of life: Comparison of performance of human infant and rhesus monkeys on a detour task with transparent barrier. *Soc. Neurosci. Abstr.* 11:832.

DIAMOND, A., and P. S. GOLDMAN-RAKIC, 1986. Comparative development in human infants and infant rhesus monkeys of cognitive functions that depend on prefrontal cortex. *Soc. Neurosci. Abstr.* 12:742.

DIAMOND, A., and P. S. GOLDMAN-RAKIC, 1989. Comparison of human infants and rhesus monkeys on Piaget's A-not-B task: Evidence for dependence on dorsolateral prefrontal cortex. *Exp. Brain Res.* 74:24–40.

DIAMOND, A., N. KIRKHAM, and D. AMSO, submitted. Conditions under which young children CAN hold two rules in mind and inhibit a prepotent response.

DIAMOND, A., and C. HERZBERG, 1996. Impaired sensitivity to visual contrast in children treated early and continuously for PKU. *Brain* 119:101–116.

DIAMOND, A., K. M. O'CRAVEN, M. DAVIDSON, C. CRUESS, R. BERGIDA, and R. L. SAVOY, 1999b. Further fMRI-based studies of memory and inhibition in prefrontal cortex of adults. Paper presented at Cognitive Neuroscience Society Annual Meeting, Washington, D.C., April.

DIAMOND, A., K. M. O'CRAVEN, and R. L. SAVOY, 1998. Dorsolateral prefrontal cortex contributions to working memory and inhibition as revealed by fMRI. *Soc. Neurosci. Abstr.* 24:1251.

DIAMOND, A., M. PREVOR, G. CALLENDER, and D. P. DRUIN, 1997. Prefrontal cortex cognitive deficits in children treated early and continuously for PKU. *Monogr. Soc. Res. Child Dev.* 62(4).

DIAMOND, A., and C. TAYLOR, 1996. Development of an aspect of executive control: Development of the abilities to remember what I said and to "Do as I say, not as I do." *Dev. Psychobiol.* 29:315–334.

DIAMOND, A., S. ZOLA-MORGAN, and L. R. SQUIRE, 1989. Successful performance by monkeys with lesions of the hippocampal formation on A-not-B and object retrieval, two tasks that mark developmental changes in human infants. *Behav. Neurosci.* 103:526–537.

DILELLA, A. G., J. MARVIT, A. S. LIDSKY, F. GÜTTLER, and S. L. C. WOO, 1986. Tight linkage between a splicing mutation and a specific DNA haplotype in phenylketonuria. *Nature* 322:799–803.

DOBSON, J. C., E. KUSHIDA, M. L. WILLIAMSON, and E. G. FRIEDMAN, 1976. Intellectual performance of 36 phenylketonuric patients and their non-affected siblings. *Pediatrics* 58:53–58.

DREWE, E. A., 1974. The effect of type and area of brain lesion on Wisconsin Card Sorting Test performance. *Cortex* 10:159–170.

FAUST, D., D. LIBON, and S. PUESCHEL, 1986. Neuropsychological functioning in treated phenylketonuria. *Intl. J. Psychiatry Med.* 16:169–177.

FERNSTROM, J. D., and M. H. FERNSTROM, 1988. Tyrosine availability and dopamine synthesis in the retina. In *Dopaminergic Mechanisms in Vision*, I. Bodis-Wollner and M. Piccolino, eds. New York: Alan R. Liss, pp. 59–70.

FERNSTROM, M. H., E. A. VOLK, and J. D. FERNSTROM, 1986. In vivo inhibition of tyrosine uptake into rat retina by large neutral, but not acidic, amino acids. *Am. J. Physiol.* 251:E393–E399.

FITTS, P. M., and C. M. SEGER, 1953. S-R compatibility: Spatial characteristics of stimulus and response codes. *J. Exp. Psychol.* 81:174–176.

FLAVELL, J. H., 1986. The development of children's knowledge about the appearance-reality distinction. *Amer. Psychologist* 41:418–425.

FLAVELL, J. H., 1993. The development of children's understanding of false belief and the appearance-reality distinction. *Intl. J. Psychol.* 28:595–604.

FOX, N. A., and M. A. BELL, 1990. Electrophysiological indices of frontal lobe development: Relations to cognitive and affective behavior in human infants over the first year of life. *Ann. N.Y. Acad. Sci.* 608:677–704.

FOX, N., J. KAGAN, and S. WEISKOPF, 1979. The growth of memory during infancy. *Genetic Psychol. Monogr.* 99:91–130.

FRITZ, A. S., 1991. Is there a reality bias in young children's emergent theories of mind? Paper presented at the biennial meeting of the Society for Research in Child Development, Seattle.

FUSTER, J. M., 1973. Unit activity in prefrontal cortex during delayed-response performance: Neuronal correlates of transient memory. *J. Neurophysiol.* 36:61–78.

FUSTER, J. M., 1980. *The Prefrontal Cortex: Anatomy, Physiology, and Neuropsychology of the Frontal Lobe*. New York: Raven Press.

FUSTER, J. M., and G.E. ALEXANDER, 1970. Delayed response deficit by cryogenic depression of frontal cortex. *Brain Res.* 61:79–91.

FUSTER, J. M., and G. E. ALEXANDER, 1971. Neuron activity related to short-term memory. *Science* 173:652–654.

GASPAR, P., B. BERGER, A. FEBVRET, A. VIGNY, and J. P. HENRY, 1989. Catecholamine innervation of the human cerebral cortex as revealed by comparative immunohistochemistry of tyrosine hydroxylase and dopamine-β-hydroxylase. *J. Comp. Neurol.* 279:249–271.

GERSTADT, C., Y. HONG, and A. DIAMOND, 1994. The relationship between cognition and action: Performance of 3.5–7 year old children on a Stroop-like day-night test. *Cognition* 53:129–153.

GILMORE, G. C., and J. A. LEVY, 1991. Spatial contrast sensitivity in Alzheimer's disease: A comparison of two methods. *Optom. Vis. Sci.* 68:790–794.

GINSBERG, A. R., 1984. A new contrast sensitivity vision test chart. *Am. J. Optom. Physiol. Optics* 61:403–407.

GOLDMAN, P. S., and W. J. H. NAUTA, 1977. An intricately patterned prefrontal-caudate projection in the rhesus monkey. *J. Comp. Neurol.* 171:369–385.

GOLDMAN, P. S., and H. E. ROSVOLD, 1970. Localization of function within the dorsolateral prefrontal cortex of the rhesus monkey. *Exp. Neurol.* 29:291–304.

GOLDMAN, P. S., H. E. ROSVOLD, and M. MISHKIN, 1970. Evidence for behavioral impairment following prefrontal lobectomy in the infant monkey. *J. Comp. Physiol. Psychol.* 70:454–463.

GOLDMAN-RAKIC, P. S., 1987. Circuitry of primate prefrontal cortex and regulation of behavior by representational memory. In *Handbook of Physiology, the Nervous System, Higher Functions of the Brain*, Vol. 5, F. Plum, ed. Bethesda, Md.: American Physiological Society, pp. 373–417.

GOLDMAN-RAKIC, P. S., and L. J. PORRINO, 1985. The primate mediodorsal (MD) nucleus and its projection to the frontal lobe. *J. Comp. Neurol.* 242:535–560.

GOLDMAN-RAKIC, P. S., and M. L. SCHWARTZ, 1982. Interdigitation of contralateral and ipsilateral columnar projections to frontal association cortex in primates. *Science* 216:755–757.

GOLDSTEIN, K., 1936. The modifications of behavior consequent to cerebral lesions. *Psychiatric Quart.* 10:586–610.

GOLDSTEIN, K., 1944. The mental changes due to frontal lobe damage. *J. Psychol.* 17:187–208.

GRATCH, G., K. J. APPEL, W. F. EVANS, G. K. LeCOMPTE, and N. A. WRIGHT, 1974. Piaget's stage IV object concept error: Evidence for forgetting or object conception? *Child Dev.* 45:71–77.

GRATCH, G., and W. F. LANDERS, 1971. Stage IV of Piaget's theory of infant's object concepts: A longitudinal study. *Child Dev.* 42:359–372.

GREENGARD, O., and C. A. BRASS, 1984. Developmental changes of cerebral phenylalanine uptake from severely elevated blood levels. *Neurochem. Res.* 9:837–848.

GREENGARD, O., M. S. YOSS, and J. A. DEL VALLE, 1976. α-Methylphenylalanine, a new inducer of chronic hyperphenylalaninemia in suckling rats. *Science* 192:1007–1008.

HARLOW, H. F., R. T. DAVIS, P. H. SETTLAGE, and D. R. MEYER, 1952. Analysis of frontal and posterior association syndroms in brain damaged monkeys. *J. Compar. Physiol. Psych.* 45:419–429.

HARRIS, P. L., 1973. Perseverative errors in search by young infants. *Child Dev.* 44:29–33.

HERBERLE, J. F., M. CLUNE, and K. KELLY, 1999. *Development of young children's understanding of the appearance-reality distinction.* Paper presented at the Biennial Meeting of the Society for Research in Child Development, Albuquerque, New Mexico.

HJELLE, J. T., J. BAIRD-LAMBERT, G. CARDINALE, S. SPECOR, and S. UDENFRIEND, 1978. Isolated microvessels: The blood-brain barrier in vitro. *Proc. Natl. Acad. Sci. USA* 75:4544–4548.

HOFSTADTER, M., and J. S. REZNICK, 1996. Response modality affects human infant delayed-response performance. *Child Dev.* 67:646–658.

HOLTZMAN, N. A., R. A. KRONMAL, W. van DOORNINK, C. AZEN, and R. KOCH, 1986. Effect of age at loss of dietary control on intellectual performance and behavior of children with phenylketonuria. *N. Engl. J. Med.* 314:593–598.

HSIA, D. Y., 1967. Phenylketonuria. *Dev. Med. Child Neurol.* 9:531–540

HUTTENLOCHER, P. R., 1979. Synaptic density in human frontal cortex—Developmental changes and effects of aging. *Brain Res.* 163:195–205.

HUTTENLOCHER, P. R., 1984. Synapse elimination and plasticity in developing human cerebral cortex. *Am. J. Mental Deficiency* 88:488–496.

HUTTENLOCHER, P. R., 1990. Morphometric study of human cerebral cortex development. *Neuropsychologia* 28:517–527.

HUTTENLOCHER, P. R., C. DE COURTEN, L. J. GAREY, and H. VAN DER LOOS, 1982. Synaptic development in human cerebral cortex. *Intl. J. Neurol.* 16/17:144–154.

IRIE, K., and R. J. WURTMAN, 1987. Release of norepinephrine from rat hypothalamic slices: Effects of desipramine and tyrosine. *Brain Res.* 432:391–394.

IUVONE, P. M., C. L. GALLI, C. K. GARRISON-GUND, and N. H. NEFF, 1978. Light stimulates tyrosine hydroxylase activity and dopamine synthesis in retinal amacrine neurons. *Science* 202:901–902.

IUVONE, P. M., M. TIGGES, A. FERNANDES, and J. TIGGES, 1989. Dopamine synthesis and metabolism in rhesus monkey retina: Development, aging, and the effects of monocular visual deprivation. *Vis. Neurosci.* 2:465–471.

JACOBSEN, C. F., 1935. Functions of the frontal association areas in primates. *Arch. Neurol. Psychiatry* 33:558–560.

JACOBSEN, C. F., 1936. Studies of cerebral function in primates: I. The functions of the frontal association areas in monkeys. *Comp. Psychol. Monogr.* 13:1–30.

JACOBSEN, C. F., and H. W. NISSEN, 1937. Studies of cerebral function in primates. The effects of frontal lobe lesions on the delayed alternation habit in monkeys. *J. Comp. Physiol. Psychol.* 23:101–112.

JACOBSON, S., N. BUTTERS, and N. J. TOVSKY, 1978. Afferent and efferent subcortical projections of behaviourally defined secotres of prefrontal granular cortex. *Brain Res.* 159:279–296.

JOHNSON, P. B., A. ANGELUCCI, M. ZIPARO, D. MINCIACCHI, M. BENTIVOGLIO, and R. CAMINTI, 1989. Segregation and overlap of callosal and association neurons in frontal and parietal cortices of primates: A spectral and coherency analysis. *J. Neurosci.* 9:2313–2326.

KEMP, J. M., and T. P. POWELL, 1970. The cortico-striate projection in the monkey. *Brain* 93:525–546.

KHOKHRYAKOVA, M., 1979. Structural organization of the prefrontal cortex in cats and its differences from that in monkeys. *Neurosci. Behav. Physiol.* 9:103–109.

KIEVIT, J., and H. G. J. M. KUYPERS, 1977. Organization of the thalamo-cortical connexions to the frontal lobe in the rhesus monkey. *Exp. Brain Res.* 29:299–322.

KIRKHAM, N., L. CRUESS, and A. DIAMOND, submitted. Helping children apply their knowledge to their behavior on a dimension-switching task.

KOCH, R., C. AZEN, E. G. FRIEDMAN, and E. L. WILLIAMSON, 1982. Preliminary report on the effects of diet discontinuation in PKU. *Pediatrics* 100:870–875.

KOCH, R., and E. WENZ, 1987. Phenylketonuria. *Annu. Rev. Nutrition* 7:117–135.

KRAUSE, W. L., M. HELMINSKI, L. MCDONALD, P. DEMBURE, R. SALVO, D. FREIDES, and L. J. ELSAS, 1985. Biochemical and neuropsychological effects of elevated plasma phenylalanine in patients with treated phenylketonuria, a model for the study of phenylalanine in brain function in man. *J. Clin. Invest.* 75:40–48.

KUBOTA, K., and H. NIKI, 1971. Prefrontal cortical unit activity and delayed alternation performance in monkeys. *J. Neurophysiol.* 34:337–347.

KÜNZLE, H., 1978. An autoradiographic analysis of the efferent connections from premotor and adjacent prefrontal regions (areas 6 and 9) in *Macaca fascicularis. Brain Behav. Evol.* 15:185–234.

KUPERSMITH, M. J., E. SHAKIN, I. M. SIEGEL, and A. LIEBERMAN, 1982. Visual system abnormalities in patients with Parkinson's disease. *Arch. Neurol.* 39:284–286.

LAJTHA, A., H. SERSHEN, and D. DUNLOP, 1987. Developmental changes in cerebral amino acids and protein metabolism. In *Amino Acid Availability and Brain Function in Health and Disease,* G. Huether, ed. Berlin: Springer-Verlag, pp. 393–402.

LAMB, M. R., L. C. ROBERTSON, and R. T. KNIGHT, 1989. Attention and inference in the processing of global and local information: Effects of unilateral temporal parietal junction lesions. *Neuropsychologia* 27:471–483.

LARSEN, J. K., and I. DIVAC, 1978. Selective ablations within the prefrontal cortex of the rat and performance on delayed alternation. *Physiol. Psychol.* 6:15–17.

LEDERER, P. J., and J. C. BOSSE, 1992. Clinical use of contrast sensitivity evaluation for general practice of optometry. *Pract. Optom.* 3:34–40.

LEGROS CLARK, W. E., 1930. The thalamus of the tarsius. *J. Anat.* 64:371–414.

LEINER, H. C., A. L. LEINER, and R. S. DOW, 1989. Reappraising the cerebellum: What does the hindbrain contribute to the forebrain? *Behav. Neurosci.* 103:998–1008.

LEVITT, M., P. RAKIC, and P. S. GOLDMAN-RAKIC, 1984. Region-specific distribution of catecholamine afferents in primate cerebral cortex: A fluorescent histochemical analysis. *J. Comp. Neurol.* 227:23–36.

LEWIS, D. A., S. L. FOOTE, M. GOLDSTEIN, and J. H. MORRISON, 1988. The dopaminergic innervation of monkey prefrontal cortex: A tyrosine hydroxylase immunohistochemical study. *Brain Res.* 565:1–13.

LEWIS, D. A., and H. W. HARRIS, 1991. Differential laminar distribution of tyrosine hydroxylase-immunoreactive axons in infant and adult monkey prefrontal cortex. *Neurosci. Lett.* 125:151–154.

LEWIS, D. A., S. R. SESACK, A. I. LEVEY, and D. R. ROSENBERG, 1998. Dopamine axons in primate prefrontal cortex: Specificity of distribution, synaptic targets, and development. *Adv. Pharmacol.* 42:703–706.

LIDOW, M. S., and P. RAKIC, 1992. Scheduling of monoaminergic neurotransmitter receptor expression in the primate neocortex during postnatal development. *Cereb. Cortex* 2:401–416.

LIDSKY, A. S., M. L. LAW, H. G. MORSE, F. T. KAO, and S. L. C. WOO, 1985. Regional mapping of the human phenylalanine hydroxylase gene and the PKU locus on chromosome 12. *Proc. Natl. Acad. Sci. USA* 82:6221–6225.

LIVESEY, D. J., and G. A. MORGAN, 1991. The development of response inhibition in 4- and 5-year-old children. *Austral. J. Psychol.* 43:133–137.

LUCIANA, M., and P. F. COLLINS, 1997. Dopaminergic modulation of working memory for spatial but not object cues in normal humans. *J. Cogn. Neurosci.* 9:330–347.

LUCIANA, M., R. A. DEPUE, P. ARBISI, and A. LEON, 1992. Facilitation of working memory in humans by a D2 dopamine receptor agonist. *J. Cogn. Neurosci.* 4:58–68.

LURIA, A. R., and E. D. HOMSKAYA, 1964. Disturbance in the regulative role of speech with frontal lobe lesions. In *The Frontal Granular Cortex and Behavior,* J. M. Warren and K. Akert, eds. New York: McGraw-Hill, pp. 353–371.

LURIA, A. R., 1966. *The Higher Cortical Functions in Man.* New York: Basic Books.

MÄNTYJÄRVI, M. I., M. H. AUTERE, A. M. SILVENNOINEN, and T. MYÖHÄNEN, 1989. Observations of the use of three different contrast sensitivity tests in children and young adults. *J. Pediatr. Ophthalmol. Strabismus* 26:113–119.

MCDONALD, J. D., V. C. BODE, W. F. DOVE, and A. SHEDLOVSKY, 1990. Pahhph-5: A mouse mutant deficient in phenylalanine hydroxylase. *Proc. Natl. Acad. Sci.* 87:1965–1967.

MCGUIRE, P. K., J. F. BATES, and P. S. GOLDMAN-RAKIC, 1991. Interhemispheric integration: I. Symmetry and convergence of the corticocortical connections of the left and the right principal sulcus (PS) and the left and the right supplementary motor area (SMA) in the rhesus monkey. *Cereb. Cortex* 1:390–407.

MCKEE, R. D., and L. R. SQUIRE, 1993. On the development of declarative memory. *J. Exp. Psych.: Learn. Mem. and Cogn.* 19:397–404.

MCLARDY, T., 1950. Thalamic projection to frontal cortex in man. *J. Neurol. Neurosurg. Psychiatry* 13:198–202.

MEUNIER, M., J. BACHEVALIER, M. MISHKIN, and E. A. MURRAY, 1993. Effects on visual recognition of combined and separate ablations of the entorhinal and perirhinal cortex in rhesus monkeys. *J. Neurosci.* 13:5418–5432.

MIDDLETON, F. A., and P. L. STRICK, 1994. Anatomical evidence for cerebellar and basal ganglia involvement in higher cognitive function. *Science* 266:458–461.

MIDDLETON, F. A., and P. L. STRICK, 1997. Cerebellar output channels. In *The Cerebellum and Cognition,* J. D. Schmahmann, ed. San Diego: Academic Press, pp. 61–82.

MILES, R. C., and A. J. BLOMQUIST, 1960. Frontal lesions and behavioral deficits in monkey. *J. Neurophysiol.* 23:471–484.

MILLER, L., L. D. BRAUN, W. M. PARDRIDGE, and W. H. OLDENDORF, 1985. Kinetic constants for blood-brain, barrier amino acid transport in conscious rats. *J. Neurochem.* 45:1427–1432.

MILNER, B., 1963. Effects of different brain lesions on card sorting: The role of the frontal lobes. *Arch. Neurol.* 9:90–100.

MILNER, B., 1964. Some effects of frontal lobectomy in man. In *The Frontal Granular Cortex and Behavior,* J. M. Warren and K. Akert, eds. New York: McGraw-Hill, pp. 313–334.

MILNER, B., 1982. Some cognitive effects of frontal-lobe lesions in man. *Phil. Trans. R. Soc. (London),* 298(suppl B):211–226.

MILNER, B., P. CORSI, and G. LEONARD, 1991. Frontal-lobe contribution to recency judgments. *Neuropsychologia* 29:601–618.

MISCHEL, H. N., and W. MISCHEL, 1983. The development of children's knowledge of self-control strategies. *Child Dev.* 54:603–619.

MORRIS, R., D. N. PANDYA, and M. PETRIDES, 1999. Fiber system linking the mid-dorsolateral frontal cortex with the retrosplenial/presubicular region in the rhesus monkey. *J. Comp. Neurol.* 407:183–192.

MORRIS, R., M. PETRIDES, and D. N. PANDYA, 1999. Architecture and connections of retrosplenial area 30 in the rhesus monkey (*Macaca mulatta*). *Eur. J. Neurosci.* 11:2506–2518.

NIKI, H., 1974. Differential activity of prefrontal units during right and left delayed response trials. *Brain Res.* 70:346–349.

NORD, A. M., L. MCCABE, and E. R. MCCABE, 1988. Biochemical and nutritional status of children with hyperphenylalaninaemia, *J. Inherit. Metab. Disorders* 11:431–432.

OLDENDORF, W. H., 1973. Stereospecificity of blood–brain barrier permeability to amino acids. *Am. J. Physiol.* 224:967–969.

ORZHEKHOVSKAYA, N. S., 1981. Fronto-striatal relationships in primate ontogeny. *Neurosci. Behav. Physiol.* 11:379–385.

OWEN, A. M., N. J. HERROD, D. K. MENON, J. C. CLARK, S. P. DOWNEY, T. A. CARPENTER, P. S. MINHAS, F. E. TURKHEIMER, E. J. WILLIAMS, T. W. ROBBINS, B. J. SAHAKIAN, M. PETRIDES, and J. D. PICKARD, 1999. Redefining the functional organization of working memory processes within human lateral prefrontal cortex. *Eur. J. Neurosci.* 11(2):567–574.

OWEN, A. M., R. G. MORRIS, B. J. SAHAKIAN, C. E. POLKEY, and T. W. ROBBINS, 1996. Double dissociations of memory and executive functions in a self-ordered working memory task following frontal lobe excision, temporal lobe excisions or amygdalahippocampectomy in man. *Brain* 119:1597–1615.

PARDRIDGE, W., 1977. Regulation of amino acid availability to the brain. In *Nutrition and the Brain,* R. J. Wurtman and J. J. Wurtman, eds. New York: Raven Press, pp. 141–204.

PARDRIDGE, W. M., and W. H. OLDENDORF, 1977. Transport of metabolic substrates through the blood-brain barrier. *J. Neurochem.* 28:5–12.

PASSLER, P. A., W. ISAAC, and G. W. HYND, 1985. Neuropsychological development of behavior attributed to frontal lobe functioning in children. *Dev. Neuropsychol.* 4:349–370.

PELLI, D. G., J. G. ROBSON, and A. J. WILKINS, 1988. The design of a new letter chart for measuring contrast sensitivity. *Clin. Vis. Sci.* 2:187–199.

PENNINGTON, B. F., and S. OZONOFF, 1996. Executive function and developmental psychopathology. *J. Child Psychol. Psychiatry* 37:51–87.

PENNINGTON, B. F., W. J. VAN DOORNICK, L. L. MCCABE, and E. R. B. MCCABE, 1985. Neuropsychological deficits in early treated phenylketonuric children. *Am. J. Mental Deficiency* 89:467–474.

PERRET, E., 1974. The left frontal lobe of man and the suppression of habitual responses in verbal categorical behaviour. *Neuropsychologia* 12:527–537.

PETRIDES, M., 1994. Frontal lobes and working memory: Evidence from investigations of the effects of cortical excisions in nonhuman primates. In *Handbook of Neuropsychology,* F. Boller and J. Grafman, eds. Amsterdam: Elsevier Science, pp. 59–82.

PETRIDES, M., 1995a. Impairments on nonspatial self-ordered and externally ordered working memory tasks after lesions of the mid-dorsal part of the lateral frontal cortex in the monkey. *J. Neurosci.* 15:359–375.

PETRIDES, M., 1995b. Functional organization of the human frontal cortex for mnemonic processing: Evidence from neuroimaging studies. *Ann. N.Y. Acad. Sci.* 769:85–96.

PETRIDES, M., B. ALIVISATOS, E. MEYER, and A. C. EVANS, 1993. Functional activation of the human frontal cortex during performance of verbal working memory tasks. *Proc. Natl. Acad. Sci. USA* 90:878–882.

PETRIDES, M., and B. MILNER, 1982. Deficits in subject-ordered tasks after frontal- and temporal-lobe lesions in man. *Neuropsychologia* 20:249–262.

PETRIDES, M., and D. N. PANDYA, 1984. Projections to the frontal cortex from the posterior parietal region in the rhesus monkey. *J. Comp. Neurol.* 228:105–116.

PETRIDES, M., and D. N. PANDYA, 1988. Association fiber pathways to the frontal cortex from the superior temporal region in the rhesus monkey. *J. Comp. Neurol.* 273:52–66.

PETRIDES, M., and D. N. PANDYA, 1999. Dorsolateral prefrontal cortex: Comparative cytoarchitectonic analysis in the human and the macaque brain and corticocortical connection patterns. *Eur. J. Neurosci.* 11:1011–1036.

PIAGET, J., 1954. *The Construction of Reality in the Child.* New York: Basic Books.

PIAGET, J., and B. INHELDER, 1941. *Le Développement Des Quantités Chez l'Enfant.* Neuchâtel: Delachaux et Niestlé.

PINES, J. L., 1927. Zur architektonik des thalamus opticus beim halbaffen (*Lemur catta*). *J. Psychol. Neurol.* 33:31–72.

PINSKER, H. M., and G. M. FRENCH, 1967. Indirect delayed reactions under various testing conditions in normal and midlateral frontal monkeys. *Neuropsychologia* 5:13–24.

POHL, W., 1973. Dissociation of spatial discrimination deficits following frontal and parietal lesions in monkeys. *J. Comp. Physiol. Psychol.* 82:227–239.

POSTLE, B. R., J. S. BERGER, and M. D'ESPOSITO, 1999. Functional neuroanatomical double dissociation of mnemonic and executive control processes contributing to working memory performance. *Proc. Natl. Acad. Sci.* 96:12959–12964.

PRICE, B. H., K. R. DAFFNER, R. M. STOWE, and M. M. MESULAM, 1990. The compartmental learning disabilities of early frontal lobe damage. *Brain* 113:1383–1393.

RAPOPORT, S. I., 1976. Sites and functions of the blood-aqueous and blood-vitreous barriers of the eye. In *Blood–Brain Barrier in Physiology and Medicine,* S. I. Rapoport, ed. New York: Raven Press, pp. 207–232.

REGAN, D., and D. NEIMA, 1983. Low-contrast letter charts as a test of visual function. *Ophthalmology* 90:1192–1200.

REGAN, D., and D. NEIMA, 1984. Low-contrast letter charts in early diabetic retinopathy, ocular hypertension, glaucoma, and Parkinson's disease. *Br. J. Ophthalmol.* 68:885–889.

RICE, C., D. KOINIS, K. SULLIVAN, H. TAGER-FLUSBERG, and E. WINNER, 1997. When 3-year-olds pass the appearance-reality test. *Dev. Psychol.* 33:54–61.

RICHER, F., A. DECARY, M. F. LAPIERRE, I. ROULEAU, and G. BOUVIER, 1993. Target detection deficits in frontal lobotomy. *Brain Cognition* 21:203–211.

RIS, M. D., S. E. WILLIAMS, M. M. HUNT, H. K. BERRY, and N. LESLIE, 1994. Early-treated phenylketonuria: Adult neuropsychologic outcome. *J. Pediatr.* 124:388–392.

ROBERTSON, L. C., M. R. LAMB, and R. T. KNIGHT, 1988. Effects of lesions of temporal-parietal junction on perceptual and attentional processing in humans. *J. Neurosci.* 8:3757–3769.

ROGERS, G. L., D. L. BREMER, and L. E. LEGUIRE, 1987. Contrast sensitivity functions in normal children with the Vistech method. *J. Pediatr. Ophthalmol. Strabismus* 24:216–219.

ROSE, J. E., and C. N. WOOLSEY, 1948. The orbitofrontal cortex and its connections with the mediodorsal nucleus in rabbit, sheep and cat. *Res. Pub. Assoc. Res. Nervous Mental Disorders* 27:210–232.

ROSENBERG, D. R., and D. A. LEWIS, 1994. Changes in the dopaminergic innervation of monkey prefrontal cortex during late postnatal development: A tyrosine hydroxylase immunohistochemical study. *Biol. Psychiatry* 15:272–277.

ROSENBERG, D. R., and D. A. LEWIS, 1995. Postnatal maturation of the dopaminergic innervation of monkey prefrontal and motor cortices: A tyrosine hydroxylase immunohistochemical analysis. *J. Comp. Neurol.* 358:383–400.

ROTH, R. H., 1984. CNS dopamine autoreceptors: Distribution, pharmacology, and function. *Ann. N.Y. Acad. Sci.* 430:27–53.

RUSSELL, J., N. MAUTHNER, S. SHARPE, and T. TIDSWELL, 1991. The "windows task" as a measure of strategic deception in preschoolers and autistic subjects. *Br. J. Dev. Psychol.* 9:101–119.

RYPMA, B., and M. D'ESPOSITO, 1999. The roles of prefrontal brain regions in components of working memory: Effects of memory load and individual differences. *Proc. Natl. Acad. Sci.* 96:6558–6563.

SAHAKIAN, B. J., G. S. SARNA, B. D. KANTAMANENI, A. JACKSON, P. H. HUTSON, and G. CURZON, 1985. Association between learning and cortical catecholamines in non-drug-treated rats. *Psychopharmacol.* 86:339–343.

SAINT-CYR, J. A., R. O. WAN, D. DOUDET, and T. G. AIGNER, 1988. Impaired detour reaching in rhesus monkeys after MPTP lesions. *Soc. Neurosci. Abstr.* 14:389.

SASAKI, K., K. JINNAI, H. GEMBA, S. HASHIMOTO, and N. MIZUNO, 1979. Projection of the cerebellar dentate nucleus onto the frontal association cortex in monkeys. *Exp. Brain Res.* 37:193–198.

SAVOY, R. L., K. M. O'CRAVEN, M. DAVIDSON, and A. DIAMOND, 1999. *Memory load and inhibition in dorsolateral prefrontal cortex.* Poster presented at the International Conference on Functional Mapping of the Human Brain, Dusseldorf, Germany.

SAWAGUCHI, T., and P. S. GOLDMAN-RAKIC, 1991. D1 dopamine receptors in prefrontal cortex: Involvement in working memory. *Science* 251:947–950.

SAWAGUCHI, T., M. MATSUMURA, and K. KUBOTA, 1988. Dopamine enhances the neuronal activity of spatial short-term memory task in the primate prefrontal cortex. *Neurosci. Res.* 5:465–473.

SAWAGUCHI, T., M. MATSUMURA, and K. KUBOTA, 1990. Effects of dopamine antagonists on neuronal activity related to a delayed response task in monkey prefrontal cortex. *J. Neurophysiol.* 63:1401–1412.

SCHMAHMANN, J. D., and D. N. PANDYA, 1995. Prefrontal cortex projections to the basilar pons in rhesus monkey: Implications for the cerebellar contribution to higher function. *Neurosci. Lett.* 199:175–178.

SCHNEIDER, J. S., and C. J. KOVELOWSKI II, 1990. Chronic exposure to low doses of MPTP. I. Cognitive deficits in motor asymptomatic monkeys. *Brain Res.* 519:122–128.

SCHNEIDER, J. S., and D. P. ROELTGEN, 1993. Delayed matching-to-sample, object retrieval, and discrimination reversal deficits in chronic low dose MPTP-treated monkeys. *Brain Res.* 615:351–354.

SCHWARTZ, M. L., and P. S. GOLDMAN-RAKIC, 1984. Callosal and intrahemispheric connectivity of the prefrontal association cortex in rhesus monkey: Relation between intraparietal and principal sulcal cortex. *J. Comp. Neurol.* 226:403–420.

SELEMON, L. D., and P. S. GOLDMAN-RAKIC, 1985. Longitudinal topography and interdigitation of corticostriatal projections in the rhesus monkey. *J. Neurosci.* 5:776–794.

SELEMON, L. D., and P. S. GOLDMAN-RAKIC, 1988. Common cortical and subcortical targets of the dorsolateral prefrontal and posterior parietal cortices in the rhesus monkey: Evidence for a distributed neural network subserving spatially guided behavior. *J. Neurosci.* 8:4049–4068.

SELTZER, B., and D. N. PANDYA, 1989. Frontal lobe connections of the superior temporal sulcus in the rhesus monkey. *J. Comp. Neurol.* 281:97–113.

SHALLICE, T., 1988. *From Neuropsychology to Mental Structure.* Cambridge: Cambridge University Press.

SHEDLOVSKY, A., J. D. MCDONALD, D. SYMULA, and W. F. DOVE, 1993. Mouse models of human phenylketonuria. *Genetics* 134:1205–1210.

SIMON, H., B. SCATTON, and M. LEMOAL, 1980. Dopaminergic A10 neurons are involved in cognitive functions. *Nature* 286:150–151.

SIMON, R. J., and K. BERBAUM, 1990. Effect of conflicting cues on information processing: the 'Stroop Effect' vs. the 'Simon Effect.' *Acta Psychol.* 73:159–170.

SIWEK, D. F., and D. F. PANDYA, 1991. Prefrontal projections to the mediodorsal nucleus of the thalamus in the rhesus monkey. *J. Comp. Neurol.* 312:509–524.

SKRANDIES, W., and I. GOTTLOB, 1986. Alterations of visual contrast sensitivity in Parkinson's disease. *Hum. Neurobiol.* 5:255–259.

SMITH, E. E., J. JONIDES, C. MARSHUETZ, and R. A. KOEPPE, 1998. Components of verbal working memory: Evidence from neuroimaging. *Proc. Natl. Acad. Sci.* 95(3):876–882.

SMITH, E. E., and J. JONIDES, 1999. Storage and executive processes in the frontal lobes. *Science* 283:1657–1661.

SMITH, I., and M. BEASLEY, 1989. Intelligence and behaviour in children with early treated phenylketonuria. *Eur. J. Clin. Nutrit.* 43:1–5.

SMITH, L. B., E. THELEN, R. TITZER, and D. MCLIN, 1999. Knowing in the context of acting: The task dynamics of the A-not-B error. *Psychol. Rev.* 106:235–260.

SMITH, M. L., P. KLIM, E. MALLOZZI, and W. B. HANLEY, 1996. A test of the frontal-specificity hypothesis in the cognitive performance of adults with phenylketonuria. *Dev. Neuropsychol.* 12:327–341.

DE SONNEVILLE, L. N. J., E. SCHMIDT, U. MICHEL, and U. BATZLER, 1990. Preliminary neuropsychological test results. *Eur. J. Pediatr.* 149(suppl. 1): S39–S44.

SOPHIAN, C., and H. M. WELLMAN, 1983. Selective information use and perseveration in the search behavior of infants and young children. *J. Exp. Child Psychol.* 35:369–390.

SOWELL, E. R., P. M. THOMPSON, C. J. HOLMES, T. L. JERNIGAN, and A. W. TOGA, 1999. In vivo evidence for post-adolescent brain maturation in frontal and striatal regions. *Nature Neurosci.* 2:859–861.

SQUIRE, L. R., S. ZOLA-MORGAN, and K. S. CHEN, 1988. Human amnesia and animal models of amnesia: Performance of amnesic patients on tests designed for the monkey. *Behav. Neurosci.* 102:210–221.

STEMERDINK, B. A., J. J. VAN DER MEERE, M. W. VAN DER MOLEN, A. F. KALVERBOER, M. M. T. HENDRIKX, J. HUISMAN, L. W. A. VAN DER SCHOT, F. M. E. SLIJPER, F. J. VAN SPRONSEN, and P. H. VERKERK, 1995. Information processing in patients with early and continuously-treated phenylketonuria. *Eur. J. Pediatr.* 154:739–746.

STUSS, D. T., and D. F. BENSON, 1986. *The Frontal Lobes.* New York: Raven Press.

STUSS, D. T., and D. F. BENSON, 1987. The frontal lobes and control of cognition and memory. In *The Frontal Lobes Revisited*, E. Perecman, ed. New York: IRBN Press, pp. 141–158.

TAM, S. Y., J. D. ELSWORTH, C. W. BRADBERRY, and R. H. ROTH, 1990. Mesocortical dopamine neurons: High basal firing frequency predicts tyrosine dependence of dopamine synthesis. *J. Neural Transmission* 81:97–110.

TAYLOR, J. R., J. D. ELSWORTH, R. H. ROTH, J. R. SLADEK, JR., and D. E. REDMOND, JR., 1990a. Cognitive and motor deficits in the acquisition of an object retrieval detour task in MPTP-treated monkeys. *Brain* 113:617–637.

TAYLOR, J. R., R. H. ROTH, J. R. SLADEK, JR., and D. E. REDMOND, JR., 1990b. Cognitive and motor deficits in the performance of the object retrieval detour task in monkeys (*Cercopithecus aethiops sabaeus*) treated with MPTP: Long-term performance and effect of transparency of the barrier. *Behav. Neurosci.* 104:564–576.

THATCHER, R. W., R. A. WALKER, and S. GIUDICE, 1987. Human cerebral hemispheres develop at different rates and ages. *Science* 230:1110–1113.

THIERRY, A. M., J. P. TASSIN, A. BLANC, L. STINUS, B. SCATTON, and J. GLOWINSKI, 1977. Discovery of the mesocortical dopaminergic system: Some pharmacological and functional characteristics. *Adv. Biomed. Psychopharmacol.* 16:5–12.

TOBIAS, T. J., 1975. Afferents to prefrontal cortex from the thalamic mediodorsal nucleus in the rhesus monkey. *Brain Res.* 83:191–212.

TORNQUIST, P., and A. ALM, 1986. Carrier-mediated transport of amino acids through the blood-retinal and blood-brain barriers. *Graefe's Arch. Clin. Exp. Ophthalmol.* 224:21–25.

TOURIAN, A. Y., and J. B. SIDBURY, 1978. Phenylketonuria. In *The Metabolic Basis of Inherited Disease*, J. D. Stanbury, J. B. Wyngaarden, and D. Fredrickson, eds. New York: McGraw-Hill, pp. 240–255.

TWETEN, S., M. WALL, and B. D. SCHWARTZ, 1990. A comparison of three clinical methods of spatial contrast-sensitivity testing in normal subjects. *Graefe's Arch. Clin. Exp. Ophthalmol.* 228:24–27.

VOGT, B. A., and D. N. PANDYA, 1987. Cingulate cortex of the rhesus monkey: II. Cortical afferents. *J. Comp. Neurol.* 262:271–289.

VOGT, B. A., D. L. ROSENE, and D. N. PANDYA, 1979. Thalamic and cortical afferents differentiate anterior from posterior cingulate cortex in the monkey. *Science* 204:205–207.

WALKER, A. E., 1940. A cytoarchitectural study of the prefrontal area of the macaque monkey. *J. Comp. Neurol.* 73:59–86.

WARREN, J. M., and K. AKERT, 1964. *The Frontal Granular Cortex and Behavior.* New York: McGraw-Hill.

WATANABE, M., T. KODAMA, and K. HIKOSAKA, 1997. Increase of extracellular dopamine in primate prefrontal cortex during a working memory task. *J. Neurophysiol.* 78:2795–2798.

WEGLAGE, J., M. PIETSCH, B. FUNDERS, H. G. KOCH, and K. ULLRICH, 1995. Neurological findings in early treated phenylketonuria. *Acta Pædiatrica* 84:411–415.

WELSH, M. C., B. F. PENNINGTON, S. OZONOFF, B. ROUSE, and E. R. B. MCCABE, 1990. Neuropsychology of early-treated phenylketonuria: Specific executive function deficits. *Child Dev.* 61:1697–1713.

WIESENDANGER, M., 1981. Organization of the secondary motor areas of the cerebral cortex. In *Handbook of Physiology: The Nervous System. Vol. 2: Motor Control*, V.B. Brooks, ed. Bethesda, Md.: American Physiological Society.

WIKMARK, R. G. E., I. DIVAC, and R. WEISS, 1973. Delayed alternation in rats with lesions in the frontal lobes: Implications for a comparative neuropsychology of the frontal system. *Brain Behav. Evol.* 8:329–339.

WILLATS, P., 1985. Adjustment of means-ends coordination and the representation of spatial relations in the production of search errors by infants. *Br. J. Dev. Psychol.* 3:259–272.

WILLIAMS, S. M., and P. S. GOLDMAN-RAKIC, 1993. Characterization of the dopaminergic innervation of the primate frontal cortex using a dopamine-specific antibody. *Cereb. Cortex* 3:199–222.

WILLIAMS, S. M., and P. S. GOLDMAN-RAKIC, 1995. Modulation of memory fields by dopamine D1 receptors in prefrontal cortex. *Nature* 376:572–575.

WILLIAMSON, M. L., R. KOCH, C. AZEN, and C. CHANG, 1981.

Correlates of intelligence test results in treated phenylketonuric children. *Pediatrics* 68:161–167.

WOO, S. L. C., A. S. LIDSKY, F. GÜTTLER, T. CHANDRA, and K. J. H. ROBSON, 1983. Cloned human phenylalanine hydroxylase gene allows prenatal diagnosis and carrier detection of classical phenylketonuria. *Nature* 306:151–155.

WURTMAN, R. J., F. LORIN, S. MOSTAFAPOUR, and J. D. FERNSTROM, 1974. Brain catechol synthesis: Control by brain tyrosine concentration. *Science* 185:183–184.

YAKOVLEV, P. I, and A. R. LECOURS, 1967. The myelogenetic cycles of regional maturation of the brain. In *Regional Development of the Brain in Early Life*, A. Minkowski, ed. Oxford: Blackwell, pp. 3–70.

YAMAMOTO, T., K. YOSHIDA, H. YOSHIKAWA, Y. KISHIMOTO, and H. OKA, 1992. The medial dorsal nucleus is one of the thalamic relays of the cerebellocerebral responses to the frontal association cortex in the monkey: Horseradish peroxidase and florescent dye double staining study. *Brain Res.* 579:315–320.

ZAGREDA, L., J. GOODMAN, D. P. DRUIN, D. MCDONALD, and A. DIAMOND, 1999. Cognitive deficits in a genetic mouse model of the most common biochemical cause of human mental retardation. *J. Neurosci.* 19:6175–6182.

ZAITCHIK, D., 1991. Is only seeing really believing?: Sources of the true belief in the false belief task. *Cogn. Dev.* 6:91–103.

ZELAZO, P. D., D. FRYE, and T. RAPUS, 1996. An age-related dissociation between knowing rules and using them. *Cogn. Dev.* 11:37–63.

ZELAZO, P. D., and J. S. REZNICK, 1991. Age-related asynchrony of knowledge and action. *Child Dev.* 62:719–735.

ZELAZO, P. D., J. S. REZNICK, and D. E. PIÑON, 1995. Response control and the execution of verbal rules. *Dev. Psychol.* 31:508–517.

ZOLA-MORGAN, S., L. R. SQUIRE, and D. G. AMARAL, 1989. Lesions of the hippocampal formation but not lesions of the fornix or mammillary nuclei produce long-lasting memory impairment in monkeys. *J. Neurosci.* 9(3):898–913.

# 30  Age-Related Changes in Working Memory and Frontal Lobe Function: A Review

MONICA FABIANI
AND EMILY WEE

ABSTRACT  The frontal lobes are considered to be an essential component of a circuit that supports working memory function. This chapter examines several aspects of the changes that occur in frontal lobe function and working memory during normal aging. We review data from cognitive, neuropsychological, and neuroimaging research that suggest the existence of diminished frontal lobe function in normal aging, leading to diminished performance in a wide variety of tasks involving working memory. These include age-related changes in the effects of memory load, in the processing of different types of stimuli, in the susceptibility to distractors, and in the ability to inhibit prepotent but unwanted responses. In addition, we discuss dissociations between performance in source memory tasks and recognition memory tasks, as well as methodological and theoretical issues pertaining to this research.

## Introduction and background

WORKING MEMORY, THE FRONTAL LOBES, AND AGING One of the most common complaints of normal older adults is a reduction in their memory capacity. Research on metamemory suggests that the elderly commonly expect memory failures, and sometimes exaggerate their likelihood of occurrence and extent (Hess and Pullen, 1996; Parr and Siegert, 1993). However, an examination of the literature concerning age-related memory changes suggests that some aspects of memory (such as direct vocabulary knowledge, priming, and recognition memory[1]) appear to remain fairly stable throughout the adult life span, whereas other aspects of memory are affected by increasing age (for reviews, see Kausler, 1991; Light, 1996; Woodruff-Pak, 1997). Among the memory functions that appear to be most affected by normal aging is "working memory," especially in situations that require the recall and "on-line" manipulation of contextual details, coupled with a fair amount of flexibility and strategic adjustments (Moscovitch and Winocur, 1992; Parkin and Walter, 1991; West, 1996).

MONICA FABIANI AND EMILY WEE  Department of Psychology, University of Missouri, Columbia, Missouri.

Working memory refers to a system for temporarily holding and manipulating information (Baddeley, 1986; Cowan, 1995). As such, working memory is likely to contribute to a wide variety of tasks, including learning and comprehension, as well as the planning and maintenance of goals and actions and the monitoring and supervision of one's own behavior. Given this view of working memory, it is not surprising that age-related changes in this function may be far-reaching and have effects on a variety of laboratory and real-life tasks.

Evidence has accumulated that suggests that the frontal lobes, and particularly the dorsolateral prefrontal cortex (Brodmann area 46), are an essential component of a circuit that sustains working memory function (Fuster, 1973; Goldman-Rakic, 1987; 1992). Damage to the frontal lobes does not necessarily lead to memory loss per se, but it may lead to impairments on tasks requiring the organization of external cues and the initiation and execution of strategic behavior (Knight, Grabowecky, and Scabini, 1995; Milner, 1995; Milner and Petrides, 1984; Moscovitch and Winocur, 1992; Shimamura, 1995; Stuss, Eskes, and Foster, 1994). In fact, patients with frontal lobe lesions show minor performance decrements in tasks involving "item memory" (memory for the items or events themselves), but are often impaired in tasks requiring "source memory" (memory for contextual details referring to the remembered items), and may lack flexibility when confronted with changing task demands. A typical task in which frontal-lesioned patients show diminished performance is the Wisconsin Card Sorting Test (WCST, Heaton, 1981; Milner, 1963). In this task patients with frontal lesions have difficulty adjusting their response strategies on the basis of feedback from the experimenter, and tend to persevere with responses that were originally correct but are no longer valid.

Recent evidence suggests that altered frontal function may frequently accompany not only pathological, but also normal aging (West, 1996). Several reports suggest that older adults' performance is diminished with respect to that of young adults in neuropsychological tests such as the WCST (e.g., Fabiani and Friedman, 1995; Fabiani, Friedman, and Cheng, 1998; Parkin and Walter, 1991), in source memory tasks (Fabiani and Friedman, 1997; Schacter et al., 1993; Trott et al., 1999), and in other tasks requiring the monitoring of strategies and/or the inhibition of prepotent responses (e.g., conflict paradigms such as the Stroop tasks; Spieler, Balota, and Faust, 1996). There is also evidence that age-related changes in brain anatomy (Haug and Eggers, 1981; for a review, see West, 1996) and function (e.g., Gur et al., 1987) are more extensive in the frontal lobes than in other areas of the brain, such as sensory and motor areas. These data are consistent with the proposal that many of the cognitive changes observed in later life may be due to reduced frontal function (Moscovitch and Winocur, 1992; Parkin and Walter, 1991; Stuss et al., 1996; West, 1996).

LAYOUT OF THE REVIEW  In summary, it is hypothesized that age-related problems in working memory may be associated, at least in part, with diminished frontal function. In this chapter, we present converging evidence of (1) changes in the working memory function of normally aging adults and (2) age-related changes in frontal lobe function in the same population. As will become apparent in the course of this review, the exact mapping and degree of overlap between working memory and frontal lobe function remain to be completely clarified.

Although by no means exhaustive, this review includes representative examples from the cognitive, neuropsychological, and brain imaging literatures, including event-related brain potentials (ERPs), positron emission tomography (PET), and functional magnetic resonance imaging (fMRI). We begin the review with a discussion of methodological issues in aging research, including the definition of "old" age and the role of individual differences, as well as some of the problems associated with the interpretation of brain imaging and neuropsychological data. These are issues that should be considered when examining literature on aging, and may guide the interpretation of the remainder of the chapter. We then describe (1) possible age-related changes in sensory memory; (2) the effects of working memory load, both in terms of the number of items to be held in memory and in terms of the number of operations to be performed on the items; (3) evidence of increased distractibility and decreased ability to inhibit prepotent, but incorrect, responses; (4) the differential effects of the type of task and material to be

processed in working memory; and (5) evidence pertaining to memory errors for contextual information (source memory). In closing, we briefly summarize some theoretical issues and future directions in this research domain.

*Methodological issues*

"OLD" AGE AND INDIVIDUAL DIFFERENCES  The definition of "old" age is a source of controversy in aging research because there is no exact correspondence between chronological age and the extent of age-related cognitive change. In an effort to increase their understanding of the aging process, researchers sometimes divide older subjects into groups characterized by more restricted age ranges, such as young-old (ages 60–74) and old-old (ages 74 and over; e.g., Parkin and Java, 1999). However, there is no universally accepted demarcation between middle age and older adulthood. The studies reviewed in this chapter mostly involve two subject groups: young adults (most often college students below the age of 30) and older adults (typically 60 years of age or older).

Individual differences tend to increase with age. Lifestyle, general health, and other factors greatly contribute to how much an individual actually ages with respect to other members of his/her cohort. For example, a number of investigators have looked at the role of physical fitness on cognitive function in aging (e.g., Bashore, 1990; Bashore and Goddard, 1993; Kramer et al., 1999). Older adults who exercise regularly tend to perform better in cognitive tasks than those who do not, especially if their exercise programs involve aerobic activities. These effects may be due to the benefits of enhanced overall health, or to more indirect effects such as an increased blood circulation to the brain.

Of course, the role of individual differences in aging begs the question of whether engaging in frequent and complex mental activity may delay or counteract some of the impairments observed in normal cognitive aging (the "use-it-or-lose-it" hypothesis). Snowdon and colleagues (1996, 1997) initiated a longitudinal study involving a group of nuns who joined the Sisters of Notre Dame in the 1920s, and were tested at regular intervals throughout old age. Data published in 1996 (Snowdon et al., 1996) suggested the possibility of predicting the onset of Alzheimer's disease in old age by examining the writing complexity of the same women at age 20. However, although very intriguing in principle, this study has been criticized for the subjectivity of the writing analysis and for the small number of subjects involved. A more general issue is that it is difficult, in studies involving individual differences, to distinguish between causes and effects (i.e., does mental activity "protect" the brain from aging, or is a more "capable" brain more resistant to aging?). In summary, the role of a more active cognitive life in preventing some of the adverse effects of aging on cognition is far from clear and difficult to address even in the context of longitudinal studies because a number of alternative explanations are usually possible.

THE INTERPRETATION OF BRAIN IMAGING DATA FROM OLDER ADULTS  Technological advances in the last two decades have greatly enhanced the tools available to investigators to examine the relationships between behavior and underlying brain function in older adults (Fabiani, Gratton, and Coles, 2000; Gratton and Fabiani, 1998; Kutas and Federmeier, 1998; Toga and Mazziotta, 1996). However, several caveats in the interpretation of brain imaging data should be considered, especially with respect to their use in aging research. For example, a number of the ERP studies described in this chapter were designed on the basis of a priori hypotheses of frontal effects and did report marked age-related changes of brain activity at frontal electrode sites. However, it is generally not possible to make inferences about the brain origin of electrical potentials only on the basis of scalp-recorded data (Fabiani, Gratton, and Coles, 2000), although some inferences can be made on the basis of converging evidence from intracranial (Fernandez et al., 1999) and brain injury (Knight, 1984) studies.

Although fMRI may provide more precise localization data than ERP recordings, there are a number of limitations in the application of fMRI to the study of aging. Some of these limitations are practical (such as the need for the subjects to be motionless for extended periods and the necessity of avoiding glasses or other prostheses containing metal), and can probably be solved for a number of older participants. There are, however, some more fundamental issues concerning the degree to which the coupling between neuronal function and blood flow remains the same in old age, and whether it remains consistent for different areas of the brain (D'Esposito et al., 1999). These problems may complicate the interpretation of hemodynamic imaging data in the study of age-related cognitive changes. Further understanding of the neuronal–hemodynamic coupling in aging may help address these issues.

THE USE OF NEUROPSYCHOLOGICAL TESTING IN AGING RESEARCH  Neuropsychological tests are typically designed to characterize patients with specific brain lesions. In aging research, they can also be used to help characterize the underlying brain source of behavioral

or ERP effects. Although this approach is potentially useful, it can be criticized because many of these tests are not sufficiently specific to the brain region whose functions they are designed to assess (Eslinger and Grattan, 1993; Mountain and Snow, 1993). In addition, it should also be kept in mind that, although the effects of normal aging may be accompanied by some cell atrophy and neurotransmitter depletion, they are not characterized by the extensive cell death typical of brain lesions. Thus, the analogy between normal aging processes and the effects of frontal lesions should not be overemphasized. For instance, Fabiani and Friedman (1995) observed an increased frontal P3 in aging, whereas Knight (1984) reported decreased frontal P3 in patients with frontal lesions. This underscores the difference that may exist between a full-fledged lesion and the microscopic, though diffuse, alterations that may occur in normal aging.

*Sensory memory*

Although this chapter mainly focuses on age-related changes in working memory and frontal function, in this section we briefly review some recent studies suggesting that early and largely preattentive stimulus processing may also show changes during normal aging. This early processing can be roughly identified with sensory memory—a memory buffer that can briefly hold large amounts of information before some of it enters attention and working memory (Näätänen, 1992). It may be hypothesized that information from the sensory systems is continuously "fed" into working memory from sensory memory (Broadbent, 1957). Regardless of the theoretical framework adopted, it follows that if the capacity and/or duration of sensory memory is in some way degraded in aging, this may, in turn, influence subsequent working memory processing.

One component of the ERP, the mismatch negativity (MMN; Näätänen and Alho, 1995; Ritter et al., 1995), has been used as an index of automatic deviance detection in auditory sensory memory. In fact, the MMN increases in amplitude in response to deviant tones (e.g., high-pitched) occasionally intermixed within a stream of homogeneous (standard) tones (e.g., low-pitched), even when the subject is ignoring the tones and reading a book (passive oddball paradigm). This amplitude increase to the rarely occurring deviant stimuli implies that the memory of the standard stimuli is maintained automatically.

The average ERP waveform elicited by the standard tones is subtracted from that of the deviant tones to yield the MMN, which, as its name indicates, is negative in polarity. The MMN has an onset latency as short as

50 ms, a peak latency of 100–200 ms, and is most likely generated in primary auditory cortex and/or immediately adjacent areas, with at least one additional contribution from the frontal lobes (Alho, Huotilainen, and Näätänen, 1995; Alho et al., 1994; Javitt et al., 1994; Rinne et al., 1999).

Because the MMN is generated in response to any discriminable change between the standard and deviant tones even when the subject is not attending to the stimuli, it is likely to reflect the automatic and preattentive processing of deviant features. In addition, because the MMN is not elicited after long (10 s or more) interstimulus intervals, it is hypothesized that it may be based on a type of memory that is transient in nature.

A few studies have investigated the effects of aging on the MMN. Some of these studies have reported a decreased MMN amplitude in the elderly, irrespective of the length of the interval interposed between standard and deviant stimuli (Czigler, Csibra, and Csontos, 1992; Gaeta et al., 1998; Kazmerski, Friedman, and Ritter, 1997; Woods, 1992; see figure 30.1) and therefore suggest a decreased sensitivity to deviance as a function of age. In contrast, others have reported a normal-amplitude MMN in the elderly when short ISIs are used, but a reduced MMN when long intervals are interposed between stimuli (Pekkonen et al., 1996; see figure 30.2). The latter finding suggests that the early sensory processing leading to tone discrimination may be intact in older subjects, at least at short intervals, but that the information required to determine whether a stimulus is deviant may decay at a faster rate in the elderly than it does in young adults. These discrepant findings may be due to methodological differences among studies. For example, a fixed tone volume was used in some studies (Czigler, Csibra, and Csontos, 1992), and adjusted in others (Woods, 1992; Pekkonen et al., 1996). Thus, peripheral hearing loss may have contributed to the MMN differences observed between young and old subjects. Similarly, eye movement artifacts may have led to increased trial rejection in the elderly with respect to the young. Finally, some of the studies used paradigms that involved some degree of attention switching (Woods, 1992), and therefore may have imposed an additional memory load, whereas others did not (Pekkonen et al., 1996). In conclusion, although it is still unclear whether or not there is decreased automatic deviance detection in aging in general, or whether this decrease is limited to conditions in which relatively long (e.g., 4 s or more) ISIs separate deviants from standard stimuli, there appears to be some amount of change in early auditory sensory memory processing in normal aging.

## Effects of working memory load

NUMBER OF ITEMS IN WORKING MEMORY A way of determining whether working memory function is impaired is to test it by increasing the amount of information (load) to be handled. It can be expected that subjects with impaired working memory would show disproportionately high performance decrements under high load conditions. A classic and widely used paradigm to test the effects of memory load is Sternberg's memory search task (Sternberg, 1966), in which memory set size (i.e., number of items stored in memory) is varied. Subjects are asked to decide whether or not probe stimuli are part of the memory set, and reaction time (RT) in response to probe stimuli is measured. As set size increases, RT to the probes also increases (typically 38 ms per item in young adults). Within an additive factor framework, the slope of the RT function is usually taken as evidence that memory scan and comparison processes last a fixed amount of time per item. Experiments conducted with older adults typically show slower overall RT (*intercept*, presumably related to delays in other types of processes, including generalized slowing) and a steeper increase in RT (*slope*) with increased set size as compared to young adults (Anders, Fozard, and Lillyquist, 1972; Bashore, Osman, and Heffley, 1989; Fisk and Rogers, 1991).

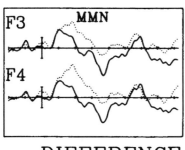

DIFFERENCE
WAVES

IGNORED
DEV–STAND

700 AND 1300 HZ
—— ELDERLY
·········· MIDDLE–AGED

FIGURE 30.1 Results from a study by Woods (1992) showing a diminished MMN amplitude in elderly subjects (solid line) with respect to middle-aged subjects (dashed line). (Reprinted with permission from Elsevier Science.)

**ISI 0.5 s**

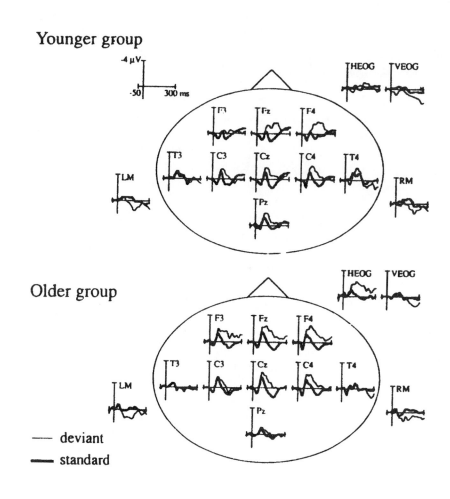

**ISI 4.5 s**

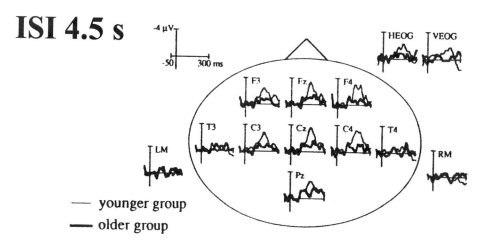

FIGURE 30.2 Results from a study by Pekkonen and colleagues (1996) showing diminished MMN amplitude in older subjects at long (bottom panel) but not at short ISIs (top panel). (Reproduced with permission from Taylor & Francis.)

Investigators have used ERPs to specify further the causes of the age-related RT delay that occurs with increased memory load in Sternberg's task. The most common approach has been to use the latency of the P300 (also called P3 or P3b; Sutton et al., 1965; Fabiani, Gratton, and Coles, 2000) elicited by the probe stimuli as an index of decision processes independent of response selection processes (McCarthy and Donchin, 1981). In other words, because the P300 is elicited by target stimuli (such as the probes in a Sternberg's task; Johnson and Donchin, 1978), it can be used as an additional measure of processing time.

Ford and colleagues (1979) reported that, in Sternberg's task, the slope of the increases in P3 latency as a function of set size was less than that for the RT in young adults. In a subsequent study, Ford and colleagues (1982) reported that, in older adults, the latency of P3 was unaffected by set size or response type, possibly suggesting strategic differences between young and older adults. Strayer, Wickens, and Braune (1987) suggested that perceptual encoding, response criterion adjustment, and response execution were affected by aging more than memory search speed per se (see also Strayer and Kramer, 1994; for a meta-analytic study, see Bashore, Osman, and Heffley, 1989). Thus, these data suggest that (1) different phenomena may contribute to the age-related changes in the RT/item slope in Sternberg's task; (2) aging produces differential effects, depending on the aspects of processing involved (see also Chao and Knight, 1997a); and (3) response selection and execution may play an important role in the slowing of RT in aging, possibly reflecting increased distractibility and consequent response conflict.

A different approach to investigating the effects of working memory load was taken recently by Wee and Fabiani (1999a,b). They used a modified 2-back task in which encoding and retrieval processes could be separated more easily than in the traditional continuous N-back task (Jonides et al., 1997). In one of the experimental conditions, subjects were asked to encode two successive stimuli, each varying on two dimensions (*shape:* square or diamond; *position:* above or below fixation). Following stimulus encoding, the subjects were given a cue indicating which of the two dimensions they should use in formulating a response. The cue was followed by two test stimuli presented one after the other. For each of these test stimuli, subjects had to indicate whether or not it matched the stimulus presented in position 2-back with respect to the dimension indicated by the cue. The sequence then ended and a new trial started again with the study stimuli. In this task, memory load during encoding was defined as the number of separate stimulus features that had to be maintained in

memory. For example, the load was defined as low when the two study stimuli were identical on both dimensions (e.g., two squares above fixation), and therefore only two features needed to be kept in working memory. The load was considered medium when the two stimuli matched on only one dimension (e.g., two squares presented in different positions). Finally, load was considered high when the two stimuli differed on both dimensions (e.g., a diamond and a square presented in different positions), requiring the maintenance of four separate features and their correct pairings. Note that subjects did not know which dimension they needed to use for the test, and therefore had to encode all relevant information. As in Sternberg's task, the RT at test increased as a function of load, especially for older adults. Although there were small P300 effects as a function of load, the most significant ERP changes consisted of variations in the amplitude of a frontally distributed slow wave elicited by the second study stimulus, which became progressively more negative as load increased from low to high. These slow-wave effects at encoding were more pronounced in older adults than in young adults. This slow-wave component may reflect encoding efforts, and, if so, these data may indicate that older adults require more effort to encode and/or maintain information in working memory as load increases.

NUMBER OF OPERATIONS TO BE PERFORMED IN WORKING MEMORY   The effects of working memory load can also be assessed with respect to the number of operations (or amount of processing) that subjects are required to perform "on-line." The WCST (Parkin and Walter, 1991) and the continuous N-back task (Jonides et al., 1997) are both tasks in which the subject has to hold several pieces of information in memory as well as complex instructions on how to handle each new item. For example, Parkin and Walter (1991) reported that, in older adults, performance on the WCST correlates with performance in the Brown-Peterson task. In the N-back task, Jonides and colleagues (1997), using PET, showed progressively poorer performance and increased activity in frontal areas as the working memory load was increased by varying the value of N in young adults (see also Braver et al., 1997). In the modified 2-back task described earlier, older adults' performance at test decreased with load more than the performance of young adults (see Wee and Fabiani, 1999a).

These data suggest that the age-related effects of load are increased further if older subjects have to maintain a number of items in memory while performing a task that involves complex instructions and/or frequent strategic adjustments and flexibility. In fact, data from Kramer, Hahn, and Gopher (1999) suggest that, with practice in a task-switching paradigm, older adults improve to the level of young adults under low load conditions. However, under conditions of high memory load, older adults are maximally affected by task switching and are not able to benefit from practice.

## Effects of type of material to be processed in working memory

An important variable in the analysis of working memory function is the type of material to be held in memory. Both fMRI (McCarthy et al., 1994) and PET studies (Jonides et al., 1993; Smith et al., 1995) have reported an increased activation in the middle frontal gyrus (Brodmann area 46) during the performance of spatial working memory tasks in young adults. This activation is predominant in the right hemisphere, and it is part of a circuit that involves occipital, parietal, and prefrontal areas. Verbal working memory tasks appear to activate regions in the left hemisphere (Smith, Jonides, and Koeppe, 1996, 1998), whereas not much prefrontal activity has been reported for object working memory tasks (Smith et al., 1995).

Only a handful of imaging data are currently available for older subjects. Jonides and colleagues (2000) reported that, in a verbal working memory task in which inhibitory activity was required, older adults (unlike young adults) failed to show increased activation in prefrontal cortex. In addition, whereas in young adults there appears to be a lateralization of working memory function depending on the type of material used (verbal vs. spatial), either bilateral activation or the opposite pattern of activation is observed in older adults (see figure 30.3 [see color plate 20]; Gabrieli, 1999; Reuter-Lorenz, 1999; Reuter-Lorenz et al., 2000).

ERP data obtained in young subjects suggest that working memory function may be indexed by negative slow waves (Mecklinger, 1998; Ruchkin et al., 1995). Wee and Fabiani (1999a,b) found a reduction in the frontal negative activity between young and older adults, and more bilateral activity in older than young adults when comparing spatial and object memory.

Taken as a whole, these blood flow and ERP data suggest that older adults may either need to recruit more brain areas than do young adults to assist in processing (bilateral vs. lateralized effects), or may be invoking processes that are inappropriate for the task at hand.

## Decreased inhibition of unwanted responses and increased susceptibility to distractors

For many years it has been known that it is often difficult for older adults to inhibit the processing of ir-

relevant stimuli (Rabbitt, 1965). It has been also hypothesized that the dorsolateral prefrontal cortex plays a crucial role in a system aimed at inhibiting prepotent but unwanted responses to irrelevant stimuli (Chao and Knight, 1997b; Cohen, Braver, and O'Reilly, 1996; Knight, Grabowecky, and Scabini, 1995). In this section we examine two different lines of evidence for this hypothesis. The first is an examination of results obtained by recording ERPs in two variants of the oddball paradigm in young and older adults, and in patients with frontal lobe lesions. The second is an examination of data obtained in paradigms in which two stimulus dimensions call for opposite responses (only one of which is correct), thereby creating a conflict in the processing of information.

AGE-RELATED CHANGES IN THE AMPLITUDE AND SCALP DISTRIBUTION OF P300   The P300 component of the ERPs is typically recorded in an active oddball paradigm, in which two types of stimuli, differing in probability of occurrence, are presented in a Bernoulli sequence, and the subjects are instructed to respond to or count the rare (target) stimuli. It has been suggested that the P300 is involved in some aspects of working memory processes (Donchin, 1981).

Several age-related changes in the P300 recorded in the oddball paradigm have been reported, including an increased latency and decreased amplitude as a function of age (Ford and Pfefferbaum, 1991; Polich, 1991, 1996; Polich, Howard, and Starr, 1985). The age-related amplitude decrease is not uniformly distributed across the scalp. The P300 is diminished in amplitude at posterior electrodes (where it is typically largest in young adults), whereas it does not change much at frontal electrode sites, thus resulting in an apparent age-related change in scalp distribution (see figure 30.4; Fabiani and Friedman, 1995; Fabiani, Friedman, and Cheng, 1998; Friedman, Kazmerski, and Fabiani, 1997).

This age-related change in the scalp distribution of the P300 has little apparent correspondence in behavioral changes: In most cases the oddball task is extremely easy, and performance is asymptotic in both young and older adults. Furthermore, RT typically is not slower in older adults in this task. However, hypotheses about the possible meaning of these changes can be derived by an examination of findings obtained in a variant of the oddball paradigm, the "novelty" oddball task.

THE P300 IN THE NOVELTY ODDBALL TASK   As in the active oddball task, in the novelty oddball task subjects are presented with a series of stimuli and asked to respond to the target (rare) stimulus. However, in addition to target and standard stimuli, novel stimuli are

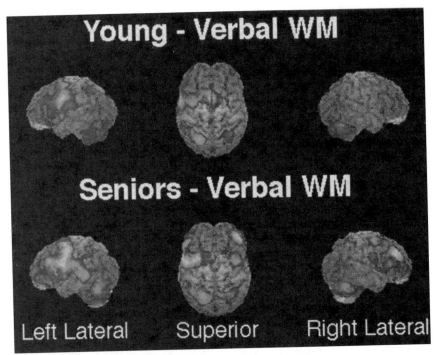

FIGURE 30.3 Data from Reuter-Lorenz (1999), showing bilateral frontal activation in the older subjects during a verbal working memory (WM) task, and left activation only in the young subjects. (Reproduced with permission from Taylor & Francis.)

also intermittently presented in the series. Much of the research in this paradigm has been done within the auditory domain (but see Courchesne, Hillyard, and Galambos, 1975; Yamaguchi and Knight, 1991a,b), and the novel stimuli are unexpected nontonal sounds (e.g., a dog bark) rarely presented within a series of tones (Fabiani and Friedman, 1995; Fabiani, Friedman, and Cheng, 1998; Fabiani et al., 1996; Friedman, Simpson and Hamberger, 1993; Knight, 1987). It is hypothesized that the rarely occurring novel stimuli may capture attention, and may therefore elicit an orienting response (which is not elicited by the rare but repeated targets). However, because no response is assigned to these stimuli, it is also hypothesized that they may elicit inhibitory processes to suppress response execution (Knight and Nakada, 1998).

Using this paradigm in control subjects and patients with frontal lesions, Knight (1984) reported that, in normal control subjects, the novel sounds elicited a P300-like activity (called novelty P3a or novelty P3) characterized by increased amplitude at frontal electrodes in comparison to the P300 elicited by rare target stimuli. However, this increased activity in response to the novel stimuli was absent in patients with lesions to the dorsolateral frontal cortex. This lends support to the hypothesis that the anterior aspect of the novelty-P3 activity may be generated in the frontal lobes (see

also Friedman, Simpson, and Fabiani, 1999). In other words, it could be hypothesized that the scalp-recorded P300 represents the summation of the activity of neural generators in a circuit encompassing frontal, parietal and temporal areas (Knight, 1997; Knight et al., 1989; Yamaguchi and Knight, 1991a,b; see also Goldman-Rakic, 1992, for a similar circuit in the monkey). Scalp distribution changes observed in lesioned patients and older adults may represent a change in the relative "weight" of the various generators within this circuit, which, in turn, may reflect functional changes.

Using this paradigm and theoretical framework in the context of normal aging research, Fabiani and Friedman (1995) found that both young and older adults showed increased frontal activity in response to nonrepeated novel sounds as compared to the P300 activity elicited by target tones (see figures 30.4 and 30.5). Although the behavior of young and older adults did not differ much in this paradigm, there was a trend for the older adults to produce more false alarms in response to the novel sounds (for which the motor response should be inhibited), at least early on in the session. In addition, older adults showed frontally oriented P300 activity in response to the rare but repeated target tones, whereas young adults had a typical parietal-maximum P3 in response to targets. Finally, when the P3 response to target stimuli was examined

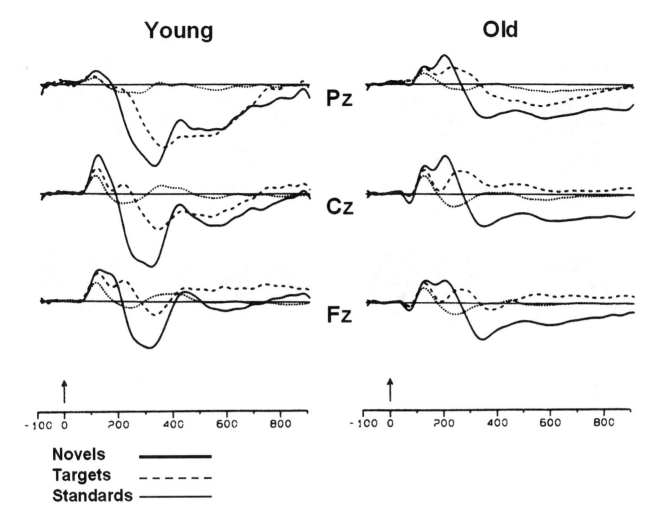

**Young**          **Old**

Pz

Cz

Fz

-100  0      200      400      600      800

**Novels** ————
**Targets** – – – – –
**Standards** ————

FIGURE 30.4 Data from Fabiani and Friedman (1995) showing changes in P3 amplitude, latency and scalp distribution in aging. Positive potentials are plotted downward. (Reprinted with permission of Cambridge University Press.)

over time, starting with the practice block, it was apparent that young adults showed a frontally oriented P3 in response to the initial presentations of the target stimuli. This response faded out with time on task and was replaced by a parietal-maximum P3 (see figure 30.6). In older adults, the frontal focus of this component in response to targets remained stable over time, regardless of repeated exposures to the target tone. This suggests that novel stimuli engage working memory/ orienting processes in both young and older adults. However, with aging, these processes may also be engaged inappropriately in response to repeated stimuli (such as the oddball targets) that should no longer require them. This may occur because working memory templates decay faster in old age, and/or because older adults are more susceptible to distractors and increased workload.

In a follow-up study, Fabiani, Friedman, and Cheng (1998) found that those older adults whose target P3 was more parietally focused (and thus more similar to the target P3 observed in young subjects) were much less impaired in tests of frontal function such as the WCST than were those older adults whose P3 was largest at the frontal electrodes (and thus more similar to a novelty P3). This relationship between brain activity and neuropsychological profile was specific to tests of frontal lobe function, as the two groups of older subjects did not differ on the basis of IQ or other "nonfrontal" variables. This suggests that the frontal portion of the P3 may represent the engagement of a working memory/orienting system that may normally be suppressed with repeated stimulus presentation. The persistence of frontal activity in response to repeated targets in older subjects may therefore signal the inappropriate elicitation of orienting responses. In turn, this may indicate the presence of working memory dysfunction and be associated with increased distractibility.

THE STROOP AND OTHER CONFLICT TASKS A more direct test of the hypothesis that older adults are more

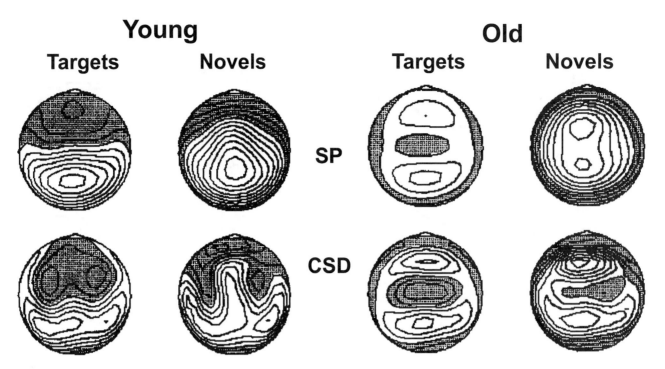

**Young**

| Targets | Novels |
|---------|--------|

**Old**

| Targets | Novels |
|---------|--------|

SP

CSD

FIGURE 30.5   Data from Fabiani and Friedman (1995) showing surface potential (SP) and current source density (CSD) maps at the peak of P3 for target and novel stimuli. (Reprinted with permission of Cambridge University Press.)

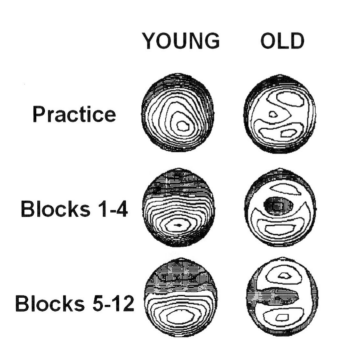

| YOUNG | OLD |
|-------|-----|

Practice

Blocks 1-4

Blocks 5-12

FIGURE 30.6   Data from Fabiani and Friedman (1995) showing surface potential (SP) maps at the peak of P3 for target stimuli over time. (Reprinted with permission of Cambridge University Press.)

susceptible to distractors and conflicting task demands is to examine age-related differences in tasks that pose conflicting demands on the information processing system. In a conflict task, two stimulus dimensions lead to two separate responses, only one of which is correct. A classic example of a conflict paradigm is the Stroop task (Stroop, 1935), in which subjects are asked to name the ink color of color name words. When the ink color and the color name are in conflict (such as when the word "yellow" is written in red ink), subjects are slower and make more errors because of the interference caused by the processing of the irrelevant dimension (i.e., the word meaning).

Recent modeling efforts and corresponding fMRI data in young adults suggest that the dorsolateral prefrontal cortex and the cingulate cortex may be involved in these tasks, and that they may be connected in a feedback system (Carter et al., 1998; Cohen and Servan-Schreiber, 1992). ERP data collected in the Stroop paradigm in young adults suggest that the interference effects are related to response selection (Duncan-Johnson and Kopell, 1981). In fact, P300 latency does not appear to be affected by conflict. This suggests that the interference may be due, at least in part, to response conflict. This idea is supported by recent data obtained with fast optical imaging (the event-related optical signal, or EROS) indicating that, during conflict trials that are responded to correctly, both motor cortices are activated simultaneously (DeSoto et al., in press), whereas only the contralateral motor cortex is activated in trials with no conflict.

Spieler, Balota, and Faust (1996) found, using ex-Gaussian analyses, that healthy older adults exhibited a disproportionate increase in Stroop interference with respect to young adults. This is consistent with the hypothesis that additional processing time may be required to resolve conflict and produce the correct response. Similarly, Duchek and colleagues (1995) found that the elderly showed deficits in the control of interfering information. This suggests that irrelevant information may be processed to a greater extent by older adults, as compared to younger subjects, leading to greater response competition.

ERP data obtained in the Stroop task by Lavoie, Bherer, and Belleville (1999) showed that, whereas young adults had an enhanced P300 in response to conflict trials, older adults did not (see also West and Alain, 2000). Similarly, Jonides and colleagues (2000) reported that, in a task requiring inhibition of prepotent responses, older adults were slower and less accurate than young adults, and, unlike young adults, did not show increased frontal activation. These data suggest that older adults may lack the resources necessary to implement inhibitory processes.

*Memory for contextual details*

In recent years much attention has been paid to age-related changes in the memory for contextual details (source of the information, relative time of occurrence, etc.). Behavioral studies comparing young and older adults suggest that older adults, although able to indicate whether or not they have been presented with the information (recognition judgments—*item memory*[1]) have increased difficulty when asked specific questions about details of their episodic memory (*source memory*; Kausler, Lichty, and Davis, 1985; Kausler, Salthouse, and Saults, 1988; Schacter et al., 1993). These results are also corroborated by findings suggesting that recognition performance (which does not show substantial age-related decrements) may be supported by different processes in young and older adults (Tulving, 1985). In fact, when asked to judge whether a correctly recognized word is "remembered" (i.e., details about the episodes are retrieved) or just "known" (i.e., accompanied by familiarity without detail), older adults tend to give more "know" responses, whereas young adults give more "remember" responses (Parkin and Walter, 1992; for a similar dissociation, see Jennings and Jacoby, 1997). These results bear similarities with data obtained in patients with frontal lobe lesions (Milner, 1995), suggesting a possible frontal contribution to these tasks.

This position is further corroborated by recent imaging data obtained with PET (Cabeza et al., 2000).

Fabiani and Friedman (1997) compared the performance of young and older adults in a continuous task that involved both recognition and recency judgments. In this task, study trials and trials testing recency and recognition memory were intermixed. The subjects' task was to indicate which of two items (either pictures or words) was presented most recently. In recognition trials only one of the pictures had been studied earlier, making that the most recent by default. In recency test trials, both pictures had been previously presented, so the subjects had to remember the relative temporal occurrence of the two in order to produce a correct response. This continuous paradigm has some characteristics that make it advantageous for studying changes in recency memory in normal aging. First, the subjects need not know whether they are performing a recency or recognition task, and therefore task differences per se are minimized. Second, by mixing study and test trials and by building an appropriate sequence, the effects of lag can be studied. Third, like all continuous paradigms, this task imposes an additional load on working memory, thereby allowing one to study encoding and retrieval of contextual attributes in a situation of increased workload, in which age-related effects should be maximized.

Using this paradigm, Fabiani and Friedman (1997) found that older subjects did not differ from young adults on the recognition trials, whereas they performed more poorly than the young subjects on the recency trials (in fact, they performed at chance level on these trials). In addition, for the old subjects (age range 65–88) the performance on the recency task, but not that on the recognition task, was correlated with performance on the Wisconsin Card Sorting Test and other tests of frontal function.

In a follow-up study in which ERPs were recorded, Fabiani and colleagues (1999) found that there were clear individual differences among the elderly in the performance of this task. Older adults with higher levels of education and professional jobs were not impaired in their recency judgments, whereas older adults with lower levels of education and socioeconomic status performed at chance levels on the recency task. In addition, highly educated older adults showed enhanced negative slow wave activity at frontal electrodes in the performance of the recency task, which was not displayed by the older adults with lower educational levels or by the young adults. This suggests the existence of compensatory activity in those older adults who achieved high performance in the recency task. Whether similar effects could be found in young adults remains unclear. This leaves open the issue of whether these phenomena may be due only to education, or to the protective role that high levels of education might have on the effects of cognitive aging.

Trott and colleagues (1997, 1999) compared young and older adults in a task in which subjects were asked to indicate in which of two lists a given noun had occurred. Compared with young adults, older adults had greater source memory (study list) performance decrements. In addition, only the young produced a frontal-maximal, late-onset old/new effect that differed as a function of subsequent source attribution (see also Senkfor and Van Petten, 1996, 1998).

The studies just described indicate that older adults have more difficulty than young adults in acquiring and/or maintaining at least some of the contextual details of the memory episode. One extreme form of source memory error is the phenomenon of false memory, which involves recalling or recognizing an event that did not actually occur. This phenomenon has received much attention in recent years owing to the use of a clever experimental paradigm that makes it possible to produce it easily in a laboratory setting (the Deese-Roediger-McDermott, or DRM paradigm; Deese, 1959; Roediger and McDermott, 1995). In this paradigm, subjects are presented with lists of words that all relate to a nonstudied "lure" (e.g., the words *slumber*, *night*, *bed*, and *snore* are all related to *sleep*, which is not presented at study). In this paradigm, even young subjects produce a large number of false alarms to the nonstudied lures when they are included at test as distractor items (the false memory effect, Roediger and McDermott, 1995). In older adults the false memory effect is increased, owing to the increased number of false alarms and the lower overall memory for studied items (true memory—Balota et al., 1999; Schacter, 1997; Schacter, Israel, and Racine, 1999). Behaviorally, it has proved difficult to distinguish between true and false memory. In fact, attempts at finding blood flow or ERP differences between these two types of items have also proved elusive (Johnson et al., 1997; Schacter et al., 1996, 1997), although recent ERP data in young adults suggest that some evidence of sensory signatures for veridical but not false memory may be found (Fabiani, Stadler, and Wessels, 2000).

## Summary and future directions

This chapter presented a brief and selective overview of research suggesting that age-related changes in frontal lobe function may underlie changes in working memory capacity that are commonly observed in normally aging adults. This view may account for a number of the memory findings in the aging literature.

Several unresolved theoretical issues are also likely to inform the research framework presented in this chapter, together with further developments of imaging methods. For example, there is evidence that many of the effects of cognitive aging can be accounted for by generalized slowing of function (Salthouse, 1996). It has also been known for a number of years that the alpha rhythm of the EEG slows down with age, probably because of diminished arousal to the cortex from the reticular formation (for a review, see Woodruff-Pak, 1997). It will be important to determine how a generalized slowing may interact with working memory functions. For instance, it is conceivable that a slower processor may require the maintenance of information for a longer period of time, or having more information available at any one time. Both conditions may result in an increased working memory load. If that happens, apparent working memory deficits may actually reflect slower processing abilities.

From the review presented in this chapter, it should be evident that a number of tasks are expected to have a substantial contribution from the frontal lobes. However, as the concept of working memory may not be unitary, the role of frontal lobes and in particular of dorsolateral prefrontal cortex may be more differentiated than currently hypothesized (Petrides et al., 1993; West, 1996).

In addition, some of the effects attributed to the frontal lobes may result from slowed down or deficient transfer of information among brain areas, as suggested by the review of the auditory sensory memory literature presented here. Methods such as diffusion tensor imaging, which allows one to examine the intactness of white matter fiber tracts, may be particularly useful in assessing age-related changes in the transfer of information between brain regions (Shimony et al., 1999). Similarly, fast optical imaging (EROS, Gratton and Fabiani, 1998) may provide a useful bridge for the integration of imaging methods based on hemodynamics and methods based on electrophysiology. Finally, the integration of existing methods is likely to afford a view of brain function over the lifespan that is not possible with any single method in isolation (Fabiani, Gratton, and Coles, 2000; Gratton and Fabiani, 1998; Kutas and Federmeier, 1998; Liu, Belliveau, and Dale, 1998).

ACKNOWLEDGMENTS We would like to acknowledge the support of a grant from the Alzheimer's Disease and Related Disorders Program (ADRD) to Monica Fabiani. We also thank David Friedman and Gabriele Gratton for reviewing an earlier version of this manuscript.

## NOTE

1. The lack of performance decrements in recognition tasks in older adults can often be attributed to a shift from recollection-based to familiarity-based processes (Jennings and Jacoby, 1997; Parkin and Walter, 1992).

## REFERENCES

ALHO, K., M. HUOTILAINEN, and R. NÄÄTÄNEN, 1995. Are memory traces for simple and complex sounds located in different regions of auditory cortex? Recent MEG studies. *Electroencephalogr. Clin. Neurophysiol.* 44(suppl.):197–203.

ALHO, K., D. L. WOODS, A. ALGAZI, R. T. KNIGHT, and R. NÄÄTÄNEN, 1994. Lesions of frontal cortex diminish the auditory mismatch negativity. *Electroencephalogr. Clin. Neurophysiol.* 91(5):353–362.

ANDERS, T. R., J. L. FOZARD, and T. D. LILLYQUIST, 1972. Effects of age upon retrieval from short-term memory. *Dev. Psychol.* 6(2):214–217.

BADDELEY, A. D., 1986. *Working Memory.* Oxford, UK: Oxford University Press.

BALOTA, D. A., M. J. CORTESE, J. M. DUCHEK, D. ADAMS, H. L. ROEDIGER III, K. B. MCDERMOTT, and B. E. YERYS, 1999. Veridical and false memories in healthy older adults and in dementia of the Alzheimer's type. *Cogn. Neuropsychol.* 16:361–384.

BASHORE, T. R., 1990. Age, physical fitness, and mental processing speed. In *Annual Review of Gerontology and Geriatrics,* Vol. 9, M. P. Lawton, ed. New York: Springer, pp. 120–144.

BASHORE, T. R., and P. H. GODDARD, 1993. Preservative and restorative effects of aerobic fitness on the age-related slowing of mental processing speed. In Cerella, J., J. Rhybash, and W. Hoyer, eds. *Adult Information Processing: Limits on Loss,* New York: Academic Press, pp. 205–228.

BASHORE, T. R., A. OSMAN, and E. F. HEFFLEY, 1989. Mental slowing in elderly persons: A cognitive psychophysiological analysis. *Psychol. Aging* 4(2):235–244.

BRAVER, T. S., J. D. COHEN, L. E. NYSTROM, J. JONIDES, E. E. SMITH, and D. C. NOLL, 1997. A parametric study of prefrontal cortex involvement in human working memory. *Neuroimage* 5(1):49–62.

BROADBENT, D. E., 1957. A mathematical model for human attention and immediate memory. *Psychol. Rev.* 64:205–215.

CABEZA, R., N. D. ANDERSON, S. HOULE, J. MANGELS, and L. NYBERG, 2000. Age-related differences in neural activity during item and temporal-order memory retrieval: A positron emission tomography study. *J. Cogn. Neurosci.* 12(1):197–206.

CARTER, C. S., T. S. BRAVER, D. M. BARCH, M. M. BOTVINICK, D. NOLL, and J. D. COHEN, 1998. Anterior cingulate cortex, error detection, and the online monitoring of performance. *Science* 280(5364):747–749.

CHAO, L. L., and R. T. KNIGHT, 1997a. Age-related prefrontal alterations during auditory memory. *Neurobiol. Aging* 18(1):87–95.

CHAO, L. L., and R. T. KNIGHT, 1997b. Prefrontal deficits in attention and inhibitory control with aging. *Cereb. Cortex* 7(1):63–69.

COHEN, J. D., T. S. BRAVER, and R. C. O'REILLY, 1996. A computational approach to prefrontal cortex, cognitive control and schizophrenia: Recent developments and current challenges. *Phil. Trans. R. Soc. Lond. [B]* 351(1346):1515–1527.

COHEN, J. D., and D. SERVAN-SCHREIBER, 1992. Context, cortex and dopamine: A connectionist approach to behavior and biology in schizophrenia. *Psychol. Rev.* 99:45–77.

COURCHESNE, E., S. A. HILLYARD, and R. GALAMBOS, 1975. Stimulus novelty, task relevance and the visual evoked potential in man. *Electroencephalogr. Clin. Neurophysiol.* 39:131–143.

COWAN, N., 1995. *Attention and Memory: An Integrated Framework.* New York: Oxford University Press.

CZIGLER, I., G. CSIBRA, and A. CSONTOS, 1992. Age and interstimulus interval effects on event-related potentials to frequent and infrequent auditory stimuli. *Biol. Psychol.* 33(2–3):195–206.

DEESE, J., 1959. On the prediction of occurrence of particular verbal intrusions in immediate recall. *J. Exp. Psychol.* 58:17–22.

DESOTO, M. C., M. FABIANI, D. C. GEARY, and G. GRATTON, in press. When in doubt, do it both ways: Brain evidence of the simultaneous activation of conflicting responses in a spatial Stroop task. *J. Cogn. Neurosci.*

D'ESPOSITO, M., E. ZARAHN, G. K. AGUIRRE, and B. RYPMA, 1999. The effect of normal aging on the coupling of neural activity to the bold hemodynamic response. *Neuroimage* 10(1):6–14.

DONCHIN, E., 1981. Surprise! . . . Surprise? *Psychophysiology* 18:493–513.

DUCHEK, J. M., D. A. BALOTA, M. E. FAUST, and F. R. FERRARO, 1995. Inhibitory processes in young and older adults in a picture-word task. *Aging Cognit.* 2(2):156–167.

DUNCAN-JOHNSON, C. C., and B. S. KOPELL, 1981. The Stroop effect: Brain potentials localize the source of interference. *Science* 214:938–940.

ESLINGER, P. J., and L. M. GRATTAN, 1993. Frontal lobe and frontal-striatal substrates for different forms of human cognitive flexibility. *Neuropsychologia* 31(1):17–28.

FABIANI, M., and D. FRIEDMAN, 1995. Changes in brain activity patterns in aging: The novelty oddball. *Psychophysiology* 32(6):579–594.

FABIANI, M., and D. FRIEDMAN, 1997. Dissociations between memory for temporal order and recognition memory in aging. *Neuropsychologia* 35(2):129–141.

FABIANI, M., D. FRIEDMAN, and J. C. CHENG, 1998. Individual differences in P3 scalp distribution in old subjects, and their relationship to frontal lobe function. *Psychophysiology* 35:698–708.

FABIANI, M., D. FRIEDMAN, J. C. CHENG, E. WEE, and C. TROTT, 1999. Use it or lose it: Effects of aging and education on brain activity in the performance of recency and recognition memory tasks. *J. Cogn. Neurosci. Suppl.* 83B:18.

FABIANI, M., G. GRATTON, and M. G. H. COLES, 2000. Event related brain potentials: Methods, theory and applications. In *Tutorials in Psychophysiology: Physical, Social and Inferential Elements,* 2nd ed., J. T. Cacioppo, L. G. Tassinary, and G. Bernston, eds. New York: Cambridge University Press, pp. 53–84.

FABIANI, M., V. A. KAZMERSKI, Y. M. CYCOWICZ, and D. FRIEDMAN, 1996. Naming norms for brief environmental sounds: Effects of age and dementia. *Psychophysiology* 33(4):462–475.

FABIANI, M., M. A. STADLER, and P. WESSELS, 2000. True memories but not false ones produce a sensory signature in human lateralized brain potentials. *J. Cogn. Neurosci.* 12(6):1–10.

FERNANDEZ, G., A. EFFERN, T. GRUNWALD, N. PEZER, K. LEHNERTZ, M. DUMPELMANN, D. VAN ROOST, and C. E. ELGER,

1999. Real-time tracking of memory formation in the human rhinal cortex and hippocampus. *Science* 285:1582–1585.

FISK, A. D., and W. A. ROGERS, 1991. Toward an understanding of age-related memory and visual search effects. *J. Exp. Psychol. Gen.* 120(2):131–149.

FORD, J. M., and A. PFEFFERBAUM, 1991. Event-related potentials and eyeblink responses in automatic and controlled processing: Effects of age. *Electroencephalogr. Clin. Neurophysiol.* 78:361–377.

FORD, J. M., A. PFEFFERBAUM, J. R. TINKLENBERG, and B. S. KOPELL, 1982. Effects of perceptual and cognitive difficulty on P3 and RT in young and old adults. *Electroencephalogr. Clin. Neurophysiol.* 54(3):311–321.

FORD, J. M., W. T. ROTH, R. C. MOHS, W. F. HOPKINS, and B. S. KOPELL, 1979. Event-related potentials recorded from young and old adults during a memory retrieval task. *Electroencephalogr. Clin. Neurophysiol.* 47(4):450–459.

FRIEDMAN, D., V. KAZMERSKI, and M. FABIANI, 1997. An overview of age-related changes in the scalp distribution of P3b. *Electroencephalogr. Clin. Neurophysiol.* 104(6):498–513.

FRIEDMAN, D., M. FABIANI, and G. SIMPSON, 1999. *J. Cogn. Neurosci.* 31A (suppl):21.

FRIEDMAN, D., G. SIMPSON, and M. HAMBERGER, 1993. Age-related changes in scalp topography to novel and target stimuli. *Psychophysiology* 30:383–396.

FUSTER, J. M., 1973. Unit activity in prefrontal cortex during delayed response performance: Neuronal correlates of transient memory. *J. Neurophysiol.* 36:61–78.

GABRIELI, J., 1999. FMRI evidence for age-associated alterations in prefrontal contributions to the encoding and retrieval of new memories. *J. Cogn. Neurosci. Suppl.* 10.

GAETA, H., D. FRIEDMAN, W. RITTER, and J. CHENG, 1998. An event-related potential study of age-related changes in sensitivity to stimulus deviance. *Neurobiol. Aging* 19(5):447–459.

GOLDMAN-RAKIC, P. S., 1987. Circuitry of primate prefrontal cortex and regulation of behavior by representational memory. In *Handbook of Physiology—The Nervous System,* Vol. 5, V. B. Mountcastle, F. Plum, and S. R. Geiger, eds. Bethesda, Md.: American Physiological Association, pp. 373–417.

GOLDMAN-RAKIC, P. S., 1992. Working memory and the mind. *Scientific American* 267(3):110–117.

GRATTON, G., and M. FABIANI, 1998. Dynamic brain imaging: Event-related optical signal (EROS) measures of the time course and localization of cognitive-related activity. *Psychonom. Bull. Rev.* 5:535–563.

GUR, R. C., R. E. GUR, W. D. OBRIST, B. E. SKOLNICK, and M. REIVICH, 1987. Age and regional cerebral blood flow at rest and during cognitive activity. *Arch. Gen. Psychiatry* 44(7):617–621.

HAUG, H., and R. EGGERS, 1991. Morphometry of the human cortex cerebri and corpus striatum during aging [comment]. *Neurobiol. Aging* 12(4):336–338; discussion 352–355.

HEATON, R. K., 1981. *Wisconsin Cards Sorting Test Manual.* Odessa, Fla.: Psychological Assessment Resources.

HESS, T. M., and S. M. PULLEN, 1996. Memory in context. In *Perspectives on Cognitive Change in Adulthood and Aging,* F. Blanchard-Fields and T. H. Hess, eds. New York: McGraw-Hill.

JAVITT, D. C., M. STEINSCHNEIDER, C. E. SCHROEDER, H. G. VAUGHAN, JR., and J. C. AREZZO, 1994. Detection of stimulus deviance within primate primary auditory cortex: Intra-

cortical mechanisms of mismatch negativity (MMN) generation. *Brain Res.* 667(2):192–200.

JENNINGS, J. M., and L. L. JACOBY, 1997. An opposition procedure for detecting age-related deficits in recollection: Telling effects of repetition. *Psychol. Aging* 12(2):352–361.

JOHNSON, M. K., S. F. NOLDE, M. MATHER, J. KOUNIOS, D. L. SCHACTER, and T. CURRAN, 1997. The similarity of brain activity associated with true and false recognition memory depends on test format. *Psychol. Sci.* 8(3):250–257.

JOHNSON, R., JR., and E. DONCHIN, 1978. On how P300 amplitude varies with the utility of the eliciting stimulus. *Electroencephalogr. Clin. Neurophysiol.* 44(4):424–437.

JONIDES, J., C. MARSHUETZ, E. E. SMITH, P. A. REUTER-LORENZ, and R. A. KOEPPER, 2000. Age differences in behavior and PET activation reveal differences in interference resolution in verbal working memory. *J. Cogn. Neurosci.* 12(1):188–196.

JONIDES, J., E. H. SCHUMACHER, E. E. SMITH, E. J. LAUBER, J. AWH, S. MINOSHIMA, and R. A. KOEPPE, 1997. Verbal working memory load affects regional brain activation as measured by PET. *J. Cogn. Neurosci.* 9(4):462–475.

JONIDES, J., E. E. SMITH, R. A. KOEPPE, E. AWH, S. MINOSHIMA, and M. A. MINTUN, 1993. Spatial working memory in humans as revealed by PET [see comments]. *Nature* 363(6430):623–625.

KAUSLER, D. H., 1991. *Experimental Psychology, Cognition and Human Aging,* 2nd ed. New York: Springer-Verlag.

KAUSLER, D. H., W. LICHTY, and R. T. DAVIS, 1985. Temporal memory for performed activities: Intentionality and adult age differences. *Dev. Psychol.* 21(6):1132–1138.

KAUSLER, D. H., T. A. SALTHOUSE, and J. S. SAULTS, 1988. Temporal memory over the adult lifespan. *Am. J. Psychol.* 101(2):207–215.

KAZMERSKI, V. A., D. FRIEDMAN, and W. RITTER, 1997. Mismatch negativity during attend and ignore conditions in Alzheimer's disease. *Biol. Psychiatry* 42(5):382–402.

KNIGHT, R. T., 1984. Decreased response to novel stimuli after prefrontal lesions in man. *Electroencephalogr. Clin. Neurophysiol.* 59:9–20.

KNIGHT, R. T., 1987. Aging decreases auditory event-related potentials to unexpected stimuli in humans. *Neurobiol. Aging* 8(2):109–113.

KNIGHT, R. T., 1997. Distributed cortical network for visual attention. *J. Cogn. Neurosci.* 9(1):75–91.

KNIGHT, R. T., M. F. GRABOWECKY, and D. SCABINI, 1995. Role of human prefrontal cortex in attention control. *Adv. Neurol.* 66:21–34; discussion 34–36.

KNIGHT, R. T., and T. NAKADA, 1998. Cortico-limbic circuits and novelty: A review of EEG and blood flow data. *Rev. Neurosci.* 9(1):57–70.

KNIGHT, R. T., D. SCABINI, and D. L. WOODS, 1989. Prefrontal cortex gating of auditory transmission in humans. *Brain Res.* 504:338–342.

KRAMER, A. F., S. HAHN, N. J. COHEN, M. T. BANICH, E. MCAULEY, C. R. HARRISON, J. CHASON, E. VAKIL, L. BARDELL, R. A. BOILEAU, and A. COLCOMBE, 1999. Ageing, fitness and neurocognitive function [letter]. *Nature* 400(6743):418–419.

KRAMER, A. F., S. HAHN, and D. GOPHER, 1999. Task coordination and aging: Explorations of executive control processes in the task switching paradigm. *Acta Psychol.,* 101(2–3):339–378.

KUTAS, M., and K. D. FEDERMEIER, 1998. Minding the body. *Psychophysiology* 35(2):135–150.

LAVOIE, M. E., L. BHERER, and S. BELLEVILLE, 1999. Effect of aging on event-related potentials topography during a Stroop task. *Psychophysiology* 36:S72.

LIGHT, L. L., 1996. Memory and aging. In *Memory. Handbook of Perception and Cognition*, Vol. xxii, 2nd ed., E. L. Bjork, ed. San Diego: Academic Press, pp. 443–490.

LIU, A. K., J. W. BELLIVEAU, and A. M. DALE, 1998. Spatiotemporal imaging of human brain activity using functional MRI constrained magnetoencephalography data: Monte Carlo simulations. *Proc. Natl. Acad. Sci. USA* 95(15):8945–8950.

MCCARTHY, G., A. M. BLAMIRE, A. PUCE, A. C. NOBRE, G. BLOCH, F. HYDER, P. GOLDMAN-RAKIC, and R. G. SHULMAN, 1994. Functional magnetic resonance imaging of human prefrontal cortex activation during a spatial working memory task. *Proc. Natl. Acad. Sci. USA* 91(18):8690–8694.

MCCARTHY, G., and E. DONCHIN, 1981. A metric for thought: A comparison of P300 latency and reaction time. *Science* 211(4477):77–80.

MECKLINGER, A., 1998. On the modularity of recognition memory for object form and spatial location: A topographic ERP analysis. *Neuropsychologia* 36(5):441–460.

MILNER, B., 1963. Effects of different brain lesions on card sorting. *Arch. Neurol.* 9:90–100.

MILNER, B., 1995. Aspects of human frontal lobe function. In *Epilepsy and the Functional Anatomy of the Frontal Lobe*, Vol. 66, H. H. Jasper, ed. New York: Raven Press, pp. 67–84.

MILNER, B., and M. PETRIDES, 1984. Behavioural effects of frontal-lobe lesions in man. *Trends Neurosci.* 7:403–407.

MOSCOVITCH, M., and G. WINOCUR, 1992. The neuropsychology of memory and aging. In *The Handbook of Aging and Cognition*, F. I. M. Craik and T. A. Salthouse, eds. Hillsdale, N.J.: Erlbaum, pp. 315–372.

MOUNTAIN, M. A., and W. G. SNOW, 1993. Wisconsin Card Sorting Test as a measure of frontal pathology: A review. *Clin. Neuropsychol.* 7(1):108–118.

NÄÄTÄNEN, R., 1992. *Attention and Brain Function.* Hillsdale, N.J.: Erlbaum.

NÄÄTÄNEN, R., and K. ALHO, 1995. Mismatch negativity—A unique measure of sensory processing in audition. *Intl. J. Neurosci.* 80(1–4):317–337.

PARKIN, A. J., and R. I. JAVA, 1999. Deterioration of frontal lobe function in normal aging: Influences of fluid intelligence versus perceptual speed. *Neuropsychology* 13(4):539–545.

PARKIN, A. J., and B. M. WALTER, 1991. Aging, short-term memory, and frontal dysfunction. *Psychobiology* 19(2):175–179.

PARKIN, A. J., and B. M. WALTER, 1992. Recollective experience, normal aging, and frontal dysfunction. *Psychol. Aging* 7(2):290–298.

PARR, W. V., and R. SIEGERT, 1993. Adults' conceptions of everyday memory failures in others: Factors that mediate the effects of target age. *Psychol. Aging* 8(4):599–605.

PEKKONEN, E., T. RINNE, K. REINIKAINEN, T. KUJALA, K. ALHO, and R. NÄÄTÄNEN, 1996. Aging effects on auditory processing: An event-related potential study. *Exp. Aging Res.* 22(2):171–184.

PETRIDES, M., B. ALIVISATOS, A. C. EVANS, and E. MEYER, 1993. Dissociation of human mid-dorsolateral from posterior dorsolateral frontal cortex in memory processing. *Proc. Natl. Acad. Sci. USA* 90(3):873–877.

POLICH, J., 1991. P300 in the evaluation of aging and dementia. In *Event-Related Brain Research (EEG Suppl. 42)*, C. H. M. Brunia, G. Mulder, and M. N. Verbaten, eds. Amsterdam: Elsevier, pp. 304–323.

POLICH, J., 1996. Meta-analysis of P300 normative aging studies. *Psychophysiology* 33(4):334–353.

POLICH, J., L. HOWARD, and A. STARR, 1985. Effects of age on the P300 component of the event-related brain potential from auditory stimuli: Peak definition, variation, and measurement. *J. Gerontol.* 40(6):721–726.

RABBITT, P., 1965. Age-decrement in the ability to ignore irrelevant information. *J. Gerontol.* 20:233–238.

REUTER-LORENZ, P. A., 1999. Cognitive neuropsychology of the aging brain. In *Cognitive Aging: A Primer*, D. C. Park and N. Schwarz, eds. Philadelphia: Psychology Press, pp. 93–114.

REUTER-LORENZ, P. A., J. JONIDES, E. E. SMITH, A. HARTLEY, A. MILLER, C. MARSHUETZ, and R. A. KOEPPE, 2000. Age differences in the frontal lateralization of verbal and spatial working memory revealed by PET. *J. Cogn. Neurosci.* 12(1):174–187.

RINNE, T., G. GRATTON, M. FABIANI, N. COWAN, E. MACLIN, A. STINARD, J. SINKKONEN, K. ALHO, and R. NÄÄTÄNEN, 1999. Scalp-recorded optical signals make sound processing from the auditory cortex visible. *Neuroimage* 10:620–624.

RITTER, W., D. DEACON, H. GOMES, D. C. JAVITT, and H. G. VAUGHAN, JR., 1995. The mismatch negativity of event-related potentials as a probe of transient auditory memory: A review. *Ear Hearing* 16(1):52–67.

ROEDIGER, H. L., and K. B. McDERMOTT, 1995. Creating false memories: Remembering words not presented in lists. *J. Exp. Psych.: Learning, Mem. & Cogn.* 21(4):803–814.

RUCHKIN, D. S., H. L. CANOUNE, R. JOHNSON, JR., and W. RITTER, 1995. Working memory and preparation elicit different patterns of slow wave event-related brain potentials. *Psychophysiology* 32(4):399–410.

SALTHOUSE, T. A., 1996. The processing-speed theory of adult age differences in cognition. *Psychol. Rev.*, 103(3):403–428.

SCHACTER, D. L., R. L. BUCKNER, W. KOUTSTAAL, A. M. DALE, and B. R. ROSEN, 1997. Late onset of anterior prefrontal activity during true and false recognition: An event-related fMRI study. *Neuroimage* 6(4):259–269.

SCHACTER, D. L., L. ISRAEL, and C. RACINE, 1999. Suppressing false recognition in younger and older adults: The distinctiveness heuristic. *J. Mem. Lang.* 40(1):1–24.

SCHACTER, D. L., J. F. KIHLSTROM, A. W. KASZNIAK, and M. VALDISERRI, 1993. Preserved and impaired memory functions in elderly adults. In *Adult Information Processing: Limits on Loss*, J. Cerella, ed. San Diego: Academic Press, pp. 327–350.

SCHACTER, D. L., W. KOUTSTAAL, M. K. JOHNSON, M. S. GROSS, and K. E. ANGELL, 1997. False recollection induced by photographs: A comparison of older and younger adults. *Psychol. Aging* 12(2):203–215.

SCHACTER, D. L., E. REIMAN, T. CURRAN, L. S. YUN, D. BANDY, K. B. McDERMOTT, and H. L. ROEDIGER III, 1996. Neuroanatomical correlates of veridical and illusory recognition memory: Evidence from positron emission. *Neuron* 17(2):267–274.

SENKFOR, A. J., and C. VAN PETTEN, 1996. ERP measures of source and item memory in young and elderly subjects. *Psychophysiology* S71.

SENKFOR, A. J., and C. VAN PETTEN, 1998. Who said what? An event-related potential investigation of source and item memory. *J. Exp. Psychol. Learn. Mem. Cogn.* 24(4):1005–1025.

SHIMAMURA, A. P., 1995. Memory and frontal lobe function. In *The Cognitive Neurosciences*, M. S. Gazzaniga, ed. Cambridge, Mass.: MIT Press, pp. 803–813.

SHIMONY, J. S., R. C. MCKINSTRY, E. AKBUDAK, J. A. ARONOVITZ, A. Z. SNYDER, N. F. LORI, T. S. CULL, and T. E. CONTURO, 1999. Quantitative diffusion-tensor anisotropy brain MR imaging: Normative human data and anatomic analysis. *Radiology* 212(3):770–784.

SMITH, E. E., J. JONIDES, and R. A. KOEPPE, 1996. Dissociating verbal and spatial working memory using PET. *Cereb. Cortex* 6(1):11–20.

SMITH, E. E., J. JONIDES, and R. A. KOEPPE, 1998. Dissociating verbal and spatial working memory using PET. Corrigendum. *Cereb. Cortex* 8(8):762.

SMITH, E. E., J. JONIDES, R. A. KOEPPE, E. AWH, E. H. SCHUMACHER, and S. MINOSHIMA, 1995. Spatial versus object working memory: PET investigations. *J. Cogn. Neurosci.* 7(3):337–356.

SNOWDON, D. A., L. H. GREINER, J. A. MORTIMER, K. P. RILEY, P. A. GREINER, and W. R. MARKESBERY, 1997. Brain infarction and the clinical expression of Alzheimer disease. The Nun Study [see comments]. *JAMA* 277(10):813–817.

SNOWDON, D. A., S. J. KEMPER, J. A. MORTIMER, L. H. GREINER, D. R. WEKSTEIN, and W. R. MARKESBERY, 1996. Linguistic ability in early life and cognitive function and Alzheimer's disease in late life. Findings from the Nun Study [see comments]. *JAMA* 275(7):528–532.

SPIELER, D. H., D. A. BALOTA, and M. E. FAUST, 1996. Stroop performance in healthy younger and older adults and in individuals with dementia of the Alzheimer's type. *J. Exp. Psychol. Hum. Percept. Perform.* 22(2):461–479.

STERNBERG, S., 1966. High-speed scanning in human memory. *Science* 153(3736):652–654.

STRAYER, D. L., and A. F. KRAMER, 1994. Aging and skill acquisition: Learning-performance distinctions. *Psychol. Aging* 9(4):589–605.

STRAYER, D. L., C. D. WICKENS, and R. BRAUNE, 1987. Adult age differences in the speed and capacity of information processing: II. An electrophysiological approach. *Psychol. Aging* 2(2):99–110.

STROOP, J. R., 1935. Studies of interference in serial verbal reactions. *J. Exp. Psychol.* 18:643–662.

STUSS, D. T., F. I. CRAIK, L. SAYER, D. FRANCHI, and M. P. ALEXANDER, 1996. Comparison of older people and patients with frontal lesions: Evidence from word list learning. *Psychol. Aging* 11(3):387–395.

STUSS, D. T., G. A. ESKES, and J. K. FOSTER, 1994. Experimental neuropsychological studies of frontal lobe function. In *Handbook of Neuropsychology*, Vol. 9, F. Boller and J. Grafman, eds. Amsterdam: Elsevier, pp. 149–185.

SUTTON, S., M. BRAREN, J. ZUBIN, and E. R. JOHN, 1965. Evoked-potential correlates of stimulus uncertainty. *Science* 150:1187–1188.

TOGA, A. W., and J. C. MAZZIOTTA (EDS.), 1996. *Brain Mapping. The Methods.* San Diego: Academic Press.

TROTT, C. T., D. FRIEDMAN, W. RITTER, and M. FABIANI, 1997. Item and source memory: Differential age effects revealed by event-related potentials. *NeuroReport* 8(15):3373–3378.

TROTT, C. T., D. FRIEDMAN, W. RITTER, M. FABIANI, and J. G. SNODGRASS, 1999. Episodic priming and memory for temporal source: Event-related potentials reveal age-related differences in prefrontal functioning. *Psychol. Aging* 14(3):390–413.

TULVING, E., 1985. Memory and consciousness. *Can. J. Psychol.* 26:1–12.

WEE, E., and M. FABIANI, 1999a. Differential effects of aging on encoding and processing of object/spatial stimuli in a modified two-back task. *Psychophysiology* 36:S123.

WEE, E., and M. FABIANI, 1999b. Aging effects on behavior and event-related brain potentials in a modified two-back task. *J. Cogn. Neurosci.* 82(suppl.):21.

WEST, R., and C. ALAIN, 2000. Age-related decline in inhibitory control contributes to the increased Stroop effect observed in older adults. *Psychophysiology* 37:179–189.

WEST, R. L., 1996. An application of prefrontal cortex function theory to cognitive aging. *Psychol. Bull.* 120(2):272–292.

WOODRUFF-PAK, D. S., 1997. *The Neuropsychology of Aging*, Vol. 352. Cambridge, Mass.: Blackwell Publishers.

WOODS, D. L., 1992. Auditory selective attention in middle-aged and elderly subjects: An event-related brain potential study. *Electroencephalogr. Clin. Neurophysiol.* 84(5):456–468.

YAMAGUCHI, S., and R. T. KNIGHT, 1991a. P300 generation by novel somatosensory stimuli. *Electroencephalogr. Clin. Neurophysiol.* 78(1):50–55.

YAMAGUCHI, S., and R. T. KNIGHT, 1991b. Age effects on the P300 to novel somatosensory stimuli. *Electroencephalogr. Clin. Neurophysiol.* 78(4):297–301.

# VII

# NEURO-
# DEVELOPMENTAL
# ASPECTS OF
# CLINICAL
# DISORDERS

# 31 The Role of Nutrition in Cognitive Development

MICHAEL K. GEORGIEFF
AND RAGHAVENDRA RAO

ABSTRACT  Nutrients are critical for optimal brain development and function. Although maintenance of adequate intake of all nutrients throughout life is important for brain health and function, certain nutrients have a more profound effect on brain development than others. The timing of nutrient supplementation or deprivation also has an important effect on brain development and function. Nutrient intakes may vary widely; yet, for certain nutrients, there must be a steady flow across the blood–brain barrier to maintain brain development and functional homeostasis. Storage and subsequent mobilization of nutrients from body pools ensure that the brain receives neither too much nor too little of each nutrient.

This chapter reviews the evidence for the role of nutrition in brain development, concentrating especially on nutrients that are important in the development of cognitive function. A short review of nutrient categories is followed by a section on how individual nutrients directly and indirectly affect developing brain structure and function. A detailed analysis of the nutrients that most profoundly affect brain development ensues, with emphasis on the importance of the timing of nutrient deprivation or supplementation.

## Nutrient categories and growth factors

MACRONUTRIENTS  Protein and energy are considered the two macronutrients. Protein is typically used by the body for somatic (tissue) protein and serum protein synthesis. Proteins also include all enzymes found within organs. Energy in the form of fat or carbohydrates is the metabolic fuel on which the body depends. The body preferentially uses carbohydrates (typically glucose) as the substrate for cellular metabolism to generate adenosine triphosphate (ATP). Neuronal metabolism is particularly dependent on glucose availability and is very sensitive to periods of carbohydrate deprivation (Volpe, 1995). Hypoglycemia has a particularly profound negative effect on the developing hippocampus (Barks et al., 1995). Fat, with its higher caloric value,

provides energy for storage (as adipose tissue), but can also be utilized more slowly than glucose to provide acute energy to the entire body, including the brain. Certain fats and lipoproteins are important for normal neuronal cell membrane integrity and myelination. For example, cholesterol, phosphatidyl choline, and certain fatty acids are essential for cell membrane synthesis and integrity. Linolenic acid, linoleic acid, arachidonic acid, and docosohexaenoic acid are essential for normal brain myelination. During starvation or periods of illness, protein can also be used as an energy substrate. When protein is utilized in such a manner, it is not available for structural tissue (including brain) synthesis.

There is an extensive literature in both humans and animal models on the isolated and combined adverse effects of protein and energy malnutrition on the developing brain (Pollitt, 1996; Pollitt and Gorman, 1994; Pollitt, Watkins, Husaini, 1997; Pollitt et al., 1993, 1995; Winick and Nobel, 1966; Winick and Rosso, 1969a,b). Pollitt and Gorman (1994) have pointed out that other nutrient deficiencies usually coexist with protein–energy malnutrition (PEM) in free-living populations.

MINERALS  The major minerals of the body are sodium, potassium (with their usual accompanying dietary anion, chloride), calcium, and phosphorus. Minerals are not classically considered essential for brain development, but deficiencies in these nutrients will lead to abnormal brain function, mostly through altering neuronal electrical function.

MICRONUTRIENTS AND TRACE ELEMENTS  This class of nutrients contains elements that are required in trace quantities by the body and are used, for the most part, in intermediary cellular metabolism. Members of this category include magnesium, manganese, iodine, zinc, copper, molybdenum, cobalt, selenium, fluoride, and iron. As with the major minerals, these elements are not classically considered to be uniquely important for normal brain development except as their deficiencies affect cellular (including neuronal) function. Two

MICHAEL K. GEORGIEFF  Professor of Pediatrics and Child Development, School of Medicine, Institute of Child Development, University of Minnesota, Minneapolis, Minnesota.
RAGHAVENDRA RAO  Instructor of Pediatrics, School of Medicine, University of Minnesota, Minneapolis, Minnesota.

elements in this group, however, are exceptional in their particularly profound effect on brain development: iron and iodine. Iron is required for enzymes that regulate central nervous system cell division (ribonucleotide reductase), dopamine synthesis (tyrosine hydroxylase), myelination (delta-9 desaturase), and oxidative metabolism (cytochromes). The effects of iron deficiency on the growing and mature brain are well documented. Iodine is essential for normal thyroid hormone synthesis. Brain development is severely compromised by hypothyroidism (cretinism) with particularly profound cognitive effects (Hetzel and Mano, 1989; Kretchmer, Beard, and Carlson, 1996). Other than the extensive literature on iron and iodine, little developmental work has been performed to assess the roles of the remaining micronutrients on brain development.

VITAMINS Vitamins are categorized as water- and fat-soluble. They generally are cofactors in intermediary metabolism, although some, like vitamin A, bind promoter regions of genes which regulate cell differentiation and neuronal growth (Mangelsdorf, 1994). As with the trace elements, vitamin deficiencies can potentially affect total body metabolism and consequently brain growth and development. Nevertheless, certain vitamins [e.g., vitamin A, folic acid, pyridoxine (B6)] appear to be more critical during certain periods of CNS development and their deficiencies present a greater risk to neurodevelopment (for review, see Pollitt, 1996). Folic acid deficiency during early pregnancy has been closely linked, both epidemiologically and in animal models, to neural tube defects such as meningomyelocele and encephalocele (Copp and Bernfield, 1994). Vitamin A deficiency is an important neuroteratogenic risk factor during the periconceptional period, but is also associated with retinal and neuronal degeneration in the postnatal period (Goodman, 1984). Pyridoxine is critical for NMDA receptor synthesis and function (Guilarte, 1993).

GROWTH FACTORS It is critical to appreciate that adequate nutrient delivery alone does not ensure normal brain growth and development. Growth factors and anabolic hormones translate potential nutritional value into tissue synthesis and function. Nutrients for the body are analogous to fuel for a car. Growth factors act as the transmission that puts the car into drive.

Starvation has a different effect than illness on somatic and cerebral metabolism. Typically, the body lowers its metabolic setpoint, thereby requiring fewer calories for maintenance of vital functions. Although insulin levels are low, counter-regulatory hormone concentrations are not typically elevated. Provision of protein and energy at a level slightly higher than that needed for maintenance will result in some, albeit suboptimal, growth. In the young child, the fascinating phenomenon of "head-sparing" occurs, where somatic growth will suffer at the expense of brain growth during periods of marginal malnutrition. The mechanism of this regional growth effect is unknown.

The brain is dependent on a host of growth factors for normal neurogenesis, synaptogenesis, dendritic arborization, and myelination. A complete review of these factors and their functions is beyond the scope of this chapter (for review, see Pleasure and Pleasure, 1998). By "growth factors" in this context, we mean small proteins that enhance proliferation of target cells either by encouraging cell division or preventing cell death. The brain contains growth factors that are found throughout the body, including insulin-like growth factor-I (IGF-I), epidermal growth factor (EGF), and fibroblast growth factor (FGF), as well as some that are specific to brain [e.g., brain-derived neurotrophic factor (BDNF) or glial growth factor (GGF)].

The expression and function of these growth factors are influenced by nutritional status. Malnutrition during fetal life (i.e., intrauterine growth retardation) downregulates IGF-I and IGF-I binding protein expression (Nishijima, 1986). IGF-I has a mitogenic and posttranscriptional effect on oligodendrocytes, stimulates neurite outgrowth, and promotes neuronal differentiation (Fellows, 1987). Reduction in IGF-I levels can thus influence myelin production (McMorris and Dubois-Dalcq, 1988; Saneto et al., 1988), as well as neuronal number and complexity. The reduction in IGF-I concentrations noted in growth-retarded fetuses may account for the high rate of microcephaly seen in this population.

A recent study in transgenic mice underscores the importance of the interaction between IGF-I and malnutrition as they influence brain growth (Lee et al., 1999). Whole brain and regional brain growth were assessed in well-nourished and malnourished suckling transgenic mice that overexpress IGF-I. Transgenic overexpression of IGF-I in well-nourished mice increased whole brain weight by 20% over well-nourished controls, predominantly due to increased myelination, a modest increase in DNA content, and increased neuronal survival due to decreased apoptosis. Whereas generalized malnutrition reduced brain weight by 10% in control mice, the IGF-I overexpressing mice had brain weights comparable to well-nourished controls, implying sparing of undernutrition effects by the IGF-I. More importantly, the malnutrition in the control group and the ameliorating effect of IGF-I in the transgenic group were regional. The hippocampus and cerebellum were more affected by malnutrition than the cortex, diencephalon, or brainstem. The brain-sparing effects of IGF-I overexpression were more prominent in the undernourished hippocampus, cortex, and diencephalon, but were not seen in the cerebellum. This regionalization of brain effects from malnutrition may be related to the metabolic demand of the areas at this time of development as well as variations in the expression of IGF-I. A similar effect in terms of iron accretion has been described in young rats (Erikson et al., 1997; deUngria et al., 2000).

## Selected nutrients and their effect on brain development

Table 31.1 categorizes the components of human nutrition and their likely relationships to central nervous system development and function. All nutrients are needed for normal somatic development, but some play a greater role in neurodevelopment than others. The following sections present the evidence for the nutrients that are most important to the developing cognitive systems of the brain.

PROTEIN—ENERGY STATUS    The effect of protein–energy nutritional status on brain growth and neurodevelopment is one of the most extensively studied subjects in nutrition. The importance of providing protein and energy to developing and mature brains has been assessed almost exclusively through studies of protein–energy insufficiency (as opposed to evaluating whether there is a beneficial effect of supplementing a replete organism). Even large-scale epidemiological studies demonstrating beneficial effects of protein and energy supplementation have been conducted in populations where protein–energy malnutrition (PEM) is endemic (Gorman, 1995). Pollitt and Gorman (1994) suggest that chronic energy rather than protein deficiency is responsible for most of the neurobehavioral changes associated with PEM. Animal models, however, strongly implicate independent roles for protein and energy in brain structural changes.

PEM can occur throughout the lifespan from fetal life through adulthood. The likely neuropathology underlying the significant changes in brain development or function seen with PEM has been elucidated using animal models.

*Effects of prenatal PEM*    As with most nutritional deficiencies, the most significant neurodevelopmental effects appear to occur when severe PEM is imposed on a rapidly growing brain. The brain grows most rapidly during fetal and early neonatal life. Restriction of mac-

ronutrients during fetal life results in deceleration of growth and bears the term "intrauterine growth retardation" (IUGR). Maternal hypertension during gestation accounts for 75% of all cases of IUGR, although intrauterine infections and chromosomal anomalies can alter fetal growth as well (Low and Galbraith, 1974). In the latter two instances, the adverse neurodevelopmental outcome associated with small brain size is not due to PEM but to the underlying pathology of the precipitating condition (e.g., viral invasion of CNS cells). In the case of maternal hypertension, high blood pressure causes atheromatous (plaque-like) changes in the vessels of the placenta, which in turn restricts blood and nutrient flow to a smaller, more calcified placenta (DeWolf, Robertson, and Brosen, 1975). Evidence of PEM resides in the smaller weight, length, and fat and muscle content of the growth-retarded fetus and newborn. Brain growth is compromised if the hypertensive insult is early (second trimester), prolonged, or severe.

The neurodevelopmental effects of restricted fetal nutritional delivery and delayed brain growth have been a subject of extensive clinical and laboratory investigation. Epidemiological studies show that poor prenatal head growth presages poor developmental outcome (Gottlieb, Biasini, and Bray, 1988; Harvey et al., 1982; Low et al., 1982; Strauss and Dietz, 1998; Winer and Tejani, 1994). Most larger trials measured relatively neurologically nonspecific outcomes such as intelligence quotient (Strauss and Dietz, 1998). Smaller studies have looked more specifically at what areas of the brain may be preferentially affected by fetal PEM. These studies demonstrate a fivefold higher prevalence of mild neurodevelopmental abnormalities at 2 years of age (Spinillo et al., 1993), weak novelty preference on visual recognition memory tasks (Gottlieb, Biasini, and Bray, 1988), and reduced verbal ability (Pollitt and Gorman, 1994) in the IUGR infants compared with appropriate-sized controls. It is important to recognize that these effects may be due to PEM alone (based on animal models), but may also be due to other micronutrient deficiencies (iron, zinc, selenium) or chronic intrauterine hypoxia. A significant postnatal confound has been the consistent finding that fetal growth retardation occurs more frequently in women of lower socioeconomic status who receive less prenatal care and in whom there is an increased incidence of smoking (Strauss and Dietz, 1998). Employing a clever study design, Strauss and Dietz (1998) matched IUGR infants to sibling controls who were of appropriate size, thus controlling for genetic and postnatal environment; they showed a significant decrement in IQ and Bender-Gestalt scores at 7 years if head growth had been compromised in the fetal period.

TABLE 31.1
*Selected nutrient effects on cognitive development at the (1) molecular, (2) biochemical, (3) structural, and (4) behavioral level\**

| Nutrient | Effect of Deficit | Targeted Brain Region |
|---|---|---|
| Protein–energy | (1) ↓ Total DNA, RNA, protein content<br>↓ mRNA for neuronal, glial proteins<br>(2) ↓ Neurotransmitter production<br>↓ Altered fatty acid profile<br>↓ Growth factor synthesis<br>(3) ↓ Synapse number<br>↓ Myelin<br>↓ Brain weight<br>(4) ↓ IQ<br>↓ Bender-Gestalt scores<br>Weak visual recognition memory<br>Weak verbal ability/reduced vocabulary<br>Decreased speed of processing | Whole brain<br><br>Cerebellar cortex<br><br>Cerebral cortex<br><br>Hippocampus |
| Iron | (1) ↓ Brain DNA, RNA protein content<br>↓ Ribonucleotide reductase activity<br>(2) ↓ Tyrosine hydroxylase activity<br>↓ Cytochrome c and c oxidase activity<br>↓ Delta-9 desaturase activity<br>(3) ↓ Dopamine activity<br>↓ Neuronal oxidative metabolism<br>↓ Myelination<br>(4) ↓ Bayley MDI<br>↓ Bayley PDI<br>↓ Spontaneous movement<br>Delayed latency on evoked responses<br>↓ Spatial working memory<br>↓ Memory and learning | Variable, based on age of<br>insult<br>(see text for details)<br><br>Hippocampus targeted at<br>young ages |
| Zinc | (1) ↓ DNA, RNA, and protein content<br>↓ Cell replication<br>(2) ↓ IGF-I activity<br>↓ Synaptic Zn release<br>Altered neurotransmitter receptor binding<br>(3) Truncated dendritic arborization<br>Reduced regional brain mass<br>↓ Inhibition of GABA<br>↓ Binding to μ and δ receptors<br>(4) ↓ Spontaneous motor activity<br>↓ Short-term visual memory<br>↓ Concept formation and abstract reasoning | Cerebellum, limbic system,<br>cerebral cortex<br><br>Many effects are<br>neurochemical/<br>neurophysiological,<br>given their reversibility<br>with treatment |

(continued)

The biochemical and neuroanatomic bases of neurodevelopmental impairment from early PEM can be found in human autopsy studies and in investigations using animal models. The human studies show significant reductions in brain DNA, RNA, and protein content (Winick and Nobel, 1966; Winick and Rosso, 1969a,b). IUGR infants have lower brain cell number, smaller cell size, and smaller head circumferences. Certain areas (e.g., the cerebellum, cerebral cortex, hippocampus) demonstrate more profound effects than others, suggesting that the developing brain in some way prioritizes protein and energy during deficiency states.

Animal models of IUGR support the human findings of lighter brain weights; reduced neuronal DNA and RNA content, mRNA for neuronal and glial structural proteins, synapse number, and neurotransmitter peptide production; and synaptic junction ultrastructural changes (Bass, Netsky, and Young, 1970; Cragg, 1972; Jones and Dyson, 1976; Wiggins, Fuller, and Enna, 1984). Fatty acid profiles are profoundly altered, with subsequent reductions in myelination, brain lipid composition, and learning ability in fat-restricted rats

| Nutrient | Effect of Deficit | Targeted Brain Region |
|---|---|---|
| Iodine[°] | (1) ↓ Brain DNA, stable protein:DNA ratio<br>↓ Membrane signaling proteins<br>↓ mRNA for microtubule proteins<br>↓ Binding of gene promoter regions for stem cell differentiation<br>(2) Abnormal fatty acid synthesis<br>↓ Axonal and dendritic microtubule protein<br>↓ Neuronal oxidative metabolism<br>(3) ↓ Brain weight<br>↓ Dendritic arborization<br>Migration defects<br>↓ Neuropil<br>Hypomyelination<br>(4) ↓ Verbal IQ<br>↓ Subset coding ability (WISC-R)<br>Motor impairment (reaction time)<br>Spastic diplegia<br>Mental retardation | |
| Selenium[‡] | (1) Downregulation of myelin genes in oligodendrocytes<br>(2) Biochemical findings of hypothyroidism (see iodine deficiency)<br>(3) Increased dopamine turnover<br>Hypomyelination (↓ myelin basic protein)<br>(4) ↓ Thermoregulation<br>Impaired motor ability | All areas, but primarily cerebellar cortex, prefrontal cortex, and hippocampus |

*The model portrayed is based on integrated human and animal behavioral, histological, and cell culture data.
[°]Iodine's effect on the CNS is strictly through its role in thyroid hormone, not elemental iodine deficiency.
[‡]Selenium's primary effects are through interaction with iodine and thyroid status.

(Yamamoto et al., 1987). Malnutrition also downregulates CNS growth factors critical for normal brain development (Nishijima, 1986). The study by Lee and colleagues (1999) in transgenic mice emphasizes the importance of maintaining IGF-I levels during periods of malnutrition in order to spare regions of the brain important for cognition.

It will be important in future research on IUGR infants to link specific regional neuropathologic or neurochemical findings (elucidated from controlled animal models of PEM) with deficits in behaviors known to be based in those regions. Thus, one should be able to relate the reduction in visual recognition memory processing in IUGR infants (Gottlieb, Biasini, and Bray, 1988) to either reduced hippocampal volume or metabolism on MRI/MRI spectroscopy.

*Effects of postnatal PEM* The postnatal brain grows rapidly during the first six postnatal months and then slows considerably during the last six months of the first year. Important regions that become functionally significant during this year include motor cortex, myelinating motor tracts, rapid cerebellar development, and hippocampal–prefrontal connections. Infants in the United States and Canada are typically fed either human milk or infant formula derived from cow's milk or soy plant products during this time. The significant, positive relationship between breastfeeding and cognitive development is intriguing, since it is unclear whether the positive effect is related to nutritional factor(s) present in human milk but not in formula, to positive maternal–infant interactions (including the propensity of higher-IQ mothers to choose breastfeeding), or both.

There is good reason to believe that multiple factors found in breast milk promote normal CNS development, and that deficiencies of these nutrients in cow's milk or soy-based formulas are responsible for slower rates of cognitive development (Lucas, 1997; Morrow-Tlucak, Haude, and Ernhart, 1988; Wang and Wu,

1996). These factors include compounds such as nucleotides (DeLucchi, Pita, and Faus, 1987) and long-chain polyunsaturated fatty acids (LCPUFA; Innis, 1992) that are simply not synthesized by cows and soy bean plants. Other neurotrophic compounds (e.g., growth factors) may be synthesized, but are destroyed in formula processing or storage (MacLean and Benson, 1989).

LCPUFAs include the omega-3 fatty acids docosohexaenoic acid (DHA; 22:6n-3) and arachidonic acid (AA; 20:4n-6). Both are transported by the placenta to the fetus and are present in human milk, but not formula (Carlson, 1997).

LCPUFAs potentially affect neurodevelopment because they are essential in all cell membranes. They are involved in intercellular communication and in signal transduction (Carlson, 1997). They are critical for visual development in primates and likely in humans (Neuringer et al., 1986; Uauy et al., 1990). Randomized trials of LCPUFA supplementation in preterm infants show transiently improved visual acuity, faster processing time on electroretinogram, better visual recognition memory, and higher scores on the Mental Developmental Index of the Bayley Scales of Infant Development at 12 months of age (Birch et al., 1992; Carlson, Werkman, and Tolley, 1996). The retinal results with respect to rod electroretinogram threshold at 36 weeks gestation and visual acuity by forced-choice preferential looking and by visual evoked potential in preterm infants fed supplemented formula approach the findings in breastfed infants, and are significantly better than those of infants fed unsupplemented formula (Uauy-Dagach and Mena, 1995). Nevertheless, most of the effects appear transient. Furthermore, the transience of the findings is not due to withdrawal of the supplementation with subsequent lack of synthesis by the infants, since the trials typically lasted well beyond the age (6 months) when infants can synthesize LCPUFAs de novo. Formulas manufactured in the United States for preterm infants are not currently supplemented with LCPUFAs because of poor growth associated with supplementation in early studies. The poor growth was most likely related to inappropriate ratios of AA to DHA (Carlson, 1997), and have not plagued subsequent studies. LCPUFA-supplemented formulas are available in Europe.

Term infants supplemented with LCPUFAs do not demonstrate nearly the beneficial effect that preterm infants show, perhaps because of an increased capacity to synthesize de novo AA and DHA at an earlier postnatal age (Jensen et al., 1997). The growth failure seen in preterm infants supplemented with LCPUFAs has not been observed in term infants.

In spite of the mixed long-term results, the data are quite convincing that LCPUFAs (administered without the remainder of trophic factors and nutrients found in breast milk) independently alter neurologic function and perhaps development, and provide clear evidence that nutrients can affect brain development and function. Although they appear to be supplementation studies, they are better considered studies of correction of deficiencies of essential nutrients in nonhuman milk formulas. There is no evidence that supplementing breastfed infants or oversupplementing formula-fed infants with LCPUFAs will result in more profound CNS changes.

Nucleotides are nitrogenous compounds derived from the combination of a nucleic acid base (adenine, guanine, cytosine, thymine, or uracil) with a phosphorylated pentose sugar. Nucleotides and their precursors (nucleosides and nucleic acids) are critical for DNA and RNA synthesis. Thus, a steady intracellular pool of nucleotides is required to ensure cell division and protein synthesis. This de novo synthetic pathway is immature in all newborns, but particularly in premature infants, raising the still unresolved issue of whether dietary nucleotides are semi-essential in the newborn period. Nucleotide supplementation of infant formula has been postulated to have an impact on the developing brain by increasing the levels of LCPUFAs such as arachidonic and docosohexaenoic acid (DeLucchi, Pita, and Faus, 1987; Gil et al., 1986).

Once infants are weaned from human milk or formula, their risk of PEM increases because they are now dependent on the same foods as their adult food providers. A child growing up in an area of the world where PEM is endemic will be placed at a risk equivalent to or greater than the adult population of that area. The effects of PEM have been extensively studied in children from age 6 months through the early teenage years in these endemic areas. Although the studies show mixed results owing to differences in degree, timing, type, and duration of malnutrition, it is safe to state that PEM of sufficient degree and duration at a critical time during a growing child's life will affect cognitive abilities. In some cases, the negative effect on the brain is reversible with nutritional rehabilitation, while in other cases the effects appear more "permanent." However, as discussed below, the assignment of nutritional causality to poorer cognitive outcomes in free-living societies has been very difficult, given concurrent confounding variables such as maternal mental health, maternal socioeconomic status, lack of infant mental stimulation, and malnutrition-induced lack of infant motivation (Stein and Susser, 1985).

Until the mid-1990s, studies assessing the role of post-natal malnutrition in cognitive development were dominated by two important theoretical concepts. The first centered on the idea of "critical periods." Winick and Noble's histopathologic studies introduced the idea that PEM during the period of rapid brain growth in the perinatal period would cause more significant and hence more permanent perturbations in brain structure and, ultimately, function (Winick and Noble, 1966). The vulnerable period was subsequently extended until at least 3 years of age as it became apparent that synaptogenesis, dendritic pruning, programmed cell death, and myelinogenesis continued well into the postnatal period. Dobbing's work codified the concept of vulnerable or critical periods (Dobbing, 1990). Based on these developmental neuroanatomic considerations, it was logical to expect that field studies of PEM in 6-month-old to 3-year-old children should demonstrate significant cognitive effects.

The other important theoretical concept centered on the role of covariates such as maternal mental status, maternal–child interactions, and infant motivation in determining the cognitive abilities of the malnourished infant (Lozoff et al., 1998; Pollitt and Gorman, 1994). Theoretically, these covariates could be highly dependent on either maternal or infant nutritional status, or they could be completely separate issues. Another example concerns the effects of individual differences in infant motivation. An infant could perform poorly on a set of cognitive measures as a function of what is perceived by the investigator as "reduced motivation." Reduced motivation could be due to depression, decreased energy due to marginal malnutrition, or poor maternal–child stimulation based on the mother's (and not the infant's) nutritional status. Lozoff has published a diagram of these complex interactions with respect to iron deficiency (Lozoff et al., 1998), but the tenets are clearly applicable to PEM as well.

Prior to the mid-1990s, studies in humans that attempted to associate mild to moderate PEM with poorer cognitive outcome were so hopelessly flawed that researchers in the field would reach diametrically opposite conclusions about the studies (see Stein and Susser, 1985). It may not be ethically possible to separate all of the nonnutritional confounding variables in a free-living human society, but studies published by Pollitt's group in the mid-1990s have given credence to the hypothesis that nutritional factors (specifically, PEM) do influence postnatal cognitive development (Pollitt and Gorman, 1994; Pollitt et al., 1995; Pollitt, Watkins, and Husaini, 1997).

In these studies, long-term cognitive effects of early supplemental feeding in children 0–7 years of age were examined in four Guatemalan villages from 1969 to 1977. Seventy percent of the children were followed up in 1988 at ages 11–26 years. The villages were in an area marked by mild to moderate PEM. Participants in two of the villages received a high-calorie/high-protein supplement that was administered to the mothers, infants, and young children. Participants in the other two villages received a supplement with 40% fewer calories and 20% less protein. Test scores on knowledge, numeracy, reading, processing time, and vocabulary at follow-up (adolescence) were significantly higher in the group receiving more robust protein–energy supplementation. Within that group, no effect of socioeconomic status was observed. Interestingly, the group that received less supplementation not only had lower scores on cognitive tasks, but demonstrated a profound socioeconomic effect as well. This result suggests that marginal nutritional status may potentiate the effects of other neurologic risk factors. A similar effect has been described in animal models of iron deficiency (Rao et al., 1999).

Pollitt and colleagues (1995) very carefully considered potential alternative explanations (including differences between the villages, intervening factors between the initial intervention and the follow-up 10 years later, compliance with the dietary supplements, and the 30% dropout rate at follow-up), and concluded that none accounted for the observed differences in cognition. They do not claim that the study provided definitive proof of the effect of early mild PEM on later cognitive ability, but felt that the evidence is compelling enough to justify nutritional intervention as sound public health policy (Pollitt and Gorman, 1994).

From a mechanistic standpoint, it would be most useful for researchers studying postnatal PEM to assess whether the neurodevelopmental abnormalities that are observed fit the expected pattern of vulnerable brain areas and processes predicted from human and animal histopathologic, neurochemical, or neurophysiologic models. Although it is laudable to demonstrate effects of mild PEM on relatively broad cognitive function, it would be interesting to know whether neurologic circuits involved in the behaviors where differences are observed between groups are particularly at risk specifically for protein or energy malnutrition. For example, the reduced speed of processing could be easily explained by nutritionally induced hypomyelination. Alternatively, the same finding at the behavioral level could be due to reduced motivation to perform the task and may be related to damage or dysfunction of limbic structures such as the amygdala. If no data support amygdaloid vulnerability to PEM, the latter may be more effectively ruled out. New tools that assess the structure and functions underlying certain cognitive capabilities (e.g., fMRI, event-related potential) now allow for more precise delineation of cause and effect of nutritional deficiencies such as early PEM.

IRON Iron is the second most commonly studied nutrient in relation to brain development, after protein–energy. Iron deficiency is common worldwide; 30% of the developing world's population and 11% of U.S. toddlers are iron-deficient due to a low-iron diet combined (especially in the developing world) with a high rate of intestinal blood loss. Iron deficiency is the world's most common nutritional cause of anemia. It is not unreasonable to study the relationship of iron to neurodevelopment and neurologic function, given the role of iron in many brain cellular metabolic processes (Cammack, Wrigglesworth, and Baum, 1990; Larkin and Rao, 1990; Thelander, 1990; Youdim, Ben-Sachar, and Yehuda, 1989). As with PEM, a convincing relationship can be drawn between this nutrient and brain development based on deficiency states.

There are three time periods when children are at particular risk for iron deficiency: the fetal/neonatal period, infancy (6–18 months of age), and following the onset of menarche (Bruner et al., 1996). Brain growth and development is relatively rapid during two of these periods, while it is complete or nearly complete during the third. This distinction allows for studying the comparative effects of a single nutrient deficiency on a growing versus a mature brain. Because of its intricate involvement in cell cycle kinetics and myelination (Larkin and Rao, 1990; Thelander, 1990), one would expect profound neuroanatomic changes in a brain that is still growing, but perhaps no effect in a relatively mature brain. Areas that are growing particularly rapidly might be expected to be most affected. Since the brain does not develop homogeneously (i.e., not all parts mature simultaneously), iron deficiency during one growth period (e.g., fetal life) may result in very different neuroanatomic and neurobehavioral deficits than iron deficiency during another growth period (e.g., infancy). Iron also has important effects on neurochemistry and neurometabolism through its effect on dopamine metabolism and oxidative phosphorylation (Cammack, Wrigglesworth, and Baum, 1990; Youdim, Ben-Sachar, and Yehuda, 1989). Iron deficiency may affect these aspects of brain function relatively similarly in developing and mature brains.

Iron deficiency most commonly occurs during infancy, between 6 and 18 months of age, due to reduced iron intake (either through low-iron formula or through cow's milk). It is not surprising that this age group has been more extensively studied than any other

iron-deficient group. Multiple well-controlled clinical studies in this age group demonstrate significant decrements in motor and mental achievement (Lozoff, 1990; Lozoff et al., 1982, 1987; Nokes, van den Bosch, and Bundy, 1998; Walter, Kowalskys, and Stekel, 1983). While the motor findings are less robust and generally reversible with iron therapy, the significant cognitive deficits that have been documented are more resistant to reversal, and in some studies are very long-term (Lozoff, 1990). The cognitive deficits include a 10- to 12-point reduction in the Mental Developmental Index of the Bayley Scales of Infant Development, significantly associated with the degree of anemia (Lozoff, 1990). The findings are not thought to be due to anemia itself, since rapid repletion of the anemia (by transfusion in animal models and by iron therapy in humans) does not affect the neurodevelopmental test scores.

The apparent permanence of these neurobehavioral findings has three important implications. First, there appears to be a differential regional effect of iron on the growing brain, perhaps mediated by differences in regional blood–brain iron transport regulation. This regionalization concept is supported by the nonhomogeneous (e.g., cognitive greater than motor) deficits induced by iron deficiency. Second, iron deficiency during this period of brain development likely changes neuroanatomy since the deficits remain extant over much longer periods of time than would be expected for neurochemical or neurophysiological alterations. Third, and perhaps of greatest concern, the results demonstrate that certain brain lesions induced by nutritional deficiencies are beyond the reach of CNS reparative or compensatory processes which may be termed "plasticity."

The human studies of this age group have utilized fairly gross measures of motor and intellectual quality primarily because they are constrained by testing resources available to the investigators in the field. These assessments typically evaluate global neurobehavioral abilities that may in turn have been affected by the specific effects of iron deficiency on the brain. For example, given enough hypomyelination from iron deficiency to reduce speed of processing, the score on the Bayley Scales of Infant Development can be expected to fall. Nevertheless, this is an indirect way to understand the effect of iron on the developing brain.

As with PEM, recent smaller cohort studies have now begun to look for iron-specific effects in these infants. These effects may be predictable based on the role of iron in neuroanatomy, neurochemistry, and neurophysiology. The presence of iron in the brain is critical for myelination (Larkin, Jarratt, and Rao, 1986). Iron deficiency in immature animal models results in a predictable loss of enzyme activity and in hypomyelination (Larkin and Rao, 1990). If the same process occurs in infants, one could predict a specific neuroanatomic effect (potentially visible with high-resolution magnetic resonance imaging) or a neurophysiologic effect (potentially detected by electrophysiologic assessment). Although the former has not been assessed, Roncagliolo and colleagues (1998) have reported delayed latencies on auditory brainstem-evoked responses in iron-deficient 6-month-old infants. They attributed this delay to the effects of iron deficiency–induced hypomyelination.

The selectivity of iron deficiency for certain areas of the brain can be similarly assessed. Dietary iron deficiency has been induced in rats from weaning (21 days) to 35 days of age in order to model iron deficiency of human infancy. CNS iron deficiency at this age results in selected regions of decreased iron uptake, with the hippocampus at particular risk for reduced brain iron content. If similar regionalization occurs in the human, deficits related to hippocampal functioning could be expected (Erikson et al., 1997). Studies of this degree of specificity have not yet been performed, but are needed to demonstrate a cause-and-effect relationship between iron deficiency and human behavior.

The neurobehavioral study of iron-deficient teenage girls provides an interesting contrast to iron-deficient infants since the brain is neuroanatomically relatively mature and myelination is complete at this age. Iron supplementation of young women with iron deficiency anemia improves memory and learning but has no effect on attention (Groner et al., 1986). These findings can be contrasted with the long-term (and perhaps permanent) deficits found in toddlers who became iron-deficient and were subsequently treated. The reversibility of the neurobehavioral deficits with iron therapy in the teenage population argue for an effect of iron on neurochemistry (e.g., dopamine) or neurophysiology (oxidative metabolism) as opposed to potential structural changes in neuroanatomy that may have occurred in the toddlers.

The final group of developing humans at risk for iron deficiency is late-gestation fetuses and newborns. Two groups have been identified: infants of mothers with diabetes mellitus during pregnancy and infants who suffered IUGR. Each group has a 50% prevalence of low iron stores at birth, 25% of which are at risk for brain iron deficiency. Autopsy studies have documented up to a 40% decrease in brain iron in the most severely affected infants. Both groups of infants are at increased risk for neurobehavioral abnormalities. Animal models of perinatal iron deficiency support the concept of regional loss of iron-dependent brain metabolic function,

with the hippocampus and its prefrontal projections demonstrating particular vulnerability (deUngria et al., 2000). Thus, a putative link between perinatal iron deficiency and newborn and long-term neurobehavioral sequelae can be proposed. Unfortunately, like all other clinical population studies, each group has other significant neurologic risk factors (e.g., hypoglycemia, hypoxia, PEM) that may affect long-term outcome and confound any attempt at causally relating perinatal iron deficiency with neurobehavioral deficits.

ZINC   A strong case can be made for the essentiality of zinc for normal brain development and function. Zinc deficiency affects neuroanatomy, neurochemistry, and neurophysiology through a variety of mechanisms. The global effects of zinc are in part due to the essential role that zinc plays in basic protein biochemistry and in cell replication. Zinc has a direct effect on brain growth and morphology through its role in enzymes that mediate protein and nucleic acid synthesis (Sandstead, 1985; Terhune and Sandstead, 1972). Profound zinc deficiency in the growing animal results in decreased brain DNA, RNA, and protein content (Duncan and Hurley, 1978; Sandstead, 1985). Zinc has an indirect effect on brain growth because its presence is needed for normal insulin-like growth factor-I (IGF-I) activity (McNall, Etherton, and Fosmire, 1995). Zinc influences brain neurochemistry (and presumably function) by inhibiting binding of opioids to $\mu$ receptors and of magnesium to $\mu$ and $\delta$ receptors in the cerebral cortex (Tejwani and Hanissian, 1990). Zinc also inhibits γ-aminobutyric acid (GABA) stimulated chloride influx into hippocampal neurons (Li, Rosenberg, and Chiu, 1994). Zinc is released into the interneuronal space from presynaptic boutons (Frederickson and Danscher, 1990). Zinc's effect on brain neurophysiology is evident in abnormal electroencephalographic tracings found in zinc-deficient rats (Hesse, 1979).

The cerebellum, limbic system and cerebral cortex are particularly rich in zinc and demonstrate the most profound effects of zinc deprivation (Frederickson and Danscher, 1990). These effects include truncated dendritic arborization and reduced regional brain mass in rats. As with iron deficiency, the neuroanatomic sequelae of zinc deficiency in young rats persist into adulthood with attendant persistent behavioral sequelae (Frederickson and Danscher, 1990). Two-year-old rhesus monkeys fed a zinc-deficient diet have reduced spontaneous motor activity and poorer short-term memory compared to the pre-deficiency baseline period (Golub et al., 1994). Similar results have been found in mice and rats.

Zinc deficiency in humans results in significant changes in neuropsychological performance on tests that tap the anatomical areas shown to be vulnerable in the animal models (Sandstead et al., 1998). Six- to nine-year-old first-graders with low zinc status were assessed biochemically and neuropsychologically before and after treatment. The tasks included design matching to assess visual perception, delayed design matching to assess short-term visual memory, a spatial orientation memory test, and Pollitt's oddity task to assess concept formation and abstract reasoning. Zinc supplementation for 10 weeks resulted in significantly better zinc status and improvement in these particular neuropsychological assessments.

IODINE  There is overwhelming evidence that iodine sufficiency is critical for normal early CNS development. An analysis of available epidemiological studies has helped elucidate the effect of severity, timing, and duration of iodine deficiency on brain development and neurologic outcome. Iodine deficiency can range from severe to mild based on the availability of iodine in the food supply (Hetzel and Mano, 1989). Endemic areas of severe dietary iodine deficiency include parts of China, Zaire, Iran, and India (Hetzel and Mano, 1989; Kretchmer, Beard, and Carlson, 1996). Classic older studies from these areas helped characterize the syndrome of endemic cretinism that, in its severest neurologic manifestation, includes mental retardation, spastic diplegia, and deaf-mutism. More recently, investigators have concentrated on describing the neuropsychological and motor effects of moderate or mild iodine deficiency and the effect of iodine prophylaxis or treatment in high-risk groups (Aghini-Lombardi et al., 1995; Azizi et al., 1993). A clear dose–response effect can be appreciated across the studies, with moderate iodine deficiency resulting in reduced verbal IQ and subset coding ability on the Wechsler Intelligence Scale for Children-Revised (WISC-R) as well as motor impairments on simple reaction time tests in children of elementary school age (Fenzi, Giusti, and Aghini-Lombardi, 1990). Mild iodine deficiency results in reduced motor ability without any apparent effect on cognition when children of the same age were assessed with the same tools (Azizi et al., 1993). It is unclear whether the latter group had early cognitive findings that were "reversed" with postnatal iodine treatment or whether they were never affected in the first place.

As with any nutrient deficiency, timing and duration are of critical importance. Interventional studies with iodine treatment clearly demonstrate that prophylaxis works. Iodine-deficient women living in endemic areas who were injected with iodinated oil prior to pregnancy did not produce infants with cretinism (Hetzel, 1987). In animal models, treatment later in pregnancy had a much less dramatic effect, and postnatal treatment of humans and animals appeared to have little effect. These observations lend credence to the hypothesis that the critical window for brain responsiveness to iodine is during early fetal life. Nevertheless, it should be noted that children and adolescents living in areas of endemic iodine deficiency will demonstrate alterations in psychomotor development with reduced IQ, even with normal physical growth (an indicator of less severe iodine deficiency) (Azizi et al., 1993). Studies that assess the effect of repletion of iodine status on psychomotor performance in children with mild to moderate iodine deficiency remain to be performed. There is reason to believe that late-onset iodine deficiency (hypothyroidism) affects brain function, but not anatomy. Smith and Ain (1995), using $^{31}$P magnetic resonance spectroscopy, demonstrated reduced oxidative metabolism in the hypothyroid brain (Pleasure and Pleasure, 1998) that was reversible with thyroid replacement therapy.

SELENIUM  Selenium is a micronutrient whose role in brain development is only now being elucidated. Although direct evidence of its effect on cognitive development in humans is lacking, its role in brain thyroid and iodine metabolism, as well as its interaction with other micronutrients (e.g., iron, copper, zinc, lead) that affect brain development, is important to note. Studies linking selenium status with behavioral development in animal models have been published (Mitchell et al., 1998; Watanabe and Satoh, 1994). Preterm infants are at relatively high risk of selenium deficiency because of their lower body stores and generally poorer antioxidant status. Thus, it is likely that research on the role of this nutrient in human brain development will be forthcoming.

*The role of timing in nutrient deprivation and subsequent repletion*

A common theme in the discussion of each of the nutrients has been the roles of timing, duration, and severity of nutrient administration or deficiency.

Clear evidence exists that brain growth and development is not an even process and that various "circuits" come on line at different times between conception and adolescence. Nutrient requirements are increased during a period of rapid growth for any organ, including the brain. Human and animal model experiments also support the concept that nutritional deprivations during a period of rapid growth result in more profound structural, chemical, and physiological changes than if the same degree of deprivation is imposed during a more quiescent period. What remains of great interest is whether these early changes are reversible.

Reversibility (or amenability to nutritional rehabilitation) can be looked at in two ways—through a large-scale population-based approach, as Pollitt has done (Pollitt and Gorman, 1994), and through further understanding of the critical nutrients required for normal ontogeny of brain development. Both approaches beg the question of "plasticity" within the developing system. Pollitt's studies clearly demonstrate that developmental benefits of nutrient supplementation are a function of the timing of that intervention (Pollitt et al., 1993). The earlier the timing, the greater the benefits. Yet, it is difficult to argue that the "critical window" is ever "closed" during childhood. Studies of children suffering from prenatal malnutrition (IUGR; Morgane et al., 1993; Strauss and Dietz, 1998) or postnatal malnutrition (Pollitt et al., 1993) clearly demonstrate recoverability of function well beyond the period of rapid brain growth.

A similar effect is seen in the growth and development of preterm infants. Greater than 50% of preterm infants become microcephalic during their hospital stay due to inadequate nutrient delivery, severe illness resulting in catabolism, and a very rapid expected rate of brain growth (Georgieff et al., 1985). Although nutritional management of preterm infants has improved substantially during the years (Georgieff et al., 1989), preterm infants leave the NICU with significant postnatal growth retardation and altered body composition which remain extant until more than 1 year of life. Catch-up growth and development has been described well into the teenage years. The developmental outcome of these infants far exceeds the expectations based on number of neurologic risk factors (including malnutrition) they encounter. A reasonable hypothesis is that the expected developmental sequelae of this "extrauterine growth retardation" is reversed postnatally with catch-up growth. Although it would be preferable never to have had a nutritional deficit in the first place, it is clear that recovery is entirely possible and, in fact, likely. Consequently, periods of rapid growth may not only confer a risk factor when nutrients are deprived, but may also offer a window of opportunity for rapid and complete repair when nutrients are subsequently provided. Pollitt (1996) notes that there is evidence for recovery following PEM in all age groups, including fetuses who receive adequate postnatal nutrition (IUGR), infants malnourished before 2 years of age who were not supplemented until after 3 years, and infants malnourished postnatally but also treated before 2 years of age.

A review of the nutrients that affect brain growth and development reveals striking differences with respect to vulnerability and timing. Deficiencies of certain nutrients, such as iodine, selenium, folate and vitamin A, exert their effects in a very narrow post-conceptional window. Later supplementation of these nutrients will do little to alter damage that occurred in the first 12 weeks post-conception. These nutrients play important roles in neuronal differentiation, cell division, protein synthesis, and neuronal migration. Other nutrients (e.g., protein, energy, iron, zinc) play a role throughout development. Deficiencies of these nutrients at different ages result in variable neuroanatomic, neurochemical, and neurobehavioral effects. These differences may be regionalized within the brain, with certain areas being spared at one age and not at another (deUngria et al., 2000; Erikson et al., 1997). In humans, nutrient deficiencies tend to cluster and are frequently prolonged, thus exposing vulnerable brain regions to multiple nutrient deficiencies over time. Only through careful modeling of each nutrient's effect on brain development combined with utilization of nutrient-specific assessments (e.g., if hypomyelination is a distinguishing hallmark of iron deficiency, the effect in a population could be studied electrophysiologically) (Roncagliolo et al., 1998) will it become possible to unravel the precise effects of nutrient deficiencies at the various stages of neurodevelopment.

ACKNOWLEDGMENTS  Supported in part by a grant from NIH (HD 29421) to MKG. We thank Ginny Lyson for editorial assistance.

## REFERENCES

AGHINI LOMBARDI, F. A., A. PINCHERA, L. ANTONANGELI, T. RAGO, L. CHIOVATO, S. BARGAGNA, B. BERTUCELLI, G. FERRETTI, B. SBRANA, and M. MARCHESCHI, 1995. Mild iodine deficiency during fetal/neonatal life and neuropsychological impairment in Tuscany. *J. Endocrinol. Invest.* 18:57–72.

AZIZI F., A. SARSHAR, M. NAFARABADI, A. GHAZI, M. KIMIAGAR, S. NOOHI, N. RAHBAR, A. BAHRAMI, and S. KALANTARI, 1993. Impairment of neuromotor and cognitive development in iodine-deficient schoolchildren with normal physical growth. *Acta Endocrinol. (Copenh.)* 129:497–500.

BARKS, J. D. E., R. SUN, C. MALINAK, and F. S. SILVERSTEIN, 1995. Gp120, an HIV-1 protein, increases susceptibility to hypoglycemic and ischemic brain injury in perinatal rats. *Exp. Neurol.* 132:123–133.

BASS, N. H., M. G. NETSKY, and E. YOUNG, 1970. Effects of neonatal malnutrition on developing cerebrum. I. Microchemical and histologic study of cellular differentiation in the rat. *Arch. Neurol.* 23:289–302.

BIRCH, E. E., D. G. BIRCH, D. R. HOFFMAN, and R. UAUY, 1992. Dietary essential fatty acid supply and visual acuity development. *Invest. Ophthalmol. Vis. Sci.* 33:3242–3253.

BRUNER, A. B., A. JOFFE, A. K. DUGGAN, J. F. CASELLA, and J. BRANDT, 1996. Randomized study of cognitive effects of iron supplementation in non-anemic iron-deficient adolescent girls. *Lancet* 348:992–996.

CAMMACK, R., J. M. WRIGGLESWORTH, and H. BAUM, 1990. Iron-dependent enzymes in mammalian systems. In *Iron Transport and Storage*, P. Ponka, H. M. Schulman, and R. C. Woodworth, eds. Boca Raton, Fla.: CRC Press, pp. 18–39.

CARLSON, S. E., 1997. Long-chain polyunsaturated fatty acid supplementation of preterm infants. In *Developing Brain and Behaviour*, J. Dobbing, ed. London: Academic Press, pp. 41–78.

CARLSON, S. E., S. H. WERKMAN, and E. A. TOLLEY, 1996. The effect of long chain n-3 fatty acid supplementation on visual acuity and growth of preterm infants with and without bronchopulmonary dysplasia. *Am. J. Clin. Nutr.* 63:687–697.

COPP, A. J., and M. BERNFIELD, 1994. Etiology and pathogenesis of human neural tube defects. *Curr. Opin. Pediatr.* 6:626–631.

CRAGG, B. G., 1972. The development of cortical synapses during starvation in the rat. *Brain* 95(1):143–150.

DELUCCHI, C., M. L. PITA, and M. J. FAUS, 1987. Effects of dietary nucleotides on the fatty acid composition of erythrocyte membrane lipids in term infants. *J. Ped. Gastroenterol. Nutr.* 6:568–574.

DEUNGRIA, M., R. RAO, J. D. WOBKEN, M. LUCIANA, C. A. NELSON, and M. K. GEORGIEFF, 2000. Perinatal iron deficiency decreases cytochrome c oxidase activity in selected regions of neonatal rat brain. *Pediatr. Res.* 48:169–176.

DEWOLF, F., W. B. ROBERTSON, and I. BROSEN, 1975. The ultrastructure of acute atherosis in hypertensive pregnancy. *Am. J. Obstet. Gynecol.* 123:164–174.

DOBBING, J., 1990. Vulnerable periods in developing brain. In *Brain, Behavior and Iron in the Infant Diet*, J. Dobbing, ed. London: Springer-Verlag, pp. 1–25.

DUNCAN, J., and L. HURLEY, 1978. Thymidine kinase and DNA polymerase activity in normal and zinc deficient developing rat embryos. *Proc. Soc. Exp. Biol. Med.* 159:39–43.

ERIKSON, K. M., D. J. PINERO, J. R. CONNOR, and J. L. BEARD, 1997. Regional brain iron, ferritin and transferrin concentrations during iron deficiency and iron repletion in developing rats. *J. Nutr.* 127:2030–2038.

FELLOWS, R., 1987. IGF-1 supports survival and differentiation of fetal rat brain neurons in serum-free, hormone-free defined medium. *Soc. Neurosci. Abstr.* 13:1615.

FENZI, G. F., L. F. GIUSTI, and F. AGHINI-LOMBARDI, 1990. Neuropsychological assessment of schoolchildren from an area of moderate iodine deficiency. *J. Endocrinol. Invest.* 13:427–432.

FREDERICKSON, C., and G. DANSCHER, 1990. Zinc-containing neurons in hippocampus and related CNS structures. *Prog. Brain Res.* 83:71–84.

GEORGIEFF, M. K., J. S. HOFFMAN, G. R. PEREIRA, J. BERNBAUM, and M. HOFFMAN-WILLIAMSON, 1985. Effect of neonatal caloric deprivation on head growth and 1-year developmental status in preterm infants. *J. Pediatr.* 107:581–587.

GEORGIEFF, M. K., M. M. MILLS, L. L. LINDEKE, S. IVERSON, D. E. JOHNSON, and T. R. THOMPSON, 1989. Changes in nutritional management and outcome of very-low-birth-weight infants. *Am. J. Dis. Child.* 143:82–85.

GIL, A., M. PITA, A. MARTINEZ, J. A. MOLINA, AND F. SANCHEZ MEDINA, 1986. Effect of dietary nucleotides on the plasma fatty acids in at-term in neonates. *Human Nutr. Clin. Nutr.* 40:185–195.

GOLUB, M. S., P. T. TAKEUCHI, C. L. KEEN, M. E. GERSHWIN, A. G. HENDRICKS, and B. LONNERDAL, 1994. Modulation of behavioral performance of prepubertal monkeys by moderate dietary zinc deprivation. *Am. J. Clin. Nutr.* 60:238–243.

GORMAN, K. S., 1995. Malnutrition and cognitive development: Evidence from experimental/quasi-experimental studies among the mild-moderately malnourished. *J. Nutr.* 125:S2239–S2244.

GOTTLIEB, S. J., F. J. BIASINI, and N. W. BRAY, 1988. Visual recognition memory in IUGR and normal birthweight infants. *Infant Behav. Dev.* 11:223–228.

GRONER, J. A., N. A. HOLTZMAN, E. CHARNEY, and E. D. MELLITS, 1986. A randomized trial of oral iron on tests of short-term memory and attention span in young pregnant women. *J. Adolesc. Health Care* 7:44–48.

GUILARTE, T. R., 1993. Vitamin B6 and cognitive development: recent research findings from human and animal studies. *Nutr. Rev.* 51:193–198.

HARVEY, D., J. PRINCE, J. BUNTON, C. PARKINSON, and S. CAMPBELL, 1982. Abilities of children who were small-for-gestational-age babies. *Pediatrics* 69:296–300.

HESSE, G., 1979. Chronic zinc deficiency alters neuronal function of hippocampal mossy fibers. *Science* 205:1005–1007.

HETZEL, B. S., 1987. An overview of the prevention and control of iodine deficiency disorders. In *The Prevention and Control of Iodine Deficiency Disorders*, B. S. Hetzel, J. T. Dunn, and J. B. Standbury, eds. Amsterdam: Elsevier, pp. 7–34.

HETZEL, B. S., and M. T. MANO, 1989. A review of experimental studies of iodine deficiency during fetal development. *J. Nutr.* 119:145–151.

INNIS, S. M., 1992. Human milk and formula fatty acids. *J. Pediatr.* 120:S55–61.

JENSEN, C. L., T. C. PRAGER, J. K. FRALEY, H. CHEN, R. E. ANDERSON, and W. C. HEIRD, 1997. Effects of dietary linoleic/alpha-linolenic acid ratio on growth and visual function of term infants. *J. Pediatr.* 131:173–175.

JONES, D. G., and S. E. DYSON, 1981. The influence of protein restriction, rehabilitation and changing nutritional status on synaptic development: A quantitative study in rat brain. *Brain Res.* 208:97–111.

KRETCHMER, N., J. L. BEARD, and S. CARLSON, 1996. The role of nutrition in the development of normal cognition. *Am. J. Clin. Nutr.* 63:997S–1001S.

LARKIN, E. C., B. A. JARRATT, and G. A. RAO, 1986. Reduction of relative levels of nervonic to lignoceric acid in the brain of rat pups due to iron deficiency. *Nutr. Res.* 6:309–314.

LARKIN, E. C., and G. A. RAO, 1990. Importance of fetal and neonatal iron: Adequacy for normal development of central nervous system. In *Brain, Behavior and Iron in the Infant Diet*, J. Dobbing, ed. London: Springer-Verlag, London, pp. 43–62.

LEE, K.-H., A. KALIKOGLU, P. YE, and A. J. D'ERCOLE, 1999. Insulin-like growth factor-I (IGF-I) ameliorates and IGF binding protein-1 (IGFBP-1) exacerbates the effects of undernutrition on brain growth during early postnatal life: Studies in IGF-I and IGFBP-1 transgenic mice. *Pediatr. Res.* 45:331–336.

LI, M., H. ROSENBERG, and T. CHIU, 1994. Zinc inhibition of GABA-stimulated $Cl^-$ flux in rat brain regions is unaffected by acute or chronic benzodiazepine. *Pharmacol. Biochem. Behav.* 49:477–482.

LOW, J. A., and R. S. GALBRAITH, 1974. Pregnancy characteristics of intrauterine growth retardation. *Obstet. Gynecol.* 44:122–126.

Low, J. A., R. S. Galbraith, D. Muir, H. Killen, B. Pater, and J. Karchmar, 1982. Intrauterine growth retardation: A study of long-term morbidity. *Am. J. Obstet. Gynecol.* 142:670–677.

Lozoff, B., 1990. Has iron deficiency been shown to cause altered behavior in infants? In *Brain, Behavior and Iron in the Infant Diet*, J. Dobbing, ed. London: Springer-Verlag, pp. 107–131.

Lozoff, B., G. M. Brittenham, F. E. Viteri, A. W. Wolf, and J. J. Urrutia, 1982. The effects of short-term oral iron therapy on developmental deficits in iron-deficient anemic infants. *J. Pediatr.* 100:351–357.

Lozoff, B., G. M. Brittenham, A. W. Wolf, D. K. McClish, P. M. Kuhnert, E. Jimenez, R. Jimenez, L. A. Mora, I. Gomez, and D. Krauskoph, 1987. Iron-deficiency anemia and iron therapy: Effects on infant developmental test performance. *Pediatrics* 79:981–995.

Lozoff, B., N. K. Klein, E. C. Nelson, D. K. McClish, M. Manuel, and M. E. Chacon, 1998. Behavior of infants with iron-deficiency anemia. *Child Dev.* 69:24–36.

Lucas, A., 1997. Long-chain polyunsaturated fatty acids, infant feeding and cognitive development. In *Developing Brain and Behaviour*, J. Dobbing, ed. London: Academic Press, pp. 3–27.

MacLean, W. C., Jr., and J. D. Benson, 1989. Theory into practice: The incorporation of new knowledge into infant formula. *Sem. Perinatol.* 13:104–111.

Mangelsdorf, D. J., 1994. Vitamin A receptors. *Nutr. Rev.* 52:S32–S37.

McMorris, F. A., and M. Dubois-Dalcq, 1988. Insulin-like growth factor I promotes cell proliferation and oligodendroglial commitment in rat glial progenitor cells developing in vitro. *J. Neurosci. Res.* 21:199–209.

McNall, A., T. Etherton, and G. Fosmire, 1995. The impaired growth induced by zinc deficiency in rats is associated with decreased expression of hepatic insulin-like growth factor I and growth hormone receptor genes. *J. Nutr.* 125:874–879.

Mitchell, J. H., F. Nicol, G. J. Beckett, and J. R. Arthur, 1998. Selenoprotein expression and brain development in preweanling selenium and iodine deficient rats. *J. Mol. Endocrinol.* 20:203–210.

Morgane, P. J., R. Austin-LaFrance, J. Bronzino, J. Tonkiss, S. Diaz-Cintra, L. Cintra, T. Kemper, and J. R. Galler, 1993. Prenatal malnutrition and development of the brain. *Neurosci. Biobehav. Rev.* 17:91–128.

Morrow-Tlucak, M., R. H. Haude, and C. B. Ernhart, 1988. Breastfeeding and cognitive development in the first 2 years of life. *Soc. Sci. Med.* 26:625–639.

Neuringer, M., W. E. Connor, D. S. Lin, L. Barstad, and S. Luck, 1986. Biochemical and functional effects of prenatal and postnatal omega-3-fatty acid deficiency on retina and brain in rhesus monkeys. *Proc. Natl. Acad. Sci. USA* 83:4021–4025.

Nishijima, M., 1986. Somatomedin-C as a fetal growth promoting factor and amino acid composition of cord blood in Japanese neonates. *J. Perinatol. Med.* 14:163–166.

Nokes, C., C. van den Bosch, and D. A. P. Bundy, 1998. Infants and young children (6–24 months). In *A Report of the International Anemia Consultative Group: The Effects of Iron Deficiency and Anemia on Mental and Motor Performance, Educational Achievement and Behavior in Children. An Annotated Bibliography.* Washington, D.C., pp. 7–22.

Pleasure, J., and D. Pleasure, 1998. Trophic factor, nutritional and hormonal regulation of brain development. In *Fetal and Neonatal Physiology*, R. A. Polin and W. W. Fox, eds. Philadelphia: W.B. Saunders, pp. 2215–2226.

Pollitt, E., 1996. Timing and vulnerability in research on malnutrition and cognition. *Nutr. Rev.* 54:S49–S55.

Pollitt, E., and K. S. Gorman, 1994. Nutritional deficiencies as developmental risk factors. In *Threats to Optimal Development. The Minnesota Symposia on Child Psychology*, Vol. 27, C. A. Nelson, ed. Hillsdale, N.J.: Erlbaum Associates, pp. 121–144.

Pollitt, E., K. S. Gorman, P. L. Engle, R. Martorell, and J. Rivera, 1993. Early supplementary feeding and cognition: Effects over two decades. *Monogr. Soc. Res. Child Dev.* 58:1–99.

Pollitt, E., K. S. Gorman, P. L. Engle, J. A. Rivera, and R. Martorell, 1995. Nutrition in early life and the fulfillment of intellectual potential. *J. Nutr.* 125: S1111–S1118.

Pollitt, E., W. E. Watkins, and M. A. Husaini, 1997. Three-month nutritional supplementation in Indonesian infants and toddlers benefits memory function 8 Y later. *Am. J. Clin. Nutr.* 66:1357–1363.

Rao, R., M. deUngria, D. Sullivan, P. Wu, J. D. Wobken, C. A. Nelson, and M. K. Georgieff, 1999. Perinatal brain iron deficiency increases the vulnerability of rat hippocampus to hypoxic ischemic insult. *J. Nutr.* 129:199–206.

Roncagliolo, M., M. Garrido, T. Walter, P. Peirano, and B. Lozoff, 1998. Evidence of altered central nervous system development in infants with iron deficiency anemia at 6 mo: Delayed maturation of auditory brainstem responses. *Am. J. Clin. Nutr.* 68:683–690.

Sandstead, H. H., 1985. Zinc: Essentiality for brain development and function. *Nutr. Rev.* 43:129–137.

Sandstead, H. H., J. G. Penland, N. W. Alcock, and H. H. Dayal, 1998. Effects of repletion with zinc and other micronutrients on neuropsychologic performance and growth of Chinese children. *Am. J. Clin. Nutr.* 68:470S–475S.

Saneto, R. P., K. G. Low, M. H. Melner, and J. de Vellis, 1988. Insulin/insulin-like growth factor I and other epigenetic modulators of myelin basic protein expression in isolated oligodendrocyte progenitor cells. *J. Neurosci. Res.* 21:210–219.

Smith, C. D., and K. B. Ain, 1995. Brain metabolism in hypothyroidism studied with $^{31}$P magnetic-resonance spectroscopy. *Lancet* 345:619–620.

Spinillo, A., M. Stronati, A. Ometto, E. Fazzi, G. Lanzi, and S. Guaschino, 1993. Infant neurodevelopmental outcome in pregnancies complicated by gestational hypertension and intrauterine growth retardation. *J. Perinatol. Med.* 21:195–203.

Stein, Z., and M. Susser, 1985. Effects of early nutrition on neurological and mental competence in human beings. *Psychol. Med.* 15:717–726.

Strauss, R. S., and W. H. Dietz, 1998. Growth and development of term children born with low birth weight: Effects of genetic and environmental factors. *J. Pediatr.* 133:67–72.

Tejwani, G., and S. Hanissian, 1990. Modulation of mu, delta and kappa opioid receptors in rat brain by metal ions and histidine. *Neuropharmacology* 29:445–452.

Terhune, M. W., and H. H. Sandstead, 1972. Decreased RNA polymerase activity in mammalian zinc deficiency. *Science* 177:68–69.

THELANDER, L., 1990. Ribonucleotide reductase. In *Iron Transport and Storage*, P. Ponka, H. M. Schulman, and R. C. Woodworth, eds. Boca Raton, Fla.: CRC Press, pp. 193–200.

UAUY, R. D., D. G. BIRCH, E. E. BIRCH, J. E. TYSON, and D. R. HOFFMAN, 1990. Effect of dietary omega-3 fatty acids on retinal function of very-low-birth-weight neonates. *Pediatr. Res.* 28:485–492.

UAUY-DAGACH, R., and P. MENA, 1995. Nutritional role of omega-3 fatty acids during the perinatal period. *Clin. Perinatol.* 22:157–176.

VOLPE, J. J., 1995. Hypoglycemia and brain injury. In *Neurology of the Newborn*, 3rd. ed., J. J. Volpe, ed. Philadelphia: W.B. Saunders, pp. 467–489.

WALTER, T., J. KOWALSKYS, and A. STEKEL, 1983. Effect of mild iron deficiency on infant mental developmental scores. *J. Pediatr.* 102:519–522.

WANG, Y. S., and S. Y. WU, 1996. The effect of exclusive breast-feeding on development and incidence of infection in infants. *J. Hum. Lactation* 12:27–30.

WATANABE, C., and H. SATOH, 1994. Brain selenium status and behavioral development in selenium-deficient preweanling mice. *Physiol. Behav.* 56:927–932.

WIGGINS, R. C., G. FULLER, and S. J. ENNA, 1984. Undernutrition and the development of brain neurotransmitter systems. *Life Sci.* 35:2085–2094.

WINER, E. K., and N. TEJANI, 1994. Four- to seven-year evaluation in two groups of small-for-gestational-age infants. In *Obstetrical Events and Developmental Sequelae,* 2nd ed., N. Tejani, ed. Boca Raton, Fla.: CRC Press, pp. 77–94.

WINICK, M., and A. NOBEL, 1966. Cellular responses in rats during malnutrition at various ages. *J. Nutr.* 89:300–306.

WINICK, M., and P. ROSSO, 1969a. Head circumference and cellular growth of the brain in normal and marasmic children. *J. Pediatr.* 74:774–778.

WINICK, M., and P. ROSSO, 1969b. The effect of severe early malnutrition on cellular growth of the human brain. *Pediatr. Res.* 3:181–184.

YAMAMOTO, N., M. SAITOH, A. MORIUCHI, M. NOMURA, and H. OKUYAMA, 1987. Effect of dietary alpha-linolenate/linoleate balance on brain lipid compositions and learning ability of rats. *J. Lipid Res.* 28:144–151.

YOUDIM, M. B. H., D. BEN-SACHAR, and S. YEHUDA 1989. Putative biological mechanisms of the effect of iron deficiency on brain biochemistry and behavior. *Am. J. Clin. Nutr.* 50:607–612.

# 32 Fetal Alcohol Syndrome and Other Effects of Prenatal Alcohol: Developmental Cognitive Neuroscience Implications

ANN P. STREISSGUTH
AND PAUL D. CONNOR

ABSTRACT  The developmental cognitive neuroscience approach offers an important framework for understanding the complexities of fetal alcohol syndrome and other prenatal alcohol effects. While the genesis of this main dysfunction lies in alcohol exposure during the prenatal period, the neurobehavioral sequelae last throughout postnatal life, during which adverse social experiences can interact with prenatal brain damage to produce secondary disabilities. Animal, clinical, and epidemiologic studies have confirmed many types of neurodevelopmental deficits caused by prenatal alcohol exposure. The challenge for the future is to integrate these findings into a meaningful body of knowledge in order to identify and intervene with affected children, reduce secondary disabilities, and promote healthy and productive lives. The magnitude of the problem of fetal alcohol–affected youth makes this a challenge worth undertaking.

## Establishing the developmental cognitive neuroscience context for fetal alcohol syndrome

Fetal alcohol syndrome (FAS) is a birth defect caused by prenatal alcohol exposure, which produces a spectrum of lifelong effects on offspring depending on the dose, timing, and conditions of exposure. In this chapter, we review and explore the developmental cognitive neuroscience implications of FAS and other fetal alcohol effects (FAE). Although prenatal alcohol increases the rate of major congenital malformations, producing a variety of physical abnormalities including characteristic facial features in childhood, it is the consequences of brain maldevelopment that are of primary focus here.

ANN P. STREISSGUTH AND PAUL D. CONNOR  Fetal Alcohol and Drug Unit, Department of Psychiatry and Behavioral Sciences, University of Washington School of Medicine, Seattle, Washington.

Our clinical experience with hundreds of patients identified as FAS or FAE leads us to believe that child and adult psychopathology is an important outcome of alcohol teratogenesis, thus relating this work to the broader fields of psychology, psychiatry, and developmental disabilities (Streissguth, 1997; Streissguth and Kanter, 1997; Streissguth and O'Malley, 2000). Conceptualizing alcohol teratogenesis within the constructs of developmental cognitive neuroscience should provide a theoretical framework supporting the types of research that need to be undertaken in order to understand these phenomena scientifically and to meet the clinical needs of individuals of all ages who are themselves affected by prenatal alcohol exposure.

Cognitive neuroscience involves the union of cognitive psychology (the study of perception, attention, language, memory, and the organization of action) with neural science (the localization within the brain of various cognitive capabilities) (Kandel and Squire, 1992). Developmental cognitive neuroscience provides the lifespan context in which the processes of neural science produce the outcomes of cognitive psychology. This approach should help us understand child psychopathology as it emerges from insults to the brain during various stages of development. For children with FAS/FAE, the relevant period of primary damage is prior to birth, during the period of gestational development and organogenesis when the developing brain is particularly vulnerable to the teratogenic effects of alcohol. The reverberations of this damage persist throughout childhood, adolescence, and into adulthood.

As Harris (1998) notes, "The developmental perspective emphasizes maturation of the brain in the context of social experience, the environmental interface" (p. 166). For FAS/FAE, there is a vast literature documenting the biological impact of alcohol as a teratogen, but little scientific documentation of the environmental context as it interacts with the primary neurological disruption produced prenatally by the teratogenic effects of alcohol. The biological mothers of children with FAS/FAE have, by definition, been using or abusing alcohol during pregnancy. The literature on children of alcoholics reveals significant levels of child neglect, abuse, out-of-home placements, and so forth, which are important, but as yet unstudied, components of the environmental/biological interface as it relates to the developmental perspective on children with FAS/FAE.

The developmental perspective also involves ethology, the biology of behavior, in terms of the form and function of behavior throughout development and in terms of the comparisons among different species. Here we find exceptional richness in the science of prenatal alcohol damage, as thousands of experimental animal studies have documented not only the primary teratogenic insults of prenatal alcohol but also their developmental and behavioral consequences across the lifespan, all in the presence of normal postnatal rearing conditions and appropriate controls including pair-fed controls and cross-fostering of young. It is clear that the biological insult from prenatal alcohol exposure can last a lifetime and is not dependent on an adverse environment. It is less clear to what extent an adverse environment further compromises the behavior of a damaged brain or how an enriched environment might enhance development.

The developmental perspective also involves the processes of emotional regulation, emotional dysregulation, and the achievement of emotional competence. Harris (1998) notes that children with developmental disabilities who are physically and sexually abused are known to be at particularly high risk of dysfunctional regulation of emotion. Children with FAS/FAE are at high risk of abuse, yet emotional regulation has not been a popularly studied outcome. Harris concludes "that for the developmentally disabled child, difficulties in emotion regulation are a particular concern because neurobiological, psychological, and environmental factors may interact in ways that lead to emotional dysregulation" (p. 211).

Although we know little about the neural processes underlying higher cognitive functions, we know clinically that even when failing to qualify as mentally retarded or developmentally disabled, individuals with FAS/FAE often fail to integrate learned information in order to function in an adaptive and independent fashion appropriate to their developmental stage. These are often called "executive functions."

Some data are available on prenatal alcohol's impact on cognitive development and executive function, but little is available on the social aspects of cognition. Yet it is the social aspects of cognition that appear most challenging to individuals with FAS/FAE as they mature (Streissguth et al., 1991). The developmental trajectory from cognitive dysfunction to maladaptive behavior to mental illness has been insufficiently explored in the research literature, although the vast majority of patients with FAS/FAE are thought by their caretakers to have mental health problems and are taken to mental health practitioners for help.

These covarying influences are far from resolved in child development research in general and in the study of alcohol teratogenesis in particular. But it is important for investigators of the postnatal conditions associated with developmental problems also to consider covarying prenatal conditions, of which the most significant in terms of magnitude is prenatal alcohol exposure.

The cognitive neuroscience of FAS and FAE is focused, of course, on understanding the neural basis of damage to the brain during prenatal development. But the developmental perspective demands that the behavioral, cognitive, and emotional outcomes be considered in the context of the broader postnatal environment, and across the entire developmental trajectory from infancy to old age. Accomplishing this will require interdisciplinary research and the integration of outcomes from both experimental animal and human studies.

FAS and FAE have tremendous implications for developmental cognitive neuroscience because alcohol is a known teratogen, affecting the developing embryo and fetus during gestation and producing consequences that influence offspring development and behavior throughout the lifespan. Unlike many other developmental disabilities for which the cause is unknown, experimental animal models of prenatal alcohol damage have been important contributors to our understanding of the central nervous system (CNS) effects of prenatal alcohol exposure in humans, and to our understanding of alcohol as a teratogen. On the other hand, children with FAS are also different from children with clear genetically linked developmental disabilities (e.g. Down syndrome, fragile X) and even from other malformation syndromes with known teratogenic causes (e.g., thalidomide, fetal hydantoin syndrome). One reason for this difference is that the teratogen (alcohol) that produces the damage to the developing embryo and fetus can also produce a dysfunctional rearing environment for the developing child.

In our work we think of the teratogenic CNS effects of alcohol as the primary disabilities and the apparent consequences of postnatal rearing conditions as the secondary disabilities. In this context, we find that the environmental conditions associated with secondary disabilities in our patients are those that ethological researchers consider primary and causative (e.g., physical and sexual abuse, neglect). Without a careful prenatal history, these two cannot be untangled. Because child abuse and neglect are more carefully recorded in social service documents than are prenatal alcohol exposure and maternal alcoholism, the teratogenic consequences of alcohol often masquerade as consequences of the shortcoming in the postnatal environment that lead to out-of-home placements (e.g., child abuse and neglect).

Here we review briefly the historical context of prenatal alcohol research and current diagnostic nomenclature, summarize the data verifying alcohol as a teratogen, and review the data documenting prenatal alcohol effects on the developing CNS in children. The brain/behavior consequences of prenatal alcohol damage, as understood from both animal and human studies, are discussed, and finally, clinical aspects of this knowledge for the developing child and adult.

As the estimated incidence of FAS is 1–3 per 1000 live births and the estimated prevalence of other clinically significant FAE is 2–3 times greater (NIAAA, 1990), FAS/FAE is clearly a significant topic for the whole field of developmental cognitive neuroscience.

## Discovering and diagnosing FAS and other prenatal alcohol effects

Prior to 1973 there was no general awareness that prenatal alcohol exposure had any associated risks. The report in an international medical journal of seven young, unrelated children with an apparent dysmorphic syndrome and associated central nervous system damage, all born to alcoholic mothers, was a surprising event (Jones et al., 1973). The second report appeared a few months later, naming the syndrome "fetal alcohol syndrome" and showing photographs of a newborn infant identified at birth, and the malformed brain of a second identified infant who died shortly after birth (Jones and Smith, 1973). A third study, fortuitously made possible by access to data from the National Perinatal Collaborative Project, revealed that, compared with nonalcoholic mothers of very similar backgrounds ($n = 46$), the children of alcoholic mothers ($n = 23$) had much worse outcomes, including a fourfold increase in low IQ scores (IQ < 75) and an eightfold increase in perinatal mortality. Children ret-

rospectively identified as having FAS based on blind chart reviews occurred only among offspring of mothers who had been identified as alcoholics by other reviewers doing blind chart reviews (Jones et al., 1974).

Historical research revealed a number of previous references in the medical literature to children who appeared to have had FAS, who were born to alcoholic mothers (Streissguth, 1997)—including one in the French language describing 120 children born to alcoholic mothers (Lemoine et al., 1968)—who had similar appearance and comportment to those described by Jones and colleagues.

The diagnosis of FAS includes three main characteristics identified in face, growth, and brain. The facial features (figure 32.1) involve a specific pattern of minor facial anomalies, including short palpebral fissures (the length of the eye slits), an indistinct philtrum (the ridges running between the nose and the mouth), a narrow upper lip, and a flat midface. The growth characteristics include prenatal onset growth deficiency for height and/or weight. The CNS characteristics involve brain damage or dysfunction, including such characteristics as microcephaly, seizures, mental retardation, fine or gross motor problems, tremulousness, hyperactivity, and poor attention spans (Clarren and Smith 1978; Jones, 1986).

Eye anomalies include ptosis (drooping eyelid) and strabismus (crossed eye), tortuosity of the retinal vessels, and hypoplasia of the optic nerve. Near-sightedness is the most common vision problem, followed by cataracts (Strömland, Miller, and Cook, 1991; Strömland and Pinazo-Duran, 1994). Low-set, malformed, and posteriorially rotated ears are sometimes noted. Functional hearing problems, thought to be of central auditory origin, but possibly related to structural abnormalities of the auditory canal, are very prevalent in children with FAS/FAE (Church and Kaltenbach, 1997).

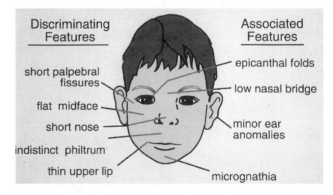

FIGURE 32.1 Diagram of the face of fetal alcohol syndrome in the young child. (From Streissguth and Little, 1994, with permission.)

Some of the differentiating characteristics of diagnostic significance in young children diminish with approaching puberty (figure 32.2). These include the short nose, the small chin, and excessive thinness. In early adolescence, females may increase body weight and their weight-to-height ratio significantly; males may show a similar increase later in adolescence or in young adulthood (Streissguth, Clarren, and Jones, 1985; Streissguth et al., 1991). Diagnosis after puberty is often difficult, but the CNS manifestations of FAS do not attenuate with age (Aronson, 1997; Lemoine and Lemoine, 1992; Löser, Bierstedt, and Blum, 1999; Spohr and Steinhausen, 1996; Streissguth et al., 1991)

Several attempts have been made to codify the necessary diagnostic criteria for FAS for research purposes (Rosett, 1980; Sokol and Clarren, 1989) or for a clinical case definition (Astley and Clarren, 1999). The Institute of Medicine (IOM, 1996) made recommendations for some changes in the nomenclature for alcohol-related birth defects, including introducing the term *alcohol-related neurodevelopmental disorder* (ARND), which was suggested for individuals having clinical conditions

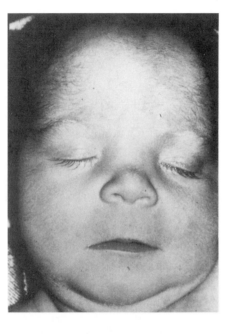
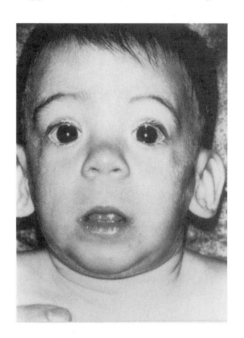
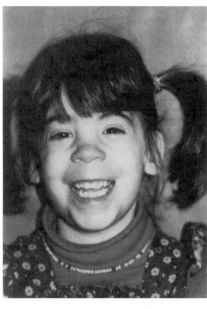

FIGURE 32.2    Photographs of individuals with FAS from childhood to adulthood. (From Streissguth et al., 1991. © 1991, AMA.)

involving CNS abnormalities or dysfunctions that research has linked to maternal alcohol ingestion. "Evidence of a complex pattern of behavior or cognitive abnormalities that are inconsistent with developmental level and cannot be explained by familial background or environment alone, such as learning difficulties; deficits in school performance; poor impulse control; problems in social perception; deficits in higher level receptive and expressive language; poor capacity for abstraction or metacognition; specific deficits in mathematical skills; or problems in memory, attention, or judgment" (IOM, 1996, p.77). There is general awareness that full-blown FAS is only part of the full spectrum of fetal alcohol disorders, but less agreement on diagnostic nomenclature for individuals who are significantly exposed but lack the full FAS. The importance of continuing to study the non-FAS components of the fetal alcohol spectrum disorders is illustrated by recent findings from our population-based longitudinal prospective study in Seattle: The incidence of FAS in a 1974/75 birth cohort of approximately 500 offspring of 1529 unselected women in prenatal care by the fifth month of pregnancy, was 3 per 1000 live births. The prevalence of ARND, determined by repeat psychological and behavioral examinations during the first 7 years of life, was 6 per 1000, resulting in an overall rate of FAS/ARND of nearly 1 per 100 live births (Sampson et al., 1997).

As used in this chapter the term *fetal alcohol effects*, or *FAE* (Clarren and Smith, 1978; Hanson, Streissguth, and Smith, 1978), refers to patients with known prenatal exposure to significant alcohol, who have been examined by a dysmorphologist, and have some characteristics of FAS, but not enough for a full diagnosis.

## Verifying alcohol as a teratogen

As maternal alcoholism is confounded by a variety of psychosocial conditions that could also affect child development, an important starting place was to establish whether it was the alcohol or the lifestyle characteristics of the mother that was responsible for the damage to the offspring. Controlled experiments on laboratory animals were an essential component of this investigation.

By 1980, it was clear that heavy doses of alcohol, administered to a variety of laboratory animals throughout pregnancy, produced all four known teratogenic endpoints: death (absorptions—the rodent equivalent of miscarriage) (Chernoff, 1977), malformations (Randall and Taylor, 1979), growth deficiency (Ellis and Pick, 1980), and functional deficits (Martin et al., 1977a). During the 1980s the focus was on the exposure

parameters and the specificity of effects. In general, animal studies indicated that it is ethanol, not the type of alcoholic beverage consumed, that causes the damage. Although alcohol dehydrogenase, a metabolite of alcohol, is also teratogenic, there is a measurable direct effect of ethanol itself. Furthermore, ethanol is teratogenic during any of the three trimesters of pregnancy.

Teratogenic effects are a function of the dose, timing, and conditions of exposure (Wilson and Fraser, 1977). In some studies utilizing a third-trimester model, massed alcohol (as in a binge-drinking pattern) produced more offspring effects than the same amount of alcohol spread evenly throughout the 24-hour period (Clarren et al., 1992; Goodlett and West, 1992). Some of the lower doses studied have produced neurochemical and behavioral outcomes, consistent with theory in terms of functional or behavioral teratology (Riley and Vorhees, 1986; Wilson, 1977). Brain damage from prenatal alcohol can occur without accompanying physical manifestations and from lower doses and frequency of exposure than appear necessary for dysmorphologic effects. Behavioral consequences of prenatal alcohol exposure are measurable at all developmental stages including old age (Dumas and Rabe, 1994; Riley, 1990). Individual differences in mother and offspring modify the effects of prenatal exposure in the individual embryo and fetus in terms of the type and severity of offspring effect (Chernoff, 1980; Streissguth and Dehaene, 1993).

By the 1990s several mechanisms for the teratogenic action of alcohol were clearly established (Randall, Ekblad, and Anton, 1990; Schenker et al., 1990). Prenatal alcohol has a direct toxic effect on cells and can produce cell death; alcohol can impede the transport of amino acids, impair placental–fetal blood flow causing hypoxia, and derange hormone and chemical regulatory systems that control the maturation and migration of nerve cells in brain (Michaelis and Michaelis, 1994).

## Neurodevelopmental consequences of prenatal alcohol exposure in humans and laboratory animals

Epidemiological studies of prenatal alcohol consumption and its consequences began in 1974 under the auspices of the newly funded National Institute on Alcohol Abuse and Alcoholism. Although a few studies were retrospective, most were prospective, in that they began during pregnancy with self-reports of maternal alcohol use, and then measured offspring outcomes at birth. Some were both prospective and longitudinal, and offspring were examined at specific developmental stages as they matured. The first studies were undertaken in

Boston (Ouellette et al., 1977; Rosett et al., 1979) and Seattle (Streissguth et al., 1981, 1993). Others have followed in Cleveland, Pittsburgh (Day, 1992), and Detroit (Jacobson et al., 1993a,b). One study was carried out in northern France (Larroque et al., 1995; Larroque et al., 2000; Larroque and Kaminski, 1998). The populations involved and the drinking habits and life circumstances of the mothers in these various studies differed greatly. These large-sample follow-up studies (sometimes involving hundreds of offspring with prenatal exposure information) were able to control or adjust for many potentially confounding factors (such as length of prenatal care, race, socioeconomic status, parental education, life stress, nutrition, medications, and other drug use) either through study design or through statistical analysis.

In studies examining children of drinking or alcohol-abusing mothers and suitable control groups, alcohol-related offspring outcomes in the domain of cognition are observed in the first few postnatal days. In the neonatal period, the findings include disruptions in typical sleep/wake cycles (Rosett et al., 1979; Scher et al., 1988); atypical EEG patterns (Ioffe and Chernick, 1988); poor state regulation and arousal (Sander et al., 1977; Streissguth, Barr, and Martin, 1983); poor operant conditioning (Martin et al., 1977b); weak Moro reflex, hypertonic passive arms reflex, hypertonic incurvation reflex, and delayed stepping reflex threshold (Streissguth et al., 1993); and increased time with eyes open but not attending, bodily tremors, head turns to the left, hand-to-face activity, and decreased vigorous bodily activity (Landesman-Dwyer, Keller, and Streissguth, 1978).

Many similarities exist between the neurobehavioral sequelae observed in animal models of prenatal alcohol exposure and those documented in human clinical or epidemiological studies (Driscoll, Streissguth, and Riley, 1990). For example, both clinical and animal studies report a weak suck and longer latency to initiate suckling after exposure to the nipple (Chen et al., 1982; Martin et al., 1979; Rockwood and Riley, 1986). Poor habituation, an important cross-species sign of CNS dysfunction, is another. Maternal alcohol use during pregnancy was related to poor habituation among neonates responding to redundant visual and auditory stimuli on day 1 of life (Streissguth, Barr, and Martin, 1983) and to neonatal rat pups responding to olfactory stimuli (Barron, Gagnon, and Riley, 1986). These neonatal CNS findings have particular relevance because they are manifested prior to contact with the home environment. The animal studies are particularly relevant for understanding the neurobiology of postnatal neurocognitive deficits because in animal models the offspring are cross-fostered to avoid postnatal confounding of prenatal teratogenic effects.

Later infancy outcomes associated with prenatal alcohol exposure have included lower mental and/or motor scores and feeding problems (Streissguth et al., 1980; Jacobson et al., 1993b; Larroque and Kaminski, 1998) as well as less efficient information processing and lower scores on elicited play (Jacobson et al., 1993a). Neurological and motor coordination problems (balance and fine motor coordination) have been associated with prenatal alcohol in young children (Barr et al., 1990; Kyllerman et al., 1985; Larroque et al., 2000) and in young rats (gait and balance) (Meyer, Kotch, and Riley, 1990; Goodlett et al., 1991). New data from our unit indicate that motor coordination problems (balance, fine motor coordination) continue into adulthood in patients with FAS and FAE (Connor et al., 2000).

Attention problems, measured with vigilance and CPT tasks (Streissguth et al., 1984, 1986, 1994b, 1995) as well as naturalistic observations (Landesman-Dwyer, Ragozin, and Little, 1981), have been associated with prenatal alcohol exposure in Seattle studies involving two different populations of children. Errors of omission (EO), errors of commission (EC), ratio of correct responses to total responses, and mean reaction time were all related to prenatal alcohol in young children. However, in older children, EC showed a stronger relationship to prenatal alcohol, particularly on the AX task of the CPT which requires withholding a response. Following reports that reaction time variability is a sensitive long-term sequela of closed head injuries (Stuss et al., 1989), we reanalyzed all our vigilance data using standard deviation of reaction time (SDRT), which proved to be the most salient attention score for prenatal alcohol in laboratory vigilance tests at 4, 7, and 14 years of age (Streissguth et al., 1994b, 1995). Reliable cross-age and cross-task consistency has been observed in attention deficits, measured over a 10-year period, with both laboratory vigilance tasks and laboratory behavior ratings, and with classroom ratings by teachers (Carmichael Olson et al., 1992; Streissguth et al., 1995). Brown and colleagues (1991) and Russell and colleagues (1991) have also found laboratory attention measures associated with prenatal alcohol exposure. Our recent research describes the relative importance of auditory versus visual attention and the broad range of individual differences in attentional errors across time (Connor et al., 1999). Because hyperactivity was one of the earliest-noted behavioral manifestations of FAS in clinical observations, many rodent studies have documented offspring hyperactivity produced by prenatal alcohol exposure (Driscoll, Streissguth, and Riley,

1990; Martin et al., 1978; Shaywitz, Griffieth, and Warshaw, 1979).

Learning deficits, particularly for arithmetic, have been associated with prenatal alcohol exposure in several studies, and across several ages, in the Seattle study (Sampson et al., 1989; Streissguth et al., 1993, 1994a). Deficits in spatial memory (stepping-stone maze), visual memory and integration (recalling and copying designs and block designs), verbal memory and integration (recalling stories and digits), auditory memory (seashore rhythm test), flexible problem solving (progressive figures test), and perceptual motor function were related to prenatal alcohol exposure at the 7-year and/or 14-year examinations (Sampson et al., 1989; Streissguth et al., 1989, 1994b). Prenatal alcohol-related learning deficits have also been demonstrated in controlled experiments with laboratory animals, particularly with respect to response inhibition. Young rats continued to run into the arms of the maze where they had been previously shocked, and continued to run into arms of the maze where the food used to be even though it was no longer available there (Riley, Barron, and Hannigan, 1986; Riley, Lochry, and Shapiro, 1979; Riley et al., 1979). In a classic study of prenatal alcohol–related learning deficits, chick embryos were injected with alcohol in dosages not high enough to cause physical malformations. When examined in a detour learning task in which they had to find a nondirect route to get to a source of food, the alcohol-exposed chicks performed much more poorly than the controls (Means, Burnette, and Pennington, 1988).

Several studies of children and adolescents with FAS/FAE have also demonstrated learning problems involving planning and problem solving deficits. On the Wisconsin Card Sort Test (WCST) or a tower planning test, they often have poorer performance compared to controls; specifically, they correctly identified fewer categories and made more perseverative errors (Carmichael Olson et al., 1998; Coles et al., 1997; Kodituwakku et al., 1995). In the latter study, the adolescents with FAS made an exceptionally high percentage of card-sorting errors, even compared to an IQ-matched comparison group. However the WCST was not a strong outcome for adolescents in our social drinking study. Recent work from our unit indicates increased frequency of bizarre responses (e.g., the length of a dollar bill is 12 inches) in adolescents and adults with FAS (Carmichael Olson et al., 1998; Kopera-Frye, Dehaene, and Streissguth, 1996) and continuing executive function deficits into adulthood (Connor et al., in press).

Studies of the damaging effects of prenatal alcohol in animal models have also focused on socialization impairments. A recent paper (Kelly, Day, and Streissguth, 2000) examines the comparability of human and animal research in this context. Prenatally exposed male rats displayed longer latency periods to achieve appropriate sexually specific behaviors such as mounting and copulation (Barron, Tieman, and Riley, 1988). Prenatally exposed female rats showed impairments in appropriate maternal behaviors, such as inferior quality of nest building, increased latency to retrieve a pup that had strayed from the nest, and poor retrieval behaviors when searching for and returning pups to the nest (Hård et al., 1985). Several studies using The Vineland Adaptive Behavior Scale have shown marked socialization and adaptive behavior problems in children and adults with FAS/FAE (Streissguth et al., 1991; Thomas et al., 1996). Aronson (1997) and Streissguth and colleagues (1997) also found that psychosocial problems were exacerbated when alcohol-affected individuals were raised in poor environments. Clinical research on our unit is documenting the types of problems that mothers with FAS/FAE are experiencing in raising their children, and the types of help and community support they need to avoid inadvertent child abuse and neglect (Grant et al., 1997). Early-onset alcohol use and abuse in offspring is another consequence of prenatal alcohol exposure that has been explored both in humans (Baer et al., 1998) and in animal models (Molina et al., 1999).

## Necropsy and brain studies in humans and animals

Since the first clinical reports of children with FAS, much attention has been focused on the damaging effects of prenatal alcohol exposure on the brain. Initial study focused on autopsy findings from children exposed to high levels of alcohol during pregnancy who died shortly after birth. The first autopsy report by Jones and Smith of an infant with FAS showed an unusually small brain with abnormal cell migration patterns, agyria (incomplete development of the cortex), enlarged ventricles, and agenesis of the corpus callosum (Jones and Smith, 1973, 1975). Clarren and colleagues (1978) reported autopsy results from four infants who were exposed to heavy doses of alcohol in utero. They found heterotopias, disorganization of cell migration, abnormalities in cerebellum development, dysplastic brainstems, and hydrocephalus in several infants. Majewski (1993) reviewed 16 published brain dissections of FAS cases, and found 10 microdysplasias and heterotopias and 5 severe brain malformations, including 3 cases with hydrocephalus, 4 cases with cerebellar hypoplasia, and 3 cases with callosal agenesis. Kovetskii and colleagues (1991) examined 44 embryos and one fetus from women whose prenatal alcohol exposure was known. Brain pathology was found in 100% (10/10) of the progeny of alcoholic mothers, with decreasing frequency in mothers reporting less frequent use.

Initial autopsy studies of infants with FAS led animal researchers to assess regions of brain damage in an animal analog of FAS. The hippocampus and cerebellum were among the first regions investigated. In one such early study (West, Hodges, and Black, 1981), rats were ethanol-exposed between gestational days 1 and 21. When the hippocampi were examined, exposed pups displayed hypertrophied mossy fibers whereas none of the control rats showed this finding. Later rat studies (Goodlett et al., 1992) documented actual cell loss in hippocampal mossy fibers caused by early postnatal ethanol exposure (which for rats is equivalent to gestational exposure during the third trimester in humans). Significant reductions in cerebellar weight compared with control pups were also demonstrated in rat pups exposed to ethanol early in this third trimester equivalent model (Meyer, Kotch, and Riley, 1990). Macaques on several prenatal dosing regimes had a dose-dependent reduction in the number of Purkinje cells in the cerebellum (Bonthius et al., 1996).

Numerous other types of brain anomalies have been produced in experimental animal models of prenatal alcohol exposure. Smaller and thinner corpora callosa have been produced by ethanol exposure on the sixth gestational day (Zimmerberg and Mickus, 1990), and it has been postulated that this reduction could be related to damage to myelin development, another outcome of prenatal ethanol exposure described by Phillips (1992) and Phillips and Krueger (1992). Neural crest cell death was studied in chick embryos exposed to a single dose of alcohol at different times during gestation (Cartwright and Smith, 1995). Various subpopulations of neural crest cells were damaged depending on the timing of exposure. Other prenatal alcohol studies in rodents have described alterations in the generation and migration of cortical neurons (Kotkoskie and Norton, 1989; Miller, 1986), as well as massive nerve cell death during synaptogenesis (Ikonomidou et al., 2000).

With the development of modern neuroimaging techniques, it has become possible to study brain structures in vivo in patients prenatally exposed to alcohol. Mattson and colleagues (1996) examined six children and adolescents with FAS using volumetric assessment of magnetic resonance imaging. The cerebral vault, the cerebellar vault, the basal ganglia, and the diencephalon were reduced significantly in volume compared to controls. The basal ganglia, and especially the caudate nucleus, were significantly reduced even when controlling for the degree of microcephaly.

A substantial reduction in the area of the anterior vermis of the cerebellum was found in children with heavy prenatal alcohol exposure (Sowell et al., 1996). (Of nine exposed patients, seven fell below the lowest of 25 controls. The two in the control range included one FAS and one FAE.) Frank agenesis of the corpus callosum was seen in three of 12 children with heavy prenatal alcohol exposure, including two without FAS. Overall in the FAS/FAE literature, 12 patients with callosal agenesis have been reported so far, suggesting that prenatal alcohol may be the leading known cause of agenesis of the corpus callosum (Riley et al., 1995).

Using morphometric methods to study shape variability in MR images of the brain, Bookstein and colleagues (in press) have revealed striking variability of callosal shape and of shape and orientation of the brain stem in adults with FAS/FAE compared with controls. These methods of MRI quantification permitted a powerful separation of exposed versus nonexposed in a sample of 90 males and females; they show promise of improving the diagnostic process with more direct relevance for neurodevelopmental processes and without separation of FAS from FAE.

## Associating structure and function

Only a few studies have linked deviations in brain structure due to prenatal alcohol exposure with functional deficits in the same animals or children. Most of these brain/behavior studies have employed animal models, but they have involved several different brain regions. Abel and colleagues (Abel, Jacobson, and Sherwin, 1983) found that rats exposed to ethanol throughout pregnancy showed structural brain changes that were linked with behavioral deficits. These animals had both disruption of the dendritic pattern of the hippocampal neurons and difficulty learning to avoid places where they had previously been shocked. In another study, optic nerve hypoplasia caused by prenatal alcohol exposure was associated with impaired vision in both rat models and humans (Strömland and Pinazo-Durán, 1994). Meyer and colleagues (1990) administered ethanol to rat pups early in the postnatal period, which resulted in reduced cerebellar size (especially in the anterior vermal region). This anatomical abnormality was associated with difficulties traversing a parallel bar pathway. Rat pups exposed to alcohol prenatally also showed reduction in the size of the corpus callosum compared with controls (Zimmerberg and Mickus, 1990). Those who had reduced callosal size were more hyperactive than controls in open field tests. In another study, female rats that were exposed to alcohol throughout pregnancy showed deficits in instinctive maternal behaviors including latency to retrieve pups and poor retrieval behaviors. When the brain chemistry of these prenatally exposed, maternally impaired rats was studied, there was a decrease of seratonin synthesis (Hård et al., 1985).

In human studies of other neurologically impaired populations including individuals with head injury, stroke, and other developmental disorders, it is becoming increasingly common to see research focusing on the relationship between structural changes and behavioral or neuropsychological deficits (Gabrielli et al., 1990; Johnson et al., 1994). We currently are aware of only one published abstract focusing on structure/function relationships in humans with FAS and FAE (Bookstein et al., 1999). Compared to age- and sex-matched controls, adult males with FAS/FAE had more variability in the thickness of the corpus callosum, and thickness and thinness were each related to different patterns of neuropsychological deficit.

## Relevance of the developmental cognitive neuroscience approach to understanding FAS

The rich animal literature on the capacity of alcohol to derail prenatal brain development, and the lasting postnatal behavioral consequences of these prenatal disruptions provides ample demonstration of a biological basis for the primary CNS dysfunctions observed in patients with FAS. Hyperactivity, inattention, memory problems, visual and auditory perceptual disorders, perseverations, temper tantrums, behavioral dysregulation including eating and sleeping disorders, fine and gross motor problems, and learning problems are all well documented outcomes of varying levels of prenatal alcohol exposure. The CNS impairments associated with prenatal alcohol exposure are not restricted to children of alcoholic mothers, and cover a broad range of prenatal exposure levels. Moreover, alcohol-affected individuals demonstrate these impairments as children, adolescents, and adults (Aronson, 1997; Aronson and Olegård, 1987; Aronson et al., 1985; Spohr and Steinhausen, 1996; Streissguth, 1997; Streissguth et al., 1991), and can experience IQ deficits and/or neuropsychological deficits even without having the growth deficiency or face of FAS (Mattson et al., 1997, 1998; Sampson et al., 1989, 1994). The neuropsychiatric implications of these fetal alcohol spectrum disorders are enormous (Streissguth and O'Malley, 2000).

What is less clear is how postnatal social experience interacts with prenatal brain insult (the primary disability) in determining postnatal functional and behavioral disruption. Here, two mechanisms seem plausible: One is the possibility that adverse postnatal rearing conditions exacerbate the primary disabilities arising from the organic insult, and increase the likelihood of secondary disabilities; the other is the possibility that even good postnatal environments may fail to provide the specialized learning experiences necessary to ensure that children with these primary organic disabilities develop their best potential and escape secondary disabilities.

Data from our secondary disabilities study (Streissguth et al., 1996, 1997) lend some support to the first possibility, but there are not yet any data to support the second possibility. Patients with FAS/FAE experience high rates of adverse environmental conditions that are associated with the original etiology of their organic brain damage, namely maternal alcohol use during pregnancy. They have high rates (80%) of not being raised by their biological mothers, high rates of out-of-home placements, and frequent household changes. High rates of such adverse environmental experiences are associated with higher rates of secondary disabilities, including major disruptions of schooling, trouble with the law, alcohol and drug problems, and mental health problems (Streissguth et al., 1996, 1997). On the other hand, very few of the patients we now study as adolescents and adults have had specialized interventions for their primary disabilities. There are no data, except for occasional anecdotal reports, on how intervention might facilitate the development of children with prenatal alcohol-related disabilities.

Research is urgently needed, not only on interventions to optimize developmental outcomes in children born with prenatal brain damage from alcohol, but also to improve the community response to the environmental insults to which these children are also vulnerable.

In summary, the intense research of the past 26 years has successfully established the organic basis for the primary CNS dysfunctions observed in individuals of all ages with FAS/FAE. The teratogenicity of alcohol has been well established, and the linkage between prenatal brain damage caused by alcohol and the resulting behavioral disruptions is being elucidated.

The magnitude of the problem of FAS/FAE and the serious societal consequences of associated secondary disabilities demand more research and community effort. The problem of understanding the presence of executive function deficits in people who are not mentally retarded poses severe challenges to the institutions that have traditionally dealt with the developmentally disabled. Organically based problems in judgment, reasoning and adaptive functioning must be further evaluated as precursors of serious secondary disabilities that can further incapacitate these children as they mature.

Finally, due to the often familial nature of alcoholism, efforts to develop effective interventions in each generation of affected offspring also can serve as prevention strategies. The accomplishment of such work will fulfill the promise of developmental cognitive neuroscience.

ACKNOWLEDGMENTS This work was funded by the National Institute on Alcohol Abuse and Alcoholism, grant numbers R37/AA01455-01-25 and R01/AA10836-01-05 and by the Centers for Disease Control and Prevention, grant number R04/CCR008515-01-04 to A. P. Streissguth. We thank Fred Bookstein, Paul Sampson, and Helen Barr for critiquing an earlier draft of this chapter. And we are grateful to Carole Lambert, Shae Richardson, and Cara Ernst for technical assistance.

# REFERENCES

ABEL, E. L., S. JACOBSON, and B. T. SHERWIN, 1983. In utero alcohol exposure: Functional and structural brain damage. *Neurobehav. Toxicol. Teratol.* 5(3):363–366.

ARONSON, M., 1997. Children of alcoholic mothers: Results from Goteborg, Sweden. In *The Challenge of Fetal Alcohol Syndrome: Overcoming Secondary Disabilities*, A. P. Streissguth and J. Kanter, eds. Seattle: University of Washington Press, pp. 15–24.

ARONSON, M., M. KYLLERMAN, K. G. SABEL, B. SANDIN, and R. OLEGÅRD, 1985. Children of alcoholic mothers: Developmental, perceptual and behavioural characteristics as compared to matched controls. *Acta Paediatr. Scand.* 74(1):27–35.

ARONSON, M., and R. OLEGÅRD, 1987. Children of alcoholic mothers. *Pediatrician* 14(1–2):57–61.

ASTLEY, S. J., and S. K. CLARREN, 1999. *Diagnostic Guide for FAS and Related Conditions: The 4-Digit Diagnostic Code*, 2nd ed. Seattle: FAS Diagnostic and Prevention Network, University of Washington.

BAER, J. S., H. M. BARR, F. L. BOOKSTEIN, P. D. SAMPSON, and A. P. STREISSGUTH, 1998. Prenatal alcohol exposure and family history of alcoholism in the etiology of adolescent alcohol problems. *J. Stud. Alcohol.* 59:533–543.

BARR, H. M., A. P. STREISSGUTH, B. L. DARBY, and P. D. SAMPSON, 1990. Prenatal exposure to alcohol, caffeine, tobacco, and aspirin: Effects on fine and gross motor performance in 4-year-old children. *Dev. Psychol.* 26(3):339–348.

BARRON, S., W. GAGNON, and E. P. RILEY, 1986. The effects of prenatal alcohol exposure on respiration rate and response to a novel odor in neonatal rats. *Soc. Neurosci. Abstr.* 12:51.

BARRON, S., S. TIEMAN, and E. P. RILEY, 1988. Effects of prenatal alcohol exposure on the sexually dimorphic nucleus of the preoptic area of the hypothalamus in male and female rats. *Alcohol Clin. Exp. Res.* 12(1):59–64.

BONTHIUS, D. J., N. E. BONTHIUS, R. M. A. NAPPER, S. J. ASTLEY, S. K. CLARREN, and J. R. WEST, 1996. Purkinje cell deficits in nonhuman primates following weekly exposure to ethanol during gestation. *Teratology* 53:230–236.

BOOKSTEIN, F. L., P. D. SAMPSON, A. P. STREISSGUTH, and P. D. CONNOR, in press. Geometric morphometrics of corpus callosum and subcortical structures in the fetal-alcohol-affected brain. *Teratology.*

BOOKSTEIN, F. L., A. P. STREISSGUTH, P. D. SAMPSON, P. D. CONNOR, and H. M. BARR, 1999. Corpus callosum shape and neuropsychological deficits in adult males with heavy fetal alcohol exposure. *Alcohol Clin. Exp. Res.* 23(5):28A.

BROWN, R. T., C. D. COLES, I. E. SMITH, K. A. PLATZMAN, J. SILVERSTEIN, S. ERICKSON, and A. FALEK, 1991. Effects of prenatal alcohol exposure at school age: II. Attention and behavior. *Neurotoxicol. Teratol.* 13(4):369–376.

CARMICHAEL OLSON, H., J. J. FELDMAN, A. P. STREISSGUTH, P. D. SAMPSON, and F. L. BOOKSTEIN, 1998. Neuropsychological deficits in adolescents with fetal alcohol syndrome: Clinical findings. *Alcohol Clin. Exp. Res.* 22:1998–2012.

CARMICHAEL OLSON, H., P. D. SAMPSON, H. M. BARR, A. P. STREISSGUTH, F. L. BOOKSTEIN, 1992. Prenatal exposure to alcohol and school problems in late childhood: A longitudinal prospective study. *Dev. Psychopathol.* 4:341–359.

CARTWRIGHT, M. M., and S. M. SMITH, 1995. Stage-dependent effects of ethanol on cranial neural crest cell development: Partial basis for the phenotypic variations observed in fetal alcohol syndrome. *Alcohol Clin. Exp. Res.* 19(6):1454–1462.

CHEN, J., C. DRISCOLL, and E. P. RILEY, 1982. Ontogeny of suckling behavior in rats exposed to alcohol prenatally. *Teratology* 26:145–153.

CHERNOFF, G. F., 1977. The fetal alcohol syndrome in mice: An animal model. *Teratology* 15(3):223–229.

CHERNOFF, G. F., 1980. The fetal alcohol syndrome in mice: Maternal variables. *Teratology* 22:71–75.

CHURCH, M. W., and J. A. KALTENBACH, 1997. Hearing, speech, language and vestibular disorders in the fetal alcohol syndrome: A literature review. *Alcohol Clin. Exp. Res.* 21:495–512.

CLARREN, S. K., E. C. ALVORD, S. M. SUMI, A. P. STREISSGUTH, and D. W. SMITH, 1978. Brain malformations related to prenatal exposure to ethanol. *J. Pediatr.* 92(1):64–67.

CLARREN, S. K., S. J. ASTLEY, V. M. GUNDERSON, and D. SPELLMAN, 1992. Cognitive and behavioral deficits in nonhuman primates associated with very early embryonic binge exposures to ethanol. *J Pediatr.* 121:789–796.

CLARREN, S. K., and D. W. SMITH, 1978. The fetal alcohol syndrome. *N. Engl. J. Med.* 298(19):1063–1067.

COLES, C. D., K. A. PLATZMAN, C. L. RASKIND-HOOD, R. T. BROWN, A. FALEK, and I. E. SMITH, 1997. A comparison of children affected by prenatal alcohol exposure and attention deficit, hyperactivity disorder. *Alcohol Clin. Exp. Res.* 21(1):150–161.

CONNOR, P. D., P. D. SAMPSON, F. L. BOOKSTEIN, H. BARR, and A. P. STREISSGUTH, in press. Direct and indirect effects of prenatal alcohol damage on executive function. *Dev. Neuropsychol.*

CONNOR, P. D., A. P. STREISSGUTH, P. D. SAMPSON, F. L. BOOKSTEIN, and H. M. BARR, 1999. Individual differences in auditory and visual attention in fetal alcohol affected adults. *Alcohol Clin. Exp. Res.* 23(8):1395–1402.

CONNOR, P. D., A. P. STREISSGUTH, P. D. SAMPSON, F. L. BOOKSTEIN, H. M. BARR, and S. K. TOTH, 2000. Motor coordination in adult males with fetal alcohol syndrome and fetal alcohol effects. *J. Int. Neuropsychol. Soc.* 6(2):237–238.

DAY, N. L., 1992. Effects of prenatal alcohol exposure. In *Maternal Substance Abuse and the Developing Nervous System*, I. S. Zagon and T. A. Slotkin, eds. San Diego: Academic Press, pp. 27–43.

DRISCOLL, C., A. P. STREISSGUTH, and E. P. RILEY, 1990. Prenatal alcohol exposure: Comparability of effects in humans and animal models. *Neurotoxicol. Teratol.* 12:231–237.

DUMAS, R. M., and A. RABE, 1994. Augmented memory loss in aging mice after one embryonic exposure to alcohol. *Neurotoxicol. Teratol.* 16:605–612.

ELLIS, F. W., and J. R. PICK, 1980. An animal model of the fetal alcohol syndrome in beagles. *Alcohol Clin. Exp. Res.* 4:123–134.

GABRIELLI, O., U. SALVOLINI, G. V. COPPA, C. CATASSI, R. ROSSI, A. MANCA, R. LANZA, and P. L. GIORGI, 1990. Magnetic resonance imaging in the malformative syndromes with mental retardation. *Pediatr. Radiol.* 21:16–19.

GOODLETT, C. R., D. J. BONTHIUS, E. A. WASSERMAN, and J. R. WEST, 1992. An animal model of CNS dysfunction associated with prenatal alcohol exposure: Behavioral and neuroanatomical correlates. In *Learning and Memory: Behavioral and Biological Processes*, I. Garmezano and E. A. Wasserman, eds. Inglewood, N.J.: Lawrence Erlbaum, pp. 183–208.

GOODLETT, C. R., J. D. THOMAS, and J. R. WEST, 1991. Long-term deficits in cerebellar growth and rotarod performance of rats following "binge-like" alcohol exposure during the neonatal brain growth spurt. *Neurotoxicol. Teratol.* 13:69–74.

GOODLETT, C. R., and J. R. WEST, 1992. Fetal alcohol effects: Rat model of alcohol exposure during the brain growth spurt. In *Maternal Substance Abuse and the Developing Nervous System*, I. S. Zagon and T. A. Slotkin, eds. San Diego: Academic Press, pp. 45–75.

GRANT, T., C. C. ERNST, A. P. STREISSGUTH, and J. PORTER, 1997. An advocacy program for mothers with FAS/FAE. In *The Challenge of Fetal Alcohol Syndrome: Overcoming Secondary Disabilities*, A. P. Streissguth and J. Kanter, eds. Seattle: University of Washington Press.

HANSON, J. W., A. P. STREISSGUTH, and D. W. SMITH, 1978. The effects of moderate alcohol consumption during pregnancy on fetal growth and morphogenesis. *J. Pediatr.* 92(3):457–460.

HÅRD, E., B. MUSI, I. L. DAHLGREN, J. ENGEL, K. LARSSON, S. LILJEQUIST, and A. S. LINDH, 1985. Impaired maternal behaviour and altered central serotonergic activity in the adult offspring of chronically ethanol treated dams. *Acta Pharmacol. Toxicol.* 56:347–353.

HARRIS, J. C., 1998. *Developmental Neuropsychiatry. Vol. 1, Fundamentals.* Oxford: Oxford University Press.

IKONOMIDOU, C., P. BITTIGAU, M. J. ISHIMARU, D. F. WOZNIAK, C. KOCH, K. GENZ, M. T. PRICE, V. STEFOVSKA, F. HÖRSTER, T. TENKOVA, K. DIKRANIAN, and J. W. OLNEY, 2000. Ethanol-induced apoptotic neurodegeneration and fetal alcohol syndrome. *Science* 11:1056–1060.

IOFFE, S., and V. CHERNICK, 1988. Development of the EEG between 30 and 40 weeks gestation in normal and alcohol-exposed infants. *Dev. Med. Neurol.* 30(6):797–807.

IOM: INSTITUTE OF MEDICINE, 1996. *Fetal Alcohol Syndrome: Diagnosis, Epidemiology, Prevention, and Treatment.* Washington, D.C.: National Academy Press.

JACOBSON, S. W., J. L. JACOBSON, R. J. SOKOL, S. S. MARTIER, and J. W. AGER, 1993a. Prenatal alcohol exposure and infant information processing ability. *Child Dev.* 64(6):1706–1721.

JACOBSON, J. L., S. W. JACOBSON, R. J. SOKOL, S. S. MARTIER, J. W. AGER, and M. G. KAPLAN-ESTRIN, 1993b. Teratogenic effects of alcohol on infant development. *Alcohol Clin. Exp. Res.* 17(1):174–183.

JOHNSON, S. C., E. D. BIGLER, R. B. BURR, and D. D. BLATTER, 1994. White matter atrophy, ventricular dilation, and intellectual functioning following traumatic brain injury. *Neuropsychology* 8(3):307–315.

JONES, K. L., 1986. Fetal alcohol syndrome. *Pediatr. Rev.* 8(4):122–126.

JONES, K. L., and D. W. SMITH, 1973. Recognition of the fetal alcohol syndrome in early infancy. *Lancet* 2:999–1001.

JONES, K. L., and D. W. SMITH, 1975. The fetal alcohol syndrome. *Teratology* 12(1):1–10.

JONES, K. L., D. W. SMITH, A. P. STREISSGUTH, and N.C. MYRIANTHOPOULOS, 1974. Outcome in offspring of chronic alcoholic women. *Lancet* 1(866):1076–1078.

JONES, K. L., D. W. SMITH, C. N. ULLELAND, and A. P. STREISSGUTH, 1973. Pattern of malformation in offspring of chronic alcoholic mothers. *Lancet* 1(815):1267–1271.

KANDEL, E., and L. SQUIRE, 1992. Cognitive neuroscience: Editorial overview. *Curr. Opin. Neurobiol.* 2:143–145.

KELLY, S. J., N. DAY, and A. P. STREISSGUTH, 2000. Effects of prenatal alcohol exposure on social behavior in humans and other species. *Neurotoxicol. Teratol.* 22:143–149.

KODITUWAKKU, P. W., N. S. HANDMAKER, S. K. CUTLER, E. K. WEATHERSBY, and S. D. HANDMAKER, 1995. Specific impairments in self-regulation in children exposed to alcohol prenatally. *Alcohol Clin. Exp. Res.* 19(6):1558–1564.

KOPERA-FRYE, K., S. DEHAENE, and A. P. STREISSGUTH, 1996. Impairments of number processing induced by prenatal alcohol exposure. *Neuropsychologia* 34(12):1187–1196.

KOTKOSKIE, L. A., and S. NORTON, 1989. Morphometric analysis of developing rat cerebral cortex following acute prenatal ethanol exposure. *Exp. Neurol.* 106(3):283–288.

KOVETSKII, N. S., G. V. KONOVALOV, D. D. ORLOVSKAIA, V. I. SEMKE, and A. V. SOLONSKII, 1991. Dysontogenesis of the brain (brain underdevelopment) of the progeny born to mothers drinking alcohol during pregnancy. *Zh. Nevropatol. Psikhiatr. S. S. Korsakova* 91(10):57–63.

KYLLERMAN, M., M. ARONSON, K. G. SABEL, E. KARLBERG, B. SANDIN, and R. OLEGÅRD, 1985. Children of alcoholic mothers: Growth and motor performance compared to matched controls. *Acta Paediatrica Scand.* 74(1):20–26.

LANDESMAN-DWYER, S., A. S. RAGOZIN, and R. E. LITTLE, 1981. Behavioral correlates of prenatal alcohol exposure: A four-year follow-up study. *Neurobehav. Toxicol. Teratol.* 3(2):187–193.

LANDESMAN-DWYER, S., L. S. KELLER, and A. P. STREISSGUTH, 1978. Naturalistic observations of newborns: Effects of maternal alcohol intake. *Alcohol Clin. Exp. Res.* 2(2):171–177.

LARROQUE, B. and M. KAMINSKI, 1998. Prenatal alcohol exposure and development at preschool age: Main results of a French study. *Alcohol Clin. Exp. Res.* 22:295–303.

LARROQUE, B., M. KAMINSKI, P. DEHAENE, D. SUBTIL, M. DELFOSSE, and D. QUERLEU, 1995. Moderate prenatal alcohol exposure and psychomotor development at preschool age. *Amer. J. Pub. Health.* 85:1654–1661.

LARROQUE, B., M. KAMINSKI, P. DEHAENE, D. SUBTIL, and D. QUERLEU, 2000. Prenatal alcohol exposure and signs of minor neurological dysfunction at preschool age. *Dev. Med. Child Neurol.* 42(8):508–514.

LEMOINE, P., H. HAROUSSEAU, J. P. BORTEYRU, and J. C. MENUET, 1968. Les enfants de parents alcooliques: Anomalies observées, à propos de 127 cas. *Ouest. Med.* 21:476–482.

LEMOINE, P., and PH. LEMOINE, 1992. Avenir des enfants de mères alcooliques (étude de 105 cas retrouvés à l'âge adulte) et quelques constatations d'intérêt prophylactique [Outcome in the offspring of alcoholic mothers (study of one hundred and five adults) and considerations with a view to prophylaxis]. *Ann. Pediatr. (Paris)* 39(4):226–235.

LÖSER, H., T. BIERSTEDT, and A. BLUM, 1999. Fetal alcohol syndrome in adults: Long-term observations on 52 patients. *Dtsch. Med. Wschr.* 124:412–418.

MAJEWSKI, F., 1993. Alcohol embryopathy: Experience in 200 patients. *Dev. Brain Dysfunct.* 6:248–265.

MARTIN, D., J. MARTIN, A. P. STREISSGUTH, and C. A. LUND, 1979. Sucking frequency and amplitude in newborns as a function of maternal drinking and smoking. In *Currents in Alcoholism, Biomedical Issues and Clinical Effects of Alcoholism,* M. Galanter, ed. New York: Grune & Stratton, pp. 359–366.

MARTIN, J. C., D. C. MARTIN, C. A. LUND, and A. P. STREISSGUTH, 1977a. Maternal alcohol ingestion and cigarette smoking and their effects on newborn conditioning. *Alcohol Clin. Exp. Res.* 1(3):243–247.

MARTIN, J. C., D. C. MARTIN, G. SIGMAN, and B. RADOW, 1978. Maternal ethanol consumption and hyperactivity in crossfostered offspring. *Physiol. Psychol.* 6:362–365.

MARTIN, J. C., D. C. MARTIN, G. SIGMAN, and B. RADOW, 1977b. Offspring survival, development, and operant performance following maternal ethanol consumption. *Dev. Psychobiol.* 10(5):435–446.

MATTSON, S. N., E. P. RILEY, L. GRAMLING, D. C. DELIS, and K. L. JONES, 1997. Heavy prenatal alcohol exposure with or without physical features of fetal alcohol syndrome leads to IQ deficits. *J. Pediatr.* 131(5):718–721.

MATTSON, S. N., E. P. RILEY, L. GRAMLING, D. C. DELIS, and K. L. JONES, 1998. Neuropsychological comparison of alcohol-exposed children with or without physical features of fetal alcohol syndrome. *Neuropsychology* 12(1):146–153.

MATTSON, S. N., E. P. RILEY, E. R. SOWELL, T. L. JERNIGAN, D. F. SOBEL, and K. L. JONES, 1996. A decrease in size of the basal ganglia in children with fetal alcohol syndrome. *Alcohol Clin. Exp. Res.* 20(6):1088–1093.

MEANS, L., M. BURNETTE, and S. N. PENNINGTON, 1988. The effect of embryonic ethanol exposure on detour learning in the chick. *Alcohol* 5(4):305–308.

MEYER, L. S., L. E. KOTCH, and E. P. RILEY, 1990. Neonatal ethanol exposure: Functional alterations associated with cerebellar growth retardation. *Neurotoxicol. Teratol.* 12:15–22.

MICHAELIS, E. K., and M. L. MICHAELIS, 1994. Cellular and molecular bases of alcohol's teratogenic effects. *Alcohol Health Res. World* 18(1):17–21.

MILLER, M. W., 1986. Effects of alcohol on the generation and migration of cerebral cortical neurons. *Science* 233(4770): 1308–1311.

MOLINA, J. C., H. D. DOMINGUEZ, M. F. LOPEZ, M. Y. PERINO, and A. E. FAAS, 1999. The role of fetal and infantile experience with alcohol in later recognition and acceptance patterns of the drug. In *Alcohol and Alcoholism Effects on Brain and Development,* J. H. Hannigan, L. P. Spear, N. E. Spear, and C. R. Goodlet, eds. London: Lawrence Erlbaum Associates, pp. 199–227.

NIAAA: NATIONAL INSTITUTE ON ALCOHOL ABUSE and ALCOHOLISM, 1990. Seventh Special Report to the U.S. Congress on Alcohol and Health. DHHS Pub. No.(ADM) 90–1656. Washington, D.C.: Supt. of Docs., U.S. Government Printing Office.

OUELLETTE, E. M., H. L. ROSETT, N. P. ROSMAN, and L. WEINER, 1977. Adverse effects on offspring of maternal alcohol abuse during pregnancy. *N. Engl. J. Med.* 297(10):528–530.

PHILLIPS, D. E., 1992. Effects of alcohol on the development of glial cells and myelin. In *Alcohol and Neurobiology,* R. R. Watson, ed. Boca Raton, Fla.: CRC Press, pp. 83–108.

PHILLIPS, D. E., and S. K. KRUEGER, 1992. Effects of combined pre- and postnatal ethanol exposure (third trimester equivalency) on glial cell development in rat optic nerve. *Int. J. Dev. Neurosci.* 10(3):197–206.

RANDALL, C. L., J. EKBLAD, and R. F. ANTON, 1990. Perspectives on the pathophysiology of fetal alcohol syndrome. *Alcohol Clin. Exp. Res.* 14:807–812.

RANDALL, C. L., and W. J. TAYLOR, 1979. Prenatal ethanol exposure in mice: Teratogenic effects. *Teratology* 19:305–312.

RILEY, E. P., 1990. The long-term behavioral effects of prenatal alcohol exposure in rats. *Alcohol Clin. Exp. Res.* 14(5):670–673.

RILEY, E. P., S. BARRON, and J. H. HANNIGAN, 1986. Response inhibition deficits following prenatal alcohol exposure: A comparison to the effects of hippocampal lesions in rats. In *Alcohol and Brain Development,* J. R. West, ed. New York: Oxford University Press, pp. 71–105.

RILEY, E. P., E. A. LOCHRY, and N. R. SHAPIRO, 1979. Lack of response inhibition in rats prenatally exposed to alcohol. *Psychopharmacology* 62(1):47–52.

RILEY, E. P., E. A. LOCHRY, N. R. SHAPIRO, and J. BALDWIN, 1979. Response perseveration in rats exposed to alcohol prenatally. *Pharmacol. Biochem. Behav.* 10(2):255–259.

RILEY, E. P., S. N. MATTSON, E. R. SOWELL, T. L. JERNIGAN, D. F. SOBEL, and K. L. JONES, 1995. Abnormalities of the corpus callosum in children prenatally exposed to alcohol. *Alcohol Clin. Exp. Res.* 19(5):1198–1202.

RILEY, E. P., and C. V. VORHEES, 1986. *Handbook of Behavioral Teratology.* New York: Plenum Press.

ROCKWOOD, G., and E. P. RILEY, 1986. Suckling deficits in rat pups exposed to alcohol in utero. *Teratology* 33:145–151.

ROSETT, H. L., 1980. A clinical perspective of the fetal alcohol syndrome. *Alcohol. Clin. Exp. Res.* 4:118.

ROSETT, H. L., P. SYNDER, L. W. SANDER, A. LEE, P. COOK, L. WEINER, and J. GOULD, 1979. Effects of maternal drinking on neonate state regulation. *Dev. Med. Child Neurol.* 21:464–473.

RUSSELL, M., D. M. CZARNECKI, R. COWAN, E. McPHERSON, and P. J. MUDAR, 1991. Measures of maternal alcohol use as predictors of development in early childhood. *Alcohol. Clin. Exp. Res.* 15(6):991–1000.

SAMPSON, P. D., F. L. BOOKSTEIN, H. M. BARR, and A. P. STREISSGUTH, 1994. Prenatal alcohol exposure, birthweight, and measures of child size from birth to age 14 years. *Amer. J. Pub. Health* 84(9):1421–1428.

SAMPSON, P. D., A. P. STREISSGUTH, H. M. BARR, and F. L. BOOKSTEIN, 1989. Neurobehavioral effects of prenatal alcohol. Part II: Partial Least Squares Analysis *Neurotoxicol. Teratol.* 11(5):477–491.

SAMPSON, P. D., A. P. STREISSGUTH, F. L. BOOKSTEIN, and H. BARR, 2000. On categorizations in analyses of alcohol teratogenesis. *Environ. Health Perspect.* 108(suppl 3):421–428.

SAMPSON, P. D., A. P. STREISSGUTH, F. L. BOOKSTEIN, R. E. LITTLE, S. K. CLARREN, P. DEHAENE, J. W. HANSON, JR., and J. M. GRAHAM, 1997. Incidence of fetal alcohol syndrome and prevalence of alcohol-related neurodevelopmental disorder. *Teratology* 56(6):317–326.

SANDER, L. W., P. A. SNYDER, H. L. ROSETT, A. LEE, J. B. GOULD, and E. OUELLETTE, 1977. Effects of alcohol intake during pregnancy on newborn state regulation: A progress report. *Alcohol Clin. Exp. Res.* 1(3):233–241.

SCHENKER, S., H. C. BECKER, C. L. RANDALL, D. K. PHILLIPS, G. S. BASKIN, and G. I. HENDERSON, 1990. Fetal alcohol syndrome: Current status of pathogenesis. *Alcohol Clin. Exp. Res.* 14(5):635–647.

SCHER, M. S., G. A. RICHARDSON, P. A. COBLE, N. L. DAY, and D. S. STOFFER, 1988. The effects of prenatal alcohol and marijuana exposure: Disturbances in neonatal sleep cycling and arousal. *Pediatr. Res.* 24(1):101–105.

SHAYWITZ, B. A., G. G. GRIFFIETH, and J. W. WARSHAW, 1979. Hyperactivity and cognitive deficits in developing rat pups born to alcoholic mothers: An experimental model of the expanded fetal alcohol syndrome (EFAS). *Neurobehav. Toxicol.* 1:113–122.

SOKOL, R. J., and S. K. CLARREN, 1989. Guidelines for use of terminology describing the impact of prenatal alcohol on the offspring. *Alcohol Clin. Exp. Res.* 13(4):597–598.

SOWELL, E. R., T. L. JERNIGAN, S. N. MATTSON, E. P. RILEY, D. F. SOBEL, and K. L. JONES, 1996. Abnormal development of the cerebellar vermis in children prenatally exposed to alcohol: Size reduction in lobules I though V. *Alcohol Clin. Exp. Res.* 20(1):31–34.

SPOHR, H. L., and H. C. STEINHAUSEN (eds.), 1996. *Alcohol, Pregnancy, and the Developing Child.* Cambridge: Cambridge University Press.

STREISSGUTH A. P., 1997. *Fetal Alcohol Syndrome: A Guide for Families and Communities.* Baltimore: Paul H. Brookes Publishing.

STREISSGUTH, A. P., J. M. AASE, S. K. CLARREN, S. P. RANDELS, R. A. LADUE, and D. F. SMITH, 1991. Fetal alcohol syndrome in adolescents and adults. *JAMA* 265(15):1961–1967.

STREISSGUTH, A. P., H. M. BARR, H. CARMICHAEL OLSON, P. D. SAMPSON, F. L. BOOKSTEIN, and D. M. BURGESS, 1994a. Drinking during pregnancy decreases word attack and arithmetic scores on standardized tests: Adolescent data from a population-based prospective study. *Alcohol Clin. Exp. Res.* 18(2):248–254.

STREISSGUTH, A. P., H. M. BARR, J. KOGAN, and F. L. BOOKSTEIN, 1996. *Understanding the Occurrence of Secondary Disabilities in Clients with Fetal Alcohol Syndrome (FAS) and Fetal Alcohol Effects (FAE).* Final Report to the Centers for Disease Control and Prevention (CDC). Seattle: University of Washington, Fetal Alcohol and Drug Unit, Tech. Rep. No. 96–06.

STREISSGUTH, A., H. BARR, J. KOGAN, and F. L. BOOKSTEIN, 1997. Primary and secondary disabilities in fetal alcohol syndrome. In *The Challenge of Fetal Alcohol Syndrome: Overcoming Secondary Disabilities,* A. Streissguth and J. Kanter, eds. Seattle: University of Washington Press, pp. 25–39.

STREISSGUTH, A. P., H. M. BARR, and D. C. MARTIN, 1983. Maternal alcohol use and neonatal habituation assessed with the Brazelton scale. *Child Dev.* 54(5):1109–1118.

STREISSGUTH, A. P., H. M. BARR, D. C. MARTIN, and C. S. HERMAN, 1980. Effects of maternal alcohol, nicotine and caffeine use during pregnancy on infant mental and motor development at 8 months. *Alcohol Clin. Exp. Res.* 4(2):152–164.

STREISSGUTH, A. P., H. M. BARR, P. D. SAMPSON, J. C. PARRISH-JOHNSON, G. L. KIRCHNER, and D. C. MARTIN, 1986. Attention, distraction and reaction time at age 7 years and prenatal alcohol exposure. *Neurobehav. Toxicol. Teratol.* 8(6):717–725.

STREISSGUTH, A. P., F. L. BOOKSTEIN, P. D. SAMPSON, and H. M. BARR, 1989. Neurobehavioral effects of prenatal alcohol. Part III: PLS analyses of neuropsychologic tests. *Neurotoxicol. Teratol.* 11(5):493–507.

STREISSGUTH, A. P., F. L. BOOKSTEIN, P. D. SAMPSON, and H. M. BARR, 1993. *The Enduring Effects of Prenatal Alcohol Exposure on Child Development: Birth through 7 Years, a Partial Least Squares Solution.* Ann Arbor: University of Michigan Press.

STREISSGUTH, A. P., F. L. BOOKSTEIN, P. D. SAMPSON, and H. M. BARR, 1995. Attention: Prenatal alcohol and continuities of vigilance and attentional problems from 4 through 14 years. *Dev. Psychopathol.* 7:419–446.

STREISSGUTH, A. P., S. K. CLARREN, and K. L. JONES, 1985. Natural history of the fetal alcohol syndrome: A ten-year follow-up of eleven patients. *Lancet* 2:85–91.

STREISSGUTH, A. P., P. DEHAENE, 1993. Fetal alcohol syndrome in twins of alcoholic mothers: Concordance of diagnosis and IQ. *Am. J. Med. Genet.* 47:857–861.

STREISSGUTH, A. P., and J. KANTER (eds.), 1997. *The Challenge of Fetal Alcohol Syndrome: Overcoming Secondary Disabilities.* Seattle: University of Washington Press.

STREISSGUTH, A. P., and R. E. LITTLE, 1994. Unit 5: Alcohol, Pregnancy, and the Fetal Alcohol Syndrome: Second Edition of the Project Cork Institute Medical School Curriculum (slide lecture series) on *Biomedical Education: Alcohol Use and Its Medical Consequences,* produced by Dartmouth Medical School. Milner-Fenwick, Inc., Timonium.

STREISSGUTH, A. P., D. C. MARTIN, H. M. BARR, B. M. SANDMAN, G. L. KIRCHNER, and B. L. DARBY, 1984. Intrauterine alcohol and nicotine exposure: Attention and reaction time in 4-year-old children. *Dev. Psychol.* 20(4):533–541.

STREISSGUTH, A. P., D. C. MARTIN, J. C. MARTIN, and H. M. BARR, 1981. The Seattle longitudinal prospective study on alcohol and pregnancy. *Neurobehav. Toxicol. Teratol.* 3:223–233.

STREISSGUTH, A. P., and K. O'MALLEY, 2000. Neuropsychiatric implications and long-term consequences of fetal alcohol spectrum disorders. *Semin. Clin. Neuropsychiatry* 5(3)177–190.

STREISSGUTH, A. P., P. D. SAMPSON, H. CARMICHAEL OLSON, F. L. BOOKSTEIN, H. M. BARR, M. SCOTT, J. FELDMAN, and A. F. MIRSKY, 1994b. Maternal drinking during pregnancy and attention/memory performance in 14-year-old children: A longitudinal prospective study. *Alcohol Clin. Exp. Res.* 18(1):202–218.

STRÖMLAND, K., M. MILLER, and C. COOK, 1991. Ocular teratology. *Surv. Ophthalmol.* 35(6):429–446.

STRÖMLAND, K., and M. D. PINAZO-DURÁN, 1994. Optic nerve hypoplasia: Comparative effects in children and rats exposed to alcohol during pregnancy. *Teratology* 50:100–111.

STUSS, D. T., L. L. STETHEM, H. HUGENHOLTZ, T. PICTON, J. PIVIK, and M. T. RICHARD, 1989. Reaction time after head injury: Fatigue, divided and focused attention, and consistency of performance. *J Neurol Neurosurg Psychiatry* 52:742–748.

THOMAS, J. D., E. A. WASSERMAN, J. R. WEST, and C. R. GOODLETT, 1996. Behavioral deficits induced by bingelike exposure to alcohol in neonatal rats: Importance of developmental timing and number of episodes. *Dev. Psychobiol.* 29(5):433–452.

WEST, J. R., C. A. HODGES, and A. C. BLACK, 1981. Prenatal alcohol exposure to ethanol alters the organization of hippocampal mossy fibers in rats. *Science* 211:957–959.

WILSON, J. G., 1977. New area of concern in teratology. *Teratology* 16:227–228.

WILSON, J. G., and F. C. FRASER eds., 1977. *Handbook of Teratology. Vol. 1: General Principles, Etiology*, New York: Plenum Press.

ZIMMERBERG, B., and L. A. MICKUS, 1990. Sex differences in corpus callosum: Influence of prenatal alcohol exposure and maternal undernutrition. *Brain Res.* 537(1–2):115–122.

# 33 The Effects of Cocaine on the Developing Nervous System

GREGG D. STANWOOD
AND PAT LEVITT

ABSTRACT  In utero drug exposure can lead to specific, targeted changes in brain structure and function through direct and indirect modification of developing neurotransmitter systems and intracellular messengers. This chapter describes aspects of cortical development that can be modulated by developing neurotransmitter systems, which, in turn can be affected by prenatal exposure to cocaine and other drugs of abuse. Also reviewed are data from animal models of gestational exposure to cocaine demonstrating permanent defects in the structure and function of limbic cortical areas known to play a role in the regulation of attention in drug-exposed offspring. We propose that similar changes in pattern formation likely underlie the complex cognitive and behavioral deficits that have been described in children exposed to cocaine and/or other drugs of abuse during prenatal development.

The development of the brain relies on the spatial and temporal regulation of cell–cell interactions that are controlled by contact-mediated and diffusible effector substances. Both the availability of molecular signals and the ability of developing cells to respond to those signals, by expression of specific receptors, are essential to ontogenetic processes (Goodman and Shatz, 1993; Levitt, 1999; Lillien, 1998; McConnell, 1995a). Transcription factors, cell adhesion molecules, and neurotrophic factors all have been established as mediators of tissue patterning, histotypic organization, and circuit formation (Aplin et al., 1998; Fields and Itoh, 1996; Katz and Shatz, 1996; Segal and Greenberg, 1996). It is clear, however, that many molecules exhibit pleiotrophic activities, serving as regulators of distinct cellular functions at different times in development and adulthood (Levitt, 1999). Neurotransmitters and neuromodulators are now recognized as exhibiting multiple activities, performing very different roles in cellular communication in the mature brain and during development (Lauder, 1993; Levitt, Rakic, and Goldman-Rakic, 1997; Mattson, 1988). Here, we focus on several features of brain development to understand the potential impact that an altered neurochemical environment may have on histogenesis. In this chapter we describe research findings that implicate monoamine systems, especially dopamine, in regulating certain aspects of neural development. These neurotransmitters are particularly susceptible to modifications by use of cocaine and other drugs of abuse during pregnancy.

## Fundamentals of cerebral cortical development

The cerebral cortex mediates higher cognitive functions and is responsible for the integration of complex sensory, motor, and homeostatic information. Defects in cortical development, therefore, can have a profound impact on mature brain functions. It has been suggested that developmental anomalies in cortical development underlie certain types of psychopathology, such as schizophrenia (Bloom, 1993; Raedler, Knable, and Weinberger, 1998; Elvevåg and Weinberger, this volume), and forms of mental retardation and autism (Charman, 1999; Wong et al., 1995). The molecular and cellular bases that tie developmental defects to cortical dysfunction in these disorders remain unknown, but we know that influences on cell–cell interactions that mediate specific developmental events are likely targets. This also seems to be true for nongenetic alterations in development, such as prenatal exposure to stress (Takahashi, 1998) and drugs of abuse (Ferriero and Dempsey, 1999; Levitt, 1998; Malanga and Kosofsky, 1999).

THE BASICS OF BRAIN DEVELOPMENT  Temporally overlapping events, grouped in five major categories, contribute to the formation of all brain structures from the neural tube (figure 33.1; see color plate 21). Progenitor cells of the germinal matrix, situated along the forerunner of the ventricular system, give rise to all neurons and macroglia in a well-controlled *proliferative* process. Postmitotic neurons *migrate* subsequently in a directed fashion from their place of origin to their final resting position. Neuronal *differentiation* involves the expression of specific gene products which, together with the

GREGG D. STANWOOD AND PAT LEVITT  Department of Neurobiology, University of Pittsburgh School of Medicine, Pittsburgh, Pennsylvania.

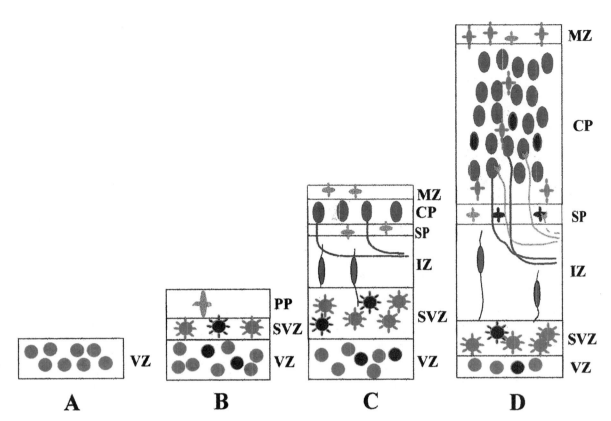

FIGURE 33.1 Schematic representation of the major stages of development of the cerebral cortex, depicting proliferation, migration, differentiation, cell death, and synaptogenesis. (A) Progenitor cells (red) proliferate in the ventricular zone and give rise mostly to neurons. (B) Specialized pioneer neurons (green; Cajal-Retzius cells) begin to differentiate in the preplate as additional cells proliferate in the ventricular and subventricular zones. The spiked red cells in the SVZ give rise mostly to glia. Cells shown in black will undergo cell death as part of a complex process to regulate cell number. (C) The preplate is divided by neurons arriving in the cortical plate into the marginal zone and the subplate. The trailing processes of differentiating neurons develop into axons (blue), and additional neurons continue to migrate through the intermediate zone to the cortical plate. (D) The cortical plate develops in an inside-out manner, such that earlier-born neurons reside deeper. Glia (red cells) begin to seed the cortical plate, afferents from subcortical and other cortical regions arrive (orange), and synaptogenesis begins. Subplate neurons receive transient synapses that eventually are lost when the neurons die. Synaptogenesis in the cortex proper continues into postnatal development through adolescence. *Abbreviations:* CP, cortical plate; IZ, intermediate zone; MZ, marginal zone; PP, preplate; SP, subplate; SVZ, subventricular zone; VZ, ventricular zone.

appearance of unique structural features (axons and dendrites), contribute to the remarkable phenotypic diversity of the nervous system. Glial cells differentiate early to form specialized migration guides, radial glia, and later to form astrocytes and oligodendrocytes. Progenitor cells, neurons, and glia undergo naturally occurring *cell death*, a complex process that appears to be a normal developmental mechanism to establish appropriate quantitative relationships between projection and target neurons and between neurons and glia. *Synaptogenesis* is a temporally extended developmental event, beginning prenatally and lasting through adolescence in the central nervous system (CNS) of all mammals, and which is critical in the formation of synapses between specific target populations of neurons.

CEREBRAL CORTICAL HISTOGENESIS The neocortex is a six-layered structure that exhibits very similar features across its tangential extent. Thus, all functional areas have repeated laminar and columnar organization that is assembled during development in well-defined temporal and spatial patterns. The first neurons produced actually are not located in the forerunner of the cortex, the cortical plate, but rather form a structure called the preplate, which eventually is split into a subplate and a supraplate in the marginal zone by the first neurons destined for the cortical plate. The process of splitting the preplate is an important first step in establishing appropriate migration patterns of neurons. In the mutant mouse reeler, in which the protein reelin is defective, this process is abnormal and the cortex is disorganized (Curran and D'Arcangelo, 1998). Subplate neurons are transient cells that serve as temporary targets for subcortical axons from the thalamus. These neurons also aid in the guidance of axons to correct target regions of the cerebral cortex (Ghosh and Shatz, 1993).

Neurons arising from the germinal matrix of the dorsal telencephalon migrate along radial glia to reach the cortical plate, with neurons born early residing deep and those born subsequently more superficial. This so-called inside-out settling pattern is a hallmark of cerebral cortical formation and allows one to define the time of origin of neurons residing in specific layers of the cortex. The trailing process of migrating cells generally forms the axon, and actually can be recognized as neurons migrate. These axons grow into the intermediate zone, the forerunner of cortical white matter, which resides between the subplate and the germinal matrix during development. Following the production of neurons destined for layers 6–4, a new, superficial zone of progenitor cells appears—the subventricular zone (SVZ). These progenitor cells maintain a position away from the luminal surface and produce the neurons of the superficial cortical layers and most of the macroglial cells (astrocytes and oligodendrocytes). The SVZ is maintained in adults in a restricted region along the rostroventral end of the lateral ventricular, and can produce new neurons and glia in the mature forebrain.

Recent studies have demonstrated that not all neurons of the cerebral cortex arise from the dorsal telencephalon. Rather, it appears that most of the GABA interneurons of the cerebral cortex are generated in the ganglionic eminence of the ventral telencephalon and migrate tangentially to reach all areas of the cerebral cortex (Anderson et al., 1997; Lavdas et al., 1999). These interneurons comprise 12–18% of all neurons in the cerebral cortex and exhibit many phenotypic properties of neurons as they migrate, including the formation of axons and dendrites and the synthesis of neurotransmitter. Because amino acids themselves can influence neuronal migration (Behar et al., 1998, 1999; Komuro and Rakic, 1993), it is possible that unique regulatory interactions between amino acid transmitter-synthesizing neurons occur during this migratory process.

Neuronal polarity reflects the asymmetry of information processing and the molecular and structural differences in the accumulation of proteins and organelles. Polarity is seen first when a neuron becomes postmitotic, with dendrite- and axon-specific proteins expressed during migration. Dendrites grow slowly over many weeks and months, whereas axons grow several orders of magnitude more rapidly, reaching target areas

in some instances prior to neurons' reaching their final resting position. Complex molecular signaling is responsible for the regulation of axonal growth. Diffusible and membrane proteins that comprise different families—including cadherins, semaphorins, the receptor tyrosine kinase ephs, members of the Ig superfamily, and netrins—are responsible for both chemoattraction and chemorepulsion (Aplin et al., 1998; Bruckner and Klein, 1998; Fields and Itoh, 1996). These signals can act locally or at a distance to direct extension of axons along specific pathways to reach their proper targets. In the cerebral cortex, axon targeting occurs prenatally, before extensive dendritic development of projection neurons. Whereas targeting occurs rapidly, quantitative analysis of synaptogenesis in the cortex indicates that only a small fraction of adult synapses are present by birth. In fact, in primates early postnatally and through adolescence, synapse number peaks, plateaus for several years, and ultimately is reduced by almost 40% of peak number through a normal process of retraction and remodeling (Bourgeois, Goldman-Rakic, and Rakic, 1999; Caviness et al., 1997).

The control of dendritic growth is complex, with neurotrophins, small GTPase signaling, and afferent-driven physiological activity among key regulators (Gallo and Letourneau, 1998; Katz and Shatz, 1996; Lo, 1998; Luo, Jan, and Jan, 1996). In the visual system, the neurotrophins brain-derived neurotrophin factor (BDNF) and neurotophin-3 (NT-3) are transported in a retrograde manner by developing thalamic neurons from the cortex and increase the complexity of dendritic branching. Modulation of GTPase signaling also has profound influences on axonal and dendritic development (Gallo and Letourneau, 1998; Luo, Jan, and Jan, 1996). In vitro studies have shown that neurotransmitter substances, in the absence of synapses, also can modulate cell migration and dendritic growth (Lauder, 1993; Lipton and Kater, 1989; Whitaker-Azmitia et al., 1996). Glutamate has complex effects on cell survival and neurite growth (Mattson, 1988). Similarly, monoamines, such as dopamine (DA), can serve as negative or positive regulators, depending upon which subtypes of receptor proteins are activated (Reinoso, Undie, and Levitt, 1996).

*Neuropharmacology of brain dopamine systems*

In order to place cocaine-induced developmental alterations in a proper context, it is necessary to understand the normal ontogeny, pharmacology, and function of mesocortical DA systems. Owing to space constraints, we are unable to describe these features of other monoamines (serotonin, norepinephrine) and the reader is referred elsewhere for reviews of these systems (Cooper,

Bloom, and Roth, 1996; Siegel et al., 1998). DA has been implicated in a variety of functions, including motor control, cognition, endocrine function, emotion, and cardiovascular regulation. Abnormalities in brain DA systems are thought to contribute to several major neurological and psychiatric disorders including schizophrenia, Parkinson's disease, Tourette's syndrome, and drug abuse (Carlsson and Carlsson, 1990; Graybiel, Hirsch, and Agid, 1990; Hyman, 1996; Zigmond et al., 1990). Many exogenously administered drugs, including cocaine, act directly on DA systems and can produce long-lasting alterations in endogenous dopaminergic and nondopaminergic functions.

SYNTHESIS, METABOLISM, AND PHARMACOLOGY  DA is synthesized from the amino acid tyrosine through the actions of tyrosine hydroxylase (TH), the rate-limiting enzyme in the process, and followed by aromatic acid decarboxylase (figure 33.2; see color plate 22). The rate at which DA is synthesized is controlled by several mechanisms, including end-product inhibition, changes in the number or structure of TH molecules, and changes in the availability of necessary cofactors for tyrosine hydroxylation. Because of these regulatory processes, neurons are usually able to match the rate of DA synthesis to the rate of DA utilization, thereby avoiding either the buildup or depletion of the transmitter.

As is the case for all neurotransmitters, DA release occurs in response to an influx of calcium into the nerve terminal, which is triggered by the arrival of an action potential. Like DA synthesis, several processes regulate DA release. For example, DA can act back on the terminal from which it was released to inhibit subsequent release. Such influences represent negative feedback loops and act to maintain the rate of DA utilization within relatively narrow limits. DA release can also be potentiated or attenuated by both local and distal actions of other neurotransmitters (Horger and Roth, 1996; Meltzer et al., 1997; Zigmond et al., 1998).

DA induces a wide range of cellular and biochemical effects in neurons by way of its interactions with specific receptor proteins (Jaber et al., 1996; Jackson and Westlind-Danielsson, 1994). These effects include relatively rapid (seconds) modulation of biochemical events in the target cell, resulting in changes in the responsiveness of the cell to other neuronal inputs, as well as more gradual (minutes to hours) alterations in gene expression (figure 33.2). DA receptors belong to a large superfamily of neurotransmitter and hormone receptors that are characterized by an extracellular N-terminus, intracellular C-terminus, seven transmembrane domains, and coupling to specific effector functions

through guanine nucleotide binding proteins (G proteins) (Birnbaumer, 1990; Gilman, 1987). DA receptors are classified into two subfamilies according to pharmacological profiles and sequence homology: the $D_1$-like receptor subtypes ($D_1$, $D_5$) and the $D_2$-like receptor subtypes ($D_2$, $D_3$, $D_4$) (Seeman and Van Tol, 1994; Sibley and Monsma, 1992).

The neurotransmitter actions of released DA and other monoamines are typically terminated by transport back into presynaptic terminals by transporter proteins that form high-affinity uptake sites. Once taken up, monoamines can be metabolized in the nerve terminal by monoamine oxidase (MAO) or further sequestered into storage vesicles for later reuse (figure 33.2).

High-affinity transporters for DA and other monoamines such as serotonin and norepinephrine serve as the primary pharmacological sites of action of cocaine. Cocaine binds to these transport proteins and blocks the reuptake of the transmitters, thus prolonging their time in the extracellular space. This permits the transmitter to bind to its receptor proteins for more sustained periods, resulting in excessive activation of these receptors. It has been suggested that the $D_1$ receptor (Gonon, 1997; Smiley et al., 1994) and DA transporter (Nirenberg et al., 1997) are primarily located extrasynaptically. Cocaine, therefore, may greatly enhance the stimulation of $D_1$ receptors by preferentially increasing extrasynaptic DA levels.

ANATOMICAL ORGANIZATION  There are several major dopaminergic pathways. Axons of DA-containing cells in the substantia nigra pars compacta form the nigrostriatal tract which provides the dopaminergic innervation of the caudate and putamen, or striatum (Beckstead, Domesick, and Nauta, 1979). The striatum is the major output component of the basal ganglia, a group of nuclei involved in motor and cognitive functions. Degeneration of nigrostriatal DA neurons is the primary pathology in Parkinson's disease (Gibb and Lees, 1991; Hirsch, Graybiel, and Agid, 1988).

Medial to the substantia nigra lies the ventral tegmental area, from which the mesolimbic and mesocortical DA systems largely arise (Beckstead, Domesick, and Nauta, 1979; Swanson, 1982), though other mesencephalic DA cell groups also contribute to cortical and limbic DA projections (Williams and Goldman-Rakic, 1998). The mesolimbic DA system innervates ventrally located subcortical regions such as the nucleus accumbens, olfactory tubercle, and amygdala. The nucleus accumbens is thought to be a site of interface between limbic and motor systems and is a critical substrate for the development and regulation of goal-

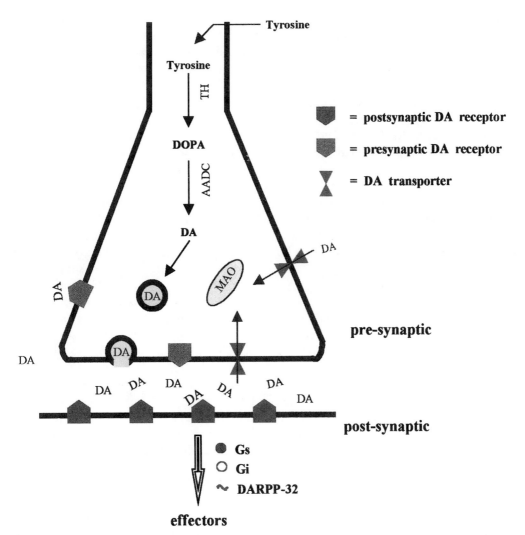

Tyrosine

Tyrosine

TH

DOPA

AADC

DA

DA

DA

MAO

DA

DA

DA

**pre-synaptic**

DA

DA    DA    DA    DA    DA

DA

**post-synaptic**

■ = postsynaptic DA receptor

■ = presynaptic DA receptor

⧖ = DA transporter

● Gs
○ Gi
∼ DARPP-32

**effectors**

FIGURE 33.2    Schematic representation of the life cycle of dopamine (DA). The amino acid precursor tyrosine is accumulated by the neuron and tyrosine is sequentially converted to DA by the actions of tyrosine hydroxylase (TH) and aromatic acid decarboxylase (AADC). DA is then accumulated into vesicles where it is protected from degradation and prepared for release. Once DA is released, it can interact with a variety of proteins including postsynaptic receptors (blue) and presynaptic autoreceptors (green) that regulate transmitter release, synthesis, or firing rate through specific effector proteins (purple). DA can also bind to sites on DA transporters (red), which are expressed on the presynaptic membrane. This leads to the termination of the extracellular actions of DA. Once accumulated by the neuron, DA can be metabolized to inactive species by degradative enzymes such as monoamine oxidase (MAO) (pink), or taken back into vesicles.

directed behaviors (Hyman, 1996; Kiyatkin, 1995; Koob, 1992; Nestler and Aghajanian, 1997). The mesocortical system provides dopaminergic afferents to the anterior cingulate (ACC) and medial prefrontal cortices (MPF). These regions have been implicated in orienting, emotional, and attentional processes (Devinsky, Morrell, and Vogt, 1995; Goldman-Rakic, 1996; Pardo, Fox, and Raichle, 1991); and disruption of mesocortical DA neurotransmission has been associated with neuropsychiatric illnesses such as schizophrenia and stress-related disorders (Deutch, 1993; Kiyatkin, 1995).

ONTOGENY OF THE MESOCORTICAL DOPAMINE SYSTEM As described earlier, cortical development involves a complicated series of regulated events. In the rabbit, the species in which we have extensively examined the effects of prenatal cocaine exposure, cells begin leaving the proliferative zones at embryonic day (E)13 and reach the deepest layers of cortex by E15 (Stensaas, 1967a). The total gestational period in this animal is approximately 30 days. By E16, approximately equivalent to a human embryo at the beginning of the third month of gestation, the cells in the cortical plate with a pyramidal morphology are evident (Stensaas, 1967b).

At E19, the cortical plate has thickened (Stensaas, 1967c), and by E22 the intermediate zone contains both subcortical afferent axons and efferents from cortical neurons (Stensaas, 1967d). Glial cells are generated by E25 and layer V is recognizable at this time with overlying cortical plate cells relatively undifferentiated (Stensaas, 1967e). Layers II–IV are still forming at the perinatal period, and complete dendritic development does not conclude until the third or fourth postnatal week. Very similar patterns of cortical development occur in all mammalian species (McConnell, 1995b). In the rat, total gestation is approximately 21 days, with the peak of cortical neurogenesis occurring at about E16. In the mouse, total gestation is about 19 days, and E15 corresponds to the peak of neuron proliferation in the cerebral cortex.

DEVELOPMENT OF DOPAMINERGIC INNERVATION AND RECEPTORS    Tyrosine hydroxylase, the rate-limiting enzyme in DA synthesis, is first apparent at E12–13 in the rat midbrain (Lauder and Bloom, 1974; Olson and Seiger, 1972; Specht et al., 1981) and E14 in the rabbit (Tennyson, Mytilineou, and Barrett, 1973). Axons of dopaminergic cells reach the cortex a few days later (Lidow and Wang, 1995; Olson and Seiger, 1972; Verney et al., 1982). Limbic cortical regions, such as the ACC and MPF, receive the densest dopaminergic innervation (Berger et al., 1976; Levitt, Rakic, and Goldman-Rakic, 1984; Reader, Masse, and de Champlain, 1979). This input is thus already present in the cortex even while more superficial cortical layers (II–IV) are beginning to form, consistent with a morphogenic role of DA. The mechanisms responsible for the proper guidance of dopaminergic afferents to the cortex and the morphogenic properties of these afferents on cortical neurons are not well understood, but recent studies suggest important roles for Eph tyrosine kinases (named for their expression in an erythropoietin-producing human hepatocellular carcinoma cell line) and their ligands (Janis, Cassidy, and Kromer, 1999; Yue et al., 1998).

The mRNA for the $D_1$, $D_2$ and $D_3$ receptors can be detected in the striatum and cortex by E14 in the rat (Cadoret, Jaber, and Bloch, 1993; Reinoso, Undie, and Levitt, 1996; Schambra et al., 1994), which corresponds to approximately E16–18 in the rabbit. $D_1$ and $D_2$ receptor proteins also are measurable prenatally, and increase throughout prenatal and early postnatal development to reach adult levels of expression between P14 and P21 in the rat (Caille et al., 1995; Sales et al., 1989; Schambra et al., 1994). DA receptors functionally couple to G proteins very soon after their appearance (Sales et al., 1989). In the human fetus, $D_1$-like and $D_2$-like receptor binding sites have been detected extraordinarily early, by gestational week 6 (Unis, 1994). Therefore, in all species examined, DA receptors are present very early in prenatal development, consistent with a role for DA in regulating neuronal differentiation.

DEVELOPMENTAL ROLES OF MONOAMINES    As described earlier, both presynaptic and postsynaptic components of central monoamines are expressed at all stages of corticogenesis. The early development of monoamine and other neurotransmitter systems has led to hypotheses concerning their trophic properties and their putative role in controlling cell proliferation and process outgrowth (Lauder, 1993; Lipton and Kater, 1989; Mattson, 1988; Whitaker-Azmitia et al., 1996). Initial in vivo studies provided only modest support for this hypothesis (Felten, Hallman, and Jonsson, 1982; Kalsbeek, Matthijssen, and Uylings, 1989). In vitro studies, on the other hand, have clearly shown that dopamine and 5-HT can greatly modify axon and dendritic outgrowth, probably through their coupling to second messenger systems (Lankford, DeMello, and Klein, 1988; Reinoso, Undie, and Levitt, 1996; Sikich, Hickok, and Todd, 1990; Todd, 1992). For example, DA can either stimulate or inhibit neurite growth in cortical neurons through actions mediated by different DA receptor subtypes (Reinoso, Undie, and Levitt, 1996). Selective $D_1$ receptor activation decreases the outgrowth of neurites in a dose-dependent manner whereas $D_2$ receptor activation induces outgrowth.

Additional evidence implicating monoamines in neurodevelopmental processes in vivo comes from work in which proteins needed for proper monoamine signaling lead to structural and functional abnormalities in the cerebral cortex. The most striking example of this is the disruption of the gene encoding monoamine oxidase A (MAO-A), an enzyme responsible for the metabolism of monoamines in nerve terminals (Cases et al., 1995, 1996; Vitalis et al., 1998). Loss of MAO-A results in increases in 5-HT and norepinephrine levels, the former being directly responsible for the failure of the development of barrel-like structures related to vibrissae representation in the somatosensory cortex. This key pattern of cytoarchitectonic organization, unique to this region of cortex, normally forms in the rodent during the first postnatal week of life. Barrel formation in the MAO-A null mice can be restored with early intervention, using a drug to inhibit 5-HT synthesis during the critical period for barrel formation. Pharmacological inhibition of MAO-A activity in wild-type mice also leads to a loss of barrel formation, clearly demonstrating the remarkable sensitivity of somatosensory pattern formation to monoamines (Cases et al.,

1996; Vitalis et al., 1998). Perhaps most intriguing is the observation that although barrels are absent in the somatosensory cortex in the mutant line, thalamic and brainstem barrel-like patterns are still evident. Cortical barrel formation is dependent upon activity arising from peripheral whisker barrels, transmitted through several synapses in the brainstem and thalamus. So why don't nonmonoaminergic afferents arising from regions with seemingly normal barrel formation produce normal barrel formation at the next synapse, in the somatosensory cortex? The work on the MAO-A knockout animals led to studies demonstrating that during normal development, the thalamic projections to somatosensory cortex transiently express the presynaptic 5-HT transporter, the vesicular monoamine transporter, and accumulate 5-HT during the critical period in the first postnatal week in mice (Lebrand et al., 1998). These studies provide the strongest evidence to date that alterations in monoamine levels during development can lead to aberrant neuronal projection patterns and target organization.

DA–GLUTAMATE INTERACTIONS   The ACC and MPF receive dopaminergic innervation from the ventral tegmental area (Levitt, Rakic, and Goldman-Rakic, 1984; Sesack, Snyder, and Lewis, 1995) and the activation of mesocortical DA neurons regulates the firing of pyramidal neurons in these regions (Yang, Seamans, and Gorelova, 1999). Pyramidal neurons predominantly use excitatory amino acids, such as glutamate, as their neurotransmitter and extend axons to many regions of the CNS, including reciprocal projections to midbrain DA cells (Sesack, Snyder, and Lewis, 1989; Sesack and Pickel, 1992). Excitatory amino acids released by these axon terminals act on glutamate receptors expressed on dopaminergic neurons to depolarize the membrane and induce burst firing patterns (Meltzer, Christoffersen, and Serpa, 1997). Glutamate also can directly regulate DA release in the cortex (Horger and Roth, 1996). Reciprocal innervation of cortex and ventral midbrain can thus serve as a feedback loop to control the activity within such circuits.

Nigrostriatal and mesolimbic DA neurons innervate subcortical structures such as the striatum and nucleus accumbens, regions that also receive glutamatergic input from the cortex. DA can reduce the release of glutamate in these regions, likely through actions on $D_2$ receptors expressed on the terminals of corticostriatal afferents (Carlsson and Carlsson, 1990; Morari et al., 1998). Glutamate can also act locally within the striatum and accumbens to increase extracellular levels of DA (Morari et al., 1998; Zigmond et al., 1998). Further interactions between these two transmitters also occur at the level of single postsynaptic cells. In this regard, activation of $D_1$ receptors potentiates glutamate signaling through the NMDA receptor, whereas $D_2$ receptor activation attenuates it (Cepeda and Levine, 1998; Yang and Seamans, 1996). In fact, $D_1$ receptor stimulation leads to phosphorylation of the NMDA receptor (Snyder et al., 1998, 2000). Interactions between DA and glutamate receptor activation on the expression or phosphorylation of intracellular signaling molecules also have been observed (Halpain, Girault, and Greengard, 1990; Konradi, Leveque, and Hyman, 1996).

Further elucidation concerning the reciprocal control of DA and glutamate neurotransmission has been obtained through studies of the neural substrates of stress. Physiological stressors, such as footshock in rodents, increase the release of DA and glutamate in the prefrontal cortex and basal ganglia (Finlay and Zigmond, 1997; Horger and Roth, 1996). Stressors can also increase drug-seeking behavior (Piazza and Le Moal, 1998). The local administration of glutamate antagonists into DA cell body–containing regions can block stress-induced increases in extracellular DA in the cortex and striatum (Karreman, Westerink, and Moghaddam, 1996; Taber, Das, and Fibiger, 1995). Conversely, the lesioning of DA axons in prefrontal cortex, which removes the inhibitory control of glutamatergic neuronal firing, results in an increased responsiveness of subcortical DA systems to stress (Deutch, Clark, and Roth, 1990; King, Zigmond, and Finlay, 1997). Dysregulation of mesocortical DA activity can thus secondarily alter dopaminergic activity in nigrostriatal and mesoaccumbens neurons, a process which may contribute to the pathophysiology of disorders such as schizophrenia, drug abuse, and attention deficit hyperactivity disorder (ADHD).

### Alterations in brain development and function due to prenatal cocaine exposure in animals

Given the modulatory influence of monoamines on certain aspects of neural development, it is understandable that prenatal exposure to drugs that affect monoamine systems, such as alcohol, nicotine, opiates, and marijuana, can have pronounced effects on the development of the cerebral cortex (Ferriero and Dempsey, 1999; Levitt, 1998; Malanga and Kosofsky, 1999; Slotkin, 1998). The current discussion will concentrate specifically on the effects of in utero cocaine.

As is evident in table 33.1, many animal models of prenatal cocaine exposure have been developed, with a multitude of distinct results reported in offspring. At high dosages, cocaine produces widespread deleterious effects on brain development. For example, oral

TABLE 33.1
*Summary of animal models of prenatal cocaine exposure*

| Species | Dose | Route | Duration | Observed Phenotype(s) | Citation(s) |
|---|---|---|---|---|---|
| Monkey | 10 mg/kg | Oral | E40–E102, 2×/day (term = 165) | Reduction in cortical cell number, inappropriate positioning of cortical cells, altered glial morphology | Lidow, 1995, 1998 |
| Monkey | 3 mg/kg | im | E20–E60, 4×/day (term = 165) | Reduced tyrosine hydroxylase and increased $D_1$ receptor mRNA in fetal midbrain, increased DA receptor mRNA in striatum, altered opioid peptides | Chai, Choi, and Ronnekleiv, 1997; Choi and Ronnekleiv, 1996; Fang, Janowsky, and Ronnekleiv, 1997; Ronnekleiv et al., 1998; Ronnekleiv and Naylor, 1995 |
| Mouse | 10–40 mg/kg | sc | E8–E17, 2×/day (term = 20) | Disruption of cortical lamination, altered gliogenesis | Gressens, Kosofsky, and Evrard, 1992; Kosofsky and Wilkins, 1998; Wilkins, Jones, and Kosofsky, 1998; Wilkins et al., 1998a,b |
| Mouse | 30 mg/kg | g.i. | E8–E19, 2×/day (term = 20) | Alterations in dopamine levels in the forebrain | Miller et al., 1995 |
| Rabbit | 2–4 mg/kg | iv | E8–E29, 2×/day (term = 30) | Altered growth of pyramidal cell dendrites, altered GABA and parvalbumin expression by cortical interneurons, reduced coupling of $D_1$ receptors and Gs$\alpha$, impaired discrimination learning, altered susceptibility to seizures, altered regulation of extracellular DA | Du et al., 1999; Friedman, Yadin, and Wang, 1996; Jones, Fischer, and Levitt, 1996; Jones et al., 2000; Murphy et al., 1995, 1997; Romano and Harvey, 1996; Romano et al., 1995; Simansky and Kachelries, 1996; Stanwood, Washington, and Levitt, 2001; Wang, Yeung, and Friedman, 1995; Wang et al., 1995a,b, 1996 |
| Rabbit | 30 mg/kg | sc | E10–birth, implant E7–E15, 1×/day (term = 32) | Altered cardiorespiratory and neurochemical responses to hypoxia | Weese-Mayer and Barkov, 1993; Weese-Mayer et al., 1993 |
| Rat | 3 mg/kg | iv | E8–E14, 1×/day E15-E20, 2X/day (term = 21) | Impaired attentional and emotional reactivity, increased cerebellar Purkinje cell number | Bayer et al., 2000; Garavan et al., 2000; Mactutus, Herman, and Booze, 1994 |
| Rat | 10–20 mg/kg | sc | E1 or E7–E21, 2×/day (term = 21) | Increased cocaine self-administration, altered regulation of DA release, 5-HT hyperinnervation of striatum, increased susceptibility to seizures, enhanced prepulse inhibition and stress responses | Keller and Snyder-Keller, 2000; Keller et al., 1996a,b; Overstreet et al., 2000; Snyder-Keller and Keller, 1993, 2000 |
| Rat | 30 mg/kg | sc | E7–E19, 2×/day (term = 21) | Reduced levels of glial cell–line derived neurotrophic factor | Lipton et al., 1999 |
| Rat | 40 mg/kg | sc | E8–E20, 2×/day (term = 21) | Deficits in Pavlovian conditioning, increased brain glycosphingolipids, decreased discriminative stimulus properties of cocaine, altered stress responsiveness | Goodwin et al., 1997; Heyser et al., 1990, 1992, 1994; Leskawa et al., 1994; Spear et al., 1989, 1998 |
| Rat | 40 mg/kg | sc | E13–birth, 1×/day (term = 21) | Increased tyrosine hydroxylase immunoreactivity, delayed maturation of the 5-HT system, altered glial development | Akbari and Azmitia, 1992; Akbari et al., 1992; Clarke et al., 1996; Whitaker-Azmitia, 1998 |
| Rat | 30–60 mg/kg | gi | E8–birth, 2×/day (term = 21) | Altered glucose metabolism | Dow-Edwards, 1989; Dow-Edwards, Freed, and Fico, 1990 |
| Rat | 40 mg/kg | sc | E8–E21, 1×/day (term = 21) | Transient decrease in striatal DA transporter expression, increase in tyrosine hydroxylase activity | Collins and Meyer, 1996; Meyer and Dupont, 1993 |

*Abbreviations:* iv, intravenous; sc, subcutaneous; im, intramuscular; ip, intraperitoneal; gi, gastric intubation; ACC, anterior cingulate cortex; DA, dopamine; 5-HT, serotonin.

administration of 10 mg/kg to pregnant rhesus monkeys for 62 days during pregnancy (E40–E102) produces profound and long-lasting abnormalities in lamination and glial differentiation throughout the cerebral cortex (Lidow, 1998; Lidow, 1995). Similar findings have been observed following 20 mg/kg cocaine injected subcutaneously into pregnant mice (Gressens, Kosofsky, and Evrard, 1992; Kosofsky and Wilkins, 1998). The results of these and other studies are fully summarized in table 33.1.

A well-characterized low-dose animal model of prenatal cocaine exposure administers the drug intravenously to rabbits to closely mimic patterns of human use (Murphy et al., 1995, 1997). This approach ensures predictable levels in the blood and highly reproducible effects on offspring, features that are difficult to attain using higher dose subcutaneous or intraperitoneal models. The rabbit was selected because of the ease in performing multiple intravenous drug injections on a daily basis, its stereotyped pattern of brain development which parallels the human (Harel et al., 1972), and the prior history of the rabbit as a model of behavioral and structural teratology following drug treatments during prenatal and perinatal periods (Gabriel et al., 1980; Hudson and Distel, 1986). The effects of prenatal cocaine on neuronal morphology, biochemical signaling, and cognitive and behavioral functioning in this model have been reviewed in detail (Levitt, 1998; Levitt et al., 1997).

Briefly, injection of low doses (2–4 mg/kg) of cocaine twice a day to pregnant rabbits during gestational days 8–29 (of a total of 30 embryonic days) produces specific changes in the structure and function of neurons in the ACC and MPF, cortical areas that receive prominent dopaminergic innervation. The alterations include aberrant dendritic development of projection neurons, such that apical dendrites of pyramidal neurons are 50% longer than normal (Jones, Fischer, and Levitt, 1996), an increase in GABA immunoreactive neurons (Wang et al., 1995a), and an increase in the dendritic expression of parvalbumin in the secondary and tertiary dendrites of interneurons (Wang et al., 1996). Moreover, offspring show a large reduction in $D_1$ DA receptor coupling to a subunit of its G protein (Gsα) in the ACC (Friedman, Yadin, and Wang, 1996) and striatum (Wang et al., 1995b). This effect appears to be specific for $D_1$-Gs coupling, because $D_2$ and muscarinic cholinergic receptor coupling to Gi/Go-proteins is normal. These alterations in prenatal cocaine-exposed rabbits are depicted in figure 33.3 (see color plate 23).

Functional outcomes of prenatal cocaine exposure in the intravenous model include anomalous behavior on motor and discriminative tasks (Romano and Harvey, 1996; Romano et al., 1995; Simansky and Kachelries, 1996), impaired neuronal activation during discriminative learning (Gabriel and Taylor, 1998), and altered regulation of DA release (Du et al., 1999; Wang, Yeung, Friedman, 1995). No changes have been detected in the visual cortex (VC) or primary somatosensory cortex, demonstrating remarkable regional specificity and suggesting dopaminergic mediation. Our most recent data indicate that cocaine exposure during gestational days 16–25 only, the period of peak cortical differentiation in the rabbit, is sufficient to induce long-term changes in the anatomical organization of the ACC (Stanwood, Washington, and Levitt, 2001). These data argue that the deleterious effects of low-dose, intravenous cocaine during brain development are specific to modulation of monoaminergic, likely dopaminergic, signaling, and not due to general teratology.

The specific and permanent uncoupling of the DA $D_1$ receptor and Gs in the rabbit model differs from the broad and time-dependent regulation of receptor signaling typically observed following chronic administration of cocaine to adult animals (Alburges, Narang, and Wamsley, 1993; Kuhar and Pilotte, 1996; Laurier, Corrigall, and George, 1994; Neisewander, Lucki, and McGonigle, 1994; Nestler and Aghajanian, 1997), though it should be pointed out that few chronic studies in adult rodents employ intravenous injections. Interestingly, similar differences in specificity have been observed in the comparison of neonatal and adult dopaminergic lesions (Joyce, Frohna, and Neal-Beliveau, 1996; Kostrzewa, Reader, and Descarries, 1998). In this regard, destruction of DA neurons in neonatal rodents leads to prominent supersensitivity of DA $D_1$ receptor-mediated responses (Joyce, Frohna, and Neal-Beliveau, 1996; Neal-Beliveau and Joyce, 1999), whereas similar lesions in adults result in changes in several receptor subtypes. Therefore, manipulations that often lead to broad changes in mature systems might not necessarily cause identical changes in developing systems.

As mentioned earlier, $D_1$ receptor activation can lead to inhibition of neurite outgrowth in cortical neurons. We have therefore hypothesized that the reduction in $D_1$ receptor coupling produced by in utero cocaine might lead to the observed increase in dendritic growth in the ACC. In fact, ACC neurons harvested from drug-exposed fetuses exhibit greater spontaneous outgrowth in vitro than ACC neurons of saline-exposed animals (Jones, Fisher, and Levitt, 2000), suggesting that a loss of $D_1$ receptor-mediated inhibition of neurite outgrowth may lead to the excessive dendritic growth following prenatal cocaine. Furthermore, similar increases in dendritic growth are observed in the ACC of mice

Saline                                    Cocaine

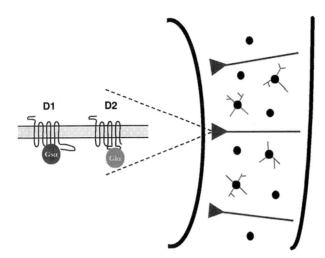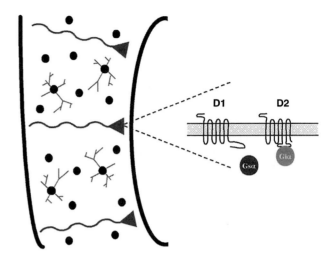

FIGURE 33.3 Schematic representation of cellular effects of in utero cocaine exposure in the rabbit. Rabbits exposed to low doses of cocaine intravenously exhibit alterations in the structure and function of neurons in the anterior cingulate cortex. The apical dendrites of pyramidal neurons (red) exhibit an undulating trajectory. The number of interneurons in which immunoreactivity for GABA is detectable (black) is increased. There also is an increase in parvalbumin (green) immunostaining in the dendrites of a subset of these neurons. $D_1$ dopamine receptor coupling to Gs protein (blue) is reduced, whereas coupling of the $D_2$ receptor to Gi (orange) is unaffected. These changes likely influence the balance of excitatory and inhibitory influences in the cingulate cortex and produce the aberrant behavioral phenotypes exhibited by these rabbits. (Modified from Levitt et al., 1997.)

lacking functional $D_1$ receptors (unpublished observations), providing further validation of this hypothesis.

The story is undoubtedly more complex, however, as the resulting changes in $D_1$ receptor signaling due to $D_1$–Gs uncoupling also likely modifies developing glutamate and GABA systems. As mentioned earlier, $D_1$ receptor stimulation can facilitate NMDA- and ameliorate AMPA/kainate-receptor responsiveness (Cepeda and Levine, 1998; Yang and Seamans, 1996) and regulate the phosphorylation state of the NMDA-receptor (Snyder et al., 1998, 2000). Prenatal cocaine-induced increases in parvalbumin-containing dendrites of cortical interneurons may indicate a greater need for calcium buffering following an increase in excitatory drive. Similarly, DA can both promote and inhibit GABA release based on the complement of activated receptor subtypes (Cameron and Williams, 1993; Harsing and Zigmond, 1997), and the increases in GABA-immunoreactive neurons in the rabbit model suggest cocaine-induced disruption of DA–GABA relationships in the developing limbic cortex.

Further interactions between dopamine and the monoamines norepinephrine and 5-HT are also likely to play a role. Cocaine blocks the reuptake of norepinephrine and 5-HT and these monoamines also influence excitatory and inhibitory activity within the cortex.

Although evidence for changes in 5-HT or norepinephrine activity has not been identified in the rabbit model, deficits in serotonergic functioning certainly have been implicated in higher dose models of prenatal cocaine exposure (Akbari et al., 1992; Battaglia et al., 1998; Snyder-Keller and Keller, 1993; Whitaker-Azmitia, 1998; Zhang, Schrott, and Sparber, 1998).

### Structural and functional deficits observed in humans exposed to cocaine in utero

Reports of the impact of prenatal cocaine exposure on newborns have been confusing, as some reports suggest gross physical malformations, others observe specific deficits in cognitive and emotional development, and yet others observe no effects whatsoever (for review, see Gingras et al., 1992; Hawley, 1994; Mayes et al., 1998). These variable outcomes are likely the result of differences in the experimental designs of these studies, some of which have been poorly controlled for important variables such as the timing and amount of cocaine use during the pregnancy, polydrug use, and extent of pre- and postnatal care.

Teratogenic effects of cocaine exposure on birth weight, body length, and head circumference have been suggested by several studies (Chasnoff et al., 1985,

1992; Chiriboga, 1998). Other investigators, however, have been unable to replicate such effects in cocaine-exposed children. The rather extreme physical deficits appear to be most apparent when the mother has abused high doses of cocaine throughout pregnancy, in some cases right up to the time at which her cocaine habit has precipitated premature delivery.

However, relatively few women abuse cocaine during later stages of pregnancy. A much more common pattern of abuse is one in which the drug is used during the first, or sometimes first and second trimesters, and at doses lower than appear to produce teratology (Richardson, 1998). It is this population that animal studies using low-dose cocaine exposure, such as our rabbits, attempt to model. Interestingly, the offspring of these relatively modest cocaine abusers show measurable functional deficits, particularly in cognitive and attentional domains.

For example, prospective studies begun at the University of Pittsburgh in the late 1980s have recruited women in a prenatal clinic and an expected subset (~8%) of women report cocaine use at some point during the pregnancy. The children of these women and demographically well-matched, non-cocaine users have now been studied at birth, one year, and three years (Richardson, 1998; Richardson, Conroy, and Day, 1996; Richardson and Day, 1991; Scher, 2000). Although no physical differences were observed at birth, by age 3 the children exposed to cocaine prenatally, even if only during the first trimester, scored lower on the Stanford-Binet Intelligence Scale and had more reported temperament and behavior problems. These deficits appear to be related to attentional difficulties and are highly reminiscent of children who develop ADHD. Deficits in recognition memory, task persistence, distractibility, and stress responsiveness also have been reported in cocaine-exposed infants and preschool-age children (Azuma and Chasnoff, 1993; Delaney-Black et al., 1996; Gingras and O'Donnell, 1998; Karmel and Gardner, 1996; Koren et al., 1998; Mayes et al., 1993, 1995, 1998). Increased risk of ADHD also has been documented in the offspring of women who smoke or consume alcohol heavily during their pregnancy (Aronson, Hagberg, and Gillberg, 1997; Milberger et al., 1998). It should be noted, however, that the clustering of other health determinants in cocaine-abusing women, such as addiction itself, makes it difficult to isolate the effects of in utero cocaine on offspring. In fact, a recent twin study has found that children exposed to cocaine prenatally, but raised by middle-upper class adopted families, show less severe deficits than those raised by their natural mothers (Koren, 1998).

Intriguingly, the ACC and MPF, the cortical regions in which we have observed in utero cocaine-induced changes in our rabbit model, contribute to the neural control of attention, and are sites of brain dysfunction in ADHD (Amen and Carmichael, 1997; Ernst et al., 1998; Faraone and Biederman, 1998; Zametkin et al., 1990). In utero cocaine-exposed children thus perform poorly on tasks that also are difficult for children diagnosed with ADHD (Richardson, Conroy, and Day, 1996; van Leeuwen et al., 1998; Verbaten et al., 1994). Animal and human studies have shown that attentional tasks depend on proper functioning of the MPF and ACC (Goldman-Rakic, 1996; Lane et al., 1998; Pardo, Fox, and Raichle, 1991). Reduced signaling through the DA $D_1$ receptor appears to underlie structural and functional deficits observed in prenatal cocaine-exposed rabbits (Friedman, Yadin, and Wang, 1996; Wang et al., 1995b), and thus it is intriguing to speculate that similar processes may be occurring in the cocaine-exposed children. The development of a therapeutic strategy to restore proper $D_1$ receptor coupling in these children might therefore be efficacious in the treatment of attentional disturbances.

Reduced $D_1$ receptor coupling could have other severe consequences for prenatal cocaine-exposed children throughout their lifetimes. $D_1$ receptor activation is an important substrate for reward pathways in the brain (Moratalla et al., 1996; Xu et al., 1994). Although not yet studied directly, one prediction is that these children would likely experience defects in endogenous reward systems that could lead to the occurrence of anhedonia and/or depression. In fact, reports from an animal model suggest that the efficacy of reinforcers is reduced following prenatal cocaine exposure (Gulley, et al., 2000; Hecht et al., 1998; Heyser et al., 1994), although this is controversial (Keller and Snyder-Keller, 2000).

In summary, severe physical abnormalities in cocaine-exposed infants appear to occur only following very prolonged and high levels of cocaine intake by the mother. However, very striking cognitive and temperamental changes are present in children exposed to relatively low doses of cocaine in the womb. These disturbances are caused by deficits in attentional processes and are likely due to improper functioning of the prefrontal and cingulate cortices and related neurotransmitter systems.

## Conclusions

Cocaine and other drugs of abuse modify neurotransmitter systems and intracellular messengers in the developing as well as adult brain. These same neurotransmitters are pleiotrophic signaling molecules that serve to regulate specific aspects of central nervous development. It is therefore not surprising that in utero drug exposure can lead to specific, targeted changes in brain structure and function. Following low-dose prenatal cocaine exposure in particular, dopamine-rich limbic cortical areas that are known to play a role in the regulation of attention, exhibit permanent alterations in brain structure and function. It is likely that similar changes in pattern formation underlie the complex cognitive and behavioral deficits described in children exposed to cocaine and/or other drugs of abuse during prenatal development.

ACKNOWLEDGMENTS   Some of the research summarized in this chapter was supported by NIDA grant DA 11165. G.D.S. is the recipient of a PhRMA Foundation fellowship.

## REFERENCES

AKBARI, H. M., and E. C. AZMITIA, 1992. Increased tyrosine hydroxylase immunoreactivity in the rat cortex following prenatal cocaine exposure. *Brain Res. Dev. Brain Res.* 66:277–281.

AKBARI, H. M., H. K. KRAMER, P. M. WHITAKER-AZMITIA, L. P. SPEAR, and E. C. AZMITIA, 1992. Prenatal cocaine exposure disrupts the development of the serotonergic system. *Brain Res.* 572:57–63.

ALBURGES, M. E., N. NARANG, and J. K. WAMSLEY, 1993. Alterations in the dopaminergic receptor system after chronic administration of cocaine. *Synapse* 14:314–323.

AMEN, D. G., and B. D. CARMICHAEL, 1997. High-resolution brain SPECT imaging in ADHD. *Ann. Clin. Psychiatry* 9:81–86.

ANDERSON, S. A., D. D. EISENSTAT, L. SHI, and J. L. RUBENSTEIN, 1997. Interneuron migration from basal forebrain to neocortex: Dependence on Dlx genes [see comments]. *Science* 278:474–476.

APLIN, A. E., A. HOWE, S. K. ALAHARI, and R. L. JULIANO, 1998. Signal transduction and signal modulation by cell adhesion receptors: The role of integrins, cadherins, immunoglobulin-cell adhesion molecules, and selectins. *Pharmacol. Rev.* 50:197–263.

ARONSON, M., B. HAGBERG, and C. GILLBERG, 1997. Attention deficits and autistic spectrum problems in children exposed to alcohol during gestation: A follow-up study. *Dev. Med. Child Neurol.* 39:583–587.

AZUMA, S. D., and I. J. CHASNOFF, 1993. Outcome of children prenatally exposed to cocaine and other drugs: A path analysis of three-year data. *Pediatrics* 92:396–402.

BATTAGLIA, G., T. M. CABRERA-VERA, L. D. VAN DE KAR, F. GARCIA, A. VICENTIC, and W. PINTO, 1998. Prenatal cocaine exposure produces long-term impairments in brain serotonin function in rat offspring. *Ann. N.Y. Acad. Sci.* 846:355–357.

BAYER, L. E., A. BROWN, C. F. MACTUTUS, R. M. BOOZE, and B. J. STRUPP, 2000. Prenatal cocaine exposure increases sensitivity to the attentional effects of the dopamine D1 agonist SKF81297. *J. Neurosci.* 20:8902–8908.

BECKSTEAD, R. M., V. B. DOMESICK, and W. J. H. NAUTA, 1979. Efferent connections of the substantia nigra and ventral tegmental area in the rat. *Brain Res.* 175:191–217.

BEHAR, T. N., A. E. SCHAFFNER, C. A. SCOTT, C. O'CONNELL, and J. L. BARKER, 1998. Differential response of cortical plate and ventricular zone cells to GABA as a migration stimulus. *J. Neurosci.* 18:6378–6387.

BEHAR, T. N., C. A. SCOTT, C. L. GREENE, X. WEN, S. V. SMITH, D. MARIC, Q. Y. LIU, C. A. COLTON, and J. L. BARKER, 1999. Glutamate acting at NMDA receptors stimulates embryonic cortical neuronal migration. *J. Neurosci.* 19:4449–4461.

BERGER, B., A. M. THIERRY, J. P. TASSIN, and M. A. MOYNE, 1976. Dopaminergic innervation of the rat prefrontal cortex: A fluorescence histochemical study. *Brain Res.* 106:133–145.

BIRNBAUMER, L., 1990. G proteins in signal transduction. *Annu. Rev. Pharmacol. Toxicol.* 30:675–705.

BLOOM, F. E., 1993. Advancing a neurodevelopmental origin for schizophrenia. *Arch. Gen. Psychiatry* 50:224–227.

BOURGEOIS, J.-P., P. S. GOLDMAN-RAKIC, and P. RAKIC, 1999. Formation, elimination, and stabilization of synapses in the primate cerebral cortex. In *The New Cognitive Neurosciences*, M. S. Gazzaniga, ed. Cambridge, Mass.: MIT Press, pp. 45–53.

BRUCKNER, K., and R. KLEIN, 1998. Signaling by Eph receptors and their ephrin ligands. *Curr. Opin. Neurobiol.* 8:375–382.

CADORET, M.-A., M. JABER, and B. BLOCH, 1993. Prenatal D1, D1b and D3 dopamine receptor gene expression in the rat forebrain: Detection by reverse polymerase chain reaction. *Neurosci. Lett.* 155:92–95.

CAILLE, I., B. DUMARTIN, C. LE MOINE, J. BEGUERET, and B. BLOCH, 1995. Ontogeny of the D1 dopamine receptor in the rat striatonigral system: An immunohistochemical study. *Eur. J. Neurosci.* 7:714–722.

CAMERON, D. L., and J. T. WILLIAMS, 1993. Dopamine D1 receptors facilitate transmitter release. *Nature* 366:344–347.

CARLSSON, M., and A. CARLSSON, 1990. Interactions between glutamatergic and monoaminergic systems within the basal ganglia—implications for schizophrenia and Parkinson's disease. *Trends Neurosci.* 13:272–276.

CASES, O., I. SEIF, J. GRIMSBY, P. GASPAR, K. CHEN, S. POURNIN, U. MULLER, M. AGUET, C. BABINET, J. C. SHIH, et al., 1995. Aggressive behavior and altered amounts of brain serotonin and norepinephrine in mice lacking MAOA [see comments]. *Science* 268:1763–1766.

CASES, O., T. VITALIS, I. SEIF, E. DE MAEYER, C. SOTELO, and P. GASPAR, 1996. Lack of barrels in the somatosensory cortex of monoamine oxidase A-deficient mice: Role of a serotonin excess during the critical period. *Neuron* 16:297–307.

CAVINESS, J. V. S., D. N. KENNEDY, J. F. BATES, and N. MAKRIS, 1997. The developing human brain: A morphometric profile. In *Developmental Neurobiology: Mapping the Development of Brain and Behavior,* R. W. Thatcher, G. R. Lyon, J. Rumsey, and N. Krasneger, eds. San Diego: Academic Press, pp. 3–14.

CEPEDA, C., and M. S. LEVINE, 1998. Dopamine and N-methyl-D-aspartate receptor interactions in the neostriatum. *Dev. Neurosci.* 20:1–18.

CHAI, L., W. S. CHOI, and O. K. RONNEKLEIV, 1997. Maternal cocaine treatment alters dynorphin and enkephalin mRNA expression in brains of fetal rhesus macaques. *J. Neurosci.* 17:1112–1121.

CHARMAN, T., 1999. Autism and the pervasive developmental disorders. *Curr. Opin. Neurol.* 12:155–159.

CHASNOFF, I. J., W. J. BURNS, S. H. SCHNOLL, and K. A. BURNS, 1985. Cocaine use in pregnancy. *N. Engl. J. Med.* 313:666–669.

CHASNOFF, I. J., D. R. GRIFFITH, C. FREIER, and J. MURRAY, 1992. Cocaine/polydrug use in pregnancy: Two-year follow-up [see comments]. *Pediatrics* 89:284–289.

CHIRIBOGA, C. A., 1998. Neurological correlates of fetal cocaine exposure. *Ann. N.Y. Acad. Sci.* 846:109–125.

CHOI, W. S., and O. K. RONNEKLEIV, 1996. Effects of in utero cocaine exposure on the expression of mRNAs encoding the dopamine transporter and the D1, D2 and D5 dopamine receptor subtypes in fetal rhesus monkey. *Brain Res. Dev. Brain Res.* 96:249–260.

CLARKE, C., K. CLARKE, J. MUNEYYIRCI, E. AZMITIA, and P. M. WHITAKER-AZMITIA, 1996. Prenatal cocaine delays astroglial maturation: Immunodensitometry shows increased markers of immaturity (vimentin and GAP-43) and decreased proliferation and production of the growth factor S-100. *Brain Res. Dev. Brain Res.* 91:268–273.

COLLINS, L. M., and J. S. MEYER, 1996. Prenatal cocaine alters dopamine transporter binding in postnatal day 10 rat striatum. *Synapse* 23:335–343.

COOPER, J. R., F. E. BLOOM, and R. H. ROTH, 1996. *The Biochemical Basis of Neuropharmacology*. New York: Oxford University Press.

CURRAN, T., and G. D'ARCANGELO, 1998. Role of reelin in the control of brain development. *Brain Res. Brain Res. Rev.* 26:285–294.

DELANEY-BLACK, V., C. COVINGTON, E. OSTREA, JR., A. ROMERO, D. BAKER, M. T. TAGLE, B. NORDSTROM-KLEE, M. A. SILVESTRE, M. L. ANGELILLI, C. HACK, and J. LONG, 1996. Prenatal cocaine and neonatal outcome: Evaluation of dose-response relationship. *Pediatrics* 98:735–740.

DEUTCH, A.Y., 1993. Prefrontal cortical dopamine systems and the elaboration of functional corticostriatal circuits: Implications for schizophrenia and Parkinson's disease. *J. Neural Transmission* 91:197–221.

DEUTCH, A. Y., W. A. CLARK, and R. H. ROTH, 1990. Prefrontal cortical dopamine depletion enhances the responsiveness of mesolimbic dopamine neurons to stress. *Brain Res.* 521:311–315.

DEVINSKY, O., M. J. MORRELL, and B. A. VOGT, 1995. Contributions of anterior cingulate cortex to behaviour. *Brain* 118:279–306.

DOW-EDWARDS, D. L., 1989. Long-term neurochemical and neurobehavioral consequences of cocaine use during pregnancy. *Ann. N.Y. Acad. Sci.* 562:280–289.

DOW-EDWARDS, D. L., L. A. FREED, and T. A. FICO, 1990. Structural and functional effects of prenatal cocaine exposure in adult rat brain. *Brain Res. Dev. Brain Res.* 57:263–268.

DU, W., V. J. ALOYO, P. S. PAZDELSKI, and J. A. HARVEY, 1999. Effects of prenatal cocaine exposure on amphetamine-induced dopamine release in the caudate nucleus of the adult rabbit. *Brain Res.* 836:194–198.

ERNST, M., A. J. ZAMETKIN, J. A. MATOCHIK, P. H. JONS, and R. M. COHEN, 1998. DOPA decarboxylase activity in attention deficit hyperactivity disorder adults. A [$^{18}$F]fluorodopa positron emission tomographic study. *J. Neurosci.* 18:5901–5907.

FANG, Y., A. JANOWSKY, and O. K. RONNEKLEIV, 1997. Cocaine exposure in fetal rhesus monkey: Consequences for dopa-mine D1- and D2-like receptor binding densities. *Brain Res. Dev. Brain Res.* 104:163–174.

FARAONE, S. V., and J. BIEDERMAN, 1998. Neurobiology of attention-deficit hyperactivity disorder. *Biol. Psychiatry* 44:951–958.

FELTEN, D. L., H. HALLMAN, and G. JONSSON, 1982. Evidence for a neurotropic role of noradrenaline neurons in the postnatal development of rat cerebral cortex. *J. Neurocytol.* 11:119–135.

FERRIERO, D. M., and D. A. DEMPSEY, 1999. Impact of addictive and harmful substances on fetal brain development. *Curr. Opin. Neurol.* 12:161–166.

FIELDS, R. D., and K. ITOH, 1996. Neural cell adhesion molecules in activity-dependent development and synaptic plasticity. *Trends Neurosci.* 19:473–480.

FINLAY, J. M., and M. J. ZIGMOND, 1997. The effects of stress on central dopaminergic neurons: Possible clinical implications. *Neurochem. Res.* 22:1387–1394.

FRIEDMAN, E., E. YADIN, and H. Y. WANG, 1996. Effect of prenatal cocaine on dopamine receptor-G protein coupling in mesocortical regions of the rabbit brain. *Neuroscience* 70:739–747.

GABRIEL, M., E. ORONA, K. FOSTER, and R. W. LAMBERT, 1980. Cingulate cortical and anterior thalamic neuronal correlates of reversal learning in rabbits. *J. Comp. Physiol. Psychol.* 94:1087–1100.

GABRIEL, M., and C. TAYLOR, 1998. Prenatal exposure to cocaine impairs neuronal coding of attention and discriminative learning. *Ann. N.Y. Acad. Sci.* 846:194–212.

GALLO, G., and P. C. LETOURNEAU, 1998. Axon guidance: GTPases help axons reach their targets. *Curr. Biol.* 8:R80–R82.

GARAVAN, H., R. E. MORGAN, C. F. MACTUTUS, D. A. LEVITSKY, R. M. BOOZE, and B. J. STRUPP, 2000. Prenatal cocaine exposure impairs selective attention: Evidence from serial reversal and extradimensional shift tasks. *Behav. Neurosci.* 114:725–738.

GHOSH, A., and C. J. SHATZ, 1993. A role for subplate neurons in the patterning of connections from thalamus to neocortex. *Development* 117:1031–1047.

GIBB, W. R. G., and A. J. LEES, 1991. Anatomy, pigmentation, ventral and dorsal subpopulations of the substantia nigra, and differential cell death in Parkinson's disease. *J. Neurol. Neurosurg. Psychiatry* 54:388–396.

GILMAN, A. G., 1987. G proteins: Transducers of receptor-generated signals. *Annu. Rev. Biochem.* 56:615–649.

GINGRAS, J. L., and K. J. O'DONNELL, 1998. State control in the substance-exposed fetus. I. The fetal neurobehavioral profile: An assessment of fetal state, arousal, and regulation competency. *Ann. N.Y. Acad. Sci.* 846:262–276.

GINGRAS, J. L., D. E. WEESE-MAYER, R. F. HUME, JR., and K. J. O'DONNELL, 1992. Cocaine and development: Mechanisms of fetal toxicity and neonatal consequences of prenatal cocaine exposure. *Early Hum. Dev.* 31:1–24.

GOLDMAN-RAKIC, P. S., 1996. Regional and cellular fractionation of working memory. *Proc. Natl. Acad. Sci. USA* 93:13473–13480.

GONON, F., 1997. Prolonged and extrasynaptic excitatory action of dopamine mediated by D1 receptors in the rat striatum in vivo. *J. Neurosci.* 17:5972–5978.

GOODMAN, C. S., and C. J. SHATZ, 1993. Developmental mechanisms that generate precise patterns of neuronal connectivity. *Cell* 72:77–98.

GOODWIN, G. A., T. BLIVEN, C. KUHN, R. FRANCIS, and L. P. SPEAR, 1997. Immediate early gene expression to examine neuronal activity following acute and chronic stressors in rat pups: Examination of neurophysiological alterations underlying behavioral consequences of prenatal cocaine exposure. *Physiol. Behav.* 61:895–902.

GRAYBIEL, A. M., E. C. HIRSCH, and Y. AGID, 1990. The nigrostriatal system in Parkinson's disease. *Adv. Neurol.* 53:17–29.

GRESSENS, P., B. E. KOSOFSKY, and P. EVRARD, 1992. Cocaine-induced disturbances of corticogenesis in the developing murine brain. *Neurosci. Lett.*140:113–116.

GULLEY, J. M., S. P. BILLMAN, D. M. GILLIAM, and F. R. GEORGE, 1999. Operant-self-administration of ethanol in mice prenatally exposed to cocaine. *J. Addict. Diseases* 18:77–89.

HALPAIN, S., J. A. GIRAULT, and P. GREENGARD, 1990. Activation of NMDA receptors induces dephosphorylation of DARPP-32 in rat striatal slices. *Nature* 343:369–372.

HAREL, S., K. WATANABE, I. LINKE, and R. J. SCHAIN, 1972. Growth and development of the rabbit brain. *Biol. Neonate* 21:381–399.

HARSING, L. G., JR., and M. J. ZIGMOND, 1997. Influence of dopamine on GABA release in striatum: Evidence for D1–D2 interactions and non-synaptic influences. *Neuroscience* 77:419–429.

HAWLEY, T. L., 1994. The development of cocaine-exposed children. *Curr. Prob. Pediatr.* 24:259–266.

HECHT, G. S., N. E. SPEAR, and L. P. SPEAR, 1998. Alterations in the reinforcing efficacy of cocaine in adult rats following prenatal exposure to cocaine. *Behav. Neurosci.* 112:410–418.

HEYSER, C. J., W. J. CHEN, J. MILLER, N. E. SPEAR, and L. P. SPEAR, 1990. Prenatal cocaine exposure induces deficits in Pavlovian conditioning and sensory preconditioning among infant rat pups. *Behav. Neurosci.* 104:955–963.

HEYSER, C. J., J. S. MILLER, N. E. SPEAR, and L. P. SPEAR, 1992. Prenatal exposure to cocaine disrupts cocaine-induced conditioned place preference in rats. *Neurotoxicol. Teratol.* 14:57–64.

HEYSER, C. J., L. RAJACHANDRAN, N. E. SPEAR, and L. P. SPEAR, 1994. Responsiveness to cocaine challenge in adult rats following prenatal exposure to cocaine. *Psychopharmacology* 116:45–55.

HIRSCH, E. C., A. M. GRAYBIEL, and Y. A. AGID, 1988. Melanized dopaminergic neurons are differentially susceptible to degeneration in Parkinson's disease. *Nature* 334:345–348.

HORGER, B. A., and R. H. ROTH, 1996. The role of mesoprefrontal dopamine neurons in stress. *Crit. Rev. Neurobiol.* 10:395–418.

HUDSON, R., and H. DISTEL, 1986. The potential of the newborn rabbit for behavioral teratological research. *Neurobehav. Toxicol. Teratol.* 8:209–212.

HYMAN, S. E., 1996. Addiction to cocaine and amphetamine. *Neuron* 16:901–904.

JABER, M., S. W. ROBINSON, C. MISSALE, and M. G. CARON, 1996. Dopamine receptors and brain function. *Neuropharmacology* 35:1503–1519.

JACKSON, D. M., and A. WESTLIND-DANIELSSON, 1994. Dopamine receptors: Molecular biology, biochemistry and behavioral aspects. *Pharmacol. Ther.* 64:291–369.

JANIS, L. S., R. M. CASSIDY, and L. F. KROMER, 1999. Ephrin-A binding and EphA receptor expression delineate the matrix compartment of the striatum. *J. Neurosci.* 19:4962–4971.

JONES, L., I. FISCHER, and P. LEVITT, 1996. Nonuniform alteration of dendritic development in the cerebral cortex following prenatal cocaine exposure. *Cereb. Cortex* 6:431–445.

JONES, L. B., G. D. STANWOOD, B. S. REINOSO, R. A. WASHINGTON, H.-Y. WANG, E. FRIEDMAN, and P. LEVITT, 2000. In utero cocaine-induced dysfunction of dopamine D1 receptor signaling and abnormal differentiation of cerebral cortical neurons. *J. Neurosci.* 20:4606–4614.

JOYCE, J. N., P. A. FROHNA, and B. S. NEAL-BELIVEAU, 1996. Functional and molecular differentiation of the dopamine system induced by neonatal denervation. *Neurosci. Biobehav. Rev.* 20:453–486.

KALSBEEK, A., M. A. MATTHIJSSEN, and H. B. UYLINGS, 1989. Morphometric analysis of prefrontal cortical development following neonatal lesioning of the dopaminergic mesocortical projection. *Exp. Brain Res.* 78:279–289.

KARMEL, B. Z., and J. M. GARDNER, 1996. Prenatal cocaine exposure effects on arousal-modulated attention during the neonatal period. *Dev. Psychobiol.* 29:463–480.

KARREMAN, M., B. H. WESTERINK, and B. MOGHADDAM, 1996. Excitatory amino acid receptors in the ventral tegmental area regulate dopamine release in the ventral striatum. *J. Neurochem.* 67:601–607.

KATZ, L. C., and C. J. SHATZ, 1996. Synaptic activity and the construction of cortical circuits. *Science* 274:1133–1138.

KELLER, R. W., JR., K. S. JOHNSON, A. M. SNYDER-KELLER, J. N. CARLSON, and S. D. GLICK, 1996a. Effects of prenatal cocaine exposure on the mesocorticolimbic dopamine system: An in vivo microdialysis study in the rat. *Brain Res.* 742:71–79.

KELLER, R. W., JR., R. LEFEVRE, J. RAUCCI, J. N. CARLSON, and S. D. GLICK, 1996b. Enhanced cocaine self-administration in adult rats prenatally exposed to cocaine. *Neurosci. Lett.* 205:153–156.

KING, D., M. J. ZIGMOND, and J. M. FINLAY, 1997. Effects of dopamine depletion in the medial prefrontal cortex on the stress-induced increase in extracellular dopamine in the nucleus accumbens core and shell. *Neuroscience* 77:141–153.

KIYATKIN, E. A., 1995. Functional significance of mesolimbic dopamine. *Neurosci. Biobehav. Rev.* 19:573–598.

KOMURO, H., and P. RAKIC, 1993. Modulation of neuronal migration by NMDA receptors. *Science* 260:95–97.

KONRADI, C., J. C. LEVEQUE, and S. E. HYMAN, 1996. Amphetamine and dopamine-induced immediate early gene expression in striatal neurons depends on postsynaptic NMDA receptors and calcium. *J. Neurosci.* 16:4231–4239.

KOOB, G. F., 1992. Neural mechanisms of drug reinforcement. *Ann. N.Y. Acad. Sci.* 654:171–191.

KOREN, G., I. NULMAN, J. ROVET, R. GREENBAUM, M. LOEBSTEIN, and T. EINARSON, 1998. Long-term neurodevelopmental risks in children exposed in utero to cocaine. The Toronto Adoption Study. *Ann. N.Y. Acad. Sci.* 846:306–313.

KOSOFSKY, B. E., and A. S. WILKINS, 1998. A mouse model of transplacental cocaine exposure. Clinical implications for exposed infants and children. *Ann. N.Y. Acad. Sci.* 846:248–261.

KOSTRZEWA, R. M., T. A. READER, and L. DESCARRIES, 1998. Serotonin neural adaptations to ontogenetic loss of dopamine neurons in rat brain. *J. Neurochem.* 70:889–898.

KUHAR, M. J., and N. S. PILOTTE, 1996. Neurochemical changes in cocaine withdrawal. *Trends Pharmacol. Sci.* 17:260–264.

LANE, R. D., E. M. REIMAN, B. AXELROD, L. S. YUN, A. HOLMES, and G. E. SCHWARTZ, 1998. Neural correlates of levels of emotional awareness. Evidence of an interaction between emotion and attention in the anterior cingulate cortex. *J. Cogn. Neurosci.* 10:525–535.

LANKFORD, K. L., F. G. DeMELLO, and W. L. KLEIN, 1988. D1-type dopamine receptors inhibit growth cone motility in cultured retina neurons: Evidence that neurotransmitters act as morphogenic growth regulators in the developing central nervous system. *Proc. Natl. Acad. Sci. USA* 85:2839–2843.

LAUDER, J., and F. BLOOM, 1974. Ontogeny of monoamine neurons in the locus coeruleus, raphe nuclei, and substantia nigra of the rat. I. Cell differentiation. *J. Comp. Neurol.* 155:469–482.

LAUDER, J. M., 1993. Neurotransmitters as growth regulatory signals: Role of receptors and second messengers. *Trends Neurosci.* 16:233–240.

LAURIER, L. G., W. A. CORRIGALL, and S. R. GEORGE, 1994. Dopamine receptor density, sensitivity and mRNA levels are altered following self-administration of cocaine in the rat. *Brain Res.* 634:31–40.

LAVDAS, A. A., M. GRIGORIOU, V. PACHNIS, and J. G. PARNAVELAS, 1999. The medial ganglionic eminence gives rise to a population of early neurons in the developing cerebral cortex. *J. Neurosci.* 19:7881–7888.

LEBRAND, C., O. CASES, R. WEHRLE, R. D. BLAKELY, R. H. EDWARDS, and P. GASPAR, 1998. Transient developmental expression of monoamine transporters in the rodent forebrain. *J. Comp. Neurol.* 401:506–524.

LESKAWA, K. C., G. H. JACKSON, C. A. MOODY, and L. P. SPEAR, 1994. Cocaine exposure during pregnancy affects rat neonate and maternal brain glycosphingolipids. *Brain Res. Bull.* 33:195–198.

LEVITT, P., 1999. Molecular determinants of regionalization of the forebrain and cerebral cortex. In *The New Cognitive Neurosciences*, M. S. Gazzaniga, ed. Cambridge, Mass.: MIT Press, pp. 23–32.

LEVITT, P., 1998. Prenatal effects of drugs of abuse on brain development. *Drug Alcohol Depend.* 51:109–125.

LEVITT, P., J. A. HARVEY, E. FRIEDMAN, K. SIMANSKY, and E. H. MURPHY, 1997. New evidence for neurotransmitter influences on brain development. *Trends Neurosci.* 20:269–274.

LEVITT, P., P. RAKIC, and P. GOLDMAN-RAKIC, 1984. Region-specific distribution of catecholamine afferents in primate cerebral cortex: A fluorescence histochemical analysis. *J. Comp. Neurol.* 227:23–36.

LIDOW, M. S., 1998. Nonhuman primate model of the effect of prenatal cocaine exposure on cerebral cortical development. *Ann. N.Y. Acad. Sci.* 846:182–193.

LIDOW, M. S., 1995. Prenatal cocaine exposure adversely affects development of the primate cerebral cortex. *Synapse* 21:332–341.

LIDOW, M. S., and F. WANG, 1995. Neurotransmitter receptors in the developing cerebral cortex. *Crit. Rev. Neurobiol.* 9:395–418.

LILLIEN, L., 1998. Neural progenitors and stem cells: Mechanisms of progenitor heterogeneity. *Curr. Opin. Neurobiol.* 8:37–44.

LIPTON, S. A., and S. B. KATER, 1989. Neurotransmitter regulation of neuronal outgrowth, plasticity and survival. *Trends Neurosci.* 12:265–270.

LIPTON, J. W., Z. LING, T. Q. VU, H. C. ROBIE, K. P. MANGAN, D. E. WEESE-MAYER, and P. M. CARVEY, 1999. Prenatal cocaine exposure reduces glial cell line-derived neurotrophic factor (GDNF) in the striatum and the carotid body of the rat: Implications for DA neurodevelopment. *Dev. Brain Res.* 118:231–235.

LO, D. C., 1998. Instructive roles of neurotrophins in synaptic plasticity. *Prog. Brain Res.* 117:65–70.

LUO, L., L. JAN, and Y. N. JAN, 1996. Small GTPases in axon outgrowth. *Perspect. Dev. Neurobiol.* 4:199–204.

MACTUTUS, C. F., A. S. HERMAN, and R. M. BOOZE, 1994. Chronic intravenous model for studies of drug (Ab)use in the pregnant and/or group-housed rat: An initial study with cocaine. *Neurotoxicol. Teratol.* 16:183–191.

MALANGA, C. J., 3RD, and B. F. KOSOFSKY, 1999. Mechanisms of action of drugs of abuse on the developing fetal brain. *Clin. Perinatol.* 26:17–37, v–vi.

MATTSON, M. P., 1988. Neurotransmitters in the regulation of neuronal cytoarchitecture. *Brain Res.* 472:179–212.

MAYES, L. C., M. H. BORNSTEIN, K. CHAWARSKA, and R. H. GRANGER, 1995. Information processing and developmental assessments in 3-month-old infants exposed prenatally to cocaine. *Pediatrics* 95:539–545.

MAYES, L. C., R. H. GRANGER, M. A. FRANK, R. SCHOTTENFELD, and M. H. BORNSTEIN, 1993. Neurobehavioral profiles of neonates exposed to cocaine prenatally. *Pediatrics* 91:778–783.

MAYES, L. C., C. GRILLON, R. GRANGER, and R. SCHOTTENFELD, 1998. Regulation of arousal and attention in preschool children exposed to cocaine prenatally. *Ann. N.Y. Acad. Sci.* 846:126–143.

McCONNELL, S. K., 1995a. Constructing the cerebral cortex: neurogenesis and fate determination. *Neuron* 15:761–768.

McCONNELL, S. K., 1995b. Strategies for the generation of neuronal diversity in the developing central nervous system. *J. Neurosci.* 15:6987–6998.

MELTZER, L. T., C. L. CHRISTOFFERSEN, and K. A. SERPA, 1997. Modulation of dopamine neuronal activity by glutamate receptor subtypes. *Neurosci. Biobehav. Rev.* 21:511–518.

MEYER, J. S., and S.A. DUPONT, 1993. Prenatal cocaine administration stimulates fetal brain tyrosine hydroxylase activity. *Brain Res.* 608:129–137.

MILBERGER, S., J. BIEDERMAN, S. V. FARAONE, and J. JONES, 1998. Further evidence of an association between maternal smoking during pregnancy and attention deficit hyperactivity disorder: Findings from a high-risk sample of siblings. *J. Clin. Child Psychol.* 27:352–358.

MILLER, M. W., R. WAZIRI, S. BARUAH, and D. M. GILLIAM, 1995. Long-term consequences of prenatal cocaine exposure on biogenic amines in the brains of mice: The role of sex. *Brain Res. Dev. Brain Res.* 87:22–28.

MORARI, M., M. MARTI, S. SBRENNA, K. FUXE, C. BIANCHI, and L. BEANI, 1998. Reciprocal dopamine-glutamate modulation of release in the basal ganglia. *Neurochem. Intl.* 33:383–397.

MORATALLA, R., M. XU, S. TONEGAWA, and A. M. GRAYBIEL, 1996. Cellular responses to psychomotor stimulant and neuroleptic drugs are abnormal in mice lacking the D1 dopamine receptor. *Proc. Natl. Acad. Sci. USA* 93:14928–14933.

MURPHY, E. H., I. FISCHER, E. FRIEDMAN, D. GRAYSON, L. JONES, P. LEVITT, A. O'BRIEN-JENKINS, H. Y. WANG, and

X. H. WANG, 1997. Cocaine administration in pregnant rabbits alters cortical structure and function in their progeny in the absence of maternal seizures. *Exp. Brain Res.* 114:433–441.

MURPHY, E. H., J. G. HAMMER, M. D. SCHUMANN, M. Y. GROCE, X. H. WANG, L. JONES, A. G. ROMANO, and J. A. HARVEY, 1995. The rabbit as a model for studies of cocaine exposure in utero. *Lab. Animal Sci.* 45:163–168.

NEAL-BELIVEAU, B. S., and J. N. JOYCE, 1999. Timing: A critical determinant of the functional consequences of neonatal 6-OHDA lesions. *Neurotoxicol. Teratol.* 21:129–140.

NEISEWANDER, J. L., I. LUCKI, and P. MCGONIGLE, 1994. Time-dependent changes in sensitivity to apomorphine and monoamine receptors following withdrawal from continuous cocaine administration in rats. *Synapse* 16:1–10.

NESTLER, E. J., and G. K. AGHAJANIAN, 1997. Molecular and cellular basis of addiction. *Science* 278:58–63.

NIRENBERG, M. J., J. CHAN, A. POHORILLE, R. A. VAUGHAN, G. R. UHL, M. J. KUHAR, and V. M. PICKEL, 1997. The dopamine transporter: Comparative ultrastructure of dopaminergic axons in limbic and motor compartments of the nucleus accumbens. *J. Neurosci.* 17:6899–6907.

OLSON, L., and A. SEIGER, 1972. Early prenatal ontogeny of central monoamine neurons in the rat: Fluorescence histochemical observations. *Zeitsch. Anat. Entwicklungs.* 137:301–316.

OVERSTREET, D. H., S. S. MOY, D. A. LUBIN, L. R. GAUSE, J. A. LIEBERMAN, and J. M. JOHNS, 2000. Enduring effects of prenatal cocaine administration on emotional behavior in rats. *Physiol. Behav.* 70:149–156.

PARDO, J. V., P. T. FOX, and M. E. RAICHLE, 1991. Localization of a human system for sustained attention by positron emission tomography. *Nature* 349:61–64.

PIAZZA, P. V., and M. LE MOAL, 1998. The role of stress in drug self-administration. *Trends Pharmacol. Sci.* 19:67–74.

RAEDLER, T. J., M. B. KNABLE, and D. R. WEINBERGER, 1998. Schizophrenia as a developmental disorder of the cerebral cortex. *Curr. Opin. Neurobiol.* 8:157–161.

READER, T. A., P. MASSE, and J. DE CHAMPLAIN, 1979. The intracortical distribution of norepinephrine, dopamine and serotonin in the cerebral cortex of the cat. *Brain Res.* 177:499–513.

REINOSO, B. S., A. S. UNDIE, and P. LEVITT, 1996. Dopamine receptors mediate differential morphological effects on cerebral cortical neurons in vitro. *J. Neurosci. Res.* 43:439–453.

RICHARDSON, G. A., 1998. Prenatal cocaine exposure: A longitudinal study of development. *Ann. N.Y. Acad. Sci.* 846:144–152.

RICHARDSON, G. A., M. L. CONROY, and N. L. DAY, 1996. Prenatal cocaine exposure: Effects on the development of school-age children. *Neurotoxicol. Teratol.* 18:627–634.

RICHARDSON, G. A., and N. L. DAY, 1991. Maternal and neonatal effects of moderate cocaine use during pregnancy. *Neurotoxicol. Teratol.* 13:455–460.

ROMANO, A. G., and J. A. HARVEY, 1996. Prenatal exposure to cocaine disrupts discrimination learning in adult rabbits. *Pharmacol. Biochem. Behav.* 53:617–621.

ROMANO, A. G., W. J. KACHELRIES, K. J. SIMANSKY, and J. A. HARVEY, 1995. Intrauterine exposure to cocaine produces a modality-specific acceleration of classical conditioning in adult rabbits. *Pharmacol. Biochem. Behav.* 52:415–420.

RONNEKLEIV, O. K., Y. FANG, W. S. CHOI, and L. CHAI, 1998. Changes in the midbrain-rostral forebrain dopamine circuitry in the cocaine-exposed primate fetal brain. *Ann. N.Y. Acad. Sci.* 846:165–181.

RONNEKLEIV, O. K., and B. R. NAYLOR, 1995. Chronic cocaine exposure in the fetal rhesus monkey: Consequences for early development of dopamine neurons. *J. Neurosci.* 15:7330–7343.

SALES, N., M. P. MARTRES, M. L. BOUTHENET, and J. C. SCHWARTZ, 1989. Ontogeny of dopaminergic D-2 receptors in the rat nervous system: Characterization and detailed autoradiographic mapping with [$^{125}$I]iodosulphide. *Neuroscience* 28:673–700.

SCHAMBRA, U. B., G. E. DUNCAN, G. R. BREESE, M. G. FORNARETTO, M. G. CARON, and R. T. J. FREMEAU, 1994. Ontogeny of D1A and D2 dopamine receptor subtypes in rat brain using in situ hybridization and receptor binding. *Neuroscience* 62:65–85.

SCHER, M. S., G. A. RICHARDSON, and N. L. DAY, 2000. Effects of prenatal cocaine/crack and other drug exposure on electroencephelographic sleep studies at birth and one year. *Peds.* 105:39–48.

SEEMAN, P., and H. H. M. VAN TOL, 1994. Dopamine receptor pharmacology. *Trends Pharmacol. Sci.* 15:264–270.

SEGAL, R. A., and M. E. GREENBERG, 1996. Intracellular signaling pathways activated by neurotrophic factors. *Annu. Rev. Neurosci.* 19:463–489.

SESACK, S. R., A. Y. DEUTCH, R. H. ROTH, and B. S. BUNNEY, 1989. Topographical organization of the efferent projections of the medial prefrontal cortex in the rat: An anterograde tract-tracing study with *Phaseolus vulgaris* leucoagglutinin. *J. Comp. Neurol.* 290:213–242.

SESACK, S. R., and V. M. PICKEL, 1992. Prefrontal cortical efferents in the rat synapse on unlabeled neuronal targets of catecholamine terminals in the nucleus accumbens septi and on dopamine neurons in the ventral tegmental area. *J. Comp. Neurol.* 320:145–160.

SESACK, S. R., C. L. SNYDER, and D. A. LEWIS, 1995. Axon terminals immunolabeled for dopamine or tyrosine hydroxylase synapse on GABA-immunoreactive dendrites in rat and monkey cortex. *J. Comp. Neurol.* 363:264–280.

SIBLEY, D. R., and F. J. MONSMA, 1992. Molecular biology of dopamine receptors. *Trends Pharmacol. Sci.* 13:61–68.

SIEGEL, G. J., B. W. AGRANOFF, R. W. ALBERS, S. K. FISHER, and M. D. UHLER, 1998. *Basic Neurochemistry.* New York: Raven Press.

SIKICH, L., J. M. HICKOK, and R. D. TODD, 1990. 5-HT1A receptors control neurite branching during development. *Brain Res. Dev. Brain Res.* 56:269–274.

SIMANSKY, K. J., and W. J. KACHELRIES, 1996. Prenatal exposure to cocaine selectively disrupts motor responding to D-amphetamine in young and mature rabbits. *Neuropharmacology* 35:71–78.

SLOTKIN, T. A., 1998. Fetal nicotine or cocaine exposure: Which one is worse? *J. Pharmacol. Exp. Ther.* 285:931–945.

SMILEY, J. F., A. I. LEVEY, B. J. CILIAX, and P. S. GOLDMAN-RAKIC, 1994. D1 dopamine receptor immunoreactivity in human and monkey cerebral cortex: Predominant and extrasynaptic localization in dendritic spines. *Proc. Natl. Acad. Sci. USA* 91:5720–5724.

SNYDER, G. L., P. B. ALLEN, A. A. FIENBERG, C. G. VALLE, R. L. HUGANIR, A. C. NAIRN, and P. GREENGARD, 2000. Regulation of phosphorylation of the GluR1 AMPA receptor in the neostriatum by dopamine and psychostimulants in vivo. *J. Neurosci.* 20:4480–4488.

SNYDER, G. L., A. A. FIENBERG, R. L. HUGANIR, and P. GREENGARD, 1998. A dopamine/D1 receptor/protein kinase A/dopamine- and cAMP-regulated phosphoprotein (Mr 32 kDa)/protein phosphatase-1 pathway regulates dephosphorylation of the NMDA receptor. *J. Neurosci.* 18:10297–10303.

SNYDER-KELLER, A., and R. W. KELLER, JR., 1998. Prenatal cocaine exposure increases susceptibility to drug-induced seizures: c-fos induction and brain cocaine levels. *Ann. N.Y. Acad. Sci.* 846:419–422.

SNYDER-KELLER, A. M., and R. W. KELLER, JR., 1993. Prenatal cocaine increases striatal serotonin innervation without altering the patch/matrix organization of intrinsic cell types. *Brain Res. Dev. Brain Res.* 74:261–267.

SNYDER-KELLER, A., C. SAM, and R. W. KELLER, JR., 2000. Enhanced susceptibility to cocaine- and pentylenetetrazol-induced seizures in prenatally cocaine-treated rats. *Neurotoxicol. Teratol.* 22:231–236.

SPEAR, L. P., J. CAMPBELL, K. SNYDER, M. SILVERI, and N. KATOVIC, 1998. Animal behavior models. Increased sensitivity to stressors and other environmental experiences after prenatal cocaine exposure. *Ann. N.Y. Acad. Sci.* 846:76–88.

SPEAR, L. P., C. L. KIRSTEIN, N. A. FRAMBES, and C. A. MOODY, 1989. Neurobehavioral teratogenicity of gestational cocaine exposure. *NIDA Res. Monogr.* 95:232–238.

SPECHT, L. A., V. M. PICKEL, T. H. JOH, and D. J. REIS, 1981. Light-microscopic immunocytochemical localization of tyrosine hydroxylase in prenatal rat brain. I. Early ontogeny. *J. Comp. Neurol.* 199:233–253.

STANWOOD, G. D., R. A. WASHINGTON, and P. LEVITT, 2001. Identification of a sensitive period of prenatal cocaine exposure that alters the development of the anterior cingulate cortex. *Cereb. Cortex* (in press).

STENSAAS, L. J., 1967a. The development of hippocampal and dorsolateral pallial regions of the cerebral hemisphere in fetal rabbits. I. Fifteen millimeter stage, spongioblast morphology. *J. Comp. Neurol.* 129:59–70.

STENSAAS, L. J., 1967b. The development of hippocampal and dorsolateral pallial regions of the cerebral hemisphere in fetal rabbits. II. Twenty millimeter stage, neuroblast morphology. *J. Comp. Neurol.* 129:71–84.

STENSAAS, L. J., 1967c. The development of hippocampal and dorsolateral pallial regions of the cerebral hemisphere in fetal rabbits. III. Twenty-nine millimeter stage, marginal lamina. *J. Comp. Neurol.* 130:149–162.

STENSAAS, L. J., 1967d. The development of hippocampal and dorsolateral pallial regions of the cerebral hemisphere in fetal rabbits. IV. Forty-one millimeter stage, intermediate lamina. *J. Comp. Neurol.* 131:409–422.

STENSAAS, L. J., 1967e. The development of hippocampal and dorsolateral pallial region of the cerebral hemisphere in fetal rabbits. V. Sixty millimeter stage, glial cell morphology. *J. Comp. Neurol.* 131:423–436.

SWANSON, L. W., 1982. The projections of the ventral tegmental area and adjacent regions: A combined retrograde tracer and immunofluoresence study in the rat. *Brain Res. Bull.* 9:321–353.

TABER, M. T., S. DAS, and H. C. FIBIGER, 1995. Cortical regulation of subcortical dopamine release: Mediation via the ventral tegmental area. *J. Neurochem.* 65:1407–1410.

TAKAHASHI, L. K., 1998. Prenatal stress: Consequences of glucocorticoids on hippocampal development and function. *Intl. J. Dev. Neurosci.* 16:199–207.

TENNYSON, V. M., C. MYTILINEOU, and R. E. BARRETT, 1973. Fluorescence and electron microscopic studies of the early development of the substantia nigra and area ventralis tegmenti in the fetal rabbit. *J. Comp. Neurol.* 149:233–258.

TODD, R. D., 1992. Neural development is regulated by classical neurotransmitters: Dopamine D2 receptor stimulation enhances neurite outgrowth. *Biol. Psychiatry* 31:794–807.

UNIS, A. S., 1994. Ontogeny of [3H]-SCH23390 and [3H]-YM09151–2 binding sites in human fetal forebrain. *Biol. Psychiatry* 35:562–569.

VAN LEEUWEN, T. H., H. C. STEINHAUSEN, C. C. OVERTOOM, R. D. PASCUAL-MARQUI, B. VAN'T KLOOSTER, A. ROTHENBERGER, J. A. SERGEANT, and D. BRANDEIS, 1998. The continuous performance test revisited with neuroelectric mapping: Impaired orienting in children with attention deficits. *Behav. Brain Res.* 94:97–110.

VERBATEN, M. N., C. C. OVERTOOM, H. S. KOELEGA, H. SWAAB-BARNEVELD, R. J. VAN DER GAAG, J. BUITELAAR, and H. VAN ENGELAND, 1994. Methylphenidate influences on both early and late ERP waves of ADHD children in a continuous performance test. *J. Abnormal Child Psychol.* 22:561–578.

VERNEY, C., B. BERGER, J. ADRIEN, A. VIGNY, and M. GAY, 1982. Development of the dopaminergic innervation of the rat cerebral cortex. A light microscopic immunocytochemical study using anti-tyrosine hydroxylase antibodies. *Brain Res.* 281:41–52.

VITALIS, T., O. CASES, J. CALLEBERT, J. M. LAUNAY, D. J. PRICE, I. SEIF, and P. GASPAR, 1998. Effects of monoamine oxidase A inhibition on barrel formation in the mouse somatosensory cortex: Determination of a sensitive developmental period. *J. Comp. Neurol.* 393:169–184.

WANG, X. H., A. O. JENKINS, L. CHOI, and E. H. MURPHY, 1996. Altered neuronal distribution of parvalbumin in anterior cingulate cortex of rabbits exposed in utero to cocaine. *Exp. Brain Res.* 112:359–371.

WANG, X. H., P. LEVITT, D. R. GRAYSON, and E. H. MURPHY, 1995a. Intrauterine cocaine exposure of rabbits: Persistent elevation of GABA-immunoreactive neurons in anterior cingulate cortex but not visual cortex. *Brain Res.* 689:32–46.

WANG, H. Y., S. RUNYAN, E. YADIN, and E. FRIEDMAN, 1995b. Prenatal exposure to cocaine selectively reduces D1 dopamine receptor-mediated activation of striatal Gs proteins. *J. Pharmacol. Exp. Ther.* 273:492–498.

WANG, H. Y., J. M. YEUNG, and E. FRIEDMAN, 1995. Prenatal cocaine exposure selectively reduces mesocortical dopamine release. *J. Pharmacol. Exp. Ther.* 273:1211–1215.

WEESE-MAYER, D. E., and G. A. BARKOV, 1993. Effect of cocaine in early gestation. Physiologic responses to hypoxia in newborn rabbits. *Am. Rev. Resp. Disease* 148:589–596.

WEESE-MAYER, D. E., J. M. SILVESTRI, D. LIN, C. M. BUHRFIEND, E. S. LO, and P. M. CARVEY, 1993. Effect of cocaine in early gestation on striatal dopamine and neurotrophic activity. *Pediatr. Res.* 34:389–392.

WHITAKER-AZMITIA, P. M., 1998. Role of the neurotrophic properties of serotonin in the delay of brain maturation induced by cocaine. *Ann. N.Y. Acad. Sci.* 846:158–164.

WHITAKER-AZMITIA, P. M., M. DRUSE, P. WALKER, and J. M. LAUDER, 1996. Serotonin as a developmental signal. *Behav. Brain Res.* 73:19–29.

WILKINS, A. S., L. M. GENOVA, W. POSTEN, and B. E. KOSOFSKY, 1998a. Transplacental cocaine exposure. 1: A rodent model. *Neurotoxicol. Teratol.* 20:215–226.

WILKINS, A. S., K. JONES, and B. E. KOSOFSKY, 1998. Transplacental cocaine exposure. 2: Effects of cocaine dose and gestational timing. *Neurotoxicol. Teratol.* 20:227–238.

WILKINS, A. S., J. J. MAROTA, E. TABIT, and B. E. KOSOFSKY, 1998b. Transplacental cocaine exposure. 3: Mechanisms underlying altered brain development. *Neurotoxicol. Teratol.* 20:239–249.

WILLIAMS, S. M., and P. S. GOLDMAN-RAKIC, 1998. Widespread origin of the primate mesofrontal dopamine system. *Cereb. Cortex* 8:321–345.

WONG, E. V., S. KENWRICK, P. WILLEMS, and V. LEMMON, 1995. Mutations in the cell adhesion molecule L1 cause mental retardation. *Trends Neurosci.* 18:168–172.

XU, M., X. T. HU, D. C. COOPER, R. MORATALLA, A. M. GRAYBIEL, F. J. WHITE, and S. TONEGAWA, 1994. Elimination of cocaine-induced hyperactivity and dopamine-mediated neurophysiological effects in dopamine D1 receptor mutant mice [see comments]. *Cell* 79:945–955.

YANG, C.R., and J. K. SEAMANS, 1996. Dopamine D1 receptor actions in layers V–VI rat prefrontal cortex neurons in vitro: Modulation of dendritic-somatic signal integration. *J. Neurosci.* 16:1922–1935.

YANG, C. R., J. K. SEAMANS, and N. GORELOVA, 1999. Developing a neuronal model for the pathophysiology of schizophrenia based on the nature of electrophysiological actions of dopamine in the prefrontal cortex. *Neuropsychopharmacology* 21:161–194.

YUE, Y., D. WIDMER, J. SU, D. P. CERRETI, G. WAGNER, J.-L. DREYER, and R. ZHOU, 1998. Specification of distinct dopaminergic neural pathways: Role of the Eph family receptor EphB1 and ligand Ephrin-B2. *Soc. Neurosci. Abstr.* 24:21.5.

ZAMETKIN, A. J., T. E. NORDAHL, M. GROSS, A. C. KING, W. E. SEMPLE, J. RUMSEY, S. HAMBURGER, and R. M. COHEN, 1990. Cerebral glucose metabolism in adults with hyperactivity of childhood onset [see comments]. *N. Engl. J. Med.* 323:1361–1366.

ZHANG, X., L. M. SCHROTT, and S. B. SPARBER, 1998. Evidence for a serotonin-mediated effect of cocaine causing vasoconstriction and herniated umbilici in chicken embryos. *Pharmacol. Biochem. Behav.* 59:585–593.

ZIGMOND, M. J., E. D. ABERCROMBIE, T. W. BERGER, A. A. GRACE, and E. M. STRICKER, 1990. Compensations after lesions of central dopaminergic neurons: Some clinical and basic implications [see comments]. *Trends Neurosci.* 13:290–296.

ZIGMOND, M. J., S. L. CASTRO, K. A. KEEFE, E. D. ABERCROMBIE, and A. F. SVED, 1998. Role of excitatory amino acids in the regulation of dopamine synthesis and release in the neostriatum. *Amino Acids* 14:57–62.

# 34 Advances in the Cognitive Neuroscience of Autism

## SALLY OZONOFF

ABSTRACT  This chapter summarizes research on the neurobiology and cognition of autism. Neurobiological investigations have yielded inconsistent and often contradictory results. No "signature" autistic anomaly has yet been discovered, nor is a single one expected, given the phenotypic heterogeneity of the disorder. It is suggested that rigorous studies at the cognitive level that define the core neuropsychological features of autism will prove informative to future neurobiological investigations. Previous studies of cognition in autism, especially executive function, are summarized, and future directions are suggested. Specifically, it appears critical that future studies employ a component process approach to any area of cognition investigated, as well as attend carefully to seemingly irrelevant, but potentially critical, task dimensions, such as administration format, response mode, and feedback provision. It is hoped that these steps will eventually bring us closer to understanding the developmental cognitive neuroscience of autism.

Autism is a lifelong developmental disorder typified by social difficulties, communicative limitations, and a restricted range of interests and behaviors. Onset of the disorder occurs before 36 months of age, although it is not always recognized at this time. Boys are more often affected than girls, with gender ratio estimates ranging from 2 to 4 males for every female with the disorder (Lord and Schopler, 1987). While once considered a rare condition, recent prevalence estimates suggest that autism occurs in approximately 1 in 1000 individuals (Bryson, Clark, and Smith, 1988). It is currently suspected that higher prevalence estimates do not indicate an actual increase in the occurrence of autism, but rather, better detection of the disorder, particularly in its milder forms (Gillberg, Steffenburg, and Schaumann, 1991).

The most commonly used diagnostic system in the United States is the *Diagnostic and Statistical Manual of Mental Disorders,* 4th edition DSM-IV), published by the American Psychiatric Association (APA, 1994). As specified in the DSM-IV, all individuals with autism demonstrate evidence of difficulties with social relatedness, verbal and nonverbal communication, and range of interests and behaviors. In the social domain, the symptoms listed in the DSM-IV include impaired use of nonverbal behaviors (e.g., eye contact, facial expression, gestures) to regulate social interaction, failure to develop age-appropriate peer relationships, little spontaneous seeking to share enjoyment or interests with other people, and limited social–emotional reciprocity. DSM-IV symptoms of communicative dysfunction include delay in or absence of spoken language, difficulty initiating or sustaining conversations, idiosyncratic or repetitive language, and imitation and pretend play deficits. In the behaviors and interests domain, there is often an encompassing preoccupation or unusual interest that is abnormal in intensity, inflexible adherence to nonfunctional routines, stereotyped body movements, and preoccupation with parts or sensory qualities of objects (APA, 1994). In order to meet criteria for a diagnosis of Autistic disorder, an individual must demonstrate at least six of the twelve symptoms listed, with at least two coming from the social domain and one each from the communication and restricted behaviors/interests categories. Additionally, at least one symptom must have been present before 36 months of age (APA, 1994). Even among individuals meeting full criteria for Autistic disorder, symptoms can vary widely in severity, spanning a continuum from easily recognized deviant behaviors to much milder presentations (Wing, 1988). There is also a wide range of cognitive ability associated with Autistic disorder. Approximately 75% of individuals with autism are diagnosed with comorbid mental retardation, but the other 25%, so-called "high-functioning" individuals, test in the borderline intellectual range or above (e.g., full scale IQ $\geq$ 70).

High-functioning autism must be distinguished from Asperger disorder, a condition sharing the social disabilities and restricted, repetitive behaviors of autism, but in which language abilities are well-developed and cognitive functioning falls in the nonretarded range. Although described more than 50 years ago by Austrian pediatrician Hans Asperger (1944), the Asperger disorder was not included in the DSM until the manual's

SALLY OZONOFF  Department of Psychology, University of Utah, Salt Lake City, Utah.

fourth edition was published in 1994. The main point of differentiation from autistic disorder, especially the higher-functioning subtype, is that those with Asperger disorder never exhibit the typical autistic symptom of severe language delay. As specified in the DSM-IV, non-echoed, communicative use of single words must be demonstrated by age 2 and meaningful phrase speech by age 3. Most parents of children with Asperger disorder are not concerned about their child's early language development and may in fact report precocious language abilities, with the child using adult-like vocabulary and phrasing from an early age. Autistic disorder must be ruled out before a diagnosis of Asperger disorder is justified. The diagnosis of autism always takes precedence over that of Asperger disorder; thus, if a child meets criteria for autistic disorder, the diagnosis must be autism even if he or she displays excellent language and cognitive skills.

## Neurobiology

Speculation about the causes of autism has existed for as long as the disorder has been recognized. Leo Kanner, the Baltimore child psychiatrist who originally coined the term "autism," was the first to propose a causal theory. He suggested that autistic children were born with "an innate inability to form the usual, biologically provided affective contacts with people" (Kanner, 1943, p. 42). Later, however, he revised his thinking, suggesting that the disorder was environmentally caused. He and his contemporaries—particularly those trained in the psychoanalytic tradition predominant in the earlier twentieth century—came to believe that autism was the result of inadequate nurturance by emotionally cold, rejecting parents (Bettelheim, 1967). More recently, however, evidence that autism is a biologically based disorder has accumulated.

Rimland (1964) was the first to suggest that autism was due to a neurological defect; and since then, a good deal of research has been focused on understanding the neural substrates of the disorder. The literature is large but often contradictory. Post-mortem studies have not revealed gross pathology, but do find abnormalities in both cell packing density and morphology in the limbic system, as well as loss of granule and Purkinje cells from the neocerebellum and archicerebellar cortex (Bauman and Kemper, 1985, 1988). Imaging studies have revealed a wide variety of structural abnormalities, from nonspecific findings of ventricular enlargement (Jacobson et al., 1988) and cortical malformations (Piven et al., 1990) to potentially more specific hypoplasia of cerebellar vermal lobules VI and VII (Courchesne et al., 1988; Ritvo et al., 1986). Inconsistent replication is the

rule, rather than the exception, in neurobiological studies of autism, however. For example, the conclusion that the cerebellar vermis is smaller in volume in autism is currently hotly debated (Courchesne, Townsend, and Saitoh, 1994; Holttum et al., 1992), and the morphological changes in the limbic system reported by Bauman and colleagues have not been found in other post-mortem investigations (Williams et al., 1980). Approximately 25% of individuals with autism demonstrate larger than average brain volume (Filipek et al., 1992; Piven et al., 1996); however, this finding does not appear specific to any particular region or structure, nor is its clinical significance understood. Neuroimaging studies have not provided evidence of structural or volumetric differences in the limbic system or neocerebellum, as autopsy studies did, suggesting that some pathological differences in the brains of autistic people will not be captured with in vivo methods.

Owing to the impairments in higher cognitive processes that are a core feature of autism (summarized in the next section), differences in the cerebral cortex have also been explored. Cognitive impairments falling within the realm of executive function have made the frontal lobes an area of intuitive interest in autism, but imaging studies of this region have so far failed to find gross abnormalities. The cognitive and behavioral similarities between individuals with autism and patients with frontal lobe disease led Damasio and Maurer (1978) to hypothesize that autism might be the result of damage to frontal cortex and related structures. So far, however, no evidence of structural abnormalities in this region has been found. Studies of cortical function, however, are somewhat more suggestive of frontal involvement. An early investigation found depressed cerebral blood flow in right frontal cortex during resting state in mentally retarded adults with autism (Sherman, Nass, and Shapiro, 1984). Similarly, a more recent single photon emission computed tomographic (SPECT) study of four young adults with autism found reduced blood flow to the right, left, and midfrontal lobes, also during resting state (George et al., 1992). Reduced frontal metabolism has also been reported in children and adolescents with high-functioning autism and Asperger syndrome (Gillberg, 1994) and preschool children with autism (Zilbovicius et al., 1995). Finally, Dawson and colleagues reported that autistic children differed from chronological and mental age controls in frontal EEG power (Dawson et al., 1995).

A second brain region of interest in autism is the medial temporal cortex and related subcortical (limbic) structures (Bachevalier, 1994; Boucher and Warrington, 1976; DeLong, 1992; Fein et al., 1986). As with the frontal theory of autism, the medial temporal hypothesis had its origins in behavioral and cognitive similarities with human brain damage syndromes, such as Kluver-Bucy and Korsakoff syndromes (Hetzler and Griffin, 1981). Damasio and Maurer (1978) posited a role for medial temporal structures (along with medial frontal structures) in their neurological theory of autism, making behavioral analogies between autism and medial temporal lobe damage in humans. The performance of people with autism is quite poor on neuropsychological tests thought to tap medial temporal cortex (e.g., delayed nonmatch to sample tasks; Barth, Fein and Waterhouse, 1995; Dawson et al., 1998). In addition, animal studies have suggested similarities between the behavior of children with autism and animals with medial temporal damage. For example, monkeys with early lesions of the hippocampus and amygdala demonstrate severe social impairment and stereotyped, self-stimulatory behavior similar to autism (Bachevalier, 1991). Finally, there are multiple case studies of individuals with medial temporal damage, secondary to viral infection (typically herpes simplex virus), who acquire autistic symptoms concomitant with the infection (DeLong, Bean, and Brown, 1981; Gillberg, 1986, 1991; Greer et al., 1989; Hauser, DeLong, and Rosman, 1975; White and Rosenbloom, 1992). However, as in the neurobiological investigations of other brain regions in autism, there are failures to replicate (Piven et al., 1998; Williams et al., 1980), as well as questions about the validity of the behavioral and cognitive analogies. For example, neuropsychological studies of autism do not find the amnesic-like cognitive profile characteristic of medial temporal damage (Bennetto, Pennington, and Rogers, 1996; Minshew and Goldstein, 1993).

Investigations of cortical glucose utilization have not yielded consistent findings either, nor do they point toward any one specific region of interest. Functional imaging studies have found evidence of global hypermetabolism (Rumsey et al., 1985), specific areas of hypometabolism (George et al., 1992; Sherman et al., 1984; Zilbovicius et al., 1995), and no metabolic differences relative to controls (Zilbovicius et al., 1992). One study found a negative correlation between frontal glucose metabolism and performance on an attention task (Siegel et al., 1995), suggesting that neuronal inefficiency in frontal regions may contribute to the attentional impairments of autism. Horwitz and colleagues (1988) examined metabolic patterns across different brain regions, looking for intercorrelations that might reflect "functional loops" important to behavior. Control subjects demonstrated large positive correlations among frontal, parietal, and subcortical regions, thought to indicate coordinated neural circuitry; individuals with autism, in contrast, demonstrated large

negative correlations. These results suggest that it may not be the structure or function of *individual* brain regions that is abnormal in autism, but their functional coordination that causes symptoms of the disorder.

In summary, the literature on the neurobiology of autism is frustratingly inconsistent. Abnormalities reported at some levels (e.g., histopathologic) are not reflected in decreased size, volume, or metabolic rate of the structures involved. Even within the same methodological approach (e.g., structural MRI), there are multiple failures to replicate. All anomalies so far reported are present in at most a minority of participants studied; no investigation has documented a signature autistic anomaly, one that even comes close to being universal and specific to the disorder. This is, at first glance, disappointing and perhaps superficially surprising, given the grave impairment that autism confers on the individual and his or her functioning. Yet the phenotype of autism is highly heterogeneous, with a number of potentially subtyping dimensions (e.g., verbal ability, cognitive level, presence of self-injury, repetitive behaviors) that may well explain the neurobiological heterogeneity and contradictory results of previous studies. In addition, many of the investigations reviewed above lacked appropriate control samples (most commonly failing to control for mental handicap), so that the results reported here must be considered provisional at best. Finally, the ability of neurobiological research to explain the cognitive impairments of autism also appears limited. Bailey (1993) and others have suggested that many or most of the neurobiological defects found so far are not necessarily the ones that are central to generating autistic symptomatology. The sophistication of imaging tools is increasing rapidly, but has likely not yet reached even close to its eventual capacity. The techniques used a decade ago, when much of the research just reported was performed, were far less powerful and may only have been able to identify the grossest and most easily detectable manifestations of more distributed central nervous system damage. Cerebellar or medial temporal abnormalities, for example, may not be critically important to producing the cognitive and behavioral symptoms of the disorder, but instead, may be neurological markers that reflect the timing of the insult during neuronal development (Gaffney et al., 1989) or may be secondary to or coexistent with abnormal innervation from other, as yet unrecognized, dysfunctional regions (Bailey, 1993).

## Cognition

Bailey (1993) has persuasively argued that neurobiological data are only as good as their capacity to explain the reliably documented psychological and cognitive impairments of autism. Luciana and Nelson (1998) suggest that the use of behavioral measures that have been firmly linked to brain anatomy or physiology can bridge the gap between psychology and neuroscience. In this section, the literature on the cognition of people with autism is reviewed, and its ability to inform the developmental neuroscience of the condition is discussed.

Children with autism, unlike those with mental retardation or other developmental disabilities, demonstrate highly variable performance across different cognitive domains. Research has demonstrated a specific neuropsychological profile that includes spared performance on tasks relying on rote, mechanical, or visual-spatial-perceptual processes and deficient performance on tasks requiring higher-order conceptual processes, such as reasoning, interpretation, integration or abstraction (Minshew, Goldstein, and Siegel, 1997). This pattern is present across multiple cognitive domains, with dissociations between simple and complex information processing demonstrated in the areas of language, memory, executive function, reading, mathematics, perspective-taking, and motor skills (Klinger and Dawson, 1995; Minshew et al., 1994; Ozonoff and Strayer, 1997; Reed and Peterson, 1990; Rumsey and Hamburger, 1988). Learning, in general, is characterized by difficulty in seeing relationships between pieces of information, identifying central patterns or themes, distinguishing relevant from irrelevant information, and deriving meaning. Individuals with autism tend to be detail-oriented, but have difficulty seeing the "big picture" and can be quite literal in their thinking. Such difficulties are apparent across the autistic continuum and are present in even very high-functioning individuals (Grandin, 1995).

Many investigations have also found attentional abnormalities in individuals with autism. Early studies, for example, suggested that arousal modulating systems were dysfunctional, leading to fluctuations between states of over- and underarousal (Hutt et al., 1964; Ornitz and Ritvo, 1968). Later work, using cortical event-related potentials, confirmed that orienting and processing of novel stimuli by autistic persons is reduced (Courchesne et al., 1985; Dawson et al., 1986). Another atypical aspect of attention in autism is an often narrowed scope of attention. This has been examined empirically using paradigms developed by Posner and colleagues, who have posited three components in the orientation of attention: disengagement from the current object of attention, movement to a new object or location, and re-engagement there (Posner, 1980). Recent studies find that the shifting or moving operation is the most problematic in autism (Casey et al.,

1993; Courchesne, Townsend, and Saitoh, 1994; Wainwright-Sharp and Bryson, 1993). This pattern of attentional dysfunction distinguishes children with autism from those with attention deficit hyperactivity disorder (ADHD), another childhood condition involving attention problems. While children with ADHD have little difficulty moving attention (Swanson et al., 1991), they demonstrate severe impairment in sustaining attention and controlling impulses (Douglas and Peters, 1979). In contrast, a number of studies have suggested that the ability to sustain attention is a relatively spared function in autism (Buchsbaum et al., 1992; Casey et al., 1993; Garretson, Fein, and Waterhouse, 1990). This research suggests that some aspects of attention are preserved in autism, but that the processes by which environmental stimuli are selected for attention and how attention is shifted between stimuli is dysfunctional.

EXECUTIVE DYSFUNCTION  Consistent with attentional shifting abnormalities is recent research finding widespread executive function impairments in autism. Executive function is a broadly defined cognitive construct originally used to describe the deficits found in patients with focal frontal lobe lesions. It refers to the many skills required to prepare for and execute complex behavior, including planning, inhibition, organization, self-monitoring, mental flexibility, and mental representation of tasks and goals. Executive dysfunction has been consistently found across different ages and ability levels of people with autism when compared with appropriate controls (for a review, see Pennington and Ozonoff, 1996). Executive function deficits have been documented in a variety of other conditions as well, including ADHD, obsessive-compulsive disorder, schizophrenia, and various dementias (Ozonoff, 1997a). One issue this raises is the so-called "discriminant validity" question (Pennington, 1994): That is, how can disorders differing in behavioral phenotype share the same cognitive underpinnings? Since the class of executive behaviors is large and diverse, it is possible that different neurodevelopmental disorders are associated with different types of executive impairment. Thus, recent research has examined separate components of executive function in autism and other disorders, as detailed following.

A second problem is that most executive tasks suffer from measurement imprecision. Most tap far more than one cognitive operation, usually without specific scoring systems that permit individual variance to be teased out and examined independently. A good example of a test that suffers from this problem is the Wisconsin Card Sorting Test (WCST), the most widely used measure of executive function in autism (Pennington and Ozonoff,

1996). While the WCST is generally considered a test of cognitive flexibility, subjects must also be able to classify stimuli according to abstract principles, inhibit previously reinforced responses, selectively attend to appropriate dimensions of the stimulus materials, and use verbal feedback provided in the context of a social interaction to perform well on the task (Ozonoff, 1995a). When an individual receives a poor score on the WCST, it is difficult to determine which cognitive operations were responsible. One way to address both the discriminant validity and measurement imprecision problems is through component process analysis (Ozonoff, 1997b).

*Component process approach*  The goal of component process analysis is decomposition of complex cognitive functions into the elementary operations that appear to underlie them; the time course and relationship of these component processes to each other; and the internal representations, schemas, or codes they act upon (Farah, 1984; Friedrich and Rader, 1996). Taking this component process approach, a series of investigations conducted in my laboratory at the University of Utah suggests that there is indeed a distinct executive function profile associated with autism, one whose peaks and valleys distinguish it from other disorders. Our first study examined flexibility in individuals with high-functioning autism, using a Go-NoGo reversal learning paradigm (Ozonoff et al., 1994). Two shapes, a circle and a square, were presented on a computer screen; participants were taught to respond to one of them, while simultaneously inhibiting responses to the other one. After several trials with this set of response contingencies, participants were given the opposite directions, now to respond to the previously inhibited dimension and ignore the previously salient stimulus. After several more trials, they had to shift back to the original response mode, then back to the opposite response set, and so forth, for several hundred trials. The need to alter cognitive set every few seconds placed a high premium on flexibility. We found robust differences between individuals with autism and both participants with Tourette syndrome (TS) and those with typical development (who did not differ from each other) on this task, suggesting that flexibility impairments are distinctive of autism.

The second study in this series examined inhibitory mechanisms in autism and TS (age- and IQ-matched). Two cognitive tasks, a stop-signal and a negative priming paradigm, were used. In the first, participants were given a primary task, in this case to categorize words as members or nonmembers of a specific target category (e.g., foods). On a subset of trials, an auditory signal was presented that told participants to inhibit the categorization response (e.g., do nothing). Individuals with autism proved able to inhibit their responses as well as typical controls (Ozonoff and Strayer, 1997), while TS participants were impaired on this task (Ozonoff et al., 1998).

In the negative priming task, a string of five letters was presented on a computer screen; participants were told to attend to the second and fourth letters in the string and ignore (e.g., inhibit the processing of) the letters in the other positions. The participants' primary task was to indicate if the second and fourth letters were the same as or different from each other, through a keypress. The primary manipulation was that on some trials, the letters to be attended to had been in the "ignored" positions on the immediately preceding trial. Research on typically developing individuals demonstrates that when stimuli have been actively inhibited on trial $x$, their processing on trial $x + 1$ is slower than if they hadn't been previously inhibited (Tipper, 1985). On this task, we again found that the autistic participants demonstrated normal inhibition (that is, their processing on trial $x + 1$ was slowed to a degree similar to that of the typical participants' processing), while the TS group demonstrated inhibitory dysfunction (Ozonoff and Strayer, 1997; Ozonoff et al., 1998).

Thus, these studies of inhibition again suggest a dissociation of the executive impairments of autism and TS, with inhibitory processing being a relative weakness for TS and a relative strength for autism. Work by other investigators using the same paradigms with ADHD children further strengthens this dissociation, with difficulty stopping or inhibiting responses evident in the ADHD group as well (Schachar and Logan, 1990).

The third study in the component process series examined yet another component of executive function, working memory (Ozonoff and Strayer, under review). Working memory is defined as the ability to maintain information in an activated, on-line state to guide cognitive processing (Baddeley, 1986). More so than other memory operations, working memory serves a dynamic function and has been referred to as a "computational workspace" (Baddeley, 1986). Typical working memory tasks require subjects to simultaneously hold information on-line, process it, and store results for later recall, thus requiring a significant amount of organization and processing of the material to be remembered.

Initial suggestion of working memory dysfunction in autism came from studies of performance on the Tower of Hanoi and closely related Tower of London tasks. These are considered classic measures of planning (Shallice, 1982) and thus, at least intuitively, of working memory. Tower tasks necessitate generating and holding potential moves in an "on-line" state while considering the consequences of each and choosing among the alternatives. The simultaneous operations of maintaining an active representation while using it to guide behavior suggest that the tasks provide at least an indirect measure of working memory performance. Five investigations using tower tasks have been conducted with autistic samples, and all have found statistically significant impairments relative to matched controls (Bennetto, Pennington, and Rogers, 1996; Hughes, Russell, and Robbins, 1994; Ozonoff and Jensen, 1999; Ozonoff and McEvoy, 1994; Ozonoff, Pennington, and Rogers, 1991). While there is overlap among the investigators of these five studies, three of the samples were completely independent (Hughes, Russell, and Robbins, 1994; Ozonoff and Jensen, 1999; Ozonoff, Pennington, and Rogers, 1991). Both low- and high-functioning individuals perform poorly on tower tasks, relative to both mentally handicapped and normally developing nonautistic individuals (Hughes, Russell, and Robbins, 1994; Ozonoff and Jensen, 1999). In fact, group differences on tower tasks are more robust and their effect size is larger than any other executive measure so far used with people with autism (Pennington and Ozonoff, 1996). One study found that performance on the Tower of Hanoi was the single best predictor of group (autistic versus learning disabled) from a broad neuropsychological battery and was able to classify 80% of the sample correctly (Ozonoff, Pennington, and Rogers, 1991).

Other investigations of working memory in autism have been less convergent, however. Two recent papers reported conflicting results. Bennetto and her colleagues found deficient performance in adolescent and adult high-functioning autistic subjects on two measures of verbal working memory capacity, a counting and a sentence span task (Bennetto, Pennington, and Rogers, 1996), but not on measures of short- and long-term recognition memory, cued recall, or new learning ability. In contrast, Russell and his team failed to find any group differences between mentally handicapped children and adolescents with autism and mentally handicapped nonautistic controls, using three measures of working memory capacity, a dice counting, an odd-man-out, and a sentence span task (Russell, Jarrold, and Henry, 1996).

Two potential explanations for the discrepant findings have been put forth. Russell and colleagues (1996) suggest that working memory deficits may be a general function of developmental handicap and not specific to autism. Therefore, when controls are also mentally handicapped, no group differences emerge. In contrast, since high-functioning individuals with autism are typically matched with nondisabled controls, group differences will be apparent. Pennington and colleagues (1997) suggest that verbal working memory may be more affected than spatial working memory in individuals with autism, who demonstrate relatively good performance on most spatial tasks.

We examined these two hypotheses with the following design (Ozonoff and Strayer, under review). We tested two different contrast groups, one clinical (TS) and one typical, permitting examination of the hypothesis that working memory impairment is a general feature of disorder rather than a specific feature of autism. We included both verbal and spatial measures of working memory, allowing exploration of the suggestion that the nature of the task (verbal vs. nonverbal) is of primary importance in producing deficient performance. The results of our study failed to support either previous hypothesis. We found no impairment across five dependent measures of working memory. Neither the autistic nor the Tourette group performed significantly less well than the controls. Within the autistic (or any) group, there was no performance differential between verbal and spatial working memory. The task designs were, however, sensitive enough to detect within-group differences as a function of working memory load, lag, and delay, discounting simple power or task sensitivity explanations for the findings. We interpreted these results as providing little evidence of working memory impairment in either autism or TS, a suggestion that has been supported by even more recent research (Griffith et al., 1999; Menard et al., 1999).

In the final investigation to date of executive profiles in neurodevelopmental disorders, Ozonoff and Jensen (1999) directly compared individuals with autism, TS, and ADHD on three measures of executive function, each tapping a separate component (flexibility, inhibition, and planning). As with the studies just summarized, the results of this investigation provided strong evidence of distinct executive profiles, with autistic participants impaired in flexibility and planning, ADHD participants deficient in inhibition, and TS participants relatively unimpaired on any executive task, relative to typically developing controls.

A recently developed computerized battery of neuropsychological tasks has permitted even more extensive dissection of executive function components. The Cambridge Neuropsychological Test Automated Battery (CANTAB) is a computer-administered, nonverbal (visually presented) set of tasks developed to examine specific components of cognition (Robbins et al., 1994). Several subtests have been used in functional imaging, animal cognition, and human lesion studies (Baker et al., 1996; Dias, Robbins, and Roberts, 1996; Owen et al.,

1996; Roberts, Robbins, and Everitt, 1988), permitting both cross-species comparison and inference about the underlying neural circuitry involved in impaired task performance. Subtests are graded in difficulty, minimizing floor and ceiling effects, and allowing use with a wide variety of ages and patient groups (Fray, Robbins, and Sahakian, 1996; Luciana and Nelson, 1998; Robbins et al., 1994, 1998).

Three recent investigations have used CANTAB with autistic individuals (Hughes, Russell, and Robbins, 1994; Ozonoff, South, and Miller, in press; Turner, 1997). Hughes and colleagues (1994) employed CANTAB's version of the Tower of London planning task with autistic participants who were also mentally handicapped. In this task, three colored balls are arranged on the computer screen in a specific configuration; participants are given three identical balls, in a different configuration, to match with the goal set and are told to do so in as few moves as possible. This demands planning and executing an optimal set of moves that transforms the initial ball configuration to the goal configuration. The autistic group took significantly more moves to solve the problems than the mentally handicapped and normally developing controls. Only 13% of the autistic group, but 49% of the mentally handicapped and 65% of the normal control group, solved the problems in the most efficient manner (e.g., in the minimum number of moves). A recent study conducted in our laboratory failed to detect any planning impairments on the CANTAB Tower of London task, however (Ozonoff, South, and Miller, in press). The primary difference between the studies appears to be the intellectual level of the participants. While the ability of the Hughes sample fell in the mentally handicapped range, ours was quite high-functioning, with a group mean full scale IQ of 111. Other potential explanations for the divergent findings are explored below.

A second subtest of much interest to autism researchers, CANTAB's intradimensional–extradimensional (IDED) task, taps the executive component of set-shifting or cognitive flexibility. A series of compound stimuli composed of colored shapes and lines is presented. Participants learn, through trial and error with computer-generated feedback, to respond to the shape; the line is effectively an irrelevant dimension. Once training to the shape is complete, the necessity to perform two kinds of shifts takes place. In the first, intradimensional, shift new shapes and lines are introduced, but shape remains the relevant response dimension. In the later, extradimensional, shift the contingencies change, with the line becoming the salient stimulus and the previously trained shape now irrelevant. Only the extradimensional shift requires conceptual flexibility

(that is, shifting from one concept or cognitive set to another); the intradimensional shift only requires perceptual flexibility, or shifting from one exemplar to another exemplar within the same cognitive set (e.g., shape). This task is functionally similar to the category shifts required by the Wisconsin Card Sorting Test, but conceptually simpler and with multiple manipulations built in to control for other sources of impairment, such as inhibitory dysfunction or discrimination learning deficits.

The first study employing the IDED subtest compared mentally handicapped autistic individuals to appropriately matched mentally handicapped but nonautistic controls (Hughes, Russell, and Robbins, 1994). Intact performance during the discrimination learning and intradimensional shifting phases of the task, but impairment at the extradimensional shift, was found. Two later investigations have had more mixed results. Turner (1997) replicated the extradimensional shifting deficit in lower-functioning (mentally handicapped) individuals with autism, but found no deficits in higher-functioning (nonretarded) autistic participants, relative to outpatient psychiatric controls. Similarly, a recent study in our laboratory (Ozonoff, South, and Miller, in press) found no extradimensional shifting difficulties in high-functioning autistic or Asperger syndrome participants relative to typically developing controls matched on IQ.

While earlier reviews (Ozonoff, 1995b; Pennington and Ozonoff, 1996) have described the widespread, almost universal, nature of executive dysfunction in autism, this chapter has highlighted a number of recent failures to replicate this general finding. Some of these recent null results are attributable to the development and refinement of experimental procedures that have permitted researchers to explore specific subcomponents of executive function. Thus, some null results are not failures to replicate or disconfirmation of the executive dysfunction hypothesis of autism, but rather clarifications of the specific nature of this executive dysfunction; the results of inhibition studies fall in this category. In other domains, such as planning and working memory impairments, the mixed pattern of results is not so straightforwardly explained. The next section explores one hypothesis for these recently obtained discrepancies.

*Executive function and social behavior* A certain level of social awareness may be necessary for successful performance on executive function tests (Ozonoff, 1995a; Ozonoff and Strayer, under review). One dimension that distinguishes most "null-result" executive function studies from investigations finding significant group differences is whether the experimental tasks were computerized or not. For example, all working memory tasks in the Ozonoff and Strayer (under review) study were computerized, as were all of Russell's (Russell, Jarrold, and Henry, 1996) working memory measures; group differences were apparent in neither investigation. Similarly, CANTAB is a computerized battery and 2 of 3 studies using it have failed to find autism-control group differences. In contrast, none of Bennetto's working memory tasks was presented by computer, and group differences were found; similarly, most versions of the Tower of Hanoi, which typically yields robust group differences, are not computerized (Ozonoff, Pennington, and Rogers, 1991). It is possible that computer administration of executive tasks attenuates group differences that might otherwise be present. In other words, tasks administered by humans, which require some degree of social interaction to indicate correct response, amplify a cognitive impairment that may otherwise be only marginal.

Some support for this "computer facilitation" hypothesis has been demonstrated by two studies that directly compared performance on computerized and noncomputerized versions of executive tasks. Ozonoff (1995a) found that when the Wisconsin Card Sorting Test was administered in the standard fashion—by humans—group differences were robust; but when it was administered by computer, group differences were greatly attenuated (although still statistically significant). Participants with autism tended to perform better on the computer than on the human-administered version of the test, while there was no difference in performance as a function of test format for normal controls. Identical within- and between-group patterns were found by Pascualvaca and colleagues (1998) using the traditional (human-administered) WCST and a computerized WCST-like matching task devised by the authors.

Computer facilitation does not explain all failures to find group differences in studies of executive function, however. Most notably, the Griffith investigation, in which performance was unimpaired on eight executive tasks, did not employ computer administration, yet still failed to find differences between young children with autism and matched controls (Griffith et al., 1999). This study has led us to suspect that the essential element distinguishing intact and deficient executive performance is not the mode of administration, but the mode of feedback delivery. In the computerized studies just summarized, administration and feedback modes were confounded; that is, they were either both performed by computer or both performed by human. The Griffith study fortuitously disentangled these typically enmeshed dimensions. Although a human examiner ad-

ministered the tasks, she did not indicate whether responses were correct, as in the WCST; instead, accuracy feedback was provided naturally, by the materials themselves. Specifically, if the response was correct, the child automatically received a reward, delivered by the test apparatus itself, whereas if the child reached for the incorrect location, he or she encountered an unbaited well and no reinforcer. At no time did the experimenter socially, verbally, or otherwise provide feedback about performance. This suggests that a central deficit in autism may be the ability to make meaningful use of feedback when it is provided in the context of a verbal, social interaction. This hypothesis is consistent with the frontal theory of autism, as orbitofrontal cortex plays an important role in stimulus-reinforcement associations and reversal learning (Dias, Robbins, and Roberts, 1996; Jones and Mishkin, 1972; Rolls, 1998).

While social-motivational factors may be important in producing executive dysfunction, there is equally strong evidence that executive factors contribute to the social-cognitive deficits of autism. Shortly after the relevance of perspective-taking deficits to autism became clear, their relationship to executive function began to be explored. In a study designed to examine strategic deception abilities (Russell et al., 1991), autistic subjects were taught to play a game in which they competed with an experimenter for a piece of candy. The candy was placed in one of two boxes with windows that revealed the contents of the box to subjects, but not to the experimenter. The objective of the task was to "fool" the experimenter into looking for the candy in the empty box. It was explained that the strategy of pointing to the empty box would be successful in winning the candy, whereas pointing to the box that actually contained the chocolate would result in losing it. Even after many trials, the autistic subjects were unable to point to the empty box, despite the consequences of this strategy. Russell and colleagues (1991) initially attributed these results to a perspective-taking deficit that caused an inability to engage in deception. In a follow-up study, however, Hughes and Russell (1993) demonstrated that significant group differences remained even after the element of social deception was removed from the task. Subjects were simply instructed to point to the empty box to get the candy. Even with no opponent present, the autistic subjects persisted in using the inappropriate strategy. On the basis of these results, Hughes and Russell (1993) reattributed the autistic participants' pattern of performance to a deficit in disengaging from the object and using internal rules to guide behavior (e.g., to an executive deficit), rather than to social or perspective-taking dysfunction.

Several other studies have highlighted the related and interdependent nature of social and executive skills (Berger et al., 1993; Grattan and Eslinger, 1989; Ozonoff, Pennington, and Rogers, 1991; Szatmari et al., 1989). Substantial correlations between executive function and theory of mind abilities have been found (Ozonoff, Pennington, and Rogers, 1991). It has been suggested that executive function and perspective-taking abilities may share a common neural substrate (Ozonoff and McEvoy, 1994; Ozonoff, 1995b), with recent functional neuroimaging research indicating that theory of mind capacities may also be subserved by prefrontal cortex (Baron-Cohen et al., 1994; Fletcher et al., 1995). Alternatively, certain executive skills, such as flexibility, may be a prerequisite for empathy and other social behaviors. These studies suggest that the social cognition and executive function deficits of autism may not be completely separable, independent islets of dysfunction. It is also clear, however, that executive difficulties cannot completely account for the social disabilities of autism, as nonautistic individuals with severe executive function disorders do not demonstrate the same magnitude or quality of social disturbance as in autism (Bishop, 1993).

## Conclusions

A strong plea for the integration of cognitive and neurobiological research was made earlier in this chapter. It has been argued that the search for neural underpinnings of autism has been delayed by the lack of consensus regarding the core cognitive impairments of the disorder (Frith, 1989). I have suggested that further dissection of apparently "core" cognitive deficits is still needed. For example, the vast majority of published studies of executive function in autism have found deficits relative to matched controls (Pennington and Ozonoff, 1996), yet there is emerging evidence of islets of spared ability within this domain, as well as noncognitive, nonexecutive contributors to the impairments that *are* present. Had robust deficits on measures of shifting or planning been consistently found, then studies examining the neural underpinnings of these tasks, using functional imaging, animal or human lesion studies, would be more straightforward. However, the findings of relatively preserved shifting and planning skills under certain task conditions suggest our job is far from simple. Functional imaging studies already necessitate changes in task administration, response mode, and feedback format to accommodate the movement and space limitations of scanners. Researchers doing this kind of work will need to wrestle further with such methodological issues as their impact on the performance of individuals with autism becomes clearer. Just a few years ago, we might have argued that the lateral prefrontal cortex (Brodmann area 9) could be a region of special investigation in neurobiological studies of autism, because of its role in performance on the IDED (Dias, Robbins, and Roberts, 1996) and Tower of London tasks (Baker et al., 1996). Yet now it appears that what we may need to study is the neural circuitry underlying the processing of various modes of contingent feedback delivery. This will require sophisticated designs that attend to and manipulate multiple task format dimensions in a controlled manner. While questions about the neural and cognitive mechanisms underlying autism remain seemingly far away, such approaches may bring answers a bit closer.

ACKNOWLEDGMENTS Work on this manuscript was supported in part by grants from the National Institutes of Health (P01 HD35476 and R29 MH52229) to the author. I am very grateful to Monica Luciana, Ph.D., for sharing normative CANTAB data for children and to my collaborator, David Strayer, Ph.D., and graduate students who helped design and execute the experiments reviewed in this chapter.

## REFERENCES

AMERICAN PSYCHIATRIC ASSOCIATION, 1994. *Diagnostic and statistical manual of mental disorders*, 4th ed. Washington, D.C.: Author.

ASPERGER, H., 1944. "Autistic psychopathy" in childhood. *Arch. Psychiat. Nervenkrank.* 117:76–136.

BACHEVALIER, J., 1991. An animal model for childhood autism: Memory loss and socio-emotional disturbances following neonatal damage of the limbic system in monkeys. In *Advances in Neuropsychiatry and Psychopharmacology*, C. A. Tamminga and S. C. Schulz, eds. New York: Raven Press, pp. 129–140.

BACHEVALIER, J., 1994. Medial temporal lobe structures and autism: A review of clinical and experimental findings. *Neuropsychologia* 32:627–648.

BADDELEY, A. D., 1986. *Working Memory*. Oxford: Clarendon Press.

BAILEY, A. J., 1993. The biology of autism. *Psychological Medicine* 23(1):7–11.

BAKER, S. C., R. D. ROGERS, A. M. OWEN, C. D. FRITH, R. J. DOLAN, R. S. J. FRACKOWIAK, and T. W. ROBBINS, 1996. Neural systems engaged by planning: A PET study of the Tower of London task. *Neuropsychologia* 34:515–526.

BARON-COHEN, S., H. RING, J. MORIARTY, B. SCHMITZ, D. COSTA, and P. ELL, 1994. Recognition of mental state terms: Clinical findings in children with autism and a functional neuroimaging study of normal adults. *Br. J. Psychiatry* 165:640–649.

BARTH, C., D. FEIN, and L. WATERHOUSE, 1995. Delayed match-to-sample performance in autistic children. *Dev. Neuropsychol.* 11:53–69.

BAUMAN, M., and T. L. KEMPER, 1985. Histoanatomic observations of the brain in early infantile autism. *Neurology* 35(6):866–874.

Bauman, M., and T. L. Kemper, 1988. Limbic and cerebellar abnormalities: Consistent findings in infantile autism. *J. Neuropath. Exper. Neurol.* 47:369.

Bennetto, L., B. F. Pennington, and S. J. Rogers, 1996. Intact and impaired memory functions in autism. *Child Dev.* 67:1816–1835.

Berger, H. J., K. P. Van Spaendonck, M. W. Horstink, E. L. Buytenhuijs, P. W. J. M. Lammers, and A. R. Cools, 1993. Cognitive shifting as a predictor of progress in social understanding in high-functioning adolescents with autism: A prospective study. *J. Autism Dev. Disorders* 23:341–359.

Bettelheim, B., 1967. *The Empty Fortress.* New York: The Free Press.

Bishop, D. V., 1993. Autism, executive functions and theory of mind: A neuropsychological perspective. *J. Child Psychol. Psychiatry* 34:279–293.

Boucher, J., and E. K. Warrington, 1976. Memory deficits in early infantile autism: Some similarities to the amnesic syndrome. *Br. J. Psychol.* 67:73–87.

Bryson, S. E., B. S. Clark, and I. M. Smith, 1988. First report of a Canadian epidemiological study of autistic syndromes. *J. Child Psychology and Psychiatry and Allied Disciplines* 29(4):433–445.

Buchsbaum, M. S., B. V. Siegel, J. C. Wu, E. Hazlett, N. Sicotte, R. Haier, P. Tanguay, R. Asarnow, T. Cadorette, D. Donoghue, M. Lagunas-Solar, I. Lott, J. Paek, and D. Sabalesky, 1992. Attention performance in autism and regional brain metabolic rate assessed by positron emission tomography. *J. Autism Dev. Disorders* 22:115–125.

Casey, B. J., C. T. Gordon, G. B. Mannheim, and J. M. Rumsey, 1993. Dysfunctional attention in autistic savants. *J. Clin. Exp. Neuropsychol.* 15:933–946.

Courchesne, E., A. J. Lincoln, B. A. Kilman, and R. Galambos, 1985. Event-related brain potential correlates of the processing of novel visual and auditory information in autism. *J. Autism Devel. Disorders* 15(1):55–76.

Courchesne, E., J. P. Townsend, and O. Saitoh, 1994. The brain in infantile autism: Posterior fossa structures are abnormal. *Neurology* 44:214–223.

Courchesne, E., R. Yeung Courchesne, G. A. Press, J. R. Hesselink, and T. L. Jernigan, 1988. Hypoplasia of cerebellar vermal lobules VI and VII in autism. *N. Engl. J. Med.* 318(21):1349–1354.

Damasio, A. R., and R. G. Maurer, 1978. A neurological model for childhood autism. *Arch. Neurol.* 35(12):777–786.

Dawson, G., A. N. Meltzoff, J. Osterling, and J. Rinaldi, 1998. Neuropsychological correlates of early symptoms in autism. *Child Dev.* 69:1276–1285.

Dawson, G., C. Finley, S. Phillips, and L. Galpert, 1986. Hemispheric specialization and the language abilities of autistic children. *Child Devel.* 57(6):1440–1453.

Dawson, G., L. G. Klinger, H. Panagiotides, A. Lewy, and P. Castelloe, 1995. Subgroups of autistic children based on social behavior display distinct patterns of brain activity. *J. Abnormal Child Psych.* 23:569–583.

DeLong, G. R., 1992. Autism, amnesia, hippocampus, and learning. *Neurosci. Biobehav. Rev.* 16:63–70.

DeLong, G. R., S. C. Bean, and F. R. Brown, 1981. Acquired reversible autistic syndrome in acute encephalopathic illness in children. *Arch. Neurol.* 38:191–194.

Dias, R., T. W. Robbins, and A. C. Roberts, 1996. Dissociation in prefrontal cortex of attentional and affective shifts. *Nature* 380:69–72.

Douglas, V. I., and K. G. Peters, 1979. Toward a clearer definition of the attentional deficit of hyperactive children. In *Attention and Cognitive Development*, G. A. Hale and M. Lewis, eds. New York: Plenum, pp. 173–247.

Farah, M. J., 1984. The neurological basis of mental imagery: A componential analysis. *Cognition* 18:245–272.

Fein, D., B. F. Pennington, P. Markowitz, M. Braverman, and L. Waterhouse, 1986. Toward a neuropsychological model of infantile autism: Are the social deficits primary? *J. Am. Acad. Child and Adol. Psychiatry* 25:198–212.

Filipek, P. A., C. Richelme, D. N. Kennedy, J. Rademacher, D. A. Pitcher, S. Zidel, and V. S. Caviness, 1992. Morphometric analysis of the brain in developmental language disorders and autism. *Ann. Neurol.* 32:475.

Fletcher, P. C., F. Happe, U. Frith, S. C. Baker, R. J. Dolan, and R. Frackowiak, 1995. Other minds in the brain: A functional imaging study of theory of mind in story comprehension. *Cognition* 57:2.

Fray, P. J., T. W. Robbins, and B. J. Sahakian, 1996. Neuropsychiatric applications of CANTAB. *Intl. J. Geriat. Psychiatry* 11:329–336.

Friedrich, F., and S. Rader, 1996. Component process analysis in experimental and clinical neuropsychology. In *Theoretical Foundations of Clinical Neuropsychology for Clinical Practicioners*, M. Marirish, and J. Moses, eds. Hillsdale, N.J.: Lawrence Erlbaum, pp. 59–79.

Frith, U., 1989. *Autism: Explaining the Enigma.* Oxford: Basil Blackwell.

Gaffney, G. R., S. Kuperman, L. Y. Tsai, and S. Minchin, 1989. Forebrain structure in autism. *J. Am. Acad. Child and Adolescent Psych.* 28:534–537.

Garretson, H. B., D. Fein, and L. Waterhouse, 1990. Sustained attention in children with autism. *J. Autism Dev. Disorders* 20:101–114.

George, M. S., D. C. Costa, K. Kouris, H. A. Ring, and P. J. Ell, 1992. Cerebral blood flow abnormalities in adults with infantile autism. *J. Nerv. and Mental Dis.* 180(7):413–417.

Gillberg, C., 1986. Brief report: Onset at age 14 of a typical autistic syndrome: A case report of a girl with herpes simplex encephalitis. *J. Autism Dev. Disorders* 16:369–375.

Gillberg, C., S. Steffenburg, and H. Schaumann, 1991. Is autism more common now than ten years ago? *Br. J. Psych.* 158(Mar):403–409.

Gillberg, I. C., 1991. Autistic syndrome with onset at age 31 years: Herpes encephalitis as a possible model for childhood autism. *Dev. Med. Child Neurol.* 33:920–924.

Grandin, T., 1995. How people with autism think. In *Learning and Cognition in Autism*, E. Schopler, and G. B. Mesibov, eds. New York: Plenum, pp. 137–156.

Grattan, L. M., and P. J. Eslinger, 1989. Higher cognition and social behavior: Changes in cognitive flexibility and empathy after cerebral lesions. *Neuropsychology* 3:175–185.

Greer, M. K., M. Lyons-Crews, L. B. Mauldin, and F. R. Brown, 1989. A case study of the cognitive and behavioral deficits of temporal lobe damage in herpes simplex encephalitis. *J. Autism Dev. Disorders* 19:317–326.

Griffith, E. M., B. F. Pennington, E. A. Wehner, and S. J. Rogers, 1999. Executive functions in young children with autism. *Child Dev.* 70:817–832.

Hauser, S. L., G. R. DeLong, and N. P. Rosman, 1975. Pneumographic findings in the infantile autism syndrome: A correlation with temporal lobe disease. *Brain* 98:677–688.

HETZLER, B. E., and J. L. GRIFFIN, 1981. Infantile autism and the temporal lobe of the brain. *J. Autism Dev. Disorders* 11:317–330.

HOLTTUM, J. R., N. J. MINSHEW, R. S. SANDERS, and N. E. PHILLIPS, 1992. Magnetic resonance imaging of the posterior fossa in autism. *Biological Psychiatry* 32:1091–1101.

HORWITZ, B., J. M. RUMSEY, C. L. GRADY, and S. I. RAPOPORT, 1988. The cerebral metabolic landscape in autism: Intercorrelations of regional glucose utilization. *Arch. Neurol.* 45:749–755.

HUGHES, C., and J. RUSSELL, 1993. Autistic children's difficulty with mental disengagement from an object: Its implications for theories of autism. *Dev. Psychol.* 29:498–510.

HUGHES, C., J. RUSSELL, and T. W. ROBBINS, 1994. Evidence for executive dysfunction in autism. *Neuropsychologia* 32: 477–492.

HUTT, S. J., C. HUTT, D. LEE, and C. OUNSTED, 1964. Arousal and childhood autism. *Nature* 204:908–909.

JACOBSON, R., A. LECOUTEUR, P. HOWLIN, and M. RUTTER, 1988. Selective subcortical anomalies in autism. *Psychologic. Med.* 18:39–48.

JONES, B., and M. MISHKIN, 1972. Limbic lesions and the problem of stimulus-reinforcement associations. *Exp. Neurol.* 36:362–377.

KANNER, L., 1943. Autistic disturbances of affective content. *Nervous Child* 2:217–250.

KLINGER, L. G., and G. DAWSON, 1995. A fresh look at categorization abilities in persons with autism. In *Learning and Cognition in Autism*, E. Schopler, and G. B. Mesibov, eds. New York: Plenum, pp. 119–136.

LORD, C., and E. SCHOPLER, 1987. Neurobiological implications of sex differences in autism. In *Neurobiological Issues in Autism*, E. Schopler, and G. B. Mesibov, eds. New York: Plenum, pp. 191–211.

LUCIANA, M., and C. A. NELSON, 1998. The functional emergence of prefrontally-guided working memory systems in four- to eight-year-old children. *Neuropsychologia* 36:272–293.

MENARD, E., S. BELLEVILLE, S. FECTEAU, and L. MOTTRON, 1999. Is there a working memory deficit in autism? Paper presented at the Society for Research in Child Development, Albuquerque, New Mexico.

MINSHEW, N. J., G. GOLDSTEIN, and D. J. SIEGEL, 1997. Neuropsychologic functioning in autism: Profile of a complex information processing disorder. *J. International Neuropsychol. Soc.* 3:303–316.

MINSHEW, N. J., G. GOLDSTEIN, H. G. TAYLOR, and D. J. SIEGEL, 1994. Academic achievement in high functioning autistic individuals. *J. Clin. Exper. Neuropsychol.* 16(2):261–270.

MINSHEW, N. J., and G. GOLDSTEIN, 1993. Is autism an amnesic disorder? Evidence from the California Verbal Learning Test. *Neuropsychology* 7:209–216.

ORNITZ, E. M., and E. R. RITVO, 1968. Perceptual inconstancy in early infantile autism. *Arch. Gen. Psychiatry* 18:76–98.

OWEN, A. M., A. C. ROBERTS, C. E. POLKEY, B. J. SAHAKIAN, and T. W. ROBBINS, 1991. Extra-dimensional versus intra-dimensional set shifting performance following frontal lobe excisions, temporal lobe excisions or amygdalo-hippocampectomy in man. *Neuropsychologia* 29:993–1006.

OWEN, A. M., J. DOYON, M. PETRIDES, and A. C. EVANS, 1996. Planning and spatial working memory: A positron emission tomography study in humans. *Eur. J. Neurosci.* 8:353–364.

OZONOFF, S., 1995a. Reliability and validity of the Wisconsin Card Sorting Test in studies of autism. *Neuropsychology* 9:491–500.

OZONOFF, S., 1995b. Executive functions in autism. In *Learning and Cognition in Autism*, E. Schopler and G. B. Mesibov, eds. New York: Plenum Press, pp. 199–219.

OZONOFF, S., 1997a. Components of executive function in autism and other disorders. In *Autism as an Executive Disorder*, J. Russell, ed. New York: Oxford University Press, pp. 179–211.

OZONOFF, S., 1997b. Causal mechanisms of autism: Unifying perspectives from an information processing framework. In *Handbook of Autism and Pervasive Developmental Disorders*, 2nd ed., D. J. Cohen and F. R. Volkmar, eds. New York: Wiley, pp. 868–879.

OZONOFF, S., and D. L. STRAYER, 1997. Inhibitory function in nonretarded children with autism. *J. Autism Dev. Disorders* 27:59–77.

OZONOFF, S., and D. L. STRAYER. Further evidence of intact working memory ability in autism. *J. Autism and Devel. Dis.* (in press).

OZONOFF, S., and J. JENSEN, 1999. Specific executive function profiles in three neurodevelopmental disorders. *J. Autism Dev. Disorders* 29:171–177.

OZONOFF, S., and R. E. McEVOY, 1994. A longitudinal study of executive function and theory of mind development in autism. *Dev. Psychopathol.* 6:415–431.

OZONOFF, S., B. F. PENNINGTON, and S. J. ROGERS, 1991. Executive function deficits in high-functioning autistic individuals: Relationship to theory of mind. *J. Child Psychol. Psychiatry* 32:1081–1105.

OZONOFF, S., D. L. STRAYER, W. M. McMAHON, and F. FILLOUX, 1994. Executive function abilities in autism and Tourette syndrome: An information processing approach. *J. Child Psychol. Psychiatry* 35:1015–1032.

OZONOFF, S., D. L. STRAYER, W. M. McMAHON, and F. FILLOUX, 1998. Inhibitory deficits in Tourette syndrome: A function of comorbidity and symptom severity. *J. Child Psychol. Psychiatry* 39:1109–1118.

OZONOFF, S., M. SOUTH, and J. N. MILLER, 2000. DSM-IV-defined Asperger syndrome: Cognitive, behavioral, and early history differentiation from high-functioning autism. *Autism: The International Journal of Research and Practice* 4:29–46.

PASCUALVACA, D. M., B. D. FANTIE, M. PAPAGEORGIOU, and A. F. MIRSKY, 1998. Attentional capacities in children with autism: Is there a general deficit in shifting focus? *J. Autism Dev. Disorders* 28:467–478.

PENNINGTON, B. F., 1994. The working memory function of the prefrontal cortices: Implications for the developmental and individual differences in cognition. In *Future-Oriented Processes in Development*, M. M. Haith, J. Benson, R. Roberts, and B. F. Pennington, eds. Chicago: University of Chicago Press, pp. 243–289.

PENNINGTON, B. F., and S. OZONOFF, 1996. Executive functions and developmental psychopathologies. *J. Child Psychol. Psychiatry* 37:51–87.

PENNINGTON, B. F., S. J. ROGERS, L. BENNETTO, E. M. GRIFFITH, D. T. REED, and V. SHYU, 1997. Validity tests of the executive dysfunction hypothesis of autism. In *Autism as an Executive Disorder*, J. Russell, ed. New York: Oxford University Press, pp. 144–178.

PIVEN, J., J. BAILEY, B. J. RANSON, and S. ARNDT, 1998. No difference in hippocampus volume detected on magnetic resonance imaging in autistic individuals. *J. Autism Dev. Disorders* 28:105–110.

PIVEN, J., M. L. BERTHIER, S. E. STARKSTEIN, E. NEHME, G. PEARLSON, and S. FOLSTEIN, 1990. Magnetic resonance imaging evidence for a defect of cerebral cortical development in autism. *Am. J. Psychiatry* 147(6):734–739.

PIVEN, J., S. ARNDT, J. BAILEY, and N. ANDREASEN, 1996. Regional brain enlargement in autism: A magnetic resonance imaging study. *J. Am. Acad. Child and Adol. Psychiatry.* 35:530–536.

POSNER, M. I., 1980. Orienting of attention. *Quart. J. Exp. Psychol.* 32:3–25.

REED, T., and C. C. PETERSON, 1990. A comparative study of autistic subjects' performance at two levels of visual and cognitive perspective taking. *J. Autism and Devel. Dis.* 20(4):555–567.

RIMLAND, E. R., 1964. *Infantile Autism: The Syndrome and Its Implications for a Neural Theory of Behavior.* New York: Appleton-Century-Crofts.

RITVO, E. R., B. J. FREEMAN, A. B. SCHEIBEL, T. DUONG, H. ROBINSON, D. GUTHRIE, and A. RITVO, 1986. Lower Purkinje cell counts in the cerebella of four autistic subjects: Initial findings of the UCLA–NSAC research report. *Am. J. Psychiatry* 143(7):862–866.

ROBBINS, T. W., M. JAMES, A. M. OWEN, B. J. SAHAKIAN, A. D. LAWRENCE, L. McINNES, and P. M. A. RABBITT, 1998. A study of performance on tests from the CANTAB battery sensitive to frontal lobe dysfunction in a large sample of normal volunteers: Implications for theories of executive functioning and cognitive aging. *J. Intl. Neuropsychol. Soc.* 4:474–490.

ROBBINS, T. W., M. JAMES, A. M. OWEN, B. J. SAHAKIAN, L. McINNES, and P. RABBITT, 1994. Cambridge Neuropsychological Test Automated Battery (CANTAB): A factor analytic study of a large sample of normal elderly volunteers. *Dementia* 5:266–281.

ROBERTS, A., T. W. ROBBINS, and B. J. EVERITT, 1988. Extra- and intradimensional shifts in man and marmoset. *Quart. J. Exp. Psychol.* 40B:321–342.

ROLLS, E. T., 1998. The orbitofrontal cortex. In *The Prefrontal Cortex: Executive and Cognitive Functions*, A. C. Roberts, T. W. Robbins, and L. Weiskrantz, eds. New York: Oxford University Press.

RUMSEY, J. M., and S. D. HAMBURGER, 1988. Neuropsychological findings in high-functioning men with infantile autism, residual state. *J. Clin. Exper. Neuropsychol.* 10(2):201–221.

RUMSEY, J. M., R. DUARA, C. GRADY, J. L. RAPOPORT, R. A. MARGOLIN, S. I. RAPOPORT, and R. N. CUTLER, 1985. Brain metabolism in autism: Resting cerebral glucose utilization rates as measured with positron emission tomography. *Arch. Gen. Psychiatry* 42:448–455.

RUSSELL, J., C. JARROLD, and L. HENRY, 1996. Working memory in children with autism and with moderate learning difficulties. *J. Child Psychol. Psychiatry* 37:673–686.

RUSSELL, J., N. MAUTHNER, S. SHARPE, and T. TIDSWELL, 1991. The "windows task" as a measure of strategic deception in preschoolers and autistic subjects. *Br. J. Dev. Psychol.* 9:331–349.

SCHACHAR, R., and G. D. LOGAN, 1990. Impulsivity and inhibitory control in normal development and childhood psychopathology. *Dev. Psychol.* 26:710–720.

SHALLICE, T., 1982. Specific impairments in planning. In *The Neuropsychology of Cognitive Function*, D. E. Broadbent and L. Weiskrantz, eds. London: Royal Society, pp. 199–209.

SHERMAN, M., R. NASS, and T. SHAPIRO, 1984. Brief report: Regional cerebral blood flow in autism. *J. Autism and Devel. Dis.* 14(4):439–446.

SIEGEL, B. V., K. H. NUECHTERLEIN, L. ABEL, J. C. WU, and M. S. BUCHSBAUM, 1995. Glucose metabolic correlates of continuous performance test performance in adults with a history of infantile autism, schizophrenics, and controls. *Schizophrenia Res.* 17:85–94.

SWANSON, J. M., M. POSNER, S. G. POTKIN, S. BONFORTE, D. YOUPA, C. FIORE, D. CANTWELL, and F. CRINELLA, 1991. Activating tasks for the study of visual-spatial attention in ADHD children: A cognitive anatomic approach. *J. Child Neurol.* 6(suppl):S119–S127.

SZATMARI, P., G. BARTOLUCCI, R. BREMNER, S. BOND, and S. RICH, 1989. A follow-up study of high-functioning autistic children. *J. Autism Dev. Disorders* 19:213–225.

TIPPER, S. P., 1985. The negative priming effect: Inhibitory priming by ignored objects. *Quart. J. Exp. Psychol. Hum. Exp. Psychol.* 37A:571–590.

TURNER, M., 1997. Towards an executive dysfunction account of repetitive behavior in autism. In *Autism as an Executive Disorder*, J. Russell, ed. New York: Oxford University Press, pp. 57–100.

WAINWRIGHT-SHARP, J. A., and S. E. BRYSON, 1993. Visual orienting deficits in high-functioning people with autism. *J. Autism Dev. Disorders* 23:1–13.

WHITE, C. P., and L. ROSENBLOOM, 1992. Temporal-lobe structures and autism. *Dev. Med. Child Neurol.* 34:558–559.

WILLIAMS, R. S., S. L. HAUSER, D. P. PURPURA, R. DeLONG, and C. N. SWISHER, 1980. Autism and mental retardation: Neuropathological studies performed in four retarded persons with autistic behavior. *Arch. Neurol.* 37:749–753.

WING, L., 1988. The continuum of autistic characteristics. In *Diagnosis and Assessment in Autism*, E. Schopler, and G. B. Mesibov, eds. New York: Plenum, pp. 91–110.

ZILBOVICIUS, M., B. GARREAU, N. TZOURIO, B. MAZOYER, B. BRUCK, J. L. MARTINOT, C. RAYNAUD, Y. SAMSON, A. SYROTA, and G. LELORD, 1992. Regional cerebral blood flow in childhood autism: A SPECT study. *Am. J. Psychiatry* 149(7):924–930.

ZILBOVICIUS, M., B. GARREAU, Y. SAMSON, P. REMY, C. BARTHELEMY, A. SYROTA, and G. LELORD, 1995. Delayed maturation of the frontal cortex in childhood autism. *Am. J. Psychiatry* 152(2):248–252.

# 35 Tics: When Habit-Forming Neural Systems Form Habits of Their Own

JAMES F. LECKMAN,
BRADLEY S. PETERSON,
ROBERT T. SCHULTZ,
AND DONALD J. COHEN

*"The motor centres and motor faculties, besides furnishing the conditions and possibilities of multiple and varied voluntary movements . . . enormously widen the field of sensory experience and complicate its results."*
—David Ferrier, 1886

*"From bad habit . . . take care my dear to guard against bad habits."*
—Samuel Johnson, discussing his tic symptoms with a curious young woman (quoted by Murray, 1982)

*"What makes a habit a habit?"*
—Anonymous

ABSTRACT Tourette's syndrome (TS) is a model developmental psychopathological disorder that has the potential to illuminate aspects of how the brain selects and maintains perceptual-emotive-cognitive-action sequences. This chapter reviews aspects of the phenomenology, neuropsychology, and natural history of TS in light of emerging knowledge concerning the role of the basal ganglia and related cortical and thalamic sites in the formation and timing of habits and other goal-directed behaviors. Advances in developmental and systems neuroscience combined with the advent of noninvasive functional brain imaging techniques make this a propitious time to study TS.

Tourette's syndrome (TS) is a chronic neuropsychiatric disorder of childhood onset that is characterized by tics that wax and wane in severity and by an array of behavioral problems that include some forms of obsessive compulsive disorder (OCD) and attention deficit hyperactivity disorder (ADHD) (American Psychiatric

JAMES F. LECKMAN Child Study Center; Children's Clinical Research Center; Departments of Pediatrics, Psychiatry, and Psychology, Yale University School of Medicine, New Haven, Connecticut.
BRADLEY S. PETERSON Child Study Center, Yale University School of Medicine, New Haven, Connecticut.
ROBERT T. SCHULTZ Child Study Center, Yale University School of Medicine, New Haven, Connecticut.
DONALD J. COHEN Child Study Center; Departments of Pediatrics, Psychiatry, and Psychology, Yale University School of Medicine, New Haven, Connecticut.

Association, 1994). Tics are sudden habitual movements, gestures, or utterances that typically mimic some fragment of normal behavior. This chapter focuses on neurobiological substrates of tics and reviews conceptual advances derived from the integration of developmental psychopathology with insights from basic and clinical neuroscience research. Points of emphasis include a review of the neural substrates of habit formation, the characterization of the clinical and neuropsychological phenotype of tic disorders, the likely role of specific neurobiological circuits in the expression and inhibition of tic symptoms, and the potential value of nonlinear dynamic systems to understand the timing of tics and the natural history of TS. Given the limits of space, the symptoms of OCD and ADHD will be addressed only in passing. Interested readers are referred to more comprehensive reviews elsewhere (Leckman and Cohen, 1998).

## Neural substrates of habit formation

Habits are assembled routines that link sensory cues with motor action. They allow us to act without thinking, as in riding a bicycle or driving a car. As such, they are enormously adaptive and part of a common evolutionary heritage that we share with other vertebrates and probably with all other species capable of goal-directed behavior. Repetitive sensory-cognitive-emotive-motor ensembles, as occur when we witness a gifted pianist playing a sonata or a surgeon suturing, have habitual elements. When we do things over and over again, we get better at it. There is less thinking about the action, and we can respond in a more nuanced manner to other internal cues or to perturbations in the external world. How does the brain manage these marvels? Ann Graybiel, following the lead of George Miller, believes that when we do something over and over, our brains compress the relevant information into "chunks" coordinating bits of behavior into action sequences

(Graybiel, 1998; Miller, 1956). It appears likely that these events involve neural loops or spirals that connect the basal ganglia with the cortex and thalamus.

NEUROANATOMIC CIRCUITS The anatomy of the motor, sensorimotor, association, and inhibitory neural circuits that course through the basal ganglia is schematically presented in figure 35.1 and table 35.1. These loops are commonly referred to by their successive processing components, and are therefore called cortical-striatal-thalamo-cortical (CSTC) circuits (Alexander, Crutcher, and DeLong, 1990). CSTC circuits are composed of multiple, partially overlapping but largely "parallel" circuits that direct information from the cerebral cortex to the subcortex, then back again to specific regions of the cortex, thereby forming multiple cortical-subcortical loops (figure 35.1). Although multiple anatomically and functionally related cortical regions provide input into a particular circuit, each circuit in turn refocuses its projections back onto only a discrete subset of the cortical regions initially contributing to that circuit's input. Within the basal ganglia and thalamus, each of the circuits appears to be microscopically segregated from others that course through the same macroscopic structure—hence the conceptualization of these pathways as parallel.

Although the number of anatomically and functionally discrete pathways is still the subject of controversy (Alexander, Crutcher, and DeLong, 1990; Goldman-Rakic and Selemon, 1990; Parent and Hazrati, 1995a,b), the current consensus holds that CSTC circuitry has at least three components—those initiating from and projecting back to sensorimotor (SM), orbitofrontal (OF), or association (AS) cortices. Other functional components of CSTC circuitry likely exist, and probably include those traditionally associated with the limbic system (table 35.1).

The largest input to the striatum is from the cortex. Cortical projections to the caudate and putamen, which together comprise the striatum, appear to be oriented in parasagittally elongated, somatotopically organized domains. As many as 10,000 cortical projection neurons converge on the dendritic arbor of a single medium spiny neuron (Wilson, 1995). From here, information leaves the basal ganglia principally through the internal segment of the globus pallidus (GPi) and its brainstem counterpart, the substantia nigra pars reticulata (SNr), before ascending to the thalamus and cortex. Striatal projections to the external segment of the globus pallidus (GPe), in contrast, give rise to projections directed primarily to the reticular thalamic nucleus, subthalamic nucleus, and GPi. Because the reticular thalamic nucleus in turn exerts powerful GABA-mediated inhibi-

tory influences on other thalamic nuclei, the GPe/reticular thalamic nucleus projection is viewed as one that can intrinsically modulate activity in CSTC pathways involving GPi (Parent and Hazrati, 1995a). The GPe projection to GPi may similarly modulate CSTC activity coursing through the GPi (Parent and Hazrati, 1995a).

Pallidal projections to the thalamus, whether of GPi or GPe origin, are tonically active and primarily GABAergic. Projections from striatum to pallidum are also GABAergic. Thus, increased striatal activity (associated with movement, for instance) will phasically silence the tonically active GPi and SNr neurons, which in turn reduces GABAergic transmission to the thalamus, thereby activating thalamic target neurons. Activation of thalamic nuclei is essential for the initiation of movement. Thus, increased striatal activity can be regarded as disinhibiting thalamic nuclei and cortical regions, since it activates the two GABAergic connections leading into and out of the GPi/SNr. Increased striatal activity in projections to GPe will similarly disinhibit reticular thalamic nuclei; but because these reticular nuclei in turn inhibit other thalamic nuclei, increased striatal activation of GPe will ultimately inhibit those same thalamic nuclei. GPe inhibition of the GPi will produce functionally similar thalamic inhibition. Therefore, increased striatal activity can either inhibit or disinhibit the same thalamic nuclei and cortical regions, depending upon whether the GPe or GPi, respectively, is the target of striatal activity (Parent and Hazrati, 1995a,b).

The subthalamic nucleus (STN) is an important element of CSTC circuitry (Gillies and Willshaw, 1998). Although the STN projects to all basal ganglia elements, excitatory projections to both pallidal segments and to the SNr are particularly massive. Individual subthalamic axons, which project to both GPi and GPe, arborize extensively throughout their rostrocaudal extent and appear to influence uniformly large subpopulations of neurons in both pallidal segments (Parent and Hazrati, 1995b). Intracellular recordings suggest that the STN may modulate the potential of pallidal neurons, thereby modifying pallidal response and sensitivity to incoming striatal signals (Kita and Kitai, 1991).

PERCEPTUALLY CUED LEARNING AND THE ESTABLISHMENT OF HABITS Based in large part on work performed in Ann Graybiel's laboratory, it appears that the response of particular medium spiny neurons in the striatum is frequently dependent upon a given set of perceptual cues and environmental conditions, suggesting that the coordinated striatal response was acquired through learning and experience (Aosaki, Graybiel, and Kimura, 1994). Inputs from ascending do-

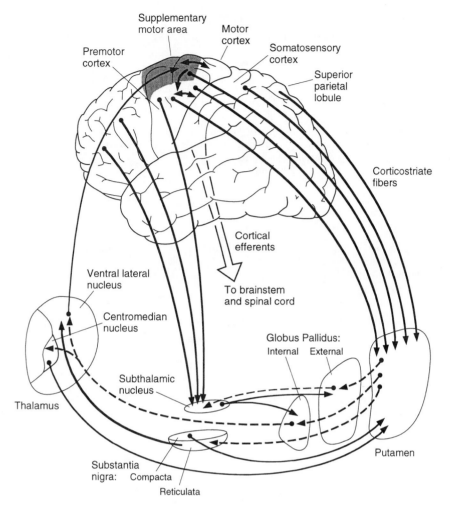

FIGURE 35.1 Corticostriatothalamocortical circuits. Excitatory projections are depicted as solid lines, while inhibitory pathways are dashed lines. Numerous cortical regions send projections to the striatum (caudate and putamen) where the inputs from as many as 10,000 cortical neurons converge on a single medium spiny (MS) neuron. Striatal neurons in turn project to the external or internal segment of the globus pallidus (GPe or GPi), or the pars reticulata of the substantia nigra (SNr). The latter two sites are way stations of the "direct" pathway while projections to the GPe form part of the "indirect" pathway. The coordinated firing of striatal MS neurons is associated with specific emotive-cognitive-action sequences. Ascending dopaminergic projections in concert with striatal interneurons sculpt these coordinated discharge patterns. Diffuse cortical inputs also converge on the subthalamic nuclei (STN). The STN also receives input from the GPe and in turn projects to the GPi and the SNr where STN inputs may serve to reset emotive-cognitive-action sequences. The tonically active ganglia output nuclei located in the GPi and SNr project to specific thalamic neurons which in turn projects to discrete cortical areas. (Adapted from Peterson et al., 1998a.)

pamine pathways originating in the substantia nigra pars compacta (SNc) play a crucial role in this learning process (Aosaki, Graybiel, and Kimura, 1994).

Ensemble recordings, in which the activity of multiple striatal neurons are recorded simultaneously, further clarify the role of the striatum and related brain circuits in the learning and production of habitual or "automatic" behavioral responses (Jog et al., 1996). Recently, Graybiel and her colleagues Yasuo Kubota and Juan Canales have recorded from ensembles of electrodes in the sensorimotor areas of rat striatum during cued learning tasks (personal communication, 1999).

Initially, a large array of neurons fired rapidly in response to the cue. But many fewer fired once the rats learned the task. Graybiel proposes that the cells that do fire may represent a chunk of behavior. Further, it has been proposed that distinct, individually coordinated, motor and cognitive action chunks are combined and implemented as more elaborate goal-directed behavior. When performed repeatedly, activity in these ensembles becomes more efficient, and through still unknown mechanisms, habits form.

Other investigators have focused on the role of the STN as a regulator of striatal output. Given the

TABLE 35.1
*CSTC circuitry implicated in habit formation and Tourette's syndrome and related disorders*

| CSTC Component | Sensorimotor (SM) | Orbitofrontal (OF) | Association (AS) | Limbic (L) |
|---|---|---|---|---|
| Cortical afferents | Somatosensory Primary motor Supplementary motor area | Orbitofrontal Superior temporal gyrus Inferior temporal gyrus Anterior cingulate | Dorsolateral prefrontal Posterior parietal Arcuate premotor | Anterior cingulate Hippocampal cortex Entorhinal cortex Superior temporal gyrus Inferior temporal gyrus |
| Striatum | Dorsolateral putamen Dorsolateral caudate Dorsolateral subthalamic Nucleus | Ventral caudate Ventral putamen | Dorsolateral caudate | Ventral caudate Ventral putamen Nucleus accumbens Olfactory tubercle |
| Pallidum/SNr | Ventrolateral GPi Caudolateral SNr | Dorsomedial GPi Rostromedial SNr | Dorsomedial GPi Rostrolateral SNr | Rostrolateral GPi Ventral pallidum Rostrodorsal SNr |
| Thalamus | Ventrolateral nucleus Centromedian intralaminar nucleus | Medial dorsal nucleus (parvocellular) | Ventral anterior nucleus (parvocellular) | Medial dorsal nucleus (posteromedial) |
| Cortical projections | Supplementary motor area | Orbitofrontal | Dorsolateral prefrontal | Anterior cingulate |

*Abbreviations:* GPi, globus pallidus, internal segment; GPe, globus pallidus, external segment; SNr, substania nigra, pars reticulata.

Adapted from Peterson et al., 1998a.

excitatory nature of the STN neurons, their threshold, and peak firing rates, a simple model of neuron responses has revealed that large regions of this highly interconnected nucleus respond to excitatory input in the form of a widespread uniform pulse (Gillies and Willshaw, 1998). These pulses of activity may act as a braking signal that resets the basal ganglia output nuclei, thus interrupting habits and setting the stage for the emergence of new goal-directed emotive-cognitive-behavioral sets.

## Tics as fragments of normal behavior?

If habits are coordinated chunks of thought and action, then conceptually tics may be best seen as those pre-wired bits of behavior that are available to be chunked together to produce habits (Leckman and Riddle, 2000). Like habits, tic action sequences often arise from a heightened and selective sensitivity to environmental cues from within the body or from the outside world

(Bliss, 1980; Leckman, Walker, and Cohen, 1993; Leckman et al., 1994; Miguel et al., 1997). These perceptual cues include faint premonitory feelings or urges that are relieved with the performance of tics (figure 35.2), and a need to perform tics or compulsions until they are felt ineffably to be "just right." Although the neural mechanisms that conspire to produce tics have yet to be elucidated, preliminary evidence suggests that they involve the same structures that underlie habit formation.

## Tics and the disregulation of the neural circuits underlying habit formation

The basal ganglia and the neural loops that they participate in have long been a focus of TS research (Balthasar, 1956; Peterson et al., 1993; Young and Penney, 1984). Advances in neuroimaging and neurophysiological techniques have made it possible to examine the activity of these circuits in living subjects.

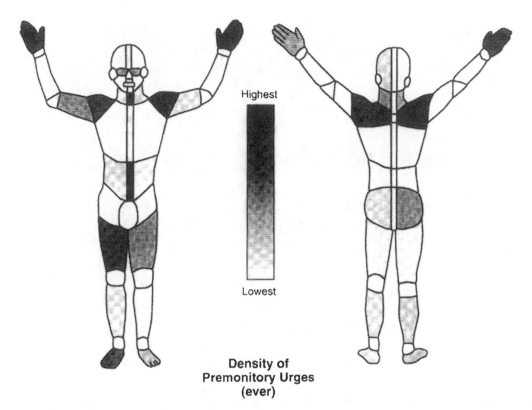

Highest

Lowest

**Density of
Premonitory Urges
(ever)**

FIGURE 35.2  Density distribution of premonitory urges. As many as 93% of individuals with TS report the presence of premonitory urges that precede their tics and that are relieved by the performance of their tics. One 21-year-old woman with TS reported, "A need to tic is an intense feeling that unless I tic or twitch I feel as if I am going to burst. Unless I can physically tic, all my mental thoughts center on ticking until I am able to let it out. It is a terrible urge that needs to be satisfied." The figure depicts the densities of premonitory urges for each of 89 arbitrarily defined anatomical regions. The highest den-sity on the scale represents 0.40 total premonitory urges per region per person. This scale is linear so the lowest density represents 0.0 total premonitory urges per region per person, and the midpoint represents 0.20 total premonitory urges per region per person. These data are based on the reports of 132 individuals with TS ranging in age from 13.8 to 51.3 years with a mean (SD) age of 29.5 years. For further details, see Leckman, Walker, and Cohen (1993). (Adapted from Leckman, Walker, and Cohen, 1993.)

CSTC CIRCUITS  In TS there is preliminary evidence that voluntary tic suppression involves activation of regions of the prefrontal cortex and the right caudate nucleus and the bilateral deactivation of the putamen and globus pallidus (figure 35.3; see color plate 24; Peterson, Skudlarski, Anderson et al., 1998b). If replicated, these findings are consistent with the well-known finding that chemical or electrical stimulation of inputs into the putamen can provoke motor and vocal responses that resemble tics (MacLean and Delgado, 1953). They also suggest that prefrontal cortex–basal ganglia circuits participate in shaping the inhibitory influence of the output neurons in the internal segment of the globus pallidus and the pars reticulata of the substantia nigra.

Most functional magnetic resonance imaging (fMRI) studies to date have employed a block design in which the activation/deactivation signal reflects a presumed continuous mental state. More recently, event-related fMRI techniques have been developed that will greatly enhance the temporal resolution of these studies (Bruckner et al., 1996). Work in progress suggests that it should be possible to monitor the progression of individual tics in the magnet. These studies should permit investigators to begin to define the temporal sequence of activity within different portions of these cortical-subcortical loops. In this regard, it will be intriguing to study the involvement of the supplementary motor area (SMA; table 35.1, figure 35.1) as electrical stimulation of the SMA elicits a variety of bodily sensations that include a premonitory sensations or "urges" to perform a movement or a sense of anticipation that a movement is about to occur (Fried et al., 1991).

DOPAMINERGIC MECHANISMS  Although controversial, age-dependent changes in central dopaminergic pathways that innervate the basal ganglia may also be characteristic of many children with TS (Ernst et al., 1999).

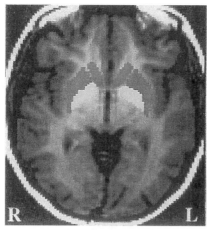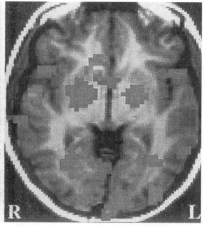

FIGURE 35.3 Single-subject activation/deactivation map of subcortical structures during voluntary tic suppression. The figure on the right depicts three regions of interest: caudate nucleus (red), putamen (blue), and globus pallidus (yellow) as defined by hand tracing on $T_1$ weighted axial MRI images. The figure on the left presents data from a single subject. Images acquired during eight 40-second epochs of voluntary tic suppression that alternated with eight 40-second epochs in which the subject was encouraged to tic freely. For each pixel, the mean difference in activity between the tic suppression epochs and the freely ticking tic epochs was normalized and transformed to a $t$-statistic. The map shows that during voluntary tic suppression this subject displayed activation of the right head of caudate (red) and a deactivation of the putamen and globus pallidus (blue), bilaterally. Remarkably, these changes were closely correlated with one another. For example, the increased activation of the head of the caudate was inversely correlated with the deactivation of both the putamen ($r = 0.86$, $P < .001$) and globus pallidus ($r = 0.84$, $P < .001$). These patterns of activation/inactivation were also found to be correlated with the subject's level of tic severity outside the magnet. Specifically, the higher activation in the caudate ($r = -0.46$, $P < .02$) and the lower the activation in the putamen and globus pallidus (range $0.54 \leq r \leq 0.40$, $P < .001$ to $P < .07$) during epochs of tic suppression, the lower the subject's level of tic severity was observed to be outside of the magnet. For further details, see Peterson et al., 1998b. (Adapted from Peterson et al., 1998b.)

Developmental shifts in the balance of tonic-phasic dopaminergic tone are likely and may influence the natural history of TS (Grace, 1995; Seeman et al., 1987). Although future ligand-based functional imaging studies in child and adolescent samples, complemented by neuropathological studies, hold considerable promise to elucidate these mechanisms, ethical concerns and logistic difficulties may limit these avenues of investigation, which in turn points to the need to develop suitable animal models for TS and related disorders.

### Neuropsychological findings implicate brain regions involved in visual-motor integration

Although motor and phonic tics constitute the core elements of the diagnostic criteria for TS, perceptual and cognitive difficulties are also common. These neuropsychological symptoms are potentially informative about the pathobiology of the disorder. Moreover, these associated difficulties can be more problematic for school and social adjustment than the primary motor symptoms (Dykens et al., 1998; Walkup et al., 1998).

Neuropsychological studies of TS have focused on a broad array of functions. Review of the literature suggests that the most consistently observed deficits occur on tasks requiring the accurate copy of geometric designs, i.e., "visual-motor integration" or "visual-graphic" ability. The ability to copy simple designs accurately has been investigated in 12 studies, excluding case reports (see Schultz et al., 1998b, for a review). For example, we studied the Beery test of visual-motor integration (VMI; Beery and Buktenica, 1989) performance of 50 children with TS (34 TS with ADHD, and 16 TS without ADHD) and 23 age-matched controls (Schultz et al., 1998a). The VMI requires subjects to copy simple designs as accurately as possible. Consistent with prior studies, we obtained significant group differences; children with TS scored approximately 1 standard deviation (SD) below the controls on the VMI. We found no evidence to suggest that comorbid ADHD or depressive symptomatology could account for the observed group differences.

As part of this study, a four-component process model of visual-motor integration (fine motor skill, visual-perceptual skill, response inhibition, and sustained attention) was also assessed. Three putative component processes—fine motor skill, visual-perceptual ability, and response inhibition—were also significant areas of weakness for children with TS, irrespective of their ADHD status. None of the measures considered separately could fully account for the deficits in visual-motor integration. Even after controlling statistically for visual-perceptual skill, intelligence, and fine motor control, children with TS continued to perform worse than controls on the VMI, suggesting that the integration of visual inputs and organized motor output is a specific area of weakness in individuals with TS.

Considerable knowledge about neural systems that support visual-motor integration and its component processes has been gleaned from lesions in adulthood. Both right and left hemisphere processes have been implicated in drawing ability, but the contributions of each to good performance is quite likely different. Right hemisphere damage typically results in drawings with sufficiently accurate detail, but distorted spatial relations among the elements and a failure to capture the gestalt, while left hemisphere lesions more often result in drawings that are slowly executed, oversimplified, and lacking detail, but spatially intact (Gainotti and Tiacci, 1970; Warrington, James, and Kinsbourne, 1966). Although both hemispheres may contribute to visual-motor integration, a more important role for the right is suggested by the greater frequency of drawing difficulties with right hemisphere lesions, especially when patients with global cognitive deficits are excluded (Damasio, 1985; Villa, Gainotti, and De Bonis, 1986).

Lesions to the parietal cortex in humans produce impaired visual perception, particularly when the injury is in the right hemisphere (for a review, see Anderson, 1987). The integration of motor movements with visual-perception is conducted with body-centered representations of space (as opposed to retinotopic) within the posterior parietal cortex (Andersen and Zipser, 1988). Single cell recording studies in nonhuman primates and functional neuroimaging studies in humans indicate that posterior parietal cortex codes for the position of body parts relative to one another and to the external world, and participates in planned movements in external space (Anderson, 1987). These processes are essential for accurate drawing. Posterior parietal lobule lesions result in reaching errors and deficits in fine motor coordination with visual guidance. Moreover, a small region within the posterior parietal cortex, the lateral intraparietal area, appears to be specialized for the visual-motor integration of saccadic eye movements, allowing location of targets in space and planning for subsequent movements (Andersen, Brotchie, and Mazzoni, 1992). Superior aspects of the right parietal lobe also subserve somatosensory processes that allow for feedback about the placement of the pencil on the fingertips and real-time adjustments for fine motor control during drawing.

Although considerable evidence documents the role of the nondominant parietal lobe in somatosensory and visual-spatial processes contributing to visual-motor integration, drawing is a complex ability involving multiple brain regions. The integration of visual-perceptual, somatosensory, and motor components in drawing is probably mediated by bidirectional exchange of information between parietal and motor areas of the frontal cortex (Quintana and Fuster, 1993), with a substantial integrative contribution from subcortical circuits (table 35.1). Indeed, visual-motor integration deficits may arise from frontal and subcortical lesions as well as parietal lobe lesions. Marshall and colleagues (1994) studied drawing dysfunction in 37 patients with right hemisphere stroke, with lesions distributed between subcortical, anterior and posterior cortical locations. When both drawing and visual-perceptual function were disturbed, lesions always involved the temporo-parietal-occipital junction. When visual-spatial functions were intact but drawings were unrecognizable, lesion location more often was subcortical, with a point of lesion overlap across subjects in the anterior limb of the internal capsule and the lateral head of the right caudate nucleus. Thus, the basal ganglia may have a specific role in the integration of motor programming and perceptual inputs. This is consistent with other reports of constructional apraxia following subcortical lesions in the nondominant hemisphere (Lazar et al., 1995).

The role of the basal ganglia in drawing disturbance is particularly intriguing because neuroimaging, neuropathological, and phenomenological studies implicate the basal ganglia and functionally related cortical and thalamic structures in the pathobiology of TS. A specific role for the right caudate in the pathobiology of TS is suggested by an MRI study of 10 pairs of monozygotic twins concordant for tics (Hyde et al., 1995). In this sample, aged 9–31 years, the size of the right caudate nucleus was significantly reduced in the more severely affected twin. Abnormalities of the right caudate, therefore, could have a primary role in both the tic behavior and the impaired visual-motor integration skills seen in TS. In recent follow-up study of these twins, Wolf and colleagues (1996) reported greater $D_2$ dopamine receptor binding in the head of the caudate bilaterally using single-photon emission computed tomography in the more severely affected co-twin. Intrapair binding differences accounted for nearly all of the variance in the corresponding within-pair differences in symptom severity. These findings are consistent with our observation that activation of the right caudate is crucially involved in voluntary tic suppression (figure 35.3; Peterson et al., 1998b).

## The fractal nature of the timing of tics

As noted by Esther Thelen and Linda Smith (1996) in their volume, *A Dynamical Systems Approach to the Development of Cognition and Action*, a central question is how complex systems, including the developing human nervous system, produce patterns that evolve in time. The application of complex, nonlinear dynamic models to the activity of biological systems may allow us to make sense of how ensembles of neurons self-organize within discrete neuroanatomical structures and centrifugally within neural loops to integrate their functioning with the functioning of other circuits to facilitate the expression of goal-directed behavior (Milton et al., 1989; Thelen and Smith, 1996).

Motor and phonic tics occur in bouts over the course of a day and wax and wane in severity over the course of weeks to months. Less well known is the "self-similarity" of these temporal patterns across different time scales. It has recently been documented that the frequency distribution of inter-tic interval durations follow an inverse power law of temporal scaling; spectral analyses similarly demonstrated that the power density of tic interval duration scales inversely with frequency (Peterson and Leckman, 1998). In addition, first return maps demonstrated "burstlike" behavior and short-term periodicity, proving that successive tic intervals are not random events (figure 35.4). These findings provide suggestive, though not conclusive, evidence for the presence of fractal and deterministic processes at work in tic time series. These analytic methods may provide insight into the temporal features of tics that commonly are described clinically, such as short-term bouts or bursting and longer-term waxing and waning. A deeper understanding of the multiplicative processes that govern these patterns may clarify both microscopic neural events occurring in millisecond time scales as well as macroscopic features of the natural history of tic disorders that unfold over the course of decades (King, Barchas, and Huberman, 1984; Leckman et al., 1998). When used in conjunction with clinician ratings of tic severity (Leckman et al., 1989), these computational methods may also prove useful in characterizing present tic severity and predicting future symptom exacerbations.

## The natural history of TS—A predictable course

In what may be a further demonstration of fractal patterning, investigators have documented a characteristic progression of tic symptom severity over the first two

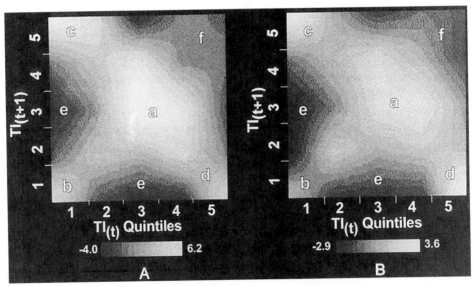

FIGURE 35.4   First return maps. (**A**) and (**B**): Probability density maps for inter-tic intervals recorded for single facial tics monitored in two men with TS aged 36 and 30 years. Each videotaped recording was 3 hours in length and was uninterrupted. Inter-tic intervals ($TI_{(t)}$) on the *x*-axis have been divided into five equal-sized bins (quintiles). The *y*-axis plots the very next inter-tic interval ($TI_{(t+1)}$). If the succession of inter-tic intervals were random, these joint probability density maps would be of uniform color. Islands of positivity, labeled "a" in both images, indicate a strong tendency for the periodicity if intermediate duration inter-tic intervals. Very short inter-tic intervals are typically followed by either very short inter-tic intervals, labeled "b" in both images, or by very long inter-tic intervals, labeled "c" in both images. Reciprocally, very long inter-tic intervals are typically followed by very short inter-tic intervals, labeled "d" in both images. The remaining regions "e" and "f" indicate regions where the joint probability is low. For further details, see Peterson and Leckman (1998).

decades of life (Leckman et al., 1998). A birth-year cohort of 42 TS patients followed at the Yale Child Study Center was recontacted an average of 7.3 years after their initial clinical evaluation. Data concerning the onset and course of tic severity until 18 years of age were available on 36 TS patients. Parents and subjects participated in four semi-structured interviews to chart the course of tic severity. Parents and patients were asked to record an annual rating of tic severity using a 6-point ordinal scale. Current and worst-ever tic severity ratings were also obtained using a widely utilized clinician-rated instrument, the Yale Global Tic Severity Scale (Leckman et al., 1989). Mean (SD) tic onset at 5.6 (2.3) years of age appeared to be followed by a progressive pattern of tic worsening. On average, the most severe period of tic severity occurred at 10.0 (2.4) years of age. In eight cases (22%), the frequency and forcefulness of the tics reached a severe level during the worst-ever period such that functioning in school was impossible or in serious jeopardy. In almost every case this period was followed by a steady decline in tic severity. By 18 years of age nearly half of the cohort was nearly tic-free. The onset of puberty was not associated with either the timing or severity of tics. A majority of TS patients displayed a consistent time course of tic severity (figure 35.5). This consistency in disease course can be accurately modeled with mathematical equations. Determination of the model parameters that describe each patient's course of tic severity may be of prognostic value and assist in the identification of factors that differentially influence the course of tic severity.

In 14% (5/36) of these cases, relative maximums other than the worst-ever point were described. Rather than seeing these as exceptional cases, it is probably better to consider the unimodal distributions of relative tic severity (seen in all the remaining cases) as being composed of multiple relative maximums in tic severity that are unresolvable using the annual ratings of tic severity employed in this study. That is, if monthly or weekly tic severity ratings were available, a sawtooth pattern of relative maximums would likely be apparent underlying these unimodal distributions. Viewed from this perspective, the unimodal tic severity curves seen in this study may be a reflection of the same multiplicative processes that underlie both the occurrence of tics in bouts (temporal scaling at the level of seconds) and their waxing and waning pattern (temporal scaling at the level of weeks to months). If true, this also implies that similar processes may govern subsequent exacerbations in adulthood. Discovery of the events that contribute to recurrence or persistence of tics may benefit those individuals, probably comprising fewer than 5% of child-

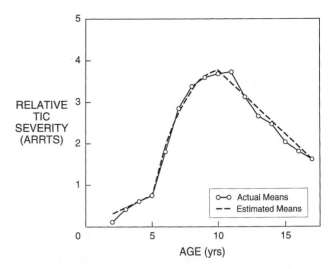

FIGURE 35.5   Plot of mean tic trajectory, ages 2–18 years. (A) Mean annual rating of relative tic severity scores (ARRTS) for 36 individuals with TS born in 1975 and evaluated at the Yale Child Study Center. Age at evaluation ranged from 5.9 to 16.9 years with a mean (SD) of 11.0 (2.9). Two systematic follow-ups were completed as the subjects reached the age of 18 years. Two inflection points are evident that correspond to the age of tic onset and the age of worst-ever tic severity respectively (solid line). (B) This line was generated using the mean values for each of the parameters included in the tic trajectory function (broken line). The tic time course, $f(t)$, is characterized by the equation:

$$f(t) = \begin{cases} \alpha t & \text{if } t \leq \tau_1 \\ \beta_0 + \beta_1 t + \beta_2 t^2 & \text{if } \tau_1 < t \leq \tau_2 \\ \gamma_0 + \gamma_1 t & \text{if } t > \tau_2 \end{cases}$$

where $\tau_1$ refers to the age-at-onset and $\tau_2$ is closely related, but not necessarily equal, to the age at which their tics were at their worst. For further details, see Leckman et al. (1998). (Adapted from Leckman et al., 1998.)

hood TS cases, who continue to experience severe bouts of tics in adulthood.

## Conclusion

Advances in the clinical phenomenology of TS have marvelously kept pace with advances in systems neuroscience and the emerging understanding of the role of the basal ganglia in responding to cues from the internal environment of the body and external world as presented by our sensory apparatus. Indeed, recent progress in neuroanatomy, systems neuroscience, and functional in vivo neuroimaging has set the stage for a major advance in our understanding of these disorders. Success in this area will lead to the targeting of specific brain circuits for more intensive study. Diagnostic and prognostic advances can also be anticipated, allowing us to address some important questions: Which circuits are involved and to what degree? How does that degree of involvement affect the patients symptomatic course and outcome?

Given this potential, TS can be considered a model disorder to study the dynamic interplay of neurobiological systems during development. It is likely that the research paradigms utilized in these studies, and many of the empirical findings resulting from them, will be relevant to other disorders of childhood onset and to our understanding of the integration of perceptual inputs with cognitive, emotive, and motor responses during normal development. For example, the application of nonlinear dynamic models may be useful in exploring the self-organizing, basal ganglia–based mechanisms required for learning to perform sequential motor tasks.

ACKNOWLEDGMENTS   This research was supported by grants from the Tourette Syndrome Association (J.F.L., B.S.P.); NIH: P01 MH49351, P01 HD03008, T32 MH18268, M01 RR06022, P30 MH30929, R01 MH59139 (B.S.P.), K08 MH01232 (B.S.P.); and the Charles A. Dana Foundation (B.S.P.). Portions of this chapter are adapted from (Leckman and Cohen, 1998) and from a recent review in *Neuron* (Leckman and Riddle, 2000).

## REFERENCES

ALEXANDER, G. E., M. D. CRUTCHER, and M. R. DeLONG, 1990. Basal ganglia-thalamocortical circuits: Parallel substrates for motor, oculomotor, "prefrontal" and "limbic" functions. *Prog. Brain Res.* 85:119–146.

AMERICAN PSYCHIATRIC ASSOCIATION, 1994. *Diagnostic and Statistical Manual of Mental Disorders*, 4th ed. Washington, D.C.

ANDERSEN, R. A., 1987. Inferior parietal lobule function in spatial perception and visuomotor integration. In *The Handbook of Physiology, Section 1: The Nervous System: Vol. V, Higher Functions of the Brain*, F. Plum, V. B. Mountcastle, and S. R. Geiger, eds. Bethesda, Md.: American Physiological Society, pp. 483–518.

ANDERSEN, R. A., P. R. BROTCHIE, and P. MAZZONI, 1992. Evidence for the lateral intraparietal area as the parietal eye field. *Curr. Opin. Neurobiol.* 2:840–846.

ANDERSEN, R. A., and D. ZIPSER, 1988. The role of the posterior parietal cortex in coordinate transformations for visual-motor integration. *Can. J. Physiol. Pharmacol.* 66:488–501.

AOSAKI, T., A. M. GRAYBIEL, and M. KIMURA, 1994. Effects of nigrostriatal dopamine system on acquired neural responses in the striatum of behaving monkey. *Science* 265:412–415.

BALTHASAR, K., 1956. Über das anatomische Substrat der generalisierten Tic-Krankheit: Entwicklungshemmung des Corpus Striatum. *Arch. Psychiat. Nervenkrankk.* 195:531–549.

BEERY, K., and N. BUKTENICA, 1989. *The Developmental Test of Visual-Motor Integration*. Toronto: Modern Curriculum Press.

BLISS, J., 1980. Sensory experiences of Gilles de la Tourette syndrome. *Arch. Gen. Psychiatry* 37:1343–1347.

BUCKNER, R. L., P. A. BANDETTINI, K. M. O'CRAVEN, R. L. SAVOY, S. E. PETERSEN, M. E. RAICHLE, and B. R. ROSEN, 1996. Detection of cortical activation during averaged single trials of a cognitive task using functional magnetic resonance imaging. *Proc. Natl. Acad. Sci. USA* 93:14878–14883.

DAMASIO, A. R., 1985. Disorders of complex visual processing: Agnosias, achromatopsia, Balint's syndrome, and related difficulties of orientation and construction. In *Principles of Behavioral Neurology*, M. M. Mesulam, ed. Philadelphia: F. A. Davis, pp. 259–288.

DYKENS, E. M., S. S. SPARROW, D. J. COHEN, L. SCAHILL, and J. F. LECKMAN, J. F., 1998. Peer acceptance and adaptive functioning. In *Tourette's Syndrome Tics, Obsessions, Compulsions—Developmental Psychopathology and Clinical Care*, J. F. Leckman and D. J. Cohen, eds. New York: John Wiley and Sons, pp.104–117.

ERNST, M., A J. ZAMETKIN, P. H. JONS, J. A. MATOCHIK, D. PASCUALVACA, and R. M. COHEN, 1999. High presynaptic dopaminergic activity in children with Tourette's disorder. *J. Am. Acad. Child Adolesc. Psychiatry* 38:86–94.

FRIED, I., A. KATZ, G. McCARTHY, K. J. SASS, P. WILLIAMSON, S. S. SPENCER, and D. D. SPENCER, 1991. Functional organization of human supplementary motor cortex studied by electrical stimulation. *J. Neurosci.* 11:3656–3666.

GAINOTTI, G., and C. TIACCI, 1970. Patterns of drawing disability in right and left hemispheric patients. *Neuropsychologia* 8:379–384.

GILLIES, A. J., and D. J. WILLSHAW, 1998. A massively connected subthalamic nucleus leads to the generation of widespread pulses. *Proc. R. Soc. Lond. [B]* 265:2101–2109.

GOLDMAN-RAKIC, P. S., and L. D. SELEMON, 1990. New frontiers in basal ganglia research. Introduction. *Trends Neurosci.* 13:241–244.

GRACE, A. A., 1995. The tonic/phasic model of dopamine system regulation: Its relevance for understanding how stimulant abuse can alter basal ganglia function. *Drug Alcohol Depend.* 37:111–129.

GRAYBIEL, A. M., 1998. The basal ganglia and chunking of action repertoires. *Neurobiol. Learn. Mem.* 70:119–136.

HYDE, T., M. STACEY, R. COPPOLA, S. HANDEL, K. RICKLER, and D. WEINBERGER, 1995. Cerebral morphometric abnormalities in Tourette's syndrome: A quantitative MRI study of monozygotic twins. *Neurology* 45:1176–1182.

JOG, M., C. CONNOLLY, V. HILLEGAART, M. WILSON, and A. M. GRAYBIEL, 1996. Ensemble recordings from striatum of freely-behaving rats. *Soc. Neurosci. Abstr.* 22:1086.

KING, R., J. D. BARCHAS, and B. A. HUBERMAN, 1984. Chaotic behavior in dopamine neurodynamics. *Proc. Natl. Acad. Sci. USA* 81:1244–1247.

KITA, H., and S. T. KITAI, 1991. Intracellular study of rat globus pallidus neurons: Membrane properties and responses to neostriatal, subthalamic and nigral stimulation. *Brain Res.* 564:296–305.

LAZAR, R. M., M. WEINER, H. S. WALD, and R. W. KULA, 1995. Visuoconstructional deficit following infarction in the right basal ganglia: A case report and some experimental data. *Arch. Clin. Neuropsychol.* 10:543–553.

LECKMAN, J. F., and D. J. COHEN, 1998. *Tourette's Syndrome: Tics, Obsessions, Compulsions—Developmental Psychopathology and Clinical Care*. New York: John Wiley and Sons.

LECKMAN, J. F., and M. A. RIDDLE, 2000. Tourette's syndrome. When habit-forming systems form habits of their own. *Neuron* 28(2):349–354.

LECKMAN, J. F., M. A. RIDDLE, M. T HARDIN, S. I. ORT, K. L. SWARTZ, J. STEVENSON, and D. J. COHEN, 1989. The Yale Global Tic Severity Scale: Initial testing of a clinician-rated scale of tic severity. *J. Am. Acad. Child Adolesc. Psychiatry* 28:566–573.

LECKMAN, J. F., D. E. WALKER, and D. J. COHEN, 1993. Premonitory urges in Tourette's syndrome. *Am. J. Psychiatry* 150:98–102.

LECKMAN, J. F., W. K. WALKER, W. K. GOODMAN, D. L. PAULS, and D. J. COHEN, 1994. "Just right" perceptions associated with compulsive behaviors in Tourette's syndrome. *Am. J. Psychiatry* 151:675–680.

LECKMAN, J. F., H. ZHANG, A. VITALE, F. LAHNIN, K. LYNCH, C. BONDI, Y. S. KIM, and B. S. PETERSON, 1998. Course of tic severity in Tourette syndrome: The first two decades. *Pediatrics* 102:14–19.

MACLEAN, P. D., and J. M. R. DELGADO, 1953. Electrical and chemical stimulation of frontotemporal portion of the limbic system in the waking animal. *Electroencephalogr. Clin. Neurophysiol.* 5:91–100.

MARSHALL, R. S., R. M. LAZAR, J. R. BINDER, D. W. DESMOND, P. M. DRUCKER, and J. P. MOHR, 1994. Interhemispheric localization of drawing dysfunction. *Neuropsychologia* 32:493–501.

MIGUEL, E. C., L. BAER, B. J. COFFEY, S. L. RAUCH, C. R. SAVAGE, R. L. O'SULLIVAN, K. PHILLIPS, C. MORETTI, J. F. LECKMAN, and M. A. JENIKE, 1997. Phenomenological differences appearing with repetitive behaviours in obsessive-compulsive disorder and Gilles de la Tourette's syndrome. *Br. J. Psychiatry* 170:140–145.

MILLER, G. A., 1956. The magic number seven, plus or minus two: Some limits on our capacity for processing information. *Psychol. Rev.* 63:81–97.

MILTON, J. G., A. LONGTIN, A. BEUTER, M. C. MACKEY, and L. GLASS, 1989. Complex dynamics and bifurcations in neurology. *J. Theor. Biol.* 138:129–147.

PARENT, A., and L. N. HAZRATI, 1995a. Functional anatomy of the basal ganglia. I. The cortico-basal ganglia-thalamo-cortical loop. *Brain Res. Brain Res. Rev.* 20:91–127.

PARENT, A., and L. N. HAZRATI, 1995b. Functional anatomy of the basal ganglia. II. The place of subthalamic nucleus and external pallidum in basal ganglia circuitry. *Brain Res. Brain Res. Rev.* 20:128–154.

PETERSON, B. S., and J. F. LECKMAN, 1998. The temporal dynamics of tics in Gilles de la Tourette syndrome. *Biol. Psychiatry* 44:1337–1348.

PETERSON, B. S., J. F. LECKMAN, A. ARNSTEN, G. M. ANDERSON, L. H. STAIB, J. C. GORE, R. A. BRONEN, R. MALISON, L. SCAHILL, and D. J. COHEN, 1998a. Neuroanatomical circuitry. In *Tourette's Syndrome: Tics, Obsessions, Compulsions—Developmental Psychopathology and Clinical Care*, J. F. Leckman and D. J. Cohen, eds. New York: John Wiley and Sons, pp. 230–260.

PETERSON, B. S., M. A. RIDDLE, D. J. COHEN, L. D. KATZ, J. C. SMITH, M. T. HARDIN, and J. F. LECKMAN, 1993. Reduced basal ganglia volumes in Tourette's syndrome using 3-dimensional reconstruction techniques from magnetic resonance images. *Neurology* 43:941–949.

PETERSON, B. S., P. SKUDLARSKI, A. W. ANDERSON, H. ZHANG, J. C. GATENBY, C. M. LACADIE, J. F. LECKMAN, and J. C. GORE, 1998b. A functional magnetic resonance imaging study of tic suppression in Tourette syndrome. *Arch. Gen. Psychiatry* 55:326–333.

QUINTANA, J., and J. M. FUSTER, 1993. Spatial and temporal factors in the role of prefrontal and parietal cortex in visuomotor integration. *Cereb. Cortex* 3:122–132.

SCHULTZ, R. T., A. S. CARTER, M. GLADSTONE, L. SCAHILL, J. F. LECKMAN, B. S. PETERSON, H. ZHANG, D. J. COHEN, and D. L. PAULS, 1998a. Visual-motor integration, visuoperceptual and fine motor functioning in children with Tourette's syndrome. *Neuropsychology* 12:134–145.

SCHULTZ, R. T., A. S. CARTER, L. SCAHILL, and J. F. LECKMAN, 1998b. Neuropsychological findings. In *Tourette's Syndrome: Tics, Obsessions, Compulsions—Developmental Psychopathology and Clinical Care*, J. F. Leckman and D. J. Cohen, eds. New York: John Wiley and Sons, pp. 80–103.

SEEMAN, P., N. H. BZOWEJ, H. C. GUAN, C. BERGERON, L. E. BECKER, G. P. REYNOLDS, E. D. BIRD, P. RIEDERER, K. JELLINGER, and S. WATANABE, 1987. Human brain dopamine receptors in children and aging adults. *Synapse* 1:399–404.

THELEN, E., and L. B. SMITH, 1996. *A Dynamical Systems Approach to the Development of Cognition and Action.* Cambridge, Mass.: MIT press.

VILLA, G., G. GAINOTTI, and C. DE BONIS, 1986. Constructive disabilities in focal brain-damaged patients. Influence of the hemispheric side, locus of lesion and coexistent mental deterioration. *Neuropsychologia* 24:497–510.

WALKUP, J. T., S. KHAN, L. SCHUERHOLZ, Y.-S. PAIK, J. F. LECKMAN, and R. T. SCHULTZ, 1998. Phenomenology and natural history of tic-related ADHD and learning disabilities. In *Tourette's Syndrome: Tics, Obsessions, Compulsions—Developmental Psychopathology and Clinical Care*, F. Leckman and D. J. Cohen, eds. New York: John Wiley and Sons, pp. 63–79.

WARRINGTON, E. K., M. JAMES, and M. KINSBOURNE, 1966. Drawing disability in relation to laterality of cerebral lesion. *Brain* 89:53–82.

WILSON, C. J., 1995. The contribution of cortical neurons to the firing pattern of medium spiny neurons. In *Models of Information Processing in the Basal Ganglia*, J. C. Houk, J. L. Davis, and D. G. Beiser, eds. Cambridge, Mass.: MIT Press, pp. 29–50.

WOLF, S. S., D. W. JONES, M. B. KNABLE, J. G. GOREY, K. S. LEE, T. M. HYDE, R. COPPOLA, and D. R. WEINBERGER, 1996. Tourette syndrome: Prediction of phenotypic variation in monozygotic twins by caudate nucleus D2 receptor binding. *Science* 273:1225–1227.

YOUNG, A. B., and J. B. PENNEY, 1984. Neurochemical anatomy of movement disorders. *Neurol. Clin.* 2:417–433.

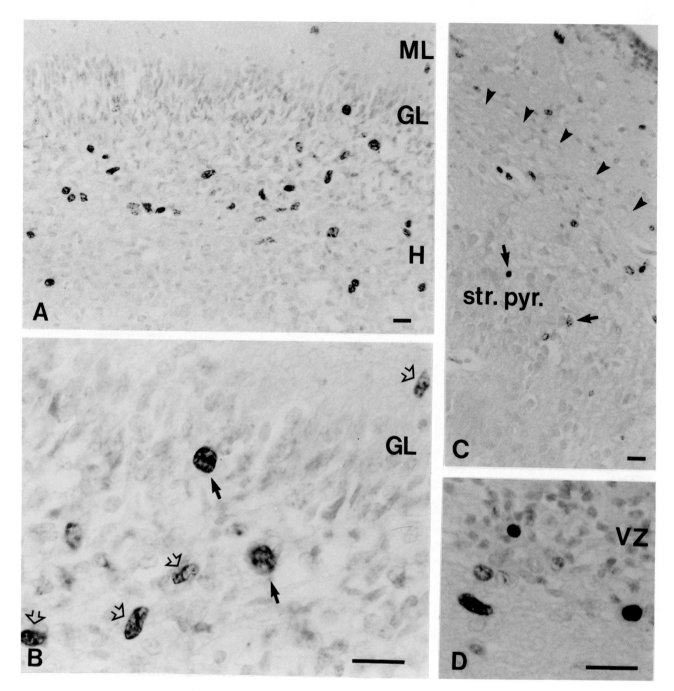

PLATE 1 Photomicrographs of Ki-67 labeled cells in cresyl violet–stained coronal sections of the hippocampal formation of the 24-week-old child. (A) Large numbers of labeled cells are in the hilus (H). (B) Higher magnification reveals differences in the nuclear structure. Some of the labeled cells appear to be neuronal precursors (arrows), whereas others are glial cells (open arrows). (C) There are a few labeled cells inside the pyramidal cell layer (str. pyr. = stratum pyramidale of Ammon's horn) of the CA1 area (arrows). Most labeled cells are in the intermediate and subplate zones, showing a band of probably migrating immature cells (arrowheads). (D) There are a few labeled cells in the ventricular zone (VZ) at the hippocampus. Calibration bar = 20 μm.

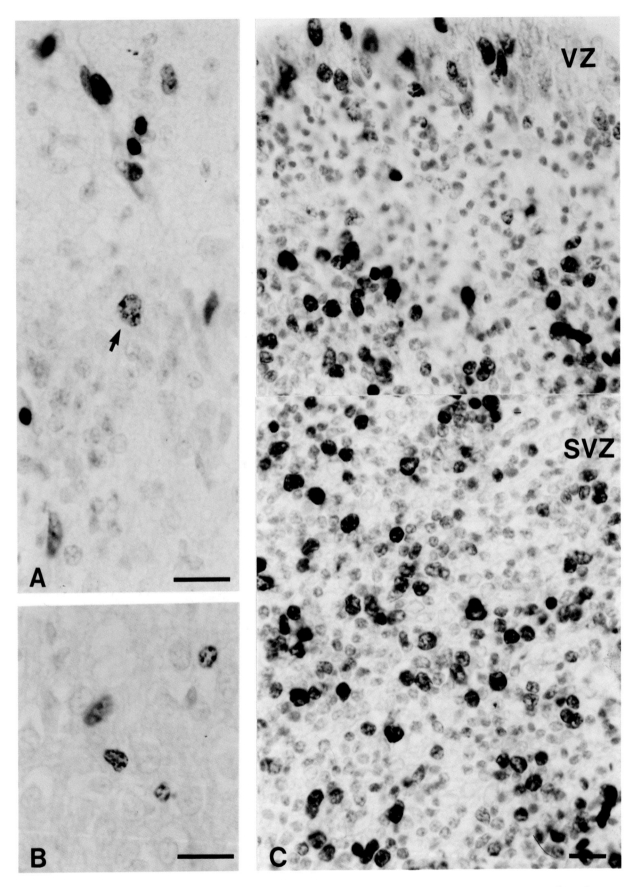

PLATE 2 Photomicrographs of Ki-67–labeled cells in cresyl violet–stained coronal sections of the entorhinal cortex (**A**), subiculum (**B**), and the subventricular zone under the temporal cortex (**C**). (**A** and **B**) Some of the labeled cells appear to be neurons (arrow on A), whereas the others are glial cells. (**C**) Large numbers of labeled cells are in the ventricular zone (VZ) as well as in the subventricular zone (SVZ) at the temporal neocortex. Calibration bar = 20 µm.

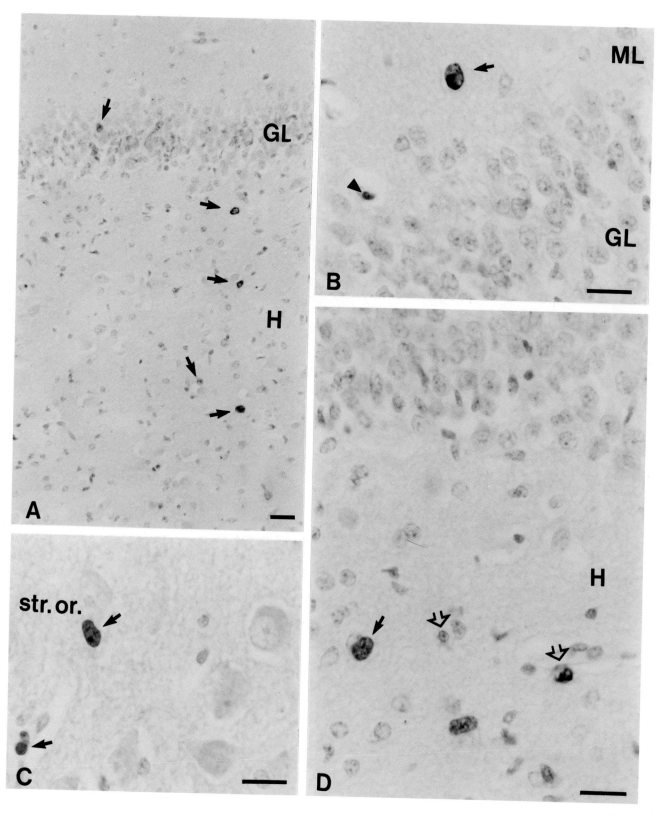

PLATE 3 Photomicrographs of Ki-67–labeled cells in cresyl violet–stained coronal sections of the dentate gyrus (**A, B,** and **D**) and Ammon's horn (**C**) of a newborn child. (**A**) There are a few labeled cells (arrows) in the hilus (H) and in the granule cells layer (GL). (**B**) Labeled glial cell (arrowhead) at the border of the granule cell layer (GL) and another that could be a nonaligned granule cell (arrow) in the molecular layer (ML). (**C**) Labeled glial cells (arrows) in the stratum oriens (str. or.) of the CA1 area of Ammon's horn. (**D**) Some of the labeled cells in the hilar region (H) of the dentate gyrus may be neuronal precursors (arrow), whereas others are glial cells (open arrows). Calibration bar = 20 μm.

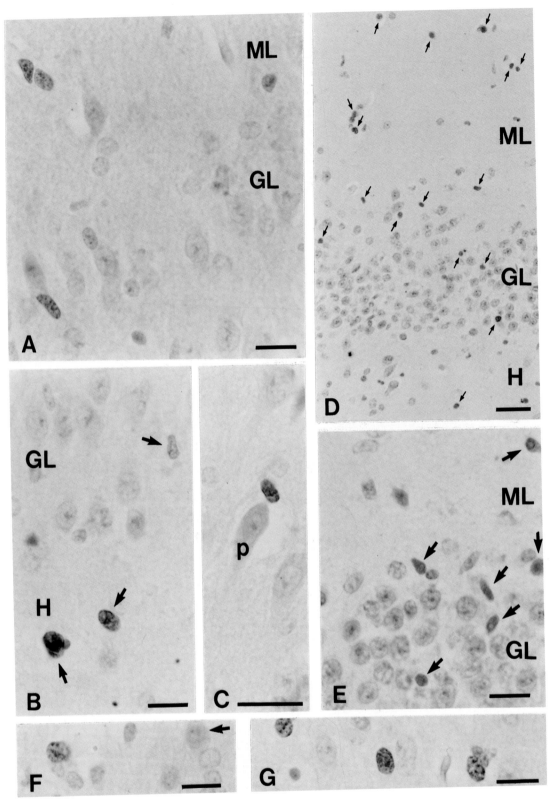

PLATE 4 Photomicrographs of Ki-67–labeled cells in different parts of the hippocampal formation of a 3-month-old (**A, B, C, F, G**) and an 11.5-month-old child (**D** and **E**). (**A**) Labeled cells appear to be glial cells in the molecular layer (ML) and granule cell layer (GL). (**B**) Labeled cells (arrows) in the granule cell layer (GL) and hilus (H). (**C**) A labeled astroglia in satellite position to a pyramidal cell (p) in the CA1 area of Ammon's horn. (**D**) Many small, darkly stained labeled cells (arrows) in the different layers of dentate gyrus of the 11.5-month-old child. (**E**) Higher magnification reveals that the Ki-67–labeled cells (arrows) are all glial elements. (**F**) An immunolabeled cell in the hilus of a 3-month-old child. Nuclear morphology of labeled cell suggests that, when compared with an unlabeled neuron (arrow), it may be a neuron. (**G**) Labeled cells in the entorhinal cortex of the 3-month-old child. Calibration bars = 40 μm for **D**, 20 μm for **A, B, C, E, F, G.**

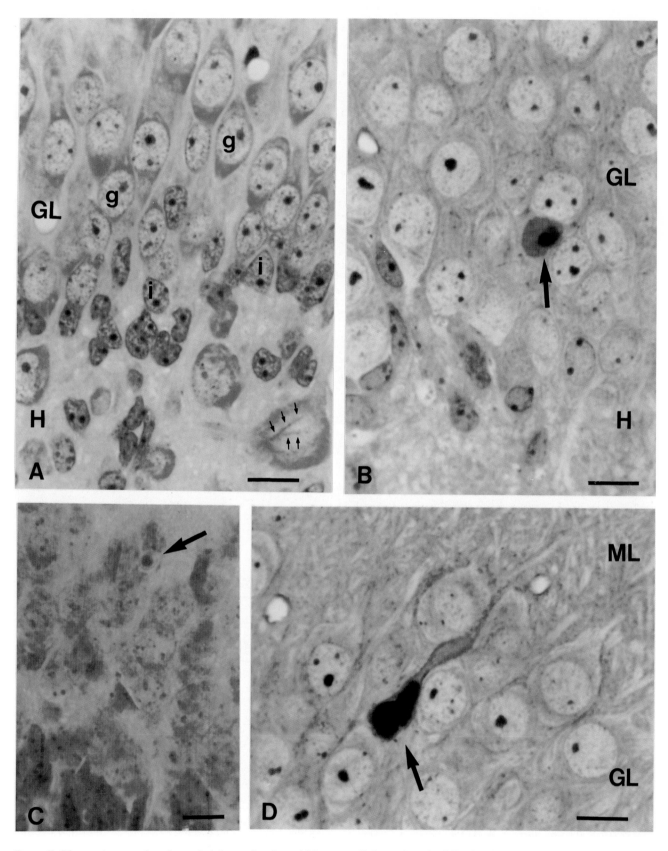

PLATE 5 Photomicrographs of cresyl violet–stained semithin sections of the dentate gyrus of a newborn monkey. (**A**) Inside the granule cell layer (GL), matured granule cells (g) display large pale cell nuclei with a purple cytoplasmic rim, whereas at the hilar (H) border many small dark immature cells (i) accumulate. Some of the large hilar neurons display deep nuclear infoldings (arrows) characteristic of matured GABAergic neurons of the hippocampus. (**B**) An apoptotic cell (arrow) at the hilar border of the granule cell layer. (**C**) A pycnotic cell nucleus (arrow) at the molecular layer border of the granule cell layer. (**D**) An apoptotic granule cell (arrow) at the molecular layer border (ML) of the granule cell layer. Note the shrunken soma and dense cell nucleus as well as the basophilic dendrite of the apoptotic cell. Calibration bar = 10 μm.

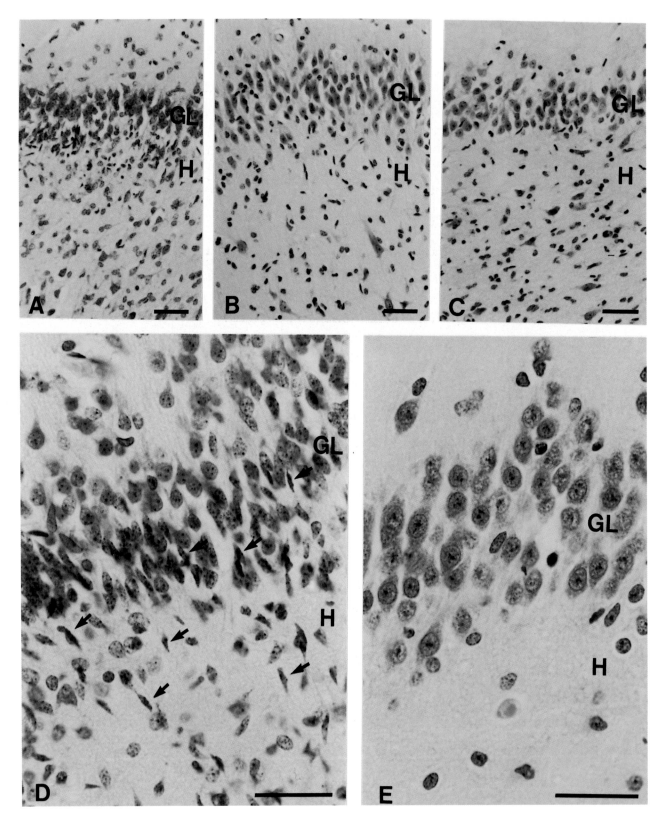

PLATE 6 Photomicrographs of cresyl violet–stained coronal sections of the human dentate gyrus. (**A**) In the newborn infant, the subgranular zone and the deep hilus contain large numbers of darkly stained small cell nuclei. (**D**) Higher magnification reveals the elongated cell nuclei (arrows) of immature neurons that are probably migrating granule cells. In 5-month-old (**B**) and 8.5-month-old (**C**) children, migrating cells are still seen in the hilus (H) and at the hilar border of the granule cell layer (GL). (**E**) In the dentate gyrus of a 1-year-old child, the subgranular zone contains only glial cells (compare **D** with **E**). Calibration bar = 50 μm.

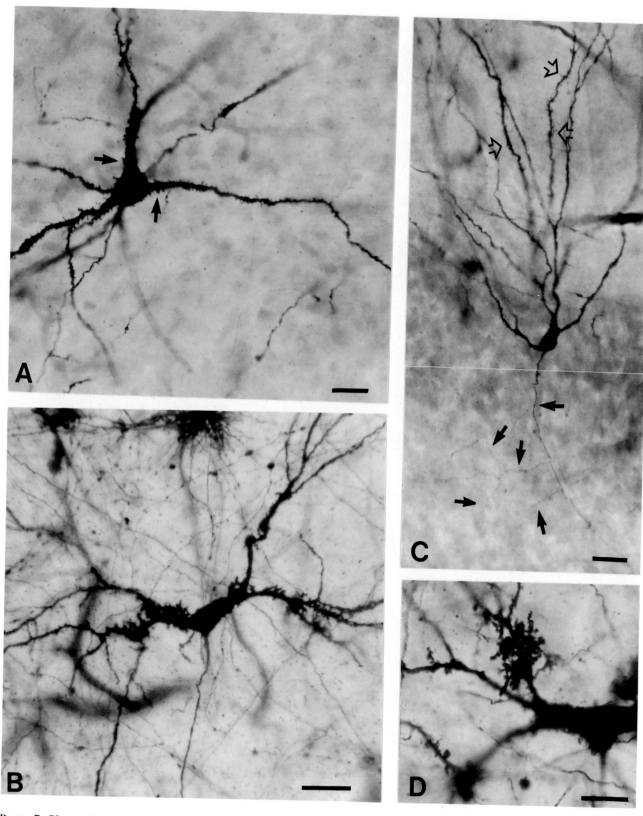

PLATE 7 Photomicrographs of Golgi-impregnated neurons in the human dentate gyrus. (A) Dendrites of the mossy cell in the newborn infant display the conventional simple spines and a few small protrusions that can be thorny excrescences (arrows). (B) Dendrites of mossy cell of the 3-year-old child display large complex spines, the so-called thorny excres-cences, that are characteristic for mossy cells of the adult brain (D). (C) Large numbers of granule cells display spiny dendrites (open arrows) and a richly arborizing axon (arrows point to the axon and its collaterals) in the dentate gyrus of the newborn child. Calibration bars = 40 μm for B and 20 μm for A, C, and D.

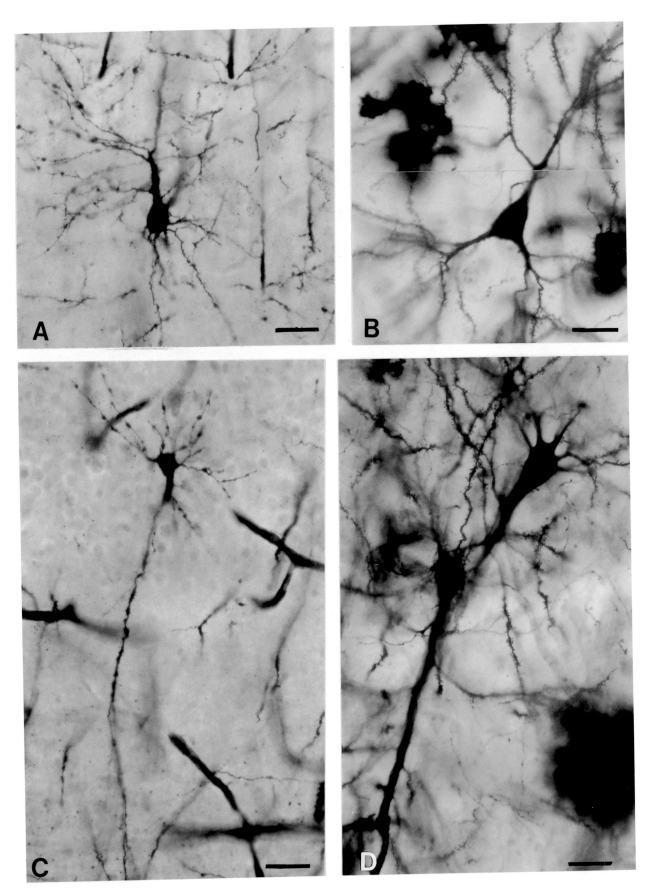

PLATE 8  Photomicrographs of Golgi-impregnated pyramidal cells in the cortex (**A** and **B**) and in Ammon's horn (**C** and **D**) of hippocampal formation in newborn (**A** and **C**) and adult (**B** and **D**) brain. Pyramidal cells in the newborn child display immature, beaded, spine-free short dendrites, whereas in the adult, pyramidal cells have large dendrites fully covered with spines. Calibration bar = 20 μm.

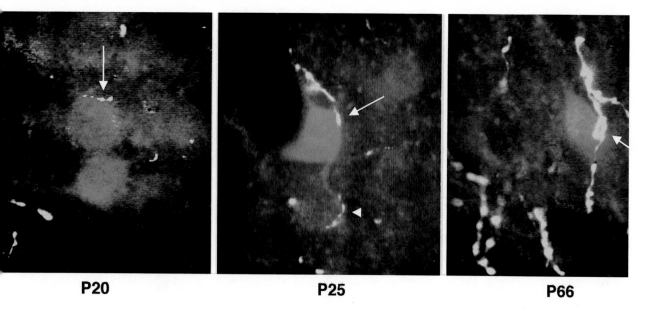

**P20**　　　　**P25**　　　　**P66**

ᴘʟᴀᴛᴇ 9　A digital confocal photomicrograph of a double-immunofluorescent localization of dopamine fibers (yellow) and GABA cell bodies in layer VI of rat medial prefrontal cortex at postnatal days P20, P25, and P66. By P20, dopamine fibers have already begun to form contacts with GABAergic neurons (arrows). Following weaning, the fibers show a subtle increase, and contacts can be seen both on the cell bodies and on large dendritic branches (arrowhead). By P66, the overall density of fibers is markedly increased and the number of interactions for any given cell is much greater. (Reprinted with permission from Benes, F. M., S. L. Vincent, R. Molloy, and Y. Khan, 1996. Increased interaction of dopamine-immunoreactive varicosities with GABA neurons of rat medial prefrontal cortex occurs during the post-weanling period. *Synapse* 23:237–245.)

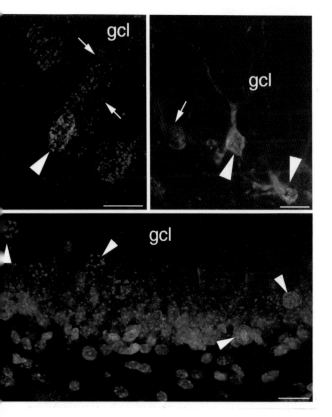

Pʟᴀᴛᴇ 10　Confocal laser scanning microscope images of new cells in the rat dentate gyrus. (*Top left*) BrdU-labeled cell (green, arrowhead) in the granule cell layer (gvcl) of an adult rat that is labeled with the retrograde tracer fluororuby. Arrows depict dendrites that are labeled with retrograde tracer. (*Top right*) BrdU-labeled cells (red, arrowheads) in the granule cell layer of an adult rat that are immunoreactive for TOAD-64 (green), a marker of immature neurons. Arrows depict TOAD-64–positive cells that are not labeled with BrdU. (*Bottom*) BrdU-labeled cells (red, arrowheads) in the dentate gyrus of a 3-week-old rat. Granule cells not labeled with BrdU are counter-stained with the DNA dye Hoechst 33342 (blue). Scale bar = 10 μm.

## Familiar Words    Pseudowords    Consonant Strings

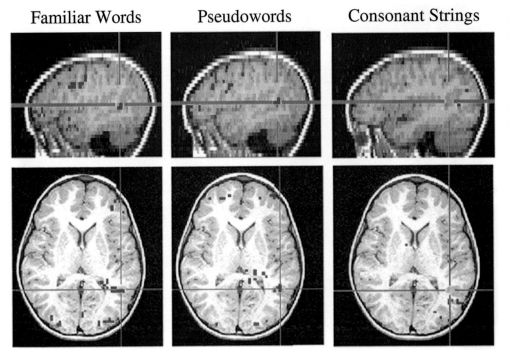

PLATE 11  fMRI results from a single session with an 8-year-old normal reading child performing a repetition detection (one-back) task on familiar words, pseudowords, and consonant strings minus an active fixation monitoring task.

## Before Intervention    After Intervention

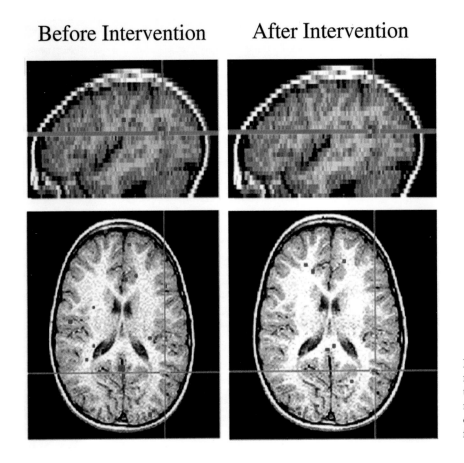

PLATE 12  fMRI results from two separate sessions (before and after intervention) with an 8-year-old child with reading impairments performing a repetition detection (one-back) task on familiar words.

B

D

ATE 13 Simulated views of the same scene as viewed at      (Reprinted with permission from Tony Young.)
th (**A**), 3 months (**B**), 6 months (**C**), and adult (**D**).

# Cholinergic

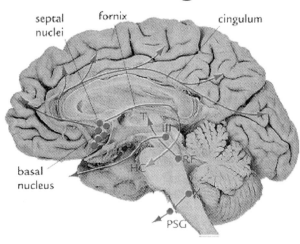

# Noradrenergic

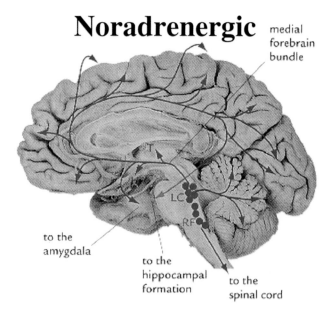

# Dopaminergic

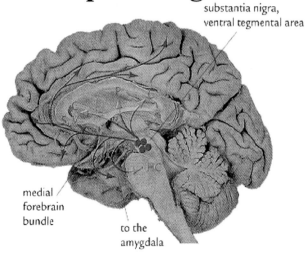

# Serotoninergic

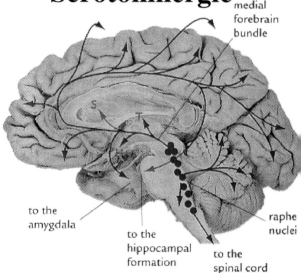

PLATE 14 The neurochemical systems involved in attention and arousal. *Abbreviations:* III, oculomotor nucleus; T, thalamus; HC, hippocampal formation; RF, reticular formation; PSG, parasympathetic ganglion cell; X, dorsal motor nucleus of the vagus; H, hypothalamus; LC, locus ceruleus; C, caudate nucleus; P, putamen; S, septal nuclei; V, ventral striatum. (Reprinted with permission from J. Nolte and J. B. Angevine, 1995. *The Human Brain.* St. Louis, MO: Mosby.)

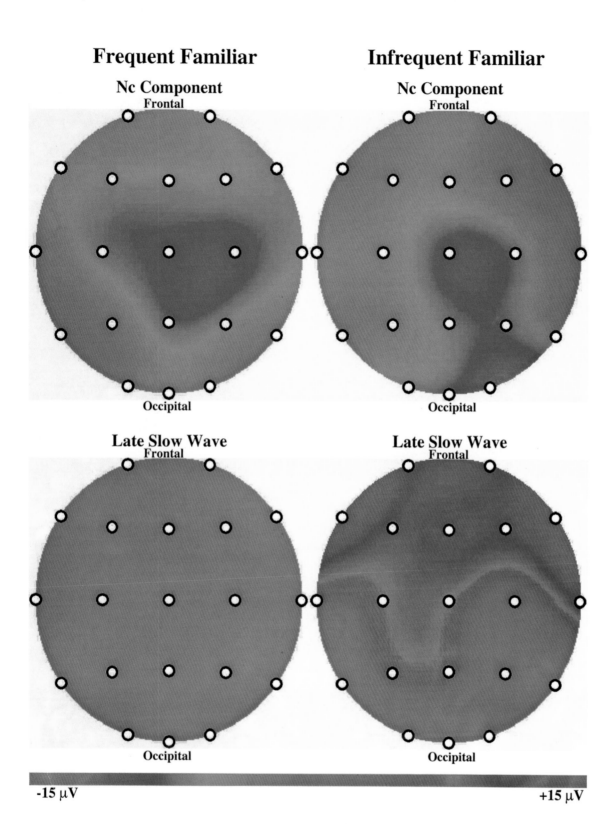

**Frequent Familiar**

**Nc Component**
Frontal
Occipital

**Late Slow Wave**
Frontal
Occipital

**Infrequent Familiar**

**Nc Component**
Frontal
Occipital

**Late Slow Wave**
Frontal
Occipital

-15 μV                                                    +15 μV

ᴛᴇ 15  A topographical mapping of the ERP components ᵤrring during sustained attention. The ERP components e the Nc (400–700 ms; top figures) and the later slow e component (700–1500 ms; bottom figures) taken dur- the presentation of the frequent familiar (left figures) the infrequent familiar (right figures) stimuli. The data ach figure represent an 80-ms average of the ERP for the

Nc (centered at 560 ms) and the slow wave (centered at 1120 ms) components for the 20 recording electrodes. The data are plotted with a cubic spline interpolation algorithm, with an averaged electrode reference, and represents absolute amplitude of the ERP for the recorded data rather than difference ERPs.

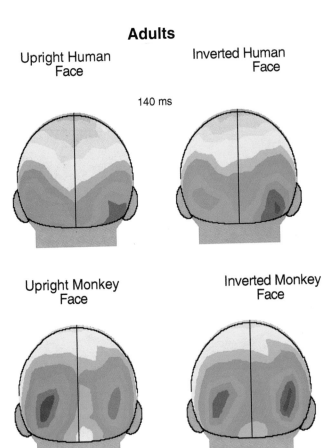

**Adults**

Upright Human
Face

Inverted Human
Face

140 ms

Upright Monkey
Face

Inverted Monkey
Face

PLATE 16 Amplitude distributions of activity at the peak of the N170 created using spherical spline interpolation. The view is looking straight on from the back of the head. The peak of the negativity of the N170 is seen in blue. The white/light areas indicate positivities. The black/dark areas indicate negativities.

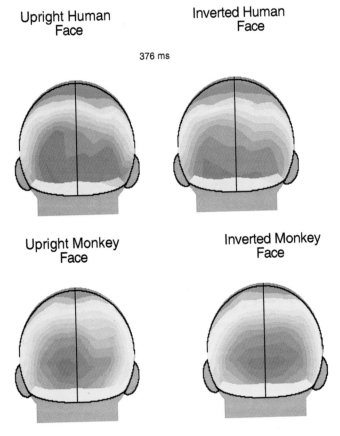

**Infants**

Upright Human
Face

Inverted Human
Face

376 ms

Upright Monkey
Face

Inverted Monkey
Face

PLATE 17 Amplitude distributions of activity at the peak of the P400 created using spherical spline interpolation. The view is looking straight on from the back of the head. The peak of the positivity of the P400 is seen in red. The white/light areas indicate positivities. The black/dark areas indicate negativities.

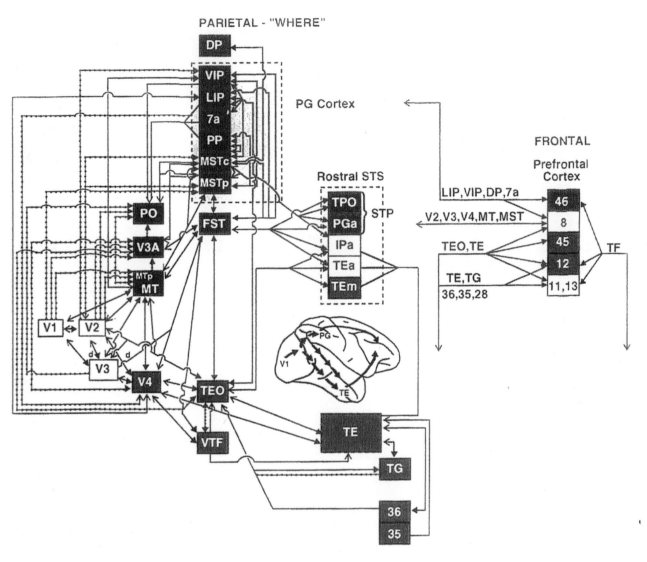

PARIETAL - "WHERE"

TEMPORAL - "WHAT"

PLATE 18 Visual processing pathways in monkeys. Solid lines indicate connections arising from both central and peripheral visual field representations; dotted lines indicate connections restricted to peripheral field representations. Red boxes indicate ventral stream areas related primarily to object vision; green boxes indicate dorsal stream areas related primarily to spatial vision; white boxes indicate areas not clearly allied with either stream. The shaded region on the lateral view of the brain represents the extent of the cortex included in the diagram. Abbreviations are as follows: DP, dorsal prelunate area; FST, fundus of superior temporal area; HIPP, hippocampus; LIP, lateral intraparietal area; MSTc, medial superior temporal area, central visual field representation; MSTp, medial superior temporal area, peripheral visual field representation; MT, middle temporal area; MTp, middle temporal area, peripheral visual field representation; PO, parietooccipital area; PP, posterior parietal sulcal zone; STP, superior temporal polysensory area; V1, primary visual cortex; V2, visual area 2; V3, visual area 3; V3A, visual area 3, part A; V4, visual area 4; and VIP, ventral intraparietal area. Inferior parietal area 7a; prefrontal areas 8, 11 to 13, 45, and 46, perirhinal areas 35 and 36; and entorhinal area 28 are from Brodmann (Brodmann, 1909). Inferior temporal areas TEO and TE, parahippocampal area TF, temporal pole area TG, and inferior parietal area PG are from von Bonin and Bailey (von Bonin and Bailey, 1947). Rostral superior temporal sulcal (STS) areas are from Seltzer and Pandya (Seltzer and Pandya, 1978) and VTF is the visually responsive portion of area TF (Boussaoud, Desimone, and Ungerleider, 1991). (Figure and caption reprinted with permission from Ungerleider, L. G., 1995. Functional brain imaging studies of cortical mechanisms for memory. *Science* 270:770.)

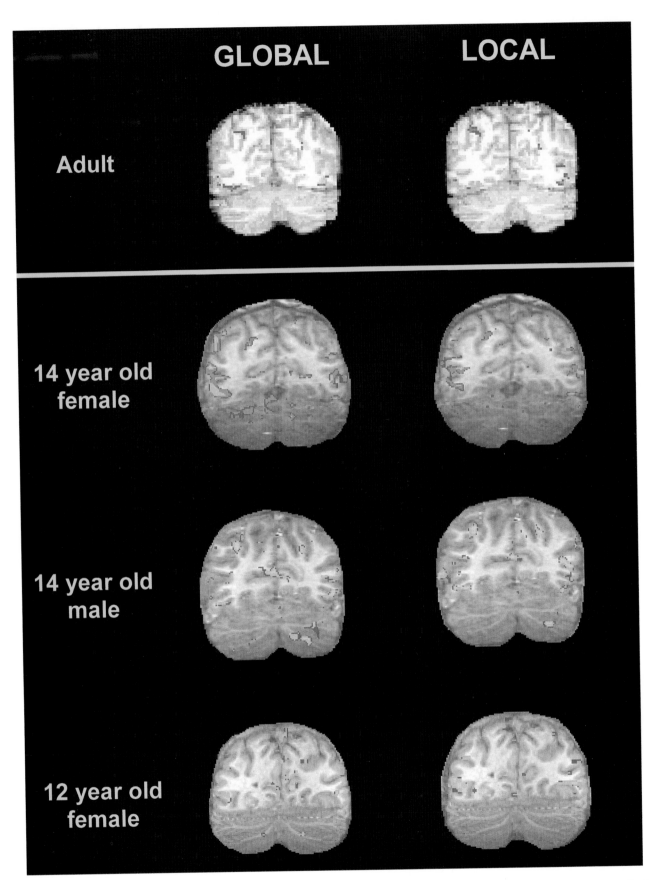

PLATE 19 Brain activation patterns from a functional MRI study of global–local processing. The top panel shows representative activation patterns for adult subjects. During the attend global condition, activation is greater on the right than on the left; during the attend local condition, activation is greater on the left. The bottom three panels show activation profiles from three representative children. Unlike adults, children show greater right than left activation for both the attend global and attend local condition.

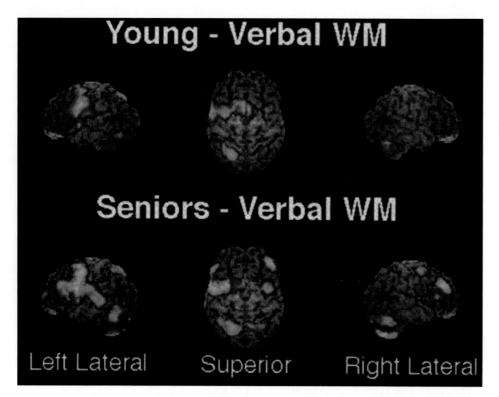

PLATE 20 Data from Reuter-Lorenz (1999), showing bilateral frontal activation in the older subjects during a verbal working memory (WM) task, and left activation only in the young subjects. (Reproduced with permission from Taylor & Francis.)

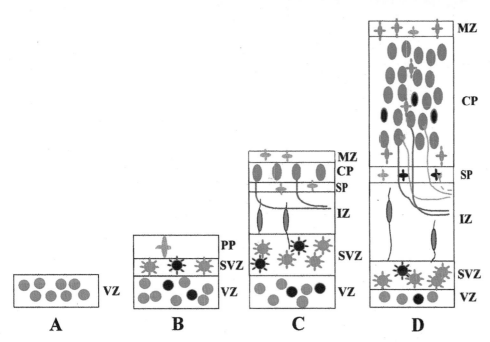

PLATE 21 Schematic representation of the major stages of development of the cerebral cortex, depicting proliferation, migration, differentiation, cell death, and synaptogenesis. (A) Progenitor cells (red) proliferate in the ventricular zone and give rise mostly to neurons. (B) Specialized pioneer neurons (green; Cajal-Retzius cells) begin to differentiate in the preplate as additional cells proliferate in the ventricular and subventricular zones. The spiked red cells in the SVZ give rise mostly to glia. Cells shown in black will undergo cell death as part of a complex process to regulate cell number. (C) The preplate is divided by neurons arriving in the cortical plate into the marginal zone and the subplate. The trailing processes of differentiating neurons develop into axons (blue), and additional neurons continue to migrate through the intermediate zone to the cortical plate. (D) The cortical plate develops in an inside-out manner, such that earlier-born neurons reside deeper. Glia (red cells) begin to seed the cortical plate, afferents from subcortical and other cortical regions arrive (orange), and synaptogenesis begins. Subplate neurons receive transient synapses that eventually are lost when the neurons die. Synaptogenesis in the cortex proper continues into postnatal development through adolescence. *Abbreviations:* CP, cortical plate; IZ, intermediate zone; MZ, marginal zone; PP, preplate; SP, subplate; SVZ, subventricular zone; VZ, ventricular zone.

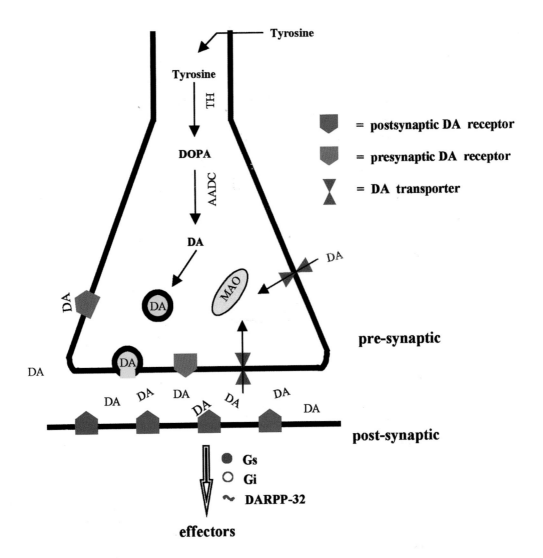

Plate 22 Schematic representation of the life cycle of dopamine (DA). The amino acid precursor tyrosine is accumulated by the neuron and tyrosine is sequentially converted to DA by the actions of tyrosine hydroxylase (TH) and aromatic acid decarboxylase (AADC). DA is then accumulated into vesicles where it is protected from degradation and prepared for release. Once DA is released, it can interact with a variety of proteins including postsynaptic receptors (blue) and presynaptic autoreceptors (green) that regulate transmitter release, synthesis, or firing rate through specific effector proteins (purple). DA can also bind to sites on DA transporters (red), which are expressed on the presynaptic membrane. This leads to the termination of the extracellular actions of DA. Once accumulated by the neuron, DA can be metabolized to inactive species by degradative enzymes such as monoamine oxidase (MAO) (pink), or taken back into vesicles.

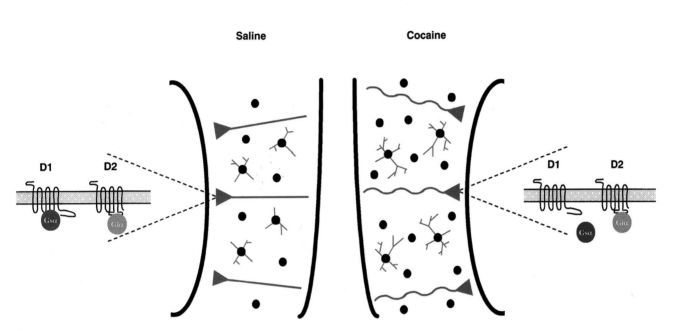

**Saline**

**Cocaine**

D1    D2

Gsα    Giα

D1    D2

Gsα    Giα

PLATE 23 Schematic representation of cellular effects of in utero cocaine exposure in the rabbit. Rabbits exposed to low doses of cocaine intravenously exhibit alterations in the structure and function of neurons in the anterior cingulate cortex. The apical dendrites of pyramidal neurons (red) exhibit an undulating trajectory. The number of interneurons in which immunoreactivity for GABA is detectable (black) is increased. There also is an increase in parvalbumin (green) immunostaining in the dendrites of a subset of these neurons. $D_1$ dopamine receptor coupling to Gs protein (blue) is reduced, whereas coupling of the $D_2$ receptor to Gi (orange) is unaffected. These changes likely influence the balance of excitatory and inhibitory influences in the cingulate cortex and produce the aberrant behavioral phenotypes exhibited by these rabbits. (Modified from Levitt et al., 1997.)

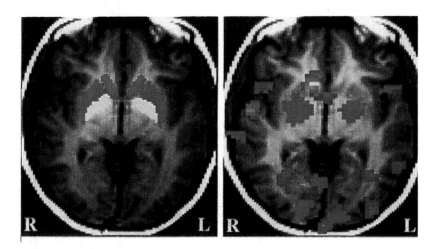

PLATE 24 Single-subject activation/deactivation map of sub-cortical structures during voluntary tic suppression. The figure on the right depicts three regions of interest: caudate nucleus (red), putamen (blue), and globus pallidus (yellow) as defined by hand tracing on $T_1$ weighted axial MRI images. The figure on the left presents data from a single subject. Images acquired during eight 40-second epochs of voluntary tic suppression that alternated with eight 40-second epochs in which the subject was encouraged to tic freely. For each pixel, the mean difference in activity between the tic suppression epochs and the freely ticking tic epochs was normalized and transformed to a $t$-statistic. The map shows that during voluntary tic suppression this subject displayed activation of the right head of caudate (red) and a deactivation of the putamen and globus pallidus (blue), bilaterally. Remarkably, these changes were closely correlated with one another. For example, the increased activation of the head of the caudate was inversely correlated with the deactivation of both the putamen ($r = 0.86$, $P < .001$) and globus pallidus ($r = 0.84$, $P < .001$). These patterns of activation/inactivation were also found to be correlated with the subject's level of tic severity outside the magnet. Specifically, the higher activation in the caudate ($r = -0.46$, $P < .02$) and the lower the activation in the putamen and globus pallidus (range $0.54 \leq r \leq 0.40$, $P < .001$ to $P < .07$) during epochs of tic suppression, the lower the subject's level of tic severity was observed to be outside of the magnet. For further details, see Peterson et al., 1998b. (Adapted from Peterson et al., 1998b.)

# 36 Developmental Disorders of Attention

CANAN KARATEKIN

ABSTRACT  The goal of the chapter is to explore different meanings of attention in the context of two neurodevelopmental disorders. Although it has been conceptualized as a unitary construct, attention refers to a variety of cognitive processes. The chapter begins with an overview of research on three commonly used meanings of attention in the cognitive neuroscience literature: selective, executive, and sustained attention. Next, a brief summary of research on these aspects of attention in schizophrenia and attention-deficit/hyperactivity disorder (ADHD) is presented. The final section concludes with a consideration of potential contributions of cognitive neuroscience to an understanding of disorders of attention and potential contributions of research on developmental disorders of attention to an understanding of the cognitive and neurobiological substrates of attentional development.

The first point to make about attention is that there is no one definition of attention. As Treisman (1998) has noted, "Attention need not be a unitary process simply because a single word is used in everyday language" (p. 1305). What researchers mean by attention is inevitably shaped by their perspective, the methods and populations they are working with, and the specific aspect of attention they are studying.

As a behavioral descriptor, attention can mean being able to sustain a high level of effort on cognitively demanding tasks (e.g., homework), refraining from being distracted by irrelevant stimuli (e.g., a noise in the background), and attending to inappropriate stimuli (e.g., internal or intrusive thoughts, hallucinations).

In cognitive neuroscience, some researchers conceptualize attention as an enhancement of processing of relevant stimuli (Posner and Dehaene, 1994), whereas others view it as akin to an executive controlling different parts of the brain (Baddeley, 1996) or a pool of resources (Kahneman, 1973). Neuropsychological studies of patients with frontal lesions emphasize the role of the frontal lobes in attention (Swick and Knight, 1998), whereas studies of patients with subcortical lesions highlight the interactions of the frontal lobes with the basal ganglia, the thalamus, and the cerebellum (Dubois et al., 1995). Finally, some researchers suggest

that attention emerges out of the synchronized activity of large-scale neuronal networks distributed across the whole brain (Dehaene, Kerszberg, and Changeux, 1998; Lumer, Edelman, and Tononi, 1997; Niebur and Koch, 1998).

Other chapters in this volume (Johnson, Mareschal, and Csibra; Rothbart and Posner; Richards) address attention and its development in healthy individuals. In this chapter, we explore the different meanings of attention within the context of two developmental disorders. The first section is a brief overview of three common meanings of attention in cognitive neuroscience: selective, executive, and sustained attention (Parasuraman, 1998; Perry and Hodges, 1999). All three types of attention are mediated by widespread neuronal networks that are vulnerable to many kinds of damage and dysfunction. Therefore, it is not surprising that attentional impairments play a significant role in many psychiatric disorders. The discussion that follows summarizes research on two of these disorders—schizophrenia and attention-deficit/hyperactivity disorder (ADHD)—and considers potential contributions of the cognitive neuroscience of attention to research on these and other disorders of attention. Missing to some extent in both of these research literatures is a genuinely developmental perspective. Thus, the chapter concludes by highlighting developmental questions that can be investigated in disorders of attention and their potential for illuminating our understanding of the cognitive and neurobiological substrates of the development of attention.

## Meanings of attention in cognitive neuroscience

SELECTIVE ATTENTION  The first meaning of attention refers to selectivity, the ability to attend to relevant stimuli and ignore irrelevant stimuli. Selective attention can be controlled in a bottom-up (e.g., by physically salient stimuli such as a bright light) or a top-down manner (e.g., by expectations and goals that determine what is "relevant").

CANAN KARATEKIN  Institute of Child Development, University of Minnesota, Minneapolis, Minnesota.

There is a long tradition of research in cognitive psychology on the top-down control, or the active and constructive nature, of visual-spatial attention (Brandt, 1945; Bruner and Minturn, 1955; James, 1890; Karpov, Luria, and Yarbus, 1968; Neisser, 1976; van Essen, Anderson, and Felleman, 1992). As psychologists since William James (1890) have argued, what we choose to attend to and what we choose to ignore defines our subjective experience of the world. Modern research techniques have now begun to delineate the cognitive and neurobiological underpinnings of top-down control of selective attention, even at the level of single cells, and demonstrate how "we often see what we expect to see" (Llewellyn-Thomas, 1969, p. 414).

One of the most influential theories of selective attention is Treisman's feature integration theory, which details how visual-spatial attention binds features of objects together and draws heavily upon data from visual search tasks. On search tasks, participants decide if a target is present among variable numbers of distractors. Treisman and her colleagues argue that when we search for the target, attention is initially spread wide over the whole display and unique features (e.g., color or orientation) can be detected in parallel. If the target does not have a unique feature distinguishing it from the distractors, attention has to be focused and the display is searched in a serial fashion (Treisman and Gelade, 1980). The original version of the theory did not include any mechanisms for top-down control of attention. Revisions of the theory (Treisman and Sato, 1990) and alternative theories by other researchers (Cave and Wolfe, 1990; Wolfe, 1994) place greater emphasis on mechanisms of attentional control through enhancement of potential targets and inhibition of potential distractors within the first few hundred milliseconds after stimulus onset.

Electrophysiological studies in adults have provided support for the notion of top-down guidance of attention. It has long been known that the same stimulus can give rise to different patterns of brain activity depending on whether the participant is attending to it or not (Hillyard, Teder-Sälerjärvi, and Münte, 1998). In the visual modality, these differences are apparent as early as 60–100 ms after stimulus onset (Luck and Girelli, 1998). Hillyard and colleagues have argued that discrete mechanisms of selective attention can operate simultaneously within the same task during these first few hundred milliseconds (Hillyard, Teder-Sälerjärvi, and Münte, 1998; Luck, 1995). These mechanisms include phasic amplification of stimulus-evoked neuronal activity, starting at extrastriate cortex, and tonic increase of neuronal activity caused by a bias toward the contents of an "attentional template." These mechanisms can be further divided into those that suppress information at unattended locations (reflected in the P1 component of evoked-response potentials), those that facilitate processing of attended stimuli (reflected in the N1 component), and a "winner-take-all" mechanism by which attention comes to be focused on a potential target and information from distractors is suppressed (reflected in the N2pc component).

Single-cell recordings in nonhuman primates also indicate that the same stimulus evokes different responses in the same cell depending on whether the organism is attending to it or not (Chelazzi, 1995). Focal attention modulates the sensitivity and the size of the functional receptive fields of neurons (Motter, 1998) and suppresses responses of individual cells to distractors even when the distractors are within the receptive fields of the cells (Moran and Desimone, 1985).

Likewise, functional imaging studies show higher levels of neuronal activity in task-relevant brain regions for attended compared to unattended stimuli. Depending on the task, these modulations can be observed as early as striate and extrastriate cortex (Brefczynski and DeYoe, 1999; Gandhi, Heeger, and Boynton, 1999; Haxby, Courtney, and Clark, 1998; Martinez et al., 1999; O'Craven et al., 1997). Studies further suggest that attention influences the baseline sensitivity of task-specific neuronal populations even prior to the onset of the stimulus to be attended (Chawla, Rees, and Friston, 1999) and increase functional interconnectivity among task-relevant regions (Büchel and Friston, 1997; Haxby, Courtney, and Clark, 1998).

What is clear from these different strands of research is that selective attention can modulate information processing even before the presentation of a stimulus and that functional interconnectivity is crucial to the efficiency of selective attention. What is not settled yet is the mechanism of this modulation (Parasuraman, 1998). That is, are there distinct neuronal networks controlling attention and influencing the activity of other, modality-specific regions (Mesulam, 1998; Posner and Petersen, 1990)? Or is attention an emergent property of competitive interactions within task-relevant populations of neurons (Desimone and Duncan, 1995; Reynolds, Chelazzi, and Desimone, 1999)?

ATTENTION AS EXECUTIVE Another meaning of attention refers to control over cognitive processes in general. Though similar to the concept of top-down control of visual-spatial attention, the concern here is more on control and integration of knowledge, thoughts, and actions than on the biasing of visual-spatial processing toward the selection of certain stimuli. This type of attention has gone under many names, including "central executive" (Baddeley, 1996), "executive" attention (Posner and Dehaene, 1994), "supervisory attention" (Shallice and Burgess, 1991), and "effortful control" (Ruff and Rothbart, 1996).

It should be noted from the start, however, that the distinctions among this type of attentional control, working memory, and executive functions are blurry. In Baddeley's model of working memory, for instance, "the central executive [is] primarily attentional in nature" (1993, p. 168). Mesulam (1998) calls working memory "a special type of attentional process" (p. 1032). Others emphasize the overlap between the neural circuits mediating working memory and attention (Desimone, 1998) and argue that spatial rehearsal in working memory is mediated by covert spatial attention (Awh and Jonides, 1998). Working memory, in turn, is crucial for most executive functions. Thus, it may be parsimonious to consider control of attention, working memory, and executive functions together.

Much of the early research on this aspect of attention was based on the dramatic dissociations observed in patients with frontal lobe lesions who were severely impaired in their ability to carry out basic activities of daily living but could perform within normal limits on IQ tests. Many of these patients had difficulty with problem solving and decision making, encoding contextual information about stimuli, working memory, strategic and goal-directed behavior, abstract thought, cognitive flexibility, inhibition, judgment, adaptation to novel circumstances, and self-regulation. Over time, the set of cognitive processes impaired in patients with frontal lesions came to be used interchangeably with the term "executive" processes (Tranel, Anderson, and Benton, 1994).

Gradually, however, there emerged an increasing number of reports of patients with subcortical lesions who showed deficits similar to those of patients with frontal lesions. These reports, along with neuroanatomical studies uncovering the rich feed-forward and -backward connections among brain regions and neuroimaging studies showing large areas of activation in many tasks, highlighted the functional interconnectivity between the frontal lobes and the rest of the brain in supporting executive functions.

These developments led to a growing number of theories of executive function based on neuronal networks that included the prefrontal cortex, the parietal lobes, the basal ganglia, the thalamus, and the cerebellum (Alexander, DeLong, and Strick, 1986; Fuster, 1995; Goldman-Rakic, 1988; Houk and Wise, 1995; Mesulam, 1998). A large portion of the data on which these theories are based came from single-cell and lesion studies with monkeys. Consequently, these theories tend to focus on a relatively limited number of executive processes whose neurobiological bases have been fairly well established in monkeys. Other theories of executive function were built on constructs from experimental cognitive psychology as well as findings from neuropsychological and neuroanatomical studies. These theories tend to encompass a greater number of executive processes that are relatively less well-specified and harder to localize within specific neural circuits or regions.

The differences among these approaches can be illustrated with a review of several major theories of working memory, which is considered to be an executive function or, at least necessary for the efficient operation of executive functions. Based on her extensive research on the prefrontal cortex in monkeys, Goldman-Rakic (1998), who defines working memory as the ability to maintain representations "on line," views it as the primary function of prefrontal cortex and regards executive functions as an emergent property of multiple integrated working memory circuits. Similarly, Fuster (1995) states that working memory is the ability to integrate memory for past events with current behavior and preparation for future goals. He argues that the prefrontal cortex is situated at the highest level of a hierarchy of information processing and that its main function is the temporal organization of behavior.

The supervisory attention model of Shallice and Burgess (1991) represents research based to a greater extent on cognitive psychology. Shallice and Burgess (1991) state that their theory of the supervisory functions of attention grew out of Luria's neuropsychological studies and his "approach to the frontal lobes as a system for the programming, regulation and verification of activity" (p. 125). They add that, "[The supervisory attention model] can be viewed as one possible realization of Luria's theory in information-processing terms. When we developed our model, we were attempting to explain not only neuropsychological findings in frontal lobe patients but also empirical phenomena in the experimental psychology of attention and in the phenomenology of attention to action. It was therefore linked directly to studies of normal subjects" (pp. 125–126). This model posits two systems that underlie attentional control of action. Routine actions (e.g., stopping at a red stoplight) are carried out by the *contention scheduling system*. When routine actions are not enough (e.g., when the situation is too novel, dangerous, or difficult), the *supervisory attention system* takes over.

Borrowing from this notion of supervisory control of attention and expanding on the older concept of short-term memory, Baddeley later proposed a model that includes (1) temporary buffers that hold information in different modalities (e.g., verbal or spatial), (2) rehearsal mechanisms that maintain the contents of these buffers in mind, and (3) a "central executive" that coordinates the activities of the buffers and controls attention. As noted earlier, the central executive is hypothesized to be attentional in nature (Baddeley, 1993; Collette et al., 1999) and is composed of a finite set of processes that include selective and divided attention (Baddeley, 1996). There is fairly strong evidence for the existence of modality-specific buffers and rehearsal mechanisms (Smith and Jonides, 1998). However, as Baddeley (1996, 1998) acknowledges, there is still much research to be done on the nature of the specific processes comprising the central executive. Although the neurobiological bases of the different aspects of the supervisory attention system and Baddeley's model of working memory have been investigated extensively, the mapping of function to location is less precise than in the neuroanatomically precise models proposed by Goldman-Rakic (1998), Fuster (1995), and others.

ATTENTION AS A RESOURCE   In contrast to the views of attention as a "spotlight" or a "chief executive officer," the dominant metaphor for a third meaning of attention is that of "energy" or "cognitive resources." According to Kahneman's (1973) model of resources, attention depends on a limited number of resources that can be recruited and allocated according to task demands. One's overall level of resources is related to level of arousal in an inverted U-shaped function. When level of arousal is too low, an inadequate amount of resources is allocated to the task; when it is too high, individuals cannot allocate resources efficiently and have difficulty making appropriate distinctions between relevant and irrelevant stimuli. Allocation of resources on a moment-to-moment basis depends on both external (e.g., stimulus salience) and internal (e.g., goals) factors. The neurobiological bases of resources are hypothesized to include interactions among the prefrontal cortex, the thalamus, and the mesencephalic reticular formation (Dehaene, Kerszberg, and Changeux, 1998; Heilman et al., 1987; Robbins, 1997). Among the key distinctions that follow from this view of attention is that between tasks requiring more versus fewer resources, or that between tasks relying on "automatic" versus "effortful" processes (Schneider and Shiffrin, 1977).

Although the notion of a limited pool of resources that places constraints on attention makes common sense and figures implicitly or explicitly in many theories of attention as an explanatory construct, it has been notoriously hard to pin down and measure. In addition, as findings contradicted the hypothesis of a limited pool

of resources, researchers began to posit the existence of a number of pools (Wickens, 1980). However, at a certain point in this endeavor to explain contradictory results, the construct of resources becomes irrefutable and scientifically useless (Meyer and Kieras, 1997; Navon, 1984).

Nevertheless, valiant researchers have made attempts to measure the amount of cognitive resources devoted to different tasks. One measure used for this purpose is task-evoked pupillary dilation, which increases systematically up to a point as a function of processing load and demands on sustained attention (Beatty, 1982). For instance, Peavler (1974) has shown that pupillary dilation in normal adults increases during digit span up to approximately 9 digits, after which it plateaus. This pattern of performance suggests that individuals expend an increasingly greater amount of attentional resources on remembering the digits, but only up to the point at which the expenditure of additional resources cannot improve memory any further. A recent study has provided converging evidence for this hypothesis. Callicott and colleagues (1999) have used the *n*-back task to investigate the physiological bases of capacity limitations using functional magnetic resonance imaging (fMRI). On the *n*-back task, participants are presented with a continuous stream of stimuli and asked to decide if the stimulus they are seeing currently is the same as the stimulus they saw *n* trials ago. Callicott and colleagues found that performance and activation in the dorsolateral prefrontal cortex were at first tightly coupled. As the memory load began to overwhelm the participants' capacity, however, the correlations dropped to nonsignificant levels. The findings of these studies are consistent with the notion that the expenditure of cognitive resources increases systematically with task demands up to the point at which the demands overwhelm the resources of the system.

A concept that is closely related to the idea of resources is sustained attention, or vigilance, which refers to control over allocation of resources over time (Parasuraman, 1998). Researchers often portray sustained attention as a continuous process and emphasize that resources are depleted by having to maintain focused attention over time. Therefore, decrements in performance on sustained attention tasks should parallel the rate of depletion of resources, and a disproportionate decrement in performance over time would suggest that an inadequate amount of resources was allocated to the task.

Research on sustained attention received a boost during World War II from concerns about vigilance in radar operators. Hence, one of the popular tests of sustained attention today, the continuous performance test

(CPT), is modeled on the typical situation that a radar operator must face: monitoring a continuous stream of rapidly flashing stimuli over a long period of time in order to detect infrequent targets (Sergeant and van der Meere, 1994). The two most useful indices of performance on the CPT are perceptual sensitivity ($d'$) and response criterion ($\beta$) as a function of time. The former refers to the ability to distinguish between targets and distractors; the latter, to the threshold set by the participant for deciding whether a stimulus is a target or not (measured by the overall probability of responding that the target is present). A decrease in perceptual sensitivity or an increase in response criterion over the course of the CPT is believed to reflect decrements in sustained attention and depletion of cognitive resources. Findings that both perceptual sensitivity and task-evoked pupillary dilation decrease over time on the CPT are consistent with the hypothesis that both measures are tapping a common pool of attentional resources (Nuechterlein and Asarnow, 1989).

Conclusions More than two decades ago, Norman Garmezy (1977) wrote an excellent review article on the psychology and psychopathology of attention. He observed that "so many different meanings have surrounded the concept of attention that its use as a global term has only served to produce confusion and to reduce any potential power inherent in the diversity" (p. 364). Has anything changed since then? The answer is both yes and no. Grouping different attentional phenomena under three clusters (control of attention over space, over other cognitive processes, or over time) may reduce some of the confusion. The evidence so far indicates that these clusters are tapping distinct cognitive processes mediated by different but overlapping neural circuits (Parasuraman, 1998). Yet, the use of attention as a global term to describe all of these processes, within and across the clusters, continues to create confusion (Grafman, 1995). For example, there is no a priori reason why being able to engage in serial search for a target among distractors should refer to the same process as being able to orient to the likely location of a target prior to its onset; yet, the term "selective attention" is used to describe both. This correspondence was established only after careful testing of the hypothesis that the two terms refer to the same process (e.g., Luck, 1995). Therefore, until relations among these processes are ascertained through empirical investigation, it may be advisable to view attention as a set of loosely related processes and not as a unitary construct (Kagan, 1984). With this caveat in mind, let us now summarize how these two types of attention have been studied in three neurodevelopmental disorders.

## Research on attention in schizophrenia and ADHD

Schizophrenia Schizophrenia is defined by the presence of two or more of the following: delusions, hallucinations, disorganized speech, grossly disorganized or catatonic behavior, and negative symptoms (e.g., flat affect, avolition). The diagnosis also requires social or occupational dysfunction or deterioration and persistence of at least some signs of the disorder for at least 6 months (American Psychiatric Association, 1994).

The lifetime prevalence of schizophrenia is approximately 1% across cultures (Jablensky et al., 1992). Although the modal age of onset for schizophrenia is in the early 20s, subtle delays and deficits in cognitive, language, social, and motor functions can be observed long before the onset of the full-blown disorder (Nuechterlein, 1986). Some individuals who develop schizophrenia recover from it to a great extent, some exhibit a fluctuating course, and some show significant deterioration in functioning. In general, the worse the premorbid functioning, the worse the prognosis tends to be (APA, 1994).

Childhood-onset schizophrenia, which has a prevalence of approximately .002 to .04%, is much less common than the adult-onset form (Burd and Kerbeshian, 1987; Russell, Bott, and Sammons, 1989). The phenomenology of the disorder is very similar in children and adults. However, the content of the psychotic symptoms in children tends to reflect age-appropriate themes (e.g., monsters) (Russell, 1994). Retrospective accounts indicate a much longer and insidious onset in children compared to adults (Asarnow, Tompson, and Goldstein, 1994; Jacobsen and Rapoport, 1998; Watkins, Asarnow, and Tanguay, 1988). The childhood-onset form of the disorder is also associated with a worse prognosis and greater genetic loading than the adult form (Asarnow, Tompson, and Goldstein, 1994; Asarnow, Asarnow, and Strandburg, 1989; Bettes and Walker, 1987; Green et al., 1992; McClellan and Werry, 1994; Schmidt et al., 1995; Werry, 1992).

There is a substantial genetic component to schizophrenia (Holzman, 1996; McGuffin, Owen, and Farmer, 1995); however, concordance is less than 100% even in monozygotic twins. Thus, it is hypothesized that in most cases, the disorder is manifested when a genetic vulnerability is combined with a high level of environmental stressors such as infections during the pre- or postnatal period (Buckley et al., 1996; Mortensen et al., 1999). The biological substrates of schizophrenia include abnormalities in the frontal and temporal lobes, the anterior cingulate, the basal ganglia, the thalamus, and the cerebellum (Andreasen, 1997). Neurotransmitters that seem to play a prominent role in the disorder include dopamine, serotonin, and glutamate (Carlsson et al., 1997; Kahn and Davis, 1995). Recent models of schizophrenia have emphasized that the disorder is associated more with abnormal or inefficient patterns of connectivity across brain regions than with a specific lesion in a particular area (Buchsbaum et al., 1996; Friston, 1998; Weinberger, 1993). For example, Jones (1997) has argued that an impairment in coordinated recruitment of ensembles of neurons in the cortex and thalamus may explain difficulties that schizophrenic individuals have in focusing on relevant stimuli. Andreasen has suggested that the fundamental impairment has to do with cortical-thalamic-cerebellar circuitry and called the resulting dysfunction "cognitive dysmetria" (Andreasen, 1999).

The vast literature on attention in schizophrenia is well beyond the scope of this chapter (see Nuechterlein and Dawson, 1984). The following, then, is a very selective review of this literature.

Selective attention in schizophrenia has been measured on visual search tasks such as the span of apprehension (SOA), which was originally designed to measure the amount of information that can be extracted from briefly presented displays of letters (Estes and Taylor, 1964). In the original, full-report version, subjects report as many letters from the display as they can recall, which is taken as an estimate of their "span of apprehension." In the partial-report version, which is more germane to schizophrenia research, subjects are presented with two target letters (e.g., T and F) and asked to decide which of these letters is present in displays that include variable numbers of nontarget letters. The primary dependent variable is the percentage of correct responses. In most studies, the number of letters in the display ranges from 1 to 12, and the displays are typically visible for 50–70 ms, too brief for eye movements to be executed (Asarnow, Granholm, and Sherman, 1991). Schizophrenic individuals perform as well as controls on the partial-report SOA when there are 1–3 letters in the display. However, when the display contains more letters, the performance of a subgroup of schizophrenic individuals (approximately 40%) deteriorates more than that of controls. Impaired performance on larger displays on the partial-report SOA has been observed in adults (Neale, 1971; Neale et al., 1969) and children (Asarnow and Sherman, 1984) with the disorder, and even in individuals in the general population who exhibit schizotypal characteristics as measured by personality tests (Asarnow, Nuechterlein, and Marder, 1983). The impairment appears to be independent of clinical state (Asarnow and Mac-Crimmon, 1981, 1982), and to have high test–retest

reliability (Asarnow et al., 1988). It is associated with the negative, but not the positive, symptoms of schizophrenia (Nuechterlein et al., 1986; Strauss, Buchanan, and Hale, 1993), and discriminates schizophrenic individuals from individuals with other psychiatric disorders (Asarnow and MacCrimmon, 1981; Neale, 1971). To do well on this task, participants must focus their attention and rapidly search the displays in a serial fashion. Impairments on this task appear to be due to a slow rate of processing the relevant information and engaging in serial search (Davidson and Neale, 1974; Karatekin and Asarnow, 1998a), and not other factors (Asarnow and Sherman, 1984). Although it is likely that schizophrenic individuals have deficits in top-down guidance of attention, this hypothesis has not yet been tested adequately.

Individuals with schizophrenia, as well as their unaffected relatives, perform poorly on most measures of executive attention. However, the nature of this impairment is still under question. Goldman-Rakic has suggested that deficits in working memory, mediated by abnormalities in the prefrontal cortex, represent a fundamental impairment in schizophrenia (Goldman-Rakic, 1994; Selemon, Rajkowska, and Goldman-Rakic, 1995). Cohen and colleagues (1996) have developed a computational model that explains the executive impairments observed in schizophrenic individuals, including deficits in working memory and inhibition, by an impairment in the representation of contextual information. On the other hand, Andreasen (1997) has argued that the fundamental deficit in schizophrenia is one of "consciousness"—"an inefficient temporal and spatial referencing of information and experience as the person attempts to determine boundaries between self and not-self and to formulate effective decisions or plans that will guide him or her through the small-scale (speaking a sentence) or large-scale (finding a job) maneuvers of daily living" (p. 1590).

Reductions in processing capacity can also explain a wide range of impairments in schizophrenia (Nuechterlein and Dawson, 1984). Consistent with this hypothesis, studies of pupillary dilation show that the pupils of schizophrenic individuals do not dilate as much as those of normal participants under high processing loads, suggesting that they have limitations in the availability of cognitive resources (Granholm et al., 1997). There is not much evidence for a vigilance decrement on the traditional CPT in schizophrenia (Nestor and O'Donnell, 1998). However, schizophrenic individuals (Cornblatt and Keilp, 1994; Nuechterlein et al., 1986) and their unaffected relatives (Maier et al., 1992) do show decrements on modified versions of the CPT that make greater demands on information processing (e.g., through perceptual degradation of the stimuli or increased memory requirements). These results are also consistent with the hypothesis of reduced resources.

ADHD    ADHD is characterized by developmentally inappropriate levels of inattention, hyperactivity, and impulsivity. For the diagnosis to be made, the symptoms must be present before 7 years of age, cause impairment in more than one setting (e.g., home and school), and not be accounted for by another mental disorder (APA, 1994). Initial labels for the disorder, such as minimal brain dysfunction, reflected the assumption that the disorder had a neurological cause. Gradually, the labels turned into behavioral descriptions that highlighted the hyperactivity dimension [e.g., hyperkinetic reaction of childhood (APA, 1968)]. In the 1970s, work by Douglas (1972) and others led to an emphasis on the attentional problems of children with the disorder and labels emphasizing the presumed "attention deficit" (APA, 1980). Definitions of the diagnosis included in earlier versions of the DSM were "heavily influenced by theories of attention in contemporary cognitive psychology that emphasize the importance of filtering out extraneous stimuli" (Nuechterlein and Asarnow, 1989, p. 241). The current label is still not very satisfactory; it implies that there is a deficit in attention, whereas a more fundamental difficulty may lie with the regulation of attention and integration of goals and actions (Shue and Douglas, 1992).

It is estimated that 3–5% of school children in the United States have ADHD. There are large differences in prevalence across cultures owing to differences in diagnostic criteria, societal tolerance for symptoms of ADHD, and treatment and educational placement options (Cantwell, 1996; Swanson et al., 1998).

The symptoms of ADHD change as the individuals grow older (Cantwell, 1996). In preschool, children with ADHD are sometimes distinguishable from their peers by their aggressive, noncompliant, argumentative, and reckless behavior. In elementary school, they tend to have difficulty finishing cognitively effortful tasks, do not get along well with peers, and start to develop comorbid symptoms (e.g., oppositional and defiant behavior). In adolescents and adults, hyperactivity gives way to an inner sense of restlessness. The predominant clinical symptoms during this period are disorganization, poor concentration, procrastination, lack of follow-through on tasks, risky behaviors, and intermittent outbursts. There appears to be diagnostic continuity between child and adolescent ADHD; however, it has been hypothesized that the form of ADHD that continues into adolescence and adulthood may be more familial than the form of ADHD that improves with age (Biederman et al., 1998a).

Roughly 30% of children with ADHD "grow out of it." In roughly 40%, symptoms continue in clinical or subclinical form into adulthood, accompanied by a variety of social and emotional difficulties. In about 30% (particularly those whose initial presentation includes symptoms of conduct disorder), ADHD deteriorates into more severe conditions, such as conduct or substance use disorder (Biederman et al., 1998b; Cantwell, 1996; Hansen, Weiss, and Last, 1999).

The neurobiological substrates of the disorder are believed to include dysregulation of activity in frontalstriatal circuits regulated by dopamine. Other structures (e.g., parietal cortex, cerebellar vermis, anterior cingulate) and neurotransmitters (e.g., norepinephrine) have also been implicated in the disorder (Arnsten, Steere, and Hunt, 1996; Berquin et al., 1998; Castellanos, 1997; Ernst et al., 1999; Faraone and Biederman, 1998; Pliszka, McCracken, and Maas, 1996; Swanson et al., 1998; Tannock, 1998). Castellanos (1997) has suggested that dopaminergic circuits connecting the prefrontal cortex, basal ganglia, and cerebellum may mature late in ADHD. Ernst and colleagues (1998) hypothesize that the primary deficit in ADHD children is in the basal ganglia but that the locus of the dysfunction shifts to the prefrontal cortex in adulthood through compensatory or developmental mechanisms or learned changes in behavior.

A large number of family, twin, adoption, and molecular genetic studies have pointed to a substantial genetic component to ADHD. In particular, several reports have linked ADHD to genes involved in dopamine regulation. However, the specific genes involved in the disorder and mode of inheritance have not yet been established (Faraone and Biederman, 1998; Hechtman, 1994; Tannock, 1998). Nonspecific factors, including chronic pregnancy complications and psychosocial adversity factors, are also associated with ADHD (Faraone and Biederman, 1998).

By definition, attention is impaired in ADHD. The following is a brief summary of studies of attention in ADHD in which DSM criteria were used to diagnose the disorder.

Fairly subtle deficits in selective visual attention have been observed on visual search tasks (Asarnow et al., 1994; Karatekin and Asarnow, 1998a), though not in all studies (Hazell et al., 1999; Øie and Rund, 1999). Some deficits are also observed on spatial cueing paradigms that measure covert orienting of attention (Nigg, Swanson, and Hinshaw, 1997; Novak, Solanto, and Abikoff, 1995; Pearson et al., 1995). These deficits tend to be due to inefficient processing of to-be-attended stimuli rather than distractibility or processing of to-be-ignored stimuli (Karatekin and Asarnow, 1998a, 1999; Satterfield, Schell, and Nicholas, 1994).

Although difficulty sustaining attention is one of the diagnostic criteria for ADHD, the performance of individuals with ADHD on the CPT has been surprisingly inconsistent and hard to interpret (Denckla, 1996). Initially, research suggested that individuals with ADHD are impaired on the CPT. In many studies, however, overall performance across the whole test has been used as the main dependent variable. As a result, sustained attention deficits have been inferred without demonstration of a performance decrement over time. Even when performance decrement over time is measured, deficits have been found in ADHD children in some studies (Börger et al., 1999), but not in others (Marakovitz and Campbell, 1998). In some studies in which ADHD individuals show a deterioration in performance on some measures, control participants show no change in performance over time (Hooks, Milich, and Lorch, 1994), which puts into question the validity of the test as a measure of sustained attention. In addition, task parameters (e.g., frequency and level of perceptual degradation of the targets, duration of the displays and inter-stimulus interval, memory demands, and response requirements) have varied widely across studies, and the effects of these variations on the performance of ADHD individuals have not been studied systematically. After an extensive review of the literature on CPTs, Corkum and Siegel (1993) concluded that there was no evidence for a sustained attention deficit in ADHD (measured by a performance decrement on the CPT). However, ADHD children make more omission errors and have lower $d'$ scores compared to control children and show lower levels of performance on CPTs that make heavy demands on cognitive processes (e.g., through frequent targets, short display times, and short inter-stimulus intervals). Corkum and Siegel suggested that this pattern of performance may be explained through deficits in general levels of arousal, activation, or effort rather than through a deficit in sustained attention.

On tests of executive attention, individuals with ADHD often differ from controls (Pennington and Ozonoff, 1996). Deficits have been found on tests of planning and response organization (Carte, Nigg, and Hinshaw, 1996; Klorman et al., 1999; Wiers, Gunning, and Sergeant, 1998), working memory (Karatekin and Asarnow, 1998b; Wiers, Gunning, and Sergeant, 1998), and on memory tests on which the use of mnemonic strategies improves recall (August, 1987; Chang et al., 1999; Hamlett, Pellegrini, and Conners, 1987; Shue and Douglas, 1992). Findings are not as clear for the Wisconsin Card Sorting Test, a measure of problem solving

and set shifting; some studies find deficits in ADHD individuals on a variety of measures (Grodzinsky and Diamond, 1992; Shue and Douglas, 1992), whereas others find only a higher rate of nonperseverative errors (Klorman et al., 1999) or no deficits at all (Øie and Rund, 1999; Seidman et al., 1997). Inhibition is another function that has been studied extensively in ADHD (Barkley, 1997). In general, individuals with ADHD have difficulty inhibiting disallowed movements on paradigms such as the go/no-go, stop, delayed saccade and anti-saccade tasks (Munoz et al., 1998; Nigg, 1999; Ross et al., 1994). However, effect sizes of differences between ADHD and control participants are fairly modest on other inhibition tests, such as the Stroop (Pennington and Ozonoff, 1996). It has been suggested that response inhibition deficits characterize children with a variety of disruptive behavior disorders, not just ADHD (Oosterlaan, Logan, and Sergeant, 1998). Like attention, the concept of inhibition is complex. Tests purported to measure inhibition could be measuring aversion to delay, readiness to respond, ability to inhibit an ongoing response or a reflexive response, or interference within working memory (Oosterlaan, Logan, and Sergeant, 1998; Tannock, 1998). The nature of inhibition deficits in ADHD and their relation to attention and executive functions are not yet well delineated.

CONCLUSIONS   The general conclusion to be drawn from studies on schizophrenia is that individuals with this disorder have widespread impairments in all three types of attention. More importantly, these impairments are observed in remitted patients as well as relatives of schizophrenic individuals, which suggests that the impairments are tapping a genetic vulnerability to the disorder.

On the other hand, individuals with ADHD appear to have minimal to mild difficulties on tests of selective and sustained attention. These difficulties do not appear to be related to distractibility or difficulty sustaining attention, but seem to reflect problems in processing to-be-attended stimuli and in maintaining a high level of attention on tasks that make heavy demands on cognitive resources. Deficits in executive control of attention and executive processes are most apparent on tasks that tap working memory, planning and organization skills, self monitoring, and inhibition.

*Potential contributions of research on the cognitive neuroscience of attention to the study of disorders of attention*

The research on the cognitive neuroscience of attention has much to offer research on disorders such as schizophrenia and ADHD. First is a more refined understanding of the construct of attention. There are detailed and elegant theories of attention, particularly selective attention, in cognitive neuroscience that can be valuable in understanding these disorders.

Second, research in cognitive psychology and cognitive neuroscience has highlighted important issues related to the measurement of attention and interpretation of test results (Baddeley et al., 1997; Pennington and Ozonoff, 1996; Perry and Hodges, 1999). For example, it is becoming obvious that many traditional neuropsychological tests that are used in research in psychopathology and that purport to measure attention or executive functions are not based on strong theoretical foundations and tap multiple cognitive processes. Many of these tests were developed to assess presence of gross brain damage long before the introduction of modern methods such as brain imaging; therefore, they have outlived their usefulness. Convergent and divergent measures of specific aspects of attention derived from current cognitive models need to be used to arrive at a more coherent picture of attention in different disorders (Diamond, 1991; Fletcher et al., 1996). Problems also arise when impairment on behavioral measures of attention and executive functions is interpreted as indicating a dysfunction in the frontal lobes. Yet, "no neuropsychological measure has been found to be sensitive and specific to frontal lobe damage" (Tranel, Anderson, and Benton, 1994, p. 134). Therefore, it is advisable to use these tests as markers of cognitive deficits rather than as instruments for localizing these deficits.

Third, cognitive neuroscience can help psychopathologists formulate better and more reliable operational definitions of terms. Many of the terms currently used to diagnose these disorders are not well defined. In the latest version of the DSM, for instance, criteria for ADHD include "fails to give close attention to details," "easily distracted by extraneous stimuli," "difficulty sustaining attention," and "reluctant to engage in tasks that require sustained mental effort." The ambiguity of these terms leaves the diagnosis to the vagaries of clinicians' idiosyncratic interpretations of these concepts. In addition, these criteria are listed separately even though they are not independent of each other, increasing the chances that the disorder will be over-diagnosed. Furthermore, the terms overlap across disorders, making differential diagnosis challenging. For instance, one of the criteria for ADHD is "difficulty organizing tasks," whereas one of the criteria for schizophrenia is "grossly disorganized behavior." Yet, it would be hard to argue that the main difference between these two disorders is simply in the extent of disorganization.

It is also helpful to remember that the terms used in diagnostic criteria reflect the predominant thinking in cognitive and clinical psychology at the time when the diagnosis was first formulated. As noted above, the criteria for ADHD were influenced by "filter" theories of attention that held sway the 1960s and 1970s, when the disorder was gaining prominence. The diagnostic criteria for schizophrenia (e.g., "loosening of associations") were influenced by associationism, a theory of mind that was ascendant when the diagnosis was being formulated around the end of the 19th century (Peters, 1991). According to this theory, the mind is composed of elementary units that are combined into larger units through rule-based associations. When Bleuler began his work with schizophrenic individuals, he characterized the fundamental symptom in this disorder as the loss of continuity of associations, meaning that the basic units of thought were combined haphazardly (Bleuler, 1911/1950). Vestiges of this framework are still apparent in the current diagnostic criteria for schizophrenia. Thus, the DSM is like an archeological site in which traces of ancient civilizations have been overlaid on top of each other through the centuries.

Conceptualizing attentional impairments within a more unified theoretical framework that reflects the current state of knowledge, conducting more direct comparisons across disorders on specific types of attention, considering subtypes based on similarities in core cognitive impairments (Andreasen, 1999) or psychophysiological or neuroanatomic variables (Gooding and Iacono, 1995) rather than imprecise phenomenological descriptions, and investigating the functional consequences of different types of attentional impairments in everyday life (Baddeley et al., 1997; Burgess et al., 1998; Green, 1996) will allow us to construct better models of the disorders and make more accurate diagnoses.

*Potential contributions of developmental research on disorders of attention to the cognitive neuroscience of attention*

Both schizophrenia and ADHD are developmental disorders in the sense that signs and symptoms of the disorders are present at a very early age and develop over time. Although neither disorder is likely to be diagnosed before the age of 6 or 7 years, individuals with both disorders show clear evidence of impairments long before the onset of the full-blown disorder. Animal studies and longitudinal studies of children at high genetic risk for developing these disorders could be used to ask key developmental questions that can reveal a great deal of information about both the disorders and the normal development of attention. In particular, what are the early manifestations of these disorders in different domains of development? When do they emerge? How can we model the cognitive and neurobiological substrates of these early manifestations and their development over time? To what extent do these early manifestations show evidence of continuity and discontinuity? How do they affect cognitive and brain development? What kinds of environmental manipulations are likely to exacerbate or alleviate the impairments observed in these disorders, and what would these findings imply about neural plasticity?

For example, up to 70–80% of individuals with childhood-onset schizophrenia show delays in learning language and motor skills. Yet, by the time the diagnosis is made, they have caught up with their peers and show evidence of impairments in these domains only on cognitively challenging tasks (Alaghband-Rad et al., 1995; Watkins, Asarnow, and Tanguay, 1988). So what might be the developmental significance of these delays? One suggestion is that delays in automatization of these skills and later difficulties on tests of attention both reflect limitations in cognitive resources. These limitations would reduce the efficiency of controlled processes that are crucial for learning new skills; they can also hinder performance later on laboratory tasks that make demands on attention (Asarnow, Brown, and Strandburg, 1995). This hypothesis has not yet been tested directly; if supported, it would provide evidence of heterotypic continuity in the development of schizophrenia. It could also contribute to our understanding of the role of cognitive resources in the development and automatization of language, motor, and attentional skills.

Similarly, ADHD is often diagnosed after the age of 7, when children begin having difficulties with the demands of the school environment. Yet, children with ADHD differ from their peers from an early age. For instance, retrospective reports hint at delays in the development of fine motor skills, particularly those involved in procedural learning, in the preschool period (Karatekin, Markiewicz, and Siegel, submitted). Children with ADHD also exhibit delays in fine motor coordination in middle childhood (Denckla and Rudel, 1978). Could these early delays be harbingers of a dysfunction in dopaminergic frontal-striatal circuits, which mediate high-level motor control and procedural learning? Could these circuits also underlie impairments in certain aspects of executive attention that emerge later in development? The answers to these questions could reveal a great deal of information on the attentional and cognitive processes mediated by dopaminergic frontal-striatal circuits during different developmental periods as well as the interrelationship of higher-order motor and attentional skills.

The research summarized above suggests that there are dissociations between and within disorders in different types of attention. What are the developmental trajectories of these types of attention in these disorders? At what point do these trajectories begin to diverge from each other and from those observed in healthy populations? What is the effect of periods of rapid brain growth and reorganization on different types of attention in these disorders? How do impairments in these different types of attention affect each other and other domains of cognition? Is it possible, as might be the case in some individuals with ADHD, for sustained and selective attention to develop normally despite deficits in executive attention? Research on these questions can yield information about the timetable of the emergence of different types of attention and the roles they play during development that may not be apparent from studies with normal adults. This developmental approach is best exemplified by the work of Baddeley, Gathercole, and Papagno (1998) who argue that a specific component of the working memory system (the phonological loop) might have evolved to aid the early acquisition of novel words. Similarly, research on the development, dissociation, and impact of attentional impairments in disorders such as ADHD and schizophrenia can yield insights into the functional roles of different types of attention in other domains of cognitive development.

As we learn more about the precise neurobiological substrates of these disorders, we will also gain greater insight into the neural bases of the development of attention. For example, it is likely that ADHD involves a dysfunction in the regulation of dopamine. How early is this dysfunction apparent and how is it manifested in attentional and other domains of functioning? Given that monoamines, including dopamine, promote axonal and dendritic growth during the prenatal period (Levitt et al., 1997), if not later, how does a dysfunction in dopamine regulation affect the development of attention and neuronal connectivity? To what extent are these effects reversible by the administration of psychostimulant medications targeting dopaminergic neurons?

We also stand to gain a lot of information on cortical-subcortical interactions by studying the development of attentional impairments in these disorders. It is possible that both disorders involve early deficits in subcortical regions, namely, the thalamus in schizophrenia (Jones,

1997) and the basal ganglia in ADHD (Lou, 1996). How do these early deficits affect the development of higher cortical regions and how are impairments manifested as attentional processes come under cortical control? Is early input from subcortical regions necessary for the normal development of cortical centers? If so, what is the mechanism of this interaction? Does the locus of the deficit gradually shift to the prefrontal cortex from the basal ganglia in ADHD or from the thalamus in schizophrenia? If so, do these shifts reflect the effects of a primary deficit in the prefrontal cortex that emerges with increasing cortical control over cognition or the deleterious impact of a subcortical dysfunction on cortical development?

Finally, both disorders involve impairments in functional interconnectivity. We know from neuroimaging (Van Bogaert et al., 1998) and neuropsychological data (Luciana and Nelson, 1998) that functional interconnectivity begins to mature around 5 years of age and continues to develop through adolescence. How do impairments in functional interconnectivity affect attention and brain development?

In conclusion, these lines of research can provide significant clues about the maturation of cortical-subcortical circuits and functional interconnectivity and their role in attentional and cognitive development.

ACKNOWLEDGMENT    I thank Lisa Scott for her helpful comments on an earlier version of this chapter.

## REFERENCES

ALAGHBAND-RAD, J., K. MCKENNA, C. T. GORDON, K. E. ALBUS, S. D. HAMBURGER, J. M. RUMSEY, J. A. FRAZIER, M. C. LENANE, and J. L. RAPOPORT, 1995. Childhood-onset schizophrenia: The severity of premorbid course. *J. Am. Acad. Child and Adolesc. Psychiatry.* 34:1273–1283.

ALEXANDER, G. E., M. R. DELONG, and P. L. STRICK, 1986. Parallel organization of functionally segregated circuits linking basal ganglia and cortex. *Annu. Rev. Neurosci.* 9:357–381.

AMERICAN PSYCHIATRIC ASSOCIATION, 1968. *Diagnostic and Statistical Manual of Mental Disorders,* 2nd ed. Washington, D.C.

AMERICAN PSYCHIATRIC ASSOCIATION, 1980. *Diagnostic and Statistical Manual of Mental Disorders,* 3rd ed. Washington, D.C.

AMERICAN PSYCHIATRIC ASSOCIATION, 1994. *Diagnostic and Statistical Manual of Mental Disorders,* 4th ed. Washington, D.C.

ANDREASEN, N. C., 1997. Linking mind and brain in the study of mental illnesses: A project for a scientific psychopathology. *Science* 275:1586–1593.

ANDREASEN, N. C., 1999. A unitary model of schizophrenia: Bleuler's "fragmented phrene" as schizencephaly. *Arch. Gen. Psychiatry* 56:781–787.

ARNSTEN, A. F. T., J. C. STEERE, and R. D. HUNT, 1996. The contribution of $\alpha_2$-noradrenergic mechanisms to prefrontal cortical cognitive function. *Arch. Gen. Psychiatry* 53:448–455.

ASARNOW, R. F., J. ASAMEN, E. GRANHOLM, T. SHERMAN, J. M. WATKINS, and M. WILLIAMS 1994. Cognitive/neuropsychological studies of children with a schizophrenic disorder. *Schizophr. Bull.* 20:647–670.

ASARNOW, R. F., J. R. ASARNOW, and R. STRANDBURG, 1989. Schizophrenia: A developmental perspective. In *The Emergence of a Discipline: Rochester Symposium on Developmental Psychopathology,* Vol. 1, D. Cicchetti, ed. Hillsdale, N.J.: Erlbaum, pp. 189–219.

ASARNOW, R. F., W. BROWN, and R. STRANDBURG, 1995. Children with a schizophrenic disorder: Neurobehavioral studies. *Eur. Arch. Psychiatry Clin. Neurosci.* 245:70–79.

ASARNOW, R. F., E. GRANHOLM, and T. SHERMAN, 1991. Span of apprehension in schizophrenia. In *Handbook of Schizophrenia: Vol. 5. Neuropsychology, Psychophysiology and Information Processing,* S. R. Steinhauer, J. H. Gruzelier, and J. Zubin, eds. New York: Elsevier, pp. 335–370.

ASARNOW, R. F., and D. J. MACCRIMMON, 1981. Span of apprehension deficits during the postpsychotic stages of schizophrenia: A replication and extension. *Arch. Gen. Psychiatry.* 38:1006–1011.

ASARNOW, R. F., and D. J. MACCRIMMON, 1982. Attention/information-processing, neuropsychological functioning, and thought disorder during the acute and partial recovery phases of schizophrenia: A longitudinal study. *Psychiatry Res.* 7:309–319.

ASARNOW, R. F., S. R. MARDER, J. MINTZ, T. VAN PUTTEN, and K. E. ZIMMERMAN, 1988. The differential effect of low and conventional doses of fluphenazine decanoate on schizophrenic outpatients with good or poor information processing abilities. *Arch. Gen. Psychiatry.* 45:822.

ASARNOW, R. F., K. H. NUECHTERLEIN, and S. R. MARDER, 1983. Span of apprehension performance, neuropsychological functioning, and indices of psychosis-proneness. *J. Nerv. Ment. Dis.* 171:662–669.

ASARNOW, R. F., and T. SHERMAN, 1984. Studies of visual information processing in schizophrenic children. *Child Dev.* 55:249–261.

ASARNOW, J. R., M. C. TOMPSON, and M. GOLDSTEIN, 1994. Childhood onset schizophrenia: A follow-up study. *Schizophr. Bull.* 20:599–617.

AUGUST, G. J., 1987. Production deficiencies in free recall: A comparison of hyperactive, learning-disabled, and normal children. *J. Abnorm. Child Psychol.* 15:429–440.

AWH, E., and J. JONIDES, 1998. Spatial working memory and spatial selective attention. In *The Attentive Brain,* R. Parasuraman, ed. Cambridge, Mass.: MIT Press, pp. 353–380.

BADDELEY, A., 1993. Working memory or working attention? In *Attention: Selection, Awareness and Control,* A. Baddeley and L. Weiskrantz, eds. Oxford: Clarendon Press, pp. 152–170.

BADDELEY, A., 1996. Exploring the central executive. *Quart. J. Exp. Psychol.* 49A:5–28.

BADDELEY, A., 1998. Recent developments in working memory. *Curr. Opin. Neurobiol.* 8:234–238.

BADDELEY, A., S. DELLA SALA, C. PAPAGNO, and H. SPINNLER, 1997. Dual-task performance in dysexecutive and nondysexecutive patients with a frontal lesion. *Neuropsychology* 11:187–194.

BADDELEY, A., S. GATHERCOLE, and C. PAPAGNO, 1998. The phonological loop as a language learning device. *Psychol. Rev.* 105:158–173.

BARKLEY, R. A., 1997. Behavioral inhibition, sustained attention, and executive functions: Constructing a unifying theory of ADHD. *Psychol. Bull.* 121:65–94.

BEATTY, J., 1982. Task-evoked pupillary responses, processing load, and the structure of processing resources. *Psychol. Bull.* 91:276–292.

BERQUIN, P. C., J. N. GIEDD, L. K. JACOBSEN, S. D. HAMBURGER, A. L. KRAIN, J. L. RAPOPORT, and F. X. CASTELLANOS, 1998. Cerebellum in attention-deficit hyperactivity disorder: A morphometric MRI study. *Neurology* 50:1087–1093.

BETTES, B. A., and E. WALKER, 1987. Positive and negative symptoms in psychotic and other psychiatrically disturbed children. *J. Child Psychol. Psychiatry* 28:555–568.

BIEDERMAN, J., S. V. FARAONE, A. TAYLOR, M. SIENNA, S. WILLIAMSON, and C. FINE, 1998a. Diagnostic continuity between child and adolescent ADHD: Findings from a longitudinal clinical sample. *J. Am. Acad. Child and Adolesc. Psychiatry* 37:305–313.

BIEDERMAN, J., T. E. WILENS, E. MICK, S. V. FARAONE, and T. SPENCER, 1998b. Does attention-deficit hyperactivity disorder impact the developmental course of drug and alcohol abuse and dependence? *Biol. Psychiatry* 44:269–273.

BLEULER, E., 1911/1950. *Dementia Praecox, or the Group of Schizophrenias.* New York: International Universities Press. [J. Zinkin, translator].

BÖRGER, N., J. VAN DER MEERE, A. RONNER, E. ALBERTS, R. GEUZE, and H. BOGTE, 1999. Heart rate variability and sustained attention in ADHD children. *J. Abnorm. Child Psychol.* 27:25–33.

BRANDT, H. F., 1945. *The Psychology of Seeing.* New York: The Philosophical Library.

BREFCZYNSKI, J. A., and E. A. DEYOE, 1999. A physiological correlate of the "spotlight" of visual attention. *Nature Neurosci.* 2:370–374.

BRUNER, J. S., and A. L. MINTURN, 1955. Perceptual identification and perceptual organization. *J. Gen. Psychol.* 53:21–28.

BÜCHEL, C., and K. J. FRISTON, 1997. Modulation of connectivity in visual pathways by attention: Cortical interactions evaluated with structural equation modeling and fMRI. *Cereb. Cortex* 7:768–778.

BUCHSBAUM, M. S., T. SOMEYA, C. Y. TENG, L. ABEL, S. CHIN, A. NAJAFI, R. J. HAIER, J. WU, and W. E. BUNNEY, 1996. PET and MRI of the thalamus in never-medicated patients with schizophrenia. *Am. J. Psychiatry* 153:191–199.

BUCKLEY, P. F., R. W. BUCHANAN, S. C. SCHULZ, and C. A. TAMMINGA, 1996. Catching up on schizophrenia. *Arch. Gen. Psychiatry* 53:456–462.

BURD, L., and J. KERBESHIAN, 1987. A North Dakota prevalence study of schizophrenia presenting in childhood. *J. Am. Acad. Child and Adolesc. Psychiatry* 26:347–350.

BURGESS, P. W., N. ALDERMAN, J. EVANS, H. EMSLIE, and B. WILSON, 1998. The ecological validity of tests of executive function. *J. Int. Neuropsychol. Soc.* 4:547–558.

CALLICOTT, J. H., V. S. MATTAY, A. BERTOLINO, K. FINN, R. COPPOLA, J. A. FRANK, T. E. GOLDBERG, and D. R. WEINBERGER, 1999. Physiological characteristics of capacity constraints in working memory as revealed by functional MRI. *Cereb. Cortex* 9:20–26.

CANTWELL, D. P., 1996. Classification of child and adolescent psychopathology. *J. Child Psychol. Psychiatry* 37:3–12.

CARLSSON, A., L. O. HANSSON, N. WATERS, and M. L. CARLSSON, 1997. Neurotransmitter aberrations in schizophrenia: New perspectives and therapeutic implications. *Life Sci.* 61:75–94.

CARTE, E. T., J. T. NIGG, and S. P. HINSHAW, 1996. Neuropsychological functioning, motor speed, and language processing in boys with and without ADHD. *J. Abnorm. Child Psychol.* 24:481–498.

CASTELLANOS, F. X., 1997. Toward a pathophysiology of attention-deficit/hyperactivity disorder. *Clin. Pediatr.* 36:381–393.

CAVE, K. R., and J. M. WOLFE, 1990. Modeling the role of parallel processing in visual search. *Cogn. Psychol.* 22:225–271.

CHANG, H. T., R. KLORMAN, S. E. SHAYWITZ, J. M. FLETCHER, K. E. MARCHIONE, J. M. HOLAHAN, K. K. STEUBING, J. T. BRUMAGHIM, and B. A. SHAYWITZ, 1999. Paired-associate learning in attention-deficit/hyperactivity disorder as a function of hyperactivity-impulsivity and oppositional defiant disorder. *J. Abnorm. Child Psychol.* 27:237–245.

CHAWLA, D., G. REES, and K. J. FRISTON, 1999. The physiological basis of attentional modulation in extrastriate visual areas. *Nature Neurosci.* 2:671–676.

CHELAZZI, L., 1995. Neural mechanisms for stimulus selection in cortical areas of the macaque subserving object vision. *Behav. Brain Res.* 71:125–134.

COHEN, J. D., T. S. BRAVER, and R. C. O'REILLY, 1996. A computational approach to prefrontal cortex, cognitive control, and schizophrenia: Recent developments and current challenges. *Phil. Trans. R. Soc. Lond. [B]* 351:1515–1527.

COLLETTE, F., E. SALMON, M. VAN DER LINDEN, C. CHICHERIO, S. BELLEVILLE, C. DEGUELDRE, G. DELFIORE, and G. FRANCK, 1999. Regional brain activity during tasks devoted to the central executive of working memory. *Brain Res. Cogn. Brain Res.* 7:411–417.

CORKUM, P. V., and L. S. SIEGEL, 1993. Is the continuous performance task a valuable research tool for use with children with attention-deficit-hyperactivity disorder? *J. Child Psychol. Psychiatry* 34:1217–1239.

CORNBLATT, B. A., and J. G. KEILP, 1994. Impaired attention, genetics, and the pathophysiology of schizophrenia. *Schizophr. Bull.* 20:31–46.

DAVIDSON, G. S., and J. M. NEALE, 1974. The effects of signal-noise similarity on visual information processing of schizophrenics. *J. Abnorm. Psychol.* 83:683–686.

DEHAENE, S., M. KERSZBERG, and J.-P. CHANGEUX, 1998. A neuronal model of a global workspace in effortful cognitive tasks. *Proc. Natl. Acad. Sci. USA* 95:14529–14534.

DENCKLA, M. B., 1996. Biological correlates of learning and attention: What is relevant to learning disability and attention-deficit hyperactivity disorder? *J. Dev. Behav. Pediatrics* 17:114–119.

DENCKLA, M. B., and R. G. RUDEL, 1978. Anomalies of motor development in hyperactive boys. *Ann. Neurol.* 3:231–233.

DESIMONE, R., 1998. Visual attention mediated by biased competition in extrastriate visual cortex. *Phil. Trans. R. Soc. Lond. [B]* 353:1245–1255.

DESIMONE, R., and J. DUNCAN, 1995. Neural mechanisms of selective visual attention. *Annu. Rev. Neurosci.* 18:193–222.

DIAMOND, A., 1991. Guidelines for the study of brain-behavior relationships during development. In *Frontal Lobe Function and Dysfunction,* H. S. Levin, H. M. Eisenberg, and A. L.

Benton, eds. New York: Oxford University Press, pp. 339–378.

DOUGLAS, V., 1972. Stop, look and listen: The problem of sustained attention and impulse control in hyperactive and normal children. *Can. J. Behav. Sci.* 4:258–282.

DUBOIS, B., B. DEFONTAINES, B. DEWEER, C. MALAPANI, and B. PILLON, 1995. Cognitive and behavioral changes in patients with focal lesions of the basal ganglia. In *Advances in Neurology*, Vol. 65, W. J. Weiner and A. E. Lang, eds. New York: Raven Press, pp. 29–41.

ERNST, M., A. J. ZAMETKIN, J. A. MATOCHIK, P. H. JONS, and R. M. COHEN, 1998. DOPA decarboxylase activity in attention deficit hyperactivity disorder adults. A [$^{18}$F]Fluorodopa positron emission tomographic study. *J. Neurosci.* 18:5901–5907.

ERNST, M., A. J. ZAMETKIN, J. A. MATOCHIK, D. PASCUALVACA, P. H. JONS, and R. M. COHEN, 1999. High midbrain [$^{18}$F]DOPA accumulation in children with attention deficit hyperactivity disorder. *Am. J. Psychiatry* 156:1209–1215.

ESTES, W. K., and H. A. TAYLOR, 1964. A detection method and probabilistic models for assessing information processing from brief visual displays. *Proc. Natl. Acad. Sci. USA* 52:446–454.

FARAONE, S. V., and J. BIEDERMAN, 1998. Neurobiology of attention-deficit hyperactivity disorder. *Biol. Psychiatry* 44:951–958.

FLETCHER, J. M., B. L. BROOKSHIRE, S. H. LANDRY, T. P. BOHAN, K. C. DAVIDSON, D. J. FRANCIS, H. S. LEVIN, M. E. BRANDT, L. A. KRAMER, and R. D. MORRIS, 1996. Attentional skills and executive functions in children with early hydrocephalus. *Dev. Neuropsychol.* 12:53–76.

FRISTON, K. J., 1998. The disconnection hypothesis. *Schizophr. Res.* 30:115–125.

FUSTER, J. M., 1995. Temporal processing. *Ann. N.Y. Acad. Sci.* 769:173–181.

GANDHI, S. P., D. J. HEEGER, and G. M. BOYNTON, 1999. Spatial attention affects brain activity in human primary visual cortex. *Proc. Natl. Acad. Sci. USA* 96:3314–3319.

GARMEZY, N., 1977. The psychology and psychopathology of attention. *Schizophr. Bull.* 3:360–368.

GOLDMAN-RAKIC, P. S., 1988. Topography of cognition: Parallel distributed networks in primate association cortex. *Annu. Rev. Neurosci.* 11:137–156.

GOLDMAN-RAKIC, P. S., 1994. Working memory dysfunction in schizophrenia. *J. Neuropsychiatry Clin. Neurosci.* 6:348–357.

GOLDMAN-RAKIC, P. S., 1998. The cortical dopamine system: Role in memory and cognition. *Adv. Pharmacol.* 42:707–711.

GOODING, D. C., and W. G. IACONO, 1995. Schizophrenia through the lens of a developmental psychopathology perspective. In *Developmental Psychopathology*, Vol. 2, D. Cicchetti and D. Cohen, eds. New York: Wiley Interscience, pp. 535–569.

GRAFMAN, J., 1995. Similarities and distinctions among current models of prefrontal cortical functions. *Ann. N.Y. Acad. Sci.* 769:337–368.

GRANHOLM, E., S. K. MORRIS, A. J. SARKIN, R. F. ASARNOW, and D. V. JESTE, 1997. Pupillary responses index overload of working memory resources in schizophrenia. *J. Abnorm. Psychol.* 106:458–467.

GREEN, M. F., 1996. What are the functional consequences of neurocognitive deficits in schizophrenia? *Am. J. Psychiatry* 153:321–330.

GREEN, W. H., M. PADRON-GAYOL, A. S. HARDESTY, and M.

BASSIRI, 1992. Schizophrenia with childhood onset: A phenomenological study of 38 cases. *J. Am. Acad. Child and Adolesc. Psychiatry* 31:968–976.

GRODZINSKY, G. M., and R. DIAMOND, 1992. Frontal lobe functioning in boys with attention-deficit hyperactivity disorder. *Dev. Neuropsychol.* 8:427–445.

HAMLETT, K. W., D. S. PELLEGRINI, and C. K. CONNERS, 1987. An investigation of executive processes in the problem-solving of attention deficit disorder/hyperactive children. *J. Pediatr. Psychol.* 12:227–240.

HANSEN, C., D. WEISS, and C. G. LAST, 1999. ADHD boys in young adulthood: Psychosocial adjustment. *J. Am. Acad. Child and Adolesc. Psychiatry* 38:165–171.

HAXBY, J. V., S. M. COURTNEY, and V. P. CLARK, 1998. Functional magnetic resonance imaging and the study of attention. In *The Attentive Brain*, R. Parasuraman, ed. Cambridge, Mass.: MIT Press, pp. 123–142.

HAZELL, P. L., V. J. CARR, T. J. LEWIN, S. A. M. DEWIS, D. M. HEATHCOTE, and B. M. BRUCKI, 1999. Effortful and automatic information processing in boys with ADHD and specific learning disorders. *J. Child Psychol. Psychiatry* 40:275–286.

HECHTMAN, L., 1994. Genetic and neurobiological aspects of attention deficit hyperactive disorder: A review. *J. Psychiatry Neurosci.* 19:193–201.

HEILMAN, K. M., R. T. WATSON, E. VALENSTEIN, and M. E. GOLDBERG, 1987. Attention: Behavior and neural mechanisms. In *Handbook of Physiology: Sect. 1. The Nervous System: Vol. 5. Higher Functions of the Brain, Part 2*, V. B. Mountcastle, ed. Bethesda, Md.: American Physiological Society, pp. 461–481.

HILLYARD, S. A., W. A. TEDER-SÄLERJÄRVI, and T. F. MÜNTE, 1998. Temporal dynamics of early perceptual processing. *Curr. Opin. Neurobiol.* 8:202–210.

HOLZMAN, P. S., 1996. On the trail of the genetics and pathophysiology of schizophrenia. *Psychiatry* 59:117–127.

HOOKS, K., R. MILICH, and E. P. LORCH, 1994. Sustained and selective attention in boys with attention deficit hyperactivity disorder. *J. Clin. Child Psychol.* 23:69–77.

HOUK, J. C., and S. P. WISE, 1995. Distributed modular architectures linking basal ganglia, cerebellum, and cerebral cortex: Their role in planning and controlling action. *Cereb. Cortex.* 2:95–110.

JABLENSKY, A., N. SARTORIUS, G. ERNBERG, M. ANKER, A. KORTEN, J. E. COOPER, R. DAY, and A. BERTELSEN, 1992. Schizophrenia: Manifestations, incidence and course in different cultures: A World Health Organization ten-country study. *Psychol. Med. Monogr.* (suppl. 20).

JACOBSEN, L. K., and J. L. RAPOPORT, 1998. Research update: Childhood-onset schizophrenia: Implications of clinical and neurobiological research. *J. Child Psychol. Psychiatry* 39:101–113.

JAMES, W., 1890/1950. *The Principles of Psychology*, Vol. 1. New York: Dover.

JONES, E. G., 1997. Cortical development and thalamic pathology in schizophrenia. *Schizophr. Bull.* 23:483–501.

KAGAN, J., 1984. *The Nature of the Child*. New York: Basic Books.

KAHN, R. S., and K. L. DAVIS, 1995. New developments in dopamine and schizophrenia. In *Psychopharmacology: The Fourth Generation of Progress*, F. E. Bloom and D. J. Kupfer, eds. New York: Raven Press, pp. 1193–1203.

KAHNEMAN, D., 1973. *Attention and Effort*. Englewood Cliffs, N.J.: Prentice-Hall.

KARATEKIN, C., and R. F. ASARNOW, 1998a. Components of visual search in childhood-onset schizophrenia and attention deficit/hyperactivity disorder (ADHD). *J. Abnorm. Child Psychol.* 26:367–380.

KARATEKIN, C., and R. F. ASARNOW, 1998b. Working memory in childhood-onset schizophrenia and attention deficit/hyperactivity disorder (ADHD). *Psychiatry Res.* 80:165–176.

KARATEKIN, C., and R. F. ASARNOW, 1999. Exploratory eye movements to pictures in childhood-onset schizophrenia and attention deficit/hyperactivity disorder (ADHD). *J. Abnorm. Child Psychol.* 27:35–49.

KARATEKIN, C., S. W. MARKIEWICZ, and M. A. SIEGEL, 2000. A retrospective developmental study of motor problems in children with attention-deficit-hyperactivity disorder (ADHD). (submitted).

KARPOV, B. A., A. R. LURIA, and A. L. YARBUS, 1968. Disturbances of the structure of active perception in lesions of the posterior and anterior regions of the brain. *Neuropsychologia* 6:157–166.

KLORMAN, R., L. A. HAZEL-FERNANDEZ, S. E. SHAYWITZ, J. M. FLETCHER, K. E. MARCHIONE, J. M. HOLAHAN, K. K. STUEBING, and B. A. SHAYWITZ, 1999. Executive functioning deficits in attention-deficit/hyperactivity disorder are independent of oppositional defiant or reading disorder. *J. Am. Acad. Child and Adolesc. Psychiatry* 38:1148–1155.

LEVITT, P., J. A. HARVEY, E. FRIEDMAN, K. SIMANSKY, and E. H. MURPHY, 1997. New evidence for neurotransmitter influences on brain development. *Trends Neurosci.* 20:269–274.

LLEWELLYN-THOMAS, E., 1969. Search behavior. *Radiol. Clin. North Am.* 7:403–417.

LOU, H. C., 1996. Etiology and pathogenesis of attention-deficit hyperactivity disorder (ADHD): Significance of prematurity and perinatal hypoxic-haemodynamic encephalopathy. *Acta Paediatr.* 85:1266–1271.

LUCIANA, M., and C. A. NELSON, 1998. The functional emergence of prefrontally-guided working memory systems in four- to eight-year-old children. *Neuropsychologia* 36:273–293.

LUCK, S., 1995. Multiple mechanisms of visual-spatial attention: Recent evidence from human electrophysiology. *Behav. Brain Res.* 71:113–123.

LUCK, S. J., and M. GIRELLI, 1998. Electrophysiological approaches to the study of selective attention in the human brain. In *The Attentive Brain,* R. Parasuraman, ed. Cambridge, Mass.: MIT Press, pp. 71–94.

LUMER, E. D., G. M. EDELMAN, and G. TONONI, 1997. Neural dynamics in a model of the thalamocortical system. I. Layers, loops, and the emergence of fast synchronous rhythms. *Cereb. Cortex* 7:207–227.

MAIER, W., P. FRANKE, C. HAIN, B. KOPP, and F. RIST, 1992. Neuropsychological indicators of the vulnerability to schizophrenia. *Prog. Neuropsychopharmacol. Biol. Psychiatry* 16:703–715.

MARAKOVITZ, S. E., and S. B. CAMPBELL, 1998. Inattention, impulsivity, and hyperactivity from preschool to school age: Performance of hard-to-manage boys on laboratory measures. *J. Child Psychol. Psychiatry* 39:841–851.

MARTINEZ, M., L. ANLLO-VENTO, M. I. SERENO, L. R. FRANK, R. B. BUXTON, D. J. DUBOWITZ, E. C. WONG, H. HINRICHS, H. J. HEINZE, and S. A. HILLYARD, 1999. Involvement of striate and extrastriate visual cortical areas in spatial attention. *Nature Neurosci.* 2:364–369.

MCCLELLAN, J., and J. WERRY, 1994. Practice parameters for the assessment and treatment of children and adolescents with schizophrenia. *J. Am. Acad. Child and Adolesc. Psychiatry* 33:616–635.

MCGUFFIN, P., M. J. OWEN, and A. E. FARMER, 1995. Genetic basis of schizophrenia. *Lancet* 346(8976):678–682.

MESULAM, M.-M., 1998. From sensation to cognition. *Brain* 121:1013–1052.

MEYER, D. E., and D. E. KIERAS, 1997. A computational theory of executive cognitive processes and multiple-task performance: Part 1. Basic mechanisms. *Psychol. Rev.* 104:3–65.

MORAN, J., and R. DESIMONE, 1985. Selective attention gates visual processing in the extrastriate cortex. *Science* 229:782–784.

MORTENSEN, P. B., C. B. PEDERSEN, T. WESTERGAARD, T. WOHLFART, H. EWALD, O. MORS, P. K. ANDERSEN, and M. MELBYE, 1999. Effects of family history and place and season of birth on the risk of schizophrenia. *N. Engl. J. Med.* 340:603–608.

MOTTER, B. C., 1998. Neurophysiology of visual attention. In *The Attentive Brain,* R. Parasuraman, ed. Cambridge, Mass.: MIT Press, pp. 51–69.

MUNOZ, D. P., J. R. BROUGHTON, J. E. GOLDRING, and I. T. ARMSTRONG, 1998. Age-related performance of human subjects on saccadic eye movement tasks. *Exp. Brain Res.* 121:391–400.

NAVON, D., 1984. Resources—A theoretical soup stone? *Psychol. Rev.* 91:216–234.

NEALE, J. M., 1971. Perceptual span in schizophrenia. *J. Abnorm. Psychol.* 77:196–204.

NEALE, J. M., C. W. MCINTYRE, R. FOX, and R. L. CROMWELL, 1969. Span of apprehension in acute schizophrenics. *J. Abnorm. Psychol.* 74:593–596.

NEISSER, U., 1976. *Cognition and Reality.* San Francisco: Freeman.

NESTOR, P. G., and B. F. O'DONNELL, 1998. The mind adrift: Attentional dysregulation in schizophrenia. In *The Attentive Brain,* R. Parasuraman, ed. Cambridge, Mass.: MIT Press, pp. 527–546.

NIEBUR, E., and C. KOCH, 1998. Computational architectures for attention. In *The Attentive Brain,* R. Parasuraman, ed. Cambridge, Mass.: MIT Press, pp. 163–186.

NIGG, J. T., 1999. The ADHD response-inhibition deficit as measured by the stop task: Replication w/DSM-IV combined type, extension, and qualification. *J. Abnorm. Child Psychol.* 27:393–402.

NIGG, J. T., J. M. SWANSON, and S. P. HINSHAW, 1997. Covert visual spatial attention in boys with attention deficit hyperactivity disorder: Lateral effects, methylphenidate response and results for parents. *Neuropsychologia* 35:165–176.

NOVAK, G. P., M. SOLANTO, and H. ABIKOFF, 1995. Spatial orienting and focused attention in attention deficit hyperactivity disorder. *Psychophysiology* 32:546–559.

NUECHTERLEIN, K. H., 1986. Childhood precursors of adult schizophrenia. *J. Child Psychol. Psychiatry* 27:133–144.

NUECHTERLEIN, K. H., and R. F. ASARNOW, 1989. Perception and cognition. In *Comprehensive Textbook of Psychiatry,* Vol. 5, H. I. Kaplan and B. J. Saddock, eds. Baltimore, Md.: Williams & Wilkins, pp. 241–256.

NUECHTERLEIN, K. H., and M. E. DAWSON, 1984. Information processing and attentional functioning in the developmental course of schizophrenic disorders. *Schizophr. Bull.* 10:160–203.

NUECHTERLEIN, K. H., W. S. EDELL, M. NORRIS, and M. E. DAWSON, 1986. Attentional vulnerability indicators, thought disorder, and negative symptoms. *Schizophr. Bull.* 12:408–426.

O'CRAVEN, K. M., B. R. ROSEN, K. K. KWONG, A. TREISMAN, and R. L. SAVOY, 1997. Voluntary attention modulates fMRI activity in human MT-MST. *Neuron* 18:591–598.

ØIE, M., and B. R. RUND, 1999. Neuropsychological deficits in adolescent-onset schizophrenia compared with attention deficit hyperactivity disorder. *Am. J. Psychiatry* 156:1216–1222.

OOSTERLAAN, J., G. D. LOGAN, and J. A. SERGEANT, 1998. Response inhibition in AD/HD, CD, comorbid AD/HD + CD, anxious, and control children: A meta-analysis of studies with the stop task. *J. Child Psychol. Psychiatry* 39:411–425.

PARASURAMAN, R., 1998. The attentive brain: Issues and prospects. In *The Attentive Brain*, R. Parasuraman, ed. Cambridge, Mass.: MIT Press, pp. 3–15.

PEARSON, D. A., L. S. YAFFEE, K. A. LOVELAND, and A. M. NORTON, 1995. Covert visual attention in children with attention deficit hyperactivity disorder: Evidence for developmental immaturity? *Dev. Psychopathol.* 7:351–367.

PEAVLER, W. S., 1974. Individual differences in pupil size and performance. In *Pupillary Dynamics and Behavior,* M. P. Janisse, ed. New York: Plenum Press, pp. 159–175.

PENNINGTON, B. F., and S. OZONOFF, 1996. Executive functions and developmental psychopathology. *J. Child Psychol. Psychiatry* 37:51–87.

PERRY, R. J., and J. R. HODGES, 1999. Attention and executive deficits in Alzheimer's disease: A critical review. *Brain* 122:383–404.

PETERS, U. H., 1991. The German classical concept of schizophrenia. In *The Concept of Schizophrenia*, J. G. Howells, ed. Washington, D.C.: American Psychiatric Press, pp. 59–73.

PLISZKA, S. R., J. T. MCCRACKEN, and J. W. MAAS, 1996. Catecholamines in attention-deficit hyperactivity disorder: Current perspectives. *J. Am. Acad. Child Adolesc. Psychiatry* 35:264–272.

POSNER, M. I., and S. DEHAENE, 1994. Attentional networks. *Trends Neurosci.* 17:75–79.

POSNER, M. I., and S. E. PETERSEN, 1990. The attention system of the human brain. *Annu. Rev. Neurosci.* 13:25–42.

REYNOLDS, J. H., L. CHELAZZI, and R. DESIMONE, 1999. Competitive mechanisms subserve attention in macaque areas V2 and V4. *J. Neurosci.* 19:1736–1753.

ROBBINS, T. W., 1997. Arousal systems and attentional processes. *Biol. Psychol.* 45:57–71.

ROSS, R. G., D. HOMMER, D. BREIGER, C. VARLEY, and A. RADANT, 1994. Eye movement task related to frontal lobe functioning in children with attention deficit disorder. *J. Am. Acad. Child and Adolesc. Psychiatry* 33:869–874.

RUFF, H. A., and M. K. ROTHBART, 1996. *Attention in Early Development*. New York: Oxford University Press.

RUSSELL, A. T., 1994. The clinical presentation of childhood onset schizophrenia. *Schizophr. Bull.* 20:631–646.

RUSSELL, A. T., L. BOTT, and C. SAMMONS, 1989. The phenomenology of schizophrenia occurring in childhood. *J. Am. Acad. Child and Adolesc. Psychiatry* 28:399–407.

SATTERFIELD, J. H., A. M. SCHELL, and T. NICHOLAS, 1994. Preferential neural processing of attended stimuli in attention-deficit hyperactivity disorder and normal boys. *Psychophysiology* 31:1–10.

SCHMIDT, M., B. BLANZ, A. DIPPE, T. KOPPE, and B. LAY, 1995. Course of patients diagnosed as having schizophrenia during first episode occurring under age 18 years. *Eur. Arch. Psychiatry Clin. Neurosci.* 245:93–100.

SCHNEIDER, W., and R. M. SHIFFRIN, 1977. Controlled and automatic human information processing: I. Detection, search, and attention. *Psychol. Rev.* 84:1–66.

SEIDMAN, L. J., J. BIEDERMAN, S. V. FARAONE, W. WEBER, AND C. OUELLETTE, 1997. Toward defining a neuropsychology of attention deficit-hyperactivity disorder. Performance of children and adolescents from a large clinically referred sample. *J. Consult. Clin. Psychol.* 65:150–160.

SELEMON, L. D., G. RAJKOWSKA, and P. S. GOLDMAN-RAKIC, 1995. Abnormally high neuronal density in the schizophrenic cortex. *Arch. Gen. Psychiatry* 52:805–818.

SERGEANT, J., and J. J. VAN DER MEERE, 1994. Toward an empirical child psychopathology. In *Disruptive Behavior Disorders in Childhood*, D. K. Routh, ed. Reading, Mass.: Perseus Books, pp. 59–85.

SHALLICE, T., and P. BURGESS, 1991. Higher-order cognitive impairments and frontal lobe lesions in man. In *Frontal Lobe Function and Dysfunction*, H. S. Levin, H. M., Eisenberg, and A. L. Benton, eds. New York: Oxford University Press, pp. 125–138.

SHUE, K. L., and V. I. DOUGLAS, 1992. Attention deficit hyperactivity disorder and the frontal lobe syndrome. *Brain Cogn.* 20:104–124.

SMITH, E. E., and J. JONIDES, 1998. Neuroimaging analyses of human working memory. *Proc. Natl. Acad. Sci. USA* 95:12061–12068.

STRAUSS, M. E., R. W. BUCHANAN, and J. HALE, 1993. Relations between attentional deficits and clinical symptoms in schizophrenic outcome. *Psychiatry Res.* 47:205–213.

SWANSON, J. M., J. A. SERGEANT, E. TAYLOR, E. J. S. SONUGA-BARKE, P. S. JENSEN, and D. P. CANTWELL, 1998. Attention-deficit hyperactivity disorder and hyperkinetic disorder. *Lancet* 351:429–433.

SWICK, D., and R. T. KNIGHT, 1998. Cortical lesions and attention. In *The Attentive Brain*, R. Parasuraman, ed. Cambridge, Mass.: MIT Press, pp. 143–162.

TANNOCK, R., 1998. Attention deficit hyperactivity disorder: Advances in cognitive, neurobiological, and genetic research. *J. Child Psychol. Psychiatry* 39:65–99.

TRANEL, D., S. W. ANDERSON, and A. BENTON, 1994. Development of the concept of "executive function" and its relationship to the frontal lobes. In *Handbook of Neuropsychology*, Vol. 9, F. Boller and J. Grafman, eds. New York: Elsevier Science, pp. 125–148.

TREISMAN, A., 1998. Feature binding, attention and object perception. *Phil. Trans. R. Soc. Lond [B]* 353:1295–1306.

TREISMAN, A. M., and G. GELADE, 1980. A feature-integration theory of attention. *Cogn. Psychol.* 12:97–136.

TREISMAN, A., and S. SATO, 1990. Conjunction search revisited. *J. Exp. Psychol. Hum. Percept. Perform.* 16:459–478.

VAN BOGAERT, P., D. WIKLER, P. DAMHAUT, H. B. SZLIWOWSKI, and S. GOLDMAN, 1998. Regional changes in glucose metabolism during brain development from the age of 6 years. *Neuroimage* 8:62–68.

VAN ESSEN, D. C., C. H. ANDERSON, and D. J. FELLEMAN, 1992. Information processing in the primate visual system: An integrated systems perspective. *Science* 255:419–423.

WATKINS, J. M., R. F. ASARNOW, and P. E. TANGUAY, 1988. Symptom development in childhood onset schizophrenia. *J. Child Psychol. Psychiatry* 29:865–878.

WEINBERGER, D. R., 1993. A connectionist approach to the prefrontal cortex. *J. Neuropsychiatry Clin. Neurosci.* 5:241–253.

WERRY, J. S., 1992. Child and adolescent (early onset) schizophrenia: A review in light of DSM-III-R. *J. Autism Dev. Dis.* 22:601–624.

WICKENS, C. D., 1980. The structure of attentional resources. In *Attention and Performance VIII,* R. S. Nickerson, ed. Hillsdale, N.J.: Erlbaum, pp. 239–257.

WIERS, R. W., W. B. GUNNING, and J. A. SERGEANT, 1998. Is a mild deficit in executive functions in boys related to childhood ADHD or to parental multigenerational alcoholism? *J. Abnorm. Child Psychol.* 26:415–430.

WOLFE, J. M., 1994. Guided Search 2.0: A revised model of visual search. *Psychonom. Bull. Rev.* 1:202–238.

# 37 The Neuropsychology of Schizophrenia and Its Relationship to the Neurodevelopmental Model

BRITA ELVEVÅG
AND DANIEL R. WEINBERGER

ABSTRACT In this chapter we explore ways in which the neuropsychological profile of schizophrenia, namely problems in attention, working memory, episodic memory, and semantic memory, can inform us of the neurodevelopmental trajectory of the illness. A large number of studies have demonstrated that schizophrenia is associated with neurocognitive weakness which is present prior to the onset of the illness and probably is due to subtle development abnormalities in critical circuitry. One of the challenging questions is why abnormal brain development might result specifically in schizophrenia rather than some other neurodevelopmental disorder. We suggest that a combination of age and specific sites of brain insult (especially the temporal-limbic and dorsolateral prefrontal cortices) produces a unique neurodevelopmental trajectory that leads to the specific neurocognitive profile associated with schizophrenia.

Schizophrenia is a devastating human illness involving changes in perception, cognition, and comportment. Research in unraveling the mystery of this disorder has met with surprisingly limited success, despite considerable commitment of people and money. Recently, the research community has shown increasing enthusiasm for the notion that neuropsychological deficits are core features of the illness that arise from abnormalities in the development of the brain and that predict long-term disability and outcome. In this chapter we address three questions that are fundamental to the exploration of the nature of neuropsychological deficits in patients with schizophrenia, and particularly how the neurodevelopmental model of schizophrenia might shed light on the neuropsychological course of the schizophrenia illness. First, we ask what affected or compromised neurocognitive systems are implicated in schizophrenia, and what this can tell us about neuro-

developmental aspects of schizophrenia. We suggest that the core cognitive deficits in schizophrenia have specific physiological correlates and thus provide crucial clues about the neurodevelopmental trajectory of the illness. Second, we ask why brain development is of interest in schizophrenia research. We argue that there is compelling evidence that schizophrenia is associated with neurocognitive weakness that is present prior to the onset of the illness. This is most probably due to an underlying abnormality of cortical development. Third, we ask why any abnormality of brain development might result specifically in schizophrenia rather than some other neurodevelopmental disorder. We present data demonstrating that it is possible for early brain injury involving the neural circuitry implicated in schizophrenia to have substantial and long-lasting effects on specific and also syndromally relevant neural systems that are quite distant from the site of original damage. Moreover, we contend that since the cognitive deficit profiles of schizophrenia are qualitatively distinct from other disorders, it is highly probable that there is a unique neurodevelopmental profile associated with schizophrenia.

## What compromised neurocognitive systems are implicated in schizophrenia?

The cardinal symptoms of schizophrenia are abnormal ideas (such as delusions); abnormal perceptions (such as hallucinations); formal thought disorder (as evidenced by disorganized speech); motor, volitional, and behavioral disorders; and emotional disorders (such as affective flattening or inappropriateness) (American Psychiatric Association, 1994). In addition to this exceedingly wide range of symptoms and behaviors, it has become increasingly apparent that schizophrenia is, to varying degrees, accompanied by a broad spectrum of cognitive deficits (for a review, see Elvevåg and Goldberg, 2001). If the cognitive deficits of schizophrenia

BRITA ELVEVÅG Clinical Brain Disorders Branch, National Institute of Mental Health/National Institutes of Health, Bethesda, Maryland.
DANIEL R. WEINBERGER Chief, Clinical Brain Disorders Branch, National Institute of Mental Health/National Institutes of Health, Bethesda, Maryland.

are to inform us about the origins of the illness, it is important to establish when they arise, how they develop, and how enduring (and debilitating) they are. We will address these issues first, and then explore the nature of the neurocognitive deficits in schizophrenia.

There is ample evidence that the cognitive deficits associated with schizophrenia are core, fundamental aspects of the disorder—specifically, that they are enduring features of the illness, and further they are not medication- or state-related, nor are they specific to clinical subtypes of the illness. First, the line of evidence that argues that cognitive deficits are more than merely epiphenomena of schizophrenia is that cognitive deficits are not correlated with the severity of the psychosis and are not ameliorated with the "removal" of symptoms: Despite marked improvement in psychiatric symptoms from antipsychotic medication, cognitive benefits appear to be limited (Gold et al., 1991; Gold and Hurt, 1990; Goldberg et al., 1993b; Medalia, Gold, and Merriam, 1988). Second, unlike psychotic symptoms that vary over time, cognitive deficits appear to be more durable and unchanging (Klonoff et al., 1970; Smith, 1964; Sweeney et al., 1991; for a review, see Rund, 1998). Moreover, the correlations between cognitive deficits and symptoms are weak, a finding that may be taken to suggest that it is not the symptoms alone that are responsible for the cognitive deficits (Faustman, Moses, and Csernansky, 1988; Goldberg et al., 1993a; Lawson, Waldman, and Weinberger, 1988). Third, despite considerable heterogeneity at the phenomenological level, patients with schizophrenia display unexpected homogeneity at the cognitive level, a finding that goes against the notion that cognitive deficits are only observed in a subgroup of patients, or that they appear with differing frequencies in various subgroups (Braff et al., 1991; Goldberg et al., 1988, 1990; Hoff et al., 1998; Sullivan et al.,1994; but see Goldstein et al., 1998, for an alternative position). In fact, it is quite possible that schizophrenic patients merely vary along a severity dimension of cognitive impairment. Moreover, the severity and manner of cognitive deficits present in schizophrenic patients provide a better predictor of functional outcome than the presence of psychotic symptoms, consistent with the fact that the later symptoms are unstable and transitory (Addington and Addington, 1993; Addington, Addington, and Maticka-Tyndale, 1991; Breier et al., 1991; Goldberg et al., 1995; Green, 1996; Harvey et al., 1998; Heaton, Baade, and Johnson, 1978; Heaton and Pendleton, 1981; Jonsson and Nyman, 1991; Newnan, Heaton, and Lehman, 1978; Perlick et al., 1992; Velligan et al., 1997). For example, neuropsychological measures such as verbal reasoning and concept formation have been shown to be significantly associated with premorbid functioning and outcome in schizophrenia (Addington and Addington, 1993). Other cognitive measures such as paired-associates learning, memory for stories, verbal fluency, and problem-solving have also been shown to be significantly related to indices of social and vocational functioning in patients with schizophrenia (Goldberg et al., 1993d). Even though it is the positive, psychotic symptoms that are most readily noticeable and often most disturbing to the patients, it is the cognitive deficits that may be related more directly to functional impairment and ultimately to the core biological foundations of the disorder. Since associations between negative symptoms and cognitive deficits are by definition substantially greater than those with positive symptoms (Addington, Addington, and Maticka-Tyndale, 1991; Breier et al., 1991), one might expect the negative symptoms to be good predictors of functional outcome. However, it is noteworthy that even negative symptoms and cognitive deficits are not synonymous with each other. Indeed, it is the cognitive deficits in schizophrenic patients that are the most reliable predictors of functional outcome (Green, 1996); thus it would seem logical to assume that a better understanding of these cognitive deficits will inform us as to the origins of the illness itself.

A rapidly expanding body of research indicates that problems in the cognitive domains of attention, working memory, episodic memory, and semantic memory are at the core of the neuropsychological dysfunction in this disease (for a review, see Elvevåg and Goldberg, 2000). Moreover, these cognitive deficits have specific physiological correlates that provide potentially crucial information concerning the neurodevelopment of the compromised neurocognitive system in schizophrenia.

ATTENTION In numerous clinical and experimental descriptions of schizophrenic performance impairments, problems in sustained and focused attention have been a prominent issue (Shakow, 1962). A sustained vigilance task, such as the continuous-performance task (CPT), has been used extensively in studies of patients with schizophrenia. In this task, participants are to monitor random series of single numbers or letters that are presented continuously, usually at a rate of approximately one per second. Participants are asked to detect a target event by pressing a response button, and to avoid responding to distracting stimuli. Schizophrenic patients consistently miss more targets than do healthy control participants (for a review, see Cornblatt and Keilp, 1994). Based upon these observations, it has been suggested that schizophrenic patients have compromised attention, although an adequate account of this basic attentional abnormality in schizophrenic patients remains elusive. In our own recent work, we found that patients with schizophrenia made disproportionately more omission errors at short delay intervals and low target probabilities (Elvevåg et al., 2000). We have taken this finding to suggest that schizophrenic patients have a specific problem in rapidly encoding information (i.e., constructing a representation of the stimuli to be attended to) under certain unengaging situations. For example, if patients were slow in constructing a representation, a short delay between stimuli would more likely lead to interference, as a second stimulus would exact a cost on ongoing processes. We have proposed that this deficit may represent the core difficulty experienced by patients with schizophrenia on this task.

Attentional deficits have been reported in groups at high risk for schizophrenia, suggesting that poor attention in patients with schizophrenia is not due solely to medication factors or transitory symptomatic states, but rather to some stable, perhaps genetic, pathogenic trait. These high-risk groups include first-degree relatives of schizophrenic patients (Gottesman, 1978; Keefe et al., 1994, 1997b; Nuechterlein, 1983), people with personality characteristics thought to be related to an increased risk for schizophrenia (Sternoko and Woods, 1978) such as schizotypal personality disorder (Roitman et al., 1997; Trestman et al., 1995), children with schizophrenic parents (Erlenmeyer-Kimling, Golden, and Cornblatt, 1989; Erlenmeyer-Kimling et al., 1993), and other family members of patients with schizophrenia (Chen et al., 1998; Lenzenweger, Cornblatt, and Putnick, 1991; Nuechterlein, 1983; for a review, see Siever and Coursey, 1985). However, it is not always clear to what extent the problems observed involve attention rather than working memory, which involves overlapping cognitive as well as neural constructs. Both processes involve large-scale neural networks of which frontal neural circuitry is especially crucial (Goldman-Rakic, 1987; Posner and Peterson, 1990).

WORKING MEMORY Memory is composed of multiple systems that vary according to the type of information being stored, the duration of storage, and capacity limitations. Working memory is a general-purpose short-duration memory system involved in a variety of cognitive tasks, such as those in which it is necessary to retain and manipulate visual or auditory information over short periods of time in the absence of external cues (Baddeley, 1986, 1996). In the digit span task, participants have to recall a sequence of various lengths of digits they had just heard or seen, either in order or in reverse order. In both visual and auditory modalities, working memory capacity is reduced in schizophrenic patients; i.e., they have a smaller span or capacity (El-

vevåg, Weinberger, and Goldberg, 2000; Fleming et al., 1995, 1997; Goldberg et al., 1998b; Keefe et al., 1995, 1997a; Park, Holzman, and Goldman-Rakic, 1995). Importantly, problems in both attention and working memory are characteristically impaired in patients with schizophrenia irrespective of their level of intelligence (Weickert et al., 2000). A working memory task adapted specifically for functional magnetic resonance imaging is the n-back task (Callicott et al., 1998b; Cohen et al., 1994, 1997). In the n-back task, participants are presented with a continual and random sequence of letters or digits (e.g., the numbers 1, 2, 3, and 4) presented at a rate of about one stimulus per two seconds. Participants are to maintain this information and resist interference from the incoming information, since they have to remember digits that were presented n stimuli ago. This task has been shown to reliably activate the dorsolateral prefrontal cortex. The degree of prefrontal activity in the 2-back task has been shown to be greater in control participants than in schizophrenic patients in some studies (Callicott et al., 1998b; Carter et al., 1998) but not in others (Callicott et al., 1999). Interestingly, at 3-back, the activity in the prefrontal cortex is reduced in healthy controls but not in patients. These data have been taken to suggest that activation of prefrontal cortex is modulated abnormally during working memory in schizophrenic patients, who may reach their psychometric capacity earlier than healthy controls but show a sustained inefficiency of the physiological response (i.e., maximum activity in the prefrontal cortex but poor behavioral performance) (Callicott et al., 1999). These neuroimaging findings fit well with the neuropsychological and neuroanatomical data which suggest that the neurobiological underpinnings for visuospatial working memory, and hence problems therein (e.g., in schizophrenia; Callicott et al., 1998b; Carter et al., 1998), include the dorsolateral prefrontal cortex and a related cortical network also including parietal and cingulate cortices (Diamond and Goldman-Rakic, 1989; Goldman-Rakic, 1987). Indeed, a substantial amount of data may be taken to suggest that those components of working memory critically dependent on the prefrontal cortex may be critically deficient in schizophrenia. The cognitive activation paradigms that reliably demonstrate abnormal activation of the prefrontal cortex in patients with schizophrenia in response to cognitive challenge are those that require working memory (for a review, see Weinberger and Berman, 1996).

For more complex information processing (such as problem-solving, planning, and shifting response sets when the older ones are no longer adaptive), an executive component of working memory is thought to be recruited (Baddeley, 1986, 1996). Impairment in this executive domain has long been viewed as the hallmark of cognitive dysfunction in schizophrenia (Goldberg et al., 1988; Sullivan et al., 1994). The Wisconsin Card Sorting Test (WCST) has been used extensively to index the process of rule learning and set-shifting (Grant and Berger, 1948); this test, which is thought to be a good measure of executive function, depends upon the integrity of the frontal lobes for optimal performance (Milner, 1963). In this task, participants are required to sort cards printed with various designs that differ along three major stimulus dimensions or categories (e.g., color, number, and shape). Participants are not given advice as to how to sort the cards, but are told whether their sort is correct or incorrect. The experimenter starts the task with one dimension as the "correct" one, then alters the reinforcement contingencies once an individual reaches a criterion number of correct responses. The performance of schizophrenic patients on this task is characterized by fewer categories being achieved and a high proportion of perseverative errors (Goldberg et al., 1988, 1994; Seidman et al., 1994). In order to explore empirically the nature of this problem in shifting response set, a componential analysis of the WCST using a visual discrimination paradigm has been developed. This task, known as the Intradimensional/ Extradimensional Set-Shifting Task (from the Cambridge Neuropsychological Test Automated Battery; Fray, Robbins, and Sahakian, 1996) is conceptually simpler than the WCST. In this test, participants are required to learn a series of discriminations and reversals (intradimensional shifts), and they are given feedback as to their accuracy. The final stages of the test are an extradimensional shift and reversal stage in which additional novel stimuli are introduced. These novel stimuli may vary along the same dimensions (e.g., shapes and lines) as those previously experienced, whereupon the task becomes one of ignoring the previously relevant dimensions and responding to the previously irrelevant dimension. Importantly, the test has been shown to be sensitive to frontal, but not temporal-lobe damage (Owen et al., 1991). Whereas some schizophrenic patients have been shown to have problems at the intradimensional stage, others (older, chronic and IQ intact schizophrenic patients) have been shown to have problems at the extradimensional stage (Elliott et al., 1995, 1998); thus the interpretation of the data is not obvious.

EPISODIC MEMORY Episodic memory is memory of longer duration referring to a specific episode that can be located temporally. Impairment in this domain is widespread in schizophrenia, although not clearly characteristic of all patients with schizophrenia, and not typically occurring in isolation (i.e., problems in attention, working memory, and general memory may also be present). Indeed, memory disturbance contributes considerably to the overall cognitive deficit profile of schizophrenic patients (Clare et al., 1993). For example, patients have been reported to display slow rates of learning (Mungas, 1983) or inefficient encoding strategies (Calev, 1984; Calev, Berlin, and Lever, 1987; Koh, 1978; Traupmann, 1980). Such elementary problems naturally result in relative deficits on numerous memory and learning tasks (Gold et al., 1992; Landrø, Ørbeck and Rund, 1993; Saykin et al., 1991, 1994), especially those that require immediate recall (Goldberg et al., 1989; McClain, 1983) or simply recognition (Calev, Venables, and Monk, 1983; Glahn et al., 1997; Heaton et al., 1994; Paulsen et al., 1995). In our own work looking at memory for temporal order in patients with schizophrenia, we found that, although compromised, this deficit was mainly due to schizophrenic patients' generally poorer item-specific memory retrieval, i.e., recall (Elvevåg, Egan, and Goldberg, 2000a). In line with this finding, another study found that susceptibility to interference effects in memory in patients with schizophrenia is not a specific problem in interference susceptibility per se, but rather one that is generally confounded by general memory problems (Elvevåg, Egan, and Goldberg, 2000b).

Episodic memory is thought to be dependent upon medial temporal lobe structures (Squire, 1992), and the deficit in the rapid acquisition of new information has been associated with problems in the hippocampal formation. Impairment in this cognitive domain in schizophrenic patients has been shown (using magnetic resonance imaging) to be correlated with volumetric reductions of the left hippocampal region (Goldberg et al., 1994). Despite some inconsistencies in this research (Torres et al., 1997), a recent meta-analytic study lends support to the notion that schizophrenia is indeed associated with a bilateral volumetric reduction of the hippocampus, and probably also of the amygdala (Nelson et al., 1998). Thus, it is very possible that the neural substrate responsible for some of the memory deficits observed in schizophrenia are due to alterations in the hippocampal formation, although restriction of range difficulties inherent in volume reductions of 5–10% limit the strength of the association (for a review of the hippocampus in schizophrenia, see Weinberger, 1999). It is important to note that while volumetric decreases in the hippocampus are prevalent in patients with schizophrenia, their direct link to memory deficits remains unestablished and thus speculative. Another in vivo method with which to measure neuronal integrity of the hippocampus is proton magnetic resonance spectroscopy ($^{1}$H MRS) to index the concentration of

*N*-acetyl aspartate (NAA), a marker of the overall abundance and integrity of neuronal processes (Cendes et al., 1997; Cheng et al., 1997; DeStefano et al., 1995; Hugg et al., 1996; Rango et al., 1995; Rubin et al., 1995; Vion-Dury et al., 1995). A growing number of studies have found decreased NAA in the hippocampal region of patients with schizophrenia (Bertolino et al., 1997, 1998; Deicken et al., 1998; Maier et al., 1995; Nasrallah et al., 1994). More specifically, a comparison of unaffected siblings of schizophrenic patients and normal controls found a significant reduction in hippocampal NAA measures in the relatives, yielding moderate to strong genetic relative risk estimates of heritability, a finding taken to suggest that these hippocampal abnormalities may represent a biological phenotype related to schizophrenia susceptibility genes (Callicott et al., 1998a).

SEMANTIC MEMORY   Semantic memory is where the postulated storage and organization of meaning resides (i.e., representations of entities in the world; see Baddeley, 1990). Whereas episodic memory refers to a specific episode that can be located temporally, semantic memory refers to knowledge about the meanings of words, objects, and concepts. Since semantic knowledge is gleaned from specific (episodic) experiences, it is obvious that there is functional interdependence between episodic and semantic memory. However, knowledge in semantic memory no longer necessarily contains information concerning the specific episode. Interestingly, despite the interdependence between the episodic and semantic subsystems, they are also separable to the extent that one can observe deficits in either system while the other remains intact (e.g., this is often the case in amnesic patients). Much evidence supports the existence of a semantic deficit in schizophrenia (Aloia et al., 1996, 1998; Chen, Wilkins, and McKenna, 1994; Clare et al., 1993; Manschreck et al., 1988; Ober, Vinogradov, and Shenaut, 1995; Tamyln et al., 1992). In these studies, schizophrenic patients' performance on a wide variety of tasks (e.g., deciding which two objects, out of three, go best together) has been interpreted as reflecting problems in semantic storage, especially in the organization of information and in the use of that information. These processes are considered to be qualitatively different in schizophrenic patients and so result in poorer performance.

The possibility that the semantic memory system is disordered in schizophrenia has potential implications for understanding the mechanisms underlying the disorganized speech and thought disorder that characterize schizophrenia (for reviews, see Elvevåg and Goldberg, 1997; Goldberg et al., 1998a). Disorganized

speech in patients with schizophrenia has to do with disturbances in the form, and not the content, of speech (e.g., tangentiality, irrelevance, illogicality, incoherence, and derailment). Aloia and colleagues (1998) found that schizophrenic patients with high levels of thought disorder (as determined by the Scale for the Assessment of Thought, Language and Communication; Andreasen, 1986) did not display priming in contrast to schizophrenic patients with no thought disorder ("priming" in this instance means that responses to a target word are faster when that word has been preceded or cued by a semantically related word). These results suggest that patients with substantial thought disorder have more difficulties accessing a word that is typically associated with its semantic context; hence there is activation of a similar but less relevant word, which is then experienced by the listener as a "loose association" (e.g., instead of "cat–dog", the thought-disordered patient might say "cat–elephant"). These findings are important because they provide a possible cognitive mechanism of thought disorder.

It has been hypothesized that the neurobiological substrate for semantic memory is in the left temporal parietal cortex (Hodges et al., 1992; Hodges, Patterson, and Tyler, 1994; Warrington, 1975). Abnormalities in the left superior temporal cortex have been reported in schizophrenia (Barta et al., 1990; Shenton et al., 1992), but not without negative reports (Kulynych et al., 1996). Functional magnetic resonance imaging techniques used to examine the association between semantic memory anomalies and disorganized speech and/or thought disorder directly, promise to provide clues as to the exact neural underpinnings of this key cognitive deficit in schizophrenia.

In summary, there are four main cognitive processes—attention, working memory, episodic memory, and semantic memory—that together comprise the specific neuropsychological deficit profile characteristic of schizophrenia. While it is tempting to attribute these deficits to a single effector system, such as the hippocampal formation or the dorsolateral prefrontal cortex (DL-PFC), this conclusion reaches beyond the current data. In the next section, we explore possible neurodevelopmental reasons for the involvement of this compromised neurocognitive system in individuals who go on to develop schizophrenia.

## Why is brain development of interest in schizophrenia research?

Until relatively recently, schizophrenia was viewed as a condition that begins in early adult life and leads to a clinical deterioration over time (i.e., premature dementia; Kraepelin, 1919). Given this presumption, the logical conclusion was that the brains of these patients are generally normal until early adulthood when the illness manifests itself. Furthermore, it seemed logical to expect that such an adult-onset brain disorder would be accompanied by an increasing amount of neuropathological change as the illness evolved. However, with the exception of symptomatic progression, there have been surprisingly scant convincing data to support the idea of adult-onset pathological changes in the brain (see Weinberger, 1999). Although this view is controversial, we suggest that the course of schizophrenia is not particularly eventful cognitively: Once the deficits have arisen, they are relatively stable; and the evidence, taken as a whole, is not compatible with the idea of a progressive dementia. Moreover, we review evidence that supports the hypothesis of cortical maldevelopment, accompanied by ideas as to how such problems could give rise to the clinical symptoms of schizophrenia.

Today the dominant theory about schizophrenia is that it is a neurodevelopmental disorder in which damage to the brain occurs many years before the illness expresses itself in a florid fashion (Murray and Lewis, 1987; Weinberger, 1987). This theory assumes that even though schizophrenia per se is an adult-emergent phenomenon, evidence of deficits in brain function are present early in life, albeit in less dramatic form. In the next section we explore the integrity of the neurocognitive system in childhood, adolescence, and early adulthood before illness onset; then in adulthood when the illness has expressed itself in a florid fashion; and finally over the long-term course of the illness, as well as its interaction with the aging brain. This survey of cognition during the lifespan of the patient with schizophrenia argues strongly for a neurodevelopmental component to the cognitive deficits.

PREMORBID DYSFUNCTION  There is a large and surprisingly consistent body of literature that has shown schizophrenia to be associated with premorbid cognitive, social, and even neuromotor dysfunction. These data are basically of two types: cognitive comparison studies of intelligence quotients (IQ), and observations of neuromotor dysfunction in early childhood of individuals who later go on to develop schizophrenia. We will address each in turn.

*Cognitive studies*  Several large birth cohort studies have shown that individuals who go on to develop schizophrenia exhibit a small but significant diminution in cognitive function prior to the onset of symptoms (Crow, Done, and Sacker, 1995; David et al., 1997; Jones et al., 1994). Jones and colleagues (1994) studied a large birth cohort (children born in Britain in a single

week in March, 1946) and found that those individuals who went on to develop schizophrenia in adulthood had significant, albeit subtle, problems early in childhood (as early as 6 months of age), including retardation in the attainment of neuromotor milestones, lower levels of educational achievement, and speech abnormalities. Crow and colleagues (1995), who conducted another large birth cohort study (children born in Britain in a single week in March, 1958), also reported that the individuals who later went on to develop schizophrenia had significantly lower (again small) intellectual abilities premorbidly (i.e., prior to the onset of the psychotic symptoms) than the individuals in the cohort who did not develop psychosis. Examining data from psychological assessments of 50,054 Swedish army conscripts upon entry into the army at the age of 18 years, David and colleagues (1997; Malmberg et al., 1998) identified 195 individuals who, by the time of follow-up 15 years later, had gone on to develop schizophrenia or other psychoses. These individuals were found to have significantly lower premorbid IQ scores than the rest of the group, and the lower the IQ, the more severe the illness. This finding was taken to suggest that the emergence of schizophrenia is related to IQ as a continuous function. Moreover, they found that the tests that were the best predictors of later schizophrenia were those composed of reasoning tasks that require working memory capacity ("mechanical knowledge" tests). In a similar vein, a recent study by Davidson and colleagues (1999), using data from the Israeli Draft Board Registry and also from the National Psychiatric Hospitalization Case Registry, found that healthy male adolescents who were later hospitalized for schizophrenia had significantly lower scores in the domain of social functioning, organizational ability, and intellectual functioning than adolescents who were not later referred to psychiatric services. Taken together, these findings from unbiased epidemiological studies suggest that early developmental anomalies may contribute substantially to the cognitive impairment observed in schizophrenia.

These epidemiological studies have generally left unexplored the question of specificity: Is a low IQ in childhood or adolescence specific to the later risk of developing schizophrenia, or does it just increase an individual's risk to a variety of possible disorders? Indeed, not all individuals who go on to develop schizophrenia have low IQs in childhood and adolescence, or even early adulthood (before the onset of the illness); nor do all individuals with low IQ go on to develop schizophrenia. Employing a cross-sectional methodology, Weickert and colleagues recently addressed aspects of this issue (Weickert et al., 2000). They administered IQ tests to a large group ($n = 117$) of schizophrenic patients. One of these tests was a four-subtest version of the Wechsler Adult Intelligence Scale (WAIS-R; Wechsler, 1981), consisting of the Arithmetic, Digit Symbol Substitution Test, Picture Completion, and Similarities subtests, in order to obtain an estimate of current full-scale IQ (as described by Kaufman, 1990; Missar et al., 1994). The other test was one of reading proficiency—the Wide Range Achievement Test or WRAT (Jastak and Wilkinson, 1984)—which is widely used as a putative measure of premorbid intellect, since the ability to pronounce words is generally a robust ability that does not decline with the onset of schizophrenia (Crawford et al., 1992; Goldberg et al., 1995). Comparison of scores from these two tests, indexing pre- and postmorbid IQ, revealed that about one third of the cohort had low WRAT-Reading scores. Taken together with the birth cohort studies, these findings are consistent with the idea that, even before the symptoms of schizophrenia emerge in early adulthood, there are subtle cognitive deficits that are present in at least some of the individuals who later become psychotic. The fact that these cognitive deficits are not present in all of the individuals who go on to develop schizophrenia clearly emphasizes that low premorbid IQ is but one part of the overall picture.

*Neuromotor dysfunction* There is an impressive body of literature suggesting that, in terms of neuromotor development, behavioral dysfunction is abnormally high in early childhood in individuals who develop florid psychotic symptomatology as adults. In a series of ingenious studies of the developmental precursors of schizophrenia, Walker and colleagues examined home movies of adult-onset schizophrenic patients and their healthy siblings filmed during their childhood (Walker and Lewine, 1990; Walker, Savoie, and Davis, 1994). Simply by observing the behavior of these children (none of whom had any psychiatric disorder in childhood), viewers were able to reliably identify the preschizophrenic children in the sibling groups. Specifically, the preschizophrenic children showed a higher rate of neuromotor abnormalities (primarily on the left side of the body) and poorer motor skills when compared to their healthy siblings or to a control sample of preaffectively disordered individuals. Interestingly, early reports of patients and of children of patients with schizophrenia included these abnormalities (e.g., choreoathetoid movements and posturing of upper limbs) (Fish, 1977; Guttman, 1936; Reiter, 1926). It is noteworthy that some of these abnormal movements (e.g., hand posture) in preschizophrenic children are similar to those found in children with known or suspected central nervous system damage. Clearly, neuromotor dysfunction per se (or the aforementioned diminution

in premorbid IQ) does not increase the risk for schizophrenia specifically, but it may represent a nonspecific sign of neurodevelopmental deviance that may be specific for schizophrenia at a more fundamental neuropathological level.

MORBID FUNCTION  Based upon the neurodevelopmental model, we would expect that once the schizophrenia illness expresses itself clinically, the neurocognitive system is already compromised. Studies of patients during their first episode of schizophrenia have shown clearly that marked cognitive abnormalities (although not always as severe as in the chronic form of the disease) are present at the very onset of illness (Bilder et al., 1991; Goldberg et al., 1988; Hoff et al., 1992; Saykin et al., 1994). These findings are important since they demonstrate that cognitive diminution is present at the initial stages of the disease, and thus the impairment cannot be attributed to the treatment process or illness duration. A question remains as to what extent the already compromised cognitive system deteriorated from its original state to the point at which the symptoms emerged.

COURSE OF ILLNESS  If the disorder is not of a neurodegenerative nature, we would expect that the damaged neurocognitive system would not progressively worsen once the illness presents itself. In other words, the additional burden of the psychotic symptomatology does not precipitate a progressive decline in cognitive function. We present three lines of evidence to support this position. This evidence is derived from longitudinal and cross-sectional cognitive (i.e., IQ) studies, and from data on the absence of brain neuropathological degeneration over the course of the illness.

*Longitudinal studies*  Longitudinal studies support the idea that schizophrenia is not associated with progressive deterioration of cognitive function (Klonoff, Hutton, and Fibiger, 1970; Smith, 1964; Sweeney et al., 1991; but see Miller, 1989, for an opposite view, and for a review see Rund, 1998). Russell and colleagues observed low pre- and postmorbid IQ scores in a sample of 34 patients with schizophrenia; these patients had had IQ measurements as children and then were measured as adults approximately 19 years later (Russell et al., 1997). In interpreting their results, these authors found an early decline in individuals who later develop schizophrenia and suggested that this deficit in intellectual function predates disease onset. It is noteworthy that this study may suffer from ascertainment bias. These children, whose IQs had been tested because they had been sent to psychiatry services, may not be truly representative of children who later manifest schizophrenia. Nonetheless, this methodological limitation does not detract from the finding that patients with schizophrenia do have measurable cognitive deficits early on in their development.

*Cross-sectional studies* Cross-sectional and pseudo–cross-sectional studies used to explore the extent of cognitive decline over the course of the illness support the notion of relative stability, at least after the first 3–5 years of the illness (Davidson and McGlashan, 1997; Goldberg et al., 1993c; Goldstein and Zubin, 1990; Heaton et al., 1994; Hyde et al., 1994; Mason et al., 1996; Mockler, Riordan, and Sharma, 1997; Weickert et al., 2000). An attempt to incorporate these findings suggesting the presence of an apparent static defect, similar to that of a static encephalopathy, within the theoretical framework of a neurodevelopmental model has led to the suggestion that the cognitive deficits in schizophrenia arise along at least two developmental trajectories (Weickert et al., 2000). The first trajectory contains a general range of cognitive deficits manifested as a result of the early developmental problems. During the second trajectory the specific (i.e., more circumscribed) cognitive deficits manifest themselves (e.g., problems in the domain of working memory, attention, and episodic memory) alongside the onset of the florid symptomatology.

*Static lesion model* The hypothesis of a static lesion is a centerpiece of the neurodevelopmental model and is consistent with the absence of progression in ventricular enlargement found in many studies of schizophrenic patients (Andreasen et al., 1982, 1990a,b; Illowsky et al., 1988; Jaskiw et al., 1994). However, other recent longitudinal magnetic resonance imaging studies seemingly do not support the idea of a static lesion in schizophrenic patients (DeLisi et al., 1995, 1997; Gur et al., 1998). These recent studies, however, while generally showing morphometric changes in 2–5-year follow-up periods, are remarkably inconsistent. For example, while DeLisi and colleagues (1995) reported increases in ventricular size and reductions in temporal lobe size, Gur and colleagues (1998) reported no change in ventricular or temporal lobe size, but reductions in frontal lobe size. Moreover, a recent longitudinal study of volume measurements of ventricles and cerebral hemispheres in schizophrenic patients rather paradoxically suggested that large ventricular size in acute onset patients may actually be predictive of good recovery (DeLisi et al., 1998). Examination of these data demonstrates a further methodological problem with these measurements in general: namely, the structural data are highly variable between patients. Moreover, and

more worrisome, is the fact that volume measurements of individual patients go up and down rather erratically, thus raising the question of the validity of MRI morphometry as a reflection of pathological change. The conclusion that changes in MRI morphometry in schizophrenia may not reflect neuropathological change is also consistent with results from postmortem tissue studies that have failed to find evidence of such degenerative neuropathology (Weinberger, 1999).

When declines in cognition have been reported during the course of the schizophrenia illness, they have been very small (1–2 Mini Mental State Examination points per decade; Folstein, Folstein, and McHugh, 1975), which would not appear compatible with a progressive dementia, or indeed the notion that age disproportionately burdens schizophrenic patients. However, there is dissent from this view. Neuropsychological assessments in first-episode and chronic schizophrenic patients found that the chronic group performed worse on measures that were considered sensitive to cognitive deterioration (Bilder et al., 1992). These results were taken to suggest that cognitive deterioration may occur after the onset of psychosis in some schizophrenic patients. Another study involving first-episode schizophrenic patients found executive impairments at the beginning of the illness (Hutton et al., 1998), but more severe executive deficits were reported in chronic patients in an earlier study (Elliott et al., 1995, 1998; Elliott and Sahakian, 1995). Thus, the authors interpreted these results to suggest a progressive cognitive decline, at least in executive function, during the course of the schizophrenia illness. We suggest that in general this dissent from the static view of the illness may be reconciled by appreciating that these studies did not control for potential intervening illnesses (hypertension, diabetes, etc.) which can compromise cognition independently of schizophrenia. Moreover, cross-sectional studies such as these do not control for the fact that chronic patients are, by definition, a more severe group than acute patients, and many of the well-functioning acute patients do not end up as chronic. Thus, the poorer functioning acute patients may simply come to represent a greater proportion of the chronic group, and really have suffered no deterioration in cognitive function. A study by Harvey and colleagues in geriatric patients with chronic schizophrenia over a 2½-year period found a significant cognitive decline for that period (Harvey et al., 1999). However, since this study was exclusively in elderly institutionalized patients, these data have no bearing on cognitive change during the principal years of the illness, and may reflect secondary factors such as poorly diagnosed or treated medical problems (e.g., hypertension, diabetes, head injury). Thus, we suggest that once the cognitive deficits have arisen, the course of schizophrenia is not particularly eventful cognitively.

In considering changes in cognition and brain structures over time, it is important to take the effects of "normal" aging into account. Age is generally thought to be a negative prognostic indicator in traumatic brain injury (TBI), the notion being that older individuals are more likely to suffer greater impairment following TBI, primarily owing to pre-injury comorbidity factors. Work on traumatic brain-injured individuals suggests that the greater neuropsychological impairment noted in older individuals with TBI is probably due to the additive effects of normal aging (Johnstone, Childers, and Hoerner, 1998). Moreover, aging does not affect all cognitive functions uniformly; a high initial education level slows the rate of decline for certain tasks (Ritchie et al., 1997). However, the extent to which education itself is a protective factor is not simple, since this factor interacts in a complex manner with lifestyle factors such as physical fitness (Houx and Jolles, 1993). The question then emerges as to whether the additional burden of age would affect patients with schizophrenia differentially. However, the relation of age-associated changes in cognition to those in schizophrenia is not well investigated. In fact, MRI studies suggest that age differentially affects the frontal lobes (Coffey et al., 1992), which could conceivably have an additional effect on frontal lobe deficits in schizophrenia.

To conclude this section, we argue that the above data provide evidence that schizophrenia is associated with neurocognitive weakness that, to a certain degree, exists from early in life. Other questions then emerge: How do the other features of schizophrenia relate to this neurocognitive analogy, and why does schizophrenia rather than some other neurodevelopmental disorder emerge at all? In other words, why do the neural events responsible for a diminution in IQ, attention, and working memory associated with schizophrenia result in schizophrenia rather than some other disorder? And are the cognitive deficits sufficient to produce the disorder?

## Why would abnormal brain development result specifically in schizophrenia rather than some other neurodevelopmental disorder? A cognitive perspective

THE SPECIFICITY OF NEURAL DEVELOPMENT TO SCHIZOPHRENIA Different stages and aspects of the complex process of brain development are differentially vulnerable to adverse events, and the manifestations of the damage vary depending on extent, timing,

and region of damage. In the process of normal brain development, problems in the first stage of forming the neural tube (*neurulation*), if major, are usually aborted, and if minor, are not specifically associated with the development of schizophrenia. The second stage of neuronal *proliferation* is a stage in which abnormal development might result in anomalies similar to some of the neuropathological findings of schizophrenia. The third stage of neuronal *migration* is a process that is very sensitive to genetic and environmental insults. Again, neuropathological data of schizophrenia are not incompatible with possible problems in the timing of some of these migratory processes. The final stage of brain development results in regional anatomical and functional *differentiation*. Again, much evidence of neuronal and regional differentiation has been implicated in neurodevelopmental models of schizophrenia. We discuss possible candidate models below.

*Windows of vulnerability* The age at which a neurological disorder presents itself is a good predictor of whether or not it will be associated with a psychosis (Weinberger, 1987), with psychosis being more likely to manifest itself in late adolescence and early adulthood than at other times of life, regardless of the specific nature of the neuropathological process. This observation has far-reaching consequences, in that simple damage to neural systems implicated in psychosis is not sufficient to cause the schizophrenia illness. Rather, what appears necessary is that the brain achieve a certain stage of development after the damage is acquired for psychosis to result. We explore this issue using a neurological analogy, namely, the rare illness metachromatic leukodystrophy; then we review how animal models have shed light on the neurodevelopmental aspects of schizophrenia.

*Metachromatic leukodystrophy* Metachromatic leukodystrophy (MLD) is an inherited disorder of myelin metabolism that can initially present during childhood, adolescence or adulthood. If the disease presents between the ages of 12 and 30 years, psychiatric symptoms appear that are clinically very similar to schizophrenia, probably more so than with any other neurologic disorder (Hyde, Ziegler, and Weinberger, 1992). However, when MLD presents outside of this age range, it rarely presents with psychosis. In other words, it would seem that an age-related factor, independent of the illness, is a required neurobiological factor for psychosis presentation. The purpose of this neurological analogy is to demonstrate that, like adolescent and early adult-onset MLD, schizophrenia may also be associated with dysfunctional connectivity of frontal cortex and this dysfunction must specifically occur at a critical period in brain maturation for it to be expressed as a psychosis. However, the analogy ends there, since there is a progressive degeneration of other neural systems in MLD (the integrity of which is ironically crucial for the continual presentation of the psychosis, which eventually recedes) which is quite different from the static course of schizophrenia.

*Animal models* Whereas the MLD model demonstrates that it is possible that brain damage involving certain neural functions during a critical period may result in psychosis, such a model does not provide evidence for the possibility that such defects might remain relatively silent until late adolescence and or early adulthood. We now discuss some animal models which make this aspect of the neurodevelopmental model of schizophrenia appear neurobiologically plausible.

Delayed emergence of hyperdopaminergic behaviors (i.e., a "psychosis" construct) has been modeled in the rat by making perinatal excitotoxic lesions of the ventral hippocampus (Lipska, Jaskiw, and Weinberger, 1993; Lipska and Weinberger, 1993a,b, 1996). Hyperdopaminergia has been assumed to be important in schizophrenia because of the effectiveness of anti-dopaminergic (neuroleptic) drugs. After damage and before puberty, there are no apparent mesolimbic or nigrostriatally mediated behavioral consequences. However, by early adulthood the effects of the perinatal lesion become very clear, with the rats being hyperresponsive to dopaminergic drugs and to a variety of environmental stresses. Although no one would suggest that these rats are "schizophrenic," they do display certain behavioral and biological abnormalities associated with schizophrenia (e.g., abnormal prepulse inhibition of startle, working memory deficits, and other evidence of prefrontal dysfunction; see Weinberger and Lipska, 1995). It is noteworthy that antipsychotic drugs ameliorate many of the abnormal behaviors displayed by rats who undergo these manipulations.

This work shows that it is neurobiologically plausible that damage to selected cortical systems implicated in schizophrenia during development may have delayed effects in the regulation of dopaminergic systems and in responses to environmental stress. Furthermore, other experiments in rats that differ genetically in their responsivity to environmental stresses have shown differential effects of neonatal lesions. Rats that are inbred to be hyperresponsive to stress (Fisher 344 strain) have been shown to display exaggerated effects of small lesions, with the same-sized lesion having a much less pronounced effect in less stress-responsive rats (Sprague-Dawley strain). Interestingly, rats that are

bred to be hyporesponsive to stress (Lewis strain) appeared to be able to compensate for many of the consequences of the lesion (Lipska and Weinberger, 1995). This work shows how genetic factors, such as susceptibility to stress, interact in a complex fashion with the effects of environmental injury, which in turn determine how responsive the mesolimbic dopaminergic system might be.

Work in monkeys to examine the highly evolved dorsolateral prefrontal cortex (DL-PFC) has also shown that damage to temporal-limbic cortical systems during neurodevelopment can result in dysregulation of dopaminergic systems—a dysregulation that could account for some of the changing life course manifestations of dysfunction in schizophrenia. In adult monkeys that had neonatal medial-temporal removals, in contrast to normal animals and animals with adult removals, prefrontal cortical regulation of striatal dopamine was dramatically abnormal (Saunders et al., 1998). Whereas adult monkeys without lesions and those with adult lesions displayed a reduction in dopamine overflow following pharmacological stimulation of DL-PFC, monkeys that had lesions as neonates showed an increase in dopamine release. Such data suggest that early lesions can have substantial effects later in life on neural systems that are quite distant and subserve functions not traditionally associated with the lesioned structure.

Other studies examining the effects of neonatal hippocampal lesions on prefrontal development in primates and rodents have evaluated in vivo neuronal integrity in the prefrontal cortex, assessed by relative concentrations of the metabolite *N*-acetylaspartate (NAA) measured with proton magnetic resonance spectroscopic imaging. These studies have found reductions specifically in the dorsolateral prefrontal cortex in rhesus monkeys with neonatal damage (Bertolino et al., 1997). Such reductions were not found in animals with similar ablations performed after they were adults. Moreover, reductions in DL-PFC NAA were predictive of the basal and amphetamine-induced release of striatal dopamine. Importantly, these measures have now been applied to compare healthy control participants with patients with schizophrenia. In the patients, NAA measures in DL-PFC selectively predicted striatal displacement of [$^{11}$C]raclopride after amphetamine infusions, unlike controls who did not show this correlation (Bertolino et al., 2000). These various findings in patients are taken to support the hypothesis that developmental neuronal pathology of the DL-PFC is directly related to abnormal subcortical dopamine function in patients with schizophrenia. The animal work clearly illustrates that cortical systems damaged during development could account for the changing life-course manifestations of dysfunction in that there can be delayed effects emerging that result in the dysregulation of dopaminergic systems—the system that is targeted through pharmaceutical intervention when the florid symptoms emerge in adulthood.

THE SPECIFICITY OF COGNITIVE IMPAIRMENT TO SCHIZOPHRENIA  Is there evidence that the cognitive deficit profile observed in schizophrenia is selectively unique? We contend that a unique neurodevelopmental profile associated with schizophrenias is highly probable because the cognitive deficit profile is qualitatively different from that of other disorders. Several neonatal cerebral insults produce a pattern of cognitive deficits reflecting the neural system's damage. Certainly, attention and working memory are often affected. Episodic and semantic memory might be affected if there is some temporal lobe damage. However, in order to appreciate how the profile of deficits and preserved functions compare with schizophrenia, it is necessary to compare these directly. This has rarely been done. We will review a few instances in which direct comparisons have been made.

*Affective disorder*  A case could be made that, from a cognitive perspective, affective disorder is just a muted form of the schizophrenia illness, and that neuropsychological differences between groups might determine, to some extent, the outcome in these disorders—schizophrenia being characterized by a chronic course and affective disorder being more episodic and less disabling. We suggest that these disorders do present with different profiles, in that the cognitive deficit profile is not only more severe in patients with schizophrenia compared to bipolar or depressed patients but also qualitatively different (for a review, see Goldberg, 1999; but see an alternative view by Zihl, Grön, and Brunnauer, 1998). In comparisons with patients with affective disorders, patients with schizophrenia have been shown to have worse performance on a degraded version of the vigilance task—the Continuous Performance Task (Nuechterlein et al., 1991)—a decline in IQ from premorbid levels, and decreased visual memory and executive function (Goldberg et al., 1993a; Gourovitch et al., 1999). Such evidence is consistent with the observations that functional outcomes are worse for patients with schizophrenia (Marneros, Rohde, and Deister, 1995, 1998). Importantly, since affective illness is more episodic, it is also less disabling, with patients generally recovering their cognitive function once an episode has resolved (i.e., state-dependent). This is quite unlike the cognitive deficits

observed in schizophrenia, which remain throughout the course of the illness.

*Temporal lobe epilepsy*  One might expect the cognitive profiles of schizophrenic patients and those with temporal lobe epilepsy to overlap to some degree. This is because patients with schizophrenia are postulated to have medial temporal lobe dysfunction. Comparing schizophrenic patients with temporal lobe epilepsy patients, Gold and colleagues (Gold et al., 1994, 1995) found that patients with schizophrenia had more attentional problems, were slower in motor tasks, and performed more poorly on the WCST. However, schizophrenic patients were not just worse overall, as they had superior semantic knowledge than patients with left temporal lobe epilepsy. In addition, Gold and colleagues (1994, 1995) found a double dissociation between IQ factors: Schizophrenic patients scored lower on measures of "freedom from distractibility" and higher on a verbal measure whereas the opposite profile was observed for patients with temporal lobe epilepsy. Thus, we suggest that the cognitive profiles of temporal lobe epilepsy and schizophrenia are very different.

HUNTINGTON'S DISEASE  Both Huntington's disease and schizophrenia have been considered to be subcortical disorders with cognitive slowing and executive-type problems. Nonetheless, the cognitive profiles of these two groups are in fact quite distinct. In a direct comparison of patients, Goldberg and colleagues (Goldberg et al., 1990) found that patients with schizophrenia performed better on visuospatial tasks after the two groups had been matched on a putative measure of frontal lobe function (the WCST), a finding taken to suggest that patients with Huntington's disease and those with schizophrenia present with different cognitive performance profiles.

*Alzheimer's disease*  Comparison of patients with Alzheimer's disease with schizophrenic patients have demonstrated that the former group are more impaired cognitively, especially as the Alzheimer's disease progresses. As discussed earlier, the cognitive courses of the illnesses are very distinct, the cognitive declines being small in schizophrenia relative to that of Alzheimer's disease. A study by Heaton and colleagues (Heaton et al., 1994) found that patients with schizophrenia did not show an increased rate of forgetting, unlike the patients with Alzheimer's disease.

*Attention deficit/hyperactivity disorder*  One of the main cognitive deficits observed in both schizophrenic patients and individuals diagnosed with attention deficit/hyperactivity disorder (ADHD) is that of attention (Øie, Rund, and Sundet, 1998; Overtoom et al., 1998; Rund, Øie, and Sundet, 1996; Rund et al., 1998), although there is disagreement over the relative severity of attentional disorders in the groups (Carter et al., 1995; Rund et al., 1998). Interestingly, patients with ADHD who are classically defined as being distractible do not display thought disorder, which is a main symptom in the schizophrenia illness. Thus, whatever the cognitive function that underlies thought disorder, attentional factors cannot be solely responsible (Elvevåg and Goldberg, 1997). Comparison of children with ADHD and children with childhood-onset schizophrenia have shown that both groups display deficits in verbal and spatial working memory, a finding which suggests that both disorders are characterized by limited executive resources (Karatekin and Asarnow, 1998b; see also Karatekin, this volume). There are also cognitive differences in these children: Unlike schizophrenic or control children, those with ADHD displayed delayed initiation of serial visual search (Karatekin and Asarnow, 1998a). A recent comparison of adolescents with schizophrenia and adolescents with ADHD found that the schizophrenic group displayed more severe deficits on tests of abstraction, visual memory, and motor function. In contrast, the ADHD group displayed the more severe deficits on tests of attention, verbal memory, and learning (Øie and Rund, 1999).

*Obsessive-compulsive disorder*   There is considerable overlap in the postulated functional circuitry thought to be involved in both schizophrenia and obsessive-compulsive disorder (OCD) (e.g., a frontostriatal network; Hollander et al., 1993; Purcell et al., 1998; Rauch et al., 1997; Schmidtke et al., 1998; Tallis, 1997; Tibbo and Warneke, 1999). Importantly, there may be a high prevalence of OCD-like features in schizophrenia (Tibbo and Warneke, 1999), with a negative relation between OCD symptoms in schizophrenia and activation of the dorsolateral prefrontal cortex (i.e., a relationship with severity; Levine et al., 1998). However, the difference between the groups is not simply a matter of severity. Abbruzzese and colleagues (Abbruzzese et al., 1995; Abbruzzese, Ferri, and Scarone, 1997) report a double dissociation in frontal lobe function of OCD patients and schizophrenic patients, with OCD patients' performance being normal on the WCST (a test thought to be sensitive to dorsolateral prefrontal cortex) but abnormalities on an object alternation test (a tool sensitive to orbitofrontal cortex). In contrast, schizophrenic patients' performance was abnormal on the WCST and normal on the object alternation test. These findings suggest a dorsolateral prefrontal cortex deficit in schizophrenia and an orbitofrontal involvement in OCD.

In summary, most forms of brain damage or dysfunction produce cognitive deficits, but patients with schizophrenia appear to have a profile that can be distinguished from other groups (i.e., not just a profile of general cognitive deficits): namely, executive and memory impairments in the context of a more general IQ decline (and independently from this decline). In the context of a neurodevelopmental model, this specific neuropsychological profile strongly supports the hypothesis that schizophrenia follows a unique neurodevelopmental trajectory.

*Conclusion*

In this chapter we have explored the ways in which the neuropsychological profile of schizophrenia (problems in attention, working memory, episodic memory, and semantic memory which have specific physiological correlates) can inform us of the neurodevelopmental trajectory of the schizophrenia illness. We have reviewed a variety of studies showing abnormalities premorbidly in the cognitive and neuromotor realms in schizophrenic patients, thus providing support for a neurodevelopmental hypothesis of schizophrenia. These findings of a neurocognitive weakness being present before the illness onset provide strong evidence for abnormal cortical development, which although debilitating to varying degrees, appears to arise from a static neuropathology. Finally, we explored possible explanations for why early brain insults result specifically in schizophrenia. We have suggested that it is a combination of age and specific sites of brain insult (especially the temporal-limbic and dorsolateral prefrontal cortices) that produces a unique neurodevelopmental trajectory leading to schizophrenia.

ACKNOWLEDGMENT   We are very grateful to Terry Goldberg, Ph.D., for useful discussions.

REFERENCES

ABBRUZZESE, M., L. BELLODI, S. FERRI, and S. SCARONE, 1995. Frontal lobe dysfunction in schizophrenia and obsessive-compulsive disorder: A neuropsychological study. *Brain Cogn.* 27:202–212.

ABBRUZZESE, M., S. FERRI, and S. SCARONE, 1997. The selective breakdown of frontal functions in patients with obsessive-compulsive disorder and in patients with schizophrenia: A double dissociation experimental finding. *Neuropsychologia* 35:907–912.

ADDINGTON, J., and D. ADDINGTON, 1993. Premorbid functioning, cognitive functioning, symptoms and outcome in schizophrenia. *J. Psychiatry Neurosci.* 18:18–23.

ADDINGTON, J., D. ADDINGTON, and E. MATICKA-TYNDALE, 1991. Cognitive functioning and positive and negative symptoms in schizophrenia. *Schizophr. Res.* 5:123–134.

ALOIA, M. S., M. L. GOUROVITCH, D. MISSAR, D. PICKAR, D. R. WEINBERGER, and T. E. GOLDBERG, 1998. Cognitive substrates of thought disorder, II: Specifying a candidate cognitive mechanism. *Am. J. Psychiatry* 155:1677–1684.

ALOIA, M. S., M. L. GOUROVITCH, D. R. WEINBERGER, and T. E. GOLDBERG, 1996. An investigation of semantic space in patients with schizophrenia. *J. Int. Neuropsychol. Soc.* 2:267–273.

AMERICAN PSYCHIATRIC ASSOCIATION, 1994. *Diagnostic and Statistical Manual of Mental Disorders,* 4th ed. Washington D.C.

ANDREASEN, N. C., 1986. Scale for the assessment of thought, language and communication (TLC). *Schizophr. Bull.* 12:473–482.

ANDREASEN, N. C., J. C. EHRHARDT, V. W. SWAYZE 2D, R. J. ALLIGER, W. T. YUH, G. COHEN, and S. ZIEBELL, 1990a. Magnetic resonance imaging of the brain in schizophrenia: The pathophysiologic significance of structural abnormalities. *Arch. Gen. Psychiatry* 47:35–44.

ANDREASEN, N. C., M. R. SMITH, C. G. JACOBY, J. W. DENNERT, and S. A. OLSEN, 1982. Ventricular enlargement in schizophrenia: Definition and prevalence. *Am. J. Psychiatry* 139:292–296.

ANDREASEN, N. C., V. W. SWAYZE 2D, M. FLAUM, W. R. YATES, S. ARNDT, and C. MCCHESNEY, 1990b. Ventricular enlargement in schizophrenia evaluated with computed tomographic scanning. Effects of gender, age, and stage of illness. *Arch. Gen. Psychiatry* 47:1008–1015.

BADDELEY, A. D., 1986. *Working Memory.* Oxford, UK: Oxford University Press.

BADDELEY, A. D., 1990. *Human Memory: Theory and Practice.* London: Lawrence Erlbaum Associates.

BADDELEY, A. D., 1996. The fractionation of working memory. *Proc. Natl. Acad. Sci. USA* 93:13468–13472.

BARTA, P. E., G. D. PEARLSON, R. E. POWERS, S. S. RICHARDS, and L. E. TUNE, 1990. Auditory hallucinations and smaller superior temporal gyral volume in schizophrenia. *Am. J. Psychiatry* 147:1457–1462.

BERTOLINO, A., A. BREIER, J. H. CALLICOTT, C. ADLER, V. S. MATTAY, M. SHAPIRO, J. A. FRANK, D. PICKAR, and D. R. WEINBERGER, 2000. The relationship between dorsolateral prefrontal neuronal N-acetylaspartate and evoked release of striatal dopamine in schizophrenia. *Neuropsycho-pharmacology* 22:125–132.

BERTOLINO, A., A. BREIER, J. H. CALLICOTT, C. ADLER, V. S. MATTAY, M. SHAPIRO, J. A. FRANK, D. PICKAR, and D. R. WEINBERGER, 1998. The relationship between dorsolateral prefrontal neuronal N-acetylaspartate and evoked release of striatal dopamine in schizophrenia. *Neuroimage* 7:S31.

BERTOLINO, A., R. C. SAUNDERS, V. S. MATTAY, J. BACHEVALIER, J. A. FRANK, and D. R. WEINBERGER, 1997. Altered development of prefrontal neurons in rhesus monkeys with neonatal mesial temporo-limbic lesions: A proton magnetic resonance spectroscopic imaging study. *Cereb. Cortex* 7:740–748.

BILDER, R. M., L. LIPSCHUTZ-BROCH, G. REITER, S. GEISLER, D. MAYERHOFF, and J. A. LIEBERMAN, 1991. Neuropsychological deficits in the early course of first episode schizophrenia. *Schizophr. Res.* 5:198–199.

BILDER, R. M., L. LIPSCHUTZ-BROCH, G. REITER, S. H. GEISLER, D. I. MAYERHOFF, and J. A. LIEBERMAN, 1992. Intellec-tual deficits in first-episode schizophrenia: Evidence for progressive deterioration. *Schizophr. Bull.* 18:437–448.

BRAFF, D. L., R. HEATON, J. KUCK, M. CULLUM, J. MORANVILLE, I. GRANT, and S. ZISOOK, 1991. The generalized pattern of neuropsychological deficits in outpatients with chronic schizophrenia with heterogeneous Wisconsin Card Sorting Test results. *Arch. Gen. Psychiatry* 48:891–898.

BREIER, A., J. L. SCHREIBER, J. DYER, and D. PICKAR, 1991. National Institute of Mental Health longitudinal study of chronic schizophrenia: Prognosis and predictors of outcome. *Arch. Gen. Psychiatry* 48:239–246.

CALEV, A., 1984. Recall and recognition in chronic nondemented schizophrenics: Use of matched tasks. *J. Abnorm. Psychol.* 93:172–177.

CALEV, A., H. BERLIN, and B. LEVER, 1987. Remote and recent memory in long hospitalized schizophrenics. *Biol. Psychiatry* 22:70–85.

CALEV, A., P. H. VENABLES, and A. F. MONK, 1983. Evidence for distinct verbal memory pathologies in severely and mildly disturbed schizophrenics. *Schizophr. Bull.* 9:247–264.

CALLICOTT, J. H., A. BERTOLINO, V. S. MATTAY, F. J. P. LANGHEIM, J. H. DUYN, R. COPPOLA, T. E. GOLDBERG, and D. R. WEINBERGER, 2000. Physiological dysfunction of the dorsolateral prefrontal cortex in schizophrenia revisited. *Cerebral Cortex* 10:1078–1092.

CALLICOTT, J. H., M. F. EGAN, A. BERTOLINO, V. S. MATTAY, F. J. LANGHEIM, J. A. FRANK, and D. R. WEINBERGER, 1998a. Hippocampal N-acetyl aspartate in unaffected siblings of patients with schizophrenia: A possible intermediate neurobiological phenotype. *Biol. Psychiatry* 44:941–950.

CALLICOTT, J. H., N. F. RAMSEY, K. TALLENT, A. BERTOLINO, M. B. KNABLE, R. COPOLLA, T. GOLDBERG, P. VAN GELDERN, V. S. MATTAY, J. A. FRANK, C. T. W. MOONEN, and D. R. WEINBERGER, 1998b. Functional magnetic resonance imaging brain mapping in psychiatry: Methodological issues illustrated in a study of working memory in schizophrenia. *Neuropsychopharmacology* 18:186–196.

CARTER, C. S., P. KRENER, M. CHADERJIAN, C. NORTHCUTT, and V. WOLFE, 1995. Abnormal processing of irrelevant information in attention deficit hyperactivity disorder. *Psychiatry Res.* 56:59–70.

CARTER, C. S., W. PERLSTEIN, R. GANGULI, J. BRAR, M. MINTUN, and J. D. COHEN, 1998. Functional hypofrontality and working memory dysfunction in schizophrenia. *Am. J. Psychiatry* 155:1285–1287.

CENDES, F., F. ANDERMANN, F. DUBEAU, P. M. MATTHEWS, and D. L. ARNOLD, 1997. Normalization of neuronal metabolic dysfunction after surgery for temporal lobe epilepsy: Evidence from proton MR spectroscopic imaging. *Neurology* 49:1525–1533.

CHEN, E. Y. H., A. J. WILKINS, and P. J. MCKENNA, 1994. Semantic memory is both impaired and anomalous in schizophrenia. *Psychol. Med.* 24:193–202.

CHEN, W. J., S. K. LIU, C.-J. CHANG, Y.-J. LIEN, Y.-H. CHANG, and H.-G. HWU, 1998. Sustained attention deficit and schizotypal personality features in nonpsychotic relatives of schizophrenic patients. *Am. J. Psychiatry* 155:1214–1219.

CHENG, L. L., M. J. MA, L. BECERRA, T. PTAK, I. TRACEY, A. LACKNER, and R. G. GONZÁLEZ, 1997. Quantitative neuropathology by high resolution magic angle spinning proton magnetic resonance spectroscopy. *PNAS* 94:6408–6413.

CLARE, L., P. J. MCKENNA, A. M. MORTIMER, and A. D. BADDELEY, 1993. Memory in schizophrenia: What is impaired and what is preserved? *Neuropsychologia* 31:1225–1241.

COFFEY, C. E., W. E. WILKINSON, I. A. PARASHOS, S. A. R. SOADY, R. J. SULLIVAN, L. J. PATTERSON, G. S. FIGIEL, M. C. WEBB, C. E. SPRITZER, and W. T. DJANG, 1992. Quantitative cerebral anatomy of the aging human brain: A cross-sectional study using magnetic resonance imaging. *Neurology* 42:527–536.

COHEN, J. D., S. D. FORMAN, T. S. BRAVER, B. J. CASEY, D. SERVAN-SCHREIBER, and D. C. NOLL, 1994. Activation of the prefrontal cortex in a nonspatial working memory task with functional MRI. *Hum. Brain Mapp.* 1:293–304.

COHEN, J. D., W. M. PERSTEIN, T. S. BRAVER, L. E. NYSTROM, D. C. NOLL, J. JONIDES, and E. E. SMITH, 1997. Temporal dynamics of brain activation during a working memory task. *Nature* 386:604–608.

CORNBLATT, B. A., and J. G. KEILP, 1994. Impaired attention, genetics, and the psychophysiology of schizophrenia. *Schizophr. Bull.* 20:31–46.

CRAWFORD, J. R., J. A. O. BESSON, K. P. EBMEIER, R. H. B. COCHRANE, and K. KIRKWOOD, 1992. Estimation of premorbid intelligence in schizophrenia. *Br. J. Psychiatry* 161:69–74.

CROW, T. J., J. BALL, S. R. BLOOM, R. BROWN, C. J. BRUTON, N. COLTER, C. D. FRITH, E. C. JOHNSTONE, D. G. C. OWENS, and G. W. ROBERTS, 1989. Schizophrenia as an anomaly of development of cerebral asymmetry. *Arch. Gen. Psychiatry* 46:1145–1150.

CROW, T. J., D. J. DONE, and A. SACKER, 1995. Childhood precursors of psychosis as clues to its evolutionary origins. *Eur. Arch. Psychiatry Clin. Neurosci.* 245:61–69.

DAVID, A. S., A. MALMBERG, L. BRANDT, P. ALLEBECK, and G. LEWSI, 1997. IQ and risk for schizophrenia: A population based cohort study. *Psychol. Med.* 27:1311–1323.

DAVIDSON, L., and T. H. MCGLASHAN, 1997. The varied outcomes of schizophrenia. *Can. J. Psychiatry* 42:34–43.

DAVIDSON, M., A. REICHENBERG, J. RABINOWITZ, M. WEISRE, Z. KAPLAN, and M. MARK, 1999. Behavioral and intellectual markers for schizophrenia in apparently healthy male adolescents. *Am. J. Psychiatry* 156:1328–1335.

DEICKEN, R. F., L. ZHOU, N. SCHUFF, G. FEIN, and M. W. WEINER, 1998. Hippocampal neuronal dysfunction in schizophrenia as measured by proton magnetic resonance spectroscopy. *Biol. Psychiatry* 43:483–488.

DELISI, L. E., M. SAKUMA, S. GE, and M. KUSHNER, 1998. Association of brain structural change with the heterogeneous course of schizophrenia from early childhood through five years subsequent to a first hospitalization. *Psychiatry Res.: Neuroimaging* 84:75–88.

DELISI, L. E., M. SAKUMA, W. TEW, M. KUSHNER, A. L. HOFF, and R. GRIMSON, 1997. Schizophrenia as a chronic active brain process: A study of progressive brain structural changes subsequent to the onset of schizophrenia. *Psychiatry Res.* 74:129–140.

DELISI, L. E., W. TEW, S. XIE, A. L. HOFF, M. SAKUMA, M. KUSHNER, G. LEE, K. SHEDLACK, A. M. SMITH, and R. GRIMSON, 1995. A prospective follow-up study of brain morphology and cognition in first-episode schizophrenic patients: Preliminary findings. *Biol. Psychiatry* 38:349–360.

DESTEFANO, N., P. MATTHEWS, J. P. ANTEL, M. PREUL, G. FRANCIS, and D. L. ARNOLD, 1995. Chemical pathology of acute demyelinating lesions and its correlations with disability. *Ann. Neurol.* 38:901–909.

DIAMOND, A., and P. S. GOLDMAN-RAKIC, 1989. Comparison of human infants and rhesus monkeys on Piaget's AB task:

Evidence for dependence on dorsolateral prefrontal cortex. *Exp. Brain Res.* 74:24–40.

ELLIOTT, R., P. J. MCKENNA, T. W. ROBBINS, and B. J. SAHAKIAN, 1995. Neuropsychological evidence for fronto-striatal dysfunction in schizophrenia. *Psychol. Med.* 25:619–630.

ELLIOTT, R., P. J. MCKENNA, T. W. ROBBINS, and B. J. SAHAKIAN, 1998. Specific neuropsychological deficits in schizophrenic patients with preserved intellectual function. *Cogn. Neuropsychiatry* 3:45–70.

ELLIOTT, R., and B. J. SAHAKIAN, 1995. The neuropsychology of schizophrenia: Relations with clinical and neurobiological dimensions. *Psychol. Med.* 25:581–594.

ELVEVÅG, B., M. F. EGAN, and T. E. GOLDBERG, 2000a. Memory for temporal order in patients with schizophrenia. *Schizophr. Res.* 46:187–193.

ELVEVÅG, B., M. F. EGAN, and T. E. GOLDBERG, 2000b. Paired-associate learning and memory interference in schizophrenia. *Neuropsychologia* 38:1565–1575.

ELVEVÅG, B., and T. E. GOLDBERG, 1997. Formal thought disorder and semantic memory in schizophrenia. *CNS Spect.* 2(8):15–25.

ELVEVÅG, B., and T. E. GOLDBERG, 2001. Cognitive impairment is the core of the disorder. *Crit. Rev. Neurobiol.* (in press)

ELVEVÅG, B., D. R. WEINBERGER, and T. E. GOLDBERG, 2001. Short-term memory for serial order in schizophrenia: A detailed examination of error types. *Neuropsychology* (in press)

ELVEVÅG, B., D. R. WEINBERGER, J. SUTER, and T. E. GOLDBERG, 2000. Continuous performance test and schizophrenia: A test of stimulus response compatibility, working memory, attention or response readiness? *Am. J. Psychiatry* 157:772–780.

ERLENMEYER-KIMLING, L., B. A. CORNBLATT, D. ROCK, S. ROBERTS, M. BELL, and A. WEST, 1993. The New York high-risk project: Anhedonia, attentional deviance, and psychopathology. *Schizophr. Bull.* 19:141–153.

ERLENMEYER-KIMLING, L., R. R. GOLDEN, and B. A. CORNBLATT, 1989. A taxometric analysis of cognitive and neuromotor variables in children at risk for schizophrenia. *J. Abnorm. Psychol.* 48:203–208.

FAUSTMAN, W. O., J. A. MOSES, and J. B. CSERNANSKY, 1988. Luria-Nebraska performance and symptomatology in unmedicated schizophrenic patients. *Psychiatry Res.* 26:29–34.

FISH, B., 1977. Neurobiologic antecedents of schizophrenia in children. *Arch. Gen. Psychiatry* 34:1297–1313.

FLEMING, K., T. E. GOLDBERG, S. BINKS, C. RANDOLPH, J. M. GOLD, and D. R. WEINBERGER, 1997. Visuospatial working memory in patients with schizophrenia. *Biol. Psychiatry* 41:43–49.

FLEMING, K., T. E. GOLDBERG, J. M. GOLD, and D. R. WEINBERGER, 1995. Verbal working memory dysfunction in schizophrenia: Use of a Brown-Peterson paradigm. *Psychiatry Res.* 56:155–161.

FOLSTEIN, M. F., S. E. FOLSTEIN, and P. R. MCHUGH, 1975. "Mini-mental state." A practical method for grading the cognitive state of patients for the clinician. *J. Psychiatr. Res.* 12:189–198.

FRAY, P. J., T. W. ROBBINS, and B. J. SAHAKIAN, 1996. Neuropsychiatric applications of CANTAB. *Int. J. Geriat. Psychiatry* 11:329–336.

GLAHN, D. C., R. C. GUR, J. D. RAGLAND, D. M. CENSITS, and R. E. GUR, 1997. Reliability, performance characteristics, construct validity, and an initial clinical application of a visual object learning test (VOLT). *Neuropsychology* 11:602–612.

GOLD, J. M., T. A. BLAXTON, B. P. HERMANN, C. RANDOLPH, P. FEDIO, T. E. GOLDBERG, W. H. THEODORE, and D. R. WEINBERGER, 1995. Memory and intelligence in lateralized temporal lobe epilepsy and schizophrenia. *Schizophr. Res.* 17:59–65.

GOLD, J. M., T. E. GOLDBERG, J. E. KLEINMAN, and D. R. WEINBERGER, 1991. The impact of symptomatic state and pharmacological treatment on cognitive functioning of patients with schizophrenia and mood disorders. In *Handbook of Clinical Trials: The Neurobehavioural and Injury Approach*, E. Mohr and P. Brouwers, eds. Amsterdam: Swets and Zeitlinger, pp. 185–214.

GOLD, J. M., B. P. HERMANN, C. RANDOLPH, A. R. WYLER, T. E. GOLDBERG, and D. R. WEINBERGER, 1994. Schizophrenia and temporal lobe epilepsy: A neuropsychological analysis. *Arch. Gen. Psychiatry* 51:265–272.

GOLD, J. M., and S. W. HURT, 1990. The effects of haloperidol on thought disorder and IQ in schizophrenia. *J. Pers. Assess.* 54:390–400.

GOLD, J. M., C. RANDOLPH, C. J. CARPENTER, T. E. GOLDBERG, and D. R. WEINBERGER, 1992. Forms of memory failure in schizophrenia. *J. Abnorm. Psychol.* 101:487–494.

GOLDBERG, T. E., 1999. Some fairly obvious distinctions between schizophrenia and bipolar disorder. *Schizophr. Res.* 39:127–132.

GOLDBERG, T. E., M. S. ALOIA, M. L. GOUROVITCH, D. MISSAR, D. PICKAR, and D. R. WEINBERGER, 1998a. Cognitive substrates of thought disorder, I: The semantic system. *Am. J. Psychiatry* 155:1671–1676.

GOLDBERG, T. E., J. M. GOLD, R. GREENBERG, S. GRIFFIN, S. C. SCHULZ, D. PICKAR, J. E. KLEINMAN, and D. R. WEINBERGER, 1993a. Contrasts between patients with affective disorders and patients with schizophrenia on a neuropsychological test battery. *Am. J. Psychiatry* 150:1355–1362.

GOLDBERG, T. E., R. D. GREENBERG, S. J. GRIFFIN, J. M. GOLD, J. E. KLEINMAN, D. PICKAR, S. C. SCHULZ, and D. R. WEINBERGER, 1993b. The effect of clozapine on cognition and psychiatric symptoms in patients with schizophrenia. *Br. J. Psychiatry* 162:43–48.

GOLDBERG, T. E., T. M. HYDE, J. E. KLEINMAN, and D. R. WEINBERGER, 1993c. Course of schizophrenia: Neuropsychological evidence for a static encephalopathy. *Schizophr. Bull.* 19:797–804.

GOLDBERG, T. E., J. R. KELSOE, D. R. WEINBERGER, N. H. PLISKIN, P. D. KIRWIN, and K. F. BERMAN, 1988. Performance of schizophrenic patients on putative neuropsychological tests of frontal lobe function. *Int. J. Neurosci.* 42:51–58.

GOLDBERG, T. E., K. J. PATTERSON, Y. TAQQU, and K. WILDER, 1998b. Capacity limitations in short-term memory in schizophrenia: Tests of competing hypotheses. *Psychol. Med.* 28:665–673.

GOLDBERG, T. E., D. R. RAGLAND, J. GOLD, L. B. BIGELOW, E. F. TORREY, and D. R. WEINBERGER, 1990. Neuropsychological assessment of monozygotic twins discordant for schizophrenia. *Arch. Gen. Psychiatry* 47:1066–1072.

GOLDBERG, T. E., E. F. TORREY, K. F. BERMAN, and D. R. WEINBERGER, 1994. Relations between neuropsychological performance and brain morphological and physiological measures in monozygotic twins discordant for schizophrenia. *Psychiatry Res.: Neuroimaging* 55:51–61.

GOLDBERG, T. E., E. F. TORREY, J. M. GOLD, L. B. BIGELOW, R. D. RAGLAND, E. TAYLOR, and D. R. WEINBERGER, 1995. Genetic risk of neuropsychological impairment in schizophrenia: A study of monozygotic twins discordant and concordant for the disorder. *Schizophr. Res.* 17:77–84.

GOLDBERG, T. E., E. F. TORREY, J. M. GOLD, J. D. RAGLAND, L. B. BIGELOW, and D. R. WEINBERGER, 1993d. Learning and memory in monozygotic twins discordant for schizophrenia. *Psychol. Med.* 23:71–85.

GOLDBERG, T. E., D. R. WEINBERGER, N. H. PLISKIN, K. F. BERMAN, and M. H. PODD, 1989. Recall memory deficit in schizophrenia. *Schizophr. Res.* 2:251–257.

GOLDMAN-RAKIC, P. S., 1987. Motor control function of the prefrontal cortex. In *Motor Areas of the Cerebral Cortex (Ciba Foundation Symposium 132)*, G. Bock, M. O'Connor, and J. Marsh, eds. Chichester: John Wiley and Sons, pp. 187–200.

GOLDSTEIN, J. M., L. J. SEIDMAN, J. M. GOODMAN, D. KOREN, H. LEE, S. WEINTRAUB, and M. T. TSUANG, 1998. Are there sex differences in neuropsychological function among patients with schizophrenia? *Am. J. Psychiatry* 155:1358–1364.

GOLDSTEIN, G., and J. ZUBIN, 1990. Neuropsychological differences between young and old schizophrenics with and without associated neurological dysfunction. *Schizophr. Res.* 3:117–126.

GOTTESMAN, I. I., 1978. Schizophrenia and genetics: Where are we? Are you sure? In *The Nature of Schizophrenia: New Approaches to Research and Treatment*, L. C. Wynne, R. L., Cromwell, and S. Matthysse, eds. New York: John Wiley and Sons, pp. 59–69.

GOUROVITCH, M. L., E. F. TORREY, J. M. GOLD, C. RANDOLPH, D. R. WEINBERGER, and T. E. GOLDBERG, 1999. Neuropsychological performance of monozygotic twins discordant for bipolar disorder. *Biol. Psychiatry* 45:639–646.

GRANT, D. A., and E. A. BERGER, 1948. A behavioral analysis of degree of reinforcement and ease of shifting to new responses in a Weigl type card sorting problem. *J. Exp. Psychol.* 38:404–411.

GREEN, M. F., 1996. What are the functional consequences of neurocognitive deficits in schizophrenia? *Am. J. Psychiatry* 153:321–330.

GUR, R. E., P. COWELL, B. I. TURETSKY, F. GALLACHER, T. CANNON, W. BILKER, and R. C. GUR, 1998. A follow-up magnetic resonance imaging study of schizophrenia: Relationship of neuroanatomical changes to clinical and neurobehavioral measures. *Arch. Gen. Psychiatry* 55:145–152.

GUTTMAN, E., 1936. On some constitutional aspects of chorea and on its sequelae. *J. Neurol. Psychopathol.* 17:16–26.

HARVEY, P. D., E. HOWANITZ, M. PARRELLA, L. WHITE, M. DAVIDSON, R. C. MOHS, J. HOBLYN, and K. L. DAVIS, 1998. Symptoms, cognitive functioning, and adaptive skills in geriatric patients with lifelong schizophrenia: A comparison across treatment sites. *Am. J. Psychiatry* 155:1080–1086.

HARVEY, P. D., M. PARRELLA, L. WHITE, R. C. MOH, M. DAVIDSON, and K. L. DAVIS, 1999. Convergence of cognitive and adaptive decline in late-life schizophrenia. *Schizophr. Res.* 35:77–84.

HEATON, R., J. S. PAULSEN, L. A. MCADAMS, J. KUCK, S. ZISOOK, D. BRAFF, J. HARRIS, and D. V. JESTE, 1994. Neuropsychological deficits in schizophrenics: Relationship to age, chronicity, and dementia. *Arch. Gen. Psychiatry* 51:469–476.

HEATON, R. K., L. E. BAADE, and K. L. JOHNSON, 1978. Neuropsychological test results associated with psychiatric disorders in adults. *Psychol. Bull.* 85:141–162.

HEATON, R. K., and M. G. PENDLETON, 1981. Use of neuropsychological tests to predict adult patients' everyday functioning. *J. Consult. Clin. Psychol.* 49:807–821.

HODGES, J. R., K. PATTERSON, S. OXBURY, and E. FUNNELL, 1992. Semantic dementia: Progressive fluent aphasia with temporal lobe atrophy. *Brain* 115:1783–1806.

HODGES, J. R., K. PATTERSON, and L. K. TYLER, 1994. Loss of semantic memory: Implications for the modularity of mind. *Cogn. Neuropsychol.* 11:505–542.

HOFF, A. L., H. RIORDAN, D. W. O'DONNELL, L. MORRIS, and L. E. DELISI, 1992. Neuropsychological functioning of first-episode schizophreniform patients. *Am. J. Psychiatry* 149:898–903.

HOFF, A. L., M. WEINEKE, W. O. FAUSTMAN, R. HORON, M. SAKUMA, H. BLANKFELD, S. EPINOZA, and L. E. DELISI, 1998. Sex differences in neuropsychological functioning of first-episode and chronically ill schizophrenic patients. *Am. J. Psychiatry* 155:1437–1439.

HOLLANDER, E., L. COHEN, M. RICHARDS, L. MULLEN, C. DECARLA, and Y. STERN, 1993. A pilot study of the neuropsychology of obsessive-compulsive disorder and Parkinson's disease: Basal ganglia disorders. *J. Neuropsychiatry Clin. Neurosci.* 5:104–107.

HOUX, P. J., and J. JOLLES, 1993. Age-related decline of psychomotor speed: Effects of age, brain health, sex and education. *Percept. Motor Skills* 76:195–211.

HUGG, J. W., R. I. KUZNIECKY, F. G. GILLIAM, R. B. MORAWETZ, R. E. FRAUGHT, and H. P. HETHERINGTON, 1996. Normalization of contralateral metabolic function following temporal lobectomy demonstrated by $^1$H magnetic resonance spectroscopic imaging. *Ann. Neurol.* 40:236–239.

HUTTON, S. B., B. K. PURI, L. J. DUNCAN, T. W. ROBBINS, T. R. BARNES, and E. M. JOYCE, 1998. Executive function in first-episode schizophrenia. *Psychol. Med.* 28:463–473.

HYDE, T. M., S. NAWROZ, T. E. GOLDBERG, L. B. BIGELOW, D. STRONG, J. L. OSTREM, D. R. WEINBERGER, and J. E. KLEINMAN, 1994. Is there a cognitive decline in schizophrenia? A cross-sectional study. *Br. J. Psychiatry* 164:494–500.

HYDE, T. M., J. C. ZIEGLER, and D. R. WEINBERGER, 1992. Psychiatric disturbances in metachromatic leukodystrophy: Insights into the neurobiology of psychosis. *Arch. Neurol.* 49:401–406.

ILLOWSKY, B. P., D. M. JULIANO, L. B. BIGELOW, and D. R. WEINBERGER, 1988. Stability of CT scan findings in schizophrenia: Results of an eight-year follow-up study. *J. Neurol. Neurosurg. Psychiatry* 51:209–213.

JASKIW, G. E., D. M. JULIANO, T. E. GOLDBERG, M. HERTZMAN, E. UROW-HAMELL, and D. R. WEINBERGER, 1994. Cerebral ventricular enlargement in schizophreniform disorder does not progress: A seven-year follow-up study. *Schizophr. Res.* 14:23–28.

JASTAK, S., and G. S. WILKINSON, 1984. *The Wide Range Achievement Test—Revised Administration Manual.* Wilmington, Del.: Jastak Assoc., Inc.

JOHNSTONE, B., M. K. CHILDERS, and J. HOERNER, 1998. The effects of normal aging on neuropsychological functioning following traumatic brain injury. *Brain Inj.* 12:569–576.

JONES, P., B. RODGERS, R. MURRAY, and M. MARMOT, 1994. Child developmental risk factors for adult schizophrenia in the British 1946 birth cohort. *Lancet* 344:1398–1402.

JONSSON, H., and A. K. NYMAN, 1991. Predicting long-term outcome in schizophrenia. *Acta Psychiatr. Scand.* 83:342–346.

KARATEKIN, C., and R. F. ASARNOW, 1998a. Components of visual search in childhood-onset schizophrenia and attention-deficit/hyperactivity disorder. *J. Abnorm. Child Psychol.* 26:367–380.

KARATEKIN, C., and R. F. ASARNOW, 1998b. Working memory in childhood-onset schizophrenia and attention-deficit/hyperactivity disorder. *Psychiatry Res.* 80:165–176.

KAUFMAN, A. S., 1990. *Assessing Adolescent and Adult Intelligence.* Needham, Mass.: Allyn & Bacon.

KEEFE, R. S., J. M. SILVERMAN, S. E. ROITMAN, P. D. HARVEY, M. A. DUNCAN, D. ALROY, L. J. SIEVER, K. L. DAVIS, and R. C. MOHS, 1994. Performance of nonpsychotic relatives of schizophrenic patients on cognitive tests. *Psychiatry Res.* 53:1–12.

KEEFE, R. S., S. E. LEES-ROITMAN, and R. L. DUPRE, 1997a. Performance of patients with schizophrenia on a pen and paper visuospatial working memory task with short delay. *Schizophr. Res.* 26:9–14.

KEEFE, R. S., S. E. ROITMAN, P. D. HARVEY, C. S. BLUM, R. L. DUPRE, D. M. PRIETO, M. DAVIDSON, and K. L. DAVIS, 1995. A pen-and-paper human analogue of a monkey prefrontal cortex activation task: Spatial working memory in patients with schizophrenia. *Schizophr. Res.* 17:25–33.

KEEFE, R. S., J. M. SILVERMAN, R. C. MOHS, L. J. SIEVER, P. D. HARVEY, L. FRIEDMAN, S. E. ROITMAN, R. L. DUPRE, C. J. SMITH, J. SCHMEIDLER, and K. L. DAVIS, 1997b. Eye tracking, attention, and schizotypal symptoms in nonpsychotic relatives of patients with schizophrenia. *Arch. Gen. Psychiatry* 54:169–176.

KLONOFF, H., G. H. HUTTON, and C. H. FIBIGER, 1970. Neuropsychological patterns in chronic schizophrenia. *J. Nerv. Ment. Dis.* 150:291–300.

KOH, S. D., 1978. Remembering of verbal material by schizophrenic young adults. In *Language and Cognition in Schizophrenia,* S. Schwartz, ed. Englewood Cliffs, N.J.: Lawrence Erlbaum, pp. 555–599.

KRAEPELIN, E., 1919. *Dementia Praecox and Paraphrenia.* G. M. Robertson, ed. [translated by R. M. Barclay, 1971]. Huntington, NY: Robert E. Krieger.

KULYNYCH, J. J., K. VLADAR, D. W. JONES, and D. R. WEINBERGER, 1996. Superior temporal gyrus volume in schizophrenia: A study using MRI morphometry assisted by surface rendering. *Am. J. Psychiatry* 153:50–56.

LANDRØ, N. I., A. L. ØRBECK, and B. R. RUND, 1993. Memory functioning in chronic and non-chronic schizophrenics, affectively disturbed patients and normal controls. *Schizophr. Res.* 10:85–92.

LAWSON, W. B., I. N. WALDMAN, and D. R. WEINBERGER, 1988. Schizophrenia dementia: Clinical and computed axial tomography correlates. *J. Nerv. Ment. Dis.* 176:207–212.

LENZENWEGER, M. F., B. A. CORNBLATT, and M. PUTNICK, 1991. Schizotypy and sustained attention. *J. Abnorm. Psychol.* 100:84–89.

LEVINE, J. B., S. A. GRUBER, A. A. BAIRD, and D. YURGELUN-TODD, 1998. Obsessive-compulsive disorder among schizophrenic patients: An exploratory study using functional magnetic resonance imaging data. *Compr. Psychiatry* 39:308–311.

LIPSKA, B. K., G. E. JASKIW, and D. R. WEINBERGER, 1993. Postpubertal emergence of hyperresponsiveness to stress and to amphetamine after neonatal excitotoxic hippocampal damage: A potential animal model of schizophrenia. *Neuropsychopharmacology* 9:67–75.

LIPSKA, B. K., and D. R. WEINBERGER, 1993a. Delayed behavioral disturbances associated with neonatal excitotoxic hippocampal damage in the rat: Effects of castration and neuroleptics. *Soc. Neurosci. Abstr.* 19:587.

LIPSKA, B. K., and D. R. WEINBERGER, 1993b. Delayed effects of neonatal hippocampal damage on haloperidol-induced catalepsy and apomorphine-induced stereotypic behaviors in the rat. *Dev. Brain Res.* 75:213–222.

LIPSKA, B. K., and D. R. WEINBERGER, 1995. Genetic variation in vulnerability to the behavioral effects of neonatal hippocampal damage in rats. *Proc. Natl. Acad. Sci. USA* 92:8906–8910.

LIPSKA, B. K., and D. R. WEINBERGER, 1996. Hippocampal damage in the neonatal rat as a model of some aspects of schizophrenia. In *The Hippocampus: Functions and Clinical Relevance*, N. Kato, ed. Amsterdam: Elsevier Science.

MAIER, M., M. A. RON, G. J. BARKER, and P. S. TOFTS, 1995. Proton magnetic spectroscopy: An *in vivo* method of estimating hippocampal neuronal depletion in schizophrenia. *Psychol. Med.* 25:1201–1209.

MALMBERG, A., G. LEWIS, A. DAVID, and P. ALLEBECK, 1998. Premorbid adjustment and personality in people with schizophrenia. *Br. J. Psychiatry* 172:308–313.

MANSCHRECK, T. C., B. A. MAHER, J. J. MILAVETZ, D. AMES, C. C. WEISSTEIN, and M. L. SCHNEYER, 1988. Semantic priming in thought disordered schizophrenic patients. *Schizophr. Res.* 1:61–66.

MARNEROS, A., A. ROHDE, and A. DEISTER, 1995. Validity of the negative/positive dichotomy of schizophrenic disorders under long-term conditions. *Psychopathology* 28:2–37.

MARNEROS, A., A. ROHDE, and A. DEISTER, 1998. Frequency and phenomenology of persisting alterations in affective, schizoaffective and schizophrenic disorders: A comparison. *Psychopathology* 31:23–28.

MASON, P., G. HARRISON, C. GLAZEBROOK, I. MEDLEY, and T. CROUDACE, 1996. The course of schizophrenia over 13 years: A report from the International Study on Schizophrenia (ISoS) coordinated by the World Health Organization. *Br. J. Psychiatry* 169:580–586.

MCCLAIN, L., 1983. Encoding and retrieval in schizophrenics' free recall. *J. Nerv. Ment. Dis.* 171:471–479.

MEDALIA, A., J. M. GOLD, and A. MERRIAM, 1988. The effects of neuroleptics on neuropsychological test results of schizophrenics. *Arch. Clin. Neuropsychology* 3:249–271.

MILLER, R., 1989. Schizophrenia as a progressive disorder: Relations to EEG, CT, neuropathological and other evidence. *Prog. Neurobiol.* 33:17–44.

MILNER, B., 1963. Effects of different brain lesions on card sorting: The role of the frontal lobes. *Arch. Neurol.* 9:100–110.

MISSAR, C. D., J. M. GOLD, and T. E. GOLDBERG, 1994. WAIS-R short forms in chronic schizophrenia. *Schizophr. Res.* 12:247–250.

MOCKLER, D., J. RIORDAN, and T. SHARMA, 1997. Memory and intellectual deficits do not decline with age in schizophrenia. *Schizophr. Res.* 26:1–7.

MUNGAS, D., 1983. Differential clinical sensitivity of specific parameters of the Rey auditory-verbal learning test. *J. Consult. Clin. Psychol.* 51:848–855.

MURRAY, R. M., and S. W. LEWIS, 1987. Is schizophrenia a neurodevelopmental disorder? *Br. Med. J.* 295:681–682.

NASRALLAH, H. A., T. E. SKINNER, P. SCHMALBROCK, and P. M. ROBITAILLE, 1994. Proton magnetic resonance spectroscopy (¹H MRS) of the hippocampal formation in schizophrenia: A pilot study. *Br. J. Psychiatry* 165:481–485.

NELSON, M. D., A. J. SAYKIN, L. A. FLASHMAN, and H. J. RIORDAN, 1998. Hippocampal volume reduction in schizophrenia as assessed by magnetic resonance imaging: A meta-analytic study. *Arch. Gen. Psychiatry* 55:433–440.

NEWNAN, O. S., R. K. HEATON, and R. A. W. LEHMAN, 1978. Neuropsychological and MMPI correlates of patients' future employment characteristics. *Percept. Motor Skills* 46:635–642.

NUECHTERLEIN, K. H., 1983. Signal detection in vigilance tasks and behavioral attributes among offspring of schizophrenic mothers and among hyperactive children. *J. Abnorm. Psychol.* 92:4–28.

NUECHTERLEIN, K. H., M. E. DAWSON, J. VENTURA, D. MIKLOWITZ, and G. KONISHI, 1991. Information processing anomalies in the early course of schizophrenia and bipolar disorder. *Schizophr. Res.* 5:195–196.

OBER, B. A., S. VINOGRADOV, and G. K. SHENAUT, 1995. Semantic priming of category relations in schizophrenia. *Neuropsychology* 9:220–228.

ØIE, M., and B. R. RUND, 1999. Neuropsychological deficits in adolescent-onset schizophrenia compared with attention deficit hyperactivity disorder. *Am. J. Psychiatry* 156:1216–1222.

ØIE, M., B. R. RUND, and K. SUNDET, 1998. Covert visual attention in patients with early-onset schizophrenia. *Schizophr. Res.* 34:195–205.

OVERTOOM, C. C., M. N. VERBATEN, C. KEMNER, J. L. KENEMANS, H. VAN ENGELAND, J. K. BUITERLAAR, G. CAMFFERMAN, and H. S. KOELEGA, 1998. Associations between event-related potentials and measures of attention and inhibition in the continuous performance task in children with ADHD and normal controls. *J. Am. Acad. Child Adolesc. Psychiatry* 37:977–985.

OWEN, A. M., A. C. ROBERTS, C. E. POLKEY, B. J. SAHAKIAN, and T. W. ROBBINS, 1991. Extra-dimensional versus intra-dimensional set shifting performance following frontal lobe excisions, temporal lobe excisions or amygdalo-hippocampectomy in man. *Neuropsychologia* 29:993–1006.

PARK, S., P. S. HOLZMAN, and P. S. GOLDMAN-RAKIC, 1995. Spatial working memory deficits in the relatives of schizophrenic patients. *Arch. Gen. Psychiatry* 52:821–828.

PAULSEN, J. S., R. K. HEATON, J. R. SADEK, W. PERRY, D. C. DELIS, D. BRAFF, J. KUCK, S. ZISOOK, and D. V. JESTE, 1995. The nature of learning and memory impairments in schizophrenia. *J. Int. Neuropsychol. Soc.* 1:88–99.

PERLICK, D., S. MATTIS, P. STASTNY, and J. TERESI, 1992. Neuropsychological discriminators of long-term inpatients or outpatients in chronic schizophrenia. *J. Neuropsychiatric Clin. Neurosci.* 4:428–434.

POSNER, M. I., and S. E. PETERSON, 1990. The attention system of the human brain. *Annu. Rev. Neurosci.* 13:25–42.

PURCELL, R., P. MARUFF, M. KYRIOS, and C. PANTELIS, 1998. Cognitive deficits in obsessive-compulsive disorder on tests of frontal-striatal function. *Biol. Psychiatry* 43:348–357.

RANGO, M., D. SPAGNOLI, G. TOMEI, F. BAMONTI, G. SCARLATO, and L. ZETTA, 1995. Central nervous system transsynaptic effects of acute axonal injury: A ¹H magnetic resonance spectroscopy study. *Magn. Reson. Med.* 33:595–600.

RAUCH, S. L., C. R. SAVAGE, N. M. ALPERT, D. DOUGHERTY, A. KENDRICK, T. CURRAN, H. D. BROWN, P. MANZO, A. J. FISCHMAN, and M. A. JENIKE, 1997. Probing striatal function in obsessive-compulsive disorder: A PET study of implicit sequence learning. *J. Neuropsychiatry Clin. Neurosci.* 9:568–573.

REITER, P. J., 1926. Extrapyramidal motor disturbances in dementia praecox. *Acta Psychiatr. Neurol. Scand.* 1:287–309.

RITCHIE, K., J. TOUCHON, B. LEDESERT, D. LEIBOVICI, and A. M. GORCE, 1997. Establishing the limits and characteristics of normal age-related cognitive decline. *Rev. Epidemiol. Sante Publique* 45:373–381.

ROITMAN, S. E., B. A. CORNBLATT, A. BERGMAN, M. OBUCHOWSKI, V. MITROPOULOU, R. S. KEEFE, J. M. SILVERMAN, and L. J. SIEVER, 1997. Attentional functioning in schizotypal personality disorder. *Am. J. Psychiatry* 154:655–660.

RUBIN, Y., M. C. LAPLACA, D. H. SMITH, L. E. THIBAULT, and R. E. LENKINSKI, 1995. The effect of *N*-acetyl-aspartate on the intracellular calcium concentration in NTera2-neurons. *Neurosci. Lett.* 198:209–212.

RUND, B. R., 1998. A review of longitudinal studies of cognitive functions in schizophrenia patients. *Schizophr. Bull.* 24:425–435.

RUND, B. R., M. ØIE, and K. SUNDET, 1996. Backward-masking deficit in adolescents with schizophrenic disorders or attention deficit hyperactivity disorder. *Am. J. Psychiatry* 153:1154–1157.

RUND, B. R., P. ZEINER, K. SUNDET, M. ØIE, and G. BRYHN, 1998. No vigilance deficit found in either young schizophrenic or ADHD subjects. *Scand. J. Psychol.* 39:101–107.

RUSSELL, A. J., J. C. MUNRO, P. B. JONES, D. R. HEMSLEY, and R. M. MURRAY, 1997. Schizophrenia and the myth of intellectual decline. *Am. J. Psychiatry* 154:635–639.

SAUNDERS, R. C., B. S. KOLACHANA, J. BACHEVALIER, and D. R. WEINBERGER, 1998. Neonatal lesions of the medial temporal lobe disrupts prefrontal cortical regulation of striatal dopamine. *Nature* 393:169–171.

SAYKIN, A. J., R. C. GUR, R. E. GUR, P. D. MOZLEY, L. H. MOZLEY, S. M. RESNICK, D. B. KESTER, and P. STAFINIAK, 1991. Neuropsychological function in schizophrenia: Selective impairment in memory and learning. *Arch. Gen. Psychiatry* 48:618–624.

SAYKIN, A. J., D. L. SHTASEL, R. E. GUR, D. B. KESTER, L. H. MOZLEY, P. STAFINIAK, and R. C. GUR, 1994. Neuropsychological deficits in neuroleptic naïve patients with first episode schizophrenia. *Arch. Gen. Psychiatry* 51:124–131.

SCHMIDTKE, K., A. SCHORB, G. WINKELMANN, and F. HOHAGEN, 1998. Cognitive frontal lobe dysfunction in obsessive-compulsive disorder. *Biol. Psychiatry* 43:666–673.

SEIDMAN, L. J., D. YURGELUN-TODD, W. S. KREMEN, B. T. WOODS, J. M. GOLDSTEIN, S. V. FARAONE, and M. T. TSUANG, 1994. Relationship of prefrontal and temporal lobe MRI measures to neuropsychological performance in chronic schizophrenia. *Biol. Psychiatry* 35:235–246.

SHAKOW, D., 1962. Segmental set: A theory of the formal psychological deficit in schizophrenia. *Arch. Gen. Psychiatry* 6:17–33.

SHENTON, M. E., R. KIKINIS, F. A. JOLESZ, S. D. POLLAK, M. LEMAY, C. G. WIBLE, H. HOKAMA, J. MARTIN, D. METCALF, M. COLEMAN, and R. W. MCCARLEY, 1992. Abnormalities of the left temporal lobe and thought disorder in schizophrenia: A quantitative magnetic resonance imaging study. *N. Engl. J. Med.* 327:604–612.

SIEVER, L. J., and R. D. COURSEY, 1985. Biological markers for schizophrenia and the biological high-risk approach. *J. Nerv. Ment Dis.* 173:4–16.

SMITH, A., 1964. Mental deterioration in chronic schizophrenia. *J. Nerv. Ment. Dis.* 39:479–487.

SQUIRE, L. R., 1992. Memory and the hippocampus: A synthesis from findings with rats, monkeys, and humans. *Psychol. Rev.* 99:195–231.

STERNOKO, R. J., and D. J. WOODS, 1978. Impairment in early stages of visual information processing in nonpsychotic schizotypal individuals. *J. Abnorm. Psychol.* 87:481–490.

SULLIVAN, E. V., P. K. SHEAR, R. B. ZIPURSKY, H. J. SAGAR, and A. PFEFFERBAUM, 1994. A deficit profile of executive, memory and motor functions in schizophrenia. *Biol. Psychiatry* 36:641–653.

SWEENEY, J. A., G. L. HAAS, J. G. KEILP, and M. LONG, 1991. Evaluation of the stability of neuropsychological functioning after acute episodes of schizophrenia: One-year follow-up study. *Psychiatry Res.* 38:63–76.

TALLIS, F., 1997. The neuropsychology of obsessive-compulsive disorder: Review and considerations of clinical implications. *Br. J. Clin. Psychol.* 36:3–20.

TAMYLN, D., P. J. MCKENNA, A. M. MORTIMER, C. E. LUND, S. HAMMOND, and A. D. BADDELEY, 1992. Memory impairment in schizophrenia: Its extent, affiliations and neuropsychological character. *Psychol. Med.* 22:101–115.

TIBBO, P., and L. WARNEKE, 1999. Obsessive-compulsive disorder in schizophrenia: Epidemiologic and biologic overlap. *J. Psychiatry Neurosci.* 24:15–24.

TORRES, I. J., L. A. FLASHMAN, D. S. O'LEARY, V. SWAYZE, and N. C. ANDREASEN, 1997. Lack of an association between delayed memory and hippocampal and temporal lobe size in patients with schizophrenia and healthy controls. *Biol. Psychiatry* 42:1087–1096.

TRAUPMANN, K. L., 1980. Encoding processes and memory for categorically related words by schizophrenic patients. *J. Abnorm. Psychol.* 89:704–716.

TRESTMAN, R. L., R. S. KEEFE, V. MITROPOULOU, P. D. HARVEY, M. L. deVEGVAR, S. LEES-ROITMAN, M. DAVIDSON, A. ARONSON, J. SILVERMAN, and L. J. SIEVER, 1995. Cognitive function and biological correlates of cognitive performance in schizotypal personality disorder. *Psychiatry Res.* 59:127–136.

VELLIGAN, D. I., R. K. MAHURIN, P. L. DIAMOND, B. C. HAZLETIN, S. L. ECKERT, and A. L. MILLER, 1997. The functional significance of symptomatology and cognitive function in schizophrenia. *Schizophr. Res.* 25:21–31.

VION-DURY, J., A. M. SALVAN, S. CONFORT-GOUNY, C. DHIVER, and P. COZZONE, 1995. Reversal of brain metabolic alterations with zidovudine detected by proton localised magnetic resonance spectroscopy. *Lancet* 345:60–61.

WALKER, E., and R. J. LEWINE, 1990. Prediction of adult-onset schizophrenia from childhood home movies of the patients. *Am. J. Psychiatry* 147:1052–1056.

WALKER, E., T. SAVOIE, and D. DAVIS, 1994. Neuromotor precursors of schizophrenia. *Schizophr. Bull.* 20:441–451.

WARRINGTON, E. K., 1975. The selective impairment of semantic memory. *Quart. J. Exp. Psychol.* 27:187–199.

WECHSLER, D., 1981. *Wechsler Adult Intelligence Scale—Revised.* San Antonio: Psychological Corporation.

WEICKERT, T. W., T. E. GOLDBERG, J. M. GOLD, L. B. BIGELOW, M. F. EGAN, and D. R. WEINBERGER, 2000. Cognitive impairments in patients with schizophrenia displaying preserved and compromised intellect. *Arch. Gen. Psychiatry* 57:907–913.

WEINBERGER, D. R., 1987. Implications of normal brain development for the pathogenesis of schizophrenia. *Arch. Gen. Psychiatry* 44:660–669.

WEINBERGER, D. R., 1999. Cell biology of the hippocampal formation in schizophrenia. *Biol. Psychiatry* 45:395–402.

WEINBERGER, D. R., and K. F. BERMAN, 1996. Prefrontal function in schizophrenia: Confounds and controversies. *Phil. Trans. R. Soc. Lond. [B]* 351:1495–1503.

WEINBERGER, D. R., and B. K. LIPSKA, 1995. Cortical maldevelopment, anti-psychotic drugs, and schizophrenia: A search for common ground. *Schizophr. Res.* 16:87–110.

WEINGARTNER, H., R. M. COHEN, D. L. MURPHY, J. MARTELLO, and C. GERDT, 1981. Cognitive processes in depression. *Arch. Gen. Psychiatry* 38:42–47.

ZIHL, J., G. GRÖN, and A. BRUNNAUER, 1998. Cognitive deficits in schizophrenia and affective disorders: Evidence for a final common pathway disorder. *Acta Psychiatr. Scand.* 97:351–357.

# VIII

# EMOTION AND
# COGNITION
# INTERACTIONS

# 38 Toward a Neurobiology of Attachment

MYRON A. HOFER
AND REGINA M. SULLIVAN

ABSTRACT  New laboratory research has begun to reveal a network of simple behavioral, physiological, and neural processes that underlie the psychological constructs of attachment theory. It has become apparent that the unique features of early infant attachment reflect certain unique features of early infant sensory and motor integration, early learning, communication, motivation, and the regulation of biobehavioral systems by the mother–infant interaction. This chapter is organized around the three major questions that gave rise to the concept of attachment: How does the infant find its own mother and stay close to her? Why does separation of the infant from its mother produce such severe physiologic and behavioral responses? How can individual differences in adult offspring and especially in their maternal behavior be related to the patterns of their early life with their parents? In each of these cases, we review the recent research that has given us new answers to these questions at the level of early behavioral and cognitive processes and their neurobiological substrates. Attachment remains useful as a concept, like hunger, that describes the output of subprocesses that work together within the frame of a vital biological function.

The word attachment has come to refer to a broad range of behavioral processes and mental states unified by a single central concept. Attachment theory envisages a unique motivational system with evolutionary survival value, on a par with hunger and sex, that is organized to maintain physical proximity to the mother/caretaker soon after birth and psychological proximity, or closeness, later in development (Bowlby, 1969). The special qualities of this bond reflect the nature of the infant's and the caretaker's mental representations of the behavioral dynamics and patterns of their many previous interactions. Much current research is concerned with identifying developmental continuities between individual differences in the patterns of parent–infant attachment and the later cognitive and emotional characteristics of the child and adult. In an extension of these longitudinal correla-

tions, there is evidence that attachment experiences in infancy strongly affect characteristics of the attachment pattern of the mother with her infant in the next generation. Several extensive reviews of this field have recently been published, covering human and nonhuman primate research (Cassidy and Shaver, 1999; Goldberg, Muir, and Kerr, 1995; Suomi, 1997) and the growing field of neurobiological studies (Carter, Lederhandler, and Kirkpatrick, 1997; Insel, 1992; Kraemer, 1992; Wilson and Sullivan, 1994).

It is curious that most of the research on attachment subsequent to Bowlby's landmark volume defining the field (Bowlby, 1969) has focused on the different patterns of early attachment and their later developmental correlates, leaving far less studied the developmental processes through which attachment is initially formed in altricial (slow-developing) mammals and the behavioral mechanisms underlying the dramatic responses of infants to separation. Meanwhile, others interested in processes underlying the early development of motor and sensory systems, perception, attention, learning, memory, communication, motivation, and emotion have developed new methods (Shair, Barr, and Hofer, 1991) and a knowledge base in each of these areas (Michel and Moore, 1995) without relation to the concept of attachment or its field of research. To these researchers, the range of associated phenomena did not appear to function as a unitary system and attachment concepts were too global to generate incisive research questions that could lead to a deeper understanding of the phenomena described.

Now that a knowledge base has been established in the various research areas just described, at least for one mammalian species, the laboratory rat, we can revisit the basic observations on which attachment theory is based, and describe some of the underlying processes responsible for them in terms that can be related to neural structure and function. When one does this, it becomes apparent that the unique features of early attachment phenomena can be shown to be the result of certain unique features of early sensory and motor

MYRON A. HOFER  Department of Developmental Psychobiology, New York State Psychiatric Institute; Department of Psychiatry, Columbia University, New York, New York.
REGINA M. SULLIVAN  Department of Zoology, University of Oklahoma, Norman, Oklahoma.

integration, of early learning, communication, motivation, and the regulation of biological and behavioral systems by the mother–infant interaction. The apparently unified nature of attachment and its function as a system are the result of the fact that for the mammalian fetus and infant, the entire environment virtually begins and ends within the confines of a unified source of stimulation, the mother. Thus attachment, like hunger, is made up of a number of subprocesses, and exists as a useful concept because it describes the output of these subprocesses as they work together within the larger scale arena of social relationships.

The observations that attachment theory was formulated to explain are used to organize this chapter. In each case, we describe recent evidence for the behavioral and physiological processes that underlie the concepts of attachment theory and relate these to the neural processes found to be responsible in laboratory studies thus far. Because we know a great deal less about the neurobiological mechanisms than about the cognitive and emotional processes, our aim is to suggest where neurobiological research methods can be used to explore this new research field.

Three major questions are raised by the basic observations that led to the field of attachment research. First, how does the infant come to know and prefer its own mother, maintain proximity with her, and continue to do so, even despite abuse and neglect at her hands? Second, why does separation from the mother produce such intense and widespread emotional responses in the infant? Third, how do individual differences arise in the characteristic patterns or qualities of the mother–infant interaction and how do these early interactions become translated into long-term effects on infant development and ultimately into similar maternal behavior in the next generation? We focus on those areas in which we have the most detailed knowledge of the underlying cognitive and neurobiological processes involved, work almost exclusively done with laboratory rats. However, we relate these to the human wherever possible. We describe in some detail the rapid and highly specific early olfactory learning processes recently discovered in infant rats and their neural substrates. This phenomenon appears to represent an altricial mammalian counterpart of avian imprinting, and some recent evidence suggesting a similar process at work in newborn babies is described.

## Initial formation of a specific attachment

Infants of mammalian species that are born in an immature state, such as the human and the laboratory rat, face a daunting cognitive task. They must eventually learn to identify, remember, and prefer their own mother; and they must learn to use these new cognitive capacities to reorganize their simple motor repertoires, long adapted to the uterine environment, so as to be able to approach, remain close, and orient themselves to their mothers for the first nursing bout. It has been assumed until recently that these processes were well beyond the capacities of newborn mammals (except in precocial species such as the sheep) and that the relationship initially depended almost entirely upon maternal behavior until well into the nursing period (Bowlby, 1982; Kraemer, 1992). Attachment has thus been supposed to be built up slowly in the weeks or days after birth in human or rat. But the last decade has produced a number of studies revealing earlier and earlier evidence of learning, even extending into the prenatal period. In addition, coordinated motor acts have been demonstrated in fetuses in response to specific stimuli that will not be encountered until after birth. Thus the solutions for the infant's cognitive tasks appear to be found much earlier than previously thought and to take place through novel developmental processes that had not been imagined until recently.

PRENATAL ORIGINS The first strong evidence for fetal learning came from studies on early voice recognition in humans, in which it was found that babies recognize and prefer their own mother's voice, even when tested within hours after birth (de Casper and Fifer, 1980). Bill Fifer continued these studies in our department using an ingenious device through which newborns can choose between two tape-recorded voices by sucking at different rates on a pacifier rigged to control an audio tape player (reviewed in Fifer and Moon, 1995). He has found that newborn infants, in the first hours after birth, prefer human voices to silence, female voices to male voices, their native language to another language, and their own mother to another mother reading the same Dr. Seuss story. In order to obtain more direct evidence for the prenatal origins of these preferences (rather than very rapid postnatal learning), Fifer filtered the high-frequency components from the tapes to make the mother's voice resemble recordings of maternal voice by hydrophone placed within the amniotic space of pregnant women. This altered recording, in which the words were virtually unrecognizable to adults, was preferred to the standard mothers' voice by newborns in the first hours after birth, a preference that tended to wane in the second and third postnatal days. Furthermore, there is now evidence that newborns prefer familiar rhythmic phrase sequences to which they have been repeatedly exposed prenatally (DeCasper and Spence, 1986).

In a striking interspecies similarity, rat pups were subsequently shown to discriminate and prefer their own dams' amniotic fluid in preference to that of another dam when offered a choice in a head-turning task (Hepper, 1987). Newborn pups were also shown to require amniotic fluid on a teat in order to find and attach to it for their first nursing attempt (Blass, 1990). Robinson and Smotherman (1995) have directly tested the hypothesis that pups begin to learn about their mothers' scent in utero. They have been able to demonstrate one-trial taste aversion learning and classical conditioning in late-term rat fetuses, using intraoral cannula infusions and perioral stimulation. Taste aversions learned in utero were expressed in the free feeding responses of weanling rats nearly 3 weeks later. They went on to determine that aversive responses to vibrissa stimulation were attenuated or blocked by intraoral milk infusion, a prenatal "comfort" effect they found to be mediated by a central kappa-opioid receptor system. Interestingly, when artificial nipple stimulation was presented as a predictive cue (CS) for intraoral milk in a learning paradigm, and a reduction in fetal responsiveness to the CS was acquired in this way, the conditioned response was blocked by a mu-opioid antagonist rather than a kappa antagonist. This suggests an important role for the opioid system in the organization of fetal behavior by redirecting and focusing responsiveness to a subset of available stimuli (Robinson and Smotherman, 1995).

These forms of fetal learning involving maternal voice in humans and amniotic fluid in rodents appear to play an adaptive role in preparing the infant for its first extrauterine encounter with its mother. They are thus the earliest origins yet found for attachment to the mother.

THE PERINATAL TRANSITION In addition to the evidence for fetal learning just described, specific adaptive motor response capabilities have also been found in later term rat fetuses using an exteriorized in vivo preparation (Smotherman and Robinson, 1992). The reflexes of licking, mouthing, and sucking necessary for postnatal nipple grasp and nursing can be elicited in late-term fetuses, as can the characteristic stretch response to oral milk and the facial wiping (rejection) response to unfamiliar tastes that are usually associated with rat pups tested several days postnatally. The emergence of these reflex responses in anticipation of the postnatal environment in which they will be expressed provides the newborn with the components needed for the transition to postnatal life and for the rapid organization of an integrated response repertoire tuned to specific characteristics of the maternal body.

The spontaneous motor acts needed for an attachment system also appear to be developing prior to birth. Rat fetuses engage in a number of spontaneous behaviors in utero, including curls, stretches, and trunk and limb movements. These acts were observed to increase markedly in frequency with progressive removal of intrauterine space constraints, as pups were observed first through the uterine wall, then through the thin amniotic sac, and finally unrestrained in a warm saline bath (Smotherman and Robinson, 1986). When newborn pups are observed prior to their first nursing bout, they resemble exteriorized fetuses until the mother lowers her ventrum over them. Their behavior then changes rapidly over the first few nursing bouts, into the complex repertoire described below.

AN ATTACHMENT SYSTEM IN THE NEWBORN When pups less than a day old are stimulated gently by soft surfaces from above, as when the mother hovers over them, they show a surprisingly vigorous repertoire of behaviors (Polan and Hofer, 1999a). These include the curling and stretching seen prenatally, but now also include locomotor movement toward the suspended surface, directed wriggling, audible vocalizations, and, most strikingly, turning upside down toward the surface above them. Evidently, these behaviors propel the pup into close contact with the ventrum, maintain it in proximity, and keep it oriented toward the surface. They thus appear to be very early attachment behaviors. In a series of experiments, we found that these are not stereotyped reflex acts, but organized responses that are graded according to the number of maternal modalities present on the surface, such as texture, warmth, and odor (Polan and Hofer 1999a). Furthermore, they are enhanced by periods of prior maternal deprivation, suggesting the rapid development of a motivational component. By 2 days of age, we found that pups discriminate their own mother's odor in preference to equally familiar nest odors (Polan and Hofer 1998) and by the first postnatal week, Hepper (1986) has shown that pups discriminate and prefer their own mother, father, and siblings to other lactating females, males, or age mates.

These results show that a highly specific "behavioral attachment system" (Bowlby, 1969), capable of approach and proximity maintenance to the mother and motivated by brief periods of separation from her, may occur much earlier in development than previously supposed. The remarkable specificity of the approach response of the infant rat to individual family members acquired within the first few postnatal days demonstrates that specificity of attachment does not require long experience or advanced cognitive and emotional capabilities. Olfaction in the rat and vision in the human provide the necessary basis for approach responses that are specific to a single individual. But this remarkable capability can develop independently of the specificity of the rat pup's contact comfort response. For even by 2 weeks of age a rat pup will show an equal comfort response to contact with any female that is available. This nonspecificity is limited, however, and a form of "stranger anxiety" develops by the second week of life, well before weaning. Pups will avoid the odor of unfamiliar adult males (but not of familiar or unfamiliar prepubertal males), and they show immobility and a brisk adrenocortical response when the stranger is too near (Takahashi, 1992). This early fear response, like approach responses to the mother, depends upon olfactory cues (Shair et al., 1997).

Recent work in humans, inspired by these findings in lower animals, has shown that human newborns, too, are capable of slowly locomoting across the bare surface of the mother's abdomen and locating the breast scented with amniotic fluid in preference to the untreated breast (Varendi, Porter, and Winberg, 1996). Although newborns are attracted to natural breast odors even before the first nursing bout (Makin and Porter, 1989), amniotic fluid can override this effect. Apparently, human newborns are not as helpless as previously thought, and possess approach and orienting behaviors that anticipate the recognized onset of maternal attachment at 6–8 months.

POSTNATAL LEARNING    Although specific olfactory and/or auditory predispositions toward the infant's own mother may be acquired prenatally, after birth the newborn mammal enters a new world where contingent events, so important for more advanced forms of learning, are now occurring with great frequency. The abrupt transition from prenatal to postnatal life appears to be eased for the newborn by the presence of prenatal stimuli continuing into the postnatal environment (i.e., the odor of amniotic fluid; Lecanuet and Schaal, 1996; Mennella et al., 1995; Schaal, Marlier, and Soussignan, 1995; Varendi et al., 1998). However, it seemed likely that the neonatal capacities for stimulus discrimination and preferential approach, orienting, and proximity-maintenance behavior described in the previous section are formed by some type of rapid postnatal learning process, resembling avian imprinting, as hypothesized by Bowlby. Yet until recently, no such process had been discovered.

When developmental psychobiologists first began assessing infant rat development, any form of learning appeared beyond the capabilities of the neonatal rat. However, as our understanding of the newborn's environment began to evolve and experimental conditions became more naturalistic, the surprising learning capabilities of rodent neonates have emerged. Since then, extensive work characterizing early learning has demonstrated that the basic laws of adult learning also apply to infant rats and that learning occurs naturally within the nest (Brunjes and Alberts, 1979; Campbell, 1984; Galef and Kaner, 1980; Leon, 1975; Miller, Jagielo, and Spear, 1989; Pedersen, Williams, and Blass, 1982; Rudy and Cheatle, 1979; Sullivan, Hofer, and Brake, 1986; Sullivan et al., 1986, 1990; Terry and Johanson, 1996).

In these studies, the use of a two-choice preference platform revealed for the first time that within 2–3 days after birth, pups are capable of learning to discriminate, prefer, approach, and maintain proximity to an odor associated with forms of stimulation that naturally occur within the early mother–infant interaction (Sullivan, Hofer, and Brake, 1986). Random presentations of the two stimuli (odor and reward) had no such effect and provided the control procedure necessary to identify the change in behavior as due to associative conditioning. Since the learning required only two or three paired presentations and since the preference was retained for many days, it seemed to qualify as an "imprinting-like process" that is likely to be central to attachment in slow-developing mammals. Indeed, a human analog of this process was found by Sullivan and colleagues (1991). These investigators presented human newborns with a novel odor, then rubbed them along their torsos to simulate maternal care; the next day, the infants became activated and turned their heads preferentially toward that odor. This suggests that rapid learning of orientation to olfactory cues is an evolutionarily conserved process in mammalian newborns.

Somatosensory information is also important in mother–infant interactions. For example, pup mortality rate (due to disturbance of nipple orientation and grasp) increases markedly when their facial somatosensory system is disrupted (Hofer, 1981). Somatosensory stimulation evokes specific orientation behaviors in 2–3-day-old pups (Polan and Hofer, 1999b), and specific contingent stimulation can be shown to alter pups responsiveness to somatosensory stimulation. Following a conditioning procedure in which whisker stimulation was paired with a reward, pups showed more vigorous responding to whisker stimulation (Landers and Sullivan, 1999a,b), resulting in enhanced responding to tactile stimulation from the mother.

From an evolutionary perspective, a reliance on learning for early attachment might appear rather risky, considering the potential for inappropriate object choice. However, considering the physical constraints of the nest and pups' immature motor system, the range of possible attachment figures is limited. Additionally, unique characteristics of infant learning appear to greatly enhance the likelihood of pups' developing odor preferences necessary for forming maternal attachment. For example, during the neonatal period, when positive associations are readily formed, inhibitory conditioning and passive avoidance do not appear to emerge until after postnatal days 10–11 (Blozovski and Cudennec, 1980; Collier et al., 1979; Goldman and Tobach, 1967; Martin and Alberts, 1979; Stehouwer and Campbell, 1978; for a review, see Myslivecek, 1997). Moreover, pre-exposure to a conditioned stimulus (CS) facilitates conditioning in infant rats at an age when maternal cues are repeatedly presented during nursing bouts, whereas it retards conditioning in weanling and adult rats (Hoffmann and Spear, 1989) at ages when novel environmental cues are presented only rarely. Furthermore, when pups do learn, they appear to be less selective learners as compared to adult rats. That is, whereas an adult will focus on a narrow range of environmental stimuli in a learning situation, pups will learn associations with a broad range of such stimuli (Spear, Kucharski, and Miller, 1989), thus promoting learned responses to multiple maternal features.

Clinical observations have taught us that attachment occurs not only to supportive caretakers, but to abusive caretakers as well. In fact, children tolerate considerable abuse while remaining strongly attached to the abusive caretaker (Helfer, Kemp, and Krugman, 1997). Initially, it seems counterproductive to form and maintain an attachment to an abusive caretaker; but from an evolutionary perspective, it may be better for an altricial infant to have a bad caretaker than no caretaker. We found that this aspect of human attachment can also be modeled in the infant rat. We and others have found that, during the first postnatal week, a surprisingly broad spectrum of stimuli can function as reinforcers to produce an odor preference in rat pups (Sullivan, Hofer, and Brake, 1986; Sullivan et al., 1986). As illustrated in figure 38.1, these stimuli range from apparently rewarding ones, such as milk and access to the mother (Alberts and May, 1984; Brake, 1981; Galef and Sherry, 1973; Johanson and Hall, 1979; Johanson and Teicher, 1980; Leon, 1975; McLean et al., 1993; Pedersen, Williams, and Blass, 1982; Weldon, Travis, and Kennedy, 1991; Wilson and Sullivan, 1994), to apparently aversive stimuli, such as moderate shock and tailpinch (Camp and Rudy, 1988; Spear 1978; Sullivan, Hofer, and Brake, 1986)—stimuli that elicit escape responses from the pups. It should be noted that threshold to shock (Stehouwer and Campbell, 1978) and behavioral response (Emerich et al., 1985) to shock does not change between the ages of 9 and 11 days. As pups mature and reach an age when leaving the nest becomes more likely (Bolles and Woods, 1965; pups begin to walk between PN9 and PN11), olfactory learning comes to resemble learning in adults more closely. Specifically, odor aversions are easily learned by 2-week olds and acquisition of odor preferences is limited to odors paired with stimuli of positive value (Camp and Rudy, 1988; Spear 1978; Sullivan and Wilson, 1995). Thus, the odor learning that underlies early attachment appears to take place in response to a very broad range of contingent events while pups are confined to the nest, but becomes more selective at a time in development when pups begin leaving the nest and encountering novel odors not associated with the mother.

Unique learning capabilities facilitating infant attachment appear throughout the animal kingdom and may have evolved to ensure that altricial animals easily form a repertoire of proximity-seeking behaviors, regardless of the specific qualities of the treatment they receive from the primary caretaker. Observations of mother–infant interactions within the rat nest demonstrate that maternal behaviors are sometimes painful to pups. For example, when the rat mother steps on pups upon entering/leaving the nest or when she retrieves pups by a leg rather than at the nape of the neck, broadband (mixed ultrasonic and audible range) vocalizations— the type associated with noxious stimuli—are elicited (White et al., 1992). It is certainly beneficial to pups not to learn an aversion to their mother's odor or inhibit approach responses to nest odors; instead, pups need to exhibit approach behaviors to procure the mother's milk, warmth, and protection. A similar phenomenon exists in avian species. Specifically, experiencing an aversive shock during exposure to an imprinting object strengthens the following response. For example, in a series of classic experiments by Hess (1962) and Salzen (1970), recently hatched chicks were shocked (3 mA for 0.5 s) while presented with a surrogate mother. The next day, chicks that were shocked showed a significantly stronger following response than chicks that were not shocked. With striking similarity to the infant rat, similar pairings in older chicks resulted in a subsequent aversion to the surrogate mother. Additional mammalian species in which similar phenomena have been documented include nonhuman primates (Harlow and Harlow, 1965), dogs (reviewed in Rajecki, Lamb, and Obmascher, 1978), and humans (for a review, Helfer, Kempe, and Krugman, 1997).

In rats, early attachment-related odors appear to retain value into adulthood, although the role of the odor in modifying behavior appears to change with development. Work done independently in the labs of Celia

# Tactile stimulation

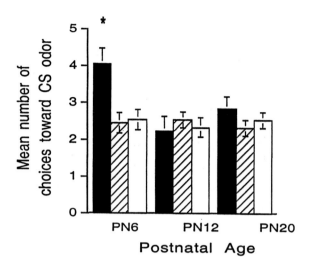

# Moderate Shock (0.5mA)

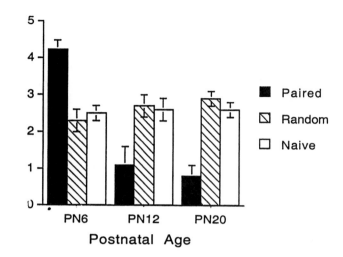

FIGURE 38.1 During the first week of life, a wide variety of stimuli can function as a reward (tactile stimulation, moderate shock). However, as pups mature, rewarding stimuli are more similar to that seen in the adult. Tactile stimulation (stroking) produces an odor preference at PN6 but not in older pups (left). Moderate-intensity shock produces an odor preference in PN6 but an aversion at older ages (right).

Moore (Moore, Jordan, and Wong, 1996) and Elliot Blass (Fillion and Blass, 1986) demonstrated that adult male rats exhibited enhanced sexual performance when exposed to the natural and artificial odors learned in infancy. These results support observations on the role of early experience on adult mate preference in other species, such as occurs in imprinting.

NEURAL PLASTICITY UNDERLYING OLFACTORY PREFERENCE LEARNING    The development of a specific olfactory-based attachment system in the rat pup during the first week and a half of life is associated with the acquisition of olfactory bulb neural changes. We found that rat pups express this modified olfactory bulb response to both natural maternal and artificial odors experienced in the nest (Sullivan et al., 1990), as well as to odors in controlled learning experiments (Johnson et al., 1995; Sullivan and Leon, 1986; Wilson and Sullivan, 1991; Wilson, Sullivan, and Leon, 1987). The modified olfactory bulb response is characterized by enhanced immediate-early gene activity (*c-fos*) and enhanced 2-deoxyglucose (2-DG) uptake in focal, odor-specific glomerular regions in response to the conditioned odor. Within the underlying neural substrate, modified single-unit response patterns of mitral/tufted cells near the enhanced glomerular foci were found (Wilson and Leon, 1988b; Wilson and Sullivan, 1990; Wilson, Sullivan, and Leon, 1987) and olfactory bulb anatomical changes reflected in enlarged glomeruli within these foci (Woo, Coopersmith, and Leon, 1987). As with the behavioral changes in attachment, these neural changes are retained into adulthood, but their acquisition is dependent upon experiences during infancy (Pager, 1974; Woo and Leon, 1988).

Many neurotransmitters have a role in early olfactory learning in neonatal rats—5-HT (McLean et al., 1993), DA (Barr and Wang, 1992; Weldon, Travis, and Kennedy, 1991), GABA (Okutani, Yagi, and Kaba, 1999), glutamate (Lincoln et al., 1988; Mickley et al., 1998), and opiates (Barr and Rossi, 1992; Kehoe and Blass, 1986). Roth and Sullivan (2000) have recently shown that PN8 pups treated with systemic naltrexone, a nonspecific opioid antagonist, do not show a subsequent odor preference after odor-shock classical conditioning, suggesting an important role for opioids in early preference formation to noxious stimuli. However, the action of norepinephrine (NE) appears particularly important in neural plasticity during early development and in the form of olfactory (Brennen and Keverne, 1997; Wilson and Sullivan, 1994) and somatosensory (Landers and Sullivan, 1999b) learning-induced plasticity used in early attachment.

Norepinephrine input to the olfactory bulb is widespread throughout the granule cell layer as early as the first postnatal week (McLean and Shipley, 1991; Woo and Leon, 1995). The granule cell layer is composed of inhibitory interneurons modulating the output of the olfactory bulb through the adjacent mitral cells (Brunjes, Smith-Craft, and McCarty, 1985; Lauder and Bloom, 1974; Trombley and Shepherd, 1992; Wilson and Leon, 1988b). Wilson has shown that activation of the NE input to the infant rat's olfactory bulb during an odor presentation maintains mitral cell responsiveness to that odor, preventing the habituation these cells normally exhibit to repeated odor presentations (Wilson and Sullivan, 1992). Subsequent work has shown that NE increases mitral cell responses to olfactory nerve input, suggesting that NE functions to increase the signal to noise ratio (Jiang et al., 1996).

The notion that this mechanism of plasticity underlies the neural and behavioral changes of the rapid, olfactory-based learning underlying rat pup attachment has received strong support from a variety of labs. First, work in Michael Leon's lab, using microdialysis, showed that olfactory bulb NE increases during infant odor learning (Rangel and Leon, 1995). Second, recordings from olfactory bulb mitral cells during learning indicate that mitral cells maintain their responsiveness to odors in the experimental learning groups, but not control groups (Wilson and Sullivan, 1992). Third, infusion of NE into the olfactory bulb during an odor presentation is sufficient for pups to acquire an odor preference (Sullivan et al., submitted). Fourth, olfactory bulb NE (Langdon, Harley, and McLean, 1997; Sullivan et al., 1992) from the noradrenergic locus coeruleus (Sullivan et al., 1994) is necessary for infant rat learning. Thus, it is the contingent events of increasing olfactory bulb NE and odor stimulation that underlie the neural plasticity responsible for the acquisition of olfactory-based attachment behavior.

PARALLEL PROCESSES IN MATERNAL ATTACHMENT Successful mother–infant interactions require the reciprocal responding of both individuals in the mother–infant dyad. Human mothers rapidly learn about their babies' characteristics and can identify their babies' cries, odors, and facial features within hours of birth (Eidelman and Kaitz, 1992; Kaitz et al., 1992; Porter, Cernoch, and McLaughin, 1983). An animal model for this rapid learning has received considerable attention (for reviews, see Brennan and Keverne, 1997; Fleming et al., 1999). Indeed, there are interesting parallels between the early attachment behavior of infants and the attachment behavior of the newly parturient mother. In rats and sheep, a temporally restricted period of post-partum olfactory learning in the mother involving NE facilitates the mother's learning about her young (Levy et al., 1990; Moffat, Suh, and Fleming, 1993; Pissonnier

et al., 1985). It is possible that mammalian mothers and pups use similar neural circuitry to form their reciprocal attachment.

CLOSING THE SENSITIVE PERIOD FOR INFANTILE OLFACTORY PREFERENCE LEARNING Olfactory bulb NE is not found in neurons intrinsic to the olfactory bulb, but arrives via direct projections from the noradrenergic pontine nucleus locus coeruleus (McLean and Shipley, 1991; Shipley, Halloran, and De la Torre, 1985). Recent evidence strongly suggests that developmental changes within the locus coeruleus may underlie the termination of the infant rat's unique learning abilities during the first week and a half of postnatal life. In neonatal rat pups, the locus coeruleus is not completely mature during the first week of postnatal life, nor is it an immature version of the adult locus coeruleus. Indeed, it has unique characteristics that result in an enhanced response of neonatal locus coeruleus neurons to sensory stimulation.

The infant locus coeruleus is more responsive to sensory stimuli than the adult locus coeruleus. Although the adult locus coeruleus is activated by sensory stimuli (Aston-Jones et al., 1994; Foote, Aston-Jones, and Bloom, 1980; Harley and Sara, 1992; Sara, Dyon-Laurent, and Herve, 1995; Vankov, Herve-Minvielle, and Sara, 1995), in comparison to the infant, it is less likely to respond to non-noxious stimuli (Kimura and Nakamura, 1985; Nakamura and Sakaguchi, 1990). Furthermore, the adult locus coeruleus habituates after repeated presentation of the stimuli (Vankov, Herve-Minvielle, and Sara, 1995) whereas the infant locus coeruleus fails to exhibit habituation (Kimura and Nakamura, 1985; Nakamura and Sakaguchi, 1990). Furthermore, a 1-second presentation of tactile stimulation is likely to cause a few millisecond response in the adult locus coeruleus, but a 20–30-second response in the first week infant locus coeruleus. Finally, the early infant locus coeruleus shows far more extensive electronic coupling through gap junctions, a process that appears to potentiate the locus coeruleus's response (Marshall et al., 1991).

At about PN10, the infant locus coeruleus begins to take on adult characteristics (Marshall et al., 1991; Nakamura and Sakaguchi, 1990). These results suggest that the infant rat's olfactory bulb receives unique input from the locus coeruleus during the first week of life and that maturational changes in the locus coeruleus during the second week, alter the properties of this input so as to bring to a close the early sensitive period for the imprinting-like learning underlying attachment in this species.

POSSIBLE ROLES OF OTHER BRAIN REGIONS IN EARLY ATTACHMENT Although the simultaneous presentation of odor and olfactory bulb NE is sufficient to produce an odor preference, it is possible that other brain areas contribute to olfactory attachments under normal conditions. As is indicated in figure 38.2, there are complex connections between the olfactory bulb and other brain areas previously shown to be important in learning, such as the amygdala and hippocampus. These brain areas may mediate the development of a close association of emotional states with events within the sphere of attachment processes. Although the exact role of the amygdala in emotional learning has been disputed, there is abundant evidence for this association (Cahill et al., 1999; Fanselow and LeDoux, 1999; Fanselow and Rudy, 1998; Schoenbaum, Chiba, and Gallagher, 1999).

The neonatal rodent amygdala does not appear to be necessary for infant olfactory learning since pups acquire specific conditioned responding and olfactory preferences without an amygdala (Blozovski and Cudennec, 1980; Blozovski and Hennocq, 1982; Sullivan and Wilson, 1993). However, in these lesioned pups, more than the usual amount of training is necessary for them to acquire olfactory preferences (Sullivan and Wilson, 1993), suggesting that the amygdala may play a facilitative role in the acquisition of attachment behaviors, possibly through its role in mediating emotional processing. As the rat pup matures, the amygdala does become more important in learning (Sananes and Campbell, 1989). Specifically, the ontogeny of both

learned (Sullivan et al., 2000) and unlearned (Takahashi, 1992) responses to aversive odors appears to emerge at the same time the amygdala appears to participate in odor aversion learning (PN10; Sullivan et al., 2000). Furthermore, the ability to learn odor aversions easily coincides with the pups' emerging ability to walk (Bolles and Woods, 1965) and leave the nest. These data suggest that there is a unique behavioral and neural response to aversive conditioning that helps optimize preference conditioning to and minimize aversive conditioning to the mother. The role of the hippocampus is likely to be negligible since the primary cortical input to the hippocampus from the entorhinal cortex is only beginning to develop during the first postnatal week (Crain et al., 1973) and does not appear to be functioning in learning until just prior to weaning or even later (Fanselow and Rudy, 1998; Rudy and Morledge, 1994; Rudy, Stadler-Morris, and Alberts, 1987; Stanton, 2000). Furthermore, connectivity between the hippocampus and other brain areas in the hippocampal system may not become functional until sometime between P12 to PN17 (Nair and Gonzalez-Lima, 1999), after the closing of the sensitive period for infantile attachment. Furthermore, at least with respect to somatosensory learning, there does not appear to be any cortical involvement in this learning (Landers and Sullivan, 1999a). However, it is also clear that brain structures other than the olfactory bulb are of great importance to pup learning. For example, work by Ku-

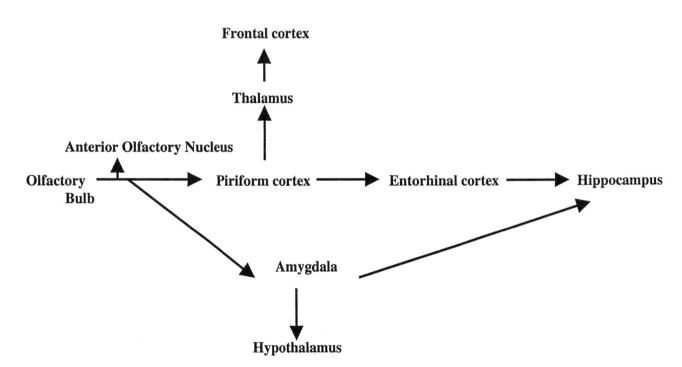

FIGURE 38.2  The adult olfactory pathway. Although many of these brain areas have been implicated in adult olfactory learning, their role in infant learning has not been determined.

charski and Hall (1988) clearly demonstrates the importance of olfactory commissural and efferent pathways in early olfactory learning.

Much more work is needed to clarify the processes by which cognitive and emotional aspects of attachment come to be related in early development. Although the neural basis for early attachment has yet to be fully documented, it is clear that the characteristics of the neonatal rat brain provide the infant with a predisposition to form attachments to their caregiver. These infant neural characteristics are not due simply to the absence or immaturity of a brain area, but rather to the brain's having unique characteristics that enable the infant to survive in the environment that is unique to the infant.

## Maternal separation responses, hidden regulators, and the emergence of emotion in attachment

Soon after birth, prenatally acquired perceptual biases and motor programs, stimulus-guided tactile responses, and associative learning create a powerful behavioral control system through which the infant maintains close proximity to its mother. But there is another important attribute of attachment from which the emotional tie of the infant to its mother has been inferred: the response to separation. This has been supposed to be an integral part of the proximity-maintenance system, one that represents the affective expression of its motivational nature. Thus, the degree or strength of attachment is thought to be responsible for the intensity of the response to separation, and the separation response itself is taken to represent a full expression of attachment behaviors in the absence of their "goal object."

Experiments in our lab led us to a very different view, in which the processes underlying attachment and the responses to separation are seen as separate and distinct early in postnatal life (Hofer, 1975a, 1983). The response of infant rats, and primates, to maternal separation has been found to involve a complex pattern of changes in a number of different behavioral and physiologic systems (Hofer, 1996a; Kraemer, 1992). We found that this pattern was not an integrated psychophysiological response, as had been supposed (the "despair" phase of the separation response), but the result of a novel mechanism. We found that, during separation, each of the individual systems of the infant rat responded to the absence of one or another of the components of the infants' previous interaction with its mother. Providing one of these components to a separated pup, for example, maternal warmth, maintained the level of brain biogenic amine function underlying the pups' general activity level (Hofer, 1980; Stone, Bonnet, and Hofer, 1976), but had no effect on other systems, for example, the pups' cardiac rate. Heart rate fell 40% after 18 hours of separation, regardless of whether supplemental heat was provided (Hofer, 1971). We found that the heart rate, normally maintained by sympathetic tone, was regulated by maternal provision of milk to neural receptors in the lining of the pup's stomach (Hofer and Weiner, 1975).

By studying a number of additional systems, such as those controlling sleep-wake states (Hofer, 1976), activity level (Hofer, 1975b), sucking pattern (Brake et al., 1982), vocalization (Hofer and Shair, 1980), and blood pressure (Shear, Brunelli, and Hofer, 1983), we concluded that in maternal separation, all these regulatory components of the mother–infant interaction are withdrawn at once. This widespread loss creates a pattern of increases or decreases in level of function of the infant's systems, depending upon whether the particular system had been up- or downregulated by the previous mother–infant interaction. We called these "hidden regulators" because they were not evident in simply observing the mother–infant interaction. Other investigators, using this approach, have discovered other maternal regulatory systems of the same sort.

For example, removal of the dam from rat pups was found to produce a rapid (30 min) fall in the pup's growth hormone (GH) levels, and vigorous tactile stroking of maternally separated pups (mimicking maternal licking) prevented the fall in GH (reviewed in Kuhn and Schanberg, 1991). Brain substrates for this effect were then investigated, and it now appears that GH levels are normally maintained by maternal licking, acting through serotonin (5-HT) 2A and 2C receptor modulation of the balance between growth hormone releasing factor (GRH) and somatostatin (SS), which together act on the anterior pituitary release of GH (Katz et al., 1996). The withdrawal of maternal licking by separation allows GRH to fall and SS to rise, resulting in a precipitous fall in GH.

There are several biological similarities between this maternal deprivation effect in rats and the growth retardation that occurs in some variants of human reactive attachment disorders of infancy. Applying this new knowledge about the regulation of GH to low-birth-weight, prematurely born babies, Tiffany Field and coworkers joined the Schanberg group. They used a combination of stroking and limb movement, administered three times a day for 15 minutes each time, and continued throughout their 2-week hospitalization. This intervention increased weight gain, head circumference, and behavior development test scores in relation to a randomly chosen control group, with beneficial effects discernible many months later (Field et al., 1986).

ATTACHMENT, EMOTION, AND THE ORIGINS OF VOCAL COMMUNICATION  One of the best known responses to maternal separation is the infant's isolation call, a behavior that occurs in a wide variety of species (Lester and Boukydis, 1985; Newman, 1998). In the rat, this call is in the ultrasonic range (40 kHz) and appears in the first or second postnatal day (Noirot, 1968). Pharmacological studies show that the ultrasonic vocalization (USV) response to isolation is attenuated or blocked in a dose-dependent manner by clinically effective anxiolytics that act at benzodiazepine and serotonin receptors; and conversely, USV rates are increased by compounds known to be anxiogenic in humans, such as benzodiazepine receptor inverse agonists (β-carboline, FG 1742) and $GABA_a$ receptor ligands such as pentylenetetrazol (Hofer, 1996b; Miczek, Tornatsky, and Vivian, 1991). Within serotonin and opioid systems, receptor subtypes known to have opposing effects on experimental anxiety in adult rats also have opposing effects on infant calling rates. Neuroanatomical studies in infant rats show that stimulation of the periaqueductal gray area produces USV and chemical lesions of this area prevent calling (Goodwin and Barr, 1998). The more distal motor pathway is through the nucleus ambiguous and both laryngeal branches of the vagus nerve (Wetzel, Kelly, and Campbell, 1980). Higher centers known to be involved in cats and primates suggest a neural substrate for isolation calls involving primarily the hypothalamus, amygdala, thalamus, and hippocampus (Jurgens, 1994)—brain areas known to be involved in adult human and adult animal anxiety and defensive responses.

This evidence strongly suggests that social isolation produces an early affective state in rat pups that is expressed overtly in the rates of infant calling and covertly by the autonomic and adrenocortical systems. How does this calling behavior, and its inferred underlying affective state, develop as a communication system between mother and pup? Infant rat USVs are powerful stimuli for the lactating rat, capable of causing her to interrupt an ongoing nursing bout, initiate searching outside the nest, and direct her search toward the source of the calls (Smotherman et al., 1978). The mother's retrieval response to the pup's vocal signals then results in renewed contact between pup and mother. This contact in turn quiets the pup. The isolation and comfort responses in attachment theory are described as expressions of interruption and re-establishment of a social bond. Such a formulation would predict that since the pup recognizes its mother by her scent, pups made acutely anosmic would fail to show a comfort response. But anosmic pups show comfort responses that are virtually unaffected by loss of the capacity to recognize their mother in this way (Hofer and Shair, 1991). Instead, we and others have found multiple regulators of infant USV within the contact between mother and pup: warmth, tactile stimuli, and milk as well as her scent (Hofer, 1996b). Provision of these modalities separately, by experimental design, and then in combination elicits a graded response, with the maximum isolation calling rates occurring when all are withdrawn at once and with the full comfort response being elicited only when all are present at once.

FROM PHYSIOLOGICAL REGULATION TO MENTAL REPRESENTATION  The early learning processes and the widespread regulatory interactions (summarized in table 38.1) are not involved in biological and behavioral development solely in rats; they are also the first experiences out of which human mental representations and their associated emotions arise. So far as we understand the process for the human, experiences made up of the infant's individual acts, parental responses, sensory impressions, and associated affects are laid down in memory during and after early parent–infant interactions (Gergeley and Watson, 1999; Stern 1985). These individual units of experience are integrated into something like a network of attributes in memory, invested with associated affect, and result in the formation of what Bowlby referred to as an "internal working model" of the relationship.

In the light of the research described in the previous sections, we can speculate that the early learning and maternal regulatory interactions described for rats occur also in human babies. For human infants, these experiences are gradually joined in memory and stored as the mental representations and related affective states that older children are able to describe in words. It seems likely that these mental structures combine the infant's newly developing capacities to anticipate events and respond to symbolic cues with the earlier biological functions of the "hidden" regulatory interactions through processes similar to the functional links involved in the classical conditioning of physiologic responses. In this way our concept of the "mental representation" can be thought to link together into a functional network within the child's brain the learned patterns of behavior and the physiological response systems previously regulated by the mother–infant interaction. In this way we can envisage the development of self-regulation of the behavioral and physiological systems underlying motivation and affect, gradually supplanting the sensorimotor, thermal, and nutrient regulatory systems found in the interactions of younger infants with their mothers. This would link biological systems with internal object representation and account

TABLE 38.1
*Maternal regulators of infant systems in 2-week-old rat pups**

| Infant Systems | Maternal Regulators and Effects |
|---|---|
| *Behavioral* | |
| Activity level | Thermal—heat ( + ) |
| | Thermal—cold (–) |
| | Tactile stimulation (–) |
| | Olfactory cues (–) |
| | |
| Sucking: | |
|    Nutritive | Gastric distension (–) |
|    Nonnutritive | Perioral—tactile/chemical (–) |
| Vocalization ultrasound | Thermal, texture, olfactory, milk (–) |
| | |
| *Autonomic* | |
| Sympathetic cardiac (β-adrenergic) | Milk at gastric receptors ( + ) |
| Vasomotor (α-adrenergic) | Milk at gastric receptors (–) |
| | |
| *Endocrine* | |
| Growth hormone | Tactile stimulation ( + ) |
| ACTH, CRH | Tactile stimulation (–) |
| Corticosterone | Milk, acting on adrenal response to ACTH (–) |
| | |
| *Sleep—wake states* | Regularly timed tactile and/or nutrient stimuli |
| |    REM duration ( + ) |
| |    Awakening frequency (–); duration (–) |

*The direction of regulation is indicated by ( + ) or (–) for up- or downregulation during normal ongoing mother–infant interaction. Upon maternal separation, release from regulation produces changes in the opposite direction in each infant system.

for the remarkable upheavals of biological as well as psychological systems that take place in adult humans in response to cues signaling impending separation or in response to losses established simply upon hearing of a death, for example, by telephone (Hofer, 1984, 1996a).

Mother–infant relationships, which differ in quality and which necessarily involve different levels and patterns of behavioral and physiological regulation in a variety of systems, will be reflected in the nature of the mental representations present in different children as they grow up. The emotions aroused during early crying responses to separation, during the profound state changes associated with the prolonged loss of all maternal regulators, and during the reunion of a separated infant with its mother are apparently intense. These emotional states have commanded our attention; they are what everyone intuitively recognizes about attachment and separation, and what we feel about the people we are close to. As inner experiences, these occur at a different level of psychobiological organization than the changes in autonomic, endocrine, and neurophysiological systems we have been able to study in rats and monkeys, as well as in younger human infants. Hidden regulators thus form a developmental as well as a conceptual bridge between the tangible and the intangible in our understanding of attachment.

*Mother–infant interaction patterns, infant development, and maternal behavior in the next generation*

The actions of maternal regulators of infant biology and behavior are not limited to the mediation of responses to maternal separation. They exert their regulatory effects continuously, throughout the preweaning period and even beyond. A good illustration is the recent discovery of a major role for the mother–infant interaction in the development of the hypothalamic-adrenocortical axis (HPA) during the preweaning period. It has long been known that in the rat from postnatal days 4 to 14, the pups' HPA response to isolation and mild stressors like saline injections are less intense than in the newborn or weaning periods; this stage is known as the "stress-hyporesponsive period" (Levine, 1994). Surprisingly, it has recently been found that this species-typical developmental stage is not the product of an intrinsic developmental program, but the result of hidden regulators at work within the ongoing mother–infant interaction. First, it was found that 9–12-day-old pups' basal corticosterone (CORT) level and the magnitude of the adrenocorticotrophic hormone (ACTH) and CORT response to isolation was increased 5-fold after 24 hours of maternal separation (Stanton, Gutierrez, and Levine, 1988). Next, by utilizing our concept of hidden regulators, Suchecki, Rosenfeld, and Levine (1993) attempted to prevent these separation-induced changes by supplying various components of the mother–infant interaction. They found that repeated stroking of the separated infants for as little as three 1-minute periods prevented the increase in ACTH response while providing milk by cheek cannula during separation prevented the separation-induced blunting of the adrenal CORT response to ACTH.

Thus the mother normally reduces infant HPA responses and separation eliminates this hyporesponsive state. Tracing these regulatory effects back to brain systems, Levine's group has recently found that stroking (representing maternal licking) regulates the intensity of the immediate-early gene *cfos* messenger RNA (mRNA) response in the paraventricular nucleus of the hypothalamus (PVN), and the corticotropin-releasing hormone (CRH) receptor mRNA expression as well, in PVN, amygdala, and other limbic system sites (Van Oers et al., 1998). It is intraorally administered milk, however, that regulates glucocorticoid receptor mRNA in the CA1 region of the hippocampus and CORT release from the adrenal in response to ACTH.

Through this anatomical and molecular neuromodulator analysis, Levine and colleagues discovered that maternal licking and milk delivery during suckling, independently exert a prolonged attenuating effect on the responsiveness of the HPA axis. This maternal regulatory effect, once established in the first few postnatal days, continues throughout most of the nursing period, finally declining as weaning occurs from day 15 to 21. These regulatory interactions achieve this effect by increasing the inhibitory feedback from hippocampal glucocorticoid receptors and by decreasing the hypothalamic stimulation of CRF and ACTH output. These regulatory effects on the pup's brain can be rapidly reversed and stress responsiveness restored by maternal separation.

LONG-TERM EFFECTS    These preweaning studies on brain mechanisms underlying maternal regulation of HPA axis function suggested that qualitative differences in the patterns of early mother–infant interaction could have long-term effects on HPA responses to stress in adults similar to those we had discovered for adult blood pressure in spontaneously hypertensive rats (SHR) (Myers et al., 1989). Meaney and his colleagues used the maternal behavior observational approach developed in those studies to directly test this implication of the discovery of maternal regulators (Liu et al., 1997). They found that dams in their colony that were observed to have naturally high levels of licking, grooming, and of the high-arched back nursing position (LG/

ABN) produced pups that were later found to be less fearful in a variety of behavioral tests and to show lower than normal HPA axis responsivity to restraint stress as adults than the offspring of dams that naturally showed the lowest levels of these early interactions.

In order to show that these differences in the offspring in adulthood were not simply reflections of a different genetic constitution in the two groups, Meaney and his colleagues handled daily the infants of the low LG/ABN group, an early intervention that is known to increase levels of the mother's concurrent LG/ABN behaviors. By doing so, he showed that the adult behavior and HPA axis responses of the offspring also changed to closely resemble the patterns that naturally occurred in the previously studied high LG/ABN group.

These results showed that an intervention that alters the mother–infant interaction pattern also changes the adult fear behavior and physiological response characteristics of the offspring. One observation that currently occupies researchers in the attachment area is how mothers in one generation can pass on to their adult female offspring the attachment pattern they experienced as infants. The experiment I have just described provided a chance to find out if this transgenerational effect occurs in nonprimate species and to explore how it comes about. By allowing the offspring of the handled litters to rear another generation under normal laboratory conditions, Meaney and his colleagues (in press) went on to find that the mother–infant interaction established by these progeny resembled the one their mothers had been induced to have in their own infancy (high LG/ABN) rather than the one characteristic of their ancestors before the handling intervention (low LG/ABN) (Francis et al., 1999). Furthermore, the unmanipulated pups in these litters also went on to show the adult behaviors and hormonal stress patterns typical of offspring of high LG/ABN litters.

These experiments show the intergenerational transmission of mother–infant interaction patterns and the developmental effect of these interaction patterns on adult behavior and physiology. They provide an animal model for the neurobiological analysis of mechanisms underlying environmental effects on the transgenerational patterns of mothering and an experimental verification of one of the central tenets of present-day human attachment research.

## Summary and perspective

We have re-examined the major propositions of attachment theory and described a series of component processes, discovered in experiments with laboratory rats, that enable us to begin to understand the behavioral mechanisms involved and to identify their underlying neural substrates. We first described the processes that bring the neonatal mammal into close proximity to the mother, continue to keep the infant close, act to reunite the separated infant with the mother, and cause a complex patterned response to prolonged maternal separation. These several components tell us that an "enduring social bond" (to use Bowlby's term) has been formed, but we can now understand the bond in terms of separate processes that can be delineated as they work independently, serially, or in parallel to produce the familiar behavioral signs of "attachment." The discovery of these component processes allows us to begin to understand what makes up the "glue" that holds the infant to the mother. The discovery of regulatory interactions within the mother–infant relationship allows us to escape the circularity of the traditional attachment model, in which the response to separation is attributed to disruption of a social bond, the existence of which is inferred from the presence of that same separation response. Some of the individual processes described allow us to understand how the infant comes to identify and orient toward the mother by different means at different stages in development. Beginning before birth and continuing in the newborn period, novel processes of associative learning have been discovered that allow us for the first time to identify and understand the mysterious "imprinting-like process" that Bowlby envisioned as the altricial mammalian equivalent of avian imprinting. And, finally, we can begin to see how one of the consequences of these early learning processes, acting within repeated regulatory interactions, is to provide a novel source of experiences for the formation of the mental representation of the infant–mother relationship.

With this enlarged view, some processes have been discovered to play an important role in the development of proximity maintenance between infant and mother that were not previously considered to be important (e.g., prenatal learning). And events that were thought to be central to attachment have been found to be produced by other, independent mechanisms (e.g., separation responses). More broadly, our understanding of the evolutionary survival value of remaining close to the mother has been expanded to include the many pathways available for regulation of the infant's physiological and behavioral systems by its interactions with the caregiver. The relationship thus provides an opportunity for the mother to shape both the developing physiology and the behavior of her offspring, through her patterned interactions with the infant. Behavioral adaptations to environmental change occurring in the life of the mother can thus lead to "antici-

patory" biological changes in the offspring—a novel evolutionary mechanism.

The discovery of regulatory interactions and the effects of their withdrawal allow us to understand not only the responses to separation in young organisms of limited cognitive-emotional capacity, but also the familiar experienced emotions and memories that can be verbally described to us by older children and adults. It is not that rat pups respond to loss of regulatory processes, while human infants respond to emotions of love, sadness, anger, and grief. Human infants, as they mature, can respond at the symbolic level *as well as* at the level of the behavioral and physiological processes of the regulatory interactions. The two levels appear to be organized as parallel and complementary response systems. Even *adult* humans continue to respond in important ways at the sensorimotor-physiologic level in their social interactions, separations and losses, continuing a process begun in infancy. A good example of this is the mutual regulation of menstrual synchrony among close female friends, an effect that takes place out of conscious awareness and has recently been found to be mediated at least in part by a pheromonal cue (Stern and McClintock, 1998). Other examples may well include the role of social interactions in entraining circadian physiological rhythms, the disorganizing effects of sensory deprivation, and the remarkable therapeutic effects of social support on the course of medical illness (reviewed in Hofer, 1984). In this way, adult love, grief, and bereavement may well contain elements of the simpler regulatory processes that we can clearly see in the attachment responses of infant animals to separation from their social companions.

This is perhaps the most challenging area for future research: to find out how to apply what we have learned in basic brain and behavior studies to the human condition. Studies on other animals cannot be used to define human nature, but many of the principles and new ways to approach the mother–infant interaction described in this chapter can be useful in studies of the human mother–infant relationship. We must take into account obvious differences between species, such as the primacy of olfaction and tactile senses in the newborn rat as contrasted to the wider range of senses available to the human newborn. For example, the learning processes regulating approach and proximity that are based on olfaction and tactile senses in the rat pup are likely to be mediated by visual and auditory systems as well as olfaction and touch in the human newborn.

At present, there is widespread use of the concept of regulation as inherent in the mother–infant interaction in humans. This word is generally used in two ways. First, it is used to refer to the graded effects of different patterns of interaction on the emotional responses of the infant, the so-called "regulation of affect" (Schore 1994). Second, it is used to refer to how the behaviors initiated by the infant or mother and/or their responses to each other act to regulate the interaction itself, its tempo or rhythm (hence its "quality"), or the distance (both psychological and physical) between the members of the dyad (Gergeley and Watson, 1999). The word "regulation" is used extensively in the literature on molecular genetic, cellular, and electrophysiological brain processes so that it serves as a useful conceptual link across wide differences in the level of organization at which developmental processes are studied.

A role for nonverbal features of the early mother–infant interaction in the specification of lasting mental representations of maternal behavior in the adult is a central hypothesis of clinical attachment theory. It would be difficult to confirm clinically this useful idea with any degree of certainty. But the transgenerational effects on maternal behavior and the HPA axis described in this chapter can serve as a research model for understanding the psychobiological mechanisms for this important effect. Prospective clinical studies from infancy to childhood would be most interesting and could reveal which residues of particular early interactions can be related to which later characteristics of the stories, play, or social relationships of older children, and eventually the parental behavior of adults.

## REFERENCES

ALBERTS, J. R. and B. MAY, 1984. Nonnutritive, thermotactile induction of filial huddling in rat pups. *Dev. Psychobiol.* 17:161–181.

ASTON-JONES, G., J. RAJKOWSKI, P. KUBIAK, and R. ALEXINSKY, 1994. Locus coeruleus neurons in the monkey are selectively activated by attended stimuli in a vigilance task. *J. Neurosci.* 14:4467–4480.

BARR, G. A., and G. ROSSI, 1992. Conditioned place preference from ventral tegmental injections of morphine in neonatal rats. *Dev. Brain Res.* 66:133–136.

BARR, G. A., and S. WANG, 1992. Peripheral and central administration of cocaine produces conditioned odor preferences in the infant rats. *Brain Res.* 599:181–185.

BLASS, E. M., 1990. Suckling: Determinants, changes, mechanisms, and lasting impressions. *Dev. Psychol.* 26(4):520–533.

BLOZOVSKI, D., and A. CUDENNEC, 1980. Passive avoidance learning in the young rat. *Dev. Psychobiol.* 13:513–518.

BLOZOVSKI, D., and N. HENNOCQ, 1982. Effects of antimuscarinic cholinergic drugs injected systemically or into the hippocampal-entorhinal area upon passive avoidance learning in young rats. *Psychopharmacology* 76:351–358.

BOLLES, R. C., and P. J. WOODS, 1965. The ontogeny of behavior in the albino rat. *Animal Behav.* 12:427–441.

BOWLBY, J., 1969. *Attachment and Loss. Vol. 1: Attachment.* New York: Basic Books.

BOWLBY, J., 1982. Attachment and loss: Retrospect and prospect. *Am. J. Orthopsychiat.* 52:664–678.

BRAKE, S., 1981. Suckling infant rats learn a preference for a novel olfactory stimulus paired with milk delivery. *Science* 211:506–508.

BRAKE, S. C., D. J. SAGER, R. SULLIVAN, AND M. A. HOFER, 1982. The role of intraoral and gastrointestinal cues in the control of sucking and milk consumption in rat pups. *Develop. Psychobiol.* 15(6):529–541.

BRENNEN, P. A., and E. B. KEVERNE, 1997. Neural mechanisms of mammalian olfactory learning. *Prog. Neurobiol.* 51:457–451.

BRUNJES, P. C., and J. R. ALBERTS, 1979. Olfactory stimulation induces filial preferences for huddling in rat pups. *J. Comp. Physiol. Psychol.* 93:548–555.

BRUNJES, P. C., L. K. SMITH-CRAFT, and R. McCARTY, 1985. Unilateral odor deprivation: Effects on the development of olfactory bulb catecholamines and behavior. *Dev. Brain Res.* 22:1–6.

CAHILL, L., N. M. WEINBERGER, B. ROOZENDAAL, and J. L. McGAUGH, 1999. Is the amygdala a locus of "conditioned fear"? Some questions and caveats. *Neuron* 23:227–228.

CAMP, L. L., and J. W. RUDY, 1988. Changes in the categorization of appetitive and aversive events during postnatal development of the rat. *Dev. Psychobiol.* 21:25–42.

CAMPBELL, B. A., 1984. Reflections on the ontogeny of learning and memory. In *Comparative Perspectives on the Development of Memory,* R. Kail and N. E. Spear, eds. Hillsdale, N.J.: Lawrence Erlbaum Associates, pp. 23–35.

CARTER, C. S., J. I. LEDERHANDLER, and B. KIRKPATRICK, 1997. *The Integrative Neurobiology of Affiliation.* New York: New York Academy of Sciences.

CASSIDY, J., and P. R. SHAVER, eds., 1999. Psychobiological origins of infant attachment and separation responses. In *Handbook of Attachment Theory and Research.* New York: Guilford Press.

COLLIER, A. C., J. MAST, D. R. MEYER, and C. E. JACOBS, 1979. Approach-avoidance conflict in preweanling rats: A developmental study. *Animal Learn. Behav.* 7:514–520.

CRAIN, B., C. COTMAN, D. TAYLOR, and G. LYNCH, 1973. A quantitative electron microscopic study of synaptogenesis in the dentate gyrus of the rat. *Brain Res.* 63:195–204.

DECASPER, A. J., and W. P. FIFER, 1980. Of human bonding: Newborns prefer their mothers' voices. *Science* 208:1174–1176.

DECASPER, A. J., and M. J. SPENCE, 1986. Prenatal maternal speech influences a newborn's perception of speech sounds. *Infant Behav. Dev.* 9:133–150.

EIDELMAN, A. I., and M. KAITZ, 1992. Olfactory recognition: A genetic or learned capacity? *Dev. Behav. Pediatr.* 13:126–127.

EMERICH, D. F., F. M. SCALZO, E. K. ENTERS, N. SPEAR, and L. SPEAR, 1985. Effects of 6-hydroxydopamine-induced catecholamine depletion on shock-precipitated wall climbing of infant rat pups. *Dev. Psychobiol.* 18:215–227.

FANSELOW, M. S., and J. E. LEDOUX, 1999. Why we think plasticity underlying Pavlovian fear conditioning occurs in the basolateral amygdala. *Neuron* 23:229–232.

FANSELOW, M. S., and J. W. RUDY, 1998. Convergence of experimental and developmental approaches to animal learning and memory processes. In *Mechanistic Relationships between Development and Learning,* T. J. Carew, R. Menzel, and C. J. Shatz, eds. New York: John Wiley and Sons, pp. 15–28.

FIELD, T. M., S. M. SCHANBERG, F. SCAFIDID, C. R. BAUER, N. VEGA-LAHR, R. GARCIA, J. NYSTROM, and C. M. KUHN, 1986.

Tactile/kinesthetic stimulation effects on preterm neonates. *Pediatrics* 77(5):654–658.

FIFER, W. P., and C. M. MOON, 1995. The effects of fetal experience with sound. In *Fetal Development—A Psychobiological Perspective,* J.-P. Lecanuet, W. P. Fifer, N. A. Krasnegor, and W. P. Smotherman, eds. Hillsdale, N.J.: Lawrence Erlbaum, pp. 351–368.

FILLION, T. J., and E. M. BLASS, 1986. Infantile experience with suckling odors determine adult sexual behavior in male rats. *Science* 231:729–731.

FLEMING, A. S., E. H. O'DAY, and G. W. KRAEMER, 1999. Neurobiology of mother-infant interactions: Experience and central nervous system plasticity across development and generations. *Neurosci. Biobehav. Rev.* 23:673–685.

FOOTE, S. L., G. ASTON-JONES, and F. E. BLOOM, 1983. Impulse activity of locus coeruleus neurons in awake rats and monkey is a function of sensory stimulation and arousal. *Proc. Natl. Acad. Sci. USA* 77:3033–3037.

FRANCIS, D., J. DIORIO, D. LIU, and M. J. MEANEY, 1999. Nongenomic transmission across generations of maternal behavior and stress responses in the rat. *Science* 286:1155–1158.

GALEF, G. G., and H. C. KANER, 1980. Establishment and maintenance of preference for natural and artificial olfactory stimuli in juvenile rats. *J. Comp. Physiol. Psychol.* 94:588–595.

GALEF, G. G., and D. F. SHERRY, 1973. Mother's milk: Medium for transmission of cues reflecting the flavor of mother's diet. *J. Comp. Physiol. Psychol.* 83:374–378.

GERGELEY, G., and J. S. WATSON, 1999. Early social-emotional development: Contingency perception and the social biofeedback model. In *Early Social Cognition,* P. Rochat, ed. Hillsdale, N.J.: Erlbaum, pp. 101–136.

GOLDBERG, S., R. MUIR, and J. KERR, 1995. *Attachment Theory: Social, Developmental, and Clinical Perspectives.* Hillsdale, N.J.: Analytic Press.

GOLDMAN, P. S., and E. TOBACH, 1967. Behavior modification in infant rats. *Animal Behav.* 15:559–562.

GOODWIN, G. A., and G. A. BARR, 1998. Behavioral and heart rate effects of infusing kainic acid into the dorsal midbrain during early development in the rat. *Dev. Brain Res.* 107:11–20.

HARLEY, C. W., and S. J. SARA, 1992. Locus coeruleus burst induced by glutamate trigger delayed perforant path spike amplitude potentiation in the dentate gyrus. *Exp. Brain Res.* 89:581–587.

HARLOW, H. F., and M. K. HARLOW, 1965. The affectional systems. In *Behavior of Nonhuman Primate,* Vol. 2, A. Schrier, H. F. Harlow, and F. Stollnitz, eds. New York: Academic Press.

HELFER, M. E., R. S. KEMPE, and R. D. KRUGMAN, 1997. *The Battered Child.* Chicago: University of Chicago Press.

HEPPER, P. G., 1986. Parental recognition in the rat. *Quart. J. Exp. Psychol.* 38B:151–160.

HEPPER, P. G., 1987. The amniotic fluid: An important priming role in kin recognition. *Animal Behav.* 35(5):1343–1346.

HESS, E. H., 1962. Ethology: An approach to the complete analysis of behavior. In *New Directions in Psychology,* R. Brown, E. Galanter, E. H. Hess, and G. Mendler, eds. New York: Holt, Rinehart, and Winston.

HOFER, M. A., 1971. Cardiac rate regulated by nutritional factor in young rats. *Science* 172:1039–1041.

HOFER, M. A., 1975a. Infant separation responses and the maternal role. *Biol. Psychiat.* 10:149–153.

HOFER, M. A., 1975b. Studies on how early maternal separation produces behavioral change in young rats. *Psychosom. Med.* 37:245–264.

HOFER, M. A., 1976. The organization of sleep and wakefulness after maternal separation in young rats. *Dev. Psychobiol.* 9:189–205.

HOFER, M. A., 1980. The effects of reserpine and amphetamine on the development of hyperactivity in maternally deprived rat pups. *Psychosom. Med.* 42:513–520.

HOFER, M. A., 1981. Effects of infraorbital nerve section on survival, growth and suckling behaviors of developing rats. *J. Comp. Physiol. Psychol.* 95:123–133.

HOFER, M. A., 1983. On the relationship between attachment and separation processes in infancy. In *Emotions in Early Development,* R. Plutchik and H. Kellerman, eds. New York: Academic Press, pp. 199–216.

HOFER, M. A., 1984. Relationships as regulators: A psychobiological perspective on bereavement. *Psychosom. Med.* 46:183–197.

HOFER, M. A., 1996a. On the nature and consequences of early loss. *Psychosom. Med.* 58(6):570–581.

HOFER, M. A., 1996b. Multiple regulators of ultrasonic vocalization in the infant rat. *Psychoneuroendocrinology* 21(2):203–217.

HOFER, M. A., and H. N. SHAIR, 1980. Sensory processes in the control of isolation-induced ultrasonic vocalization by 2 week old rats. *J. Comp. Physiol. Psychol.* 94:271–279.

HOFER, M. A., and H. N. SHAIR, 1991. Trigeminal and olfactory pathways mediating isolation distress and companion comfort responses in rat pups. *Behav. Neurosci.* 105:699–706.

HOFER, M. A., and H. WEINER, 1975. Physiological mechanisms for cardiac control by nutritional intake after early maternal separation in the young rat. *Psychosom. Med.* 37:8–24.

HOFFMANN, H., and N. E. SPEAR, 1989. Facilitation and impairment of conditioning in the preweanling rat after prior exposure to the conditioned stimulus. *Animal Learn. Behav.* 17:63–69.

INSEL, T. R., 1992. Oxytocin—a neuropeptide for affiliation: Evidence from behavioral, receptor autoradiographic and comparative studies. *Psychoneuroendocrinology* 17:3–35.

JIANG, M. R., E. R. GRIFF, M. ENNIS, L. A. ZIMMER, and M. T. SHIPLEY, 1996. Activation of locus coeruleus enhances the responses of olfactory bulb mitral cells to weak olfactory nerve input. *J. Neurosci.* 16:6319–6329.

JOHANSON, I. B., and W. G. HALL, 1979. Appetitive learning in 1-day-old rat pups. *Science* 205:419–421.

JOHANSON, I. B., and M. TEICHER, 1980. Classical conditioning of an odor preference in 3-day-old rats. *Behav. Neural Biol.* 29:132–136.

JOHNSON, B. A., C. C. WOO, H. DUONG, V. NGUYEN, and M. LEON, 1995. A learned odor evokes an enhanced Fos-like glomerular response in the olfactory bulb of young rats. *Brain Res.* 699:192–200.

JURGENS, U., 1994. The role of periaqueductal grey in vocal behaviour. *Behav. Brain Res.* 62:107–117.

KAITZ, M., P. LAPIDOT, and R. BRONNER, 1992. Parturient women can recognize their infants by touch. *Dev. Psychol.* 1:35–39.

KATZ, L. M., L. NATHAN, C. M. KUHN, and S. M. SCHANBERG, 1996. Inhibition of GH in maternal separation may be mediated through altered serotonergic activity at 5HT$_{2A}$ and 5HT$_{2C}$ receptors. *Psychoneuroendocrinology* 21(2):219–235.

KEHOE, P., and E. BLASS, 1986. Central nervous system mediation of positive and negative reinforcement in neonatal albino rats. *Brain Res.* 392:69–75.

KIMURA, F., and S. NAKAMURA, 1985. Locus coeruleus neurons in the neonatal rat: Electrical activity and responses to sensory stimulation. *Dev. Brain Res.* 23:301–305.

KRAEMER, G. W., 1992. A psychobiological theory of attachment. *Behav. Brain Sci.* 15(3):493–511.

KUCHARSKI, D., and W. G. HALL, 1988. Developmental changes in the access to olfactory memories. *Behav. Neurosci.* 102:340–348.

KUHN, C. M., and S. M. SCHANBERG, 1991. Stimulation in infancy and brain development. In *Psychopathology and the Brain,* B.J. Carroll, ed. New York: Raven Press.

LANDERS, M., and R. M. SULLIVAN, 1999a. Vibrissae evoked behavior and conditioning before functional ontogeny of the somatosensory vibrissae cortex. *J. Neurosci.* 19:5131–5137.

LANDERS, M., and R. M. SULLIVAN, 1999b. Norepinephrine and associative conditioning in the neonatal rat somatosensory system. *Dev. Brain Res.* 114:261–264.

LANGDON, P. E., C. W. HARLEY, and J. H. MCLEAN, 1997. Increased ß adrenoceptor activation overcomes conditioned olfactory learning induced by serotonin depletion. *Dev. Brain Res.* 102:291–293.

LAUDER, J. M., and F. E. BLOOM, 1974. Ontogeny of monoamine neurons in the locus coeruleus, raphe nuclei and substantia nigra of the rat. *J. Comp. Neurol.* 155:469–482.

LECANUET, J., and B. SCHAAL, 1996. Fetal sensory competencies. *Eur. J. Obstet. Gynecol. Reprod. Biol.* 68:1–23.

LEON, M., 1975. Dietary control of maternal pheromone in the lactating rat. *Physiol. Behav.* 14:311–319.

LESTER, B. M., and C. F. BOUKYDIS, eds., 1985. *Infant Crying: Theoretical and Research Perspectives.* New York: Plenum Press.

LEVINE, A., 1994. The ontogeny of the hypothalamic-pituitary-adrenal axis: The influence of maternal factors. *Ann. N.Y. Acad. Sci.* 746:275–293.

LEVY, F., R. GERVAIS, U. KINDERMANN, P. ORGEUR, and V. PIKETTY, 1990. Importance of ß adrenergic receptors in the olfactory bulb of sheep for recognition of lambs. *Behav. Neurosci.* 104:464–469.

LINCOLN, J., R. COOPERSMITH, E. W. HARRIS, C. W. COTMAN, and M. LEON, 1988. NMDA receptor activation and early olfactory learning. *Brain Res.* 467:309–312.

LIU, D., J. DIORIO, B. TANNENBAUM, C. CALDJI, D. FRANCIS, A. FREEDMAN, S. SHARMA, D. PEARSON, P. M. PLOTSKY, and M. J. MEANEY, 1997. Maternal care, hippocampal glucocorticoid receptors, and hypothalamic-pituitary-adrenal responses to stress. *Science* 277:1659–1661.

MAKIN, J. W., and R. H. PORTER, 1989. Attractiveness of lactating females' breast odors to neonates. *Child Dev.* 60:803–810.

MARSHALL, K. C., M. M. CHRISTI, P. G. FINLAYSON, and J. T. WILLIAMS, 1991. Developmental aspects of the locus coeruleus-noradrenaline system. *Prog. Brain Res.* 88:173–185.

MARTIN, L. T., and J. R. ALBERTS, 1979. Taste aversion to mother's milk: The age-related role of nursing in acquisition and expression of a learned association. *J. Comp. Physiol. Psychol.* 93:430–445.

MCLEAN, J. H., A. DARBY-KING, R. M. SULLIVAN, and S. R. KING, 1993. Serotonergic influences on olfactory learning in the neonatal rat. *Behav. Neural Biol.* 60:152–162.

MCLEAN, J. H., and M. T. SHIPLEY, 1991. Postnatal develop-

ment of the noradrenergic projection from the locus coeruleus to the olfactory bulb in the rat. *J. Comp. Neurol.* 304:467–477.

MENNELLA, J., A. JOHNSON, and G. BEAUCHAMP, 1995. Garlic ingestion by pregnant women alters the odor of amniotic fluid. *Chem. Senses* 20:207–209.

MICHEL, G. F., and C. L. MOORE, 1995. *Developmental Psychobiology: An Interdisciplinary Science.* Cambridge, Mass.: MIT Press.

MICKLEY, G. A., M. A. SCHALDACH, K. J. SNYDER, S. A. BALAGH, T. LEN, K. NEIMANIS, P. GAULIS, J. HUG, K. SAUCHAK, D. R. REMMERS-ROEBER, C. WALKER, and B. K. YAMAMOTO, 1998. Ketamine blocks a conditioned taste aversion in neonatal rats. *Physiol. Behav.* 64:381–390.

MICZEK, K. A., W. TORNATSKY, and J. VIVIAN, 1991. Ethology and neuropharmacology: Rodent ultrasounds. *Advances in Pharmacologic Sciences.* Basel: Birkhauser, pp. 409–429.

MILLER, J. S., J. A. JAGIELO, and N. E. SPEAR, 1989. Age-related differences in short-term retention of separable elements of an odor aversion. *J. Exp. Psychol.* 15:194–201.

MOFFAT, S. D., E. J. SUH, and A. FLEMING, 1993. Noradrenergic involvement in the consolidation of maternal experience in postpartum rats. *Physiol. Behav.* 53:805–811.

MOORE, C. L., L. JORDAN, and L. WONG, 1996. Early olfactory experience, novelty and choice of sexual partner by male rats. *Physiol. Behav.* 60:1361–1367.

MYERS, M. M., S. A. BRUNELLI, J. M. SQUIRE, R. SHINDELDECKER, and M. A. HOFER, 1989. Maternal behavior of SHR rats and its relationship to offspring blood pressure. *Dev. Psychobiol.* 22(1):29–53.

MYSLIVECEK, J., 1997. Inhibitory learning and memory in newborn rats. *Prog. Neurobiol.* 53:399–430.

NAIR, H. P., and F. GONZALEZ-LIMA, 1999. Extinction of behavior in infant rats: Development of functional coupling between septal, hippocampal, and ventral tegmental regions. *J. Neurosci.* 19:8646–8655.

NAKAMURA, S. T., and T. SAKAGUCHI, 1990. Development and plasticity of the locus coeruleus. A review of recent physiological and pharmacological experimentation. *Prog. Neurobiol.* 34:505–526.

NEWMAN, J. D. (ed.), 1988. *The Physiological Control of Mammalian Vocalization.* New York: Plenum Press.

NOIROT, E., 1968. Ultrasounds in young rodents: II. Changes with age in albino rats. *Animal. Behav.* 16:129–134.

OKUTANI, F., F. YAGI, and H. KABA, 1999. GABAergic control of olfactory learning in young rats. *Neuroscience* 93:1297–1300.

PAGER, J., 1974. A selective modulation of olfactory bulb electrical activity in relation to the learning of palatability in hungry and satiated rats. *Physiol. Behav.* 12:189–195.

PEDERSEN, P., C. L. WILLIAMS, and E. M. BLASS, 1982. Activation and odor conditioning of suckling behavior in 3-day-old albino rats. *J. Exp. Psychol. Anim. Behav. Proc.* 8:329–341.

PISSONNIER, D., J. C. THIERY, C. FABRE-NYS, P. POINDRON, and E. B. KEVERNE, 1985. The importance of olfactory bulb noradrenaline for maternal recognition in sheep. *Physiol. Behav.* 35:361–363.

POLAN, H. J., and M. A. HOFER, 1998. Olfactory preference for mother over home nest shavings by newborn rats. *Dev. Psychobiol.* 33:5–20.

POLAN, H. J., and M. A. HOFER, 1999a. Maternally directed orienting behaviors of newborn rats. *Dev. Psychobiol.* 34:269–280.

POLAN, H. J., and M. A. HOFER, 1999b. Psychobiological origins of infant attachment and separation response. In *Handbook of Attachment Theory and Research*, J. Cassidy and P. R. Shaver, eds. New York: Guilford Publications, pp. 162–180.

PORTER, M. J., J. M. CERNOCH, and F. J. McLAUGHLIN, 1983. Maternal recognition of neonates through olfactory cues. *Physiol. Behav.* 30:151–154.

PORTER, R. H., and J. WINBERG, 1999. Unique salience of maternal breast odors for newborn infants. *Neurosci. Biobehav. Rev.* 23:439–449.

RAJECKI, D. W., M. E. LAMB, and P. OBMASCHER, 1978. Toward a general theory of infantile attachment: A comparative view of the social bond. *Behav. Brain Sci.* 3:417–464.

RANGEL, S., and M. LEON, 1995. Early odor preference training increases olfactory bulb norepinephrine. *Dev. Brain Res.* 85:187–191.

ROBINSON, S. R., and W. P. SMOTHERMAN, 1995. Habituation and classical conditioning in the rat fetus: Opioid involvements. In *Fetal Development—A Psychobiological Perspective*, J.-P. Lecanuet, W. P. Fifer, N. A. Krasnegor, and W. P. Smotherman, eds. Hillsdale, N.J.: Lawrence Erlbaum Associates, pp. 295–314.

ROTH, T., and R. M. SULLIVAN, 2000. Endogenous opioids are necessary for an odor preference during odor-shock conditioning. Paper presented at the annual meeting of the International Society for Developmental Psychobiology, New Orleans.

RUDY, J. W., and M. D. CHEATLE, 1979. Odor aversion learning in neonatal rats. *Science* 198:845–846.

RUDY, J. W., and P. MORLEDGE, 1994. The ontogeny of contextual fear conditioning: Implications for consolidation, infantile amnesia, and hippocampal system function. *Behav. Neurosci.* 108:227–234.

RUDY, J. W., S. STADLER-MORRIS, and P. A. ALBERTS, 1987. Ontogeny of spatial navigation behaviors in the rat: Dissociation of "proximal-" and "distal-cue" based behaviors. *Behav. Neurosci.* 101:62–73.

SALZEN, E. A., 1970. Imprinting and environmental learning. In *Development and Evolution of Behavior*, L. R. Aronson, E. Tobach, D. S. Lehrman, and J. Rosenblatt, eds. San Francisco: W. H. Freeman.

SANANES, C. B., and B. A. CAMPBELL, 1989. Role of the central nucleus of the amygdala in olfactory heart rate conditioning. *Behav. Neurosci.* 103:519–525.

SARA, S. J., D. DYON-LAURENT, and A. HERVE, 1995. Novelty seeking behavior in the rat is dependent upon the integrity of the noradrenergic system. *Cogn. Brain Res.* 2:181–187.

SCHAAL, B., L. MARLIER, and R. SOUSSIGNAN, 1995. Responsiveness to the odour of amniotic fluid in the human neonate. *Biol. Neonate* 67:396–406.

SCHOENBAUM, G., A. A. CHIBA, and M. GALLAGHER, 1999. Neural encoding in orbitofrontal cortex and basolateral amygdala during olfactory discrimination learning. *J. Neurosci.* 19:1876–1884.

SCHORE, A. N., 1994. *Affect Regulation and the Origin of the Self.* Hillsdale, N.J.: Lawrence Erlbaum Associates.

SHAIR, H. N., G. A. BARR, and M. A. HOFER, eds., 1991. *Developmental Psychobiology, New Methods and Changing Concepts.* Oxford: Oxford University Press.

SHAIR, H. N., J. R. MASMELA, S. A. BRUNELLI, and M. A. HOFER, 1997. Potentiation and inhibition of ultrasonic vocalization of rat pups: Regulation by social cues. *Dev. Psychobiol.* 30:195–200.

SHEAR, M. K., S. A. BRUNELLI, AND M. A. HOFER, 1983. The effects of maternal deprivation and of refeeding on the blood pressure of infant rats. *Psychosom. Med.* 45:3–9.

SHIPLEY, M. T., F. J. HALLORAN, and J. DE LA TORRE, 1985. Surprisingly rich projection from locus coeruleus to the olfactory bulb in the rat. *Brain Res.* 239:294–299.

SMOTHERMAN, W. P., R. W. BELL, W. A. HERSHBERGER, and G. D. COOVER, 1978. Orientation to rat pup cues: Effects of maternal experiential history. *Animal Behav.* 26:265–273.

SMOTHERMAN, W. P., and S. R. ROBINSON, 1986. Environmental determinants of behaviour in the rat fetus. *Animal Behav.* 34:1859–1873.

SMOTHERMAN, W. P., and S. R. ROBINSON, 1992. Prenatal experience with milk: Fetal behavior and endogenous opioid systems. *Neurosci. Biobehav. Rev.* 16:351–364.

SPEAR, N. E., 1978. *Processing Memories: Forgetting and Retention.* Hillsdale, N.J.: Erlbaum.

SPEAR, N. E., D. KUCHARSKI, and J. S. MILLER, 1989. The CS-effect in simple conditioning and stimulus selection during development. *Animal Learn. Behav.* 17:70–82.

STANTON, M. E., 2000. Multiple memory systems, development and conditioning. *Behav. Brain Res.* 110:25–37.

STANTON, M. D., Y. R. GUTIERREZ, and S. LEVINE, 1988. Maternal deprivation potentiates pituitary-adrenal stress responses in infant rats. *Behav. Neurosci.* 102:692–700.

STEHOUWER, D. J., and B. A. CAMPBELL, 1978. Habituation of the forelimb-withdrawal response in neonatal rats. *J. Exp. Psychol. Anim. Behav. Proc.* 4:104–119.

STERN, D. N., 1985. *The Interpersonal World of the Infant: A View from Psychoanalysis and Developmental Psychology.* New York: Basic Books.

STERN, K., and M. K. McCLINTOCK, 1998. Regulation of ovulation by human pheromones. *Nature* 392:177–179.

STONE, E., K. BONNET, and M. A. HOFER, 1976. Survival and development of maternally deprived rat pups: Role of body temperature. *Psychosom. Med.* 38:242–249.

SUCHECKI, D., P. ROSENFELD, and S. LEVINE, 1993. Maternal regulation of the hypothalamic-pituitary-adrenal axis in the infant rat: The roles of feeding and stroking. *Dev. Brain Res.* 75:185–192.

SULLIVAN, R. M., S. C. BRAKE, M. A. HOFER, and C. L. WILLIAMS, 1986. Huddling and independent feeding of neonatal rats can be facilitated by a conditioned change in behavioral state. *Dev. Psychobiol.* 19:625–635.

SULLIVAN, R. M., M. A. HOFER, and S. C. BRAKE, 1986. Olfactory-guided orientation in neonatal rats is enhanced by a conditioned change in behavioral state. *Dev. Psychobiol.* 19:615–623.

SULLIVAN, R. M., M. LANDERS, B. YEAGER, and D. A. WILSON, 2000. Good memories of bad events in infancy. *Nature* 407:38–39.

SULLIVAN, R. M., and M. LEON, 1986. Early olfactory learning induces an enhanced olfactory bulb response in young rats. *Dev. Brain Res.* 27:278–282.

SULLIVAN, R. M., G. STACKENWALT, F. NASR, C. LEMON, and D. A. WILSON, 2000. Association of an odor with activation of olfactory bulb noradrenergic ß-receptors or locus coeruleus stimulation is sufficient to produce learned approach response to that odor in neonatal rats. *Behav. Neurosci.* 114:957–962.

SULLIVAN, R. M., S. TABORSKY-BARBA, R. MENDOZA, A. ITANO, M. LEON, C. COTMAN, T. F. PAYNE, and I. LOTT, 1991. Olfactory classical conditioning in neonates. *Pediatrics* 87:511–518.

SULLIVAN, R. M., and D. A. WILSON, 1993. Role of the amygdala complex in early olfactory associative learning. *Behav. Neurosci.* 107:254–263.

SULLIVAN, R. M., and D. A. WILSON, 1995. Dissociation of behavioral and neural correlates of early associative learning. *Dev. Psychobiol.* 28:213–219.

SULLIVAN, R. M., D. A. WILSON, C. LEMON, and G. A. GERHARDT, 1994. Bilateral 6-OHDA lesions of the locus coeruleus impair associative olfactory learning in newborn rats. *Brain Res.* 643:306–309.

SULLIVAN, R. M., D. A. WILSON, R. WONG, A. CORREA, and M. LEON, 1990. Modified behavioral olfactory bulb responses to maternal odors in preweanling rats. *Dev. Brain Res.* 53:243–247.

SULLIVAN, R. M., D. ZYZAK, P. SKIERKOWSKI, and D. A. WILSON, 1992. The role of olfactory bulb norepinephrine in early olfactory learning. *Dev. Brain Res.* 70:279–282.

SUOMI, S. J., 1997. Early determinants of behaviour: Evidence from primate studies. *Br. Med. Bull.* 53(1):170–184.

TAKAHASHI, L. K., 1992. Developmental expression of defensive responses during exposure to conspecific adults in preweanling rats (*Rattus norvegicus*). *J. Comp. Psychol.* 106:69–77.

TERRY, L. M., and I. B. JOHANSON, 1996. Effects of altered olfactory experiences on the development of infant rats' responses to odors. *Dev. Psychobiol.* 29:353–377.

TROMBLEY, P. Q., and G. M. SHEPHERD, 1992. Noradrenergic inhibition of synaptic transmission between mitral and granule cells in mammalian olfactory bulb cultures. *J. Neurosci.* 12:3985–3991.

VANKOV, A., A. HERVE-MINVIELLE, and S. J. SARA, 1995. Response to novelty and its rapid habituation in locus coeruleus neurons of the freely exploring rat. *Eur. J. Neurosci.* 7:1180–1187.

VAN OERS, H. J. J., E. R. DE KLOET, T. WHELAN, and S. LEVINE, 1998. Maternal deprivation effect on the infant's neural stress markers is reversed by tactile stimulation and feeding but not by suppressing corticosterone. *J. Neurosci.* 18(23):10171–10179.

VARENDI, H., K. CHRISTENSON, R. H. PORTER, and J. WINBERG, 1998. Soothing effect of amniotic fluid smell in newborn infants. *Early Hum. Dev.* 51:47–55.

VARENDI, H., R. H. PORTER, and J. WINBERG, 1996. Attractiveness of amniotic fluid odor: Evidence of prenatal olfactory learning? *Acta Paediatr.* 85:1223–1227.

WELDON, D. A., M. L. TRAVIS, and D. A. KENNEDY, 1991. Post-training D1 receptor blockade impairs odor conditioning in neonatal rats. *Behav. Neurosci.* 105:450–458.

WETZEL, D. M., D. B. KELLEY, and B. A. CAMPBELL, 1980. Central control of ultrasonic vocalizations in neonatal rats: I. Brain stem motor nuclei. *J. Comp. Physiol. Psychol.* 94:596–605.

WHITE, N. R., R. ADOX, A. REDDY, and R. J. BARFIELD, 1992. Regulation of rat maternal behavior by broadband pup vocalizations. *Behav. Neural Biol.* 58:131–137.

WILSON, D. A., and M. LEON, 1988b. Noradrenergic modulation of olfactory bulb excitability in the postnatal rat. *Dev. Brain Res.* 42:69–75.

WILSON, D. A., and R. M. SULLIVAN, 1990. Olfactory associative conditioning in infant rats with brain stimulation as reward. I. Neurobehavioral consequences. *Dev. Brain Res.* 53:215–221.

WILSON, D. A., and R. M. SULLIVAN, 1991. Olfactory associative conditioning in infant rats with brain stimulation as reward. II. Norepinephrine mediates a specific component of the bulb response to reward. *Behav. Neurosci.* 105:843–849.

WILSON, D. A., and R. M. SULLIVAN, 1992. Blockade of mitral/tufted cell habituation to odors by association with reward: A preliminary note. *Brain Res.* 594:143–145.

WILSON, D. A., and R. M. SULLIVAN, 1994. Neurobiology of associative learning in the neonate: Early olfactory learning. *Behav. Neural Biol.* 61:1–18.

WILSON, D. A., R. M. SULLIVAN, and M. LEON, 1987. Single-unit analysis of postnatal olfactory learning: Modified olfactory bulb output response patterns to learned attractive odors. *J. Neurosci.* 7:3154–3162.

WOO, C. C., R. COOPERSMITH, and M. LEON, 1987. Localized changes in olfactory bulb morphology associated with early olfactory learning. *J. Comp. Neurol.* 263:113–125.

WOO, C. C., and M. LEON, 1988. Sensitive period for neural and behavioral responses to learned odors. *Dev. Brain Res.* 36:309–313.

WOO, C. C., and M. LEON, 1995. Distribution and development of β-adrenergic receptors in the rat olfactory bulb. *J. Comp. Neurol.* 352:1–10.

# 39 Effects of Early Deprivation: Findings from Orphanage-Reared Infants and Children

MEGAN R. GUNNAR

ABSTRACT This chapter briefly summarizes the state of our current understanding of the development of children from deprived, orphanage backgrounds, considering, where relevant, the results of animal studies. Three levels of deprivation are contrasted that differ in whether health and nutrition, social and physical stimulation, and relationship needs are met. Emphasis is placed on relating the relatively large literature on deprivation and behavioral development to the more limited literature on deprivation and neurobiological development in humans and other primates.

The effects of early deprivation have seen renewed interest recently. As will be discussed, deprivation can be multifaceted, involving various failures in the caregiving environment: failure to provide adequate nutrition, medical care, stimulation, and/or enduring and supportive relationships. Such failures constitute neglect, and there is a mounting belief that neglect or deprivation may confer as significant a risk for psychopathology as physical and sexual abuse (National Research Council, 1993). Our renewed interest and deepening concern about the effects of early deprivation comes at a time when the tools of neuroscience offer promise that we may be able to understand deprivation effects in ways not previously possible. Nonetheless, the impact of early deprivation is difficult to isolate unless the period of deprivation is circumscribed. In most cases, deprivation early in life is followed by life events that also threaten healthy physical, emotional, and cognitive development, making it difficult to disentangle early from later threats to normal brain development. Children adopted from orphanages offer a dramatic contrast; their early deprivation is typically followed by development within often enriched environments (Rutter, 1981). The last decade also has seen an increasing flow of these children from orphanages in the developing world and Eastern Europe into middle- and upper-middle class families in the

United States, Canada, and Western Europe. Because these children offer a dramatic case in point, in considering the impact of early deprivation in this chapter, I will focus on information obtained in studies of orphanage-reared children—in particular, those fostered or adopted into families after spending some or all of their first two years in institutions. The term "orphanage," while evocative, is a misnomer, as most of these children are not orphaned, but abandoned or removed from families who cannot care for them adequately. As yet, there have been few neurobiological studies of these children (Chugani et al., 2001). Nonetheless, there is a long history of behavioral research on orphanage rearing. There is also a related body of nonhuman primate research, some of which includes neurobiological data (Kraemer et al., 1989). This earlier work should serve as a starting point for future neurobiological studies. With this in mind, the goal of this chapter is to briefly summarize the state of our current understanding of the development of children from deprived, orphanage backgrounds, considering, where relevant, the results of animal, and in particular, primate studies.

## History of orphanage-rearing studies and conceptual issues

Current studies of orphanage-reared children focus on the wave of Romanian children adopted into families following the fall of the Romanian communist regime in the early 1990s (Benoit et al., 1996; Groze and Ileana, 1996; Morison, Ames, and Chisholm, 1995; Rutter, 1998). Future studies are likely to deal with the thousands of children arriving yearly from orphanages in Russia, the former Soviet Republics, Eastern Europe, and China (Albers et al., 1997). The work on the Romanian children adds to information from research on orphanage rearing that spanned the decades of the 1930s through the 1970s (Rutter, 1981). This work is credited with the closing of most orphanages in western

MEGAN R. GUNNAR  Institute of Child Development, University of Minnesota, Minneapolis, Minnesota.

industrialized countries in favor of expanding the foster-care system for young wards of the state. There have been many excellent reviews of this early work (see especially Rutter, 1981) and the reader is encouraged to consult these sources.

LEVELS OF PRIVATION A critical caveat, based on all of the work on orphanage-rearing, is the evidence that the orphanage experience is heterogeneous and cannot be encompassed, as it often was, by reference to maternal deprivation (Rutter, 1981). Despite the heterogeneity of institutional environments, these environments can be ordered by establishing a hierarchy of needs met or not met in institutional settings. Health and nutrition can be considered the most basic of needs, followed by stimulation supporting sensorimotor, cognitive and language development, adult–child and child–child social stimulation, and finally relationships (i.e., stable, consistent, interpersonal associations in which emotional attachments are likely to develop). While these levels of need can be differentiated, typically they do not vary independently. Thus, institutions that fail to meet the most basic needs also tend to fail on all the remaining levels. Those that provide adequate cognitive and sensorimotor stimulation, for reasons discussed below, tend also to provide adequate social and linguistic stimulation. We have no information on the impact of orphanages that manage to supply adequate relationship experiences, as none of the ones previously studied, irrespective of how adequately staffed and financed, is known to have met this level of need. Thus in reviewing the data, I will consider the impact of three levels of privation: (1) what Rutter (1998) has called global privation (privation of health, nutrition, stimulation, and relationship needs); (2) institutions that provide adequate health and nutrition support, but fail to meet the child's need for stimulation and relationships; and (3) institutions that appear to meet all needs except the need for stable, long-term relationships with consistent caregivers.

Of course, for children arriving from abroad we often lack the information needed to determine which level of privation they have experienced. Indeed, even within the same orphanage different children may experience different levels of privation (Frank et al., 1996). This problem is not that different from the problem we face in studying maltreated and neglected children, as our data on what these children have experienced is usually either missing or dependent on the reports of those whose actions produced or allowed the maltreatment (Cicchetti and Lynch, 1995). Nonetheless, to deal with the missing information problem, I will emphasize early studies that tested children while they were still in the orphanage environment and followed them after being fostered or adopted into homes. Two of these early studies will be used as exemplars of more general findings. These studies were chosen because they allow examination of the impact of the second and third levels of privation described above. Their results will be contrasted with those from the recent work on post-institutionalized, Romanian-adopted children for whom we can be fairly certain that most experienced the first or global privation level of orphanage experience.

EXEMPLAR STUDIES The first exemplar study was conducted by Provence and Lipton (1962) who traced the developmental decline of 75 full-term, healthy newborns over the course of their first 2 years of institutional life. This study provides evidence that, even in the context of adequate health and nutritional support, failure to meet stimulation and relationship needs produces marked developmental delays in human infants. Provence and Lipton conducted their study in a U.S. orphanage that was fairly typical for its time. It provided its charges with a clean, albeit fairly sterile environment, competent, albeit perfunctory caretaking, good medical care, and adequate nutrition. Social stimulation was negligible, feedings were from propped bottles, only a few toys were available, and motor development was not especially encouraged. High staff turnover and high child-to-staff ratio hindered the establishment of relationships. Using Gesell's scales of sensorimotor development, infants were only slightly delayed by 3–6 months (mean full-scale scores of 102) compared to infants in foster or family care (mean 116), although both groups scored within the normal range on this test. However, by 10–13 months, the orphanage-reared infants were significantly delayed (scores of 84 versus 107). In detailed notes Provence and Lipton documented the delays as they emerged. Their notes clearly document a striking and increasing apathy among the infants, as indicated in repeated comments about lack of fussing, crying, cooing, laughing, babbling, motor activity, and busyness. We will return to the issue of apathy later. Importantly, despite adequate medical care and nutrition, the developmental decline noted by Provence and Lipton was similar in degree to the typical decline noted for the current wave of Romanian children adopted after experiencing global privation (Rutter, 1998). Clearly, the failure to thrive seen in orphanage-reared infants and toddlers cannot be attributed solely to poor health and nutrition, although health and nutrition must be considered in modeling the neurobiological effects of early deprivation.

The second study that will be emphasized was conducted by Tizard and colleagues (Hodges and Tizard,

1989a,b; Tizard and Hodges, 1978; Tizard and Joseph, 1970; Tizard and Rees, 1974). They studied children reared in institutions in England that served as training institutes for nurses. These institutions were clearly exemplary in providing adequate, developmentally appropriate stimulation in addition to health and nutritional support. This study demonstrates that many of the cognitive, sensorimotor, and linguistic delays for orphanage-reared children can be prevented when stimulation is adequate. Unlike the institutions studied by Provence and Lipton, those studied by Tizard and colleagues had staff:child ratios of 1:1.4. Children lived in small, stable living groups, in rooms well-stocked with developmentally appropriate books and toys. They took many outings and often spent weekends with staff members. Because these were training sites, however, staff turnover was high, with children experiencing an average of 24 caregivers in 24 months. The development of these children allows us to examine the impact of relationship privation, in the absence of privation of health, nutrition, and cognitive-social support. Under these conditions, the failure to develop behaviorally and physically was not observed. Although there was some slight delay in language at 2 years, development at 24 months of age averaged only 2 months delayed, compared to the more typical 9–12-month delay noted by this age for infants in low-stimulating institutions (Tizard and Joseph, 1970). Clearly, relationships are not required to halt the physical decline and to support many of the sensorimotor, cognitive, and linguistic accomplishments of the early years. However, these children, like many with more deprived orphanage experiences, did display certain long-term effects that will be highlighted in this chapter.

Framing Questions about Stimulation What is it about inadequate stimulation that is so devastating early in life? The temptation is to start answering this question by attempting to map particular types of stimulation to particular aspects of neurobehavioral development. Indeed, as evidenced in the work on visual stimulation and the organization of the visual cortex, such specificity does exist (Hubel and Wiesel, 1965). However, to begin at this level misses a most profound phenomenon. In stimulation-poor environments human infants experience massive delays in both physical and behavioral growth (Hostetter et al., 1991; Johnson et al., 1992; Spitz, 1946). Furthermore, they appear to be much more vulnerable to these delays than do even our close primate relatives. It is striking that even if the monkey infant is reared in complete social isolation, it does not show anything like the decline in functioning routinely described for human infants and toddlers

(Harlow, Harlow, and Suomi, 1971). Numerous studies of monkeys reared under conditions of isolation have shown that compared to mother-reared captive monkeys or feral-reared monkeys, they continue to grow physically and they achieve the expected motor milestones. In cognitive functioning they differ only slightly from mother-reared infants, showing deficits in one series of studies only on highly complex, oddity-learning problems (Harlow, Harlow, and Suomi, 1971; Singh, 1969). This finding is in sharp contrast to what has been observed in human infants (Spitz, 1946). Something beyond the lack of stimulation needs to be considered in explaining these differences.

Models of the role of experience in neural development, and the mounting information on molecular processes in neural plasticity, indicate that neural activity (i.e., activity-dependent processes) is critical to brain development (Purvis, 1997). This implies that, in addition to the stimuli available in the environment, effects on neural development will depend on the neural activity the stimuli engender. In this regard, active engagement of the environment may be essential in order for some, perhaps many, aspects of stimulation-dependent neural development to occur. Indeed, long ago Held and Hein (1963) demonstrated this for the visual system in their study contrasting visual development for kittens whose own activity produced changes in visual stimulation compared to those who passively experienced the same visual environment. Recent work with human infants on the onset of independent locomotion and its impact on perceptual-motor development and the maturation of EEG patterns (Bai and Bertenthal, 1992; Bell and Fox, 1996) makes a similar point. This work has been discussed in the larger framework of the critical role of agency and intentionality in motivation (White, 1959) and cognitive development (Russell, 1996). Accordingly, the motivation to produce actions is viewed as dependent on the experience of response-contingent stimulation (White, 1959). Likewise, the development of concepts of the physical world, of one's mental self, and of the mental lives of others is viewed as dependent on the exercise of agency, or the power to alter at will one's perceptual inputs (Russell, 1996).

For much of the first year of life the human infant can do little to produce effects on the environment without the active intervention and mediation of adults. Thus depriving environments deprive the human infant not only of passive stimulation, but of response-contingent stimulation as well. Indeed, most stimulation received in a low-stimulating orphanage is response-independent (Provence and Lipton, 1962). Children reared in families rapidly develop sensitivity to both response-contingent and response-independent stimulation and appear capable, by as early as 3–4 months, of learning when outcomes are response-independent (Rovee-Collier and Capatides, 1979). Learning that events are response-independent (i.e., learned helplessness) decreases the likelihood of detection of response contingencies when they do exist (Seligman, 1972). Learned helplessness in animal studies has also been associated with heightened stress hormone responses to threatening stimuli and heightened risk of depression (Altar, 1999; Rulcovius and Reinhard, 1990). Indeed, the apathy and developmental decline of infants in institutional settings has been described as a form of infantile depression (i.e., hospitalism or anaclitic depression; Bowlby, 1951; Spitz, 1946).

As noted, nonhuman primate models do not appear to produce the same massive delays in behavioral and physical growth. However, primates, especially the monkey species used most often in deprivation studies, differ markedly in motor competence from human infants. Soon after birth they can move about on their own, climb, reach, grasp, bring objects to mouth, cling, and otherwise produce effects on the environment. This disparity in motor competence means that it may be impossible to develop primate models as bereft of opportunities to self-produce alterations in perceptual input as the typical orphanage environment is for the human infant. Nonhuman primate models thus may help, but cannot fully explicate the experiential and therefore neurobiological processes of human infant deprivation. Ultimately, we may need to find ways of studying the institutionalized infant while still in the orphanage in order to understand the neurobiology of these developmental declines. This is because there is evidence that the biology of growth failure begins to revert within only a few days and weeks once the child is removed from the depriving environment (Alanese et al., 1994). This pattern of reactivation of growth processes may correspond to what adoptive parents describe anecdotally as a startling change in demeanor, "It was as if she suddenly came alive."

## Domains of development

With this discussion as background, let us now turn to the data on domains of development associated with early deprivation experiences. Cognition and language, physical growth, and socio-emotional development will be described. Woven throughout this brief review is evidence that in stimulation-rich orphanage contexts much of behavioral development appears to proceed adequately. However, even in these contexts, certain types of functioning still seem to be delayed or impaired.

COGNITION AND LANGUAGE

*General intelligence* As already noted, sensorimotor development is grossly delayed in stimulation-poor environments. Unfortunately, little is known about specific cognitive functions as in most cases only gross or general measures of developmental quotient and/or general intelligence have been used (Carlson and Earls, 1997; see Rutter, 1981, for review of the early work). With regard to these global measures, duration of deprivation correlates with the degree of retardation, as do measures of the severity of deprivation (Ames, 1997; Dennis, 1973; Provence and Lipton, 1962; Rutter, 1998). In contexts of severe or global privation, by 2 years development may be 50% delayed (Carlson and Earls, 1997), while by 5 years 2–3-year delays have been reported (Kaler and Freeman, 1994). The delays span domains rather than being domain-specific (Ames, 1997). However, this may be because, as noted earlier, social mediation is typically needed to allow the kind of stimulation that supports sensorimotor and cognitive development. Once human adults become involved in stimulating infants, typically all forms of stimulation are enhanced; when they are not involved, all forms are depressed.

Importantly, there appears to be a wide window during which transition to enriched environments can produce remarkable catch-up growth. Current studies on Romanian orphans show no reason to alter this conclusion, which is based on the earlier work (Rutter, 1972). For example, using a stratified, random sample of all Romanian children adopted into the United Kingdom (UK study), Rutter and his colleagues (1998) report that despite marked developmental delays at adoption, after several years in middle- to upper-middle-class family environments, the majority of children were functioning intellectually within the normal range. Similar results have been reported for a sample of all Romanian children adopted into British Columbia, Canada (BC study; Ames, 1997). However, both the BC and UK studies also point to the problem of using averages to describe the intellectual functioning of post-institutionalized children. While most post-institutionalized children exhibit rapid intellectual catching up and some eventually show superior intellectual functioning, a persistent minority across all studies and samples fails to show this dramatic recovery. Malnutrition, assessed using measures of weight at adoption, does not appear to predict which children will fail to exhibit marked cognitive catch-up (Rutter, 1998). Importantly, there is some evidence that facets of the post-institutionalized context may be predictive of the degree or rate of cognitive catch-up. These facets are similar to ones that are associated with cognitive competence in children reared in their families of origin (e.g., maternal education, family economic resources, and factors affecting the amount of time and attention devoted to the child; Ames, 1997). Finally, duration of deprivation appears to continue to predict outcomes several years post-adoption, at least for children coming from conditions of global privation. Thus in the BC study, most of the children who exhibited markedly low IQs (< 85) several years post-adoption arrived in their families after 20+ months of institutional experience (Ames, 1997). We should be leery of inferring from such findings that there is a critical or sensitive period for general cognitive growth. This is because the duration of institutional experience is a marker for a number of adverse experiences that increase in probability the longer the orphanage stay (e.g., undetected medical problems, physical abuse, sexual abuse, multiple transitions in care) (Verhulst, Althaus, and Versluis-Den Bieman, 1990a).

*Specific cognitive functions* Because of the assessment tools that have been used in previous studies, little is known about specific cognitive impairments. Some guidance, however, can be found in the clinical notes on these children and in the data on the types of behavioral problems they exhibit. Thus, for example, Provence and Lipton (1962), who followed 14 of the children from their study after being fostered into families at around 2 years of age, noted that by age 5 many still showed numerous impairments in thinking, all of which seemed to target aspects of executive function: rigidity in thinking, difficulties in generalizing problem solutions, difficulties with logical and sequential reasoning, and excessive concreteness of thought. The last is also mentioned in other clinical descriptions of post-institutionalized children (Goldfarb, 1944). The behavior problem literature on post-institutionalized children is also consistent with problems in executive functions (Ames, 1997; Hodges and Tizard, 1989b; Tizard and Hodges, 1978). Thus, many years post-institutionalization these children were noted to be at enhanced risk for problems with concentration, attention regulation, and inhibitory control.

Importantly, these problems have been noted even for children reared in the kind of enriched orphanage contexts that support normal general intelligence and sensorimotor development (Hodges and Tizard, 1989b; Tizard and Hodges, 1978). Even in Tizard's sample of children raised under nearly optimal orphanage conditions, problems with concentration, inhibition of inappropriate behavior, and attention were noted. Specifically, when the children were 8 years of age,

teachers reported significantly more problems with restlessness and fidgeting, while at 16 years of age teachers described 29% as being above the clinical cut-off for problems with concentration and settling into tasks. These kinds of problems are also often noted for children from neglecting and maltreating family environments (Cicchetti, 1991). They suggest that aspects of executive function, presumably reflecting frontal lobe development (Smith, Kates, and Vriezen, 1993), may be highly sensitive to early experience. Furthermore, because these problems were apparent even in Tizard's children, they raise the possibility that aspects of stimulation associated with the opportunity to form and maintain relationships with caregivers early in life may be involved (Schore, 1996). The animal studies of early deprivation would tend to support this conclusion, as they show that social deprivation produces long-term alterations, for example, in neurotransmitter activity (e.g., dopamine) that might impact executive functions mediated by areas and pathways in the frontal lobe (Hall et al., 1998).

The animal research also strongly suggests that deprivation should affect the hippocampus and associated cognitive processes (Heim et al., 1997). The specific effects are complex, and vary with the timing of deprivation (Vazquez, 1998). Studies in rodents have shown that stimulation typically received during mother–pup interaction (i.e., licking and grooming) supports the development of the hippocampus, possibly through the mediating activity of thyroid hormone and serotonin (Caldji et al., 1998). Similarly, deprivation of this stimulation produces as much as a 50% increase in cell death in the hippocampus (Zhang et al., 1997). Tactile stimulation (i.e., handling) has also frequently been shown to increase hippocampal glucocorticoid receptors (Meaney et al., 1996). Higher glucocorticoid receptor numbers are credited with the enhanced capacity of stimulated pups to contain glucocorticoid responses to stressors in adulthood. Behaviorally, in rodents early deprivation has been associated with more inhibition in response to novelty and greater difficulty with hippocampally mediated tasks (Meaney et al., 1988). Primate studies of early deprivation also point to larger and more prolonged elevations in glucocorticoids in response to stressors and enhanced reactivity to novelty (Higley, Suomi, and Linnoila, 1992; Laurens et al., 1973; Suomi, 1991). Recently, immunocytochemical studies of 19–27-month-old rhesus monkeys (equivalent roughly to 7–8-year-old children) reared in total social isolation revealed that compared to mother-reared monkeys, these animals exhibited increased optical density in the dentate gyrus granule layer of the hippocampus (Siegel et al., 1993). Cells were stained more darkly and appeared to be more numerous. Further examination of phosphorylated neurofilament proteins in the dentate suggested more of these proteins in socially deprived monkeys. The authors argue that these proteins may index neuronal vulnerability.

The measures that so far have been used to study post-institutionalized children do not allow specific examination of functions subserved by the hippocampus and parahippocampal regions. Thus, it is difficult to speculate on whether we might expect similar effects in children. However, there is evidence that 6–7 years after adoption, children reared for 8 months or more under global privation in Romanian orphanages had elevated levels of cortisol under home baseline conditions, relative to Romanian children adopted under 4 months of age and children reared in their families of origin (Gunnar, 2000). Furthermore, evening levels were highly correlated with duration of orphanage experience. Finding increased basal, especially evening, glucocorticoid levels might well reflect a reduction in the type of hippocampal glucocorticoid receptor involved in basal regulation of the hormone (i.e., Type I receptors; see de Kloet et al., 1998). If so, this supports the possibility that early deprivation in humans may also target the hippocampus. Clearly, more work is needed examining potential impacts on the hippocampus and its development.

*Language development*  Outside of what is measured on standard developmental and IQ tests, language development has not been studied in post-institutionalized children (but see Tizard et al., 1972). Language development is markedly delayed in low-stimulating institutional settings (for review, see Rutter, 1981, pp. 185–187). Once placed in families, post-institutionalized children do appear to be capable of developing language, even though in most cases of international adoption the child is learning a new language. The evidence of resilience in language development despite wide variations in linguistic input is consistent with conclusions derived from deaf children of hearing parents (Golden-Meadow, 1998). Clinical notes on language development in post-institutionalized children, however, suggest that these children, while developing language, may not use language as readily for expressing emotion, requesting aid from adults, and expressing ideas and fantasy (Provence and Lipton, 1962). Whether they are as likely to use language to guide problem-solving has not been examined, but this may be one route to the poorer executive functioning discussed earlier.

GROWTH FAILURE AND CATCH-UP GROWTH  It has been estimated that infants and toddlers lose approxi-

mately 1 month of linear growth for every 3 months in institutional care (Johnson, in press). This growth failure is likely due to multiple causes, including lack of provision of adequate nutrition, lack of intake due to poor health and apathy, poor absorption of nutrients due, in part, to intestinal parasites, and/or depression of growth hormone and other growth factors and resistance of cells to these factors resulting from lack of adequate psychosocial and/or response-contingent stimulation. Previously, researchers studying early deprivation in humans attempted to downplay the importance of malnutrition in producing developmental delays in order to highlight the importance of stimulation in early development (Rutter, 1981). But clearly, any attempt to model deprivation effects on brain development needs to incorporate growth failure and its various pathways.

In this regard, the possibility that the neurobiology of apathy and infantile depression encompasses neurobiological changes that inhibit physical growth deserves special attention. The pattern of growth failure most often described for institutionalized infants is one where growth of the long bones (i.e., length) is suppressed, while weight remains fairly proportional to length (Johnson, 2000). This is the pattern associated with what has been variously termed "psychological short stature" or "psychosocial dwarfism" (Skuse, 1993). Based on recent research, it is now clear that conditions associated with psychosocial deprivation can inhibit growth processes in human infants and young children (Skuse et al., 1996). The syndrome involves reduced pituitary secretion of growth hormone (GH), blunted GH responses to provocative challenge, and cell resistance to growth factors. Similarities between psychosocial dwarfism and depression have been noted, including blunted GH responses to provocative challenge, one of the few neuroendocrine markers found in childhood or early-onset depression to parallel major depression in adulthood (Brendt et al., 1995; Ryan and Dahl, 1993; Stables et al., 1998). The dynamics of these neuroendocrine changes revert quickly upon removing the child from the depriving environment, showing alteration after 1 week and returning to near normal functioning within 3 weeks (Alanese et al., 1994). Interestingly, although nursery-reared rhesus infants do not show the growth failure observed in orphanage-reared human infants, within the first month of birth, they also show reduced pituitary production of growth hormone and blunted growth hormone to pharmacologic challenge, along with elevated cortisol levels compared to mother-reared animals (Champoux et al., 1989).

While the consequences of these alterations are clear for linear growth, the question of how they relate to brain development is only beginning to receive explication. Poor cognitive outcome is associated with psychosocial dwarfism in the clinical cases that have been studied (Elmer, Gregg, and Ellison, 1969). Extrapituitary GH appears to play a role in modulation of the immune system, with depletion of GH reducing immune competence (Clark, 1997). In addition, there is evidence that suppressed GH has effects that mimic the central impacts of malnutrition (Gustina and Veldhuis, 1998). Furthermore, the multiple neurotransmitter pathways and feedback signals that regulate the growth system interact with growth hormone–releasing hormone (GHRH) and growth hormone–releasing peptides at the level of the hypothalamus (Arvat, Camanni, and Rhigo, 1997). Combined, these alterations suggest that the neurobiology of psychosocial dwarfism might well intersect broadly with processes influencing brain growth and development (Gustina and Veldhuis, 1998; Vazquez, personal communication, 1999). Interestingly, children diagnosed with psychosocial dwarfism show alterations in behavior related to food sometimes long after the neuroendocrine functioning appears to have returned to normal (Skuse et al., 1996). These behaviors include hyperphagia, difficulties in identifying and responding to cues of satiation, food hoarding, and panic/distress at any threat to food access. These behaviors have also been described for some post-institutionalized children (Ames, 1997), although they are said, based on little firm evidence, to wane with time in enriched environments.

Perhaps related to deprivation-induced alterations in growth processes, early-onset puberty has also been described for post-institutionalized children (Proos, Hofvander, and Turvemo, 1991). While epidemiological and neurobiological studies of this phenomenon are sorely needed, the possibility that physical growth and pubertal timing are altered for post-institutionalized children reared under conditions of deprivation early in life suggests that these early environments may produce significant, long-term alterations in hypothalamic systems regulating food intake, physical growth, and the biology of puberty. While neuroanatomical and neurochemical changes in hypothalamic nuclei involved in the regulation of feeding and sex hormones have not been examined, it is perhaps noteworthy that studies of rhesus monkeys who were socially deprived early in life have shown few neuroanatomical changes in hypothalamic nuclei (Ginsberg et al., 1993a,b). However, the absence of significant growth failure in socially deprived monkeys should caution us against using data such as these to direct attention away from potential alterations in hypothalamic neuroanatomy and functioning in children who experience significant growth failure and developmental delay as a consequence of early deprivation.

## Socio-Emotional Development

*Behavior problems* In contrast to the apparent rapid amelioration of gross cognitive and language deficits, post-institutionalized children appear to be at enhanced risk for psychosocial problems that may persist and even increase over time after the child is moved into a family context (Ames, 1997; Hoksbergen, 1981; Rutter, 1998; Tizard and Rees, 1974; Verhulst, Althaus, and Versluis-Den Bieman, 1990b, 1992). The research on stress and deprivation in animals strongly suggests that early deprivation results in enhanced fear of novelty, behavioral inhibition in novel contexts, and heightened anxiety and stress-reactivity (Meyer et al., 1975; Siegel et al., 1993; Sutanto et al., 1996). These data suggest that post-institutionalized children might have problems in the internalizing spectrum. Notably, most studies of post-institutionalized children do not report problems with anxiety and depression (Ames, 1997; Verhulst, Althaus, and Versluis-Den Bieman, 1990a,b, 1992). Instead, those post-institutionalized children with clinically significant behavior problems appear to experience problems of an externalizing nature.

As noted earlier, at least when children remain in these settings until they are 2 years or older, these risks appear to be enhanced even when the orphanage setting appears to deprive them only of consistent relationships with adults. In addition to the problems with attention and inhibitory control mentioned earlier, the most frequent concern appears to lie in the domain of emotion regulation, in particular the regulation of anger and aggression (Fisher et al., 1997; Verhulst, Althaus, and Versluis-Den Bieman, 1992). For example, at 8 and again at 16 years, teacher reports for the post-institutionalized children Tizard studied indicated that many exceeded the clinical cut-off on behaviors such as "likely to be resentful and aggressive when corrected," "irritable," and "likely to argue and fight with peers" (Hodges and Tizard, 1989b; Tizard and Hodges, 1978). Similar, although perhaps more severe, problems have been reported for the current wave of Romanian adopted children (Ames, 1997). It is perhaps noteworthy that attention regulation and inhibitory control are believed to be important cognitive functions contributing to the adequate regulation of emotions (Posner and Rothbart, 1994). Thus, these two domains of problematic behavior (poor attention and poor emotion regulation) may be functionally related.

*Peer problems* Externalizing problems seem to be associated with some of the difficulties these children experience with peers (Ames, 1997; Verhulst, Althaus, and Versluis-Den Bieman, 1992). These problems develop even when only relationship privation characterized the orphanage environment. Indeed, at age 16, 43% of the children studied by Tizard were described as above the clinical cut-off on "not being much liked by peers" and on being "solitary" (Hodges and Tizard, 1989b; Tizard and Hodges, 1978). As will be discussed, Rutter (1981) has noted that by adolescence some of these peer difficulties may reflect problems with intimacy. Some, as noted, may reflect problems with regulating anger and aggression (Groze and Ileana, 1996). In addition, however, some may reflect problems that some of these children have in reading and responding appropriately to social cues. Again using Tizard's data, the lack of responsiveness to social cues can be detected clearly in teacher reports on these children at age 8 (Tizard and Hodges, 1978). These descriptions appear in response to questions about attention seeking from adults, but are also mirrored in comments about these children's lack of adherence to social rules in peer interaction. The teachers noted that "it is not that these children seek attention through being especially naughty, rather they make excessive social approaches" (presumably in the presence of cues to inhibit approach such as the teacher concentrating on a task or another child), "tells you unnecessary things," "persists in conversations about self, family and possessions," and "tries to help even when not asked." Anecdotally, these children often fail to realize when they are being subtly rebuffed through the use of socially appropriate cues (turning your back on them, failing to respond to conversational bids, etc.), requiring other children to use often cruel techniques to inhibit their advances. Rutter (1998) argues that this type of insensitivity to social boundaries and social cues is observed in many post-institutionalized toddlers and preschoolers and may underlie what has been called "indiscriminate friendliness" in the younger child. Speculation about underlying neurobiology is always tenuous; however, these behaviors do seem to suggest alterations in amygdala-orbital frontal pathways (Schore, 1996). That these changes can be observed even in post-institutionalized children whose intellectual functioning is within the normal range suggests that they result from deprivation-induced changes that impact fairly specific, rather than grossly general, aspects of brain development. Because many of these problems could be generated by deficits in understanding the psychological perspective of others, it is tempting to speculate that they may reflect, at least partially, the absence of experiences that support the development of "theory of mind" (Wellman, 1990), although the performance of these children on theory-of-mind tasks has not been examined experimentally. This would be consistent with concerns about decreased opportunities for experiences supporting a sense of agency or intentionality as these are now hypothesized to contribute importantly as precursors to many aspects of "theory of mind" (Russell, 1996).

*Attachment* Concerns with whether infants deprived of specific attachment figures could form emotional bonds with others after the presumed sensitive period for attachment has passed (2 years of age) drove much of the early research on orphanage-reared children (Rutter, 1972, 1981). This issue is still one of intense focus in the current wave of research on orphanage-reared children (Chisholm, 1998; Sabbagh, 1995). The question really exists in three parts, the first of which has just been stated. A second or corollary question is whether these children are able to form secure relationships despite early experiences that should result in "inner working models" (i.e., expectations about relationships) of attachment figures as rejecting, unreliable, and likely to abandon them. A third question is whether attachment relations, once formed, will be as deep. This latter question actually merges with the first as issues of depth of relationship center around whether the person or the functions they serve form the basis for the child's attachment-like behavior.

With the emergence of attachment behaviors organized around one or a few specific individuals, most family-reared infants appear to base their attempts to maintain and re-establish contact with attachment figures increasingly on the person more so than the person's function (Ainsworth, 1969). This is apparent from the infant's earliest distress reactions to separation, as these reactions typically appear even when alternative caregivers are doing their utmost to duplicate the functions served by the primary attachment figures (Bowlby, 1969). It is also apparent in the longevity of attachment relationship, existing over time even as the functions served by members of the relationship change or even reverse in the normal course of parental aging. It is also apparent in the experience of loss and grief when death severs the possibility of reunion, and among individuals who live at great distances and only periodically interact (Bowlby, 1973). While the capacity to maintain emotional bonds despite distance and intermittent contact undoubtedly requires cognitive capacities beyond the scope of infants and young children, some of the emotional quality of this specificity is seen as the basis upon which grief reactions to permanent or prolonged separations are based.

Unfortunately, it is difficult to tell whether a young child preferentially seeks contact with an adult because he/she has been reinforced for doing so (i.e., his/her needs are being met) or because the child has formed a relationship in which the adult has become more important than the needs served. In part for this reason, our tests of attachment are not designed to test whether the child is attached, but rather to assess attachment security or quality, presuming the existence of a person-based, rather than function-based, bond (Ainsworth, Bell, and Stayton, 1971; Lamb et al., 1985). Importantly, conclusions about whether post-institutionalized children can form emotional bonds have been based on these quality-of-attachment rather than existence-of-attachment measures (Chisholm, 1998; Sabbagh, 1995) or on parents' reporting that the child seems attached to them (Groze and Ileana, 1996). Based on these types of data, the current view is that the window for forming specific attachment relationships is wide and that specific attachments can form for the first time across a wide swath of the child's early life (Chisholm, 1998). Even secure attachment relationships do not seem to be precluded by inhibiting the first formation of any specific relationship until after the child's second birthday. Nonetheless, there appears to be clear evidence that it is more difficult for children to form secure attachment relationships when they experience global privation early in development (Chisholm, 1998). Indeed, among the children adopted from Romanian institutions after more than 8 months of institutional experiences, only 37% exhibited secure attachment behavior with their adoptive mothers several years after adoption, compared to 58% of the family-reared, non-adopted children and 66% of the Romanian children adopted by 4 months of age. Furthermore, many of those with 8 months or more of orphanage experience exhibited atypical insecure attachment behavior, behavior more often seen among maltreated children than among children from supportive family environments (Lieberman and Zeanah, 1995). It is perhaps noteworthy that this type of atypical attachment behavior was associated in the BC sample with low intellectual functioning (mean Stanford Binet IV scores of 73 versus 88 for typically insecure and 90 for typically secure children, with all subtests exhibiting similar depression in functioning for the atypically insecure children). The strong association with IQ raises questions about the meaning of these data. Unfortunately, we do not have attachment quality scoring systems specifically developed to evaluate attachment security among children with significantly depressed cognitive functioning.

The final question about the depth of the relationship reflects a commonly described phenomenon for post-institutionalized children (Rutter, 1981). This phenomenon is also noted among maltreated, family-reared children (Lieberman and Zeanah, 1995). Specifically, a significant number of these children are described as indiscriminately social, indiscriminately friendly, and as having diffuse or nonselective attachment relationships. As Rutter and his colleagues argue (O'Connor, Bredenkamp, and Rutter, 1999), terms like "indiscriminate friendliness" or "sociability" are misnomers, as the core behavior is neither friendly nor sociable in the traditional sense, nor are the children completely indiscriminate. Instead, the friendliness is superficial, impersonal, and rarely reciprocal. In Tizard's sample even as late as age 16 nearly 50% of the children exhibited 4 or 5 characteristics that reflected lack of social competence combined with a lack of a special, intimate friendship relationship that involved the sharing of confidences (Hodges and Tizard, 1989b). In the studies of adopted Romanian children, similar findings have been reported. Thus, several years after adoption, around 25% of the BC sample adopted after 8 months or more of orphanage experience were described as exhibiting 4 or 5 (of 5) "indiscriminately friendly" behaviors, including approaching new adults without hesitation, evincing willingness to go home with a stranger, and wandering away from the parent in public without distress (Chisholm, 1998). Similarly, approximately 20% in the UK sample of children adopted between 7 and 24 months from Romanian institutions scored between 4 and 6 (of 6) on similar behaviors studied as indices of attachment disorder (O'Connor, Bredenkamp, and Rutter, 1999). These included a definite lack of differentiation in seeking help and comfort from adults as well as clear indications that they would readily go off with a stranger and fail to check back with parents.

Several characteristics of these behaviors are highly consistent across studies. First, these behaviors, unlike measures of attachment security, are uncorrelated with IQ. This has been found in both the BC and UK samples of Romanian adopted children, and is suggested by the presence of these behaviors in the Tizard sample despite the fact that those children had largely normal, or even superior, general intelligence. Second, these behaviors seem somewhat resistant to change. In the BC sample, only a slight decrease in the percentage of children showing the most extreme behaviors (i.e., those most atypical of family-reared children) were noted from one to three or more years post-adoption. Third, the pattern of association with duration of institutional care differs markedly for these behaviors as compared to, say, general intelligence. For general intelligence there is little evidence that less than 6 months of low-stimulating orphanage rearing has long-term impact, while longer periods seem to confer more risk for intellectual impairment (Ames, 1997; Rutter, 1998). In contrast, in the UK sample an increased likelihood of scoring in the moderate to severe range on these "shallowness of relationship" measures was observed for Romanian infants adopted before 6 months (i.e., 10% of the sample), with an increase in probability noted for those adopted between 7 and 24 months (i.e., 20%), but no increase risk for the period between 7 and 24 months. In the BC sample, no increase in frequency of indiscriminate friendliness was noted for those children adopted prior to 4 months; however, most of the early adopted Romanian children in that study were adopted at birth, and thus experienced little to no early privation. For those adopted after 8 months, duration of institutionalization was uncorrelated with scores on indiscriminate friendliness. Combined with the data from Tizard's study, these results suggest the following: Events early in life, probably before 12 months and probably those correlated with consistent caregiver–infant relationships, are involved in organizing competencies that support the development of relationships where persons, more so than the functions they serve, emerge as the salient element over time.

It is unclear whether the factors associated with increased risk of shallowness in relating to others bear any relation to those associated with the increased risk of autistic-like behaviors recently reported for the Romanian children adopted into the UK (Rutter et al., 1999). Rutter and his colleagues have described around 12% of their sample as exhibiting either quasi-autism or isolated autistic features. Like the pattern of shallowness of relationships described above, these children displayed friendly behavior that lacks social awareness and appreciation of normal social boundaries, limited empathy, and sometimes little use of their parents for security and comfort, in addition to features more characteristic of autism (e.g., intense, focused, stereotyped interests). All of the children had experienced orphanage-rearing and all had been in orphanages until at least 12 months of age. Unlike the case for "simple" indiscriminate friendliness or shallow relationships, however, in most instances a markedly lower IQ was noted, and autistic behavior tended to diminish over time as general intellectual functioning improved. Autistic-like behaviors were not described for children in Tizard's sample. Thus it seems that more than relationship privation was probably involved in the development of these autistic-like characteristics in the UK sample of Romanian adopted children.

## Conclusions

Deprivation has profound effects on human development during the first years of life. While it is likely that privation of health and nutritional needs plays a role in many cases of neglect and orphanage rearing, privation of stimulation appears to be sufficient to produce both physical and behavioral growth retardation. Although it is possible that passive stimulation may halt or reverse some of these declines, it seems likely that stimulation that supports the infant's developing capacity to produce effects on the environment (i.e., response-contingent stimulation) is critical. In this regard, the profound motor helplessness of the human infant may make our species particularly vulnerable to the impact of privation and neglect early in life. Because for many months the infant is dependent on the mediation of adults in order to regulate stimulation, conditions that provide adequate developmentally appropriate perceptual-cognitive stimulation also provide enhanced social stimulation, and vice versa. Many aspects of cognitive and sensorimotor development appear dependent on such stimulation; however, the windows for provision of this stimulation seem to be quite wide, with rapid catch-up growth to relatively normal developmental ranges being observed even after prolonged periods of privation. Stimulation adequate for supporting sensorimotor, cognitive, and even linguistic development may not be adequate in fully supporting the development of neural processes involved in aspects of executive functioning, emotion regulation, the capacity to respond appropriately to social cues and boundaries, and the capacity to establish person-based, more so than function-based, relationships with others. While still quite tenuous, the evidence seems to point to experiences within consistent adult–infant relationships as being important in the development of these latter cognitive-emotional capacities. Furthermore, unlike the data on general intelligence, sensorimotor development, and language, the window for these relationship-associated aspect of early experience may be more circumscribed and/or the post-institutional experiences needed to organize these functions later in development may be less likely to be present in the environments of post-institutionalized children. Theoretically, many of the capacities seemingly influenced by early privation of consistent relationships (i.e. attention regulation, social awareness, inhibitory control) involve structures and pathways in the frontal cortex. One reasonable hypothesis, then, is that development of aspects of the frontal functioning may be highly dependent on early experiences in ways that are not readily recoverable if privation continues beyond the first year or so of life. Whether stable relationships are required or are merely more closely associated with the experiences that are necessary to support the development of these functions cannot be determined from the literature just reviewed. Nonetheless, examining the role of early experience, and particularly relationship-associated experiences, in the development of emotion and attention regulation, inhibitory control, social awareness, and so on may prove to be fruitful in future neurobehavioral studies.

ACKNOWLEDGMENT   This manuscript was supported by an Independent Scientist Research Award from the National Institute of Mental Health (MH00946). The author wishes to thank Bonny Donzella for her help in manuscript preparation.

## REFERENCES

AINSWORTH, M. D., 1969. Object relations, dependency, and attachment: A theoretical review of the infant-mother relationship. *Child Dev.* 40:969–1025.

AINSWORTH, M., S. BELL, and D. STAYTON, 1971. Individual differences in strange-situation behavior of one-year-olds. In *The Origins of Human Social Relations*, H. Schaffer, ed. New York: Academic Press, pp. 17–57.

ALANESE, A., G. HAMILL, J. JONES, D. SKUSE, D. R. MATTHEWS, and R. STANHOPE, 1994. Reversibility of physiological growth hormone secretion in children with psychosocial dwarfism. *Clin. Endocrinol.* 40(5):687–692.

ALBERS, L., D. JOHNSON, M. K. HOSTETTER, S. IVERSON, and L. C. MILLER, 1997. Health of children adopted from the former Soviet Union and Eastern Europe. *JAMA* 278:922–924.

ALTAR, C. A., 1999. Neurotrophins and depression. *Trends Psychopharmacol. Sci.* 20:59–61.

AMES, E., 1997. *The Development of Romanian Orphanage Children Adopted to Canada* (Final Report to the National Welfare Grants Program: Human Resources Development Canada). Burnaby, British Columbia: Simon Fraser University.

ARVAT, E., F. CAMANNI, and E. RHIGO, 1997. Age-related growth hormone-releasing activity and growth hormone secretagogues in humans. *Acta Paediatr. Suppl.* 423:92–96.

BAI, D. L., and B. I. BERTENTHAL, 1992. Locomotor status and the development of spatial search skills. *Child Dev.* 63:215–226.

BELL, M. A., and N. A. FOX, 1996. Crawling experience is related to changes in cortical organization during infancy: Evidence from EEG coherence. *Dev. Psychobiol.* 29: 551–561.

BENOIT, T. C., L. J. JOCELYN, D. M. MODDEMAN, and J. E. EMBREE, 1996. Romanian adoption: The Manitoba experience. *Arch. Pediatr. Adoles. Med.* 150:1278–1282.

BOWLBY, J., 1951. *Maternal Care and Mental Health.* Geneva: World Health Organization.

BOWLBY, J., 1969. *Attachment and Loss. Vol. 1: Attachment.* New York: Basic Books.

BOWLBY, J., 1973. *Attachment and Loss. Vol. 1: Separation.* New York: Basic Books.

BRENDT, D. A., N. RYAN, R. DAHL, and B. BORIS, 1995. Early-onset mood disorder. In *Psychopharmacology: The Fourth Generation of Progress*, F. Bloom and D. Kupfer, eds. New York: Raven Press, pp. 1631–1642.

CALDJI, C., B. TANNENBAUM, S. SHARMA, D. FRANCIS, P. M. PLOTSKY, and M. J. MEANEY, 1998. Maternal care during infancy regulates the development of neural systems mediating the expression of fearfulness in the rat. *Proc. Natl. Acad. Sci. USA* 95(9):5445–5340.

CARLSON, M., and F. EARLS, 1997. Psychological and neuroendocrinological sequelae of early deprivation in institutionalized children in Romania. *Ann. N.Y. Acad. Sci.* 807:419–428.

CHAMPOUX, M., C. L. COE, S. M. SCHANBERG, C. M. KUHN, and S. J. SUOMI, 1989. Hormonal effects of early rearing conditions in the infant rhesus monkey. *Am. J. Primatol.* 19:111–117.

CHUGANI, H. T., M. E. BEHEN, O. MUZIK, C. JUHASZ, F. NAGY and D. C. CHUGANI, 2001. Local Brain Functional Activity Following Early Deprivation: A Study of Post-Institutionalized Romanian Orphans. (manuscript under review)

CHISHOLM, K., 1998. A three year follow-up of attachment and indiscriminate friendliness in children adopted from Romanian orphanages. *Child Dev.* 69(4):1092–1106.

CICCHETTI, D., 1991. Fractures in the crystal: Developmental psychopathology and the emergence of self. *Dev. Rev.* 11:271–287.

CICCHETTI, D., and M. LYNCH, 1995. Failures in the expectable environment and their impact on individual development: The case of child maltreatment. In *Developmental Psychopathology*, Vol. 2, D. Cicchetti and D. J. Cohen, eds. New York: Wiley, pp. 32–71.

CLARK, R., 1997. The somatogenic hormones and insulin-like growth factor-1: Stimulators of lymphopoiesis and immune function. *Endocr. Rev.* 18:157–179.

DE KLOET, R., E. VREUGDENHIL, M. OITZL, and A. JOELS, 1998. Brain corticosteroid receptor balance in health and disease. *Endocr. Rev.* 19:269–301.

DENNIS, W., 1973. *Children of the Creche.* New York: Appleton-Century-Crofts.

ELMER, E., G. S. GREGG, and P. ELLISON, 1969. Late results of the "failure to thrive" syndrome. *Clin. Pediatr.* 8:584–592.

FISHER, L., E. W. AMES, K. CHISHOLM, and L. SAVOIE, 1997. Problems reported by parents of Romanian orphans adopted to British Columbia. *Int. J. Behav. Dev.* 20:67–82.

FRANK, D. A., P. E. KLASS, F. EARLS, and L. EISENBERG, 1996. Infants and young children in orphanages: One view from pediatrics and child psychiatry. *Pediatrics* 97:569–578.

GINSBERG, S. D., P. R. HOF, W. T. MCKINNEY, and J. H. MORRISON, 1993a. The noradrenergic innervation density of the monkey paraventricular nucleus is not altered by early social deprivation. *Neurosci. Lett.* 1993:130–134.

GINSBERG, S. D., P. R. HOF, W. T. MCKINNEY, and J. H. MORRISON, 1993b. Quantitative analysis of tuberoinfundibular tyrosine hydroxylase- and corticotropin-releasing factor-immunoreactive neurons in monkeys raised with differential rearing conditions. *Exp. Neurol.* 120:95–105.

GOLDEN-MEADOW, S., 1998. The resilience of language in humans. In *Social Influences on Vocal Development*, C. T. Snowdon and M. Hausberger, eds. Cambridge, UK: Cambridge University Press, pp. 293–311.

GOLDFARB, W., 1944. Psychological privation in infancy and subsequent adjustment. *Am. J. Orthopsychiatry* 15:247–255.

GROZE, V., and D. ILEANA, 1996. A follow-up study of adopted children from Romania. *Child Adoles. Soc. Work J.* 13:541–565.

GUNNAR, M. R., 2000. Early adversity and the development of stress reactivity and regulation. In *The Effects of Adversity on Neurobehavioral Development:Minnesota Symposia on Child Psychology*, Vol. 31, C. A. Nelson, ed. Mahwah, N.J.: Lawrence Erlbaum Associates, pp. 163–200.

GUSTINA, A., and J. D. VELDHUIS, 1998. Pathophysiology of the neuroregulation of growth hormone secretion in experimental animals and the human. *Endocr. Rev.* 19:717–797.

HALL, F. S., L. S. WILKINSON, T. HUMBY, W. INGLIS, D. A. KENDALL, C. A. MARSDEN, and T. W. ROBBINS, 1998. Isolation rearing in rats: Pre- and postsynaptic changes in striatal dopaminergic systems. *Pharmacol. Biochem. Behav.* 59(4):859–872.

HARLOW, H. F., M. K. HARLOW, and S. J. SUOMI, 1971. From thought to therapy: Lessons from a primate laboratory. *Am. Sci.* 59:538–549.

HEIM, C., M. J. OWEN, P. M. PLOTSKY, and C. B. NEMEROFF, 1997. The role of early adverse life events in the etiology of depression and posttraumatic stress disorder: Focus on corticotropin-releasing factor. *Ann. N.Y. Acad. Sci.* 821:194–207.

HELD, R., and A. HEIN, 1963. Movement-produced stimulation in the development of visually guided behavior. *J. Comp. Physiol. Psychol.* 56:872–876.

HIGLEY, J. D., S. J. SUOMI, and M. LINNOILA, 1992. A longitudinal study of CSF monoamine metabolite and plasma cortisol concentrations in young rhesus monkeys: Effects of early experience, age, sex, and stress on continuity of individual differences. *Biol. Psychiatry* 32:127–145.

HODGES, J., and B. TIZARD, 1989a. IQ and behavioural adjustment of ex-institutional adolescents. *J. Child Psychol. Psychiatry* 30:53–75.

HODGES, J., and B. TIZARD, 1989b. Social and family relationships of ex-institutional adolescents. *J. Child Psychol. Psychiatry* 30:77–97.

HOKSBERGEN, R. A. C., 1981. Adoption of foreign children in the Netherlands. *Int. Child Welfare Rev.* 49:28–37.

HOSTETTER, M. K., S. IVERSON, W. THOMAS, D. McKENZIE, K. DOLE, and D. E. JOHNSON, 1991. Medical evaluation of internationally adopted children. *N. Engl. J. Med.* 325:479–485.

HUBEL, D. H., and T. N. WIESEL, 1965. Binocular interaction in striate cortex of kittens reared with artificial squint. *J. Neurophysiol.* 28:1041–1059.

JOHNSON, D. E., 2000. The impact of orphanage rearing on growth and development. In *The Effects of Adversity on Neurobehavioral Development: Minnesota Symposia on Child Psychology*, Vol. 31, C. A. Nelson, ed. Mahwah, N.J.: Lawrence Erlbaum Associates, pp. 113–162.

JOHNSON, D. E., L. C. MILLER, S. IVERSON, W. THOMAS, B. FRANCHINO, K. DOLE, M. T. KIERNAN, M. K. GEORGIEFF, and M. K. HOSTETTER, 1992. The health of children adopted from Romania. *JAMA* 268(24):3446–3451.

KALER, S. R., and B. J. FREEMAN, 1994. An analysis of environmental deprivation: Cognitive and social development in Romanian orphans. *J. Child Psychol. Psychiatry* 35:769–781.

KRAEMER, G. W., M. H. EBERT, D. E. SCHMIDT, and W. T. McKINNEY, 1989. A longitudinal study of the effect of different social rearing conditions on cerebrospinal fluid norepinephrine and biogenic amine metabolites in rhesus monkeys. *Neuropsychopharmacology* 2:175–189.

LAMB, M. E., R. A. THOMPSON, W. P. GARDNER, E. L. CHARNOV, and D. ESTES, eds., 1985. *Security of Infantile Attachment as Assessed in the "Strange Situation": Its Study and Biological Interpretation.* New York: Brunner/Mazel.

LAURENS, D. Y., S. J. SUOMI, H. F. HARLOW, and W. T. McKINNEY, 1973. Early stress and later response to separation in rhesus monkeys. *Am. J. Psychiatry* 130(4):400–405.

LIEBERMAN, A. F., and C. H. ZEANAH, 1995. Disorders of attachment in infancy. *Infant Psychiatry* 4:571–587.

MEANEY, M. J., D. H. AITKEN, C. VAN BERKEL, S. BHATNAGAR, and R. M. SAPOLSKY, 1988. Effect of neonatal handling on age-related impairments associated with the hippocampus. *Science* 239:766–768.

MEANEY, M. J., J. DIORIO, D. FRANCIS, J. WIDDOWSON, P. LA PLANTE, C. CALDUI, D. SHARMA, J. SECKL, and P. M. PLOTSKY, 1996. Early environmental regulation of forebrain glucocorticoid receptor gene expression: Implications for adrenocortical responses to stress. *Dev. Neurosci.* 18:49–72.

MEYER, J. S., M. A. NOVAK, R. E. BOWMAN, and H. F. HARLOW, 1975. Behavioral and hormonal effects of attachment object separation in surrogate-peer-reared and mother-reared infant rhesus monkeys. *Dev. Psychobiol.* 8(5):425–435.

MORISON, S. J., E. W. AMES, and K. CHISHOLM, 1995. The development of children adopted from Romanian orphanages. *Merrill-Palmer Quart.* 41:411–430.

NATIONAL RESEARCH COUNCIL, 1993. *Understanding Child Abuse and Neglect.* Washington D.C.: National Academy Press.

O'CONNOR, T. G., D. BREDENKAMP, and M. RUTTER, 1999. Attachment disturbances and disorders in children exposed to early severe deprivation. *Infant Ment. Health J.* 20:10–29.

POSNER, M. I., and M. K. ROTHBART, 1994. Attentional regulation: From mechanism to culture. In *International Perspectives on Psychological Science*, Vol. 1, P. Bertelson, P. Elen, and G. d'Ydewalle, eds. Hillsdale, N.J.: Lawrence Erlbaum Associates, pp. 41–54.

PROOS, L. A., R. HOFVANDER, and T. TURVEMO, 1991. Menarcheal age and growth pattern of Indian girls adopted in Sweden. I. Menarcheal age. *Acta Paediatr. Scand.* 80:852–858.

PROVENCE, S., and R. C. LIPTON, 1962. *Infants in Institutions.* New York: International Universities Press.

PURVIS, D. 1997. *Neuroscience.* Sunderland, Mass.: Sinauer.

ROVEE-COLLIER, C. K., and J. B. CAPATIDES, 1979. Positive behavioral contrast in 3-month-old infants on multiple conjugate reinforcement schedules. *J. Exp. Anal. Behav.* 32(1):15–27.

RULCOVIUS, G., and H. G. REINHARD, 1990. Cognitive theories of depression: Implications for the investigation of emotional disturbances in childhood and adolescence. *Acta Paedopsychiat.* 53:62–70.

RUSSELL, J., 1996. *Agency: Its Role in Mental Development.* East Sussex, UK: Erlbaum (UK) Taylor and Francis, Ltd.

RUTTER, M., 1972. Maternal deprivation reconsidered. *J. Psychosom. Res.* 16:241–250.

RUTTER, M., 1981. *Maternal Deprivation Reassessed.* New York: Penguin Books.

RUTTER, M., 1998. Developmental catch-up, and deficit, following adoption after severe global early privation. *J. Child Psychol. Psychiatry* 39:465–476.

RUTTER, M., L. ANDERSEN-WOOD, C. BECKETT, D. BREDEN-KAMP, J. CASTLE, C. GROOTHUES, J. KREPPNER, L. KEAVENEY, C. LORD, and T. G. O'CONNOR, 1999. Quasi-autistic patterns following severe early global privation. *J. Child Psychol. Psychiatry* 40(4):537–549.

RYAN, N. D., and R. E. DAHL, 1993. The biology of depression in children and adolescents. In *Biology of Depressive Disorders*, J. J. Mann and D. J. Kupfer, eds. New York: Plenum Press, pp. 37–58.

SABBAGH, R., 1995. *Attachment and behavior towards strangers in Romanian preschoolers adopted into Canadian families.* Unpublished Masters thesis, University of Toronto, Ontario, Canada.

SCHORE, A. N., 1996. The experience-dependent maturation of a regulatory system in the orbital prefrontal cortex and the origin of developmental psychopathology. *Dev. Psychopathol.* 8:59–87.

SELIGMAN, M. E., 1972. Learned helplessness. *Annu. Rev. Med.* 23:407–412.

SIEGEL, S. J., S. D. GINSBERG, P. R. HOF, S. L. FOOTE, W. G. YOUNG, G. W. DRAEMER, W. T. MCKINNEY, and J. H. MORRISON, 1993. Effects of social deprivation in prepubescent rhesus monkeys: Immunohistochemical analysis of the neurofilament protein triplet in the hippocampal formation. *Brain Res.* 619:299–305.

SINGH, S. D., 1969. Urban monkeys. *Sci. Am.* 24:108–115.

SKUSE, D., 1993. Epidemiological and definitional issues in failure to thrive. *Child Adoles. Psychiatr. Clin. N. Am.* 2:37–59.

SKUSE, D., A. ALBANESE, R. STANHOPE, J. GILMOUR, and L. VOSS, 1996. A new stress-related syndrome of growth failure and hyperphagia in children associated with reversibility of growth-hormone insufficiency. *Lancet* 348(9024):353–358.

SMITH, M. L., M. H. KATES, and E. R. VRIEZEN, 1993. The development of frontal-lobe functions. In *Handbook of Neuropsychology*, Vol. 7, S. J. Segalowitz and I. Rapin, eds. New York: Elsevier Science.

SPITZ, R. A., 1946. Hospitalism: A follow-up report. *The Psychoanalytic Study of the Child*, Vol. 2. New York: International Universities Press.

STABLES, B., T. SIEGEL, N. R. CLOPPER, C. E. STOPPANI, P. G. COMPTON, and L. E. UNDERWOOD, 1998. Behavioral change after growth hormone treatment of children with short stature. *J. Pediatr.* 133:366–373.

SUOMI, S. J., 1991. *Early stress and adult emotional reactivity in rhesus monkeys.* Paper presented at The Childhood Environment and Adult Disease: Ciba Foundation Symposium.

SUTANTO, W., P. ROSENFELD, E. R. DE KLOET, and S. LEVINE, 1996. Longterm effects of neonatal maternal deprivation and ACTH on hippocampal mineralocorticoid and glucocorticoid receptors. *Brain Res. Dev. Brain Res.* 92:156–163.

TIZARD, B., O. COOPERMAN, A. JOSEPH, and J. TIZARD, 1972. Environmental effects on language development: A study of young children in long-stay residential nurseries. *Child Dev.* 43:337–358.

TIZARD, B., and J. HODGES, 1978. The effect of early institutional rearing on the development of eight-year-old children. *J. Child Psychol. Psychiatry* 19:99–118.

TIZARD, B., and A. JOSEPH, 1970. Cognitive development of young children in residential care: A study of children aged 24 months. *J. Child Psychol. Psychiatry* 11:177–186.

TIZARD, B., and J. REES, 1974. A comparison of the effects of adoption, restoration to the natural mother, and continued institutionalization on the cognitive development of four-year-old children. *Child Dev.* 45:92–99.

VAZQUEZ, D. M., 1998. Stress and the developing limbic-hypothalamic-pituitary-adrenal axis. *Psychoneuroendocrinology* 23(7):663–700.

VERHULST, F., M. ALTHAUS, and H. J. VERSLUIS-DEN BIEMAN, 1990a. Problem behavior in international adoptees: I. An epidemiological study. *J. Am. Acad. Child Adoles. Psychol.* 29(1):94–103.

VERHULST, F., M. ALTHAUS, and H. J. VERSLUIS-DEN BIEMAN, 1990b. Problem behavior in international adoptees: II. Age at placement. *J. Am. Acad. Child Adoles. Psychol.* 29(1):104–111.

VERHULST, F., M. ALTHAUS, and H. J. VERSLUIS-DEN BIEMAN, 1992. Damaging backgrounds: Later adjustment of international adoptees. *J. Am. Acad. Child Adoles. Psychol.* 31(3):518–524.

WELLMAN, H., 1990. *The Child's Theory of Mind.* Cambridge, Mass.: MIT Press.

WHITE, R. W., 1959. Motivation reconsidered: The concept of competence. *Psychol. Rev.* 66:297–333.

ZHANG L. X., G. O. XING, S. LEVINE, R. M. POST, and M. A. SMITH, 1997. Maternal deprivation induces neuronal death. *Soc. Neurosci. [Abstr.]* October:1113.

# 40 The Biology of Temperament: An Integrative Approach

NATHAN A. FOX,
HEATHER A. HENDERSON,
AND PETER J. MARSHALL

ABSTRACT Temperament refers to a style or pattern of behavior that characterizes young infants' ongoing interaction
with the world. Individual differences in this behavioral style
are thought to reflect biologically based dispositions (Goldsmith et al., 1987). The precise nature of these biological differences has, however, only recently been investigated. In part,
current research on the biological bases of temperament
stems from an articulation of models of individual differences
that emphasize the role of the nervous system in the expression of behavioral styles (Kagan, 1994; Rothbart and Derryberry, 1981). This work reflects a developing synthesis of
research in the neurosciences and developmental psychology
toward an understanding of the biology of behavior. This
chapter provides the reader with a view of the different models
of temperament that have guided the field of developmental
research. We present our own conceptualization of infant temperament, one that focuses on the concepts of reactivity and
regulation but emphasizes as well the overlay of emotional
valence in the expression of individual differences in reactivity. The final section of this chapter presents a brief review of
the work on behavioral inhibition as an example of the new
synthesis of biological and behavioral research toward an understanding of individual differences in temperament.

## Psychobiological models of temperament

The notion of a biological basis to individual differences
in personality appears as early as the Greek philoso-
phers, with their division of temperament into types
(Kagan, 1994). The twentieth-century neurophysiolo-
gist Pavlov noted differences in speed of conditioning
and suggested that these effects were a result of individual differences in strength of the nervous system (Pavlov, 1927). Eastern European personality psychologists
subsequently adopted the notion of strength of the nervous system and constructed typologies of personality
based upon this notion of individual differences (e.g.,
Strelau, 1983).

A second influential stream of work on the biology
of individual differences in personality emerged from

the work of Gray. Gray (1982, 1987) articulated a
motivation-based view of temperament and proposed
three fundamental motivation systems, each defined by
a set of behavioral input–output relations and each associated with a particular subsystem in the brain. These
three systems are the behavioral inhibition system, the
fight–flight system, and the behavioral approach system. There are a number of comprehensive reviews of
the comparative behavioral evidence and the underlying neural bases for each system (Gray, 1991). Much of
the behavioral work examining Gray's model and its relation to temperament/personality has centered on the
use of Eysenck's model of personality (Eysenck and
Eysenck, 1985). This model makes specific predictions
about the susceptibility to conditioning and arousal of
introverts and extroverts. Gray's model predicts the efficacy of certain types of reinforcement for introverts
and extroverts.

Mary Rothbart expanded on the ideas of Pavlov and
the Eastern European personality psychologists as well
as the notions of activation and inhibition of Gray to
articulate a psychobiological model of infant temperament. Rothbart's theory of temperament has as its foundation the notion that infants differ early in life in the
manner in which they respond to sensory stimulation
(Rothbart and Derryberry, 1981). In addition, infants
differ in their ability to return to homeostasis following
a reactive response.

Growth of interest in individual differences in infant
temperament has been paralleled by research in the
development of emotions as well as individual differences in expression and control of emotion (Fox,
1994a). Goldsmith and Campos (1986), for example,
posit that temperament may be viewed as individual differences among infants in the expression of specific
emotions in reaction to specific contexts. For example,
some infants may be predisposed to respond with the
emotion of fear to novelty or uncertainty. The work on
behavioral inhibition has utilized an emotion-based
temperament approach toward understanding the

NATHAN A. FOX, HEATHER A. HENDERSON, AND PETER J.
MARSHALL    Department of Human Development, University
of Maryland, College Park, Maryland.

etiology of this pattern of behavior (Kagan, Reznick, and Snidman, 1987).

The emotion-based approach to behavioral inhibition has found an important link to the neuroscience work on the fear system. This work has in large part been motivated by the potentiated startle paradigm. First described by Brown, Kalish, and Farber (1951), the paradigm involves the classical conditioning of an animal to a light (or tone) and electric shock. The affective state of the animal after classical conditioning (paired light or tone and shock) has been termed "fear." Brown and colleagues (1951) demonstrated that the acoustic startle reflex (an unconditioned response) could be augmented or potentiated by presenting the acoustic startle stimulus in the presence of a cue that had previously been paired with the shock. This state potentiates the acoustic startle reflex. In a series of elegant experiments, Michael Davis and his colleagues have identified the neural circuitry involved in the acoustic reflex in the rat and have mapped the circuitry involved in the augmentation of that reflex (Davis, 1986, 1989; Davis, Hitchcock, and Rosen, 1987; Davis et al., 1993). These studies have shown that the acoustic startle pathway consists of only three synapses and that a single nucleus in the amygdala, the central nucleus, is involved in the potentiation of the reflex (LeDoux, Farb, and Ruggiero, 1990; LeDoux et al., 1988).

Davis and colleagues recognized the possible limitations of a neural model of conditioned fear with regard to its association with certain clinical states in humans, in particular, anxiety. A fear state is assumed to have a specific elicitor, whereas anxiety is a more generalized state with no specific eliciting stimulus. Thus, in their more recent work they have attempted to examine the neural circuits associated with non–fear-potentiated startle (Davis, 1998). In fear-potentiated startle the central nucleus of the amygdala played a critical role in the augmentation of the reflex. However, Davis and colleagues showed a clear distinction between the central nucleus of the amygdala and the bed nucleus of the stria terminalis (a site adjacent to but anatomically distinct from the amygdala) in relation to fear-potentiated startle versus non–fear-enhanced startle (Walker and Davis, 1997). While lesions of the central nucleus blocked expression of fear-potentiated startle, they had no effect on light-enhanced startle. Conversely, lesions of the bed nucleus of the stria terminalis significantly attenuated light-enhanced startle without any effect on fear-potentiated startle.

Additionally, Davis and colleagues found that the bed nucleus of the stria terminalis (along with other limbic structures) but not the central nucleus was involved in startle enhanced by corticotrophin-releasing hormone (CRH), a neuropeptide involved in stress reactivity (Lee and Davis, 1997). Davis and colleagues believe these findings to be critical to their model differentiating conditioned fear and its location to the central nucleus from anxiety and its location to the stria terminalis. A CRH-enhanced state has a longer time course, and this longer action may be more akin to a model of anxiety than to conditioned fear. Importantly for the study of temperament, both neural systems (central nucleus of the amygdala and bed nucleus) have similar outputs to autonomic and motor targets.

AN INTEGRATIVE APPROACH TO THE BIOLOGY OF TEMPERAMENT  Our model of temperament incorporates Rothbart's behavioral elements while attempting to integrate the findings from neuroscience research such as that of Davis and LeDoux. In our view, temperament reflects differences in infant response to different sensory or social stimuli. Overlaying these behavioral and physiological responses is the infant's affective display. Thus, reactivity has multiple components including motoric (excluding movements involved in facial expressions), physiological, and affective (facial, vocal) responses. In this model, it is critical to identify which sensory modality elicits reactive responses. Infants may vary in their threshold or intensity of reactions to auditory, visual, tactile, or olfactory stimuli. These individual differences in sensitivity to one sensory modality over others may have implications for caregiver–infant interactions. Moreover, the affective bias, or predisposition to respond with a particular emotion or set of emotions may be modality-specific. That is, infants may more likely display negative or positive affect in response to stimulation specific to one modality over another. These initial affective dispositions are reflected in certain patterns of central nervous system activity which are evident early in the first year of life and which may bias the infant in its response to the social world.

Infant modulation of reactive responses develops over the first years of life. In the first months of life infants have only primitive capacities for self-regulation, often falling asleep in the most stimulus-intensive environments (Turkewitz, Gardner, and Lewkowicz, 1984). In addition, infants display elementary motor behaviors such as hand-to-mouth movement and sucking that they use for self-regulation of reactive state. On the other hand, in the first year of life infants rely primarily on external support, particularly caregivers, for physiological and behavioral regulation (Kopp, 1982). Caregivers, with knowledge of the stimulus conditions that elicit intense reactivity, may manipulate the context so as to decrease the intensity or eliminate entirely the source of aversive stimulation. Caregivers may also provide the infant with artificial (e.g., pacifier) or natural (e.g., the mother's breast) means to self-soothe. Rhythmic sucking behavior, even nonnutritive sucking, has been found to modulate and decrease infant distress (DiPietro et al., 1994).

Through the end of the first year and into the second year, infants continue to depend upon caregivers as immediate regulators of sensory reactivity and distress. One interactive system that develops in the first two years of life and which provides initial support is the attachment system (Bowlby, 1969). When stressed, infants will seek the caregiver's proximity and contact to modulate their distress. This will occur when the infant is frustrated, or overwhelmed by sensory stimulation, or in the case of the attachment model, when the infant is separated from the mother.

As reactive responses increase in complexity, so do the competencies that are involved in the regulation of these responses. Behavioral competencies that have been nominated to play a role in emotion regulation include use of language (both private speech and its internalization), motor inhibition, attentional skills, and the ability to switch set and goal planfulness (Dodge, 1991; Kopp, 1982; Thompson, 1990). These latter skills have also been investigated under the rubric of executive functions, and there is some discussion in the literature on the significance of the coincidental development of these executive function skills and behaviors involved in regulation of emotion (Kopp, 1989; Welsh and Pennington, 1988). In our view, individual differences in maturation of the frontal lobes play an important role in understanding the development of regulatory behaviors, particularly behaviors associated with regulation of emotional reactivity. Areas of the prefrontal cortex have been implicated as subserving skills necessary for executive attention tasks. These same skills may play a role in regulation of emotion.

The role of cognitive processes as modulators of temperamental reactivity also corresponds to neural models, which view cortical regions as inhibitory of lower level limbic emotional responses. This "top-down" model emphasizes the activity of regions in the cerebral cortex as playing an executive role vis-à-vis basic sensory reactivity. In this model, responses to sensory stimuli are modulated by the control of higher order cortical processes in a unidirectional manner. Deficits in cortical control thus contribute to disinhibition of these more primitive limbic responses.

There are, of course, multiple approaches to understanding relations between reactive and regulatory processes. One view is that intense emotion may flood or overwhelm the cognitive system, interfering with its efficient production (Lazarus and Folkman, 1984; Mandler, 1982). Individuals may not necessarily differ in their cognitive skills (under non–intense affect conditions), but under stress their reactive response produces interference in the performance of certain cognitive competencies. It may be helpful to speculate on the development of such interference effects among young children. Developmentally, the experience of intense negative affect might occur prior to the appearance of cognitive skills thought important in the regulation of reactivity. As general cognitive skills emerge, there may be attempts to utilize them in the service of regulation of distress or negative affect. If the negative affect is intense, these cognitive skills may not be successfully evoked to produce successful regulation of negative affect. One would thus expect normative performance on cognitive tasks thought to subsume regulation (e.g., attention or executive function skills) in temperamentally negative reactive children in the absence of emotional challenge. In contrast, a decrement in performance on these tasks might be expected when they are overlaid with a negative affect component.

A neural model of this account might include the influence of subcortical activation on those areas of cortex thought to involve these higher order cognitive skills. This bottom-up view might account for the disruption of ongoing cognitive activity thought to occur during periods of intense negative affect. A variety of data indicate that limbic areas modulate cortical activity (Derryberry and Tucker, 1991). In a recent report, Garcia and colleagues (1999) found that in a fear conditioning paradigm, amygdala activity modulated the activity of prefrontal cortex. The authors speculate that abnormal amygdala-induced modulation of prefrontal neuronal activity may be involved in the pathophysiology of certain forms of anxiety disorder. In all probability, neither the top-down model, in which cortical processes modulate limbic areas, nor the bottom up model, in which activation of limbic regions modulate cortex, is sufficient to explain relations between emotional reactivity and regulation. The behavioral work of Rothbart and others, including Kochanska (Kochanska, Murray, and Coy, 1997) and Eisenberg (Eisenberg et al., 1994), clearly indicates that certain cognitive processes involving attention and inhibition are critical in regulating emotional distress. On the other hand, in individuals with temperamental biases to express negative affect in response to novelty or stress, cognitive processes may be insufficient to downregulate intense emotional arousal.

## Components of temperament I: Reactivity

Physiological models of temperament state that individual variation in behavioral reactivity reflects individual differences in the physiological response systems defining internal organization and adjustment in response to environmental challenges. Two measures and their accompanying models of reactivity have dominated the developmental literature: vagal tone as an index of autonomic responsivity and cortisol as a measure of the activity of the hypothalamic-pituitary-adrenal axis.

VAGAL TONE—AN INDEX OF AUTONOMIC RESPONSIVITY Porges developed a psychophysiological model of temperament that focuses on the central regulation of autonomic reflexes and the mediating role of the nervous system in coordinating such reflexes to deal with internal need states and external challenges (Porges, 1983; Porges and Doussard-Roosevelt, 1997a). Central to Porges's model is respiratory sinus arrhythmia (RSA), which refers to the transient decreases and increases in heart period that occur with inspiration and expiration (Katona and Jih, 1975). RSA is often quantified by applying a high-pass filter to a series of heart period data in order to remove unwanted slow trends, and then using spectral analytic techniques or bandpass filters to quantify the residual variance in the appropriate frequency band (Porges, 1986). RSA is determined almost exclusively by the nucleus ambiguus (NA) portion of the right vagus (Porges, 1995), and has therefore been referred to as Vna. Porges views baseline measures of Vna as assessing the successful regulation of internal bodily processes via neural negative-feedback systems, and he has suggested that the organization of reactive responses is a function of the level of baseline Vna. Infants with low Vna would be expected to exhibit more disorganized responses to moderate levels of novelty or stress, and infants with high levels of Vna would be expected to react with appropriate, organized responses.

In neonates, higher baseline Vna is associated with increased reactivity to noxious and invasive procedures such as circumcision (Porter, Porges, and Marshall, 1988) and gavage feeding (DiPietro and Porges, 1991). High Vna has also been associated with increased behavioral reactivity and irritability during less stressful procedures such as the administration of the Neonatal Behavioral Assessment Scale (NBAS; Brazelton, 1984; DiPietro, Larson, and Porges, 1987).

Early Vna has been found to predict cognitive and behavioral outcomes in later infancy. Higher neonatal Vna has been associated with higher scores on cognitive development indices in later infancy (Fox and Porges, 1985; Porges and Doussard-Roosevelt, 1997b). At 5 months of age, Fox and Stifter (1989) found that infants with high Vna were more reactive to both positive (peek-a-boo) and negative (arm restraint) stimuli compared to infants with low Vna. Furthermore, infants with high Vna at 5 months of age had shorter latencies to approach a stranger and novel toy in a laboratory assessment of behavioral inhibition at 14 months of age.

The association of Vna with high reactivity to aversive stimuli in early infancy suggests that higher levels of Vna may facilitate affective responses to emotion-eliciting stimuli. When appropriately expressed in response to aversive events, negative reactivity can be an effective signal to a caregiver of the infant's emotional state (Porges, Doussard-Roosevelt, and Maiti, 1994; Stifter, 1995). Frequent and effective soothing from caregivers in combination with the high vagal tone of these infants may result in more optimal neurobehavioral organization. In later infancy, these infants may be more able both to respond to stimuli and to efficiently return to a less aroused state.

Vna is generally suppressed during conditions of stress, attention, or effort. This removal of the "vagal brake" (Porges et al., 1996) facilitates an instantaneous increase in cardiac output. Vna suppression may be directed by higher subcortical and cortical structures that connect with the NA, providing the potential for the influence of cognitive and affective processes on Vna suppression. Appropriate suppression of Vna to stimuli would therefore be expected to be associated with more optimal behavioral responses. Huffman and colleagues (1998) found that 3-month-olds who suppressed Vna during a series of laboratory episodes were rated by their mothers as having longer durations of orienting, more frequent smiling and laughing, and greater ease of soothability, compared with infants who failed to suppress Vna. Conversely, a consistent failure to regulate Vna in tasks requiring effort or attention may lead to difficulties in the development of appropriate social interaction patterns. Porges and colleagues (1996) reported that infants who had difficulties in decreasing Vna during a social attention task at 9 months of age had significantly more behavioral problems at 3 years of age compared to those infants who showed efficient Vna suppression to the task.

CORTISOL—AN INDEX OF STRESS REACTIVITY Another physiological system that has been extensively studied in relation to infant and child temperament is the hypothalamic-pituitary-adrenal (HPA) system. The activity of the HPA system can be assessed using salivary concentrations of cortisol (Stansbury and Gunnar, 1994). HPA activity has been theoretically related to affective responses to environmental challenge (Mason, 1975), which leads to a simple prediction that increases in cortisol should be associated with negative emotional reactivity and distressed behavior. This question has been addressed in studies with newborns and also over infancy and early childhood.

In healthy newborns, elevations in cortisol have been associated with a number of events that produce behavioral distress. Gunnar and colleagues (1988) examined behavioral and adrenocortical responses of healthy neonates to circumcision, blood sampling, weighing and measuring, as well as to a discharge examination. Each of the four events elicited fussing and crying and elevations in cortisol. However, if less noxious events such as a discharge exam or weighing and measuring are repeated on two consecutive days, the adrenocortical response is smaller on the second day, even though the newborns continue to exhibit a similar degree of behavioral distress (Gunnar, Connors, and Isensee, 1989; Gunnar et al., 1992). Such dissociation can also be seen in cases where soothing procedures diminish behavioral distress in the newborn, but do not reduce cortisol levels (Gunnar et al., 1988).

Given such dissociations, it is not surprising that both positive and negative correlations have been found between cortisol responses and behavioral distress in newborns. Crying and increases in cortisol are positively correlated in response to noxious stimulation (e.g., heel-stick, circumcision); but for less stressful procedures, different patterns of reactivity emerge. Gunnar, Isensee, and Fust (1987) found negative correlations between cortisol increases and crying during administration of the Brazelton NBAS neonatal exam. One explanation for this finding is that increases in cortisol during the NBAS are not related to behavioral distress, but instead relate to increased self-calming activity. Consistent with this hypothesis, Spangler and Scheubeck (1993) found only inconsistent correlations between newborn irritability and the adrenocortical response during NBAS, but found that higher orientation as assessed by the NBAS was associated with a larger increase in cortisol. A related finding is that of Spangler, Meindl, and Grossman (1988), who found that high baseline cortisol was associated with low irritability in newborns. Newborns with high baseline cortisol also showed less of a cortisol response to the Brazelton exam, and were less irritable in the nursery. The suggestion is that a high-cortisol newborn may in fact be more prepared to cope with stimulation than a newborn with low cortisol (Gunnar, 1989). Studies with infants have also found negative relations between negative emotionality and

cortisol levels. Gunnar and colleagues (1989) found that negative emotional temperament was negatively correlated with baseline cortisol levels in 13-month-old infants, although negative emotional temperament was positively associated with elevations in cortisol during maternal separation at 9 and 13 months.

Dissociations between HPA activity and negative emotional responses have led researchers to suggest that novelty or discrepancy may be more important than the expression of negative affect in the activation of the HPA system (Hennessy and Levine, 1979). However, various studies have suggested that novelty or uncertainty also may not be the primary psychological determinant of elevated cortisol levels (Stansbury and Gunnar, 1994). Gunnar and colleagues have suggested that the critical aspect of uncertainty may not be novelty or unfamiliarity, but rather uncertainty about how to control or influence the stressful event and one's reactions to it (Gunnar et al., 1989). Gunnar and colleagues (1992) found that ratings by mothers of distress in response to limitations predicted distress and cortisol responses on separation from mother at 9 months of age.

Other studies of older infants have suggested that cortisol levels may be related to the maintenance or failure of coping strategies (Gunnar, 1994). For example, Nachmias and colleagues (1996) examined cortisol responses of 18-month-olds to the Ainsworth Strange Situation and a challenging coping episode. Analyses also included attachment classification and an index of behavioral inhibition for each child. Infants who were highly inhibited and insecurely attached showed greater cortisol responses to the Strange Situation and the challenging coping episode, compared to children who were also highly inhibited but who were securely attached. The cortisol increase for inhibited-insecure infants was also greater than that for the uninhibited infants, whether securely or insecurely attached. The authors suggest that mothers in insecure dyads who have inhibited children may interfere with their children's strategies for coping with an unfamiliar and/or stressful situation. This disruption of an inhibited child's coping strategy is then reflected in a greater increase in cortisol compared to an inhibited and secure child whose coping strategy is not disrupted.

## Components of temperament II: Affective bias

A second component of our model of infant temperament involves the overlay of affective response that infants display as part of their reactive response. We have investigated the physiological correlates of this affective response by measuring patterns of EEG from infants and young children during a series of stimulus challenge situations. The motivation for examining EEG patterning and affect derives from a variety of data including work with clinical adult populations, normative adult, and developmental studies (see Fox, 1994b; Silberman and Weingartner, 1986). There has long been interest in the finding that unilateral lesion or stroke, particularly in anterior portions of cortex, seems to differentially affect mood state. Left anterior lesions are often associated with depressive symptoms and negative affect (Morris et al., 1996) while right anterior lesions are associated with mania and inappropriate positive affect (Sackeim et al., 1982). There are, as well, reports on differential mood states achieved during Wada procedures that are consonant with the lateralization of mood (see Snyder and Harris, 1997, for a review). These clinical findings have prompted theorists to speculate as to the functional implications of lateralization for emotions. One prominent model, postulated by Davidson (1992) and Fox (1991), is that anterior regions of the two hemispheres are lateralized for the behavioral/motivational systems involved in either approach or withdrawal. The left anterior region is specialized for the integration and control of those motor and cognitive behaviors associated with approach, novelty seeking, and reward, including most positive affects and fine motor and exploratory behavior. The right anterior region is specialized for the integration and control of those motor and cognitive behaviors associated with withdrawal, flight, or aversive responses.

There are experimental data that support these associations. For example, Davidson and colleagues found that subjects exhibiting right frontal asymmetry were more likely to rate video clips as negative compared to subjects exhibiting left frontal asymmetry (Wheeler, Davidson, and Tomarken, 1993). Sobotka, Davidson, and Senulis (1992) found increased left frontal asymmetry during a task designed to enhance approach and reward motivation. And Sutton and Davidson (1997) report an association between frontal asymmetry and subject scores on a scale measuring behavioral approach or withdrawal motivations. Subjects self-rated as high on behavioral approach were more likely to display left frontal EEG asymmetry.

There are developmental data supporting the relation between frontal EEG asymmetry and affective bias. Davidson and Fox (1989) found that 10-month-old infants who exhibited left frontal EEG asymmetry were less likely to cry and show distress to immediate, brief, maternal separation compared to infants displaying right frontal EEG asymmetry. Fox and colleagues replicated this finding and reported that the pattern of frontal asymmetry appeared to be a stable characteristic in infants over the course of the second half of the first year of life (Fox, Bell, and Jones, 1992). Davidson's work with clinical populations further elaborated the relation of frontal EEG asymmetry to affective bias. Henriques and Davidson (1991) report associations between frontal EEG asymmetry and depression, noting that patients exhibiting depressive symptoms were more likely to exhibit right frontal asymmetry. Work in our laboratory has identified patterns of frontal EEG asymmetry, as well, that appear to reflect an affective bias (Fox et al., 1995). In particular, infants who were highly reactive to novel stimuli and expressed negative affect were more likely to exhibit right frontal EEG asymmetry compared to reactive infants who did not show the same negative affect bias (Calkins, Fox, and Marshall, 1996). The combination of behavioral reactivity and negative affect bias as reflected in the pattern of frontal EEG asymmetry is, as well, the best predictor of temperamental outcome in infants across the first four years of life (Henderson and Fox, 2001).

## Components of temperament III: Regulation

From birth, infants have rudimentary behavioral and physiological capacities that support the expression of emotion and serve to maintain a state of homeostasis. These capacities are primarily reflexive, however, and are elicited in response to changes in the external or internal milieu, and thus have been studied under the rubric of temperamental reactivity. With development, increasing cognitive capacities (e.g., working memory, response inhibition, attentional control) allow for the implementation of more intentional strategies for managing behavior and emotion in support of both physiological and psychological homeostasis, and have been studied as components of temperamental self-regulation. The development of the frontal cortex over the first several years of life, including synaptogenesis and pruning, and the refinement in corticocortical and corticolimbic connections, allows for increasingly efficient and integrated strategies for regulation. In the following section we review the literature on the development of self-regulation, with a special focus on fundamental cognitive capacities and their neuroanatomical bases that may provide the basis for both normative developmental increases and individual differences in self-regulation across early childhood.

The concept of self-regulation plays a central theoretical role in diverse domains of developmental psychology including the study of temperament (Rothbart and Derryberry, 1981), socialization processes (Grusec and Goodnow, 1994), moral development (Kochanska, Murray, and Coy, 1997), and academic achievement (Pintrich and De Groot, 1990; Zimmerman, 1994). Self-regulation is considered such a key aspect of normal development that deficits in various aspects of regulation are the defining features of numerous developmental disabilities including attention deficit hyperactivity disorder (Barkley, 1997), autism (Ozonoff, Pennington, and Rogers, 1991), and conduct disorder (White et al., 1994).

In the most general sense, self-regulation refers to the ability to generate and voluntarily direct goal-oriented, adaptive responses in the absence of external monitors or supports (Kopp, 1982; Welsh and Pennington, 1988). In the temperament literature, self-regulation is used to describe processes that function to modulate the timing and intensity of patterns of reactivity. Self-regulatory processes occur at many levels of functioning including neurophysiological, autonomic, cognitive, and behavioral. Changes at any of these levels can serve to increase, decrease, maintain, or restructure patterns of reactivity (Rothbart and Derryberry, 1981). The goal of self-regulation in the temperament and personality literatures is to promote adaptation through the maintenance of physiological and psychological well-being (Block and Block, 1980; Rothbart and Bates, 1998). In addition to behavioral control, emotional reactions become better regulated across development. Thompson (1990) described well-regulated emotional experiences as those that "flexibly change in response to changing conditions, and rise and fall in intensity in a manner that permits a productive accommodation to changing situational demands" (p. 373). In the model of temperament proposed by Rothbart and Derryberry (1981), self-regulative and reactive processes are simultaneously interactive, such that behavior patterns can be thought of as reflecting the intersection or combined influence of relative levels of reactivity and self-regulation.

Despite the wide range of use and application of the concept of self-regulation, there is a general consensus that self-regulation emerges gradually over childhood (Kopp, 1982). Across all domains of development, regulation is initially mediated through external sources as is reflected in infants' and young children's almost exclusive reliance on others to satisfy their needs. With age, regulation becomes increasingly internally mediated, likely due to the accumulation of learning experiences and the development of higher-order cognitive processes that allow children to exert control over their surroundings and states. Vaughn, Kopp, and Krakow (1984) conducted a cross-sectional study of 18–30-month-old children's performance on several tasks tapping two aspects of self-control (compliance with maternal directives and delay/response inhibition). In addition to age-related increases in performance within

each domain, there was an increased coherence in task performance, both within each of the domains, and across the two domains (compliance vs. response inhibition). The greater coherence across domains of self-control across the toddler years was interpreted as reflecting the increasing global influence of internal, or within-child, factors on self-control.

The idea that self-regulation emerges over the first several years of life may seem at odds with traditional models of temperament, in which it has been emphasized that individual differences in temperament are present at, or very soon after, birth (Goldsmith et al., 1987). This restrictive requirement appears to be a result of the notion that temperament is biologically based and therefore not dependent upon learning experiences. The fact that there is a biological, and specifically neurological, basis for self-regulation, however, is precisely the reason that individual differences emerge gradually over the first several years of life (see Derryberry and Rothbart, 1997; Rothbart, 1989). This would suggest that in thinking of the biological bases for temperament, eligible systems need not be functional at birth, but may also follow a specified developmental time course. Understanding the normal developmental time course for such systems will allow for a better description of the emergence of individual differences in functioning. Several lines of evidence suggest that the emergence of self-regulation is dependent upon the development and integration of internal inhibitory systems associated with and involving the prefrontal cortex.

Speculation about the neurological origins of self-regulation in humans is based in part on detailed observations of changes in behavior and personality resulting from lesions to the brain caused by disease or trauma. The sequelae of frontal lobe damage have been documented in great detail and include deficits in the control of attention, including increased distractibility, disorders of motility including both hypokinesis and hyperkinesis, and perhaps most notably, deficits in initiating and implementing goal-directed patterns of behavior. In addition to the cognitive impairments attributed to frontal lobe damage, changes in affect and emotion have been documented. These changes range from extreme affective lability, evidenced in mood swings between unbridled rage and states of euphoria, to a complete blunting of emotion or apathy (for detailed reviews of cognitive and affective changes associated with damage to the frontal cortex, see Fuster, 1989; Levin, Eisenberg, and Benton, 1991; Stuss and Benson, 1986). Together, the cognitive and emotional changes following damage to the frontal lobes have been attributed to a disruption in the normal inhibitory influences exerted by the frontal cortex on subcortical regions including the hypothalamus and the amygdala.

There are clear similarities between the disinhibited behaviors of adults following damage to the prefrontal cortex and the behaviors and emotions of infants and young children during the normal developmental transition toward self-regulation. Because the development of the prefrontal cortex and self-regulation occur during similar timeframes across the first several years of life (Huttenlocher and Dabholkar, 1997), the progressive stages of self-regulation may be mapped onto the emerging cognitive competencies governed by the prefrontal cortex. Across domains of development and approaches to the study of self-regulation, it is evident that a certain level of cognitive development is required for the transfer of control of regulation from external to internal sources. For example, Kopp (1982) described fundamental cognitive abilities that are required before a child can internalize caregiver expectations for self-initiated behavioral control. These cognitive abilities include intentionality or goal-directedness, object-permanence, differentiation of self from others, representational thought, evocative or recall memory, self-monitoring, and self-initiated motor and language inhibition. For example, in order to comply with a caregiver's rule for behaving, a child must be able to hold the rule in memory in a meaningful way that allows the rule to be selectively retrieved and applied in appropriate situations (representational thought and recall memory). Additionally, a child must be able to monitor his/her behavior in order to recognize transgressions (self-monitoring), efficiently stop inappropriate behaviors (response inhibition), and flexibly implement alternative responses that are deemed more acceptable (planning and monitoring outcomes). Similar to the regulation of behavior, the regulation of emotion can be broken down into component processes, including the recognition, definition, and representation of the cause of distress; the appraisal of contextual features of the event; and the formation of a plan for a sequence of actions in order to change the situation so that distress is modified (Kopp, 1989; Thompson, 1990).

Such cognitive processes are part of a larger group of cognitive functions referred to as executive, highlighting their higher-order control, or regulation, over more basic reaction tendencies (see Diamond, this volume; Rothbart and Posner, this volume). Developments in executive functioning are attributed to structural and functional changes within the prefrontal cortex over the first several years of life (Welsh, Pennington, and Groisser, 1991). Although the terms "self-regulation" and "executive function" are often used almost interchangeably, we believe that executive functions are nec-

essary but not sufficient for effective self-regulation. Specifically, self-regulation is a behavioral reflection of the adaptive implementation of executive control processes; but additional motivational processes, specifically levels of emotional arousal or reactivity, will influence the implementation and perhaps development of these control processes. Indeed, self-regulation, particularly in the context of temperament research, reflects the intersection of emotion and cognition. This idea is supported at both neuroanatomical and behavioral levels by the reciprocal innervation between centers implicated in temperamental reactivity (e.g., limbic structures including the amygdala) and regulation (e.g., regions of the prefrontal cortex and the anterior cingulate cortex) (Alexander, Crutcher, and De Long, 1990; Masterman and Cummings, 1997; Nauta, 1986; Pandya and Barnes, 1987; Tucker, 1992) and by findings with patient populations in which high levels of emotion essentially flood the system, preventing the effective implementation of control strategies (Johanson et al., 1992; Tucker and Derryberry, 1992).

Two cognitive processes, executive attention and response inhibition, appear critical for the emergence of and/or individual differences in regulation. For a detailed review of the development and relevance of executive attention to the emergence of self-regulation, see Rothbart and Posner (this volume). In summary, individual differences in the flexible focusing and shifting of attention have been related to indices of temperamental self-regulation from infancy through adulthood. For example, 4-month-old infants who quickly disengaged their attention from a central fixation point upon presentation of another stimulus in the periphery were rated by their mothers as less easily distressed and more easily soothed compared to infants who disengaged their attention less easily (Johnson, Posner, and Rothbart, 1991).

The development of executive attention, and the ability to implement executive attention in a purposeful manner, likely depends on a combination of neurological maturation and social learning experiences. Specifically, increases in executive attention are attributed to developments in a network of anterior cortical structures, including parts of the prefrontal cortex, the anterior cingulate cortex, and the supplementary motor area (see Rothbart and Posner, this volume). The anterior cingulate may be particularly relevant to the study of temperament, because it appears to serve as a point of integration for the visceral, attentional, and affective information that forms the basis of self-regulation (Devinsky, Morrell, and Vogt, 1995; Lane et al., 1998; Thayer and Lane, 2000). In addition, the flexible and intentional employment of attention characterizes many of the early interactions that take place between caregivers and infants. During adult–infant interactions, adults engage and disengage infants' attention in order to manage the infants' level of arousal. States of engaged attention between infants and their caregivers tend to be associated with play, states of joy, and general states of positive affect (Gottman, Katz, and Hooven, 1997). Adults also tend to be sensitive to infants' needs to disengage their attention in order to damp or reduce levels of arousal. When attention is engaged, arousal is heightened; and by disengaging attention, adults give infants the opportunity to damp their levels of arousal. When parents respond contingently to their infants' needs to disengage and re-engage interactions, infants learn about the efficacy of attentional control as a means of self-regulation (Gottman, Katz, and Hooven, 1997).

Another component of executive functioning with close conceptual connections to self-regulation is the ability to control actions, or inhibit prepotent action tendencies. The use of action-oriented plans affords young children reflective control over their behavior and their environment (Zelazo, Reznick, and Pinon, 1995). This involves two processes. The first is the understanding and representation of a rule or contingency specifying the relation between a stimulus condition and the expected response. The second process involves using the representation of the rule to guide behavior. This translation of representation into action depends on the maturation of cortical processes, particularly those relating to the inhibition of inappropriate responses and behaviors (Bell and Livesey, 1983).

The ability to exert conscious control over behaviors based on cognitive representations of the stimulus conditions emerges gradually over the first several years of life, with rapid increases in the ability to use rules to guide behaviors occurring during the third year of life (Bell and Livesey, 1983; Vaughn, Kopp, and Krakow, 1984; Zelazo, Reznick, and Pinon, 1995). Zelazo and colleagues (1995) reported that young children could hold in working memory a simple set of rules by which they were asked to sort a set of picture cards into piles, then use this set of rules to tell the experimenter where a card belonged with good accuracy. However, up until the age of 36 months, children could not use such rules to guide their own behavior. Thus, performance on such tasks appears to be restricted not because of an inability to understand or represent the contingencies cognitively, or to hold the contingencies in working memory, but rather, on the ability to use this understanding to control behavior. Similar dissociations between knowledge and action have been reported in several studies of the development of response control

(Becker, Isaac, and Hynd, 1987; Bell and Livesey, 1983; Luria, 1973). Many studies of response inhibition with children and adults involve conflict tasks such as the traditional Stroop task in which prepotent responses must be inhibited for successful performance. Conflict tasks with less demanding language requirements have been developed for younger children (see Diamond, this volume; Rothbart and Posner, this volume). Similar to the findings of Zelazo and colleagues (1995), Diamond and colleagues concluded that 3½- and 4-year-old children's poor performance on conflict tasks was due to an inability to inhibit prepotent responses rather than an inability to learn and remember the rules (Gerstadt, Hong, and Diamond, 1994). Using an even more simplified conflict task with children as young as 24 months of age, Rothbart and colleagues (Gerardi, 1996, as cited by Posner and Rothbart, 1998) noted a transition point around 30 months of age, in terms of children's abilities to inhibit responding, a developmental period that is consistent with others' reports of rapid changes in self-regulation (e.g., Vaughn, Kopp, and Krakow, 1984). Of particular interest for the study of the development of self-regulation, performance on the modified Stroop task was positively correlated with children's performance on several laboratory tasks requiring inhibitory control and parental reports of effortful control and negatively correlated with parental reports of negative affect (Rothbart and Bates, 1998).

Luria (1973) speculated on the cortical mechanisms involved in the inhibition of prepotent responses based on the finding that young children and adults with prefrontal injury had difficulty using rules to guide behaviors due to a tendency to perseverate on a particular motor response. Based on lesion data and PET studies during performance of conflict tasks, the inhibition of prepotent responding appears to be mediated by regions of the prefrontal cortex, particularly the dorsolateral prefrontal cortex, and the anterior cingulate cortex (see Casey, Thomas, and McCandliss, this volume; Pardo et al., 1990). As is the case with executive attention, the involvement of the anterior cingulate may account for the relations reported between individual differences in response inhibition and measures of negative affect (see Rothbart and Posner, this volume).

Although higher-order cognitive abilities such as executive attention control and response inhibition are usually thought of as modulators of early-appearing patterns of temperamental reactivity (i.e., a top-down model), temperamental reactivity may influence the development of regulatory mechanisms in at least two ways. First, given the bidirectional innervations between structures in the prefrontal cortex and the limbic system, it is possible that individual differences in limbic, particularly amygdala, reactivity that are thought to underlie differences in temperamental reactivity, will influence the development of inhibitory connections between the prefrontal cortex and other limbic structures. Second, individual differences in temperamental reactivity will influence the quantity and quality of social interactions with caregivers. As such, it would be expected that temperamentally diverse infants would have varied learning histories with respect to both the engagement and disengagement of attention and the ability to use rules to guide behavior allowing for the inhibition of prepotent behavioral and emotional reactions.

### Behavioral inhibition: Integration of behavioral and neuroscience approaches to temperament

Behaviorally inhibited children display characteristic behaviors when confronted with novelty such as motor quieting, long latencies to approach, active avoidance, decreased vocalizations, and increased proximity to caregivers (Garcia Coll, Kagan, and Reznick, 1984). These behaviors may reflect an active fear state in the child or a state of heightened vigilance in which the child is prepared to respond to threat. Linking the neuroscience work of Davis and LeDoux on the physiology of the fear system to behavioral observations of inhibited children, Kagan hypothesized that temperamental inhibition reflected overarousal of the fear system. As such, he predicted that inhibited children should be negatively reactive to novel stimuli compared to non-fearful age-matched controls and that their behavioral and physiological pattern should parallel the physiological changes reported by Davis in the fear-potentiated animals (Kagan, 1994). In particular, Davis describes multiple target outputs from the central nucleus (or bed nucleus) which may be expected to result in changes in heart rate, cortisol production, behavioral freezing, and startle response.

In order to examine the temperamental origins of behavioral inhibition (BI), both Kagan (Kagan and Snidman, 1991) and Fox (Calkins, Fox, and Marshall, 1996) in two independent studies selected infants at 4 months of age who were highly reactive and displayed high negative affect to novel auditory and visual stimuli. A significant percentage of these infants displayed signs of behavioral inhibition at one year of age in both samples. Fox and colleagues (2001) reported that 25% of the infants selected for these reactivity patterns remained inhibited through 4 years of age.

The physiological and behavioral data from inhibited children seem to confirm to the predicted pattern as well. For example, Schmidt and Fox (1998) found that infants selected for precursors of temperamental inhibition were more likely at 9 months of age to show potentiated startle responses to the approach of an unfamiliar adult. Significant autonomic findings have been reported as well. At 21 months, 4 years, and 5.5 years, children who were classed as inhibited at 21 months had significantly lower HP than uninhibited children across a range of laboratory tasks (Garcia Coll, Kagan, and Reznick, 1984; Kagan et al., 1984; Reznick et al., 1986). In addition to tonic between-group differences in HP, Kagan also found that inhibited children tended to show larger decreases in HP to stressors compared to uninhibited children. At every age of assessment (from 21 months to 7.5 years of age), children who were classified as inhibited at 21 months were more likely than uninhibited children to show a decrease in HP across a battery of cognitive tests (Kagan et al., 1988). As well as relating HP at each age to the initial 21-month behavioral assessment, Kagan also examined the concurrent relations of HP and inhibition. At each age of assessment (21 months; 4, 5.5, and 7.5 years), HP during quiet or active tasks was significantly negatively correlated with BI as assessed at that age (Kagan et al., 1984; Reznick et al., 1986; Kagan et al., 1988). Furthermore, children who were inhibited at all four assessment ages had the lowest levels of mean HP at each age, while consistently uninhibited children had the highest levels of mean HP at each. Marshall and Stevenson-Hinde (1998) examined relations between BI and HP in a sample of children who were selected at 4 years according to criteria for high or low BI on the basis of both a maternal questionnaire and interviewer ratings at home. Subsequent laboratory assessments at 4.5 and 7 years involved further BI ratings as well as the measurement of HP over a series of episodes. No significant relations emerged between BI and HP over the whole sample. However, HP predicted which of the children in the high inhibition group would remain inhibited at 7 years: HP at 4.5 years was significantly lower for children with high BI ratings at 4.5 who remained highly inhibited at 7 years compared with children with high BI at 4.5 years who were less inhibited at 7 years. Contemporaneous relations between inhibition and HP at 4.5 years were found only when attachment security was considered in combination with inhibition grouping (Stevenson-Hinde and Marshall, 1999).

With regard to the HPA axis, Kagan, Reznick, and Snidman (1987) found elevated cortisol levels in 5.5-year-olds who had been classified as behaviorally inhibited at 21 months of age, compared to those who had been classified as uninhibited at 21 months. Inhibited behavior at 5.5 years of age was also associated with high levels of cortisol as measured at the same age. In addition, Schmidt and colleagues (1997) found that 4-year-olds who showed high levels of anxious and unoccupied behavior in laboratory play sessions with unfamiliar peers showed significantly higher morning salivary cortisol levels compared to less wary children.

Other work by Gunnar has provided alternative insights into the relation of socially withdrawn, fearful behavior in childhood and reactivity of the HPA axis. For instance, de Haan and colleagues (1998) found home cortisol levels to be associated with more anxious, internalizing behavior in 2-year-olds, but found that the cortisol response to starting preschool was correlated with more assertive, angry, and aggressive behavior rather than with socially inhibited or anxious behavior. Gunnar (1994) suggests one possible reason why inhibited children may not show elevated cortisol reactivity during such transitions. Unlike less fearful children, inhibited children tend to avoid the kinds of social and physical activities that would elicit elevations in cortisol. Another interesting suggestion raised by Gunnar is that adrenocortical activity may not map neatly onto fear- or stress-related constructs, but rather that cortisol reactivity may be related to the maintenance or failure of coping strategies.

In our own work, we have observed similar physiological patterns in certain school-age children (Schmidt et al., 1997, 1999). We have labeled these children "socially reticent," as they spend their time watching other children when put in a group of unfamiliar peers. They tend to hover on the fringe of the social activity, display behavioral signs of anxiety, and remain unengaged in any other activities. These children appear to be unable to disengage their attention to the other children and make few attempts to join in group activities. This fixation not only appears to be ineffective in reducing wariness, but it may also increase wariness over the course of the play period.

These socially reticent children appear to be unsuccessful at cognitive tasks that require working memory if they are tested within a social situation. Within our peer group situation, children are asked to sort cards by color. In order to complete the task, the children must remember the instructions, systematically select one card of each color from the bigger pile, put the four cards together, and put them in the envelope, therefore requiring basic executive functions including working memory, response inhibition, and planning. Across numerous independent cohorts, we have found that the display of socially reticent behavior in the free-play session is highly correlated with off-task, unoccupied behavior during the ticket-sorting task. We believe that the reticent children are flooded by their reactions

to the novel social context and with unfamiliar peers, which prevents them from executing the simple rules of the card-sorting game. Such an interpretation would be consistent with a bottom-up model of emotion and cognition described earlier (Mandler, 1982), and with findings from adult populations in which decision-making processes are compromised under conditions of stress (Keinan, Friedland, and Ben-Porath, 1987).

In a more direct test of the association between behavioral inhibition and basic executive function abilities, we examined the relation between three neuropsychological tests (Tower of Hanoi, Wisconsin Card Sorting Task, and Matching Familiar Figures Test) and children's behaviors with unfamiliar peers at the age of 7 (Fox and Henderson, 1997). These tasks were presented to the children on a separate visit when they were alone with an experimenter. Socially reticent children did not differ from their more sociable peers on performance in these tasks. This suggests that socially reticent children, when not in conditions that might be expected to elicit temperamental reactivity, were able to perform equally well on tests of basic executive functioning. An interesting test of the emotion-flooding model would be to examine the relative decrement in performance on these tasks for children differing in temperamental profile under conditions of stress (e.g., in the presence of unfamiliar peers).

In sum, the data on behavioral and physiological reactivity in inhibited infants and children seems to mimic the patterns that are described for animals in the fear-potentiated paradigm of Davis and LeDoux. At this point, it is not clear whether the model of fear-potentiated startle and its neural circuits through the central nucleus of the amygdala or non–fear-conditioned startle and its neural circuits through the bed nucleus of the stria terminalis best describes the condition of temperamental inhibition. Although there are no direct empirical tests among inhibited children of either neural model, this work has served as an important heuristic for thinking about the pattern of their behavioral and physiological responses to novelty and mild stress. In addition, the work of Posner and Rothbart and others on the neural bases of attention and response inhibition may provide insights into the development of regulatory mechanisms as it affects temperamental reactivity and emotion. These links between neuroscience and temperamental inhibition may serve as a model for examining other temperamental types. For example, Fox and colleagues (in press) report on the behavior and physiology of exuberant infants who display high reactivity coupled with positive affect in response to novelty and mild stress. These children display positive social behaviors, high exploratory behavior, and low fear in novel settings. Future research should attempt to find connections between the neuroscience work and human temperamental behavior in describing and ultimately understanding unique individual differences.

ACKNOWLEDGMENTS    Preparation for this chapter was supported in part by a grant from the National Institutes of Health (HD#17899) to Nathan A. Fox.

REFERENCES

ALEXANDER, G. E., M. D. CRUTCHER, and M. R. DE LONG, 1990. Basal ganglia-thalamo-cortical circuits: Parallel substrates for motor, oculomotor, "prefrontal" and "limbic" functions. *Prog. Brain Res.* 85:119–146.

BARKLEY, R. A., 1997. Behavioral inhibition, sustained attention, and executive functions: Constructing a unifying theory of ADHD. *Psychol. Bull.* 121:65–94.

BECKER, M. G., W. ISAAC, and G. W. HYND, 1987. Neuropsychological development of nonverbal behaviors attributed to "frontal lobe" functioning. *Dev. Neuropsychol.* 3:275–298.

BELL, J. A., and P. J. LIVESEY, 1983. Cue significance and response regulation in 3- to 6-year-old children's learning of multiple choice discrimination tasks. *Dev. Psychobiol.* 18:229–245.

BLOCK, J. H., and J. BLOCK, 1980. The role of ego-control and ego-resiliency in the organization of behavior. In *Minnesota Symposium on Child Psychology*, Vol. 13, W. A. Collins, ed. Hillsdale, N.J.: Erlbaum, pp. 39–101.

BOWLBY, J., 1969. *Attachment and Loss. Vol. 1: Attachment.* New York: Basic Books.

BRAZELTON, T. B., 1984. *Neonatal Behavioral Assessment Scale*, 2nd ed. Philadelphia: J.B. Lippincott.

BROWN, J. S., H. I. KALISH, and I. E. FARBER, 1951. Conditioned fear as revealed by magnitude of startle response to an auditory stimulus. *J. Exp. Psychol.* 41:317–328.

CALKINS, S. D., N. A. FOX, and T. R. MARSHALL, 1996. Behavioral and physiological antecedents of inhibited and uninhibited behavior. *Child Dev.* 67:523–540.

DAVIDSON, R. J., 1992. Anterior cerebral asymmetry and the nature of emotion. *Brain Cognit.* 20:125–151.

DAVIDSON, R. J., and N. A. FOX, 1989. Frontal brain asymmetry predicts infants' response to maternal separation. *J. Abnorm. Psychol.* 98:127–131.

DAVIS, M., 1986. Pharmacological and anatomical analysis of fear conditioning using the fear-potentiated startle paradigm. *Behav. Neurosci.* 100:814–824.

DAVIS, M., 1989. Sensitization of the acoustic startle reflex by footshock. *Behav. Neurosci.* 103:495–503.

DAVIS, M., 1998. Are different parts of the extended amygdala involved in fear versus anxiety? *Biol. Psychiatry* 44:1239–1247.

DAVIS, M., W. A. FALLS, S. CAMPEAU, and M. KIM, 1993. Fear-potentiated startle: A neural and pharmacological analysis. *Behav. Brain Res.* 58:175–198.

DAVIS, M., J. HITCHCOCK, and J. ROSEN, 1987. Anxiety and the amygdala: Pharmacological and anatomical analysis of the fear potentiated startle paradigm. In *Psychology of Learning and Motivation*, Vol. 21, G. H. Bower, ed. New York: Academic Press, pp. 263–305.

DE HAAN, M., M. R. GUNNAR, K. TOUT, J. HART, and K. STANSBURY, 1998. Familiar and novel contexts yield different associations between cortisol and behavior among 2-year-old children. *Dev. Psychobiol.* 33:93–101.

DERRYBERRY, D., and M. K. ROTHBART, 1997. Reactive and effortful processes in the organization of temperament. *Development and Psychopathology,* 9:633–652.

DERRYBERRY, D., and D. M. TUCKER, 1991. The adaptive base of the neural hierarchy: Elementary motivational controls on network function. In *Nebraska Symposium on Motivation. Vol. 38: Perspectives on Motivation,* R. Dienstbier, ed. Lincoln: University of Nebraska Press, pp. 289–342.

DEVINSKY, O., M. J. MORRELL, and B. A. VOGT, 1995. Contributions of the anterior cingulate cortex to behaviour. *Brain* 118:279–306.

DIPIETRO J. A., R. M. CUSSON, M. O. CAUGHY, and N. A. FOX, 1994. Behavioral and physiologic effects of nonnutritive sucking during gavage feeding in preterm infants. *Pediatr. Res.* 36:207–214.

DIPIETRO, J. A., S. K. LARSON, and S. W. PORGES, 1987. Behavioral and heart-rate patterns between breast-fed and bottle-fed neonates. *Dev. Psychol.* 23:467–474.

DIPIETRO, J. A., and S. W. PORGES, 1991. Vagal responsiveness to gavage feeding as an index of preterm stress. *Pediatr. Res.* 29:231–236.

DODGE, K. A., 1991. Emotion and social information processing. In *The Development of Emotion Regulation and Dysregulation,* J. Garber and K. A. Dodge, eds. Cambridge: Cambridge University Press, pp. 159–181.

EISENBERG, N., R. A. FABES, M. NYMAN, J. BERNZWEIG, and A. PINUELAS, 1994. The relations of emotionality and regulation to children's anger-related reactions. *Child Dev.* 65:109–128.

EYSENCK, H. J., and M. W. EYSENCK, 1985. *Personality and Individual Differences: A Natural Science Approach.* New York: Plenum.

FOX, N. A., 1991. If it's not left, it's right. Electroencephalograph asymmetry and the development of emotion. *American Psychologist* 46:863–872.

FOX, N. A., ed., 1994a. *The Development of Emotion Regulation: Biological and Behavioral Considerations.* Monographs of the Society for Research in Child Development, Vol. 59 (2–3, Serial No. 240).

FOX, N. A., 1994b. Dynamic cerebral processes underlying emotion regulation. In *The Development of Emotion Regulation: Biological and Behavioral Considerations,* N. A. Fox, ed. Monographs of the Society for Research in Child Development, Vol. 59 (2–3, Serial No. 240), pp. 152–166.

FOX, N. A., M. A. BELL, and N. A. JONES, 1992. Individual differences in response to stress and cerebral asymmetry. *Dev. Neuropsychol.* 8:161–184.

FOX, N. A., and H. A. HENDERSON, 1997. Emotion regulation: Distinguishing between subtypes of behavioral inhibition. In *Emotion Regulation: Theory and Research.* Symposium conducted at the 9th Annual Convention of the American Psychological Society, May 1997. Washington, DC.

FOX, N. A., H. A. HENDERSON, K. RUBIN, S. D. CALKINS, and L. A. SCHMIDT, 2001. Continuity and discontinuity of behavioral inhibition and exuberance: Psychophysiological and behavioral influences across the first 4 years of life. *Child Dev.* 72:1–21.

FOX, N. A., and S. W. PORGES, 1985. The relation between neonatal heart period patterns and developmental outcome. *Child Dev.* 56:28–37.

Fox, N. A., K. H. Rubin, S. D. Calkins, T. R. Marshall, R. J. Coplan, S. W. Porges, J. M. Long, and S. Stewart, 1995. Frontal activation asymmetry and social competence at four years of age. *Child Dev.* 66:1770–1784.

Fox, N. A., and C. A. Stifter, 1989. Biological and behavioral differences in infant reactivity and regulation. In *Temperament in Childhood*, G. A. Kohnstamm, J. E. Bates, and M. K. Rothbart, eds. Chichester: John Wiley, pp. 169–183.

Fuster, J. M., 1989. *The Prefrontal Cortex: Anatomy, Physiology, and Neuropsychology of the Frontal Lobe*. New York: Raven Press.

Garcia, R., R. M. Vouimba, M. Baudry, and R. F. Thompson, 1999. The amygdala modulates prefrontal cortex activity relative to conditioned fear. *Nature* 402:294–296.

Garcia Coll, C., J. Kagan, and J. S. Reznick, 1984. Behavioral inhibition to the unfamiliar. *Child Dev.* 55:1005–1019.

Gerardi, G., M. K. Rothbart, M. I. Posner, and S. Kepler, 1996, April. The development of attentional control: Performance on a spatial Stroop-like task at 24, 30, and 36–38-months-of-age. Poster presented at the annual meeting of the International Society for Infant Studies, Providence, RI.

Gerstadt, C. L., Y. J. Hong, and A. Diamond, 1994. The relationship between cognition and action: Performance of children 3½–7 years old on a Stroop-like day-night task. *Cognition* 53:129–153.

Goldsmith, H. H., A. H. Buss, R. Plomin, M. K. Rothbart, A. Thomas, S. Chess, R. A. Hinde, and R. B. McCall, 1987. Roundtable: What is temperament? Four approaches. *Child Dev.* 58:505–529.

Goldsmith, H. H., and J. J. Campos, 1986. Fundamental issues in the study of early temperament: The Denver Twin Temperament Study. In *Advances in Developmental Psychology*, Vol. 4, M. E. Lamb, A. L. Brown, and B. Rogoff, eds. Hillsdale, N.J.: Lawrence Erlbaum, pp. 231–283.

Gottman, J. M., L. F. Katz, and C. Hooven, 1997. *Meta-emotion: How Families Communicate Emotionally*. Mahwah, N.J.: Lawrence Erlbaum Associates.

Gray, J. A., 1982. *The Neuropsychology of Anxiety: An Enquiry into the Functions of the Septo-hippocampal System*. New York: Oxford University Press.

Gray, J. A., 1987. *The Psychology of Fear and Stress*, 2nd ed. Cambridge: Cambridge University Press, 1987.

Gray, J. A., 1991. The neuropsychology of temperament. In *Explorations in Temperament: International Perspectives on Theory and Measurement*, J. Strelau and A. Angleneitner, eds. New York: Plenum, pp. 105–128.

Grusec, J. E., and J. J. Goodnow, 1994. The impact of parental discipline methods on the child's internalization of values: A reconceptualization of current points of view. *Dev. Psychol.* 30:4–19.

Gunnar, M. R., 1989. The psychobiology of infant temperament. In *Individual Differences in Infancy: Reliability, Stability, Prediction*, J. Columbo and J. Fagen, eds. Hillsdale, N.J.: Lawrence Erlbaum Associates, pp. 387–409.

Gunnar, M. R., 1994. Psychoendocrine studies of temperament and stress in early childhood: Expanding current models. In *Temperament: Individual Differences at the Interface of Biology and Behavior*, J. E. Bates and T. D. Wachs, eds. Washington, D.C.: American Psychological Association, pp.175–198.

Gunnar, M. R., J. Connors, and J. Isensee, 1989. Lack of stability in neonatal adrenocortical reactivity because of rapid habituation of the adrenocortical response. *Dev. Psychobiol.* 22:221–233.

Gunnar, M. R., J. Connors, J. Isensee, and L. Wall, 1988. Adrenocortical reactivity and behavioral distress in newborns. *Dev. Psychobiol.* 21:279–310.

Gunnar, M. R., L. Hertsgaard, M. Larson, and J. Rigatuso, 1992. Cortisol and behavioral responses to repeated stressors in the human newborn. *Dev. Psychobiol.* 24:487–505.

Gunnar, M. R., J. Isensee, and L. S. Fust, 1987. Adrenocortical activity and the Brazelton Neonatal Assessment Scale: Moderating effects of the newborn's biomedical status. *Child Dev.* 58:1448–1458.

Gunnar, M. R., M. Larson, L. Hertsgaard, M. Harris, and L. Broderson, 1992. The stressfulness of separation among 9-month-old infants: Effects of social context variables and infant temperament. *Child Dev.* 63:290–303.

Gunnar, M. R., S. Mangelsdorf, M. Larson, and L. Hertsgaard, 1989. Attachment, temperament, and adrenocortical activity in infancy: A study of psychoendocrine regulation. *Dev. Psychol.* 25:355–363.

Gunnar, M. R., D. Marvinney, J. Isensee, and R. P. Fisch, 1989. Coping with uncertainty: New models of the relations between behavioral, cognitive, and hormonal processes. In *Coping with Uncertainty: Biological, Behavioral, and Developmental Perspectives*, D. Palermo, ed. Hillsdale, N.J.: Lawrence Erlbaum Associates.

Henderson, H. A., and N. A. Fox, 2001. Temperamental contributions to social behavior: The moderating roles of frontal EEG asymmetry and gender. *J. Am. Acad. Child Adolesc. Psychiatry* 40:68–74.

Hennessy, J., and S. Levine, 1979. Stress, arousal, and the pituitary-adrenal system: A psychoendocrine model. In *Progress in Psychobiological and Physiological Psychology*, Vol. 8, J. Sprague and A. Epstein, eds. New York: Academic Press.

Henriques, J. B., and R. J. Davidson, 1991. Left frontal hypoactivation in depression. *J. Abnorm. Psychol.* 100:535–545.

Huffman, L. C., Y. E. Bryan, R. del Carmen, F. A. Pedersen, J. A. Doussard-Roosevelt, and S. W. Porges, 1998. Infant temperament and cardiac vagal tone: Assessments at twelve weeks of age. *Child Dev.* 69:624–635.

Huttenlocher, P. R., A. S. Dabholkar, 1997. Developmental anatomy of prefrontal cortex. In *Development of the Prefrontal Cortex: Evolution, Neurobiology, and Behavior*, N. A. Krasnegor, G. R. Lyon, and P. S. Goldman-Rakic, eds. Baltimore, Md.: Paul H. Brookes, pp. 69–84.

Johanson, A., G. Smith, J. Risberg, P. Silfverskiold, and D. Tucker, 1992. Left orbital frontal activation in pathological anxiety. *Anxiety Stress Coping* 5:313–328.

Johnson, M. H., M. I. Posner, and M. K. Rothbart, 1991. Components of visual orienting in early infancy: Contingency learning, anticipatory looking, and disengaging. *J. Cogn. Neurosci.* 3:335–344.

Kagan, J., 1994. *Galen's Prophecy*. New York: Basic Books.

Kagan, J., J. S. Reznick, C. Clarke, N. Snidman, and C. Garcia Coll, 1984. Behavioral inhibition to the unfamiliar. *Child Dev.* 55:2212–2225.

Kagan, J., J. S. Reznick, and N. Snidman, 1987. The physiology and psychology of behavioral inhibition in children. *Child Dev.* 58:1459–1473.

Kagan, J., J. S. Reznick, N. Snidman, J. Gibbons, and M. O. Johnson, 1988. Childhood derivatives of inhibition and lack of inhibition to the unfamiliar. *Child Dev.* 59:1580–1589.

Kagan, J., and N. Snidman, 1991. Temperamental factors in human development. *American Psychologist* 46:856–862.

Katona, P. G., and F. Jih, 1975. Respiratory sinus arrhythmia:

Non-invasive measure of parasympathetic cardiac control. *J. Appl. Physiol.* 39:801–805.

KEINAN, G., N. FRIEDLAND, and Y. BEN-PORATH, 1987. Decision making under stress: Scanning of alternatives under physical threat. *Acta Psychol.* 64:219–228.

KOCHANSKA, G., K. MURRAY, and K. C. COY, 1997. Inhibitory control as a contributor to conscience in childhood: From toddler to early school age. *Child Dev.* 68:263–277.

KOPP, C. B., 1982. Antecedents of self-regulation: A developmental perspective. *Dev. Psychol.* 18:199–214.

KOPP, C. B., 1989. Regulation of distress and negative emotions: A developmental view. *Dev. Psychol.* 25:343–354.

LANE, R. D., E. M. REIMAN, V. B. B. AXELROD, L.-S. YUN, A. HOLMES, and G. E. SCHWARTZ, 1998. Neural correlates of levels of emotional awareness: Evidence of an interaction between emotion and attention in the anterior cingulated. *J. Cogn. Neurosci.* 10:525–535.

LAZARUS, R. S., and S. FOLKMAN, 1984. *Stress, Appraisal, and Coping.* New York: Springer.

LEDOUX, J. E., C. F. FARB, and D. A. RUGGIERO, 1990. Topographic organization of neurons in the acoustic thalamus that project to the amygdala. *J. Neurosci.* 10:1043–1054.

LEDOUX, J. E., J. IWATA, P. CICCHETTI, and D. J. REIS, 1988. Different projections of the central amygdaloid nucleus mediate autonomic and behavioral correlates of conditioned fear. *J. Neurosci.* 8:2517–2529.

LEE, Y., and M. DAVIS, 1997. Role of the hippocampus, bed nucleus of the stria terminalis and amygdala in the excitatory effect of corticotrophin releasing hormone (CRH) on the acoustic startle reflex. *J. Neuroscience* 17:6434–6446.

LEVIN, H. S., H. M. EISENBERG, and A. L. BENTON, 1991. *Frontal Lobe Function and Dysfunction.* New York: Oxford University Press.

LURIA, A. R., 1973. *The Working Brain. An Introduction to Neuropsychology* [B. Haigh, translator]. New York: Basic Books.

MANDLER, G., 1982. Stress and thought processes. In *Handbook of Stress: Theoretical and Clinical Aspects*, L. Goldberger and S. Breznitz, eds. New York: Free Press, pp. 88–104.

MARSHALL, P. J., and J. STEVENSON-HINDE, 1998. Behavioral inhibition, heart period, and respiratory sinus arrhythmia in young children. *Dev. Psychobiol.* 33:283–292.

MASON, J. W., 1975. A historical view of the stress field. *J. Hum. Stress* 1:22–36.

MASTERMAN, D. L., and J. L. CUMMINGS, 1997. Frontal-subcortical circuits: The anatomical basis of executive, social, and motivated behaviors. *J. Psychopharmacol.* 11:107–114.

MORRIS, P. L., R. G. ROBINSON, B. RAPHAEL, and M. J. HOPWOOD, 1996. Lesion location and poststroke depression. *J. Neuropsychiatry Clin. Neurosci.* 8:399–403.

NACHMIAS, M., M. GUNNAR, S. MANGELSDORF, R. H. PARRITZ, and K. BUSS, 1996. Behavioral inhibition and stress reactivity: The moderating role of attachment security. *Child Dev.* 67:508–522.

NAUTA, W. J. H., 1986. Circuitous connections linking cerebral cortex, limbic system, and corpus striatum. In *The Limbic System: Functional Organization and Clinical Disorders*, B. K. Doane and K. E. Livingston, eds. New York: Raven Press, pp. 43–54.

OZONOFF, S., B. F. PENNINGTON, and S. J. ROGERS, 1991. Executive function deficits in high-functioning autistic individuals: Relationship to theory of mind. *J. Child Psychol. Psychiatry* 32:1081–1105.

PANDYA, D. N., and C. L. BARNES, 1987. Architecture and connections of the frontal lobe. In *The Frontal Lobes Revisited*, E. Perecman, ed. New York: IRBN Press, pp. 41–72.

PARDO, J. V., P. J. PARDO, K. W. JANER, and M. E. RAICHLE, 1990. The anterior cingulate cortex mediates processing selection in the Stroop attentional conflict paradigm. *Proc. Natl. Acad. Sci. USA* 89:5951–5955.

PAVLOV, I. P., 1927. *Conditioned Reflexes.* New York: Dover.

PINTRICH, P. R., and E. V. DE GROOT, 1990. Motivational and self-regulated learning components of classroom academic performance. *J. Edu. Psychol.* 82:33–40.

PORGES, S. W., 1983. Heart rate patterns in neonates: A potential diagnostic window to the brain. In *Infants Born at Risk: Psychological, Perceptual, and Cognitive Processes*, T. Field and A. Sostek, eds. New York: Grune & Stratton, pp. 3–22.

PORGES, S. W., 1986. Respiratory sinus arrhythmia: Physiological basis, quantitative methods, and clinical implications. In *Cardiorespiratory and Cardiosomatic Psychophysiology*, P. Grossman, K. Janssen, and D. Vaitl, eds. New York: Plenum Press, pp. 101–115.

PORGES, S. W., 1995. Orienting in a defensive world: Mammalian modifications of our evolutionary heritage. A polyvagal theory. *Psychophysiology* 32:301–318.

PORGES, S. W., and J. A. DOUSSARD-ROOSEVELT, 1997a. The psychophysiology of temperament. In *The Handbook of Child and Adolescent Psychiatry. Vol. 1: Infants and Preschoolers: Development and Syndromes*, J. D. Noshpitz, S. Greenspan, S. Wieder, and J. Osofsky, eds. New York: Wiley, pp. 250–268.

PORGES, S. W., and J. A. DOUSSARD-ROOSEVELT, 1997b. Early psychophysiological response patterns and later psychological development. In *Life-Span Developmental Psychology: Biological and Neuropsychological Mechanisms*, H. W. Reese and M. D. Franzen, eds. Hillsdale, N.J.: Lawrence Erlbaum Associates, pp. 163–179.

PORGES, S. W., J. A. DOUSSARD-ROOSEVELT, and A. K. MAITI, 1994. Vagal tone and the physiological regulation of emotion. In *The Development of Emotion Regulation: Biological and Behavioral Considerations*, N. A. Fox, ed. Monographs of the Society for Research in Child Development, Vol. 59(2–3, Serial No. 240), pp. 167–188.

PORGES, S. W., J. A. DOUSSARD-ROOSEVELT, A. L. PORTALES, and S. I. GREENSPAN, 1996. Infant regulation of the vagal brake predicts child behavior problems—A psychobiological model of social behavior. *Dev. Psychobiol.* 29:697–712.

PORTER, F. L., S. W. PORGES, and R. E. MARSHALL, 1988. Newborn pain cries and vagal tone: Parallel changes in response to circumcision. *Child Dev.* 59:495–505.

POSNER, M. I., and M. K. ROTHBART, 1998. Attention, self-regulation and consciousness. *Phil. Trans. R. Soc. Lond. [B]* 353(1377):1915–1927.

REZNICK, J. S., J. KAGAN, N. SNIDMAN, M. GERSTEN, K. BAAK, and A. RODENBERG, 1986. Inhibited and uninhibited children: A follow-up study. *Child Dev.* 57:660–680.

ROTHBART, M. K., 1989. Temperament and development. In *Temperament in Childhood*, G. A. Kohnstamm, J. A. Bates, and M. K. Rothbart, eds. New York: Wiley, pp. 187–247.

ROTHBART, M. K., and J. E. BATES, 1998. Temperament. In *Handbook of Child Psychology: Vol. 3: Social, Emotional, and Personality Development*, 5th ed., N. Eisenberg and W. Damon, eds. New York: Wiley, pp. 105–176.

ROTHBART, M. K., and D. DERRYBERRY, 1981. Development of individual differences in temperament. In *Advances in Developmental Psychology*, Vol. 1, M. Lamb and A. Brown, eds. Hillsdale, N.J.: Erlbaum, pp. 37–86.

SACKEIM, H. A., M. S. GREENBERG, A. L. WEIMAN, R. C. GUR, J. P. HUNGERBUHLER, and N. GESCHWIND, 1982. Hemispheric asymmetry in the expression of positive and negative emotions. *Arch. Neurol.* 39:210–218.

SCHMIDT, L. A., and N. A. FOX, 1998. Fear-potentiated startle responses in temperamentally different human infants. *Dev. Psychobiol.* 32:113–120.

SCHMIDT, L. A., N. A. FOX, K. H. RUBIN, E. STERNBERG, P. W. GOLD, C. SMITH, and J. SCHULKIN, 1997. Behavioral and neuroendocrine responses in shy children. *Dev. Psychobiol.* 30:127–140.

SCHMIDT, L. A., N. A. FOX, J. SCHULKIN, and P. W. GOLD, 1999. Behavioral and psychophysiological correlates of self-presentation in temperamentally shy children. *Dev. Psychobiol.* 35:119–135.

SILBERMAN, E. K., and H. WEINGARTNER, 1986. Hemispheric lateralization of functions related to emotion. *Brain Cognit.* 5:322–353.

SNYDER, P. J., and L. J. HARRIS, 1997. The intracarotid amobarbital procedure: An historical perspective. *Brain Cognit.* 33:18–32.

SOBOTKA, S. S., R. J. DAVIDSON, and J. A. SENULIS, 1992. Anterior brain electrical asymmetries in response to reward and punishment. *Electroencephalogr. Clin. Neurophysiol.* 83:236–247.

SPANGLER, G., E. MEINDL, and K. GROSSMAN, 1988. Behavioral organization and adrenocortical activity in newborns. *Infant Behav. Dev.* 11:295.

SPANGLER, G., and R. SCHEUBECK, 1993. Behavioral organization in newborns and its relation to adrenocortical and cardiac activity. *Child Dev.* 64:622–633.

STANSBURY, K., and M. R. GUNNAR, 1994. Adrenocortical activity and emotion regulation. In *The Development of Emotion Regulation: Biological and Behavioral Considerations*, N. A. Fox, ed. Monographs of the Society for Research in Child Development, 59(2–3, Serial No. 240), pp. 108–134.

STEVENSON-HINDE, J., and P. J. MARSHALL, 1999. Behavioral inhibition, heart period, and respiratory sinus arrhythmia: An attachment perspective. *Child Dev.* 70:805–816.

STIFTER, C. A., 1995. Approach/withdrawal processes in infancy: The relationship between parasympathetic tone and infant temperament: In *Behavioral Development: Concepts of Approach/Withdrawal and Integrative Levels. Research in Developmental and Comparative Psychology*, Vol. 1, E. Hood and G. Greenberg, eds. New York: Garland Publishing, pp. 371–395.

STRELAU, J., 1983. Pavlov's nervous system typology and beyond. In *Physiological Correlates of Human Behavior: Individual Differences and Psychopathology*, Vol. 3, A. Gale and J. A. Edwards, eds. New York: Academic Press, pp. 139–154.

STUSS, D. T., and D. F. BENSON, 1986. *The Frontal Lobes*. New York: Raven Press.

SUTTON, S. K., and R. J. DAVIDSON, 1997. Prefrontal brain asymmetry: A biological substrate of the behavioral approach and inhibition systems. *Psychol. Sci.* 8:204–210.

THAYER, J. F., and R. D. LANE, 2000. A model of neurovisceral integration in emotion regulation and dysregulation. *J. Affective Dis.* 61:201–216.

THOMPSON, R. A., 1990. Emotion and self-regulation. In *Socioemotional Development: Nebraska Symposium on Motivation*, Vol. 36, R. A. Thompson, ed. Lincoln, Neb.: University of Nebraska Press, pp. 367–467.

TUCKER, D. M., 1992. Development of emotion and cortical networks. In *Minnesota Symposium on Child Development: Developmental Neuroscience*, M. Gunnar and C. Nelson, eds. New York: Oxford University Press.

TUCKER, D. M., and D. DERRYBERRY, 1992. Motivated attention: Anxiety and the frontal executive functions. *Neuropsychiatry Neuropsychol. Behav. Neurol.* 5:233–252.

TURKEWITZ, G., J. GARDNER, and D. J. LEWKOWICZ, 1984. Sensory and perceptual functioning during early infancy: The implications of a quantitative basis for responding. In *Behavioral Evolution and Integrative Levels*, G. Greenberg and E. Tobach, eds. Hillsdale, N.J.: Lawrence Erlbaum Associates, pp. 167–195.

VAUGHN, B. E., C. B. KOPP, and J. B. KRAKOW, 1984. The emergence and consolidation of self-control from eighteen to thirty months of age: Normative trends and individual differences. *Child Dev.* 55:990–1004.

WALKER, D. L., and M. DAVIS, 1997. Double dissociation between the involvement of the bed nucleus of the stria terminalis and the central nucleus of the amygdala in light-enhanced versus fear-potentiated startle. *J. Neurosci.* 17:9375–9938.

WELSH, M. C., and B. F. PENNINGTON, 1988. Assessing frontal lobe functioning in children: Views from developmental psychology. *Dev. Neuropsychol.* 4:199–230.

WELSH, M. C., B. F. PENNINGTON, and D. B. GROISSER, 1991. A normative developmental study of executive function: A window on prefrontal function in children. *Dev. Neuropsychol.* 7:131–149.

WHITE, J. L., T. W. MOFFIT, A. CASPI, D. J. BARTUSCH, D. J. NEEDLES, and M. STOUTHAMER-LOEBER, 1994. Measuring impulsivity and examining its relationship to delinquency. *J. Abnorm. Psychol.* 103:192–205.

WHEELER, R. E., R. J. DAVIDSON, and A. J. TOMARKEN, 1993. Frontal brain asymmetry and emotional reactivity: A biological substrate of affective style. *Psychophysiology* 30:82–89.

ZELAZO, P. D., J. S. REZNICK, and D. E. PINON, 1995. Response control and the execution of verbal rules. *Dev. Psychol.* 31:508–517.

ZIMMERMAN, B., 1994. Dimensions of academic self-regulation: A conceptual framework for education. In *Self-Regulation of Learning and Performance: Issues and Educational Applications*, D. H. Schunk and B. J. Zimmerman, eds. Hillsdale, N.J.: Lawrence Erlbaum Associates, pp. 3–21.

# 41 Dopamine-Opiate Modulations of Reward-Seeking Behavior: Implications for the Functional Assessment of Prefrontal Development

MONICA LUCIANA

ABSTRACT  Much of human behavior is organized around stimuli that we conceptualize as worthy of approach (e.g., positive reinforcers) or emotional attachment (natural rewards). Two separable emotional systems have been described that contribute to these reward-related processes. One of these is a system involved in approach to distal rewards, and the other mediates consummatory aspects of reward acquisition. In addition to their emotional functions, each of these systems is proposed to guide specific cognitive processes. Spatial working memory is viewed as the cognitive extension of an emotional system underlying anticipatory reward and approach to incentive stimuli. Both aspects of behavior share a common neurobiological substrate in the functioning of ascending brain dopamine systems. In contrast, the type of affective state that accompanies reward acquisition is consummatory in nature and serves to keep the organism close to objects and places of attachment. When this system is activated, behaviors promoted by the approach system, including spatial working memory, are inhibited. The consummatory system is mediated, at least in part, by endogenous opiates. In this chapter, the implications of a DA-based incentive system and an opiate-based consummatory attachment system are discussed in relation to the developmental assessment of spatial working memory skills as exemplified by Piaget's A-not-B task. Specifically, it is proposed that young infants are predominantly guided by an opiate-based attachment system, leading to the A-not-B error and conditioned place preferences when they perform spatial memory tasks. Hence, the resolution of the A-not-B error may represent an affective, rather than a cognitive, milestone reflecting increasing maturity of brain dopamine systems underlying agency and approach to positive stimuli.

One critical challenge in deciphering what is reflected in discrete measures of cognitive skill is to account for the manner in which motivational variables can influence performance. It is a longstanding tenet in neuropsychological assessment that when motivation is insufficient, individuals demonstrate inconsistent patterns of performance, sometimes doing better on more difficult (presumably more demanding) task items or otherwise demonstrating a performance pattern that is not easily accounted for by a task's cognitive demands (Lezak, 1983). In most instances of adult assessment, it is a fundamental assumption that a test taker's motivational resources are appropriately engaged and that task performance can be attributed more or less solely to cognitive abilities. That is, there is often an assumed equivalence between performance and overall ability. When we test children, psychiatric patients, or individuals with neurological injuries, this basic assumption may be particularly flawed because integration between the cortical areas that perform distinct cognitive computations and other brain regions that mediate intrinsic motivational states and sensitivity to external rewards is not maximally adaptive.

The general objective of this chapter is to consider cognition from this expanded behavioral perspective, by emphasizing the motivational conditions under which it occurs, and using spatial working memory as an exemplar. Herein, spatial working memory is understood as a component of dopamine-driven reward-seeking behavior and will be discussed in that context (Depue and Iacono, 1989; Depue and Collins, 1999; Depue et al., 1994; Luciana, 1994; Luciana and Collins, 1997; Luciana et al., 1992). I will begin by describing the phenomenological structure of reward-seeking behavior and dopamine's role in promoting positive incentive motivation. Cognitive extensions of this emotional repertoire, including spatial working memory and its modulation by prefrontal dopamine, will then

MONICA LUCIANA  Department of Psychology, University of Minnesota, Minneapolis, Minnesota.

be described. Then, the covariance between positive incentive motivation and spatial working memory as two types of behavior that are DA-modulated and integral to reward seeking will be discussed relative to infant emotional development and patterns of performance on the A-not-B task.

## The structure of reward-seeking behavior

Modern inquiry into the neurobiological structure of emotion was revolutionized by Gray's assertion that variations in individuals' responses to positive and negative reinforcement contingencies represent the activity of intrinsic motivational systems that are neurobiologically based (Gray, 1973). Since then, efforts to validate the existence of the systems described by Gray have proliferated, as has the search for basic emotional systems of behavior that are neurobiologically linked (Depue and Collins, 1999; Panksepp, 1998). Panksepp (1992, 1998) expanded upon Gray's framework by proposing the existence of a number of basic emotional systems, each of which has (a) an evolutionary link in the development of modern mammalian behavior, (b) an identifiable neural substrate or set of substrates, and (c) a well-defined pattern of neurochemical modulation. The crux of this approach to behavior rests on what has been recently referred to as "Darwinian medicine," defined as "the enterprise of seeking evolutionary explanations for design characteristics that make organisms vulnerable to disorders" (Nesse and Berridge, 1997, p. 63). Inherent to this evolutionary approach is the understanding that emotional behaviors and their sequelae, which include visceral, motor, and subjective responses as well as higher order processes of decision-making, have been shaped by natural selection to promote genetic fitness in the face of eliciting situations that threatened survival in the course of an organism's evolutionary history. Hence, it has been proposed that there exist a set of emotional primes that underlie critical aspects of human experience and are therefore systematized within the mammalian neural architecture.

One of the proposed systems, most recently described as a *seeking* system (Panksepp, 1998), is particularly relevant to this discussion. The seeking system underlies appetitive motivation, serving to guide behavior toward rewarding experiences or stimuli. This system is not a new construct and has been described under various labels, including Schneirla's approach system (Schneirla, 1959), Gray's behavioral activation system (Gray, 1987), MacLean's search system (MacLean, 1986), Panksepp's foraging/expectancy system (Panksepp, 1992), and Depue's behavioral facilitation system (Depue and Iacono, 1989). Despite these nominal

distinctions, there has been general agreement that this system provides positive energy or activation that motivates an organism to approach distal sources of reward. This system is distinct from that which mediates the consummatory state accompanying reward attainment (Blackburn, Phillips, and Fibiger, 1989; Panksepp, 1998). Thus, in addition to the seeking system that mediates feelings of "wanting," it has been suggested that reward-directed behavior also includes an affective "attachment-based" component that underlies the feelings and behaviors that occur when a reward has been attained. The subjective emotional state that accompanies reward attainment has been variously referred to by different authors as "liking," "consummatory behavior," and "satiety" (Nesse and Berridge, 1997; Panksepp, 1998).

## The seeking system in humans

The seeking system, as represented in trait descriptions of human personality, is characterized by subjective feelings of excitation, positive engagement, and a desire for environmental exploration or approach. It may be partially reflected by the dimension referred to as "extraversion" in trait descriptions of human personality (see Depue and Collins, 1999, for discussion) and by temperamental descriptors such as "surgency" or "activity" or "high-intensity pleasure" in infant studies (Derryberry and Rothbart, 1988). In adults, this affective state serves to recruit behavior under conditions where positive rewards are needed or desired, but not present. Such conditions might include aversive or unsafe circumstances where basic needs (e.g., food, shelter, clothing, interpersonal bonding) are not being met, or they might include relatively enriched circumstances where conditioned cues signal the potential presence of positive reinforcers. Accordingly, in humans, this state underlies achievement motivation that serves the cross-temporal function of driving immediate behavior toward the attainment of future goals, and in this sense is accompanied by subjective feelings of mastery, dominance, and potency (Depue and Collins, 1999; Tellegen and Waller, 1997). Whether guided by more immediate needs or by distal goals, the individual is motivated to *want* something that is not immediately present. Accordingly, this state can be conceptualized as one of psychological craving (Nesse and Berridge, 1997), and specific objects of desire can vary, based on an individual's reinforcement history. Accordingly, the specific features of objects are not in themselves critical to seeking system activation, but their reward salience and their spatial and temporal locations relative to the organism's current context are critical. That is, in order for this system to function most adaptively, the organism must not only want something, but s/he must be able to localize him/herself in space and time relative to the desired object.

Before turning to a discussion of this system's neurobiology, I will consider the functioning of human infants within this system. On the one hand, given that infants are helpless beings, they are frequently in some state of primary need, whether driven by hunger, thirst, temperature changes, fatigue, or a desire for contact comfort. Obviously, these need states are aversive and disruptive to internal homeostasis. On the other hand, prior to achieving independent locomotion, the infant is relatively powerless to actively seek out or anticipate the sources of reward that will satisfy these wants, unless potential sources of reward are immediately present (typically in the form of a proximal caregiver). Although the infant can direct a limited range of responses (e.g., sucking, grasping, molding to the body of a caretaker) to reward objects immediately present (e.g., the nipple, mother's body, an interesting toy) in order to alleviate a need state, s/he is unable to actively *move toward* positive reinforcement when rewards are distal. On the basis of this phenomenology, then, one could argue that the seeking system cannot attain functional maturity until independent locomotion is achieved. Prior to this time, the infant's responsivity in the context of desired or immediately present reward objects is more attachment-based or consummatory in nature.

Given its reliance on motor functions, it is not surprising that the neural underpinnings of the seeking system rely on the integration between the motor system and limbic and cortical structures that promote positive incentive-guided behavior.

NEUROBIOLOGY OF THE SEEKING SYSTEM  The neuroanatomy and neurochemical characterization of specific behavioral processes comprising the seeking system have been extensively examined in the animal literature (see Panksepp, 1998). Our group has expanded upon these findings to suggest a role for the neurotransmitter dopamine (DA) in promoting core affective components of this system in human behavior (Collins and Depue, 1992; Depue and Collins, 1999; Depue and Iacono, 1989; Luciana, 1994; Luciana et al., 1992).

Currently, at least nine major DA cell groups have been identified in the mammalian brain, referred to by the nomenclature of Dahlstrom and Fuxe (1964) as A8 to A15, plus a retinal system. These cell groups are located mainly in the mesencephalic and diencephalic regions of the brain and can be divided into ascending,

descending, and local neuron systems (Fuxe et al., 1985). The mesencephalic DA cell groups are composed largely of major ascending DA projection systems, and two of these groups are of primary interest. The first group originates in the substantia nigra, comprising the A9 DA system and projecting primarily to the dorsal and ventral striatum. The second source originates in the midbrain ventral tegmental area (VTA), referred to as the A10 DA system. VTA afferents are primarily directed to limbic structures, including the olfactory tubercle, nucleus accumbens, amygdala, hippocampus, and septum, and have been traditionally linked under the label "mesolimbic" DA projections (Haas, 1983; Koob, Balcom, and Meyerhoff, 1975; Moore and Bloom, 1978; Oades and Halliday, 1987; Oades et al., 1986; Simon, Scatton, and LeMoal, 1980). VTA projections to the cortex are relatively sparse, with the exception of those that innervate primary motor and prefrontal regions. Additionally, the mesocortical DA system includes the transitional entorhinal, cingulate, and orbitofrontal cortices. These are collectively referred to as the "mesocortical" DA projections, although the prefrontal system has been most extensively studied (Brown and Goldman, 1977; Goldman-Rakic, 1987, 1988; 1999; Levitt, Rakic, and Goldman-Rakic, 1984; Lewis et al., 1988; Porrino and Goldman-Rakic, 1982). The prefrontal DA projection system is unique in several respects, including its site of origin in the VTA, the cellular basal firing rate and degree of bursting activity, amount of DA turnover, sensitivity to DA agonists and antagonists, and the development of tolerance following chronic neuroleptic administration (Bannon and Roth, 1983; Beckstead, 1979a,b; Fallon and Moore, 1978; Glowinski, Tassin, and Thierry, 1984; Lindvall and Bjorklund, 1978; Oades and Halliday, 1987; Tam and Roth, 1997). Many of these distinctions are attributed to a distinct pattern of neuroregulation in prefrontal DA neurons, including a lack of impulse– and nerve-terminal synthesis–modulating autoreceptors. Additionally, under acutely stressful conditions, DA metabolism accelerates in the prefrontal cortex, a finding that is hypothesized to occur because this system has a low threshold for phasic activation by other modulatory afferents to the VTA, including the serotonin, norepinephrine, acetylcholine, GABA, and opiate transmitter systems.

DOPAMINE AND APPETITIVE MOTIVATION  While nigrostriatal DA projections mediate various aspects of sensorimotor integration, those projecting to limbic forebrain structures underlie appetitive motivation, and this fact is demonstrated by DA's role in decreasing the threshold for intracranial and stimulant self-stimulation of the VTA-nucleus accumbens pathway, and in facilitating locomotor initiation. DA's role in these functions, through VTA-NAS circuitry, has been validated through the use of several methodologies including direct injections of DA agonists/antagonists into the brains of behaving animals, neurotoxic lesions of DA-innervated regions, single-cell recording studies under pharmacological challenge conditions, and operant conditioning paradigms. Through interconnections with other basal forebrain sites, including the amygdala, hippocampus, and orbitofrontal cortex, the VTA-DA system integrates incentive motivation with other aspects of behavior (Depue and Collins, 1999). A complete review of this literature is beyond the scope of this chapter, but suffice it to say that numerous studies link subcortical brain DA activity to two major behavioral processes: (a) sensorimotor integration and (b) incentive-reward motivation. These functions can be linked, in turn, by their roles in appetitive responding. Hence, the importance of appropriately translating positively valenced incentive motivation into behavioral action (Mogenson, Jones, and Yim, 1980) cannot be overemphasized as the critical component of seeking system function. Moreover, because this system is anticipatory in nature, localization of rewards in extrapersonal (and perhaps temporal) space is paramount to its adaptive function.

COGNITIVE EXTENSIONS OF THE SEEKING SYSTEM Because humans are highly evolved species, emotional systems are likely to have cognitive counterparts—that is, cognitive behaviors that have developed over phylogeny to guide each system's expression in a manner than is maximally appropriate to the stimulus context and, ultimately, to species preservation. This view is grounded in the notion that the neocortical structures characteristic of late mammalian development, including the prefrontal cortex and other association regions, have elaborated upon the more primitive brain structures that mediate emotional responding (e.g., the classically-defined "limbic system"; MacLean, 1952, 1990). If this is the case, then emotional drives serve as primitive and fundamental forces around which advanced cognition has become organized through phylogeny and recapitulated in ontogeny.

Given that the primary objective of seeking system activation is to bring an organism into proximity with distal sources of reward, its cognitive extensions would be similarly guided. For instance, to ensure that approach behavior is adaptively related to stimulus events, there will be the need to serially search an environment for relevant sources of reward, a widening of attentional resources (even to the point of distractibility under extreme conditions) to facilitate such searching, spatial skill in order to construct maps of extrapersonal space and to retrieve identified reward objects, memory in order that spatial information can be bridged across time, and strategic future-directed thinking that would allow an individual to cross the spatial and temporal gaps separating the self from the desired object. Relevant updating of response-reinforcement contingencies in the course of search behavior would also ensure that behavior would be appropriate to the current environmental context.

These features closely correspond to the manner in which spatial working memory as a hierarchical executive function has been described by various researchers (Baddeley, 1992; Fuster, 1989; Goldman-Rakic, 1987; Luciana and Collins, 1997; Luciana and Nelson, 1998). Indeed, the most consistently employed measure of prefrontal function in experimental studies has been the spatial delayed response (DR) task (Jacobson, 1936). In traditional versions of this task, an animal subject is presented with two identical "wells," one of which is baited with a desired object within full view. Following a brief delay interval (e.g., in the range of 1–10 seconds), the subject must retrieve the object without the benefit of object cues to facilitate recognition. On subsequent trials, the side of hiding is randomly determined. Since the discovery that frontal lobe lesions impaired DR performance (Jacobsen, 1936), the task has become the focus of experimental inquiry and theoretical debate; and to some extent, it can be said that spatial working memory may be equated in many researchers' minds with functioning of the dorsolateral prefrontal cortex.

From the standpoint of behavioral cognition, this view lacks precision. Although the dorsolateral PFC may function as the central executive (Baddeley, 1992) that orchestrates working memory, spatial working memory is a complex behavior, involving integration across multiple cortical and subcortical regions (Selemon and Goldman-Rakic, 1988). These regions minimally include the thalamus, superior colliculus, cingulate gyrus, parietal cortex, and striatum. The challenge is to determine how it is that the nervous system functions to link these regions in the service of a behavioral goal. Here it is suggested that dopamine may provide the neural "gel" that links these regions in the service of appetitive approach. Hence, the functioning of DA within the PFC may be but one component of some, but not all, PFC-regulated behaviors. Indeed, a recent study concluded that the only instance in which prefrontal and DA-prefrontal lesions overlap in their behavioral effects is when the task involves *spatial* working memory (Collins et al., 1998). Hence, dopamine's role within the PFC and with respect to prefrontally mediated behaviors may be more specific than has been previously emphasized (Luciana and Collins, 1997).

Integrated spatial working memory function not only assumes adequate sensory, perceptual, and motor processing skills, but also operates as a gestalt—the overall function being greater than the sum of its component parts. The development of many of these component parts is the subject of several chapters in this volume and will not be considered here. What has not been emphasized in the cognitive neuroscience literature is that spatial working memory has, as its fundamental underpinning, a pronounced affective component, one that serves to appropriately link stimulus and reward, maintain this linkage across spatial and temporal delays, and update contingencies when they change. This affective component is grounded in the seeking system described above. Furthermore, it may be a specific design of nature that both positive incentive behavior and spatial working memory are DA-modulated. This design allows an organism's motivational and cognitive resources to be engaged in a covariate manner under salient conditions.

MESOCORTICAL DOPAMINE AND SPATIAL WORKING MEMORY  The explosive growth of the neocortex in mammalian species is paralleled by a phenomenal increase in DA cell number as one moves up the phylogenetic ladder. Particularly remarkable is the phylogenetic growth of frontal cortex and of the mesocortical DA projections to it (Oades and Halliday, 1987). The neural architecture and physiology of PFC cells involved in spatial working memory processes have been increasingly well-characterized. Single-unit recordings from the primate dorsolateral prefrontal cortex, in the region of the principal sulcus, have identified several subtypes of task-related neurons during spatial WM performance. These neurons differentially increase in firing rate during cue presentation, during the delay period, and spanning the interval between the temporal delay and the response initiation periods (Funahashi, Bruce and Goldman-Rakic, 1989; Fuster and Alexander, 1971; Kojima and Goldman-Rakic, 1982). Within the PFC, VTA DA neurons synapse on the shafts and spines of pyramidal neurons, the neurons that appear to be most critical for working memory functions. These cells appear to code specific items of information related to peripheral events (such as an object's location, its identity, and the direction of prior responses toward the object) and are characterized by the presence of what Goldman-Rakic (1999) describes as "memory fields," a preferential pattern of responding corresponding to the mnemonic representations of par-

ticular spatial locations. Because the spiny shafts of pyramidal cells are the targets of other neurotransmitters (glutamate, in particular), DA projections are uniquely situated to modulate activity patterns among excitatory and inhibitory PFC afferents (Goldman-Rakic, 1999).

The functional importance of the A10 DA system to spatial mnemonic processes has been demonstrated by several findings. VTA lesions impair spatial working memory function (Simon, Scatton, and LeMoal, 1980), and the DA projections to the prefrontal cortex appear to be critical in mediating this effect. It has been demonstrated through in vivo microdialysis that extracellular concentrations of DA increase in the dorsolateral, but not orbital, prefrontal cortex in monkeys as they perform a delayed alteration task (Watanabe, Kodama, and Hikosaka, 1997). Neurotoxic (6-hydroxydopamine) lesions of the PFC's dorsolateral convexity have produced impaired spatial delayed alternation performance in rhesus monkeys that was reversed by DA agonists (Brozoski et al., 1979). Additionally, iontophoretic applications of DA enhance PFC neuronal activity associated with the sequence of WM processes, including cellular responses to the spatial cue, the delay, and/or memory-guided response initiation (Sawaguchi, Matsumura, and Kubota, 1988, 1990a,b). Conversely, pharmacological blockade of $D_1$ DA receptors in monkeys results in reversible decrements in accuracy and latency of an oculomotor DR task (Sawaguchi and Goldman-Rakic, 1991). Williams and Goldman-Rakic (1995) have demonstrated through the use of iontophoretic injections of $D_1$ and $D_2$ receptor antagonists into the non-human primate prefrontal cortex that dopamine's facilitatory effects on the cellular processes that support working memory are dose-dependent. The $D_1$ receptor system appears to specifically generate delay-related cellular activity, but only when stimulated at an optimal level. The $D_1$ DA modulation of cellular activity appears to be specific to cellular activity during the delay period and only in relation to a specific neuron's preferred memory field. Finally, alterations in multiple DA receptor systems appear to contribute to the cognitive decline associated with normal aging in primates (Arnsten et al., 1995; Cai and Arnsten, 1997).

The nature of the signal provided by DA to prefrontal cells has been debated. Schultz (1998) recently dissociated the role that VTA DA cells play in reward prediction in monkeys from that played by other neurons in the frontal-basal ganglia system. He found that dopamine neurons responded phasically to the presence of primary rewards and in the context of reward prediction but only when reward delivery was not habitual (e.g., was unpredictable). Additionally, DA neurons did not differentially represent distinct rewards, but fired in a similar manner to the presence or anticipated presence of all stimuli that signaled reward. Hence, DA appears to play a specific role in the anticipation of reward when the organism is in a state of uncertainty regarding reward delivery, as would be the case during the temporal stimulus-response intervals in delayed response tasks.

This role for DA is contrasted by patterns of firing in non-DA cells in the striatum and frontal cortex during reward learning. Non-DA striatal neurons appear to be transiently activated when animals expect reward delivery. These neurons magnify their signals throughout the course of learning and do not show the trend, present in DA neurons, of decreasing activation once rewards have become predictable. In contrast, neurons in the orbitofrontal cortex respond differentially to distinct rewards and appear to code specifics of "task rules," or the context in which reward delivery takes place. It has been demonstrated that the orbitofrontal cortex plays a critical role in enabling the organism to update his/her responding when the context or task contingencies change (Dias, Robbins, and Roberts, 1996; Rosenkilde, 1979).

Human studies are generally consistent with these findings. There are several clinical populations in which DA neurotransmission is either known or theorized to be disrupted, including schizophrenia (Park and Holtzmann, 1992), phenylketonuria (PKU) (see Diamond, this volume), and Parkinson's disease (Gotham, Brown, and Marsden, 1988). Deficient spatial working memory function has been reported in all three disorders. Connectionist modeling that includes a gain parameter to represent DA activity in cortical circuits accurately accounts for the types of cognitive deficits displayed by schizophrenics as they perform working memory tasks (Cohen and Servan-Schreiber, 1992, 1993). This model did not originally account for DA's role in limbic as well as cortical regions. However, it has been recently elaborated, in keeping with the extensive behavioral and theoretical literature linking dopamine activity to reward-related behaviors, to propose "that the function of the DA system is to provide a means for the organism to learn about, predict, and respond appropriately to events that lead to reward" (Braver and Cohen, 1999, p. 331).

Our research group has demonstrated that pharmacological activation of $D_2$ DA receptors in normal humans through the use of the selective $D_2$ dopamine receptor agonist bromocriptine facilitates spatial working memory and the nonspecific DA antagonist haloperidol inhibits it (Luciana et al., 1992; Luciana and Collins, 1997; Luciana, Collins, and Depue, 1998). Muller and colleagues (Muller, von Cramon, and Pollmann, 1998) examined performance on a forced-choice delayed matching to location task in healthy adults using both $D_1$ and $D_2$ receptor manipulations (including bromocriptine) and demonstrated a facilitatory effect of the $D_1$ agent.

Based on our finding that bromocriptine did not appear to affect forced-choice responding in a nonspatial working memory task (Luciana and Collins, 1997), we concur with Goldman-Rakic's view (1988) that dopamine plays a rather specific role within the dorsolateral PFC in modulating behaviors that demand the cross-temporal modulation of more complex motor-guided behaviors. Hence, *DA's role in the dorsolateral PFC is a mirror of the general function that it plays throughout the brain in integrating the localization and motoric aspects of reward-seeking behavior.* These DA effects are maximal in times of uncertainty (including the delay period in delayed response tasks that demand representational memory for spatial cues) regarding reward delivery, consistent with the seeking system's involvement in approach to distal (but not immediately present) goals.

INDIVIDUAL DIFFERENCES IN DA FUNCTIONAL ACTIVITY Some individuals tolerate uncertainty more adaptively than others. To the extent that DA cells continue to fire in the context of reward uncertainty, "affective permanence" (herein defined as the maintenance of incentive-motivation under conditions of spatial or temporal distance) will be maintained. Kimberg, D'Esposito and Farah (1997) further extended the work of Luciana and colleagues (Luciana et al., 1992; Luciana and Collins, 1997; Luciana, Collins, and Depue, 1998) by demonstrating that the optimal threshold of DA activation may differ within individuals. Individual differences in DA reactivity would be consistent with the differential patterns of inhibition versus excitation found under conditions of high versus low levels of receptor stimulation in monkeys (Williams and Goldman-Rakic, 1995). Additionally, two labs have successfully used bromocriptine in brain-injured populations, one to treat behavioral perseveration in individuals with dementia (Imamura et al., 1998) and the other to evaluate executive function in traumatic brain injury patients with frontal lobe injuries (McDowell, Whyte, and D'Esposito, 1998).

Recently, there have been several attempts to link either central nervous system DA functioning (Depue et al., 1994) or genetically determined allelic variations in genes coding for DA receptor subtypes (Cloninger, 1996) with the self-reported personality trait of extraversion (or similar derivatives, including "novelty seeking") in humans. The overall pattern of findings is not definitive, but has been encouraging, particularly given researchers' disagreements as to the manner in which the psychometrically derived extraversion construct should best be represented neurobiologically (Depue and Collins, 1999). The cellular mechanisms supporting individual differences in DA reactivity likely involve DA cell numbers and receptors (Fink and Reis, 1981; Fink and Smith, 1980; Smith et al., 1998). Animals bred for high versus low numbers of DA cells demonstrate an increased vigor of reward-seeking behaviors.

These findings with respect to DA's influence over individual differences in emotional and cognitive behaviors lead to several testable hypotheses. First, individual differences in endogenous DA activity and reactivity exist and are measurable through genetic, neurobiological, and behavioral means. These differences should be reflected in patterns of emotional trait-edness with respect to emotional behaviors that are consistent with the seeking system construct (see Collins and Depue, 1992; Depue et al., 1994) and will also be reflected in discrete behavioral states. Thus, individuals who function at different levels along this emotional continuum at any given point in time should display different patterns of DA-modulated cognition, particularly spatial working memory. Individuals who are characterized by high levels of anticipatory motivation should perform better on spatial search and working memory tasks because of covarying levels of DA activation in prefrontal and limbic/striatal regions. Those who exemplify low trait levels should perform more poorly due either to low levels of limbic DA (leading to deficient motivation) or to disruptions in integrating this information within the prefrontal cortex. If there is biological preparedness for a covariance between DA-modulated emotional and cognitive behaviors, then these individual differences, which will extend to influence performance in discrete circumstances, will have implications for any laboratory study that involves testing subjects under motivationally salient conditions. Indeed, the relatively poor test–retest stability of some frontal lobe tasks in human studies (Lowe and Rabbitt, 1998) may partially reflect the fact that session-to-session performance is highly influenced by motivational state. This difficulty is circumvented in animal studies where it is nearly always a given that testing is conducted under highly salient conditions of food deprivation, using food rewards to encourage performance. Few human studies have considered the association between personality traits and cognitive function from a neuromodulatory perspective, measuring both affect and affect-specific cognition in relation to changes in neurotransmitter activity. Nor have developmental accounts regarding the emergence of spatial working memory skills explored the mechanisms that might guide affective biases that contribute to task performance.

## The development of spatial working memory

THE A-NOT-B TASK AND ITS AFFECTIVE DEMANDS   The classic DR task as described above is formally similar to Piaget's Stage IV object permanence task (Piaget, 1954), in which it has been demonstrated that infants and young toddlers make a classic error referred to as the A-not-B error. This error occurs when the object is first hidden at one of two locations (location A) where it is correctly retrieved, then hidden at the second location B on a subsequent trial. Instead of searching at location B to retrieve the object, infants sometimes return perseveratively to location A. The A-not-B error has been one of the most frequently researched phenomena in cognitive development (see Diamond, this volume, for detailed discussion). Numerous explanations have been offered to account for why the AB error occurs, including failure of memory, lack of inhibitory control over prepotent responding, and motor system immaturity. As Thelen and Smith (1994) suggest, none of these explanations is completely satisfactory, and research in this area may be hampered by the tendency to search for single explanations of the error and by making distinctions between children's performance on the task and their competence. I would suggest that a third hindrance has been the notion that the AB task is "frontal" without a more thorough consideration of the many behavioral subroutines that lead to successful task performance. Given the correspondence between reward-seeking behavior and brain DA activity, we perhaps gain more explanatory power by conceptualizing the task as "dopaminergic," encompassing a broader range of motor, motivational, and mnemonic functions that involve the entire brain operating in the service of a specific emotional system under the orchestration of the PFC. That is, given DA's role in promoting affective behavior, it may be that the AB error is informative as to the nature of an individual's affective as well as cognitive development. If this is the case, then successful performance on the task should relate to the emergence of other behaviors that are guided by the DA-based seeking system. Additionally, task errors should be attributed to a lack of functional maturity in this system. In the discussion that follows, I will attempt to argue that infants' failures on the A-not-B task are due to deficient DA neurotransmission within limbic-prefrontal circuitry, and that in the absence of a fully functional DA system, performance is guided by an attachment-based behavioral system.

POSSIBLE BEHAVIORAL EXPLANATIONS FOR THE A-NOT-B ERROR  Poor performance on the task is understandable if we deconstruct the task into its component parts, as summarized in table 41.1. As indicated in the table, in the context of neurobehavioral development, this very simple task suddenly does not seem so simple. A great deal of multitasking, particularly in terms of updating relevant information, is required. Since the infant is said to be successful at the task either when there is no delay or when s/he is allowed to visually or kinesthetically orient toward the correct location even at longer delays (Diamond, 1990), then there must be something about the delay interval that is crucial. However, that "something" cannot be basic memory, since performance is fine when the location of hiding remains unchanged, even at long delays. Also, given that the infant can remember to physically "orient" him/herself toward the object at long delays (if permitted), there seems to be adequate memory for the object per se (Diamond, 1990). What is not necessarily correctly regulated is the trial-by-trial updating of the nature of the reward as linked to the object but not to the place, or what will here be termed an error of "affective permanence" versus "object permanence." Put another way, the place or location seems to acquire more affective salience than does the object, and with subsequent trials, the reward–place association appears difficult for the infant to disengage, while keeping the reward–object association intact. Accordingly, the error is not one of faulty object-concept *formation* but one that represents an inability to *disengage* a place-reinforcement association that has developed over the course of successive trials. Hence, this error is *attachment-based*, which, as discussed above, is a primitive behavioral mode that may characterize infants' responding to rewards prior to seeking system maturation.

How is this observed? When the location of hiding changes from A to B trials, the reward contingency changes. That is, location A is no longer rewarded. Location B is now rewarded. That the same object is maintained as the stimulus that provides reinforcement is not at issue. What is at issue is how the object–reward association is integrated with other reward associations that have been developed in the course of learning the task. Consider possible outcomes if the infant is attaching reward significance to the location (or perhaps to his/her reaching response to that location) rather than to the object itself. On the first trials of the task, the linking of [reward = location] and [reward = object] cannot be distinguished. By transitory logic, the object and location are linked by a common reward association, and when the infant correctly retrieves the object from location A, linkage forms between the two. Both associations have guided the response, and both are reinforced. Establishing the basic reward associations inherent to the task does not appear to be a problem. Rather, it appears that on A-to-B trials, the [reward = object] association remains intact (as it should) but so does the [reward = location] association (when it shouldn't). This does not lead to a simple location preference (e.g., always responding to location A), because after a number of repetitions, the infant will eventually respond correctly to location B, only to get "stuck" there and fail to return to A when the side of hiding again changes.

Does this mean that the infant does not know that the object is permanent? I suggest not. The infant might be well aware of "object permanence" on a purely computational level. Does this mean that the infant does not want the object? On the contrary, the infant likely finds the object to be quite interesting, and researchers take pains to make sure that this is the case (Diamond, 1990). However, it may be that an *affective constraint* pre-

TABLE 41.1
*Components of the A-not-B task*

| Experimenter Action | Requires |
| --- | --- |
| *Step 1: A-Trials* | |
| Presentation of the cue | Adequate sensory perception |
| | Attention |
| Cue deemed desirable to infant | Cue linked with incentive motivation |
| Cue is hidden in location A | Attention to the hiding of the cue |
| | Linking of cue + location |
| | Linking of reward + location |
| Delay interval | Memory for the cue |
| | Memory for side of hiding |
| | Maintenance of cue–reward association |
| | Maintenance of cue–location association |
| | Sustained interest/attention |
| Lids removed from hiding wells; retrieval allowed | Reinforced cue–reward association |
| | Reinforced location–reward association |
| | Reaching to retrieve the cue |
| *Step 2: B-Trials* | |
| Cue hidden at location B | Extinguish previous cue–location association* |
| | Extinguish previous cue–response association* |
| | Extinguish previous location–response association* |
| | Maintenance of cue–reward association |
| | Establishment of new cue–location association* |

*Indicates failures that would lead to nonrandom errors.

cludes the infant from correctly separating the object-as-reward from the location-as-reward contingency and updating his/her responses accordingly on a trial-by-trial basis. Moreover, this deficiency may not be due so much to dorsolateral prefrontal immaturity but to deficient, or inconsistent, patterns of DA-seeking system activity (specifically, the signaling of a phasic contextual change) that indicates reward uncertainty, in the context of optimally functioning attachment system activity. This attachment activity may be based on interactions between the VTA-DA system and other neurochemical systems involved in attachment-consummatory behavior. A candidate system that might be particularly important in this respect is the opiate peptide system.

## Opiates and consummatory attachment

When reward has been attained, activity in several ascending neuromodulatory systems is inhibited, and motor behavior slows down so that consummatory behavior can occur (Depue and Collins, 1999; Panksepp, 1998). DA activity decreases, at least in part, because reward acquisition is no longer an uncertain proposition (Schultz, Tremblay, and Hollerman, 1998). Moreover, because the phasic bursts of VTA DA cell firing serve to activate the organism in preparation for motor approach, such activity would be counterproductive in the presence of reward stimuli. Hence, the balance of behavioral control must shift under conditions of reward attainment to a repertoire that encourages relative relaxation, a narrowing of attentional focus, and the onset of consummatory behavior.

In contrast to the dopaminergic mediation of anticipatory reward, the post-reward consummatory state is at least partially mediated by endogenous opiate neuropeptides (Panksepp, 1998). The endogenous opiates refer to a class of naturally occurring neuropeptides that produce behavioral effects when they bind to one of at least three major types of receptors. Three families of naturally occurring opiate compounds have been discovered, and the three associated receptor subtypes that have been identified in mammals are the mu, delta, and kappa receptors, all of which are abundant within the basolateral limbic forebrain. The mu receptor is most abundant, and is diffusely distributed throughout the midbrain and limbic system (Self and Stein, 1992; Shippenberg and Elmer, 1998).

Many of the opiate drugs of abuse, including morphine, codeine, and heroin, have strong affinities for the mu receptor subtype, and this subtype has been the most intensively studied. Indeed, most human studies that have examined opioid effects have concentrated on individuals who are addicts. Animal studies have been more informative as to the effects of endogenous ligands for opiate receptors. Whether or not an organism is addicted, the opiates are positive behavioral reinforcers (mediated through mu receptor activation), and organisms will not only self-administer opiates to avoid withdrawal from opiate administration but they will perform other behaviors to escape injection with opiate antagonists. Because nondependent animals will perform operant behaviors to escape a pharmacologically induced low-opiate state, the suggestion has been made that there is an active endogenous opiate reward pathway that is disrupted when antagonists are administered (McKim, 2000; Shippenberg and Elmer, 1998).

The opiates are perhaps best known for their peripheral analgesic effects, mediated through descending actions of mu receptors in the midbrain periaqueductal gray, that interact with ascending sensory pathways from the spinal cord. In addition to this role in visceral nociception, the opiates also reduce psychic or emotional pain (McKim, 2000). Recent speculation centers on the role of the endogenous opiates in promoting social reward in mammals under naturally occurring circumstances. Following gratifying consummatory behaviors including the ingestion of food, sexual climax, maternal bonding, social grooming, and rough-and-tumble play, endogenous opiates are released (Panksepp, 1998; Panksepp, Nelson, and Bekkedal, 1999). Accordingly, endogenous opiate activity may form a neural bridge that is responsible for the pleasure associated with obtaining natural rewards, leading to the formation of attachments to the rewarding objects. Panksepp has emphasized the importance of this system in mediating responses to social separation, noting biochemical similarities between animals that are in states of separation distress (e.g., as a result of maternal separation) and those who are in the midst of opiate withdrawal. Indeed, administration of morphine to animals in the midst of maternal separation attenuates the expression of distress vocalizations in a dose-dependent manner. Opiate administration also attenuates other psychobiological indicators of emotional stress, including the response of the HPA axis, resulting in decreased CRF (and cortisol) secretion. Conversely, administration of opiate antagonists enhances these behaviors and HPA activity. Based on these findings, Panksepp (1998; Panksepp, Nelson, and Bekkedal, 1999) proposes that opiates underlie a system mediating social need. When an individual is in a "low-opiate state," a natural state of separation distress is present and the organism is motivated to solicit social comfort. An exceptionally low state of endogenous opiate activity might promote behavior that we would consider pathologically needy. On the other hand, a state of extremely high opiate activity would result in a condition of "natural opiate addiction" in which circulating opiate activity would substitute for that gained by social experience. Individuals in this state would have little need for social contact comfort and would appear aloof or even autistic. The optimal state of endogenous opiate activity would thus be one in which levels would fluctuate in response to social cues, driving behavior toward social interaction when levels drop but then increasing in activation in the presence of peers, caregivers, or other loved ones. In order to re-experience the feeling of social contact comfort (and endogenous opiate secretion) that accompanies being in the presence of significant others, contact with these significant objects must be maintained, and pair bonding occurs. With re-exposure to familiar individuals, places, or things that provide social and other contact comforts, the idea is that we literally become addicted to their presence and experience a state of natural opiate depletion in their absence. Roles for other neuropeptides, including oxytocin, arginine-vasopressin, and gonadal hormones are also critical for social selectivity and interpersonal bonding, particularly in the context of infant-mother attachment (Panksepp, Nelson, and Bekkedal, 1999). As described previously in this chapter, the behaviors of young infants are primarily attachment-based, and it may be that their cognitive abilities are similarly biased.

COGNITIVE EXTENSIONS OF A CONSUMMATORY-ATTACHMENT SYSTEM In order to maintain proximity to attachment figures, it is necessary to maintain behaviors that maximize recognition of familiar stimuli and maintenance of proximity to them (Bowlby, 1982). Relevant stimuli might include familiar people, objects, or places. Opiate effects on recognition learning and memory have not been exhaustively examined. Nonetheless, it has been observed in several animal studies that appetitive learning and memory, and spatial working memory in particular, are disrupted by administration of opiate agonists (Braida, Gori, and Sala, 1994; Levin, 1988; Stone et al., 1991; Terman and Loeser, 1992) and facilitated by antagonist administration (Canli, Cook, and Miczek, 1990; Collier and Routtenberg, 1984; Fanelli, Rosenberg, and Gallagher, 1985; Gallagher, 1982; Gallagher, King, and Young, 1983; Izquierdo, 1982; Mickley and Cobb, 1998). The mechanisms underlying these amnestic actions of opiate agonists are not fully known, although morphine appears to induce a state-dependent form of learning where information can only be recalled within the same context in which it was learned (Bruins and Colpaert, 1999). If this is the case, then a high-opiate state might preclude updating of learned associations when environmental contingencies change. Consistent with this conjecture, morphine administration to anesthetized rats has been shown to modulate cellular firing in the medial prefrontal cortex. Observed changes are both inhibitory and excitatory and reversible by naloxone administration (Giacchino and Henriksen, 1996).

One robust phenomenon that is associated with opiate administration in experimental research is conditioned place preference (CPP) (Bozarth, 1987; Shippenberg and Elmer, 1998; Tzchentke, 1998). In CPP paradigms, an animal is first permitted to freely roam a shuttle box that consists of two compartments. Ideally, no particular side preference is demonstrated, but if there is a place preference, it is recorded. Subsequently, the animal is administered opiate drugs while in the nonpreferred side. Following several drug treatment sessions (where it is expected that the animal will come to associate the rewarding effects of the drug with the environment in which drug administration occurred), the animal is tested again under nondrug conditions to examine whether a preference has developed for the side of the shuttle box where the drug was administered. CPP forms when animals are permitted to self-administer opiate drugs that act upon the mu receptor system. Intracranial self-administration into specific brain regions has identified that the source of this opiate-reward pathway involves the VTA, the nucleus accumbens, the hypothalamus, and the hippocampus. Concordant activation of the mesolimbic DA system potentiates these opiate effects on behavioral conditioning (Gysling and Wang, 1983; Kalivas and Abhold, 1987; Shippenberg and Elmer, 1998). As a possible mechanism to keep reward systems in balance, morphine administration also has been shown to increase release of dopamine in the VTA system (Wood and Rao, 1991). The time course of such effects would be important to determine in order to understand dopamine-opiate interactions in the ongoing maintenance of reward seeking behavior and the switching of reward-relevant states from the consummatory to the seeking phases and vice versa.

## Interactions between the cognitive seeking and consummatory-attachment systems

The seeking and consummatory systems are contrasted in table 41.2. In an ideal world in which reward acquisition proceeds unimpeded, an organism behaves in a manner that suggests balance between preparatory-seeking and consummatory-attachment behaviors. Following a period of goal-directed search, the animal presumably finds what s/he is looking for and settles down to enjoy it. As the consummatory gusto fades,

## TABLE 41.2
*Affective and cognitive aspects of reward-seeking behavior*

|  | Seeking Phase | Consummatory Phase |
|---|---|---|
| Neurobiology | Dopamine | Opiates? |
| Affect | Anticipation/desire incentive | Well-being/contentedness |
| Cognition | Search<br>Expansion of attention<br>Spatial coordination<br>Cross-temporal memory<br>Strategic thinking<br>Contingency updating | ?Tunnel vision<br>Narrowing of attention<br>Object recognition<br>Immediate encoding<br>Place + object preference |
| Motor | Diffuse/active exploration | Localized/consummatory |

s/he will once again become reactivated to begin the search anew. Neuromodulatory systems would be designed such that activity in one branch of this overall reward system is accompanied by decreased activity in the other branch, and that as activity in one branch was decreasing, the other would begin a gradual ascent. However, if one or the other piece of this overall reward system is "locked in" or otherwise biased, as may be the case within discrete developmental periods, this balance of behavior will be altered to favor one repertoire or the other.

With respect to cognition, organisms in a high-DA state will be pulled by search processes that maximize novelty and demand representational thought for anticipated events. On the other hand, if the organism is dominated by a high attachment-consummatory state, s/he will perform better on tasks that maximize responses to familiarity, habituation, and contact comfort. This state is one of inherent contentment and well-being, whereby behavioral activation is at a relative low. With respect to DA-modulated behaviors, individuals in this state would perform relatively poorly. It is suggested that infants are affectively biased toward attachment-consummatory activation and that, until the DA system is more mature, this bias has predictable implications for A-not-B task performance.

### The A-not-B error and consummatory-attachment behavior

The A-not-B error has been described as a perseverative response, similar to that made by frontal patients on the Wisconsin Card Sort Task or other measures that require shifting of response sets in response to external feedback. Diamond (1990; this volume) discusses these tasks in terms of their requirements for inhibitory control. Her argument is that in order to be correct on each A-to-B trial, the infant must not only remember where

the object is hidden but must inhibit prepotent responding in order to correctly guide that memory. This review extends Diamond's observations by offering an explanation of the affective processing mechanism underlying the infants' prepotent responding. When the adult encounters a reversal contingency on the Wisconsin Card Sort, s/he presumably does not have other reward associations that have been guiding his/her responses. A perseverative error that occurs after one has been clearly told "Wrong" is particularly hard to fathom. Similarly, it has been assumed that when the infant makes the A-not-B error, s/he has behaved illogically. The perseverative response is viewed as an automatism (Diamond, 1988). However, what has perhaps been overlooked is that the infant may be drawn by a legitimate reward association—one that, until correctly updated, links the desired object with a specific location. The observation that the AB error occurs only at increasingly long delay intervals depending on the age of the child might again relate to how behavior is modulated under conditions of uncertainty, and the response of the developing DA system under such conditions. A delay interval, however small, puts reward acquisition into question. If the DA-modulated seeking system is immature, cellular firing patterns in limbic and cortical structures that hold incentive-guided motor behaviors on-line will fail. Under such conditions, one's reward-respondent behavior might be biased by attachment-based principles (Bowlby, 1982). On a neural level, this would mean that the neurochemical environment is more conducive to attachment-consummatory behavior, which as described above, may increase the likelihood that responses will be conditioned as the task unfolds to discrete locations.

Infants' performance on the A-not-B task can be reinterpreted from this framework, whereby the gradual elimination of the A-not-B error is a marker of an affective milestone in which the infant transitions from being governed primarily by attachments to specific places and objects in times of doubt to a more confident self-directed mastery of the environment. In terms of system-level guidance of behavior, the transition would be from an emotional system that primarily serves to promote attachment to discrete locations and places to the DA-mediated seeking system that serves to encourage motor exploration and reward-seeking. In this regard, it may be a critical observation that infants with increased locomotor proficiency perform better on the task than infants with less experience (Thelen and Smith, 1994; Clearfield and Thelen, this volume).

The infants' pattern of responding on AB trials would be similar to the phenomenon of conditioned place preference that has been associated with endogenous opiate activity in many studies. Moreover, Panksepp (1998) discusses place preference as a cognitive outgrowth of an attachment-based system that serves to maintain close proximity between the mother and her offspring. Place preferences would theoretically decrease the likelihood of exploration of novel environments, and therefore may represent a covert cognitive regulator (Hofer, 1994) of infant attachment behavior.

When we consider what would be an appropriate survival strategy for an infant who has recently acquired the capacity for independent locomotion, it is obvious that maintenance of attachment to caregivers and safe places is paramount (Bowlby, 1982). Accordingly, what is observed in cognitive testing of infants can be accounted for by this psychobiological constraint: *Despite the fact that mnemonic resources are clearly adequate to the task at hand, the infant is motivationally constrained, in the face of an immature DA system, to maintain attachment to specific places.* As the infant matures, s/he becomes motorically independent and must juggle two motivational demands—one being the need to maintain proximity to caregivers, and the other the desire to explore a novel and interesting environment. It is at this point that a "battle" will occur between the attachment system (already in place) and the emergent dopaminergic-seeking system that underlies reward-seeking behavior. Any parent of a 2–3-year-old is familiar with the behavioral manifestation of this interplay, often referred to as the "terrible twos" because of the child's apparent oppositional behavior. S/he is distractable, often hyperactive, and highly responsive to novelty. Interestingly, this is also the time period when A-not-B performance becomes more accurate at increasingly long delays (Diamond, this volume).

Although frontally guided cognitive systems may be generally immature, it may be the case that resolution of the A-not-B error indicates that a milestone has been achieved within the affective domain, and that behavior can now be guided more efficiently by consciously guided appetitive drives. Given the pronounced individual differences in mastery of the AB task that exist and around which age-based developmental trajectories have been described (Diamond, 1988, 1990), stable neurochemical variations in reward-seeking behavior may ultimately represent trait factors around which normal development proceeds and around which an individual's potential performance level is restricted.

## Conclusions

Evolutionary psychology emphasizes the primacy of affective states around which higher order cognitive functions have developed. Accordingly, affective states are important modulators of cognitive ability, serving to guide cognition in the service of biologically salient objectives. This relationship has been difficult to consistently observe and describe within the context of laboratory-based research. Nonetheless, most animal studies take place under highly salient motivational conditions of food deprivation. When we study the cognition of animals in that context, we are studying behavior under the influence of an emotional system that drives an animal to obtain distal, but greatly desired, rewards. When we study humans, similar conditions of deprivation are not the norm, but cognition may still be modulated by individual differences in affective state. If cognitive functions are specific outgrowths of functioning within basic emotional systems, then there should be covariance in function between emotions governed by that system and its cognitive counterparts. This relationship was illustrated here for spatial working memory, which may be a cognitive extension of a dopamine-based seeking system that serves to bring an organism into proximity with desired objects. However, if cognition that is specific to one system is demanded of an organism that is in a different affective state, performance will be adversely affected. It may be that with respect to reward-related activity, infants are governed more by a consummatory/attachment-based system than by a seeking system. Their errors on spatial working memory tasks may reflect a bias toward cognitive processes inherent to the attachment system, proposed here to be mediated by endogenous opiate neuropeptides.

This account is not perfect, and there are multiple avenues for interaction between the seeking and consummatory systems in determining final behavioral outcome. For example, dopamine activity has also been associated with CPP in animal studies (Bozarth, 1987). However, if this theoretical model holds when subjected to empirical study, then developmental cognitive neuroscientists may reconceptualize their measures of specific cognitive processes in light of the motivational conditions under which the measures have been obtained. For instance, it would seem critical to examine whether infants' A-not-B task performance would be improved by using highly salient and already-familiar stimuli, such as pacifiers, or perhaps even the mother herself as an object. This account would predict that when the stimulus object becomes more attachment-based, infants' performance on the task will improve. When the stimulus calls for self-guided motor exploration to seek novel stimuli or when the task takes place under conditions where the infant is in a "high attachment" mode (e.g., sitting on the mother's lap), performance will deteriorate. In the future, it is hoped that neurobiological techniques will become increasingly less invasive from the standpoint of ascertaining functioning within discrete neurochemical systems that underlie complex behavioral tasks. As illustrated here, we cannot understand the functioning of a neurochemical, such as dopamine, within the human brain by considering only its role in motor behavior, emotional reward-seeking, or working memory. An integrative systems-level approach, as applied to the study of cognitive development, is needed.

## REFERENCES

Arnsten, A. F. T., J. X. Cai, J. C. Steere, and P. S. Goldman-Rakic, 1995. Dopamine D2 receptor mechanisms contribute to age-related cognitive decline: The effects of quinpirole on memory and motor performance in monkeys. *J. Neurosci.* 15(5):3429–3439.

Baddeley, A. D., 1992. Working memory. *Science* 255:556–559.

Bannon, M. J., and R. H. Roth, 1983. Pharmacology of mesocortical dopamine neurons. *Pharmacol. Rev.* 35(1):53–68.

Beckstead, R. M., 1979a. An autoradiographic examination of corticocortical and subcortical projections of the mediodorsal projection (prefrontal) cortex in the rat. *J. Comp. Neurol.* 184:43–62.

Beckstead, R. M., 1979b. Convergent prefrontal and nigral projections to the striatum in the rat. *Neurosci. Lett.* 12: 59–64.

Blackburn, J. R., A. G. Philips, and H. C. Fibiger, 1989. Dopamine and preparatory behavior. I: Effects of pimozide. *Behav. Neurosci.* 101:352–360.

Bowlby, J., 1982. *Attachment.* New York: Basic Books.

Bozarth, M. A., 1987. Ventral tegmental reward system. In *Brain Reward Systems and Abuse,* J. Engel and L. Oreland, eds. New York: Raven Press, pp. 1–17.

Braida, D., E. Gori, and M. Sala, 1994. Relationship between morphine and etoniazene-induced working memory impairments and analgesia. *Eur. J. Pharmacol.* 271(2–3):497–504.

Braver, T. S., and J. D. Cohen, 1999. Dopamine, cognitive control, and schizophrenia: The gating model. *Prog. Brain Res.* 121:327–349.

Brown, R. M., and P. S. Goldman, 1977. Catecholamines in neocortex of rhesus monkeys: Regional distribution and ontogenetic development. *Brain Res.* 124:576–580.

Brozoski, T. J., R. M. Brown, H. E. Rosvold, and P. Goldman, 1979. Cognitive deficit caused by regional depletion of dopamine in prefrontal cortex of rhesus monkey. *Science* 205:929–931.

Bruins, L. A., and F. C. Colpaert, 1999. Recall rendered dependent on an opiate state. *Behav. Neurosci.* 113(2):337–344.

Cai, J. X., and A. F. T. Arnsten, 1997. Dose-dependent effects of the dopamine D1 receptor agonists A77636 or SKF81297 on spatial working memory in aged monkeys. *J. Pharmacol. Exp. Ther.* 283(1):183–189.

Canli, T., R. G. Cook, and K. A. Miczek, 1990. Opiate antagonists enhance the working memory of rats in the radial maze. *Pharmacol. Biochem. Behav.* 36:521–525.

Cloninger, C. R., 1996. Mapping genes for human personality. *Nature Genetics* 12:3–4.

Cohen, J. D., and D. Servan-Schreiber, 1992. Context, cortex, and dopamine: A connectionist approach to behavior and biology in schizophrenia. *Psychol. Reports* 1992:45–75.

Cohen, J. D., and D. Servan-Schreiber, 1993. A theory of dopamine function and its role in cognitive deficits in schizophrenia. *Schizophr. Bull.* 19(1):85–104.

Collier, T. J., and A. Routtenberg, 1984. Selective impairment of declarative memory following stimulation of dentate gyrus granule cells: A naloxone-sensitive effect. *Brain Res.* 310:384–387.

Collins, P. F., and R. A. Depue, 1992. A neurobehavioral systems approach to developmental psychopathology: Implications for disorders of affect. In *Rochester Symposium on Developmental Psychopathology. Vol. 4: Developmental Perspectives on Depression,* D. Cicchetti and S. L. Toth, eds. Rochester, N.Y.: University of Rochester Press, pp. 29–101.

Collins, P., A. C. Roberts, R. Dias, B. J. Everitt, and T. W. Robbins, 1998. Perseveration and strategy in a novel spatial self-ordered sequencing task for nonhuman primates: Effects of excitotoxic lesions and dopamine depletions of the prefrontal cortex. *J. Cogn. Neurosci.* 10(3):332–354.

Dahlstrom, A., and K. Fuxe, 1964. Evidence for the existence of monoamine-containing neurons in the central nervous system. I: Demonstrations of monoamines in the cell bodies of brain stem neurons. *Acta Physiol. Scand.* 62(suppl. 232): 1–55.

Depue, R. A., and P. F. Collins, 1999. Neurobiology of the structure of personality: Dopamine, facilitation of incentive motivation, and extraversion. *Behav. Brain Sci.* 22(3):491–569.

Depue, R. A., and W. G. Iacono, 1989. Neurobehavioral aspects of affective disorders. *Annu. Rev. Psychol.* 40:457–492.

Depue, R. A., M. Luciana, P. Arbisi, P. F. Collins, and A. Leon, 1994. Relation of agonist-induced dopamine activity to personality. *J. Personality Soc. Psychol.* 67(3):485–498.

Derryberry, D., and M. K. Rothbart, 1988. Arousal, affect, and attention as components of temperament. *J. Personality Soc. Psychol.* 55(6):958–966.

Diamond, A., 1988. The abilities and neural mechanisms underlying AB performance. *Child Dev.* 59:523–527.

Diamond, A., 1990. The development and neural bases of memory formation as indexed by the AB and delayed response tasks in human infants and infant monkeys. *Ann. N.Y. Acad. Sci.* 608:267–317.

DIAS, R., T. W. ROBBINS, and A. C. ROBERTS, 1996. Dissociation in prefrontal cortex of attentional and affective shifts. *Nature* 380:69–72.

FALLON, J. H., and R. Y. MOORE, 1978. Catecholamine innervation of the basal forebrain. IV: Topography of the dopamine projection to the basal forebrain and neostriatum. *J. Comp. Neurol.* 180:545–580.

FANELLI, R. J., R. A. ROSENBERG, and M. GALLAGHER, 1985. Role of noradrenergic function in the opiate antagonist facilitation of spatial memory. *Behav. Neurosci.* 99(4):751–755.

FINK, J. S., and D. J. REIS, 1981. Genetic variations in midbrain dopamine cell number: Parallel with differences in responses to dopaminergic agonists and in naturalistic behaviors mediated by dopaminergic systems. *Brain Res.* 222:335–349.

FINK, J. S., and G. P. SMITH, 1980. Mesolimbic and mesocortical dopaminergic systems are necessary for normal exploratory behavior in the rat. *Neurosci. Lett.* 17:61–65.

FUNAHASHI, S., C. J. BRUCE, and P. S. GOLDMAN-RAKIC, 1989. Mnemonic coding of visual space in the monkey's dorsolateral prefrontal cortex. *J. Neurophysiol.* 61:331–349.

FUSTER, J. M., 1989. *The Prefrontal Cortex.* New York: Raven Press.

FUSTER, J. M., and G. E. ALEXANDER, 1971. Neuron activity related to short-term memory. *Science* 173:652–654.

FUXE, K., L. F. AGNATI, M. KALIA, M. GOLDSTEIN, K. ANDERSSON, and A. HARFSTRAND, 1985. Dopaminergic systems in the brain and pituitary. In *The Dopaminergic System*, E. Fluckiger, E. E. Muller, and M. O. Thorner, eds. New York: Springer-Verlag, pp. 11–26.

GALLAGHER, M., 1982. Naloxone enhancement of memory processes: Effects of other opiate antagonists. *Behav. Neural Biol.* 35:375–382.

GALLAGHER, M., R. A. KING, and N. B. YOUNG, 1983. Opiate antagonists improve spatial memory. *Science* 221:975–976.

GIACCHINO, J. L., and S. J. HENRIKSEN, 1996. Systemic morphine and local opioid effects on neuronal activity in the medial prefrontal cortex. *Neuroscience* 70(4):941–949.

GLOWINSKI, J., J. P. TASSIN, and A. M. THIERRY, 1984. Mesocortico-prefrontal dopaminergic neurons. *Trends Neurosci.* 415–418.

GOLDMAN-RAKIC, P. S., 1987. Circuitry of primate prefrontal cortex and regulation of behavior by representational memory. In *Handbook of Physiology: The Nervous System.* Bethesda, Md.: *Am. Physiol. Soc.* 5:373–417.

GOLDMAN-RAKIC, P. S., 1988. Topography of cognition: Parallel distributed networks in primate association cortex. *Ann. Rev. Neurosci.* 11:137–156.

GOLDMAN-RAKIC, P. S., 1999. The "psychic" neuron of the cerebral cortex. *Ann. N.Y. Acad. Sci.* 868:13–26.

GOTHAM, A. M., R. G. BROWN, and C. P. MARSDEN, 1988. Frontal cognitive deficits in patients with Parkinson's disease on and off levodopa. *Brain* 111:299–321.

GRAY, J., 1973. Causal theories of personality and how to test them. In *Multivariate Analysis and Psychological Theory. The 3rd Banff Conference on Theoretical Psychology*, J. Royce, ed. New York: Academic Press.

GRAY, J., 1987. The neuropsychology of emotion and personality. In *Cognitive Neurochemistry*, S. M. Stahl, S. Iversen, and E. Goodman, eds. Oxford: Oxford University Press.

GYSLING, K., and R. Y. WANG, 1983. Morphine-induced activation of A10 dopamine neurons in the rat. *Brain Res.* 277:119–127.

HAAS, H. L., 1983. Amine neurotransmitter action in the hippocampus. In *Neurobiology of the Hippocampus*, W. Seifert, ed. New York: Academic Press, pp. 139–155.

HOFER, M. A., 1994. Hidden regulators in attachment, separation, and loss. *Monographs of the Society for Research in Child Development*, pp. 192–207.

IMAMURA, T., M. TAKANASHI, N. HATTORI, M. FUJIMORI, H. YAMSHITA, K. ISHII, and A. YAMATORI, 1998. Bromocriptine treatment for perseveration in demented patients. *Alzheimer Disease Assoc. Disorders* 12(2):109–113.

IZQUIERDO, I., 1982. The role of an endogenous amnesic mechanism mediated by brain beta-endorphins in memory modulation. *Brazil. J. Med. Biol. Res.* 159(2–3):119–134.

JACOBSEN, C. F., 1936. Studies of cerebral function in primates. I: The functions of the frontal association areas in monkeys. *Comp. Psychol. Monogr.* 13:3–60.

KALIVAS, P. W., and R. ABHOLD, 1987. Enkephalin release into the ventral tegmental area in response to stress: Modulation of mesocorticolimbic dopamine. *Brain Res.* 414:339–348.

KIMBERG, D. Y., M. D. D'ESPOSITO, and M. J. FARAH, 1997. Effects of bromocriptine on human subjects depend on working memory capacity. *NeuroReport* 8:3581–3583.

KOJIMA, S., and P. S. GOLDMAN-RAKIC, 1982. Delay-related activity of prefrontal neurons in rhesus monkeys performing delayed response. *Brain Res.* 248:43–49.

KOOB, G. F., G. J. BALCOM, and J. L. MEYERHOFF, 1975. Dopamine and norepinephrine levels in the nucleus accumbens, olfactory tubercle, and corpus striatum following lesions in the ventral tegmental area. *Brain Res.* 94:45–55.

LEVIN, E. D., 1988. Psychopharmacological effects in the radial-arm maze. *Neurosci. Biobehav. Rev.* 12(2):169–175.

LEVITT, P., P. RAKIC, and P. S. GOLDMAN-RAKIC, 1984. Region-specific distribution of catecholamine afferents in primate cerebral cortex. A fluorescence analysis. *J. Comp. Neurol.* 27:23–36.

LEWIS, D. A., S. L. FOOTE, M. GOLDSTEIN, and J. H. MORRISON, 1988. The dopaminergic innervation of monkey prefrontal cortex: A tyrosine hydroxylase immunohistochemical study. *Brain Res.* 449:225–243.

LEZAK, M. D., 1983. *Neuropsychological Assessment.* New York: Oxford University Press.

LINDVALL, O., and A. BJORKLUND, 1978. Organization of catecholamine neurons in the rat central nervous system. In *Handbook of Psychopharmacology*, Vol. 9, L. L. Iversen, S. D. Iversen, and S. H. Snyder, eds. New York: Plenum Press, pp.139–231.

LOWE, C., and P. RABBITT, 1998. Test/re-test reliability of the CANTAB and ISPOCD neuropsychological batteries: Theoretical and practical issues. *Neuropsychologia* 36(9):915–923.

LUCIANA, M., 1994. The functional role of dopamine in cognitive and emotional aspects of reward-seeking behavior. *Dissertation Abstracts International.*

LUCIANA, M., and P. F. COLLINS, 1997. Dopamine modulates working memory for spatial but not object cues in normal humans. *J. Cogn. Neurosci.* 9(3):330–347.

LUCIANA, M., P. F. COLLINS, and R. A. DEPUE, 1998. Opposing roles for dopamine and serotonin in the modulation of human spatial working memory functions. *Cereb. Cortex* 8(3):218–226.

LUCIANA, M., R. A. DEPUE, P. ARBISI, and A. LEON, 1992. Facilitation of working memory in humans by a D2 dopamine receptor agonist. *J. Cogn. Neurosci.* 4:58–68.

LUCIANA, M., and C. A. NELSON, 1998. The functional emergence of prefrontally-guided working memory systems in four-to-eight-year-old children. *Neuropsychologia* 36(3):273–293.

MACLEAN, P. D., 1952. Some psychiatric implications of physiological studies on frontotemporal portion of limbic system (visceral brain). *Electroencephalogr. Clin. Neurophysiol.* 4:407–418.

MACLEAN, P. D., 1986. Ictal symptoms relating to the nature of affects and their cerebral substrate. In *Emotion: Theory, Research, and Experience. Vol. 3: Biological Foundations of Emotion*, E. Plutchik and H. Kellerman, eds. New York: Academic Press, pp. 61–90.

MACLEAN, P. D., 1990. *The Triune Brain in Evolution. Role in Paleocerebral Functions.* New York: Plenum Press.

MCDOWELL, S., J. WHYTE, and M. D. D'ESPOSITO, 1998. Differential effect of a dopaminergic agonist on prefrontal function in traumatic brain injury patients. *Brain* 121:1155–1164.

MCKIM, W. A., 2000. *Drugs and Behavior: An Introduction to Behavioral Pharmacology*, 4th ed. Upper Saddle River, N.J.: Prentice Hall, pp. 246–266.

MICKLEY, G. A., and B. L. COBB, 1998. Thermal tolerance reduces hyperthermia-induced disruption of working memory: A role for endogenous opiates? *Physiol. Behav.* 63(5):855–865.

MOGENSON, G. H., D. L. JONES, and C. Y. YIM, 1980. From motivation to action: Functional interface between the limbic system and the motor system. *Prog. Neurobiol.* 14:69–77.

MOORE, R. Y., and F. E. BLOOM, 1978. Central catecholamine neuron systems: Anatomy and physiology of the dopamine system. *Ann. Rev. Neurosci.* 1:129–169.

MULLER, U., D. Y. VON CRAMON, and S. POLLMANN, 1998. D1- versus D2 receptor modulation of visuospatial working memory in humans. *J. Neurosci.* 18(7):2720–2728.

NESSE, R. M., and K. C. BERRIDGE, 1997. Psychoactive drug use in evolutionary perspective. *Science* 278(3):63–66.

OADES, R. D., and G. M. HALLIDAY, 1987. Ventral tegmental A10 system. Neurobiology I: Anatomy and connectivity. *Brain Res. Rev.* 12:117–165.

OADES, R. D., K. TAGHZOUTI, J. M. RIVER, H. SIMON, and M. LEMOAL, 1986. Locomotor activity in relation to dopamine and adrenaline in the nucleus accumbens, septal and frontal areas: A 6-hydroxydopamine study. *Neuropsychobiology* 16:37–43.

PANKSEPP, J., 1998. *Affective Neuroscience: The Foundations of Human and Animal Emotions.* Oxford: Oxford University Press.

PANKSEPP, J., 1992. A critical role for "affective neuroscience" in resolving what is basic about basic emotions. *Psychol. Rev.* 99(3):554–560.

PANKSEPP, J., E. NELSON, and M. BEKKEDAL, 1999. Brain systems for the mediation of social separation-distress and social-reward: Evolutionary antecedents and neuropeptide intermediaries. In *The Integrative Neurobiology of Affiliation*, C. S. Carter, I. Lederhendler, and B. Kirkpatrick, eds. Cambridge, Mass.: MIT Press.

PARK, S., and P. S. HOLTZMANN, 1992. Schizophrenics show spatial working memory deficits. *Arch. Gen. Psychiatry* 49:975–982.

PIAGET, J., 1954. *The Construction of Reality in the Child.* New York: Basic Books.

PORRINO, L. J., and P. S. GOLDMAN-RAKIC, 1982. Brainstem innervation of prefrontal and anterior cingulate cortex in the rhesus monkey revealed by retrograde transport of HRP. *J. Comp. Neurol.* 205:63–76.

ROSENKILDE, C. E., 1979. Functional heterogeneity of the prefrontal cortex in the monkey. A review. *Behav. Neural Biol.* 25:301–345.

SAWAGUCHI, T., and P. S. GOLDMAN-RAKIC, 1991. D$_1$ dopamine receptors in prefrontal cortex: Involvement in working memory. *Science* 251:947–950.

SAWAGUCHI, T., M. MATSUMURA, and K. KUBOTA, 1988. Dopamine enhances the neuronal activity of spatial short-term memory task in the primate prefrontal cortex. *Neurosci. Res.* 5:465–473.

SAWAGUCHI, T., M. MATSUMURA, and K. KUBOTA, 1990a. Catecholamine effects on neuronal activity related to a delayed response task in monkey prefrontal cortex. *J. Neurophysiol.* 63(6):1385–1400.

SAWAGUCHI, T., M. MATSUMURA, and K. KUBOTA, 1990b. Effects of dopamine antagonists on neuronal activity related to a delayed response task in monkey prefrontal cortex. *J. Neurophysiol.* 63(6):1401–1412.

SCHNEIRLA, T., 1959. An evolutionary and developmental theory of biphasic processes underlying approach and withdrawal. In *Nebraska Symposium on Motivation*, M. Jones, ed. University of Nebraska Press.

SCHULTZ, W., L. TREMBLAY, and J. R. HOLLERMAN, 1998. Reward prediction in primate basal ganglia and frontal cortex. *Neuropharmacology* 37:421–429.

SELEMON, L. D., and P. S. GOLDMAN-RAKIC, 1988. Common cortical and subcortical target areas of the dorsolateral prefrontal and posterior parietal cortices in the rhesus monkey. Evidence for a distributed neural network subserving spatially-guided behavior. *J. Neurosci.* 8:4049–4068.

SELF, D. W., and L. STEIN, 1992. Receptor subtypes in opioid and stimulant reward. *Pharmacol. Toxicol.* 70:87–94.

SHIPPENBERG, T. S., and G. I. ELMER, 1998. The neurobiology of opiate reinforcement. *Crit. Rev. Neurobiol.* 12(4):267–303.

SIMON, H., B. SCATTON, and M. LEMOAL, 1980. Dopaminergic A10 neurons are involved in cognitive functions. *Nature* 288:150–151.

SMITH, D. R., C. D. STRIPLIN, A. M. GELLER, R. B. MAILMAN, J. DRAGO, C. P. LAWLER, and M. GALLAGHER, 1998. Behavioural assessment of mice lacking D1A dopamine receptors. *Neuroscience* 86(1):135–146.

STONE, W. S., B. WALSER, S. D. GOLD, and P. E. GOLD, 1991. Scopolamine and morphine-induced impairments of spontaneous alternation behavior in mice: Reversal with glucose and with cholinergic and adrenergic agonists. *Behav. Neurosci.* 105:264–271.

TAM, S. Y., and R. H. ROTH, 1997. Mesoprefrontal dopaminergic neurons: Can tyrosine availability influence their functions? *Biochem. Pharmacol.* 53(4):441–453.

TELLEGEN, A., and N. G. WALLER, 1997. Exploring personality through test construction: Development of the multidimensional personality questionnaire. In *Personality Measures: Development and Evaluation*, Vol. 1, S. R. Briggs and J. M. Cheek, eds. Greenwich, Conn.: JAI Press.

TERMAN, G. W., and J. D. LOESER, 1992. A case of opiate-sensitive pain: Malignant treatment of benign pain. *Clin. J. Pain* 8(3):255–259.

THELEN, E., and L. B. SMITH, 1994. *A Dynamic Systems Approach to the Development of Cognition and Action*, 2nd ed., Cambridge, Mass.: MIT Press, pp. 279–310.

Tzschentke, T. M., 1998. Measuring reward with the conditioned place preference paradigm: A comprehensive review of drug effects, recent progress and new issues. *Prog. Neurobiol.* 56:513–672.

Watanabe, M., T. Kodama, and K. Hikosaka, 1997. Increase of extracellular dopamine in primate prefrontal cortex during a working memory task. *J. Neurophysiol.* 78(5):2795–2798.

Williams, G. V., and P. S. Goldman-Rakic, 1995. Modulation of memory fields by dopamine D1 receptors in prefrontal cortex. *Nature* 376:572–575.

Wood, P. L., and T. S. Rao, 1991. Morphine stimulation of mesolimbic and mesocortical but not nigrostriatal dopamine release in the rat as reflected by changes in 3-methyxytyramine levels. *Neuropharmacology* 30(4):399–401.

# CONTRIBUTORS

RICHARD N. ASLIN, PH.D.    Department of Brain and Cognitive Sciences, University of Rochester, Rochester, New York

JOCELYNE BACHEVALIER, PH.D.    Department of Neurobiology and Anatomy, University of Texas Health Science Center, Houston, Texas

ELIZABETH BATES, PH.D.    Center for Research in Language, University of California at San Diego, La Jolla, California

GAIL C. BEDI, PH.D.    Director, Manhattan Neuropsychology; Assistant Clinical Professor, Mount Sinai School of Medicine, New York, New York

FRANCINE M. BENES, M.D., PH.D.    Laboratory for Structural Neuroscience, McClean Hospital, Belmont, Massachusetts; Program in Neuroscience and Department of Psychiatry, Harvard Medical School, Boston, Massachusetts

J.-P. BOURGEOIS, PH.D.    Laboratoire de Récepteurs et Cognition, Département des Biotechnologies, Institut Pasteur, Paris, France

JOHN BRUER, PH.D.    James S. McDonnell Foundation, St. Louis, Missouri

JUDY L. CAMERON, PH.D.    Departments of Psychiatry, Neuroscience, and Cell Biology & Physiology, University of Pittsburgh, Pittsburgh Pennsylvania; Oregon Regional Primate Research Center, Oregon Health Sciences University, Beaverton, Oregon

SUSAN CAREY, PH.D.    Department of Psychology, New York University, New York, New York

B. J. CASEY, PH.D.    Sackler Institute for Developmental Psychobiology, Joan and Sanford I. Weill Medical College of Cornell University, New York, New York

V. S. CAVINESS, JR., M.D., PH.D.    Department of Neurology, Massachusetts General Hospital, Harvard Medical School, Boston, Massachusetts

MELISSA W. CLEARFIELD, B.A.    Department of Psychology, Indiana University, Bloomington, Indiana

DONALD J. COHEN, M.D.    Child Study Center; Departments of Pediatrics, Psychiatry, and Psychology, Yale University School of Medicine, New Haven, Connecticut

PAUL D. CONNER, PH.D.    Fetal Alcohol and Drug Unit, Department of Psychiatry and Behavioral Sciences, University of Washington School of Medicine, Seattle, Washington

GERGELY CSIBRA, PH.D.    Centre for Brain and Cognitive Development, Department of Psychology, Birkbeck College, University of London, London, England

JAMES L. DANNEMILLER, PH.D.    Department of Psychology, University of Wisconsin at Madison, Madison, Wisconsin

MICHELLE DE HAAN, PH.D.    Cognitive Neuroscience Unit, Institute of Child Health and Great Ormond Street Hospital, University College London Medical School, The Wolfson Centre, London, England

ADELE DIAMOND, PH.D.    Director, Center for Developmental Cognitive Neuroscience, Eunice Kennedy Shriver Center; Professor, Department of Psychiatry, University of Massachusetts School of Medicine, Waltham, Massachusetts

THOMAS ELBERT, PH.D.    Department of Psychology, University of Konstanz, Konstanz, Germany

BRITA ELVEVÅG, PH.D.    Clinical Brain Disorders Branch, National Institute of Mental Health/National Institutes of Health, Bethesda, Maryland

MONICA FABIANI, PH.D.    Department of Psychology, University of Missouri, Columbia, Missouri

NATHAN A. FOX, PH.D.    Department of Human Development, University of Maryland, College Park, Maryland

MICHAEL K. GEORGIEFF, M.D.    School of Medicine, Institute of Child Development, Department of Pediatrics, University of Minnesota, Minneapolis, Minnesota

ROBBIN GIBB, M.SC.    Departments of Psychology and Neuroscience, University of Lethbridge, Lethbridge, Canada

ELIZABETH GOULD, PH.D.    Department of Psychology, Princeton University, Princeton, New Jersey

MEGAN R. GUNNAR, PH.D.    Institute of Child Development, University of Minnesota, Minneapolis, Minnnesota

NICHOLAS B. HASTINGS, PH.D.    Department of Psychology, Princeton University, Princeton, New Jersey

SABINE HEIM, PH.D.    Department of Psychology, University of Konstanz, Konstanz, Germany

HEATHER A. HENDERSON, B.A.    Department of Human Development, University of Maryland, College Park, Maryland

MYRON A. HOFER, M.D.    Department of Developmental Psychobiology, New York State Psychiatric Institute; Department of Psychiatry, Columbia University, New York, New York

RUSKIN H. HUNT, B.A.    Department of Brain and Cognitive Sciences, University of Rochester, Rochester, New York

MARK H. JOHNSON, PH.D.    Centre for Brain and Cognitive Development, Department of Psychology, Birkbeck College, University of London, London, England

CANAN KARATEKIN, PH.D.    Institute of Child Development, University of Minnesota, Minneapolis, Minnesota

BRYAN KOLB, PH.D.    Departments of Psychology and Neuroscience, University of Lethbridge, Lethbridge, Canada

JAMES F. LECKMAN, M.D.    Child Study Center; Children's Clinical Research Center; Departments of Pediatrics, Psychiatry, and Psychology, Yale University School of Medicine, New Haven, Connecticut

PAT LEVITT, PH.D.    Department of Neurobiology, University of Pittsburgh School of Medicine, Pittsburgh, Pennsylvania

TERRI L. LEWIS, PH.D.    Department of Psychology, McMaster University, Hamilton, Ontario; Department of Ophthalmology, The Hospital for Sick Children, Toronto; Department of Opthalmology, University of Toronto, Toronto, Canada

MONICA LUCIANA, PH.D.    Department of Psychology, University of Minnesota, Minneapolis, Minnesota

DENIS MARESCHAL, PH.D.    Centre for Brain and Cognitve Development, Department of Psychology, Birkbeck College, University of London, London, England

PETER J. MARSHALL, PH.D.    Department of Human Development, University of Maryland, College Park, Maryland

DAPHNE MAURER, PH.D.    Department of Psychology, McMaster University, Hamilton, Ontario; Department of Ophthalmology, The Hospital for Sick Children, Toronto, Canada

BRUCE MCCANDLISS, PH.D.    Sackler Institute for Developmental Psychobiology, Joan and Sanford I. Weill Medical College of Cornell University, New York, New York

CHRISTOPHER S. MONK, PH.D.    Institute of Child Development, University of Minnesota, Minneapolis, Minnesota

YUKO MUNAKATA, PH.D.    Department of Psychology, University of Denver, Denver, Colorado

CHARLES A. NELSON, PH.D.    Institute of Child Development and Department of Pediatrics, University of Minnesota, Minneapolis, Minnesota

R. S. NOWAKOWSKI, PH.D.    Department of Neuroscience and Cell Biology, UMDNJ–Robert Wood Johnson Medical School, Piscataway, New Jersey

WILLIAM H. OVERMAN, PH.D.    Psychology Department, University of North Carolina at Wilmington, Wilmington, North Carolina

SALLY OZONOFF, PH.D.    Department of Psychology, University of Utah, Salt Lake City, Utah

BRUCE F. PENNINGTON, PH.D.    Department of Psychology, University of Denver, Denver, Colorado

BRADLEY S. PETERSON, M.D.    Child Study Center, Yale University School of Medicine, New Haven, Connecticut

MICHAEL I. POSNER, PH.D.    Sackler Institute for Developmental Psychobiology, Weill Medical College of Cornell University, New York, New York

RAGHAVENDRA RAO, MD    Department of Pediatrics, School of Medicine, University of Minnesota, Minneapolis, Minnesota

JOHN E. RICHARDS, PH.D.    Department of Psychology, University of South Carolina, Columbia, South Carolina

BRIGITTE ROCKSTROH, PH.D.    Department of Psychology, University of Konstanz, Konstanz, Germany

KATHERINE ROE, B.A.    Center for Research in Language, University of California at San Diego, La Jolla, California

MARY K. ROTHBART, PH.D.    Department of Psychology, University of Oregon, Eugene, Oregon

RICARDO C. SAMPAIO, M.D.    Department of Radiology, University of Minnesota, Minneapolis, Minnesota

ROBERT T. SCHULTZ, PH.D.    Child Study Center, Yale University School of Medicine, New Haven, Connecticut

LÁSZLÓ SERESS, M.D., PH.D.    Central Electron Microscopic Laboratory, Faculty of Medicine, University of Pécs, Pécs, Szigeti, Hungary

GREGG D. STANWOOD, PH.D.    Department of Neurobiology, University of Pittsburgh School of Medicine, Pittsburgh, Pennsylvania

JENNIFER MERVA STEDRON, B.A.    Department of Psychology, University of Denver, Denver, Colorado

JOAN STILES, PH.D.    Department of Cognitive Science, University of California at San Diego, La Jolla, California

ANN P. STREISSGUTH, PH.D.    Fetal Alcohol and Drug Unit, Department of Psychiatry and Behavioral Sciences, University of Washington School of Medicine, Seattle, Washington

REGINA M. SULLIVAN, PH.D.    Department of Zoology, University of Oklahoma, Norman, Oklahoma

T. TAKAHASHI, M.D.    Department of Neurology, Massachusetts General Hospital, Harvard Medical School, Boston, Massachusetts; Department of Pediatrics, Keio University School of Medicine, Tokyo, Japan

PATIMA TANAPAT, PH.D.    Department of Psychology, Princeton University, Princeton, New Jersey

ESTHER THELEN, PH.D.    Department of Psychology, Indiana University, Bloomington, Indiana

KATHLEEN M. THOMAS, PH.D.    Sackler Institute for Developmental Psychobiology, Joan and Sanford I. Weill Medical College of Cornell University, New York, New York

CHARLES L. TRUWIT, M.D.    Department of Radiology, University of Minnesota, Minneapolis, Minnesota

ATHENA VOULOUMANOS, B.SC.    Department of Psychology, University of British Columbia, Vancouver, British Columbia, Canada

EMILY WEE, M.A., M.H.S.    Department of Psychology, University of Missouri, Columbia, Missouri

DANIEL R. WEINBERGER, M.D.    Chief, Clinical Brain Disorders Branch, National Institute of Mental Health/National Institutes of Health, Bethesda, Maryland

JANET F. WERKER, PH.D.    Department of Psychology, University of British Columbia, Vancouver, British Columbia, Canada

# INDEX

Cortex (continued)
  plasticity of (continued)
    and auditory development, 213–216
    behavioral relevance and, 194–195, 312
    deafferentation and, 193–194
    in musicians, 193–196, 196f
    principles of, 194–195
    in representational zones, 191–196
    sensitive periods for, 192, 199
    temporal dynamics of, 194
    in treatment of specific language impairment
      and dyslexia, 314–316
    use-dependent, 193–195
  sexual dimorphism in, 66, 69–71, 70f
  synaptic connections in, formation of, 82, 519–
    521, 520f
  in temperament, 633
  in Tourette's syndrome, 553, 554f
Cortical face areas hypothesis, 382
Cortical parcellation hypothesis, of visual
  development, 231
Cortical-striatal-thalamo-cortical (CSTC) circuits
  in habit formation, 550–552, 551f, 552t
  in Tourette's syndrome, 553, 554f
Corticofugal pathways, early brain injury and, 180
Corticolimbic pathways, myelination of, 82
Corticopontine tracts, myelination of, 43
Corticospinal tracts, myelination of, magnetic
  resonance imaging of, 38f
Corticosterone, infant levels of, mother-child
  interactions and, 609–610
Corticostriatal system, in procedural learning,
  111–112
Corticotropin-releasing factor, opiates and, 655
Corticotropin-releasing hormone, mother-infant
  interactions and, 610
Cortisol levels
  in behaviorally inhibited children, 640–641
  early deprivation/orphanage rearing and, 622
  as measure of reactivity, 634–635
CPP. See Conditioned place preference
CPT. See Continuous performance test
Cranial nerves, myelination of, 42
Critical periods
  developmental, neural network model of, 164–
    165
  for language development, 165, 282
  for nutrition, in brain development, 497, 500–
    501
  in synaptogenesis phase 3, 27–28
  for visual development, 211–212
Crowding hypothesis, of language development in
  children with unilateral brain injury, 296
CSTC circuits. See Cortical-striatal-thalamo-cortical
  circuits
Cue(s)
  in radial-arm maze testing, 116–117
  in spatial-relational learning, 115
Cuneus gyrus, development of, 80t
Cyclic adenosine monophosphate (cAMP), as
  second messenger, estrogen and, 64
Cyclin D, in neurogenesis, 14
Cyclin E, in neurogenesis, 14–15
Cyclin-dependent kinases, in neuronogenesis,
  14–15

### D

Darwinian medicine, 648
Day-night Stroop-like task, 449t
  in dorsolateral prefrontal cortex studies, 442–
    443, 443f, 448, 451f
  PKU treatment and, 448, 451f
Deaf
  cortical plasticity in, 215–216
  sensory compensation in, 215–216

Deafferentation, and cortical plasticity, 193–194
Declarative learning
  inferences about, from animal cognition tests
    applied to children, 111–112
  neural basis for, 111
Declarative memory, 365–366
  adult abilities in, emergence of, 368–371
  development of, 368–371, 374
    in monkeys and humans, 375t
  inferences about, from animal cognition tests
    applied to children, 111–112
  neural circuits mediating, maturation of, 369–
    371, 374
Delay of gratification paradigm, in dorsolateral
  prefrontal cortex studies, 442
Delayed alternation task
  in animal model of cognitive effects of PKU,
    455, 456f
  in working memory assessment, 371–374, 375t
Delayed response task
  affective demands of, 653
  as diagnostic marker of dorsolateral prefrontal
    cortex injury, 417
  in dopamine-dorsolateral prefrontal cortex
    studies, 435–440, 438f–439f, 441t, 459
  performed by children treated for PKU, 454,
    455t
  in working memory assessment, 371–374, 375t
Delayed-nonmatch-to-sample (DNMS) tasks, 449t
  for children, 111–112, 120t
  in recognition memory testing, 369–370, 375t
Deltoid muscles, in reaching skills, 258, 258f–259f
Dendrite(s)
  development of
    in cortex, 80, 521
    early brain injury and, 179–180, 186–188,
      187f
    experience-dependent changes in, 177–178,
      178f
    in hippocampal formation, 52–54, 53f–54f,
      119
    in normal brain, 176–177
    nutrition and, 492, 499
    and visual development, 226, 227f, 230
  orientation of, and event-related potentials, 126,
    127f
  sex hormones and, 65
Dentate gyrus
  cell death in, evidence of, 47–49, 51f
  cell migration in, 49–52, 51f, 56
  development of, 96f, 96–97, 369, 371
  early deprivation/orphanage rearing and, 621
  estrogen receptors in, 60
  hormones and, 68–69, 93, 97
  in learning and memory, 56–57
  neuronal connections of, development of, 52,
    56–57
  neuronal development in, of principal and
    nonprincipal neurons, 52–54, 53f, 56
  neuronogenesis in, 45–47, 48f–50f, 369, 371
    in adults, 93–103
  synapse formation in, 52, 54–56, 55f
2-Deoxyglucose metabolic labeling, in dorsolateral
  prefrontal cortex studies, 436
Depression, infantile, and growth, 622–623
Depression, long-term, synaptic, 192, 247
Deprivation, early
  and attachment, 624–626
  and behavior problems, 623
  catch-up growth after, 620–623
  and domains of development, 620–626
  effects of, 617–627
  exemplar studies of, 618–619

and general intelligence, 620–621
  and growth failure, 622–623
  and language development, 622
  levels of privation in, 618
  orphanage-reared studies of, history and
    conceptual issues of, 617–620
  and peer problems, 624
  and socio-emotional development, 623–626
Depth of processing hypothesis, of face
  processing, 390–391
Depth vision, development of, 229
Development. See also Brain development;
  Cognitive development
  plasticity and, 191–199
Developmental cognitive neuroscience
  advances in, 339
  fetal alcohol syndrome studies in, 505–513
  goals of, 149, 417
  neural network models in, 159–170, 339
  number representations in, 418–425
  understanding of mind in, 415, 418
Developmental neuroscience
  and cognition, bridging gap between, 415–429
  structural analogy in, 415–417
DF method, 153–154
Diagnostic and Statistical Manual of Mental Disorders,
  fourth edition (DSM-IV), diagnostic criteria in
  for Asperger disorder, 537–538
  for attention-deficit/hyperactivity disorder, 569
  for autism, 537
Diagnostic markers, 417
Diencephalic dopamine, 649
Diencephalon
  development of, nutrition and, 493
  in fetal alcohol syndrome, 512
  medial, in declarative memory, 368
Differential maturation hypothesis
  subtleties of, 230–232
  of visual development, 226–232
Differential regression to mean, 153
Diffusion anisotropy, 37, 41
Diffusion tensor imaging, 484
Diffusion-weighted imaging
  Brownian movement and, 37
  of myelination, 37, 39, 43
Digit span task, in schizophrenia, 579
Digits, cortical representational zones for
  fusion of, 193–194
  plasticity of, 193–194
Dihydrotestosterone, testosterone transformation
  to, by 5α-reductase, 62f, 63–64, 65f
Dipole, in event-related potentials, 126, 127f
Directional selectivity, visual, development of, 229
Directional Stroop task, in dopamine-dorsolateral
  prefrontal cortex studies, 462t, 462–463,
    463f–464f
Discriminant validity, 540
Disparity sensitivity, visual, development of, 229
Distal pathways, myelination of, 35–36
Distinctiveness effects, in face processing, 390
Distractors, susceptibility to, aging and, 479–483
Distress keeper, in infants, 358
Divided visual field studies, of face processing,
  382, 388
DL-PFC. See Dorsolateral prefrontal cortex
Docosohexaenoic acid
  and brain development, 491
  nutritional need for, 496
Dopamine
  in A-not-B task, 435–440, 438f–439f, 441t, 447–
    448, 449t, 451f, 459, 459f, 653–655
  in appetitive motivation, 649–650

in attention, 322–323, 323*f*, 325
in attention-deficit/hyperactivity disorder, 156–157, 525, 567
brain systems
abnormalities in, disorders associated with, 522
anatomical organization of, 522–523
neuropharmacology of, 521–525
sex dimorphism in, 67
cocaine and, 519, 522, 525–528
in conditioned place preference, 658–659
in consummatory attachment, 655–656
in cortical development, 521
developmental roles of, 524–525
diencephalic, 649
functional activity of, individual differences in, 652–653
functions of, 522
and glutamate, interactions between, 525
innervation, development of, 524
iron and, 492, 498
major cell groups of, 649
mesencephalic, 649
mesocortical, 521–525, 649, 651–652
ontogeny of, 523–524
mesolimbic, 649
metabolism, 522, 523*f*
as neurotransmitter, 522
interaction and convergence of, with serotonin, 79, 88–89
interaction with GABA, 86–89, 87*f*–88*f*
maturation of, 79, 85–86, 86*f*
opiates and, 655–656
pharmacology, 522, 523*f*
in prefrontal cortex
and cognition, 435–456, 459–463
early and continuous treatment of PKU model of, 434, 444–463, 447*f*
evidence from visual psychophysics confirming hypothesis of, 456–459, 457*f*–458*f*
and inhibitory control, 436–440, 448–450
role of, 433–463, 523, 525, 647–659
selective deficit in, with PKU treatment, 444–447, 445*f*
and progesterone receptors, in sexual behavior, 65, 72
in retinal function, 456–461, 457*f*–458*f*
in reward-seeking behavior, 647–659
in schizophrenia, 523, 525, 565–566, 586–587, 652
synthesis of, 522, 523*f*
in Tourette's syndrome, 553–555
tyrosine levels and, 446–447, 447*f*, 460, 522, 523*f*
in working memory, 436, 440–444, 448–454, 459–463
spatial, 650–652
Dopamine receptors, 87, 373, 522
in attention-deficit/hyperactivity disorder, 156–157, 525
development of, 524
pharmacological activation of, and cognition, 436
in prefrontal cortex, 434
subtypes of, 522
in ventral tegmental area, 436, 446–447
Dorsal putamen, myelination of, magnetic resonance imaging of, 40
Dorsal visual pathway, 339–349, 399, 400*f*
anatomy of, 399–401, 400*f*
and body-centered frames of reference, 344, 345*f*, 348–349

computational model of object processing in, 346*f*, 346–348
development of, 341–348
dissociation of, with ventral pathway, behavioral evidence of, 344–346, 349
and eye movement control, 339–340, 342*f*–343*f*, 342–344, 349, 401
function of, 399
high-density ERP studies of, 342–344, 343*f*–344*f*
neurocomputational properties of, 339–341
plasticity of, 348–349
processing in, 340–341
spatial processes associated with, development of, 401–406
in visual processing, 339–341
as where or action pathway, 340, 399
Dorsolateral prefrontal cortex
anatomy of, 434–435, 435*f*
in attention, 436
in cognition
in childhood, improvement of, 440–444, 443*f*
in infancy, evidence of, 435–440, 438*f*–440*f*, 441*t*
phenylalanine levels and, 450–452
in conflict tasks, 482
connections and interactions of, 435
damage
cognitive effects of, 436–440
diagnostic marker for, 417
dopamine in
and cognition, 435–456, 459–463
early and continuous treatment of PKU model of, 434, 444–463, 447*f*
evidence from visual psychophysics confirming hypothesis of, 456–459, 457*f*–458*f*
role of, 433–463, 651–652
selective deficit in, with PKU treatment, 444–447, 445*f*
tyrosine levels and, 446–447, 447*f*, 460
functions of, 433, 459
in inhibitory control, 436–440, 448–454, 459–463, 479
maturation of, 373–374, 417, 433
in schizophrenia, 586–587
in self-regulation, 639
size of, evolutionary increase in, 434–435
in spatial localization, 401–404
in spatial working memory, 650–652
in working memory, 366, 371–374, 436, 440–444, 448–454, 459–463, 473
Down syndrome
genetic studies of, 150–151
microcephaly in, 157
Drawing tasks, in Tourette's syndrome, 555–556
Dwarfism, psychosocial, 622–623
Dyscalculia, 422
Dyslexia, 310
auditory/speech development and, 198–199, 309–311
functional magnetic resonance imaging in, 141–143
genetic studies of, 151–152, 154–156
temporal processing deficits in, 198–199, 309–311
treatment of, 309
experience-driven plasticity in, 314–316

## E

Early brain injury. *See* Brain injury, early
Early deprivation, effects of, 617–627

Ease of learning argument, against continuity hypothesis of number representation, 419–421
Echoes, suppression of, 213
Echolocation, 210–211
Echopractic errors, 444
E2F, in neuronogenesis, 14
Effortful control, 562–563
during childhood, 360–361
Elderly
brain imaging data from, interpretation of, 475
event-related potentials in
mismatch negativity amplitude in, 475–476, 476*f*–477*f*
novelty P3 in, 479–481, 481*f*–482*f*
P300 amplitude and scalp distribution in, 479
individual differences and cognitive function in, 474–475
inhibitory control in, 479–483
memory in
for contextual detail, 483–484
frontal cortex activation patterns in, during working memory task, 479, 480*f*
frontal lobe function and, 473–484
future directions for study of, 484
item, 473, 483
number of operations to be performed in working memory and, 478–479
sensory, 474–475
source, 473–474, 483–484
type of material to be processed in working memory and, 479
working, 473–484
working memory load and, 476–478
methodological issues in studies of, 474–475
susceptibility to distractors in, 479–483
Electrode(s)
10/20 system of, 126
high-density arrays of, 126–127
for recording event-related potentials, 126
Electroencephalography (EEG)
in affective bias studies, 635–636
aging and, 484
in attention studies, 326–327, 334–336
event-related potentials in, 125–133. *See also* Event-related potentials
Electrooculogram, of infant eye movements, 329
Emergentist view, of children with unilateral brain injury, 282, 297, 299–304
Emotion(s)
A-not-B task and, 653
in attachment, emergence of, 607–609
hemisphere specialization in, 635
perception of, in face processing
autism and, 392–393
categorical, 388–389, 392–393
in infants, 388–389
in newborns, 384
regulation of
attention and, 353–354, 358–360, 638–639
cognitive prerequisites for, 638
early deprivation/orphanage rearing and, 623–626
fetal alcohol syndrome and, 506
and temperament, 632–634, 636–640
and reward-seeking behavior, 648, 653, 658
and temperament, 631–632
Emotional development, early deprivation/orphanage rearing and, 623–626
Emotional reactivity
hypothalamic-pituitary-adrenal axis in, 634–635
and temperament, 632–635
vagal tone as measure of, 634

visual capacities of, 228–230
visual development in, 221–232, 225*f*
  absolute thresholds in, 222–223
  acuity in, 223–224, 229–230, 237–248
  contrast sensitivity in, 223–224, 229–231,
    237–248
  cortical, 221, 224–232, 240
  differential maturation in, 226–232
  dorsal and ventral pathways in, 339–349
  effort required for tasks in, 231
  retinal, 221–224, 239–240
  word learning in, 274–276
Inferior cerebellar peduncle, myelination of, 42
  magnetic resonance imaging of, 37*t*, 39
Inferior colliculi, brachia of, myelination of, 42
Inferior temporal gyrus, development of, 80*t*
Infundibular nucleus, progesterone receptors
  in, 60
Inhibition, behavioral, 631–632, 640–642
Inhibition of return, 357–358, 404–405
Inhibitory control, 403
  aging and, 479–483
  in A-not-B task, 657
  in attention-deficit/hyperactivity disorder, 568
  dorsolateral prefrontal cortex in, 479
    dopamine and, 436–440, 448–454, 459–463
  early deprivation/orphanage rearing and, 621–
    623
  PKU treatment and, 448–450, 449*t*–450*t*, 451*f*
  in schizophrenia, 566
  and self-regulation, 638–640
  in Tourette's syndrome, 554–556
Inhibitory input, and event-related potentials,
  125–126, 127*f*
Input units, in neural network models, 160, 161*f*
Insulin-like growth factor-I
  and brain development, 492–493, 495
  zinc and, 499
Integer-list representation
  bootstrapping mechanism for, 426–429
  construction of, 421, 425–426
  as new representational resource, 425
  object-file representations versus, 423
  sketch of one proposal for, 426
Intelligence. *See also* IQ
  early deprivation/orphanage rearing and, 620–
    621
Intensity discrimination, auditory, 206–207
Interaural level difference, 211
Interaural time difference, 211–212
Internal capsule
  myelination of, 43, 82
    magnetic resonance imaging of, 37*t*, 38*f*, 40*f*,
      40–41
  sex hormones and, 72
Internal working models, in attachment, 608, 624
Interval mapping, 155
Intervention, magnetic resonance imaging in,
  139–140
  functional, 141–143
Intradimensional-extradimensional (IDED) task,
  543, 545, 580
Intrauterine growth restriction, and brain
  development, 492–495
Intrinsic neurotransmitters
  developmental changes in, 84–85
  interactions of, with extrinsic neurotransmitters,
    86–88
Introverts, 631
Iodine, and brain development, 491–492, 495*t*,
  500
Ipsilateral corticospinal pathway, early brain injury
  and, 180

IQ
  early deprivation/orphanage rearing and, 620–
    621
  focal brain injury and, 284*t*–287*t*, 296–298, 300
  intrauterine growth restriction and, 493
  PKU treatment and, 446, 461–462
  schizophrenia and, 582–584
Iron
  and brain development, 491–492, 494*t*, 497–499
  regionalization effect of, 498–499
Irreversible determinism, in children with
  unilateral brain injury, 282–297
Isolation call, of infants, 607–608
Item memory, aging and, 473, 483

## K

Kanner, Leo, 538
Kennard principle, 178–180
Ki-67, as proliferation marker, in hippocampus,
  46–47, 47*t*, 48*f*–50*f*
Knowledge, neural network models of, 160, 163–
  166

## L

Lambda wave, in ERP studies of eye movement,
  343–344
Language
  event-related potentials in, 129–130
  native versus foreign, 269, 272–274, 276–277
  verbal, sexual dimorphism and, 66, 70*f*, 70–71
Language development
  analytic style in, 303
  in children with unilateral brain injury, 281–
    305, 316
    age of onset and, 296–299
    crowding hypothesis of, 296
    developmental sensitivity in studies of, 299
    emergentist view of, 282, 297, 299–304
    equipotentiality in, 282–283
    fresh-start hypothesis of, 298
    IQ data from studies of, 284*t*–287*t*, 296–298,
      300
    irreversible determinism in, 282–297
    language assessment data on, 288*t*–295*t*
    lesion etiology and, 298
    lesion neurocorrelates and, 298
    methodological confounds in studying, 292,
      297–299
    prospective studies of, 299
    retrospective studies of, 299
    sample size in studies of, 298–299
    seizures and, 296, 298
    timing of language testing for, 299
    type, site and size of lesion and, 296, 298
  critical period for, 282
    neural network model of, 165
  early deprivation/orphanage rearing and, 622
  experience and, 192
  holistic style in, 303
  left hemisphere as specialized organ for, 281–
    282, 304
  nominal style in, 303
  otitis media and, 304
  plasticity and, 192, 196–199, 276
  pronominal style in, 303
  schizophrenia and, 570
  sensitive period for, 197–198
  vowel triangle in, 197–198, 198*f*
Language disorders, 309–316
  auditory development and, 198–199, 208, 309–
    311

Language organ hypothesis, 281–282
Language processing
  experience and, 276–277
  foundations of, 269–271
  in infancy, neurocognitive approach to, 269–277
Laplacian analysis, of event-related potentials, 127
Lateral geniculate nucleus (LGN), 399
  neurotransmitters in, glutamate, maturation of,
    83
  visual deprivation and, 246–247
  in visual development, 226–227, 228*f*, 229–231,
    239–240
Lateral orbital gyrus, development of, 80*t*
Lateral weights, in neural network models, 160,
  161*f*
LCPUFA. *See* Long-chain polyunsaturated fatty
  acids
Learned helplessness, 620
Learning
  adult-generated neurons and, 100–103
  attention and, 359
  auditory, 205–216
  autism and, 540
  declarative
    inferences about, from animal cognition tests
      applied to children, 111–112
    neural basis for, 111
  ease of, in number representation, 419–421
  estrogen and, 68–69, 102–103
  fetal alcohol syndrome and, 511–512
  functional magnetic resonance imaging in, 142
  hippocampus in, 45, 56–57, 67–69, 100–103,
    111–112, 115, 119
  long-term potentiation in, 68, 83
  and neuronogenesis, 93, 99–100, 99*f*–101*f*
  nucleus basalis and, 194
  olfactory preference
    and attachment, 602–605
    neural plasticity underlying, 604–605
    sensitive period for, closing, 605
  perceptually cued, and habit establishment,
    550–552
  place, 115
  plasticity and, 199
  postnatal, and attachment, 602–604
  procedural
    attention-deficit/hyperactivity disorder and,
      570
    inferences about, from animal cognition tests
      applied to children, 111–112
    neural basis for, 111
  sexual dimorphism and, 66–69, 112–115
  spatial-relational, 115–120
    neural circuit mediating, maturation of, 371
  stress and, 102
  types of, 111
  word, 274–277
Learning algorithms
  error-driven, 162
  in neural network models, 162–163
  in object processing model, 346–347
  self-organizing, 162
Left hemisphere
  damage
    and adult aphasia, 281–282
    and language development, 281–305, 300*f*,
      302*f*
    and neglect, 405–406
    versus right hemisphere damage, 282–297,
      300*f*, 300–304
    and spatial analysis, 406–410

Left hemisphere (continued)
  perceptual detail advantage of, 304
  in spatial analysis, 406–407, 408*f*
  as specialized organ for language development, 281–282, 304
Lesion paradigm, 150
LGN. *See* Lateral geniculate nucleus
Light, detection of, absolute thresholds of, 222–223
Limbic system
  aromatase activity in, 63
  in attention, 321–322, 322*f*
  in autism, 538
  in temperament, 633
  zinc deprivation and, 499
Line bisection task, 450*t*
Linear synergy, and reaching skills, 256–258, 257*f*
Lingual gyrus, development of, 80*t*
Linguistic processing, event-related potentials in, 129–130
Linkage analysis, 152, 153*t*, 154–156
  nonparametric, 153*t*, 154–155
  parametric, 153*t*, 154–155
Linkage, versus linkage disequilibrium, 155
Linking propositions, in visual development, 221
Linoleic acid, and brain development, 491
Linolenic acid, and brain development, 491
Lipoproteins, and brain development, 491
Liquid conservation task, in dorsolateral prefrontal cortex studies, 442
Listening, preferences, in infants, 208–209, 216, 271
Localization
  auditory
    in human infants, 212–213, 216
    in nonhumans, 210–211
  spatial, development of, 401–404
Locus coeruleus
  in attention, 354
  in closing of sensitive period for olfactory preference learning, 605
Long-chain polyunsaturated fatty acids (LCPUFA), nutritional need for, 496
Long-term depression, synaptic, 192, 247
Long-term potentiation, 192
  estrogen and, 68
  glutamate receptors in, 83
Looking
  obligatory, 356
  preferential
    and attention, 357–358
    at eyes, 385
    at faces, 383–385, 387, 416
    in global-local task, 449*t*
    in studies of dorsal and ventral visual pathways, 344–346
    in visual assessment, 237
Lordosis, in rats, sex hormones and, 61–62

## M

Macrocephaly, 157
Macronutrients, and brain development, 491
Magnesium, and brain development, 491
Magnetic resonance imaging (MRI), 137–140
  of behavioral development, 138–139
  of brain development
    applications of, 137–145, 138*f*
    postnatal, 36–41
  of cognitive functioning, 70
  of fetal alcohol syndrome, 512
  functional, 137, 140–143
    of behavioral development, 141, 141*f*
    of brain development, 140–141, 141*f*

of children, difficulties with, 315
  combination of, with event-related potentials, 133
  in face processing, 382, 385
  in older adults, interpretation of, 475
  in phonetic perception, 273–274
  in reading disorders, 141–143, 143*f*–144*f*
  in remediation/intervention, 141–143
  in Tourette's syndrome, 553, 554*f*
  of myelination, 35–43, 38*f*–40*f*
    appearance in T1-weighted images, 36
    appearance in T2-weighted images, 36
    milestones in, 37*t*
  in obsessive compulsive disorder, 139–140, 140*f*
  versus other imaging modalities, 137
  pharmacologic, 143–145
  of remediation/intervention, 139–140
  rescanning, reliability of, 139
  in schizophrenia, 581, 584
  terminology, 36
Magnetoencephalography, in phonetic perception, 273
Magnocellular pathway, 226–227, 228*f*. *See also* Dorsal visual pathway
  development of, 221, 229–232
  visual deprivation and, 246
Malnutrition
  and brain development, 491–498, 501
  protein-energy, 491, 493–498, 494*t*, 501
    postnatal, effects of, 495–498
    prenatal, effects of, 493–495
    weaning, and risk of, 496
Mammillothalamic tract, myelination of, 82
Manganese, and brain development, 491
MAO-A. *See* Monoamine oxidase A
Marginal zone, 80
Marker tasks, 326
  of attention in young infants, 326–327
Masking, auditory, 207
Mass action, principle of, 298
Maternal attachment, parallel processes in, 605
Maternal separation responses, 607–609
Mean, differential regression to, 153
Medial diencephalon, in declarative memory, 368
Medial frontal gyrus, development of, 79
Medial geniculate nuclei, myelination of, 42
Medial lemniscus, myelination of, 82
Medial longitudinal fasciculus, myelination of, 82
Medial orbital gyrus, development of, 80*t*
Medial prefrontal cortex
  in attention-deficit/hyperactivity disorder, 529
  cocaine and, 527, 529
  dopamine in, 523, 525
Medial preoptic area
  androgen receptors in, 60
  sexual dimorphism in, 66
Medial temporal lobe
  in autism, 538–539
  in declarative learning/memory, 111–112, 365, 368–371
  in schizophrenia, 580–581
Medium-wavelength sensitive cones, development of, 221
Melody perception, 209–210
Memory
  aging and
    effects of working memory load and, 476–478
    frontal cortex activation patterns in, 479, 480*f*
    frontal lobe changes and, 473–484
    future directions for study of, 484
    number of operations to be performed and, 478–479
    type of material to be processed and, 479
  categories of, 365–366

for contextual detail, aging and, 483–484
declarative, 365–366
  adult abilities in, emergence of, 368–371
  development of, 368–371, 374, 375*t*
  inferences about, from animal cognition tests applied to children, 111–112
  neural circuits mediating, maturation of, 369–371, 374
episodic, 580
  in schizophrenia, 577, 580–581
event-related potentials in, 130–131
false, 484
fetal alcohol syndrome and, 511, 513
hippocampus in, 45, 56–57, 111, 119–120, 369–372, 374
item, aging and, 473, 483
long-term, 365–366
long-term potentiation in, 68, 83
neural bases of, insights into, from neuropsychological studies in primates, 365–375
plasticity and, 199
procedural, 365–366
  adult abilities in, emergence of, 366–367
  development of, 366–368, 374, 375*t*
  inferences about, from animal cognition tests applied to children, 111–112
  neural circuits mediating, maturation of, 367–368, 374
recognition
  adult abilities in, emergence of, 368–369
  aging and, 483–484
  attention and, 330–334, 332*f*, 334*f*
  Corsi-Milner test of, 450*t*
  development of, in monkeys and humans, 375*t*
  neural circuits mediating, maturation of, 369–370
  visual, 119–120
relational
  adult abilities in, emergence of, 370–371
  development of, 375*t*
  neural circuit mediating, maturation of, 371
semantic, in schizophrenia, 577, 581
sensory, aging and, 475–476
sexual dimorphism and, 66–69
short-term, 365–366
source, aging and, 473–474, 483–484
types of, 111
working, 365–366, 541, 579
  adult level of proficiency in, emergence of, 372–373
  age-related changes in frontal cortex and, 473–484
  aging and, 473–484
  attention and, 563–564
  in attention-deficit/hyperactivity disorder, 568
  in autism, 541–543
  development of, 371–374, 375*t*
  dopamine and, 436, 440–444, 448–454, 459–463
  dorsolateral prefrontal cortex in, 366, 371–374, 436, 440–444, 448–454, 459–463, 473
  PKU treatment and, 448–453, 449*t*–450*t*, 451*f*, 459–463
  in schizophrenia, 566–567, 578–580, 582
  spatial, 647, 650–655
Memory fields, 651
Menopause, behavioral changes in, 71–72
Menstrual synchrony, 611
Mental retardation, phenylketonuria and, 445
Mesencephalic dopamine, 649

Neural network models (continued)
learning algorithms in, 162–163
limitations of and improvements to, 169–170
net input and activation functions in, 161–162, 162f
of origin of knowledge, 163–164
understanding behavior from, 159, 169
units and weights in, 160, 161f
Neural plasticity. See Plasticity
Neural tube defects, folic acid deficiency and, 492
Neurogenesis. See Neuronogenesis
Neuromodulators, and recovery from early brain injury, 175, 185–186, 186f, 188
Neuromotor system, interconnectedness and redundancy in, 254–255, 264–265
Neuron(s)
aromatase activity in, 63
changes in, during development, 175–177, 176f
connections, development of, in hippocampus, 52
cortical, maturation of, 80–82, 81f
face-responsive, in monkeys, 382
formation of. See Neuronogenesis
neocortical, classes of, 3, 4f, 4t
number of, genetics and, 157
sex hormones and, 61, 63–69
size of, experience and, 177
substance P-containing, testosterone and, 61
as units in neural network models, 160, 161f
Neuronal specific enolase, 96
Neuronogenesis
abbreviations related to, 7t
adult, 93–103
discovery of, in mammalian brain, 94f–95f, 94–96
functional significance of, 100–103
new method for detection of, 94f, 95–96
in cerebellum, 93, 367–368
cortical, 80–82, 81f, 519–520, 520f
prefrontal, 373
early brain injury and, 176, 180–183, 182f, 187
experience and, 93, 98–100, 103, 177–178
hippocampal, 45–47, 48f–50f, 56, 369, 371
in adults, 93–103
hormones and, 65–69, 93, 97, 102–103
learning and, 93, 99–100, 99f–101f, 103
neocortical, 3–19
algorithm, 7–19
cell cycle and, 7, 9f, 10, 11f, 15–18, 17f
equations in, 10
master integrator of, 14–15
output domain of, 11–12
parameters in, 10, 11f
in pseudostratified ventricular epithelium, 4–5, 6f, 7–19, 11f
restriction point of, 9f, 14–15
and structural variation, 15–18, 16f
temporospatial domain of, 11–14, 13f
in normal brain, 175–176, 176f
nutrition and, 492
stress and, 93, 97–98, 99f, 102–103
in visual system, 230
Neuronogenetic sequence, 6f, 8–10
Neuropeptides, sex hormones and, 64–65, 72
Neuropil, increase of, in cortex, 80, 81f
Neuroscience
cognitive
genetics and, 149–150
meanings of attention in, 561–565
developmental
and cognition, bridging gap between, 415–429
structural analogy in, 415–417

developmental cognitive
advances in, 339
fetal alcohol syndrome studies in, 505–513
goals of, 149, 417
neural network models in, 159–170, 339
number representations in, 418–425
understanding of mind in, 415, 418
systems
in closing gap between biology and psychology, 417
integrating cognitive development with, 427–429
Neurosteroids, 64, 65f
Neurotransmitter(s)
activity, pharmacologic magnetic resonance imaging of, 144
in attention-deficit/hyperactivity disorder, 567
convergence of, 88–89
functional implications of, 88–89
cortical, maturation and interactions of, 79, 82–88
developmental changes in, 79, 82–85
developmental similarities among systems of, 85–86
extrinsic
developmental changes in, 84–85
interactions of, with intrinsic neurotransmitters, 86–88
genetics and, 157
intrinsic
developmental changes in, 83–84
interactions of, with extrinsic neurotransmitters, 86–88
in schizophrenia, 565–566
sex hormones and, 64–65, 72
Neurotrophin(s)
in cortical development, 521
visual deprivation and, 247
Neurotrophin-3, 521
Newborns. See also Infants
attachment system in, 601–602
auditory development in, 205–216
face processing in, 383–384
Conspec/Conlern hypothesis of, 383
externality effect in, 384
limitations of, 384
mental representation of facedness in, 383
perception of emotion in, 384
recognition of identity in, 383–384
sensory hypothesis of, 383
social hypothesis of, 383
listening preferences in, 208–209, 216, 271
neocortical synaptogenesis in, 23–32
Nigrostriatal tract, dopamine in, 522, 525, 649
NMDA receptors
cocaine and, 528
estrogen and, 68
subunit 1, as marker of neuronogenesis, 96
NMR. See Nuclear magnetic resonance
Noise, sensory, in infants, 206–207, 221, 224
Nominal style, in language development, 303
Nonparametric linkage analysis, 153t, 154–155
Noradrenaline, and recovery from early brain injury, 175, 185–186, 186f, 188
Noradrenergic system
and attention, 322–323, 323f
maturation of, 84–85
Norepinephrine
cocaine and, 528
as neurotransmitter, maturation of, 84–85
in olfactory preference learning and attachment, 604–605

Norm-based encoding hypothesis, of face processing, 390–391
Novelty
behavioral inhibition and, 640
fear of, early deprivation/orphanage rearing and, 623
Novelty P3, 131
in older adults, 479–481, 481f–482f
Novelty preference
and attention, 330–334, 357–358
in recognition memory testing, 330–334, 368–370
NSW (negative slow wave), in event-related potentials, 129
in infants, 131, 131f
Nuclear magnetic resonance (NMR), 137
Nucleotides, nutritional need for, 496
Nucleus accumbens
dopamine in, 522–523, 525, 649–650
in opiate reward pathway, 656
Nucleus basalis, 194
Number representation
analog-magnitude, 421–425, 427–429
choice experiment on, 419, 420f, 422, 424
disorders of, 422, 427–428
as example of bridging gap between cognition and developmental neuroscience, 418–425
Gelman and Gallistel's continuity hypothesis of, 419
Wynn's ease of learning argument against, 419–421
infant, format of, 424–425
integer-list
bootstrapping mechanism for, 426–429
construction of, 421, 425–426
as new representational resource, 425
sketch of one proposal for, 426
object-file, 423–425, 427–429
prelinguistic, 418–425
possible systems for, 421–424
structural analogy from, 426–429
Numerons, 419
Nutrients
categories of, 491–493
role of timing in deprivation and subsequent repletion of, 500–501
selected, and brain development, 493–500, 494t–495t
Nutrition, and cognitive development, 491–501
critical periods for, 497, 500–501
role of covariates in studies of, 497

## O

Object continuity, neural network model of, 163–164, 169
Object permanence, 428
neural network model of, 164, 169
Object processing
dorsal and ventral visual pathways in, 339–349
computational model of, 346f, 346–348
versus face processing, 381–383
movement and, 344–345
Object recognition module, in object processing model, 346f, 346–347
Object retrieval task, 449t
in dopamine-dorsolateral prefrontal cortex studies, 435–440, 440f, 441t, 447–448, 451f
PKU treatment and, 448, 451f
Object reversal discrimination task
for children, 112–115, 114f, 120t
gender specificity in, 112–115, 114f
gonadal hormones and, 113
neural basis of, 113

Photoreceptors, development of, 222–224
Physical fitness, and cognitive effects of aging, 474
Piaget, Jean, 402
PKU. *See* Phenylketonuria
Place learning, 115
Planum temporale, sexual dimorphism in, 70, 70*f*
Plasticity
  acetylcholine and, 185–186
  adaptive and maladaptive, 194
  in amputees, 193, 193*f*, 195, 195*f*
  of auditory system, 195–196, 196*f*, 205, 210–216
    in humans, 215–216
    in nonhumans, 213–215
  basic aspects of, 193–194
  behavioral relevance and, 194–195, 312
  in blind, 194, 215–216
  in children, capacity for, versus adult capacity
    for, 194, 316
  in deaf, 215–216
  deafferentation and, 193–194
  and development, 191–199
  early brain injury and, 175–188, 281–282, 297–
    299
  early deprivation and, 619
  experience-driven or training-induced, 311–312
    after speech perception training, 313
    for aphasia, 316
    characteristics of training necessary to induce,
      312–313, 315
  Hebbian mechanisms in, 192
  and language development, 196–199, 276
  and learning, 199
  and memory, 199
  in musicians, 193–196, 196*f*
  noradrenaline and, 185–186
  in normal developing brain, 175–178
  in olfactory preference learning, 604–605
  principles of, 194–195
  regulation of, 192–193
  of representational zones, 191–194
    examples of, 195–196
  sensitive periods for, 192, 199
  of somatosensory system, 192–193, 193*f*, 195,
    195*f*
  in spatial cognitive development, 410–411
  subcortical, vertical, 228–229
  temporal dynamics of, 194
  use-dependent, 193–195
  of visual system, 240–248, 348–349
Pleiotropy, 156
PN. *See* Processing negativity
Pointing tasks, self-ordered, preservation of
  performance on, in children treated for PKU,
  453–454, 455*t*
Poles, myelination of, 35–36
Polygeny, 156
Polymorphic genes, 149
Polysialylated form of neural cell adhesion
  molecule (PSA-NCAM), 96
Positive slow wave. *See* PSW
Positron emission tomography (PET)
  of children, difficulties with, 315
  in obsessive compulsive disorder, following
    pharmacologic treatment, 144
  of visual development, 227–228
Posterior attention system, 322, 324, 404
Posterior cerebellar peduncle, myelination of,
  magnetic resonance imaging of, 37*t*
Posterior cingulate cortex, dorsolateral prefrontal
  cortex connection to, 435
Posterior fossa structures, myelination of,
  magnetic resonance imaging of, 39–40
Posterior orbital gyrus, development of, 80*t*

Posterior parietal cortex, dorsolateral prefrontal
  cortex connection to, 435
Post-rolandic gyrus, development of, 80*t*
Posture, and reaching skills, 258–259
Potassium, and brain function, 491
Precentral gyrus, representation of motor
  responses in, 192
Precentral sulcus, 434, 435*f*
Preferential listening, in infants, 208–209, 216,
  271
Preferential looking
  and attention, 357–358
  at eyes, 385
  at faces, 383–385, 387, 416
  in global-local task, 449*t*
  in studies of dorsal and ventral visual pathways,
    344–346
  in visual assessment, 237
Prefrontal cortex
  anatomy of, 434–435, 435*f*
  in attention, 436, 563–564
  in attention-deficit/hyperactivity disorder, 567,
    570–571
    Ritalin and, 144
  cocaine and, 527
  cytoarchitectural maturation of, 80–82, 81*f*
  in declarative memory, 370–371
  development of, 79–89
  dopamine in
    and cognition, 435–456, 438*f*–440*f*, 441*t*,
      459–463
    early and continuous treatment of PKU
      model of, 434, 444–463, 447*f*
    evidence from visual psychophysics
      confirming hypothesis of, 456–459, 457*f*–
      458*f*
    and inhibitory control, 436–440, 448–450
    and reward-seeking behavior, 647–659
    role of, 433–463, 523, 525
    selective deficit in, with PKU treatment, 444–
      447, 445*f*
    tyrosine levels and, 446–447, 447*f*, 460
    and working memory, 436, 440–444
  dorsolateral. *See* Dorsolateral prefrontal cortex
  functions of, 434
  in go/no-go task, magnetic resonance imaging
    in, 140–141, 141*f*
  in learning, 111–113
  in motor skill acquisition, 262–263
  myelination of, 82
  neurotransmitters in
    convergence of, 88–89
    developmental similarities among systems of,
      85–86
    extrinsic, 84–85
    interactions of, 79, 86–88
    intrinsic, 83–84
    maturation of, 79, 82–85
  in schizophrenia, 579
  in self-regulation, 638–640
  size of, evolutionary increase in, 434–435
  in spatial working memory, 650–652
  synaptic connections in, formation of, 82
  in temperament, 633
  in Tourette's syndrome, 553, 554*f*
Pregnenolone, and brain development, 64, 65*f*
Premonitory urges, in tic disorders, 552–553, 553*f*
Premotor cortex, dorsolateral prefrontal cortex
  connection to, 435
Preoptic area
  aromatase activity in, 63
  estrogen receptors in, 60

  medial
    androgen receptors in, 60
    sexual dimorphism in, 66
    progesterone receptors in, 60
Preplate, 520–521
Pre-rolandic gyrus, development of, 80*t*
Prism studies
  of reaching skills, 254
  of sensory development, in owls, 211–212
Privation, levels of, in orphanages, 618
Probabilistic epigenesis, 150, 156
Procedural learning
  attention-deficit/hyperactivity disorder and, 570
  inferences about, from animal cognition tests
    applied to children, 111–112
  neural basis for, 111
Procedural memory, 365–366
  adult abilities in, emergence of, 366–367
  development of, 366–368, 374
    in monkeys and humans, 375*t*
  inferences about, from animal cognition tests
    applied to children, 111–112
  neural circuits mediating, maturation of, 367–
    368, 374
Processing negativity (PN), in event-related
  potentials, 128
Progenitor cells
  development of, in normal brain, 175–176,
    176*f*, 519–521, 520*f*
  early brain injury and, 183
Progesterone
  and brain development, 60–62, 64, 65*f*,
    67–68, 72
  and dopamine, 67
  organizational and activational effects of, 61–62
  and verbal abilities, 70
Progesterone receptors
  in brain, 60
  dopamine and, 65, 72
Projection pathways, myelination of, 35–36
Pronominal style, in language development, 303
Propositional memory. *See* Declarative memory
Prosopagnosia, 382
  developmental, 392
Prostate, 5α-reductase metabolism of testosterone
  and, 63–64
Protein, and brain development, 491, 493–498,
  494*t*
Protein-energy malnutrition (PEM)
  and brain development, 491, 493–498, 494*t*, 501
  postnatal, effects of, 495–498
  prenatal, effects of, 493–495
  weaning, and risk of, 496
Protein-energy status, and brain development,
  493–498, 494*t*
Proteolipid protein, 35
Proton magnetic resonance spectroscopy, in
  schizophrenia, 580–581
Proximal pathways, myelination of, 35–36
Proximity, with mother, and attachment, 601–602,
  611, 656
Pruning, synaptic, 82, 373, 393
Pseudostratified ventricular epithelium (PVE),
  7–10
  architecture of, 7–10, 8*f*
  cell cycle of, 7, 9*f*, 10, 11*f*, 15–17, 18*f*
  neuronogenesis in, 4–5, 6*f*, 7–19
    algorithm for, 10–19
    equations in, 10
    master integrator of, 14–15
    output domain of, 11–12
    parameters in, 10, 11*f*
    temporospatial domain of, 11–14, 13*f*
  operational properties of, 7–10

Stages, developmental, neural network model of, 164–166, 169
Startle paradigm, 632
Starvation, and brain development, 492
Static lesion model, of schizophrenia, 584–585
Stem cells
    development of, in normal brain, 175–176, 176f
    early brain injury and, 181–183
Stereopsis, development of, 226, 226f, 231
Stereoscopic vision, 192
Sternberg's memory search task, in older adults, 476–478
Steroid hormone(s)
    metabolism of, and effect of sex hormones on brain, 62–64, 62f–63f, 65f
    and neuronogenesis, 65–69, 93, 97, 102–103
    sex. See Sex hormone(s)
Stimulation, framing questions about, 619
Stimulus onset asychrony, 404–405
Stress
    and learning, 102
    and neuronogenesis, 93, 97–98, 99f, 102
Stress responses
    early deprivation/orphanage rearing and, 623
    mother-infant interactions and, 609–610
Stress-hyporesponsive period, 609
Stria terminalis, bed nucleus of
    androgen receptors in, 60
    aromatase activity in, 63
    estrogen receptors in, 59–60
    in fear system, 632, 641
    sex hormones and, 59–61, 63
    sexual dimorphism in, 66
Striatum
    in attention-deficit/hyperactivity disorder, 567
    dopamine in, 522, 525
    in habit formation, 550–552, 551f, 552t
    in memory, 366, 374
    sexual dimorphism in, 66–67
Stroke, cortical reorganization after, functional magnetic resonance imaging of, 142
Stroop tasks
    aging and, 481–483
    control condition, 450t
    in dopamine-dorsolateral prefrontal cortex studies, 462–463, 462t, 463f–464f
    in dorsolateral prefrontal cortex studies, 442
    in executive control, 359
Structural analogy, 415–417
    from number representation, 426–429
Structural parallels, 415–417
Subcortical mechanisms, in face processing, 383
Subcortical plasticity, vertical, 228–229
Subcortical visual development, 221, 226–232
Subcortical white matter, myelination of, magnetic resonance imaging of, 41
Subicular complex
    cell migration in, 49–52, 56
    neuronal cell formation in, 45–47, 48f–49f, 56
Substance P-containing neurons, testosterone and, 61
Substantia nigra
    dopamine in, 522
    in habit formation, 550–552, 551f, 552t
    in Tourette's syndrome, 553, 554f
Subthalamic nuclei, in habit formation, 551f, 551–552
Subthalamic region, myelination of, 42
Subventricular zone (SVZ), cell formation and migration in, 49, 49f, 521
Sulcus, 434
Superior cerebellar peduncle, myelination of, 42
    magnetic resonance imaging of, 37t, 39

Superior colliculus, 211, 213–214
    and spatial attention, 404–405
    in visual development, 226–229, 228f, 356
Superior frontal gyrus, development of, 80t
Superior medullary lamina, myelination of, 82
Superior temporal cortex, dorsolateral prefrontal cortex connection to, 435
Superior temporal gyrus, development of, 79, 80t
Superior temporale, sexual dimorphism in, 70–71, 70f
Supervisory attention, 562–564
Supplementary motor area (SMA), 434, 435f
    in attention, 354–355
    in self-regulation, 638
    in Tourette's syndrome, 551f, 552t, 553
Supramarginal gyrus, development of, 79, 80t
Supraoptic nucleus, estrogen receptors in, 60
Supratentorial brain, myelination of, 42
    magnetic resonance imaging of, 40
Surface features, perception of, ventral visual pathway and, 341, 344–349
Sustained attention, 324–325, 327–329, 437, 561, 564–565
SVZ. See Subventricular zone
Syllable discrimination, 270, 314–315
Synapse(s)
    density of
        days after conception and, 26f
        decline in, with age, 24–25, 28–29, 82
        and visual development, 225–226, 226f–227f, 230, 240
    formation of. See Synaptogenesis
    mismatch of pre- and postsynaptic activity of, visual deprivation and, 247
    number of, genetics and, 157
    plasticity of, regulation of, 192–193
    as weights in neural network models, 160, 161f
Synaptic pruning, 82, 373, 393
Synaptic scaling, 192–193
Synaptic space, early brain injury and, 179–180
Synaptogenesis
    cortical, 82, 519–521, 520f
    distinct waves of, 25–26, 25f, 32
    early brain injury and, 179–180
    environment and, 24f, 27–29, 31–32, 150
    epigenesis and, 23, 31–32
    experience-dependent, 24f, 27–28, 177–178
    experience-expectant, 24f, 27
    experience-independent, 24f, 27
    genetics of, new perspectives on, 31–32
    heterochronic epigenesis hypothesis of, 32
    in hippocampus, 52, 54–57, 55f, 68, 371
    and individuation, 31–32
    kinetics of, 24–25, 24f–25f, 31
    levels of, 23
    neocortical
        in newborn, 23–32
        and structural variation, 18
    in normal brain, 176–177
    nutrition and, 492
    phase 1 of, 24–25, 24f, 27
    phase 2 of, 24–25, 24f, 27
    phase 3 of, 24, 24f, 31–32
        critical periods in, 27–28
        days after conception and, 26f, 29–30
        in diverse cortical areas, 26
        duration of, 30–31, 31t
        evolution of, in neocortex, 29–31, 30f, 31t
        genetic hypothesis of, 30
        modifiability of, 26–27
        morphofunctional hypothesis of, 30–31
    phase 4 (plateau) of, 24–25, 24f, 28
    phase 5 of, 24–25, 24f, 28

regulation of, 23
selectionist versus constructivist hypothesis of, 29
sex hormones and, 65
Systems neuroscience
    in closing gap between biology and psychology, 417
    integrating cognitive development with, 427–429

## T

T1, in magnetic resonance imaging
    T1 relaxation time, 137
    T1-weighted images, of myelination, 36–41, 38f–40f
T2, in magnetic resonance imaging
    T2 relaxation time, 137–138
    T2-weighted images, 140
        of myelination, 36–41, 38f–40f
Tapping task, 449t
    in dorsolateral prefrontal cortex studies, 442–444, 443f, 448, 451f
    PKU treatment and, 448, 451f
Tectal visual system, 399
Telencephalon
    androgen receptors in, 60
    myelination of, 35–36, 42–43
Temperament
    affective bias in, 635–636
    and attention, 353–354, 360–361
    behavioral inhibition in, 631–632, 640–642
    biology of, 631–642
        integrative approach to, 632–633
    bottom-up regulation of, 633
    components of, 634–640
    emotion-based approach to, 631–632
    motivation-based view of, 631
    reactivity in, 632–635
    Rothbart's theory of, 631
    self-regulation in, 632–634, 636–640
    strength of nervous system and, 631
    top-down regulation of, 633
Temporal dynamics, of plasticity, 194
Temporal lobe
    in autism, 538–539
    in declarative learning/memory, 111–112, 365, 368–371
    dorsolateral prefrontal cortex connection to, 435
    in schizophrenia, 565, 580–581
    volume of, 138
Temporal lobe epilepsy, cognitive deficits of schizophrenia versus, 587
Temporal order memory tasks, 450t
    preservation of performance on, in children treated for PKU, 453–454
    in schizophrenia, 580
Temporal pole, myelination of, 35–36
Temporal processing
    deficits, in speech and language disorders, 208, 309–311
    training
        for aphasia, 316
        for specific language impairment and dyslexia, 314–316
Temporal resolution, auditory, 207–208
Temporal theory, of speech processing, 208, 309–310
Temporal-directed stream, visual, 227. See also Parvocellular pathway
Temporospatial domain, of neuronogenetic operation, 11–14, 13f